www.wileyplus.com

This online teaching and learning environment integrates the **entire digital textbook** with the most effective instructor and student resources to fit every learning style.

With **WileyPLUS:**

D0139066

○ Students achieve concept mastery in a rich, structured environment that's available 24/7

○ Instructors personalize and manage their course more effectively with assessment, assignments, grade tracking, and more

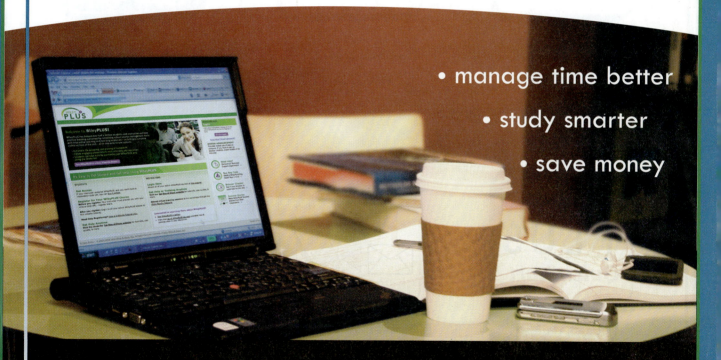

• manage time better

• study smarter

• save money

From multiple study paths, to self-assessment, to a wealth of interactive visual and audio resources, *WileyPLUS* gives you everything you need to personalize the teaching and learning experience.

»Find out how to MAKE IT YOURS»

www.wiley**plus**.com

ALL THE HELP, RESOURCES, AND PERSONAL SUPPORT YOU AND YOUR STUDENTS NEED!

2-Minute Tutorials and all of the resources you & your students need to get started
www.wileyplus.com/firstday

Student support from an experienced student user Ask your local representative for details!

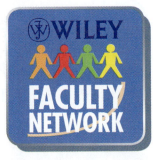

Collaborate with your colleagues, find a mentor, attend virtual and live events, and view resources
www.WhereFacultyConnect.com

Pre-loaded, ready-to-use assignments and presentations
www.wiley.com/college/quickstart

Technical Support 24/7 FAQs, online chat, and phone support
www.wileyplus.com/support

Your *WileyPLUS* Account Manager Training and implementation support
www.wileyplus.com/accountmanager

www.wileyplus.com

MAKE IT YOURS!

Big Java

4th edition

Big Java

4th edition

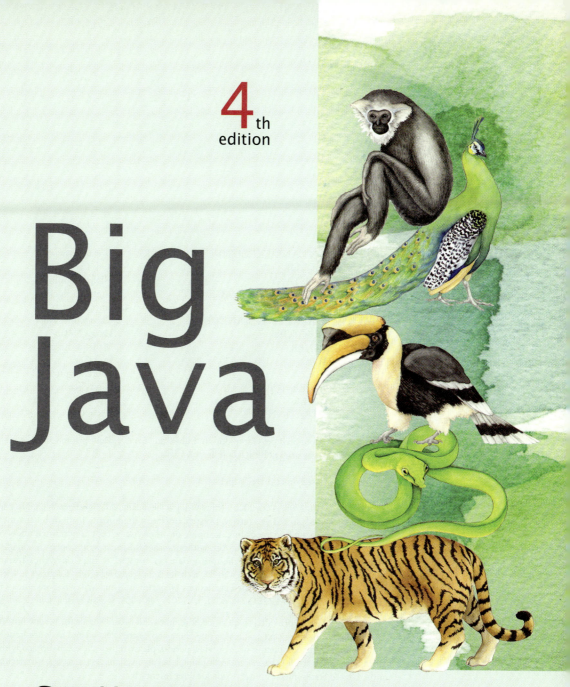

Cay Horstmann SAN JOSE STATE UNIVERSITY

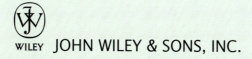

WILEY JOHN WILEY & SONS, INC.

VICE PRESIDENT AND EXECUTIVE PUBLISHER	Donald Fowley
EXECUTIVE EDITOR	Beth Lang Golub
EDITORIAL ASSISTANT	Michael Berlin
PRODUCTION SERVICES MANAGER	Dorothy Sinclair
PRODUCTION EDITOR	Janet Foxman
EXECUTIVE MARKETING MANAGER	Christopher Ruel
CREATIVE DIRECTOR	Harry Nolan
SENIOR DESIGNER	Madelyn Lesure
PHOTO EDITOR	Lisa Gee
MEDIA EDITOR	Lauren Sapira
PRODUCTION SERVICES	Cindy Johnson
COVER DESIGNER	Howard Grossman
COVER ILLUSTRATION	Susan Cyr

This book was set in Stempel Garamond by Publishing Services, and printed and bound by RRD Jefferson City. The cover was printed by RRD Jefferson City.

This book is printed on acid-free paper. ∞

Library of Congress Cataloging-in-Publication Data:
Horstmann, Cay S., 1959–
  Big Java : compatible with Java 5, 6 and 7 / Cay Horstmann. -- 4th ed.
    p. cm.
  Includes index.
  ISBN 978-0-470-50948-7 (pbk. : alk. paper)
  1. Java (Computer program language) I. Title.
  QA76.73.J38H674 2010
  005.13'3--dc22
                                    2009042604
ISBN 978-0-470-50948-7

Printed in the United States of America

10 9 8 7 6 5 4 3 2 1

PREFACE

This book is an introductory text in computer science, focusing on the principles of programming and software engineering. Here are its key features:

- **Teach objects gradually.**

    In Chapter 2, students learn how to use objects and classes from the standard library. Chapter 3 shows the mechanics of implementing classes *from a given specification*. Students then use simple objects as they master branches, loops, and arrays. Object-oriented design starts in Chapter 8. This gradual approach allows students to use objects throughout their study of the core algorithmic topics, without teaching bad habits that must be un-learned later.

- **Reinforce sound engineering practices.**

    A focus on test-driven development encourages students to test their programs systematically. A multitude of useful tips on software quality and common errors encourage the development of good programming habits.

- **Help students with guidance and worked examples.**

    Beginning programmers often ask "How do I start? Now what do I do?" Of course, an activity as complex as programming cannot be reduced to cookbook-style instructions. However, step-by-step guidance is immensely helpful for building confidence and providing an outline for the task at hand. The book contains a large number of "How To" guides for common tasks, with pointers to additional worked examples on the Web.

- **Focus on the essentials while being technically accurate.**

    An encyclopedic coverage is not helpful for a beginning programmer, but neither is the opposite—reducing the material to a list of simplistic bullet points that give an illusion of knowledge. In this book, the essentials of each subject are presented in digestible chunks, with separate notes that go deeper into good practices or language features when the reader is ready for the additional information.

- **Use standard Java.**

    The book teaches the standard Java language—not a specialized "training wheels" environment. The Java language, library, and tools are presented at a depth that is sufficient to solve real-world programming problems. The final chapters of the book cover advanced techniques such as multithreading, database storage, XML, and web programming.

- **Provide an optional graphics track.**

    Graphical shapes are splendid examples of objects. Many students enjoy writing programs that create drawings or use graphical user interfaces. If desired, these topics can be integrated into the course by using the materials at the end of Chapters 2, 3, 9, and 10.

New in This Edition

This is the fourth edition of *Big Java,* and the book has once again been carefully revised and updated. The new and improved features include:

More Help for Beginning Programmers

- The How To sections have been updated and expanded, and four new ones have been added. Fifteen new Worked Examples (on the companion web site and in WileyPLUS) walk students through the steps required for solving complex and interesting problems.

- The treatment of algorithm design, planning, and the use of pseudocode has been enhanced. Students learn to use pseudocode to define the solution algorithm in Chapter 1.

- Chapters have been revised to focus each section on a specific learning objective. These learning objectives also organize the chapter summary to help students assess their progress.

Annotated Examples

- Syntax diagrams now call out features of typical example code to draw student attention to the key elements of the syntax. Additional annotations point out special cases, common errors, and good practice associated with the syntax.

- New example tables clearly present a variety of typical and special cases in a compact format. Each example is accompanied by a brief note explaining the usage shown and the values that result from it.

- The gradual introduction of objects has been further improved by providing additional examples and insights in the early chapters.

Updated for Java 7

- Features introduced in Java 7 are covered as Special Topics so that students can prepare for them. In this edition, we use Java 5 or 6 for the main discussion.

More Opportunities for Practice

- The test bank has been greatly expanded and improved. (See page xi.)

- A new set of lab assignments enables students to practice solving complex problems one step at a time.

- The LabRat code evaluation feature, enhanced for this edition, gives students instant feedback on their programming assignments. (See page xvi.)

A Tour of the Book

The book can be naturally grouped into four parts, as illustrated by Figure 1. The organization of chapters offers the same flexibility as the previous edition; dependencies among the chapters are also shown in the figure.

Part A: Fundamentals (Chapters 1–7)

Chapter 1 contains a brief introduction to computer science and Java programming. Chapter 2 shows how to manipulate objects of predefined classes. In Chapter 3, you will build your own simple classes from given specifications.

Fundamental data types, branches, loops, and arrays are covered in Chapters 4–7.

Part B: Object-Oriented Design (Chapters 8–12)

Chapter 8 takes up the subject of class design in a systematic fashion, and it introduces a very simple subset of the UML notation.

The discussion of polymorphism and inheritance is split into two chapters. Chapter 9 covers interfaces and polymorphism, whereas Chapter 10 covers inheritance. Introducing interfaces before inheritance pays off in an important way: Students immediately see polymorphism before getting bogged down with technical details such as superclass construction.

Exception handling and basic file input/output are covered in Chapter 11. The exception hierarchy gives a useful example for inheritance.

Chapter 12 contains an introduction to object-oriented design, including two significant case studies.

Part C: Data Structures and Algorithms (Chapters 13–17)

Chapters 13 through 17 contain an introduction to algorithms and data structures, covering recursion, sorting and searching, linked lists, binary trees, and hash tables. These topics may be outside the scope of a one-semester course, but can be covered as desired after Chapter 7 (see Figure 1).

Recursion is introduced from an object-oriented point of view: An object that solves a problem recursively constructs another object of the same class that solves a simpler problem. The idea of having the other object do the simpler job is more intuitive than having a function call itself.

Each data structure is presented in the context of the standard Java collections library. You will learn the essential abstractions of the standard library (such as iterators, sets, and maps) as well as the performance characteristics of the various collections. However, a detailed discussion of the implementation of advanced data structures is beyond the scope of this book.

Chapter 17 introduces Java generics. This chapter is suitable for advanced students who want to implement their own generic classes and methods.

Part D: Advanced Topics (Chapters 18–24)

Chapters 18 through 24 cover advanced Java programming techniques that definitely go beyond a first course in Java. Although, as already mentioned, a comprehensive coverage of the Java library would span many volumes, many instructors prefer that a textbook should give students additional reference material valuable beyond their first course. Some institutions also teach a second-semester course that

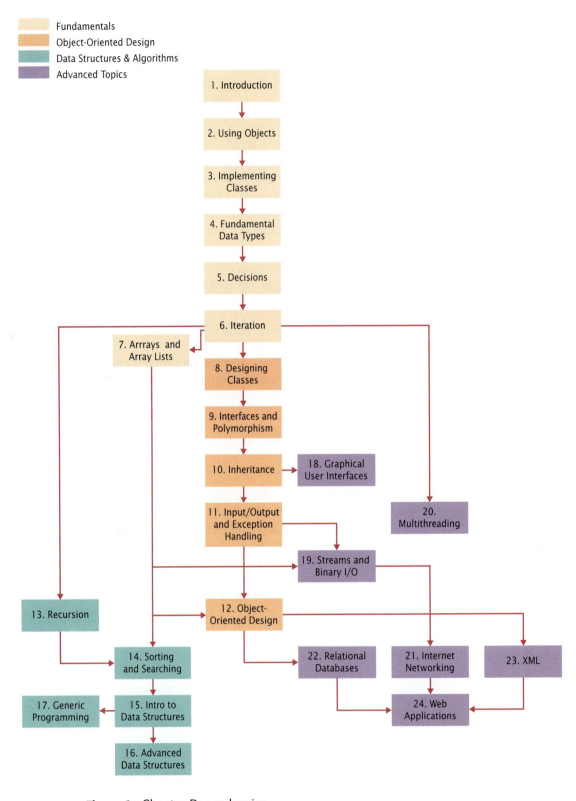

Fundamentals
Object-Oriented Design
Data Structures & Algorithms
Advanced Topics

1. Introduction

2. Using Objects

3. Implementing Classes

4. Fundamental Data Types

5. Decisions

6. Iteration

7. Arrrays and Array Lists

8. Designing Classes

9. Interfaces and Polymorphism

10. Inheritance

18. Graphical User Interfaces

11. Input/Output and Exception Handling

20. Multithreading

19. Streams and Binary I/O

13. Recursion

12. Object-Oriented Design

22. Relational Databases

21. Internet Networking

23. XML

14. Sorting and Searching

17. Generic Programming

15. Intro to Data Structures

24. Web Applications

16. Advanced Data Structures

Figure 1 Chapter Dependencies

covers more practical programming aspects such as database and network programming, rather than the more traditional in-depth material on data structures and algorithms. This book can be used in a two-semester course to give students an introduction to programming fundamentals and broad coverage of applications. Alternatively, the material in the final chapters can be useful for student projects.

The advanced topics include graphical user-interface design, advanced file handling, multithreading, and those technologies that are of particular interest to server-side programming: networking, databases, XML, and web applications. The Internet has made it possible to deploy many useful applications on servers, often accessed by nothing more than a browser. This server-centric approach to application development was in part made possible by the Java language and libraries, and today, much of the industrial use of Java is in server-side programming.

Appendices

Appendix A lists character escape sequences and the Basic Latin and Latin-1 subsets of Unicode. Appendices B and C summarize Java reserved words and operators. Appendix D documents all of the library methods and classes used in this book.

Additional appendices contain quick references on Java syntax, HTML, Java tools, binary numbers, and UML.

Appendix L contains a style guide for use with this book. Many instructors find it highly beneficial to require a consistent style for all assignments. If this style guide conflicts with instructor sentiment or local customs, however, it is available in electronic form so that it can be modified.

Web Resources

This book is complemented by a complete suite of online resources and a robust WileyPLUS course.

Go to www.wiley.com/college/horstmann to visit the online companion site, which includes

- Source code for all examples in the book.
- Worked Examples that apply the problem-solving steps in the book to other realistic examples.
- Laboratory exercises (and solutions for instructors only).
- Lecture presentation slides (in HTML and PowerPoint formats).
- Solutions to all review and programming exercises (for instructors only).
- A test bank that focuses on skills, not just terminology (for instructors only).

WileyPLUS is an online teaching and learning environment that integrates the digital textbook with instructor and student resources. See page xvi for details.

Web resources are summarized at chapter end for easy reference.

Media Resources

PLUS
www.wiley.com/
college/
horstmann

- ***Worked Example*** How Many Days Have You Been Alive?
- ***Worked Example*** Working with Pictures
- Lab Exercises
- ⊕ ***Animation*** Variable Initialization and Assignment
- ⊕ ***Animation*** Parameter Passing
- ⊕ ***Animation*** Object References
- ⊕ Practice Quiz
- ⊕ Code Completion Exercises

A Walkthrough of the Learning Aids

The pedagogical elements in this book work together to make the book accessible to beginners as well as those learning Java as a second language.

Throughout each chapter, **margin notes** show where new concepts are introduced and provide an outline of key ideas.

Annotated **syntax boxes** provide a quick, visual overview of new language constructs.

Annotations explain required components and point to more information on common errors or best practices associated with the syntax.

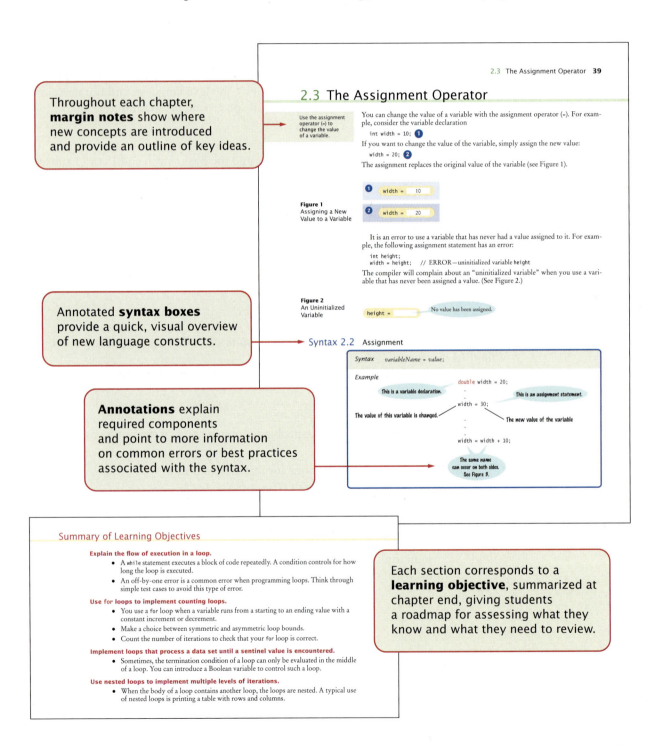

2.3 The Assignment Operator

Use the assignment operator (=) to change the value of a variable.

You can change the value of a variable with the assignment operator (=). For example, consider the variable declaration

```
int width = 10;  ①
```

If you want to change the value of the variable, simply assign the new value:

```
width = 20;  ②
```

The assignment replaces the original value of the variable (see Figure 1).

① width =   10
② width =   20

Figure 1
Assigning a New Value to a Variable

It is an error to use a variable that has never had a value assigned to it. For example, the following assignment statement has an error:

```
int height;
width = height;    // ERROR—uninitialized variable height
```

The compiler will complain about an "uninitialized variable" when you use a variable that has never been assigned a value. (See Figure 2.)

Figure 2
An Uninitialized Variable

height =   No value has been assigned.

Syntax 2.2   Assignment

```
Syntax      variableName = value;
```

```
Example                              double width = 20;
         This is a variable declaration.          This is an assignment statement.
                                     .
                                     .
                                  width = 30;
   The value of this variable is changed.          The new value of the variable
                                     .
                                     .
                               width = width + 10;
                                The same name
                               can occur on both sides.
                                  See Figure 3.
```

Summary of Learning Objectives

Explain the flow of execution in a loop.
- A while statement executes a block of code repeatedly. A condition controls for how long the loop is executed.
- An off-by-one error is a common error when programming loops. Think through simple test cases to avoid this type of error.

Use for loops to implement counting loops.
- You use a for loop when a variable runs from a starting to an ending value with a constant increment or decrement.
- Make a choice between symmetric and asymmetric loop bounds.
- Count the number of iterations to check that your for loop is correct.

Implement loops that process a data set until a sentinel value is encountered.
- Sometimes, the termination condition of a loop can only be evaluated in the middle of a loop. You can introduce a Boolean variable to control such a loop.

Use nested loops to implement multiple levels of iterations.
- When the body of a loop contains another loop, the loops are nested. A typical use of nested loops is printing a table with rows and columns.

Each section corresponds to a **learning objective**, summarized at chapter end, giving students a roadmap for assessing what they know and what they need to review.

How To 1.1   Developing and Describing an Algorithm

This is the first of many "How To" sections in this book that give you step-by-step proce-dures for carrying out important tasks in developing computer programs.

Before you are ready to write a program in Java, you need to develop an algorithm—a method for arriving at a solution for a particular problem. Describe the algorithm in pseudocode: a sequence of precise steps formulated in English.

For example, consider this problem: You have the choice of buying two cars. One is more fuel efficient than the other, but also more expensive. You know the price and fuel efficiency (in miles per gallon, mpg) of both cars. You plan to keep the car for ten years. Assume a price of $4 per gallon of gas and usage of 15,000 miles per year. You will pay cash for the car and not worry about financing costs. Which car is the better deal?

Step 1   Determine the inputs and outputs.

In our sample problem, we have these inputs:

- purchase price1 and fuel efficiency1, the price and fuel efficiency (in mpg) of the first car.
- purchase price2 and fuel efficiency2, the price and fuel efficiency of the second car.

We simply want to know which car is the better buy. That is the desired output.

Step 2   Break down the problem into smaller tasks.

For each car, we need to know the total cost of driving it. Let's do this computation sepa-rately for each car. Once we have the total cost for each car, we can decide which car is the better deal.

The total cost for each car is purchase price + operating cost.

We assume a constant usage and gas price for ten years, so the operating cost depends on the cost of driving the car for one year.

The operating cost is 10 x annual fuel cost.

The annual fuel cost is price per gallon x annual fuel consumed.

The annual fuel consumed is annual miles driven / fuel efficiency. For example, if you drive the for 15,000 miles and the fuel efficiency is 15 miles/gallon, the car consumes 1,000 gallons

Step 3   Describe each subtask in pseudocode.

In your description, arrange the steps so that any intermediate values are computed be they are needed in other computations. For example, list the step

total cost = purchase price + operating cost

after you have computed operating cost.

Here is the algorithm for deciding which car to buy.

For each car, compute the total cost as follows:
    annual fuel consumed = annual miles driven / fuel efficiency
    annual fuel cost = price per gallon x annual fuel consumed
    operating cost = 10 x annual fuel cost
    total cost = purchase price + operating cost

+ **Worked Example 1.1**   **Writing an Algorithm for Tiling a Floor**

This Worked Example shows how to develop an algorithm for laying tile in an alternating pattern of colors.

+ **Worked Example 6.1**   **Credit Card Processing**

This Worked Example uses a loop to remove spaces from a credit card number.

How To guides give step-by-step guidance for common programming tasks, emphasizing planning and testing. They answer the beginner's question, "Now what do I do?" and integrate key concepts into a problem-solving sequence.

Worked Examples apply the steps in the How To to a different example, illustrating how they can be used to plan, implement, and test a solution to another programming problem.

Example tables support beginners with multiple, concrete examples. These tables point out common errors and present another quick reference to the section's topic.

Table 1 Relational Operator Examples		
Expression	**Value**	**Comment**
3 <= 4	true	3 is less than 4; <= tests for "less than or equal".
🚫 3 =< 4	**Error**	The "less than or equal" operator is <=, not =<, with the "less than" symbol first.
3 > 4	false	> is the opposite of <=.
4 < 4	false	The left-hand side must be strictly smaller than the right-hand side.
4 <= 4	true	Both sides are equal; <= tests for "less than or equal".
3 == 5 - 2	true	== tests for equality.
3 != 5 - 1	true	!= tests for inequality. It is true that 3 is not 5 – 1.
🚫 3 = 6 / 2	**Error**	Use == to test for equality.
1.0 / 3.0 == 0.333333333	false	Although the values are very close to one another, they are not exactly equal. See Common Error 4.3.
🚫 "10" > 5	**Error**	You cannot compare a string to a number.
"Tomato".substring(0, 3).equals("Tom")	true	Always use the equals method to check whether two strings have the same contents.
"Tomato".substring(0, 3) == ("Tom")	false	Never use == to compare strings; it only checks whether the strings are stored in the same location. See Common Error 5.2 on page 180.
"Tom".equalsIgnoreCase("TOM")	true	Use the equalsIgnoreCase method if you don't want to distinguish between uppercase and lowercase letters.

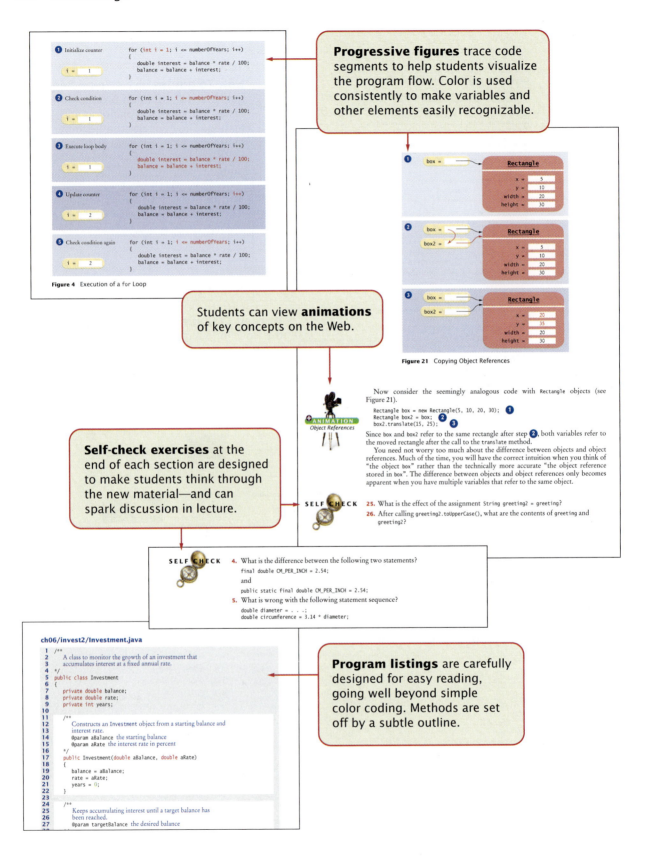

Progressive figures trace code segments to help students visualize the program flow. Color is used consistently to make variables and other elements easily recognizable.

Figure 4   Execution of a for Loop

Students can view **animations** of key concepts on the Web.

Figure 21   Copying Object References

Now consider the seemingly analogous code with Rectangle objects (see Figure 21).

```
Rectangle box = new Rectangle(5, 10, 20, 30); 1
Rectangle box2 = box; 2  3
box2.translate(15, 25);
```

Since box and box2 refer to the same rectangle after step 2, both variables refer to the moved rectangle after the call to the translate method.

You need not worry too much about the difference between objects and object references. Much of the time, you will have the correct intuition when you think of "the object box" rather than the technically more accurate "the object reference stored in box". The difference between objects and object references only becomes apparent when you have multiple variables that refer to the same object.

Self-check exercises at the end of each section are designed to make students think through the new material—and can spark discussion in lecture.

SELF CHECK

25. What is the effect of the assignment String greeting2 = greeting?
26. After calling greeting2.toUpperCase(), what are the contents of greeting and greeting2?

SELF CHECK

4. What is the difference between the following two statements?
   ```
   final double CM_PER_INCH = 2.54;
   ```
   and
   ```
   public static final double CM_PER_INCH = 2.54;
   ```
5. What is wrong with the following statement sequence?
   ```
   double diameter = . . .;
   double circumference = 3.14 * diameter;
   ```

ch06/invest2/Investment.java

```
1   /**
2      A class to monitor the growth of an investment that
3      accumulates interest at a fixed annual rate.
4   */
5   public class Investment
6   {
7      private double balance;
8      private double rate;
9      private int years;
10
11     /**
12        Constructs an Investment object from a starting balance and
13        interest rate.
14        @param aBalance the starting balance
15        @param aRate the interest rate in percent
16     */
17     public Investment(double aBalance, double aRate)
18     {
19        balance = aBalance;
20        rate = aRate;
21        years = 0;
22     }
23
24     /**
25        Keeps accumulating interest until a target balance has
26        been reached.
27        @param targetBalance the desired balance
```

Program listings are carefully designed for easy reading, going well beyond simple color coding. Methods are set off by a subtle outline.

Common Errors describe the kinds of errors that students often make, with an explanation of why the errors occur, and what to do about them.

Common Error 7.3

Length and Size

Unfortunately, the Java syntax for determining the number of elements in an array, an array list, and a string is not at all consistent. It is a common error to confuse these. You just have to remember the correct syntax for every data type.

Data Type	Number of Elements
Array	a.length
Array list	a.size()
String	a.length()

Quality Tips explain good programming practices. These notes carefully motivate the reason behind the advice, and explain why the effort will be repaid later.

Quality Tip 4.1

Do Not Use Magic Numbers

A magic number is a numeric constant that appears in your code without explanation. For example, consider the following scary example that actually occurs in the Java library source:

```
h = 31 * h + ch;
```

Why 31? The number of days in January? One less than the number of bits in an integer? Actually, this code computes a "hash code" from a string—a number that is derived from the characters in such a way that different strings are likely to yield different hash codes. The value 31 turns out to scramble the character values nicely.

A better solution is to use a named constant:

```
final int HASH_MULTIPLIER = 31;
h = HASH_MULTIPLIER * h + ch;
```

You should never use magic numbers in your code. Any number that is not completely self-explanatory should be declared as a named constant. Even the most reasonable cosmic constant is going to change one day. You think there are 365 days in a year? Your customers on Mars are going to be pretty unhappy about your silly prejudice. Make a constant

```
final int DAYS_PER_YEAR = 365;
```

By the way, the device

```
final int THREE_HUNDRED_AND_SIXTY_FIVE = 365;
```

Productivity Hints teach students how to use their time and tools more effectively. They encourage students to be more productive with tips and techniques such as hand-tracing.

Productivity Hint 6.1

Hand-Tracing Loops

In Programming Tip 5.2, you learned about the method of hand tracing. This method is particularly effective for understanding how a loop works.

Consider this example loop. What value is displayed?

```
int n = 1729;  ❶
int sum = 0;
while (n > 0)  ❷
{
    int digit = n % 10;  ❸ ❹ ❺ ❻
    sum = sum + digit;
    n = n / 10;
}
System.out.println(sum);  ❼
```

1. There are three variables: n, sum, and digit. The first two variables are initialized with 1729 and 0 before the loop is entered.

n	sum	digit
1729	0	

Special Topics present optional topics and provide additional explanation of others. New features of Java 7 are also covered in these notes.

Special Topic 7.2

ArrayList Syntax Enhancements in Java 7

Java 7 introduces several convenient syntax enhancements for array lists.

When you declare and construct an array list, you need not repeat the type parameter in the constructor. That is, you can write

```
ArrayList<String> names = new ArrayList<>();
```

instead of

```
ArrayList<String> names = new ArrayList<String>();
```

Random Facts provide historical and social information on computing—for interest and to fulfill the "historical and social context" requirements of the ACM/IEEE curriculum guidelines.

Random Fact 6.1

The First Bug

According to legend, the first bug was one found in 1947 in the Mark II, a huge electro-mechanical computer at Harvard University. It really was caused by a bug—a moth was trapped in a relay switch. Actually, from the note that the operator left in the log book next to the moth (see the figure), it appears as if the term "bug" had already been in active use at the time.

The First Bug

The pioneering computer scientist Maurice Wilkes wrote: "Somehow, at the Moore School and afterwards, one had always assumed there would be no particular difficulty in getting programs right. I can remember the exact instant in time at which it dawned on me

WileyPLUS

WileyPLUS is an online environment that supports students and instructors. This book's WileyPLUS course can complement the printed text or replace it altogether.

For Students

Different learning styles, different levels of proficiency, different levels of preparation—each student is unique. WileyPLUS empowers all students to take advantage of their individual strengths.

Integrated, multi-media resources—including audio and visual exhibits and demonstration problems—encourage active learning and provide multiple study paths to fit each student's learning preferences.

- Worked Examples apply the problem-solving steps in the book to another realistic example.
- Screencast Videos present the author explaining the steps he is taking and showing his work as he solves a programming problem.
- Animations of key concepts allow students to replay dynamic explanations that instructors usually provide on a whiteboard.

Self-assessments are linked to relevant portions of the text. Students can take control of their own learning and practice until they master the material.

- Practice quizzes can reveal areas where students need to focus.
- Lab exercises can be assigned for self-study or for use in the lab.
- "Code completion" questions enable students to practice programming skills by filling in small code snippets and getting immediate feedback.
- LabRat provides instant feedback on student solutions to all programming exercises in the book.

For Instructors

WileyPLUS includes all of the instructor resources found on the companion site, and more.

WileyPLUS gives you tools for identifying those students who are falling behind, allowing you to intervene accordingly, without having to wait for them to come to office hours.

- Practice quizzes for pre-reading assessment, self-quizzing, or additional practice can be used as-is or modified for your course needs.
- Multi-step laboratory exercises can be used in lab or assigned for extra student practice.

WileyPLUS simplifies and automates student performance assessment, making assignments, and scoring student work.

- An extensive set of multiple-choice questions for quizzing and testing have been developed to focus on skills, not just terminology.
- "Code completion" questions can also be added to online quizzes.
- LabRat can track student work on all programming exercises in the book, adding the student solution and a record of completion to the gradebook.
- Solutions to all review and programming exercises are provided.

With WileyPLUS ...

Students can read the book online and take advantage of searching and cross-linking.

Instructors can assign drill-and-practice questions to check that students did their reading and grasp basic concepts.

Students can practice programming by filling in small code snippets and getting immediate feedback.

Students can play and replay dynamic explanations of concepts and program flow.

Students can check that their programming assignments fulfill the specifications.

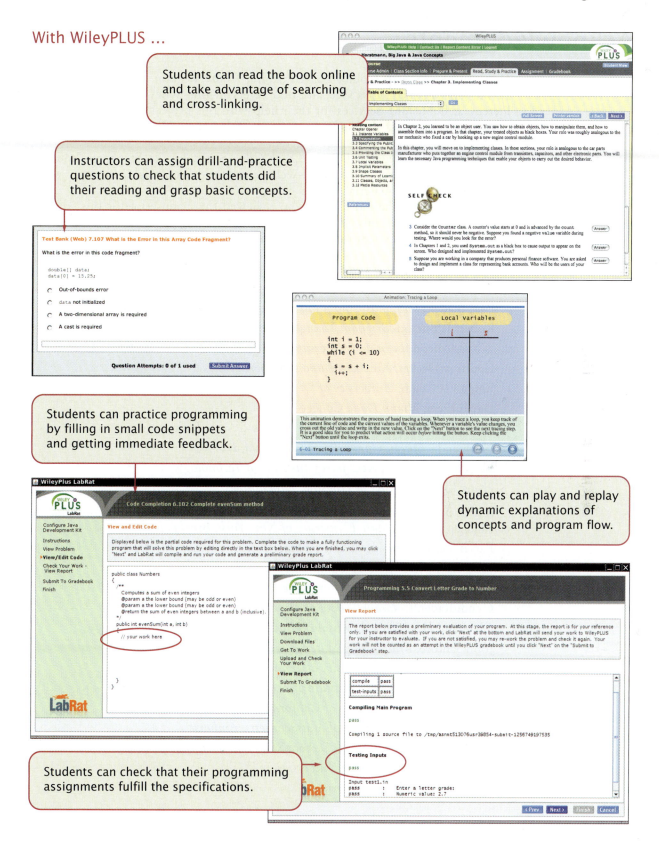

To order *Big Java* with its WileyPLUS course for your students, use ISBN 978-0-470-57827-8.

Acknowledgments

Many thanks to Beth Golub, Lauren Sapira, Andre Legaspi, Don Fowley, Mike Berlin, Janet Foxman, Lisa Gee, and Bud Peters at John Wiley & Sons, and Vickie Piercey at Publishing Services for their help with this project. An especially deep acknowledgment and thanks goes to Cindy Johnson for her hard work, sound judgment, and amazing attention to detail.

I am grateful to Suzanne Dietrich, Rick Giles, Kathy Liszka, Stephanie Smullen, Julius Dichter, Patricia McDermott-Wells, and David Woolbright, for their work on the supplemental material.

Many thanks to the individuals who reviewed the manuscript for this edition, made valuable suggestions, and brought an embarrassingly large number of errors and omissions to my attention. They include:

Ian Barland, *Radford University*

Rick Birney, *Arizona State University*

Paul Bladek, *Edmonds Community College*

Robert P. Burton, *Brigham Young University*

Teresa Cole, *Boise State University*

Geoffrey Decker, *Northern Illinois University*

Eman El-Sheikh, *University of West Florida*

David Freer, *Miami Dade College*

Ahmad Ghafarian, *North Georgia College & State University*

Norman Jacobson, *University of California, Irvine*

Mugdha Khaladkar, *New Jersey Institute of Technology*

Hong Lin, *University of Houston, Downtown*

Jeanna Matthews, *Clarkson University*

Sandeep R. Mitra, *State University of New York, Brockport*

Parviz Partow-Navid, *California State University, Los Angeles*

Jim Perry, *Ulster County Community College*

Kai Qian, *Southern Polytechnic State University*

Cyndi Rader, *Colorado School of Mines*

Chaman Lal Sabharwal, *Missouri University of Science and Technology*

John Santore, *Bridgewater State College*

Stephanie Smullen, *University of Tennessee, Chattanooga*

Monica Sweat, *Georgia Institute of Technology*

Shannon Tauro, *University of California, Irvine*

Russell Tessier, *University of Massachusetts, Amherst*

Jonathan L. Tolstedt, *North Dakota State University*

David Vineyard, *Kettering University*

Lea Wittie, *Bucknell University*

Every new edition builds on the suggestions and experiences of prior reviewers and users. I am grateful for the invaluable contributions these individuals have made to this book:

Tim Andersen, *Boise State University*

Ivan Bajic, *San Diego State University*

Ted Bangay, *Sheridan Institute of Technology*

George Basham, *Franklin University*

Sambit Bhattacharya, *Fayetteville State University*

Joseph Bowbeer, *Vizrea Corporation*

Timothy A. Budd, *Oregon State University*

Frank Butt, *IBM*

Jerry Cain, *Stanford University*

Adam Cannon, *Columbia University*

Nancy Chase, *Gonzaga University*

Archana Chidanandan, *Rose-Hulman Institute of Technology*

Vincent Cicirello, *The Richard Stockton College of New Jersey*

Deborah Coleman, *Rochester Institute of Technology*

Valentino Crespi, *California State University, Los Angeles*

Jim Cross, *Auburn University*

Russell Deaton, *University of Arkansas*

H. E. Dunsmore, *Purdue University*

Robert Duvall, *Duke University*

Henry A. Etlinger, *Rochester Institute of Technology*

John Fendrich, *Bradley University*

John Fulton, *Franklin University*

David Geary, *Sabreware, Inc.*

Margaret Geroch, *Wheeling Jesuit University*

Rick Giles, *Acadia University*

Stacey Grasso, *College of San Mateo*

Jianchao Han, *California State University, Dominguez Hills*

Lisa Hansen, *Western New England College*

Elliotte Harold

Eileen Head, *Binghamton University*

Cecily Heiner, *University of Utah*

Brian Howard, *Depauw University*

Lubomir Ivanov, *Iona College*

Curt Jones, *Bloomsburg University*

Aaron Keen, *California Polytechnic State University, San Luis Obispo*

Elliot Koffman, *Temple University*

Kathy Liszka, *University of Akron*

Hunter Lloyd, *Montana State University*

Youmin Lu, *Bloomsburg University*

John S. Mallozzi, *Iona College*

John Martin, *North Dakota State University*

Scott McElfresh, *Carnegie Mellon University*

Joan McGrory, *Christian Brothers University*

Carolyn Miller, *North Carolina State University*

Teng Moh, *San Jose State University*

John Moore, *The Citadel*

Faye Navabi, *Arizona State University*

Kevin O'Gorman, *California Polytechnic State University, San Luis Obispo*

Michael Olan, *Richard Stockton College*

Kevin Parker, *Idaho State University*

Cornel Pokorny, *California Polytechnic State University, San Luis Obispo*

Roger Priebe, *University of Texas, Austin*

C. Robert Putnam, *California State University, Northridge*

Neil Rankin, *Worcester Polytechnic Institute*

Brad Rippe, *Fullerton College*

Pedro I. Rivera Vega, *University of Puerto Rico, Mayaguez*

Daniel Rogers, *SUNY Brockport*

Carolyn Schauble, *Colorado State University*

Christian Shin, *SUNY Geneseo*

Jeffrey Six, *University of Delaware*

Don Slater, *Carnegie Mellon University*

Ken Slonneger, *University of Iowa*

Peter Stanchev, *Kettering University*

Ron Taylor, *Wright State University*

Joseph Vybihal, *McGill University*

Xiaoming Wei, *Iona College*

Todd Whittaker, *Franklin University*

Robert Willhoft, *Roberts Wesleyan College*

David Womack, *University of Texas at San Antonio*

Catherine Wyman, *DeVry University*

Arthur Yanushka, *Christian Brothers University*

Salih Yurttas, *Texas A&M University*

CONTENTS

ALPHABETICAL LIST OF SYNTAX BOXES

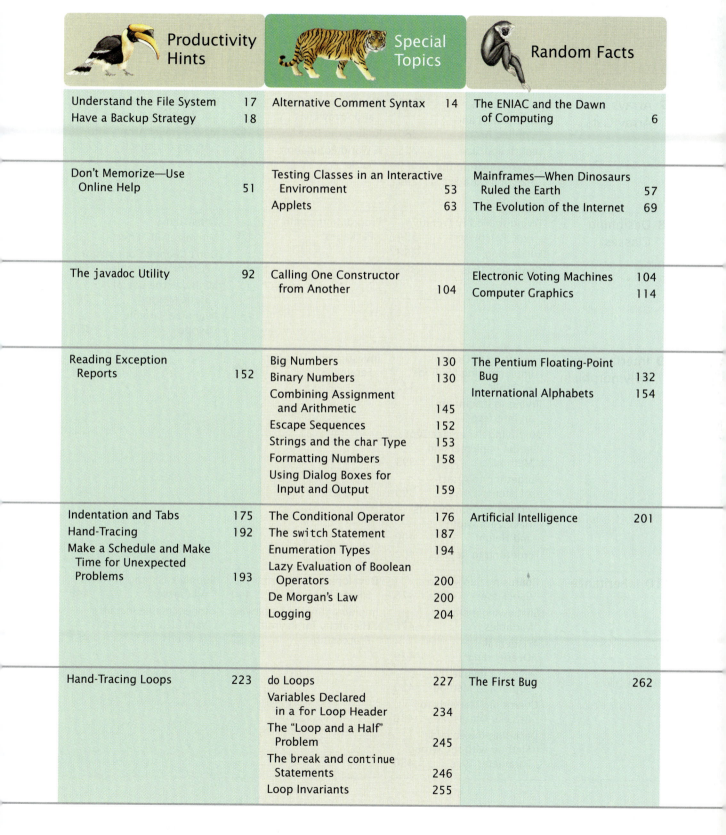

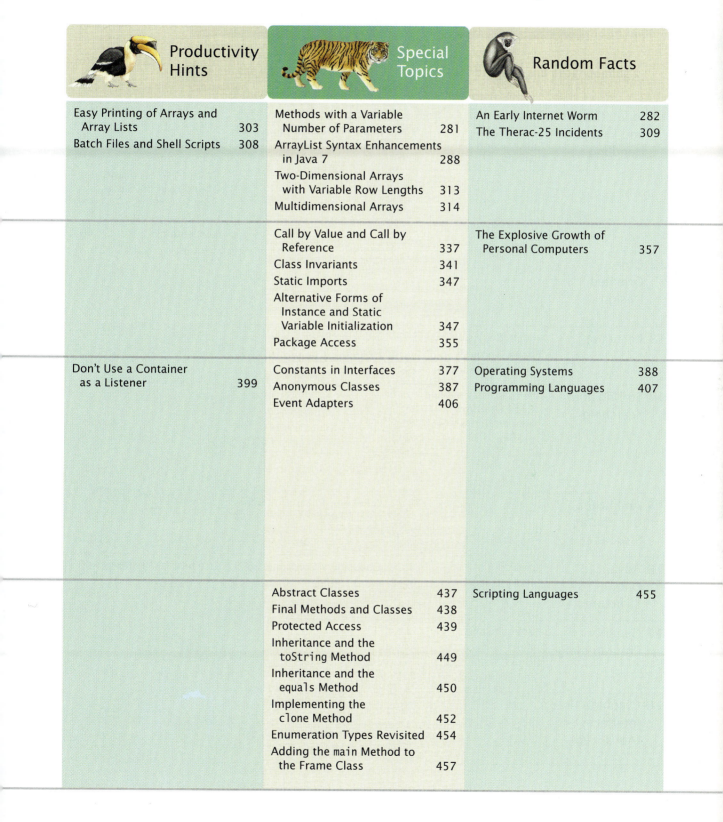

 Productivity Hints

 Special Topics

 Random Facts

Chapter	Common Errors	How Tos and Worked Examples	Quality Tips
19 Streams and Binary Input/ Output (Advanced)	Negative byte Values 782	Using Files and Streams 793	
20 Multi-threading (Advanced)	Calling await Without Calling signalAll 822 Calling signalAll Without Locking the Object 823		Use the Runnable Interface 806 Check for Thread Interruptions in the run Method of a Thread 809
21 Internet Networking (Advanced)		Designing Client/Server Programs 855	
22 Relational Databases (Advanced)	Joining Tables Without Specifying a Link Condition 879 Delimiters in Manually Constructed Queries 892		Don't Hardwire Database Connection Parameters into Your Program 892
23 XML (Advanced)	XML Elements Describe Objects, Not Classes 919	Designing an XML Document Format 909 Writing an XML Document 928 Writing a DTD 936	Prefer XML Elements over Attributes 911 Avoid Children with Mixed Elements and Text 912
24 Web Applications (Advanced)		Designing a Managed Bean 962	

Chapter 1

Introduction

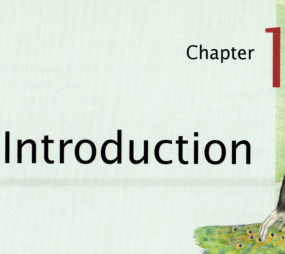

CHAPTER GOALS

- To understand the activity of programming
- To learn about the architecture of computers
- To learn about machine code and high-level programming languages
- To become familiar with the structure of simple Java programs
- To compile and run your first Java program
- To recognize compile-time and run-time errors
- To write pseudocode for simple algorithms

The purpose of this chapter is to familiarize you with the concepts of programming and program development. It reviews the architecture of a computer and discusses the difference between machine code and high-level programming languages. You will see how to compile and run your first Java program, and how to diagnose errors that may occur when a program is compiled or executed. Finally, you will learn how to formulate simple algorithms using pseudocode notation.

CHAPTER CONTENTS

1.1 What Is Programming?

You have probably used a computer for work or fun. Many people use computers for everyday tasks such as balancing a checkbook or writing a term paper. Computers are good for such tasks. They can handle repetitive chores, such as totaling up numbers or placing words on a page, without getting bored or exhausted. Computers also make good game machines because they can play sequences of sounds and pictures, involving the human user in the process.

The flexibility of a computer is quite an amazing phenomenon. The same machine can balance your checkbook, print your term paper, and play a game. In contrast, other machines carry out a much narrower range of tasks—a car drives and a toaster toasts.

A computer must be programmed to perform tasks. Different tasks require different programs.

To achieve this flexibility, the computer must be *programmed* to perform each task. A computer itself is a machine that stores data (numbers, words, pictures), interacts with devices (the monitor screen, the sound system, the printer), and executes programs. Programs are sequences of instructions and decisions that the computer carries out to achieve a task. One program balances checkbooks; a different program, perhaps designed and constructed by a different company, processes words; and a third program, probably from yet another company, plays a game.

A computer program executes a sequence of very basic instructions in rapid succession.

Today's computer programs are so sophisticated that it is hard to believe that they are all composed of extremely primitive instructions. A typical instruction may be one of the following:

- Put a red dot onto this screen position.
- Get a number from this location in memory.
- Add up two numbers.
- If this value is negative, continue the program at that instruction.

A computer program contains the instruction sequences for all tasks that it can execute.

A computer program tells a computer, in minute detail, the sequence of steps that are needed to complete a task. A program contains a huge number of simple instructions, and the computer executes them at great speed. The computer has no intelligence—it simply executes instruction sequences that have been prepared in advance.

To use a computer, no knowledge of programming is required. When you write a term paper with a word processor, that computer program has been developed by the manufacturer and is ready for you to use. That is only to be expected—you can drive a car without being a mechanic and toast bread without being an electrician.

A primary purpose of this book is to teach you how to design and implement computer programs. You will learn how to formulate instructions for all tasks that your programs need to execute.

Keep in mind that programming a sophisticated computer game or word processor requires a team of many highly skilled programmers, graphic artists, and other professionals. Your first programming efforts will be more mundane. The concepts and skills you learn in this book form an important foundation, but you should not expect to immediately produce professional software. A typical college degree in computer science or software engineering takes four years to complete; this book is intended as a text for an introductory course in such a program.

Many students find that there is an immense thrill even in simple programming tasks. It is an amazing experience to see the computer carry out a task precisely and quickly that would take you hours of drudgery.

SELF CHECK

1. What is required to play a music CD on a computer?
2. Why is a CD player less flexible than a computer?
3. Can a computer program develop the initiative to execute tasks in a better way than its programmers envisioned?

1.2 The Anatomy of a Computer

To understand the programming process, you need to have a rudimentary understanding of the building blocks that make up a computer. This section will describe a personal computer. Larger computers have faster, larger, or more powerful components, but they have fundamentally the same design.

> At the heart of the computer lies the central processing unit (CPU).

At the heart of the computer lies the **central processing unit (CPU)** (see Figure 1). It consists of a single *chip* (integrated circuit) or a small number of chips. A computer chip is a component with a plastic or metal housing, metal connectors,

Figure 1
Central Processing Unit

Figure 2
A Memory Module with
Memory Chips

and inside wiring made principally from silicon. For a CPU chip, the inside wiring is enormously complicated. For example, the Intel Core processor (a popular CPU for inexpensive laptops at the time of this writing) contains several hundred million structural elements called *transistors*—the elements that enable electrical signals to control other electrical signals, making automatic computing possible. The CPU locates and executes the program instructions; it carries out arithmetic operations such as addition, subtraction, multiplication, and division; and it fetches data from storage and input/output devices and sends data back.

The computer keeps data and programs in *storage*. There are two kinds of storage. *Primary storage*, also called *random-access memory* (RAM) or simply *memory*, is fast but expensive; it is made from memory chips (see Figure 2). Primary storage loses all its data when the power is turned off. *Secondary storage*, usually a *hard disk* (see Figure 3), provides less expensive storage that persists without electricity. A hard disk consists of rotating platters, which are coated with a magnetic material, and read/write heads, which can detect and change the patterns of varying magnetic flux on the platters.

> Data and programs are stored in primary storage (memory) and secondary storage (such as a hard disk).

Some computers are self-contained units, whereas others are interconnected through *networks*. Home computers are usually intermittently connected to the Internet via a dialup or broadband connection. The computers in your computer lab are probably permanently connected to a local area network. Through the network cabling, the computer can read programs from central storage locations or send data to other computers. For the user of a networked computer, it may not even be obvious which data reside on the computer itself and which are transmitted through the network.

Most computers have *removable storage* devices that can access data or programs on media such as memory sticks or optical disks.

To interact with a human user, a computer requires other peripheral devices. The computer transmits information to the user through a display screen, loudspeakers, and printers. The user can enter information and directions to the computer by using a keyboard or a pointing device such as a mouse.

Figure 3 A Hard Disk

The CPU, the RAM, and the electronics controlling the hard disk and other devices are interconnected through a set of electrical lines called a *bus.* Data travel along the bus from the system memory and peripheral devices to the CPU and back. Figure 4 shows a *motherboard,* which contains the CPU, the RAM, and connectors to peripheral devices.

Figure 4 A Motherboard

Figure 5 Schematic Diagram of a Computer

The CPU reads machine instructions from memory. The instructions direct it to communicate with memory, secondary storage, and peripheral devices.

Figure 5 gives a schematic overview of the architecture of a computer. Program instructions and data (such as text, numbers, audio, or video) are stored on the hard disk, on an optical disk (such as a DVD), or on a network. When a program is started, it is brought into memory where it can be read by the CPU. The CPU reads the program one instruction at a time. As directed by these instructions, the CPU reads data, modifies it, and writes it back to RAM or to secondary storage. Some program instructions will cause the CPU to interact with the devices that control the display screen or the speaker. Because these actions happen many times over and at great speed, the human user will perceive images and sound. Similarly, the CPU can send instructions to a printer to mark the paper with patterns of closely spaced dots, which a human recognizes as text characters and pictures. Some program instructions read user input from the keyboard or mouse. The program analyzes these inputs and then executes the next appropriate instructions.

SELF CHECK

4. Where is a program stored when it is not currently running?
5. Which part of the computer carries out arithmetic operations, such as addition and multiplication?

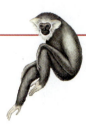

Random Fact 1.1

The ENIAC and the Dawn of Computing

The ENIAC (*electronic numerical integrator and computer*) was the first usable electronic computer. It was designed by J. Presper Eckert and John Mauchly at the University of Pennsylvania and was completed in 1946. Instead of transistors, which were not invented until two years after it was built, the ENIAC contained about 18,000 *vacuum tubes* in many cabinets housed in a large room. Vacuum tubes burned out at the rate of several tubes per day.

The ENIAC

An attendant with a shopping cart full of tubes constantly made the rounds and replaced defective ones. The computer was programmed by connecting wires on panels. Each wiring configuration would set up the computer for a particular problem. To have the computer work on a different problem, the wires had to be replugged.

Work on the ENIAC was supported by the U.S. Navy, which was interested in computations of ballistic tables that would give the trajectory of a projectile, depending on the wind resistance, initial velocity, and atmospheric conditions. To compute the trajectories, one must find the numerical solutions of certain differential equations; hence the name "numerical integrator". Before machines like ENIAC were developed, humans did this kind of work, and until the 1950s the word "computer" referred to these people. The ENIAC was later used for peaceful purposes, such as the tabulation of U.S. census data.

1.3 Translating Human-Readable Programs to Machine Code

Generally, machine code depends on the CPU type. However, the instruction set of the Java virtual machine (JVM) can be executed on different CPUs.

On the most basic level, computer instructions are extremely primitive. The processor executes *machine instructions*. CPUs from different vendors, such as the Intel Pentium or the Sun SPARC, have different sets of machine instructions. To enable Java applications to run on different CPUs without modification, Java programs contain machine instructions for a so-called "Java virtual machine" (JVM), an idealized CPU that is simulated by a program run on the actual CPU.

Instructions for actual and virtual machines are very simple and can be executed very quickly. A typical sequence of machine instructions is

1. Load the contents of memory location 40.
2. Load the value 100.
3. If the first value is greater than the second value, continue with the instruction that is stored in memory location 240.

Actually, machine instructions are encoded as numbers so that they can be stored in memory. On the Java virtual machine, this sequence of instructions is encoded as the sequence of numbers

```
21 40
16 100
163 240
```

When the virtual machine fetches this sequence of numbers, it decodes them and executes the associated sequence of commands.

How can you communicate the command sequence to the computer? The most direct method is to place the actual numbers into the computer memory. This is, in fact, how the very earliest computers worked. However, a long program is composed of thousands of individual commands, and it is tedious and error-prone to look up the numeric codes for all commands and manually place the codes into memory. As we said before, computers are really good at automating tedious and error-prone activities, and it did not take long for computer programmers to realize that computers could be harnessed to help in the programming process.

In the mid-1950s, *high-level* programming languages began to appear. In these languages, the programmer expresses the idea behind the task that needs to be performed, and a special computer program, called a **compiler**, translates the high-level description into machine instructions for a particular processor.

For example, in Java, the high-level programming language that you will use in this book, you might give the following instruction:

```
if (intRate > 100)
    System.out.println("Interest rate error");
```

This means, "If the interest rate is over 100, display the message *Interest rate error*". It is then the job of the compiler program to look at the sequence of characters if (intRate > 100) . . . and translate that into

```
21 40 16 100 163 240 . . .
```

Compilers are quite sophisticated programs. They translate logical statements, such as the if statement, into sequences of computations, tests, and jumps. They assign memory locations for **variables**—items of information identified by symbolic names—like intRate. In this course, we will generally take the existence of a compiler for granted. If you decide to become a professional computer scientist, you may well learn more about compiler-writing techniques later in your studies.

Because machine instructions are encoded as numbers, it is difficult to write programs in machine code.

High-level languages allow you to describe tasks at a higher conceptual level than machine code.

A compiler translates programs written in a high-level language into machine code.

SELF CHECK

6. What is the code for the Java virtual machine instruction "Load the contents of memory location 100"?

7. Does a person who uses a computer for office work ever run a compiler?

1.4 The Java Programming Language

Java was originally designed for programming consumer devices, but it was first used successfully to write Internet applets.

In 1991, a group led by James Gosling and Patrick Naughton at Sun Microsystems designed a programming language that they code-named "Green" for use in consumer devices, such as intelligent television "set-top" boxes. The language was designed to be simple and architecture neutral, so that it could be executed on a variety of hardware. No customer was ever found for this technology.

Gosling recounts that in 1994 the team realized, "We could write a really cool browser. It was one of the few things in the client/server mainstream that needed some of the weird things we'd done: architecture neutral, real-time, reliable, secure." Java was introduced to an enthusiastic crowd at the SunWorld exhibition in 1995.

Java was designed to be safe and portable, benefiting both Internet users and students.

Since then, Java has grown at a phenomenal rate. Programmers have embraced the language because it is simpler than its closest rival, C++. In addition, Java has a rich *library* that makes it possible to write portable programs that can bypass proprietary operating systems—a feature that was eagerly sought by those who wanted to be independent of those proprietary systems and was bitterly fought by their vendors. A "micro edition" and an "enterprise edition" of the Java library make Java programmers at home on hardware ranging from smart cards and cell phones to the largest Internet servers.

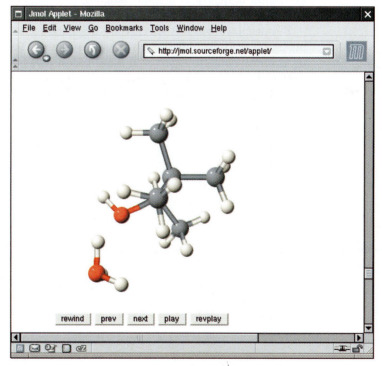

Figure 6 An Applet for Visualizing Molecules Running in a Browser (*http://jmol.sourceforge.net/applet/*)

Because Java was designed for the Internet, it has two attributes that make it very suitable for beginners: safety and portability. If you visit a web page that contains Java code (so-called *applets*—see Figure 6 for an example), the code automatically starts running. It is important that you can trust that applets are inherently safe. If an applet could do something evil, such as damaging data or reading personal information on your computer, then you would be in real danger every time you browsed the Web—an unscrupulous designer might put up a web page containing dangerous code that would execute on your machine as soon as you visited the page. The Java language has an assortment of security features that guarantees that no malicious applets can run on your computer. As an added benefit, these features also help you to learn the language faster. The Java virtual machine can catch many kinds of beginners' mistakes and report them accurately. (In contrast, many beginners' mistakes in the C++ language merely produce programs that act in random and confusing ways.) The other benefit of Java is portability. The same Java program will run, without change, on Windows, UNIX, Linux, or the Macintosh. This too is a requirement for applets. When you visit a web page, the web server that serves up the page contents has no idea what computer you are using to browse the Web. It simply returns the portable code that was generated by the Java compiler. The virtual machine on your computer executes that portable code. Again, there is a benefit for the student. You do not have to learn how to write programs for different platforms.

At this time, Java is firmly established as one of the most important languages for general-purpose programming as well as for computer science instruction. However, although Java is a good language for beginners, it is not perfect, for three reasons.

Because Java was not specifically designed for students, no thought was given to making it really simple to write basic programs. You must master a certain amount of technical detail to write even the simplest Java program. This is not a problem for professional programmers, but it is a drawback for beginning students. As you learn how to program in Java, there will be times when you will be asked to be

Table 1	Java Versions	
Version	**Year**	**Important New Features**
1.0	1996	
1.1	1997	Inner classes
1.2	1998	Swing, Collections framework
1.3	2000	Performance enhancements
1.4	2002	Assertions, XML support
5	2004	Generic classes, enhanced for loop, auto-boxing, enumerations, annotations
6	2006	Library improvements
7	2010	Small language changes and library improvements

satisfied with a preliminary explanation and wait for complete information in a later chapter.

Java was revised and extended many times during its life—see Table 1. In this book, we assume that you have Java version 5 or later.

Finally, you cannot hope to learn all of Java in one term. The Java language itself is relatively simple, but Java has a vast library with support for graphics, user interface design, cryptography, networking, sound, database storage, and many other purposes. Even expert Java programmers cannot hope to know the contents of the entire library—they just use those parts that they need for particular projects.

> Java has a very large library. Focus on learning those parts of the library that you need for your programming projects.

Using this book, you should expect to learn a good deal about the Java language and about the most important parts of the Java library. Keep in mind that the central goal of this book is not to make you memorize Java minutiae, but to teach you how to think about programming.

 **SELF CHECK**

8. What are the two most important benefits of the Java language?

9. How long does it take to learn the entire Java library?

1.5 The Structure of a Simple Program

When learning a new programming language, it is traditional to start with a "Hello, World!" program—a program that displays a greeting. Here is this program in Java:

ch01/hello/HelloPrinter.java

```java
1  public class HelloPrinter
2  {
3     public static void main(String[] args)
4     {
5        // Display a greeting in the console window
6
7        System.out.println("Hello, World!");
8     }
9  }
```

Program Run

```
Hello, World!
```

In the next section, you will see how to compile and run this program. But let us first understand how it is structured.

The line,

```
public class HelloPrinter
```

> Classes are the fundamental building blocks of Java programs.

starts a new **class**. Classes are a fundamental concept in Java, and you will begin to study them in Chapter 2. In Java, every program consists of one or more classes.

The word `public` denotes that the class is usable by the "public", that is, everywhere in your program. You will later encounter `private` features.

In Java, every source file can contain at most one public class, and the name of the public class must match the name of the file containing the class. For example, the class `HelloPrinter` *must* be contained in a file named `HelloPrinter.java`.

Every Java application contains a class with a main method. When the application starts, the instructions in the main method are executed.

The construction

```
public static void main(String[] args)
{
    . . .
}
```

declares a **method** called `main`. A method contains a collection of programming instructions that describe how to carry out a particular task. Every Java application must have a `main` method. Most Java programs contain other methods besides `main`, and you will see in Chapter 3 how to write other methods.

We will fully explain the word `static` and the declaration `String[] args` in Chapters 8 and 11. At this time, you should simply consider

```
public class ClassName
{
    public static void main(String[] args)
    {
        . . .
    }
}
```

as a part of the "plumbing" that is required to write any Java program.

The first line inside the `main` method is a **comment**:

```
// Display a greeting in the console window
```

Use comments to help human readers understand your program.

This comment is purely for the benefit of the human reader, to explain in more detail what the next statement does. Any text enclosed between `//` and the end of the line is completely ignored by the compiler. Comments are used to explain the program to other programmers or to yourself.

The instructions or **statements** in the *body* of the `main` method—that is, the statements inside the curly brackets ({})—are executed one by one. Each statement ends in a semicolon (;). Our method has a single statement:

```
System.out.println("Hello, World!");
```

This statement prints a line of text, namely "Hello, World!". However, there are many places where a program can send that text: to a window, to a file, or to a networked computer on the other side of the world. You need to specify that the destination is the *system output*—that is, a console window. The console window is represented in Java by an object called `System.out`. An **object** is an entity that you manipulate in your programs.

In Java, each object belongs to a class, and the class declares methods that specify what you can do with the objects. The `System.out` object belongs to the `PrintStream` class. The `PrintStream` class has a method called `println` for printing a line of text.

You do not have to implement this method—the programmers who wrote the Java library already did that for us—but you do need to *call* the method.

A method is called by specifying an object, the method name, and the method parameters.

Whenever you call a method in Java, you need to specify three items (see Figure 7):

1. The object that you want to use (in this case, `System.out`).
2. The name of the method you want to use (in this case, `println`).
3. A pair of parentheses, containing any other information the method needs (in this case, `"Hello, World!"`). The technical term for this information is a **parameter**.

Figure 7
Calling a Method

Object   Method   Parameters

```
System.out.println("Hello, World!")
```

A sequence of characters enclosed in double quotation marks

```
"Hello, World!"
```

A string is a
sequence of
characters enclosed
in quotation marks.

is called a **string**. You must enclose the contents of the string inside quotation marks so that the compiler knows you literally mean `"Hello, World!"`. There is a reason for this requirement. Suppose you need to print the word *main*. By enclosing it in quotation marks, `"main"`, the compiler knows you mean the sequence of characters m a i n, not the method named `main`. The rule is simply that you must enclose all text strings in quotation marks, so that the compiler considers them plain text and does not try to interpret them as program instructions.

You can also print numerical values. For example, the statement

```
System.out.println(3 + 4);
```

displays the number 7.

The `println` method prints a string or a number and then starts a new line. For example, the sequence of statements

```
System.out.println("Hello");
System.out.println("World!");
```

prints two lines of text:

```
Hello
World!
```

There is a second method, called `print`, that you can use to print an item without starting a new line. For example, the output of the two statements

```
System.out.print("00");
System.out.println(3 + 4);
```

is the single line

```
007
```

Syntax 1.1   Method Call

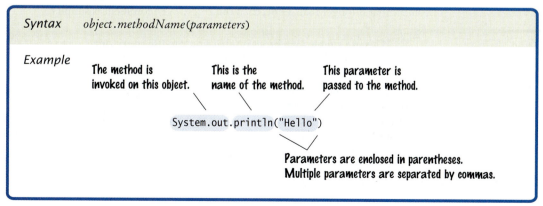

Syntax   *object.methodName(parameters)*

Example

The method is
invoked on this object.

This is the
name of the method.

This parameter is
passed to the method.

```
System.out.println("Hello")
```

Parameters are enclosed in parentheses.
Multiple parameters are separated by commas.

10. How would you modify the `HelloPrinter` program to print the words "Hello," and "World!" on two lines?

11. Would the program continue to work if you omitted the line starting with //?

12. What does the following set of statements print?

```
System.out.print("My lucky number is");
System.out.println(3 + 4 + 5);
```

Common Error 1.1

Omitting Semicolons

In Java every statement must end in a semicolon. Forgetting to type a semicolon is a common error. It confuses the compiler, because the compiler uses the semicolon to find where one statement ends and the next one starts. The compiler does not use line breaks or closing braces to recognize the end of statements. For example, the compiler considers

```
System.out.println("Hello")
System.out.println("World!");
```

a single statement, as if you had written

```
System.out.println("Hello") System.out.println("World!");
```

Then it doesn't understand that statement, because it does not expect the word `System` following the closing parenthesis after `"Hello"`. The remedy is simple. Scan every statement for a terminating semicolon, just as a writer would check that every English sentence ends in a period.

Special Topic 1.1

Alternative Comment Syntax

In Java there are two methods for writing comments. You already learned that the compiler ignores anything that you type between // and the end of the current line. The compiler also ignores any text between a /* and */.

```
/* A simple Java program */
```

The // comment is easier to type if the comment is only a single line long. If you have a comment that is longer than a line, then the /* . . . */ comment is simpler:

```
/*
   This is a simple Java program that you can use to try out
   your compiler and virtual machine.
*/
```

It would be somewhat tedious to add the // at the beginning of each line and to move them around whenever the text of the comment changes.

In this book, we use // for comments that will never grow beyond a line, and /* . . . */ for longer comments. If you prefer, you can always use the // style. The readers of your code will be grateful for *any* comments, no matter which style you use.

1.6 Compiling and Running a Java Program

> Set aside some time to become familiar with the computer system and the Java compiler that you will use for your class work.

Many students find that the tools that they need as programmers are very different from the software with which they familiar. You should spend some time making yourself familiar with your programming environment. Instructions for several popular environments are available in WileyPLUS.

Some Java development environments are very convenient to use. Enter the code in one window, click on a button to compile, and click on another button to execute your program. Error messages show up in a second window, and the program runs in a third window. With such an environment you are completely shielded from the details of the compilation process. On other systems you must carry out every step manually, by typing commands into a console window.

> An editor is a program for entering and modifying text, such as a Java program.

No matter which development environment you use, you begin your activity by typing in the program statements. The program that you use for entering and modifying the program text is called an *editor*. The first step for creating a Java program, such as the HelloPrinter program of the preceding section, is to start your editor. Make a new program file and call it HelloPrinter.java. (If your environment requires that you supply a project name in addition to the file name, use the name hello for the project.) Enter the program instructions exactly as they are given above. Alternatively, locate an electronic copy and paste it into your editor.

> Java is case sensitive. You must be careful about distinguishing between upper- and lowercase letters.

Java is **case sensitive**. You must enter upper- and lowercase letters in the same way as they appear in the program listing. You cannot type MAIN or PrintLn. If you are not careful, you will run into problems—see Common Error 1.2 on page 20. On the other hand, Java has *free-form layout*. You can use any number of spaces and line breaks to separate words. You can cram as many words as possible into each line,

```
public class HelloPrinter{public static void main(String[]
args){// Display a greeting in the console window
System.out.println("Hello, World!");}}
```

> Lay out your programs so that they are easy to read.

Of course, this is not a good idea. It is important to format your programs neatly so that you and other programmers can read them easily. We will give you recommendations for good layout throughout this book. Appendix L contains a summary of our recommendations.

Now find out how to run the test program. The message

```
Hello, World!
```

will appear somewhere on the screen (see Figures 8 and 9). The exact location depends on your programming environment.

Figure 8 Running the HelloPrinter Program in a Console Window

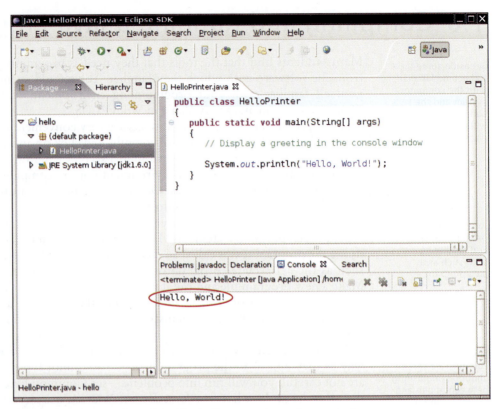

Figure 9 Running the `HelloPrinter` Program in an Integrated Development Environment

> The Java compiler translates source code into class files that contain instructions for the Java virtual machine.

Running your program takes two steps. (Some development environments automatically carry out both steps when you ask to run a program.)

The first step is to *compile* your program. The compiler translates the Java **source code** (that is, the statements that you wrote) into *class files*, which consist of virtual machine instructions and other information that is required for execution. The class files have the extension `.class`. For example, the virtual machine instructions for the

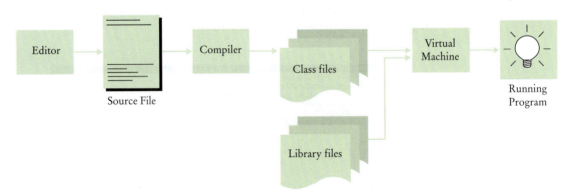

Figure 10 From Source Code to Running Program

`HelloPrinter` program are stored in a file `HelloPrinter.class`. Note that the compiler does not produce a class file if it has found errors in your program.

The class file contains merely the translation of the instructions that you wrote. That is not enough to actually run the program. To display a string in a window, quite a bit of low-level activity is necessary. The authors of the `System` and `PrintStream` classes (which declare the out object and the `println` method) have implemented all necessary actions and placed the required class files into a **library**. A library is a collection of code that has been programmed and translated by someone else, ready for you to use in your program.

The Java virtual machine loads the instructions for the program that you wrote, starts your program, and loads the necessary library files as they are required.

The steps of compiling and running your program are outlined in Figure 10.

The Java virtual machine loads program instructions from class files and library files.

SELF CHECK

13. Can you use a word processor for writing Java programs?

14. What do you expect to see when you load a class file into your text editor?

Productivity Hint 1.1

Understand the File System

In recent years, computers have become easier to use for home or office users. Many inessential details are now hidden from casual users. For example, many users simply place all their work inside a default folder (such as "Home" or "My Documents") and are blissfully ignorant about details of the file system.

For your programming work, you need to understand that files are stored in *folders* or **directories**, and that these file containers can be *nested*. That is, a folder can contain not only files but also other folders, which themselves can contain more files and folders (see Figure 11).

You need to know how to impose an organization on the data that you create. You also need to be able to locate files and inspect their contents.

If you are not comfortable with files and folders, be sure to set aside some time to learn about these concepts.

Figure 11
A Folder Hierarchy

Have a Backup Strategy

You will spend many hours typing Java program code and improving it. The resulting program files have some value, and you should treat them as you would other important property. A conscientious safety strategy is particularly important for computer files. They are more fragile than paper documents or other more tangible objects. It is easy to delete a file accidentally, and occasionally files are lost because of a computer malfunction. Unless you keep a copy, you must then retype the contents. Because you probably won't remember the entire file, you will likely find yourself spending almost as much time as you did to enter and improve it in the first place. This costs time, and it may cause you to miss deadlines. It is therefore crucial that you learn how to safeguard files and that you get in the habit of doing so *before* disaster strikes. You can make safety or *backup* copies of files by saving copies into another folder, on a thumb drive, or on the Internet.

> Develop a strategy for keeping backup copies of your work before disaster strikes.

Here are a few pointers to keep in mind.

- *Back up often.* Backing up a file takes only a few seconds, and you will hate yourself if you have to spend many hours recreating work that you easily could have saved.

- *Rotate backups.* Use more than one place for backups, and rotate between them. That is, first back up onto the first backup destination, then to the second and third, and then go back to the first. That way you always have three recent backups. Even if one of them has a defect, you can use one of the others.

- *Back up source files only.* The compiler translates the files that you write into files consisting of machine code. There is no need to back up the machine code files, because you can recreate them easily by running the compiler again. Focus your backup activity on those files that represent your effort. That way your backups won't fill up with files that you don't need.

- *Pay attention to the backup direction.* Backing up involves copying files from one place to another. It is important that you do this right—that is, copy from your work location to the backup location. If you do it the wrong way, you will overwrite a newer file with an older version.

- *Check your backups once in a while.* Double-check that your backups are where you think they are. There is nothing more frustrating than finding out that the backups are not there when you need them.

- *Relax before restoring.* When you lose a file and need to restore it from backup, you are likely to be in an unhappy, nervous state. Take a deep breath and think through the recovery process before you start. It is not uncommon for an agitated computer user to wipe out the last backup when trying to restore a damaged file.

1.7 Errors

Experiment a little with the `HelloPrinter` program. What happens if you make a typing error such as

```
System.ou.println("Hello, World!");
System.out.println("Hello, Word!");
```

> A compile-time error is a violation of the programming language rules that is detected by the compiler.

In the first case, the compiler will complain. It will say that it has no clue what you mean by `ou`. The exact wording of the error message is dependent on the compiler, but it might be something like "Cannot find symbol *ou*". This is a **compile-time**

error, also called a *syntax error*. Something is wrong according to the language rules and the compiler finds it. When the compiler finds one or more errors, it refuses to translate the program to Java virtual machine instructions, and as a consequence you have no program that you can run. You must fix the error and compile again. In fact, the compiler is quite picky, and it is common to go through several rounds of fixing compile-time errors before compilation succeeds for the first time.

If the compiler finds an error, it will not simply stop and give up. It will try to report as many errors as it can find, so you can fix them all at once.

Sometimes, an error throws the compiler off track. Suppose, for example, you forget the quotation marks around a string: `System.out.println(Hello, World!)`. The compiler will not complain about the missing quotation marks. Instead, it will report "Cannot find symbol Hello". It is up to you to realize that you need to enclose strings in quotation marks.

The error in the second line is of a different kind. The program will compile and run, but its output will be wrong. It will print

```
Hello, Word!
```

A run-time error causes a program to take an action that the programmer did not intend.

This is a **run-time error**, also called a *logic error*. The program is syntactically correct and does something, but it doesn't do what it is supposed to do.

This particular run-time error did not include an error message. It simply produced the wrong output. Some kinds of run-time errors are so severe that they generate an *exception*: an error message from the Java virtual machine. For example, if your program includes the statement

```
System.out.println(1/0);
```

you will get a run-time error message "Division by zero".

During program development, errors are unavoidable. Once a program is longer than a few lines, it requires superhuman concentration to enter it correctly without slipping up once. You will find yourself omitting semicolons or quotes more often than you would like, but the compiler will track down these problems for you.

Run-time errors are more troublesome. The compiler will not find them—in fact, the compiler will cheerfully translate any program as long as its syntax is correct—but the resulting program will do something wrong. It is the responsibility of the program author to test the program and find any run-time errors. Testing programs is an important topic that you will encounter many times in this book. Another important aspect of good craftsmanship is *defensive programming*: structuring programs and development processes in such a way that an error in one part of a program does not trigger a disastrous response.

The error examples that you saw so far were not difficult to diagnose or fix, but as you learn more sophisticated programming techniques, there will also be much more room for error. It is an uncomfortable fact that locating all errors in a program is very difficult. Even if you can observe that a program exhibits faulty behavior, it may not at all be obvious what part of the program caused it and how you can fix it. Special software tools (so-called **debuggers**) let you trace through a program to find *bugs*—that is, run-time errors. In Chapter 6 you will learn how to use a debugger effectively.

Note that these errors are different from the types of errors that you are likely to make in calculations. If you total up a column of numbers, you may miss a minus sign or accidentally drop a carry, perhaps because you are bored or tired. Computers do not make these kinds of errors.

This book uses a three-part error management strategy. First, you will learn about common errors and how to avoid them. Then you will learn defensive programming strategies to minimize the likelihood and impact of errors. Finally, you will learn testing and debugging strategies to flush out those errors that remain.

SELF CHECK

15. Suppose you omit the `//` characters from the `HelloPrinter.java` program but not the remainder of the comment. Will you get a compile-time error or a run-time error?

16. When you used your computer, you may have experienced a program that "crashed" (quit spontaneously) or "hung" (failed to respond to your input). Is that behavior a compile-time error or a run-time error?

17. Why can't you test a program for run-time errors when it has compiler errors?

Common Error 1.2

Misspelling Words

If you accidentally misspell a word, then strange things may happen, and it may not always be completely obvious from the error messages what went wrong. Here is a good example of how simple spelling errors can cause trouble:

```java
public class HelloPrinter
{
    public static void Main(String[] args)
    {
        System.out.println("Hello, World!");
    }
}
```

This class declares a method called `Main`. The compiler will not consider this to be the same as the `main` method, because `Main` starts with an uppercase letter and the Java language is case sensitive. Upper- and lowercase letters are considered to be completely different from each other, and to the compiler `Main` is no better match for `main` than `rain`. The compiler will cheerfully compile your `Main` method, but when the Java virtual machine executes the compiled file, it will complain about the missing `main` method and refuse to run the program. Of course, the message "missing main method" should give you a clue where to look for the error.

If you get an error message that seems to indicate that the compiler is on the wrong track, it is a good idea to check for spelling and capitalization. If you misspell the name of a symbol (for example, `ou` instead of `out`), the compiler will produce an error message such as "Cannot find symbol ou". That error message is usually a good clue that you made a spelling error.

1.8 Algorithms

You will soon learn how to program calculations and decision making in Java. But before we look at the mechanics of implementing computations in the next chapter, let's consider the planning process that precedes implementation.

You may have run across advertisements that encourage you to pay for a computerized service that matches you up with a love partner. Think how this might work. You fill out a form and send it in. Others do the same. The data are processed by a computer program. Is it reasonable to assume that the computer can perform the task of finding the best match for you? Suppose your younger brother, not the computer, had all the forms on his desk. What instructions could you give him? You can't say, "Find the best-looking person who likes inline skating and browsing the Internet". There is no objective standard for good looks, and your brother's opinion (or that of a computer program analyzing the digitized photo) will likely be different from yours. If you can't give written instructions for someone to solve the problem, there is no way the computer can magically find the right solution. The computer can only do what you tell it to do. It just does it faster, without getting bored or exhausted.

For that reason, a computerized match-making service cannot guarantee to find the optimal match for you. Instead, it may present a set of potential partners who share common interests with you. That is a task that a computer program can solve.

Now consider the following investment problem:

> You put $10,000 into a bank account that earns 5 percent interest per year. How many years does it take for the account balance to be double the original?

Could you solve this problem by hand? Sure, you could. You figure out the balance as follows:

year	balance
0	10000
1	10000.00 x 1.05 = 10500.00
2	10500.00 x 1.05 = 11025.00
3	11025.00 x 1.05 = 11576.25
4	11576.25 x 1.05 = 12155.06

You keep going until the balance is at least $20,000. Then the last number in the year column is the answer.

Of course, carrying out this computation is intensely boring to you or your younger brother. But computers are very good at carrying out repetitive calculations quickly and flawlessly. What is important to the computer is a description of the steps for finding the solution. Each step must be clear and unambiguous, requiring no guesswork. Here is such a description:

Start with a year value of 0 and a balance of $10,000.

year	balance
0	10000

Repeat the following steps while the balance is less than $20,000.
    Add 1 to the year value.
    Multiply the balance value by 1.05 (a 5 percent increase).

year	balance
0	10000
1	10500
14	19799.32
⑮	20789.28

Report the final year value as the answer.

Of course, these steps are not yet in a language that a computer can understand, but you will soon learn how to formulate them in Java. This informal description is called **pseudocode**.

There are no strict requirements for pseudocode because it is read by human readers, not a computer program. Here are the kinds of pseudocode statements that we will use in this book:

> Pseudocode is an informal description of a sequence of steps for solving a problem.

- Use statements such as the following to describe how a value is set or changed:

  total cost = purchase price + operating cost

  or

  Multiply the balance value by 1.05.

  or

  Remove the first and last character from the word.

- Describe decisions and repetitions as follows:

  If total cost 1 < total cost 2

  or

  While the balance is less than $20,000

  or

  For each picture in the sequence

  Use indentation to indicate which statements should be selected or repeated.

  For each car
      operating cost = 10 x annual fuel cost
      total cost = purchase price + operating cost

  Here, the indentation indicates that both statements should be executed for each car.

- Indicate results with statements such as

  Choose car1.
  Report the final year value as the answer.

The exact wording is not important. What is important is that the pseudocode describes a sequence of steps that is

- Unambiguous
- Executable
- Terminating

The step sequence is *unambiguous* when there are precise instructions for what to do at each step and where to go next. There is no room for guesswork or personal opinion. A step is *executable* when it can be carried out in practice. Had we asked to use the actual interest rate that will be charged in years to come, and not a fixed rate of 5 percent per year, that step would not have been executable, because there is no way for anyone to know what that interest rate will be. A sequence of steps is *terminating* if it will eventually come to an end. In our example, it requires a bit of thought to see that the sequence will not go on forever: With every step, the balance goes up by at least $500, so eventually it must reach $20,000.

An algorithm for solving a problem is a sequence of steps that is unambiguous, executable, and terminating.

A sequence of steps that is unambiguous, executable, and terminating is called an **algorithm**. We have found an algorithm to solve our investment problem, and thus we can find the solution by programming a computer. The existence of an algorithm is an essential prerequisite for programming a task. You need to first discover and describe an algorithm for the task that you want to solve before you start programming (see Figure 12).

> Understand the problem
>
> Develop and describe an algorithm
>
> Test the algorithm with different inputs
>
> Translate the algorithm into Java
>
> Compile and test your program

Figure 12
The Program Development Process

SELF CHECK

18. Suppose the interest rate was 20 percent. How long would it take for the investment to double?

19. Suppose your cell phone carrier charges you $29.95 for up to 300 minutes of calls, and $0.45 for each additional minute, plus 12.5 percent taxes and fees. Give an algorithm to compute the monthly charge for a given number of minutes.

How To 1.1   Developing and Describing an Algorithm

This is the first of many "How To" sections in this book that give you step-by-step procedures for carrying out important tasks in developing computer programs.

Before you are ready to write a program in Java, you need to develop an algorithm—a method for arriving at a solution for a particular problem. Describe the algorithm in pseudocode: a sequence of precise steps formulated in English.

For example, consider this problem: You have the choice of buying two cars. One is more fuel efficient than the other, but also more expensive. You know the price and fuel efficiency (in miles per gallon, mpg) of both cars. You plan to keep the car for ten years. Assume a price of $4 per gallon of gas and usage of 15,000 miles per year. You will pay cash for the car and not worry about financing costs. Which car is the better deal?

Step 1 Determine the inputs and outputs.

In our sample problem, we have these inputs:

- purchase price1 and fuel efficiency1, the price and fuel efficiency (in mpg) of the first car.
- purchase price2 and fuel efficiency2, the price and fuel efficiency of the second car.

We simply want to know which car is the better buy. That is the desired output.

Step 2 Break down the problem into smaller tasks.

For each car, we need to know the total cost of driving it. Let's do this computation separately for each car. Once we have the total cost for each car, we can decide which car is the better deal.

The total cost for each car is purchase price + operating cost.

We assume a constant usage and gas price for ten years, so the operating cost depends on the cost of driving the car for one year.

The operating cost is 10 x annual fuel cost.

The annual fuel cost is price per gallon x annual fuel consumed.

The annual fuel consumed is annual miles driven / fuel efficiency. For example, if you drive the car for 15,000 miles and the fuel efficiency is 15 miles/gallon, the car consumes 1,000 gallons.

Step 3 Describe each subtask in pseudocode.

In your description, arrange the steps so that any intermediate values are computed before they are needed in other computations. For example, list the step

total cost = purchase price + operating cost

after you have computed operating cost.

Here is the algorithm for deciding which car to buy.

```
For each car, compute the total cost as follows:
    annual fuel consumed = annual miles driven / fuel efficiency
    annual fuel cost = price per gallon x annual fuel consumed
    operating cost = 10 x annual fuel cost
    total cost = purchase price + operating cost
If total cost1 < total cost2
    Choose car1.
Else
    Choose car2.
```

Step 4 Test your pseudocode by working problems.

We will use these sample values:

Car 1: $25,000, 50 miles/gallon
Car 2: $20,000, 30 miles/gallon

Here is the calculation for the cost of the first car.

```
annual fuel consumed = annual miles driven / fuel efficiency = 15000 / 50 = 300
annual fuel cost = price per gallon x annual fuel consumed = 4 x 300 = 1200
operating cost = 10 x annual fuel cost = 10 x 1200 = 12000
total cost = purchase price + operating cost = 25000 + 12000 = 37000
```

Similarly, the total cost for the second car is $40,000. Therefore, the output of the algorithm is to choose car 1.

⊕ *Worked
Example 1.1*

Writing an Algorithm for Tiling a Floor

This Worked Example shows how to develop an algorithm for laying tile in an alternating pattern of colors.

Summary of Learning Objectives

Define "computer program" and "programming".

- A computer must be programmed to perform tasks. Different tasks require different programs.
- A computer program executes a sequence of very basic instructions in rapid succession.
- A computer program contains the instruction sequences for all tasks that it can execute.

Describe the components of a computer.

- At the heart of the computer lies the central processing unit (CPU).
- Data and programs are stored in primary storage (memory) and secondary storage (such as a hard disk).
- The CPU reads machine instructions from memory. The instructions direct it to communicate with memory, secondary storage, and peripheral devices.

Describe the process of translating high-level languages to machine code.

- Generally, machine code depends on the CPU type. However, the instruction set of the Java virtual machine (JVM) can be executed on different CPUs.
- Because machine instructions are encoded as numbers, it is difficult to write programs in machine code.
- High-level languages allow you to describe tasks at a higher conceptual level than machine code.
- A compiler translates programs written in a high-level language into machine code.

Describe the history and design principles of the Java programming language.

- Java was originally designed for programming consumer devices, but it was first used successfully to write Internet applets.
- Java was designed to be safe and portable, benefiting both Internet users and students.
- Java has a very large library. Focus on learning those parts of the library that you need for your programming projects.

Describe the building blocks of a simple program and the structure of a method call.

- Classes are the fundamental building blocks of Java programs.
- Every Java application contains a class with a main method. When the application starts, the instructions in the main method are executed.
- Use comments to help human readers understand your program.

⊕ Available online in WileyPLUS and at www.wiley.com/college/horstmann.

- A method is called by specifying an object, the method name, and the method parameters.
- A string is a sequence of characters enclosed in quotation marks.

Use your programming environment to write and run Java programs.

- Set aside some time to become familiar with the computer system and the Java compiler that you will use for your class work.
- An editor is a program for entering and modifying text, such as a Java program.
- Java is case sensitive. You must be careful about distinguishing between upper- and lowercase letters.
- Lay out your programs so that they are easy to read.
- The Java compiler translates source code into class files that contain instructions for the Java virtual machine.
- The Java virtual machine loads program instructions from class files and library files.
- Develop a strategy for keeping backup copies of your work before disaster strikes.

Classify program errors as compile-time and run-time errors.

- A compile-time error is a violation of the programming language rules that is detected by the compiler.
- A run-time error causes a program to take an action that the programmer did not intend.

Write pseudocode for simple algorithms.

- Pseudocode is an informal description of a sequence of steps for solving a problem.
- An algorithm for solving a problem is a sequence of steps that is unambiguous, executable, and terminating.

Classes, Objects, and Methods Introduced in this Chapter

Here is a list of all classes, objects, and methods introduced in this chapter. Turn to the documentation in Appendix D for more information.

```
java.io.PrintStream          class
    print   method
    println method
```

```
java.lang.System    class
    out   object
```

Media Resources

- ***Worked Example*** Writing an Algorithm for Tiling a Floor
- ➕ Practice Quiz
- ➕ Code Completion Exercises

www.wiley.com/
college/
horstmann

Review Exercises

★   **R1.1** Explain the difference between using a computer program and programming a computer.

★   **R1.2** What distinguishes a computer from a typical household appliance?

★★   **R1.3** Describe *exactly* what steps you would take to back up your work after you have typed in the HelloPrinter.java program.

★★   **R1.4** On your own computer or on a lab computer, find the exact location (folder or directory name) of

     a. The sample file HelloPrinter.java, which you wrote with the editor.

     b. The Java program launcher java.exe or java.

     c. The library file rt.jar that contains the run-time library.

★   **R1.5** How do you discover syntax errors? How do you discover logic errors?

★★   **R1.6** Write three versions of the HelloPrinter.java program that have different compile-time errors. Write a version that has a run-time error.

★★★ **R1.7** What do the following statements print? Don't guess; write programs to find out.

     a. System.out.println("3 + 4");

     b. System.out.println(3 + 4);

     c. System.out.println(3 + "4");

★★   **R1.8** Write an algorithm to settle the following question: A bank account starts out with $10,000. Interest is compounded monthly at 6 percent per year (0.5 percent per month). Every month, $500 is withdrawn to meet college expenses. After how many years is the account depleted?

★★★ **R1.9** Consider the question in Exercise R1.8. Suppose the numbers ($10,000, 6 percent, $500) were user selectable. Are there values for which the algorithm you developed would not terminate? If so, change the algorithm to make sure it always terminates.

★★★ **R1.10** In order to estimate the cost of painting a house, a painter needs to know the surface area of the exterior. Develop an algorithm for computing that value. Your inputs are the width, length, and height of the house, the number of windows and doors, and their dimensions. (Assume the windows and doors have a uniform size.)

★★   **R1.11** You want to decide whether you should drive your car to work or take the train. You know the one-way distance from your home to your place of work, and the fuel efficiency of your car (in miles per gallon). You also know the one-way price of a train ticket. You assume the cost of gas at $4 per gallon, and car maintenance at 5 cents per mile. Write an algorithm to decide which commute is cheaper.

★★   **R1.12** You want to find out which fraction of your car use is for commuting to work, and which is for personal use. You know the one-way distance from your home to your place of work. For a particular period, you recorded the beginning and ending mileage on the odometer and the number of work days. Write an algorithm to settle this question.

★ **R1.13** In the problem described in How To 1.1 on page 23, you made assumptions about the price of gas and the annual usage. Ideally, you would like to know which car is the better deal without making these assumptions. Why can't a computer program solve that problem?

Programming Exercises

★ **P1.1** Write a program `NamePrinter` that displays your name inside a box on the console screen, like this:

```
+----+
|Dave|
+----+
```

Do your best to approximate lines with characters, such as |, -, and +.

★★★ **P1.2** Write a program that prints your name in large letters, such as

```
*   *    **    ****    ****    *     *
*   *   *  *   *   *    *   *    *   *
*****   *    *  ****    ****      * *
*   *   ******  *   *    *  *       *
*   *   *    *  *   *    *   *      *
```

★ **P1.3** Write a program `FacePrinter` that prints a face, using text characters, hopefully better looking than this one:

```
 /////
| o o |
(|  ^  |)
 | [_] |
  -----
```

Use *comments* to indicate the statements that print the hair, ears, mouth, and so on.

★★★ **P1.4** Write a program that prints an animal speaking a greeting, similar to (but different from) the following

```
/\_/\      -----
( ' ' )  / Hello \
(  -  ) <  Junior |
| | |    \ Coder!/
(_|_)      -----
```

★ **P1.5** Write a program `TicTacToeBoardPrinter` that prints a tic-tac-toe board:

```
+---+---+---+
|   |   |   |
+---+---+---+
|   |   |   |
+---+---+---+
|   |   |   |
+---+---+---+
```

★ **P1.6** Write a program StaircasePrinter that prints a staircase:

★ **P1.7** Write a program that prints three items, such as the names of your three best friends or favorite movies, on three separate lines.

★★ **P1.8** Write a program that computes the sum of the first ten positive integers, $1 + 2 + \cdots + 10$. *Hint:* Write a program of the form

```
public class Sum10
{
    public static void main(String[] args)
    {
        System.out.println(           );
    }
}
```

★★ **P1.9** Type in and run the following program:

```
import javax.swing.JOptionPane;

public class DialogViewer
{
    public static void main(String[] args)
    {
        JOptionPane.showMessageDialog(null, "Hello, World!");
        System.exit(0);
    }
}
```

Then modify the program to show the message "Hello, *your name!*".

★★ **P1.10** Type in and run the following program:

```
import javax.swing.JOptionPane;

public class DialogViewer
{
    public static void main(String[] args)
    {
        String name = JOptionPane.showInputDialog("What is your name?");
        System.out.println(name);
        System.exit(0);
    }
}
```

Then modify the program to print "Hello, *name!*", displaying the name that the user typed in.

★★ **P1.11** Run the following program:

```
import java.net.URL;
import javax.swing.ImageIcon;
import javax.swing.JOptionPane;

public class Test
{
    public static void main(String[] args) throws Exception
    {
        URL imageLocation = new URL(
            "http://horstmann.com/bigjava/duke.gif");
        JOptionPane.showMessageDialog(null, "Hello", "Title",
            JOptionPane.PLAIN_MESSAGE, new ImageIcon(imageLocation));
        System.exit(0);
    }
}
```

Then modify it to show a different greeting and image.

Programming Projects

Project 1.1 This project builds on Exercises P1.9 and P1.10. Your program should read the user's name, then show a sequence of two dialog boxes:

- First, an input dialog box that asks: "What would you like me to do?"
- Then a message dialog box that says: "I'm sorry, *your name*. I'm afraid I can't do that."

Answers to Self-Check Questions

1. A program that reads the data on the CD and sends output to the speakers and the screen.
2. A CD player can do one thing—play music CDs. It cannot execute programs.
3. No—the program simply executes the instruction sequences that the programmers have prepared in advance.
4. In secondary storage, typically a hard disk.
5. The central processing unit.
6. 21 100
7. No—a compiler is intended for programmers, to translate high-level programming instructions into machine code.
8. Safety and portability.
9. No one person can learn the entire library—it is too large.
10. `System.out.println("Hello,"); System.out.println("World!");`
11. Yes—the line starting with // is a comment, intended for human readers. The compiler ignores comments.
12. The printout is `My lucky number is12`. It would be a good idea to add a space after the is.

13. Yes, but you must remember to save your file as "plain text."

14. A sequence of random characters, some funny-looking. Class files contain virtual machine instructions that are encoded as binary numbers.

15. A compile-time error. The compiler will not know what to do with the word `Display`.

16. It is a run-time error. After all, the program had been compiled in order for you to run it.

17. When a program has compiler errors, no class file is produced, and there is nothing to run.

18. 4 years:

0 10,000

1 12,000

2 14,400

3 17,280

4 20,736

19. Is the number of minutes at most 300?

a. If so, the answer is $29.95 × 1.125 = $33.70.

b. If not,

1. Compute the difference: (number of minutes) − 300.

2. Multiply that difference by 0.45.

3. Add $29.95.

4. Multiply the total by 1.125. That is the answer.

Chapter 2

Using Objects

CHAPTER GOALS

- To learn about variables
- To understand the concepts of classes and objects
- To be able to call methods
- To learn about parameters and return values
- To be able to browse the API documentation
- **T** To implement test programs
- To understand the difference between objects and object references
- **G** To write programs that display simple shapes

Most useful programs don't just manipulate numbers and strings.
Instead, they deal with data items that are more complex and that more closely represent entities in the real world. Examples of these data items include bank accounts, employee records, and graphical shapes.

The Java language is ideally suited for designing and manipulating such data items, or **objects**. In Java, you implement **classes** that describe the behavior of these objects. In this chapter, you will learn how to manipulate objects that belong to classes that have already been implemented. This knowledge will prepare you for the next chapter in which you will learn how to implement your own classes.

CHAPTER CONTENTS

2.1 Types

Before we start with the main topic of this chapter, we need to go over some basic programming terminology. In the first three sections of this chapter, you will learn about the concepts of types, variables, and assignment.

A type specifies a set of values and the operations that can be carried out with the values.

A computer program processes values: numbers, strings, and more complex data items. In Java, every value has a **type**. For example, the number 13 has the type int (an abbreviation for "integer"), "Hello, World" has the type String, and the object System.out has the type PrintStream. The type tells you what operations you can carry out with the values. For example, you can compute the sum or product of any two integers. You can call println on any object of type PrintStream.

Java has separate types for **integers** and **floating-point numbers**. Integers are whole numbers; floating-point numbers can have fractional parts. For example, 13 is an integer and 1.3 is a floating-point number.

The name "floating-point" describes the representation of the number in the computer as a sequence of the significant digits and an indication of the position of the decimal point. For example, the numbers 13000.0, 1.3, 0.00013 all have the same decimal digits: 13. When a floating-point number is multiplied or divided by 10, only the position of the decimal point changes; it "floats". This representation is related to the "scientific" notation 1.3×10^{-4}. (Actually, the computer represents numbers in base 2, not base 10, but the principle is the same.)

The double type denotes floating-point numbers that can have fractional parts.

If you need to process numbers with a fractional part, you should use the type called double, which stands for "double precision floating-point number". Think of a number in double format as any number that can appear in the display panel of a calculator, such as 1.3 or –0.333333333.

	Table 1 Number Literals in Java		
Number	**Type**	**Comment**	
6	`int`	An integer has no fractional part.	
–6	`int`	Integers can be negative.	
0	`int`	Zero is an integer.	
0.5	`double`	A number with a fractional part has type `double`.	
1.0	`double`	An integer with a fractional part .0 has type `double`.	
1E6	`double`	A number in exponential notation: 1×10^6 or 1000000. Numbers in exponential notation always have type `double`.	
2.96E-2	`double`	Negative exponent: $2.96 \times 10^{-2} = 2.96 / 100 = 0.0296$	
🚫 100,000		**Error:** Do not use a comma as a decimal separator.	
🚫 3 1/2		**Error:** Do not use fractions; use decimal notation: 3.5.	

When a value such as 13 or 1.3 occurs in a Java program, it is called a **number literal**. Do not use commas when you write number literals in Java. For example, 13,000 must be written as 13000. To write numbers in exponential notation in Java, use the notation En instead of "$\times 10^n$". For example, 1.3×10^{-4} is written as 1.3E-4. Table 1 shows how to write integer and floating-point literals in Java.

You may wonder why Java has separate integer and floating-point number types. Pocket calculators don't need a separate integer type; they use floating-point numbers for all calculations. However, integers have several advantages over floating-point numbers. They take less storage space, are processed faster, and don't cause rounding errors. You will want to use the `int` type for quantities that can never have fractional parts, such as the length of a string. Use the `double` type for quantities that can have fractional parts, such as a grade point average.

There are several other number types in Java that are not as commonly used. We will discuss these types in Chapter 4. For most programs in this book, however, the `int` and `double` types are all you need for processing numbers.

In Java, the number types are primitive types, and numbers are not objects.

In Java, the number types (`int`, `double`, and the less commonly used types) are **primitive types**. Numbers are not objects. The number types have no methods.

However, you can combine numbers with operators such as + and -, as in 10 + n or n - 1. To multiply two numbers, use the * operator. For example, $10 \times n$ is written as 10 * n.

A combination of variables, literals, operators, and/or methods (which you will see in Section 2.4) is called an *expression*. A typical example of an expression is

```
x + y * 2
```

Numbers can be combined by arithmetic operators such as +, -, and *.

As in mathematics, the * operator binds more strongly than the + operator. That is, x + y * 2 means the sum of x and y * 2. If you want to multiply the sum of x and y by 2, use parentheses:

```
(x + y) * 2
```

1. What are the types of the values 0 and "0"?

2. Which number type would you use for storing the area of a circle?

3. Why is the expression 13.println() an error?

4. Write an expression to compute the average of the values x and y.

2.2 Variables

You often want to store values so that you can use them at a later time. To remember a value, you need to hold it in a **variable**. A variable is a storage location in the computer's memory that has a type, name, and contents. For example, here we declare three variables:

```
String greeting = "Hello, World!";
PrintStream printer = System.out;
int width = 20;
```

> You use variables to store values that you want to use at a later time. A variable has a type, a name, and a value.

The first variable is called greeting. It can be used to store String values, and it is set to the value "Hello, World!". The second variable, printer, stores a PrintStream value, and the third stores an integer.

Variables can be used in place of the values that they store:

```
printer.println(greeting); // Same as System.out.println("Hello, World!")
printer.println(width); // Same as System.out.println(20)
```

When you declare your own variables, you need to make two decisions.

- What type should you use for the variable?
- What name should you give the variable?

The type depends on the intended use. If you need to store a string, use the String type for your variable. If you need a number, choose the int or double type.

It is an error to store a value whose type does not match the type of the variable. For example, the following is an error:

```
String greeting = 20; // ERROR: Types don't match
```

Table 2 Variable Declarations in Java

Variable Name	Comment
`int width = 10;`	Declares an integer variable and initializes it with 10.
`int area = width * height;`	The initial value can depend on other variables. (Of course, width and height must have been previously declared.)
🚫 `height = 5;`	**Error:** The type is missing. This statement is not a declaration but an assignment of a new value to an existing variable—see Section 2.3.
🚫 `int height = "5";`	**Error:** You cannot initialize a number with a string.
`int width, height;`	Declares two integer variables in a single statement. In this book, we will declare each variable in a separate statement.

You cannot use a `String` variable to store an integer. The compiler checks type mismatches to protect you from errors.

When deciding on a name for a variable, you should make a choice that describes the purpose of the variable. For example, the variable name `greeting` is a better choice than the name `g`.

An *identifier* is the name of a variable, method, or class. Java imposes the following rules for identifiers:

> Identifiers for variables, methods, and classes are composed of letters, digits, and the underscore character.

- Identifiers can be made up of letters, digits, and the underscore (_) and dollar sign ($) characters. They cannot start with a digit, though.
- You cannot use spaces or symbols such as ? or %.
- Furthermore, you cannot use **reserved words**, such as `public`, as names; these words are reserved exclusively for their special Java meanings. (See Appendix C for all reserved words in Java.)

These are firm rules of the Java language. If you violate one of them, the compiler will report an error. Moreover, there are a couple of *conventions* that you should follow so that other programmers will find your programs easy to read:

> By convention, variable names should start with a lowercase letter.

- Variable and method names should start with a lowercase letter. It is OK to use an occasional uppercase letter, such as `farewellMessage`. This mixture of lowercase and uppercase letters is sometimes called "camel case" because the uppercase letters stick out like the humps of a camel.
- Class names should start with an uppercase letter. For example, `Greeting` would be an appropriate name for a class, but not for a variable.
- You should not use the $ symbol in names. It is intended for names that are automatically generated by tools.

If you violate these conventions, the compiler won't complain, but you will confuse other programmers who read your code.

Syntax 2.1   Variable Declaration

Syntax   *typeName variableName* = *value*;
            or
            typeName variableName;

Example

See pages 37–38 for rules and examples of valid names.

The type specifies what can be done with values stored in this variable.

`String greeting = "Hello, Dave!";`

A variable declaration ends with a semicolon.

Use a descriptive variable name. See page 38.

Supplying an initial value is optional, but it is usually a good idea.

Table 3	Variable Names in Java
Variable Name	**Comment**
farewellMessage	Use "camel case" for variable names consisting of multiple words.
x	In mathematics, you use short variable names such as x or y. This is legal in Java, but not very common, because it can make programs harder to understand.
⚠ Greeting	**Caution:** Variable names are case-sensitive. This variable name is different from greeting.
🚫 6pack	**Error:** Variable names cannot start with a number.
🚫 farewell message	**Error:** Variable names cannot contain spaces.
🚫 public	**Error:** You cannot use a reserved word as a variable name.

Table 3 shows examples of legal and illegal variable names in Java.

S E L F   C H E C K

5. Which of the following are legal identifiers?

```
Greeting1
g
void
101dalmatians
Hello, World
<greeting>
```

6. Declare a variable to hold your name. Use camel case in the variable name.

Quality Tip 2.1

Choose Descriptive Names for Variables

In algebra, variable names are usually just one letter long, such as p or A, maybe with a subscript such as p_1. You might be tempted to save yourself a lot of typing by using short variable names in your Java programs:

```
int A = w * h;
```

Compare this with the following statement:

```
int area = width * height;
```

The advantage is obvious. Reading width is much easier than reading w and then figuring out that it must mean "width".

In practical programming, descriptive variable names are particularly important when programs are written by more than one person. It may be obvious to you that w stands for width, but is it obvious to the person who needs to update your code years later? For that matter, will you yourself remember what w means when you look at the code a month from now?

2.3 The Assignment Operator

Use the assignment operator (=) to change the value of a variable.

You can change the value of a variable with the assignment operator (=). For example, consider the variable declaration

```
int width = 10;
```

If you want to change the value of the variable, simply assign the new value:

```
width = 20;
```

The assignment replaces the original value of the variable (see Figure 1).

Figure 1
Assigning a New Value to a Variable

It is an error to use a variable that has never had a value assigned to it. For example, the following assignment statement has an error:

```
int height;
width = height;    // ERROR—uninitialized variable height
```

The compiler will complain about an "uninitialized variable" when you use a variable that has never been assigned a value. (See Figure 2.)

Figure 2
An Uninitialized Variable

Syntax 2.2   Assignment

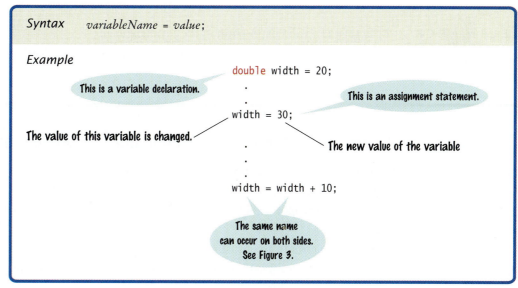

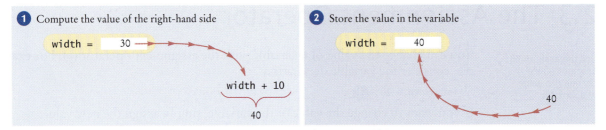

Figure 3 Executing the Statement `width = width + 10`

The remedy is to assign a value to the variable before you use it:

```
int height = 30;
width = height; // OK
```

Or, even better, initialize the variable when you declare it.

```
int height = 30;
int width = height; // OK
```

The right-hand side of the = symbol can be a mathematical expression. For example,

```
width = height + 10;
```

This means "compute the value of `height + 10` and store that value in the variable `width`".

In the Java programming language, the = operator denotes an *action*, to replace the value of a variable. This usage differs from the mathematical usage of the = symbol, as a statement about equality. For example, in Java, the following statement is entirely legal:

```
width = width + 10;
```

This means "compute the value of `width + 10` ❶ and store that value in the variable `width` ❷" (see Figure 3).

In Java, it is not a problem that the variable `width` is used on both sides of the = symbol. Of course, in mathematics, the equation *width = width* + 10 has no solution.

SELF CHECK

7. Is `12 = 12` a valid expression in the Java language?

8. How do you change the value of the `greeting` variable to `"Hello, Nina!"`?

Common Error 2.1

Confusing Variable Declarations and Assignment Statements

Suppose your program declares a variable as follows:

```
int width = 20;
```

If you want to change the value of the variable, you use an assignment statement:

```
width = 30;
```

It is a common error to accidentally use another variable declaration:

```
int width = 30; // ERROR—starts with int and is therefore a declaration
```

But there is already a variable named width. The compiler will complain that you are trying to declare another variable with the same name.

2.4   Objects, Classes, and Methods

> Objects are entities in your program that you manipulate by calling methods.

> A method is a sequence of instructions that accesses the data of an object.

We now come to the main purpose of this chapter: a closer understanding of objects. An **object** is a value that you can manipulate by calling one or more of its **methods**. A method consists of a sequence of instructions that can access the internal data of an object. When you call the method, you do not know exactly what those instructions are, or even how the object is organized internally. However, the behavior of the method is well-defined, and that is what matters to us when we use it.

For example, you saw in Chapter 1 that System.out refers to an object. You manipulate it by calling the println method. When the println method is called, some activities occur inside the object, and the ultimate effect is that text appears in the console window. You don't know how that happens, and that's OK. What matters is that the method carries out the work that you requested.

Figure 4 shows a representation of the System.out object. The internal data is symbolized by a sequence of zeroes and ones. Think of each method (symbolized by the gears) as a piece of machinery that carries out its assigned task.

In Chapter 1, you encountered two objects:

- System.out
- "Hello, World!"

The type of an object is a **class**. The System.out object belongs to the class Print-Stream. The "Hello, World!" object belongs to the class String. A class specifies the methods that you can apply to its objects.

> A class declares the methods that you can apply to its objects.

You can use the println method with any object that belongs to the PrintStream class. System.out is one such object. It is possible to obtain other objects of the Print-Stream class. For example, you can construct a PrintStream object to send output to a file. However, we won't discuss files until Chapter 11.

Just as the PrintStream class provides methods such as println and print for its objects, the String class provides methods that you can apply to String objects. One of them is the length method. The length method counts the number of characters in

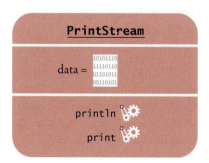

Figure 4   Representation of the System.out Object

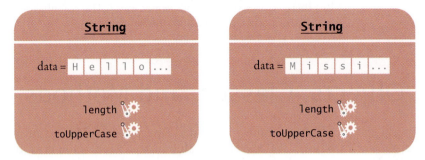

Figure 5 A Representation of Two String Objects

a string. You can apply that method to any object of type String. For example, the sequence of statements

```
String greeting = "Hello, World!";
int n = greeting.length();
```

sets n to the number of characters in the String object "Hello, World!". After the instructions in the length method are executed, n is set to 13. (The quotation marks are not part of the string, and the length method does not count them.)

The length method—unlike the println method—requires no input inside the parentheses. However, the length method yields an output, namely the character count.

In the next section, you will see in greater detail how to supply method inputs and obtain method outputs.

Let us look at another method of the String class. When you apply the toUpperCase method to a String object, the method creates another String object that contains the characters of the original string, with lowercase letters converted to uppercase. For example, the sequence of statements

```
String river = "Mississippi";
String bigRiver = river.toUpperCase();
```

sets bigRiver to the String object "MISSISSIPPI".

When you apply a method to an object, you must make sure that the method is declared in the appropriate class. For example, it is an error to call

```
System.out.length(); // This method call is an error
```

The PrintStream class (to which System.out belongs) has no length method.

Let us summarize. In Java, *every object belongs to a class. The class declares the methods for the objects.* For example, the String class declares the length and toUpperCase methods (as well as other methods—you will learn about most of them in Chapter 4). The methods form the *public interface* of the class, telling you what you can do with the objects of the class. A class also declares a *private implementation*, describing the data inside its objects and the instructions for its methods. Those details are hidden from the programmers who use objects and call methods.

Figure 5 shows two objects of the String class. Each object stores its own data (drawn as boxes that contain characters). Both objects support the same set of methods—the interface that is specified by the String class.

The public interface of a class specifies what you can do with its objects. The hidden implementation describes how these actions are carried out.

Occasionally, a class declares two methods with the same name and different parameter types. For example, the `PrintStream` class declares a second method, also called `println`, as

```
public void println(int output)
```

That method is used to print an integer value. We say that the `println` name is **overloaded** because it refers to more than one method.

9. How can you compute the length of the string `"Mississippi"`?

10. How can you print out the uppercase version of `"Hello, World!"`?

11. Is it legal to call `river.println()`? Why or why not?

2.5 Method Parameters and Return Values

Methods are fundamental building blocks of Java programs. A program performs useful work by calling methods. In this section, we will examine how to provide inputs into a method, and how to obtain the result of the method.

> A parameter is an input to a method.

Most methods require inputs that give details about the work that the method needs to do. For example, the `println` method has an input: the string that should be printed. Computer scientists use the technical term parameter for method inputs. We say that the string `greeting` is a parameter of the method call

```
System.out.println(greeting);
```

Figure 6 illustrates passing of the parameter to the method.

> The implicit parameter of a method call is the object on which the method is invoked. All other parameters are explicit parameters.

Technically speaking, the `greeting` parameter is an **explicit parameter** of the `println` method. The object on which you invoke the method is also considered a parameter of the method call; it is called the **implicit parameter**. For example, `System.out` is the implicit parameter of the method call

```
System.out.println(greeting);
```

Some methods require multiple explicit parameters, others don't require any explicit parameters at all. An example of the latter is the `length` method of the `String` class (see Figure 7). All the information that the `length` method requires to do its job—namely, the character sequence of the string—is stored in the implicit parameter object.

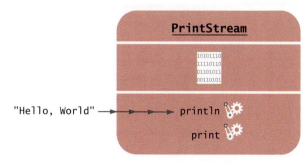

Figure 6 Passing a Parameter to the `println` Method

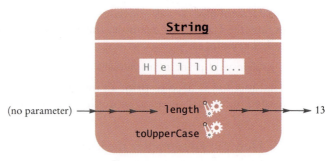

Figure 7 Invoking the `length` Method on a `String` Object

ANIMATION
Parameter Passing

> The return value of a method is a result that the method has computed for use by the code that called it.

The `length` method differs from the `println` method in another way: it has an output. We say that the method *returns a value*, namely the number of characters in the string. You can store the return value in a variable:

```
int n = greeting.length();
```

You can also use the return value as a parameter of another method:

```
System.out.println(greeting.length());
```

The method call `greeting.length()` returns a value—the integer 13. The return value becomes a parameter of the `println` method. Figure 8 shows the process.

Not all methods return values. One example is the `println` method. The `println` method interacts with the operating system, causing characters to appear in a window. But it does not return a value to the code that calls it.

Let us analyze a more complex method call. Here, we will call the `replace` method of the `String` class. The `replace` method carries out a search-and-replace operation, similar to that of a word processor. For example, the call

```
river.replace("issipp", "our")
```

constructs a new string that is obtained by replacing all occurrences of `"issipp"` in `"Mississippi"` with `"our"`. (In this situation, there was only one replacement.) The method returns the `String` object `"Missouri"`. You can save that string in a variable:

```
river = river.replace("issipp", "our");
```

Or you can pass it to another method:

```
System.out.println(river.replace("issipp", "our"));
```

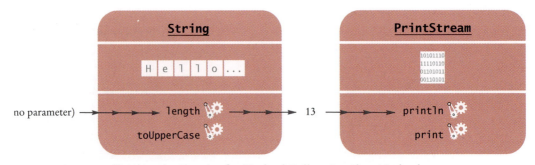

Figure 8 Passing the Result of a Method Call to Another Method

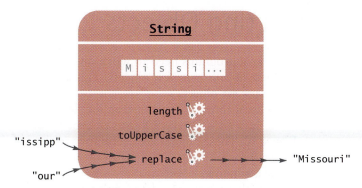

Figure 9 Calling the `replace` Method

As Figure 9 shows, this method call has

- one implicit parameter: the string `"Mississippi"`
- two explicit parameters: the strings `"issipp"` and `"our"`
- a return value: the string `"Missouri"`

When a method is declared in a class, the declaration specifies the types of the explicit parameters and the return value. For example, the `String` class declares the `length` method as

```
public int length()
```

That is, there are no explicit parameters, and the return value has the type int. (For now, all the methods that we consider will be "public" methods—see Chapter 10 for more restricted methods.)

The type of the implicit parameter is the class that declares the method—`String` in our case. It is not mentioned in the method declaration—hence the term "implicit".

The `replace` method is declared as

```
public String replace(String target, String replacement)
```

To call the `replace` method, you supply two explicit parameters, `target` and `replacement`, which both have type `String`. The returned value is another string.

When a method returns no value, the return type is declared with the reserved word void. For example, the `PrintStream` class declares the `println` method as

```
public void println(String output)
```

SELF CHECK

12. What are the implicit parameters, explicit parameters, and return values in the method call `river.length()`?

13. What is the result of the call `river.replace("p", "s")`?

14. What is the result of the call `greeting.replace("World", "Dave").length()`?

15. How is the `toUpperCase` method declared in the `String` class?

2.6 Constructing Objects

Most Java programs need to work on a variety of objects. In this section, you will see how to *construct* new objects. This allows you to go beyond String objects and the System.out object.

To learn about object construction, let us turn to another class: the Rectangle class in the Java class library. Objects of type Rectangle describe rectangular shapes—see Figure 10. These objects are useful for a variety of purposes. You can assemble rectangles into bar charts, and you can program simple games by moving rectangles inside a window.

Note that a Rectangle object isn't a rectangular shape—it's an object that contains a set of numbers. The numbers *describe* the rectangle (see Figure 11). Each rectangle is described by the *x*- and *y*-coordinates of its top-left corner, its width, and its height.

It is very important that you understand this distinction. In the computer, a Rectangle object is a block of memory that holds four numbers, for example $x = 5$, $y = 10$, *width* $= 20$, *height* $= 30$. In the imagination of the programmer who uses a Rectangle object, the object describes a geometric figure.

To make a new rectangle, you need to specify the *x*, *y*, *width*, and *height* values. Then *invoke the* new *operator*, specifying the name of the class and the parameters that are required for constructing a new object. For example, you can make a new rectangle with its top-left corner at (5, 10), width 20, and height 30 as follows:

> Use the new operator, followed by a class name and parameters, to construct new objects.

```
new Rectangle(5, 10, 20, 30)
```

Here is what happens in detail:

1. The new operator makes a Rectangle object.
2. It uses the parameters (in this case, 5, 10, 20, and 30) to initialize the data of the object.
3. It returns the object.

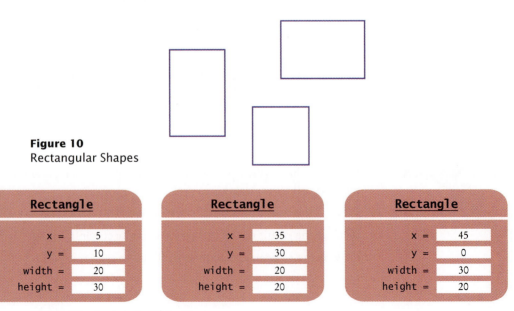

Figure 10
Rectangular Shapes

Figure 11 Rectangle Objects

Syntax 2.3 Object Construction

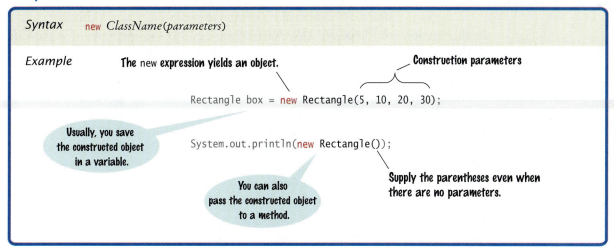

Syntax new *ClassName(parameters)*

Example

The new expression yields an object.   Construction parameters

Rectangle box = new Rectangle(5, 10, 20, 30);

Usually, you save the constructed object in a variable.

System.out.println(new Rectangle());

You can also pass the constructed object to a method.

Supply the parentheses even when there are no parameters.

The process of creating a new object is called **construction**. The four values 5, 10, 20, and 30 are called the *construction parameters*.

The new expression yields an object, and you need to store the object if you want to use it later. Usually you assign the output of the new operator to a variable. For example,

```
Rectangle box = new Rectangle(5, 10, 20, 30);
```

Some classes let you construct objects in multiple ways. For example, you can also obtain a Rectangle object by supplying no construction parameters at all (but you must still supply the parentheses):

```
new Rectangle()
```

This expression constructs a (rather useless) rectangle with its top-left corner at the origin (0, 0), width 0, and height 0.

SELF CHECK

16. How do you construct a square with center (100, 100) and side length 20?

17. The getWidth method returns the width of a Rectangle object. What does the following statement print?

```
System.out.println(new Rectangle().getWidth());
```

Common Error 2.2

Trying to Invoke a Constructor Like a Method

Constructors are not methods. You can only use a constructor with the new operator, not to reinitialize an existing object:

```
box.Rectangle(20, 35, 20, 30); // Error—can't reinitialize object
```

The remedy is simple: Make a new object and overwrite the current one stored by box.

```
box = new Rectangle(20, 35, 20, 30); // OK
```

2.7 Accessor and Mutator Methods

> An accessor method does not change the internal data of its implicit parameter. A mutator method changes the data.

In this section we introduce a useful terminology for the methods of a class. A method that accesses an object and returns some information about it, without changing the object, is called an **accessor method**. In contrast, a method whose purpose is to modify the internal data of an object is called a **mutator method**.

For example, the `length` method of the `String` class is an accessor method. It returns information about a string, namely its length. But it doesn't modify the string at all when counting the characters.

The `Rectangle` class has a number of accessor methods. The `getX`, `getY`, `getWidth`, and `getHeight` methods return the x- and y-coordinates of the top-left corner, the width, and the height values. For example,

```
double width = box.getWidth();
```

Now let us consider a mutator method. Programs that manipulate rectangles frequently need to move them around, for example, to display animations. The `Rectangle` class has a method for that purpose, called `translate`. (Mathematicians use the term "translation" for a rigid motion of the plane.) This method moves a rectangle by a certain distance in the x- and y-directions. The method call,

```
box.translate(15, 25);
```

moves the rectangle by 15 units in the x-direction and 25 units in the y-direction (see Figure 12). Moving a rectangle doesn't change its width or height, but it changes the top-left corner. Afterward, the rectangle that had its top-left corner at (5, 10) now has it at (20, 35).

This method is a mutator because it modifies the implicit parameter object.

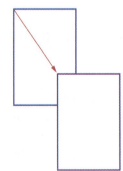

Figure 12
Using the `translate` Method
to Move a Rectangle

SELF CHECK

18. Is the `toUpperCase` method of the `String` class an accessor or a mutator?

19. Which call to `translate` is needed to move the rectangle declared by `Rectangle box = new Rectangle(5, 10, 20, 30)` so that its top-left corner is the origin (0, 0)?

2.8 The API Documentation

The classes and methods of the Java library are listed in the **API documentation**. The API is the "application programming interface". A programmer who uses the Java classes to put together a computer program (or *application*) is an *application programmer*. That's you. In contrast, the programmers who designed and implemented the library classes such as PrintStream and Rectangle are *system programmers*.

> The API (Application Programming Interface) documentation lists the classes and methods of the Java library.

You can find the API documentation on the Web. Point your web browser to http://java.sun.com/javase/7/docs/api/index.html. Appendix D contains an abbreviated version of the API documentation that may be easier to use at first. It is fine if you rely on the abbreviated documentation for your first programs, but you should eventually move on to the real thing.

The API documentation documents all classes in the Java library—there are thousands of them (see Figure 13). Most of the classes are rather specialized, and only a few are of interest to the beginning programmer.

Locate the Rectangle link in the left pane, preferably by using the search function of your browser. Click on the link, and the right pane shows all the features of the Rectangle class (see Figure 14).

Figure 13   The API Documentation of the Standard Java Library

Figure 14   The API Documentation for the Rectangle Class

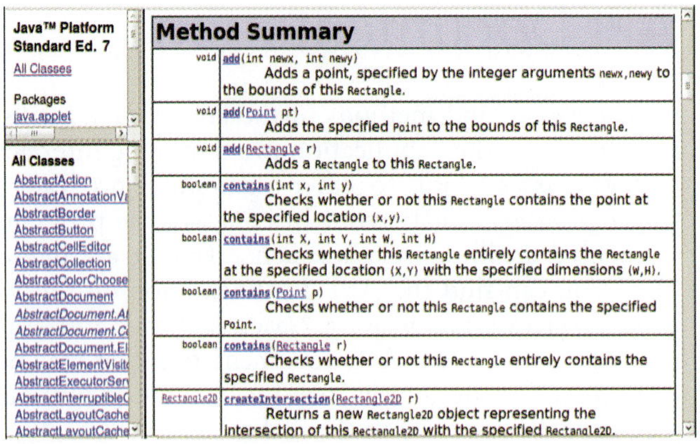

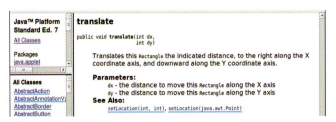

Figure 15 The Method Summary for the Rectangle Class

Figure 16 The API Documentation of the `translate` Method

The API documentation for each class starts out with a section that describes the purpose of the class. Then come summary tables for the constructors and methods (see Figure 15). Click on the link of a method to get a detailed description (see Figure 16).

The detailed description of a method shows

- The action that the method carries out.
- The parameters that the method receives.
- The value that it returns (or the reserved word `void` if the method doesn't return any value).

As you can see, the `Rectangle` class has quite a few methods. While occasionally intimidating for the beginning programmer, this is a strength of the standard library. If you ever need to do a computation involving rectangles, chances are that there is a method that does all the work for you.

For example, suppose you want to change the width or height of a rectangle. If you browse through the API documentation, you will find a `setSize` method with the description "Sets the size of this `Rectangle` to the specified width and height." The method has two parameters, described as

- `width` - the new width for this `Rectangle`
- `height` - the new height for this `Rectangle`

Now let us use this information to change the box object so that it is a square of side length 40. The name of the method is `setSize`, and we supply two parameters: the new width and height:

```
box.setSize(40, 40);
```

Syntax 2.4 Importing a Class from a Package

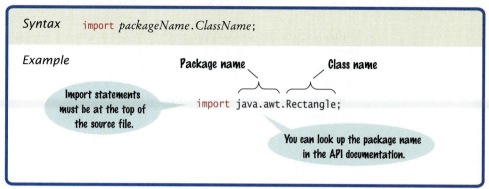

Syntax import *packageName.ClassName;*

Example

Package name   Class name

Import statements must be at the top of the source file.

import java.awt.Rectangle;

You can look up the package name in the API documentation.

The API documentation contains another important piece of information about each class. The classes in the standard library are organized into **packages**. A package is a collection of classes with a related purpose. The Rectangle class belongs to the package java.awt (where awt is an abbreviation for "Abstract Windowing Toolkit"), which contains many classes for drawing windows and graphical shapes. You can see the package name java.awt in Figure 14, just above the class name.

To use the Rectangle class from the java.awt package, you must *import* the package. Simply place the following line at the top of your program:

```
import java.awt.Rectangle;
```

Why don't you have to import the System and String classes? Because the System and String classes are in the java.lang package, and all classes from this package are automatically imported, so you never need to import them yourself.

> Java classes are grouped into packages. Use the import statement to use classes that are declared in other packages.

SELF CHECK

20. Look at the API documentation of the String class. Which method would you use to obtain the string "hello, world!" from the string "Hello, World!"?

21. In the API documentation of the String class, look at the description of the trim method. What is the result of applying trim to the string " Hello, Space ! "? (Note the spaces in the string.)

22. The Random class is declared in the java.util package. What do you need to do in order to use that class in your program?

Productivity Hint 2.1

Don't Memorize—Use Online Help

The Java library has thousands of classes and methods. It is neither necessary nor useful trying to memorize them. Instead, you should become familiar with using the API documentation. Because you will need to use the API documentation all the time, it is best to download and install it onto your computer, particularly if your computer is not always connected to the Internet. You can download the documentation from http://java.sun.com/javase/downloads/index.html.

2.9 Implementing a Test Program

In this section, we discuss the steps that are necessary to implement a test program. The purpose of a test program is to verify that one or more methods have been implemented correctly. A test program calls methods and checks that they return the expected results. Writing test programs is a very important skill.

In this section, we will develop a simple program that tests a method in the Rectangle class. The program performs the following steps:

1. Provide a tester class.
2. Supply a main method.
3. Inside the main method, construct one or more objects.
4. Apply methods to the objects.
5. Display the results of the method calls.
6. Display the values that you expect to get.

> A test program verifies that methods behave as expected.

Our sample test program tests the behavior of the translate method. Here are the key steps (which have been placed inside the main method of the MoveTester class).

```
Rectangle box = new Rectangle(5, 10, 20, 30);

// Move the rectangle
box.translate(15, 25);

// Print information about the moved rectangle
System.out.print("x: ");
System.out.println(box.getX());
System.out.println("Expected: 20");
```

We print the value that is returned by the getX method, and then we print a message that describes the value we expect to see.

> Determining the expected result in advance is an important part of testing.

This is a very important step. You want to spend some time thinking about the expected result before you run a test program. This thought process will help you understand how your program should behave, and it can help you track down errors at an early stage. Finding and fixing errors early is a very effective strategy that can save you a great deal of time.

In our case, the rectangle has been constructed with the top-left corner at (5, 10). The x-direction is moved by 15, so we expect an x-value of $5 + 15 = 20$ after the move.

Here is a complete program that tests the moving of a rectangle.

ch02/rectangle/MoveTester.java

```
1  import java.awt.Rectangle;
2
3  public class MoveTester
4  {
5     public static void main(String[] args)
6     {
7        Rectangle box = new Rectangle(5, 10, 20, 30);
8
9        // Move the rectangle
10       box.translate(15, 25);
11
```

```
12          // Print information about the moved rectangle
13          System.out.print("x: ");
14          System.out.println(box.getX());
15          System.out.println("Expected: 20");
16
17          System.out.print("y: ");
18          System.out.println(box.getY());
19          System.out.println("Expected: 35");
20      }
21  }
```

Program Run

```
x: 20
Expected: 20
y: 35
Expected: 35
```

S E L F C H E C K

23. Suppose we had called box.translate(25, 15) instead of box.translate(15, 25). What are the expected outputs?

24. Why doesn't the MoveTester program need to print the width and height of the rectangle?

Special Topic 2.1

Testing Classes in an Interactive Environment

Some development environments are specifically designed to help students explore objects without having to provide tester classes. These environments can be very helpful for gaining insight into the behavior of objects, and for promoting object-oriented thinking. The BlueJ environment (shown in the figure) displays objects as blobs on a workbench. You can

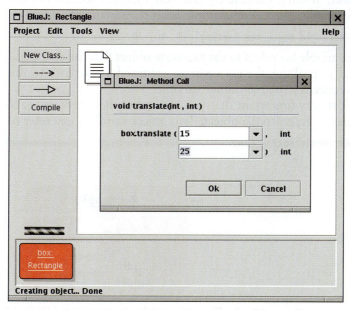

Testing a Method Call in BlueJ

construct new objects, put them on the workbench, invoke methods, and see the return values, all without writing a line of code. You can download BlueJ at no charge from www.bluej.org. Another excellent environment for interactively exploring objects is Dr. Java at drjava.sourceforge.net.

➕ **Worked Example 2.1**

How Many Days Have You Been Alive?

In this Worked Example, you explore the API of a class Day that represents a calendar day, and you write a program that computes how many days have elapsed since the day you were born.

➕ **Worked Example 2.2**

Working with Pictures

In this Worked Example, you use the API of a Picture class to edit photos.

2.10 Object References

In Java, a variable whose type is a class does not actually hold an object. It merely holds the memory *location* of an object. The object itself is stored elsewhere—see Figure 17.

There is a reason for this behavior. Objects can be very large. It is more efficient to store only the memory location instead of the entire object.

An object reference describes the location of an object.

We use the technical term **object reference** to denote the memory location of an object. When a variable contains the memory location of an object, we say that it *refers* to an object. For example, after the statement

```
Rectangle box = new Rectangle(5, 10, 20, 30);
```

the variable box refers to the Rectangle object that the new operator constructed. Technically speaking, the new operator returned a reference to the new object, and that reference is stored in the box variable.

It is very important that you remember that the box variable *does not contain* the object. It *refers* to the object. Two object variables can refer to the same object:

```
Rectangle box2 = box;
```

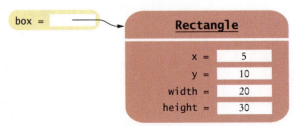

Figure 17 An Object Variable Containing an Object Reference

➕ Available online in WileyPLUS and at www.wiley.com/college/horstmann.

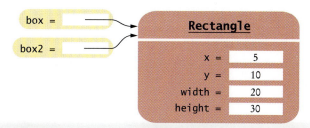

Figure 18   Two Object Variables Referring to the Same Object

Now you can access the same Rectangle object both as box and as box2, as shown in Figure 18.

> Multiple object variables can contain references to the same object.

However, number variables actually store numbers. When you declare

```
int luckyNumber = 13;
```

then the luckyNumber variable holds the number 13, not a reference to the number (see Figure 19). The reason is again efficiency. Because numbers require little storage, it is more efficient to store them directly in a variable.

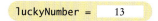

Figure 19   A Number Variable Stores a Number

> Number variables store numbers. Object variables store references.

You can see the difference between number variables and object variables when you make a copy of a variable. When you copy a number, the original and the copy of the number are independent values. But when you copy an object reference, both the original and the copy are references to the same object.

Consider the following code, which copies a number and then changes the copy (see Figure 20):

```
int luckyNumber = 13; ❶
int luckyNumber2 = luckyNumber; ❷
luckyNumber2 = 12; ❸
```

Now the variable luckyNumber contains the value 13, and luckyNumber2 contains 12.

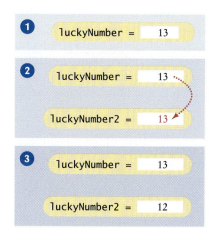

Figure 20
Copying Numbers

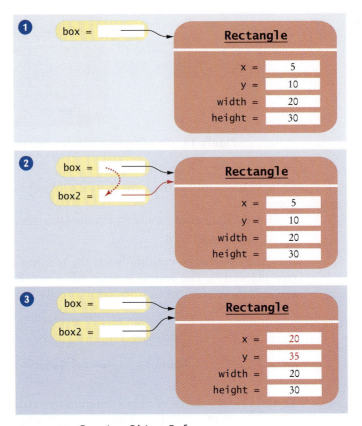

Figure 21 Copying Object References

Now consider the seemingly analogous code with `Rectangle` objects (see Figure 21).

ANIMATION
Object References

```
Rectangle box = new Rectangle(5, 10, 20, 30);   ①
Rectangle box2 = box;   ②
box2.translate(15, 25);   ③
```

Since `box` and `box2` refer to the same rectangle after step ②, both variables refer to the moved rectangle after the call to the `translate` method.

You need not worry too much about the difference between objects and object references. Much of the time, you will have the correct intuition when you think of "the object box" rather than the technically more accurate "the object reference stored in box". The difference between objects and object references only becomes apparent when you have multiple variables that refer to the same object.

SELF CHECK

25. What is the effect of the assignment `String greeting2 = greeting`?

26. After calling `greeting2.toUpperCase()`, what are the contents of `greeting` and `greeting2`?

Random Fact 2.1

Mainframes—When Dinosaurs Ruled the Earth

When International Business Machines Corporation (IBM), a successful manufacturer of punched-card equipment for tabulating data, first turned its attention to designing computers in the early 1950s, its planners assumed that there was a market for perhaps 50 such devices, for installation by the government, the military, and a few of the country's largest corporations. Instead, they sold about 1,500 machines of their System 650 model and went on to build and sell more powerful computers.

The so-called mainframe computers of the 1950s, 1960s, and 1970s were huge. They filled rooms, which had to be climate-controlled to protect the delicate equipment (see figure). Today, because of miniaturization technology, even mainframes are getting smaller, but they are still very expensive. (At the time of this writing, the cost for a typical mainframe is several million dollars.)

A Mainframe Computer

These huge and expensive systems were an immediate success when they first appeared, because they replaced many roomfuls of even more expensive employees, who had previously performed the tasks by hand. Few of these computers do any exciting computations. They keep mundane information, such as billing records or airline reservations; they just keep lots of them.

IBM was not the first company to build mainframe computers; that honor belongs to the Univac Corporation. However, IBM soon became the major player, partially because of technical excellence and attention to customer needs and partially because it exploited its strengths and structured its products and services in a way that made it difficult for customers to mix them with those of other vendors. In the 1960s, IBM's competitors, the so-called "Seven Dwarfs"—GE, RCA, Univac, Honeywell, Burroughs, Control Data, and NCR—fell on hard times. Some went out of the computer business altogether, while others tried unsuccessfully to combine their strengths by merging their computer operations. It was generally predicted that they would eventually all fail. It was in this atmosphere that the U.S. government brought an antitrust suit against IBM in 1969. The suit went to trial in 1975 and dragged on until 1982, when the Reagan Administration abandoned it, declaring it "without merit".

Of course, by then the computing landscape had changed completely. Just as the dinosaurs gave way to smaller, nimbler creatures, three new waves of computers had appeared: the minicomputers, workstations, and microcomputers, all engineered by new companies, not the Seven Dwarfs. Today, the importance of mainframes in the marketplace has diminished, and IBM, while still a large and resourceful company, no longer dominates the computer market.

Mainframes are still in use today for two reasons. They still excel at handling large data volumes. More importantly, the programs that control the business data have been refined over the last 30 or more years, fixing one problem at a time. Moving these programs to less expensive computers, with different languages and operating systems, is difficult and error-prone. In the 1990s, Sun Microsystems, a leading manufacturer of workstations and servers—and the inventor of Java—was eager to prove that its mainframe system could be "downsized" and replaced by its own equipment. Sun eventually succeeded, but it took over five years—far longer than it expected.

2.11 Graphical Applications and Frame Windows

This is the first of several optional sections that teach you how to write *graphical applications:* applications that display drawings inside a window. Graphical applications look more attractive than the console applications that show plain text in a console window.

> To show a frame, construct a JFrame object, set its size, and make it visible.

A graphical application shows information inside a **frame**: a window with a title bar, as shown in Figure 22. In this section, you will learn how to display a frame. In Section 3.9, you will learn how to create a drawing inside the frame.

Figure 22
A Frame Window

To show a frame, carry out the following steps:

1. Construct an object of the JFrame class:

   ```
   JFrame frame = new JFrame();
   ```

2. Set the size of the frame:

   ```
   frame.setSize(300, 400);
   ```

   This frame will be 300 pixels wide and 400 pixels tall. If you omit this step the frame will be 0 by 0 pixels, and you won't be able to see it. (Pixels are the tiny dots from which digital images are composed.)

3. If you'd like, set the title of the frame:

   ```
   frame.setTitle("An Empty Frame");
   ```

   If you omit this step, the title bar is simply left blank.

4. Set the "default close operation":

   ```
   frame.setDefaultCloseOperation(JFrame.EXIT_ON_CLOSE);
   ```

   When the user closes the frame, the program automatically exits. Don't omit this step. If you do, the program continues running even after the frame is closed.

5. Make the frame visible:

   ```
   frame.setVisible(true);
   ```

The simple program below shows all of these steps. It produces the empty frame shown in Figure 22.

The JFrame class is a part of the javax.swing package. Swing is the nickname for the graphical user interface library in Java. The "x" in javax denotes the fact that Swing started out as a Java *extension* before it was added to the standard library.

We will go into much greater detail about Swing programming in Chapters 3, 9, 10, and 18. For now, consider this program to be the essential plumbing that is required to show a frame.

ch02/emptyframe/EmptyFrameViewer.java

```java
1   import javax.swing.JFrame;
2
3   public class EmptyFrameViewer
4   {
5      public static void main(String[] args)
6      {
7         JFrame frame = new JFrame();
8
9         frame.setSize(300, 400);
10        frame.setTitle("An Empty Frame");
11        frame.setDefaultCloseOperation(JFrame.EXIT_ON_CLOSE);
12
13        frame.setVisible(true);
14     }
15  }
```

S E L F   C H E C K

27. How do you display a square frame with a title bar that reads "Hello, World!"?

28. How can a program display two frames at once?

2.12 Drawing on a Component

This section continues the optional graphics track. You will learn how to make shapes appear inside a frame window. The first drawing will be exceedingly modest: just two rectangles (see Figure 23). You'll soon see how to produce more interesting drawings. The purpose of this example is to show you the basic outline of a program that creates a drawing. You cannot draw directly onto a frame. Whenever you want to show anything inside a frame, be it a button or a drawing, you have to construct a **component** object and add it to the frame. In the Swing toolkit, the JComponent class represents a blank component.

> In order to display a drawing in a frame, declare a class that extends the JComponent class.

Since we don't want to add a blank component, we have to modify the JComponent class and specify how the component should be painted. The solution is to declare a new class that extends the JComponent class. You will learn about the process of extending classes in Chapter 10. For now, simply use the following code as a template.

```
public class RectangleComponent extends JComponent
{
    public void paintComponent(Graphics g)
    {
        Drawing instructions
    }
}
```

The extends reserved word indicates that our component class, RectangleComponent, can be used like a JComponent. However, the RectangleComponent class will be different from the plain JComponent class in one respect: Its paintComponent method will contain instructions to draw the rectangles.

> Place drawing instructions inside the paintComponent method. That method is called whenever the component needs to be repainted.

When the component is shown for the first time, the paintComponent method is called automatically. The method is also called when the window is resized, or when it is shown again after it was hidden.

The paintComponent method receives an object of type Graphics. The Graphics object stores the graphics state—the current color, font, and so on, that are used for

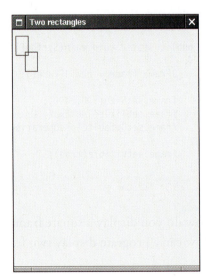

Figure 23
Drawing Rectangles

Use a cast to recover the Graphics2D object from the Graphics parameter of the paintComponent method.

drawing operations. However, the Graphics class is primitive. When programmers clamored for a more object-oriented approach for drawing graphics, the designers of Java created the Graphics2D class, which extends the Graphics class. Whenever the Swing toolkit calls the paintComponent method, it actually passes a parameter of type Graphics2D. Because we want to use the more sophisticated methods to draw two-dimensional graphics objects, we need to use the Graphics2D class. This is accomplished by using a **cast**:

```java
public class RectangleComponent extends JComponent
{
    public void paintComponent(Graphics g)
    {
        // Recover Graphics2D
        Graphics2D g2 = (Graphics2D) g;
        . . .
    }
}
```

We cover the concepts of extending classes and of casting in Chapter 10. For now, you should simply include the cast at the top of your paintComponent methods.

Now you are ready to draw shapes. The draw method of the Graphics2D class can draw shapes, such as rectangles, ellipses, line segments, polygons, and arcs. Here we draw a rectangle:

```java
public class RectangleComponent extends JComponent
{
    public void paintComponent(Graphics g)
    {
        . . .
        Rectangle box = new Rectangle(5, 10, 20, 30);
        g2.draw(box);
        . . .
    }
}
```

Following is the source code for the RectangleComponent class. Note that the paintComponent method of the RectangleComponent class draws two rectangles.

As you can see from the import statements, the Graphics and Graphics2D classes are part of the java.awt package.

ch02/rectangles/RectangleComponent.java

```java
 1  import java.awt.Graphics;
 2  import java.awt.Graphics2D;
 3  import java.awt.Rectangle;
 4  import javax.swing.JComponent;
 5
 6  /*
 7     A component that draws two rectangles.
 8  */
 9  public class RectangleComponent extends JComponent
10  {
11     public void paintComponent(Graphics g)
12     {
13        // Recover Graphics2D
14        Graphics2D g2 = (Graphics2D) g;
15
```

```
16        // Construct a rectangle and draw it
17        Rectangle box = new Rectangle(5, 10, 20, 30);
18        g2.draw(box);
19
20        // Move rectangle 15 units to the right and 25 units down
21        box.translate(15, 25);
22
23        // Draw moved rectangle
24        g2.draw(box);
25    }
26 }
```

In order to see the drawing, one task remains. You need to display the frame into which you added a component object. Follow these steps:

1. Construct a frame as described in the preceding section.

2. Construct an object of your component class:

   ```
   RectangleComponent component = new RectangleComponent();
   ```

3. Add the component to the frame:

   ```
   frame.add(component);
   ```

4. Make the frame visible, as described in the preceding section.

The following listing shows the complete process.

ch02/rectangles/RectangleViewer.java

```
1   import javax.swing.JFrame;
2
3   public class RectangleViewer
4   {
5       public static void main(String[] args)
6       {
7           JFrame frame = new JFrame();
8
9           frame.setSize(300, 400);
10          frame.setTitle("Two rectangles");
11          frame.setDefaultCloseOperation(JFrame.EXIT_ON_CLOSE);
12
13          RectangleComponent component = new RectangleComponent();
14          frame.add(component);
15
16          frame.setVisible(true);
17      }
18  }
```

Note that the rectangle drawing program consists of two classes:

- The `RectangleComponent` class, whose `paintComponent` method produces the drawing.
- The `RectangleViewer` class, whose `main` method constructs a frame and a `RectangleComponent`, adds the component to the frame, and makes the frame visible.

 **SELF CHECK**

29. How do you modify the program to draw two squares?

30. How do you modify the program to draw one rectangle and one square?

31. What happens if you call `g.draw(box)` instead of `g2.draw(box)`?

Special Topic 2.2

Applets

In the preceding section, you learned how to write a program that displays graphical shapes. Some people prefer to use **applets** for learning about graphics programming. Applets have two advantages. They don't need separate component and viewer classes; you only implement a single class. And, more importantly, applets run inside a web browser, allowing you to place your creations on a web page for all the world to admire.

To implement an applet, use this code outline:

```
public class MyApplet extends JApplet
{
   public void paint(Graphics g)
   {
      // Recover Graphics2D
      Graphics2D g2 = (Graphics2D) g;

      // Drawing instructions go here
      . . .
   }
}
```

This is almost the same outline as for a component, with two minor differences:

1. You extend JApplet, not JComponent.

2. You place the drawing code inside the paint method, not inside paintComponent.

The following applet draws two rectangles:

ch02/applet/RectangleApplet.java

```java
 1  import java.awt.Graphics;
 2  import java.awt.Graphics2D;
 3  import java.awt.Rectangle;
 4  import javax.swing.JApplet;
 5
 6  /*
 7     An applet that draws two rectangles.
 8  */
 9  public class RectangleApplet extends JApplet
10  {
11     public void paint(Graphics g)
12     {
13        // Prepare for extended graphics
14        Graphics2D g2 = (Graphics2D) g;
15
16        // Construct a rectangle and draw it
17        Rectangle box = new Rectangle(5, 10, 20, 30);
18        g2.draw(box);
19
20        // Move rectangle 15 units to the right and 25 units down
21        box.translate(15, 25);
22
23        // Draw moved rectangle
24        g2.draw(box);
25     }
26  }
```

To run an applet, you need an HTML file with the applet tag.

To run this applet, you need an HTML file with an `applet` tag. HTML, the hypertext markup language, is the language used to describe web pages. (See Appendix F for more information on HTML.) Here is the simplest possible file to display the rectangle applet:

ch02/applet/RectangleApplet.html

```
1  <applet code="RectangleApplet.class" width="300" height="400">
2  </applet>
```

If you know HTML, you can proudly explain your creation, by adding text and more HTML tags:

ch02/applet/RectangleAppletExplained.html

```
1  <html>
2     <head>
3        <title>Two rectangles</title>
4     </head>
5     <body>
6        <p>Here is my <i>first applet</i>:</p>
7        <applet code="RectangleApplet.class" width="300" height="400">
8        </applet>
9     </body>
10  </html>
```

An HTML file can have multiple applets. Simply add a separate `applet` tag for each applet.

You can give the HTML file any name you like. It is easiest to give the HTML file the same name as the applet. But some development environments already generate an HTML file with the same name as your project to hold your project notes; then you must give the HTML file containing your applet a different name.

An Applet in the Applet Viewer

An Applet in a Web Browser

To run the applet, you have two choices. You can use the applet viewer, a program that is included with the Java Software Development Kit from Sun Microsystems. You simply start the applet viewer, giving it the name of the HTML file that contains your applets:

```
appletviewer RectangleApplet.html
```

The applet viewer only shows the applet, not the HTML text (see the left figure).

> You view applets with the applet viewer or a Java-enabled browser.

You can also show the applet inside any Java-enabled web browser, such as Firefox or Safari. (If you use Internet Explorer, you probably need to configure it. By default, Microsoft supplies either an outdated version of Java or no Java at all. Go to the java.com web site and install the Java plugin.) The second figure shows the applet running in a browser. As you can see, both the text and the applet are displayed.

2.13 Ellipses, Lines, Text, and Color

In Section 2.12 you learned how to write a program that draws rectangles. In this section you will learn how to draw other shapes: ellipses and lines. With these graphical elements, you can draw quite a few interesting pictures.

2.13.1 Ellipses and Circles

To draw an ellipse, you specify its bounding box (see Figure 24) in the same way that you would specify a rectangle, namely by the x- and y-coordinates of the top-left corner and the width and height of the box.

> The Ellipse2D.Double and Line2D.Double classes describe graphical shapes.

However, there is no simple Ellipse class that you can use. Instead, you must use one of the two classes Ellipse2D.Float and Ellipse2D.Double, depending on whether you want to store the ellipse coordinates as single- or double-precision floating-point values. Because the latter are more convenient to use in Java, we will always use the Ellipse2D.Double class. Here is how you construct an ellipse:

```
Ellipse2D.Double ellipse = new Ellipse2D.Double(x, y, width, height);
```

The class name Ellipse2D.Double looks different from the class names that you have encountered up to now. It consists of two class names Ellipse2D and Double separated

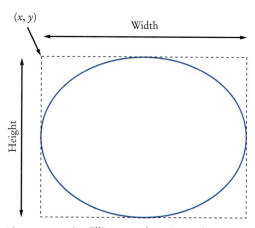

Figure 24 An Ellipse and Its Bounding Box

by a period (.). This indicates that Ellipse2D.Double is a so-called **inner class** inside Ellipse2D. When constructing and using ellipses, you don't actually need to worry about the fact that Ellipse2D.Double is an inner class—just think of it as a class with a long name. However, in the import statement at the top of your program, you must be careful that you import only the outer class:

```
import java.awt.geom.Ellipse2D;
```

Drawing an ellipse is easy: Use exactly the same draw method of the Graphics2D class that you used for drawing rectangles.

```
g2.draw(ellipse);
```

To draw a circle, simply set the width and height to the same values:

```
Ellipse2D.Double circle = new Ellipse2D.Double(x, y, diameter, diameter);
g2.draw(circle);
```

Notice that (x, y) is the top-left corner of the bounding box, not the center of the circle.

2.13.2 Lines

To draw a line, use an object of the Line2D.Double class. A line is constructed by specifying its two end points. You can do this in two ways. Simply give the *x*- and *y*-coordinates of both end points:

```
Line2D.Double segment = new Line2D.Double(x1, y1, x2, y2);
```

Or specify each end point as an object of the Point2D.Double class:

```
Point2D.Double from = new Point2D.Double(x1, y1);
Point2D.Double to = new Point2D.Double(x2, y2);

Line2D.Double segment = new Line2D.Double(from, to);
```

The second option is more object-oriented and is often more useful, particularly if the point objects can be reused elsewhere in the same drawing.

2.13.3 Drawing Text

> The drawString method draws a string, starting at its basepoint.

You often want to put text inside a drawing, for example, to label some of the parts. Use the drawString method of the Graphics2D class to draw a string anywhere in a window. You must specify the string and the *x*- and *y*-coordinates of the basepoint of the first character in the string (see Figure 25). For example,

```
g2.drawString("Message", 50, 100);
```

Figure 25   Basepoint and Baseline

2.13.4 Colors

When you first start drawing, all shapes and strings are drawn with a black pen. To change the color, you need to supply an object of type Color. Java uses the RGB color model. That is, you specify a color by the amounts of the primary colors—red, green, and blue—that make up the color. The amounts are given as integers between 0 (primary color not present) and 255 (maximum amount present). For example,

```
Color magenta = new Color(255, 0, 255);
```

constructs a Color object with maximum red, no green, and maximum blue, yielding a bright purple color called magenta.

For your convenience, a variety of colors have been declared in the Color class. Table 4 shows those colors and their RGB values. For example, Color.PINK has been declared to be the same color as new Color(255, 175, 175).

To draw a shape in a different color, first set the color of the Graphics2D object, then call the draw method:

```
g2.setColor(Color.RED);
g2.draw(circle); // Draws the shape in red
```

If you want to color the inside of the shape, use the fill method instead of the draw method. For example,

```
g2.fill(circle);
```

fills the inside of the circle with the current color.

> When you set a new color in the graphics context, it is used for subsequent drawing operations.

Table 4	Predefined Colors	
Color		**RGB Value**
Color.BLACK		0, 0, 0
Color.BLUE		0, 0, 255
Color.CYAN		0, 255, 255
Color.GRAY		128, 128, 128
Color.DARKGRAY		64, 64, 64
Color.LIGHTGRAY		192, 192, 192
Color.GREEN		0, 255, 0
Color.MAGENTA		255, 0, 255
Color.ORANGE		255, 200, 0
Color.PINK		255, 175, 175
Color.RED		255, 0, 0
Color.WHITE		255, 255, 255
Color.YELLOW		255, 255, 0

Figure 26
An Alien Face

The following program puts all these shapes to work, creating a simple drawing (see Figure 26).

ch02/face/FaceComponent.java

```java
1   import java.awt.Color;
2   import java.awt.Graphics;
3   import java.awt.Graphics2D;
4   import java.awt.Rectangle;
5   import java.awt.geom.Ellipse2D;
6   import java.awt.geom.Line2D;
7   import javax.swing.JComponent;
8
9   /*
10     A component that draws an alien face.
11  */
12  public class FaceComponent extends JComponent
13  {
14     public void paintComponent(Graphics g)
15     {
16        // Recover Graphics2D
17        Graphics2D g2 = (Graphics2D) g;
18
19        // Draw the head
20        Ellipse2D.Double head = new Ellipse2D.Double(5, 10, 100, 150);
21        g2.draw(head);
22
23        // Draw the eyes
24        g2.setColor(Color.GREEN);
25        Rectangle eye = new Rectangle(25, 70, 15, 15);
26        g2.fill(eye);
27        eye.translate(50, 0);
28        g2.fill(eye);
29
30        // Draw the mouth
31        Line2D.Double mouth = new Line2D.Double(30, 110, 80, 110);
32        g2.setColor(Color.RED);
33        g2.draw(mouth);
34
35        // Draw the greeting
36        g2.setColor(Color.BLUE);
37        g2.drawString("Hello, World!", 5, 175);
38     }
39  }
```

ch02/face/FaceViewer.java

```java
1  import javax.swing.JFrame;
2
3  public class FaceViewer
4  {
5     public static void main(String[] args)
6     {
7        JFrame frame = new JFrame();
8        frame.setSize(150, 250);
9        frame.setTitle("An Alien Face");
10       frame.setDefaultCloseOperation(JFrame.EXIT_ON_CLOSE);
11
12       FaceComponent component = new FaceComponent();
13       frame.add(component);
14
15       frame.setVisible(true);
16    }
17 }
```

SELF CHECK

32. Give instructions to draw a circle with center (100, 100) and radius 25.

33. Give instructions to draw a letter "V" by drawing two line segments.

34. Give instructions to draw a string consisting of the letter "V".

35. What are the RGB color values of `Color.BLUE`?

36. How do you draw a yellow square on a red background?

Random Fact 2.2

The Evolution of the Internet

In 1962, J.C.R. Licklider was head of the first computer research program at DARPA, the Defense Advanced Research Projects Agency. He wrote a series of papers describing a "galactic network" through which computer users could access data and programs from other sites. This was well before computer networks were invented. By 1969, four computers—three in California and one in Utah—were connected to the ARPANET, the precursor of the Internet. The network grew quickly, linking computers at many universities and research organizations. It was originally thought that most network users wanted to run programs on remote computers. Using remote execution, a researcher at one institution would be able to access an underutilized computer at a different site. It quickly became apparent that remote execution was not what the network was actually used for. Instead, the "killer application" was electronic mail: the transfer of messages between computer users at different locations.

In 1972, Bob Kahn proposed to extend ARPANET into the *Internet:* a collection of interoperable networks. All networks on the Internet share common *protocols* for data transmission. Kahn and Vinton Cerf developed a protocol, now called TCP/IP (Transmission Control Protocol/Internet Protocol). On January 1, 1983, all hosts on the Internet simultaneously switched to the TCP/IP protocol (which is used to this day).

Over time, researchers, computer scientists, and hobbyists published increasing amounts of information on the Internet. For example, the GNU (GNU's Not UNIX) project is producing a free set of high-quality operating system utilities and program development tools (www.gnu.org). Project Gutenberg makes available the text of important classical books, whose copyright has expired, in computer-readable form (www.gutenberg.org). In 1989, Tim Berners-Lee started work on hyperlinked documents, allowing users to browse by following links to related documents. This infrastructure is now known as the World Wide Web (WWW).

The first interfaces to retrieve this information were, by today's standards, unbelievably clumsy and hard to use. In March 1993, WWW traffic was 0.1% of all Internet traffic. All that changed when Marc Andreesen, then a graduate student working for NCSA (the National Center for Supercomputing Applications), released Mosaic. Mosaic displayed web pages in graphical form, using images, fonts, and colors (see the figure). Andreesen went on to fame and fortune at Netscape, and Microsoft licensed the Mosaic code to create Internet Explorer. By 1996, WWW traffic accounted for more than half of the data transported on the Internet.

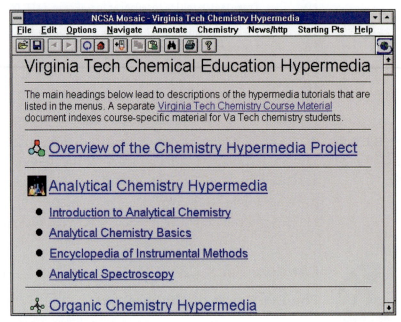

The NCSA Mosaic Browser

Summary of Learning Objectives

Use integers and floating-point numbers.

- A type specifies a set of values and the operations that can be carried out with the values.
- The double type denotes floating-point numbers that can have fractional parts.
- In Java, the number types are primitive types, and numbers are not objects.
- Numbers can be combined by arithmetic operators such as +, -, and *.

Write variable declarations in Java.

- You use variables to store values that you want to use at a later time. A variable has a type, a name, and a value.
- Identifiers for variables, methods, and classes are composed of letters, digits, and the underscore character.
- By convention, variable names should start with a lowercase letter.

Explain the processes of variable assignment and initialization.
- Use the assignment operator (=) to change the value of a variable.
- All variables must be initialized before you access them.

Declare objects, classes, and methods.
- Objects are entities in your program that you manipulate by calling methods.
- A method is a sequence of instructions that accesses the data of an object.
- A class declares the methods that you can apply to its objects.
- The public interface of a class specifies what you can do with its objects. The hidden implementation describes how these actions are carried out.

Recognize implicit parameters, explicit parameters, and return values of methods.
- A parameter is an input to a method.
- The implicit parameter of a method call is the object on which the method is invoked. All other parameters are explicit parameters.
- The return value of a method is a result that the method has computed for use by the code that called it.

Use constructors to construct new objects.
- Use the new operator, followed by a class name and parameters, to construct new objects.

Classify methods as accessor and mutator methods.
- An accessor method does not change the internal data of its implicit parameter. A mutator method changes the data.

Use the API documentation for finding method descriptions and packages.
- The API (Application Programming Interface) documentation lists the classes and methods of the Java library.
- Java classes are grouped into packages. Use the import statement to use classes that are declared in other packages.

Write programs that test behavior of methods.
- A test program verifies that methods behave as expected.
- Determining the expected result in advance is an important part of testing.

Describe how multiple object references can refer to the same object.
- An object reference describes the location of an object.
- Multiple object variables can contain references to the same object.
- Number variables store numbers. Object variables store references.

Write programs that display frame windows.
- To show a frame, construct a JFrame object, set its size, and make it visible.
- In order to display a drawing in a frame, declare a class that extends the JComponent class.
- Place drawing instructions inside the paintComponent method. That method is called whenever the component needs to be repainted.

- Use a cast to recover the Graphics2D object from the Graphics parameter of the paintComponent method.
- Applets are programs that run inside a web browser.
- To run an applet, you need an HTML file with the applet tag.
- You view applets with the applet viewer or a Java-enabled browser.

Use the Java API for drawing simple figures.

- The Ellipse2D.Double and Line2D.Double classes describe graphical shapes.
- The drawString method draws a string, starting at its basepoint.
- When you set a new color in the graphics context, it is used for subsequent drawing operations.

Classes, Objects, and Methods Introduced in this Chapter

```
java.awt.Color                          java.awt.Rectangle
java.awt.Component                         getX
   getHeight                               getY
   getWidth                                getHeight
   setSize                                 getWidth
   setVisible                              setSize
java.awt.Frame                             translate
   setTitle                             java.lang.String
java.awt.geom.Ellipse2D.Double             length
java.awt.geom.Line2D.Double                replace
java.awt.geom.Point2D.Double               toLowerCase
java.awt.Graphics                          toUpperCase
   setColor                             javax.swing.JComponent
java.awt.Graphics2D                        paintComponent
   draw                                 javax.swing.JFrame
   drawString                             setDefaultCloseOperation
   fill
```

Media Resources

www.wiley.com/
college/
horstmann

- ***Worked Example*** How Many Days Have You Been Alive?
- ***Worked Example*** Working with Pictures
- Lab Exercises
- ⊕ ***Animation*** Variable Initialization and Assignment
- ⊕ ***Animation*** Parameter Passing
- ⊕ ***Animation*** Object References
- ⊕ Practice Quiz
- ⊕ Code Completion Exercises

Review Exercises

★   **R2.1** Explain the difference between an object and an object reference.

★   **R2.2** Explain the difference between an object and an object variable.

★ **R2.3** Explain the difference between an object and a class.

★★ **R2.4** Give the Java code for constructing an *object* of class `Rectangle`, and for declaring an *object variable* of class `Rectangle`.

★★ **R2.5** Explain the difference between the = symbol in Java and in mathematics.

★★ **R2.6** Give Java code for objects with the following descriptions:

    a. A rectangle with center (100, 100) and all side lengths equal to 50

    b. A string with the contents "Hello, Dave"

Create objects, not object variables.

★★ **R2.7** Repeat Exercise R2.6, but now declare object variables that are initialized with the required objects.

★★ **R2.8** Write a Java statement to initialize a variable `square` with a rectangle object whose top left corner is (10, 20) and whose sides all have length 40. Then write a statement that replaces `square` with a rectangle of the same size and top left corner (20, 20).

★★ **R2.9** Write Java statements that initialize two variables `square1` and `square2` to refer to the same square with center (20, 20) and side length 40.

★★ **R2.10** Write Java statements that initialize a string `message` with `"Hello"` and then change it to `"HELLO"`. Use the `toUpperCase` method.

★★ **R2.11** Write Java statements that initialize a string `message` with `"Hello"` and then change it to `"hello"`. Use the `replace` method.

★★ **R2.12** Find the errors in the following statements:

    a. `Rectangle r = (5, 10, 15, 20);`

    b. `double width = Rectangle(5, 10, 15, 20).getWidth();`

    c. `Rectangle r;`
       `r.translate(15, 25);`

    d. `r = new Rectangle();`
       `r.translate("far, far away!");`

★ **R2.13** Name two accessor methods and two mutator methods of the `Rectangle` class.

★★ **R2.14** Look into the API documentation of the `Rectangle` class and locate the method

```
void add(int newx, int newy)
```

Read through the method documentation. Then determine the result of the following statements:

```
Rectangle box = new Rectangle(5, 10, 20, 30);
box.add(0, 0);
```

If you are not sure, write a small test program.

★G **R2.15** What is the difference between a console application and a graphical application?

★★G **R2.16** Who calls the `paintComponent` method of a component? When does the call to the `paintComponent` method occur?

★★G **R2.17** Why does the parameter of the `paintComponent` method have type `Graphics` and not `Graphics2D`?

★★G **R2.18** What is the purpose of a graphics context?

★★G **R2.19** Why are separate viewer and component classes used for graphical programs?

★G **R2.20** How do you specify a text color?

Programming Exercises

★T **P2.1** Write an AreaTester program that constructs a Rectangle object and then computes and prints its area. Use the getWidth and getHeight methods. Also print the expected answer.

★T **P2.2** Write a PerimeterTester program that constructs a Rectangle object and then computes and prints its perimeter. Use the getWidth and getHeight methods. Also print the expected answer.

★★ **P2.3** Write a program called FourRectanglePrinter that constructs a Rectangle object, prints its location by calling System.out.println(box), and then translates and prints it three more times, so that, if the rectangles were drawn, they would form one large rectangle:

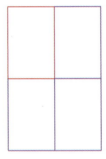

Your program will not produce a drawing. It will simply print the locations of the four rectangles.

★★ **P2.4** Write a GrowSquarePrinter program that constructs a Rectangle object square representing a square with top-left corner (100, 100) and side length 50, prints its location by calling System.out.println(square), applies the translate and grow methods and calls System.out.println(square) again. The calls to translate and grow should modify the square so that it has twice the size and the same top-left corner as the original. If the squares were drawn, they would look like this:

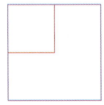

Your program will not produce a drawing. It will simply print the locations of square before and after calling the mutator methods.

Look up the description of the grow method in the API documentation.

★★★ **P2.5** The `intersection` method computes the *intersection* of two rectangles—that is, the rectangle that would be formed by two overlapping rectangles if they were drawn:

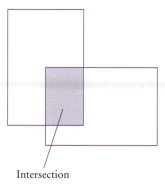

Intersection

You call this method as follows:

```
Rectangle r3 = r1.intersection(r2);
```

Write a program `IntersectionPrinter` that constructs two rectangle objects, prints them as described in Exercise P2.3, and then prints the rectangle object that describes the intersection. Then the program should print the result of the `intersection` method when the rectangles do not overlap. Add a comment to your program that explains how you can tell whether the resulting rectangle is empty.

★★★ **P2.6** In this exercise, you will explore a simple way of visualizing a `Rectangle` object. The `setBounds` method of the `JFrame` class moves a frame window to a given rectangle. Complete the following program to visually show the `translate` method of the `Rectangle` class:

```java
import java.awt.Rectangle;
import javax.swing.JFrame;
import javax.swing.JOptionPane;

public class TranslateDemo
{
    public static void main(String[] args)
    {
        // Construct a frame and show it
        JFrame frame = new JFrame();
        frame.setDefaultCloseOperation(JFrame.EXIT_ON_CLOSE);
        frame.setVisible(true);

        // Your work goes here:
        // Construct a rectangle and set the frame bounds

        JOptionPane.showMessageDialog(frame, "Click OK to continue");

        // Your work goes here:
        // Move the rectangle and set the frame bounds again
    }
}
```

★★ **P2.7** In the Java library, a color is specified by its red, green, and blue components between 0 and 255 (see Table 4 on page 67). Write a program `BrighterDemo` that constructs a `Color` object with red, green, and blue values of 50, 100, and 150. Then apply the brighter method and print the red, green, and blue values of the resulting color. (You won't actually see the color—see the next exercise on how to display the color.)

★★ P2.8 Repeat Exercise P2.7, but place your code into the following class. Then the color will be displayed.

```java
import java.awt.Color;
import javax.swing.JFrame;

public class BrighterDemo
{
    public static void main(String[] args)
    {
        JFrame frame = new JFrame();
        frame.setSize(200, 200);
        Color myColor = ...;
        frame.getContentPane().setBackground(myColor);
        frame.setDefaultCloseOperation(JFrame.EXIT_ON_CLOSE);
        frame.setVisible(true);
    }
}
```

★★ P2.9 Repeat Exercise P2.7, but apply the `darker` method twice to the object `Color.RED`. Call your class `DarkerDemo`.

★★ P2.10 The `Random` class implements a *random number generator*, which produces sequences of numbers that appear to be random. To generate random integers, you construct an object of the `Random` class, and then apply the `nextInt` method. For example, the call `generator.nextInt(6)` gives you a random number between 0 and 5.

Write a program `DieSimulator` that uses the `Random` class to simulate the cast of a die, printing a random number between 1 and 6 every time that the program is run.

★★★ P2.11 Write a program `LotteryPrinter` that picks a combination in a lottery. In this lottery, players can choose 6 numbers (possibly repeated) between 1 and 49. (In a real lottery, repetitions aren't allowed, but we haven't yet discussed the programming constructs that would be required to deal with that problem.) Your program should print out a sentence such as "Play this combination—it'll make you rich!", followed by a lottery combination.

★★T P2.12 Write a program `ReplaceTester` that encodes a string by replacing all letters `"i"` with `"!"` and all letters `"s"` with `"$"`. Use the `replace` method. Demonstrate that you can correctly encode the string `"Mississippi"`. Print both the actual and expected result.

★★★ P2.13 Write a program `HollePrinter` that switches the letters `"e"` and `"o"` in a string. Use the `replace` method repeatedly. Demonstrate that the string `"Hello, World!"` turns into `"Holle, Werld!"`

★★G P2.14 Write a graphics program that draws your name in red, contained inside a blue rectangle. Provide a class `NameViewer` and a class `NameComponent`.

★★G P2.15 Write a graphics program that draws 12 strings, one each for the 12 standard colors, besides `Color.WHITE`, each in its own color. Provide a class `ColorNameViewer` and a class `ColorNameComponent`.

★★G P2.16 Write a program that draws two solid squares: one in pink and one in purple. Use a standard color for one of them and a custom color for the other. Provide a class `TwoSquareViewer` and a class `TwoSquareComponent`.

★★★G **P2.17** Write a program that fills the window with a large ellipse, with a black outline and filled with your favorite color. The ellipse should touch the window boundaries, even if the window is resized.

★★G **P2.18** Write a program to plot the following face.

Provide a class FaceViewer and a class FaceComponent.

Programming Projects

Project 2.1 The GregorianCalendar class describes a point in time, as measured by the Gregorian calendar, the standard calendar that is commonly used throughout the world today. You construct a GregorianCalendar object from a year, month, and day of the month, like this:

```
GregorianCalendar cal = new GregorianCalendar(); // Today's date
GregorianCalendar eckertsBirthday = new GregorianCalendar(1919,
    Calendar.APRIL, 9);
```

Use the values Calendar.JANUARY . . . Calendar.DECEMBER to specify the month.

The add method can be used to add a number of days to a GregorianCalendar object:

```
cal.add(Calendar.DAY_OF_MONTH, 10); // Now cal is ten days from today
```

This is a mutator method—it changes the cal object.

The get method can be used to query a given GregorianCalendar object:

```
int dayOfMonth = cal.get(Calendar.DAY_OF_MONTH);
int month = cal.get(Calendar.MONTH);
int year = cal.get(Calendar.YEAR);
int weekday = cal.get(Calendar.DAY_OF_WEEK);
    // 1 is Sunday, 2 is Monday, . . . , 7 is Saturday
```

Your task is to write a program that prints the following information:

- The date and weekday that is 100 days from today
- The weekday of your birthday
- The date that is 10,000 days from your birthday

Use the birthday of a computer scientist if you don't want to reveal your own birthday.

Project 2.2 Run the following program:

```
import java.awt.Color;
import javax.swing.JFrame;
import javax.swing.JLabel;

public class FrameViewer
{
    public static void main(String[] args)
    {
```

```
                JFrame frame = new JFrame();
                frame.setSize(200, 200);
                JLabel label = new JLabel("Hello, World!");
                label.setOpaque(true);
                label.setBackground(Color.PINK);
                frame.add(label);
                frame.setDefaultCloseOperation(JFrame.EXIT_ON_CLOSE);
                frame.setVisible(true);
            }
        }
```

Modify the program as follows:

- Double the frame size.
- Change the greeting to "Hello, *your name*!".
- Change the background color to pale green (see Exercise P2.7).
- For extra credit, add an image of yourself. (*Hint:* Construct an `ImageIcon`.)

Answers to Self-Check Questions

1. `int` and `String`
2. `double`
3. An `int` is not an object, and you cannot call a method on it.
4. `(x + y) * 0.5`
5. Only the first two are legal identifiers.
6. `String myName = "John Q. Public";`
7. No, the left-hand side of the = operator must be a variable.
8. `greeting = "Hello, Nina!";`
   Note that
   `String greeting = "Hello, Nina!";`
   is not the right answer—that statement declares a new variable.
9. `river.length()` or `"Mississippi".length()`
10. `System.out.println(greeting.toUpperCase());`
    or
    `System.out.println("Hello, World!".toUpperCase());`
11. It is not legal. The variable `river` has type `String`. The `println` method is not a method of the `String` class.
12. The implicit parameter is `river`. There is no explicit parameter. The return value is 11.
13. `"Missississi"`
14. 12
15. As `public String toUpperCase()`, with no explicit parameter and return type `String`.
16. `new Rectangle(90, 90, 20, 20)`
17. 0
18. An accessor—it doesn't modify the original string but returns a new string with uppercase letters.

19. `box.translate(-5, -10)`, provided the method is called immediately after storing the new rectangle into `box`.

20. `toLowerCase`

21. `"Hello, Space !"`—only the leading and trailing spaces are trimmed.

22. Add the statement `import java.util.Random;` at the top of your program.

23. `x: 30, y: 25`

24. Because the `translate` method doesn't modify the shape of the rectangle.

25. Now `greeting` and `greeting2` both refer to the same `String` object.

26. Both variables still refer to the same string, and the string has not been modified. Recall that the `toUpperCase` method constructs a new string that contains uppercase characters, leaving the original string unchanged.

27. Modify the `EmptyFrameViewer` program as follows:

```
frame.setSize(300, 300);
frame.setTitle("Hello, World!");
```

28. Construct two `JFrame` objects, set each of their sizes, and call `setVisible(true)` on each of them.

29. `Rectangle box = new Rectangle(5, 10, 20, 20);`

30. Replace the call to `box.translate(15, 25)` with

```
box = new Rectangle(20, 35, 20, 20);
```

31. The compiler complains that `g` doesn't have a `draw` method.

32. `g2.draw(new Ellipse2D.Double(75, 75, 50, 50));`

33.
```
Line2D.Double segment1 = new Line2D.Double(0, 0, 10, 30);
g2.draw(segment1);
Line2D.Double segment2 = new Line2D.Double(10, 30, 20, 0);
g2.draw(segment2);
```

34. `g2.drawString("V", 0, 30);`

35. `0, 0, 255`

36. First fill a big red square, then fill a small yellow square inside:

```
g2.setColor(Color.RED);
g2.fill(new Rectangle(0, 0, 200, 200));
g2.setColor(Color.YELLOW);
g2.fill(new Rectangle(50, 50, 100, 100));
```

Chapter 3

Implementing Classes

CHAPTER GOALS

- To become familiar with the process of implementing classes
- To be able to implement simple methods
- To understand the purpose and use of constructors
- To understand how to access instance variables and local variables
- To be able to write javadoc comments
- G To implement classes for drawing graphical shapes

In this chapter, you will learn how to implement your own classes. You will start with a given design that specifies the public interface of the class—that is, the methods through which programmers can manipulate the objects of the class. Then you will learn the steps to completing the class. You need to implement the methods, which requires that you find a data representation for the objects, and supply the instructions for each method. You need to document your efforts so that other programmers can understand and use your creation. And you need to provide a tester to validate that your class works correctly.

CHAPTER CONTENTS

3.1 Instance Variables

In Chapter 2, you learned how to use objects from existing classes. In this chapter, you will start implementing your own classes. We begin with a very simple example that shows you how objects store their data, and how methods access the data of an object. You will then learn a systematic process for implementing classes.

Our first example is a class that models a *tally counter*, a mechanical device that is used to count people—for example, to find out how many people attend a concert or board a bus (see Figure 1).

Whenever the operator pushes a button, the counter value advances by one. We model this operation with a count method. A physical counter has a display to show the current value. In our simulation, we use a getValue method instead. For example,

```
Counter tally = new Counter();
tally.count();
tally.count();
int result = tally.getValue(); // Sets result to 2
```

When implementing the Counter class, we need to determine the data that each counter object contains. In this simple example, that is very straightforward. Each counter needs to store a variable that keeps track of how many times the counter has been advanced.

Figure 1 A Tally Counter

82

Syntax 3.1 Instance Variable Declaration

Syntax
```
accessSpecifier class ClassName
{
    accessSpecifier typeName variableName;
    . . .
}
```

Example

Instance variables should always be private.

```
public class Counter
{
    private int value;
    . . .
}
```

Each object of this class has a separate copy of this instance variable.

Type of the variable

An object's instance variables store the data required for executing its methods.

An object stores its data in **instance variables**. An *instance* of a class is an object of the class. Thus, an instance variable is a storage location that is present in each object of the class.

You specify instance variables in the class declaration:

```
public class Counter
{
    private int value;
    . . .
}
```

An instance variable declaration consists of the following parts:

- An **access specifier** (private)
- The **type** of the instance variable (such as int)
- The name of the instance variable (such as value)

Each object of a class has its own set of instance variables.

Each object of a class has its own set of instance variables. For example, if concert-Counter and boardingCounter are two objects of the Counter class, then each object has its own value variable (see Figure 2). As you will see in Section 3.7, the instance variable value is set to 0 when a Counter object is constructed.

In order to gain a better understanding of how methods affect instance variables, we will have a quick look at the implementation of the methods of the Counter class.

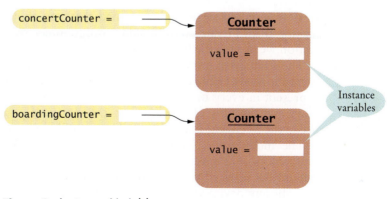

Figure 2 Instance Variables

The `count` method advances the counter value by 1. We will cover the syntax of the method header in Section 3.3. For now, focus on the body of the method inside the braces:

```
public void count()
{
    value = value + 1;
}
```

Note how the `count` method accesses the instance variable `value`. *Which* instance variable? The one belonging to the object on which the method is invoked. For example, consider the call

```
concertCounter.count();
```

This call advances the `value` variable of the `concertCounter` object.

The `getValue` method returns the current value:

```
public int getValue()
{
    return value;
}
```

The `return` statement is a special statement that terminates the method call and returns a result to the method's caller.

> Private instance variables can only be accessed by methods of the same class.

Instance variables are generally declared with the access specifier `private`. That specifier means that they can be accessed only by the methods of the *same class*, not by any other method. For example, the `value` variable can be accessed by the `count` and `getValue` methods of the `Counter` class but not a method of another class. Those other methods need to use the `Counter` class methods if they want to manipulate a counter's value.

In the next section, we discuss the reason for making instance variables private.

SELF CHECK

1. Supply the body of a method `public void reset()` that resets the counter back to zero.

2. Suppose you use a class `Clock` with private instance variables `hours` and `minutes`. How can you access these variables in your program?

3.2 Encapsulation

In the preceding section, you learned that you should hide instance variables by making them private. Why would a programmer want to hide something? In this section we discuss the benefits of information hiding.

The strategy of information hiding is not unique to computer programming—it is used in many engineering disciplines. Consider the electronic control module that is present in every modern car. It is a device that controls the timing of the spark plugs and the flow of gasoline into the motor. If you ask your mechanic what is inside the electronic control module, you will likely get a shrug.

The module is a *black box*, something that magically does its thing. A car mechanic would never open the control module—it contains electronic parts that can only be serviced at the factory. In general, engineers use the term "black box" to describe any device whose inner workings are hidden. Note that a black box is not totally mysterious. Its interface with the outside world is well-defined. For example, the car mechanic understands how the electronic control module must be connected with sensors and engine parts.

The process of hiding implementation details while publishing an interface is called **encapsulation**. In Java, the class construct provides encapsulation. The public methods of a class are the interface through which the private implementation is manipulated.

> Encapsulation is the process of hiding implementation details and providing methods for data access.

Why do car manufacturers put black boxes into cars? The black box greatly simplifies the work of the car mechanic. Before engine control modules were invented, gasoline flow was regulated by a mechanical device called a carburetor, and car mechanics had to know how to adjust the springs and latches inside. Nowadays, a mechanic no longer needs to know what is inside the module.

Similarly, a programmer using a class is not burdened by unnecessary detail, as you know from your own experience. In Chapter 2, you used classes for strings, streams, and windows without worrying how these classes are implemented.

> Encapsulation allows a programmer to use a class without having to know its implementation.

Encapsulation also helps with diagnosing errors. A large program may consist of hundreds of classes and thousands of methods, but if there is an error with the internal data of an object, you only need to look at the methods of one class. Finally, encapsulation makes it possible to change the implementation of a class without having to tell the programmers who use the class.

> Information hiding makes it simpler for the implementor of a class to locate errors and change implementations.

In Chapter 2, you learned to be an object user. You saw how to obtain objects, how to manipulate them, and how to assemble them into a program. In that chapter, your treated objects as black boxes. Your role was roughly analogous to the car mechanic who fixed a car by hooking up a new engine control module.

In this chapter, you will move on to implementing classes. In these sections, your role is analogous to the car parts manufacturer who puts together an engine control module from transistors, capacitors, and other electronic parts. You will learn the necessary Java programming techniques that enable your objects to carry out the desired behavior.

SELF CHECK

3. Consider the Counter class. A counter's value starts at 0 and is advanced by the count method, so it should never be negative. Suppose you found a negative value variable during testing. Where would you look for the error?

4. In Chapters 1 and 2, you used System.out as a black box to cause output to appear on the screen. Who designed and implemented System.out?

5. Suppose you are working in a company that produces personal finance software. You are asked to design and implement a class for representing bank accounts. Who will be the users of your class?

3.3 Specifying the Public Interface of a Class

In this section, we will discuss the process of specifying the public interface of a class. Imagine that you are a member of a team that works on banking software. A fundamental concept in banking is a *bank account*. Your task is to understand the design of a BankAccount class so that you can implement it, which in turn allows other programmers on the team to use it.

In order to implement a class, you first need to know which methods are required.

You need to know exactly what features of a bank account need to be implemented. Some features are essential (such as deposits), whereas others are not important (such as the gift that a customer may receive for opening a bank account). Deciding which features are essential is not always an easy task. We will revisit that issue in Chapters 8 and 12. For now, we will assume that a competent designer has decided that the following are considered the essential operations of a bank account:

- Deposit money
- Withdraw money
- Get the current balance

In Java, operations are expressed as method calls. To figure out the exact specification of the method calls, imagine how a programmer would carry out the bank account operations. We'll assume that the variable harrysChecking contains a reference to an object of type BankAccount. We want to support method calls such as the following:

```
harrysChecking.deposit(2240.59);
harrysChecking.withdraw(500);
double currentBalance = harrysChecking.getBalance();
```

The first two methods are mutators. They modify the balance of the bank account and don't return a value. The third method is an accessor. It returns a value that you store in a variable or pass to a method.

As you can see from the sample calls, the BankAccount class should declare three methods:

- public void deposit(double amount)
- public void withdraw(double amount)
- public double getBalance()

Recall from Chapter 2 that double denotes the double-precision floating-point type, and void indicates that a method does not return a value.

Here we only give the method *headers*. When you declare a method, you also need to provide the method *body*, consisting of statements that are executed when the method is called.

```
public void deposit(double amount)
{
    implementation—filled in later
}
```

We will supply the method bodies in Section 3.5.

Every method header contains the following parts:

In a method header, you specify the return type, method name, and the types and names of the parameters.

- An **access specifier** (usually public)
- The *return type* (the type of the value returned, such as void or double)
- The name of the method (such as deposit)
- A list of the **parameter variables** of the method (if any), enclosed in parentheses (such as double amount)

The access specifier controls which other methods can call this method. Most methods should be declared as public. That way, all other methods in a program can call them. (Occasionally, it can be useful to have private methods. They can only be called from other methods of the same class.)

The return type is the type of the value that the method returns. The `deposit` method does not return a value, whereas the `getBalance` method returns a value of type `double`.

Each parameter of the method has both a type and a name that describes its purpose. For example, the `deposit` method has a single parameter named `amount` of type `double`.

Next, you need to supply **constructors**. A constructor initializes the instance variables of an object. In Java, a constructor is very similar to a method, with two important differences.

- The name of the constructor is always the same as the name of the class (e.g., `BankAccount`).
- Constructors have no return type (not even `void`).

We want to construct bank accounts that initially have a zero balance, as well as accounts that have a given initial balance. For this purpose, we specify two constructors.

- `public BankAccount()`
- `public BankAccount(double initialBalance)`

They are used as follows:

```
BankAccount harrysChecking = new BankAccount();
BankAccount momsSavings = new BankAccount(5000);
```

Constructors set the initial data for objects. The constructor name is always the same as the class name.

Just like a method, a constructor also has a body—a sequence of statements that is executed when a new object is constructed.

```
public BankAccount()
{
    implementation—filled in later
}
```

The statements in the constructor body will set the instance variables of the object that is being constructed—see Section 3.5.

Don't worry about the fact that there are two constructors with the same name—*all* constructors of a class have the same name, that is, the name of the class. The compiler can tell them apart because they take different parameters.

When declaring a class, you place all constructor and method declarations inside, like this:

```
public class BankAccount
{
    private instance variables—filled in later

    // Constructors
    public BankAccount()
    {
        implementation—filled in later
    }

    public BankAccount(double initialBalance)
    {
        implementation—filled in later
    }
```

```
// Methods
public void deposit(double amount)
{
    implementation—filled in later
}

public void withdraw(double amount)
{
    implementation—filled in later
}

public double getBalance()
{
    implementation—filled in later
}
}
```

The public constructors and methods of a class form the **public interface** of the class. These are the operations that any programmer can use to create and manipulate BankAccount objects.

Our BankAccount class is simple, but it allows programmers to carry out all of the important operations that commonly occur with bank accounts. For example, consider this program segment, authored by a programmer who uses the BankAccount class. These statements transfer an amount of money from one bank account to another:

```
// Transfer from one account to another
double transferAmount = 500;
momsSavings.withdraw(transferAmount);
harrysChecking.deposit(transferAmount);
```

And here is a program segment that adds interest to a savings account:

```
double interestRate = 5; // 5% interest
double interestAmount
    = momsSavings.getBalance() * interestRate / 100;
momsSavings.deposit(interestAmount);
```

Syntax 3.2   Class Declaration

Syntax	*accessSpecifier* class *ClassName*
	{
	    instance variables
	    constructors
	    methods
	}

Example

```
public class Counter
{
    private int value; ─────────────────────────┐ Private
                                                   implementation
    public Counter(int initialValue) { value = initialValue; }

    public void count() { value = value + 1; }
    public int getValue() { return value; }
}
```

Public interface

As you can see, programmers can use objects of the BankAccount class to carry out meaningful tasks, without knowing how the BankAccount objects store their data or how the BankAccount methods do their work.

Of course, as implementors of the BankAccount class, we will need to supply the private implementation. We will do so in Section 3.5. First, however, an important step remains: *documenting* the public interface. That is the topic of the next section.

SELF CHECK

6. How can you use the methods of the public interface to *empty* the harrysChecking bank account?

7. What is wrong with this sequence of statements?

```
BankAccount harrysChecking = new BankAccount(10000);
System.out.println(harrysChecking.withdraw(500));
```

8. Suppose you want a more powerful bank account abstraction that keeps track of an *account number* in addition to the balance. How would you change the public interface to accommodate this enhancement?

Common Error 3.1

Declaring a Constructor as void

Do not use the void reserved word when you declare a constructor:

```
public void BankAccount()   // Error—don't use void!
```

This would declare a method with return type void and *not* a constructor. Unfortunately, the Java compiler does not consider this a syntax error.

3.4 Commenting the Public Interface

When you implement classes and methods, you should get into the habit of thoroughly *commenting* their behaviors. In Java there is a very useful standard form for **documentation comments**. If you use this form in your classes, a program called javadoc can automatically generate a neat set of HTML pages that describe them. (See Productivity Hint 3.1 on page 92 for a description of this utility.)

A documentation comment is placed before the class or method declaration that is being documented. It starts with a /**, a special comment delimiter used by the javadoc utility. Then you describe the method's *purpose*. Then, for each method parameter, you supply a line that starts with @param, followed by the parameter name and a short explanation. Finally, you supply a line that starts with @return, describing the return value. You omit the @param tag for methods that have no parameters, and you omit the @return tag for methods whose return type is void.

> Use documentation comments to describe the classes and public methods of your programs.

The javadoc utility copies the *first* sentence of each comment to a summary table in the HTML documentation. Therefore, it is best to write that first sentence with some care. It should start with an uppercase letter and end with a period. It does not have to be a grammatically complete sentence, but it should be meaningful when it is pulled out of the comment and displayed in a summary.

Here are two typical examples.

```
/**
    Withdraws money from the bank account.
    @param amount  the amount to withdraw
*/
public void withdraw(double amount)
{
    implementation—filled in later
}

/**
    Gets the current balance of the bank account.
    @return  the current balance
*/
public double getBalance()
{
    implementation—filled in later
}
```

The comments you have just seen explain individual *methods*. Supply a brief comment for each *class*, explaining its purpose. The comment syntax for class comments is very simple: Just place the documentation comment above the class.

```
/**
    A bank account has a balance that can be changed by
    deposits and withdrawals.
*/
public class BankAccount
{
    . . .
}
```

Your first reaction may well be "Whoa! Am I supposed to write all this stuff?" These comments do seem pretty repetitive. But you should take the time to write them, even if it feels silly.

It is always a good idea to write the method comment *first*, before writing the code in the method body. This is an excellent test to see that you firmly understand what you need to program. If you can't explain what a class or method does, you aren't ready to implement it.

What about very simple methods? You can easily spend more time pondering whether a comment is too trivial to write than it takes to write it. In practical programming, very simple methods are rare. It is harmless to have a trivial method overcommented, whereas a complicated method without any comment can cause real grief to future maintenance programmers. According to the standard Java documentation style, *every* class, *every* method, *every* parameter, and *every* return value should have a comment.

The javadoc utility formats your comments into a neat set of documents that you can view in a web browser. It makes good use of the seemingly repetitive phrases. The first sentence of the comment is used for a *summary table* of all methods of your class (see Figure 3). The @param and @return comments are neatly formatted in the detail description of each method (see Figure 4). If you omit any of the comments, then javadoc generates documents that look strangely empty.

This documentation format should look familiar. The programmers who implement the Java library use javadoc themselves. They too document every class, every

Provide documentation comments for every class, every method, every parameter, and every return value.

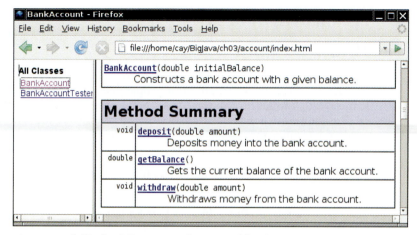

Figure 3 A Method Summary Generated by javadoc

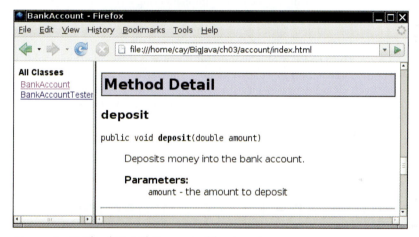

Figure 4 Method Detail Generated by javadoc

method, every parameter, and every return value, and then use javadoc to extract the documentation in HTML format.

SELF CHECK

9. Provide documentation comments for the Counter class of Section 3.1.

10. Suppose we enhance the BankAccount class so that each account has an account number. Supply a documentation comment for the constructor

```
public BankAccount(int accountNumber, double initialBalance)
```

11. Why is the following documentation comment questionable?

```
/**
    Each account has an account number.
    @return  the account number of this account
*/
public int getAccountNumber()
```

Productivity Hint 3.1

The javadoc Utility

Always insert documentation comments in your code, whether or not you use javadoc to produce HTML documentation. Most people find the HTML documentation convenient, so it is worth learning how to run javadoc. Some programming environments (such as BlueJ) can execute javadoc for you. Alternatively, you can invoke the javadoc utility from a shell window, by issuing the command

```
javadoc MyClass.java
```

or, if you want to document multiple Java files,

```
javadoc *.java
```

The javadoc utility produces files such as MyClass.html in HTML format, which you can inspect in a browser. If you know HTML (see Appendix F), you can embed HTML tags into the comments to specify fonts or add images. Perhaps most importantly, javadoc automatically provides *hyperlinks* to other classes and methods.

You can run javadoc before implementing any methods. Just leave all the method bodies empty. Don't run the compiler—it would complain about missing return values. Simply run javadoc on your file to generate the documentation for the public interface that you are about to implement.

The javadoc tool is wonderful because it does one thing right: It allows you to put the documentation *together with your code*. That way, when you update your programs, you can see right away which documentation needs to be updated. Hopefully, you will update it right then and there. Afterward, run javadoc again and get updated information that is timely and nicely formatted.

3.5 Providing the Class Implementation

Now that you understand the specification of the public interface of the BankAccount class, let's provide the implementation.

First, we need to determine the data that each bank account object contains. In the case of our simple bank account class, each object needs to store a single value, the current balance. (A more complex bank account class might store additional data—perhaps an account number, the interest rate paid, the date for mailing out the next statement, and so on.)

> The private implementation of a class consists of instance variables, and the bodies of constructors and methods.

```
public class BankAccount
{
    private double balance;
    . . .
}
```

Now that we have determined the instance variables, let's complete the BankAccount class by supplying the bodies of the constructors and methods. Each body contains a sequence of statements. We'll start with the constructors because they are very straightforward. A constructor has a simple job: to initialize the instance variables of an object.

Recall that we designed the BankAccount class to have two constructors. The first constructor simply sets the balance to zero:

```
public BankAccount()
{
    balance = 0;
}
```

The second constructor sets the balance to the value supplied as the construction parameter:

```
public BankAccount(double initialBalance)
{
    balance = initialBalance;
}
```

To see how these constructors work, let us trace the statement

```
BankAccount harrysChecking = new BankAccount(1000);
```

one step at a time.

Here are the steps that are carried out when the statement executes.

- Create a new object of type BankAccount.
- Call the second constructor (because a parameter value is supplied in the constructor call).
- Set the parameter variable initialBalance to 1000.
- Set the balance instance variable of the newly created object to initialBalance.
- Return an object reference, that is, the memory location of the object, as the value of the new expression.
- Store that object reference in the harrysChecking variable.

Let's move on to implementing the BankAccount methods. Here is the deposit method:

```
public void deposit(double amount)
{
    balance = balance + amount;
}
```

To understand exactly what the method does, consider this statement:

```
harrysChecking.deposit(500);
```

This statement carries out the following steps:

- Set the parameter variable amount to 500.
- Fetch the balance instance variable of the object whose location is stored in harrysChecking.
- Add the value of amount to balance
- Store the sum in the balance instance variable, overwriting the old value.

The withdraw method is very similar to the deposit method:

```
public void withdraw(double amount)
{
    balance = balance - amount;
}
```

Syntax 3.3 Method Declaration

Syntax   *accessSpecifier returnType methodName(parameterType parameterName, . . .)*
            {
                method body
            }

Example

This method does
not return a value.

public void deposit(double amount)
{
    balance = balance + amount;
}

A mutator method modifies
an instance variable.

These methods
are part of the
public interface.

This method has
no parameters.

public double getBalance()
{
    return balance;
}

An accessor method returns a value.

There is only one method left, getBalance. Unlike the deposit and withdraw methods, which modify the instance variables of the object on which they are invoked, the getBalance method returns a value:

```
public double getBalance()
{
    return balance;
}
```

We have now completed the implementation of the BankAccount class—see the code listing below. There is only one step remaining: testing that the class works correctly. That is the topic of the next section.

ch03/account/BankAccount.java

```
 1  /**
 2      A bank account has a balance that can be changed by
 3      deposits and withdrawals.
 4  */
 5  public class BankAccount
 6  {
 7      private double balance;
 8
 9      /**
10          Constructs a bank account with a zero balance.
11      */
12      public BankAccount()
13      {
14          balance = 0;
15      }
16
```

```
17      /**
18          Constructs a bank account with a given balance.
19          @param initialBalance  the initial balance
20      */
21      public BankAccount(double initialBalance)
22      {
23          balance = initialBalance;
24      }
25
26      /**
27          Deposits money into the bank account.
28          @param amount  the amount to deposit
29      */
30      public void deposit(double amount)
31      {
32          balance = balance + amount;
33      }
34
35      /**
36          Withdraws money from the bank account.
37          @param amount  the amount to withdraw
38      */
39      public void withdraw(double amount)
40      {
41          balance = balance - amount;
42      }
43
44      /**
45          Gets the current balance of the bank account.
46          @return  the current balance
47      */
48      public double getBalance()
49      {
50          return balance;
51      }
52  }
```

 **SELF CHECK**

12. Suppose we modify the BankAccount class so that each bank account has an account number. How does this change affect the instance variables?

13. Why does the following code not succeed in robbing mom's bank account?

```
public class BankRobber
{
    public static void main(String[] args)
    {
        BankAccount momsSavings = new BankAccount(1000);
        momsSavings.balance = 0;
    }
}
```

14. The Rectangle class has four instance variables: x, y, width, and height. Give a possible implementation of the getWidth method.

15. Give a possible implementation of the translate method of the Rectangle class.

How To 3.1

Implementing a Class

This "How To" section tells you how you implement a class from a given specification.

For example, a homework assignment might ask you to implement a class that models a cash register. Your class should allow a cashier to enter item prices and the amount of money that the customer paid. It should then calculate the change due.

Step 1 Find out which methods you are asked to supply.

In the cash register example, you won't have to provide every feature of a real cash register—there are too many. The assignment tells you, in plain English, *which aspects* of a cash register your class should simulate. Make a list of them:

- Ring up the sales price for a purchased item.
- Enter the amount of payment.
- Calculate the amount of change due to the customer.

Step 2 Specify the public interface.

Turn the list in Step 1 into a set of methods, with specific types for the parameters and the return values. Many programmers find this step simpler if they write out method calls that are applied to a sample object, like this:

```
CashRegister register = new CashRegister();
register.recordPurchase(29.95);
register.recordPurchase(9.95);
register.enterPayment(50);
double change = register.giveChange();
```

Now we have a specific list of methods.

- `public void recordPurchase(double amount)`
- `public void enterPayment(double amount)`
- `public double giveChange()`

To complete the public interface, you need to specify the constructors. Ask yourself what information you need in order to construct an object of your class. Sometimes you will want two constructors: one that sets all instance variables to a default and one that sets them to user-supplied values.

In the case of the cash register example, we can get by with a single constructor that creates an empty register. A more realistic cash register would start out with some coins and bills so that we can give exact change, but that is beyond the scope of our assignment.

Thus, we add a single constructor:

- `public CashRegister()`

Step 3 Document the public interface.

Here is the documentation, with comments, that describes the class and its methods:

```
/**
    A cash register totals up sales and computes change due.
*/
public class CashRegister
{
    /**
        Constructs a cash register with no money in it.
    */
    public CashRegister()
    {
    }
```

```
/**
    Records the sale of an item.
    @param amount  the price of the item
*/
public void recordPurchase(double amount)
{
}

/**
    Enters the payment received from the customer.
    @param amount  the amount of the payment
*/
public void enterPayment(double amount)
{
}

/**
    Computes the change due and resets the machine for the next customer.
    @return  the change due to the customer
*/
public double giveChange()
{
}
}
```

Step 4   Determine instance variables.

Ask yourself what information an object needs to store to do its job. Remember, the methods can be called in any order! The object needs to have enough internal memory to be able to process every method using just its instance variables and the method parameters. Go through each method, perhaps starting with a simple one or an interesting one, and ask yourself what you need to carry out the method's task. Make instance variables to store the information that the method needs.

In the cash register example, you would want to keep track of the total purchase amount and the payment. You can compute the change due from these two amounts.

```
public class CashRegister
{
    private double purchase;
    private double payment;
    . . .
}
```

Step 5   Implement constructors and methods.

Implement the constructors and methods in your class, one at a time, starting with the easiest ones. For example, here is the implementation of the recordPurchase method:

```
public void recordPurchase(double amount)
{
    purchase = purchase + amount;
}
```

Here is the giveChange method. Note that this method is a bit more sophisticated—it computes the change due, and it also resets the cash register for the next sale.

```
public double giveChange()
{
    double change = payment - purchase;
    purchase = 0;
    payment = 0;
    return change;
}
```

If you find that you have trouble with the implementation, you may need to rethink your choice of instance variables. It is common for a beginner to start out with a set of instance variables that cannot accurately reflect the state of an object. Don't hesitate to go back and add or modify instance variables.

Once you have completed the implementation, compile your class and fix any compile-time errors.

You can find the complete implementation in the ch03/cashregister directory of the book code.

Step 6 Test your class.

Write a short tester program and execute it. The tester program can carry out the method calls that you found in Step 2.

```java
public class CashRegisterTester
{
    public static void main(String[] args)
    {
        CashRegister register = new CashRegister();

        register.recordPurchase(29.50);
        register.recordPurchase(9.25);
        register.enterPayment(50);

        double change = register.giveChange();

        System.out.println(change);
        System.out.println("Expected: 11.25");
    }
}
```

The output of this test program is:

```
11.25
Expected: 11.25
```

Alternatively, if you use a program that lets you test objects interactively, such as BlueJ, construct an object and apply the method calls.

Worked Example 3.1

Making a Simple Menu

Worked Example 3.1 shows how to implement a class that constructs simple menus.

3.6 Unit Testing

In the preceding section, we completed the implementation of the BankAccount class. What can you do with it? Of course, you can compile the file BankAccount.java. However, you can't *execute* the resulting BankAccount.class file. It doesn't contain a main method. That is normal—most classes don't contain a main method.

In the long run, your class may become a part of a larger program that interacts with users, stores data in files, and so on. However, before integrating a class into a program, it is always a good idea to test it in isolation. Testing in isolation, outside a complete program, is called **unit testing**.

> A unit test verifies that a class works correctly in isolation, outside a complete program.

+ Available online in WileyPLUS and at www.wiley.com/college/horstmann.

Figure 5
The Return Value of the
getBalance Method in BlueJ

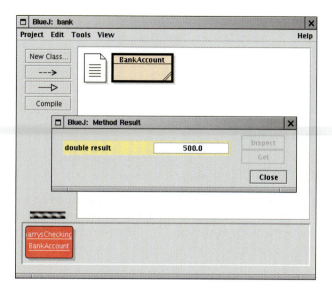

To test your class, you have two choices. Some interactive development environments have commands for constructing objects and invoking methods (see Special Topic 2.1). Then you can test a class simply by constructing an object, calling methods, and verifying that you get the expected return values. Figure 5 shows the result of calling the getBalance method on a BankAccount object in BlueJ.

Alternatively, you can write a *tester class*. A tester class is a class with a main method that contains statements to run methods of another class. As discussed in Section 2.9, a tester class typically carries out the following steps:

1. Construct one or more objects of the class that is being tested.
2. Invoke one or more methods.
3. Print out one or more results.
4. Print the expected results.

The MoveTester class in Section 2.9 is a good example of a tester class. That class runs methods of the Rectangle class—a class in the Java library.

Here is a class to run methods of the BankAccount class. The main method constructs an object of type BankAccount, invokes the deposit and withdraw methods, and then displays the remaining balance on the console.

We also print the value that we expect to see. In our sample program, we deposit $2,000 and withdraw $500. We therefore expect a balance of $1,500.

ch03/account/BankAccountTester.java

```
1   /**
2       A class to test the BankAccount class.
3   */
4   public class BankAccountTester
5   {
6      /**
7          Tests the methods of the BankAccount class.
8          @param args not used
9      */
10     public static void main(String[] args)
11     {
```

Gregorich

```
12      BankAccount harrysChecking = new BankAccount();
13      harrysChecking.deposit(2000);
14      harrysChecking.withdraw(500);
15      System.out.println(harrysChecking.getBalance());
16      System.out.println("Expected: 1500");
17    }
18  }
```

Program Run

```
1500
Expected: 1500
```

To produce a program, you need to combine the BankAccount and the BankAccount-Tester classes. The details for building the program depend on your compiler and development environment. In most environments, you need to carry out these steps:

1. Make a new subfolder for your program.
2. Make two files, one for each class.
3. Compile both files.
4. Run the test program.

Many students are surprised that such a simple program contains two classes. However, this is normal. The two classes have entirely different purposes. The Bank-Account class describes objects that compute bank balances. The BankAccountTester class runs a test that puts a BankAccount object through its paces.

SELF CHECK

16. When you run the BankAccountTester program, how many objects of class Bank-Account are constructed? How many objects of type BankAccountTester?

17. Why is the BankAccountTester class unnecessary in development environments that allow interactive testing, such as BlueJ?

3.7 Local Variables

Local variables are declared in the body of a method.

ANIMATION
Lifetime of Variables

In this section, we discuss the behavior of *local* variables. A **local variable** is a variable that is declared in the body of a method. For example, the giveChange method in How To 3.1 on page 96 declares a local variable change:

```
public double giveChange()
{
    double change = payment - purchase;
    purchase = 0;
    payment = 0;
    return change;
}
```

Parameter variables are similar to local variables, but they are declared in method headers. For example, the following method declares a parameter variable amount:

```
public void enterPayment(double amount)
```

When a method
exits, its local
variables are
removed.

Local and parameter variables belong to methods. When a method runs, its local and parameter variables come to life. When the method exits, they are removed immediately. For example, if you call `register.giveChange()`, then a variable `change` is created. When the method exits, that variable is removed.

In contrast, instance variables belong to objects, not methods. When an object is constructed, its instance variables are created. The instance variables stay alive until no method uses the object any longer. (The Java virtual machine contains an agent called a **garbage collector** that periodically reclaims objects when they are no longer used.)

Instance variables
are initialized to a
default value, but
you must initialize
local variables.

An important difference between instance variables and local variables is **initialization**. You must initialize all local variables. If you don't initialize a local variable, the compiler complains when you try to use it. (Note that parameter variables are initialized when the method is called.)

Instance variables are initialized with a default value before a constructor is invoked. Instance variables that are numbers are initialized to 0. Object references are set to a special value called `null`. If an object reference is `null`, then it refers to no object at all. We will discuss the `null` value in greater detail in Section 5.2.5.

SELF CHECK

18. What do local variables and parameter variables have in common? In which essential aspect do they differ?

19. Why was it necessary to introduce the local variable `change` in the `giveChange` method? That is, why didn't the method simply end with the statement

```
return payment - purchase;
```

Common Error 3.2

Forgetting to Initialize Object References in a Constructor

Just as it is a common error to forget to initialize a local variable, it is easy to forget about instance variables. Every constructor needs to ensure that all instance variables are set to appropriate values.

If you do not initialize an instance variable, the Java compiler will initialize it for you. Numbers are initialized with 0, but object references—such as string variables—are set to the `null` reference.

Of course, 0 is often a convenient default for numbers. However, `null` is hardly ever a convenient default for objects. Consider this "lazy" constructor for a modified version of the BankAccount class:

```java
public class BankAccount
{
    private double balance;
    private String owner;
    . . .
    public BankAccount(double initialBalance)
    {
        balance = initialBalance;
    }
}
```

Then `balance` is initialized, but the `owner` variable is set to a `null` reference. This can be a problem—it is illegal to call methods on the `null` reference.

To avoid this problem, it is a good idea to initialize every instance variable:

```
public BankAccount(double initialBalance)
{
    balance = initialBalance;
    owner = "None";
}
```

3.8 Implicit Parameters

In Section 2.4, you learned that a method has an **implicit parameter** (the object on which the method is invoked) in addition to the **explicit parameters**, which are enclosed in parentheses. In this section, we will examine implicit parameters in greater detail.

Have a look at a particular invocation of the deposit method:

```
momsSavings.deposit(500);
```

Here, the implicit parameter is momsSavings and the explicit parameter is 500.

Now look again at the code of the deposit method:

```
public void deposit(double amount)
{
    balance = balance + amount;
}
```

What does balance mean exactly? After all, our program may have multiple Bank-Account objects, and *each of them* has its own balance.

> Use of an instance variable name in a method denotes the instance variable of the implicit parameter.

Of course, since we are depositing the money into momsSavings, balance must mean momsSavings.balance. In general, when you refer to an instance variable inside a method, it means the instance variable of the implicit parameter.

If you need to, you can access the implicit parameter—the object on which the method is called—with the reserved word this. For example, in the preceding method invocation, this refers to the same object as momsSavings (see Figure 6).

> The this reference denotes the implicit parameter.

The statement

```
balance = balance + amount;
```

actually means

```
this.balance = this.balance + amount;
```

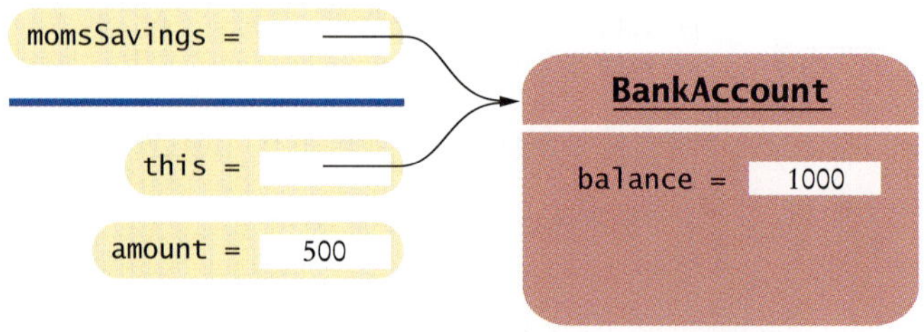

Figure 6 The Implicit Parameter of a Method Call

When you refer to an instance variable in a method, the compiler automatically applies it to the `this` reference. Some programmers actually prefer to manually insert the `this` reference before every instance variable because they find it makes the code clearer. Here is an example:

```
public BankAccount(double initialBalance)
{
    this.balance = initialBalance;
}
```

You may want to try it out and see if you like that style.

The `this` reference can also be used to distinguish between instance variables and local or parameter variables. Consider the constructor

```
public BankAccount(double balance)
{
    this.balance = balance;
}
```

The expression `this.balance` clearly refers to the `balance` instance variable. However, the expression `balance` by itself seems ambiguous. It could denote either the parameter variable or the instance variable. In Java, local and parameter variables are considered first when looking up variable names. Therefore,

```
this.balance = balance;
```

means: "Set the instance variable `balance` to the parameter variable `balance`".

There is another situation in which it is important to understand the implicit parameter. Consider the following modification to the `BankAccount` class. We add a method to apply the monthly account fee:

```
public class BankAccount
{
    . . .
    public void monthlyFee()
    {
        withdraw(10); // Withdraw $10 from this account
    }
}
```

A method call without an implicit parameter is applied to the same object.

That means to withdraw from the *same* bank account object that is carrying out the `monthlyFee` operation. In other words, the implicit parameter of the `withdraw` method is the (invisible) implicit parameter of the `monthlyFee` method.

If you find it confusing to have an invisible parameter, you can use the `this` reference to make the method easier to read:

```
public class BankAccount
{
    . . .
    public void monthlyFee()
    {
        this.withdraw(10); // Withdraw $10 from this account
    }
}
```

You have now seen how to use objects and implement classes, and you have learned some important technical details about variables and method parameters. The remainder of this chapter continues the optional graphics track. In the next chapter, you will learn more about the most fundamental data types of the Java language.

20. How many implicit and explicit parameters does the `withdraw` method of the `BankAccount` class have, and what are their names and types?

21. In the `deposit` method, what is the meaning of `this.amount`? Or, if the expression has no meaning, why not?

22. How many implicit and explicit parameters does the `main` method of the `Bank-AccountTester` class have, and what are they called?

Special Topic 3.1

Calling One Constructor from Another

Consider the `BankAccount` class. It has two constructors: a constructor without parameters to initialize the balance with zero, and another constructor to supply an initial balance. Rather than explicitly setting the balance to zero, one constructor can call another constructor of the same class instead. There is a shorthand notation to achieve this result:

```java
public class BankAccount
{
   public BankAccount (double initialBalance)
   {
      balance = initialBalance;
   }

   public BankAccount()
   {
      this(0);
   }
   . . .
}
```

The command `this(0);` means "Call another constructor of this class and supply the value 0". Such a call to another constructor can occur only as the *first line in a constructor*.

This syntax is a minor convenience. We will not use it in this book. Actually, the use of the reserved word `this` is a little confusing. Normally, `this` denotes a reference to the implicit parameter, but if `this` is followed by parentheses, it denotes a call to another constructor of this class.

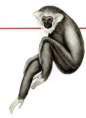

Random Fact 3.1

Electronic Voting Machines

In the 2000 presidential elections in the United States, votes were tallied by a variety of machines. Some machines processed cardboard "punch card" ballots into which voters punched holes to indicate their choices. When voters were not careful, remains of paper—the now infamous "chads"—were partially stuck in the punch cards, causing votes to be miscounted. A manual recount was necessary, but it was not carried out everywhere due to time constraints and procedural wrangling. The election was very close, and there remain doubts in the minds of many people whether the election outcome would have been different if the voting machines had accurately counted the intent of the voters.

Subsequently, voting machine manufacturers have argued that electronic voting machines would avoid the problems caused by punch cards or optically scanned forms. In an electronic voting machine, voters indicate their preferences by pressing buttons or touching

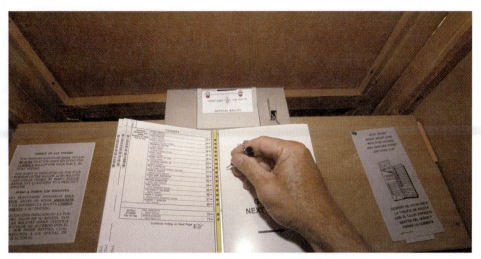

Punch Card Ballot

icons on a computer screen. Typically, each voter is presented with a summary screen for review before casting the ballot. The process is very similar to using an automatic bank teller machine.

It seems plausible that these machines make it more likely that a vote is counted in the same way that the voter intends. However, there has been significant controversy surrounding some types of electronic voting machines. If a machine simply records the votes and prints out the totals after the election has been completed, then how do you know that the machine worked correctly? Inside the machine is a computer that executes a program, and, as you may know from your own experience, programs can have bugs.

In fact, some electronic voting machines do have bugs. There have been isolated cases where machines reported tallies that were impossible. When a machine reports far more or far fewer votes than voters, then it is clear that it malfunctioned. Unfortunately, it is then impossible to find out the actual votes. Over time, one would expect these bugs to be fixed in the software. More insidiously, if the results are plausible, nobody may ever investigate.

Many computer scientists have spoken out on this issue and confirmed that it is impossible, with today's technology, to tell that software is error free and has not been tampered with. Many of them recommend that electronic voting machines should be complemented

Touch Screen Voting Machine

by a *voter verifiable audit trail*. (A good source of information is `http://verifiedvoting.org`.) Typically, a voter-verifiable machine prints out the choices that are being tallied. Each voter has a chance to review the printout, and then deposits it in an old-fashioned ballot box. If there is a problem with the electronic equipment, the printouts can be counted by hand.

As this book is written, this concept is strongly resisted both by manufacturers of electronic voting machines and by their customers, the cities and counties that run elections. Manufacturers are reluctant to increase the cost of the machines because they may not be able to pass the cost increase on to their customers, who tend to have tight budgets. Election officials fear problems with malfunctioning printers, and some of them have publicly stated that they actually prefer equipment that eliminates bothersome recounts.

What do you think? You probably use an automatic bank teller machine to get cash from your bank account. Do you review the paper record that the machine issues? Do you check your bank statement? Even if you don't, do you put your faith in other people who double-check their balances, so that the bank won't get away with widespread cheating?

Is the integrity of banking equipment more important or less important than that of voting machines? Won't every voting process have some room for error and fraud anyway? Is the added cost for equipment, paper, and staff time reasonable to combat a potentially slight risk of malfunction and fraud? Computer scientists cannot answer these questions—an informed society must make these tradeoffs. But, like all professionals, they have an obligation to speak out and give accurate testimony about the capabilities and limitations of computing equipment.

3.9 Shape Classes

In this section, we continue the optional graphics track by discussing how to organize complex drawings in a more object-oriented fashion.

It is a good idea to make a class for any part of a drawing that can occur more than once.

When you produce a drawing that is composed of complex parts, such as the one in Figure 7, it is a good idea to make a separate class for each part. Provide a draw method that draws the shape, and provide a constructor to set the position of the shape. For example, here is the outline of the Car class.

```
public class Car
{
    public Car(int x, int y)
    {
        // Remember position
        . . .
    }

    public void draw(Graphics2D g2)
    {
        // Drawing instructions
        . . .
    }
}
```

To figure out how to draw a complex shape, make a sketch on graph paper.

You will find the complete class declaration at the end of this section. The draw method contains a rather long sequence of instructions for drawing the body, roof, and tires. The coordinates of the car parts seem a bit arbitrary. To come up with suitable values, draw the image on graph paper and read off the coordinates (Figure 8).

Figure 7
The Car Component Draws Two Car Shapes

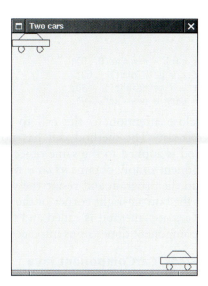

The program that produces Figure 7 is composed of three classes.

- The Car class is responsible for drawing a single car. Two objects of this class are constructed, one for each car.
- The CarComponent class displays the drawing.
- The CarViewer class shows a frame that contains a CarComponent.

Let us look more closely at the CarComponent class. The paintComponent method draws two cars. We place one car in the top-left corner of the window, and the other car in the bottom right. To compute the bottom right position, we call the getWidth and getHeight methods of the JComponent class. These methods return the dimensions of

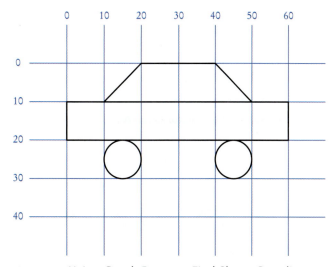

Figure 8 Using Graph Paper to Find Shape Coordinates

the component. We subtract the dimensions of the car to determine the position of car2:

```
Car car1 = new Car(0, 0);
int x = getWidth() - 60;
int y = getHeight() - 30;
Car car2 = new Car(x, y);
```

Pay close attention to the call to getWidth inside the paintComponent method of CarComponent. The method call has no implicit parameter, which means that the method is applied to the same object that executes the paintComponent method. The component simply obtains *its own* width.

Run the program and resize the window. Note that the second car always ends up at the bottom-right corner of the window. Whenever the window is resized, the paintComponent method is called and the car position is recomputed, taking the current component dimensions into account.

ch03/car/CarComponent.java

```java
 1   import java.awt.Graphics;
 2   import java.awt.Graphics2D;
 3   import javax.swing.JComponent;
 4
 5   /**
 6       This component draws two car shapes.
 7   */
 8   public class CarComponent extends JComponent
 9   {
10      public void paintComponent(Graphics g)
11      {
12         Graphics2D g2 = (Graphics2D) g;
13
14         Car car1 = new Car(0, 0);
15
16         int x = getWidth() - 60;
17         int y = getHeight() - 30;
18
19         Car car2 = new Car(x, y);
20
21         car1.draw(g2);
22         car2.draw(g2);
23      }
24   }
```

ch03/car/Car.java

```java
 1   import java.awt.Graphics2D;
 2   import java.awt.Rectangle;
 3   import java.awt.geom.Ellipse2D;
 4   import java.awt.geom.Line2D;
 5   import java.awt.geom.Point2D;
 6
 7   /**
 8       A car shape that can be positioned anywhere on the screen.
 9   */
10   public class Car
11   {
```

```
12    private int xLeft;
13    private int yTop;
14
15    /**
16       Constructs a car with a given top left corner.
17       @param x the x coordinate of the top left corner
18       @param y the y coordinate of the top left corner
19    */
20    public Car(int x, int y)
21    {
22       xLeft = x;
23       yTop = y;
24    }
25
26    /**
27       Draws the car.
28       @param g2 the graphics context
29    */
30    public void draw(Graphics2D g2)
31    {
32       Rectangle body
33             = new Rectangle(xLeft, yTop + 10, 60, 10);
34       Ellipse2D.Double frontTire
35             = new Ellipse2D.Double(xLeft + 10, yTop + 20, 10, 10);
36       Ellipse2D.Double rearTire
37             = new Ellipse2D.Double(xLeft + 40, yTop + 20, 10, 10);
38
39       // The bottom of the front windshield
40       Point2D.Double r1
41             = new Point2D.Double(xLeft + 10, yTop + 10);
42       // The front of the roof
43       Point2D.Double r2
44             = new Point2D.Double(xLeft + 20, yTop);
45       // The rear of the roof
46       Point2D.Double r3
47             = new Point2D.Double(xLeft + 40, yTop);
48       // The bottom of the rear windshield
49       Point2D.Double r4
50             = new Point2D.Double(xLeft + 50, yTop + 10);
51
52       Line2D.Double frontWindshield
53             = new Line2D.Double(r1, r2);
54       Line2D.Double roofTop
55             = new Line2D.Double(r2, r3);
56       Line2D.Double rearWindshield
57             = new Line2D.Double(r3, r4);
58
59       g2.draw(body);
60       g2.draw(frontTire);
61       g2.draw(rearTire);
62       g2.draw(frontWindshield);
63       g2.draw(roofTop);
64       g2.draw(rearWindshield);
65    }
66 }
```

ch03/car/CarViewer.java

```
 1  import javax.swing.JFrame;
 2
 3  public class CarViewer
 4  {
 5     public static void main(String[] args)
 6     {
 7        JFrame frame = new JFrame();
 8
 9        frame.setSize(300, 400);
10        frame.setTitle("Two cars");
11        frame.setDefaultCloseOperation(JFrame.EXIT_ON_CLOSE);
12
13        CarComponent component = new CarComponent();
14        frame.add(component);
15
16        frame.setVisible(true);
17     }
18  }
```

SELF CHECK

23. Which class needs to be modified to have the two cars positioned next to each other?

24. Which class needs to be modified to have the car tires painted in black, and what modification do you need to make?

25. How do you make the cars twice as big?

How To 3.2   **Drawing Graphical Shapes**

You can write programs that display a wide variety of graphical shapes. These instructions give you a step-by-step procedure for decomposing a drawing into parts and implementing a program that produces the drawing. In this How To, we will create a program to draw a national flag.

Step 1   Determine the shapes that you need for the drawing.

You can use the following shapes:

- Squares and rectangles
- Circles and ellipses
- Lines

The outlines of these shapes can be drawn in any color, and you can fill the insides of these shapes with any color. You can also use text to label parts of your drawing.

Some national flag designs consist of three equally wide sections of different colors, side by side:

You could draw such a flag using three rectangles. But if the middle rectangle is white, as it is, for example, in the flag of Italy (green, white, red), it is easier and looks better to draw a line on the top and bottom of the middle portion:

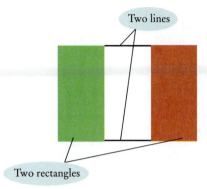

Step 2 Find the coordinates for the shapes.

You now need to find the exact positions for the geometric shapes.

- For rectangles, you need the *x*- and *y*-position of the top-left corner, the width, and the height.
- For ellipses, you need the top-left corner, width, and height of the bounding rectangle.
- For lines, you need the *x*- and *y*-positions of the starting point and the end point.
- For text, you need the *x*- and *y*-position of the basepoint.

A commonly-used size for a window is 300 by 300 pixels. You may not want the flag crammed all the way to the top, so perhaps the upper-left corner of the flag should be at point (100, 100).

Many flags, such as the flag of Italy, have a width : height ratio of 3 : 2. (You can often find exact proportions for a particular flag by doing a bit of Internet research on one of several Flags of the World sites.) For example, if you make the flag 90 pixels wide, then it should be 60 pixels tall. (Why not make it 100 pixels wide? Then the height would be $100 \cdot 2 / 3 \approx 67$, which seems more awkward.)

Now you can compute the coordinates of all the important points of the shape:

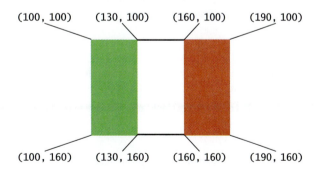

Step 3 Write Java statements to draw the shapes.

In our example, there are two rectangles and two lines:

```
Rectangle leftRectangle
      = new Rectangle(100, 100, 30, 60);
Rectangle rightRectangle
      = new Rectangle(160, 100, 30, 60);
```

```
Line2D.Double topLine
    = new Line2D.Double(130, 100, 160, 100);
Line2D.Double bottomLine
    = new Line2D.Double(130, 160, 160, 160);
```

If you are more ambitious, then you can express the coordinates in terms of a few variables. In the case of the flag, we have arbitrarily chosen the top-left corner and the width. All other coordinates follow from those choices. If you decide to follow the ambitious approach, then the rectangles and lines are determined as follows:

```
Rectangle leftRectangle = new Rectangle(
    xLeft, yTop,
    width / 3, width * 2 / 3);
Rectangle rightRectangle = new Rectangle(
    xLeft + 2 * width / 3, yTop,
    width / 3, width * 2 / 3);
Line2D.Double topLine = new Line2D.Double(
    xLeft + width / 3, yTop,
    xLeft + width * 2 / 3, yTop);
Line2D.Double bottomLine = new Line2D.Double(
    xLeft + width / 3, yTop + width * 2 / 3,
    xLeft + width * 2 / 3, yTop + width * 2 / 3);
```

Now you need to fill the rectangles and draw the lines. For the flag of Italy, the left rectangle is green and the right rectangle is red. Remember to switch colors before the filling and drawing operations:

```
g2.setColor(Color.GREEN);
g2.fill(leftRectangle);
g2.setColor(Color.RED);
g2.fill(rightRectangle);
g2.setColor(Color.BLACK);
g2.draw(topLine);
g2.draw(bottomLine);
```

Step 4 Combine the drawing statements with the component "plumbing".

```
public class MyComponent extends JComponent
{
    public void paintComponent(Graphics g)
    {
        Graphics2D g2 = (Graphics2D) g;
        // Drawing instructions
        . . .
    }
}
```

In our example, you can simply add all shapes and drawing instructions inside the paintComponent method:

```
public class ItalianFlagComponent extends JComponent
{
    public void paintComponent(Graphics g)
    {
        Graphics2D g2 = (Graphics2D) g;
        Rectangle leftRectangle
            = new Rectangle(100, 100, 30, 60);
        . . .
        g2.setColor(Color.GREEN);
        g2.fill(leftRectangle);
        . . .
    }
}
```

That approach is acceptable for simple drawings, but it is not very object-oriented. After all, a flag is an object. It is better to make a separate class for the flag. Then you can draw different flags at different positions. Specify the sizes in a constructor and supply a draw method:

```java
public class ItalianFlag
{
   private int xLeft;
   private int yTop;
   private int width;

   public ItalianFlag(int x, int y, int aWidth)
   {
      xLeft = x;
      yTop = y;
      width = aWidth;
   }

   public void draw(Graphics2D g2)
   {
      Rectangle leftRectangle = new Rectangle(
           xLeft, yTop,
           width / 3, width * 2 / 3);
      . . .
      g2.setColor(Color.GREEN);
      g2.fill(leftRectangle);
      . . .
   }
}
```

You still need a separate class for the component, but it is very simple:

```java
public class ItalianFlagComponent extends JComponent
{
   public void paintComponent(Graphics g)
   {
      Graphics2D g2 = (Graphics2D) g;
      ItalianFlag flag = new ItalianFlag(100, 100, 90);
      flag.draw(g2);
   }
}
```

Step 5 Write the viewer class.

Provide a viewer class, with a main method in which you construct a frame, add your component, and make your frame visible. The viewer class is completely routine; you only need to change a single line to show a different component.

```java
public class ItalianFlagViewer
{
   public static void main(String[] args)
   {
      JFrame frame = new JFrame();

      frame.setSize(300, 400);
      frame.setDefaultCloseOperation(JFrame.EXIT_ON_CLOSE);

      ItalianFlagComponent component = new ItalianFlagComponent();
      frame.add(component);

      frame.setVisible(true);
   }
}
```

Random Fact 3.2

Computer Graphics

Generating and manipulating visual images is one of the most exciting applications of the computer. We distinguish different kinds of graphics.

Diagrams, such as numeric charts or maps, are artifacts that convey information to the viewer. They do not directly depict anything that occurs in the natural world, but are a tool for visualizing information.

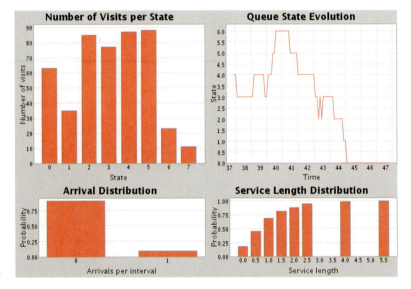

Diagrams

Scenes are computer-generated images that attempt to depict images of the real or an imagined world. It turns out to be quite challenging to render light and shadows accurately. Special effort must be taken so that the images do not look too neat and simple; clouds,

Scene

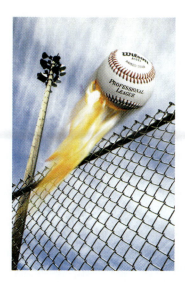

Manipulated Image

rocks, leaves, and dust in the real world have a complex and somewhat random appearance. The degree of realism in these images is constantly improving.

Manipulated Images are photographs or film footage of actual events that have been converted to digital form and edited by the computer. For example, film sequences in the movie *Apollo 13* were produced by starting from actual images and changing the perspective, showing the launch of the rocket from a more dramatic viewpoint.

Computer graphics is one of the most challenging fields in computer science. It requires processing of massive amounts of information at very high speed. New algorithms are constantly invented for this purpose. Displaying an overlapping set of three-dimensional objects with curved boundaries requires advanced mathematical tools. Realistic modeling of textures and biological entities requires extensive knowledge of mathematics, physics, and biology.

Summary of Learning Objectives

Understand instance variables and the methods that access them.

- An object's instance variables store the data required for executing its methods.
- Each object of a class has its own set of instance variables.
- Private instance variables can only be accessed by methods of the same class.

Explain the concept and benefits of encapsulation.

- Encapsulation is the process of hiding implementation details and providing methods for data access.
- Encapsulation allows a programmer to use a class without having to know its implementation.
- Information hiding makes it simpler for the implementor of a class to locate errors and change implementations.

Write method and constructor headers that describe the public interface of a class.

- In order to implement a class, you first need to know which methods are required.
- In a method header, you specify the return type, method name, and the types and names of the parameters.
- Constructors set the initial data for objects. The constructor name is always the same as the class name.

Write class documentation in javadoc format.

- Use documentation comments to describe the classes and public methods of your programs.
- Provide documentation comments for every class, every method, every parameter, and every return value.

Provide the private implementation of a class.

- The private implementation of a class consists of instance variables, and the bodies of constructors and methods.

Write tests that verify that a class works correctly.

- A unit test verifies that a class works correctly in isolation, outside a complete program.

Compare lifetime and initialization of instance, local, and parameter variables.

- Local variables are declared in the body of a method.
- When a method exits, its local variables are removed.
- Instance variables are initialized to a default value, but you must initialize local variables.

Recognize the use of the implicit parameter in method declarations.

- Use of an instance variable name in a method denotes the instance variable of the implicit parameter.
- The this reference denotes the implicit parameter.
- A method call without an implicit parameter is applied to the same object.

Implement classes that draw graphical shapes.

- It is a good idea to make a class for any part of a drawing that can occur more than once.
- To figure out how to draw a complex shape, make a sketch on graph paper.

Media Resources

www.wiley.com/
college/
horstmann

- ***Worked Example*** Making a Simple Menu
- Lab Exercises
- ⊕ ***Animation*** Lifetime of Variables
- ⊕ Practice Quiz
- ⊕ Code Completion Exercises

Review Exercises

★ **R3.1** What is the interface of a class? How does it differ from the implementation of a class?

★ **R3.2** What is encapsulation? Why is it useful?

★ **R3.3** Instance variables are a part of the hidden implementation of a class, but they aren't actually hidden from programmers who have the source code of the class. Explain to what extent the private reserved word provides information hiding.

★ **R3.4** Consider a class Grade that represents a letter grade, such as A+ or B. Give two choices of instance variables that can be used for implementing the Grade class.

★★ **R3.5** Consider a class Time that represents a point in time, such as 9 A.M. or 3:30 P.M. Give two different sets of instance variables that can be used for implementing the Time class.

★ **R3.6** Suppose the implementor of the Time class of Exercise R3.5 changes from one implementation strategy to another, keeping the public interface unchanged. What do the programmers who use the Time class need to do?

★★ **R3.7** You can read the value instance variable of the Counter class with the getValue accessor method. Should there be a setValue mutator method to change it? Explain why or why not.

★★ **R3.8** **a.** Show that the BankAccount(double initialBalance) constructor is not strictly necessary. That is, if we removed that constructor from the public interface, how could a programmer still obtain BankAccount objects with an arbitrary balance?
b. Conversely, could we keep only the BankAccount(double initialBalance) constructor and remove the BankAccount() constructor?

★★ **R3.9** Why does the BankAccount class not have a reset method?

★ **R3.10** What happens in our implementation of the BankAccount class when more money is withdrawn from the account than the current balance?

★★ **R3.11** What is the this reference? Why would you use it?

★★ **R3.12** What does the following method do? Give an example of how you can call the method.

```
public class BankAccount
{
    public void mystery(BankAccount that, double amount)
    {
        this.balance = this.balance - amount;
        that.balance = that.balance + amount;
    }
    . . . // Other bank account methods
}
```

★★ **R3.13** Suppose you want to implement a class `TimeDepositAccount`. A time deposit account has a fixed interest rate that should be set in the constructor, together with the initial balance. Provide a method to get the current balance. Provide a method to add the earned interest to the account. This method should have no parameters because the interest rate is already known. It should have no return value because you already provided a method for obtaining the current balance. It is not possible to deposit additional funds into this account. Provide a `withdraw` method that removes the entire balance. Partial withdrawals are not allowed.

★ **R3.14** Consider the following implementation of a class `Square`:

```
public class Square
{
    private int sideLength;
    private int area; // Not a good idea

    public Square(int length)
    {
        sideLength = length;
    }

    public int getArea()
    {
        area = sideLength * sideLength;
        return area;
    }
}
```

Why is it not a good idea to introduce an instance variable for the area? Rewrite the class so that area is a local variable.

★★ **R3.15** Consider the following implementation of a class `Square`:

```
public class Square
{
    private int sideLength;
    private int area;

    public Square(int initialLength)
    {
        sideLength = initialLength;
        area = sideLength * sideLength;
    }

    public int getArea() { return area; }
    public void grow() { sideLength = 2 * sideLength(); }
}
```

What error does this class have? How would you fix it?

★★T **R3.16** Provide a unit test class for the `Counter` class in Section 3.1.

★★T **R3.17** Read Exercise P3.7, but do not implement the `Car` class yet. Write a tester class that tests a scenario in which gas is added to the car, the car is driven, more gas is added, and the car is driven again. Print the actual and expected amount of gas in the tank.

★★G **R3.18** Suppose you want to extend the car viewer program in Section 3.9 to show a suburban scene, with several cars and houses. Which classes do you need?

★★★G **R3.19** Explain why the calls to the getWidth and getHeight methods in the CarComponent class have no explicit parameter.

★★G **R3.20** How would you modify the Car class in order to show cars of varying sizes?

Programming Exercises

★T **P3.1** Write a BankAccountTester class whose main method constructs a bank account, deposits $1,000, withdraws $500, withdraws another $400, and then prints the remaining balance. Also print the expected result.

★ **P3.2** Add a method

```
public void addInterest(double rate)
```

to the BankAccount class that adds interest at the given rate. For example, after the statements

```
BankAccount momsSavings = new BankAccount(1000);
momsSavings.addInterest(10); // 10% interest
```

the balance in momsSavings is $1,100. Also supply a BankAccountTester class that prints the actual and expected balance.

★★ **P3.3** Write a class SavingsAccount that is similar to the BankAccount class, except that it has an added instance variable interest. Supply a constructor that sets both the initial balance and the interest rate. Supply a method addInterest (with no explicit parameter) that adds interest to the account. Write a SavingsAccountTester class that constructs a savings account with an initial balance of $1,000 and an interest rate of 10%. Then apply the addInterest method and print the resulting balance. Also compute the expected result by hand and print it.

★★★ **P3.4** Add a feature to the CashRegister class for computing sales tax. The tax rate should be supplied when constructing a CashRegister object. Add recordTaxablePurchase and getTotalTax methods. (Amounts added with recordPurchase are not taxable.) The giveChange method should correctly reflect the sales tax that is charged on taxable items.

★★ **P3.5** After closing time, the store manager would like to know how much business was transacted during the day. Modify the CashRegister class to enable this functionality. Supply methods getSalesTotal and getSalesCount to get the total amount of all sales and the number of sales. Supply a method reset that resets any counters and totals so that the next day's sales start from zero.

★★ **P3.6** Implement a class Employee. An employee has a name (a string) and a salary (a double). Provide a constructor with two parameters

```
public Employee(String employeeName, double currentSalary)
```

and methods

```
public String getName()
public double getSalary()
public void raiseSalary(double byPercent)
```

These methods return the name and salary, and raise the employee's salary by a certain percentage. Sample usage:

```
Employee harry = new Employee("Hacker, Harry", 50000);
harry.raiseSalary(10); // Harry gets a 10% raise
```

Supply an `EmployeeTester` class that tests all methods.

★★ **P3.7** Implement a class `Car` with the following properties. A car has a certain fuel efficiency (measured in miles/gallon or liters/km—pick one) and a certain amount of fuel in the gas tank. The efficiency is specified in the constructor, and the initial fuel level is 0. Supply a method `drive` that simulates driving the car for a certain distance, reducing the amount of gasoline in the fuel tank. Also supply methods `getGasInTank`, returning the current amount of gasoline in the fuel tank, and `addGas`, to add gasoline to the fuel tank. Sample usage:

```
Car myHybrid = new Car(50); // 50 miles per gallon
myHybrid.addGas(20); // Tank 20 gallons
myHybrid.drive(100); // Drive 100 miles
double gasLeft = myHybrid.getGasInTank(); // Get gas remaining in tank
```

You may assume that the `drive` method is never called with a distance that consumes more than the available gas. Supply a `CarTester` class that tests all methods.

★★ **P3.8** Implement a class `Student`. For the purpose of this exercise, a student has a name and a total quiz score. Supply an appropriate constructor and methods `getName()`, `addQuiz(int score)`, `getTotalScore()`, and `getAverageScore()`. To compute the latter, you also need to store the *number of quizzes* that the student took.

Supply a `StudentTester` class that tests all methods.

★ **P3.9** Implement a class `Product`. A product has a name and a price, for example new `Product("Toaster", 29.95)`. Supply methods `getName`, `getPrice`, and `reducePrice`. Supply a program `ProductPrinter` that makes two products, prints the name and price, reduces their prices by $5.00, and then prints the prices again.

★★ **P3.10** Provide a class for authoring a simple letter. In the constructor, supply the names of the sender and the recipient:

```
public Letter(String from, String to)
```

Supply a method

```
public void addLine(String line)
```

to add a line of text to the body of the letter.

Supply a method

```
public String getText()
```

that returns the entire text of the letter. The text has the form:

Dear *recipient name*:
blank line
first line of the body
second line of the body

. . .

last line of the body
blank line
Sincerely,
blank line
sender name

Also supply a class `LetterPrinter` that prints this letter.

```
Dear John:

I am sorry we must part.
I wish you all the best.

Sincerely,

Mary
```

Construct an object of the `Letter` class and call `addLine` twice.

Hints: (1) Use the `concat` method to form a longer string from two shorter strings.
(2) The special string "\n" represents a new line. For example, the statement

```
body = body.concat("Sincerely,").concat("\n");
```

adds a line containing the string "Sincerely," to the body.

★★ **P3.11** Write a class `Bug` that models a bug moving along a horizontal line. The bug moves either to the right or left. Initially, the bug moves to the right, but it can turn to change its direction. In each move, its position changes by one unit in the current direction. Provide a constructor

```
public Bug(int initialPosition)
```

and methods

```
public void turn()
public void move()
public int getPosition()
```

Sample usage:

```
Bug bugsy = new Bug(10);
bugsy.move(); // now the position is 11
bugsy.turn();
bugsy.move(); // now the position is 10
```

Your `BugTester` should construct a bug, make it move and turn a few times, and print the actual and expected position.

★★ **P3.12** Implement a class `Moth` that models a moth flying across a straight line. The moth has a position, the distance from a fixed origin. When the moth moves toward a point of light, its new position is halfway between its old position and the position of the light source. Supply a constructor

```
public Moth(double initialPosition)
```

and methods

```
public void moveToLight(double lightPosition)
public double getPosition()
```

Your `MothTester` should construct a moth, move it toward a couple of light sources, and check that the moth's position is as expected.

★★ **P3.13** Implement a class `RoachPopulation` that simulates the growth of a roach population. The constructor takes the size of the initial roach population. The `breed` method simulates a period in which the roaches breed, which doubles their population. The `spray` method simulates spraying with insecticide, which reduces the population by

10 percent. The `getRoaches` method returns the current number of roaches. A program called `RoachSimulation` simulates a population that starts out with 10 roaches. Breed, spray, and print the roach count. Repeat three more times.

★★ **P3.14** Implement a `VotingMachine` class that can be used for a simple election. Have methods to clear the machine state, to vote for a Democrat, to vote for a Republican, and to get the tallies for both parties. Extra credit if your program gives the nod to your favored party if the votes are tallied after 8 P.M. on the first Tuesday in November, but acts normally on all other dates. (*Hint:* Use the `GregorianCalendar` class — see Programming Project 2.1.)

★★G **P3.15** Draw a "bull's eye"—a set of concentric rings in alternating black and white colors. *Hint:* Fill a black circle, then fill a smaller white circle on top, and so on.

Your program should be composed of classes `BullsEye`, `BullsEyeComponent`, and `BullsEyeViewer`.

★★G **P3.16** Write a program that draws a picture of a house. It could be as simple as the accompanying figure, or if you like, make it more elaborate (3-D, skyscraper, marble columns in the entryway, whatever).

Implement a class `House` and supply a method `draw(Graphics2D g2)` that draws the house.

★★G **P3.17** Extend Exercise P3.16 by supplying a `House` constructor for specifying the position and size. Then populate your screen with a few houses of different sizes.

★★G **P3.18** Change the car viewer program in Section 3.9 to make the cars appear in different colors. Each `Car` object should store its own color. Supply modified `Car` and `CarComponent` classes.

★★G **P3.19** Change the `Car` class so that the size of a car can be specified in the constructor. Change the `CarComponent` class to make one of the cars appear twice the size of the original example.

★★G **P3.20** Write a program to plot the string "HELLO", using only lines and circles. Do not call `drawString`, and do not use `System.out`. Make classes `LetterH`, `LetterE`, `LetterL`, and `LetterO`.

★★G   **P3.21**   Write a program that displays the Olympic rings. Color the rings in the Olympic colors.

Provide a class OlympicRingViewer and a class OlympicRingComponent.

★★G   **P3.22**   Make a bar chart to plot the following data set. Label each bar. Make the bars horizontal for easier labeling.

Bridge Name	Longest Span (ft)
Golden Gate	4,200
Brooklyn	1,595
Delaware Memorial	2,150
Mackinac	3,800

Provide a class BarChartViewer and a class BarChartComponent.

Programming Projects

Project 3.1   In this project, you will enhance the BankAccount class and see how abstraction and encapsulation enable evolutionary changes to software.

Begin with a simple enhancement: charging a fee for every deposit and withdrawal. Supply a mechanism for setting the fee and modify the deposit and withdraw methods so that the fee is levied. Test your resulting class and check that the fee is computed correctly.

Now make a more complex change. The bank will allow a fixed number of free transactions (deposits or withdrawals) every month, and charge for transactions exceeding the free allotment. The charge is not levied immediately but at the end of the month.

Supply a new method deductMonthlyCharge to the BankAccount class that deducts the monthly charge and resets the transaction count. (*Hint:* Use Math.max(actual transaction count, free transaction count) in your computation.)

Produce a test program that verifies that the fees are calculated correctly over several months.

Project 3.2   In this project, you will explore an object-oriented alternative to the "Hello, World" program in Chapter 1.

Begin with a simple Greeter class that has a single method, sayHello. That method should *return* a string, not print it. Use BlueJ to create two objects of this class and invoke their sayHello methods.

That is boring—of course, both objects return the same answer.

Enhance the Greeter class so that each object produces a customized greeting. For example, the object constructed as new Greeter("Dave") should say "Hello, Dave". (Use the concat method to combine strings to form a longer string, or peek ahead at Section 4.6 to see how you can use the + operator for the same purpose.)

Add a method sayGoodbye to the Greeter class.

Finally, add a method refuseHelp to the Greeter class. It should return a string such as "I am sorry, Dave. I am afraid I can't do that."

Test your class in BlueJ. Make objects that greet the world and Dave, and invoke methods on them.

Answers to Self-Check Questions

1.
```
public void reset()
{
    value = 0;
}
```

2. You can only access them by invoking the methods of the Clock class.

3. In one of the methods of the Counter class.

4. The programmers who designed and implemented the Java library.

5. Other programmers who work on the personal finance application.

6. `harrysChecking.withdraw(harrysChecking.getBalance())`

7. The withdraw method has return type void. It doesn't return a value. Use the getBalance method to obtain the balance after the withdrawal.

8. Add an accountNumber parameter to the constructors, and add a getAccount-Number method. There is no need for a setAccountNumber method—the account number never changes after construction.

9.
```
/**
    This class models a tally counter.
*/
public class Counter
{
    private int value;

    /**
        Gets the current value of this counter.
        @return the current value
    */
    public int getValue()
    {
        return value;
    }

    /**
        Advances the value of this counter by 1.
    */
    public void count()
    {
        value = value + 1;
```

```
        }
    }
```

10. ```
    /**
       Constructs a new bank account with a given initial balance.
       @param accountNumber the account number for this account
       @param initialBalance the initial balance for this account
    */
    ```

11. The first sentence of the method description should describe the method—it is displayed in isolation in the summary table.

12. An instance variable

    ```
    private int accountNumber;
    ```

    needs to be added to the class.

13. Because the `balance` instance variable is accessed from the `main` method of `BankRobber`. The compiler will report an error because it is not a method of the `BankAccount` class.

14. ```
    public int getWidth()
    {
        return width;
    }
    ```

15. There is more than one correct answer. One possible implementation is as follows:

    ```
    public void translate(int dx, int dy)
    {
        int newx = x + dx;
        x = newx;
        int newy = y + dy;
        y = newy;
    }
    ```

16. One `BankAccount` object, no `BankAccountTester` object. The purpose of the `BankAccountTester` class is merely to hold the `main` method.

17. In those environments, you can issue interactive commands to construct `BankAccount` objects, invoke methods, and display their return values.

18. Variables of both categories belong to methods—they come alive when the method is called, and they die when the method exits. They differ in their initialization. Parameter variables are initialized with the call values; local variables must be explicitly initialized.

19. After computing the change due, `payment` and `purchase` were set to zero. If the method returned `payment - purchase`, it would always return zero.

20. One implicit parameter, called `this`, of type `BankAccount`, and one explicit parameter, called `amount`, of type `double`.

21. It is not a legal expression. `this` is of type `BankAccount` and the `BankAccount` class has no instance variable named `amount`.

22. No implicit parameter—the `main` method is not invoked on any object—and one explicit parameter, called `args`.

23. `CarComponent`

24. In the `draw` method of the `Car` class, call

    ```
    g2.fill(frontTire);
    g2.fill(rearTire);
    ```

25. Double all measurements in the `draw` method of the `Car` class.

Chapter 4

Fundamental Data Types

CHAPTER GOALS

- To understand integer and floating-point numbers
- To recognize the limitations of the numeric types
- To become aware of causes for overflow and roundoff errors
- To understand the proper use of constants
- To write arithmetic expressions in Java
- To use the String type to manipulate character strings
- To learn how to read program input and produce formatted output

This chapter teaches how to manipulate numbers and character strings in Java. The goal of this chapter is to gain a firm understanding of these fundamental data types in Java.

You will learn about the properties and limitations of the number types in Java. You will see how to manipulate numbers and strings in your programs. Finally, we cover the important topic of input and output, which enables you to implement interactive programs.

CHAPTER CONTENTS

4.1 Number Types

> Java has eight primitive types, including four integer types and two floating-point types.

In Java, every value is either a reference to an object, or it belongs to one of the eight **primitive types** shown in Table 1.

Six of the primitive types are number types; four of them for integers and two for floating-point numbers.

Each of the integer types has a different range—Special Topic 4.2 on page 130 explains why the range limits are related to powers of two. The largest number that can be represented in an int is denoted by Integer.MAX_VALUE. Its value is about 2.14 billion. Similarly, Integer.MIN_VALUE is the smallest integer, about –2.14 billion.

Generally, you will use the int type for integer quantities. However, occasionally, calculations involving integers can *overflow*. This happens if the result of a computation exceeds the range for the number type. For example:

> A numeric computation overflows if the result falls outside the range for the number type.

```
int n = 1000000;
System.out.println(n * n);   // Prints –727379968, which is clearly wrong
```

The product n * n is 10^{12}, which is larger than the largest integer (about $2 \cdot 10^9$). The result is truncated to fit into an int, yielding a value that is completely wrong. Unfortunately, there is no warning when an integer overflow occurs.

If you run into this problem, the simplest remedy is to use the long type. Special Topic 4.1 on page 130 shows you how to use the BigInteger type in the unlikely event that even the long type overflows.

Overflow is not usually a problem for double-precision floating-point numbers. The double type has a range of about $\pm 10^{308}$ and about 15 significant digits. However, you want to avoid the float type—it has less than 7 significant digits. (Some programmers use float to save on memory if they need to store a huge set of numbers that do not require much precision.)

Table 1 Primitive Types

Type	Description	Size
int	The integer type, with range −2,147,483,648 (Integer.MIN_VALUE) ... 2,147,483,647 (Integer.MAX_VALUE, about 2.14 billion)	4 bytes
byte	The type describing a single byte, with range −128 ... 127	1 byte
short	The short integer type, with range −32,768 ... 32,767	2 bytes
long	The long integer type, with range −9,223,372,036,854,775,808 ... 9,223,372,036,854,775,807	8 bytes
double	The double-precision floating-point type, with a range of about $\pm10^{308}$ and about 15 significant decimal digits	8 bytes
float	The single-precision floating-point type, with a range of about $\pm10^{38}$ and about 7 significant decimal digits	4 bytes
char	The character type, representing code units in the Unicode encoding scheme (see Special Topic 4.5 on page 153)	2 bytes
boolean	The type with the two truth values false and true (see Chapter 5)	1 bit

> Rounding errors occur when an exact conversion between numbers is not possible.

Rounding errors are a more serious issue with floating-point values. Rounding errors can occur when you convert between binary and decimal numbers, or between integers and floating-point numbers. When a value cannot be converted exactly, it is rounded to the nearest match. Consider this example:

```
double f = 4.35;
System.out.println(100 * f); // Prints 434.99999999999994
```

This problem is caused because computers represent numbers in the binary number system. In the binary number system, there is no exact representation of the fraction 1/10, just as there is no exact representation of the fraction 1/3 = 0.33333 in the decimal number system. (See Special Topic 4.2 on page 130 for more information.)

For this reason, the double type is not appropriate for financial calculations. In this book, we will continue to use double values for bank balances and other financial quantities so that we keep our programs as simple as possible. However, professional programs need to use the BigDecimal type for this purpose—see Special Topic 4.1 on page 130.

In Java, it is legal to assign an integer value to a floating-point variable:

```
int dollars = 100;
double balance = dollars; // OK
```

But the opposite assignment is an error: You cannot assign a floating-point expression to an integer variable.

```
double balance = 13.75;
int dollars = balance; // Error
```

You will see in Section 4.3.5 how to convert a value of type double into an integer.

1. Which are the most commonly used number types in Java?

2. Suppose you want to write a program that works with population data from various countries. Which Java data type should you use?

3. Which of the following initializations are incorrect, and why?

   a. `int dollars = 100.0;`

   b. `double balance = 100;`

Special Topic 4.1

Big Numbers

If you want to compute with really large numbers, you can use big number objects. Big number objects are objects of the `BigInteger` and `BigDecimal` classes in the `java.math` package. Unlike the number types such as `int` or `double`, big number objects have essentially no limits on their size and precision. However, computations with big number objects are much slower than those that involve number types. Perhaps more importantly, you can't use the familiar arithmetic operators such as (+ - *) with them. Instead, you have to use methods called `add`, `subtract`, and `multiply`. Here is an example of how to create a `BigInteger` object and how to call the `multiply` method.

```
BigInteger n = new BigInteger("1000000");
BigInteger r = n.multiply(n);
System.out.println(r); // Prints 1000000000000
```

The `BigDecimal` type carries out floating-point computation without roundoff errors. For example,

```
BigDecimal d = new BigDecimal("4.35");
BigDecimal e = new BigDecimal("100");
BigDecimal f = d.multiply(e);
System.out.println(f); // Prints 435.00
```

Special Topic 4.2

Binary Numbers

You are familiar with decimal numbers, which use the digits 0, 1, 2, . . . , 9. Each digit has a place value of 1, 10, 100 = 10^2, 1000 = 10^3, and so on. For example,

$$435 = 4 \cdot 10^2 + 3 \cdot 10^1 + 5 \cdot 10^0$$

Fractional digits have place values with negative powers of ten: 0.1 = 10^{-1}, 0.01 = 10^{-2}, and so on. For example,

$$4.35 = 4 \cdot 10^0 + 3 \cdot 10^{-1} + 5 \cdot 10^{-2}$$

Computers use binary numbers instead, which have just two digits (0 and 1) and place values that are powers of 2. Binary numbers are easier for computers to manipulate, because it is easier to build logic circuits that differentiate between "off" and "on" than it is to build circuits that can accurately tell ten different voltage levels apart.

It is easy to transform a binary number into a decimal number. Just compute the powers of two that correspond to ones in the binary number. For example,

$$1101 \text{ binary} = 1 \cdot 2^3 + 1 \cdot 2^2 + 0 \cdot 2^1 + 1 \cdot 2^0 = 8 + 4 + 1 = 13$$

Fractional binary numbers use negative powers of two. For example,

$$1.101 \text{ binary} = 1 \cdot 2^0 + 1 \cdot 2^{-1} + 0 \cdot 2^{-2} + 1 \cdot 2^{-3} = 1 + 0.5 + 0.125 = 1.625$$

Converting decimal numbers to binary numbers is a little trickier. Here is an algorithm that converts a decimal integer into its binary equivalent: Keep dividing the integer by 2, keeping track of the remainders. Stop when the number is 0. Then write the remainders as a binary number, starting with the last one. For example,

$$100 \div 2 = 50 \text{ remainder } 0$$
$$50 \div 2 = 25 \text{ remainder } 0$$
$$25 \div 2 = 12 \text{ remainder } 1$$
$$12 \div 2 = 6 \text{ remainder } 0$$
$$6 \div 2 = 3 \text{ remainder } 0$$
$$3 \div 2 = 1 \text{ remainder } 1$$
$$1 \div 2 = 0 \text{ remainder } 1$$

Therefore, 100 in decimal is 1100100 in binary.

To convert a fractional number <1 to its binary format, keep multiplying by 2. If the result is >1, subtract 1. Stop when the number is 0. Then use the digits before the decimal points as the binary digits of the fractional part, starting with the first one. For example,

$$0.35 \cdot 2 = 0.7$$
$$0.7 \cdot 2 = 1.4$$
$$0.4 \cdot 2 = 0.8$$
$$0.8 \cdot 2 = 1.6$$
$$0.6 \cdot 2 = 1.2$$
$$0.2 \cdot 2 = 0.4$$

Here the pattern repeats. That is, the binary representation of 0.35 is 0.01 0110 0110 0110...

To convert any floating-point number into binary, convert the whole part and the fractional part separately. For example, 4.35 is 100.01 0110 0110 0110... in binary.

You don't actually need to know about binary numbers to program in Java, but at times it can be helpful to understand a little about them. For example, knowing that an `int` is represented as a 32-bit binary number explains why the largest integer that you can represent in Java is 0111 1111 1111 1111 1111 1111 1111 1111 binary = 2,147,483,647 decimal. (The first bit is the sign bit. It is off for positive values.)

To convert an integer into its binary representation, you can use the static `toString` method of the `Integer` class. The call `Integer.toString(n, 2)` returns a string with the binary digits of the integer n. Conversely, you can convert a string containing binary digits into an integer with the call `Integer.parseInt(digitString, 2)`. In both of these method calls, the second parameter denotes the base of the number system. It can be any number between 0 and 36. You can use these two methods to convert between decimal and binary integers. However, the Java library has no convenient method to do the same for floating-point numbers.

Now you can see why we had to fight with a roundoff error when computing 100 times 4.35. If you actually carry out the long multiplication, you get:

```
1 1 0 0 1 0 0 * 1 0 0.0 1|0 1 1 0|0 1 1 0|0 1 1 0 ...

1 0 0.0 1|0 1 1 0|0 1 1 0|0 1 1 0 ...
  1 0 0.0 1|0 1 1 0|0 1 1 0|0 1 1 ...
      0
        0
          1 0 0.0 1|0 1 1 0|0 1 1 0 ...
              0
                0
  _____
1 1 0 1 1 0 0 1 0.1 1 1 1 1 1 1 1 ...
```

That is, the result is 434, followed by an infinite number of 1s. The fractional part of the product is the binary equivalent of an infinite decimal fraction 0.999999 . . . , which is equal to 1. But the CPU can store only a finite number of 1s, and it discards some of them when converting the result to a decimal number.

Random Fact 4.1

The Pentium Floating-Point Bug

In 1994, Intel Corporation released what was then its most powerful processor, the first of the Pentium series. Unlike previous generations of Intel's processors, the Pentium had a built-in floating-point unit. Intel's goal was to compete aggressively with the makers of higher-end processors for engineering workstations. The Pentium was an immediate success.

In the summer of 1994, Dr. Thomas Nicely of Lynchburg College in Virginia ran an extensive set of computations to analyze the sums of reciprocals of certain sequences of prime numbers. The results were not always what his theory predicted, even after he took into account the inevitable roundoff errors. Then Dr. Nicely noted that the same program did produce the correct results when run on the slower 486 processor, which preceded the Pentium in Intel's lineup. This should not have happened. The roundoff behavior of floating-point calculations had been standardized by the Institute of Electrical and Electronics Engineers (IEEE), and Intel claimed to adhere to the IEEE standard in both the 486 and the Pentium processors. Upon further checking, Dr. Nicely discovered that indeed there was a very small set of numbers for which the product of two numbers was computed differently on the two processors. For example,

$$4,195,835 = ((4,195,835 \, / \, 3,145,727) \times 3,145,727)$$

is mathematically equal to 0, and it did compute as 0 on a 486 processor. On a Pentium processor, however, the result was 256.

As it turned out, Intel had independently discovered the bug in its testing and had started to produce chips that fixed it. (Subsequent versions of the Pentium, such as the Pentium III and IV, are free of the problem.) The bug was caused by an error in a table that was used to

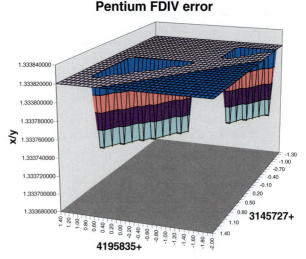

This graph shows a set of numbers for which the original Pentium processor obtained the wrong quotient.

speed up the floating-point multiplication algorithm of the processor. Intel determined that the problem was exceedingly rare. They claimed that under normal use a typical consumer would only notice the problem once every 27,000 years. Unfortunately for Intel, Dr. Nicely had not been a normal user.

Now Intel had a real problem on its hands. It figured that replacing all the Pentium processors that it had already sold would cost it a great deal of money. Intel already had more orders for the chip than it could produce, and it would be particularly galling to have to give out the scarce chips as free replacements instead of selling them. Initially, Intel's management offered to replace the processors only for those customers who could prove that their work required absolute precision in mathematical calculations. Naturally, that did not go over well with the hundreds of thousands of customers who had paid retail prices of $700 and more for a Pentium chip and did not want to live with the nagging feeling that perhaps, one day, their income tax program would produce a faulty return. In the end, Intel gave in to public demand and replaced the defective chips, at a cost of about 475 million dollars.

4.2 Constants

In many programs, you need to use numerical **constants**—values that do not change and that have a special significance for a computation.

A typical example for the use of constants is a computation that involves coin values, such as the following:

```
payment = dollars + quarters * 0.25 + dimes * 0.1
    + nickels * 0.05 + pennies * 0.01;
```

Most of the code is self-documenting. However, the four numeric quantities, 0.25, 0.1, 0.05, and 0.01 are included in the arithmetic expression without any explanation. Of course, in this case, you know that the value of a nickel is five cents, which explains the 0.05, and so on. However, the next person who needs to maintain this code may live in another country and may not know that a nickel is worth five cents.

Thus, it is a good idea to use symbolic names for all values, even those that appear obvious. Here is a clearer version of the computation of the total:

```
double quarterValue = 0.25;
double dimeValue = 0.1;
double nickelValue = 0.05;
double pennyValue = 0.01;
payment = dollars + quarters * quarterValue + dimes * dimeValue
    + nickels * nickelValue + pennies * pennyValue;
```

There is another improvement we can make. There is a difference between the `nickels` and `nickelValue` variables. The `nickels` variable can truly vary over the life of the program, as we calculate different payments. But `nickelValue` is always 0.05.

In Java, constants are identified with the reserved word `final`. A variable tagged as `final` can never change after it has been set. If you try to change the value of a `final` variable, the compiler will report an error and your program will not compile.

Many programmers use all-uppercase names for constants (`final` variables), such as `NICKEL_VALUE`. That way, it is easy to distinguish between variables (with mostly lowercase letters) and constants. We will follow this convention in this book. However, this rule is a matter of good style, not a requirement of the Java language. The compiler will not complain if you give a `final` variable a name with lowercase letters.

A final variable is a constant. Once its value has been set, it cannot be changed.

Use named constants to make your programs easier to read and maintain.

Here is an improved version of the code that computes the value of a payment.

```java
final double QUARTER_VALUE = 0.25;
final double DIME_VALUE = 0.1;
final double NICKEL_VALUE = 0.05;
final double PENNY_VALUE = 0.01;
payment = dollars + quarters * QUARTER_VALUE + dimes * DIME_VALUE
        + nickels * NICKEL_VALUE + pennies * PENNY_VALUE;
```

Frequently, constant values are needed in several methods. Then you should declare them together with the instance variables of a class and tag them as `static` and `final`. As before, `final` indicates that the value is a constant. The `static` reserved word means that the constant belongs to the class—this is explained in greater detail in Chapter 8.)

```java
public class CashRegister
{
    // Constants
    public static final double QUARTER_VALUE = 0.25;
    public static final double DIME_VALUE = 0.1;
    public static final double NICKEL_VALUE = 0.05;
    public static final double PENNY_VALUE = 0.01;

    // Instance variables
    private double purchase;
    private double payment;

    // Methods
    . . .
}
```

We declared the constants as `public`. There is no danger in doing this because constants cannot be modified. Methods of other classes can access a public constant by first specifying the name of the class in which it is declared, then a period, then the name of the constant, such as `CashRegister.NICKEL_VALUE`.

Syntax 4.1   Constant Declaration

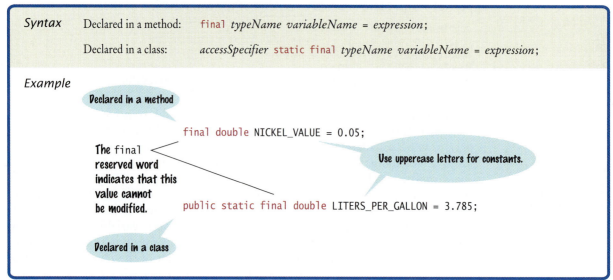

Syntax   Declared in a method: `final` *typeName* *variableName* = *expression*;

Declared in a class: *accessSpecifier* `static final` *typeName* *variableName* = *expression*;

Example

Declared in a method

`final double NICKEL_VALUE = 0.05;`

Use uppercase letters for constants.

The `final` reserved word indicates that this value cannot be modified.

`public static final double LITERS_PER_GALLON = 3.785;`

Declared in a class

The Math class from the standard library declares a couple of useful constants:

```
public class Math
{
    . . .
    public static final double E = 2.7182818284590452354;
    public static final double PI = 3.14159265358979323846;
}
```

You can refer to these constants as Math.PI and Math.E in any of your methods. For example,

```
double circumference = Math.PI * diameter;
```

The sample program at the end of this section puts constants to work. The program shows a refinement of the CashRegister class of How To 3.1. The public interface of that class has been modified in order to solve a common business problem.

Busy cashiers sometimes make mistakes totaling up coin values. Our Cash-Register class features a method whose inputs are the *coin counts.* For example, the call

```
register.enterPayment(1, 2, 1, 1, 4);
```

enters a payment consisting of one dollar, two quarters, one dime, one nickel, and four pennies. The enterPayment method figures out the total value of the payment, $1.69. As you can see from the code listing, the method uses named constants for the coin values.

ch04/cashregister/CashRegister.java

```
1   /**
2       A cash register totals up sales and computes change due.
3   */
4   public class CashRegister
5   {
6       public static final double QUARTER_VALUE = 0.25;
7       public static final double DIME_VALUE = 0.1;
8       public static final double NICKEL_VALUE = 0.05;
9       public static final double PENNY_VALUE = 0.01;
10
11      private double purchase;
12      private double payment;
13
14      /**
15          Constructs a cash register with no money in it.
16      */
17      public CashRegister()
18      {
19          purchase = 0;
20          payment = 0;
21      }
22
23      /**
24          Records the purchase price of an item.
25          @param amount the price of the purchased item
26      */
27      public void recordPurchase(double amount)
28      {
29          purchase = purchase + amount;
```

```java
30      }
31
32      /**
33          Enters the payment received from the customer.
34          @param dollars the number of dollars in the payment
35          @param quarters the number of quarters in the payment
36          @param dimes the number of dimes in the payment
37          @param nickels the number of nickels in the payment
38          @param pennies the number of pennies in the payment
39      */
40      public void enterPayment(int dollars, int quarters,
41              int dimes, int nickels, int pennies)
42      {
43          payment = dollars + quarters * QUARTER_VALUE + dimes * DIME_VALUE
44              + nickels * NICKEL_VALUE + pennies * PENNY_VALUE;
45      }
46
47      /**
48          Computes the change due and resets the machine for the next customer.
49          @return the change due to the customer
50      */
51      public double giveChange()
52      {
53          double change = payment - purchase;
54          purchase = 0;
55          payment = 0;
56          return change;
57      }
58  }
```

ch04/cashregister/CashRegisterTester.java

```java
1   /**
2       This class tests the CashRegister class.
3   */
4   public class CashRegisterTester
5   {
6       public static void main(String[] args)
7       {
8           CashRegister register = new CashRegister();
9
10          register.recordPurchase(0.75);
11          register.recordPurchase(1.50);
12          register.enterPayment(2, 0, 5, 0, 0);
13          System.out.print("Change: ");
14          System.out.println(register.giveChange());
15          System.out.println("Expected: 0.25");
16
17          register.recordPurchase(2.25);
18          register.recordPurchase(19.25);
19          register.enterPayment(23, 2, 0, 0, 0);
20          System.out.print("Change: ");
21          System.out.println(register.giveChange());
22          System.out.println("Expected: 2.0");
23      }
24  }
```

Program Run

```
Change: 0.25
Expected: 0.25
Change: 2.0
Expected: 2.0
```

SELF CHECK

4. What is the difference between the following two statements?

```
final double CM_PER_INCH = 2.54;
```

and

```
public static final double CM_PER_INCH = 2.54;
```

5. What is wrong with the following statement sequence?

```
double diameter = . . .;
double circumference = 3.14 * diameter;
```

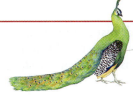

Quality Tip 4.1

Do Not Use Magic Numbers

A magic number is a numeric constant that appears in your code without explanation. For example, consider the following scary example that actually occurs in the Java library source:

```
h = 31 * h + ch;
```

Why 31? The number of days in January? One less than the number of bits in an integer? Actually, this code computes a "hash code" from a string—a number that is derived from the characters in such a way that different strings are likely to yield different hash codes. The value 31 turns out to scramble the character values nicely.

A better solution is to use a named constant:

```
final int HASH_MULTIPLIER = 31;
h = HASH_MULTIPLIER * h + ch;
```

You should never use magic numbers in your code. Any number that is not completely self-explanatory should be declared as a named constant. Even the most reasonable cosmic constant is going to change one day. You think there are 365 days in a year? Your customers on Mars are going to be pretty unhappy about your silly prejudice. Make a constant

```
final int DAYS_PER_YEAR = 365;
```

By the way, the device

```
final int THREE_HUNDRED_AND_SIXTY_FIVE = 365;
```

is counterproductive and frowned upon.

4.3 Arithmetic Operations and Mathematical Functions

In the following sections, you will learn how to carry out arithmetic calculations in Java.

4.3.1 Arithmetic Operators

Java supports the same four basic arithmetic operations as a calculator—addition, subtraction, multiplication, and division. As you have already seen, addition and subtraction use the familiar + and - operators, and the * operator denotes multiplication. Division is indicated with a /, not a fraction bar.
For example,

$$\frac{a + b}{2}$$

becomes

```
(a + b) / 2
```

Parentheses are used just as in algebra: to indicate in which order the subexpressions should be computed. For example, in the expression (a + b) / 2, the sum a + b is computed first, and then the sum is divided by 2. In contrast, in the expression

```
a + b / 2
```

only b is divided by 2, and then the sum of a and b / 2 is formed. Just as in regular algebraic notation, multiplication and division bind more strongly than addition and subtraction. For example, in the expression a + b / 2, the / is carried out first, even though the + operation occurs farther to the left.

4.3.2 Increment and Decrement

Incrementing a value by 1 is so common when writing programs that there is a special shorthand for it, namely

```
items++;
```

The ++ and -- operators increment and decrement a variable.

This statement adds 1 to items. It is easier to type and read than the equivalent assignment statement

```
items = items + 1;
```

As you might have guessed, there is also a decrement operator --. The statement

```
items--;
```

subtracts 1 from items.

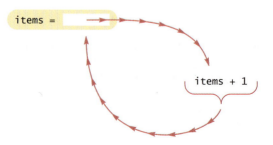

Figure 1   Incrementing a Variable

4.3.3 Integer Division

If both arguments of the / operator are integers, the result is an integer and the remainder is discarded.

Division works as you would expect, as long as at least one of the numbers involved is a floating-point number. That is,

```
7.0 / 4.0
7 / 4.0
7.0 / 4
```

all yield 1.75. However, if both numbers are integers, then the result of the division is always an integer, with the remainder discarded. That is,

```
7 / 4
```

evaluates to 1, because 7 divided by 4 is 1 with a remainder of 3 (which is discarded). Discarding the remainder is often useful, but it can also be a source of subtle programming errors — see Common Error 4.1 on page 142.

The % operator computes the remainder of a division.

If you are interested only in the remainder of an integer division, use the % operator:

```
7 % 4
```

is 3, the remainder of the integer division of 7 by 4. The % symbol has no analog in algebra. It was chosen because it looks similar to /, and the remainder operation is related to division.

Here is a typical use for the integer / and % operations. Suppose you want to know how much change a cash register should give, using separate values for dollars and cents. You can compute the value as an integer, denominated in cents, and then compute the whole dollar amount and the remaining change:

```
final int PENNIES_PER_NICKEL = 5;
final int PENNIES_PER_DIME = 10;
final int PENNIES_PER_QUARTER = 25;
final int PENNIES_PER_DOLLAR = 100;

// Compute total value in pennies
int total = dollars * PENNIES_PER_DOLLAR + quarters * PENNIES_PER_QUARTER
      + nickels * PENNIES_PER_NICKEL + dimes * PENNIES_PER_DIME + pennies;

// Use integer division to convert to dollars, cents
int dollars = total / PENNIES_PER_DOLLAR;
int cents = total % PENNIES_PER_DOLLAR;
```

For example, if total is 243, then dollars is set to 2 and cents to 43.

4.3.4 Powers and Roots

The Math class contains methods sqrt and pow to compute square roots and powers.

To compute x^n, you write Math.pow(x, n). However, to compute x^2 it is significantly more efficient simply to compute x * x.

To take the square root of a number, you use the Math.sqrt method. For example, $\sqrt{x}$ is written as Math.sqrt(x).

In algebra, you use fractions, superscripts for exponents, and radical signs for roots to arrange expressions in a compact two-dimensional form. In Java, you have to write all expressions in a linear arrangement.

$$(\text{-b + Math.sqrt(b * b - 4 * a * c)) / (2 * a)}$$

Figure 2 Analyzing an Expression

For example, the subexpression

$$\frac{-b + \sqrt{b^2 - 4ac}}{2a}$$

of the quadratic formula becomes

```
(-b + Math.sqrt(b * b - 4 * a * c)) / (2 * a)
```

Figure 2 shows how to analyze such an expression. With complicated expressions like these, it is not always easy to keep the parentheses ( ) matched—see Common Error 4.2 on page 143.

Table 2 shows additional methods of the Math class. Inputs and outputs are floating-point numbers.

4.3.5 Casting and Rounding

Occasionally, you have a value of type double that you need to convert to the type int. Use the *cast* operator (int) for this purpose. You write the cast operator before the expression that you want to convert:

```
double balance = total + tax;
int dollars = (int) balance;
```

Syntax 4.2 Cast

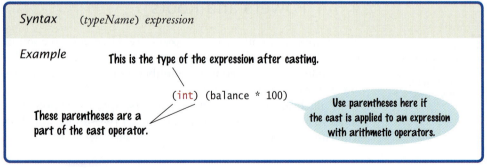

Table 2 Mathematical Methods	
Function	Returns
`Math.sqrt(x)`	Square root of x (≥ 0)
`Math.pow(x, y)`	x^y ($x > 0$, or $x = 0$ and $y > 0$, or $x < 0$ and y is an integer)
`Math.sin(x)`	Sine of x (x in radians)
`Math.cos(x)`	Cosine of x
`Math.tan(x)`	Tangent of x
`Math.asin(x)`	Arc sine ($\sin^{-1}x \in [-\pi/2, \pi/2], x \in [-1, 1]$)
`Math.acos(x)`	Arc cosine ($\cos^{-1}x \in [0, \pi], x \in [-1, 1]$)
`Math.atan(x)`	Arc tangent ($\tan^{-1}x \in [-\pi/2, \pi/2]$)
`Math.atan2(y, x)`	Arc tangent ($\tan^{-1}y/x \in [-\pi, \pi]$), x may be 0
`Math.toRadians(x)`	Convert x degrees to radians (i.e., returns $x \cdot \pi/180$)
`Math.toDegrees(x)`	Convert x radians to degrees (i.e., returns $x \cdot 180/\pi$)
`Math.exp(x)`	e^x
`Math.log(x)`	Natural log ($\ln(x), x > 0$)
`Math.log10(x)`	Decimal log ($\log_{10}(x), x > 0$)
`Math.round(x)`	Closest integer to x (as a `long`)
`Math.ceil(x)`	Smallest integer $\geq x$ (as a `double`)
`Math.floor(x)`	Largest integer $\leq x$ (as a `double`)
`Math.abs(x)`	Absolute value $|x|$
`Math.max(x, y)`	The larger of x and y
`Math.min(x, y)`	The smaller of x and y

You use a cast (*typeName*) to convert a value to a different type.

The cast (`int`) converts the floating-point value `balance` to an integer by discarding the fractional part. For example, if `balance` is 13.75, then `dollars` is set to 13.

The cast tells the compiler that you agree to *information loss,* in this case, to the loss of the fractional part. You can also cast to other types, such as (`float`) or (`byte`).

If you want to round a floating-point number to the nearest whole number, use the `Math.round` method. This method returns a `long` integer, because large floating-point numbers cannot be stored in an `int`.

Use the `Math.round` method to round a floating-point number to the nearest integer.

```
long rounded = Math.round(balance);
```

If `balance` is 13.75, then `rounded` is set to 14.

Table 3 Arithmetic Expressions

Mathematical Expression	Java Expression	Comments
$\dfrac{x+y}{2}$	`(x + y) / 2`	The parentheses are required; `x + y / 2` computes $x + \dfrac{y}{2}$.
$\dfrac{xy}{2}$	`x * y / 2`	Parentheses are not required; operators with the same precedence are evaluated left to right.
$\left(1 + \dfrac{r}{100}\right)^n$	`Math.pow(1 + r / 100, n)`	Complex formulas are "flattened" in Java.
$\sqrt{a^2 + b^2}$	`Math.sqrt(a * a + b * b)`	`a * a` is simpler than `Math.pow(a, 2)`.
$\dfrac{i+j+k}{3}$	`(i + j + k) / 3.0`	If i, j, and k are integers, using a denominator of 3.0 forces floating-point division.

SELF CHECK

6. What is the value of n after the following sequence of statements?

```
n--;
n++;
n--;
```

7. What is the value of 1729 / 100? Of 1729 % 100?

8. Why doesn't the following statement compute the average of s1, s2, and s3?

```
double average = s1 + s2 + s3 / 3; // Error
```

9. What is the value of `Math.sqrt(Math.pow(x, 2) + Math.pow(y, 2))` in mathematical notation?

10. When does the cast `(long) x` yield a different result from the call `Math.round(x)`?

11. How do you round the `double` value x to the nearest `int` value, assuming that you know that it is less than $2 \cdot 10^9$?

Common Error 4.1

Integer Division

It is unfortunate that Java uses the same symbol, namely /, for both integer and floating-point division. These are really quite different operations. It is a common error to use integer division by accident. Consider this program segment that computes the average of three integers.

```
int s1 = 5; // Score of test 1
int s2 = 6; // Score of test 2
int s3 = 3; // Score of test 3
double average = (s1 + s2 + s3) / 3;  // Error
```

```
System.out.print("Your average score is ");
System.out.println(average);
```

What could be wrong with that? Of course, the average of s1, s2, and s3 is

$$\frac{s_1 + s_2 + s_3}{3}$$

Here, however, the / does not mean division in the mathematical sense. It denotes integer division, because the values s1 + s2 + s3 and 3 are both integers. For example, if the scores add up to 14, the average is computed to be 4, the result of the integer division of 14 by 3. That integer 4 is then moved into the floating-point variable average. The remedy is to make either the numerator or denominator into a floating-point number:

```
double total = s1 + s2 + s3;
double average = total / 3;
```

or

```
double average = (s1 + s2 + s3) / 3.0;
```

Common Error 4.2

Unbalanced Parentheses

Consider the expression

```
1.5 * ((-(b - Math.sqrt(b * b - 4 * a * c)) / (2 * a))
```

What is wrong with it? Count the parentheses. There are five opening parentheses (and four closing parentheses). The parentheses are unbalanced. This kind of typing error is very common with complicated expressions. Now consider this expression.

```
1.5 * (Math.sqrt(b * b - 4 * a * c))) - ((b / (2 * a))
```

This expression has five opening parentheses (and five closing parentheses), but it is still not correct. In the middle of the expression,

```
1.5 * (Math.sqrt(b * b - 4 * a * c))) - ((b / (2 * a))
```

there are only two opening parentheses (but three closing parentheses), which is an error. In the middle of an expression, the count of opening parentheses must be greater than or equal to the count of closing parentheses, and at the end of the expression the two counts must be the same.

Here is a simple trick to make the counting easier without using pencil and paper. It is difficult for the brain to keep two counts simultaneously, so keep only one count when scanning the expression. Start with 1 at the first opening parenthesis; add 1 whenever you see an opening parenthesis; subtract 1 whenever you see a closing parenthesis. Say the numbers aloud as you scan the expression. If the count ever drops below zero, or if it is not zero at the end, the parentheses are unbalanced. For example, when scanning the previous expression, you would mutter

```
1.5 * (Math.sqrt(b * b - 4 * a * c) )   ) - ((b / (2 * a))
        1        2                1 0 -1
```

and you would find the error.

Quality Tip 4.2

White Space

The compiler does not care whether you write your entire program onto a single line or place every symbol onto a separate line. The human reader, though, cares very much. You should use blank lines to group your code visually into sections. For example, you can signal to the reader that an output prompt and the corresponding input statement belong together by inserting a blank line before and after the group. You will find many examples in the source code listings in this book.

White space inside expressions is also important. It is easier to read

```
x1 = (-b + Math.sqrt(b * b - 4 * a * c)) / (2 * a);
```

than

```
x1=(-b+Math.sqrt(b*b-4*a*c))/(2*a);
```

Simply put spaces around all operators + - * / % =. However, don't put a space after a unary minus: a - used to negate a single quantity, as in -b. That way, it can be easily distinguished from a binary minus, as in a - b. Don't put spaces between a method name and the parentheses, but do put a space after every Java reserved word. That makes it easy to see that the sqrt in Math.sqrt(x) is a method name, whereas the if in if (x > 0) . . . is a reserved word.

Quality Tip 4.3

Factor Out Common Code

Suppose you want to find both solutions of the quadratic equation $ax^2 + bx + c = 0$. The quadratic formula tells us that the solutions are

$$x_{1,2} = \frac{-b \pm \sqrt{b^2 - 4ac}}{2a}$$

In Java, there is no analog to the ± operation, which indicates how to obtain two solutions simultaneously. Both solutions must be computed separately:

```
x1 = (-b + Math.sqrt(b * b - 4 * a * c)) / (2 * a);
x2 = (-b - Math.sqrt(b * b - 4 * a * c)) / (2 * a);
```

This approach has two problems. First, the computation of Math.sqrt(b * b - 4 * a * c) is carried out twice, which wastes time. Second, whenever the same code is replicated, the possibility of a typing error increases. The remedy is to factor out the common code:

```
double root = Math.sqrt(b * b - 4 * a * c);
x1 = (-b + root) / (2 * a);
x2 = (-b - root) / (2 * a);
```

You could go even further and factor out the computation of 2 * a, but the gain from factoring out very simple computations is too small to warrant the effort.

Common Error 4.3

Roundoff Errors

Roundoff errors are a fact of life when calculating with floating-point numbers. You probably have encountered this phenomenon yourself with manual calculations. If you calculate 1/3 to two decimal places, you get 0.33. Multiplying again by 3, you obtain 0.99, not 1.00.

In the processor hardware, numbers are represented in the binary number system, not in decimal. You still get roundoff errors when binary digits are lost. They just may crop up at different places than you might expect. Here is an example:

```
double f = 4.35;
int n = (int) (100 * f);
System.out.println(n); // Prints 434!
```

Of course, one hundred times 4.35 is 435, but the program prints 434.

Computers represent numbers in the binary system (see Special Topic 4.2 on page 130). In the binary system, there is no exact representation for 4.35, just as there is no exact representation for 1/3 in the decimal system. The representation used by the computer is just a little less than 4.35, so 100 times that value is just a little less than 435. When a floating-point value is converted to an integer, the entire fractional part is discarded, even if it is almost 1. As a result, the integer 434 is stored in n. Remedy: Use Math.round to convert floating-point numbers to integers. The round method returns the *closest* integer.

```
int n = (int) Math.round(100 * f);   // OK, n is 435
```

Special Topic 4.3

Combining Assignment and Arithmetic

In Java you can combine arithmetic and assignment. For example, the instruction

```
balance += amount;
```

is a shortcut for

```
balance = balance + amount;
```

Similarly,

```
items *= 2;
```

is another way of writing

```
items = items * 2;
```

Many programmers find this a convenient shortcut. If you like it, go ahead and use it in your own code. For simplicity, we won't use it in this book.

4.4 Calling Static Methods

In the preceding section, you encountered the Math class, which contains a collection of helpful methods for carrying out mathematical computations. These methods have a special form: they are *static methods* that do not operate on an object.

That is, you don't call

```
double root = 100.sqrt(); // Error
```

In Java, numbers are not objects, so you can never invoke a method on a number. Instead, you pass a number as an explicit parameter to a method, enclosing the number in parentheses after the method name:

```
double root = Math.sqrt(100);
```

Syntax 4.3   Static Method Call

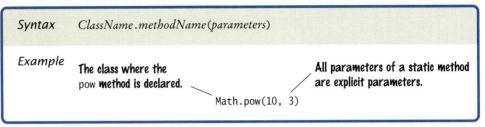

Syntax	*ClassName*.*methodName*(*parameters*)

Example

The class where the pow **method is declared.**

All parameters of a static method are explicit parameters.

```
Math.pow(10, 3)
```

A static method does not operate on an object.

This call makes it appear as if the sqrt method is applied to an object called Math. However, Math is a class, not an object. A method such as Math.sqrt that does not operate on any object is called a static method. (The term "static" is a historical holdover from the C and C++ programming languages. It has nothing to do with the usual meaning of the word.) In contrast, a method that is invoked on an object is class, is called an *instance method*:

```
harrysChecking.deposit(100); // deposit is an instance method
```

Static methods do not operate on objects, but they are still declared inside classes. When calling the method, you specify the class to which the sqrt method belongs— hence the call is Math.sqrt(100).

How can you tell that Math is a class and not an object? By convention, class names start with an uppercase letter (such as Math or BankAccount). Objects and methods start with a lowercase letter (such as harrysChecking and println). Therefore, harrysChecking.deposit(100) denotes a call of the deposit method on the harrysChecking object inside the System class. On the other hand, Math.sqrt(100) denotes a call to the sqrt method inside the Math class.

This use of upper- and lowercase letters is merely a convention, not a rule of the Java language. It is, however, a convention that the authors of the Java class libraries follow consistently. You should do the same in your programs so that you don't confuse your fellow programmers.

S E L F   C H E C K

12. Why can't you call x.pow(y) to compute x^y?

13. Is the call System.out.println(4) a static method call?

How To 4.1

Carrying Out Computations

Many programming problems require that you use mathematical formulas to compute values. This How To shows how to turn a problem statement into a sequence of mathematical formulas and, ultimately, a class in the Java programming language.

Step 1   Understand the problem: What are the inputs? What are the desired outputs?

For example, suppose you are asked to simulate a postage stamp vending machine. A customer inserts money into the vending machine. Then the customer pushes a "First class stamps" button. The vending machine gives out as many first-class stamps as the customer paid for. (A first-class stamp cost 44 cents at the time this book was written.) Finally, the customer pushes a "Penny stamps" button. The machine gives the change in penny (1-cent) stamps.

In this problem, there is one input:

- The amount of money the customer inserts

There are two desired outputs:

- The number of first-class stamps the machine returns
- The number of penny stamps the machine returns

Step 2 Work out examples by hand.

This is a very important step. If you can't compute a couple of solutions by hand, it's unlikely that you'll be able to write a program that automates the computation.

Let's assume that a first-class stamp costs 44 cents and the customer inserts $1.00. That's enough for two stamps (88 cents) but not enough for three stamps ($1.32). Therefore, the machine returns two first-class stamps and 12 penny stamps.

Step 3 Design a class that carries out your computations.

How To 3.1 explains how to develop a class by finding methods and instance variables. In our case, the problem statement yields three methods:

- `public void insert(int dollars)`
- `public int giveFirstClassStamps()`
- `public int givePennyStamps()`

A bigger challenge is to determine instance variables that describe the state of the machine. In this example, an excellent choice is to keep a single variable, the customer balance. (See Exercise P4.12 for another choice.)

That balance is incremented by the `insert` method and decremented by the `giveFirst-ClassStamps` and `givePennyStamps` methods.

Step 4 Write pseudocode for implementing the methods.

Given an amount of money and the price of a first-class stamp, how can you compute how many first-class stamps can be purchased with the money? Clearly, the answer is related to the quotient

$$\frac{\text{amount of money}}{\text{price of first-class stamp}}$$

For example, suppose the customer paid $1.00. Use a pocket calculator to compute the quotient: $1.00/$0.44 ≈ 2.27.

How do you get "2 stamps" out of 2.27? It's the integer part. In Java, this is easy to compute if both arguments are integers. Therefore, let's switch our computation to pennies. Then we have

number of first-class stamps = 100 / 44 (integer division, without remainder)

What if the user inputs two dollars? Then the numerator becomes 200. What if the price of a stamp goes up? A more general equation is

input in pennies = 100 x dollars

number of first-class stamps = input in pennies / price of first-class stamps in pennies (without remainder)

How about the remaining balance after dispensing the first class stamps? Here is one way of computing it. When the customer gets the stamps, the remaining balance is the original balance, reduced by the value of the stamps purchased. In our example, the remainder is 12 cents—the difference between 100 and 2 · 44. Here is the general formula:

remaining balance = input in pennies – number of first-class stamps x price of first-class stamp in pennies

Step 5 Implement the class.

In Step 3, we decided that the state of the vending machine can be represented by the customer balance. In Step 4, it became clear that the balance is best represented in pennies.

It is a good idea to rewrite the pseudocode in terms of this newly found variable. We now use the instance variable balance for what was previously called **input in pennies**. When money is inserted, the balance increases:

```
balance = balance + 100 * dollars
```

When the first class stamps are requested, the balance decreases.

```
firstClassStamps = balance / FIRST_CLASS_STAMP_PRICE;
balance = balance - firstClassStamps * FIRST_CLASS_STAMP_PRICE;
```

What was previously called **remaining balance** is now simply the value of the balance instance variable.

Here is the implementation of the StampMachine class:

```java
public class StampMachine
{
    public static final double FIRST_CLASS_STAMP_PRICE = 44;
    private int balance;

    public StampMachine()
    {
        balance = 0;
    }

    public void insert(int dollars)
    {
        balance = balance + 100 * dollars;
    }

    public int giveFirstClassStamps()
    {
        int firstClassStamps = balance / FIRST_CLASS_STAMP_PRICE;
        balance = balance - firstClassStamps * FIRST_CLASS_STAMP_PRICE;
        return firstClassStamps;
    }

    public int givePennyStamps()
    {
        int pennyStamps = balance;
        balance = 0;
        return pennyStamps;
    }
}
```

Step 6 Test your class.

Run a test program (or use an integrated environment such as BlueJ) to verify that the values that your class computes are the same values that you computed by hand.

Here is a test program:

```java
public class StampMachineTester
{
    public static void main(String[] args)
    {
        StampMachine machine = new StampMachine();
        machine.insert(1);
        System.out.print("First class stamps: ");
        System.out.println(machine.giveFirstClassStamps());
```

```
            System.out.println("Expected: 2");
            System.out.print("Penny stamps: ");
            System.out.println(machine.givePennyStamps());
            System.out.println("Expected: 12");
        }
    }
```

Program Run

```
First class stamps: 2
Expected: 2
Penny stamps: 12
Expected: 12
```

⊕ Worked Example 4.1

Computing the Volume and Surface Area of a Pyramid

This Worked Example shows how to design a class for computing the volume and surface area of a pyramid.

4.5 Strings

Many programs process text that consists of characters: letters, numbers, punctuation, spaces, and so on. A string is a sequence of characters, such as "Hello, World!". In the following sections, you will learn how to work with strings in Java.

4.5.1 The String Class

> A string is a sequence of characters. Strings are objects of the String class.

In Java, strings are objects that belong to the class String. (You can tell that String is a class name because it starts with an uppercase letter. The primitive types int and double start with lowercase letters.)

You do not need to call a constructor to create a string object. You can obtain a string *literal* simply by enclosing a sequence of characters in double quotation marks. For example, the string literal "Harry" is an object of the String class.

The number of characters in a string is called the *length* of the string. As you have seen in Chapter 2, you can use the length method to obtain the length of a string. For example, "Hello".length() is 5, and the length of "Hello, World!" is 13. (The quotation marks are not part of the string and do not contribute to the length, but you must count spaces and punctuation marks.)

A string of length zero, containing no characters, is called the *empty string* and is written as "".

4.5.2 Concatenation

You can use the + operator to put strings together to form a longer string.

```
String name = "Dave";
String message = "Hello, " + name;
```

⊕ Available online in WileyPLUS and at www.wiley.com/college/horstmann.

This process is called **concatenation**.

The + operator concatenates two strings, provided one of the expressions, either to the left or the right of a + operator, is a string. The other one is automatically forced to become a string as well, and both strings are concatenated.

For example, consider this code:

```
String a = "Agent";
int n = 7;
String bond = a + n;
```

> Strings can be concatenated, that is, put end to end to yield a new longer string. String concatenation is denoted by the + operator.

Because a is a string, n is converted from the integer 7 to the string "7". Then the two strings "Agent" and "7" are concatenated to form the string "Agent7".

This concatenation is very useful to reduce the number of System.out.print instructions. For example, you can combine

```
System.out.print("The total is ");
System.out.println(total);
```

to the single call

```
System.out.println("The total is " + total);
```

> Whenever one of the arguments of the + operator is a string, the other argument is converted to a string.

The concatenation "The total is " + total computes a single string that consists of the string "The total is ", followed by the string equivalent of the number total.

4.5.3 Converting Strings to Numbers

Sometimes you have a string that contains a number, usually from user input. For example, suppose that the string variable input has the value "19". To get the integer value 19, you use the static parseInt method of the Integer class.

```
int count = Integer.parseInt(input);
    // count is the integer 19
```

> If a string contains the digits of a number, you use the Integer.parseInt or Double.parseDouble method to obtain the number value.

To convert a string containing floating-point digits to its floating-point value, use the static parseDouble method of the Double class. For example, suppose input is the string "3.95".

```
double price = Double.parseDouble(input);
    // price is the floating-point number 3.95
```

However, if the string contains spaces or other characters that cannot occur inside numbers, an error occurs. For now, we will always assume that user input does not contain invalid characters.

4.5.4 Substrings

The substring method computes substrings of a string. The call

> Use the substring method to extract a part of a string.

```
s.substring(start, pastEnd)
```

returns a string that is made up of the characters in the string s, starting at position start, and containing all characters up to, but not including, the position pastEnd. Here is an example:

```
String greeting = "Hello, World!";
String sub = greeting.substring(0, 5); // sub is "Hello"
```

The `substring` operation makes a string that consists of five characters taken from the string `greeting`. A curious aspect of the `substring` operation is the numbering of the starting and ending positions. The first string position is labeled 0, the second one 1, and so on. For example, Figure 3 shows the position numbers in the `greeting` string.

String positions are counted starting with 0.

Figure 3 String Positions

The position number of the last character (12 for the string `"Hello, World!"`) is always 1 less than the length of the string.

Let us figure out how to extract the substring `"World"`. Count characters starting at 0, not 1. You find that `W`, the eighth character, has position number 7. The first character that you don't want, `!`, is the character at position 12 (see Figure 4).

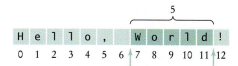

Figure 4 Extracting a Substring

Therefore, the appropriate substring command is

```
String sub2 = greeting.substring(7, 12);
```

It is curious that you must specify the position of the first character that you do want and then the first character that you don't want. There is one advantage to this setup. You can easily compute the length of the substring: It is `pastEnd - start`. For example, the string `"World"` has length $12 - 7 = 5$.

If you omit the second parameter of the `substring` method, then all characters from the starting position to the end of the string are copied. For example,

```
String tail = greeting.substring(7); // Copies all characters from position 7 on
```

sets `tail` to the string `"World!"`.

If you supply an illegal string position (a negative number, or a value that is larger than the length of the string), then your program terminates with an error message.

In this section, we have made the assumption that each character in a string occupies a single position. Unfortunately, that assumption is not quite correct. If you process strings that contain characters from international alphabets or special symbols, some characters may occupy two positions—see Special Topic 4.5 on page 153.

S E L F C H E C K

14. Assuming the `String` variable `s` holds the value `"Agent"`, what is the effect of the assignment `s = s + s.length()`?

15. Assuming the `String` variable `river` holds the value `"Mississippi"`, what is the value of `river.substring(1, 2)`? Of `river.substring(2, river.length() - 3)`?

Productivity Hint 4.1

Reading Exception Reports

You will often have programs that terminate and display an error message, such as

```
Exception in thread "main" java.lang.StringIndexOutOfBoundsException:
    String index out of range: -4
  at java.lang.String.substring(String.java:1444)
  at Homework1.main(Homework1.java:16)
```

An amazing number of students simply give up at that point, saying "it didn't work", or "my program died", without ever reading the error message. Admittedly, the format of the exception report is not very friendly. But it is actually easy to decipher it.

When you have a close look at the error message, you will notice two pieces of useful information:

1. The name of the exception, such as `StringIndexOutOfBoundsException`
2. The line number of the code that contained the statement that caused the exception, such as `Homework1.java:16`

The name of the exception is always in the first line of the report, and it ends in `Exception`. If you get a `StringIndexOutOfBoundsException`, then there was a problem with accessing an invalid position in a string. That is useful information.

The line number of the offending code is a little harder to determine. The exception report contains the entire stack trace—that is, the names of all methods that were pending when the exception hit. The first line of the stack trace is the method that actually generated the exception. The last line of the stack trace is a line in `main`. Often, the exception was thrown by a method that is in the standard library. Look for the first line in your code that appears in the exception report. For example, skip the line that refers to

```
java.lang.String.substring(String.java:1444)
```

The next line in our example mentions a line number in your code, `Homework1.java`. Once you have the line number in your code, open up the file, go to that line, and look at it! Also look at the name of the exception. In most cases, these two pieces of information will make it completely obvious what went wrong, and you can easily fix your error.

Special Topic 4.4

Escape Sequences

Suppose you want to display a string containing quotation marks, such as

```
Hello, "World"!
```

You can't use

```
System.out.println("Hello, "World"!");
```

As soon as the compiler reads `"Hello, "`, it thinks the string is finished, and then it gets all confused about `World` followed by two quotation marks. A human would probably realize that the second and third quotation marks were supposed to be part of the string, but a compiler has a one-track mind. If a simple analysis of the input doesn't make sense to it, it just refuses to go on, and reports an error. Well, how do you then display quotation marks on the screen? You precede the quotation marks inside the string with a *backslash* character. Inside a string, the sequence `\"` denotes a literal quote, not the end of a string. The correct display statement is, therefore

```
System.out.println("Hello, \"World\"!");
```

The backslash character is used as an *escape* character; the character sequence \" is called an escape sequence. The backslash does not denote itself; instead, it is used to encode other characters that would otherwise be difficult to include in a string.

Now, what do you do if you actually want to print a backslash (for example, to specify a Windows file name)? You must enter two \\ in a row, like this:

```
System.out.println("The secret message is in C:\\Temp\\Secret.txt");
```

This statement prints

```
The secret message is in C:\Temp\Secret.txt
```

Another escape sequence occasionally used is \n, which denotes a *newline* or line feed character. Printing a newline character causes the start of a new line on the display. For example, the statement

```
System.out.print("*\n**\n***\n");
```

prints the characters

```
*
**
***
```

on three separate lines. Of course, you could have achieved the same effect with three separate calls to println.

Finally, escape sequences are useful for including international characters in a string. For example, suppose you want to print "All the way to San José!", with an accented letter (é). If you use a U.S. keyboard, you may not have a key to generate that letter. Java uses the *Unicode* encoding scheme to denote international characters. For example, the é character has Unicode encoding 00E9. You can include that character inside a string by writing \u, followed by its Unicode encoding:

```
System.out.println("All the way to San Jos\u00E9!");
```

You can look up the codes for the U.S. English and Western European characters in Appendix A, and codes for thousands of characters at www.unicode.org.

Special Topic 4.5

Strings and the char Type

Strings are sequences of Unicode characters (see Random Fact 4.2 on page 154). Character literals look like string literals, except that character literals are delimited by single quotes: 'H' is a character, "H" is a string containing a single character.

Characters have numeric values. For example, if you look at Appendix A, you can see that the character 'H' is actually encoded as the number 72.

You can use escape sequences (see Special Topic 4.4 on page 152) inside character literals. For example, '\n' is the newline character, and '\u00E9' is the character é.

When Java was first designed, each Unicode character was encoded as a two-byte quantity. The char type was intended to hold the code of a Unicode character. However, as of 2003, Unicode had grown so large that some characters needed to be encoded as pairs of char values. Thus, you can no longer think of a char value as a character. Technically speaking, a char value is a *code unit* in the UTF-16 encoding of Unicode. That encoding represents the most common characters as a single char value, and less common or *supplementary* characters as a pair of char values.

The `charAt` method of the `String` class returns a code unit from a string. As with the substring method, the positions in the string are counted starting at 0. For example, the statement

```
String greeting = "Hello";
char ch = greeting.charAt(0);
```

sets ch to the value 'H'.

However, if you use char variables, your programs may fail with some strings that contain international or symbolic characters. For example, the single character ℤ (the mathematical symbol for the set of integers) is encoded by the two code units `'\uD835'` and `'\uDD6B'`.

If you call `charAt(0)` on the string containing the single character ℤ (that is, the string `"\uD835\uDD6B"`), you only get the first half of a supplementary character.

Therefore, you should only use char values if you are absolutely sure that you won't need to encode supplementary characters.

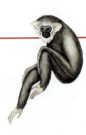

Random Fact 4.2

International Alphabets

The English alphabet is pretty simple: upper- and lowercase a to z. Other European languages have accent marks and special characters. For example, German has three umlaut characters (ä, ö, ü) and a double-s character (ß). These are not optional frills; you couldn't write a page of German text without using these characters. German computer keyboards have keys for these characters.

A German Keyboard

Many countries don't use the Roman script at all. Russian, Greek, Hebrew, Arabic, and Thai letters, to name just a few, have completely different shapes (see The Thai Alphabet). To complicate matters, scripts like Hebrew and Arabic are written from right to left instead of from left to right, and many of these scripts have characters that stack above or below other characters, as those marked with a dotted circle do in Thai. Each of these alphabets has between 30 and 100 letters.

The situation is much more dramatic in languages that use Chinese script: the Chinese dialects, Japanese, and Korean. The Chinese script is not alphabetic but ideographic—a character represents an idea or thing rather than a single sound. Tens of thousands of ideographs are in active use.

The inconsistencies among character encodings have been a major nuisance for international electronic communication and for software manufacturers vying for a global market. Between 1988 and 1991 a consortium of hardware and software manufacturers developed a uniform encoding scheme called Unicode that is expressly designed to encode text in all

จ	ฐ	ธ	ภ	ศ	ะ	◌ิ	เ	◌ุ	O	๘	เ◌
ก	ฑ	ท	น	ม	ษ	◌ั	◌ู	แ	◌ฺ	๑	๙	แ◌
ข	ฒ	ฒ	บ	ย	ส	า	◌.	โ	◌๎	๒	ๆ	โ◌
ฃ	ช	ณ	ป	ร	ห	◌ำ	ใ	◌๎	๓	ฯ	ใ◌
ค	ฌ	ด	ผ	ฤ	ฬ	◌ี	ไ	◌๋	๔	ไ◌
ฅ	ญ	ต	ฝ	ล	อ	◌ึ	ๅ	◌๐	๕
ฆ	ฎ	ถ	พ	ฦ	ฮ	◌ื	◌่	◌	๖
ง	ฏ	ท	ฟ	ว	ฯ	◌ุ	◌้	๗

The Thai Alphabet

written languages of the world (see www.unicode.org). In the first version of Unicode, about 39,000 characters were given codes, including 21,000 Chinese ideographs. A 2-byte code (which can encode over 65,000 characters) was chosen. It was thought to leave ample space for expansion for esoteric scripts, such as Egyptian hieroglyphs and the ancient script used on the island of Java.

Java was one of the first programming languages to embrace Unicode. All Unicode characters can be stored in Java strings, but which ones can actually be displayed depends on your computer system. The primitive type char denotes a 2-byte Unicode character.)

Unfortunately, in 2003, the inevitable happened. Another large batch of Chinese ideographs had to be added to Unicode, pushing it beyond the 16-bit limit. Now, some characters need to be encoded with a pair of char values (see Special Topic 4.5).

Chinese Ideographs

4.6 Reading Input

The Java programs that you have made so far have constructed objects, called methods, printed results, and exited. They were not interactive and took no user input. In this section, you will learn one method for reading user input.

Because output is sent to System.out, you might think that you use System.in for input. Unfortunately, it isn't quite that simple. When Java was first designed, not much attention was given to reading keyboard input. It was assumed that all programmers would produce graphical user interfaces with text fields and menus. System.in was given a minimal set of features—it can only read one byte at a time. Finally, in Java version 5, a Scanner class was added that lets you read keyboard input in a convenient manner.

To construct a Scanner object, simply pass the System.in object to the Scanner constructor:

> Use the Scanner class to read keyboard input in a console window.

```java
Scanner in = new Scanner(System.in);
```

You can create a scanner out of any input stream (such as a file), but you will usually want to use a scanner to read keyboard input from System.in.

Once you have a scanner, you use the nextInt or nextDouble methods to read the next integer or floating-point number.

```java
System.out.print("Enter quantity: ");
int quantity = in.nextInt();

System.out.print("Enter price: ");
double price = in.nextDouble();
```

When the nextInt or nextDouble method is called, the program waits until the user types a number and hits the Enter key. You should always provide instructions for the user (such as "Enter quantity:") before calling a Scanner method. Such an instruction is called a **prompt**.

If the user supplies an input that is not a number, then a run-time exception occurs. You will see in the next chapter how you can check whether the user supplied a numeric input.

The nextLine method returns the next line of input (until the user hits the Enter key) as a String object. The next method returns the next *word*, terminated by any **white space**, that is, a space, the end of a line, or a tab.

```java
System.out.print("Enter city: ");
String city = in.nextLine();

System.out.print("Enter state code: ");
String state = in.next();
```

Here, we use the nextLine method to read a city name that may consist of multiple words, such as San Francisco. We use the next method to read the state code (such as CA), which consists of a single word.

Here is an example of a program that takes user input. This program uses the CashRegister class and simulates a transaction in which a user purchases an item, pays for it, and receives change.

We call this class CashRegisterSimulator, not CashRegisterTester. We reserve the Tester suffix for classes whose sole purpose is to test other classes.

ch04/cashregister/CashRegisterSimulator.java

```java
1  import java.util.Scanner;
2
3  /**
4      This program simulates a transaction in which a user pays for an item
5      and receives change.
6  */
7  public class CashRegisterSimulator
8  {
```

```
 9    public static void main(String[] args)
10    {
11       Scanner in = new Scanner(System.in);
12
13       CashRegister register = new CashRegister();
14
15       System.out.print("Enter price: ");
16       double price = in.nextDouble();
17       register.recordPurchase(price);
18
19       System.out.print("Enter dollars: ");
20       int dollars = in.nextInt();
21       System.out.print("Enter quarters: ");
22       int quarters = in.nextInt();
23       System.out.print("Enter dimes: ");
24       int dimes = in.nextInt();
25       System.out.print("Enter nickels: ");
26       int nickels = in.nextInt();
27       System.out.print("Enter pennies: ");
28       int pennies = in.nextInt();
29       register.enterPayment(dollars, quarters, dimes, nickels, pennies);
30
31       System.out.print("Your change: ");
32       System.out.println(register.giveChange());
33    }
34 }
```

Program Run

```
Enter price: 7.55
Enter dollars: 10
Enter quarters: 2
Enter dimes: 1
Enter nickels: 0
Enter pennies: 0
Your change: 3.05
```

SELF CHECK

16. Why can't input be read directly from System.in?

17. Suppose in is a Scanner object that reads from System.in, and your program calls

   String name = in.next();

What is the value of name if the user enters John Q. Public?

**Worked Example 4.2**

Extracting Initials

This Worked Example shows how to read names and print a set of corresponding initials.

 Available online in WileyPLUS and at www.wiley.com/college/horstmann.

Special Topic 4.6

Formatting Numbers

The default format for printing numbers is not always what you would like. For example, consider the following code segment:

```
double total = 3.50;
final double TAX_RATE = 8.5; // Tax rate in percent
double tax = total * TAX_RATE / 100; // tax is 0.2975
System.out.println("Total: " + total);
System.out.println("Tax:    " + tax);
```

The output is

```
Total: 3.5
Tax:   0.2975
```

You may prefer the numbers to be printed with two digits after the decimal point, like this:

```
Total: 3.50
Tax:   0.30
```

You can achieve this with the printf method of the PrintStream class. (Recall that System.out is an instance of PrintStream.) The first parameter of the printf method is a *format string* that shows how the output should be formatted. The format string contains characters that are simply printed, and *format specifiers:* codes that start with a % character and end with a letter that indicates the format type. There are quite a few formats—Table 4 shows the most important ones. The remaining parameters of printf are the values to be formatted. For example,

```
System.out.printf("Total:%5.2f", total);
```

prints the string Total:, followed by a floating-point number with a *width* of 5 and a *precision* of 2. The width is the total number of characters to be printed: in our case, a space, the digit 3, a period, and two digits. If you increase the width, more spaces are added. The precision is the number of digits after the decimal point.

Table 4 Format Types

Code	Type	Example
d	Decimal integer	123
x	Hexadecimal integer	7B
o	Octal integer	173
f	Fixed floating-point	12.30
e	Exponential floating-point	1.23e+1
g	General floating-point (exponential notation is used for very large or very small values)	12.3
s	String	Tax:
n	Platform-independent line end	

Table 5 Format Flags

Flag	Meaning	Example
-	Left alignment	1.23 followed by spaces
0	Show leading zeroes	001.23
+	Show a plus sign for positive numbers	+1.23
(	Enclose negative numbers in parentheses	(1.23)
,	Show decimal separators	12,300
^	Convert letters to uppercase	1.23E+1

This simple use of `printf` is sufficient for most formatting needs. Once in a while, you may see a more complex example, such as this one:

```
System.out.printf("%-6s%5.2f%n", "Tax:", total);
```

Here, we have three format specifiers. The first one is `%-6s`. The `s` indicates a string. The hyphen is a *flag,* modifying the format. (See Table 5 for the most common format flags. The flags immediately follow the `%` character.) The hyphen indicates left alignment. If the string to be formatted is shorter than the width, it is placed to the left, and spaces are added to the right. (The default is right alignment, with spaces added to the left.) Thus, `%-6s` denotes a left-aligned string of width 6.

You have already seen `%5.2f`: a floating-point number of width 5 and precision 2. The final specifier is `%n`, indicating a platform-independent line end. In Windows, lines need to be terminated by *two* characters: a carriage return `'\r'` and a newline `'\n'`. In other operating systems, a `'\n'` suffices. The `%n` format emits the appropriate line terminators.

Moreover, this call to `printf` has two parameters. You can supply any number of parameter values to the `printf` method. Of course, they must match the format specifiers in the format string.

The `format` method of the `String` class is similar to the `printf` method. However, it returns a string instead of producing output. For example, the call

```
String message = String.format("Total:%5.2f", total);
```

sets the `message` variable to the string `"Total: 3.50"`.

Special Topic 4.7

Using Dialog Boxes for Input and Output

Most program users find the console window rather old-fashioned. The easiest alternative is to create a separate pop-up window for each input (see the figure).

An Input Dialog Box

Call the static showInputDialog method of the JOptionPane class, and supply the string that prompts the input from the user. For example,

```
String input = JOptionPane.showInputDialog("Enter price:");
```

That method returns a String object. Of course, often you need the input as a number. Use the Integer.parseInt and Double.parseDouble methods to convert the string to a number:

```
double price = Double.parseDouble(input);
```

You can also display output in a dialog box:

```
JOptionPane.showMessageDialog(null, "Price: " + price);
```

Finally, whenever you call the showInputDialog or showMessageDialog method in a program that does not show any other frame windows, you need to add a line

```
System.exit(0);
```

to the end of your main method. The showInputDialog method starts a user interface thread to handle user input. When the main method reaches the end, that thread is still running, and your program won't exit automatically. To force the program to exit, you need to call the exit method of the System class. The parameter of the exit method is the status code of the program. A code of 0 denotes successful completion; you can use nonzero status codes to denote various error conditions.

Summary of Learning Objectives

Choose appropriate types for representing numeric data.

- Java has eight primitive types, including four integer types and two floating-point types.
- A numeric computation overflows if the result falls outside the range for the number type.
- Rounding errors occur when an exact conversion between numbers is not possible.

Write code that uses constants to document the purpose of numeric values.

- A final variable is a constant. Once its value has been set, it cannot be changed.
- Use named constants to make your programs easier to read and maintain.

Write arithmetic expressions in Java.

- The ++ and -- operators increment and decrement a variable.
- If both arguments of the / operator are integers, the result is an integer and the remainder is discarded.
- The % operator computes the remainder of a division.
- The Math class contains methods sqrt and pow to compute square roots and powers.
- You use a cast (*typeName*) to convert a value to a different type.
- Use the Math.round method to round a floating-point number to the nearest integer.

Distinguish between static methods and instance methods.

- A static method does not operate on an object.

Process strings in Java programs.

- A string is a sequence of characters. Strings are objects of the String class.
- Strings can be concatenated, that is, put end to end to yield a new longer string. String concatenation is denoted by the + operator.
- Whenever one of the arguments of the + operator is a string, the other argument is converted to a string.
- If a string contains the digits of a number, you use the Integer.parseInt or Double.parseDouble method to obtain the number value.
- Use the substring method to extract a part of a string.
- String positions are counted starting with 0.

Write programs that read user input.

- Use the Scanner class to read keyboard input in a console window.

Classes, Objects, and Methods Introduced in this Chapter

```
java.io.PrintStream          max                      java.util.Scanner
   printf                    min                         next
java.lang.Double             pow                         nextDouble
   parseDouble               round                       nextInt
java.lang.Integer            sin                         nextLine
   MAX_VALUE                 sqrt                     javax.swing.JOptionPane
   MIN_VALUE                 tan                         showInputDialog
   parseInt                  toDegrees                   showMessageDialog
   toString                  toRadians
java.lang.Math            java.lang.String
   E                         format
   PI                        substring
   abs                    java.lang.System
   acos                      in
   asin                   java.math.BigDecimal
   atan                      add
   atan2                     multiply
   ceil                      subtract
   cos                    java.math.BigInteger
   exp                       add
   floor                     multiply
   log                       subtract
   log10
```

Media Resources

www.wiley.com/
college/
horstmann

- ***Worked Example*** Computing the Volume and Surface Area of a Pyramid
- ***Worked Example*** Extracting Initials
- Lab Exercises
- ⊕ Practice Quiz
- ⊕ Code Completion Exercises

Review Exercises

★★ **R4.1** Write the following mathematical expressions in Java.

$$s = s_0 + v_0 t + \frac{1}{2} g t^2$$

$$G = 4\pi^2 \frac{a^3}{P^2 (m_1 + m_2)}$$

$$FV = PV \cdot \left(1 + \frac{INT}{100}\right)^{YRS}$$

$$c = \sqrt{a^2 + b^2 - 2ab \cos \gamma}$$

★★ **R4.2** Write the following Java expressions in mathematical notation.

a. `dm = m * (Math.sqrt(1 + v / c) / (Math.sqrt(1 - v / c) - 1));`

b. `volume = Math.PI * r * r * h;`

c. `volume = 4 * Math.PI * Math.pow(r, 3) / 3;`

d. `p = Math.atan2(z, Math.sqrt(x * x + y * y));`

★★★ **R4.3** What is wrong with this version of the quadratic formula?

```
x1 = (-b - Math.sqrt(b * b - 4 * a * c)) / 2 * a;
x2 = (-b + Math.sqrt(b * b - 4 * a * c)) / 2 * a;
```

★★ **R4.4** Give an example of integer overflow. Would the same example work correctly if you used floating-point?

★★ **R4.5** Give an example of a floating-point roundoff error. Would the same example work correctly if you used integers and switched to a sufficiently small unit, such as cents instead of dollars, so that the values don't have a fractional part?

★★ **R4.6** Consider the following code:

```
CashRegister register = new CashRegister();
register.recordPurchase(19.93);
register.enterPayment(20, 0, 0, 0, 0);
System.out.print("Change: ");
System.out.println(register.giveChange());
```

The code segment prints the total as 0.07000000000000028. Explain why. Give a recommendation to improve the code so that users will not be confused.

★ **R4.7** Let n be an integer and x a floating-point number. Explain the difference between

```
n = (int) x;
```

and

```
n = (int) Math.round(x);
```

★★★ **R4.8** Let n be an integer and x a floating-point number. Explain the difference between

```
n = (int) (x + 0.5);
```

and

```
n = (int) Math.round(x);
```

For what values of x do they give the same result? For what values of x do they give different results?

★ **R4.9** Consider the vending machine implementation in How To 4.1 on page 146. What happens if the givePennyStamps method is invoked before the giveFirstClassStamps method?

★ **R4.10** Explain the differences between 2, 2.0, '2', "2", and "2.0".

★ **R4.11** Explain what each of the following two program segments computes:

```
int x = 2;
int y = x + x;
```

and

```
String s = "2";
String t = s + s;
```

★★ **R4.12** True or false? (x is an int and s is a String)

a. `Integer.parseInt("" + x)` is the same as x

b. `"" + Integer.parseInt(s)` is the same as s

c. `s.substring(0, s.length())` is the same as s

★★ **R4.13** How do you get the first character of a string? The last character? How do you remove the first character? The last character?

★★★ **R4.14** How do you get the last digit of an integer? The first digit? That is, if n is 23456, how do you find out that the first digit is 2 and the last digit is 6? Do not convert the number to a string. *Hint:* %, Math.log.

★★ **R4.15** This chapter contains several recommendations regarding variables and constants that make programs easier to read and maintain. Summarize these recommendations.

★★★ **R4.16** What is a final variable? Can you declare a final variable without supplying its value? (Try it out.)

★ **R4.17** What are the values of the following expressions? In each line, assume that

```
double x = 2.5;
double y = -1.5;
int m = 18;
int n = 4;
```

a. `x + n * y - (x + n) * y`

b. `m / n + m % n`

c. `5 * x - n / 5`

d. `Math.sqrt(Math.sqrt(n))`

e. `(int) Math.round(x)`

f. `(int) Math.round(x) + (int) Math.round(y)`

g. `1 - (1 - (1 - (1 - (1 - n))))`

★ **R4.18** What are the values of the following expressions? In each line, assume that

```
int n = 4;
String s = "Hello";
String t = "World";
```

a. s + t

b. s + n

c. n + t

d. s.substring(1, n)

e. s.length() + t.length()

Programming Exercises

★ **P4.1** Enhance the CashRegister class by adding separate methods enterDollars, enterQuarters, enterDimes, enterNickels, and enterPennies.

Use this tester class:

```
public class CashRegisterTester
{
    public static void main (String[] args)
    {
        CashRegister register = new CashRegister();
        register.recordPurchase(20.37);
        register.enterDollars(20);
        register.enterQuarters(2);
        System.out.println("Change: " + register.giveChange());
        System.out.println("Expected: 0.13");
    }
}
```

★ **P4.2** Enhance the CashRegister class so that it keeps track of the total number of items in a sale. Count all recorded purchases and supply a method

```
int getItemCount()
```

that returns the number of items of the current purchase. Remember to reset the count at the end of the purchase.

★★ **P4.3** Implement a class IceCreamCone with methods getSurfaceArea() and getVolume(). In the constructor, supply the height and radius of the cone. Be careful when looking up the formula for the surface area—you should only include the outside area along the side of the cone since the cone has an opening on the top to hold the ice cream.

★★ — **P4.4** Write a program that prompts the user for two numbers, then prints

- The sum
- The difference
- The product
- The average
- The distance (absolute value of the difference)
- The maximum (the larger of the two)
- The minimum (the smaller of the two)

To do so, implement a class

```
public class Pair
{
    /**
        Constructs a pair.
        @param aFirst the first value of the pair
        @param aSecond the second value of the pair
    */
    public Pair(double aFirst, double aSecond) { . . . }

    /**
        Computes the sum of the values of this pair.
        @return the sum of the first and second values
    */
    public double getSum() { . . . }
    . . .
}
```

Then implement a class `PairTester` that constructs a `Pair` object, invokes its methods, and prints the results.

★ **P4.5** Declare a class `DataSet` that computes the sum and average of a sequence of integers. Supply methods

- `void addValue(int x)`
- `int getSum()`
- `double getAverage()`

Hint: Keep track of the sum and the count of the values.

Then write a test program `DataSetTester` that calls `addValue` four times and prints the expected and actual results.

★★ **P4.6** Write a class `DataSet` that computes the largest and smallest values in a sequence of numbers. Supply methods

- `void addValue(int x)`
- `int getLargest()`
- `int getSmallest()`

Keep track of the smallest and largest values that you've seen so far. Then use the `Math.min` and `Math.max` methods to update them in the `addValue` method. What should you use as initial values? *Hint:* `Integer.MIN_VALUE`, `Integer.MAX_VALUE`.

Write a test program `DataSetTester` that calls `addValue` four times and prints the expected and actual results.

★ **P4.7** Write a program that prompts the user for a measurement in meters and then converts it into miles, feet, and inches. Use a class

```
public class Converter
{
    /**
        Constructs a converter that can convert between two units.
        @param aConversionFactor the factor by which to multiply
            to convert to the target unit
    */
    public Converter(double aConversionFactor) { . . . }
```

```
/**
   Converts from a source measurement to a target measurement.
   @param fromMeasurement  the measurement
   @return  the input value converted to the target unit
*/
public double convertTo(double fromMeasurement) { . . . }

/**
   Converts from a target measurement to a source measurement.
   @param toMeasurement  the target measurement
   @return  the value whose conversion is the target measurement
*/
public double convertFrom(double toMeasurement) { . . . }
}
```

In your `ConverterTester` class, construct and test the following `Converter` object:

```
final double MILE_TO_KM = 1.609;
Converter milesToMeters = new Converter(1000 * MILE_TO_KM);
```

★ **P4.8** Write a class `Square` whose constructor receives the length of the sides. Then supply methods to compute

- The area and perimeter of the square
- The length of the diagonal (use the Pythagorean theorem)

★★ **P4.9** Implement a class `SodaCan` whose constructor receives the height and diameter of the soda can. Supply methods `getVolume` and `getSurfaceArea`. Supply a `SodaCanTester` class that tests your class.

★★★ **P4.10** Implement a class `Balloon` that models a spherical balloon that is being filled with air. The constructor constructs an empty balloon. Supply these methods:

- `void addAir(double amount)` adds the given amount of air
- `double getVolume()` gets the current volume
- `double getSurfaceArea()` gets the current surface area
- `double getRadius()` gets the current radius

Supply a `BalloonTester` class that constructs a balloon, adds 100 cm³ of air, tests the three accessor methods, adds another 100 cm³ of air, and tests the accessor methods again.

★★ **P4.11** *Giving change.* Enhance the `CashRegister` class so that it directs a cashier how to give change. The cash register computes the amount to be returned to the customer, in pennies.

Add the following methods to the `CashRegister` class:

- `int giveDollars()`
- `int giveQuarters()`
- `int giveDimes()`
- `int giveNickels()`
- `int givePennies()`

Each method computes the number of dollar bills or coins to return to the customer, and reduces the change due by the returned amount. You may assume that the methods are called in this order. Here is a test class:

```java
public class CashRegisterTester
{
   public static void main(String[] args)
   {
      CashRegister register = new CashRegister();

      register.recordPurchase(8.37);
      register.enterPayment(10, 0, 0, 0, 0);
      System.out.println("Dollars: " + register.giveDollars());
      System.out.println("Expected: 1");
      System.out.println("Quarters: " + register.giveQuarters());
      System.out.println("Expected: 2");
      System.out.println("Dimes: " + register.giveDimes());
      System.out.println("Expected: 1");
      System.out.println("Nickels: " + register.giveNickels());
      System.out.println("Expected: 0");
      System.out.println("Pennies: " + register.givePennies());
      System.out.println("Expected: 3");
   }
}
```

★★ **P4.12** In How To 4.1 on page 146, we represented the state of the vending machine by storing the balance in pennies. This is ingenious, but it is perhaps not the most obvious solution. Another possibility is to store the number of dollars that the customer inserted and the change that remains after giving out the first class stamps. Reimplement the vending machine in this way. Of course, the public interface should remain unchanged.

★★★ **P4.13** Write a program that reads in an integer and breaks it into a sequence of individual digits in reverse order. For example, the input 16384 is displayed as

```
4
8
3
6
1
```

You may assume that the input has no more than five digits and is not negative.

Declare a class DigitExtractor:

```java
public class DigitExtractor
{
   /**
      Constructs a digit extractor that gets the digits
      of an integer in reverse order.
      @param anInteger the integer to break up into digits
   */
   public DigitExtractor(int anInteger) { . . . }

   /**
      Returns the next digit to be extracted.
      @return the next digit
   */
   public int nextDigit() { . . . }
}
```

In your main class DigitPrinter, call System.out.println(myExtractor.nextDigit()) five times.

★★ **P4.14** Implement a class QuadraticEquation whose constructor receives the coefficients a, b, c of the quadratic equation $ax^2 + bx + c = 0$. Supply methods getSolution1 and getSolution2 that get the solutions, using the quadratic formula. Write a test class QuadraticEquationTester that constructs a QuadraticEquation object, and prints the two solutions.

★★★ **P4.15** Write a program that reads two times in military format (0900, 1730) and prints the number of hours and minutes between the two times. Here is a sample run. User input is in color.

```
Please enter the first time: 0900
Please enter the second time: 1730
8 hours 30 minutes
```

Extra credit if you can deal with the case where the first time is later than the second:

```
Please enter the first time: 1730
Please enter the second time: 0900
15 hours 30 minutes
```

Implement a class TimeInterval whose constructor takes two military times. The class should have two methods getHours and getMinutes.

★ **P4.16** *Writing large letters.* A large letter H can be produced like this:

```
*   *
*   *
*****
*   *
*   *
```

Use the class

```
public class LetterH
{
    public String toString()
    {
        return "*   *\n*   *\n*****\n*   *\n*   *\n";
    }
}
```

Declare similar classes for the letters E, L, and O. Then write the message

```
H
E
L
L
O
```

in large letters.

★★ **P4.17** Write a class ChristmasTree whose toString method yields a string depicting a Christmas tree:

Remember to use escape sequences.

★★   **P4.18** Your job is to transform numbers 1, 2, 3, . . ., 12 into the corresponding month names `January`, `February`, `March`, . . ., `December`. Implement a class `Month` whose constructor parameter is the month number and whose `getName` method returns the month name. *Hint:* Make a very long string `"January February March . . . "`, in which you add spaces such that each month name has the same length. Then use `substring` to extract the month you want.

★★   **P4.19** Write a class to compute the date of Easter Sunday. Easter Sunday is the first Sunday after the first full moon of spring. Use this algorithm, invented by the mathematician Carl Friedrich Gauss in 1800:

1. Let y be the year (such as 1800 or 2001).
2. Divide y by 19 and call the remainder a. Ignore the quotient.
3. Divide y by 100 to get a quotient b and a remainder c.
4. Divide b by 4 to get a quotient d and a remainder e.
5. Divide 8 * b + 13 by 25 to get a quotient g. Ignore the remainder.
6. Divide 19 * a + b - d - g + 15 by 30 to get a remainder h. Ignore the quotient.
7. Divide c by 4 to get a quotient j and a remainder k.
8. Divide a + 11 * h by 319 to get a quotient m. Ignore the remainder.
9. Divide 2 * e + 2 * j - k - h + m + 32 by 7 to get a remainder r. Ignore the quotient.
10. Divide h - m + r + 90 by 25 to get a quotient n. Ignore the remainder.
11. Divide h - m + r + n + 19 by 32 to get a remainder p. Ignore the quotient.

Then Easter falls on day p of month n. For example, if y is 2001:

```
a = 6              g = 6              r = 6
b = 20             h = 18             n = 4
c = 1              j = 0, k = 1       p = 15
d = 5, e = 0       m = 0
```

Therefore, in 2001, Easter Sunday fell on April 15. Write a class `Easter` with methods `getEasterSundayMonth` and `getEasterSundayDay`.

Programming Projects

Project 4.1 In this project, you will perform calculations with triangles. A triangle is defined by the *x*- and *y*-coordinates of its three corner points.

Your job is to compute the following properties of a given triangle:

- the lengths of all sides
- the angles at all corners
- the perimeter
- the area

Of course, you should implement a `Triangle` class with appropriate methods. Supply a program that prompts a user for the corner point coordinates and produces a nicely formatted table of the triangle properties.

This is a good team project for two students. Both students should agree on the `Triangle` interface. One student implements the `Triangle` class, the other simultaneously implements the user interaction and formatting.

Project 4.2 The CashRegister class has an unfortunate limitation: It is closely tied to the coin system in the United States and Canada. Research the system used in most of Europe. Your goal is to produce a cash register that works with euros and cents. Rather than designing another limited CashRegister implementation for the European market, you should design a separate Coin class and a cash register that can work with coins of all types.

Answers to Self-Check Questions

1. int and double.
2. The world's most populous country, China, has about 1.2×10^9 inhabitants. Therefore, individual population counts could be held in an int. However, the world population is over 6×10^9. If you compute totals or averages of multiple countries, you can exceed the largest int value. Therefore, double is a better choice. You could also use long, but there is no benefit because the exact population of a country is not known at any point in time.
3. The first initialization is incorrect. The right hand side is a value of type double, and it is not legal to initialize an int variable with a double value. The second initialization is correct—an int value can always be converted to a double.
4. The first declaration is used inside a method, the second inside a class.
5. (1) You should use a named constant, not the "magic number" 3.14.
   (2) 3.14 is not an accurate representation of π.
6. One less than it was before.
7. 17 and 29.
8. Only s3 is divided by 3. To get the correct result, use parentheses. Moreover, if s1, s2, and s3 are integers, you must divide by 3.0 to avoid integer division:

   (s1 + s2 + s3) / 3.0

9. $\sqrt{x^2 + y^2}$
10. When the fractional part of x is ≥ 0.5.
11. By using a cast: (int) Math.round(x).
12. x is a number, not an object, and you cannot invoke methods on numbers.
13. No—the println method is called on the object System.out.
14. s is set to the string "Agent5".
15. The strings "i" and "ssissi".
16. The class only has a method to read a single byte. It would be very tedious to form characters, strings, and numbers from those bytes.
17. The value is "John". The next method reads the next *word*.

Chapter 5

Decisions

CHAPTER GOALS

- To be able to implement decisions using if statements
- To effectively group statements into blocks
- To learn how to compare integers, floating-point numbers, strings, and objects
- To correctly order decisions in multiple branches and nested branches
- To program conditions using Boolean operators and variables
- T To be able to design tests that cover all parts of a program

The programs we have seen so far were able to do fast computations and render graphs, but they were very inflexible. Except for variations in the input, they worked the same way with every program run. One of the essential features of nontrivial computer programs is their ability to make decisions and to carry out different actions, depending on the nature of the inputs. The goal of this chapter is to learn how to program simple and complex decisions.

CHAPTER CONTENTS

5.1 The if Statement

Computer programs often need to make *decisions*, taking different actions depending on a condition.

Consider the bank account class of Chapter 3. The withdraw method allows you to withdraw as much money from the account as you like. The balance just moves ever further into the negatives. That is not a realistic model for a bank account. Let's implement the withdraw method so that you cannot withdraw more money than you have in the account. That is, the withdraw method must make a *decision:* whether to allow the withdrawal or not.

The if statement lets a program carry out different actions depending on a condition.

The if statement is used to implement a decision. The if statement has two parts: a condition and a body. If the *condition* is true, the *body* of the statement is executed. The body of the if statement consists of a statement:

```
if (amount <= balance)  // Condition
   balance = balance - amount;   // Body
```

The assignment statement is carried out only when the amount to be withdrawn is less than or equal to the balance (see Figure 1).

Let us make the withdraw method of the BankAccount class even more realistic. Most banks not only disallow withdrawals that exceed your account balance; they also charge you a penalty for every attempt to do so.

This operation can't be programmed simply by providing two complementary if statements, such as:

```
if (amount <= balance)
   balance = balance - amount;
if (amount > balance) // Use if/else instead
   balance = balance - OVERDRAFT_PENALTY;
```

172

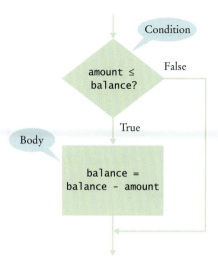

Figure 1
Flowchart for an if Statement

Figure 2
Flowchart for an if/else Statement

There are two problems with this approach. First, if you need to modify the condition amount <= balance for some reason, you must remember to update the condition amount > balance as well. If you do not, the logic of the program will no longer be correct. More importantly, if you modify the value of balance in the body of the first if statement (as in this example), then the second condition uses the new value.

To implement a choice between alternatives, use the if/else statement:

```
if (amount <= balance)
   balance = balance - amount;
else
   balance = balance - OVERDRAFT_PENALTY;
```

Now there is only one condition. If it is satisfied, the first statement is executed. Otherwise, the second is executed. The flowchart in Figure 2 gives a graphical representation of the branching behavior.

Quite often, however, the body of the if statement consists of multiple statements that must be executed in sequence whenever the condition is true. These statements must be grouped together to form a **block** statement by enclosing them in braces { }. Here is an example.

> A block statement groups several statements together.

```
if (amount <= balance)
{
   double newBalance = balance - amount;
   balance = newBalance;
}
```

In general, the body of an if statement must be a block statement, a *simple* statement, such as

```
balance = balance - amount;
```

or a *compound* statement (another if statement or a loop—see Chapter 6). The else alternative also must be a statement—that is, a simple statement, a compound statement, or a block statement.

Syntax 5.1 The if Statement

Syntax
```
if (condition)          if (condition)
    statement               statement₁
                        else
                            statement₂
```

Example

A condition that is true or false.
Often uses relational operators: == != < <= > >= (See page 177.)

Braces are not required if the body contains a single statement.

Don't put a semicolon here! See page 176.

```
if (amount <= balance)
{
    balance = balance - amount;
}
else
{
    System.out.println("Insufficient funds");
    balance = balance - OVERDRAFT_PENALTY;
}
```

If the condition is true, the statement(s) in this branch are executed in sequence; if the condition is false, they are skipped.

Omit the else branch if there is nothing to do.

If condition is false, the statement(s) in this branch are executed in sequence; if the condition is true, they are skipped.

Lining up braces is a good idea. See page 174.

S E L F   C H E C K

1. Why did we use the condition amount <= balance and not amount < balance in the example for the if/else statement?

2. What is logically wrong with the statement

```
if (amount <= balance)
    newBalance = balance - amount; balance = newBalance;
```

and how do you fix it?

Quality Tip 5.1

Brace Layout

The compiler doesn't care where you place braces, but we strongly recommend that you follow a simple rule: *Line up { and }.*

```
if (amount <= balance)
{
    double newBalance = balance - amount;
    balance = newBalance;
}
```

This scheme makes it easy to spot matching braces.

Some programmers put the opening brace on the same line as the if:

```
if (amount <= balance) {
   double newBalance = balance - amount;
   balance = newBalance;
}
```

This saves a line of code, but it makes it harder to match the braces.

It is important that you pick a layout scheme and stick with it. Which scheme you choose may depend on your personal preference or a coding style guide that you must follow.

Productivity Hint 5.1

Indentation and Tabs

When writing Java programs, use indentation to indicate nesting levels:

```
public class BankAccount
{
|  . . .
|  public void withdraw(double amount)
|  {
|  |  if (amount <= balance)
|  |  {
|  |  |  double newBalance = balance - amount;
|  |  |  balance = newBalance;
|  |  }
|  }
|  . . .
}
0  1  2  3
```
Indentation level

How many spaces should you use per indentation level? Some programmers use eight spaces per level, but that isn't a good choice:

```
public class BankAccount
{

        . . .
        public void withdraw(double amount)
        {
                if (amount <= balance)
                {
                        double newBalance =
                                balance - amount;
                        balance = newBalance;
                }
        }
        . . .

}
```

It crowds the code too much to the right side of the screen. As a consequence, long expressions frequently must be broken into separate lines. More common values are two, three, or four spaces per indentation level.

How do you move the cursor from the leftmost column to the appropriate indentation level? A perfectly reasonable strategy is to hit the space bar a sufficient number of times. However, many programmers use the Tab key instead. A tab moves the cursor to the next tab stop. By default, there are tab stops every eight columns, but most editors let you change that value; you should find out how to set your editor's tab stops to, say, every three columns.

Some editors help you out with an *autoindent* feature. They automatically insert as many tabs or spaces as the preceding line because the new line is quite likely to belong to the same logical indentation level. If it isn't, you must add or remove a tab, but that is still faster than tabbing all the way from the left margin.

While the Tab *key* is nice, some editors use *tab characters* for alignment, which is not so nice. Tab characters can lead to problems when you send your file to another person or a printer. There is no universal agreement on the width of a tab character, and some software will ignore tab characters altogether. It is therefore best to save your files with spaces instead of tabs. Most editors have settings to automatically convert all tabs to spaces. Look at your development environment's documentation to find out how to activate this useful setting.

Common Error 5.1

A Semicolon After the `if` Condition

The following code fragment has an unfortunate error:

```
if (input < 0) ; // ERROR
    System.out.println("Bad input");
```

There should be no semicolon after the `if` condition. The compiler interprets this statement as follows: If `input` is less than 0, execute the statement that is denoted by a single semicolon, that is, the do-nothing statement. The statement that follows the semicolon is no longer a part of the `if` statement. It is always executed—the error message appears for all inputs.

Special Topic 5.1

The Conditional Operator

Java has a conditional operator of the form

> *condition* ? *value*$_1$: *value*$_2$

The value of that expression is either *value*$_1$ if the condition is true or *value*$_2$ if it is false. For example, we can compute the absolute value as

```
y = x >= 0 ? x : -x;
```

which is a convenient shorthand for

```
if (x >= 0) y = x; else y = -x;
```

The conditional operator is similar to the `if/else` statement, but it works on a different syntactical level. The conditional operator combines *values* and yields another value. The `if/else` statement combines *statements* and yields another statement.

For example, it would be an error to write

```
y = if (x > 0) x; else -x; // Error
```

The `if/else` construct is a statement, not a value, and you cannot assign it to a variable.

We don't use the conditional operator in this book, but it is a convenient and legitimate construct that you will find in many Java programs.

5.2 Comparing Values

5.2.1 Relational Operators

Relational operators compare values. The == operator tests for equality.

A **relational operator** tests the relationship between two values. An example is the <= operator that we used in the test

```
if (amount <= balance)
```

Java has six relational operators:

Java	Math Notation	Description
>	>	Greater than
>=	≥	Greater than or equal
<	<	Less than
<=	≤	Less than or equal
==	=	Equal
!=	≠	Not equal

As you can see, only two relational operators (> and <) look as you would expect from the mathematical notation. Computer keyboards do not have keys for ≥, ≤, or ≠, but the >=, <=, and != operators are easy to remember because they look similar.

The == operator is initially confusing to most newcomers to Java. In Java, the = symbol already has a meaning, namely assignment. The == operator denotes equality testing:

```
a = 5; // Assign 5 to a
if (a == 5) . . . // Test whether a equals 5
```

You will have to remember to use == for equality testing, and to use = for assignment.

The relational operators have a lower precedence than the arithmetic operators. That means, you can write arithmetic expressions on either side of the relational operator without using parentheses. For example, in the expression

```
amount + fee <= balance
```

both sides (amount + fee and balance) of the < operator are evaluated, and the results are compared. Appendix B shows a table of the Java operators and their precedence.

5.2.2 Comparing Floating-Point Numbers

You have to be careful when comparing floating-point numbers, in order to cope with roundoff errors. For example, the following code multiplies the square root of 2 by itself and then subtracts 2.

```
double r = Math.sqrt(2);
double d = r * r - 2;
if (d == 0)
    System.out.println("sqrt(2) squared minus 2 is 0");
else
    System.out.println(
        "sqrt(2) squared minus 2 is not 0 but " + d);
```

Even though the laws of mathematics tell us that $\left(\sqrt{2}\right)^2 - 2$ equals 0, this program fragment prints

```
sqrt(2) squared minus 2 is not 0 but 4.440892098500626E-16
```

Unfortunately, such roundoff errors are unavoidable. It plainly does not make sense in most circumstances to compare floating-point numbers exactly. Instead, test whether they are *close enough*.

To test whether a number x is close to zero, you can test whether the absolute value $|x|$ (that is, the number with its sign removed) is less than a very small threshold number. That threshold value is often called ε (the Greek letter epsilon). It is common to set ε to 10^{-14} when testing double numbers.

Similarly, you can test whether two numbers are approximately equal by checking whether their difference is close to 0.

$$|x - y| \le \varepsilon$$

In Java, we program the test as follows:

```
final double EPSILON = 1E-14;
if (Math.abs(x - y) <= EPSILON)
    // x is approximately equal to y
```

> When comparing floating-point numbers, don't test for equality. Instead, check whether they are close enough.

Syntax 5.2   Comparisons

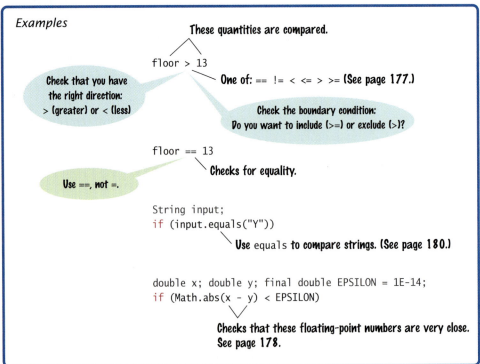

Examples

These quantities are compared.

`floor > 13`

Check that you have the right direction:
> (greater) or < (less)

One of: == != < <= > >= (See page 177.)

Check the boundary condition:
Do you want to include (>=) or exclude (>)?

`floor == 13`

Checks for equality.

Use ==, not =.

```
String input;
if (input.equals("Y"))
```

Use equals to compare strings. (See page 180.)

```
double x; double y; final double EPSILON = 1E-14;
if (Math.abs(x - y) < EPSILON)
```

Checks that these floating-point numbers are very close.
See page 178.

5.2.3 Comparing Strings

To test whether two strings are equal to each other, you must use the method called `equals`:

```
if (string1.equals(string2)) . . .
```

Do not use the `==` operator to compare strings. The expression

```
if (string1 == string2) // Not useful
```

has an unrelated meaning. It tests whether the two string variables refer to the identical string object. You can have strings with identical contents stored in different objects, so this test never makes sense in actual programming; see Common Error 5.2 on page 180.

In Java, letter case matters. For example, `"Harry"` and `"HARRY"` are not the same string. To ignore the letter case, use the `equalsIgnoreCase` method:

```
if (string1.equalsIgnoreCase(string2)) . . .
```

If two strings are not identical to each other, you still may want to know the relationship between them. The `compareTo` method compares strings in dictionary order. If

```
string1.compareTo(string2) < 0
```

then the string `string1` comes before the string `string2` in the dictionary. For example, this is the case if `string1` is `"Harry"`, and `string2` is `"Hello"`. If

```
string1.compareTo(string2) > 0
```

then `string1` comes after `string2` in dictionary order. Finally, if

```
string1.compareTo(string2) == 0
```

then `string1` and `string2` are equal.

Actually, the "dictionary" ordering used by Java is slightly different from that of a normal dictionary. Java is case sensitive and sorts characters by putting numbers first, then uppercase characters, then lowercase characters. For example, `1` comes before `B`, which comes before `a`. The space character comes before all other characters.

Let us investigate the comparison process closely. When Java compares two strings, corresponding letters are compared until one of the strings ends or the first difference is encountered. If one of the strings ends, the longer string is considered the later one. If a character mismatch is found, the characters are compared to determine which string comes later in the dictionary sequence. This process is called lexicographic comparison. For example, let's compare `"car"` with `"cargo"`. The first three letters match, and we reach the end of the first string. Therefore `"car"` comes before `"cargo"` in the lexicographic ordering. Now compare `"cathode"` with `"cargo"`. The first two letters match. In the third character position, `t` comes after `r`, so the string `"cathode"` comes after `"cargo"` in lexicographic ordering. (See Figure 3.)

Figure 3
Lexicographic Comparison

Table 1	Relational Operator Examples	
Expression	Value	Comment
`3 <= 4`	true	3 is less than 4; `<=` tests for "less than or equal".
🚫 `3 =< 4`	**Error**	The "less than or equal" operator is `<=`, not `=<`, with the "less than" symbol first.
`3 > 4`	false	`>` is the opposite of `<=`.
`4 < 4`	false	The left-hand side must be strictly smaller than the right-hand side.
`4 <= 4`	true	Both sides are equal; `<=` tests for "less than or equal".
`3 == 5 - 2`	true	`==` tests for equality.
`3 != 5 - 1`	true	`!=` tests for inequality. It is true that 3 is not 5 − 1.
🚫 `3 = 6 / 2`	**Error**	Use `==` to test for equality.
`1.0 / 3.0 == 0.333333333`	false	Although the values are very close to one another, they are not exactly equal. See Common Error 4.3.
🚫 `"10" > 5`	**Error**	You cannot compare a string to a number.
`"Tomato".substring(0, 3).equals("Tom")`	true	Always use the `equals` method to check whether two strings have the same contents.
`"Tomato".substring(0, 3) == ("Tom")`	false	Never use `==` to compare strings; it only checks whether the strings are stored in the same location. See Common Error 5.2 on page 180.
`"Tom".equalsIgnoreCase("TOM")`	true	Use the `equalsIgnoreCase` method if you don't want to distinguish between uppercase and lowercase letters.

Common Error 5.2

Using == to Compare Strings

It is an extremely common error in Java to write `==` when `equals` is intended. This is particularly true for strings. If you write

```
if (nickname == "Rob")
```

then the test succeeds only if the variable `nickname` refers to the exact same string object as the string constant `"Rob"`. For efficiency, Java makes only one string object for every string constant. Therefore, the following test will pass:

```
String nickname = "Rob";
. . .
if (nickname == "Rob") // Test is true
```

However, if the string with the letters R o b has been assembled in some other way, then the test will fail:

```
String name = "Robert";
String nickname = name.substring(0, 3);
. . .
if (nickname == "Rob") // Test is false
```

This is a particularly distressing situation: The wrong code will sometimes do the right thing, sometimes the wrong thing. Because string objects are always constructed by the compiler, you never have an interest in whether two string objects are shared. You must remember never to use == to compare strings. Always use equals or compareTo to compare strings.

5.2.4 Comparing Objects

If you compare two object references with the == operator, you test whether the references refer to the same object. Here is an example:

```
Rectangle box1 = new Rectangle(5, 10, 20, 30);
Rectangle box2 = box1;
Rectangle box3 = new Rectangle(5, 10, 20, 30);
```

The comparison

```
box1 == box2
```

is true. Both object variables refer to the same object. But the comparison

```
box1 == box3
```

is false. The two object variables refer to different objects (see Figure 4). It does not matter that the objects have identical contents.

You can use the equals method to test whether two rectangles have the same contents, that is, whether they have the same upper-left corner and the same width and height. For example, the test

> The == operator tests whether two object references are identical. To compare the contents of objects, you need to use the equals method.

```
box1.equals(box3)
```

is true.

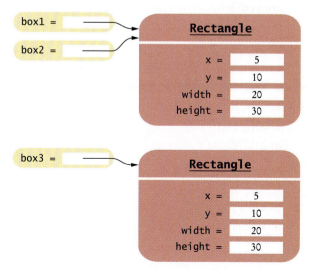

Figure 4
Comparing Object References

However, you must be careful when using the equals method. It works correctly only if the implementors of the class have supplied it. The Rectangle class has an equals method that is suitable for comparing rectangles.

For your own classes, you need to supply an appropriate equals method. You will learn how to do that in Chapter 10. Until that point, you should not use the equals method to compare objects of your own classes.

5.2.5 Testing for null

The null reference refers to no object.

An object reference can have the special value null if it refers to no object at all. It is common to use the null value to indicate that a value has never been set. For example,

```
String middleInitial = null; // Not set
if ( . . . )
    middleInitial = middleName.substring(0, 1);
```

You use the == operator (and not equals) to test whether an object reference is a null reference:

```
if (middleInitial == null)
    System.out.println(firstName + " " + lastName);
else
    System.out.println(firstName + " " + middleInitial + ". " + lastName);
```

Note that the null reference is not the same as the empty string "". The empty string is a valid string of length 0, whereas a null indicates that a string variable refers to no string at all.

SELF CHECK

3. What is the value of s.length() if s is
   a. the empty string ""?
   b. the string " " containing a space?
   c. null?

4. Which of the following comparisons are syntactically incorrect? Which of them are syntactically correct, but logically questionable?
   ```
   String a = "1";
   String b = "one";
   double x = 1;
   double y = 3 * (1.0 / 3);
   ```
   a. a == "1"
   b. a == null
   c. a.equals("")
   d. a == b
   e. a == x
   f. x == y
   g. x - y == null
   h. x.equals(y)

Quality Tip 5.2

Avoid Conditions with Side Effects

In Java, it is legal to nest assignments inside test conditions:

```
if ((d = b * b - 4 * a * c) >= 0) r = Math.sqrt(d);
```

It is legal to use the decrement operator inside other expressions:

```
if (n-- > 0) . . .
```

These are bad programming practices, because they mix a test with another activity. The other activity (setting the variable d, decrementing n) is called a **side effect** of the test.

As you will see in Special Topic 6.3, conditions with side effects can occasionally be helpful to simplify loops; for if statements they should always be avoided.

How To 5.1

Implementing an `if` Statement

This How To walks you through the process of implementing an if statement. We will illustrate the steps with the following example problem:

The university bookstore has a Kilobyte Day sale every October 24, giving an 8 percent discount on all computer accessory purchases if the price is less than $128, and a 16 percent discount if the price is at least $128. Write a program that asks the cashier for the original price and then prints the discounted price.

Step 1   In our sample problem, the obvious choice for the condition is:

original price < 128?

That is just fine, and we will use that condition in our solution.

But you could equally well come up with a correct solution if you choose the opposite condition: Is the original price at least $128? You might choose this condition if you put yourself into the position of a shopper who wants to know when the bigger discount applies.

Step 2   Give pseudocode for the work that needs to be done when the condition is fulfilled.

In this step, you list the action or actions that are taken in the "positive" branch. The details depend on your problem. You may want to print a message, compute values, or even exit the program.

In our example, we need to apply an 8 percent discount:

discounted price = 0.92 x original price

Step 3   Give pseudocode for the work (if any) that needs to be done when the condition is *not* fulfilled.

What do you want to do in the case that the condition of Step 1 is not fulfilled? Sometimes, you want to do nothing at all. In that case, use an if statement without an else branch.

In our example, the condition tested whether the price was less than $128. If that condition is *not* fulfilled, the price is at least $128, so the higher discount of 16 percent applies to the sale:

discounted price = 0.84 x original price

Step 4   Double-check relational operators.

First, be sure that the test goes in the right *direction*. It is a common error to confuse > and <. Next, consider whether you should use the < operator or its close cousin, the <= operator.

What should happen if the original price is exactly $128? Reading the problem carefully, we find that the lower discount applies if the original price is *less than* $128, and the higher discount applies when it is *at least* $128. A price of $128 should therefore *not* fulfill our condition, and we must use <, not <=.

Step 5 Remove duplication.

Check which actions are common to both branches, and move them outside. (See Quality Tip 4.3.)

In our example, we have two statements of the form

discounted price = ___ x original price

They only differ in the discount rate. It is best to just set the rate in the branches, and to do the computation afterwards:

If original price < 128
    discount rate = 0.92
Else
    discount rate = 0.84
discounted price = discount rate x original price

Step 6 Test both branches.

Formulate two test cases, one that fulfills the condition of the if statement, and one that does not. Ask yourself what should happen in each case. Then follow the pseudocode and act each of them out.

In our example, let us consider two scenarios for the original price: $100 and $200. We expect that the first price is discounted by $8, the second by $32.

When the original price is 100, then the condition 100 < 128 is true, and we get

discount rate = 0.92
discounted price = 0.92 x 100 = 92

When the original price is 200, then the condition 200 < 128 is false, and

discount rate = 0.84
discounted price = 0.84 x 200 = 168

In both cases, we get the expected answer.

Step 7 Assemble the if statement in Java.

Type the skeleton

```
if ()
{
}
else
{
}
```

and fill it in, as shown in Syntax 5.1 on page 174. Omit the else branch if it is not needed.

In our example, the completed statement is

```
double HIGH_DISCOUNT_THRESHOLD = 128;
double HIGH_DISCOUNT = 0.92;
double LOW_DISCOUNT = 0.84;

if (originalPrice < HIGH_DISCOUNT_THRESHOLD)
{
    discountRate = HIGH_DISCOUNT;
}
else
{
```

```
        discountRate = LOW_DISCOUNT;
    }
    discountedPrice = discountRate * originalPrice;
```

Here we used named constants to make the program more maintainable (see Quality Tip 4.1).

⊕ *Worked Example 5.1*

Extracting the Middle

This Worked Example shows how to extract the middle character from a string, or the two middle characters if the length of the string is even.

5.3 Multiple Alternatives

5.3.1 Sequences of Comparisons

Many computations require more than a single if/else decision. Sometimes, you need to make a series of related comparisons.

> Multiple conditions can be combined to evaluate complex decisions. The correct arrangement depends on the logic of the problem to be solved.

The following program asks for a value describing the magnitude of an earthquake on the Richter scale and prints a description of the likely impact of the quake. The Richter scale is a measurement for the strength of an earthquake. Every step in the scale, for example from 6.0 to 7.0, signifies a tenfold increase in the strength of the quake. The 1989 Loma Prieta earthquake that damaged the Bay Bridge in San Francisco and destroyed many buildings in several Bay area cities registered 7.1 on the Richter scale.

ch05/quake/Earthquake.java

```
 1  /**
 2      A class that describes the effects of an earthquake.
 3  */
 4  public class Earthquake
 5  {
 6      private double richter;
 7
 8      /**
 9          Constructs an Earthquake object.
10          @param magnitude the magnitude on the Richter scale
11      */
12      public Earthquake(double magnitude)
13      {
14          richter = magnitude;
15      }
16
17      /**
18          Gets a description of the effect of the earthquake.
19          @return the description of the effect
20      */
21      public String getDescription()
22      {
```

⊕ Available online in WileyPLUS and at www.wiley.com/college/horstmann.

```
23      String r;
24      if (richter >= 8.0)
25          r = "Most structures fall";
26      else if (richter >= 7.0)
27          r = "Many buildings destroyed";
28      else if (richter >= 6.0)
29          r = "Many buildings considerably damaged, some collapse";
30      else if (richter >= 4.5)
31          r = "Damage to poorly constructed buildings";
32      else if (richter >= 3.5)
33          r = "Felt by many people, no destruction";
34      else if (richter >= 0)
35          r = "Generally not felt by people";
36      else
37          r = "Negative numbers are not valid";
38      return r;
39   }
40 }
```

ch05/quake/EarthquakeRunner.java

```
 1  import java.util.Scanner;
 2
 3  /**
 4     This program prints a description of an earthquake of a given magnitude.
 5  */
 6  public class EarthquakeRunner
 7  {
 8      public static void main(String[] args)
 9      {
10          Scanner in = new Scanner(System.in);
11
12          System.out.print("Enter a magnitude on the Richter scale: ");
13          double magnitude = in.nextDouble();
14          Earthquake quake = new Earthquake(magnitude);
15          System.out.println(quake.getDescription());
16      }
17  }
```

Program Run

```
Enter a magnitude on the Richter scale: 7.1
Many buildings destroyed
```

Here we must sort the conditions and test against the largest cutoff first. Suppose we reverse the order of tests:

```
if (richter >= 0) // Tests in wrong order
    r = "Generally not felt by people";
else if (richter >= 3.5)
    r = "Felt by many people, no destruction";
else if (richter >= 4.5)
    r = "Damage to poorly constructed buildings";
else if (richter >= 6.0)
    r = "Many buildings considerably damaged, some collapse";
else if (richter >= 7.0)
    r = "Many buildings destroyed";
else if (richter >= 8.0)
    r = "Most structures fall";
```

This does not work. All nonnegative values of richter fall into the first case, and the other tests will never be attempted.

In this example, it is also important that we use an if/else if/else test, not just multiple independent if statements. Consider this sequence of independent tests:

```
if (richter >= 8.0) // Didn't use else
   r = "Most structures fall";
if (richter >= 7.0)
   r = "Many buildings destroyed";
if (richter >= 6.0)
   r = "Many buildings considerably damaged, some collapse";
if (richter >= 4.5)
   r = "Damage to poorly constructed buildings";
if (richter >= 3.5)
   r = "Felt by many people, no destruction";
if (richter >= 0)
   r = "Generally not felt by people";
```

Now the alternatives are no longer exclusive. If richter is 6.0, then the last four tests all match, and r is set four times.

Special Topic 5.2

The switch Statement

A sequence of if/else if/else that compares a single value against several constant alternatives can be implemented as a switch statement. For example,

```
int digit;
. . .
switch (digit)
{
   case 1: System.out.print("one"); break;
   case 2: System.out.print("two"); break;
   case 3: System.out.print("three"); break;
   case 4: System.out.print("four"); break;
   case 5: System.out.print("five"); break;
   case 6: System.out.print("six"); break;
   case 7: System.out.print("seven"); break;
   case 8: System.out.print("eight"); break;
   case 9: System.out.print("nine"); break;
   default: System.out.print("error"); break;
}
```

This is a shortcut for

```
int digit;
. . .
if (digit == 1) System.out.print("one");
else if (digit == 2) System.out.print("two");
else if (digit == 3) System.out.print("three");
else if (digit == 4) System.out.print("four");
else if (digit == 5) System.out.print("five");
else if (digit == 6) System.out.print("six");
else if (digit == 7) System.out.print("seven");
else if (digit == 8) System.out.print("eight");
else if (digit == 9) System.out.print("nine");
else System.out.print("error");
```

Using the switch statement has one advantage. It is obvious that all branches test the same value, namely digit.

The switch statement can be applied only in narrow circumstances. The values in the case clauses must be constants. They must be integers, characters, or enumeration constants—or, as of Java 7, strings. You cannot use a switch to branch on floating-point values.

Note how every branch of the switch was terminated by a break instruction. If the break is missing, execution falls through to the next branch, and so on, until finally a break or the end of the switch is reached. For example, consider the following switch statement:

```
switch (digit)
{
   case 1: System.out.print("one"); // Oops—no break
   case 2: System.out.print("two"); break;
   . . .
}
```

If digit has the value 1, then the statement after the case 1: label is executed. Because there is no break, the statement after the case 2: label is executed as well. The program prints "onetwo".

There are a few cases in which this fall-through behavior is actually useful, but they are very rare. Peter van der Linden (*Expert C Programming*, Prentice-Hall 1994, p. 38) describes an analysis of the switch statements in the Sun C compiler front end. Of the 244 switch statements, each of which had an average of 7 cases, only 3 percent used the fall-through behavior. That is, the default—falling through to the next case unless stopped by a break—was wrong 97 percent of the time. Forgetting to type the break is an exceedingly common error, yielding incorrect code.

We leave it to you to decide whether or not to use the switch statement. At any rate, you need to have a reading knowledge of switch in case you find it in the code of other programmers.

5.3.2 Nested Branches

Some computations have multiple *levels* of decision making. You first make one decision, and each of the outcomes leads to another decision. Here is a typical example.

In the United States, taxpayers pay federal income tax at different rates depending on their incomes and marital status. There are two main tax schedules: one for single taxpayers and one for married taxpayers "filing jointly", meaning that the married taxpayers add their incomes together and pay taxes on the total. Table 2 gives the tax rate computations for each of the filing categories, using a simplified version of the values for the 2008 federal tax return.

Table 2 Federal Tax Rate Schedule (2008, simplified)			
If your filing status is Single:		If your filing status is Married:	
Tax Bracket	Percentage	Tax Bracket	Percentage
$0 . . . $32,000	10%	$0 . . . $64,000	10%
Amount over $32,000	25%	Amount over $64,000	25%

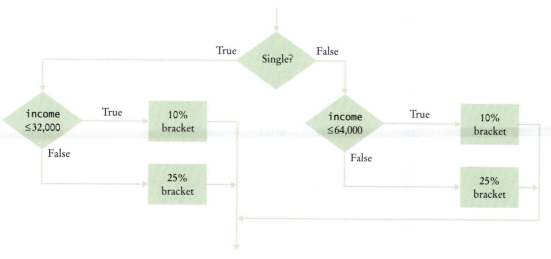

Figure 5 Income Tax Computation Using Simplified 2008 Schedule

Now let us compute the taxes due, given a filing status and an income figure. First, we must branch on the filing status. Then, for each filing status, we must have another branch on income level.

The two-level decision process is reflected in two levels of if statements. We say that the income test is *nested* inside the test for filing status. (See Figure 5 for a flowchart.)

ch05/tax/TaxReturn.java

```java
1   /**
2       A tax return of a taxpayer in 2008.
3   */
4   public class TaxReturn
5   {
6      public static final int SINGLE = 1;
7      public static final int MARRIED = 2;
8
9      private static final double RATE1 = 0.10;
10     private static final double RATE2 = 0.25;
11     private static final double RATE1_SINGLE_LIMIT = 32000;
12     private static final double RATE1_MARRIED_LIMIT = 64000;
13
14     private double income;
15     private int status;
16
17     /**
18         Constructs a TaxReturn object for a given income and
19         marital status.
20         @param anIncome the taxpayer income
21         @param aStatus either SINGLE or MARRIED
22     */
23     public TaxReturn(double anIncome, int aStatus)
24     {
25        income = anIncome;
26        status = aStatus;
27     }
28
```

```
29    public double getTax()
30    {
31       double tax1 = 0;
32       double tax2 = 0;
33
34       if (status == SINGLE)
35       {
36          if (income <= RATE1_SINGLE_LIMIT)
37          {
38             tax1 = RATE1 * income;
39          }
40          else
41          {
42             tax1 = RATE1 * RATE1_SINGLE_LIMIT;
43             tax2 = RATE2 * (income - RATE1_SINGLE_LIMIT);
44          }
45       }
46       else
47       {
48          if (income <= RATE1_MARRIED_LIMIT)
49          {
50             tax1 = RATE1 * income;
51          }
52          else
53          {
54             tax1 = RATE1 * RATE1_MARRIED_LIMIT;
55             tax2 = RATE2 * (income - RATE1_MARRIED_LIMIT);
56          }
57       }
58
59       return tax1 + tax2;
60    }
61 }
```

ch05/tax/TaxCalculator.java

```
1  import java.util.Scanner;
2
3  /**
4     This program calculates a simple tax return.
5  */
6  public class TaxCalculator
7  {
8     public static void main(String[] args)
9     {
10        Scanner in = new Scanner(System.in);
11
12        System.out.print("Please enter your income: ");
13        double income = in.nextDouble();
14
15        System.out.print("Are you married? (Y/N) ");
16        String input = in.next();
17        int status;
18        if (input.equalsIgnoreCase("Y"))
19           status = TaxReturn.MARRIED;
20        else
21           status = TaxReturn.SINGLE;
22        TaxReturn aTaxReturn = new TaxReturn(income, status);
23
```

```
24        System.out.println("Tax: "
25            + aTaxReturn.getTax());
26    }
27 }
```

Program Run

```
Please enter your income: 80000
Are you married? (Y/N) Y
Tax: 10400.0
```

SELF CHECK

5. The if/else/else statement for the earthquake strength first tested for higher values, then descended to lower values. Can you reverse that order?

6. Some people object to higher tax rates for higher incomes, claiming that you might end up with *less* money after taxes when you get a raise for working hard. What is the flaw in this argument?

Common Error 5.3

The Dangling else Problem

When an if statement is nested inside another if statement, the following error may occur.

```
if (richter >= 0)
    if (richter <= 4)
        System.out.println("The earthquake is harmless");
else // Pitfall!
    System.out.println("Negative value not allowed");
```

The indentation level seems to suggest that the else is grouped with the test richter >= 0. Unfortunately, that is not the case. The compiler ignores all indentation and follows the rule that an else always belongs to the closest if, like this:

```
if (richter >= 0)
    if (richter <= 4)
        System.out.println("The earthquake is harmless");
    else // Pitfall!
        System.out.println("Negative value not allowed");
```

That isn't what we want. We want to group the else with the first if. For that, we must use braces.

```
if (richter >= 0)
{
    if (richter <= 4)
        System.out.println("The earthquake is harmless");
}
else
    System.out.println("Negative value not allowed");
```

To avoid having to think about the pairing of the else, we recommend that you *always* use a set of braces when the body of an if contains another if. In the following example, the braces are not strictly necessary, but they help clarify the code:

```
if (richter >= 0)
{
    if (richter <= 4)
        System.out.println("The earthquake is harmless");
```

```
      else
         System.out.println("Damage may occur");
   }
```

The ambiguous else is called a *dangling* else, and it is enough of a syntactical blemish that some programming language designers developed an improved syntax that avoids it altogether. For example, Algol 68 uses the construction

   if *condition* then *statement* else *statement* fi;

The else part is optional, but since the end of the if statement is clearly marked, the grouping is unambiguous if there are two ifs and only one else. Here are the two possible cases:

   if c_1 then if c_2 then s_1 else s_2 fi fi;
   if c_1 then if c_2 then s_1 fi else s_2 fi;

By the way, fi is just if backwards. Other languages use endif, which has the same purpose but is less fun.

Productivity Hint 5.2

Hand-Tracing

A very useful technique for understanding whether a program works correctly is called *hand-tracing*. You simulate the program's activity on a sheet of paper. You can use this method with pseudocode or Java code.

Get an index card, a cocktail napkin, or whatever sheet of paper is within reach. Make a column for each variable. Have the program code ready. Use a marker, such as a paper clip, to mark the current statement. In your mind, execute statements one at a time. Every time the value of a variable changes, cross out the old value and write the new value below the old one.

For example, let's trace the getTax method with the data from the program run on page 191.

When the TaxReturn object is constructed, the income instance variable is set to 80,000 and status is set to MARRIED. Then the getTax method is called. In lines 31 and 32 of TaxReturn.java, tax1 and tax2 are initialized to 0.

```
29 public double getTax()
30 {
31    double tax1 = 0;
32    double tax2 = 0;
33
```

income	status	tax1	tax2
80000	MARRIED	0	0

Because status is not SINGLE, we move to the else branch of the outer if statement (line 46).

```
34    if (status == SINGLE)
35    {
36       if (income <= RATE1_SINGLE_LIMIT)
37       {
38          tax1 = RATE1 * income;
39       }
40       else
41       {
42          tax1 = RATE1 * RATE1_SINGLE_LIMIT;
43          tax2 = RATE2 * (income - RATE1_SINGLE_LIMIT);
44       }
45    }
46    else
47    {
```

Since income is not <= 64000, we move to the else branch of the inner if statement (line 52).

```
48       if (income <= RATE1_MARRIED_LIMIT)
49       {
50          tax1 = RATE1 * income;
51       }
```

```
52    else
53    {
54        tax1 = RATE1 * RATE1_MARRIED_LIMIT;
55        tax2 = RATE2 * (income - RATE1_MARRIED_LIMIT);
56    }
```

The values of tax1 and tax2 are updated.

```
53    {
54        tax1 = RATE1 * RATE1_MARRIED_LIMIT;
55        tax2 = RATE2 * (income - RATE1_MARRIED_LIMIT);
56    }
57    }
```

income	status	tax1	tax2
80000	MARRIED	0̸	0̸
		6400	4000

Their sum is returned and the method ends.

```
58
59    return tax1 + tax2;
60 }
```

Because the program trace shows the expected return value ($10,400), it successfully demonstrates that this test case works correctly.

income	status	tax1	tax2	return value
80000	MARRIED	0̸	0̸	
		6400	4000	10400

Productivity Hint 5.3

Make a Schedule and Make Time for Unexpected Problems

Commercial software is notorious for being delivered later than promised. For example, Microsoft originally promised that its Windows Vista operating system would be available late in 2003, then in 2005, then in March 2006; it was finally released in January 2007. Some of the early promises might not have been realistic. It is in Microsoft's interest to let prospective customers expect the imminent availability of the product, so that they do not switch to a different product in the meantime. Undeniably, though, Microsoft had not anticipated the full complexity of the tasks it had set itself to solve.

Microsoft can delay the delivery of its product, but it is likely that you cannot. As a student or a programmer, you are expected to manage your time wisely and to finish your assignments on time. You can probably do simple programming exercises the night before the due date, but an assignment that looks twice as hard may well take four times as long, because more things can go wrong. You should therefore make a schedule whenever you start a programming project.

First, estimate realistically how much time it will take you to

• Design the program logic.

• Develop test cases.

• Type the program in and fix compile-time errors.

• Test and debug the program.

For example, for the income tax program I might estimate 30 minutes for the design, because it is mostly done; 30 minutes for developing test cases; one hour for data entry and fixing compile-time errors; and 2 hours for testing and debugging. That is a total of 4 hours. If I work 2 hours a day on this project, it will take me two days.

Then think of things that can go wrong. Your computer might break down. The lab might be crowded. You might be stumped by a problem with the computer system. (That is a particularly important concern for beginners. It is *very* common to lose a day over a trivial problem just because it takes time to track down a person who knows the "magic" command to overcome it.) As a rule of thumb, *double* the time of your estimate. That is, you should start four days, not two days, before the due date. If nothing goes wrong, great; you have the program done two days early. When the inevitable problem occurs, you have a cushion of time that protects you from embarrassment and failure.

Special Topic 5.3

Enumeration Types

In many programs, you use variables that can hold one of a finite number of values. For example, in the tax return class, the status instance variable holds one of the values SINGLE or MARRIED. We arbitrarily declared SINGLE as the number 1 and MARRIED as 2. If, due to some programming error, the status variable is set to another integer value (such as –1, 0, or 3), then the programming logic may produce invalid results.

In a simple program, this is not really a problem. But as programs grow over time, and more cases are added (such as the "married filing separately" and "head of household" categories), errors can slip in. Java version 5.0 introduces a remedy: **enumeration types**. An enumeration type has a finite set of values, for example

```
public enum FilingStatus { SINGLE, MARRIED }
```

You can have any number of values, but you must include them all in the enum declaration.

You can declare variables of the enumeration type:

```
FilingStatus status = FilingStatus.SINGLE;
```

If you try to assign a value that isn't a FilingStatus, such as 2 or "S", then the compiler reports an error.

Use the == operator to compare enumeration values, for example:

```
if (status == FilingStatus.SINGLE) . . .
```

It is common to nest an enum declaration inside a class, such as

```
public class TaxReturn
{
    public TaxReturn(double anIncome, FilingStatus aStatus) { . . . }
    . . .
    public enum FilingStatus { SINGLE, MARRIED }
    private FilingStatus status;
}
```

To access the enumeration outside the class in which it is declared, use the class name as a prefix:

```
TaxReturn return = new TaxReturn(income, TaxReturn.FilingStatus.SINGLE);
```

Syntax 5.3   Declaring an Enumeration Type

Syntax   *accessSpecifier* enum *TypeName* { *value₁*, *value₂*, . . . }

Example

Type declaration

```
public enum FilingStatus { SINGLE, MARRIED }
```

Variable declaration

```
FilingStatus status;
```

> This variable can have values FilingStatus.SINGLE, FilingStatus.MARRIED, or null.

An enumeration type variable can be null. For example, the status variable in the previous example can actually have three values: SINGLE, MARRIED, and null. This can be useful, for example to identify an uninitialized variable, or a potential pitfall.

5.4 Using Boolean Expressions

5.4.1 The boolean Type

In Java, an expression such as amount < 1000 has a value, just as the expression amount + 1000 has a value. The value of a relational expression is either true or false. For example, if amount is 500, then the value of amount < 1000 is true. Try it out: The program fragment

```
double amount = 0;
System.out.println(amount < 1000);
```

> The boolean type has two values: true and false.

prints true. The values true and false are not numbers, nor are they objects of a class. They belong to a separate type, called boolean. The **Boolean type** is named after the mathematician George Boole (1815–1864), a pioneer in the study of logic.

5.4.2 Predicate Methods

A **predicate method** is a method that returns a boolean value. Here is an example of a predicate method:

> A predicate method returns a boolean value.

```
public class BankAccount
{
    public boolean isOverdrawn()
    {
        return balance < 0; // Returns true or false
    }
}
```

You can use the return value of the method as the condition of an `if` statement:

```
if (harrysChecking.isOverdrawn()) . . .
```

There are several useful static predicate methods in the `Character` class:

```
isDigit
isLetter
isUpperCase
isLowerCase
```

that let you test whether a character is a digit, a letter, an uppercase letter, or a lowercase letter:

```
if (Character.isUpperCase(ch)) . . .
```

It is a common convention to give the prefix "`is`" or "`has`" to the name of a predicate method.

The `Scanner` class has useful predicate methods for testing whether the next input will succeed. The `hasNextInt` method returns `true` if the next character sequence denotes an integer. It is a good idea to call that method before calling `nextInt`:

```
if (in.hasNextInt()) input = in.nextInt();
```

Similarly, the `hasNextDouble` method tests whether a call to `nextDouble` will succeed.

5.4.3 The Boolean Operators

Suppose you want to find whether `amount` is between 0 and 1000. Then two conditions have to be true: `amount` must be greater than 0, *and* it must be less than 1000. In Java you use the `&&` operator to represent the *and* when combining test conditions. That is, you can write the test as follows:

```
if (0 < amount && amount < 1000) . . .
```

The `&&` (*and*) operator combines several tests into a new test that passes only when all conditions are true. An operator that combines Boolean values is called a **Boolean operator.**

The `&&` operator has a lower precedence than the relational operators. For that reason, you can write relational expressions on either side of the `&&` operator without using parentheses. For example, in the expression

```
0 < amount && amount < 1000
```

the expressions `0 < amount` and `amount < 1000` are evaluated first. Then the `&&` operator combines the results. Appendix B shows a table of the Java operators and their precedence.

The `||` (*or*) logical operator also combines two or more conditions. The resulting test succeeds if at least one of the conditions is true. For example, here is a test to check whether the string `input` is an `"S"` or `"M"`:

```
if (input.equals("S") || input.equals("M")) . . .
```

Figure 6 shows flowcharts for these examples.

Sometimes you need to *invert* a condition with the `!` (*not*) logical operator. For example, we may want to carry out a certain action only if two strings are *not* equal:

```
if (!input.equals("S")) . . .
```

> You can form complex tests with the Boolean operators && (*and*), || (*or*), and ! (*not*).

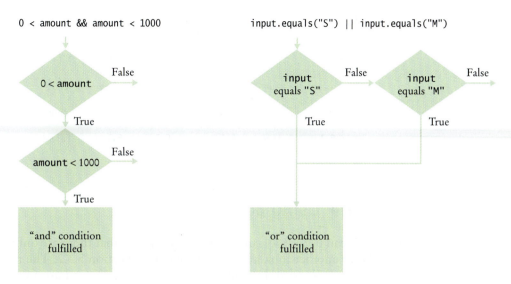

Figure 6 Flowcharts for && and || Combinations

The ! operator takes a single condition and evaluates to true if that condition is false and to false if the condition is true.

Table 3	Boolean Operators	
Expression	**Value**	**Comment**
0 < 200 && 200 < 100	false	Only the first condition is true.
0 < 200 || 200 < 100	true	The first condition is true.
0 < 200 || 100 < 200	true	The || is not a test for "either-or". If both conditions are true, the result is true.
🚫 0 < 100 < 200	Syntax error	**Error:** The expression 0 < 100 is true, which cannot be compared against 200.
🚫 0 < x || x < 100	true	**Error:** This condition is always true. The programmer probably intended 0 < x && x < 100. (See Common Error 5.5).
0 < x && x < 100 || x == -1	(0 < x && x < 100) || x == -1	The && operator binds more strongly than the || operator. (See Appendix B.)
!(0 < 200)	false	0 < 200 is true, therefore its negation is false.
frozen == true	frozen	There is no need to compare a Boolean variable with true.
frozen == false	!frozen	It is clearer to use ! than to compare with false.

Here is a summary of the three logical operations:

A	B	A && B
true	true	true
true	false	false
false	*Any*	false

A	B	A || B
true	*Any*	true
false	true	true
false	false	false

A	!A
true	false
false	true

5.4.4 Using Boolean Variables

You can use a Boolean variable if you know that there are only two possible values. Have another look at the tax program in Section 5.3.2. The marital status is either single or married. Instead of using an integer, you can use a variable of type boolean:

```
private boolean married;
```

> You can store the outcome of a condition in a Boolean variable.

The advantage is that you can't accidentally store a third value in the variable.

Then you can use the Boolean variable in a test:

```
if (married)
    . . .
else
    . . .
```

Sometimes Boolean variables are called *flags* because they can have only two states: "up" and "down".

It pays to think carefully about the naming of Boolean variables. In our example, it would not be a good idea to give the name maritalStatus to the Boolean variable. What does it mean that the marital status is true? With a name like married there is no ambiguity; if married is true, the taxpayer is married.

By the way, it is considered gauche to write a test such as

```
if (married == true) . . . // Don't
```

Just use the simpler test

```
if (married) . . .
```

In Chapter 6 we will use Boolean variables to control complex loops.

SELF CHECK

7. When does the statement
   ```
   System.out.println(x > 0 || x < 0);
   ```
   print false?

8. Rewrite the following expression, avoiding the comparison with false:
   ```
   if (Character.isDigit(ch) == false) . . .
   ```

Common Error 5.4

Multiple Relational Operators

Consider the expression

```
if (0 < amount < 1000) . . . // Error
```

This looks just like the mathematical notation for "amount is between 0 and 1000". But in Java, it is a syntax error.

Let us dissect the condition. The first half, 0 < amount, is a test with outcome true or false. The outcome of that test (true or false) is then compared against 1000. This seems to make no sense. Is true larger than 1000 or not? Can one compare truth values and numbers? In Java, you cannot. The Java compiler rejects this statement.

Instead, use && to combine two separate tests:

```
if (0 < amount && amount < 1000) . . .
```

Another common error, along the same lines, is to write

```
if (ch == 'S' || 'M') . . . // Error
```

to test whether ch is 'S' or 'M'. Again, the Java compiler flags this construct as an error. You cannot apply the || operator to characters. You need to write two Boolean expressions and join them with the || operator:

```
if (ch == 'S' || ch == 'M') . . .
```

Common Error 5.5

Confusing && and || Conditions

It is a surprisingly common error to confuse *and* and *or* conditions. A value lies between 0 and 100 if it is at least 0 *and* at most 100. It lies outside that range if it is less than 0 *or* greater than 100. There is no golden rule; you just have to think carefully.

Often the *and* or *or* is clearly stated, and then it isn't too hard to implement it. Sometimes, though, the wording isn't as explicit. It is quite common that the individual conditions are nicely set apart in a bulleted list, but with little indication of how they should be combined. The instructions for the 1992 tax return say that you can claim single filing status if any one of the following is true:

- You were never married.
- You were legally separated or divorced on December 31, 1992.
- You were widowed before January 1, 1992, and did not remarry in 1992.

Because the test passes if *any one* of the conditions is true, you must combine the conditions with *or*. Elsewhere, the same instructions state that you may use the more advantageous status of married filing jointly if all five of the following conditions are true:

- Your spouse died in 1990 or 1991 and you did not remarry in 1992.
- You have a child whom you can claim as dependent.
- That child lived in your home for all of 1992.
- You paid over half the cost of keeping up your home for this child.
- You filed (or could have filed) a joint return with your spouse the year he or she died.

Because *all* of the conditions must be true for the test to pass, you must combine them with an *and*.

Special Topic 5.4

Lazy Evaluation of Boolean Operators

The && and || operators in Java are computed using *lazy* (or *short circuit*) evaluation. In other words, logical expressions are evaluated from left to right, and evaluation stops as soon as the truth value is determined. When an *and* is evaluated and the first condition is false, then the second condition is skipped—no matter what it is, the combined condition must be false. When an *or* is evaluated and the first condition is true, the second condition is not evaluated, because it does not matter what the outcome of the second test is. Here is an example:

```
if (input != null && Integer.parseInt(input) > 0) . . .
```

If input is null, then the first condition is false, and thus the combined statement is false, no matter what the outcome of the second test. The second test is never evaluated if input is null, and there is no danger of parsing a null string (which would cause an exception).

If you do need to evaluate both conditions, then use the & and | operators (see Appendix B). When used with Boolean arguments, these operators always evaluate both arguments.

Special Topic 5.5

De Morgan's Law

In the preceding section, we programmed a test to see whether amount was between 0 and 1000. Let's find out whether the opposite is true:

```
if (!(0 < amount && amount < 1000)) . . .
```

De Morgan's law shows how to simplify expressions in which the not operator (!) is applied to terms joined by the && or || operators.

This test is a little bit complicated, and you have to think carefully through the logic. "When it is *not* true that 0 < amount and amount < 1000 . . ." Huh? It is not true that some people won't be confused by this code.

The computer doesn't care, but humans generally have a hard time comprehending logical conditions with *not* operators applied to *and/or* expressions. De Morgan's law, named after the mathematician Augustus de Morgan (1806–1871), can be used to simplify these Boolean expressions. De Morgan's law has two forms: one for the negation of an *and* expression and one for the negation of an *or* expression:

$$!(A\ \&\&\ B) \text{ is the same as } !A\ ||\ !B$$

$$!(A\ ||\ B) \text{ is the same as } !A\ \&\&\ !B$$

Pay particular attention to the fact that the *and* and *or* operators are *reversed* by moving the *not* inwards. For example, the negation of "the input is S or the input is M",

```
!(input.equals("S") || input.equals("M"))
```

is "the input is not S *and* the input is not M"

```
!input.equals("S") && !input.equals("M")
```

Let us apply the law to the negation of "the amount is between 0 and 1000":

```
!(0 < amount && amount < 1000)
```

is equivalent to

```
!(0 < amount) || !(amount < 1000)
```

which can be further simplified to

```
0 >= amount || amount >= 1000
```

Note that the opposite of < is >=, not >!

Random Fact 5.1

Artificial Intelligence

When one uses a sophisticated computer program such as a tax preparation package, one is bound to attribute some intelligence to the computer. The computer asks sensible questions and makes computations that we find a mental challenge. After all, if doing one's taxes were easy, we wouldn't need a computer to do it for us.

As programmers, however, we know that all this apparent intelligence is an illusion. Human programmers have carefully "coached" the software in all possible scenarios, and it simply replays the actions and decisions that were programmed into it.

Would it be possible to write computer programs that are genuinely intelligent in some sense? From the earliest days of computing, there was a sense that the human brain might be nothing but an immense computer, and that it might well be feasible to program computers to imitate some processes of human thought. Serious research into *artificial intelligence* began in the mid-1950s, and the first twenty years brought some impressive successes. Programs that play chess—surely an activity that appears to require remarkable intellectual powers—have become so good that they now routinely beat all but the best human players. As far back as 1975, an *expert-system* program called Mycin gained fame for being better in diagnosing meningitis in patients than the average physician.

However, there were serious setbacks as well. From 1982 to 1992, the Japanese government embarked on a massive research project, funded at over 40 billion Japanese yen. It was known as the *Fifth-Generation Project*. Its goal was to develop new hardware and software to greatly improve the performance of expert system software. At its outset, the project created fear in other countries that the Japanese computer industry was about to become the undisputed leader in the field. However, the end results were disappointing and did little to bring artificial intelligence applications to market.

From the very outset, one of the stated goals of the AI community was to produce software that could translate text from one language to another, for example from English to Russian. That undertaking proved to be enormously complicated. Human language appears to be much more subtle and interwoven with the human experience than had originally been thought. Even the grammar-checking tools that come with word-processing programs today are more of a gimmick than a useful tool, and analyzing grammar is just the first step in translating sentences.

The CYC (from en*cyc*lopedia) project, started by Douglas Lenat in 1984, tries to codify the implicit assumptions that underlie human speech and writing. The team members started

The Winner of the 2007 DARPA Urban Challenge

out analyzing news articles and asked themselves what unmentioned facts are necessary to actually understand the sentences. For example, consider the sentence "Last fall she enrolled in Michigan State". The reader automatically realizes that "fall" is not related to falling down in this context, but refers to the season. While there is a state of Michigan, here Michigan State denotes the university. A priori, a computer program has none of this knowledge. The goal of the CYC project is to extract and store the requisite facts—that is, (1) people enroll in universities; (2) Michigan is a state; (3) many states have universities named X State University, often abbreviated as X State; (4) most people enroll in a university in the fall. By 1995, the project had codified about 100,000 common-sense concepts and about a million facts of knowledge relating them. Even this massive amount of data has not proven sufficient for useful applications.

In recent years, artificial intelligence technology has seen substantial advances. One of the most astounding examples is the outcome of a series of "grand challenges" for autonomous vehicles posed by the Defense Advanced Research Projects Agency (DARPA). Competitors were invited to submit a computer-controlled vehicle that had to complete an obstacle course without a human driver or remote control. The first event, in 2004, was a disappointment, with none of the entrants finishing the route. In 2005, five vehicles completed a grueling 212 km course in the Mojave desert. Stanford's Stanley came in first, with an average speed of 30 km/h. In 2007, DARPA moved the competition to an "urban" environment, an abandoned air force base. Vehicles had to be able to interact with each other, following California traffic laws. As Stanford's Sebastian Thrun explained: "In the last Grand Challenge, it didn't really matter whether an obstacle was a rock or a bush, because either way you'd just drive around it. The current challenge is to move from just sensing the environment to understanding the environment."

5.5 Code Coverage

Black-box testing describes a testing method that does not take the structure of the implementation into account.

Testing the functionality of a program without consideration of its internal structure is called **black-box testing**. This is an important part of testing, because, after all, the users of a program do not know its internal structure. If a program works perfectly on all inputs, then it surely does its job.

However, it is impossible to ensure absolutely that a program will work correctly on all inputs just by supplying a finite number of test cases. As the famous computer scientist Edsger Dijkstra pointed out, testing can show only the presence of bugs—not their absence. To gain more confidence in the correctness of a program, it is useful to consider its internal structure. Testing strategies that look inside a program are called **white-box testing**. Performing unit tests of each method is a part of white-box testing.

White-box testing uses information about the structure of a program.

Code coverage is a measure of how many parts of a program have been tested.

You want to make sure that each part of your program is exercised at least once by one of your test cases. This is called **code coverage**. If some code is never executed by any of your test cases, you have no way of knowing whether that code would perform correctly if it ever were executed by user input. That means that you need to look at every if/else branch to see that each of them is reached by some test case. Many conditional branches are in the code only to take care of strange and abnormal inputs, but they still do something. It is a common phenomenon that they end up doing something incorrectly, but those faults are never discovered during testing, because nobody supplied the strange and abnormal inputs. Of course, these flaws become immediately apparent when the program is released and the first user types in an unusual input and is incensed when the program misbehaves. The remedy is to ensure that each part of the code is covered by some test case.

For example, in testing the getTax method of the TaxReturn class, you want to make sure that every if statement is entered for at least one test case. You should test both single and married taxpayers, with incomes in each of the three tax brackets.

When you select test cases, you should make it a habit to include *boundary test cases:* legal values that lie at the boundary of the set of acceptable inputs.

Boundary test cases are test cases that are at the boundary of acceptable inputs.

For example, what happens when you compute the taxes for an income of 0 or if a bank account has an interest rate of 0 percent? Boundary cases are still legitimate inputs, and you expect that the program will handle them correctly—often in some trivial way or through special cases. Testing boundary cases is important, because programmers often make mistakes dealing with boundary conditions. Division by zero, extracting characters from empty strings, and accessing null references are common symptoms of boundary errors.

SELF CHECK

9. How many test cases do you need to cover all branches of the getDescription method of the Earthquake class?

10. Give a boundary test case for the EarthquakeRunner program. What output do you expect?

Quality Tip 5.3

Calculate Sample Data Manually

It is usually difficult or impossible to prove that a given program functions correctly in all cases. For gaining confidence in the correctness of a program, or for understanding why it does not function as it should, manually calculated sample data are invaluable. If the program arrives at the same results as the manual calculation, our confidence in it is strengthened. If the manual results differ from the program results, we have a starting point for the debugging process.

Surprisingly, many programmers are reluctant to perform any manual calculations as soon as a program carries out the slightest bit of algebra. Their math phobia kicks in, and they irrationally hope that they can avoid the algebra and beat the program into submission by random tinkering, such as rearranging the + and - signs. Random tinkering is always a great time sink, but it rarely leads to useful results.

You should calculate test cases by hand to double-check that your application computes the correct answer.

Let's have another look at the TaxReturn class. Suppose a single taxpayer earns $50,000. The rules in Table 2 on page 188 state that the first $32,000 are taxed at 10 percent. Compute $32,000 \times 0.10 = 3,200$. The amount above $32,000, is taxed at 25 percent. It is time to take out your calculator—real world numbers are usually nasty. That is $(50,000 - 32,000) \times 0.25 = 4,500$. The total tax is the sum, $3,200 + 4,500 = 7,700$. Now, that wasn't so hard.

Run the program and compare the results. Because the results match, we have an increased confidence in the correctness of the program.

It is even better to make manual calculations before writing the program. Doing so helps you understand the task at hand, and you will be able to implement your solution more quickly.

Quality Tip 5.4

Prepare Test Cases Ahead of Time

Let us consider how we can test the tax computation program. Of course, we cannot try out all possible inputs of filing status and income level. Even if we could, there would be no point in trying them all. If the program correctly computes one or two tax amounts in a given bracket, then we have a good reason to believe that all amounts within that bracket will be correct. We want to aim for complete *coverage* of all cases.

There are two possibilities for the filing status and three tax brackets for each status. That makes six test cases. Then we want to test *boundary conditions*, such as zero income or incomes that are at the boundary between two brackets. That makes six test cases. Compute manually the answers you expect (See Quality Tip 5.3). Write down the test cases before you start coding.

Test Case	Married	Expected Output	Comment
30,000	N	3,000	10% bracket
72,000	N	13,200	3,200 + 25% of 40,000
50,000	Y	5,000	10% bracket
104,000	Y	16,400	6,400 + 25% of 40,000
32,000	N	3,200	boundary case
0		0	boundary case

Should you really test six inputs for this simple program? You certainly should. Furthermore, if you find an error in the program that wasn't covered by one of the test cases, make another test case and add it to your collection. After you fix the known mistakes, *run all test cases again.* Experience has shown that the cases that you just tried to fix are probably working now, but that errors that you fixed two or three iterations ago have a good chance of coming back! If you find that an error keeps coming back, that is usually a reliable sign that you did not fully understand some subtle interaction between features of your program.

It is always a good idea to design test cases *before* starting to code. There are two reasons for this. Working through the test cases gives you a better understanding of the algorithm that you are about to program. Furthermore, it has been noted that programmers instinctively shy away from testing fragile parts of their code. That seems hard to believe, but you will often make that observation about your own work. Watch someone else test your program. There will be times when that person enters input that makes you very nervous because you are not sure that your program can handle it, and you never dared to test it yourself. This is a well-known phenomenon, and making the test plan before writing the code offers some protection.

Special Topic 5.6

Logging

Sometimes you run a program and you are not sure where it spends its time. To get a print-out of the program flow, you can insert trace messages into the program, such as this one:

```java
public double getTax()
{
```

```
   . . .
   if (status == SINGLE)
   {
      System.out.println("status is SINGLE");
      . . .
   }
   . . .
}
```

However, there is a problem with using System.out.println for trace messages. When you are done testing the program, you need to remove all print statements that produce trace messages. If you find another error, however, you need to stick the print statements back in.

To overcome this problem, you should use the Logger class, which allows you to turn off the trace messages without removing them from the program.

Instead of printing directly to System.out, use the global logger object that is returned by the call Logger.getGlobal(). (Prior to Java 7, you obtained the global logger as Logger.getLogger("global").) Then call the info method:

```
Logger.getGlobal().info("status is SINGLE");
```

By default, the message is printed. But if you call

```
Logger.getGlobal().setLevel(Level.OFF);
```

Logging messages can be deactivated when testing is complete.

at the beginning of the main method of your program, all log message printing is suppressed. Set the level to Level.INFO to turn logging of info messages on again. Thus, you can turn off the log messages when your program works fine, and you can turn them back on if you find another error. In other words, using Logger.getGlobal().info is just like System.out.println, except that you can easily activate and deactivate the logging.

A common trick for tracing execution flow is to produce log messages when a method is called, and when it returns. At the beginning of a method, print out the parameters:

```
public TaxReturn(double anIncome, int aStatus)
{
   Logger.getGlobal().info("Parameters: anIncome = " + anIncome
         + " aStatus = " + aStatus);
   . . .
}
```

At the end of a method, print out the return value:

```
public double getTax()
{
   . . .
   Logger.getGlobal().info("Return value = " + tax);
   return tax;
}
```

The Logger class has many other options for industrial-strength logging. Check out the API documentation if you want to have more control over logging.

Summary of Learning Objectives

Use the if statement to implement a decision.

- The if statement lets a program carry out different actions depending on a condition.
- A block statement groups several statements together.

Implement comparisons of numbers and objects.

- Relational operators compare values. The == operator tests for equality.
- When comparing floating-point numbers, don't test for equality. Instead, check whether they are close enough.
- Do not use the == operator to compare strings. Use the equals method instead.
- The compareTo method compares strings in dictionary order.
- The == operator tests whether two object references are identical. To compare the contents of objects, you need to use the equals method.
- The null reference refers to no object.

Implement complex decisions that require multiple if statements.

- Multiple conditions can be combined to evaluate complex decisions. The correct arrangement depends on the logic of the problem to be solved.

Use the Boolean data type to store and combine conditions that can be true or false.

- The boolean type has two values: true and false.
- A predicate method returns a boolean value.
- You can form complex tests with the Boolean operators && (*and*), || (*or*), and ! (*not*).
- De Morgan's law shows how to simplify expressions in which the *not* operator (!) is applied to terms joined by the && or || operators.
- You can store the outcome of a condition in a Boolean variable.

Design test cases that cover all parts of a program.

- Black-box testing describes a testing method that does not take the structure of the implementation into account.
- White-box testing uses information about the structure of a program.
- Code coverage is a measure of how many parts of a program have been tested.
- Boundary test cases are test cases that are at the boundary of acceptable inputs.
- You should calculate test cases by hand to double-check that your application computes the correct answer.

Use the Java logging library for messages that can be easily turned on or off.

- Logging messages can be deactivated when testing is complete.

Classes, Objects, and Methods Introduced in this Chapter

```
java.lang.Character                 java.util.Scanner
    isDigit                             hasNextDouble
    isLetter                            hasNextInt
    isLowerCase                     java.util.logging.Level
    isUpperCase                         INFO
java.lang.Object                        OFF
    equals                          java.util.logging.Logger
java.lang.String                        getGlobal
    equals                              info
    equalsIgnoreCase                    setLevel
    compareTo
```

Media Resources

www.wiley.com/
college/
horstmann

- • **_Worked Example_** Extracting the Middle
- • Lab Exercises
- ✚ Practice Quiz
- ✚ Code Completion Exercises

Review Exercises

★ **R5.1** What is the value of each variable after the if statement?

    a. `int n = 1; int k = 2; int r = n; if (k < n) r = k;`
    b. `int n = 1; int k = 2; int r; if (n < k) r = k; else r = k + n;`
    c. `int n = 1; int k = 2; int r = k; if (r < k) n = r; else k = n;`
    d. `int n = 1; int k = 2; int r = 3; if (r < n + k) r = 2 * n; else k = 2 * r;`

★★ **R5.2** Find the errors in the following if statements.

    a. `if (1 + x > Math.pow(x, Math.sqrt(2)) y = y + x;`
    b. `if (x = 1) y++; else if (x = 2) y = y + 2;`
    c. `int x = Integer.parseInt(input);`
       `if (x != null) y = y + x;`

★★ **R5.3** Find the error in the following if statement that is intended to select a language from a given country and state/province.

```
language = "English";
if (country.equals("Canada"))
    if (stateOrProvince.equals("Quebec")) language = "French";
else if (country.equals("China"))
    language = "Chinese";
```

★★ **R5.4** Find the errors in the following if statements.

    a. `if (x && y == 0) { x = 1; y = 1; }`
    b. `if (1 <= x <= 10)`
       `System.out.println(x);`
    c. `if (!s.equals("nickels") || !s.equals("pennies")`
         `|| !s.equals("dimes") || !s.equals("quarters"))`
       `System.out.print("Input error!");`
    d. `if (input.equalsIgnoreCase("N") || "NO")`
       `return;`

★ **R5.5** Explain the following terms, and give an example for each construct:

    a. Expression
    b. Condition
    c. Statement
    d. Simple statement
    e. Compound statement
    f. Block

★ **R5.6** Explain the difference between an `if` statement with multiple `else` branches and nested `if` statements. Give an example for each.

★ **R5.7** Give an example for an `if/else if/else` statement where the order of the tests does not matter. Give an example where the order of the tests matters.

★ **R5.8** Of the following pairs of strings, which comes first in lexicographic order?

    a. `"Tom"`, `"Jerry"`
    b. `"Tom"`, `"Tomato"`
    c. `"church"`, `"Churchill"`
    d. `"car manufacturer"`, `"carburetor"`
    e. `"Harry"`, `"hairy"`
    f. `"C++"`, `" Car"`
    g. `"Tom"`, `"Tom"`
    h. `"Car"`, `"Carl"`
    i. `"car"`, `"bar"`
    j. `"101"`, `"11"`
    k. `"1.01"`, `"10.1"`

★ **R5.9** Complete the following truth table by finding the truth values of the Boolean expressions for all combinations of the Boolean inputs p, q, and r.

p	q	r	(p && q) || !r	!(p && (q || !r))
false	false	false		
false	false	false		
false	false	false		
...	...	...		
5 more combinations				
	...			

★★ **R5.10** Each square on a chess board can be described by a letter and number, such as g5 in this example:

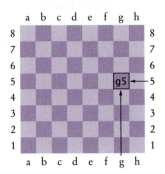

The following pseudocode describes an algorithm that determines whether a square with a given letter and number is dark (black) or light (white).

```
If the letter is an a, c, e, or g
    If the number is odd
        color = "black"
    Else
        color = "white"
Else
    If the number is even
        color = "black"
    Else
        color = "white"
```

Using the procedure in Productivity Hint 5.2 on page 192, trace this pseudocode with input g5.

★ **R5.11** Give a set of four test cases for the algorithm of Exercise R5.10 that covers all branches.

★★ **R5.12** In a scheduling program, we want to check whether two appointments overlap. For simplicity, appointments start at a full hour, and we use military time (with hours 0–24). The following pseudocode describes an algorithm that determines whether the appointment with start time **start1** and end time **end1** overlaps with the appointment with start time **start2** and end time **end2**.

```
If start1 > start2
    s = start1
Else
    s = start2
If end1 < end2
    e = end1
Else
    e = end2
If s < e
    The appointments overlap.
Else
    The appointments don't overlap.
```

Trace this algorithm with an appointment from 10–12 and one from 11–13, then with an appointment from 10–11 and one from 12–13.

★ **R5.13** Write pseudocode for a program that prompts the user for a month and day and prints out whether it is one of the following four holidays:

- New Year's Day (January 1)
- Independence Day (July 4)
- Veterans Day (November 11)
- Christmas Day (December 25)

★★★ **R5.14** True or false? A && B is the same as B && A for any Boolean conditions A and B.

★ **R5.15** Explain the difference between

```
s = 0;
if (x > 0) s++;
if (y > 0) s++;
```

and

```
s = 0;
if (x > 0) s++;
else if (y > 0) s++;
```

★★ **R5.16** Use de Morgan's law to simplify the following Boolean expressions.

    a. `!(x > 0 && y > 0)`

    b. `!(x != 0 || y != 0)`

    c. `!(country.equals("US") && !state.equals("HI")`
          `&& !state.equals("AK"))`

    d. `!(x % 4 != 0 || !(x % 100 == 0 && x % 400 == 0))`

★★ **R5.17** Make up another Java code example that shows the dangling `else` problem, using the following statement: A student with a GPA of at least 1.5, but less than 2, is on probation; with less than 1.5, the student is failing.

★ **R5.18** Explain the difference between the `==` operator and the `equals` method when comparing strings.

★★ **R5.19** Explain the difference between the tests

```
r == s
```

and

```
r.equals(s)
```

where both r and s are of type `Rectangle`.

★★★ **R5.20** What is wrong with this test to see whether r is `null`? What happens when this code runs?

```
Rectangle r;
. . .
if (r.equals(null))
    r = new Rectangle(5, 10, 20, 30);
```

★ **R5.21** Explain how the lexicographic ordering of strings differs from the ordering of words in a dictionary or telephone book. *Hint:* Consider strings, such as IBM, `wiley.com`, `Century 21`, `While-U-Wait`, and `7-11`.

★★★ **R5.22** Write Java code to test whether two objects of type `Line2D.Double` represent the same line when displayed on the graphics screen. *Do not* use `a.equals(b)`.

```
Line2D.Double a;
Line2D.Double b;

if (your condition goes here)
    g2.drawString("They look the same!", x, y);
```

Hint: If p and q are points, then `Line2D.Double(p, q)` and `Line2D.Double(q, p)` look the same.

★ **R5.23** Explain why it is more difficult to compare floating-point numbers than integers. Write Java code to test whether an integer n equals 10 and whether a floating-point number x is approximately equal to 10.

★★ **R5.24** Consider the following test to see whether a point falls inside a rectangle.

```
Point2D.Double p = . . .
Rectangle r = . . .
```

```
boolean xInside = false;
if (r.getX() <= p.getX() && p.getX() <= r.getX() + r.getWidth())
    xInside = true;
boolean yInside = false;
if (r.getY() <= p.getY() && p.getY() <= r.getY() + r.getHeight())
    yInside = true;
if (xInside && yInside)
    g2.drawString("p is inside the rectangle.",
        p.getX(), p.getY());
```

Rewrite this code to eliminate the explicit `true` and `false` values, by setting `xInside` and `yInside` to the values of Boolean expressions.

★T   **R5.25** Give a set of test cases for the earthquake program in Section 5.3.1. Ensure coverage of all branches.

★T   **R5.26** Give an example of a boundary test case for the earthquake program in Section 5.3.1. What result do you expect?

Programming Exercises

★★   **P5.1** Write a program that prints all real solutions to the quadratic equation $ax^2 + bx + c = 0$. Read in a, b, c and use the quadratic formula. If the *discriminant* $b^2 - 4ac$ is negative, display a message stating that there are no real solutions.

Implement a class `QuadraticEquation` whose constructor receives the coefficients a, b, c of the quadratic equation. Supply methods `getSolution1` and `getSolution2` that get the solutions, using the quadratic formula, or 0 if no solution exists. The `getSolution1` method should return the smaller of the two solutions.

Supply a method

```
boolean hasSolutions()
```

that returns `false` if the discriminant is negative.

★★   **P5.2** Write a program that takes user input describing a playing card in the following shorthand notation:

Notation	Meaning
A	Ace
2 ... 10	Card values
J	Jack
Q	Queen
K	King
D	Diamonds
H	Hearts
S	Spades
C	Clubs

Your program should print the full description of the card. For example,

```
Enter the card notation:
4S
Four of spades
```

Implement a class Card whose constructor takes the card notation string and whose getDescription method returns a description of the card. If the notation string is not in the correct format, the getDescription method should return the string "Unknown".

★★ **P5.3** Write a program that reads in three floating-point numbers and prints the three inputs in sorted order. For example:

```
Please enter three numbers:
4
9
2.5
The inputs in sorted order are:
2.5
4
9
```

★ **P5.4** Write a program that translates a letter grade into a number grade. Letter grades are A B C D F, possibly followed by + or -. Their numeric values are 4, 3, 2, 1, and 0. There is no F+ or F-. A + increases the numeric value by 0.3, a - decreases it by 0.3. However, an A+ has the value 4.0. All other inputs have value –1.

```
Enter a letter grade:
B-
Numeric value: 2.7.
```

Use a class Grade with a method getNumericGrade.

★ **P5.5** Write a program that translates a number into the closest letter grade. For example, the number 2.8 (which might have been the average of several grades) would be converted to B-. Break ties in favor of the better grade; for example, 2.85 should be a B. Any value ≥ 4.15 should be an A+.

Use a class Grade with a method getLetterGrade.

★ **P5.6** Write a program that reads in three strings and prints them in lexicographically sorted order:

```
Please enter three strings:
Tom
Dick
Harry
The inputs in sorted order are:
Dick
Harry
Tom
```

★★ **P5.7** Change the implementation of the getTax method in the TaxReturn class, by setting a variable rate1Limit, depending on the marital status. Then have a single formula that computes the tax, depending on the income and the limit. Verify that your results are identical to that of the TaxReturn class in this chapter.

★★★   **P5.8**   The original U.S. income tax of 1913 was quite simple. The tax was

- 1 percent on the first $50,000.
- 2 percent on the amount over $50,000 up to $75,000.
- 3 percent on the amount over $75,000 up to $100,000.
- 4 percent on the amount over $100,000 up to $250,000.
- 5 percent on the amount over $250,000 up to $500,000.
- 6 percent on the amount over $500,000.

There was no separate schedule for single or married taxpayers. Write a program that computes the income tax according to this schedule.

★★   **P5.9**   Write a program that prompts for the day and month of the user's birthday and then prints a horoscope. Make up fortunes for programmers, like this:

```
Please enter your birthday (month and day): 6 16
Gemini are experts at figuring out the behavior of complicated programs.
You feel where bugs are coming from and then stay one step ahead. Tonight,
your style wins approval from a tough critic.
```

Each fortune should contain the name of the astrological sign. (You will find the names and date ranges of the signs at a distressingly large number of sites on the Internet.)

★   **P5.10**   When two points in time are compared, each given as hours (in military time, ranging from 0 and 23) and minutes, the following pseudocode determines which comes first.

```
If hour1 < hour2
    time1 comes first.
Else if hour1 and hour2 are the same
    If minute1 < minute2
        time1 comes first.
    Else if minute1 and minute2 are the same
        time1 and time2 are the same.
    Else
        time2 comes first.
Else
    time2 comes first.
```

Write a program that prompts the user for two points in time and prints the time that comes first, then the other time.

★   **P5.11**   The following algorithm yields the season (Spring, Summer, Fall, or Winter) for a given month and day.

```
If month is 1, 2, or 3, season = "Winter"
Else if month is 4, 5, or 6, season = "Spring"
Else if month is 7, 8, or 9, season = "Summer"
Else if month is 10, 11, or 12, season = "Fall"
If month is divisible by 3 and day >= 21
    If season is "Winter", season = "Spring"
    Else if season is "Spring", season = "Summer"
    Else if season is "Summer", season = "Fall"
    Else season = "Winter"
```

Write a program that prompts the user for a month and day and then prints the season, as determined by this algorithm.

★ **P5.12** A year with 366 days is called a *leap year*. A year is a leap year if it is divisible by 4 (for example, 1980). However, since the introduction of the Gregorian calendar on October 15, 1582, a year is not a leap year if it is divisible by 100 (for example, 1900); however, it is a leap year if it is divisible by 400 (for example, 2000). Write a program that asks the user for a year and computes whether that year is a leap year. Implement a class Year with a predicate method boolean isLeapYear().

★ **P5.13** Write a program that asks the user to enter a month (1 = January, 2 = February, and so on) and then prints the number of days of the month. For February, print "28 days".

```
Enter a month (1-12):
5
31 days
```

Implement a class Month with a method int getDays(). Do not use a separate if or else statement for each month. Use Boolean operators.

★★★ **P5.14** Write a program that reads in two floating-point numbers and tests (a) whether they are the same when rounded to two decimal places and (b) whether they differ by less than 0.01. Here are two sample runs.

```
Enter two floating-point numbers:
2.0
1.99998
They are the same when rounded to two decimal places.
They differ by less than 0.01.
```

```
Enter two floating-point numbers:
0.999
0.991
They are different when rounded to two decimal places.
They differ by less than 0.01.
```

★ **P5.15** Enhance the BankAccount class of Chapter 3 by
- Rejecting negative amounts in the deposit and withdraw methods
- Rejecting withdrawals that would result in a negative balance

★ **P5.16** Write a program that reads in the hourly wage of an employee. Then ask how many hours the employee worked in the past week. Be sure to accept fractional hours. Compute the pay. Any overtime work (over 40 hours per week) is paid at 150 percent of the regular wage. Solve this problem by implementing a class Paycheck.

★★ **P5.17** Write a unit conversion program that asks users to identify the unit from which they want to convert and the unit to which they want to convert. Legal units are *in*, *ft*, *mi*, *mm*, *cm*, *m*, and *km*. Declare two objects of a class UnitConverter that convert between meters and a given unit.

```
Convert from:
in
Convert to:
mm
Value:
10
10 in = 254 mm
```

★★★ **P5.18** A line in the plane can be specified in various ways:
- by giving a point (x, y) and a slope m
- by giving two points $(x_1, y_1), (x_2, y_2)$
- as an equation in slope-intercept form $y = mx + b$
- as an equation $x = a$ if the line is vertical

Implement a class Line with four constructors, corresponding to the four cases above. Implement methods

```
boolean intersects(Line other)
boolean equals(Line other)
boolean isParallel(Line other)
```

★★G **P5.19** Write a program that draws a circle with radius 100 and center (200, 200). Ask the user to specify the x- and y-coordinates of a point. Draw the point as a small circle. If the point lies inside the circle, color the small circle green. Otherwise, color it red. In your exercise, declare a class Circle and a method boolean isInside(Point2D.Double p).

★★★G **P5.20** Write a graphics program that asks the user to specify the radii of two circles. The first circle has center (100, 200), and the second circle has center (200, 100). Draw the circles. If they intersect, then color both circles green. Otherwise, color them red. *Hint:* Compute the distance between the centers and compare it to the radii. Your program should draw nothing if the user enters a negative radius. In your exercise, declare a class Circle and a method boolean intersects(Circle other).

Programming Projects

Project 5.1 Implement a *combination lock* class. A combination lock has a dial with 26 positions labeled A . . . Z. The dial needs to be set three times. If it is set to the correct combination, the lock can be opened. When the lock is closed again, the combination can be entered again. If a user sets the dial more than three times, the last three settings determine whether the lock can be opened. An important part of this exercise is to implement a suitable interface for the CombinationLock class.

Project 5.2 Get the instructions for last year's form 1040 from http://www.irs.ustreas.gov. Find the tax brackets that were used last year for all categories of taxpayers (single, married filing jointly, married filing separately, and head of household). Write a program that computes taxes following that schedule. Ignore deductions, exemptions, and credits. Simply apply the tax rate to the income.

Answers to Self-Check Questions

1. If the withdrawal amount equals the balance, the result should be a zero balance and no penalty.
2. Only the first assignment statement is part of the `if` statement. Use braces to group both assignment statements into a block statement.
3. (a) 0; (b) 1; (c) An exception occurs.
4. Syntactically incorrect: e, g, h. Logically questionable: a, d, f
5. Yes, if you also reverse the comparisons:

```
if (richter < 3.5)
    r = "Generally not felt by people";
else if (richter < 4.5)
    r = "Felt by many people, no destruction";
else if (richter < 6.0)
    r = "Damage to poorly constructed buildings";
. . .
```

6. The higher tax rate is only applied on the income in the higher bracket. Suppose you are single and make $31,900. Should you try to get a $200 raise? Absolutely: you get to keep 90 percent of the first $100 and 75 percent of the next $100.
7. When x is zero.
8. `if (!Character.isDigit(ch)) . . .`
9. Seven
10. An input of 0 should yield an output of "Generally not felt by people". (If the output is "Negative numbers are not allowed", there is an error in the program.)

Chapter 6

Iteration

CHAPTER GOALS

- To be able to program loops with the while and for statements
- To avoid infinite loops and off-by-one errors
- To be able to use common loop algorithms
- To understand nested loops
- To implement simulations
- **T** To learn about the debugger

This chapter presents the various iteration constructs of the Java language. These constructs execute one or more statements repeatedly until a goal is reached. You will see how the techniques that you learn in this chapter can be applied to the processing of input data and the programming of simulations.

CHAPTER CONTENTS

6.1 while Loops

In this chapter you will learn how to write programs that repeatedly execute one or more statements. We will illustrate these concepts by looking at typical investment situations. Consider a bank account with an initial balance of $10,000 that earns 5 percent interest. The interest is computed at the end of every year on the current balance and then deposited into the bank account. For example, after the first year, the account has earned $500 (5 percent of $10,000) of interest. The interest gets added to the bank account. Next year, the interest is $525 (5 percent of $10,500), and the balance is $11,025.

How many years does it take for the balance to reach $20,000? Of course, it won't take longer than 20 years, because at least $500 is added to the bank account each year. But it will take less than 20 years, because interest is computed on increasingly larger balances. To know the exact answer, we will write a program that repeatedly adds interest until the balance is reached.

In Java, the while statement implements such a repetition. The construct

```
while (condition)
    statement
```

> A while statement executes a block of code repeatedly. A condition controls how long the loop is executed.

keeps executing the statement while the condition is true.

Most commonly, the statement is a block statement, that is, a set of statements delimited by { }.

In our case, we want to know when the bank account has reached a particular balance. While the balance is less, we keep adding interest and incrementing the years counter:

```
while (balance < targetBalance)
{
    years++;
    double interest = balance * rate / 100;
    balance = balance + interest;
}
```

Figure 1 shows the flow of execution of this loop.

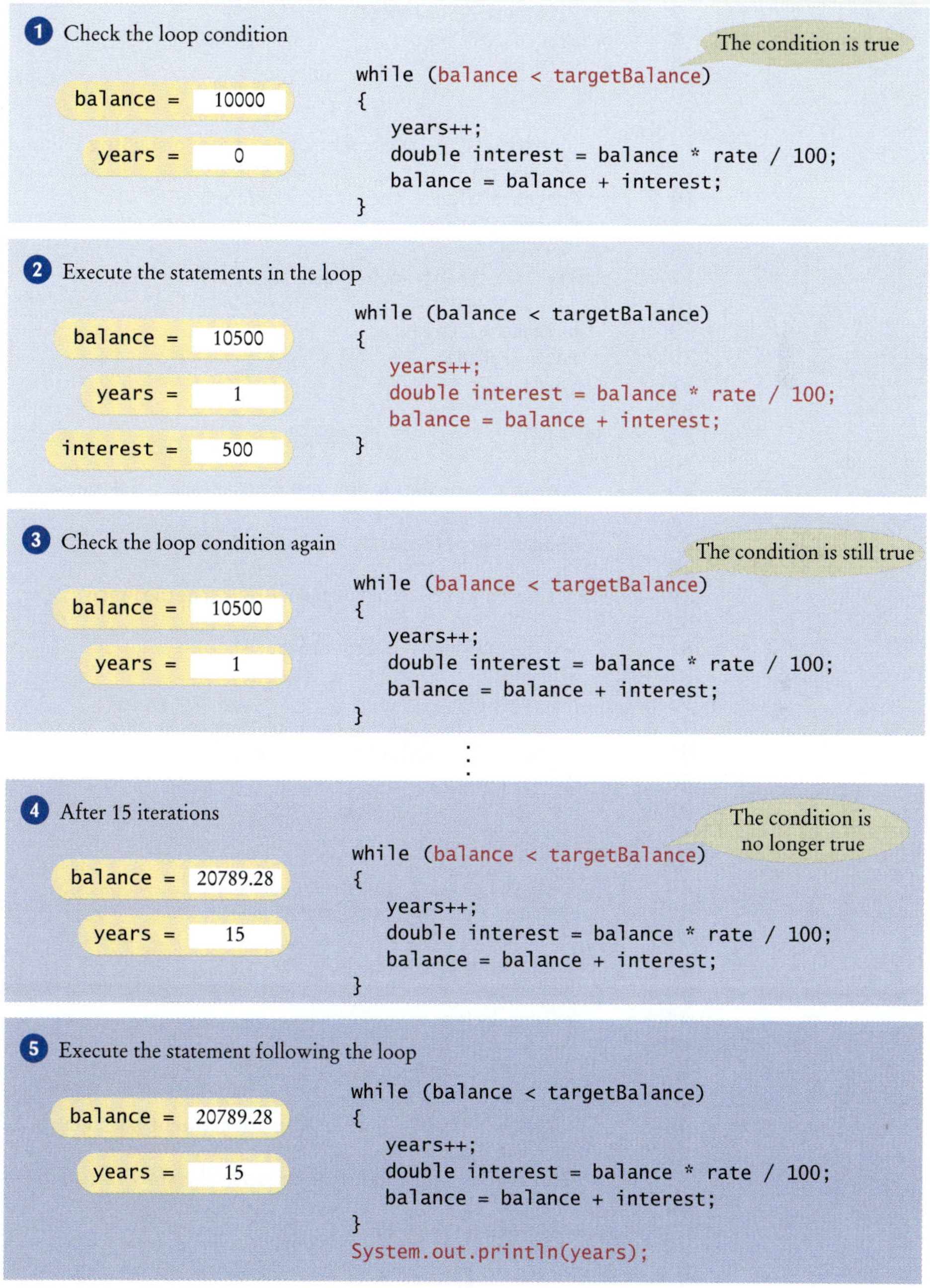

1 Check the loop condition

```
                                                        The condition is true
balance =   10000      while (balance < targetBalance)
                       {
years =       0            years++;
                           double interest = balance * rate / 100;
                           balance = balance + interest;
                       }
```

2 Execute the statements in the loop

```
balance =   10500      while (balance < targetBalance)
                       {
years =       1            years++;
                           double interest = balance * rate / 100;
interest =    500          balance = balance + interest;
                       }
```

3 Check the loop condition again

```
                                                        The condition is still true
balance =   10500      while (balance < targetBalance)
                       {
years =       1            years++;
                           double interest = balance * rate / 100;
                           balance = balance + interest;
                       }
```

⋮

4 After 15 iterations

```
                                                        The condition is
                                                        no longer true
balance =  20789.28    while (balance < targetBalance)
                       {
years =      15            years++;
                           double interest = balance * rate / 100;
                           balance = balance + interest;
                       }
```

5 Execute the statement following the loop

```
balance =  20789.28    while (balance < targetBalance)
                       {
years =      15            years++;
                           double interest = balance * rate / 100;
                           balance = balance + interest;
                       }
                       System.out.println(years);
```

Figure 1 Execution of a while Loop

Here is the program that solves our investment problem.

ch06/invest1/Investment.java

```
1   /**
2       A class to monitor the growth of an investment that
3       accumulates interest at a fixed annual rate.
4   */
5   public class Investment
6   {
7       private double balance;
8       private double rate;
9       private int years;
10
11      /**
12          Constructs an Investment object from a starting balance and
13          interest rate.
14          @param aBalance the starting balance
15          @param aRate the interest rate in percent
16      */
17      public Investment(double aBalance, double aRate)
18      {
19          balance = aBalance;
20          rate = aRate;
21          years = 0;
22      }
23
24      /**
25          Keeps accumulating interest until a target balance has
26          been reached.
27          @param targetBalance the desired balance
28      */
29      public void waitForBalance(double targetBalance)
30      {
31          while (balance < targetBalance)
32          {
33              years++;
34              double interest = balance * rate / 100;
35              balance = balance + interest;
36          }
37      }
38
39      /**
40          Gets the current investment balance.
41          @return the current balance
42      */
43      public double getBalance()
44      {
45          return balance;
46      }
47
48      /**
49          Gets the number of years this investment has accumulated
50          interest.
51          @return the number of years since the start of the investment
52      */
53      public int getYears()
54      {
55          return years;
```

```
56        }
57  }
```

ch06/invest1/InvestmentRunner.java

```java
1   /**
2      This program computes how long it takes for an investment
3      to double.
4   */
5   public class InvestmentRunner
6   {
7      public static void main(String[] args)
8      {
9         final double INITIAL_BALANCE = 10000;
10        final double RATE = 5;
11        Investment invest = new Investment(INITIAL_BALANCE, RATE);
12        invest.waitForBalance(2 * INITIAL_BALANCE);
13        int years = invest.getYears();
14        System.out.println("The investment doubled after "
15              + years + " years");
16     }
17  }
```

Program Run

```
The investment doubled after 15 years
```

ANIMATION
Tracing a Loop

A `while` statement is often called a *loop.* If you draw a flowchart, you will see that the control loops backwards to the test after every iteration (see Figure 2).

When you declare a variable *inside* the loop body, the variable is created for each iteration of the loop and removed after the end of each iteration. For example, consider the `interest` variable in this loop:

```java
while (balance < targetBalance)
{
    years++;
    double interest = balance * rate / 100;
        // A new interest variable is created
        // in each iteration
    balance = balance + interest;
} // interest no longer declared here
```

If a variable needs to be updated in multiple loop iterations, do not declare it inside the loop. For example, it would not make sense to declare the `balance` variable inside this loop.

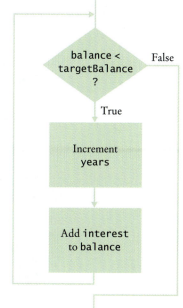

Figure 2 Flowchart of a `while` Loop

The following loop,

```
while (true)
    statement
```

executes the statement over and over, without terminating. Whoa! Why would you want that? The program would never stop. There are two reasons. Some programs indeed never stop; the software controlling an automated teller machine, a telephone switch, or a microwave oven doesn't ever stop (at least not until the device is turned off). Our programs aren't usually of that kind, but even if you can't terminate the loop, you can exit from the method that contains it. This can be helpful when the termination test naturally falls in the middle of the loop (see Special Topic 6.3 on page 245).

Table 1	while Loop Examples	
Loop	**Output**	**Explanation**

`i = 0; sum = 0;`
`while (sum < 10)`
`{`
`    i++; sum = sum + i;`
`    Print i and sum;`
`}`
	1 1
	2 3
	3 6
	4 10
		When sum is 10, the loop condition is false, and the loop ends.

`i = 0; sum = 0;`
`while (sum < 10)`
`{`
`    i++; sum = sum - i;`
`    Print i and sum;`
`}`
	1 -1
	2 -3
	3 -6
	4 -10
	. . .
		Because sum never reaches 10, this is an "infinite loop" (see Common Error 6.1 on page 225).

`i = 0; sum = 0;`
`while (sum < 0)`
`{`
`    i++; sum = sum - i;`
`    Print i and sum;`
`}`
	(No output)	The statement sum < 0 is false when the condition is first checked, and the loop is never executed.

`i = 0; sum = 0;`
`while (sum >= 10)`
`{`
`    i++; sum = sum + i;`
`    Print i and sum;`
`}`
	(No output)	The programmer probably thought, "Stop when the sum is at least 10." However, the loop condition controls when the loop is executed, not when it ends.

`i = 0; sum = 0;`
`while (sum < 10) ;`
`{`
`    i++; sum = sum + i;`
`    Print i and sum;`
`}`
	(No output, program does not terminate)	Note the semicolon before the {. This loop has an empty body. It runs forever, checking whether sum < 10 and doing nothing in the body (see Common Error 6.4 on page 233).

Syntax 6.1 The while Statement

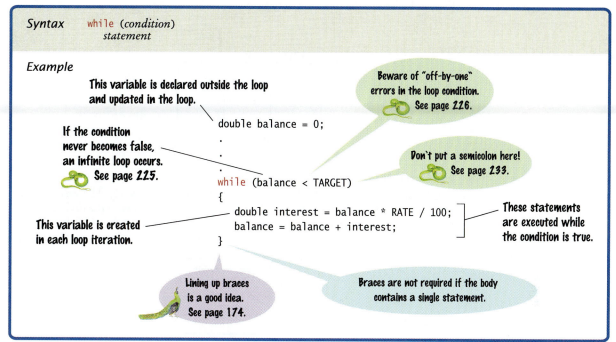

Syntax
```
while (condition)
    statement
```

Example

This variable is declared outside the loop and updated in the loop.

If the condition never becomes false, an infinite loop occurs. See page 225.

This variable is created in each loop iteration.

Beware of "off-by-one" errors in the loop condition. See page 226.

Don't put a semicolon here! See page 233.

```
double balance = 0;
   .
   .
   .
while (balance < TARGET)
{
    double interest = balance * RATE / 100;
    balance = balance + interest;
}
```

These statements are executed while the condition is true.

Lining up braces is a good idea. See page 174.

Braces are not required if the body contains a single statement.

SELF CHECK

1. How many times is the following statement in the loop executed?

   ```
   while (false) statement;
   ```

2. What would happen if RATE was set to 0 in the main method of the InvestmentRunner program?

Productivity Hint 6.1

Hand-Tracing Loops

In Programming Tip 5.2, you learned about the method of hand-tracing. This method is particularly effective for understanding how a loop works.

Consider this example loop. What value is displayed?

```
int n = 1729;  ①
int sum = 0;
while (n > 0)  ②
{
    int digit = n % 10;  ③ ④ ⑤ ⑥
    sum = sum + digit;
    n = n / 10;
}
System.out.println(sum);  ⑦
```

1. There are three variables: n, sum, and digit. The first two variables are initialized with 1729 and 0 before the loop is entered.

n	sum	digit
1729	0	

2. Because n is positive, enter the loop.

3. The variable digit is set to 9 (the remainder of dividing 1729 by 10). The variable sum is set to 0 + 9 = 9. Finally, n becomes 172. (Recall that the remainder in the division 1729 / 10 is discarded because both arguments are integers.). Cross out the old values and write the new ones under the old ones.

n	sum	digit
~~1729~~	~~0~~	
172	9	9

4. Because n > 0, we repeat the loop. Now digit becomes 2, sum is set to 9 + 2 = 11, and n is set to 17.

n	sum	digit
~~1729~~	~~0~~	
~~172~~	~~9~~	~~9~~
17	11	2

5. Because n is still not zero, we repeat the loop, setting digit to 7, sum to 11 + 7 = 18, and n to 1.

n	sum	digit
~~1729~~	~~0~~	
~~172~~	~~9~~	~~9~~
~~17~~	~~11~~	~~2~~
1	18	7

6. We enter the loop one last time. Now digit is set to 1, sum to 19, and n becomes zero.

n	sum	digit
1729	0	
172	9	9
17	11	2
1	18	7
0	19	1

7. The condition n > 0 is now false, and we continue with the output statement after the loop. The value that is output is 19.

Of course, you can get the same answer simply by running the code. The hope is that by hand-tracing, you gain an *insight*. Consider again what happens in each iteration:

- We extract the last digit of n.
- We add that digit to sum.
- We strip the digit off n.

In other words, the loop forms the sum of the digits in n. You now know what the loop does for any value of n, not just the one in the example.

Why would anyone want to form the sum of the digits? Operations of this kind are useful for checking the validity of credit card numbers and other forms of ID number—see Exercise P6.2.

Common Error 6.1

Infinite Loops

One of the most annoying loop errors is an infinite loop: a loop that runs forever and can be stopped only by killing the program or restarting the computer. If there are output statements in the loop, then reams and reams of output flash by on the screen. Otherwise, the program just sits there and hangs, seeming to do nothing. On some systems you can kill a hanging program by hitting Ctrl+Break or Ctrl+C. On others, you can close the window in which the program runs.

A common reason for infinite loops is forgetting to advance the variable that controls the loop:

```
int years = 0;
while (years < 20)
{
    double interest = balance * rate / 100;
    balance = balance + interest;
}
```

Here the programmer forgot to add a statement for incrementing years in the loop. As a result, the value of years always stays 0, and the loop never comes to an end.

Another common reason for an infinite loop is accidentally incrementing a counter that should be decremented (or vice versa). Consider this example:

```
int years = 20;
while (years > 0)
{
```

```
        years++; // Oops, should have been years--
        double interest = balance * rate / 100;
        balance = balance + interest;
    }
```

The years variable really should have been decremented, not incremented. This is a common error, because incrementing counters is so much more common than decrementing that your fingers may type the ++ on autopilot. As a consequence, years is always larger than 0, and the loop never terminates. (Actually, years eventually will exceed the largest representable positive integer and wrap around to a negative number. Then the loop exits—of course, that takes a long time, and the result is completely wrong.)

Common Error 6.2

Off-by-One Errors

Consider our computation of the number of years that are required to double an investment:

```
int years = 0;
while (balance < 2 * initialBalance)
{
    years++;
    double interest = balance * rate / 100;
    balance = balance + interest;
}
System.out.println("The investment reached the target after "
    + years + " years.");
```

Should years start at 0 or at 1? Should you test for balance < 2 * initialBalance or for balance <= 2 * initialBalance? It is easy to be *off by one* in these expressions.

Some people try to solve off-by-one errors by randomly inserting +1 or -1 until the program seems to work. That is, of course, a terrible strategy. It can take a long time to compile and test all the various possibilities. Expending a small amount of mental effort is a real time saver.

Fortunately, off-by-one errors are easy to avoid, simply by thinking through a couple of test cases and using the information from the test cases to come up with a rationale for the correct loop condition.

year	balance
0	$100
1	$150
2	$225

Should years start at 0 or at 1? Look at a scenario with simple values: an initial balance of $100 and an interest rate of 50 percent. After year 1, the balance is $150, and after year 2 it is $225, or over $200. So the investment doubled after 2 years. The loop executed two times, incrementing years each time. Hence years must start at 0, not at 1.

In other words, the balance variable denotes the balance *after* the end of the year. At the outset, the balance variable contains the balance after year 0 and not after year 1.

Next, should you use a < or <= comparison in the test? That is harder to figure out, because it is rare for the balance to be exactly twice the initial balance. Of course, there is one case when this happens, namely when the interest is 100 percent. The loop executes once. Now years is 1, and balance is exactly equal to 2 * initialBalance. Has the investment doubled after one year? It has. Therefore, the loop should *not* execute again. If the test condition is balance < 2 * initialBalance, the loop stops, as it should. If the test condition had been balance <= 2 * initialBalance, the loop would have executed once more.

In other words, you keep adding interest while the balance *has not yet doubled*.

An off-by-one error is a common error when programming loops. Think through simple test cases to avoid this type of error.

Special Topic 6.1

do **Loops**

Sometimes you want to execute the body of a loop at least once and perform the loop test after the body was executed. The do loop serves that purpose:

```
do
    statement
while (condition);
```

The *statement* is executed while the *condition* is true. The condition is tested after the statement is executed, so the statement is executed at least once.

For example, suppose you want to make sure that a user enters a positive number. As long as the user enters a negative number or zero, just keep prompting for a correct input. In this situation, a do loop makes sense, because you need to get a user input before you can test it.

```java
double value;
do
{
    System.out.print("Please enter a positive number: ");
    value = in.nextDouble();
}
while (value <= 0);
```

The figure shows a flowchart of this loop.

In practice, do loops are not very common. (The library code in Java 6 contains about 10,000 loop statements, but only about 2 percent are do loops.) Consider again the example of prompting for a positive value. In practice, you also need to guard against users who provide an input that isn't a number. Now the loop becomes so complex that you are better off controlling it with a Boolean variable:

```java
boolean valid = false;
while (!valid)
{
    System.out.print("Please enter a positive number: ");
    if (in.hasNextDouble())
    {
        value = in.nextDouble();
        if (value > 0) valid = true;
    }
    else
        in.nextLine(); // Consume input
}
```

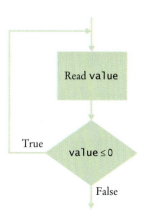

Flowchart of a do Loop

6.2 for Loops

One of the most common loop types has the form

```
i = start;
while (i <= end)
{
   . . .
   i++;
}
```

Because this loop is so common, there is a special form for it that emphasizes the pattern:

```
for (i = start; i <= end; i++)
{
   . . .
}
```

You can also declare the loop counter variable inside the for loop header. That convenient shorthand restricts the use of the variable to the body of the loop (as will be discussed further in Special Topic 6.2 on page 234).

```
for (int i = start; i <= end; i++)
{
   . . .
}
```

A for loop can be used to find out the size of our $10,000 investment if 5 percent interest is compounded for 20 years. Of course, the balance will be larger than $20,000, because at least $500 is added every year. You may be surprised to find out just how much larger the balance is.

> You use a for loop when a variable runs from a starting to an ending value with a constant increment or decrement.

In our loop, we let i go from 1 to numberOfYears, the number of years for which we want to compound interest.

```
for (int i = 1; i <= numberOfYears; i++)
{
   double interest = balance * rate / 100;
   balance = balance + interest;
}
```

Figure 3 shows the corresponding flowchart. Figure 4 shows the flow of execution. The complete program is on page 230.

Another common use of the for loop is to traverse all characters of a string:

```
for (int i = 0; i < str.length(); i++)
{
   char ch = str.charAt(i);
   Process ch
}
```

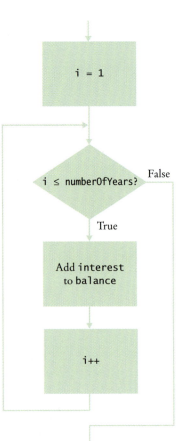

Figure 3 Flowchart of a for Loop

1 Initialize counter

```
for (int i = 1; i <= numberOfYears; i++)
{
    double interest = balance * rate / 100;
    balance = balance + interest;
}
```

i = 1

2 Check condition

```
for (int i = 1; i <= numberOfYears; i++)
{
    double interest = balance * rate / 100;
    balance = balance + interest;
}
```

i = 1

3 Execute loop body

```
for (int i = 1; i <= numberOfYears; i++)
{
    double interest = balance * rate / 100;
    balance = balance + interest;
}
```

i = 1

4 Update counter

```
for (int i = 1; i <= numberOfYears; i++)
{
    double interest = balance * rate / 100;
    balance = balance + interest;
}
```

i = 2

5 Check condition again

```
for (int i = 1; i <= numberOfYears; i++)
{
    double interest = balance * rate / 100;
    balance = balance + interest;
}
```

i = 2

Figure 4 Execution of a for Loop

ANIMATION
The for Loop

Note that the counter variable i starts at 0, and the loop is terminated when i reaches the length of the string. For example, if str has length 5, i takes on the values 0, 1, 2, 3, and 4. These are the valid positions in the string.

Note too that the three slots in the for header can contain any three expressions. You can count down instead of up:

```
for (int i = 10; i > 0; i--)
```

The increment or decrement need not be in steps of 1:

```
for (int i = -10; i <= 10; i = i + 2) . . .
```

It is possible—but a sign of unbelievably bad taste—to put unrelated conditions into the loop header:

```
for (rate = 5; years-- > 0; System.out.println(balance))
    . . . // Bad taste
```

We won't even begin to decipher what that might mean. You should stick with for loops that initialize, test, and update a single variable.

Syntax 6.2 The for Statement

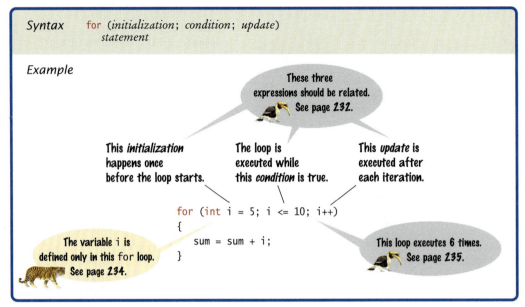

Syntax	`for (initialization; condition; update)`
	`    statement`

Example

These three expressions should be related. See page 232.

This *initialization* happens once before the loop starts.

The loop is executed while this *condition* is true.

This *update* is executed after each iteration.

```
for (int i = 5; i <= 10; i++)
{
    sum = sum + i;
}
```

The variable i is defined only in this for loop. See page 234.

This loop executes 6 times. See page 235.

ch06/invest2/Investment.java

```java
1  /**
2     A class to monitor the growth of an investment that
3     accumulates interest at a fixed annual rate.
4  */
5  public class Investment
6  {
7     private double balance;
8     private double rate;
9     private int years;
10
11    /**
12       Constructs an Investment object from a starting balance and
13       interest rate.
14       @param aBalance the starting balance
15       @param aRate the interest rate in percent
16    */
17    public Investment(double aBalance, double aRate)
18    {
19       balance = aBalance;
20       rate = aRate;
21       years = 0;
22    }
23
24    /**
25       Keeps accumulating interest until a target balance has
26       been reached.
27       @param targetBalance the desired balance
28    */
29    public void waitForBalance(double targetBalance)
30    {
31       while (balance < targetBalance)
32       {
33          years++;
```

```
34            double interest = balance * rate / 100;
35            balance = balance + interest;
36        }
37    }
38
39    /**
40        Keeps accumulating interest for a given number of years.
41        @param numberOfYears the number of years to wait
42    */
43    public void waitYears(int numberOfYears)
44    {
45        for (int i = 1; i <= numberOfYears; i++)
46        {
47            double interest = balance * rate / 100;
48            balance = balance + interest;
49        }
50        years = years + n;
51    }
52
53    /**
54        Gets the current investment balance.
55        @return the current balance
56    */
57    public double getBalance()
58    {
59        return balance;
60    }
61
62    /**
63        Gets the number of years this investment has accumulated
64        interest.
65        @return the number of years since the start of the investment
66    */
67    public int getYears()
68    {
69        return years;
70    }
71 }
```

ch06/invest2/InvestmentRunner.java

```
1  /**
2      This program computes how much an investment grows in
3      a given number of years.
4  */
5  public class InvestmentRunner
6  {
7      public static void main(String[] args)
8      {
9          final double INITIAL_BALANCE = 10000;
10         final double RATE = 5;
11         final int YEARS = 20;
12         Investment invest = new Investment(INITIAL_BALANCE, RATE);
13         invest.waitYears(YEARS);
14         double balance = invest.getBalance();
15         System.out.printf("The balance after %d years is %.2f\n",
16             YEARS, balance);
17     }
18 }
```

Program Run

The balance after 20 years is 26532.98

SELF CHECK

3. Rewrite the `for` loop in the `waitYears` method as a `while` loop.

4. How many times does the following `for` loop execute?

```
for (i = 0; i <= 10; i++)
    System.out.println(i * i);
```

Table 2   for Loop Examples

Loop	Values of i	Comment
`for (i = 0; i <= 5; i++)`	0 1 2 3 4 5	Note that the loop is executed 6 times. (See Quality Tip 6.4 on page 235.)
`for (i = 5; i >= 0; i--)`	5 4 3 2 1 0	Use i-- for decreasing values.
`for (i = 0; i < 9; i = i + 2)`	0 2 4 6 8	Use i = i + 2 for a step size of 2.
`for (i = 0; i != 9; i = i + 2)`	0 2 4 6 8 10 12 14 ... (infinite loop)	You can use < or <= instead of != to avoid this problem.
`for (i = 1; i <= 20; i = i * 2)`	1 2 4 8 16	You can specify any rule for modifying i, such as doubling it in every step.
`for (i = 0; i < str.length(); i++)`	0 1 2 ... until the last valid index of the string str	In the loop body, use the expression `str.charAt(i)` to get the ith character.

Quality Tip 6.1

Use for **Loops for Their Intended Purpose**

A for loop is an *idiom* for a while loop of a particular form. A counter runs from the start to the end, with a constant increment:

```
for (Set counter to start; Test whether counter at end; Update counter by increment)
{   . . .
    // counter, start, end, increment not changed here
}
```

If your loop doesn't match this pattern, don't use the for construction. The compiler won't prevent you from writing idiotic for loops:

```
// Bad style—unrelated header expressions
for (System.out.println("Inputs:");
        (x = in.nextDouble()) > 0;
        sum = sum + x)
    count++;

for (int i = 1; i <= years; i++)
{
```

```
        if (balance >= targetBalance)
            i = years;      // Bad style—modifies counter
        else
        {
            double interest = balance * rate / 100;
            balance = balance + interest;
        }
    }
```

These loops will work, but they are plainly bad style. Use a while loop for iterations that do not fit the for pattern.

Common Error 6.3

Forgetting a Semicolon

Occasionally all the work of a loop is already done in the loop header. Suppose you ignored Quality Tip 6.1 on page 232; then you could write an investment doubling loop as follows:

```
for (years = 1;
        (balance = balance + balance * rate / 100) < targetBalance;
        years++)
    ;
System.out.println(years);
```

The body of the for loop is completely empty, containing just one empty statement terminated by a semicolon.

If you do run into a loop without a body, it is important that you make sure the semicolon is not forgotten. If the semicolon is accidentally omitted, then the next line becomes part of the loop statement!

```
for (years = 1;
        (balance = balance + balance * rate / 100) < targetBalance;
        years++)
System.out.println(years);
```

You can avoid this error by using an empty block { } instead of an empty statement.

Common Error 6.4

A Semicolon Too Many

What does the following loop print?

```
sum = 0;
for (i = 1; i <= 10; i++);
    sum = sum + i;
System.out.println(sum);
```

Of course, this loop is supposed to compute $1 + 2 + \cdots + 10 = 55$. But actually, the print statement prints 11!

Why 11? Have another look. Did you spot the semicolon at the end of the for loop header? This loop is actually a loop with an empty body.

```
for (i = 1; i <= 10; i++)
    ;
```

The loop does nothing 10 times, and when it is finished, sum is still 0 and i is 11. Then the statement

```
sum = sum + i;
```

is executed, and sum is 11. The statement was indented, which fools the human reader. But the compiler pays no attention to indentation.

Of course, the semicolon at the end of the statement was a typing error. Someone's fingers were so used to typing a semicolon at the end of every line that a semicolon was added to the for loop by accident. The result was a loop with an empty body.

Quality Tip 6.2

Don't Use != to Test the End of a Range

Here is a loop with a hidden danger:

```
for (i = 1; i != n; i++)
```

The test i != n is a poor idea. How does the loop behave if n happens to be zero or negative? The test i != n is never false, because i starts at 1 and increases with every step.

The remedy is simple. Use <= rather than != in the condition:

```
for (i = 1; i <= n; i++)
```

Special Topic 6.2

Variables Declared in a for Loop Header

As mentioned, it is legal in Java to declare a variable in the header of a for loop. Here is the most common form of this syntax:

```
for (int i = 1; i <= n; i++)
{
   . . .
}

// i no longer defined here
```

The scope of the variable extends to the end of the for loop. Therefore, i is no longer defined after the loop ends. If you need to use the value of the variable beyond the end of the loop, then you need to declare it outside the loop. In this loop, you don't need the value of i—you know it is n + 1 when the loop is finished. (Actually, that is not quite true—it is possible to break out of a loop before its end; see Special Topic 6.4 on page 246). When you have two or more exit conditions, though, you may still need the variable. For example, consider the loop

```
for (i = 1; balance < targetBalance && i <= n; i++)
{
   . . .
}
```

You want the balance to reach the target, but you are willing to wait only a certain number of years. If the balance doubles sooner, you may want to know the value of i. Therefore, in this case, it is not appropriate to declare the variable in the loop header.

Note that the variables named i in the following pair of for loops are independent:

```
for (int i = 1; i <= 10; i++)
   System.out.println(i * i);
```

```
for (int i = 1; i <= 10; i++) // Declares a new variable i
    System.out.println(i * i * i);
```

In the loop header, you can declare multiple variables, as long as they are of the same type, and you can include multiple update expressions, separated by commas:

```
for (int i = 0, j = 10; i <= 10; i++, j--)
{
    . . .
}
```

However, many people find it confusing if a for loop controls more than one variable. I recommend that you not use this form of the for statement (see Quality Tip 6.1 on page 232). Instead, make the for loop control a single counter, and update the other variable explicitly:

```
int j = 10;
for (int i = 0; i <= 10; i++)
{
    . . .
    j--;
}
```

Quality Tip 6.3

Symmetric and Asymmetric Bounds

It is easy to write a loop with i going from 1 to n:

```
for (i = 1; i <= n; i++) . . .
```

The values for i are bounded by the relation $1 \le i \le n$. Because there are $\le$ comparisons on both bounds, the bounds are called **symmetric**.

When traversing the characters in a string, the bounds are **asymmetric**.

```
for (i = 0; i < str.length(); i++) . . .
```

Make a choice between symmetric and asymmetric loop bounds.

The values for i are bounded by $0 \le i < \text{str.length()}$, with a $\le$ comparison to the left and a $<$ comparison to the right. That is appropriate, because str.length() is not a valid position.

It is not a good idea to force symmetry artificially:

```
for (i = 0; i <= str.length() - 1; i++) . . .
```

That is more difficult to read and understand.

For every loop, consider which form is most natural for the problem, and use that.

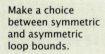

Quality Tip 6.4

Count Iterations

Finding the correct lower and upper bounds for an iteration can be confusing. Should I start at 0? Should I use <= b or < b as a termination condition?

Counting the number of iterations is a very useful device for better understanding a loop. Counting is easier for loops with asymmetric bounds. The loop

```
for (i = a; i < b; i++) . . .
```

is executed b - a times. For example, the loop traversing the characters in a string,

```
for (i = 0; i < str.length(); i++) . . .
```

runs str.length() times. That makes perfect sense, because there are str.length() characters in a string.

The loop with symmetric bounds,

```
for (i = a; i <= b; i++)
```

is executed b - a + 1 times. That "+ 1" is the source of many programming errors. For example,

```
for (n = 0; n <= 10; n++)
```

runs 11 times. Maybe that is what you want; if not, start at 1 or use < 10.

One way to visualize this "+ 1" error is to think of the posts and sections of a fence. Suppose the fence has ten sections (=). How many posts (|) does it have?

|=|=|=|=|=|=|=|=|=|=|

A fence with ten sections has *eleven* posts. Each section has one post to the left, *and* there is one more post after the last section. Forgetting to count the last iteration of a "<=" loop is often called a "fence post error".

If the increment is a value c other than 1, and c divides b - a, then the counts are

$$(b - a) / c \qquad \text{for the asymmetric loop}$$

$$(b - a) / c + 1 \qquad \text{for the symmetric loop}$$

For example, the loop for (i = 10; i <= 40; i += 5) executes $(40 - 10)/5 + 1 = 7$ times.

> **Count the number of iterations to check that your for loop is correct.**

6.3 Common Loop Algorithms

In the following sections, we discuss some of the most common algorithms that are implemented as loops. You can use them as starting points for your loop designs.

6.3.1 Computing a Total

Computing the sum of a number of inputs is a very common task. Keep a *running total:* a variable to which you add each input value. Of course, the total should be initialized with 0.

```
double total = 0;
while (in.hasNextDouble())
{
    double input = in.nextDouble();
    total = total + input;
}
```

6.3.2 Counting Matches

You often want to know how many values fulfill a particular condition. For example, you may want to count how many uppercase letters are in a string. Keep a *counter*, a variable that is initialized with 0 and incremented whenever there is a match.

```
int upperCaseLetters = 0;
for (int i = 0; i < str.length(); i++)
{
```

```
        char ch = str.charAt(i);
        if (Character.isUpperCase(ch))
        {
            upperCaseLetters++;
        }
    }
}
```

For example, if `str` is the string `"Hello, World!"`, `upperCaseLetters` is incremented twice (when `i` is 0 and 7).

6.3.3 Finding the First Match

When you count the values that fulfill a condition, you need to look at all values. However, if your task is to find a match, then you can stop as soon as the condition is fulfilled.

Here is a loop that finds the first lowercase letter in a string. Because we do not visit all elements in a string, a `while` loop is a better choice than a `for` loop:

```
boolean found = false;
char ch = '?';
int position = 0;
while (!found && position < str.length())
{
    ch = str.charAt(position);
    if (Character.isLowerCase(ch)) { found = true; }
    else { position++; }
}
```

If a match was found, then `found` is `true`, `ch` is the first matching character, and its index is stored in the variable `position`. If the loop did not find a match, then `found` remains `false` and the loop continues until `position` reaches `str.length()`.

Note that the variable `ch` is declared *outside* the `while` loop because you may want to use it after the loop has finished.

6.3.4 Prompting Until a Match is Found

In the preceding example, we searched a string for a character that matches a condition. You can apply the same process to user input. Suppose you are asking a user to enter a positive value < 100. Keep asking until the user provides a correct input:

```
boolean valid = false;
double input = 0;
while (!valid)
{
    System.out.print("Please enter a positive value < 100: ");
    input = in.nextDouble();
    if (0 < input && input < 100) { valid = true; }
    else { System.out.println("Invalid input."); }
}
```

As in the preceding example, the variable `input` is declared outside the `while` loop so that you can use it after the loop has finished.

6.3.5 Comparing Adjacent Values

When processing a sequence of values in a loop, you sometimes need to compare a value with the value that just preceded it. For example, suppose you want to check whether a sequence of inputs contains adjacent duplicates such as 1 7 2 9 9 4 9.

Now you face a challenge. Consider the typical loop for reading a value:

```
double input = 0;
while (in.hasNextDouble())
{
    input = in.nextDouble();
    . . .
}
```

How can you compare the current input with the preceding one? At any time, input contains the current input, overwriting the previous one.

The answer is to store the previous input, like this:

```
double input = 0;
while (in.hasNextDouble())
{
    double previous = input;
    input = in.nextDouble();
    if (input == previous) { System.out.println("Duplicate input"); }
}
```

One problem remains. When the loop is entered for the first time, there is no previous input value. You can solve this problem with an initial input operation outside the loop:

```
double input = in.nextDouble();
while (in.hasNextDouble())
{
    double previous = input;
    input = in.nextDouble();
    if (input == previous) { System.out.println("Duplicate input"); }
}
```

6.3.6 Processing Input with Sentinel Values

Suppose you want to process a set of values, for example a set of measurements. Your goal is to analyze the data and display properties of the data set, such as the average or the maximum value. You prompt the user for the first value, then the second value, then the third, and so on. When does the input end?

One common method for indicating the end of a data set is a **sentinel** value, a value that is not part of the data. Instead, the sentinel value indicates that the data has come to an end.

Some programmers choose numbers such as 0 or –1 as sentinel values. But that is not a good idea. These values may well be valid inputs. A better idea is to use an input that is not a number, such as the letter Q. Here is a typical program run:

```
Enter value, Q to quit: 1
Enter value, Q to quit: 2
Enter value, Q to quit: 3
Enter value, Q to quit: 4
Enter value, Q to quit: Q
```

```
Average = 2.5
Maximum = 4.0
```

Of course, we need to read each input as a string, not a number. Once we have tested that the input is not the letter Q, we convert the string into a number.

```
System.out.print("Enter value, Q to quit: ");
String input = in.next();
if (input.equalsIgnoreCase("Q"))
    We are done
else
{
    double x = Double.parseDouble(input);
    . . .
}
```

Now we have another problem. The test for loop termination occurs in the *middle* of the loop, not at the top or the bottom. You must first try to read input before you can test whether you have reached the end of input. In Java, there isn't a ready-made control structure for the pattern "do work, then test, then do more work". Therefore, we use a combination of a `while` loop and a `boolean` variable.

Sometimes, the termination condition of a loop can only be evaluated in the middle of a loop. You can introduce a Boolean variable to control such a loop.

```
boolean done = false;
while (!done)
{
    Print prompt
    String input = read input;
    if (end of input indicated)
        done = true;
    else
    {
        Process input
    }
}
```

This pattern is sometimes called "loop and a half". Some programmers find it clumsy to introduce a control variable for such a loop. Special Topic 6.3 on page 245 shows several alternatives.

Here is a complete program that reads input and analyzes the data. We separate the input handling from the computation of the data set properties by using two classes, DataAnalyzer and DataSet. The DataAnalyzer class handles the input and adds values to a DataSet object with the add method. It then calls the getAverage method and the getMaximum method to obtain the average and maximum of all added data.

ch06/dataset/DataAnalyzer.java

```java
 1  import java.util.Scanner;
 2
 3  /**
 4      This program computes the average and maximum of a set
 5      of input values.
 6  */
 7  public class DataAnalyzer
 8  {
 9      public static void main(String[] args)
10      {
11          Scanner in = new Scanner(System.in);
12          DataSet data = new DataSet();
13
```

```
14       boolean done = false;
15       while (!done)
16       {
17          System.out.print("Enter value, Q to quit: ");
18          String input = in.next();
19          if (input.equalsIgnoreCase("Q"))
20             done = true;
21          else
22          {
23             double x = Double.parseDouble(input);
24             data.add(x);
25          }
26       }
27
28       System.out.println("Average = " + data.getAverage());
29       System.out.println("Maximum = " + data.getMaximum());
30    }
31 }
```

ch06/dataset/DataSet.java

```
1  /**
2        Computes information about a set of data values.
3  */
4  public class DataSet
5  {
6     private double sum;
7     private double maximum;
8     private int count;
9
10    /**
11          Constructs an empty data set.
12    */
13    public DataSet()
14    {
15       sum = 0;
16       count = 0;
17       maximum = 0;
18    }
19
20    /**
21          Adds a data value to the data set.
22          @param x a data value
23    */
24    public void add(double x)
25    {
26       sum = sum + x;
27       if (count == 0 || maximum < x) maximum = x;
28       count++;
29    }
30
31    /**
32          Gets the average of the added data.
33          @return the average or 0 if no data has been added
34    */
35    public double getAverage()
36    {
```

```
37        if (count == 0) return 0;
38        else return sum / count;
39     }
40
41     /**
42        Gets the largest of the added data.
43        @return the maximum or 0 if no data has been added
44     */
45     public double getMaximum()
46     {
47        return maximum;
48     }
49  }
```

Program Run

```
Enter value, Q to quit: 10
Enter value, Q to quit: 0
Enter value, Q to quit: -1
Enter value, Q to quit: Q
Average = 3.0
Maximum = 10.0
```

SELF CHECK

5. How do you compute the total of all positive inputs?
6. What happens with the algorithm in Section 6.3.5 when no input is provided at all? How can you overcome that problem?
7. Why does the DataAnalyzer class call in.next and not in.nextDouble?
8. Would the DataSet class still compute the correct maximum if you simplified the update of the maximum variable in the add method to the following statement?

   ```
   if (maximum < x) maximum = x;
   ```

HOW TO 6.1

Writing a Loop

This How To walks you through the process of implementing a loop statement. We will illustrate the steps with the following example problem:

Read twelve temperature values (one for each month), and display the number of the month with the highest temperature. For example, according to http://worldclimate.com, the average maximum temperatures for Death Valley are (in order by month):

18.2 22.6 26.4 31.1 36.6 42.2
45.7 44.5 40.2 33.1 24.2 17.6

In this case, the month with the highest temperature (45.7 degrees Celsius) is July, and the program should display 7.

Step 1   Decide what work must be done *inside* the loop.

Every loop needs to do some kind of repetitive work, such as

- Reading another item.
- Updating a value (such as a bank balance or total).
- Incrementing a counter.

If you can't figure out what needs to go inside the loop, start by writing down the steps that you would take if you solved the problem by hand. For example, with the temperature reading problem, you might write

> Read first value.
> Read second value.
> If second value is higher than the first, set highest temperature to that value, highest month to 2.
> Read next value.
> If value is higher than the first and second, set highest temperature to that value, highest month to 3.
> Read next value.
> If value is higher than the highest temperature seen so far, set highest temperature to that value,
>   highest month to 4.
> . . .

Now look at these steps and reduce them to a set of *uniform* actions that can be placed into the loop body. The first action is easy:

> Read next value.

The next action is trickier. In our description, we used tests "higher than the first", "higher than the first and second", "higher than the highest temperature seen so far". We need to settle on one test that works for all iterations. The last formulation is the most general.

Similarly, we must find a general way of setting the highest month. We need a variable that stores the current month, running from 1 to 12. Then we can formulate the second loop action:

> If value is higher than the highest temperature, set highest temperature to that value,
>   highest month to current month.

Altogether our loop is

> Loop
>   Read next value.
>   If value is higher than the highest temperature, set highest temperature to that value,
>   highest month to current month.
>   Increment current month.

Step 2 Specify the loop condition.

What goal do you want to reach in your loop? Typical examples are

- Has a counter reached its final value?
- Have you read the last input value?
- Has a value reached a given threshold?

In our example, we simply want the current month to reach 12.

Step 3 Determine the loop type.

We distinguish between two major loop types. A *definite* or *count-controlled* loop is executed a definite number of times. In an *indefinite* or *event-controlled* loop, the number of iterations is not known in advance—the loop is executed until some event happens. A typical example of the latter is a loop that reads data until a sentinel is encountered.

Definite loops can be implemented as for statements. When you have an indefinite loop, consider the loop condition. Does it involve values that are only set inside the loop body? In that case, you should choose a do loop to ensure that the loop is executed at least once before the loop condition is be evaluated. Otherwise, use a while loop.

Sometimes, the condition for terminating a loop changes in the middle of the loop body. In that case, you can use a Boolean variable that specifies when you are ready to leave the loop. Follow this pattern:

```
boolean done = false;
while (!done)
{
    Do some work
    If all work has been completed
    {
        done = true;
    }
    else
    {
        Do more work
    }
}
```

Such a variable is called a *flag*.

In summary,

- If you know in advance how many times a loop is repeated, use a for loop.
- If the loop must be executed at least once, use a do loop.
- Otherwise, use a while loop.

In our example, we read 12 temperature values. Therefore, we choose a for loop.

Step 4   Set up variables for entering the loop for the first time.

List all variables that are used and updated in the loop, and determine how to initialize them. Commonly, counters are initialized with 0 or 1, totals with 0.

In our example, the variables are

```
current month
highest value
highest month
```

We need to be careful how we set up the highest temperature value. We can't simply set it to 0. After all, our program needs to work with temperature values from Antarctica, all of which may be negative.

A good option is to set the highest temperature value to the first input value. Of course, then we need to remember to only read in another 11 values, with the current month starting at 2.

We also need to initialize the highest month with 1. After all, in an Australian city, we may never find a month that is warmer than January.

Step 5   Process the result after the loop has finished.

In many cases, the desired result is simply a variable that was updated in the loop body. For example, in our temperature program, the result is the highest month. Sometimes, the loop computes values that contribute to the final result. For example, suppose you are asked to average the temperatures. Then the loop should compute the sum, not the average. After the loop has completed, you are ready compute the average: divide the sum by the number of inputs.

Here is our complete loop.

```
Read first value; store as highest value.
highest month = 1
```

```
for (current month = 2; current month <= 12; current month++)
   Read next value.
   If value is higher than the highest value, set highest value to that value,
      highest month to current month.
```

Step 6 Trace the loop with typical examples.

Hand trace your loop code, as described in Productivity Hint 6.1 on page 223. Choose example values that are not too complex—executing the loop 3–5 times is enough to check for the most common errors. Pay special attention when entering the loop for the first and last time.

Sometimes, you want to make a slight modification to make tracing feasible. For example, when hand tracing the investment doubling problem, use an interest rate of 20 percent rather than 5 percent. When hand tracing the temperature loop, use 4 data values, not 12.

Let's say the data are 22.6 36.6 44.5 24.2. Here is the walkthrough:

current month	current value	highest month	highest value
		~~1~~	~~22.6~~
~~2~~	36.6	~~2~~	~~36.6~~
~~3~~	44.5	3	44.5
4	24.2		

The trace demonstrates that **highest month** and **highest value** are properly set.

Step 7 Implement the loop in Java.

Here's the loop for our example. Exercise P6.1 asks you to complete the program.

```java
double highestValue = in.nextDouble();
int highestMonth = 1;
for (int currentMonth = 2; currentMonth <= 12; currentMonth++)
{
   double nextValue = in.nextDouble();
   if (nextValue > highestValue)
   {
      highestValue = nextValue;
      highestMonth = currentMonth;
   }
}
```

➕ *Worked
Example 6.1*

Credit Card Processing

This Worked Example uses a loop to remove spaces from a credit card number.

➕ Available online in WileyPLUS and at www.wiley.com/college/horstmann.

Special Topic 6.3

The "Loop and a Half" Problem

Reading input data sometimes requires a loop such as the following, which is somewhat unsightly:

```java
boolean done = false;
while (!done)
{
   String input = in.next();
   if (input.equalsIgnoreCase("Q"))
      done = true;
   else
   {
      Process data
   }
}
```

The true test for loop termination is in the middle of the loop, not at the top. This is called a "loop and a half", because one must go halfway into the loop before knowing whether one needs to terminate.

Some programmers dislike the introduction of an additional Boolean variable for loop control. Two Java language features can be used to alleviate the "loop and a half" problem. I don't think either is a superior solution, but both approaches are fairly common, so it is worth knowing about them when reading other people's code.

You can combine an assignment and a test in the loop condition:

```java
while (!(input = in.next()).equalsIgnoreCase("Q"))
{
   Process data
}
```

The expression

```java
(input = in.next()).equalsIgnoreCase("Q")
```

means, "First call `in.next()`, then assign the result to `input`, then test whether it equals `"Q"`". This is an expression with a side effect. The primary purpose of the expression is to serve as a test for the `while` loop, but it also does some work—namely, reading the input and storing it in the variable `input`. In general, it is a bad idea to use side effects, because they make a program hard to read and maintain. In this case, however, that practice is somewhat seductive, because it eliminates the control variable `done`, which also makes the code hard to read and maintain.

The other solution is to exit the loop from the middle, either by a `return` statement or by a `break` statement (see Special Topic 6.4 on page 246).

```java
public void processInput(Scanner in)
{
   while (true)
   {
      String input = in.next();
      if (input.equalsIgnoreCase("Q"))
         return;
      Process data
   }
}
```

Special Topic 6.4

The break and continue Statements

You already encountered the break statement in Special Topic 5.2, where it was used to exit a switch statement. In addition to breaking out of a switch statement, a break statement can also be used to exit a while, for, or do loop. For example, the break statement in the following loop terminates the loop when the end of input is reached.

```
while (true)
{
    String input = in.next();
    if (input.equalsIgnoreCase("Q"))
        break;
    double x = Double.parseDouble(input);
    data.add(x);
}
```

In general, a break is a very poor way of exiting a loop. In 1990, a misused break caused an AT&T 4ESS telephone switch to fail, and the failure propagated through the entire U.S. network, rendering it nearly unusable for about nine hours. A programmer had used a break to terminate an if statement. Unfortunately, break cannot be used with if, so the program execution broke out of the enclosing switch statement, skipping some variable initializations and running into chaos (*Expert C Programming*, Peter van der Linden, Prentice-Hall 1994, p.38). Using break statements also makes it difficult to use *correctness proof* techniques (see Special Topic 6.5 on page 255).

However, when faced with the bother of introducing a separate loop control variable, some programmers find that break statements are beneficial in the "loop and a half" case. This issue is often the topic of heated (and quite unproductive) debate. In this book, we won't use the break statement, and we leave it to you to decide whether you like to use it in your own programs.

In Java, there is a second form of the break statement that is used to break out of a nested statement. The statement break *label*; immediately jumps to the *end* of the statement that is tagged with a label. Any statement (including if and block statements) can be tagged with a label—the syntax is

label: *statement*

The labeled break statement was invented to break out of a set of nested loops.

```
outerloop:
while (outer loop condition)
{  . . .
    while (inner loop condition)
    {  . . .
        if (something really bad happened)
            break outerloop;
    }
}
Jumps here if something really bad happened
```

Naturally, this situation is quite rare. We recommend that you try to introduce additional methods instead of using complicated nested loops.

Finally, there is the continue statement, which jumps to the end of the *current iteration* of the loop. Here is a possible use for this statement:

```
while (!done)
{
    String input = in.next();
    if (input.equalsIgnoreCase("Q"))
    {
```

```
        done = true;
        continue; // Jump to the end of the loop body
    }
    double x = Double.parseDouble(input);
    data.add(x);
    // continue statement jumps here
}
```

By using the `continue` statement, you don't need to place the remainder of the loop code inside an `else` clause. This is a minor benefit. Few programmers use this statement.

6.4 Nested Loops

> When the body of a loop contains another loop, the loops are nested. A typical use of nested loops is printing a table with rows and columns.

Sometimes, the body of a loop is again a loop. We say that the inner loop is **nested** inside an outer loop. This happens often when you process two-dimensional structures, such as tables.

Let's look at an example that looks a bit more interesting than a table of numbers. We want to generate the following triangular shape:

```
[]
[][]
[][][]
[][][][]
[][][][][]
[][][][][][]
[][][][][][][]
```

The basic idea is simple. We generate a sequence of rows:

```
for (int i = 1; i <= width; i++)
{
    // Make triangle row
    . . .
}
```

How do you make a triangle row? Use another loop to concatenate the squares `[]` for that row. Then add a newline character at the end of the row. The `i`th row has `i` symbols, so the loop counter goes from 1 to `i`.

```
for (int j = 1; j <= i; j++)
    r = r + "[]";
r = r + "\n";
```

Putting both loops together yields two *nested loops:*

```
String r = "";
for (int i = 1; i <= width; i++)
{
    // Make triangle row
    for (int j = 1; j <= i; j++)
        r = r + "[]";
    r = r + "\n";
}
return r;
```

Here is the complete program:

ch06/triangle1/Triangle.java

```java
1  /**
2      This class describes triangle objects that can be displayed
3      as shapes like this:
4      []
5      [][]
6      [][][].
7  */
8  public class Triangle
9  {
10     private int width;
11
12     /**
13         Constructs a triangle.
14         @param aWidth the number of [] in the last row of the triangle
15     */
16     public Triangle(int aWidth)
17     {
18        width = aWidth;
19     }
20
21     /**
22         Computes a string representing the triangle.
23         @return a string consisting of [] and newline characters
24     */
25     public String toString()
26     {
27        String r = "";
28        for (int i = 1; i <= width; i++)
29        {
30           // Make triangle row
31           for (int j = 1; j <= i; j++)
32              r = r + "[]";
33           r = r + "\n";
34        }
35        return r;
36     }
37  }
```

ch06/triangle1/TriangleRunner.java

```java
1  /**
2      This program prints two triangles.
3  */
4  public class TriangleRunner
5  {
6     public static void main(String[] args)
7     {
8        Triangle small = new Triangle(3);
9        System.out.println(small.toString());
10
11        Triangle large = new Triangle(15);
12        System.out.println(large.toString());
13     }
14  }
```

Program Run

```
[]
[] []
[] [] []

[]
[] []
[] [] []
[] [] [] []
[] [] [] [] []
[] [] [] [] [] []
[] [] [] [] [] [] []
[] [] [] [] [] [] [] []
[] [] [] [] [] [] [] [] []
[] [] [] [] [] [] [] [] [] []
[] [] [] [] [] [] [] [] [] [] []
[] [] [] [] [] [] [] [] [] [] [] []
[] [] [] [] [] [] [] [] [] [] [] [] []
[] [] [] [] [] [] [] [] [] [] [] [] [] []
```

Table 3   Nested Loop Examples

Nested Loops	Output	Explanation
``for (i = 1; i <= 3; i++)
{
for (j = 1; j <= 4; j++) { Print "*" }
System.out.println();
}```	```****
****
****```	Prints 3 rows of 4 asterisks each.
``for (i = 1; i <= 4; i++)
{
for (j = 1; j <= 3; j++) { Print "*" }
System.out.println();
}```	```***
***
***
***```	Prints 4 rows of 3 asterisks each.
``for (i = 1; i <= 4; i++)
{
for (j = 1; j <= i; j++) { Print "*" }
System.out.println();
}```	```*
**
***
****```	Prints 4 rows of lengths 1, 2, 3, and 4.
``for (i = 1; i <= 3; i++)
{
for (j = 1; j <= 5; j++)
{
if (j % 2 == 0) { Print "*" }
else { Print "-" }
}
System.out.println();
}```	```-*-*-
-*-*-
-*-*-```	Prints asterisks in even columns, dashes in odd columns.

Table 3 Nested Loop Examples, continued		
Nested Loops	**Output**	**Explanation**
``for (i = 1; i <= 3; i++)
{
for (j = 1; j <= 5; j++)
{
if ((i + j) % 2 == 0) { Print "*" }
else { Print " " }
}
System.out.println();
}```	* * * * * * * *	Prints a checkerboard pattern.

SELF CHECK

9. How would you modify the nested loops so that you print a square instead of a triangle?

10. What is the value of n after the following nested loops?

```
int n = 0;
for (int i = 1; i <= 5; i++)
   for (int j = 0; j < i; j++)
      n = n + j;
```

➕ **Worked Example 6.2**

Manipulating the Pixels in an Image

This Worked Example shows how to use nested loops for manipulating the pixels in an image. The outer loop traverses the rows of the image, and the inner loop accesses each pixel of a row.

6.5 Application: Random Numbers and Simulations

In a simulation, you repeatedly generate random numbers and use them to simulate an activity.

A *simulation program* uses the computer to simulate an activity in the real world (or an imaginary one). Simulations are commonly used for predicting climate change, analyzing traffic, picking stocks, and many other applications in science and business. In many simulations, one or more loops are used to modify the state of a system and observe the changes.

Here is a typical problem that can be decided by running a simulation: the *Buffon needle experiment*, devised by Comte Georges-Louis Leclerc de Buffon (1707–1788), a French naturalist. On each *try*, a one-inch long needle is dropped onto paper that is ruled with lines 2 inches apart. If the needle drops onto a line, count it as a hit. (See Figure 5.) Buffon conjectured that the quotient *tries/hits* approximates π.

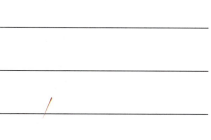

Figure 5 The Buffon Needle Experiment

Now, how can you run this experiment in the computer? You don't actually want to build a robot that drops needles on paper. The Random class of the Java library implements a *random number generator*, which produces numbers that appear to be completely random. To generate random numbers, you construct an object of the Random class, and then apply one of the following methods:

Method	Returns
nextInt(n)	A random integer between the integers 0 (inclusive) and n (exclusive)
nextDouble()	A random floating-point number between 0 (inclusive) and 1 (exclusive)

For example, you can simulate the cast of a die as follows:

```
Random generator = new Random();
int d = 1 + generator.nextInt(6);
```

The call generator.nextInt(6) gives you a random number between 0 and 5 (inclusive). Add 1 to obtain a number between 1 and 6.

To give you a feeling for the random numbers, run the following program a few times.

ch06/random1/Die.java

```java
 1  import java.util.Random;
 2
 3  /**
 4     This class models a die that, when cast, lands on a random
 5     face.
 6  */
 7  public class Die
 8  {
 9     private Random generator;
10     private int sides;
11
12     /**
13        Constructs a die with a given number of sides.
14        @param s the number of sides, e.g., 6 for a normal die
15     */
16     public Die(int s)
17     {
```

```
18        sides = s;
19        generator = new Random();
20     }
21
22     /**
23        Simulates a throw of the die.
24        @return the face of the die
25     */
26     public int cast()
27     {
28        return 1 + generator.nextInt(sides);
29     }
30  }
```

ch06/random1/DieSimulator.java

```
1  /**
2     This program simulates casting a die ten times.
3  */
4  public class DieSimulator
5  {
6     public static void main(String[] args)
7     {
8        Die d = new Die(6);
9        final int TRIES = 10;
10       for (int i = 1; i <= TRIES; i++)
11       {
12          int n = d.cast();
13          System.out.print(n + " ");
14       }
15       System.out.println();
16    }
17 }
```

Typical Program Run

```
6 5 6 3 2 6 3 4 4 1
```

Typical Program Run (Second Run)

```
3 2 2 1 6 5 3 4 1 2
```

As you can see, this program produces a different stream of simulated die casts every time it is run.

Actually, the numbers are not completely random. They are drawn from very long sequences of numbers that don't repeat for a long time. These sequences are computed from fairly simple formulas; they just behave like random numbers. For that reason, they are often called **pseudorandom numbers**. Generating good sequences of numbers that behave like truly random sequences is an important and well-studied problem in computer science. We won't investigate this issue further, though; we'll just use the random numbers produced by the Random class.

To run the Buffon needle experiment, we have to work a little harder. When you throw a die, it has to come up with one of six faces. When throwing a needle, however, there are many possible outcomes. You must generate *two* random numbers: one to describe the starting position and one to describe the angle of the needle with

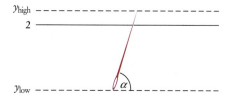

Figure 6 When Does the Needle Fall on a Line?

the x-axis. Then you need to test whether the needle touches a grid line. Stop after 10,000 tries.

Let us agree to generate the *lower* point of the needle. Its x-coordinate is irrelevant, and you may assume its y-coordinate y_{low} to be any random number between 0 and 2. However, because it can be a random **floating-point number**, we use the nextDouble method of the Random class. It returns a random floating-point number between 0 and 1. Multiply by 2 to get a random number between 0 and 2.

The angle α between the needle and the x-axis can be any value between 0 degrees and 180 degrees. The upper end of the needle has y-coordinate

$$y_{high} = y_{low} + \sin(\alpha)$$

The needle is a hit if y_{high} is at least 2. See Figure 6.

Here is the program to carry out the simulation of the needle experiment.

ch06/random2/Needle.java

```java
1   import java.util.Random;
2
3   /**
4       This class simulates a needle in the Buffon needle experiment.
5   */
6   public class Needle
7   {
8       private Random generator;
9       private int hits;
10      private int tries;
11
12      /**
13          Constructs a needle.
14      */
15      public Needle()
16      {
17          hits = 0;
18          tries = 0;
19          generator = new Random();
20      }
21
```

```
22   /**
23       Drops the needle on the grid of lines and
24       remembers whether the needle hit a line.
25   */
26   public void drop()
27   {
28       double ylow = 2 * generator.nextDouble();
29       double angle = 180 * generator.nextDouble();
30
31       // Computes high point of needle
32
33       double yhigh = ylow + Math.sin(Math.toRadians(angle));
34       if (yhigh >= 2) hits++;
35       tries++;
36   }
37
38   /**
39       Gets the number of times the needle hit a line.
40       @return the hit count
41   */
42   public int getHits()
43   {
44       return hits;
45   }
46
47   /**
48       Gets the total number of times the needle was dropped.
49       @return the try count
50   */
51   public int getTries()
52   {
53       return tries;
54   }
55 }
```

ch06/random2/NeedleSimulator.java

```
1  /**
2      This program simulates the Buffon needle experiment
3      and prints the resulting approximations of pi.
4  */
5  public class NeedleSimulator
6  {
7      public static void main(String[] args)
8      {
9          Needle n = new Needle();
10         final int TRIES1 = 10000;
11         final int TRIES2 = 1000000;
12
13         for (int i = 1; i <= TRIES1; i++)
14             n.drop();
15         System.out.printf("Tries = %d, Tries / Hits = %8.5f\n",
16             TRIES1, (double) n.getTries() / n.getHits());
17
18         for (int i = TRIES1 + 1; i <= TRIES2; i++)
19             n.drop();
20         System.out.printf("Tries = %d, Tries / Hits = %8.5f\n",
21             TRIES2, (double) n.getTries() / n.getHits());
22     }
23 }
```

Program Run

```
Tries = 10000, Tries / Hits =  3.08928
Tries = 1000000, Tries / Hits =  3.14204
```

The point of this program is not to compute π—there are far more efficient ways to do that. Rather, the point is to show how a physical experiment can be simulated on the computer. Buffon had to physically drop the needle thousands of times and record the results, which must have been a rather dull activity. The computer can execute the experiment quickly and accurately.

Simulations are very common computer applications. Many simulations use essentially the same pattern as the code of this example: In a loop, a large number of sample values are generated, and the values of certain observations are recorded for each sample. When the simulation is completed, the averages, or other statistics of interest from the observed values are printed out.

A typical example of a simulation is the modeling of customer queues at a bank or a supermarket. Rather than observing real customers, one simulates their arrival and their transactions at the teller window or checkout stand in the computer. One can try different staffing or building layout patterns in the computer simply by making changes in the program. In the real world, making many such changes and measuring their effects would be impossible, or at least, very expensive.

 **SELF CHECK**

11. How do you use a random number generator to simulate the toss of a coin?

12. Why is the NeedleSimulator program not an efficient method for computing π?

Special Topic 6.5

Loop Invariants

Consider the task of computing a^n, where a is a floating-point number and n is a positive integer. Of course, you can multiply $a \cdot a \cdot \ldots \cdot a$, n times, but if n is large, you'll end up doing a lot of multiplication. The following loop computes a^n in far fewer steps:

```
double a = . . .;
int n = . . .;
double r = 1;
double b = a;
int i = n;
while (i > 0)
{
   if (i % 2 == 0) // n is even
   {
      b = b * b;
      i = i / 2;
   }
   else
   {
      r = r * b;
      i--;
   }
}
// Now r equals a to the nth power
```

Consider the case n = 100. The method performs the steps shown in the table below.

Computing a^{100}		
b	**i**	**r**
a	100	1
a^2	50	
a^4	25	
	24	a^4
a^8	12	
a^{16}	6	
a^{32}	3	
	2	a^{36}
a^{64}	1	
	0	a^{100}

Amazingly enough, the algorithm yields exactly a^{100}. Do you understand why? Are you convinced it will work for all values of n? Here is a clever argument to show that the method always computes the correct result. It demonstrates that whenever the program reaches the top of the while loop, it is true that

$$r \cdot b^i = a^n \qquad\qquad (I)$$

Certainly, it is true the first time around, because b = a and i = n. Suppose that (I) holds at the beginning of the loop. Label the values of r, b, and i as "old" when entering the loop, and as "new" when exiting the loop. Assume that upon entry

$$r_{old} \cdot b_{old}^{i_{old}} = a^n$$

In the loop you must distinguish two cases: i_{old} even and i_{old} odd. If i_{old} is even, the loop performs the following transformations:

$$r_{new} = r_{old}$$
$$b_{new} = b_{old}^2$$
$$i_{new} = i_{old}/2$$

Therefore,

$$r_{new} \cdot b_{new}^{i_{new}} = r_{old} \cdot \left(b_{old}\right)^{2 \cdot i_{old}/2}$$
$$= r_{old} \cdot b_{old}^{i_{old}}$$
$$= a^n$$

On the other hand, if i_{old} is odd, then

$$r_{new} = r_{old} \cdot b_{old}$$
$$b_{new} = b_{old}$$
$$i_{new} = i_{old} - 1$$

Therefore,

$$r_{new} \cdot b_{new}{}^{i_{new}} = r_{old} \cdot b_{old} \cdot b_{old}{}^{i_{old}-1}$$
$$= r_{old} \cdot b_{old}{}^{i_{old}}$$
$$= a^n$$

In either case, the new values for r, b, and i fulfill the *loop invariant* (I). So what? When the loop finally exits, (I) holds again:

$$r \cdot b^i = a^n$$

Furthermore, we know that i = 0, because the loop is terminating. But because i = 0, $r \cdot b^i = r \cdot b^0 = r$. Hence r = a^n, and the method really does compute the nth power of a.

This technique is quite useful, because it can explain an algorithm that is not at all obvious. The condition (I) is called a **loop invariant** because it is true when the loop is entered, at the top of each pass, and when the loop is exited. If a loop invariant is chosen skillfully, you may be able to deduce correctness of a computation. See *Programming Pearls* (Jon Bentley, Addison-Wesley 1986, Chapter 4) for another nice example.

6.6 Using a Debugger

As you have undoubtedly realized by now, computer programs rarely run perfectly the first time. At times, it can be quite frustrating to find the bugs. Of course, you can insert print commands, run the program, and try to analyze the printout. If the printout does not clearly point to the problem, you may need to add and remove print commands and run the program again. That can be a time-consuming process.

> A debugger is a program that you can use to execute another program and analyze its run-time behavior.

Modern development environments contain special programs, called **debuggers**, that help you locate bugs by letting you follow the execution of a program. You can stop and restart your program and see the contents of variables whenever your program is temporarily stopped. At each stop, you have the choice of what variables to inspect and how many program steps to run until the next stop.

Some people feel that debuggers are just a tool to make programmers lazy. Admittedly some people write sloppy programs and then fix them up with a debugger, but the majority of programmers make an honest effort to write the best program they can before trying to run it through a debugger. These programmers realize that a debugger, while more convenient than print commands, is not cost-free. It does take time to set up and carry out an effective debugging session.

In actual practice, you cannot avoid using a debugger. The larger your programs get, the harder it is to debug them simply by inserting print commands. You will find that the time investment to learn about a debugger is amply repaid in your programming career.

Like compilers, debuggers vary widely from one system to another. On some systems they are quite primitive and require you to memorize a small set of arcane commands; on others they have an intuitive window interface. The screen shots in this chapter show the debugger in the Eclipse development environment, downloadable for free from the Eclipse Foundation web site (eclipse.org). Other integrated environments, such as BlueJ, also include debuggers. A free standalone debugger called JSwat is available from www.bluemarsh.com/java/jswat.

You will have to find out how to prepare a program for debugging and how to start a debugger on your system. If you use an integrated development environment, which contains an editor, compiler, and debugger, this step is usually very easy. You just build the program in the usual way and pick a menu command to start debugging. On some systems, you must manually build a debug version of your program and invoke the debugger.

Once you have started the debugger, you can go a long way with just three debugging commands: "set breakpoint", "single step", and "inspect variable". The names and keystrokes or mouse clicks for these commands differ widely between debuggers, but all debuggers support these basic commands. You can find out how, either from the documentation or a lab manual, or by asking someone who has used the debugger before.

When you start the debugger, it runs at full speed until it reaches a **breakpoint**. Then execution stops, and the breakpoint that causes the stop is displayed (see Figure 7). You can now inspect variables and step through the program a line at a time, or continue running the program at full speed until it reaches the next breakpoint. When the program terminates, the debugger stops as well.

Breakpoints stay active until you remove them, so you should periodically clear the breakpoints that you no longer need.

> You can make effective use of a debugger by mastering just three concepts: breakpoints, single-stepping, and inspecting variables.

> When a debugger executes a program, the execution is suspended whenever a breakpoint is reached.

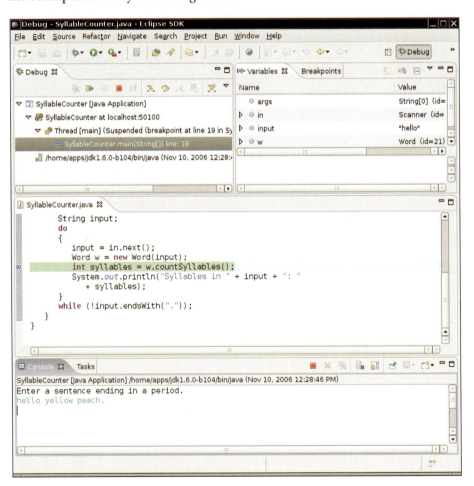

Figure 7 Stopping at a Breakpoint

Figure 8
Inspecting Variables

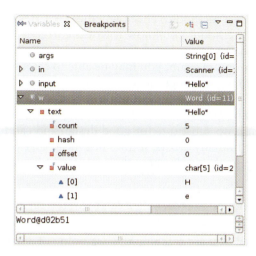

Once the program has stopped, you can look at the current values of variables. Again, the method for selecting the variables differs among debuggers. Some debuggers always show you a window with the current local variables. On other debuggers you issue a command such as "inspect variable" and type in or click on the variable. The debugger then displays the contents of the variable. If all variables contain what you expected, you can run the program until the next point where you want to stop.

When inspecting objects, you often need to give a command to "open up" the object, for example by clicking on a tree node. Once the object is opened up, you see its instance variables (see Figure 8).

Running to a breakpoint gets you there speedily, but you don't know how the program got there. You can also step through the program a line at a time. Then you know how the program flows, but it can take a long time to step through it. The *single-step command* executes the current line and stops at the next program line. Most debuggers have two single-step commands, one called *step into*, which steps inside method calls, and one called *step over*, which skips over method calls.

For example, suppose the current line is

> The single-step command executes the program one line at a time.

```
String input = in.next();
Word w = new Word(input);
int syllables = w.countSyllables();
System.out.println("Syllables in " + input + ": " + syllables);
```

When you step over method calls, you get to the next line:

```
String input = in.next();
Word w = new Word(input);
int syllables = w.countSyllables();
System.out.println("Syllables in " + input + ": " + syllables);
```

However, if you step into method calls, you enter the first line of the countSyllables method.

```
public int countSyllables()
{
    int count = 0;
    int end = text.length() - 1;
    . . .
}
```

You should step *into* a method to check whether it carries out its job correctly. You should step *over* a method if you know it works correctly.

Finally, when the program has finished running, the debug session is also finished. To run the program again, you may be able to reset the debugger, or you may need to exit the debugging program and start over. Details depend on the particular debugger.

A debugger can be an effective tool for finding and removing bugs in your program. However, it is no substitute for good design and careful programming. If the debugger does not find any errors, it does not mean that your program is bug-free. Testing and debugging can only show the presence of bugs, not their absence.

A debugger can be used only to analyze the presence of bugs, not to show that a program is bug-free.

SELF CHECK

13. In the debugger, you are reaching a call to System.out.println. Should you step into the method or step over it?

14. In the debugger, you are reaching the beginning of a method with a couple of loops inside. You want to find out the return value that is computed at the end of the method. Should you set a breakpoint, or should you step through the method?

How To 6.2   **Debugging**

Now you know about the mechanics of debugging, but all that knowledge may still leave you helpless when you fire up a debugger to look at a sick program. There are a number of strategies that you can use to recognize bugs and their causes.

Step 1   Reproduce the error.

As you test your program, you notice that it sometimes does something wrong. It gives the wrong output, it seems to print something completely random, it goes in an infinite loop, or it crashes. Find out exactly how to reproduce that behavior. What numbers did you enter? Where did you click with the mouse?

Run the program again; type in exactly the same numbers, and click with the mouse on the same spots (or as close as you can get). Does the program exhibit the same behavior? If so, then it makes sense to fire up a debugger to study this particular problem. Debuggers are good for analyzing particular failures. They aren't terribly useful for studying a program in general.

Step 2   Simplify the error.

Before you fire up a debugger, it makes sense to spend a few minutes trying to come up with a simpler input that also produces an error. Can you use shorter words or simpler numbers and still have the program misbehave? If so, use those values during your debugging session.

Step 3   Divide and conquer.

Use the divide-and-conquer technique to locate the point of failure of a program.

Now that you have a particular failure, you want to get as close to the failure as possible. The key point of debugging is to locate the code that produces the failure. Just as with real insect pests, finding the bug can be hard, but once you find it, squashing it is usually the easy part. Suppose your program dies with a division by 0. Because there are many division operations in a typical program, it is often not feasible to set breakpoints to all of them. Instead, use a technique of divide and conquer. Step over the methods in main, but don't step inside them. Eventually, the failure will happen again. Now you know which method contains the bug: It is the last method that was called from main before the program died. Restart the debugger and go back to that line in main, then step inside that method. Repeat the process.

Eventually, you will have pinpointed the line that contains the bad division. Maybe it is completely obvious from the code why the denominator is not correct. If not, you need to find the location where it is computed. Unfortunately, you can't go back in the debugger. You need to restart the program and move to the point where the denominator computation happens.

Step 4 Know what your program should do.

During debugging, compare the actual contents of variables against the values you know they should have.

A debugger shows you what the program does. You must know what the program *should* do, or you will not be able to find bugs. Before you trace through a loop, ask yourself how many iterations you expect the program to make. Before you inspect a variable, ask yourself what you expect to see. If you have no clue, set aside some time and think first. Have a calculator handy to make independent computations. When you know what the value should be, inspect the variable. This is the moment of truth. If the program is still on the right track, then that value is what you expected, and you must look further for the bug. If the value is different, you may be on to something. Double-check your computation. If you are sure your value is correct, find out why your program comes up with a different value.

In many cases, program bugs are the result of simple errors such as loop termination conditions that are off by one. Quite often, however, programs make computational errors. Maybe they are supposed to add two numbers, but by accident the code was written to subtract them. Unlike your calculus instructor, programs don't make a special effort to ensure that everything is a simple integer (and neither do real-world problems). You will need to make some calculations with large integers or nasty floating-point numbers. Sometimes these calculations can be avoided if you just ask yourself, "Should this quantity be positive? Should it be larger than that value?" Then inspect variables to verify those theories.

Step 5 Look at all details.

When you debug a program, you often have a theory about what the problem is. Nevertheless, keep an open mind and look around at all details. What strange messages are displayed? Why does the program take another unexpected action? These details count. When you run a debugging session, you really are a detective who needs to look at every clue available.

If you notice another failure on the way to the problem that you are about to pin down, don't just say, "I'll come back to it later". That very failure may be the original cause for your current problem. It is better to make a note of the current problem, fix what you just found, and then return to the original mission.

Step 6 Make sure you understand each bug before you fix it.

Once you find that a loop makes too many iterations, it is very tempting to apply a "Band-Aid" solution and subtract 1 from a variable so that the particular problem doesn't appear again. Such a quick fix has an overwhelming probability of creating trouble elsewhere. You really need to have a thorough understanding of how the program should be written before you apply a fix.

It does occasionally happen that you find bug after bug and apply fix after fix, and the problem just moves around. That usually is a symptom of a larger problem with the program logic. There is little you can do with the debugger. You must rethink the program design and reorganize it.

➕ *Worked Example 6.3*

A Sample Debugging Session

This Worked Example shows how to find bugs in an algorithm for counting the syllables of a word.

➕ Available online in WileyPLUS and at www.wiley.com/college/horstmann.

Random Fact 6.1

The First Bug

According to legend, the first bug was one found in 1947 in the Mark II, a huge electro-mechanical computer at Harvard University. It really was caused by a bug—a moth was trapped in a relay switch. Actually, from the note that the operator left in the log book next to the moth (see the figure), it appears as if the term "bug" had already been in active use at the time.

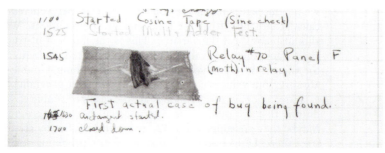

The First Bug

The pioneering computer scientist Maurice Wilkes wrote: "Somehow, at the Moore School and afterwards, one had always assumed there would be no particular difficulty in getting programs right. I can remember the exact instant in time at which it dawned on me that a great part of my future life would be spent finding mistakes in my own programs."

Summary of Learning Objectives

Explain the flow of execution in a loop.

- A `while` statement executes a block of code repeatedly. A condition controls for how long the loop is executed.
- An off-by-one error is a common error when programming loops. Think through simple test cases to avoid this type of error.

Use for loops to implement counting loops.

- You use a `for` loop when a variable runs from a starting to an ending value with a constant increment or decrement.
- Make a choice between symmetric and asymmetric loop bounds.
- Count the number of iterations to check that your `for` loop is correct.

Implement loops that process a data set until a sentinel value is encountered.

- Sometimes, the termination condition of a loop can only be evaluated in the middle of a loop. You can introduce a Boolean variable to control such a loop.

Use nested loops to implement multiple levels of iterations.

- When the body of a loop contains another loop, the loops are nested. A typical use of nested loops is printing a table with rows and columns.

Apply loops to the implementation of simulations that involve random values.

- In a simulation, you repeatedly generate random numbers and use them to simulate an activity.

Use a debugger to locate errors in a running program.

- A debugger is a program that you can use to execute another program and analyze its run-time behavior.
- You can make effective use of a debugger by mastering just three concepts: breakpoints, single-stepping, and inspecting variables.
- When a debugger executes a program, the execution is suspended when-ever a breakpoint is reached.
- The single-step command executes the program one line at a time.
- A debugger can be used only to analyze the presence of bugs, not to show that a program is bug-free.
- Use the divide-and-conquer technique to locate the point of failure of a program.
- During debugging, compare the actual contents of variables against the values you know they should have.

Classes, Objects, and Methods Introduced in this Chapter

```
java.util.Random
    nextDouble
    nextInt
```

Media Resources

www.wiley.com/ college/ horstmann

- ***Worked Example*** Credit Card Processing
- ***Worked Example*** Manipulating the Pixels in an Image
- ***Worked Example*** A Sample Debugging Session
- Lab Exercises
- ⊕ ***Animation*** Tracing a Loop
- ⊕ ***Animation*** The for Loop
- ⊕ Practice Quiz
- ⊕ Code Completion Exercises

Review Exercises

★★ **R6.1** Which loop statements does Java support? Give simple rules when to use each loop type.

★★ **R6.2** What does the following code print?

```
for (int i = 0; i < 10; i++)
{
```

```
        for (int j = 0; j < 10; j++)
            System.out.print(i * j % 10);
        System.out.println();
    }
```

★★ **R6.3** How many iterations do the following loops carry out? Assume that i is an integer variable that is not changed in the loop body.

a. for (i = 1; i <= 10; i++) . . .
b. for (i = 0; i < 10; i++) . . .
c. for (i = 10; i > 0; i--) . . .
d. for (i = -10; i <= 10; i++) . . .
e. for (i = 10; i >= 0; i++) . . .
f. for (i = -10; i <= 10; i = i + 2) . . .
g. for (i = -10; i <= 10; i = i + 3) . . .

★ **R6.4** Rewrite the following for loop into a while loop.

```
int s = 0;
for (int i = 1; i <= 10; i++) s = s + i;
```

★★ **R6.5** Rewrite the following do loop into a while loop.

```
int n = 1;
double x = 0;
double s;
do
{
    s = 1.0 / (n * n);
    x = x + s;
    n++;
}
while (s > 0.01);
```

★ **R6.6** What is an infinite loop? On your computer, how can you terminate a program that executes an infinite loop?

★★★ **R6.7** Give three strategies for implementing the following "loop and a half":

```
Loop
    Read name of bridge.
    If not OK, exit loop.
    Read length of bridge in feet.
    If not OK, exit loop.
    Convert length to meters.
    Print bridge data.
```

Use a Boolean variable, a break statement, and a method with multiple return statements. Which of these three approaches do you find clearest?

★ **R6.8** Implement a loop that prompts a user to enter a number between 1 and 10, giving three tries to get it right.

★ **R6.9** Sometimes students write programs with instructions such as "Enter data, 0 to quit" and that exit the data entry loop when the user enters the number 0. Explain why that is usually a poor idea.

★ **R6.10** How would you use a random number generator to simulate the drawing of a playing card?

★ **R6.11** What is an "off-by-one error"? Give an example from your own programming experience.

★★ **R6.12** Give an example of a for loop in which symmetric bounds are more natural. Give an example of a for loop in which asymmetric bounds are more natural.

★ **R6.13** What are nested loops? Give an example where a nested loop is typically used.

★T **R6.14** Explain the differences between these debugger operations:
- Stepping into a method
- Stepping over a method

★★T **R6.15** Explain in detail how to inspect the string stored in a String object in your debugger.

★★T **R6.16** Explain in detail how to inspect the information stored in a Rectangle object in your debugger.

★★T **R6.17** Explain in detail how to use your debugger to inspect the balance stored in a Bank-Account object.

★★T **R6.18** Explain the divide-and-conquer strategy to get close to a bug in a debugger.

Programming Exercises

★ **P6.1** Complete the program in How To 6.1 on page 241. Your program should read twelve temperature values and print the month with the highest temperature.

★★★ **P6.2** *Credit Card Number Check*. The last digit of a credit card number is the *check digit*, which protects against transcription errors such as an error in a single digit or switching two digits. The following method is used to verify actual credit card numbers but, for simplicity, we will describe it for numbers with 8 digits instead of 16:

- Starting from the rightmost digit, form the sum of every other digit. For example, if the credit card number is 4358 9795, then you form the sum $5 + 7 + 8 + 3 = 23$.
- Double each of the digits that were not included in the preceding step. Add all digits of the resulting numbers. For example, with the number given above, doubling the digits, starting with the next-to-last one, yields 18 18 10 8. Adding all digits in these values yields $1 + 8 + 1 + 8 + 1 + 0 + 8 = 27$.
- Add the sums of the two preceding steps. If the last digit of the result is 0, the number is valid. In our case, $23 + 27 = 50$, so the number is valid.

Write a program that implements this algorithm. The user should supply an 8-digit number, and you should print out whether the number is valid or not. If it is not valid, you should print out the value of the check digit that would make the number valid.

★ **P6.3** *Currency conversion*. Write a program CurrencyConverter that asks the user to enter today's price of one dollar in euro. Then the program reads U.S. dollar values and converts each to euro values. Stop when the user enters Q.

★★★ **P6.4** *Projectile flight.* Suppose a cannonball is propelled vertically into the air with a starting velocity v_0. Any calculus book will tell us that the position of the ball after t seconds is $s(t) = -0.5 \cdot g \cdot t^2 + v_0 \cdot t$, where $g = 9.81$ m/sec^2 is the gravitational force of the earth. No calculus book ever mentions why someone would want to carry out such an obviously dangerous experiment, so we will do it in the safety of the computer.

In fact, we will confirm the theorem from calculus by a simulation. In our simulation, we will consider how the ball moves in very short time intervals Δt. In a short time interval the velocity v is nearly constant, and we can compute the distance the ball moves as $\Delta s = v \cdot \Delta t$. In our program, we will simply set

```
double deltaT = 0.01;
```

and update the position by

```
s = s + v * deltaT;
```

The velocity changes constantly—in fact, it is reduced by the gravitational force of the earth. In a short time interval, v decreases by $g \cdot \Delta t$, and we must keep the velocity updated as

```
v = v - g * deltaT;
```

In the next iteration the new velocity is used to update the distance.

Now run the simulation until the cannonball falls back to the earth. Get the initial velocity as an input (100 m/sec is a good value). Update the position and velocity 100 times per second, but only print out the position every full second. Also print out the values from the exact formula $s(t) = -0.5 \cdot g \cdot t^2 + v_0 \cdot t$ for comparison. Use a class Cannonball.

What is the benefit of this kind of simulation when an exact formula is available? Well, the formula from the calculus book is *not* exact. Actually, the gravitational force diminishes the farther the cannonball is away from the surface of the earth. This complicates the algebra sufficiently that it is not possible to give an exact formula for the actual motion, but the computer simulation can simply be extended to apply a variable gravitational force. For cannonballs, the calculus-book formula is actually good enough, but computers are necessary to compute accurate trajectories for higher-flying objects such as ballistic missiles.

★★ **P6.5** Write a program that prints the powers of ten

```
1.0
10.0
100.0
1000.0
10000.0
100000.0
1000000.0
1.0E7
1.0E8
1.0E9
1.0E10
1.0E11
```

Implement a class

```
public class PowerGenerator
{
```

```
/**
    Constructs a power generator.
    @param aFactor  the number that will be multiplied by itself
*/
public PowerGenerator(double aFactor) { . . . }

/**
    Computes the next power.
*/
public double nextPower() { . . . }
    . . .
}
```

Then supply a test class `PowerGeneratorRunner` that calls `System.out.println(myGenerator.nextPower())` twelve times.

★★ **P6.6** The *Fibonacci sequence* is defined by the following rule. The first two values in the sequence are 1 and 1. Every subsequent value is the sum of the two values preceding it. For example, the third value is $1 + 1 = 2$, the fourth value is $1 + 2 = 3$, and the fifth is $2 + 3 = 5$. If f_n denotes the nth value in the Fibonacci sequence, then

$$f_1 = 1$$
$$f_2 = 1$$
$$f_n = f_{n-1} + f_{n-2} \quad \text{if } n > 2$$

Write a program that prompts the user for n and prints the first n values in the Fibonacci sequence. Use a class `FibonacciGenerator` with a method `nextNumber`.

Hint: There is no need to store all values for f_n. You only need the last two values to compute the next one in the series:

```
fold1 = 1;
fold2 = 1;
fnew = fold1 + fold2;
```

After that, discard `fold2`, which is no longer needed, and set `fold2` to `fold1` and `fold1` to `fnew`.

Your generator class will be tested with this runner program:

```
public class FibonacciRunner
{
    public static void main(String[] args)
    {
        Scanner in = new Scanner(System.in);

        System.out.println("Enter n:");
        int n = in.nextInt();

        FibonacciGenerator fg = new FibonacciGenerator();

        for (int i = 1; i <= n; i++)
            System.out.println(fg.nextNumber());
    }
}
```

★★ **P6.7** *Mean and standard deviation.* Write a program that reads a set of floating-point data values from the input. When the user indicates the end of input, print out the count of the values, the average, and the standard deviation. The average of a data set $x_1, \ldots, x_n$ is

$$\bar{x} = \frac{\sum x_i}{n}$$

where $\sum x_i = x_1 + \cdots + x_n$ is the sum of the input values. The standard deviation is

$$s = \sqrt{\frac{\sum (x_i - \bar{x})^2}{n - 1}}$$

However, that formula is not suitable for our task. By the time you have computed the mean, the individual x_i are long gone. Until you know how to save these values, use the numerically less stable formula

$$s = \sqrt{\frac{\sum x_i^2 - \frac{1}{n}\left(\sum x_i\right)^2}{n - 1}}$$

You can compute this quantity by keeping track of the count, the sum, and the sum of squares in the DataSet class as you process the input values.

★★ **P6.8** *Factoring of integers.* Write a program that asks the user for an integer and then prints out all its factors in increasing order. For example, when the user enters 150, the program should print

```
2
3
5
5
```

Use a class FactorGenerator with a constructor FactorGenerator(int numberToFactor) and methods nextFactor and hasMoreFactors. Supply a class FactorPrinter whose main method reads a user input, constructs a FactorGenerator object, and prints the factors.

★★ **P6.9** *Prime numbers.* Write a program that prompts the user for an integer and then prints out all prime numbers up to that integer. For example, when the user enters 20, the program should print

```
2
3
5
7
11
13
17
19
```

Recall that a number is a prime number if it is not divisible by any number except 1 and itself.

Supply a class PrimeGenerator with a method nextPrime.

★★ **P6.10** The *Heron method* is a method for computing square roots that was known to the ancient Greeks. If x is a guess for the value $\sqrt{a}$, then the average of x and a/x is a better guess.

$$\underset{\underset{\text{Midpoint}}{\uparrow}}{\overline{\begin{array}{ccc} a/x & \sqrt{a} & x \end{array}}}$$

Implement a class `RootApproximator` that starts with an initial guess of 1 and whose `nextGuess` method produces a sequence of increasingly better guesses. Supply a method `hasMoreGuesses` that returns `false` if two successive guesses are sufficiently close to each other (that is, they differ by no more than a small value ε). Then test your class like this:

```
RootApproximator approx = new RootApproximator(a, EPSILON);
while (approx.hasMoreGuesses())
    System.out.println(approx.nextGuess());
```

★★ **P6.11** The best known iterative method for computing the roots of a function f (that is, the x-values for which $f(x)$ is 0) is Newton-Raphson approximation. To find the zero of a function whose derivative is also known, compute

$$x_{\text{new}} = x_{\text{old}} - f(x_{\text{old}})/f'(x_{\text{old}}).$$

For this exercise, write a program to compute nth roots of floating-point numbers. Prompt the user for a and n, then obtain $\sqrt[n]{a}$ by computing a zero of the function $f(x) = x^n - a$. Follow the approach of Exercise P6.10.

★★ **P6.12** The value of e^x can be computed as the power series

$$e^x = \sum_{n=0}^{\infty} \frac{x^n}{n!}$$

where $n! = 1 \cdot 2 \cdot 3 \cdot \ldots \cdot n$.

Write a program that computes e^x using this formula. Of course, you can't compute an infinite sum. Just keep adding values until an individual summand (term) is less than a certain threshold. At each step, you need to compute the new term and add it to the total. Update these terms as follows:

```
term = term * x / n;
```

Follow the approach of the preceding two exercises, by implementing a class `ExpApproximator`. Its first guess should be 1.

★ **P6.13** Write a program `RandomDataAnalyzer` that generates 100 random numbers between 0 and 1000 and adds them to a `DataSet`. Print out the average and the maximum.

★★ **P6.14** Program the following simulation: Darts are thrown at random points onto the square with corners (1,1) and (−1,−1). If the dart lands inside the unit circle (that is, the circle with center (0,0) and radius 1), it is a hit. Otherwise it is a miss. Run this simulation and use it to determine an approximate value for π. Extra credit if you explain why this is a better method for estimating π than the Buffon needle program.

★★★G **P6.15** *Random walk.* Simulate the wandering of an intoxicated person in a square street grid. Draw a grid of 20 streets horizontally and 20 streets vertically. Represent the simulated drunkard by a dot, placed in the middle of the grid to start. For 100 times, have the simulated drunkard randomly pick a direction (east, west, north, south), move one block in the chosen direction, and draw the dot. (One might expect that on average the person might not get anywhere because the moves to different directions cancel one another out in the long run, but in fact it can be shown with probability 1 that the person eventually moves outside any finite region. Use classes for the grid and the drunkard.

★★★G **P6.16** This exercise is a continuation of Exercise P6.4. Most cannonballs are not shot upright but at an angle. If the starting velocity has magnitude v and the starting angle is α, then the velocity is a vector with components $v_x = v \cdot \cos(\alpha)$, $v_y = v \cdot \sin(\alpha)$. In the x-direction the velocity does not change. In the y-direction the gravitational force takes its toll. Repeat the simulation from the previous exercise, but update the x and y components of the location and the velocity separately. In every iteration, plot the location of the cannonball on the graphics display as a tiny circle. Repeat until the cannonball has reached the earth again.

This kind of problem is of historical interest. The first computers were designed to carry out just such ballistic calculations, taking into account the diminishing gravity for high-flying projectiles and wind speeds.

★G **P6.17** Write a graphical application that displays a checkerboard with 64 squares, alternating white and black.

★★G **P6.18** Write a graphical application that prompts a user to enter a number n and that draws n circles with random diameter and random location. The circles should be completely contained inside the window.

★★★G **P6.19** Write a graphical application that draws a spiral, such as the following:

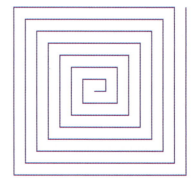

★★G **P6.20** It is easy and fun to draw graphs of curves with the Java graphics library. Simply draw 100 line segments joining the points $(x, f(x))$ and $(x + d, f(x + d))$, where x ranges from x_{min} to x_{max} and $d = (x_{max} - x_{min})/100$.

Draw the curve $f(x) = 0.00005x^3 - 0.03x^2 + 4x + 200$, where x ranges from 0 to 400 in this fashion.

★★★G **P6.21** Draw a picture of the "four-leaved rose" whose equation in polar coordinates is $r = \cos(2\theta)$. Let θ go from 0 to 2π in 100 steps. Each time, compute r and then compute the (x,y) coordinates from the polar coordinates by using the formula

$$x = r \cdot \cos(\theta), \, y = r \cdot \sin(\theta)$$

Programming Projects

Project 6.1 *Flesch Readability Index.* The following index was invented by Rudolf Flesch as a tool to gauge the legibility of a document without linguistic analysis.

- Count all words in the file. A *word* is any sequence of characters delimited by white space, whether or not it is an actual English word.
- Count all syllables in each word. To make this simple, use the following rules: Each *group* of adjacent vowels (a, e, i, o, u, y) counts as one syllable (for example, the "ea" in "real" contributes one syllable, but the "e . . . a" in "regal" count as two syllables). However, an "e" at the end of a word doesn't count as a syllable. Also, each word has at least one syllable, even if the previous rules give a count of 0.
- Count all sentences. A sentence is ended by a period, colon, semicolon, question mark, or exclamation mark.
- The index is computed by

$$\text{Index} = 206.835$$
$$- 84.6 \times \left(\text{Number of syllables}/\text{Number of words}\right)$$
$$- 1.015 \times \left(\text{Number of words}/\text{Number of sentences}\right)$$

rounded to the nearest integer.

The purpose of the index is to force authors to rewrite their text until the index is high enough. This is achieved by reducing the length of sentences and by removing long words. For example, the sentence

> The following index was invented by Flesch as a simple tool to estimate the legibility of a document without linguistic analysis.

can be rewritten as

> Flesch invented an index to check whether a text is easy to read. To compute the index, you need not look at the meaning of the words.

This index is a number, usually between 0 and 100, indicating how difficult the text is to read. Some example indices for random material from various publications are:

Comics	95
Consumer ads	82
Sports Illustrated	65
Time	57
New York Times	39
Auto insurance policy	10
Internal Revenue Code	−6

Translated into educational levels, the indices are:

91–100	5th grader
81–90	6th grader
71–80	7th grader
66–70	8th grader
61–65	9th grader
51–60	High school student
31–50	College student
0–30	College graduate
Less than 0	Law school graduate

Your program should read a text file in, compute the legibility index, and print out the equivalent educational level. Use classes Word and Document.

Project 6.2 *The game of Nim.* This is a well-known game with a number of variants. We will consider the following variant, which has an interesting winning strategy. Two players alternately take marbles from a pile. In each move, a player chooses how many marbles to take. The player must take at least one but at most half of the marbles. Then the other player takes a turn. The player who takes the last marble loses.

Write a program in which the computer plays against a human opponent. Generate a random integer between 10 and 100 to denote the initial size of the pile. Generate a random integer between 0 and 1 to decide whether the computer or the human takes the first turn. Generate a random integer between 0 and 1 to decide whether the computer plays *smart* or *stupid*. In stupid mode, the computer simply takes a random legal value (between 1 and $n/2$) from the pile whenever it has a turn. In smart mode the computer takes off enough marbles to make the size of the pile a power of 2 minus 1 — that is, 3, 7, 15, 31, or 63. That is always a legal move, except if the size of the pile is currently one less than a power of 2. In that case, the computer makes a random legal move.

Note that the computer cannot be beaten in smart mode when it has the first move, unless the pile size happens to be 15, 31, or 63. Of course, a human player who has the first turn and knows the winning strategy can win against the computer.

When you implement this program, be sure to use classes Pile, Player, and Game. A player can be either stupid, smart, or human. (Human Player objects prompt for input.)

Answers to Self-Check Questions

1. Never.

2. The `waitForBalance` method would never return due to an infinite loop.

3.
```
int i = 1;
while (i <= numberOfYears)
{
    double interest = balance * rate / 100;
    balance = balance + interest;
    i++;
}
```

4. 11 times.

5.
```
double total = 0;
while (in.hasNextDouble())
{
    double input = in.nextDouble();
    if (value > 0) total = total + input;
}
```

6. The initial call to `in.nextDouble()` fails, terminating the program. One solution is to do all input in the loop and introduce a Boolean variable that checks whether the loop is entered for the first time.

```
double input = 0;
boolean first = true;
while (in.hasNextDouble())
{
    double previous = input;
    input = in.nextDouble();
    if (first) { first = false; }
    else if (input == previous) { System.out.println("Duplicate input"); }
}
```

7. Because we don't know whether the next input is a number or the letter Q.

8. No. If *all* input values are negative, the maximum is also negative. However, the `maximum` variable is initialized with 0. With this simplification, the maximum would be falsely computed as 0.

9. Change the inner loop to `for (int j = 1; j <= width; j++)`.

10. 20.

11. `int n = generator.nextInt(2); // 0 = heads, 1 = tails`

12. The program repeatedly calls `Math.toRadians(angle)`. You could simply call `Math.toRadians(180)` to compute π.

13. You should step over it because you are not interested in debugging the internals of the `println` method.

14. You should set a breakpoint. Stepping through loops can be tedious.

Arrays and Array Lists

CHAPTER GOALS

- To become familiar with using arrays and array lists
- To learn about wrapper classes, auto-boxing, and the enhanced for loop
- To study common array algorithms
- To learn how to use two-dimensional arrays
- To understand when to choose array lists and arrays in your programs
- To implement partially filled arrays
- **T** To understand the concept of regression testing

In order to process large quantities of data, you need to have a mechanism for collecting values. In Java, arrays and array lists serve this purpose. In this chapter, you will learn how to construct arrays and array lists, fill them with values, and access the stored values. We introduce the enhanced for loop, a convenient statement for processing all elements of a collection. You will see how to use the enhanced for loop, as well as ordinary loops, to implement common array algorithms. The chapter concludes with a discussion of two-dimensional arrays, which are useful for handling rows and columns of data.

7.1 Arrays

In many programs, you need to manipulate collections of related values. It would be impractical to use a sequence of variables such as value1, value2, value3, . . . , and so on. The array construct provides a better way of storing a collection of values.

An **array** is a sequence of values of the same type. The values that are stored in an array are called its "elements". For example, here is how you construct an array of 10 floating-point numbers:

> An array is a sequence of values of the same type.

```
new double[10]
```

The number of elements (here, 10) is called the length of the array.

The new operator merely constructs the array. You will want to store a reference to the array in a variable so that you can access it later.

The type of an array variable is the element type, followed by []. In this example, the type is double[], because the element type is double. Here is the declaration of an array variable:

```
double[] values = new double[10];
```

That is, values is a reference to an array of floating-point numbers. It is initialized with an array of 10 numbers (see Figure 1).

You can also form arrays of objects, for example

```
BankAccount[] accounts = new BankAccount[10];
```

When an array is first created, all elements are initialized with 0 (for an array of numbers such as int[] or double[]), false (for a boolean[] array), or null (for an array of object references).

Figure 1
An Array Reference
and an Array

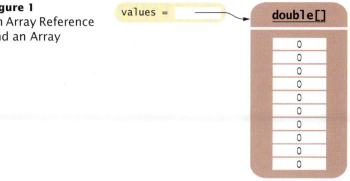

Alternatively, you can initialize an array with other values. List all elements that you want to include in the array, enclosed in braces and separated by commas:

```
int[] primes = { 2, 3, 5, 7, 11 };
```

The Java compiler counts how many elements you want to place in the array, allocates an array of the correct size, and fills it with the elements that you specify.

Each element in the array is specified by an integer index that is placed inside square brackets ([]). For example, the expression

```
values[4]
```

denotes the element of the `values` array with index 4.

You can store a value at a location with an assignment statement, such as the following.

```
values[2] = 29.95;
```

Now the position with index 2 of `values` is filled with 29.95 (see Figure 2).

> You access an array element with an integer index, using the [] operator.

To read the element at index 2, simply use the expression `values[2]` as you would any variable of type `double`:

```
System.out.println("The element at index 2 is " + values[2]);
```

If you look closely at Figure 2, you will notice that the index values start at 0. That is,

`values[0]` is the first element

`values[1]` is the second element

`values[2]` is the third element

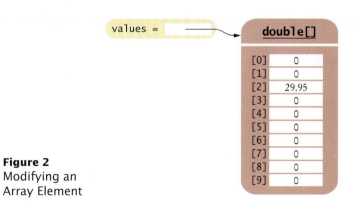

Figure 2
Modifying an
Array Element

and so on. This convention can be a source of grief for the newcomer, so you should pay close attention to the index values. In particular, the *last* element in the array has an index *one less than* the array length. For example, values refers to an array with length 10. The last element is values[9].

If you try to access an element that does not exist, then an "array index out of bounds" exception occurs. For example, the statement

```
values[10] = 29.95; // ERROR
```

is a **bounds error**.

To avoid bounds errors, you will want to know how many elements are in an array. The expression

```
values.length
```

is the length of the values array. Note that there are no parentheses following length—it is an instance variable of the array object, not a method. However, you cannot modify this instance variable. In other words, length is a final public instance variable. This is quite an anomaly. Normally, Java programmers use a method to inquire about the properties of an object. You just have to remember to omit the parentheses in this case.

The following code ensures that you only access the array when the index variable i is within the legal bounds:

```
if (0 <= i && i < values.length) values[i] = value;
```

Arrays suffer from a significant limitation: *their length is fixed*. If you start out with an array of 10 elements and later decide that you need to add additional elements, then you need to make a new array and copy all elements of the existing array into the new array. We will discuss this process in detail in Section 7.6.

> Index values of an array range from 0 to length - 1.

> Accessing a nonexistent element results in a bounds error.

> The expression *array*.length yields the number of elements in an array.

Table 1 Declaring Arrays

`int[] numbers = new int[10];`	An array of ten integers. All elements are initialized with zero.
`final int NUMBERS_LENGTH = 10;` `int[] numbers = new int[NUMBERS_LENGTH];`	It is a good idea to use a named constant instead of a "magic number".
`int valuesLength = in.nextInt();` `double[] values = new double[valuesLength];`	The length need not be a constant.
`int[] squares = { 0, 1, 4, 9, 16 };`	An array of five integers, with initial values.
`String[] names = new String[3];`	An array of three string references, all initially null.
`String[] friends = { "Emily", "Bob", "Cindy" };`	Another array of three strings.
`double[] values = new int[10]`	**Error:** You cannot initialize a double[] variable with an array of type int[].

Syntax 7.1   Arrays

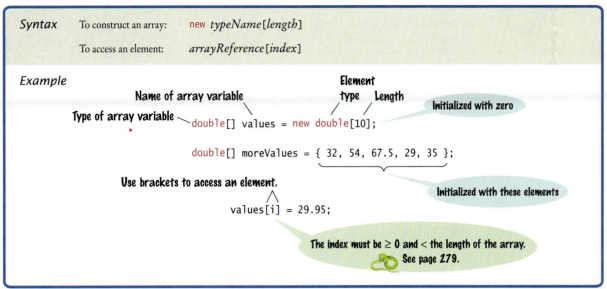

Syntax   To construct an array: new *typeName*[*length*]

To access an element: *arrayReference*[*index*]

Example

Element
type   Length

Name of array variable

Type of array variable

Initialized with zero

`double[] values = new double[10];`

`double[] moreValues = { 32, 54, 67.5, 29, 35 };`

Initialized with these elements

Use brackets to access an element.

`values[i] = 29.95;`

The index must be ≥ 0 and < the length of the array.
See page 279.

SELF CHECK

1. What elements does the values array contain after the following statements?

```
double[] values = new double[10];
for (int i = 0; i < values.length; i++) values[i] = i * i;
```

2. What do the following program segments print? Or, if there is an error, describe the error and specify whether it is detected at compile-time or at run-time.

a.
```
double[] a = new double[10];
System.out.println(a[0]);
```

b.
```
double[] b = new double[10];
System.out.println(b[10]);
```

c.
```
double[] c;
System.out.println(c[0]);
```

Common Error 7.1

Bounds Errors

A very common array error is attempting to access a nonexistent position.

```
double[] data = new double[10];
data[10] = 29.95;   // Error—only have elements with index values 0 . . . 9
```

When the program runs, an out-of-bounds index generates an exception and terminates the program.

This is a great improvement over languages such as C and C++. With those languages there is no error message; instead, the program will quietly (or not so quietly) corrupt the memory location that is 10 elements away from the start of the array. Sometimes that corruption goes unnoticed, but at other times, the program will act flaky or die a horrible death many instructions later. These are serious problems that make C and C++ programs difficult to debug. Bounds errors in C and C++ programs are a major cause of security vulnerabilities—see Random Fact 7.1 on page 282.

Common Error 7.2

Uninitialized and Unfilled Arrays

A common error is to allocate an array reference, but not an actual array.

```
double[] values;
values[0] = 29.95; // Error—values not initialized
```

Array variables work exactly like object variables—they are only references to the actual array. To construct the actual array, you must use the new operator:

```
double[] values = new double[10];
```

Another common error is to allocate an array of objects and expect it to be filled with objects.

```
BankAccount[] accounts = new BankAccount[10]; // Contains ten null references
```

This array contains null references, not default bank accounts. You need to remember to fill the array, for example:

```
for (int i = 0; i < 10; i++)
{
   accounts[i] = new BankAccount();
}
```

Quality Tip 7.1

Use Arrays for Sequences of Related Values

Arrays are intended for storing sequences of values with the same meaning. For example, an array of test scores makes perfect sense:

```
int[] scores = new int[NUMBER_OF_SCORES];
```

But it is a bad design to use an array

```
double[] personalData = new double[3];
```

that holds a person's age, bank balance, and shoe size as personalData[0], personalData[1], and personalData[2]. It would be tedious for the programmer to remember which of these data items is stored in which array location. In this situation, it is far better to use three variables

```
int age;
double bankBalance;
double shoeSize;
```

Quality Tip 7.2

Make Parallel Arrays into Arrays of Objects

Programmers who are familiar with arrays, but unfamiliar with object-oriented programming, sometimes distribute information across separate arrays. Here is a typical example. A program needs to manage bank data, consisting of account numbers and balances. Don't store the account numbers and balances in separate arrays.

```
// Don't do this
int[] accountNumbers;
double[] balances;
```

Arrays such as these are called parallel arrays (see Figure 3). The ith slice (accountNumbers[i] and balances[i]) contains data that need to be processed together.

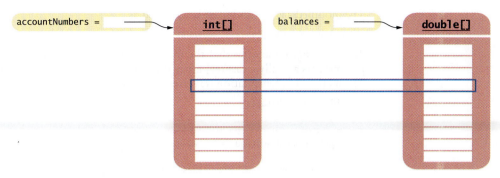

Figure 3 Avoid Parallel Arrays

Avoid parallel arrays by changing them into arrays of objects.

If you find yourself using two arrays that have the same length, ask yourself whether you couldn't replace them with a single array of a class type. Look at a slice and find the concept that it represents. Then make the concept into a class. In our example each slice contains an account number and a balance, describing a bank account. Therefore, it is an easy matter to use a single array of objects

```
BankAccount[] accounts;
```

(See Figure 4.)

Why is this beneficial? Think ahead. Maybe your program will change and you will need to store the owner of the bank account as well. It is a simple matter to update the BankAccount class. It may well be quite complicated to add a new array and make sure that all methods that accessed the original two arrays now also correctly access the third one.

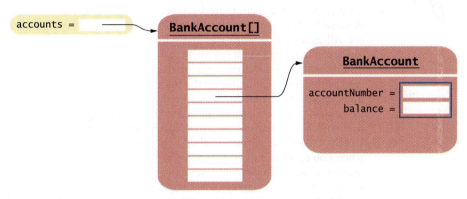

Figure 4 Reorganizing Parallel Arrays into an Array of Objects

Special Topic 7.1

Methods with a Variable Number of Parameters

Starting with Java version 5.0, it is possible to declare methods that receive a variable number of parameters. For example, we can modify the add method of the DataSet class of Chapter 6 so that one can add any number of values:

```
data.add(1, 3, 7);
data.add(4);
data.add(); // OK but not useful
```

The modified `add` method must be declared as

```
public void add(double... values)
```

The `...` symbol indicates that the method can receive any number of `double` values. The `xs` parameter is actually a `double[]` array that contains all values that were passed to the method. The method implementation traverses the parameter array and processes the values:

```java
public class DataSet
{
    . . .
    public void add(double... values)
    {
        for (int i = 0; i < values.length; i++) // values is a double[]
        {
            double x = values[i];
            sum = sum + x;
            if (count == 0 || maximum < x) maximum = x;
            count++;
        }
    }
}
```

Random Fact 7.1

An Early Internet Worm

In November 1988, a graduate student at Cornell University launched a virus program that infected about 6,000 computers connected to the Internet across the United States. Tens of thousands of computer users were unable to read their e-mail or otherwise use their computers. All major universities and many high-tech companies were affected. (The Internet was much smaller then than it is now.)

The particular kind of virus used in this attack is called a worm. The virus program crawled from one computer on the Internet to the next. The entire program is quite complex; however, one of the methods used in the attack is of interest here. The worm would attempt to connect to `finger`, a program in the UNIX operating system for finding information on a user who has an account on a particular computer on the network. Like many programs in UNIX, `finger` was written in the C language. C does not have array lists, only arrays, and when you construct an array in C, as in Java, you have to make up your mind how many elements you need. To store the user name to be looked up (say, `walters@cs.sjsu.edu`), the `finger` program allocated an array of 512 characters, under the assumption that nobody would ever provide such a long input. Unfortunately, C, unlike Java, does not check that an array index is less than the length of the array. If you write into an array, using an index that is too large, you simply overwrite memory locations that belong to some other objects.

In some versions of the `finger` program, the programmer had been lazy and had not checked whether the array holding the input characters was large enough to hold the input. So the worm program purposefully filled the 512-character array with 536 bytes. The excess 24 bytes would overwrite a return address, which the attacker knew was stored just after the line buffer. When that function was finished, it didn't return to its caller but to code supplied by the worm (see the figure). That code ran under the same super-user privileges as `finger`, allowing the worm to gain entry into the remote system.

Had the programmer who wrote `finger` been more conscientious, this particular attack would not have been possible. In C++ and C, all programmers must be especially careful to protect array boundaries. In Java, the virtual machine takes care of this protection automatically.

One may well speculate what would possess the virus author to spend many weeks to plan the antisocial act of breaking into thousands of computers and disabling them. It appears that the break-in was fully intended by the author, but the disabling of the computers was a bug, caused by continuous reinfection. The author was sentenced to 3 years probation, 400 hours of community service, and a $10,000 fine.

In recent years, computer attacks have intensified and the motives have become more sinister. Instead of disabling computers, viruses often steal financial data or use the attacked computers for sending spam e-mail. Sadly, many of these attacks continue to be possible because of poorly written programs that are susceptible to buffer overrun errors.

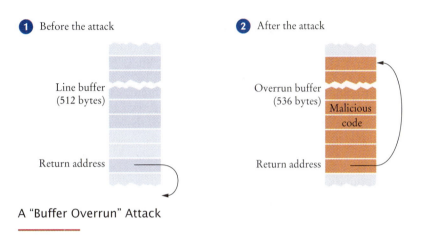

A "Buffer Overrun" Attack

7.2 Array Lists

> The ArrayList class manages a sequence of objects whose size can change.

The array construct is rather primitive. In this section, we introduce the ArrayList class. It lets you collect objects, just like an array does, but array lists offer two significant benefits:

- Array lists can grow and shrink as needed.
- The ArrayList class supplies methods for many common tasks, such as inserting and removing elements.

You declare an array list of strings as follows:

```
ArrayList<String> names = new ArrayList<String>();
```

> The ArrayList class is a generic class: ArrayList<*TypeName*> collects objects of the given type.

The type ArrayList<String> denotes an array list of strings. The angle brackets around the String type tell you that String is a **type parameter**. You can replace String with any other class and get a different array list type. For that reason, ArrayList is called a **generic class**. You will learn more about generic classes in Chapter 17. For now, simply use an ArrayList<T> whenever you want to collect objects of type T. However, keep in mind that you cannot use primitive types as type parameters—there is no ArrayList<int> or ArrayList<double>. You will see in Section 7.4 how to overcome that limitation.

When you construct an ArrayList object, it has size 0. You use the add method to add an object to the end of the array list. The size increases after each call to add (see Figure 5). The size method yields the current size of the array list.

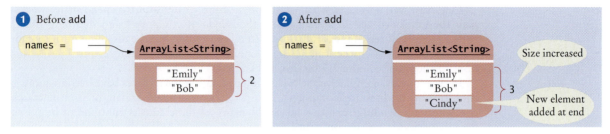

Figure 5 Adding an Element with add

```
names.add("Emily"); // Now names has size 1 and element "Emily"
names.add("Bob"); // Now names has size 2 and elements "Emily", "Bob"
names.add("Cindy"); // names has size 3 and elements "Emily", "Bob", and "Cindy"
```

To obtain the value of an array list element, use the get method, not the [ ] operator. As with arrays, index values start at 0. For example, names.get(2) retrieves the element with index 2, the third element in the array list:

```
String name = names.get(2);
```

As with arrays, it is an error to access a nonexistent element. A very common bounds error is to use the following:

```
int i = names.size();
name = names.get(i); // Error
```

The last valid index is names.size() - 1.

To set an array list element to a new value, use the set method.

```
names.set(2, "Carolyn");
```

This call sets position 2 of the names array list to "Carolyn", overwriting whatever value was there before.

Syntax 7.2 Array Lists

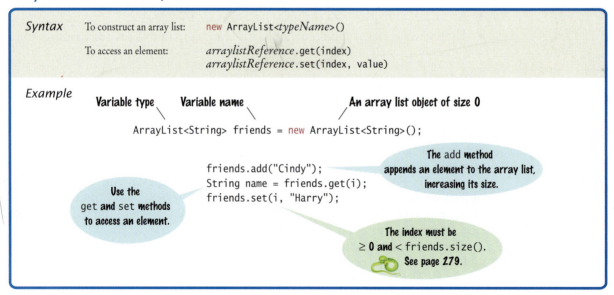

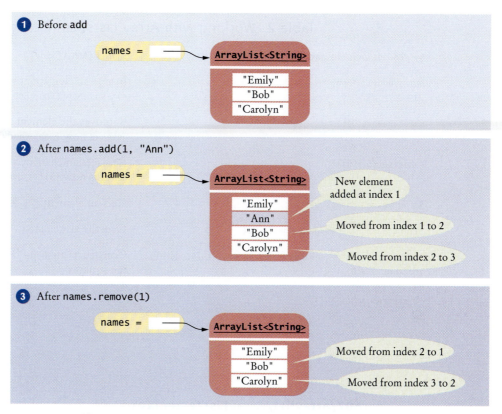

Figure 6 Adding and Removing Elements in the Middle of an Array List

The set method can only overwrite existing values. It is different from the add method, which adds a new object to the end of the array list.

You can also insert an object in the middle of an array list. The call names.add(1, "Ann") moves all elements with index 1 or larger by one position and adds the string "Ann" at index 1 (see Figure 6). After each call to the add method, the size of the array list increases by 1.

Conversely, the remove method removes the element at a given index, moves all elements after the removed element to the next lower index, and reduces the size of the array list by 1. Part 3 of Figure 6 illustrates the call names.remove(1).

The following program demonstrates how to use ArrayList class for collecting BankAccount objects. The BankAccount class has been enhanced from the version in Chapter 3. Each bank account has an account number. Note that you import the generic class java.util.ArrayList, without the type parameter.

Table 2 Working with Array Lists

`ArrayList<String> names = new ArrayList<String>();`	Constructs an empty array list that can hold strings.
`names.add("Ann");` `names.add("Cindy");`	Adds elements to the end.

Table 2 Working with Array Lists, continued	
`System.out.println(names);`	Prints [Ann, Cindy].
`names.add(1, "Bob");`	Inserts an element at index 1. names is now [Ann, Bob, Cindy].
`names.remove(0);`	Removes the element at index 0. names is now [Bob, Cindy].
`names.set(0, "Bill");`	Replaces an element with a different value. names is now [Bill, Cindy].
`String name = names.get(i);`	Gets an element.
`String last = names.get(names.size() - 1);`	Gets the last element.

`ArrayList<Integer> squares = new ArrayList<Integer>();`
`for (int i = 0; i < 10; i++)`
`{`
`    squares.add(i * i);`
`}`
	Constructs an array list holding the first ten squares.

ch07/arraylist/ArrayListTester.java

```java
 1  import java.util.ArrayList;
 2
 3  /**
 4      This program tests the ArrayList class.
 5  */
 6  public class ArrayListTester
 7  {
 8     public static void main(String[] args)
 9     {
10        ArrayList<BankAccount> accounts = new ArrayList<BankAccount>();
11        accounts.add(new BankAccount(1001));
12        accounts.add(new BankAccount(1015));
13        accounts.add(new BankAccount(1729));
14        accounts.add(1, new BankAccount(1008));
15        accounts.remove(0);
16
17        System.out.println("Size: " + accounts.size());
18        System.out.println("Expected: 3");
19        BankAccount first = accounts.get(0);
20        System.out.println("First account number: "
21               + first.getAccountNumber());
22        System.out.println("Expected: 1008");
23        BankAccount last = accounts.get(accounts.size() - 1);
24        System.out.println("Last account number: "
25               + last.getAccountNumber());
26        System.out.println("Expected: 1729");
27     }
28  }
```

ch07/arraylist/BankAccount.java

```java
1   /**
2       A bank account has a balance that can be changed by
3       deposits and withdrawals.
4   */
5   public class BankAccount
6   {
7       private int accountNumber;
8       private double balance;
9
10      /**
11          Constructs a bank account with a zero balance.
12          @param anAccountNumber the account number for this account
13      */
14      public BankAccount(int anAccountNumber)
15      {
16          accountNumber = anAccountNumber;
17          balance = 0;
18      }
19
20      /**
21          Constructs a bank account with a given balance.
22          @param anAccountNumber the account number for this account
23          @param initialBalance the initial balance
24      */
25      public BankAccount(int anAccountNumber, double initialBalance)
26      {
27          accountNumber = anAccountNumber;
28          balance = initialBalance;
29      }
30
31      /**
32          Gets the account number of this bank account.
33          @return the account number
34      */
35      public int getAccountNumber()
36      {
37          return accountNumber;
38      }
39
40      /**
41          Deposits money into the bank account.
42          @param amount the amount to deposit
43      */
44      public void deposit(double amount)
45      {
46          double newBalance = balance + amount;
47          balance = newBalance;
48      }
49
50      /**
51          Withdraws money from the bank account.
52          @param amount the amount to withdraw
53      */
54      public void withdraw(double amount)
55      {
56          double newBalance = balance - amount;
57          balance = newBalance;
58      }
```

```
59
60      /**
61          Gets the current balance of the bank account.
62          @return the current balance
63      */
64      public double getBalance()
65      {
66          return balance;
67      }
68  }
```

Program Run

```
Size: 3
Expected: 3
First account number: 1008
Expected: 1008
Last account number: 1729
Expected: 1729
```

SELF CHECK

3. How do you construct an array of 10 strings? An array list of strings?

4. What is the content of names after the following statements?

```
ArrayList<String> names = new ArrayList<String>();
names.add("A");
names.add(0, "B");
names.add("C");
names.remove(1);
```

Common Error 7.3

Length and Size

Unfortunately, the Java syntax for determining the number of elements in an array, an array list, and a string is not at all consistent. It is a common error to confuse these. You just have to remember the correct syntax for every data type.

Data Type	Number of Elements
Array	a.length
Array list	a.size()
String	a.length()

Special Topic 7.2

ArrayList Syntax Enhancements in Java 7

Java 7 introduces several convenient syntax enhancements for array lists.

When you declare and construct an array list, you need not repeat the type parameter in the constructor. That is, you can write

```
ArrayList<String> names = new ArrayList<>();
```

instead of

```
ArrayList<String> names = new ArrayList<String>();
```

This shortcut is called the "diamond syntax" because the empty brackets <> look like a diamond shape.

You can supply initial values as follows:

```
ArrayList<String> names = new ArrayList<>(["Ann", "Cindy", "Bob"]);
```

In Java 7, you can access array list elements with the [] operator instead of the get and put methods. That is, the compiler translates

```
String name = names[i];
```

into

```
String name = names.get(i);
```

and

```
names[i] = "Fred";
```

into

```
names.set(i, "Fred");
```

7.3 Wrappers and Auto-boxing

To treat primitive type values as objects, you must use wrapper classes.

Because numbers are not objects in Java, you cannot directly insert them into array lists. For example, you cannot form an ArrayList<double>. To store sequences of numbers in an array list, you must turn them into objects by using **wrapper classes**. There are wrapper classes for all eight primitive types:

Primitive Type	Wrapper Class
byte	Byte
boolean	Boolean
char	Character
double	Double
float	Float
int	Integer
long	Long
short	Short

Note that the wrapper class names start with uppercase letters, and that two of them differ from the names of the corresponding primitive type: Integer and Character.

Each wrapper class object contains a value of the corresponding primitive type. For example, an object of the class Double contains a value of type double (see Figure 7).

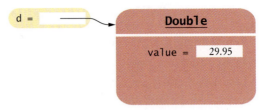

Figure 7 An Object of a Wrapper Class

Wrapper objects can be used anywhere that objects are required instead of primitive type values. For example, you can collect a sequence of floating-point numbers in an ArrayList<Double>.

Conversion between primitive types and the corresponding wrapper classes is automatic. This process is called **auto-boxing** (even though *auto-wrapping* would have been more consistent).

For example, if you assign a number to a Double object, the number is automatically "put into a box", namely a wrapper object.

```
Double d = 29.95; // Auto-boxing; same as Double d = new Double(29.95);
```

Conversely, wrapper objects are automatically "unboxed" to primitive types.

```
double x = d; // Auto-unboxing; same as double x = d.doubleValue();
```

Auto-boxing even works inside arithmetic expressions. For example, the statement

```
d = d + 1;
```

is perfectly legal. It means:

- Auto-unbox d into a double
- Add 1
- Auto-box the result into a new Double
- Store a reference to the newly created wrapper object in d

In order to collect numbers in an array list, simply remember to use the wrapper type as the type parameter, and then rely on auto-boxing.

```
ArrayList<Double> values = new ArrayList<Double>();
values.add(29.95);
double x = values.get(0);
```

Keep in mind that storing wrapped numbers is quite inefficient. The use of wrappers is acceptable if you only collect a few numbers, but you should use arrays for long sequences of numbers or characters.

S E L F   C H E C K

5. What is the difference between the types double and Double?

6. Suppose values is an ArrayList<Double> of size > 0. How do you increment the element with index 0?

7.4 The Enhanced for Loop

Java version 5.0 introduces a very convenient shortcut for a common loop type. Often, you need to iterate through a sequence of elements—such as the elements of an array or array list. The enhanced for loop makes this process particularly easy to program.

Suppose you want to total up all elements in an array values. Here is how you use the enhanced for loop to carry out that task.

```java
double[] values = . . .;
double sum = 0;
for (double element : values)
{
    sum = sum + element;
}
```

The loop body is executed for each element in the array values. At the beginning of each loop iteration, the next element is assigned to the variable element. Then the loop body is executed. You should read this loop as "for each element in values".

You may wonder why Java doesn't let you write "for each (element in values)". Unquestionably, this would have been neater, and the Java language designers seriously considered this. However, the "for each" construct was added to Java several years after its initial release. Had new reserved words each and in been added to the language, then older programs that happened to use those identifiers as variable or method names (such as System.in) would no longer have compiled correctly.

You don't have to use the "for each" construct to loop through all elements in an array. You can implement the same loop with a straightforward for loop and an explicit index variable:

```java
double[] values = . . .;
double sum = 0;
for (int i = 0; i < values.length; i++)
{
    double element = values[i];
    sum = sum + element;
}
```

Syntax 7.3 The "for each" Loop

Syntax   for (*typeName variable* : *collection*)
        statement

Example

This variable is set in each loop iteration.
It is only defined inside the loop.

An array or array list

```java
for (double element : values)
{
    sum = sum + element;
}
```

These statements are executed for each element.

The variable contains an element, not an index.

In an enhanced for loop, the loop variable contains an element, not an index.

Note an important difference between the "for each" loop and the ordinary for loop. In the "for each" loop, the loop variable e is assigned *elements:* values[0], values[1], and so on. In the ordinary for loop, the loop variable i is assigned *index values:* 0, 1, and so on.

You can also use the enhanced for loop to visit all elements of an array list. For example, the following loop computes the total of the balances of all accounts:

```java
ArrayList<BankAccount> accounts = . . . ;
double sum = 0;
for (BankAccount account : accounts)
{
    sum = sum + account.getBalance();
}
```

This loop is equivalent to the following ordinary for loop:

```java
double sum = 0;
for (int i = 0; i < accounts.size(); i++)
{
    BankAccount account = accounts.get(i);
    sum = sum + account.getBalance();
}
```

Keep in mind that the "for each" loop has a very specific purpose: getting the elements of a collection, from the beginning to the end. It is not suitable for all array algorithms. In particular, the "for each" loop does not allow you to modify the contents of an array. The following loop does *not* fill an array with zeroes:

```java
for (double element : values)
{
    element = 0; // ERROR—this assignment does not modify array elements
}
```

When the loop is executed, the variable element is first set to values[0]. Then element is set to 0, then to values[1], then to 0, and so on. The values array is not modified. The remedy is simple: Use an ordinary for loop

```java
for (int i = 0; i < values.length; i++)
{
    values[i] = 0; // OK
}
```

SELF CHECK

7. Write a "for each" loop that prints all elements in the array values.

8. What does this "for each" loop do?

```java
int counter = 0;
for (BankAccount a : accounts)
{
    if (a.getBalance() == 0) { counter++; }
}
```

7.5 Partially Filled Arrays

Suppose you write a program that reads a sequence of numbers into an array. How many numbers will the user enter? You can't very well ask the user to count the items before entering them—that is just the kind of work that the user expects the computer to do. Unfortunately, you now run into a problem. You need to set the size of the array before you know how many elements you need. Once the array size is set, it cannot be changed.

To solve this problem, make an array that is guaranteed to be larger than the largest possible number of entries, and partially fill it. For example, you can decide that the user will never provide more than 100 input values. Then allocate an array of size 100:

```java
final int VALUES_LENGTH = 100;
double[] values = new double[VALUES_LENGTH];
```

With a partially filled array, keep a companion variable to track how many elements are used.

Then keep a companion variable that tells how many elements in the array are actually used. It is an excellent idea always to name this companion variable by adding the suffix Size to the name of the array.

```java
int valuesSize = 0;
```

Now `values.length` is the capacity of the array values, and `valuesSize` is the current size of the array (see Figure 8). Keep adding elements into the array, incrementing the `valuesSize` variable each time.

```java
values[valuesSize] = x;
valuesSize++;
```

This way, `valuesSize` always contains the correct element count.

The following code segment shows how to read numbers into a partially filled array.

```java
int valuesSize = 0;
Scanner in = new Scanner(System.in);
while (in.hasNextDouble())
{
   if (valuesSize < values.length)
   {
      values[valuesSize] = in.nextDouble();
      valuesSize++;
   }
}
```

At the end of this loop, `valuesSize` contains the actual number of elements in the array. Note that you have to stop accepting inputs if the `valuesSize` companion variable reaches the array length. Section 7.6 shows how you can overcome that limitation by growing the array.

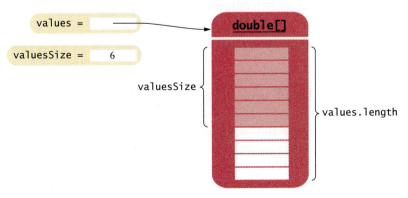

Figure 8 A Partially Filled Array

To process the gathered array elements, you again use the companion variable, not the array length. This loop prints the partially filled array:

```java
for (int i = 0; i < valuesSize; i++)
{
   System.out.println(values[i]);
}
```

Array lists use this technique behind the scenes. An array list contains an array of objects. When the array runs out of space, the array list allocates a larger array and copies the elements. However, all of this happens inside the array list methods, so you never need to think about it.

SELF CHECK

9. Write a loop to print the elements of the partially filled array values in reverse order, starting with the last element.

10. How do you remove the last element of the partially filled array values?

11. Why would a programmer use a partially filled array of numbers instead of an array list?

Common Error 7.4

Underestimating the Size of a Data Set

Programmers frequently underestimate the amount of input data that a user will pour into an unsuspecting program. A common problem results from the use of fixed-sized arrays. Suppose you write a program to search for text in a file. You store each line in a string, and keep an array of strings. How big do you make the array? Surely nobody is going to challenge your program with an input that is more than 100 lines. Really? It is easy to feed in the entire text of *Alice in Wonderland* or *War and Peace* (which are available on the Internet). All of a sudden, your program has to deal with tens or hundreds of thousands of lines. What will it do? Will it handle the input? Will it politely reject the excess input? Will it crash and burn?

A famous article (Barton P. Miller, Louis Fericksen, and Bryan So, "An Empirical Study of the Reliability of Unix Utilities", *Communications of the ACM*, vol. 33, no. 12, pp. 32–44) analyzed how several UNIX programs reacted when they were fed large or random data sets. Sadly, about a quarter didn't do well at all, crashing or hanging without a reasonable error message. For example, in some older versions of UNIX the tape backup program tar was not able to handle file names longer than 100 characters, which is a pretty unreasonable limitation. Many of these shortcomings are caused by features of the C language that, unlike Java, make it difficult to store strings and collections of arbitrary size.

7.6 Common Array Algorithms

In the following sections, we discuss some of the most common algorithms for working with arrays and array lists.

In the examples, we show a mixture of arrays and array lists so that you become familiar with the syntax for both constructs.

7.6.1 Filling

This loop fills an array with zeroes:

```
for (int i = 0; i < values.length; i++)
{
    values[i] = 0;
}
```

Here, we fill an array list with squares (0, 1, 4, 9, 16, ...). Note that the element with index 0 contains 0^2, the element with index 1 contains 1^2, and so on.

```
for (int i = 0; i < values.size(); i++)
{
    values.set(i, i * i);
}
```

7.6.2 Computing Sum and Average Values

To compute the sum of all elements, simply keep a running total.

```
double total = 0;
for (double element : values)
{
    total = total + element;
}
```

To obtain the average, divide by the number of elements:

```
double average = total / values.size(); // For an array list
```

Be sure to check that the size is not zero.

7.6.3 Counting Matches

To count values, check all elements and count the matches until you reach the end.

Suppose you want to find how many accounts of a certain type you have. Then you must go through the entire collection and increment a counter each time you find a match. Here we count the number of accounts whose balance is at least as much as a given threshold:

```
public class Bank
{
    private ArrayList<BankAccount> accounts;

    public int count(double atLeast)
    {
        int matches = 0;
        for (BankAccount account : accounts)
        {
            if (account.getBalance() >= atLeast) matches++; // Found a match
        }
        return matches;
    }
    . . .
}
```

7.6.4 Finding the Maximum or Minimum

To compute the maximum or minimum value, initialize a candidate with the starting element. Then compare the candidate with the remaining elements and update it if you find a larger or smaller value.

Suppose you want to find the account with the largest balance in the bank. Keep a candidate for the maximum. If you find an element with a larger value, then replace the candidate with that value. When you have reached the end of the sequence, you have found the maximum.

There is just one problem. When you visit the starting element, you don't yet have a candidate for the maximum. One way to overcome that is to set the candidate to the starting element and make the first comparison with the next element.

```
BankAccount largestYet = accounts.get(0);
for (int i = 1; i < accounts.size(); i++)
{
    BankAccount a = accounts.get(i);
    if (a.getBalance() > largestYet.getBalance())
        largestYet = a;
}
return largestYet;
```

Here we use an explicit for loop because the loop no longer visits all elements—it skips the starting element.

Of course, this approach works only if there is at least one element. It doesn't make a lot of sense to ask for the largest element of an empty collection. We can return null in that case:

```
if (accounts.size() == 0) return null;
BankAccount largestYet = accounts.get(0);
. . .
```

See Exercises R7.5 and R7.6 for slight modifications to this algorithm.

To compute the minimum of a data set, keep a candidate for the minimum and replace it whenever you encounter a *smaller* value. At the end of the sequence, you have found the minimum.

7.6.5 Searching for a Value

To find a value, check all elements until you have found a match.

Suppose you want to know whether there is a bank account with a particular account number in your bank. Simply inspect each element until you find a match or reach the end of the sequence. Note that the loop might fail to find an answer, namely if none of the accounts match. This search process is called a **linear search**.

```
public class Bank
{
    . . .
    public BankAccount find(int accountNumber)
    {
        for (BankAccount account : accounts)
        {
            if (account.getAccountNumber() == accountNumber) // Found a match
                return account;
        }
        return null; // No match in the entire array list
    }
    . . .
}
```

Note that the method returns null if no match is found.

7.6.6 Locating the Position of an Element

You often need to locate the position of an element so that you can replace or remove it. Use a variation of the linear search algorithm, but remember the position instead of the matching element. Here we locate the position of the first element that is larger than 100.

```java
int pos = 0;
boolean found = false;
while (pos < values.size() && !found)
{
   if (values.get(pos) > 100)
   {
      found = true;
   }
   else
   {
      pos++;
   }
}
if (found) { System.out.println("Position: " + pos); }
else { System.out.println("Not found"); }
```

7.6.7 Removing an Element

ANIMATION
Removing from an Array

Removing an element from an array list is very easy—simply use the remove method. With an array, you have to work harder.

Suppose you want to remove the element with index pos from the array values. First off, you need to keep a companion variable for tracking the number of elements in the array, as explained in Section 7.5.

If the elements in the array are not in any particular order, simply overwrite the element to be removed with the *last* element of the array, then decrement the variable tracking the size of the array. (See Figure 9.)

```java
values[pos] = values[valuesSize - 1];
valuesSize--;
```

The situation is more complex if the order of the elements matters. Then you must move all elements following the element to be removed to a lower index, and then decrement the variable holding the size of the array. (See Figure 10.)

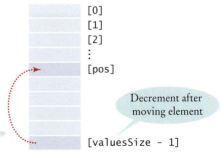

Figure 9
Removing an Element in an Unordered Array

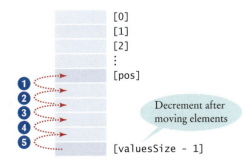

Figure 10
Removing an Element in an Ordered Array

```
for (int i = pos; i < valuesSize - 1; i++)
{
    values[i] = values[i + 1];
}
valuesSize--;
```

7.6.8 Inserting an Element

To insert an element into an array list, simply use the add method.

In this section, you will see how to insert an element into an array. Note that you need a companion variable for tracking the array size, as explained in Section 7.5. If the order of the elements does not matter, you can simply insert new elements at the end, incrementing the variable tracking the size.

```
if (valuesSize < values.length)
{
    values[valuesSize] = newElement;
    valuesSize++;
}
```

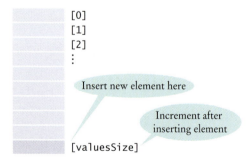

ANIMATION
Inserting into an Array

It is more work to insert an element at a particular position in the middle of an array. First, move all elements above the insertion location to a higher index. Then insert the new element.

Note the order of the movement: When you remove an element, you first move the next element down to a lower index, then the one after that, until you finally get to the end of the array. When you insert an element, you start at the end of the array, move that element to a higher index, then move the one before that, and so on until you finally get to the insertion location (see Figure 12).

```
if (valuesSize < values.length)
{
    for (int i = valuesSize; i > pos; i--)
    {
        values[i] = values[i - 1];
    }
    values[pos] = newElement;
    valuesSize++;
}
```

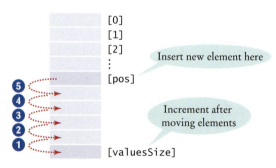

Figure 11
Inserting an Element in an Unordered Array

Figure 12
Inserting an Element in an Ordered Array

7.6.9 Copying and Growing Arrays

An array variable stores a reference to the array. Copying the variable yields a second reference to the same array.

Array variables work just like object variables—they hold a reference to the actual array. If you copy the reference, you get another reference to the same array (see Figure 13):

```
double[] values = new double[6];
. . . // Fill array
double[] prices = values; ①
```

If you want to make a true copy of an array, call the `Arrays.copyOf` method.

Use the `Arrays.copyOf` method to copy the elements of an array.

```
double[] prices = Arrays.copyOf(values, values.length); ②
```

Another use for `Arrays.copyOf` is to grow an array that has run out of space. The following statement has the effect of doubling the length of an array:

```
values = Arrays.copyOf(values, 2 * values.length);
```

See Figure 14.

For example, here is how you can read an arbitrarily long sequence numbers into an array, without running out of space:

```
int valuesSize = 0;
while (in.hasNextDouble())
{
   if (valuesSize == values.length)
      values = Arrays.copyOf(values, 2 * values.length);
   values[valuesSize] = in.nextDouble();
   valuesSize++;
}
```

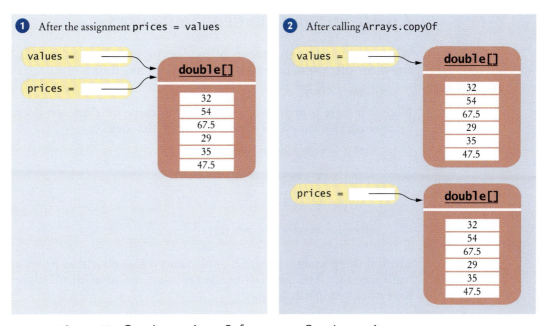

Figure 13 Copying an Array Reference vs. Copying an Array

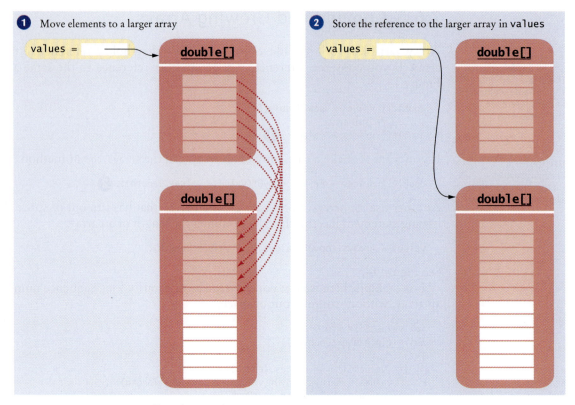

Figure 14 Growing an Array

7.6.10 Printing Element Separators

When you display the elements of an array or array list, you usually want to separate them, often with commas or vertical lines, like this:

```
Ann | Bob | Cindy
```

Note that there is one fewer separator than there are elements. Print the separator before each element *except the initial one* (with index 0):

```java
for (int i = 0; i < names.size(); i++)
{
   if (i > 0)
   {
      System.out.print(" | ");
   }
   System.out.print(names.get(i));
}
```

The following sample program implements a Bank class that stores an array list of bank accounts. The methods of the Bank class use some of the algorithms that we have discussed in this section.

ch07/bank/Bank.java

```java
1   import java.util.ArrayList;
2
3   /**
4       This bank contains a collection of bank accounts.
5   */
6   public class Bank
7   {
8       private ArrayList<BankAccount> accounts;
9
10      /**
11          Constructs a bank with no bank accounts.
12      */
13      public Bank()
14      {
15          accounts = new ArrayList<BankAccount>();
16      }
17
18      /**
19          Adds an account to this bank.
20          @param a the account to add
21      */
22      public void addAccount(BankAccount a)
23      {
24          accounts.add(a);
25      }
26
27      /**
28          Gets the sum of the balances of all accounts in this bank.
29          @return the sum of the balances
30      */
31      public double getTotalBalance()
32      {
33          double total = 0;
34          for (BankAccount a : accounts)
35          {
36              total = total + a.getBalance();
37          }
38          return total;
39      }
40
41      /**
42          Counts the number of bank accounts whose balance is at
43          least a given value.
44          @param atLeast the balance required to count an account
45          @return the number of accounts having at least the given balance
46      */
47      public int countBalancesAtLeast(double atLeast)
48      {
49          int matches = 0;
50          for (BankAccount a : accounts)
51          {
52              if (a.getBalance() >= atLeast) matches++; // Found a match
53          }
54          return matches;
55      }
56
```

```java
57    /**
58        Finds a bank account with a given number.
59        @param accountNumber the number to find
60        @return the account with the given number, or null if there
61        is no such account
62    */
63    public BankAccount find(int accountNumber)
64    {
65        for (BankAccount a : accounts)
66        {
67            if (a.getAccountNumber() == accountNumber) // Found a match
68                return a;
69        }
70        return null; // No match in the entire array list
71    }
72
73    /**
74        Gets the bank account with the largest balance.
75        @return the account with the largest balance, or null if the
76        bank has no accounts
77    */
78    public BankAccount getMaximum()
79    {
80        if (accounts.size() == 0) return null;
81        BankAccount largestYet = accounts.get(0);
82        for (int i = 1; i < accounts.size(); i++)
83        {
84            BankAccount a = accounts.get(i);
85            if (a.getBalance() > largestYet.getBalance())
86                largestYet = a;
87        }
88        return largestYet;
89    }
90 }
```

ch07/bank/BankTester.java

```java
1    /**
2        This program tests the Bank class.
3    */
4    public class BankTester
5    {
6        public static void main(String[] args)
7        {
8            Bank firstBankOfJava = new Bank();
9            firstBankOfJava.addAccount(new BankAccount(1001, 20000));
10           firstBankOfJava.addAccount(new BankAccount(1015, 10000));
11           firstBankOfJava.addAccount(new BankAccount(1729, 15000));
12
13           double threshold = 15000;
14           int count = firstBankOfJava.countBalancesAtLeast(threshold);
15           System.out.println("Count: " + count);
16           System.out.println("Expected: 2");
17
18           int accountNumber = 1015;
19           BankAccount account = firstBankOfJava.find(accountNumber);
20           if (account == null)
21               System.out.println("No matching account");
```

```
22        else
23           System.out.println("Balance of matching account: "
24              + account.getBalance());
25        System.out.println("Expected: 10000");
26
27        BankAccount max = firstBankOfJava.getMaximum();
28        System.out.println("Account with largest balance: "
29           + max.getAccountNumber());
30        System.out.println("Expected: 1001");
31     }
32 }
```

Program Run

```
Count: 2
Expected: 2
Balance of matching account: 10000.0
Expected: 10000
Account with largest balance: 1001
Expected: 1001
```

SELF CHECK

12. What does the find method do if there are two bank accounts with a matching account number?

13. Would it be possible to use a "for each" loop in the getMaximum method?

14. When printing separators, we skipped the separator before the initial element. Rewrite the loop so that the separator is printed *after* each element, except for the last element.

15. The following replacement has been suggested for the algorithm in Section 7.6.10.

```
System.out.print(names.get(0));
for (int i = 1; i < names.size(); i++) System.out.print(" | " + names.get(i));
```

What is problematic about this suggestion?

Productivity Hint 7.1

Easy Printing of Arrays and Array Lists

If values is an array, the expression

```
Arrays.toString(values)
```

returns a string describing the elements, using a format that looks like this:

```
[32, 54, 67.5, 29, 35, 47.5]
```

The elements are surrounded by a pair of brackets and separated by commas. This can be convenient for debugging:

```
System.out.println("values=" + Arrays.toString(values));
```

With an array list, it is even easier to get a quick printout. Simply pass the array list to the println method:

```
System.out.println(names); // Prints [Ann, Bob, Cindy]
```

How To 7.1

Working with Arrays and Array Lists

When you process a sequence of values, you usually need to use array lists or arrays. (In some very simple situations, you can process data as you read them in, without storing them.) This How To walks you through the necessary steps.

Consider this example problem: You are given the quiz scores of a student. You are to compute the final quiz score, which is the sum of all scores after dropping the lowest one. For example, if the scores are

    8 7 8.5 9.5 7 5 10

then the final score is 50.

However, if there is only one score, it would seem cruel to remove it. In that case, that score will be the final score. If there is no score, the final score should be 0.

Step 1   Decompose your task into steps.

You will usually want to break down your task into multiple steps, such as

- Reading the data into an array list or array.
- Processing the data in one or more steps.
- Displaying the results.

When deciding how to process the data, you should be familiar with the array algorithms in Section 7.6. Most processing tasks can be solved by using one or more of these algorithms.

In our sample problem, we will want to read the data. Then we will remove the minimum and compute the total. For example, if the input is 8 7 8.5 9.5 7 5 10, we will remove the minimum of 5, yielding 8 7 8.5 9.5 7 10. The sum of those values is the final score of 50.

Thus, we have identified three steps:

    Read inputs.
    Remove the minimum.
    Calculate the sum.

Step 2   Choose between array lists and arrays.

Generally, array lists are more convenient than arrays. You would choose arrays if one of the following applies:

- You know in advance how many elements you will collect, and the size will not change.
- You collect a large sequence of numbers.

None of these cases applies here, so we will store the scores in an array list. An alternate solution using arrays is included with the companion code for the book (ch07/scores2 directory).

Step 3   Determine which algorithm(s) you need.

Sometimes, a step corresponds to exactly one of the basic array algorithms. That is the case with calculating the sum. At other times, you need to combine several algorithms. To remove the minimum value, you can find the minimum value (Section 7.6.4), find its position (Section 7.6.6), and remove the element at that position (Section 7.6.7).

We have now refined our plan as follows:

    Read inputs.
    Find the minimum.
    Find its position.
    Remove the minimum.
    Calculate the sum.

This plan will work, but it is possible to do a bit better. It is easier to compute the sum and subtract the minimum. Then we don't have to find its position. The revised plan is

Read inputs.
Find the minimum.
Calculate the sum.
Subtract the minimum.

Step 4 Use classes and methods to structure the program.

Even though it may be possible to put all steps into the main method, this is rarely a good idea. It is better to carry out each processing step in a separate method. It is also a good idea to come up with a class that is responsible for collecting and processing the data, such as the DataSet class in Chapter 6 or the Bank class in the preceding section.

In our example, let's collect the scores in a GradeBook class.

```java
public class GradeBook
{
    private ArrayList<Double> scores;
    . . .
    public void addScore(double score) { . . . }
    public double finalScore() { . . . }
}
```

A second class, ScoreAnalyzer, is responsible for reading the user input and displaying the result. Its main method simply calls the GradeBook methods:

```java
GradeBook book = new GradeBook();
System.out.println("Please enter values, Q to quit:");
while (in.hasNextDouble())
{
    book.addScore(in.nextDouble());
}
System.out.println("Final score: " + book.finalScore());
```

Now the finalScore method must do the heavy lifting. It too should not have to do all the work. Instead, we will supply helper methods

```java
public double sum()
public double minimum()
```

These methods simply implement the algorithms in Section 7.6.2 and Section 7.6.4. Then the finalScore method becomes

```java
public double finalScore()
{
    if (scores.size() == 0)
        return 0;
    else if (scores.size() == 1)
        return scores.get(0);
    else
        return sum() - minimum();
}
```

Step 5 Assemble and test the program.

Implement your classes and test them, as described in How To 3.1. Review your code and check that you handle both normal and exceptional situations. What happens with an empty array or array list? One that contains a single element? When no match is found? When there are multiple matches? Consider these boundary conditions and make sure that your program works correctly.

In our example, it is impossible to compute the minimum if the array list is empty. In that case, we should determine the special score of 0 *before* attempting to call the minimum method.

What if the minimum value occurs more than once? That means that a student had more than one test with the same low score. We subtract only one of the occurrences of that low score, and that is the desired behavior.

The following table shows test cases and their expected output:

Test Case	Expected Output	Comment
8 7 8.5 9.5 7 5 10	50	See Step 1.
8 7 7 9	24	Only one instance of the low score should be removed.
8	8	Don't remove the lowest score if there is only one.
(no inputs)	0	An empty grade book has score 0.

The complete program is in the ch07/scores directory of the book's companion code.

Worked Example 7.1

Rolling the Dice

This Worked Example shows how to analyze a set of die tosses to see whether the die is "fair".

7.7 Regression Testing

A test suite is a set of tests for repeated testing.

Regression testing involves repeating previously run tests to ensure that known failures of prior versions do not appear in new versions of the software.

It is a common and useful practice to make a new test whenever you find a program bug. You can use that test to verify that your bug fix really works. Don't throw the test away; feed it to the next version after that and all subsequent versions. Such a collection of test cases is called a **test suite**.

You will be surprised how often a bug that you fixed will reappear in a future version. This is a phenomenon known as *cycling*. Sometimes you don't quite understand the reason for a bug and apply a quick fix that appears to work. Later, you apply a different quick fix that solves a second problem but makes the first problem appear again. Of course, it is always best to think through what really causes a bug and fix the root cause instead of doing a sequence of "Band-Aid" solutions. If you don't succeed in doing that, however, you at least want to have an honest appraisal of how well the program works. By keeping all old test cases around and testing them against every new version, you get that feedback. The process of checking each version of a program against a test suite is called **regression testing**.

How do you organize a suite of tests? An easy technique is to produce multiple tester classes, such as BankTester1, BankTester2, and so on.

Another useful approach is to provide a generic tester, and feed it inputs from multiple files. Consider this tester for the Bank class of Section 7.6:

Available online in WileyPLUS and at www.wiley.com/college/horstmann.

ch07/regression/BankTester.java

```java
1   import java.util.Scanner;
2
3   /**
4       This program tests the Bank class.
5   */
6   public class BankTester
7   {
8       public static void main(String[] args)
9       {
10          Bank firstBankOfJava = new Bank();
11          firstBankOfJava.addAccount(new BankAccount(1001, 20000));
12          firstBankOfJava.addAccount(new BankAccount(1015, 10000));
13          firstBankOfJava.addAccount(new BankAccount(1729, 15000));
14
15          Scanner in = new Scanner(System.in);
16
17          double threshold = in.nextDouble();
18          int c = firstBankOfJava.count(threshold);
19          System.out.println("Count: " + c);
20          int expectedCount = in.nextInt();
21          System.out.println("Expected: " + expectedCount);
22
23          int accountNumber = in.nextInt();
24          BankAccount a = firstBankOfJava.find(accountNumber);
25          if (a == null)
26              System.out.println("No matching account");
27          else
28          {
29              System.out.println("Balance of matching account: " + a.getBalance());
30              int matchingBalance = in.nextInt();
31              System.out.println("Expected: " + matchingBalance);
32          }
33      }
34  }
```

Rather than using fixed values for the threshold and the account number to be found, the program reads these values, and the expected responses. By running the program with different inputs, we can test different scenarios, such as the ones for diagnosing off-by-one errors discussed in Common Error 6.2.

Of course, it would be tedious to type in the input values by hand every time the test is executed. It is much better to save the inputs in a file, such as the following:

ch07/regression/input1.txt

```
15000
2
1015
10000
```

The command line interfaces of most operating systems provide a way to link a file to the input of a program, as if all the characters in the file had actually been typed by a user. Type the following command into a shell window:

```
java BankTester < input1.txt
```

The program is executed, but it no longer reads input from the keyboard. Instead, the `System.in` object (and the `Scanner` that reads from `System.in`) gets the input from the file `input1.txt`. This process is called *input redirection*.

The output is still displayed in the console window:

Program Run

```
Count: 2
Expected: 2
Balance of matching account: 10000
Expected: 10000
```

You can also redirect output. To capture the output of a program in a file, use the command

```
java BankTester < input1.txt > output1.txt
```

This is useful for archiving test cases.

SELF CHECK

16. Suppose you modified the code for a method. Why do you want to repeat tests that already passed with the previous version of the code?

17. Suppose a customer of your program finds an error. What action should you take beyond fixing the error?

18. Why doesn't the `BankTester` program contain prompts for the inputs?

Productivity Hint 7.2

Batch Files and Shell Scripts

If you need to perform the same tasks repeatedly on the command line, then it is worth learning about the automation features offered by your operating system.

Under Windows, you use batch files to execute a number of commands automatically. For example, suppose you need to test a program by running three testers:

```
java BankTester1
java BankTester2
java BankTester3 < input1.txt
```

Then you find a bug, fix it, and run the tests again. Now you need to type the three commands once more. There has to be a better way. Under Windows, put the commands in a text file and call it `test.bat`:

File test.bat

```
1   java BankTester1
2   java BankTester2
3   java BankTester3 < input1.txt
```

Then you just type

```
test.bat
```

and the three commands in the batch file execute automatically.

Batch files are a feature of the operating system, not of Java. On Linux, Mac OS, and UNIX, shell scripts are used for the same purpose. In this simple example, you can execute the commands by typing

```
sh test.bat
```

There are many uses for batch files and shell scripts, and it is well worth it to learn more about their advanced features, such as parameters and loops.

Random Fact 7.2

The Therac-25 Incidents

The Therac-25 is a computerized device to deliver radiation treatment to cancer patients (see the figure). Between June 1985 and January 1987, several of these machines delivered serious overdoses to at least six patients, killing some of them and seriously maiming the others.

The machines were controlled by a computer program. Bugs in the program were directly responsible for the overdoses. According to Leveson and Turner ("An Investigation of the Therac-25 Accidents," *IEEE Computer*, July 1993, pp. 18–41), the program was written by a single programmer, who had since left the manufacturing company producing the device and could not be located. None of the company employees interviewed could say anything about the educational level or qualifications of the programmer.

The investigation by the federal Food and Drug Administration (FDA) found that the program was poorly documented and that there was neither a specification document nor a formal test plan. (This should make you think. Do you have a formal test plan for your programs?)

The overdoses were caused by an amateurish design of the software that had to control different devices concurrently, namely the keyboard, the display, the printer, and of course the radiation device itself. Synchronization and data sharing between the tasks were done in an ad hoc way, even though safe multitasking techniques were known at the time. Had the programmer enjoyed a formal education that involved these techniques, or taken the effort to study the literature, a safer machine could have been built. Such a machine would have probably involved a commercial multitasking system, which might have required a more expensive computer.

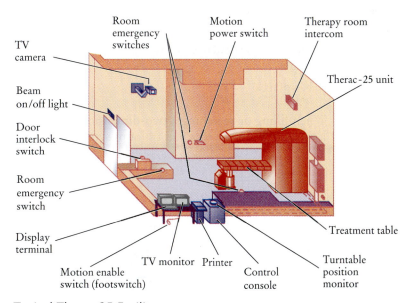

Typical Therac-25 Facility

The same flaws were present in the software controlling the predecessor model, the Therac-20, but that machine had hardware interlocks that mechanically prevented overdoses. The hardware safety devices were removed in the Therac-25 and replaced by checks in the software, presumably to save cost.

Frank Houston of the FDA wrote in 1985: "A significant amount of software for life-critical systems comes from small firms, especially in the medical device industry; firms that fit the profile of those resistant to or uninformed of the principles of either system safety or software engineering".

Who is to blame? The programmer? The manager who not only failed to ensure that the programmer was up to the task but also didn't insist on comprehensive testing? The hospitals that installed the device, or the FDA, for not reviewing the design process? Unfortunately, even today there are no firm standards of what constitutes a safe software design process.

7.8 Two-Dimensional Arrays

Arrays and array lists can store linear sequences. Occasionally you want to store collections that have a two-dimensional layout. The traditional example is the tic-tac-toe board (see Figure 15).

> Two-dimensional arrays form a tabular, two-dimensional arrangement. You access elements with an index pair a[i][j].

Such an arrangement, consisting of rows and columns of values, is called a **two-dimensional array** or matrix. When constructing a two-dimensional array, you specify how many rows and columns you need. In this case, ask for 3 rows and 3 columns:

```
final int ROWS = 3;
final int COLUMNS = 3;
String[][] board = new String[ROWS][COLUMNS];
```

This yields a two-dimensional array with 9 elements

```
board[0][0]    board[0][1]    board[0][2]
board[1][0]    board[1][1]    board[1][2]
board[2][0]    board[2][1]    board[2][2]
```

To access a particular element, specify two index values in separate brackets. For example:

```
board[1][1] = "x";
board[2][1] = "o";
```

When filling or searching a two-dimensional array, it is common to use two nested loops. For example, this pair of loops sets all elements in the array to spaces.

```
for (int i = 0; i < ROWS; i++)
    for (int j = 0; j < COLUMNS; j++)
        board[i][j] = " ";
```

Figure 15 A Tic-Tac-Toe Board

In this loop, we used constants for the number of rows and columns. You can also recover the array dimensions from the array variable:

- `board.length` is the number of rows.
- `board[0].length` is the number of columns. (See Special Topic 7.3 on page 313 for an explanation of this expression.)

You can rewrite the loop for filling the tic-tac-toe board as

```
for (int i = 0; i < board.length; i++)
   for (int j = 0; j < board[0].length; j++)
      board[i][j] = " ";
```

Here is a class and a test program for playing tic-tac-toe. This class does not check whether a player has won the game. That is left as an exercise—see Exercise P7.13.

ch07/twodim/TicTacToe.java

```java
1  /**
2     A 3 x 3 tic-tac-toe board.
3  */
4  public class TicTacToe
5  {
6     private String[][] board;
7     private static final int ROWS = 3;
8     private static final int COLUMNS = 3;
9
10    /**
11       Constructs an empty board.
12    */
13    public TicTacToe()
14    {
15       board = new String[ROWS][COLUMNS];
16       // Fill with spaces
17       for (int i = 0; i < ROWS; i++)
18          for (int j = 0; j < COLUMNS; j++)
19             board[i][j] = " ";
20    }
21
22    /**
23       Sets a field in the board. The field must be unoccupied.
24       @param i the row index
25       @param j the column index
26       @param player the player ("x" or "o")
27    */
28    public void set(int i, int j, String player)
29    {
30       if (board[i][j].equals(" "))
31          board[i][j] = player;
32    }
33
34    /**
35       Creates a string representation of the board, such as
36       |x o|
37       | x |
38       | o|.
39       @return the string representation
40    */
41    public String toString()
42    {
```

```
43        String r = "";
44        for (int i = 0; i < ROWS; i++)
45        {
46           r = r + "|";
47           for (int j = 0; j < COLUMNS; j++)
48              r = r + board[i][j];
49           r = r + "|\n";
50        }
51        return r;
52     }
53  }
```

ch07/twodim/TicTacToeRunner.java

```
1   import java.util.Scanner;
2
3   /**
4      This program runs a TicTacToe game. It prompts the
5      user to set positions on the board and prints out the
6      result.
7   */
8   public class TicTacToeRunner
9   {
10     public static void main(String[] args)
11     {
12        Scanner in = new Scanner(System.in);
13        String player = "x";
14        TicTacToe game = new TicTacToe();
15        boolean done = false;
16        while (!done)
17        {
18           System.out.print(game.toString());
19           System.out.print(
20              "Row for " + player + " (-1 to exit): ");
21           int row = in.nextInt();
22           if (row < 0) done = true;
23           else
24           {
25              System.out.print("Column for " + player + ": ");
26              int column = in.nextInt();
27              game.set(row, column, player);
28              if (player.equals("x"))
29                 player = "o";
30              else
31                 player = "x";
32           }
33        }
34     }
35  }
```

Program Run

```
|  |  |
|  |  |
|  |  |
Row for x (-1 to exit): 1
Column for x: 2
|  |  |
|  x|
|  |  |
```

```
Row for o (-1 to exit): 0
Column for o: 0
|o  |
|  x|
|   |
Row for x (-1 to exit): -1
```

19. How do you declare and initialize a 4-by-4 array of integers?

20. How do you count the number of spaces in the tic-tac-toe board?

Worked Example 7.2

A World Population Table

This Worked Example shows how to print world population data in a table with row and column headers, and totals for each of the data columns.

Special Topic 7.3

Two-Dimensional Arrays with Variable Row Lengths

When you declare a two-dimensional array with the command

```
int[][] a = new int[3][3];
```

then you get a 3-by-3 matrix that can store 9 elements:

```
a[0][0] a[0][1] a[0][2]
a[1][0] a[1][1] a[1][2]
a[2][0] a[2][1] a[2][2]
```

In this matrix, all rows have the same length.

In Java it is possible to declare arrays in which the row length varies. For example, you can store an array that has a triangular shape, such as:

```
b[0][0]
b[1][0] b[1][1]
b[2][0] b[2][1] b[2][2]
```

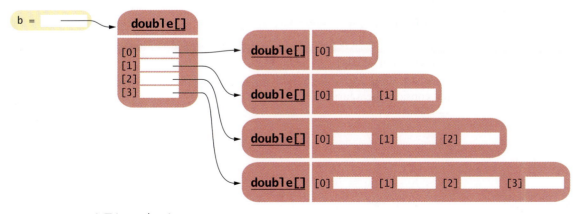

A Triangular Array

➕ Available online in WileyPLUS and at www.wiley.com/college/horstmann.

To allocate such an array, you must work harder. First, you allocate space to hold three rows. Indicate that you will manually set each row by leaving the second array index empty:

```
int[][] b = new int[3][];
```

Then allocate each row separately.

```
for (int i = 0; i < b.length; i++)
    b[i] = new int[i + 1];
```

See the figure.

You can access each array element as b[i][j]. The expression b[i] selects the ith row, and the [j] operator selects the jth element in that row.

Note that the number of rows is b.length, and the length of the ith row is b[i].length. For example, the following pair of loops prints a ragged array:

```
for (int i = 0; i < b.length; i++)
{
    for (int j = 0; j < b[i].length; j++)
        System.out.print(b[i][j]);
    System.out.println();
}
```

Alternatively, you can use two "for each" loops:

```
for (double[] row : b)
{
    for (double element : row)
        System.out.print(element);
    System.out.println();
}
```

Naturally, such "ragged" arrays are not very common.

Java implements plain two-dimensional arrays in exactly the same way as ragged arrays: as arrays of one-dimensional arrays. The expression new int[3][3] automatically allocates an array of three rows, and three arrays for the rows' contents.

Special Topic 7.4

Multidimensional Arrays

You can declare arrays with more than two dimensions. For example, here is a three-dimensional array:

```
int[][][] rubiksCube = new int[3][3][3];
```

Each array element is specified by three index values,

```
rubiksCube[i][j][k]
```

However, these arrays are quite rare, particularly in object-oriented programs, and we will not consider them further.

Summary of Learning Objectives

Use arrays for collecting values.

- An array is a sequence of values of the same type.
- You access an array element with an integer index, using the [] operator.
- Index values of an array range from 0 to length - 1.
- Accessing a nonexistent element results in a bounds error.
- The expression *array*.length yields the number of elements in an array.
- Avoid parallel arrays by changing them into arrays of objects.

Use array lists for managing collections whose size can change.

- The ArrayList class manages a sequence of objects whose size can change.
- The ArrayList class is a generic class: ArrayList<*TypeName*> collects objects of the given type.

Use wrapper classes when working with array lists of numbers.

- To treat primitive type values as objects, you must use wrapper classes.

Use the for loop to visit all elements of a collection.

- The enhanced for loop traverses all elements of a collection.
- In an enhanced for loop, the loop variable contains an element, not an index.

Work with arrays that are partially filled.

- With a partially filled array, keep a companion variable to track how many elements are used.

Be able to use common array algorithms.

- To count values, check all elements and count the matches until you reach the end.
- To compute the maximum or minimum value, initialize a candidate with the starting element. Then compare the candidate with the remaining elements and update it if you find a larger or smaller value.
- To find a value, check all elements until you have found a match.
- An array variable stores a reference to the array. Copying the variable yields a second reference to the same array.
- Use the Arrays.copyOf method to copy the elements of an array.

Describe the process of regression testing.

- A test suite is a set of tests for repeated testing.
- Regression testing involves repeating previously run tests to ensure that known failures of prior versions do not appear in new versions of the software.

Use two-dimensional arrays for data that is arranged in rows and columns.

- Two-dimensional arrays form a tabular, two-dimensional arrangement. You access elements with an index pair a[i][j].

Classes, Objects, and Methods Introduced in this Chapter

```
java.lang.Boolean
    booleanValue
java.lang.Double
    doubleValue
java.lang.Integer
    intValue
java.util.Arrays
    copyOf
    toString
```

```
java.util.ArrayList<E>
    add
    get
    remove
    set
    size
```

Media Resources

www.wiley.com/
college/
horstmann

- • ***Worked Example*** Rolling the Dice
- • ***Worked Example*** A World Population Table
- • Lab Exercises
- ➕ ***Animation*** Removing from an Array
- ➕ ***Animation*** Inserting into an Array
- ➕ Practice Quiz
- ➕ Code Completion Exercises

Review Exercises

★ **R7.1** What is an index? What are the bounds of an array or array list? What is a bounds error?

★ **R7.2** Write a program that contains a bounds error. Run the program. What happens on your computer? How does the error message help you locate the error?

★★ **R7.3** Write Java code for a loop that simultaneously computes the maximum and minimum values of an array list. Use an array list of accounts as an example.

★ **R7.4** Write a loop that reads 10 strings and inserts them into an array list. Write a second loop that prints out the strings in the opposite order from which they were entered.

★★ **R7.5** Consider the algorithm that we used for determining the maximum value in an array list. We set largestYet to the starting element, which meant that we were no longer able to use the "for each" loop. An alternate approach is to initialize largestYet with null, then loop through all elements. Of course, inside the loop you need to test whether largestYet is still null. Modify the loop that finds the bank account with the largest balance, using this technique. Is this approach more or less efficient than the one used in the text?

★★★ **R7.6** Consider another variation of the algorithm for determining the maximum value. Here, we compute the maximum value of an array of numbers.

```
double max = 0; // Contains an error!
for (double element : values)
{
    if (element > max) max = element;
}
```

However, this approach contains a subtle error. What is the error, and how can you fix it?

★ **R7.7** For each of the following sets of values, write code that fills an array a with the values.

    a. 1 2 3 4 5 6 7 8 9 10

    b. 0 2 4 6 8 10 12 14 16 18 20

    c. 1 4 9 16 25 36 49 64 81 100

    d. 0 0 0 0 0 0 0 0 0 0

    e. 1 4 9 16 9 7 4 9 11

Use a loop when appropriate.

★★ **R7.8** Write a loop that fills an array a with 10 random numbers between 1 and 100. Write code (using one or more loops) to fill a with 10 different random numbers between 1 and 100.

★ **R7.9** What is wrong with the following loop?

```
double[] values = new double[10];
for (int i = 1; i <= 10; i++) values[i] = i * i;
```

Explain two ways of fixing the error.

★★★T **R7.10** Write a program that constructs an array of 20 integers and fills the first ten elements with the numbers 1, 4, 9, . . . , 100. Compile it and launch the debugger. After the array has been filled with three numbers, inspect it. What are the contents of the elements in the array beyond those that you filled?

★★ **R7.11** Rewrite the following loops without using the "for each" construct. Here, values has type double.

    a. `for (double element : values) sum = sum + element;`

    b. `for (double element : values) if (element == target) return true;`

    c. `int i = 0;`
       `for (double element : values) { values[i] = 2 * element; i++; }`

★★ **R7.12** Rewrite the following loops, using the "for each" construct. Here, values has type double.

    a. `for (int i = 0; i < values.length; i++) sum = sum + values[i];`

    b. `for (int i = 1; i < values.length; i++) sum = sum + values[i];`

    c. `for (int i = 0; i < values.length; i++)`
          `if (values[i] == target) return i;`

★★ **R7.13** What is wrong with these statements for printing an array list with separators?

```
System.out.print(values.get(0));
for (int i = 1; i < values.size(); i++)
{
    System.out.print(", " + values.get(i));
}
```

★★ **R7.14** When finding the position of a match in Section 7.6.6, we used a `while` loop, not a `for` loop. What is wrong with using this loop instead?

```
for (pos = 0; pos < values.size() && !found; pos++)
{
   if (values.get(pos) > 100)
   {
      found = true;
   }
}
```

★★ **R7.15** When inserting an element into an array in Section 7.6.8, we moved the elements with larger index values, starting at the end of the array. Why is it wrong to start at the insertion location, like this?

```
for (int i = pos; i < size - 1; i++)
{
   values[i + 1] = values[i];
}
```

★★ **R7.16** In Section 7.6.9, we doubled the length of the array when growing it. Why didn't we just increase the size by one element?

★ **R7.17** What are parallel arrays? Why are parallel arrays indications of poor programming? How can they be avoided?

★ **R7.18** True or false?

    a. All elements of an array are of the same type.

    b. An array index must be an integer.

    c. Arrays cannot contain string references as elements.

    d. Arrays cannot contain `null` references as elements.

    e. Parallel arrays must have equal length.

    f. Two-dimensional arrays always have the same numbers of rows and columns.

    g. Two parallel arrays can be replaced by a two-dimensional array.

    h. Elements of different columns in a two-dimensional array can have different types.

★T **R7.19** Define the terms *regression testing* and *test suite*.

★T **R7.20** What is the debugging phenomenon known as *cycling*? What can you do to avoid it?

Programming Exercises

★ **P7.1** Implement a class `Purse`. A purse contains a collection of coins. For simplicity, we will only store the coin names in an `ArrayList<String>`. (We will discuss a better representation in Chapter 8.) Supply a method

```
void addCoin(String coinName)
```

Add a method `toString` to the `Purse` class that prints the coins in the purse in the format

```
Purse[Quarter,Dime,Nickel,Dime]
```

★ **P7.2** Write a method reverse that reverses the sequence of coins in a purse. Use the toString method of the preceding assignment to test your code. For example, if reverse is called with a purse

```
Purse[Quarter,Dime,Nickel,Dime]
```

then the purse is changed to

```
Purse[Dime,Nickel,Dime,Quarter]
```

★ **P7.3** Add a method to the Purse class

```
public void transfer(Purse other)
```

that transfers the contents of one purse to another. For example, if a is

```
Purse[Quarter,Dime,Nickel,Dime]
```

and b is

```
Purse[Dime,Nickel]
```

then after the call a.transfer(b), a is

```
Purse[Quarter,Dime,Nickel,Dime,Dime,Nickel]
```

and b is empty.

★ **P7.4** Write a method for the Purse class

```
public boolean sameContents(Purse other)
```

that checks whether the other purse has the same coins in the same order.

★★ **P7.5** Write a method for the Purse class

```
public boolean sameCoins(Purse other)
```

that checks whether the other purse has the same coins, perhaps in a different order. For example, the purses

```
Purse[Quarter,Dime,Nickel,Dime]
```

and

```
Purse[Nickel,Dime,Dime,Quarter]
```

should be considered equal.

You will probably need one or more helper methods.

★★ **P7.6** A Polygon is a closed curve made up from line segments that join the polygon's corner points. Implement a class Polygon with methods

```
public double perimeter()
```

and

```
public double area()
```

that compute the circumference and area of a polygon. To compute the perimeter, compute the distance between adjacent points, and total up the distances. The area of a polygon with corners $(x_0, y_0), \ldots, (x_{n-1}, y_{n-1})$ is

$$\frac{1}{2}\left(x_0 y_1 + x_1 y_2 + \cdots + x_{n-1} y_0 - y_0 x_1 - y_1 x_2 - \cdots - y_{n-1} x_0\right)$$

As test cases, compute the perimeter and area of a rectangle and of a regular hexagon. *Note:* You need not draw the polygon — that is done in Exercise P7.18.

★ **P7.7** Write a program that reads a sequence of integers into an array and that computes the alternating sum of all elements in the array. For example, if the program is executed with the input data

$$1 \quad 4 \quad 9 \quad 16 \quad 9 \quad 7 \quad 4 \quad 9 \quad 11$$

then it computes

$$1 - 4 + 9 - 16 + 9 - 7 + 4 - 9 + 11 = -2$$

★★ **P7.8** Write a program that produces random permutations of the numbers 1 to 10. To generate a random permutation, you need to fill an array with the numbers 1 to 10 so that no two entries of the array have the same contents. You could do it by brute force, by calling Random.nextInt until it produces a value that is not yet in the array. Instead, you should implement a smart method. Make a second array and fill it with the numbers 1 to 10. Then pick one of those at random, remove it, and append it to the permutation array. Repeat 10 times. Implement a class PermutationGenerator with a method

```
int[] nextPermutation
```

★★ **P7.9** A *run* is a sequence of adjacent repeated values. Write a program that generates a sequence of 20 random die tosses and that prints the die values, marking the runs by including them in parentheses, like this:

1 2 (5 5) 3 1 2 4 3 (2 2 2 2) 3 6 (5 5) 6 3 1

Use the following pseudocode:

```
Set a boolean variable inRun to false.
For each valid index i in the array list
    If inRun
        If values[i] is different from the preceding value
            Print )
            inRun = false
    Else
        If values[i] is the same as the following value
            Print (
            inRun = true
    Print values[i]
If inRun, print )
```

★★★ **P7.10** Write a program that generates a sequence of 20 random die tosses and that prints the die values, marking only the longest run, like this:

1 2 5 5 3 1 2 4 3 (2 2 2 2) 3 6 5 5 6 3 1

If there is more than one run of maximum length, mark the first one.

★★ **P7.11** It is a well-researched fact that men in a restroom generally prefer to maximize their distance from already occupied stalls, by occupying the middle of the longest sequence of unoccupied places.

For example, consider the situation where ten stalls are empty.

_ _ _ _ _ _ _ _ _ _

The first visitor will occupy a middle position:

_ _ _ _ _ X _ _ _ _

The next visitor will be in the middle of the empty area at the left.

    _ _ X _ _ X _ _ _ _

Write a program that reads the number of stalls and then prints out diagrams in the format given above when the stalls become filled, one at a time. *Hint:* Use an array of boolean values to indicate whether a stall is occupied.

★★★ **P7.12** In this assignment, you will model the game of *Bulgarian Solitaire*. The game starts with 45 cards. (They need not be playing cards. Unmarked index cards work just as well.) Randomly divide them into some number of piles of random size. For example, you might start with piles of size 20, 5, 1, 9, and 10. In each round, you take one card from each pile, forming a new pile with these cards. For example, the sample starting configuration would be transformed into piles of size 19, 4, 8, 10, and 5. The solitaire is over when the piles have size 1, 2, 3, 4, 5, 6, 7, 8, and 9, in some order. (It can be shown that you always end up with such a configuration.)

In your program, produce a random starting configuration and print it. Then keep applying the solitaire step and print the result. Stop when the solitaire final configuration is reached.

★★ **P7.13** Add a method getWinner to the TicTacToe class of Section 7.8. It should return "x" or "o" to indicate a winner, or " " if there is no winner yet. Recall that a winning position has three matching marks in a row, column, or diagonal.

★★★ **P7.14** Write an application that plays tic-tac-toe. Your program should draw the game board, change players after every successful move, and pronounce the winner.

★★ **P7.15** *Magic squares.* An $n \times n$ matrix that is filled with the numbers $1, 2, 3, \ldots, n^2$ is a magic square if the sum of the elements in each row, in each column, and in the two diagonals is the same value. For example,

16	3	2	13
5	10	11	8
9	6	7	12
4	15	14	1

Write a program that reads in n^2 values from the keyboard and tests whether they form a magic square when arranged as a square matrix. You need to test three features:

- Did the user enter n^2 numbers for some n?
- Do each of the numbers $1, 2, \ldots, n^2$ occur exactly once in the user input?
- When the numbers are put into a square, are the sums of the rows, columns, and diagonals equal to each other?

If the size of the input is a square, test whether all numbers between 1 and n^2 are present. Then compute the row, column, and diagonal sums. Implement a class Square with methods

```
public void add(int i)
public boolean isMagic()
```

★★ **P7.16** Implement the following algorithm to construct magic n-by-n^2 squares; it works only if n is odd. Place a 1 in the middle of the bottom row. After k has been placed in the (i, j) square, place $k + 1$ into the square to the right and down, wrapping around the borders. However, if the square to the right and down has already been filled, or if you are in the lower-right corner, then you must move to the square straight up instead. Here is the 5 × 5 square that you get if you follow this method:

11	18	25	2	9
10	12	19	21	3
4	6	13	20	22
23	5	7	14	16
17	24	1	8	15

Write a program whose input is the number n and whose output is the magic square of order n if n is odd. Implement a class MagicSquare with a constructor that constructs the square and a toString method that returns a representation of the square.

★G **P7.17** Implement a class Cloud that contains an array list of Point2D.Double objects. Support methods

```
public void add(Point2D.Double aPoint)
public void draw(Graphics2D g2)
```

Draw each point as a tiny circle.

Write a graphical application that draws a cloud of 100 random points.

★★G **P7.18** Implement a class Polygon that contains an array list of Point2D.Double objects. Support methods

```
public void add(Point2D.Double aPoint)
public void draw(Graphics2D g2)
```

Draw the polygon by joining adjacent points with a line, and then closing it up by joining the end and start points.

Write a graphical application that draws a square and a pentagon using two Polygon objects.

★G **P7.19** Write a class Chart with methods

```
public void add(int value)
public void draw(Graphics2D g2)
```

that displays a stick chart of the added values, like this:

You may assume that the values are pixel positions.

★★G **P7.20** Write a class BarChart with methods

```
public void add(double value)
public void draw(Graphics2D g2)
```

that displays a chart of the added values. You may assume that all added values are positive. Stretch the bars so that they fill the entire area of the screen. You must figure out the maximum of the values, and then scale each bar.

★★★**G** **P7.21** Improve the `BarChart` class of Exercise P7.20 to work correctly when the data contains negative values.

★★**G** **P7.22** Write a class `PieChart` with methods

```
public void add(double value)
public void draw(Graphics2D g2)
```

that displays a pie chart of the added values. You may assume that all data values are positive.

Programming Projects

Project 7.1 *Poker Simulator.* In this assignment, you will implement a simulation of a popular casino game usually called video poker. The card deck contains 52 cards, 13 of each suit. At the beginning of the game, the deck is shuffled. You need to devise a fair method for shuffling. (It does not have to be efficient.) Then the top five cards of the deck are presented to the player. The player can reject none, some, or all of the cards. The rejected cards are replaced from the top of the deck. Now the hand is scored. Your program should pronounce it to be one of the following:

- No pair—The lowest hand, containing five separate cards that do not match up to create any of the hands below.
- One pair—Two cards of the same value, for example two queens.
- Two pairs—Two pairs, for example two queens and two 5's.
- Three of a kind—Three cards of the same value, for example three queens.
- Straight—Five cards with consecutive values, not necessarily of the same suit, such as 4, 5, 6, 7, and 8. The ace can either precede a 2 or follow a king.
- Flush—Five cards, not necessarily in order, of the same suit.
- Full House—Three of a kind and a pair, for example three queens and two 5's
- Four of a Kind—Four cards of the same value, such as four queens.
- Straight Flush—A straight and a flush: Five cards with consecutive values of the same suit.
- Royal Flush—The best possible hand in poker. A 10, jack, queen, king, and ace, all of the same suit.

If you are so inclined, you can implement a wager. The player pays a `JavaDollar` for each game, and wins according to the following payout chart:

Hand	Payout	Hand	Payout
Royal Flush	250	Straight	4
Straight Flush	50	Three of a Kind	3
Four of a Kind	25	Two Pair	2
Full House	6	Pair of Jacks or Better	1
Flush	5		

Project 7.2 *The Game of Life* is a well-known mathematical game that gives rise to amazingly complex behavior, although it can be specified by a few simple rules. (It is not actually a game in the traditional sense, with players competing for a win.) Here are the rules. The game is played on a rectangular board. Each square can be either empty or occupied. At the beginning, you can specify empty and occupied cells in some way; then the game runs automatically. In each *generation*, the next generation is computed. A new cell is born on an empty square if it is surrounded by exactly three occupied neighbor cells. A cell dies of overcrowding if it is surrounded by four or more neighbors, and it dies of loneliness if it is surrounded by zero or one neighbor. A neighbor is an occupant of an adjacent square to the left, right, top, or bottom or in a diagonal direction. Figure 16 shows a cell and its neighbor cells.

Many configurations show interesting behavior when subjected to these rules. Figure 17 shows a *glider*, observed over five generations. Note how it moves. After four generations, it is transformed into the identical shape, but located one square to the right and below.

One of the more amazing configurations is the glider gun: a complex collection of cells that, after 30 moves, turns back into itself and a glider (see Figure 18).

Program the game to eliminate the drudgery of computing successive generations by hand. Use a two-dimensional array to store the rectangular configuration. Write a program that shows successive generations of the game. You may get extra credit if you implement a graphical application that allows the user to add or remove cells by clicking with the mouse.

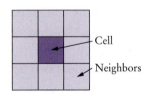

Figure 16
Neighborhood of a Cell

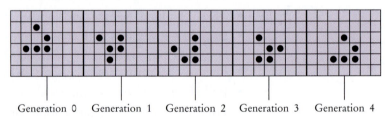

Generation 0   Generation 1   Generation 2   Generation 3   Generation 4

Figure 17
Glider

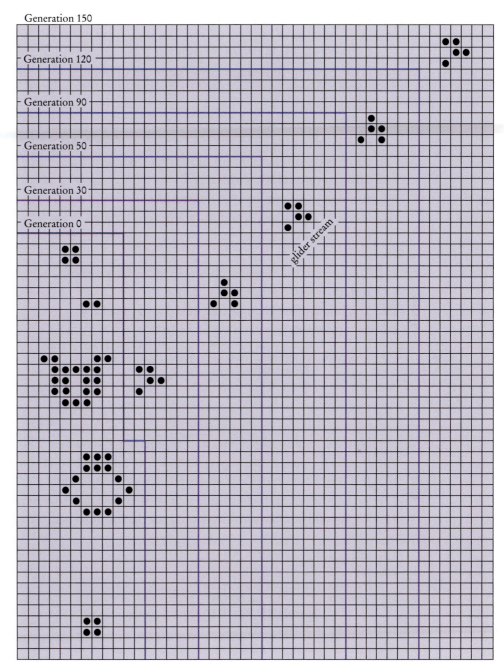

Figure 18 Glider Gun

Answers to Self-Check Questions

1. 0, 1, 4, 9, 16, 25, 36, 49, 64, 81, but *not* 100.
2. (a) 0; (b) a run-time error: array index out of bounds; (c) a compile-time error: c is not initialized.
3. ```
   new String[10];
   new ArrayList<String>();
   ```
4. names contains the strings "B" and "C" at positions 0 and 1.
5. double is one of the eight primitive types. Double is a class type.
6. `values.set(0, values.get(0) + 1);`
7. `for (double element : values) System.out.println(element);`
8. It counts how many accounts have a zero balance.
9. `for (int i = valuesSize - 1; i >= 0; i--) System.out.println(values[i]);`
10. `valuesSize--;`
11. You need to use wrapper objects in an ArrayList<Double>, which is less efficient.
12. It returns the first match that it finds.
13. Yes, but the first comparison would always fail.
14. ```
    for (int i = 0; i < values.size(); i++)
    {
        System.out.print(values.get(i));
        if (i < values.size() - 1)
        {
            System.out.print(" | ");
        }
    }
    ```
    Now you know why we set up the loop the other way.
15. If names happens to be empty, the first line causes a bounds error.
16. It is possible to introduce errors when modifying code.
17. Add a test case to the test suite that verifies that the error is fixed.
18. There is no human user who would see the prompts because input is provided from a file.
19. `int[][] array = new int[4][4];`
20. ```
    int count = 0;
    for (int i = 0; i < ROWS; i++)
        for (int j = 0; j < COLUMNS; j++)
            if (board[i][j].equals(" ")) count++;
    ```
    ```

Chapter 8

Designing Classes

CHAPTER GOALS

- To learn how to choose appropriate classes for a given problem
- To understand the concepts of cohesion and coupling
- To minimize the use of side effects
- To document the responsibilities of methods and their callers with preconditions and postconditions
- To understand static methods and variables
- To understand the scope rules for local variables and instance variables
- To learn about packages
- T To learn about unit testing frameworks

In this chapter you will learn more about designing classes. First, we will discuss the process of discovering classes and declaring methods. Next, we will discuss how the concepts of pre- and postconditions enable you to specify, implement, and invoke methods correctly. You will also learn about several more technical issues, such as static methods and variables. Finally, you will see how to use packages to organize your classes.

CHAPTER CONTENTS

8.1 Discovering Classes

You have used a good number of classes in the preceding chapters and probably designed a few classes yourself as part of your programming assignments. Designing a class can be a challenge—it is not always easy to tell how to start or whether the result is of good quality.

What makes a good class? Most importantly, a class should *represent a single concept* from a problem domain. Some of the classes that you have seen represent concepts from mathematics:

A class should represent a single concept from a problem domain, such as business, science, or mathematics.

- Point
- Rectangle
- Ellipse

Other classes are abstractions of real-life entities:

- BankAccount
- CashRegister

For these classes, the properties of a typical object are easy to understand. A Rectangle object has a width and height. Given a BankAccount object, you can deposit and withdraw money. Generally, concepts from the part of the universe that a program concerns, such as science, business, or a game, make good classes. The name for such a class should be a noun that describes the concept. In fact, a simple rule of thumb for getting started with class design is to look for nouns in the problem description.

One useful category of classes can be described as *actors*. Objects of an actor class carry out certain tasks for you. Examples of actors are the Scanner class of

Chapter 4 and the Random class in Chapter 6. A Scanner object scans a stream for numbers and strings. A Random object generates random numbers. It is a good idea to choose class names for actors that end in "-er" or "-or". (A better name for the Random class might be RandomNumberGenerator.)

Very occasionally, a class has no objects, but it contains a collection of related static methods and constants. The Math class is a typical example. Such a class is called a *utility class*.

Finally, you have seen classes with only a main method. Their sole purpose is to start a program. From a design perspective, these are somewhat degenerate examples of classes.

What might not be a good class? If you can't tell from the class name what an object of the class is supposed to do, then you are probably not on the right track. For example, your homework assignment might ask you to write a program that prints paychecks. Suppose you start by trying to design a class PaycheckProgram. What would an object of this class do? An object of this class would have to do everything that the homework needs to do. That doesn't simplify anything. A better class would be Paycheck. Then your program can manipulate one or more Paycheck objects.

Another common mistake is to turn a single operation into a class. For example, if your homework assignment is to compute a paycheck, you may consider writing a class ComputePaycheck. But can you visualize a "ComputePaycheck" object? The fact that "ComputePaycheck" isn't a noun tips you off that you are on the wrong track. On the other hand, a Paycheck class makes intuitive sense. The word "paycheck" is a noun. You can visualize a paycheck object. You can then think about useful methods of the Paycheck class, such as computeTaxes, that help you solve the assignment.

SELF CHECK

1. What is a simple rule of thumb for finding classes?
2. Your job is to write a program that plays chess. Might ChessBoard be an appropriate class? How about MovePiece?

8.2 Cohesion and Coupling

In this section you will learn two useful criteria for analyzing the quality of a class—qualities of its public interface.

A class should represent a single concept. The public methods and constants that the public interface exposes should be *cohesive*. That is, all interface features should be closely related to the single concept that the class represents.

> The public interface of a class is cohesive if all of its features are related to the concept that the class represents.

If you find that the public interface of a class refers to multiple concepts, then that is a good sign that it may be time to use separate classes instead. Consider, for example, the public interface of the CashRegister class in Chapter 4:

```
public class CashRegister
{
    public static final double NICKEL_VALUE = 0.05;
    public static final double DIME_VALUE = 0.1;
    public static final double QUARTER_VALUE = 0.25;
    . . .
```

```
    public void enterPayment(int dollars, int quarters,
        int dimes, int nickels, int pennies)
    . . .
}
```

There are really two concepts here: a cash register that holds coins and computes their total, and the values of individual coins. (For simplicity, we assume that the cash register only holds coins, not bills. Exercise P8.1 discusses a more general solution.)

It makes sense to have a separate Coin class and have coins responsible for knowing their values.

```
public class Coin
{
    . . .
    public Coin(double aValue, String aName) { . . . }
    public double getValue() { . . . }
    . . .
}
```

Then the CashRegister class can be simplified:

```
public class CashRegister
{
    . . .
    public void enterPayment(int coinCount, Coin coinType) { . . . }
    . . .
}
```

Now the CashRegister class no longer needs to know anything about coin values. The same class can equally well handle euros or zorkmids!

This is clearly a better solution, because it separates the responsibilities of the cash register and the coins. The only reason we didn't follow this approach in Chapter 4 was to keep the CashRegister example simple.

Many classes need other classes in order to do their jobs. For example, the restructured CashRegister class now depends on the Coin class to determine the value of the payment.

> A class depends on another class if it uses objects of that class.

To visualize relationships, such as dependence between classes, programmers draw class diagrams. In this book, we use the UML ("Unified Modeling Language") notation for objects and classes. UML is a notation for object-oriented analysis and design invented by Grady Booch, Ivar Jacobson, and James Rumbaugh, three leading researchers in object-oriented software development. The

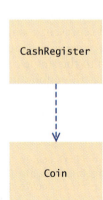

Figure 1
Dependency Relationship Between the CashRegister and Coin Classes

Figure 2   High and Low Coupling Between Classes

UML notation distinguishes between *object diagrams* and class diagrams. In an object diagram the class names are underlined; in a class diagram the class names are not underlined. In a class diagram, you denote dependency by a dashed line with a ➤-shaped open arrow tip that points to the dependent class. Figure 1 shows a class diagram indicating that the CashRegister class depends on the Coin class.

Note that the Coin class does *not* depend on the CashRegister class. Coins have no idea that they are being collected in cash registers, and they can carry out their work without ever calling any method in the CashRegister class.

If many classes of a program depend on each other, then we say that the **coupling** between classes is high. Conversely, if there are few dependencies between classes, then we say that the coupling is low (see Figure 2).

Why does coupling matter? If the Coin class changes in the next release of the program, all the classes that depend on it may be affected. If the change is drastic, the coupled classes must all be updated. Furthermore, if we would like to use a class in another program, we have to take with it all the classes on which it depends. Thus, we want to remove unnecessary coupling between classes.

> It is a good practice to minimize the coupling (i.e., dependency) between classes.

SELF CHECK

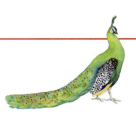

3. Why is the CashRegister class from Chapter 4 not cohesive?
4. Why does the Coin class not depend on the CashRegister class?
5. Why should coupling be minimized between classes?

Quality Tip 8.1

Consistency

In this section you learned of two criteria for analyzing the quality of the public interface of a class. You should maximize cohesion and remove unnecessary coupling. There is another criterion that we would like you to pay attention to—*consistency*. When you have a set of methods, follow a consistent scheme for their names and parameters. This is simply a sign of good craftsmanship.

Sadly, you can find any number of inconsistencies in the standard library. Here is an example. To show an input dialog box, you call

```
JOptionPane.showInputDialog(promptString)
```

To show a message dialog box, you call

```
JOptionPane.showMessageDialog(null, messageString)
```

What's the `null` parameter? It turns out that the `showMessageDialog` method needs a parameter to specify the parent window, or `null` if no parent window is required. But the `showInputDialog` method requires no parent window. Why the inconsistency? There is no reason. It would have been an easy matter to supply a `showMessageDialog` method that exactly mirrors the `showInputDialog` method.

Inconsistencies such as these are not fatal flaws, but they are an annoyance, particularly because they can be so easily avoided.

8.3 Immutable Classes

When analyzing a program that consists of many classes, it is not only important to understand which parts of the program use a given class. We also want to understand who *modifies* objects of a class. The following sections are concerned with this aspect of class design.

Recall that a **mutator method** modifies the object on which it is invoked, whereas an **accessor method** merely accesses information without making any modifications. For example, in the `BankAccount` class, the `deposit` and `withdraw` methods are mutator methods. Calling

```
account.deposit(1000);
```

modifies the state of the account object, but calling

```
double balance = account.getBalance();
```

does not modify the state of account.

> An immutable class has no mutator methods.

You can call an accessor method as many times as you like—you always get the same answer, and the method does not change the state of your object. That is clearly a desirable property, because it makes the behavior of such a method very predictable.

Some classes have been designed to have only accessor methods and no mutator methods at all. Such classes are called **immutable**. An example is the `String` class. Once a string has been constructed, its content never changes. No method in the `String` class can modify the contents of a string. For example, the `toUpperCase` method does not change characters from the original string. Instead, it constructs a *new* string that contains the uppercase characters:

```
String name = "John Q. Public";
String uppercased = name.toUpperCase(); // name is not changed
```

> References to objects of an immutable class can be safely shared.

An immutable class has a major advantage: It is safe to give out references to its objects freely. If no method can change the object's value, then no code can modify the object at an unexpected time. In contrast, if you give out a `BankAccount` reference to any other method, you have to be aware that the state of your object may change—the other method can call the `deposit` and `withdraw` methods on the reference that you gave it.

SELF CHECK

6. Is the `substring` method of the `String` class an accessor or a mutator?

7. Is the `Rectangle` class immutable?

8.4 Side Effects

A side effect of a method is any externally observable data modification.

A **side effect** of a method is any kind of modification of data that is observable outside the method. Mutator methods have a side effect, namely the modification of the implicit parameter. For example, when you call

```
harrysChecking.deposit(1000);
```

you can tell that something changed by calling `harrysChecking.getBalance()`.

Now consider the explicit parameter of a method, such as `studentNames` here:

```
public class GradeBook
{
   . . .
   /**
      Adds student names to this grade book.
      @param studentNames a list of student names
   */
   public void addStudents(ArrayList<String> studentNames)
   {
      while (studentNames.size() > 0)
      {
         String name = studentNames.remove(0); // Not recommended
         Add name to gradebook
      }
   }
}
```

This method *removes* all names from the `studentNames` parameter as it adds them to the grade book. That too is a side effect. After a call

```
book.addStudents(listOfNames);
```

the call `listOfNames.size()` returns 0. Such a side effect would not be what most programmers expect. It is better if the method reads the names from the list without modifying it.

Now consider the following method:

```
public class BankAccount
{
   . . .
   /**
      Transfers money from this account to another account.
      @param amount the amount of money to transfer
      @param other the account into which to transfer the money
   */
   public void transfer(double amount, BankAccount other)
   {
      balance = balance - amount;
      other.deposit(amount);
   }
}
```

This method modifies both the implicit parameter and the explicit parameter `other`. Neither side effect is surprising for a `transfer` method, and there is no reason to avoid them.

Another example of a side effect is output. Consider how we have always printed a bank balance:

```
System.out.println("The balance is now $" + momsSavings.getBalance());
```

Why don't we simply have a printBalance method?

```
public void printBalance() // Not recommended
{
    System.out.println("The balance is now $" + balance);
}
```

That would be more convenient when you actually want to print the value. But, of course, there are cases when you want the value for some other purpose. Thus, you can't simply drop the getBalance method in favor of printBalance.

More importantly, the printBalance method forces strong assumptions on the BankAccount class.

- The message is in English—you assume that the user of your software reads English. The majority of people on the planet don't.
- You rely on System.out. A method that relies on System.out won't work in an embedded system, such as the computer inside an automatic teller machine.

In other words, this design violates the rule of minimizing the coupling of the classes. The printBalance method couples the BankAccount class with the System and PrintStream classes. It is best to decouple input/output from the actual work of your classes.

SELF CHECK

8. If a refers to a bank account, then the call a.deposit(100) modifies the bank account object. Is that a side effect?

9. Consider the DataSet class of Chapter 6. Suppose we add a method

```
void read(Scanner in)
{
    while (in.hasNextDouble())
        add(in.nextDouble());
}
```

Does this method have a side effect other than mutating the data set?

Common Error 8.1

Trying to Modify Primitive Type Parameters

Methods can't update parameters of primitive type (numbers, char, and boolean). To illustrate this point, let's try to write a method that updates a number parameter:

```
public class BankAccount
{
    . . .
    /**
        Transfers money from this account and tries to add it to a balance.
        @param amount  the amount of money to transfer
        @param otherBalance  balance to add the amount to
    */
    void transfer(double amount, double otherBalance)   ❷
    {
        balance = balance - amount;
        otherBalance = otherBalance + amount;
            // Won't work
    }   ❸
}
```

This doesn't work. Let's consider a method call.

```
double savingsBalance = 1000;
harrysChecking.transfer(500, savingsBalance);   ①
System.out.println(savingsBalance);   ④
```

As the method starts, the parameter variable otherBalance is set to the same value as savingsBalance (see Figure 3). Then the value of the otherBalance value is modified, but that modification has no effect on savingsBalance, because otherBalance is a separate variable. When the method terminates, the otherBalance variable dies, and savingsBalance isn't increased.

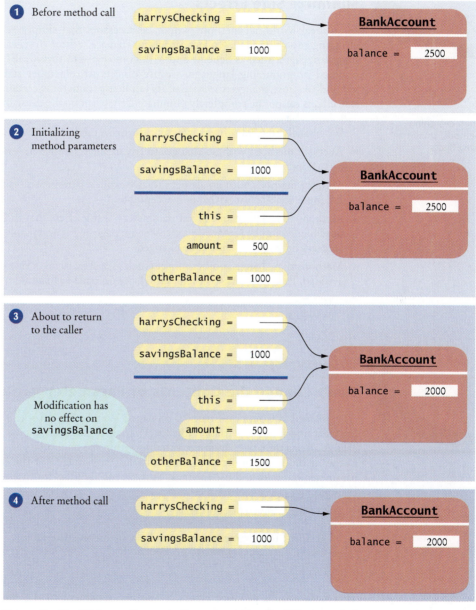

Figure 3 Modifying a Numeric Parameter Has No Effect on Caller

In Java, a method can never change parameters of primitive type.

Why did the example at the beginning of Section 8.4 work, where the second explicit parameter was a `BankAccount` reference? Then the parameter variable contained a *copy* of the object reference. Through that reference, the method is able to modify the object.

You already saw this difference between objects and primitive types in Chapter 2. As a consequence, a Java method can *never* modify numbers that are passed to it.

Quality Tip 8.2

Minimize Side Effects

In an ideal world, all methods would be accessors that simply return an answer without changing any value at all. (In fact, programs that are written in so-called *functional* programming languages, such as Scheme and ML, come close to this ideal.) Of course, in an object-oriented programming language, we use objects to remember state changes. Therefore, a method that just changes the state of its implicit parameter is certainly acceptable. Although side effects cannot be completely eliminated, they can be the cause of surprises and problems and should be minimized.

When designing methods, minimize side effects.

When analyzing side effects, we can categorize methods as follows:

- Accessor methods with no changes to any explicit parameters—no side effects. Example: `getBalance`.
- Mutator methods with no changes to any explicit parameters—an acceptable side effect. Example: `BankAccount.withdraw` is acceptable.
- Methods that change an explicit parameter—a side effect that should be avoided when possible. Example: `BankAccount.transfer` on page 333 is acceptable, but `GradeBook.addStudents` on page 333 should be changed.
- Methods that change another object (such as `System.out`)—a side effect that should be avoided. Example: `BankAccount.printBalance` on page 334 should not be implemented.

Quality Tip 8.3

Don't Change the Contents of Parameter Variables

As explained in Common Error 8.1 on page 334 and Special Topic 8.1 on page 337, a method can treat its parameter variables like local variables and change their contents. However, that change affects only the parameter variable within the method itself—not any values supplied in the method call. Some programmers take "advantage" of the temporary nature of the parameter variables and use them as "convenient" holders for intermediate results, as in this example:

```
public void deposit(double amount)
{
    // Using the parameter variable to hold an intermediate value
    amount = balance + amount;  // Poor style
    . . .
}
```

That code would produce errors if another statement in the method referred to `amount` expecting it to be the value of the parameter, and it will confuse later programmers maintaining this method. You should always treat the parameter variables as if they were constants. Don't assign new values to them. Instead, introduce a new local variable.

```
public void deposit(double amount)
{
    double newBalance = balance + amount;
    . . .
}
```

Special Topic 8.1

Call by Value and Call by Reference

In Java, parameter variables are initialized with the values that are supplied in the method call when a method starts. Computer scientists refer to this call mechanism as "call by value". There are some limitations to the "call by value" mechanism. As you saw in Common Error 8.1 on page 334, it is not possible to implement methods that modify the contents of number variables. Other programming languages such as C++ support an alternate mechanism, called "call by reference". For example, in C++ it would be an easy matter to write a method that modifies a number, by using a so-called *reference parameter.* Here is the C++ code, for those of you who know C++:

```
// This is C++
class BankAccount
{
public:
    void transfer(double amount, double& otherBalance)
        // otherBalance is a double&, a reference to a double
    {
        balance = balance - amount;
        otherBalance = otherBalance + amount; // Works in C++
    }
    . . .
};
```

You will sometimes read in Java books that "numbers are passed by value, objects are passed by reference". That is technically not quite correct. In Java, objects themselves are never passed as parameters; instead, both numbers and *object references* are passed by value. To see this clearly, let us consider another scenario. This method tries to set the otherAccount parameter to a new object:

```
public class BankAccount
{
    public void transfer(double amount, BankAccount otherAccount)
    {
        balance = balance - amount;
        double newBalance = otherAccount.balance + amount;
        otherAccount = new BankAccount(newBalance); // Won't work
    }
}
```

In Java, a method can change the state of an object reference parameter, but it cannot replace the object reference with another.

In this situation, we are not trying to change the state of the object to which the parameter variable otherAccount refers; instead, we are trying to replace the object with a different one (see the figure on page 338). Now the parameter variable otherAccount is replaced with a reference to a new account. But if you call the method with

```
harrysChecking.transfer(500, savingsAccount);
```

then that change does not affect the savingsAccount variable that is supplied in the call.

As you can see, a Java method can update an object's state, but it cannot *replace* the contents of an object reference. This shows that object references are passed by value in Java.

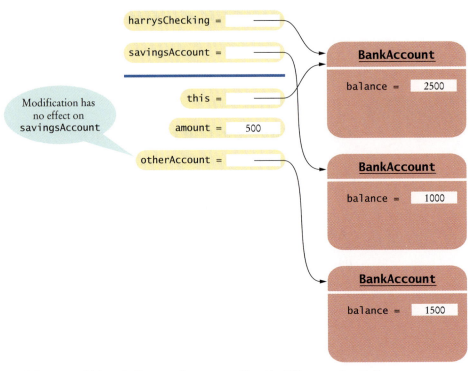

Modifying an Object Reference Parameter Has No Effect on the Caller

8.5 Preconditions and Postconditions

A precondition is a
requirement that the
caller of a method
must meet.

A **precondition** is a requirement that the caller of a method must obey. For example, the deposit method of the BankAccount class has a precondition that the amount to be deposited should not be negative. It is the responsibility of the caller never to call a method if one of its preconditions is violated. If the method is called anyway, it is not responsible for producing a correct result.

Therefore, a precondition is an important part of the method, and you must document it. Here we document the precondition that the amount parameter must not be negative.

```
/**
   Deposits money into this account.
   @param amount  the amount of money to deposit
   (Precondition: amount >= 0)
*/
```

Some javadoc extensions support a @precondition or @requires tag, but it is not a part of the standard javadoc program. Because the standard javadoc tool skips all unknown tags, we simply add the precondition to the method explanation or the appropriate @param tag.

Preconditions are typically provided for one of two reasons:

1. To restrict the parameters of a method
2. To require that a method is only called when it is in the appropriate *state*

For example, once a Scanner has run out of input, it is no longer legal to call the next method. Thus, a precondition for the next method is that the hasNext method returns true.

> If a method is called in violation of a precondition, the method is not responsible for computing the correct result.

A method is responsible for operating correctly only when its caller has fulfilled all preconditions. The method is free to do *anything* if a precondition is not fulfilled. What should a method actually do when it is called with inappropriate inputs? For example, what should account.deposit(-1000) do? There are two choices.

1. A method can check for the violation and **throw an exception**. Then the method does not return to its caller; instead, control is transferred to an exception handler. If no handler is present, then the program terminates. We will discuss exceptions in Chapter 11.
2. A method can skip the check and work under the assumption that the preconditions are fulfilled. If they aren't, then any data corruption (such as a negative balance) or other failures are the caller's fault.

The first approach can be inefficient, particularly if the same check is carried out many times by several methods. The second approach can be dangerous. The *assertion mechanism* was invented to give you the best of both approaches.

> An assertion is a logical condition in a program that you believe to be true.

An **assertion** is a condition that you believe to be true at all times in a particular program location. An assertion check tests whether an assertion is true. Here is a typical assertion check that tests a precondition:

```
public double deposit (double amount)
{
    assert amount >= 0;
    balance = balance + amount;
}
```

In this method, the programmer expects that the quantity amount can never be negative. When the assertion is correct, no harm is done, and the program works in the normal way. If, for some reason, the assertion fails, *and assertion checking is enabled*, then the program terminates with an AssertionError.

However, if assertion checking is disabled, then the assertion is never checked, and the program runs at full speed. By default, assertion checking is disabled when

Syntax 8.1 Assertion

Syntax   assert *condition*;

Example   assert amount >= 0;

If the condition is false and assertion checking is enabled, an exception occurs.

Condition that is claimed to be true.

you execute a program. To execute a program with assertion checking turned on, use this command:

```
java -enableassertions MainClass
```

You can also use the shortcut -ea instead of -enableassertions. You definitely want to turn assertion checking on during program development and testing.

You don't have to use assertions for checking preconditions—throwing an exception is another reasonable option. But assertions have one advantage: You can turn them off after you have tested your program, so that it runs at maximum speed. That way, you never have to feel bad about putting lots of assertions into your code. You can also use assertions for checking conditions other than preconditions.

Many beginning programmers think that it isn't "nice" to abort the program when a precondition is violated. Why not simply return to the caller instead?

```
public void deposit(double amount)
{
    if (amount < 0)
        return; // Not recommended
    balance = balance + amount;
}
```

That is legal—after all, a method can do anything if its preconditions are violated. But it is not as good as an assertion check. If the program calling the deposit method has a few bugs that cause it to pass a negative amount as an input value, then the version that generates an assertion failure will make the bugs very obvious during testing—it is hard to ignore when the program aborts. The quiet version, on the other hand, will not alert you, and you may not notice that it performs some wrong calculations as a consequence. Think of assertions as the "tough love" approach to precondition checking.

When a method is called in accordance with its preconditions, then the method promises to do its job correctly. A different kind of promise that the method makes is called a **postcondition**. There are two kinds of postconditions:

> If a method has been called in accordance with its preconditions, then it must ensure that its postconditions are valid.

1. The return value is computed correctly.

2. The object is in a certain state after the method call is completed.

Here is a postcondition that makes a statement about the object state after the deposit method is called.

```
/**
    Deposits money into this account.
    (Postcondition: getBalance() >= 0)
    @param amount the amount of money to deposit
    (Precondition: amount >= 0)
*/
```

As long as the precondition is fulfilled, this method guarantees that the balance after the deposit is not negative.

Some javadoc extensions support a @postcondition or @ensures tag. However, just as with preconditions, we simply add postconditions to the method explanation or the @return tag, because the standard javadoc program skips all tags that it doesn't know.

Some programmers feel that they must specify a postcondition for every method. When you use javadoc, however, you already specify a part of the postcondition in the @return tag, and you shouldn't repeat it in a postcondition.

```
// This postcondition statement is overly repetitive.
/**
    Returns the current balance of this account.
    @return the account balance
    (Postcondition: The return value equals the account balance.)
*/
```

Note that we formulate pre- and postconditions only in terms of the *interface* of the class. Thus, we state the precondition of the `withdraw` method as `amount <= getBalance()`, not `amount <= balance`. After all, the caller, which needs to check the precondition, has access only to the public interface, not the private implementation.

Preconditions and postconditions are often compared to *contracts*. In real life, contracts spell out the obligations of the contracting parties. For example, a car dealer may promise you a car in good working order, and you promise in turn to pay a certain amount of money. If either party breaks the promise, then the other is not bound by the terms of the contract. In the same fashion, pre- and postconditions are contractual terms between a method and its caller. The method promises to fulfill the postcondition for all inputs that fulfill the precondition. The caller promises never to call the method with illegal inputs. If the caller fulfills its promise and gets a wrong answer, it can take the method to "programmer's court". If the caller doesn't fulfill its promise and something terrible happens as a consequence, it has no recourse.

SELF CHECK

10. Why might you want to add a precondition to a method that you provide for other programmers?

11. When you implement a method with a precondition and you notice that the caller did not fulfill the precondition, do you have to notify the caller?

Special Topic 8.2

Class Invariants

Special Topic 6.5 introduced the concept of **loop invariants**. A loop invariant is established when the loop is first entered, and it is preserved by all loop iterations. We then know that the loop invariant must be true when the loop exits, and we can use that information to reason about the correctness of a loop.

Class invariants fulfill a similar purpose. A class invariant is a statement about an object that is true after every constructor and that is preserved by every mutator (provided that the caller respects all preconditions). We then know that the class invariant must always be true, and we can use that information to reason about the correctness of our program.

Here is a simple example. Consider a `BankAccount` class with the following preconditions for the constructor and the mutators:

```
public class BankAccount
{
    . . .
    /**
        Constructs a bank account with a given balance.
        @param initialBalance the initial balance
        (Precondition: initialBalance >= 0)
    */
    public BankAccount(double initialBalance) { . . . }
    {
        balance = initialBalance;
```

```
    }

    /**
        Deposits money into the bank account.
        @param amount the amount to deposit
        (Precondition: amount >= 0)
    */
    public void deposit(double amount) { . . . }

    /**
        Withdraws money from the bank account.
        @param amount the amount to withdraw
        (Precondition: amount <= getBalance())
    */
    public void withdraw(double amount) { . . . }
}
```

Now we can formulate the following class invariant:

```
getBalance() >= 0
```

To see why this invariant is true, first check the constructor; because the precondition of the constructor is

```
initialBalance >= 0
```

we can prove that the invariant is true after the constructor has set `balance` to `initialBalance`.

Next, check the mutators. The precondition of the `deposit` method is

```
amount >= 0
```

We can assume that the invariant condition holds before calling the method. Thus, we know that `balance >= 0` before the method executes. The laws of mathematics tell us that the sum of two nonnegative numbers is again nonnegative, so we can conclude that `balance >= 0` after the completion of the `deposit`. Thus, the `deposit` method preserves the invariant.

A similar argument shows that the `withdraw` method preserves the invariant.

Because the invariant is a property of the class, you document it with the class description:

```
/**
    A bank account has a balance that can be changed by
    deposits and withdrawals.
    (Invariant: getBalance() >= 0)
*/
public class BankAccount
{
    . . .
}
```

8.6 Static Methods

A static method is not invoked on an object.

Sometimes you need a method that is not invoked on an object. Such a method is called a **static method** or a *class method*. In contrast, the methods that you have written up to now are often called **instance methods** because they operate on a particular instance of an object.

A typical example of a static method is the `sqrt` method in the `Math` class. When you call `Math.sqrt(x)`, you don't supply any implicit parameter. (Recall that `Math` is the name of a class, not an object.)

Why would you want to write a method that does not operate on an object? The most common reason is that you want to encapsulate some computation that involves only numbers. Because numbers aren't objects, you can't invoke methods on them. For example, the call `x.sqrt()` can never be legal in Java.

Here is a typical example of a static method that carries out some simple algebra: to compute `p` percent of the amount `a`. Because the parameters are numbers, the method doesn't operate on any objects at all, so we make it into a static method:

```
/**
    Computes a percentage of an amount.
    @param p  the percentage to apply
    @param a  the amount to which the percentage is applied
    @return p percent of a
*/
public static double percentOf(double p, double a)
{
    return (p / 100) * a;
}
```

When you design a static method, you must find a class into which it should be placed.

You need to find a home for this method. Let us come up with a new class (similar to the `Math` class of the standard Java library). Because the `percentOf` method has to do with financial calculations, we'll design a class `Financial` to hold it. Here is the class:

```
public class Financial
{
    public static double percentOf(double p, double a)
    {
        return (p / 100) * a;
    }
    // More financial methods can be added here.
}
```

When calling a static method, you supply the name of the class containing the method so that the compiler can find it. For example,

```
double tax = Financial.percentOf(taxRate, total);
```

Note that you do not supply an object of type `Financial` when you call the method.

There is another reason why static methods are sometimes necessary. If a method manipulates a class that you do not own, you cannot add it to that class. Consider a method that computes the area of a rectangle. The `Rectangle` class in the standard library has no such feature, and we cannot modify that class. A static method solves this problem:

```
public class Geometry
{
    public static double area(Rectangle rect)
    {
        return rect.getWidth() * rect.getHeight();
    }
    // More geometry methods can be added here.
}
```

Now we can tell you why the `main` method is static. When the program starts, there aren't any objects. Therefore, the *first* method in the program must be a static method.

You may well wonder why these methods are called static. The normal meaning of the word *static* ("staying fixed at one place") does not seem to have anything to do with what static methods do. Indeed, it's used by accident. Java uses the static reserved word because C++ uses it in the same context. C++ uses static to denote class methods because the inventors of C++ did not want to invent another reserved word. Someone noted that there was a relatively rarely used reserved word, static, that denotes certain variables that stay in a fixed location for multiple method calls. (Java does not have this feature, nor does it need it.) It turned out that the reserved word could be reused to denote class methods without confusing the compiler. The fact that it can confuse humans was apparently not a big concern. You'll just have to live with the fact that "static method" means "class method": a method that has only explicit parameters.

SELF CHECK

12. Suppose that Java had no static methods. How would you use the Math.sqrt method for computing the square root of a number x?

13. The following method computes the average of an array list of numbers:

```java
public static double average(ArrayList<Double> values)
```

Why must it be a static method?

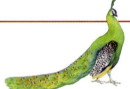

Quality Tip 8.4

Minimize the Use of Static Methods

It is possible to solve programming problems by using classes with only static methods. In fact, before object-oriented programming was invented, that approach was quite common. However, it usually leads to a design that is not object-oriented and makes it hard to evolve a program.

Consider the task of How To 7.1. A program reads scores for a student and prints the final score, which is obtained by dropping the lowest one. We solved the problem by implementing a GradeBook class that stores student scores. Of course, we could have simply written a program with a few static methods:

```java
public class ScoreAnalyzer
{
    public static double[] readInputs() { . . . }
    public static double sum(double[] values) { . . . }
    public static double minimum(double[] values) { . . . }
    public static double finalScore(double[] values)
    {
        if (values.length == 0) return 0;
        else if (values.length == 1) return 1;
        else return sum(values) - minimum(values);
    }

    public static void main(String[] args)
    {
        System.out.println(finalScore(readInputs()));
    }
}
```

That solution is fine if one's sole objective is to solve a simple homework problem. But suppose you need to modify the program so that it deals with multiple students. An object-oriented program can evolve the GradeBook class to store grades for many students. In contrast, adding more functionality to static methods gets messy quickly (see Exercise P8.7).

8.7 Static Variables

Sometimes, a value properly belongs to a class, not to any object of the class. You use a **static variable** for this purpose. Here is a typical example. We want to assign bank account numbers sequentially. That is, we want the bank account constructor to construct the first account with number 1001, the next with number 1002, and so on. Therefore, we must store the last assigned account number somewhere.

Of course, it makes no sense to make this value into an instance variable:

```
public class BankAccount
{
   private double balance;
   private int accountNumber;
   private int lastAssignedNumber = 1000; // NO—won't work
   . . .
}
```

In that case each *instance* of the BankAccount class would have its own value of last-AssignedNumber.

> A static variable belongs to the class, not to any object of the class.

Instead, we need to have a single value of lastAssignedNumber that is the same for the entire *class*. Such a variable is called a static variable, because you declare it using the static reserved word.

```
public class BankAccount
{
   private double balance;
   private int accountNumber;
   private static int lastAssignedNumber = 1000;
   . . .
}
```

Every BankAccount object has its own balance and accountNumber instance variables, but there is only a single copy of the lastAssignedNumber variable (see Figure 4). That variable is stored in a separate location, outside any BankAccount objects.

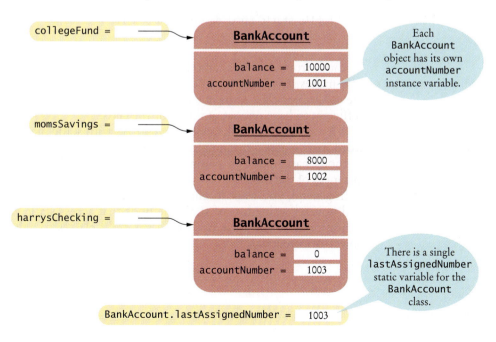

Figure 4
A Static Variable and Instance Variables

A static variable is sometimes called a *class variable* because there is a single variable for the entire class.

Every method of a class can access its static variables. Here is the constructor of the BankAccount class, which increments the last assigned number and then uses it to initialize the account number of the object to be constructed:

```java
public class BankAccount
{
   . . .
   public BankAccount()
   {
      lastAssignedNumber++; // Updates the static variable
      accountNumber = lastAssignedNumber; // Sets the instance variable
   }
}
```

There are three ways to initialize a static variable:

1. Do nothing. The static variable is then initialized with 0 (for numbers), false (for boolean values), or null (for objects).

2. Use an explicit initializer, such as

   ```java
   public class BankAccount
   {
      private static int lastAssignedNumber = 1000;
      . . .
   }
   ```

3. Use a static initialization block (see Special Topic 8.4 on page 347).

Like instance variables, static variables should always be declared as private to ensure that methods of other classes do not change their values. The exception to this rule are static *constants*, which may be either private or public. For example, the BankAccount class may want to declare a public constant value, such as

```java
public class BankAccount
{
   public static final double OVERDRAFT_FEE = 29.95;
   . . .
}
```

Methods from any class can refer to such a constant as BankAccount.OVERDRAFT_FEE.

It makes sense to declare constants as static—you wouldn't want every object of the BankAccount class to have its own set of variables with these constant values. It is sufficient to have one set of them for the class.

Why are class variables called static? As with static methods, the static reserved word itself is just a meaningless holdover from C++. But static variables and static methods have much in common: They apply to the entire *class*, not to specific instances of the class.

In general, you want to minimize the use of static methods and variables. If you find yourself using lots of static methods that access static variables, then that's an indication that you have not found the right classes to solve your problem in an object-oriented way.

SELF CHECK

14. Name two static variables of the System class.

15. Harry tells you that he has found a great way to avoid those pesky objects: Put all code into a single class and declare all methods and variables static. Then main can call the other static methods, and all of them can access the static variables. Will Harry's plan work? Is it a good idea?

Special Topic 8.3

Static Imports

Starting with Java version 5.0, there is a variant of the import directive that lets you use static methods and variables without class prefixes. For example,

```
import static java.lang.System.*;
import static java.lang.Math.*;

public class RootTester
{
   public static void main(String[] args)
   {
      double r = sqrt(PI); // Instead of Math.sqrt(Math.PI)
      out.println(r);       // Instead of System.out
   }
}
```

Static imports can make programs easier to read, particularly if they use many mathematical functions.

Special Topic 8.4

Alternative Forms of Instance and Static Variable Initialization

As you have seen, instance variables are initialized with a default value (0, false, or null, depending on their type). You can then set them to any desired value in a constructor, and that is the style that we prefer in this book.

However, there are two other mechanisms to specify an initial value. Just as with local variables, you can specify initialization values for instance variables. For example,

```
public class Coin
{
   private double value = 1;
   private String name = "Dollar";
   . . .
}
```

These default values are used for *every* object that is being constructed.

There is also another, much less common, syntax. You can place one or more *initialization blocks* inside the class declaration. All statements in that block are executed whenever an object is being constructed. Here is an example:

```
public class Coin
{
   private double value;
```

```
        private String name;
        {
            value = 1;
            name = "Dollar";
        }
        . . .
    }
```

For static variables, you use a static initialization block:

```
public class BankAccount
{
    private static int lastAssignedNumber;
    static
    {
        lastAssignedNumber = 1000;
    }
    . . .
}
```

All statements in the static initialization block are executed once when the class is loaded. Initialization blocks are rarely used in practice.

When an object is constructed, the initializers and initialization blocks are executed in the order in which they appear. Then the code in the constructor is executed. Because the rules for the alternative initialization mechanisms are somewhat complex, we recommend that you simply use constructors to do the job of construction.

8.8 Scope

The scope of a variable is the region of a program in which the variable can be accessed.

The **scope** of a variable is the part of the program in which the variable can be accessed. It is considered good design to minimize the scope of a variable. This reduces the possibility of accidental modification and name conflicts.

In the following sections, you will learn how to determine the scopes of local and instance variables, and how to resolve name conflicts if the scopes overlap.

8.8.1 Scope of Variables

The scope of a local variable extends from the point of its declaration to the end of the block or for loop that encloses it. The scope of a parameter variable is the entire method.

```
public static void process(double[] values) // values is a parameter variable
{
    for (int i = 0; i < 10; i++) // i is a local variable declared in a for loop
    {
        if (values[i] == 0)
        {
            double r = Math.random(); // r is a local variable declared in a block
            values[i] = r;
        } // Scope of r ends here
    } // Scope of i ends here
} // Scope of values ends here
```

In Java, the scope of a local variable can never contain the declaration of another local variable with the same name. For example, the following is an error:

> **The scope of a local variable cannot contain the declaration of another local variable with the same name.**

```java
public static void main(String[] args)
{
    double r = Math.random();
    if (r > 0.5)
    {
        Rectangle r = new Rectangle(5, 10, 20, 30);
        // Error—can't declare another variable called r here
        . . .
    }
}
```

However, you can have local variables with identical names if their scopes do not overlap, such as

```java
if (Math.random() > 0.5)
{
    Rectangle r = new Rectangle(5, 10, 20, 30);
    . . .
} // Scope of r ends here
else
{
    int r = 5;
    // OK—it is legal to declare another r here
    . . .
}
```

These variables are independent from each other, or, in other words, their scopes are disjoint. You can have local variables with the same name r in different methods, just as you can have different motels with the same name "Bates Motel" in different cities.

In contrast, the scope of instance variables and static variables consists of the entire class in which they are declared.

8.8.2 Overlapping Scope

Problems arise if you have two identical variable names with overlapping scope. This can never occur with local variables, but the scopes of identically named local variables and instance variables can overlap. Here is a purposefully bad example.

```java
public class Coin
{
    private String name;
    private double value; // Instance variable
    . . .
    public double getExchangeValue(double exchangeRate)
    {
        double value; // Local variable with the same name
        . . .
        return value;
    }
}
```

Inside the getExchangeValue method, the variable name value could potentially have two meanings: the **local variable** or the **instance variable**. The Java language specifies that in this situation the *local* variable wins out. It *shadows* the instance variable.

A local variable can shadow an instance variable with the same name. You can access the shadowed variable name through the this reference.

This sounds pretty arbitrary, but there is actually a good reason: You can still refer to the instance variable as `this.value`.

```
value = this.value * exchangeRate;
```

Of course, it is not a good idea to write code like this. You can easily change the name of the local variable to something else, such as `result`.

However, there is one situation where overlapping scope is acceptable. When implementing constructors or setter methods, it can be awkward to come up with different names for instance variables and parameters. Here is how you can use the same name for both:

```
public Coin(double value, String name)
{
    this.value = value;
    this.name = name;
}
```

The expression `this.value` refers to the instance variable, and `value` is the parameter.

SELF CHECK

16. Consider the following program that uses two variables named r. Is this legal?

```
public class RectangleTester
{
    public static double area(Rectangle rect)
    {
        double r = rect.getWidth() * rect.getHeight();
        return r;
    }

    public static void main(String[] args)
    {
        Rectangle r = new Rectangle(5, 10, 20, 30);
        double a = area(r);
        System.out.println(r);
    }
}
```

17. What is the scope of the `balance` variable of the `BankAccount` class?

Common Error 8.2

Shadowing

Accidentally using the same name for a local variable and an instance variable is a surprisingly common error. As you saw in the preceding section, the local variable then *shadows* the instance variable. Even though you may have meant to access the instance variable, the local variable is quietly accessed. Look at this example of an incorrect constructor:

```
public class Coin
{
    private double value;
    private String name;
    . . .
```

```
public Coin(double aValue, String aName)
{
   value = aValue;
   String name = aName; // Oops . . .
}
}
```

The programmer declared a local variable `name` in the constructor. In all likelihood, that was just a typo—the programmer's fingers were on autopilot and typed the reserved word `String`, even though the programmer all the time intended to access the instance variable. Unfortunately, the compiler gives no warning in this situation and quietly sets the local variable to the value of `aName`. The instance variable of the object that is being constructed is never touched, and remains `null`.

Some programmers give all instance variable names a special prefix to distinguish them from other variables. A common convention is to prefix all instance variable names with the prefix `my`, such as `myValue` or `myName`.

Another way of avoiding this problem is to use the `this` parameter when accessing an instance variable:

```
this.name = aName;
```

You should give each variable the smallest scope that it needs.

Quality Tip 8.5

Minimize Variable Scope

When you make the scope of a variable as small as possible, it becomes less likely that the variable is accidentally corrupted. It also becomes easier to modify or eliminate the variable as you reorganize your code.

As already mentioned, don't make an instance variable public. (The Java library has a few classes with public instance variables, but their creators later regretted their decision when they were unable to make optimizations later.)

When you have a constant, ask yourself who needs it. Everybody (`public static final`)? Only the class (`private static final`)? Only a single method (a `final` local variable)? Choose the smallest scope.

Beware of unnecessary instance variables. For example, consider the `Pyramid` class in Worked Example 4.1. You would not want an instance variable for the volume:

```
public class Pyramid
{
   private double height;
   private double baseLength;
   private double volume; // Not a good idea to use class scope for this variable
   . . .
}
```

Instead, compute the volume when it is needed in the `getVolume` method. That way, no other method can accidentally modify the `volume` variable, or forget to modify it when changing the height or base length.

Finally, with local variables, declare them only when you need them.

8.9 Packages

A package is a set of related classes.

A Java program consists of a collection of classes. So far, most of your programs have consisted of a small number of classes. As programs get larger, however, simply distributing the classes over multiple files isn't enough. An additional structuring mechanism is needed.

In Java, packages provide this structuring mechanism. A Java **package** is a set of related classes. For example, the Java library consists of several hundred packages, some of which are listed in Table 1.

Table 1 Important Packages in the Java Library		
Package	**Purpose**	**Sample Class**
java.lang	Language support	Math
java.util	Utilities	Random
java.io	Input and output	PrintStream
java.awt	Abstract Windowing Toolkit	Color
java.applet	Applets	Applet
java.net	Networking	Socket
java.sql	Database access through Structured Query Language	ResultSet
javax.swing	Swing user interface	JButton
omg.w3c.dom	Document Object Model for XML documents	Document

8.9.1 Organizing Related Classes into Packages

To put one of your classes in a package, you must place a line

```
package packageName;
```

as the first instruction in the source file containing the class. A package name consists of one or more identifiers separated by periods. (See Section 8.9.3 for tips on constructing package names.)

For example, let's put the Financial class introduced in this chapter into a package named com.horstmann.bigjava. The Financial.java file must start as follows:

```
package com.horstmann.bigjava;
public class Financial
{
   . . .
}
```

In addition to the named packages (such as java.util or com.horstmann.bigjava), there is a special package, called the *default package*, which has no name. If you did not include any package statement at the top of your source file, its classes are placed in the default package.

Syntax 8.2   Package Specification

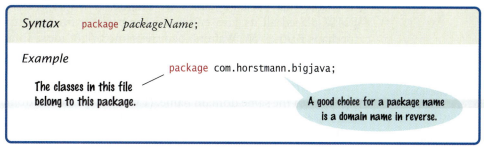

Syntax   package *packageName*;

Example

package com.horstmann.bigjava;

The classes in this file
belong to this package.

A good choice for a package name
is a domain name in reverse.

8.9.2 Importing Packages

If you want to use a class from a package, you can refer to it by its full name (package name plus class name). For example, java.util.Scanner refers to the Scanner class in the java.util package:

    java.util.Scanner in = new java.util.Scanner(System.in);

> The import directive lets you refer to a class of a package by its class name, without the package prefix.

Naturally, that is somewhat inconvenient. You can instead *import* a name with an import statement:

    import java.util.Scanner;

Then you can refer to the class as Scanner without the package prefix.

You can import *all classes* of a package with an import statement that ends in .*. For example, you can use the statement

    import java.util.*;

to import all classes from the java.util package. That statement lets you refer to classes like Scanner or Random without a java.util prefix.

However, you never need to import the classes in the java.lang package explicitly. That is the package containing the most basic Java classes, such as Math and Object. These classes are always available to you. In effect, an automatic import java.lang.*; statement has been placed into every source file.

Finally, you don't need to import other classes in the same package. For example, when you implement the class homework1.Tester, you don't need to import the class homework1.Bank. The compiler will find the Bank class without an import statement because it is located in the same package, homework1.

8.9.3 Package Names

Placing related classes into a package is clearly a convenient mechanism to organize classes. However, there is a more important reason for packages: to avoid **name clashes**. In a large project, it is inevitable that two people will come up with the same name for the same concept. This even happens in the standard Java class library (which has now grown to thousands of classes). There is a class Timer in the java.util package and another class called Timer in the javax.swing package. You can still tell the Java compiler exactly which Timer class you need, simply by referring to them as java.util.Timer and javax.swing.Timer.

Of course, for the package-naming convention to work, there must be some way to ensure that package names are unique. It wouldn't be good if the car maker BMW placed all its Java code into the package bmw, and some other programmer (perhaps Britney M. Walters) had the same bright idea. To avoid this problem, the inventors of Java recommend that you use a package-naming scheme that takes advantage of the uniqueness of Internet domain names.

For example, I have a domain name horstmann.com, and there is nobody else on the planet with the same domain name. (I was lucky that the domain name horstmann.com had not been taken by anyone else when I applied. If your name is Walters, you will sadly find that someone else beat you to walters.com.) To get a package name, turn the domain name around to produce a package name prefix, such as com.horstmann.

> Use a domain name in reverse to construct an unambiguous package name.

If you don't have your own domain name, you can still create a package name that has a high probability of being unique by writing your e-mail address backwards. For example, if Britney Walters has an e-mail address walters@cs.sjsu.edu, then she can use a package name edu.sjsu.cs.walters for her own classes.

Some instructors will want you to place each of your assignments into a separate package, such as homework1, homework2, and so on. The reason is again to avoid name collision. You can have two classes, homework1.Bank and homework2.Bank, with slightly different properties.

8.9.4 Packages and Source Files

> The path of a class file must match its package name.

A source file must be located in a subdirectory that matches the package name. The parts of the name between periods represent successively nested directories. For example, the source files for classes in the package com.horstmann.bigjava would be placed in a subdirectory com/horstmann/bigjava. You place the subdirectory inside the *base directory* holding your program's files. For example, if you do your homework assignment in a directory /home/britney/hw8/problem1, then you can place the class files for the com.horstmann.bigjava package into the directory /home/britney/hw8/problem1/com/horstmann/bigjava, as shown in Figure 5. (Here, we are using UNIX-style file names. Under Windows, you might use c:\Users\Britney\hw8\problem1\com\horstmann\bigjava.)

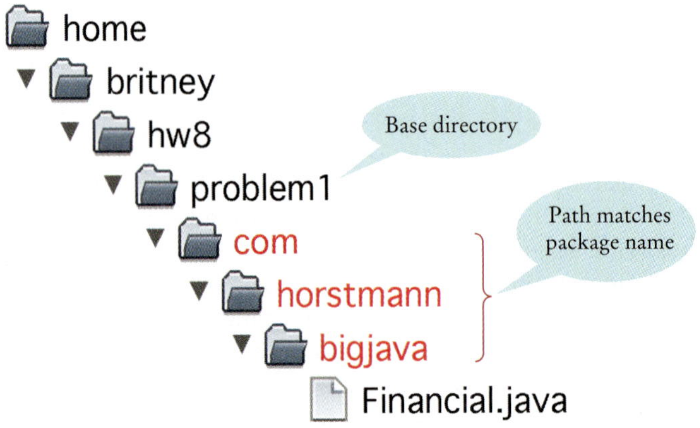

Figure 5
Base Directories and Subdirectories for Packages

18. Which of the following are packages?

    a. java

    b. java.lang

    c. java.util

    d. java.lang.Math

19. Is a Java program without `import` statements limited to using the default and `java.lang` packages?

20. Suppose your homework assignments are located in the directory /home/me/cs101 (c:\Users\Me\cs101 on Windows). Your instructor tells you to place your homework into packages. In which directory do you place the class `hw1.problem1.TicTacToeTester`?

Common Error 8.3

Confusing Dots

In Java, the dot symbol (.) is used as a separator in the following situations:

- Between package names (`java.util`)
- Between package and class names (`homework1.Bank`)
- Between class and inner class names (`Ellipse2D.Double`)
- Between class and instance variable names (`Math.PI`)
- Between objects and methods (`account.getBalance()`)

When you see a long chain of dot-separated names, it can be a challenge to find out which part is the package name, which part is the class name, which part is an instance variable name, and which part is a method name. Consider

```
java.lang.System.out.println(x);
```

Because `println` is followed by an opening parenthesis, it must be a method name. Therefore, `out` must be either an object or a class with a static `println` method. (Of course, we know that `out` is an object reference of type `PrintStream`.) Again, it is not at all clear, without context, whether `System` is another object, with a public variable `out`, or a class with a `static` variable. Judging from the number of pages that the Java language specification devotes to this issue, even the compiler has trouble interpreting these dot-separated sequences of strings.

To avoid problems, it is helpful to adopt a strict coding style. If class names always start with an uppercase letter, and variable, method, and package names always start with a lower-case letter, then confusion can be avoided.

Special Topic 8.5

Package Access

If a class, field, or method has no `public` or `private` modifier, then all methods of classes in the same package can access the feature. For example, if a class is declared as `public`, then all other classes in all packages can use it. But if a class is declared without an access modifier, then only the other classes in the *same* package can use it. Package access is a reasonable default for classes, but it is extremely unfortunate for instance variables.

It is a common error to *forget* the reserved word `private`, thereby opening up a potential security hole. For example, at the time of this writing, the `Window` class in the `java.awt` package contained the following declaration:

```
public class Window extends Container
{
    String warningString;
    . . .
}
```

There actually was no good reason to grant package access to the `warningString` instance variable—no other class accesses it.

Package access for instance variables is rarely useful and always a potential security risk. Most instance variables are given package access by accident because the programmer simply forgot the `private` reserved word. It is a good idea to get into the habit of scanning your instance variable declarations for missing `private` modifiers.

> A field or method that is not declared as `public` or `private` can be accessed by all classes in the same package, which is usually not desirable.

How To 8.1

Programming with Packages

This How To explains in detail how to place your programs into packages. For example, your instructor may ask you to place each homework assignment into a separate package. That way, you can have classes with the same name but different implementations in separate packages (such as `homework1.problem1.Bank` and `homework1.problem2.Bank`).

Step 1 Come up with a package name.

Your instructor may give you a package name to use, such as `homework1.problem2`. Or, perhaps you want to use a package name that is unique to you. Start with your e-mail address, written backwards. For example, `walters@cs.sjsu.edu` becomes `edu.sjsu.cs.walters`. Then add a subpackage that describes your project, such as `edu.sjsu.cs.walters.cs1project`.

Step 2 Pick a *base directory*.

The base directory is the directory that contains the directories for your various packages, for example, `/home/britney` or `c:\Users\Britney`.

Step 3 Make a subdirectory from the base directory that matches your package name.

The subdirectory must be contained in your base directory. Each segment must match a segment of the package name. For example,

```
mkdir -p /home/britney/homework1/problem2 (in UNIX)
```
or
```
mkdir /s c:\Users\Britney\homework1\problem2 (in Windows)
```

Step 4 Place your source files into the package subdirectory.

For example, if your homework consists of the files `Tester.java` and `Bank.java`, then you place them into

```
/home/britney/homework1/problem2/Tester.java
/home/britney/homework1/problem2/Bank.java
```
or
```
c:\Users\Britney\homework1\problem2\Tester.java
c:\Users\Britney\homework1\problem2\Bank.java
```

Step 5 Use the package statement in each source file.

The first noncomment line of each file must be a package statement that lists the name of the package, such as

```
package homework1.problem2;
```

Step 6 Compile your source files from the *base directory.*

Change to the base directory (from Step 2) to compile your files. For example,

```
cd /home/britney
javac homework1/problem2/Tester.java
```

or

```
c:
cd \Users\Britney
javac homework1\problem2\Tester.java
```

Note that the Java compiler needs the *source file name and not the class name. That is, you need to supply file separators* (/ on UNIX, \ on Windows) *and a file extension* (.java).

Step 7 Run your program from the *base directory.*

Unlike the Java compiler, the Java interpreter needs the *class name (and not a file name) of the class containing the* main *method.* That is, use periods as package separators, and don't use a file extension. For example,

```
cd /home/britney
java homework1.problem2.Tester
```

or

```
c:
cd \Users\Britney
java homework1.problem2.Tester
```

Random Fact 8.1

The Explosive Growth of Personal Computers

In 1971, Marcian E. "Ted" Hoff, an engineer at Intel Corporation, was working on a chip for a manufacturer of electronic calculators. He realized that it would be a better idea to develop a *general-purpose* chip that could be *programmed* to interface with the keys and display of a calculator, rather than to do yet another custom design. Thus, the *microprocessor* was born. At the time, its primary application was as a controller for calculators, washing machines, and the like. It took years for the computer industry to notice that a genuine central processing unit was now available as a single chip.

Hobbyists were the first to catch on. In 1974 the first computer *kit,* the Altair 8800, was available from MITS Electronics for about $350. The kit consisted of the microprocessor, a circuit board, a very small amount of memory, toggle switches, and a row of display lights. Purchasers had to solder and assemble it, then program it in machine language through the toggle switches. It was not a big hit.

The first big hit was the Apple II. It was a real computer with a keyboard, a monitor, and a floppy disk drive. When it was first released, users had a $3000 machine that could play Space Invaders, run a primitive bookkeeping program, or let users program it in BASIC. The original Apple II did not even support lowercase letters, making it worthless for word processing. The breakthrough came in 1979 with a new spreadsheet program, VisiCalc. In a spreadsheet, you enter data and their relationships into a grid of rows and columns (see the figure). Then you modify some of the data and watch in real time how the others change. For example, you can see how changing the mix of widgets in a manufacturing plant might affect estimated costs and profits. Middle managers in companies, who understood computers and were fed up with having to wait for hours or days to get their data runs back from the computing center, snapped up VisiCalc and the computer that was needed to run it. For them, the computer was a spreadsheet machine.

A *VISICALC*™ Screen:

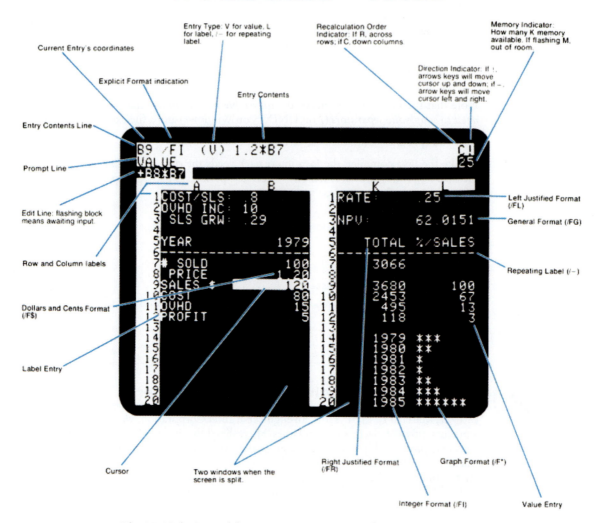

The VisiCalc Spreadsheet Running on an Apple II

The next big hit was the IBM Personal Computer, ever after known as the PC. It was the first widely available personal computer that used Intel's 16-bit processor, the 8086, whose successors are still being used in personal computers today. The success of the PC was based not on any engineering breakthroughs but on the fact that it was easy to *clone*. IBM published specifications for plug-in cards, and it went one step further. It published the exact source code of the so-called BIOS (Basic Input/Output System), which controls the keyboard, monitor, ports, and disk drives and must be installed in ROM form in every PC. This allowed third-party vendors of plug-in cards to ensure that the BIOS code, and third-party extensions of it, interacted correctly with the equipment. Of course, the code itself was the property of IBM and could not be copied legally. Perhaps IBM did not foresee that functionally equivalent versions of the BIOS nevertheless could be recreated by others. Compaq, one of the first clone vendors, had fifteen engineers, who certified that they had never seen the original IBM code, write a new version that conformed precisely to the IBM specifications. Other companies did the same, and soon a variety of vendors were selling computers that ran the same software as IBM's PC but distinguished themselves by a lower price, increased portability, or better performance. In time, IBM lost its dominant position in the PC market, and it sold its personal computer division to the Chinese manufacturer Lenovo in 2005.

IBM never produced an *operating system* for its PCs—that is, the software that organizes the interaction between the user and the computer, starts application programs, and manages disk storage and other resources. Instead, IBM offered customers the option of three separate operating systems for its original PC. Most customers couldn't care less about the operating system. They chose the system that was able to launch most of the few applications that existed at the time. It happened to be DOS (Disk Operating System) by Microsoft. Microsoft cheerfully licensed the same operating system to other hardware vendors and encouraged software companies to write DOS applications. A huge number of useful application programs for PC-compatible machines was the result.

PC applications were certainly useful, but they were not easy to learn. Every vendor developed a different *user interface:* the collection of keystrokes, menu options, and settings that a user needed to master to use a software package effectively. Data exchange between applications was difficult, because each program used a different data format. The Apple Macintosh changed all that in 1984. The designers of the Macintosh had the vision to supply an intuitive user interface with the computer and to force software developers to adhere to it. It took Microsoft and PC-compatible manufacturers years to catch up.

Today, most personal computers are used for accessing information from online sources, entertainment, word processing, and home finance (banking, budgeting, taxes). Some analysts predict that the personal computer will merge with the television set and cable network into an entertainment and information appliance.

8.10 Unit Test Frameworks

Up to now, we have used a very simple approach to testing. We provided tester classes whose main method computes values and prints actual and expected values. However, that approach has limitations. The main method gets messy if it contains many tests. And if an exception occurs during one of the tests, the remaining tests are not executed.

Unit test frameworks simplify the task of writing classes that contain many test cases.

Unit testing frameworks were designed to quickly execute and evaluate test suites, and to make it easy to incrementally add test cases. One of the most popular testing frameworks is JUnit. It is freely available at http://junit.org, and it is also built into a number of development environments, including BlueJ and Eclipse. Here we describe JUnit 4, the most current version of the library as this book is written.

When you use JUnit, you design a companion test class for each class that you develop. You provide a method for each test case that you want to have executed. You use "annotations" to mark the test methods. An annotation is an advanced Java feature that places a marker into the code that is interpreted by another tool. In the case of JUnit, the @Test annotation is used to mark test methods.

In each test case, you make some computations and then compute some condition that you believe to be true. You then pass the result to a method that communicates a test result to the framework, most commonly the assertEquals method. The assertEquals method takes as parameters the expected and actual values and, for floating-point numbers, a tolerance value.

Figure 6
Unit Testing with JUnit

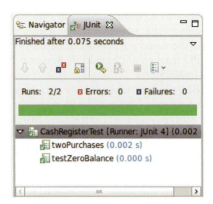

It is also customary (but not required) that the name of the test class ends in `Test`, such as `CashRegisterTest`. Here is a typical example:

```
import org.junit.Test;
import org.junit.Assert;

public class CashRegisterTest
{
    @Test public void twoPurchases()
    {
        CashRegister register = new CashRegister();
        register.recordPurchase(0.75);
        register.recordPurchase(1.50);
        register.enterPayment(2, 0, 5, 0, 0);
        double expected = 0.25;
        Assert.assertEquals(expected, register.giveChange(), EPSILON);
    }
    // More test cases
    . . .
}
```

If all test cases pass, the JUnit tool shows a green bar (see Figure 6). If any of the test cases fail, the JUnit tool shows a red bar and an error message.

Your test class can also have other methods (whose names should not be annotated with `@Test`). These methods typically carry out steps that you want to share among test methods.

> The JUnit philosophy is to run all tests whenever you change your code.

The JUnit philosophy is simple. Whenever you implement a class, also make a companion test class. You design the tests as you design the program, one test method at a time. The test cases just keep accumulating in the test class. Whenever you have detected an actual failure, add a test case that flushes it out, so that you can be sure that you won't introduce that particular bug again. Whenever you modify your class, simply run the tests again.

If all tests pass, the user interface shows a green bar and you can relax. Otherwise, there is a red bar, but that's also good. It is much easier to fix a bug in isolation than inside a complex program.

SELF CHECK

21. Provide a JUnit test class with one test case for the `Earthquake` class in Chapter 5.

22. What is the significance of the `EPSILON` parameter in the `assertEquals` method?

Summary of Learning Objectives

Find classes that are appropriate for solving a programming problem.

- A class should represent a single concept from a problem domain, such as business, science, or mathematics.

Analyze cohesiveness and coupling of classes.

- The public interface of a class is cohesive if all of its features are related to the concept that the class represents.
- A class depends on another class if it uses objects of that class.
- It is a good practice to minimize the coupling (i.e., dependency) between classes.

Recognize immutable classes and their benefits.

- An immutable class has no mutator methods.
- References to objects of an immutable class can be safely shared.

Recognize side effects and the need to minimize them.

- A side effect of a method is any externally observable data modification.
- In Java, a method can never change parameters of primitive type.
- When designing methods, minimize side effects.
- In Java, a method can change the state of an object reference parameter, but it cannot replace the object reference with another.

Document preconditions and postconditions of methods.

- A precondition is a requirement that the caller of a method must meet.
- If a method is called in violation of a precondition, the method is not responsible for computing the correct result.
- An assertion is a logical condition in a program that you believe to be true.
- If a method has been called in accordance with its preconditions, then it must ensure that its postconditions are valid.

Implement static methods that do not operate on objects.

- A static method is not invoked on an object.
- When you design a static method, you must find a class into which it should be placed.

Use static variables to describe properties of a class.

- A static variable belongs to the class, not to any object of the class.

Determine the scopes of local variables and instance variables.

- The scope of a variable is the region of a program in which the variable can be accessed.
- The scope of a local variable cannot contain the declaration of another local variable with the same name.
- A local variable can shadow an instance variable with the same name. You can access the shadowed variable name through the this reference.
- You should give each variable the smallest scope that it needs.

Use packages to organize sets of related classes.

- A package is a set of related classes.
- The `import` directive lets you refer to a class of a package by its class name, without the package prefix.
- Use a domain name in reverse to construct an unambiguous package name.
- The path of a class file must match its package name.
- A field or method that is not declared as `public` or `private` can be accessed by all classes in the same package, which is usually not desirable.

Use JUnit for writing unit tests.

- Unit test frameworks simplify the task of writing classes that contain many test cases.
- The JUnit philosophy is to run all tests whenever you change your code.

Media Resources

www.wiley.com/ college/ horstmann

- Lab Exercises
- **Animation** A Method Cannot Modify a Numeric Parameter
- Practice Quiz
- Code Completion Exercises

Review Exercises

★★ **R8.1** Consider the following problem description:

> Users place coins in a vending machine and select a product by pushing a button. If the inserted coins are sufficient to cover the purchase price of the product, the product is dispensed and change is given. Otherwise, the inserted coins are returned to the user.

What classes should you use to implement it?

★★ **R8.2** Consider the following problem description:

> Employees receive their biweekly paychecks. They are paid their hourly rates for each hour worked; however, if they worked more than 40 hours per week, they are paid at 150 percent of their regular wage for those overtime hours.

What classes should you use to implement it?

★★★ **R8.3** Consider the following problem description:

> Customers order products from a store. Invoices are generated to list the items and quantities ordered, payments received, and amounts still due. Products are shipped to the shipping address of the customer, and invoices are sent to the billing address.

What classes should you use to implement it?

★★★ **R8.4** Look at the public interface of the `java.lang.System` class and discuss whether or not it is cohesive.

★★ **R8.5** Suppose an Invoice object contains descriptions of the products ordered, and the billing and shipping addresses of the customer. Draw a UML diagram showing the dependencies between the classes Invoice, Address, Customer, and Product.

★★ **R8.6** Suppose a vending machine contains products, and users insert coins into the vending machine to purchase products. Draw a UML diagram showing the dependencies between the classes VendingMachine, Coin, and Product.

★★ **R8.7** On which classes does the class Integer in the standard library depend?

★★ **R8.8** On which classes does the class Rectangle in the standard library depend?

★ **R8.9** Classify the methods of the class Scanner that are used in this book as accessors and mutators.

★ **R8.10** Classify the methods of the class Rectangle as accessors and mutators.

★ **R8.11** Which of the following classes are immutable?

    a. Rectangle

    b. String

    c. Random

★ **R8.12** Which of the following classes are immutable?

    a. PrintStream

    b. Date

    c. Integer

★★ **R8.13** What side effect, if any, do the following three methods have:

```java
public class Coin
{
   . . .
   public void print()
   {
      System.out.println(name + " " + value);
   }

   public void print(PrintStream stream)
   {
      stream.println(name + " " + value);
   }

   public String toString()
   {
      return name + " " + value;
   }
}
```

★★★ **R8.14** Ideally, a method should have no side effects. Can you write a program in which no method has a side effect? Would such a program be useful?

★★ **R8.15** Write preconditions for the following methods. Do not implement the methods.

    a. public static double sqrt(double x)

    b. public static String romanNumeral(int n)

    c. public static double slope(Line2D.Double a)

    d. public static String weekday(int day)

★★ **R8.16** What preconditions do the following methods from the standard Java library have?

   a. `Math.sqrt`
   b. `Math.tan`
   c. `Math.log`
   d. `Math.pow`
   e. `Math.abs`

★★ **R8.17** What preconditions do the following methods from the standard Java library have?

   a. `Integer.parseInt(String s)`
   b. `StringTokenizer.nextToken()`
   c. `Random.nextInt(int n)`
   d. `String.substring(int m, int n)`

★★★ **R8.18** When a method is called with parameters that violate its precondition(s), it can terminate (by throwing an exception or an assertion error), or it can return to its caller. Give two examples of library methods (standard or the library methods used in this book) that return some result to their callers when called with invalid parameters, and give two examples of library methods that terminate.

★★ **R8.19** Consider a `CashRegister` class with methods

   • `public void enterPayment(int coinCount, Coin coinType)`
   • `public double getTotalPayment()`

   Give a reasonable postcondition of the `enterPayment` method. What preconditions would you need so that the `CashRegister` class can ensure that postcondition?

★★ **R8.20** Consider the following method that is intended to swap the values of two floating-point numbers:

```java
public static void falseSwap(double a, double b)
{
   double temp = a;
   a = b;
   b = temp;
}

public static void main(String[] args)
{
   double x = 3;
   double y = 4;
   falseSwap(x, y);
   System.out.println(x + " " + y);
}
```

   Why doesn't the method swap the contents of x and y?

★★★ **R8.21** How can you write a method that swaps two floating-point numbers?
   Hint: `Point2D.Double`.

★★ **R8.22** Draw a memory diagram that shows why the following method can't swap two `BankAccount` objects:

```java
public static void falseSwap(BankAccount a, BankAccount b)
{
   BankAccount temp = a;
   a = b;
   b = temp;
}
```

★ **R8.23** Consider an enhancement of the Die class of Chapter 6 with a static variable

```
public class Die
{
    private int sides;
    private static Random generator = new Random();
    public Die(int s) { . . . }
    public int cast() { . . . }
}
```

Draw a memory diagram that shows three dice:

```
Die d4 = new Die(4);
Die d6 = new Die(6);
Die d8 = new Die(8);
```

Be sure to indicate the values of the sides and generator variables.

★ **R8.24** Try compiling the following program. Explain the error message that you get.

```
public class Print13
{
    public void print(int x)
    {
        System.out.println(x);
    }

    public static void main(String[] args)
    {
        int n = 13;
        print(n);
    }
}
```

★ **R8.25** Look at the methods in the Integer class. Which are static? Why?

★★ **R8.26** Look at the methods in the String class (but ignore the ones that take a parameter of type char[]). Which are static? Why?

★★ **R8.27** The in and out variables of the System class are public static variables of the System class. Is that good design? If not, how could you improve on it?

★★ **R8.28** In the following class, the variable n occurs in multiple scopes. Which declarations of n are legal and which are illegal?

```
public class X
{
    private int n;

    public int f()
    {
        int n = 1;
        return n;
    }

    public int g(int k)
    {
        int a;
        for (int n = 1; n <= k; n++)
            a = a + n;
        return a;
    }
```

```
public int h(int n)
{
   int b;
   for (int n = 1; n <= 10; n++)
      b = b + n;
   return b + n;
}

public int k(int n)
{
   if (n < 0)
   {
      int k = -n;
      int n = (int) (Math.sqrt(k));
      return n;
   }
   else return n;
}

public int m(int k)
{
   int a;
   for (int n = 1; n <= k; n++)
      a = a + n;
   for (int n = k; n >= 1; n++)
      a = a + n;
   return a;
}
}
```

★★ **R8.29** Every Java program can be rewritten to avoid import statements. Explain how, and rewrite RectangleComponent.java from Chapter 2 to avoid import statements.

★ **R8.30** What is the default package? Have you used it before this chapter in your programming?

★★T **R8.31** What does JUnit do when a test method throws an exception? Try it out and report your findings.

Programming Exercises

★★ **P8.1** Implement the Coin class described in Section 8.2. Modify the CashRegister class so that coins can be added to the cash register, by supplying a method

```
void enterPayment(int coinCount, Coin coinType)
```

The caller needs to invoke this method multiple times, once for each type of coin that is present in the payment.

★★ **P8.2** Modify the giveChange method of the CashRegister class so that it returns the number of coins of a particular type to return:

```
int giveChange(Coin coinType)
```

The caller needs to invoke this method for each coin type, in decreasing value.

★ **P8.3** Real cash registers can handle both bills and coins. Design a single class that expresses the commonality of these concepts. Redesign the CashRegister class and provide a method for entering payments that are described by your class. Your primary challenge is to come up with a good name for this class.

★ **P8.4** Enhance the BankAccount class by adding preconditions for the constructor and the deposit method that require the amount parameter to be at least zero, and a precondition for the withdraw method that requires amount to be a value between 0 and the current balance. Use assertions to test the preconditions.

★★ **P8.5** Write static methods

- `public static double sphereVolume(double r)`
- `public static double sphereSurface(double r)`
- `public static double cylinderVolume(double r, double h)`
- `public static double cylinderSurface(double r, double h)`
- `public static double coneVolume(double r, double h)`
- `public static double coneSurface(double r, double h)`

that compute the volume and surface area of a sphere with radius r, a cylinder with circular base with radius r and height h, and a cone with circular base with radius r and height h. Place them into a class Geometry. Then write a program that prompts the user for the values of r and h, calls the six methods, and prints the results.

★★ **P8.6** Solve Exercise P8.5 by implementing classes Sphere, Cylinder, and Cone. Which approach is more object-oriented?

★★ **P8.7** Modify the grade book application of How To 7.1 so that it can deal with multiple students. First, ask the user for all student names. Then read in the scores for all quizzes, prompting for the score of each student. Finally, print the names of all students and their final scores. Use a single class and only static methods.

★★★ **P8.8** Repeat Exercise P8.7, using multiple classes. Modify the GradeBook class so that it collects objects of type Student. Each such object should have a list of scores.

★★★ **P8.9** Write methods

```
public static double perimeter(Ellipse2D.Double e);
public static double area(Ellipse2D.Double e);
```

that compute the area and the perimeter of the ellipse e. Add these methods to a class Geometry. The challenging part of this assignment is to find and implement an accurate formula for the perimeter. Why does it make sense to use a static method in this case?

★★ **P8.10** Write methods

```
public static double angle(Point2D.Double p, Point2D.Double q)
public static double slope(Point2D.Double p, Point2D.Double q)
```

that compute the angle between the *x*-axis and the line joining two points, measured in degrees, and the slope of that line. Add the methods to the class Geometry. Supply suitable preconditions. Why does it make sense to use a static method in this case?

★★★ **P8.11** Write methods

```
public static boolean isInside(Point2D.Double p, Ellipse2D.Double e)
public static boolean isOnBoundary(Point2D.Double p, Ellipse2D.Double e)
```

that test whether a point is inside or on the boundary of an ellipse. Add the methods to the class Geometry.

★ **P8.12** Write a method

```
public static int readInt(
        Scanner in, String prompt, String error, int min, int max)
```

that displays the prompt string, reads an integer, and tests whether it is between the minimum and maximum. If not, print an error message and repeat reading the input. Add the method to a class `Input`.

★★ **P8.13** Consider the following algorithm for computing x^n for an integer n. If $n < 0$, x^n is $1/x^{-n}$. If n is positive and even, then $x^n = (x^{n/2})^2$. If n is positive and odd, then $x^n = x^{n-1} \cdot x$. Implement a static method `double intPower(double x, int n)` that uses this algorithm. Add it to a class called `Numeric`.

★★ **P8.14** Improve the `Needle` class of Chapter 6. Turn the `generator` variable into a static variable so that all needles share a single random number generator.

★★ **P8.15** Implement a `Coin` and `CashRegister` class as described in Exercise P8.1. Place the classes into a package called `money`. Keep the `CashRegisterTester` class in the default package.

★ **P8.16** Place a `BankAccount` class in a package whose name is derived from your e-mail address, as described in Section 8.9. Keep the `BankAccountTester` class in the default package.

★★T **P8.17** Provide a JUnit test class `BankTest` with three test methods, each of which tests a different method of the `Bank` class in Chapter 7.

★★T **P8.18** Provide JUnit test class `TaxReturnTest` with three test methods that test different tax situations for the `TaxReturn` class in Chapter 5.

★G **P8.19** Write methods

- `public static void drawH(Graphics2D g2, Point2D.Double p);`
- `public static void drawE(Graphics2D g2, Point2D.Double p);`
- `public static void drawL(Graphics2D g2, Point2D.Double p);`
- `public static void drawO(Graphics2D g2, Point2D.Double p);`

that show the letters H, E, L, O on the graphics window, where the point p is the top-left corner of the letter. Then call the methods to draw the words "HELLO" and "HOLE" on the graphics display. Draw lines and ellipses. Do not use the `drawString` method. Do not use `System.out`.

★★G **P8.20** Repeat Exercise P8.17 by designing classes `LetterH`, `LetterE`, `LetterL`, and `LetterO`, each with a constructor that takes a `Point2D.Double` parameter (the top-left corner) and a method `draw(Graphics2D g2)`. Which solution is more object-oriented?

Programming Projects

Project 8.1 Implement a program that prints paychecks for a group of student assistants. Deduct federal and Social Security taxes. (You may want to use the tax computation used in Chapter 5. Find out about Social Security taxes on the Internet.) Your program should prompt for the names, hourly wages, and hours worked of each student.

Project 8.2 For faster sorting of letters, the United States Postal Service encourages companies that send large volumes of mail to use a bar code denoting the ZIP code (see Figure 7).

The encoding scheme for a five-digit ZIP code is shown in Figure 8. There are full-height frame bars on each side. The five encoded digits are followed by a check digit, which is computed as follows: Add up all digits, and choose the check digit to make the sum a multiple of 10. For example, the sum of the digits in the ZIP code 95014 is 19, so the check digit is 1 to make the sum equal to 20.

Each digit of the ZIP code, and the check digit, is encoded according to the table at right, where 0 denotes a half bar and 1 a full bar. Note that they represent all combinations of two full and three half bars. The digit can be computed easily from the bar code using the column weights 7, 4, 2, 1, 0. For example, 01100 is

	7	4	2	1	0
1	0	0	0	1	1
2	0	0	1	0	1
3	0	0	1	1	1
4	0	1	0	0	0
5	0	1	0	1	1
6	0	1	1	0	0
7	1	0	0	0	0
8	1	0	0	1	1
9	1	0	1	0	0
0	1	1	0	0	0

$$0 \cdot 7 + 1 \cdot 4 + 1 \cdot 2 + 0 \cdot 1 + 0 \cdot 0 = 6$$

The only exception is 0, which would yield 11 according to the weight formula.

Write a program that asks the user for a ZIP code and prints the bar code. Use : for half bars, | for full bars. For example, 95014 becomes

```
||:|:::|:|:||:::::||:|::|:::|||
```

(Alternatively, write a graphical application that draws real bars.)

Your program should also be able to carry out the opposite conversion: Translate bars into their ZIP code, reporting any errors in the input format or a mismatch of the digits.

✶✶✶✶✶✶✶✶✶✶✶✶✶✶✶✶ ECRLOT ✶✶ CO57

CODE C671RTS2
JOHN DOE   CO57
1009 FRANKLIN BLVD
SUNNYVALE   CA 95014 – 5143

Figure 7 A Postal Bar Code

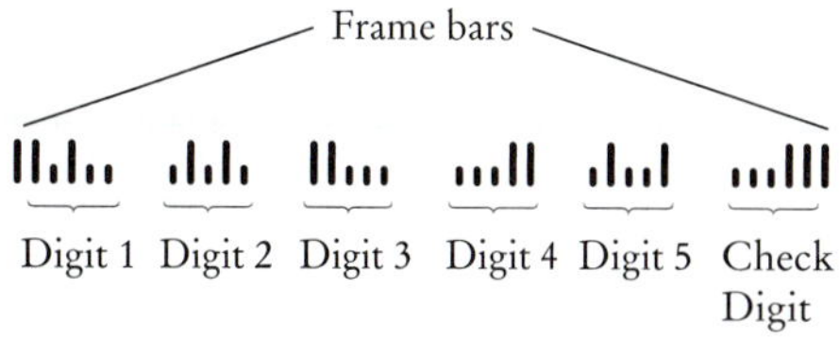

Frame bars

Digit 1 Digit 2 Digit 3 Digit 4 Digit 5 Check Digit

Figure 8 Encoding for Five-Digit Bar Codes

Answers to Self-Check Questions

1. Look for nouns in the problem description.
2. Yes (ChessBoard) and no (MovePiece).
3. Some of its features deal with payments, others with coin values.
4. None of the coin operations require the CashRegister class.
5. If a class doesn't depend on another, it is not affected by interface changes in the other class.
6. It is an accessor—calling substring doesn't modify the string on which the method is invoked. In fact, all methods of the String class are accessors.
7. No—translate is a mutator.
8. It is a side effect; this kind of side effect is common in object-oriented programming.
9. Yes—the method affects the state of the Scanner parameter.
10. Then you don't have to worry about checking for invalid values—it becomes the caller's responsibility.
11. No—you can take any action that is convenient for you.
12. `Math m = new Math(); y = m.sqrt(x);`
13. You cannot add a method to the ArrayList class—it is a class in the standard Java library that you cannot modify.
14. System.in and System.out.
15. Yes, it works. Static methods can access static variables of the same class. But it is a terrible idea. As your programming tasks get more complex, you will want to use objects and classes to organize your programs.
16. Yes. The scopes are disjoint.
17. It starts at the beginning of the class and ends at the end of the class.
18. (a) No; (b) Yes; (c) Yes; (d) No
19. No—you simply use fully qualified names for all other classes, such as java.util.Random and java.awt.Rectangle.
20. /home/me/cs101/hw1/problem1 or, on Windows, c:\Users\Me\cs101\hw1\problem1.
21. Here is one possible answer.

```java
public class EarthquakeTest
{
    @Test public void testLevel4()
    {
        Earthquake quake = new Earthquake(4);
        Assert.assertEquals("Felt by many people, no destruction",
            quake.getDescription());
    }
}
```

22. It is a tolerance threshold for comparing floating-point numbers. We want the equality test to pass if there is a small roundoff error.

Chapter 9

Interfaces and Polymorphism

CHAPTER GOALS

- To be able to declare and use interface types
- To understand the concept of polymorphism
- To appreciate how interfaces can be used to decouple classes
- To learn how to implement helper classes as inner classes
- **G** To implement event listeners in graphical applications

In order to increase programming productivity, we want to be able to *reuse* software components in multiple projects. However, some adaptations are often required to make reuse possible. In this chapter, you will learn an important strategy for separating the reusable part of a computation from the parts that vary in each reuse scenario. The reusable part invokes methods of an *interface*. It is combined with a class that implements the interface methods. To produce a different application, you simply plug in another class that implements the same interface. The program's behavior varies according to the implementation that is plugged in—this phenomenon is called *polymorphism*.

CHAPTER CONTENTS

9.1 Using Interfaces for Algorithm Reuse

It is often possible to make a service available to a wider set of inputs by focusing on the essential operations that the service requires. *Interface types* are used to express these common operations.

Consider the DataSet class of Chapter 6. That class provides a service, namely computing the average and maximum of a set of input values. Unfortunately, the class is suitable only for computing the average of a set of *numbers*. If we wanted to process bank accounts to find the bank account with the highest balance, we could not use the class in its current form. We could modify the class, like this:

```
public class DataSet // Modified for BankAccount objects
{
    private double sum;
    private BankAccount maximum;
    private int count;
    . . .
    public void add(BankAccount x)
    {
        sum = sum + x.getBalance();
        if (count == 0 || maximum.getBalance() < x.getBalance())
            maximum = x;
        count++;
    }
}
```

```java
   public BankAccount getMaximum()
   {
      return maximum;
   }
}
```

Or suppose we wanted to find the coin with the highest value among a set of coins. We would need to modify the DataSet class again.

```java
public class DataSet // Modified for Coin objects
{
   private double sum;
   private Coin maximum;
   private int count;
   . . .
   public void add(Coin x)
   {
      sum = sum + x.getValue();
      if (count == 0 || maximum.getValue() < x.getValue())
         maximum = x;
      count++;
   }

   public Coin getMaximum()
   {
      return maximum;
   }
}
```

Clearly, the algorithm for the data analysis service is the same in all cases, but the details of measurement differ. We would like to provide a *single* class that provides this service to any objects that can be measured.

Suppose that the various classes agree on a method getMeasure that obtains the measure to be used in the data analysis. For bank accounts, getMeasure returns the balance. For coins, getMeasure returns the coin value, and so on. Then we can implement a DataSet class whose add method looks like this:

```java
sum = sum + x.getMeasure();
if (count == 0 || maximum.getMeasure() < x.getMeasure())
   maximum = x;
count++;
```

What is the type of the variable x? Ideally, x should refer to any class that has a getMeasure method.

> A Java interface type declares methods but does not provide their implementations.

In Java, an **interface type** is used to specify required operations. We will declare an interface type that we call Measurable:

```java
public interface Measurable
{
   double getMeasure();
}
```

The interface declaration lists all methods that the interface type requires. The Measurable interface type requires a single method, but in general, an interface type can require multiple methods.

Note that the Measurable type is not a type in the standard library—it is a type that was created specifically for this book, in order to make the DataSet class more reusable.

Syntax 9.1   Declaring an Interface

Syntax   public interface *InterfaceName*
    {
       method signatures
    }

Example

```
                                public interface Measurable
                                {
The methods of an interface       double getMeasure();   ── No implementation is provided.
are automatically public.       }
```

The methods of an interface are automatically public.

No implementation is provided.

Unlike a class, an interface type provides no implementation.

An interface type is similar to a class, but there are several important differences:

- All methods in an interface type are *abstract*; that is, they have a name, parameters, and a return type, but they don't have an implementation.
- All methods in an interface type are automatically public.
- An interface type does not have instance variables.

Now we can use the interface type Measurable to declare the variables x and maximum.

```java
public class DataSet
{
    private double sum;
    private Measurable maximum;
    private int count;

    . . .
    public void add(Measurable x)
    {
        sum = sum + x.getMeasure();
        if (count == 0 || maximum.getMeasure() < x.getMeasure())
            maximum = x;
        count++;
    }

    public Measurable getMaximum()
    {
        return maximum;
    }
}
```

Use the implements reserved word to indicate that a class implements an interface type.

This DataSet class is usable for analyzing objects of any class that implements the Measurable interface. A class **implements an interface** type if it declares the interface in an implements clause. It should then implement the method or methods that the interface requires.

```java
public class BankAccount implements Measurable
{
    . . .
    public double getMeasure()
    {
        return balance;
    }
}
```

Figure 1
Attachments Conform to the
Mixer's Interface

Note that the class must declare the method as `public`, whereas the interface need not—all methods in an interface are public.

Similarly, it is an easy matter to modify the `Coin` class to implement the `Measurable` interface.

```
public class Coin implements Measurable
{
    public double getMeasure()
    {
        return value;
    }
    . . .
}
```

In summary, the `Measurable` interface expresses what all measurable objects have in common. This commonality makes the flexibility of the improved `DataSet` class possible. A data set can analyze objects of *any* class that implements the `Measurable` interface.

This is a typical usage for interface types. A service provider—in this case, the `DataSet`—specifies an interface for participating in the service. Any class that conforms to that interface can then be used with the service. This is similar to the way a mixer will provide rotation to any attachment that fits its interface (see Figure 1).

> Use interface types to make code more reusable.

Syntax 9.2   Implementing an Interface

Syntax	`public class` *ClassName* `implements` *InterfaceName*, *InterfaceName*, . . .
	{
	    instance variables
	    methods
	}

Example

```
                              public class BankAccount implements Measurable
                              {
                                  . . .
                                  public double getMeasure()
                                  {
                                      return balance;
                                  }
                                  . . .
                              }
```

List all interface types that this class implements.

BankAccount *instance variables*

Other BankAccount *methods*

This method provides the implementation for the method declared in the interface.

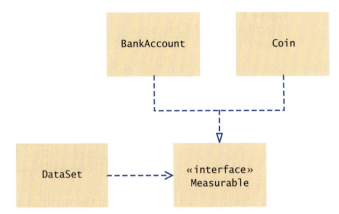

Figure 2 UML Diagram of the DataSet Class and the Classes that Implement the Measurable Interface

Figure 2 shows the relationships between the DataSet class, the Measurable interface, and the classes that implement the interface. Note that the DataSet class depends only on the Measurable interface. It is decoupled from the BankAccount and Coin classes.

In the UML notation, interfaces are tagged with an indicator «interface». A dotted arrow with a triangular tip denotes the "*is-a*" relationship between a class and an interface. You have to look carefully at the arrow tips—a dotted line with an open arrow tip (>) denotes the "*uses*" relationship or dependency.

ch09/measure1/DataSetTester.java

```
1  /**
2      This program tests the DataSet class.
3  */
4  public class DataSetTester
5  {
6     public static void main(String[] args)
7     {
8        DataSet bankData = new DataSet();
9
10       bankData.add(new BankAccount(0));
11       bankData.add(new BankAccount(10000));
12       bankData.add(new BankAccount(2000));
13
14       System.out.println("Average balance: " + bankData.getAverage());
15       System.out.println("Expected: 4000");
16       Measurable max = bankData.getMaximum();
17       System.out.println("Highest balance: " + max.getMeasure());
18       System.out.println("Expected: 10000");
19
20       DataSet coinData = new DataSet();
21
22       coinData.add(new Coin(0.25, "quarter"));
23       coinData.add(new Coin(0.1, "dime"));
24       coinData.add(new Coin(0.05, "nickel"));
25
```

```
26      System.out.println("Average coin value: " + coinData.getAverage());
27      System.out.println("Expected: 0.133");
28      max = coinData.getMaximum();
29      System.out.println("Highest coin value: " + max.getMeasure());
30      System.out.println("Expected: 0.25");
31   }
32 }
```

Program Run

```
Average balance: 4000.0
Expected: 4000
Highest balance: 10000.0
Expected: 10000
Average coin value: 0.13333333333333333
Expected: 0.133
Highest coin value: 0.25
Expected: 0.25
```

SELF CHECK

1. Suppose you want to use the DataSet class to find the Country object with the largest population. What condition must the Country class fulfill?
2. Why can't the add method of the DataSet class have a parameter of type Object?

Common Error 9.1

Forgetting to Declare Implementing Methods as Public

The methods in an interface are not declared as public, because they are public by default. However, the methods in a class are not public by default—their default access level is "package" access, which we discuss in Chapter 8. It is a common error to forget the public reserved word when declaring a method from an interface:

```
public class BankAccount implements Measurable
{
   . . .
   double getMeasure() // Oops—should be public
   {
      return balance;
   }
}
```

Then the compiler complains that the method has a weaker access level, namely package access instead of public access. The remedy is to declare the method as public.

Special Topic 9.1

Constants in Interfaces

Interfaces cannot have instance variables, but it is legal to specify *constants*. For example, the SwingConstants interface declares various constants, such as SwingConstants.NORTH, SwingConstants.EAST, and so on.

When declaring a constant in an interface, you can (and should) omit the reserved words public static final, because all variables in an interface are automatically public static final.

For example,

```
public interface SwingConstants
{
    int NORTH = 1;
    int NORTHEAST = 2;
    int EAST = 3;
    . . .
}
```

9.2 Converting Between Class and Interface Types

Interfaces are used to express the commonality between classes. In this section, we discuss when it is legal to convert between class and interface types.

Have a close look at the call

```
bankData.add(new BankAccount(1000));
```

from the test program of the preceding section. Here we pass an object of type BankAccount to the add method of the DataSet class. However, that method has a parameter of type Measurable:

```
public void add(Measurable x)
```

> You can convert from a class type to an interface type, provided the class implements the interface.

It it legal to convert from the BankAccount type to the Measurable type. In general, you can convert from a class type to the type of any interface that the class implements. For example,

```
BankAccount account = new BankAccount(1000);
Measurable meas = account; // OK
```

Alternatively, a Measurable variable can refer to an object of the Coin class of the preceding section because that class also implements the Measurable interface.

```
Coin dime = new Coin(0.1, "dime");
Measurable meas = dime; // Also OK
```

However, the Rectangle class from the standard library doesn't implement the Measurable interface. Therefore, the following assignment is an error:

```
Measurable meas = new Rectangle(5, 10, 20, 30); // Error
```

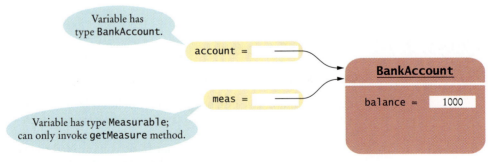

Figure 3 Variables of Class and Interface Types

Occasionally, it happens that you store an object in an interface reference and you need to convert its type back. This happens in the getMaximum method of the DataSet class. The DataSet stores the object with the largest measure, *as a* Measurable *reference*.

```
DataSet coinData = new DataSet();
coinData.add(new Coin(0.25, "quarter"));
coinData.add(new Coin(0.1, "dime"));
coinData.add(new Coin(0.05, "nickel"));
Measurable max = coinData.getMaximum();
```

Now what can you do with the max reference? *You* know it refers to a Coin object, but the compiler doesn't. For example, you cannot call the getName method:

```
String coinName = max.getName(); // Error
```

That call is an error, because the Measurable type has no getName method.

However, as long as you are absolutely sure that max refers to a Coin object, you can use the **cast** notation to convert its type back:

```
Coin maxCoin = (Coin) max;
String name = maxCoin.getName();
```

> You need a cast to convert from an interface type to a class type.

If you are wrong, and the object doesn't actually refer to a coin, a run-time exception will occur.

This cast notation is the same notation that you saw in Chapter 4 to convert between number types. For example, if x is a floating-point number, then (int) x is the integer part of the number. The intent is similar—to convert from one type to another. However, there is one big difference between casting of number types and casting of class types. When casting number types, you may *lose information*, and you use the cast to tell the compiler that you agree to the potential information loss. When casting object types, on the other hand, you *take a risk* of causing an exception, and you tell the compiler that you agree to that risk.

S E L F   C H E C K

3. Can you use a cast (BankAccount) meas to convert a Measurable variable meas to a BankAccount reference?

4. If both BankAccount and Coin implement the Measurable interface, can a Coin reference be converted to a BankAccount reference?

Common Error 9.2

Trying to Instantiate an Interface

You can declare variables whose type is an interface, for example:

```
Measurable meas;
```

However, you can *never* construct an object of an interface type:

```
Measurable meas = new Measurable(); // Error
```

Interfaces aren't classes. There are no objects whose types are interfaces. If an interface variable refers to an object, then the object must belong to some class—a class that implements the interface:

```
Measurable meas = new BankAccount(); // OK
```

9.3 Polymorphism

When multiple classes implement the same interface, each class can implement the methods of the interface in different ways. How is the correct method executed when the interface method is invoked? We will answer that question in this section.

It is worth emphasizing once again that it is perfectly legal—and in fact very common—to have variables whose type is an interface, such as

```
Measurable meas;
```

Just remember that the object to which meas refers doesn't have type Measurable. In fact, *no object* has type Measurable. Instead, the type of the object is some class that implements the Measurable interface. This might be an object of the BankAccount or Coin class, or some other class with a getMeasure method.

```
meas = new BankAccount(1000); // OK
meas = new Coin(0.1, "dime"); // OK
```

ANIMATION
Polymorphism

What can you do with an interface variable, given that you don't know the class of the object that it references? You can invoke the methods of the interface:

```
double m = meas.getMeasure();
```

The DataSet class took advantage of this capability by computing the measure of the added object, without knowing exactly what kind of object was added.

Now let's think through the call to the getMeasure method more carefully. *Which* getMeasure method? The BankAccount and Coin classes provide two *different* implementations of that method. How did the correct method get called if the caller didn't even know the exact class to which meas belongs?

The Java virtual machine locates the correct method by first looking at the class of the actual object, and then calling the method with the given name in that class. That is, if meas refers to a BankAccount object, then the BankAccount.getMeasure method is called. If meas refers to a Coin object, then the Coin.getMeasure method is called. This means that one method call

> When the virtual machine calls an instance method, it locates the method of the implicit parameter's class. This is called dynamic method lookup.

```
double m = meas.getMeasure();
```

can invoke different methods depending on the momentary contents of meas. This mechanism for locating the appropriate method is called *dynamic method lookup*.

> Polymorphism denotes the ability to treat objects with differences in behavior in a uniform way.

Dynamic method lookup enables a programming technique called **polymorphism**. The term "polymorphism" comes from the Greek words for "many shapes". The same computation works for objects of many shapes, and adapts itself to the nature of the objects.

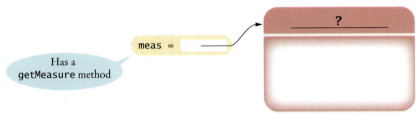

Figure 4 An Interface Reference Can Refer to an Object of Any Class that Implements the Interface

5. Why is it impossible to construct a `Measurable` object?

6. Why can you nevertheless declare a variable whose type is `Measurable`?

7. What does this code fragment print? Why is this an example of polymorphism?

```
DataSet data = new DataSet();
data.add(new BankAccount(1000));
data.add(new Coin(0.1, "dime"));
System.out.println(data.getAverage());
```

➕ **Worked Example 9.1**

Investigating Number Sequences

Worked Example 9.1 uses a `Sequence` interface to investigate properties of arbitrary number sequences.

9.4 Using Interfaces for Callbacks

In this section, we introduce the notion of a callback, show how it leads to a more flexible `DataSet` class, and study how a callback can be implemented in Java by using interface types.

To understand why a further improvement to the `DataSet` class is desirable, consider these limitations of the `Measurable` interface:

- You can add the `Measurable` interface only to classes under your control. If you want to process a set of `Rectangle` objects, you cannot make the `Rectangle` class implement another interface—it is a system class, which you cannot change.

- You can measure an object in only one way. If you want to analyze a set of savings accounts both by bank balance and by interest rate, you are stuck.

Therefore, let's rethink the `DataSet` class. The data set needs to measure the objects that are added. When the objects are required to be of type `Measurable`, the responsibility of measuring lies with the added objects themselves, which is the cause of the limitations that we noted.

It would be better if we could give a method for measuring objects to a data set. When collecting rectangles, we might give it a method for computing the area of a rectangle. When collecting savings accounts, we might give it a method for getting the account's interest rate.

Such a method is called a **callback**. A callback is a mechanism for bundling up a block of code so that it can be invoked at a later time.

In some programming languages, it is possible to specify callbacks directly, as blocks of code or names of methods. But Java is an object-oriented programming language. Therefore, you turn callbacks into objects. This process starts by declaring an interface for the callback:

> A callback is a mechanism for specifying code that is executed at a later time.

```
public interface Measurer
{
    double measure(Object anObject);
}
```

➕ Available online in WileyPLUS and at www.wiley.com/college/horstmann.

The measure method measures an object and returns its measurement. Here we use the fact that all objects can be converted to the type Object, the "lowest common denominator" of all classes in Java. We will discuss the Object type in greater detail in Chapter 10.

The code that makes the call to the callback receives an object of a class that implements this interface. In our case, the improved DataSet class is constructed with a Measurer object (that is, an object of some class that implements the Measurer interface). That object is saved in a measurer instance variable.

```java
public DataSet(Measurer aMeasurer)
{
    sum = 0;
    count = 0;
    maximum = null;
    measurer = aMeasurer;
}
```

The measurer variable is used to carry out the measurements, like this:

```java
public void add(Object x)
{
    sum = sum + measurer.measure(x);
    if (count == 0 || measurer.measure(maximum) < measurer.measure(x))
        maximum = x;
    count++;
}
```

The DataSet class simply makes a callback to the measure method whenever it needs to measure any object.

Finally, a specific callback is obtained by implementing the Measurer interface. For example, here is how you can measure rectangles by area. Provide a class

```java
public class RectangleMeasurer implements Measurer
{
    public double measure(Object anObject)
    {
        Rectangle aRectangle = (Rectangle) anObject;
        double area = aRectangle.getWidth() * aRectangle.getHeight();
        return area;
    }
}
```

Note that the measure method must accept a parameter of type Object, even though this particular measurer just wants to measure rectangles. The method parameter types must match those of the measure method in the Measurer interface. Therefore, the Object parameter is cast to the Rectangle type:

```java
Rectangle aRectangle = (Rectangle) anObject;
```

What can you do with a RectangleMeasurer? You need it for a DataSet that compares rectangles by area. Construct an object of the RectangleMeasurer class and pass it to the DataSet constructor.

```java
Measurer m = new RectangleMeasurer();
DataSet data = new DataSet(m);
```

Next, add rectangles to the data set.

```java
data.add(new Rectangle(5, 10, 20, 30));
data.add(new Rectangle(10, 20, 30, 40));
    . . .
```

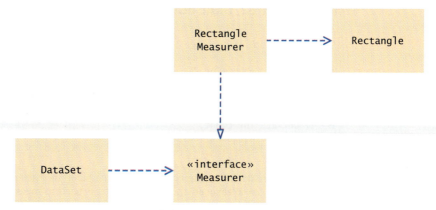

Figure 5 UML Diagram of the DataSet Class and the Measurer Interface

The data set will ask the RectangleMeasurer object to measure the rectangles. In other words, the data set uses the RectangleMeasurer object to carry out callbacks.

Figure 5 shows the UML diagram of the classes and interfaces of this solution. As in Figure 2, the DataSet class is decoupled from the Rectangle class whose objects it processes. However, unlike in Figure 2, the Rectangle class is no longer coupled with another class. Instead, to process rectangles, you provide a small "helper" class RectangleMeasurer. This helper class has only one purpose: to tell the DataSet how to measure its objects.

ch09/measure2/Measurer.java

```
1   /**
2        Describes any class whose objects can measure other objects.
3   */
4   public interface Measurer
5   {
6        /**
7            Computes the measure of an object.
8            @param anObject the object to be measured
9            @return the measure
10       */
11       double measure(Object anObject);
12   }
```

ch09/measure2/RectangleMeasurer.java

```
1   import java.awt.Rectangle;
2
3   /**
4        Objects of this class measure rectangles by area.
5   */
6   public class RectangleMeasurer implements Measurer
7   {
8        public double measure(Object anObject)
9        {
10           Rectangle aRectangle = (Rectangle) anObject;
11           double area = aRectangle.getWidth() * aRectangle.getHeight();
12           return area;
13       }
14   }
```

ch09/measure2/DataSet.java

```java
1   /**
2       Computes the average of a set of data values.
3   */
4   public class DataSet
5   {
6      private double sum;
7      private Object maximum;
8      private int count;
9      private Measurer measurer;
10
11     /**
12         Constructs an empty data set with a given measurer.
13         @param aMeasurer the measurer that is used to measure data values
14     */
15     public DataSet(Measurer aMeasurer)
16     {
17        sum = 0;
18        count = 0;
19        maximum = null;
20        measurer = aMeasurer;
21     }
22
23     /**
24         Adds a data value to the data set.
25         @param x a data value
26     */
27     public void add(Object x)
28     {
29        sum = sum + measurer.measure(x);
30        if (count == 0 || measurer.measure(maximum) < measurer.measure(x))
31           maximum = x;
32        count++;
33     }
34
35     /**
36         Gets the average of the added data.
37         @return the average or 0 if no data has been added
38     */
39     public double getAverage()
40     {
41        if (count == 0) return 0;
42        else return sum / count;
43     }
44
45     /**
46         Gets the largest of the added data.
47         @return the maximum or 0 if no data has been added
48     */
49     public Object getMaximum()
50     {
51        return maximum;
52     }
53  }
```

ch09/measure2/DataSetTester2.java

```java
1   import java.awt.Rectangle;
2
```

```
3   /**
4       This program demonstrates the use of a Measurer.
5   */
6   public class DataSetTester2
7   {
8      public static void main(String[] args)
9      {
10        Measurer m = new RectangleMeasurer();
11
12        DataSet data = new DataSet(m);
13
14        data.add(new Rectangle(5, 10, 20, 30));
15        data.add(new Rectangle(10, 20, 30, 40));
16        data.add(new Rectangle(20, 30, 5, 15));
17
18        System.out.println("Average area: " + data.getAverage());
19        System.out.println("Expected: 625");
20
21        Rectangle max = (Rectangle) data.getMaximum();
22        System.out.println("Maximum area rectangle: " + max);
23        System.out.println("Expected: "
24              + "java.awt.Rectangle[x=10,y=20,width=30,height=40]");
25     }
26  }
```

Program Run

```
Average area: 625
Expected: 625
Maximum area rectangle: java.awt.Rectangle[x=10,y=20,width=30,height=40]
Expected: java.awt.Rectangle[x=10,y=20,width=30,height=40]
```

SELF CHECK

8. Suppose you want to use the DataSet class of Section 9.1 to find the longest String from a set of inputs. Why can't this work?

9. How can you use the DataSet class of this section to find the longest String from a set of inputs?

10. Why does the measure method of the Measurer interface have one more parameter than the getMeasure method of the Measurable interface?

9.5 Inner Classes

The RectangleMeasurer class is a very trivial class. We need this class only because the DataSet class needs an object of some class that implements the Measurer interface. When you have a class that serves a very limited purpose, such as this one, you can declare the class inside the method that needs it:

```
public class DataSetTester3
{
   public static void main(String[] args)
   {
      class RectangleMeasurer implements Measurer
      {
         . . .
```

```
            }

            Measurer m = new RectangleMeasurer();
            DataSet data = new DataSet(m);
            . . .
        }
    }
```

An inner class is declared inside another class.

A class that is declared inside another class, such as the RectangleMeasurer class in this example, is called an **inner class**. This arrangement signals to the reader of your program that the RectangleMeasurer class is not interesting beyond the scope of this method. Since an inner class inside a method is not a publicly accessible feature, you don't need to document it as thoroughly.

Inner classes are commonly used for utility classes that should not be visible elsewhere in a program.

You can also declare an inner class inside an enclosing class, but outside of its methods. Then the inner class is available to all methods of the enclosing class.

```
public class DataSetTester3
{
    class RectangleMeasurer implements Measurer
    {
        . . .
    }

    public static void main(String[] args)
    {

        Measurer m = new RectangleMeasurer();
        DataSet data = new DataSet(m);
        . . .
    }
}
```

When you compile the source files for a program that uses inner classes, have a look at the class files in your program directory—you will find that the inner classes are stored in files with curious names, such as DataSetTester3$1RectangleMeasurer.class. The exact names aren't important. The point is that the compiler turns an inner class into a regular class file.

ch09/measure3/DataSetTester3.java

```java
 1  import java.awt.Rectangle;
 2
 3  /**
 4      This program demonstrates the use of an inner class.
 5  */
 6  public class DataSetTester3
 7  {
 8      public static void main(String[] args)
 9      {
10          class RectangleMeasurer implements Measurer
11          {
12              public double measure(Object anObject)
13              {
14                  Rectangle aRectangle = (Rectangle) anObject;
15                  double area
16                      = aRectangle.getWidth() * aRectangle.getHeight();
17                  return area;
18              }
19          }
20
```

```
21          Measurer m = new RectangleMeasurer();
22
23          DataSet data = new DataSet(m);
24
25          data.add(new Rectangle(5, 10, 20, 30));
26          data.add(new Rectangle(10, 20, 30, 40));
27          data.add(new Rectangle(20, 30, 5, 15));
28
29          System.out.println("Average area: " + data.getAverage());
30          System.out.println("Expected: 625");
31
32          Rectangle max = (Rectangle) data.getMaximum();
33          System.out.println("Maximum area rectangle: " + max);
34          System.out.println("Expected: "
35              + "java.awt.Rectangle[x=10,y=20,width=30,height=40]");
36      }
37   }
```

SELF CHECK

11. Why would you use an inner class instead of a regular class?

12. How many class files are produced when you compile the DataSetTester3 program?

Special Topic 9.2

Anonymous Classes

An entity is *anonymous* if it does not have a name. In a program, something that is only used once doesn't usually need a name. For example, you can replace

```
Coin aCoin = new Coin(0.1, "dime");
data.add(aCoin);
```

with

```
data.add(new Coin(0.1, "dime"));
```

if the coin is not used elsewhere in the same method. The object new Coin(0.1, "dime") is an **anonymous object**. Programmers like anonymous objects, because they don't have to go through the trouble of coming up with a name. If you have struggled with the decision whether to call a coin c, dime, or aCoin, you'll understand this sentiment.

Inner classes often give rise to a similar situation. After a single object of the Rectangle-Measurer has been constructed, the class is never used again. In Java, it is possible to declare **anonymous classes** if all you ever need is a single object of the class.

```
public static void main(String[] args)
{
   // Construct an object of an anonymous class
   Measurer m = new Measurer()
      // Class declaration starts here
      {
         public double measure(Object anObject)
         {
            Rectangle aRectangle = (Rectangle) anObject;
            return aRectangle.getWidth() * aRectangle.getHeight();
         }
      };

   DataSet data = new DataSet(m);
```

    . . .
    }

This means: Construct an object of a class that implements the `Measurer` interface by declaring the measure method as specified. Many programmers like this style, but we will not use it in this book.

Random Fact 9.1

Operating Systems

Without an operating system, a computer would not be useful. Minimally, you need an operating system to locate files and to start programs. The programs that you run need services from the operating system to access devices and to interact with other programs. Operating systems on large computers need to provide more services than those on personal computers do.

Here are some typical services:

- *Program loading.* Every operating system provides some way of launching application programs. The user indicates what program should be run, usually by typing the name of the program or by clicking on an icon. The operating system locates the program code, loads it into memory, and starts it.

- *Managing files.* A storage device, such as a hard disk is, electronically, simply a device capable of storing a huge sequence of zeroes and ones. It is up to the operating system to bring some structure to the storage layout and organize it into files, folders, and so on. The operating system also needs to impose some amount of security and redundancy into the file system so that a power outage does not jeopardize the contents of an entire hard disk. Some operating systems do a better job in this regard than others.

A Graphical Software Environment for the Linux Operating System

- *Virtual memory.* RAM is expensive, and few computers have enough RAM to hold all programs and their data that a user would like to run simultaneously. Most operating systems extend the available memory by storing some data on the hard disk. The application programs do not realize whether a particular data item is in memory or in the virtual memory disk storage. When a program accesses a data item that is currently not in RAM, the processor senses this and notifies the operating system. The operating system swaps the needed data from the hard disk into RAM, simultaneously swapping out a memory block of equal size that had not been accessed for some time.

- *Handling multiple users.* The operating systems of large and powerful computers allow simultaneous access by multiple users. Each user is connected through a separate terminal. The operating system authenticates users by checking that each one has a valid account and password. It gives each user a small slice of processor time, then serves the next user.

- *Multitasking.* Even if you are the sole user of a computer, you may want to run multiple applications—for example, to read your e-mail in one window and run the Java compiler in another. The operating system is responsible for dividing processor time between the applications you are running, so that each can make progress.

- *Printing.* The operating system queues up the print requests that are sent by multiple applications. This is necessary to make sure that the printed pages do not contain a mixture of words sent simultaneously from separate programs.

- *Windows.* Many operating systems present their users with a desktop made up of multiple windows. The operating system manages the location and appearance of the window frames; the applications are responsible for the interiors.

- *Fonts.* To render text on the screen and the printer, the shapes of characters must be defined. This is especially important for programs that can display multiple type styles and sizes. Modern operating systems contain a central font repository.

- *Communicating between programs.* The operating system can facilitate the transfer of information between programs. That transfer can happen through *cut and paste* or *interprocess communication.* Cut and paste is a user-initiated data transfer in which the user copies data from one application into a transfer buffer (often called a "clipboard") managed by the operating system and inserts the buffer's contents into another application. Interprocess communication is initiated by applications that transfer data without direct user involvement.

- *Networking.* The operating system provides protocols and services for enabling applications to reach information on other computers attached to the network.

Today, the most popular operating systems for personal computers are Linux (see the figure), the Macintosh OS, and Microsoft Windows.

9.6 Mock Objects

When you work on a program that consists of multiple classes, you often want to test some of the classes before the entire program has been completed. A very effective technique for this purpose is the use of **mock objects**. A mock object provides the same services as another object, but in a simplified manner.

Consider a grade book application that manages quiz scores for students. This calls for a class GradeBook with methods such as

> A mock object provides the same services as another object, but in a simplified manner.

```
public void addScore(int studentId, double score)
public double getAverageScore(int studentId)
public void save(String filename)
```

Now consider the class GradingProgram that manipulates a GradeBook object. That class calls the methods of the GradeBook class. We would like to test the GradingProgram class without having a fully functional GradeBook class.

To make this work, declare an interface type with the same methods that the GradeBook class provides. A common convention is to use the letter I as the prefix for such an interface:

```
public interface IGradeBook
{
    void addScore(int studentId, double score);
    double getAverageScore(int studentId);
    void save(String filename);
    . . .
}
```

The GradingProgram class should *only* use this interface, never the GradeBook class. Of course, the GradeBook class implements this interface, but as already mentioned, it may not be ready for some time.

In the meantime, provide a mock implementation that makes some simplifying assumptions. Saving is not actually necessary for testing the user interface. We can temporarily restrict to the case of a single student.

Both the mock class and the actual class implement the same interface.

```
public class MockGradeBook implements IGradeBook
{
    private ArrayList<Double> scores;

    public void addScore(int studentId, double score)
    {
        // Ignore studentId
        scores.add(score);
    }
    double getAverageScore(int studentId)
    {
        double total = 0;
        for (double x : scores) { total = total + x; }
        return total / scores.size();
    }
    void save(String filename)
    {
        // Do nothing
    }
    . . .
}
```

Now construct an instance of MockGradeBook and use it in the GradingProgram class. You can immediately test the GradingProgram class. When you are ready to test the actual class, simply use a GradeBook instance instead. Don't erase the mock class—it will still come in handy for regression testing.

SELF CHECK

13. Why is it necessary that the real class and the mock class implement the same interface type?

14. Why is the technique of mock objects particularly effective when the GradeBook and GradingProgram class are developed by two programmers?

9.7 Events, Event Sources, and Event Listeners

This and the following sections continue the book's graphics track. You will learn how interfaces are used when programming graphical user interfaces.

In the applications that you have written so far, user input was under control of the *program*. The program asked the user for input in a specific order. For example, a program might ask the user to supply first a name, then a dollar amount. But the programs that you use every day on your computer don't work like that. In a program with a graphical user interface, the *user* is in control. The user can use both the mouse and the keyboard and can manipulate many parts of the user interface in any desired order. For example, the user can enter information into text fields, pull down menus, click buttons, and drag scroll bars in any order. The program must react to the user commands, in whatever order they arrive. Having to deal with many possible inputs in random order is quite a bit harder than simply forcing the user to supply input in a fixed order.

In the following sections, you will learn how to write Java programs that can react to user-interface events, such as menu selections and mouse clicks. The Java windowing toolkit has a very sophisticated mechanism that allows a program to specify the events in which it is interested and which objects to notify when one of these events occurs.

> User-interface events include key presses, mouse moves, button clicks, menu selections, and so on.

Whenever the user of a graphical program types characters or uses the mouse anywhere inside one of the windows of the program, the Java windowing toolkit sends a notification to the program that an **event** has occurred. The windowing toolkit generates huge numbers of events. For example, whenever the mouse moves a tiny interval over a window, a "mouse move" event is generated. Whenever the mouse button is clicked, a "mouse pressed" and a "mouse released" event are generated. In addition, higher level events are generated when a user selects a menu item or button.

Most programs don't want to be flooded by boring events. For example, consider what happens when selecting a menu item with the mouse. The mouse moves over the menu item, then the mouse button is pressed, and finally the mouse button is released. Rather than receiving lots of irrelevant mouse events, a program can indicate that it only cares about menu selections, not about the underlying mouse events. However, if the mouse input is used for drawing shapes on a virtual canvas, it is necessary to closely track mouse events.

> An event listener belongs to a class that is provided by the application programmer. Its methods describe the actions to be taken when an event occurs.

Every program must indicate which events it needs to receive. It does that by installing **event listener** objects. An event listener object belongs to a class that you provide. The methods of your event listener classes contain the instructions that you want to have executed when the events occur.

> Event sources report on events. When an event occurs, the event source notifies all event listeners.

To install a listener, you need to know the **event source**. The event source is the user-interface component that generates a particular event. You add an event listener object to the appropriate event sources. Whenever the event occurs, the event source calls the appropriate methods of all attached event listeners.

This sounds somewhat abstract, so let's run through an extremely simple program that prints a message whenever a button is clicked (see Figure 6).

Figure 6 Implementing an Action Listener

> Use JButton components for buttons. Attach an ActionListener to each button.

Button listeners must belong to a class that implements the `ActionListener` interface:

```
public interface ActionListener
{
    void actionPerformed(ActionEvent event);
}
```

This particular interface has a single method, `actionPerformed`. It is your job to supply a class whose `actionPerformed` method contains the instructions that you want executed whenever the button is clicked. Here is a very simple example of such a listener class:

ch09/button1/ClickListener.java

```java
1   import java.awt.event.ActionEvent;
2   import java.awt.event.ActionListener;
3
4   /**
5       An action listener that prints a message.
6   */
7   public class ClickListener implements ActionListener
8   {
9       public void actionPerformed(ActionEvent event)
10      {
11          System.out.println("I was clicked.");
12      }
13  }
```

We ignore the `event` parameter of the `actionPerformed` method—it contains additional details about the event, such as the time at which it occurred.

Once the listener class has been declared, we need to construct an object of the class and add it to the button:

```
ActionListener listener = new ClickListener();
button.addActionListener(listener);
```

Whenever the button is clicked, it calls

```
listener.actionPerformed(event);
```

As a result, the message is printed.

You can think of the `actionPerformed` method as another example of a callback, similar to the `measure` method of the `Measurer` class. The windowing toolkit calls the actionPerformed method whenever the button is pressed, whereas the DataSet calls the measure method whenever it needs to measure an object.

The ButtonViewer class, whose source code is provided at the end of this section, constructs a frame with a button and adds a ClickListener to the button. You can test this program out by opening a console window, starting the ButtonViewer program from that console window, clicking the button, and watching the messages in the console window.

ch09/button1/ButtonViewer.java

```java
 1  import java.awt.event.ActionListener;
 2  import javax.swing.JButton;
 3  import javax.swing.JFrame;
 4
 5  /**
 6     This program demonstrates how to install an action listener.
 7  */
 8  public class ButtonViewer
 9  {
10     private static final int FRAME_WIDTH = 100;
11     private static final int FRAME_HEIGHT = 60;
12
13     public static void main(String[] args)
14     {
15        JFrame frame = new JFrame();
16        JButton button = new JButton("Click me!");
17        frame.add(button);
18
19        ActionListener listener = new ClickListener();
20        button.addActionListener(listener);
21
22        frame.setSize(FRAME_WIDTH, FRAME_HEIGHT);
23        frame.setDefaultCloseOperation(JFrame.EXIT_ON_CLOSE);
24        frame.setVisible(true);
25     }
26  }
```

SELF CHECK

15. Which objects are the event source and the event listener in the ButtonViewer program?

16. Why is it legal to assign a ClickListener object to a variable of type ActionListener?

Common Error 9.3

Modifying Parameter Types in the Implementing Method

When you implement an interface, you must declare each method *exactly* as it is specified in the interface. Accidentally making small changes to the parameter types is a common error. Here is the classic example,

```java
class MyListener implements ActionListener
{
   public void actionPerformed()
   // Oops . . . forgot ActionEvent parameter
   {
      . . .
```

```
        }
    }
```

As far as the compiler is concerned, this class fails to provide the method

```
public void actionPerformed(ActionEvent event)
```

You have to read the error message carefully and pay attention to the parameter and return types to find your error.

9.8 Using Inner Classes for Listeners

In the preceding section, you saw how the code that is executed when a button is clicked is placed into a listener class. It is common to implement listener classes as inner classes like this:

```
JButton button = new JButton(". . .");

// This inner class is declared in the same method as the button variable
class MyListener implements ActionListener
{
    . . .
};

ActionListener listener = new MyListener();
button.addActionListener(listener);
```

There are two reasons for this arrangement. The trivial listener class is located exactly where it is needed, without cluttering up the remainder of the project. Moreover, inner classes have a very attractive feature: Their methods can access variables that are declared in surrounding blocks. In this regard, method declarations of inner classes behave similarly to nested blocks.

Recall that a block is a statement group enclosed by braces. If a block is nested inside another, the inner block has access to all variables from the surrounding block:

```
{   // Surrounding block
    BankAccount account = new BankAccount();
    if (. . .)
    {   // Inner block
        . . .
        // OK to access variable from surrounding block
        account.deposit(interest);
        . . .
    }   // End of inner block
    . . .
}   // End of surrounding block
```

> Methods of an inner class can access local and instance variables from the surrounding scope.

The same nesting works for inner classes. Except for some technical restrictions, which we will examine later in this section, the methods of an inner class can access the variables from the enclosing scope. This feature is very useful when implementing event handlers. It allows the inner class to access variables without having to pass them as constructor or method parameters.

Let's look at an example. Suppose we want to add interest to a bank account whenever a button is clicked.

```java
JButton button = new JButton("Add Interest");
final BankAccount account = new BankAccount(INITIAL_BALANCE);

// This inner class is declared in the same method as the account and button variables.
class AddInterestListener implements ActionListener
{
   public void actionPerformed(ActionEvent event)
   {
      // The listener method accesses the account variable
      // from the surrounding block
      double interest = account.getBalance() * INTEREST_RATE / 100;
      account.deposit(interest);
   }
};

ActionListener listener = new AddInterestListener();
button.addActionListener(listener);
```

Local variables that are accessed by an inner class method must be declared as final.

There is a technical wrinkle. An inner class can access surrounding *local* variables only if they are declared as final. That sounds like a restriction, but it is usually not an issue in practice. Keep in mind that an object variable is final when the variable always refers to the same object. The state of the object can change, but the variable can't refer to a different object. For example, in our program, we never intended to have the account variable refer to multiple bank accounts, so there was no harm in declaring it as final.

An inner class can also access *instance* variables of the surrounding class, again with a restriction. The instance variable must belong to the object that constructed the inner class object. If the inner class object was created inside a static method, it can only access static variables.

Here is the source code for the program.

ch09/button2/InvestmentViewer1.java

```java
 1  import java.awt.event.ActionEvent;
 2  import java.awt.event.ActionListener;
 3  import javax.swing.JButton;
 4  import javax.swing.JFrame;
 5
 6  /**
 7     This program demonstrates how an action listener can access
 8     a variable from a surrounding block.
 9  */
10  public class InvestmentViewer1
11  {
12     private static final int FRAME_WIDTH = 120;
13     private static final int FRAME_HEIGHT = 60;
14
15     private static final double INTEREST_RATE = 10;
16     private static final double INITIAL_BALANCE = 1000;
17
18     public static void main(String[] args)
19     {
20        JFrame frame = new JFrame();
21
22        // The button to trigger the calculation
23        JButton button = new JButton("Add Interest");
24        frame.add(button);
25
```

```
26        // The application adds interest to this bank account
27        final BankAccount account = new BankAccount(INITIAL_BALANCE);
28
29        class AddInterestListener implements ActionListener
30        {
31           public void actionPerformed(ActionEvent event)
32           {
33              // The listener method accesses the account variable
34              // from the surrounding block
35              double interest = account.getBalance() * INTEREST_RATE / 100;
36              account.deposit(interest);
37              System.out.println("balance: " + account.getBalance());
38           }
39        }
40
41        ActionListener listener = new AddInterestListener();
42        button.addActionListener(listener);
43
44        frame.setSize(FRAME_WIDTH, FRAME_HEIGHT);
45        frame.setDefaultCloseOperation(JFrame.EXIT_ON_CLOSE);
46        frame.setVisible(true);
47     }
48  }
```

Program Run

```
balance: 1100.0
balance: 1210.0
balance: 1331.0
balance: 1464.1
```

SELF CHECK

17. Why would an inner class method want to access a variable from a surrounding scope?
18. If an inner class accesses a local variable from a surrounding scope, what special rule applies?

9.9 Building Applications with Buttons

In this section, you will learn how to structure a graphical application that contains buttons. We will put a button to work in our simple investment viewer program. Whenever the button is clicked, interest is added to a bank account, and the new balance is displayed (see Figure 7).

First, we construct an object of the JButton class. Pass the button label to the constructor:

```
JButton button = new JButton("Add Interest");
```

We also need a user-interface component that displays a message, namely the current bank balance. Such a component is called a *label*. You pass the initial message string to the JLabel constructor, like this:

```
JLabel label = new JLabel("balance: " + account.getBalance());
```

Use a JPanel container to group multiple user-interface components together.

The frame of our application contains both the button and the label. However, we cannot simply add both components directly to the frame—they would be placed

Figure 7   An Application with a Button

on top of each other. The solution is to put them into a **panel**, a container for other user-interface components, and then add the panel to the frame:

```
JPanel panel = new JPanel();
panel.add(button);
panel.add(label);
frame.add(panel);
```

Now we are ready for the hard part—the event listener that handles button clicks. As in the preceding section, it is necessary to provide a class that implements the ActionListener interface, and to place the button action into the actionPerformed method. Our listener class adds interest and displays the new balance:

You specify button click actions through classes that implement the ActionListener interface.

```
class AddInterestListener implements ActionListener
{
    public void actionPerformed(ActionEvent event)
    {
        double interest = account.getBalance() * INTEREST_RATE / 100;
        account.deposit(interest);
        label.setText("balance: " + account.getBalance());
    }
}
```

There is just a minor technicality. The actionPerformed method manipulates the account and label variables. These are local variables of the main method of the investment viewer program, not instance variables of the AddInterestListener class. We therefore need to declare the account and label variables as final so that the action-Performed method can access them.

Let's put the pieces together.

```
public static void main(String[] args)
{
    . . .
    JButton button = new JButton("Add Interest");
    final BankAccount account = new BankAccount(INITIAL_BALANCE);
    final JLabel label = new JLabel("balance: " + account.getBalance());

    class AddInterestListener implements ActionListener
    {
        public void actionPerformed(ActionEvent event)
        {
            double interest = account.getBalance() * INTEREST_RATE / 100;
            account.deposit(interest);
            label.setText("balance: " + account.getBalance());
        }
    }

    ActionListener listener = new AddInterestListener();
    button.addActionListener(listener);
    . . .
}
```

With a bit of practice, you will learn to glance at this code and translate it into plain English: "When the button is clicked, add interest and set the label text."

Here is the complete program. It demonstrates how to add multiple components to a frame, by using a panel, and how to implement listeners as inner classes.

ch09/button3/InvestmentViewer2.java

```java
1  import java.awt.event.ActionEvent;
2  import java.awt.event.ActionListener;
3  import javax.swing.JButton;
4  import javax.swing.JFrame;
5  import javax.swing.JLabel;
6  import javax.swing.JPanel;
7  import javax.swing.JTextField;
8
9  /**
10     This program displays the growth of an investment.
11  */
12  public class InvestmentViewer2
13  {
14     private static final int FRAME_WIDTH = 400;
15     private static final int FRAME_HEIGHT = 100;
16
17     private static final double INTEREST_RATE = 10;
18     private static final double INITIAL_BALANCE = 1000;
19
20     public static void main(String[] args)
21     {
22        JFrame frame = new JFrame();
23
24        // The button to trigger the calculation
25        JButton button = new JButton("Add Interest");
26
27        // The application adds interest to this bank account
28        final BankAccount account = new BankAccount(INITIAL_BALANCE);
29
30        // The label for displaying the results
31        final JLabel label = new JLabel("balance: " + account.getBalance());
32
33        // The panel that holds the user-interface components
34        JPanel panel = new JPanel();
35        panel.add(button);
36        panel.add(label);
37        frame.add(panel);
38
39        class AddInterestListener implements ActionListener
40        {
41           public void actionPerformed(ActionEvent event)
42           {
43              double interest = account.getBalance() * INTEREST_RATE / 100;
44              account.deposit(interest);
45              label.setText("balance: " + account.getBalance());
46           }
47        }
48
49        ActionListener listener = new AddInterestListener();
50        button.addActionListener(listener);
51
```

```
52        frame.setSize(FRAME_WIDTH, FRAME_HEIGHT);
53        frame.setDefaultCloseOperation(JFrame.EXIT_ON_CLOSE);
54        frame.setVisible(true);
55     }
56  }
```

SELF CHECK

19. How do you place the "balance: . . ." message to the left of the "Add Interest" button?

20. Why was it not necessary to declare the button variable as final?

Common Error 9.4

Forgetting to Attach a Listener

If you run your program and find that your buttons seem to be dead, double-check that you attached the button listener. The same holds for other user-interface components. It is a surprisingly common error to program the listener class and the event handler action without actually attaching the listener to the event source.

Productivity Hint 9.1

Don't Use a Container as a Listener

In this book, we use inner classes for event listeners. That approach works for many different event types. Once you master the technique, you don't have to think about it anymore. Many development environments automatically generate code with inner classes, so it is a good idea to be familiar with them.

However, some programmers bypass the event listener classes and instead turn a container (such as a panel or frame) into a listener. Here is a typical example. The actionPerformed method is added to the viewer class. That is, the viewer implements the ActionListener interface.

```
public class InvestmentViewer
       implements ActionListener // This approach is not recommended
{
   public InvestmentViewer()
   {
      JButton button = new JButton("Add Interest");
      button.addActionListener(this);
      . . .
   }

   public void actionPerformed(ActionEvent event)
   {
      . . .
   }
   . . .
}
```

Now the actionPerformed method is a part of the InvestmentViewer class rather than part of a separate listener class. The listener is installed as this.

This technique has two major flaws. First, it separates the button declaration from the button action. Also, it doesn't *scale* well. If the viewer class contains two buttons that each generate action events, then the actionPerformed method must investigate the event source, which leads to code that is tedious and error-prone.

Common Error 9.5

By Default, Components Have Zero Width and Height

You must be careful when you add a painted component to a panel, such as a component displaying a car. You add the component in the same way as a button or label:

```
panel.add(button);
panel.add(label);
panel.add(carComponent);
```

However, the default size for a component is 0 by 0 pixels, and the car component will not be visible. The remedy is to call the setPreferredSize method, like this:

```
carComponent.setPreferredSize(new Dimension(CAR_COMPONENT_WIDTH, CAR_COMPONENT_HEIGHT));
```

9.10 Processing Timer Events

In this section we will study timer events and show how they allow you to implement simple animations.

The Timer class in the javax.swing package generates a sequence of action events, spaced apart at even time intervals. (You can think of a timer as an invisible button that is automatically clicked.) This is useful whenever you want to have an object updated in regular intervals. For example, in an animation, you may want to update a scene ten times per second and redisplay the image, to give the illusion of movement.

> A timer generates timer events at fixed intervals.

When you use a timer, you specify the frequency of the events and an object of a class that implements the ActionListener interface. Place whatever action you want to occur inside the actionPerformed method. Finally, start the timer.

```
class MyListener implements ActionListener
{
    public void actionPerformed(ActionEvent event)
    {
        Action that is executed at each timer event
    }
}

MyListener listener = new MyListener();
Timer t = new Timer(interval, listener);
t.start();
```

Then the timer calls the actionPerformed method of the listener object every interval milliseconds.

Our sample program will display a moving rectangle. We first supply a Rectangle-Component class with a moveBy method that moves the rectangle by a given amount.

ch09/timer/RectangleComponent.java

```java
1  import java.awt.Graphics;
2  import java.awt.Graphics2D;
3  import java.awt.Rectangle;
4  import javax.swing.JComponent;
5
6  /**
7     This component displays a rectangle that can be moved.
8  */
9  public class RectangleComponent extends JComponent
10 {
11     private static final int BOX_X = 100;
12     private static final int BOX_Y = 100;
13     private static final int BOX_WIDTH = 20;
14     private static final int BOX_HEIGHT = 30;
15
16     private Rectangle box;
17
18     public RectangleComponent()
19     {
20        // The rectangle that the paint method draws
21        box = new Rectangle(BOX_X, BOX_Y, BOX_WIDTH, BOX_HEIGHT);
22     }
23
24     public void paintComponent(Graphics g)
25     {
26        Graphics2D g2 = (Graphics2D) g;
27
28        g2.draw(box);
29     }
30
31     /**
32        Moves the rectangle by a given amount.
33        @param x the amount to move in the x-direction
34        @param y the amount to move in the y-direction
35     */
36     public void moveBy(int dx, int dy)
37     {
38        box.translate(dx, dy);
39        repaint();
40     }
41 }
```

> The repaint method causes a component to repaint itself. Call repaint whenever you modify the shapes that the paintComponent method draws.

Note the call to repaint in the moveBy method. This call is necessary to ensure that the component is repainted after the state of the rectangle object has been changed. Keep in mind that the component object does not contain the pixels that show the drawing. The component merely contains a Rectangle object, which itself contains four coordinate values. Calling translate updates the rectangle coordinate values. The call to repaint forces a call to the paintComponent method. The paintComponent method redraws the component, causing the rectangle to appear at the updated location.

The actionPerformed method of the timer listener simply calls component.moveBy(1, 1). This moves the rectangle one pixel down and to the right. Since the actionPerformed method is called many times per second, the rectangle appears to move smoothly across the frame.

ch09/timer/RectangleMover.java

```java
 1  import java.awt.event.ActionEvent;
 2  import java.awt.event.ActionListener;
 3  import javax.swing.JFrame;
 4  import javax.swing.Timer;
 5
 6  /**
 7      This program moves the rectangle.
 8  */
 9  public class RectangleMover
10  {
11     private static final int FRAME_WIDTH = 300;
12     private static final int FRAME_HEIGHT = 400;
13
14     public static void main(String[] args)
15     {
16        JFrame frame = new JFrame();
17
18        frame.setSize(FRAME_WIDTH, FRAME_HEIGHT);
19        frame.setTitle("An animated rectangle");
20        frame.setDefaultCloseOperation(JFrame.EXIT_ON_CLOSE);
21
22        final RectangleComponent component = new RectangleComponent();
23        frame.add(component);
24
25        frame.setVisible(true);
26
27        class TimerListener implements ActionListener
28        {
29           public void actionPerformed(ActionEvent event)
30           {
31              component.moveBy(1, 1);
32           }
33        }
34
35        ActionListener listener = new TimerListener();
36
37        final int DELAY = 100; // Milliseconds between timer ticks
38        Timer t = new Timer(DELAY, listener);
39        t.start();
40     }
41  }
```

S E L F   C H E C K

21. Why does a timer require a listener object?

22. What would happen if you omitted the call to repaint in the moveBy method?

Common Error 9.6

Forgetting to Repaint

You have to be careful when your event handlers change the data in a painted component. When you make a change to the data, the component is not automatically painted with the new data. You must call the repaint method of the component, either in the event handler or in the component's mutator methods. Your component's paintComponent method will then be invoked with an appropriate Graphics object. Note that you should not call the paintComponent method directly.

This is a concern only for your own painted components. When you make a change to a standard Swing component such as a JLabel, the component is automatically repainted.

9.11 Mouse Events

> You use a mouse listener to capture mouse events.

If you write programs that show drawings, and you want users to manipulate the drawings with a mouse, then you need to process mouse events. Mouse events are more complex than button clicks or timer ticks.

A mouse listener must implement the MouseListener interface, which contains the following five methods:

```java
public interface MouseListener
{
    void mousePressed(MouseEvent event);
        // Called when a mouse button has been pressed on a component
    void mouseReleased(MouseEvent event);
        // Called when a mouse button has been released on a component
    void mouseClicked(MouseEvent event);
        // Called when the mouse has been clicked on a component
    void mouseEntered(MouseEvent event);
        // Called when the mouse enters a component
    void mouseExited(MouseEvent event);
        // Called when the mouse exits a component
}
```

The mousePressed and mouseReleased methods are called whenever a mouse button is pressed or released. If a button is pressed and released in quick succession, and the mouse has not moved, then the mouseClicked method is called as well. The mouseEntered and mouseExited methods can be used to paint a user-interface component in a special way whenever the mouse is pointing inside it.

The most commonly used method is mousePressed. Users generally expect that their actions are processed as soon as the mouse button is pressed.

You add a mouse listener to a component by calling the addMouseListener method:

```java
public class MyMouseListener implements MouseListener
{
    // Implements five methods
}

MouseListener listener = new MyMouseListener();
component.addMouseListener(listener);
```

In our sample program, a user clicks on a component containing a rectangle. Whenever the mouse button is pressed, the rectangle is moved to the mouse location. We first enhance the RectangleComponent class and add a moveTo method to move the rectangle to a new position.

ch09/mouse/RectangleComponent.java

```java
1   import java.awt.Graphics;
2   import java.awt.Graphics2D;
3   import java.awt.Rectangle;
4   import javax.swing.JComponent;
5
```

```
6   /**
7       This component displays a rectangle that can be moved.
8   */
9   public class RectangleComponent extends JComponent
10  {
11      private static final int BOX_X = 100;
12      private static final int BOX_Y = 100;
13      private static final int BOX_WIDTH = 20;
14      private static final int BOX_HEIGHT = 30;
15
16      private Rectangle box;
17
18      public RectangleComponent()
19      {
20          // The rectangle that the paint method draws
21          box = new Rectangle(BOX_X, BOX_Y, BOX_WIDTH, BOX_HEIGHT);
22      }
23
24      public void paintComponent(Graphics g)
25      {
26          Graphics2D g2 = (Graphics2D) g;
27
28          g2.draw(box);
29      }
30
31      /**
32          Moves the rectangle to the given location.
33          @param x the x-position of the new location
34          @param y the y-position of the new location
35      */
36      public void moveTo(int x, int y)
37      {
38          box.setLocation(x, y);
39          repaint();
40      }
41  }
```

Note the call to repaint in the moveTo method. As explained in the preceding section, this call causes the component to repaint itself and show the rectangle in the new position.

Now, add a mouse listener to the component. Whenever the mouse is pressed, the listener moves the rectangle to the mouse location.

```
class MousePressListener implements MouseListener
{
    public void mousePressed(MouseEvent event)
    {
        int x = event.getX();
        int y = event.getY();
        component.moveTo(x, y);
    }

    // Do-nothing methods
    public void mouseReleased(MouseEvent event) {}
    public void mouseClicked(MouseEvent event) {}
    public void mouseEntered(MouseEvent event) {}
    public void mouseExited(MouseEvent event) {}
}
```

Figure 8
Clicking the Mouse
Moves the Rectangle

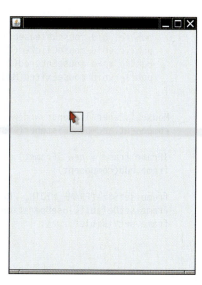

It often happens that a particular listener specifies actions only for one or two of the listener methods. Nevertheless, all five methods of the interface must be implemented. The unused methods are simply implemented as do-nothing methods.

Go ahead and run the RectangleComponentViewer program. Whenever you click the mouse inside the frame, the top-left corner of the rectangle moves to the mouse pointer (see Figure 8).

ch09/mouse/RectangleComponentViewer.java

```java
 1   import java.awt.event.MouseListener;
 2   import java.awt.event.MouseEvent;
 3   import javax.swing.JFrame;
 4
 5   /**
 6      This program displays a RectangleComponent.
 7   */
 8   public class RectangleComponentViewer
 9   {
10      private static final int FRAME_WIDTH = 300;
11      private static final int FRAME_HEIGHT = 400;
12
13      public static void main(String[] args)
14      {
15         final RectangleComponent component = new RectangleComponent();
16
17         // Add mouse press listener
18
19         class MousePressListener implements MouseListener
20         {
21            public void mousePressed(MouseEvent event)
22            {
23               int x = event.getX();
24               int y = event.getY();
25               component.moveTo(x, y);
26            }
27
```

```
28              // Do-nothing methods
29              public void mouseReleased(MouseEvent event) {}
30              public void mouseClicked(MouseEvent event) {}
31              public void mouseEntered(MouseEvent event) {}
32              public void mouseExited(MouseEvent event) {}
33          }
34
35          MouseListener listener = new MousePressListener();
36          component.addMouseListener(listener);
37
38          JFrame frame = new JFrame();
39          frame.add(component);
40
41          frame.setSize(FRAME_WIDTH, FRAME_HEIGHT);
42          frame.setDefaultCloseOperation(JFrame.EXIT_ON_CLOSE);
43          frame.setVisible(true);
44      }
45  }
```

SELF CHECK

23. Why was the moveBy method in the RectangleComponent replaced with a moveTo method?

24. Why must the MousePressListener class supply five methods?

Special Topic 9.3

Event Adapters

In the preceding section you saw how to install a mouse listener into a mouse event source and how the listener methods are called when an event occurs. Usually, a program is not interested in all listener notifications. For example, a program may only be interested in mouse clicks and may not care that these mouse clicks are composed of "mouse pressed" and "mouse released" events. Of course, the program could supply a listener that implements all those methods in which it has no interest as "do-nothing" methods, for example:

```
class MouseClickListener implements MouseListener
{
    public void mouseClicked(MouseEvent event)
    {
        Mouse click action
    }

    // Four do-nothing methods
    public void mouseEntered(MouseEvent event) {}
    public void mouseExited(MouseEvent event) {}
    public void mousePressed(MouseEvent event) {}
    public void mouseReleased(MouseEvent event) {}
}
```

This is boring. For that reason, some friendly soul has created a MouseAdapter class that implements the MouseListener interface such that all methods do nothing. You can *extend* that class, inheriting the do-nothing methods and overriding the methods that you care about, like this:

```
class MouseClickListener extends MouseAdapter
{
    public void mouseClicked(MouseEvent event)
    {
```

```
                    Mouse click action
          }
       }
```

See Chapter 10 for more information on the process of extending classes.

Random Fact 9.2

Programming Languages

Many hundreds of programming languages exist today, which is actually quite surprising. The idea behind a high-level programming language is to provide a medium for programming that is independent from the instruction set of a particular processor, so that one can move programs from one computer to another without rewriting them. Moving a program from one programming language to another is a difficult process, however, and it is rarely done. Thus, it seems that there would be little use for so many programming languages.

Unlike human languages, programming languages are created with specific purposes. Some programming languages make it particularly easy to express tasks from a particular problem domain. Some languages specialize in database processing; others in "artificial intelligence" programs that try to infer new facts from a given base of knowledge; others in multimedia programming. The Pascal language was purposefully kept simple because it was designed as a teaching language. The C language was developed to be translated efficiently into fast machine code, with a minimum of housekeeping overhead. The C++ language builds on C by adding features for object-oriented programming. The Java language was designed for securely deploying programs across the Internet.

The initial version of the C language was designed around 1972. As different compiler writers added incompatible features, the language sprouted various dialects. Some programming instructions were understood by one compiler but rejected by another. Such divergence is an immense pain to a programmer who wants to move code from one computer to another, and an effort got underway to iron out the differences and come up with a standard version of C. The design process ended in 1989 with the completion of the ANSI (American National Standards Institute) Standard. In the meantime, Bjarne Stroustrup of AT&T added features of the language Simula (an object-oriented language designed for carrying out simulations) to C. The resulting language was called C++. From 1985 on, C++ grew by the addition of many features, and a standardization process was completed in 1998. C++ has been enormously popular because programmers can take their existing C code and move it to C++ with only minimal changes. In order to keep compatibility with existing code, every innovation in C++ had to work around the existing language constructs, yielding a language that is powerful but somewhat cumbersome to use.

In 1995, Java was designed by James Gosling to be conceptually simpler and more internally consistent than C++, while retaining the syntax that is familiar to millions of C and C++

James Gosling,
Designer of the Java
Programming Language

programmers. The Java language was an immediate success, not only because it eliminated many of the cumbersome aspects of C++, but also because it included a powerful library.

However, programming language evolution has not come to an end. There are aspects of programming that Java does not handle well. Computers with multiple processors are becoming increasingly common, and it is difficult to write *concurrent* Java programs that use multiple processors correctly and efficiently. Also, as you have seen in this chapter, it can be rather cumbersome in Java to deal with small blocks of code such as the code for measuring an object. In Java, you have to make an interface with a method for that code, and then provide a class that implements the interface. In *functional* programming languages, you can manipulate functions in the same way as objects, and such tasks becomes much easier. For example, in Scala, a hybrid functional/object-oriented language, you can simply construct a DataSet with a function, without having to use an interface:

```
data = new DataSet((x : Rectangle) => x.getWidth() * x.getHeight())
```

Could the Java language be enhanced for concurrent and functional programming? Some attempts have been made, but they were not encouraging because they interacted with existing language features in complex ways. Some new languages (such as Scala) run on the same virtual machine as Java and can easily call existing Java code. Nobody can tell which languages will be most successful in the years to come, but most software developers should expect to work with multiple programming languages during their career.

Summary of Learning Objectives

Use interfaces for making a service available to multiple classes.

- A Java interface type declares methods but does not provide their implementations.
- Unlike a class, an interface type provides no implementation.
- Use the implements reserved word to indicate that a class implements an interface type.
- Use interface types to make code more reusable.

Describe how to convert between class and interface types.

- You can convert from a class type to an interface type, provided the class implements the interface.
- You need a cast to convert from an interface type to a class type.

Describe dynamic method lookup and polymorphism.

- When the virtual machine calls an instance method, it locates the method of the implicit parameter's class. This is called dynamic method lookup.
- Polymorphism denotes the ability to treat objects with differences in behavior in a uniform way.

Describe how to use interface types for providing callbacks.

- A callback is a mechanism for specifying code that is executed at a later time.

Use inner classes to limit the scope of a utility class.

- An inner class is declared inside another class.
- Inner classes are commonly used for utility classes that should not be visible elsewhere in a program.

Use mock objects for supplying test versions of classes.
- A mock object provides the same services as another object, but in a simplified manner.
- Both the mock class and the actual class implement the same interface.

Recognize the use of events and event listeners in user-interface programming.
- User-interface events include key presses, mouse moves, button clicks, menu selections, and so on.
- An event listener belongs to a class that is provided by the application programmer. Its methods describe the actions to be taken when an event occurs.
- Event sources report on events. When an event occurs, the event source notifies all event listeners.
- Use JButton components for buttons. Attach an ActionListener to each button.

Implement event listeners as inner classes.
- Methods of an inner class can access local and instance variables from the surrounding scope.
- Local variables that are accessed by an inner class method must be declared as final.

Build graphical applications that use buttons.
- Use a JPanel container to group multiple user-interface components together.
- You specify button click actions through classes that implement the ActionListener interface.

Use a timer for drawing animations.
- A timer generates timer events at fixed intervals.
- The repaint method causes a component to repaint itself. Call repaint whenever you modify the shapes that the paintComponent method draws.

Write programs that process mouse events.
- You use a mouse listener to capture mouse events.

Classes, Objects, and Methods Introduced in this Chapter

java.awt.Component
  addMouseListener
  repaint
  setPreferredSize
java.awt.Container
  add
java.awt.Dimension
java.awt.Rectangle
  setLocation
java.awt.event.ActionListener
  actionPerformed
java.awt.event.MouseEvent
  getX
  getY

java.awt.event.MouseListener
  mouseClicked
  mouseEntered
  mouseExited
  mousePressed
  mouseReleased
javax.swing.AbstractButton
  addActionListener
javax.swing.JButton
javax.swing.JLabel
javax.swing.JPanel
javax.swing.Timer
  start
  stop

Media Resources

www.wiley.com/
college/
horstmann

- ● **_Worked Example_** Investigating Number Sequences
- ● Lab Exercises
- ⊕ **_Animation_** Polymorphism
- ⊕ Practice Quiz
- ⊕ Code Completion Exercises

Review Exercises

★ **R9.1** Suppose C is a class that implements the interfaces I and J. Which of the following assignments require a cast?

```
C c = . . .;
I i = . . .;
J j = . . .;
```

a. c = i;

b. j = c;

c. i = j;

★ **R9.2** Suppose C is a class that implements the interfaces I and J, and suppose i is declared as

```
I i = new C();
```

Which of the following statements will throw an exception?

a. C c = (C) i;

b. J j = (J) i;

c. i = (I) null;

★ **R9.3** Suppose the class Sandwich implements the Edible interface, and you are given the variable declarations

```
Sandwich sub = new Sandwich();
Rectangle cerealBox = new Rectangle(5, 10, 20, 30);
Edible e = null;
```

Which of the following assignment statements are legal?

a. e = sub;

b. sub = e;

c. sub = (Sandwich) e;

d. sub = (Sandwich) cerealBox;

e. e = cerealBox;

f. e = (Edible) cerealBox;

g. e = (Rectangle) cerealBox;

h. e = (Rectangle) null;

★★ **R9.4** How does a cast such as (BankAccount) x differ from a cast of number values such as (int) x?

★★ **R9.5** The classes Rectangle2D.Double, Ellipse2D.Double, and Line2D.Double implement the Shape interface. The Graphics2D class depends on the Shape interface but not on the rectangle, ellipse, and line classes. Draw a UML diagram denoting these facts.

★★ **R9.6** Suppose r contains a reference to a new Rectangle(5, 10, 20, 30). Which of the following assignments is legal? (Look inside the API documentation to check which interfaces the Rectangle class implements.)

    a. Rectangle a = r;
    b. Shape b = r;
    c. String c = r;
    d. ActionListener d = r;
    e. Measurable e = r;
    f. Serializable f = r;
    g. Object g = r;

★★ **R9.7** Classes such as Rectangle2D.Double, Ellipse2D.Double and Line2D.Double implement the Shape interface. The Shape interface has a method

```
Rectangle getBounds()
```

that returns a rectangle completely enclosing the shape. Consider the method call:

```
Shape s = . . .;
Rectangle r = s.getBounds();
```

Explain why this is an example of polymorphism.

★★★ **R9.8** In Java, a method call such as x.f() uses dynamic method lookup—the exact method to be called depends on the type of the object to which x refers. Give two kinds of method calls that do not look dynamic method lookup in Java.

★★ **R9.9** Suppose you need to process an array of employees to find the average and the highest salaries. Discuss what you need to do to use the implementation of the DataSet class in Section 9.1 (which processes Measurable objects). What do you need to do to use the second implementation (in Section 9.4)? Which is easier?

★★★ **R9.10** What happens if you add a String object to the implementation of the DataSet class in Section 9.1? What happens if you add a String object to a DataSet object of the implementation in Section 9.4 that uses a RectangleMeasurer class?

★ **R9.11** How would you reorganize the DataSetTester3 program if you needed to make RectangleMeasurer into a top-level class (that is, not an inner class)?

★★ **R9.12** What is a callback? Can you think of another use for a callback for the DataSet class? (*Hint:* Exercise P9.12.)

★★ **R9.13** Consider this top-level and inner class. Which variables can the f method access?

```
public class T
{
    private int t;

    public void m(final int x, int y)
    {
        int a;
        final int b;

        class C implements I
        {
            public void f()
            {
                . . .
```

```
          }
        }

        final int c;
          . . .
      }
    }
```

★★ **R9.14** What happens when an inner class tries to access a non-`final` local variable? Try it out and explain your findings.

★★★G **R9.15** How would you reorganize the `InvestmentViewer1` program if you needed to make `AddInterestListener` into a top-level class (that is, not an inner class)?

★G **R9.16** What is an event object? An event source? An event listener?

★G **R9.17** From a programmer's perspective, what is the most important difference between the user interfaces of a console application and a graphical application?

★G **R9.18** What is the difference between an `ActionEvent` and a `MouseEvent`?

★★G **R9.19** Why does the `ActionListener` interface have only one method, whereas the `MouseListener` has five methods?

★★G **R9.20** Can a class be an event source for multiple event types? If so, give an example.

★★G **R9.21** What information does an action event object carry? What additional information does a mouse event object carry?

★★★G **R9.22** Why are we using inner classes for event listeners? If Java did not have inner classes, could we still implement event listeners? How?

★★G **R9.23** What is the difference between the `paintComponent` and `repaint` methods?

★G **R9.24** What is the difference between a frame and a panel?

Programming Exercises

★ **P9.1** Have the `Die` class of Chapter 6 implement the `Measurable` interface. Generate dice, cast them, and add them to the implementation of the `DataSet` class in Section 9.1. Display the average.

★ **P9.2** Implement a class `Quiz` that implements the `Measurable` interface. A quiz has a score and a letter grade (such as B+). Use the implementation of the `DataSet` class in Section 9.1 to process a collection of quizzes. Display the average score and the quiz with the highest score (both letter grade and score).

★ **P9.3** A person has a name and a height in centimeters. Use the implementation of the `DataSet` class in Section 9.4 to process a collection of `Person` objects. Display the average height and the name of the tallest person.

★ **P9.4** Modify the implementation of the `DataSet` class in Section 9.1 (the one processing `Measurable` objects) to also compute the minimum data element.

★ **P9.5** Modify the implementation of the `DataSet` class in Section 9.4 (the one using a `Measurer` object) to also compute the minimum data element.

★ **P9.6** Using a different Measurer object, process a set of Rectangle objects to find the rectangle with the largest perimeter.

★★★ **P9.7** Enhance the DataSet class so that it can either be used with a Measurer object or for processing Measurable objects. *Hint:* Supply a constructor with no parameters that implements a Measurer that processes Measurable objects.

★ **P9.8** Modify the display method of the LastDigitDistribution class of Worked Example 9.1 so that it produces a histogram, like this:

```
0: *************
1: ******************
2: *************
```

Scale the bars so that widest one has length 40.

★★ **P9.9** Write a class PrimeSequence that implements the Sequence interface of Worked Example 9.1, producing the sequence of prime numbers.

★ **P9.10** Add a method hasNext to the Sequence interface of Worked Example 9.1 that returns false if the sequence has no more values. Implement a class MySequence producing a sequence of real data of your choice, such as populations of cities or countries, temperatures, or stock prices. Obtain the data from the Internet and reformat the values so that they are placed into an array. Return one value at a time in the next method, until you reach the end of the data. Your SequenceTester class should display all data in the sequence and check whether the last digits are randomly distributed.

★ **P9.11** Provide a class FirstDigitDistribution that works just like the LastDigitDistribution class of Worked Example 9.1, except that it counts the distribution of the first digit of each value. (It is a well-known fact that the first digits of random values are *not* uniformly distributed. This fact has been used to detect accounting fraud, when sequences of transaction amounts had an unnatural distribution of their first digits.)

★★ **P9.12** Declare an interface Filter as follows:

```
public interface Filter
{
    boolean accept(Object x);
}
```

Modify the implementation of the DataSet class in Section 9.4 to use both a Measurer and a Filter object. Only objects that the filter accepts should be processed. Demonstrate your modification by having a data set process a collection of bank accounts, filtering out all accounts with balances less than $1,000.

★★ **P9.13** The standard Java library provides a Comparable interface:

```
public interface Comparable
{
    /**
        Compares this object with another.
        @param other the object to be compared
        @return a negative integer, zero, or a positive integer if this object
        is less than, equal to, or greater than, other
    */
    public int compareTo(Object other);
}
```

Modify the DataSet class of Section 9.1 to accept Comparable objects. With this interface, it is no longer meaningful to compute the average. The DataSet class should record the minimum and maximum data values. Test your modified DataSet class by adding a number of String objects. (The String class implements the Comparable interface.)

★ **P9.14** Modify the Coin class to have it implement the Comparable interface described in Exercise P9.13.

★★ **P9.15** The System.out.printf method has predefined formats for printing integers, floating-point numbers, and other data types. But it is also extensible. If you use the S format, you can print any class that implements the Formattable interface. That interface has a single method:

```
void formatTo(Formatter formatter, int flags, int width, int precision)
```

In this exercise, you should make the BankAccount class implement the Formattable interface. Ignore the flags and precision and simply format the bank balance, using the given width. In order to achieve this task, you need to get an Appendable reference like this:

```
Appendable a = formatter.out();
```

Appendable is another interface with a method

```
void append(CharSequence sequence)
```

CharSequence is yet another interface that is implemented by (among others) the String class. Construct a string by first converting the bank balance into a string and then padding it with spaces so that it has the desired width. Pass that string to the append method.

★★★ **P9.16** Enhance the formatTo method of Exercise P9.15 by taking into account the precision.

★T **P9.17** Consider the task of writing a program that plays TicTacToe against a human opponent. A user interface TicTacToeUI reads the user's moves and displays the computer's moves and the board. A class TicTacToeStrategy determines the next move that the computer makes. A class TicTacToeBoard represents the current state of the board. Complete all classes except for the strategy class. Instead, use a mock class that simply picks the first available empty square.

★★T **P9.18** Consider the task of translating a plain text book from Project Gutenberg (http://gutenberg.org) to HTML. For example, here is the start of the first chapter of Tolstoy's Anna Karenina:

```
Chapter 1

Happy families are all alike; every unhappy family is unhappy in
its own way.

Everything was in confusion in the Oblonskys' house. The wife
had discovered that the husband was carrying on an intrigue with
a French girl, who had been a governess in their family, and she
had announced to her husband that she could not go on living in
the same house with him ...
```

The equivalent HTML is:

```
<h1>Chapter 1</h1>
<p>Happy families are all alike; every unhappy family is unhappy in
its own way.</p>
<p>Everything was in confusion in the Oblonskys&rsquo; house. The wife
had discovered that the husband was carrying on an intrigue with
```

a French girl, who had been a governess in their family, and she
had announced to her husband that she could not go on living in
the same house with him ...</p>

The HTML conversion can be carried out in two steps. First, the plain text is
assembled into *segments*, blocks of text of the same kind (heading, paragraph, and
so on). Then each segment is converted, by surrounding it with the HTML tags and
converting special characters.

Plain Text	HTML
" "	“ (left) *or* ” (right)
' '	‘ (left) *or* ’ (right)
—	&emdash;
<	&lt;
>	&gt;
&	&amp;

Fetching the text from the Internet and breaking it into segments is a challenging
task. Provide an interface and a mock implementation. Combine it with a class that
uses the mock implementation to finish the formatting task.

★★★G **P9.19** Write a method randomShape that randomly generates objects implementing the Shape
interface: some mixture of rectangles, ellipses, and lines, with random positions.
Call it 10 times and draw all of them.

★G **P9.20** Enhance the ButtonViewer program so that it prints a message "I was clicked *n*
times!" whenever the button is clicked. The value *n* should be incremented with
each click.

★★G **P9.21** Enhance the ButtonViewer program so that it has two buttons, each of which prints a
message "I was clicked *n* times!" whenever the button is clicked. Each button
should have a separate click count.

★★G **P9.22** Enhance the ButtonViewer program so that it has two buttons labeled A and B, each
of which prints a message "Button *x* was clicked!", where *x* is A or B.

★★G **P9.23** Implement a ButtonViewer program as in Exercise P9.22, using only a single listener
class.

★G **P9.24** Enhance the ButtonViewer program so that it prints the time at which the button was
clicked.

★★★G **P9.25** Implement the AddInterestListener in the InvestmentViewer1 program as a regular class
(that is, not an inner class). *Hint:* Store a reference to the bank account. Add a constructor to the listener class that sets the reference.

★★★G **P9.26** Implement the AddInterestListener in the InvestmentViewer2 program as a regular class
(that is, not an inner class). *Hint:* Store references to the bank account and the label
in the listener. Add a constructor to the listener class that sets the references.

★★**G** **P9.27** Write a program that demonstrates the growth of a roach population. Start with two roaches and double the number of roaches with each button click.

★★**G** **P9.28** Write a program that uses a timer to print the current time once a second. *Hint:* The following code prints the current time:

```
Date now = new Date();
System.out.println(now);
```

The Date class is in the java.util package.

★★★**G** **P9.29** Change the RectangleComponent for the animation program in Section 9.10 so that the rectangle bounces off the edges of the component rather than simply moving outside.

★★**G** **P9.30** Write a program that animates a car so that it moves across a frame.

★★★**G** **P9.31** Write a program that animates two cars moving across a frame in opposite directions (but at different heights so that they don't collide.)

★**G** **P9.32** Change the RectangleComponent for the mouse listener program in Section 9.11 so that a new rectangle is added to the component whenever the mouse is clicked. *Hint:* Keep an ArrayList<Rectangle> and draw all rectangles in the paintComponent method.

★**G** **P9.33** Write a program that prompts the user to enter the x- and y-positions of the center and a radius, using JOptionPane dialogs. When the user clicks a "Draw" button, draw a circle with that center and radius in a component.

★★**G** **P9.34** Write a program that allows the user to specify a circle by typing the radius in a JOptionPane and then clicking on the center. Note that you don't need a "Draw" button.

★★★**G** **P9.35** Write a program that allows the user to specify a circle with two mouse presses, the first one on the center and the second on a point on the periphery. *Hint:* In the mouse press handler, you must keep track of whether you already received the center point in a previous mouse press.

Programming Projects

Project 9.1 Design an interface MoveableShape that can be used as a generic mechanism for animating a shape. A moveable shape must have two methods: move and draw. Write a generic AnimationPanel that paints and moves any MoveableShape (or array list of MoveableShape objects if you covered Chapter 7). Supply moveable rectangle and car shapes.

Project 9.2 Your task is to design a general program for managing board games with two players. Your program should be flexible enough to handle games such as tic-tac-toe, chess, or the Game of Nim of Project 6.2.

Design an interface Game that describes a board game. Think about what your program needs to do. It asks the first player to input a move—a string in a game-specific format, such as Be3 in chess. Your program knows nothing about specific games, so the Game interface must have a method such as

```
boolean isValidMove(String move)
```

Once the move is found to be valid, it needs to be executed—the interface needs another method executeMove. Next, your program needs to check whether the game is over. If not, the other player's move is processed. You should also provide some mechanism for displaying the current state of the board.

Design the Game interface and provide two implementations of your choice—such as Nim and Chess (or TicTacToe if you are less ambitious). Your GamePlayer class should manage a Game reference without knowing which game is played, and process the moves from both players. Supply two programs that differ only in the initialization of the Game reference.

Answers to Self-Check Questions

  1. It must implement the Measurable interface, and its getMeasure method must return the population.
  2. The Object class doesn't have a getMeasure method, and the add method invokes the getMeasure method.
  3. Only if x actually refers to a BankAccount object.
  4. No—a Coin reference can be converted to a Measurable reference, but if you attempt to cast that reference to a BankAccount, an exception occurs.
  5. Measurable is an interface. Interfaces have no instance variables and no method implementations.
  6. That variable never refers to a Measurable object. It refers to an object of some class—a class that implements the Measurable interface.
  7. The code fragment prints 500.05. Each call to add results in a call x.getMeasure(). In the first call, x is a BankAccount. In the second call, x is a Coin. A different getMeasure method is called in each case. The first call returns the account balance, the second one the coin value.
  8. The String class doesn't implement the Measurable interface.
  9. Implement a class StringMeasurer that implements the Measurer interface.
  10. A measurer measures an object, whereas getMeasure measures "itself", that is, the implicit parameter.
  11. Inner classes are convenient for insignificant classes. Also, their methods can access local and instance variables from the surrounding scope.
  12. Four: one for the outer class, one for the inner class, and two for the DataSet and Measurer classes.
  13. You want to implement the GradingProgram class in terms of that interface so that it doesn't have to change when you switch between the mock class and the actual class.
  14. Because the developer of GradingProgram doesn't have to wait for the GradeBook class to be complete.
  15. The button object is the event source. The listener object is the event listener.
  16. The ClickListener class implements the ActionListener interface.
  17. Direct access is simpler than the alternative—passing the variable as a parameter to a constructor or method.
  18. The local variable must be declared as final.

19. First add `label` to the `panel`, then add `button`.

20. The `actionPerformed` method does not access that variable.

21. The timer needs to call some method whenever the time interval expires. It calls the `actionPerformed` method of the listener object.

22. The moved rectangles won't be painted, and the rectangle will appear to be stationary until the frame is repainted for an external reason.

23. Because you know the current mouse position, not the amount by which the mouse has moved.

24. It implements the `MouseListener` interface, which has five methods.

Chapter 10

Inheritance

CHAPTER GOALS

- To learn about inheritance
- To understand how to inherit and override superclass methods
- To be able to invoke superclass constructors
- To learn about protected and package access control
- To understand the common superclass Object and how to override its toString and equals methods
- **G** To use inheritance for customizing user interfaces

In this chapter, we discuss the important concept of inheritance. Specialized classes can be created that inherit behavior from more general classes. You will learn how to implement inheritance in Java, and how to make use of the Object class—the most general class in the inheritance hierarchy.

CHAPTER CONTENTS

10.1 Inheritance Hierarchies

In the real world, you often categorize concepts into *hierarchies*. Hierarchies are frequently represented as trees, with the most general concepts at the root of the hierarchy and more specialized ones towards the branches. Figure 1 shows a typical example.

In Java it is equally common to group classes in *inheritance hierarchies*. The classes representing the most general concepts are near the root, more specialized classes towards the branches. For example, Figure 2 shows part of the hierarchy of Swing user-interface components in Java.

We must introduce some more terminology for expressing the relationship between the classes in an inheritance hierarchy. The more general class is called the **superclass**. The more specialized class that inherits from the superclass is called the **subclass**. In our example, JPanel is a subclass of JComponent.

Figure 2 uses the UML notation for inheritance. In a class diagram, you denote inheritance by a solid arrow with a "hollow triangle" tip that points to the superclass.

When designing a hierarchy of classes, you ask yourself which features and behaviors are common to all the classes that you are designing. Those common properties are placed in a superclass. For example, all user-interface components have a width and height, and the getWidth and getHeight methods of the JComponent

> Sets of classes can form complex inheritance hierarchies.

Figure 1
A Hierarchy of Vehicle Types

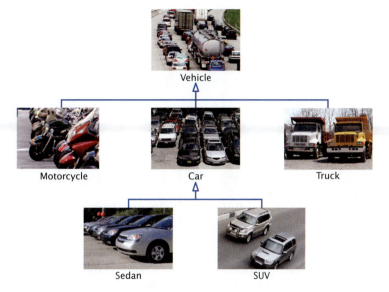

class return the component's dimensions. More specialized properties can be found in subclasses. For example, buttons can have text and icon labels. The class Abstract-Button, but not the superclass JComponent, has methods to set and get the button text and icon, and instance variables to store them. The individual button classes (such

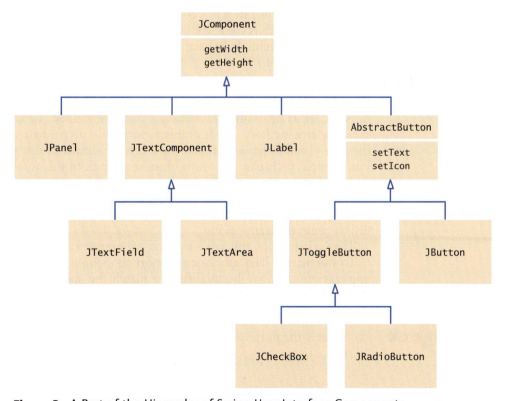

Figure 2 A Part of the Hierarchy of Swing User-Interface Components

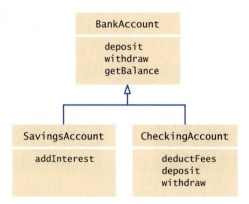

Figure 3 Inheritance Hierarchy for Bank Account Classes

as JButton, JRadioButton, and JCheckBox) inherit these properties. In fact, the Abstract-Button class was created to express the commonality among these buttons.

We will use a simpler example of a hierarchy in our study of inheritance concepts. Consider a bank that offers its customers the following account types:

1. The checking account has no interest, gives you a small number of free transactions per month, and charges a transaction fee for each additional transaction.

2. The savings account earns interest that compounds monthly. (In our implementation, the interest is compounded using the balance of the last day of the month, which is somewhat unrealistic. Typically, banks use either the average or the minimum daily balance. Exercise P10.1 asks you to implement this enhancement.)

Figure 3 shows the inheritance hierarchy. Exercise P10.2 asks you to add another class to this hierarchy.

Next, let us determine the behavior of these classes. All bank accounts support the getBalance method, which simply reports the current balance. They also support the deposit and withdraw methods, although the details of the implementation differ. For example, a checking account must keep track of the number of transactions to account for the transaction fees.

The checking account needs a method deductFees to deduct the monthly fees and to reset the transaction counter. The deposit and withdraw methods must be overridden to count the transactions.

The savings account needs a method addInterest to add interest.

To summarize: The subclasses support all methods from the superclass, but their implementations may be modified to match the specialized purposes of the subclasses. In addition, subclasses are free to introduce additional methods.

S E L F   C H E C K

1. What is the purpose of the JTextComponent class in Figure 2?
2. Why don't we place the addInterest method in the BankAccount class?

10.2 Implementing Subclasses

Inheritance is a mechanism for extending existing classes by adding instance variables and methods.

In this section, we begin building the inheritance hierarchy of bank account classes. You will learn how to form a subclass from a given superclass. Let's start with the SavingsAccount class. Here is the syntax for the class declaration:

```
public class SavingsAccount extends BankAccount
{
    added instance variables
    new methods
}
```

A subclass inherits the methods of its superclass.

In the SavingsAccount class declaration you specify only new methods and instance variables. The SavingsAccount class *automatically inherits* the methods of the BankAccount class. For example, the deposit method automatically applies to savings accounts:

```
SavingsAccount collegeFund = new SavingsAccount(10);
    // Savings account with 10% interest
collegeFund.deposit(500);
    // OK to use BankAccount method with SavingsAccount object
```

Let's see how savings account objects are different from BankAccount objects. We will set an interest rate in the constructor, and we need a method to apply that interest periodically. That is, in addition to the three methods that can be applied to every account, there is an additional method addInterest. The new method and instance variable must be declared in the subclass.

```
public class SavingsAccount extends BankAccount
{
    private double interestRate;

    public SavingsAccount(double rate)
    {
        Constructor implementation
    }

    public void addInterest()
    {
        Method implementation
    }
}
```

The instance variables declared in the superclass are present in subclass objects.

A subclass object automatically has the instance variables declared in the superclass. For example, a SavingsAccount object has an instance variable balance that was declared in the BankAccount class.

Any new instance variables that you declare in the subclass are present only in subclass objects. For example, every SavingsAccount object has an instance variable interestRate. Figure 4 shows the layout of a SavingsAccount object.

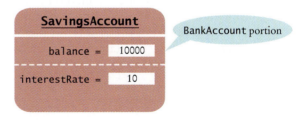

Figure 4
Layout of a
Subclass Object

Syntax 10.1 Inheritance

Syntax   class *SubclassName* extends *SuperclassName*
{
    instance variables
    methods
}

Example

Subclass   Superclass

```
public class SavingsAccount extends BankAccount
```

Declare instance variables
that are added to
the subclass.

```
{
    private double interestRate;
    . . .
```

The reserved word extends
denotes inheritance.

Declare methods that are
specific to the subclass.

```
    public void addInterest()
    {
        double interest = getBalance() * interestRate / 100;
        deposit(interest);
    }
}
```

Next, you need to implement the new addInterest method. The method computes the interest due on the current balance and deposits that interest to the account.

```
public class SavingsAccount extends BankAccount
{
    private double interestRate;

    public SavingsAccount(double rate)
    {
        interestRate = rate;
    }

    public void addInterest()
    {
        double interest = getBalance() * interestRate / 100;
        deposit(interest);
    }
}
```

A subclass has no
access to private
instance variables of
its superclass.

The addInterest method calls the getBalance and deposit methods rather than directly updating the balance variable of the superclass. This is a consequence of **encapsulation**. The balance variable was declared as private in the BankAccount class. The addInterest method is declared in the SavingsAccount class. It does not have the right to access a private instance variable of another class.

Note how the addInterest method calls the inherited getBalance and deposit methods without specifying an implicit parameter. This means that the calls apply to the implicit parameter of the addInterest method.

In other words, the statements in the addInterest method are a shorthand for the following statements:

```
double interest = this.getBalance() * this.interestRate / 100;
this.deposit(interest);
```

This completes the implementation of the SavingsAccount class. You will find the complete source code below.

You may wonder at this point in what way inheritance differs from implementing an interface. An interface is not a class. It has *no behavior*. It merely tells you which methods you should implement. A superclass has behavior that the subclasses inherit.

> Inheriting from a class differs from implementing an interface: The subclass inherits behavior from the superclass.

ch10/accounts/SavingsAccount.java

```java
1  /**
2      An account that earns interest at a fixed rate.
3  */
4  public class SavingsAccount extends BankAccount
5  {
6     private double interestRate;
7
8     /**
9         Constructs a bank account with a given interest rate.
10        @param rate the interest rate
11     */
12     public SavingsAccount(double rate)
13     {
14        interestRate = rate;
15     }
16
17     /**
18         Adds the earned interest to the account balance.
19     */
20     public void addInterest()
21     {
22        double interest = getBalance() * interestRate / 100;
23        deposit(interest);
24     }
25  }
```

SELF CHECK

3. Which instance variables does an object of class SavingsAccount have?
4. Name four methods that you can apply to SavingsAccount objects.
5. If the class Manager extends the class Employee, which class is the superclass and which is the subclass?

Common Error 10.1

Confusing Super- and Subclasses

If you compare an object of type SavingsAccount with an object of type BankAccount, then you find that

- The reserved word extends suggests that the SavingsAccount object is an extended version of a BankAccount.
- The SavingsAccount object is larger; it has an added instance variable interestRate.
- The SavingsAccount object is more capable; it has an addInterest method.

It seems a superior object in every way. So why is SavingsAccount called the *subclass* and BankAccount the *superclass*?

The *super/sub* terminology comes from set theory. Look at the set of all bank accounts. Not all of them are SavingsAccount objects; some of them are other kinds of bank accounts. Therefore, the set of SavingsAccount objects is a *subset* of the set of all BankAccount objects, and the set of BankAccount objects is a *superset* of the set of SavingsAccount objects. The more specialized objects in the subset have a richer state and more capabilities.

Common Error 10.2

Shadowing Instance Variables

A subclass has no access to the private instance variables of the superclass. For example, the methods of the SavingsAccount class cannot access the balance instance variable:

```java
public class SavingsAccount extends BankAccount
{
   public void addInterest()
   {
      double interest = getBalance() * interestRate / 100;
      balance = balance + interest; // Error
   }
   . . .
}
```

It is a common beginner's error to "solve" this problem by adding *another* instance variable with the same name.

```java
public class SavingsAccount extends BankAccount
{
   private double balance; // Don't
   . . .
   public void addInterest()
   {
      double interest = getBalance() * interestRate / 100;
      balance = balance + interest; // Compiles but doesn't update the correct balance
   }
}
```

Sure, now the addInterest method compiles, but it doesn't update the correct balance! Such a SavingsAccount object has two instance variables, both named balance (see Figure 5). The getBalance method of the superclass retrieves one of them, and the addInterest method of the subclass updates the other.

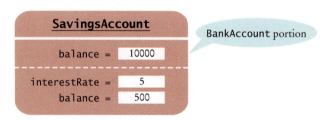

Figure 5   Shadowing Instance Variables

10.3 Overriding Methods

A subclass can inherit a superclass method or override it by providing another implementation.

A subclass method **overrides** a superclass method if it has the same name and parameter types as a superclass method. When such a method is applied to a subclass object, the overriding method, and not the original method, is executed.

We turn to the CheckingAccount class for an example of overriding methods. Recall that the BankAccount class has three methods:

```java
public class BankAccount
{
   . . .
   public void deposit(double amount) { . . . }
   public void withdraw(double amount) { . . . }
   public double getBalance() { . . . }
}
```

The CheckingAccount class declares these methods:

```java
public class CheckingAccount extends BankAccount
{
   . . .
   public void deposit(double amount) { . . . }
   public void withdraw(double amount) { . . . }
   public void deductFees() { . . . }
}
```

These methods override BankAccount methods.

The deposit and withdraw methods of the CheckingAccount class override the deposit and withdraw methods of the BankAccount class to handle transaction fees. However, the deductFees method does not override another method, and the getBalance method is not overridden.

Let's implement the deposit method of the CheckingAccount class. It increments the transaction count and deposits the money:

```java
public class CheckingAccount extends BankAccount
{
   . . .
   public void deposit(double amount)
   {
      transactionCount++;
      // Now add amount to balance
      . . .
   }
}
```

Now we have a problem. We can't simply add amount to balance:

```java
public class CheckingAccount extends BankAccount
{
   . . .
   public void deposit(double amount)
   {
      transactionCount++;
      // Now add amount to balance
      balance = balance + amount; // Error
   }
}
```

Although every CheckingAccount object has a balance instance variable, that instance variable is *private* to the superclass BankAccount. Subclass methods have no more

Syntax 10.2   Calling a Superclass Method

Syntax   super.*methodName*(*parameters*);

Example

Calls the method of the superclass instead of the method of the current class.

```
public void deposit(double amount)
{
   transactionCount++;
   super.deposit(amount);
}
```

If you omit super, this method calls itself. See page 430.

access rights to the private data of the superclass than any other methods. If you want to modify a private superclass instance variable, you must use a public method of the superclass.

How can we add the deposit amount to the balance, using the public interface of the BankAccount class? There is a perfectly good method for that purpose—namely, the deposit method of the BankAccount class. So we must invoke the deposit method on some object. On which object? The checking account into which the money is deposited—that is, the implicit parameter of the deposit method of the Checking-Account class. To invoke another method on the implicit parameter, you don't specify the parameter but simply write the method name, like this:

```
public class CheckingAccount extends BankAccount
{
   public void deposit(double amount)
   {
      transactionCount++;
      // Now add amount to balance
      deposit(amount); // Not complete
   }
   . . .
}
```

But this won't quite work. The compiler interprets

```
deposit(amount);
```

as

```
this.deposit(amount);
```

The this parameter is of type CheckingAccount. There is a method called deposit in the CheckingAccount class. Therefore, that method will be called—but that is just the method we are currently writing! The method will call itself over and over, and the program will die in an infinite recursion (discussed in Chapter 13).

Instead, we must be specific that we want to invoke only the *superclass's* deposit method. There is a special reserved word super for this purpose:

```
public class CheckingAccount extends BankAccount
{
   public void deposit(double amount)
   {
```

Use the super reserved word to call a method of the superclass.

```
        transactionCount++;
        // Now add amount to balance
        super.deposit(amount);
    }
    . . .
}
```

This version of the deposit method is correct. To deposit money into a checking account, update the transaction count and call the deposit method of the superclass. The remaining methods of the CheckingAccount class also invoke a superclass method.

```java
public class CheckingAccount extends BankAccount
{
    private static final int FREE_TRANSACTIONS = 3;
    private static final double TRANSACTION_FEE = 2.0;

    private int transactionCount;
    . . .
    public void withdraw(double amount)
    {
        transactionCount++;
        // Now subtract amount from balance
        super.withdraw(amount);
    }

    public void deductFees()
    {
        if (transactionCount > FREE_TRANSACTIONS)
        {
            double fees = TRANSACTION_FEE * (transactionCount - FREE_TRANSACTIONS);
            super.withdraw(fees);
        }
        transactionCount = 0;
    }
    . . .
}
```

SELF CHECK

6. Categorize the methods of the SavingsAccount class as inherited, new, and over-ridden.

7. Why does the withdraw method of the CheckingAccount class call super.withdraw?

8. Why does the deductFees method set the transaction count to zero?

Common Error 10.3

Accidental Overloading

Recall from Section 2.4 that two methods can have the same name, provided they have *different* method parameters. For example, the PrintStream class has methods called println with headers

```java
void println(int x)
```

and

```java
void println(String x)
```

These are different methods, each with its own implementation. The Java compiler considers them to be completely unrelated. We say that the `println` name is **overloaded**. This is different from overriding, where a subclass method provides an implementation of a method with the *same* method parameters.

If you mean to override a method but supply a different parameter type, then you accidentally introduce an overloaded method. For example,

```java
public class CheckingAccount extends BankAccount
{
    . . .
    public void deposit(int amount) // Error: should be double
    {
        . . .
    }
}
```

The compiler will not complain. It thinks that you want to provide a `deposit` method just for `int` parameters, while inheriting another `deposit` method for `double` parameters.

When overriding a method, be sure to check that the parameter types match exactly.

Common Error 10.4

Failing to Invoke the Superclass Method

A common error in extending the functionality of a superclass method is to forget the `super` qualifier. For example, to withdraw money from a checking account, update the transaction count and then withdraw the amount:

```java
public void withdraw(double amount)
{
    transactionCount++;
    withdraw(amount);
    // Error—should be super.withdraw(amount)
}
```

Here `withdraw(amount)` refers to the `withdraw` method applied to the implicit parameter of the method. The implicit parameter is of type `CheckingAccount`, and the `CheckingAccount` class has a `withdraw` method, so that method is called. Of course, that calls the current method all over again, which will call itself yet again, over and over, until the program runs out of memory. Instead, you must precisely identify which `withdraw` method you want to call.

Another common error is to forget to call the superclass method altogether. Then the functionality of the superclass mysteriously vanishes.

10.4 Subclass Construction

In this section, we discuss the implementation of constructors in subclasses. As an example, let's declare a constructor to set the initial balance of a checking account.

We want to invoke the `BankAccount` constructor to set the balance to the initial balance. There is a special instruction to call the superclass constructor from a subclass constructor. You use the reserved word super, followed by the construction parameters in parentheses:

```java
public class CheckingAccount extends BankAccount
{
    public CheckingAccount(double initialBalance)
    {
        // Construct superclass
        super(initialBalance);
        // Initialize transaction count
        transactionCount = 0;
    }
    . . .
}
```

To call the superclass constructor, you use the super reserved word in the first statement of the subclass constructor.

When the reserved word super is immediately followed by a parenthesis, it indicates a call to the superclass constructor. When used in this way, the constructor call must be *the first statement of the subclass constructor*. If super is followed by a period and a method name, on the other hand, it indicates a call to a superclass method, as you saw in the preceding section. Such a call can be made anywhere in any subclass method.

The dual use of the super reserved word is analogous to the dual use of the this reserved word (see Special Topic 3.1).

If a subclass constructor does not call the superclass constructor, the superclass must have a constructor without parameters. That constructor is used to initialize the superclass data. However, if all constructors of the superclass require parameters, then the compiler reports an error.

For example, you can implement the CheckingAccount constructor without calling the superclass constructor. Then the BankAccount class is constructed with its BankAccount() constructor, which sets the balance to zero. Of course, then the CheckingAccount constructor must explicitly deposit the initial balance.

Most commonly, however, subclass constructors have some parameters that they pass on to the superclass and others that they use to initialize subclass instance variables.

Syntax 10.3   Calling a Superclass Constructor

Syntax
```
accessSpecifier ClassName(parameterType parameterName, . . .)
{
    super(parameters);
    . . .
}
```

Example

Invokes the constructor of the superclass.

Must be the first statement of the subclass constructor.

```
public CheckingAccount(double initialBalance)
{
    super(initialBalance);
    transactionCount = 0;
}
```

Subclass constructor

If not present, the superclass constructor with no parameters is called.

ch10/accounts/CheckingAccount.java

```java
1   /**
2       A checking account that charges transaction fees.
3   */
4   public class CheckingAccount extends BankAccount
5   {
6      private static final int FREE_TRANSACTIONS = 3;
7      private static final double TRANSACTION_FEE = 2.0;
8
9      private int transactionCount;
10
11     /**
12         Constructs a checking account with a given balance.
13         @param initialBalance the initial balance
14     */
15     public CheckingAccount(double initialBalance)
16     {
17         // Construct superclass
18         super(initialBalance);
19
20         // Initialize transaction count
21         transactionCount = 0;
22     }
23
24     public void deposit(double amount)
25     {
26         transactionCount++;
27         // Now add amount to balance
28         super.deposit(amount);
29     }
30
31     public void withdraw(double amount)
32     {
33         transactionCount++;
34         // Now subtract amount from balance
35         super.withdraw(amount);
36     }
37
38     /**
39         Deducts the accumulated fees and resets the
40         transaction count.
41     */
42     public void deductFees()
43     {
44         if (transactionCount > FREE_TRANSACTIONS)
45         {
46             double fees = TRANSACTION_FEE *
47                 (transactionCount - FREE_TRANSACTIONS);
48             super.withdraw(fees);
49         }
50         transactionCount = 0;
51     }
52  }
```

SELF CHECK

9. Why didn't the SavingsAccount constructor in Section 10.2 call its superclass constructor?

10. When you invoke a superclass method with the super reserved word, does the call have to be the first statement of the subclass method?

10.5 Converting Between Subclass and Superclass Types

It is often necessary to convert a subclass type to a superclass type. Occasionally, you need to carry out the conversion in the opposite direction. This section discusses the conversion rules.

> Subclass references can be converted to superclass references.

The class SavingsAccount extends the class BankAccount. In other words, a SavingsAccount object is a special case of a BankAccount object. Therefore, a reference to a SavingsAccount object can be converted to a BankAccount reference.

```
SavingsAccount collegeFund = new SavingsAccount(10);
BankAccount anAccount = collegeFund; // OK
```

Furthermore, all references can be converted to the type Object.

```
Object anObject = collegeFund; // OK
```

Now the three object references stored in collegeFund, anAccount, and anObject all refer to the same object of type SavingsAccount (see Figure 6).

However, the variables anAccount and anObject know less than the full story about the object references that they store. Because anAccount is a variable of type BankAccount, you can invoke the deposit and withdraw methods. You cannot use the addInterest method, though—it is not a method of the BankAccount class:

```
anAccount.deposit(1000); // OK
anAccount.addInterest(); // No—not a method of the type of the anAccount variable
```

And, of course, the variable anObject knows even less. You can't even invoke the deposit method on it—deposit is not a method of the Object class.

Why would anyone *want* to know less about an object reference and use a variable whose type is a superclass? This can happen if you want to *reuse code* that knows about the superclass but not the subclass. Here is a typical example. Consider a transfer method that transfers money from one account to another:

```
public void transfer(double amount, BankAccount other)
{
   withdraw(amount);
   other.deposit(amount);
}
```

You can use this method to transfer money from one bank account to another:

```
BankAccount momsAccount = . . . ;
BankAccount harrysAccount = . . . ;
momsAccount.transfer(1000, harrysAccount);
```

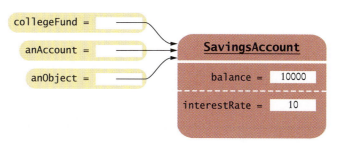

Figure 6
Variables of Different Types Can Refer to the Same Object

You can *also* use the method to transfer money into a CheckingAccount:

```
CheckingAccount harrysChecking = . . . ;
momsAccount.transfer(1000, harrysChecking);
    // OK to pass a CheckingAccount reference to a method expecting a BankAccount
```

The transfer method expects a reference to a BankAccount, and it gets a reference to a CheckingAccount object. That is perfectly legal. The transfer method doesn't actually know that, in this case, the parameter variable other contains a reference to a CheckingAccount object. All it cares about is that the object can carry out the deposit method. This is assured because the other variable has the type BankAccount.

Very occasionally, you need to carry out the opposite conversion, from a superclass type to a subclass type. For example, you may have a variable of type Object, and you know that it actually holds a BankAccount reference. In that case, you can use a cast to convert the type:

```
BankAccount anAccount = (BankAccount) anObject;
```

However, this cast is somewhat dangerous. If you are wrong, and anObject actually refers to an object of an unrelated type, then an exception is thrown.

The instanceof operator tests whether an object belongs to a particular type.

To protect against bad casts, you can use the instanceof operator. It tests whether an object belongs to a particular type. For example,

```
anObject instanceof BankAccount
```

returns true if the type of anObject is convertible to BankAccount. This happens if anObject refers to an actual BankAccount or a subclass such as SavingsAccount. Using the instanceof operator, a safe cast can be programmed as follows:

```
if (anObject instanceof BankAccount)
{
    BankAccount anAccount = (BankAccount) anObject;
    . . .
}
```

Syntax 10.4 The instanceof Operator

Syntax   *object* instanceof *TypeName*

Example

If anObject is null,
instanceof **returns** false.

Returns true **if** anObject
can be cast to a BankAccount.

The object may belong to a
subclass of BankAccount.

```
if (anObject instanceof BankAccount)
{
    BankAccount anAccount = (BankAccount) anObject;
    . . .
}
```

You can invoke BankAccount
methods on this variable.

Two references
to the same object.

11. Why did the second parameter of the transfer method have to be of type Bank-Account and not, for example, SavingsAccount?

12. Why can't we change the second parameter of the transfer method to the type Object?

10.6 Polymorphism and Inheritance

In Java, the type of a variable does not determine the type of the object to which it refers. For example, a variable of type BankAccount can hold a reference to an actual BankAccount object or a subclass object such as SavingsAccount. You already encountered this phenomenon in Chapter 9 with variables whose type was an interface. A variable whose type is Measurable holds a reference to an object of a class that implements the Measurable interface, perhaps a Coin object or an object of an entirely different class.

What happens when you invoke a method on a variable of type BankAccount? For example,

```
BankAccount anAccount = new CheckingAccount();
anAccount.deposit(1000);
```

Which deposit method is called? The anAccount variable has type BankAccount, so it would appear as if BankAccount.deposit is called. On the other hand, the CheckingAccount class provides its own deposit method that updates the transaction count. The reference stored in the anAccount variable actually refers to an object of the subclass CheckingAccount, so it would be appropriate if the CheckingAccount.deposit method were called instead.

Java uses *dynamic method lookup* to determine which method to invoke. The method to be called is always determined by the type of the actual object, not the type of the variable. That is, if the actual object has the type CheckingAccount, then the CheckingAccount.deposit method is called. It does not matter that the object reference is stored in a variable of type BankAccount.

> When the virtual machine calls an instance method, it locates the method of the implicit parameter's class. This is called dynamic method lookup.

Have another look at the transfer method:

```
public void transfer(double amount, BankAccount other)
{
   withdraw(amount);
   other.deposit(amount);
}
```

Suppose you call

```
anAccount.transfer(1000, anotherAccount);
```

Two method calls are the result:

```
anAccount.withdraw(1000);
anotherAccount.deposit(1000);
```

Depending on the actual types of the objects whose references are stored in anAccount and anotherAccount, different versions of the withdraw and deposit methods are called. This is an example of *polymorphism*. As we discussed in Chapter 9, polymorphism is the ability to treat objects with differences in behavior in a uniform way.

If you look into the implementation of the transfer method, it may not be imme-diately obvious that the first method call

```
withdraw(amount);
```

depends on the type of an object. However, that call is a shortcut for

```
this.withdraw(amount);
```

The this parameter holds a reference to the implicit parameter, which can refer to a BankAccount or a subclass object.

The following program calls the polymorphic withdraw and deposit methods. You should manually calculate what the program should print for each account balance, and confirm that the correct methods have in fact been called.

ch10/accounts/AccountTester.java

```java
1  /**
2     This program tests the BankAccount class and
3     its subclasses.
4  */
5  public class AccountTester
6  {
7     public static void main(String[] args)
8     {
9        SavingsAccount momsSavings = new SavingsAccount(0.5);
10
11       CheckingAccount harrysChecking = new CheckingAccount(100);
12
13       momsSavings.deposit(10000);
14
15       momsSavings.transfer(2000, harrysChecking);
16       harrysChecking.withdraw(1500);
17       harrysChecking.withdraw(80);
18
19       momsSavings.transfer(1000, harrysChecking);
20       harrysChecking.withdraw(400);
21
22       // Simulate end of month
23       momsSavings.addInterest();
24       harrysChecking.deductFees();
25
26       System.out.println("Mom's savings balance: "
27             + momsSavings.getBalance());
28       System.out.println("Expected: 7035");
29
30       System.out.println("Harry's checking balance: "
31             + harrysChecking.getBalance());
32       System.out.println("Expected: 1116");
33    }
34 }
```

Program Run

```
Mom's savings balance: 7035.0
Expected: 7035
Harry's checking balance: 1116.0
Expected: 1116
```

13. If a is a variable of type BankAccount that holds a non-null reference, what do you know about the object to which a refers?

14. If a refers to a checking account, what is the effect of calling a.transfer(1000, a)?

Special Topic 10.1

Abstract Classes

When you extend an existing class, you have the choice whether or not to override the methods of the superclass. Sometimes, it is desirable to *force* programmers to override a method. That happens when there is no good default for the superclass, and only the subclass programmer can know how to implement the method properly.

Here is an example. Suppose the First National Bank of Java decides that every account type must have some monthly fees. Therefore, a deductFees method should be added to the BankAccount class:

```
public class BankAccount
{
    public void deductFees() { . . . }
    . . .
}
```

But what should this method do? Of course, we could have the method do nothing. But then a programmer implementing a new subclass might simply forget to implement the deductFees method, and the new account would inherit the do-nothing method of the superclass. There is a better way—declare the deductFees method as an **abstract method**:

```
public abstract void deductFees();
```

> An abstract method is a method whose implementation is not specified.

An abstract method has no implementation. This forces the implementors of subclasses to specify concrete implementations of this method. (Of course, some subclasses might decide to implement a do-nothing method, but then that is their choice—not a silently inherited default.)

You cannot construct objects of classes with abstract methods. For example, once the BankAccount class has an abstract method, the compiler will flag an attempt to create a new BankAccount() as an error. Of course, if the CheckingAccount subclass overrides the deductFees method and supplies an implementation, then you can create CheckingAccount objects.

> An abstract class is a class that cannot be instantiated.

A class for which you cannot create objects is called an **abstract class**. A class for which you can create objects is sometimes called a **concrete class**. In Java, you must declare all abstract classes with the reserved word abstract:

```
public abstract class BankAccount
{
    public abstract void deductFees();
    . . .
}
```

A class that declares an abstract method, or that inherits an abstract method without overriding it, *must* be declared as abstract. You can also declare classes with no abstract methods as abstract. Doing so prevents programmers from creating instances of that class but allows them to create their own subclasses.

Note that you cannot construct an *object* of an abstract class, but you can still have a *variable* whose type is an abstract class. Of course, the actual object to which it refers must be an instance of a concrete subclass:

```
BankAccount anAccount; // OK
anAccount = new BankAccount(); // Error—BankAccount is abstract
```

```
anAccount = new SavingsAccount(); // OK
anAccount = null; // OK
```

The reason for using abstract classes is to force programmers to create subclasses. By specifying certain methods as abstract, you avoid the trouble of coming up with useless default methods that others might inherit by accident.

Abstract classes differ from interfaces in an important way—they can have instance variables, and they can have concrete methods and constructors.

Special Topic 10.2

Final Methods and Classes

In Special Topic 10.1 on page 437 you saw how you can force other programmers to create subclasses of abstract classes and override abstract methods. Occasionally, you may want to do the opposite and *prevent* other programmers from creating subclasses or from overriding certain methods. In these situations, you use the final reserved word. For example, the String class in the standard Java library has been declared as

```
public final class String { . . . }
```

That means that nobody can extend the String class.

The String class is meant to be *immutable*—string objects can't be modified by any of their methods. Since the Java language does not enforce this, the class designers did. Nobody can create subclasses of String; therefore, you know that all String references can be copied without the risk of mutation.

You can also declare individual methods as final:

```
public class SecureAccount extends BankAccount
{
    . . .
    public final boolean checkPassword(String password)
    {
        . . .
    }
}
```

This way, nobody can override the checkPassword method with another method that simply returns true.

Common Error 10.5

Overriding Methods to Be Less Accessible

If a superclass declares a method to be publicly accessible, you cannot override it to be more private. For example,

```
public class BankAccount
{
    public void withdraw(double amount) { . . . }
    . . .
}
```

```
public class CheckingAccount extends BankAccount
{
   private void withdraw(double amount) { . . . }
      // Error—subclass method cannot be more private
   . . .
}
```

The compiler does not allow this, because the increased privacy would conflict with polymorphism. Suppose the `AccountTester` class has this method call:

```
BankAccount account = new CheckingAccount();
account.withdraw(100000); // Should CheckingAccount.withdraw be called?
```

Polymorphism dictates that `CheckingAccount.withdraw` should be called, but that is a private method that should not be accessible in `AccountTester`.

Therefore, the compiler reports an error if you override a public method and make it private or give it package access. The latter is a common oversight. If you forget the `public` modifier, your subclass method has package access, which is more restrictive. Simply restore the `public` modifier, and the error will go away.

Special Topic 10.3

Protected Access

We ran into a hurdle when trying to implement the `deposit` method of the `CheckingAccount` class. That method needed access to the `balance` instance variable of the superclass. Our remedy was to use the appropriate method of the superclass to set the balance.

Java offers another solution to this problem. The superclass can declare an instance variable as *protected*:

```
public class BankAccount
{
   . . .
   protected double balance;
}
```

> Protected features can be accessed by all subclasses and by all classes in the same package.

Protected data in an object can be accessed by the methods of the object's class and all its subclasses. For example, `CheckingAccount` inherits from `BankAccount`, so its methods can access the protected instance variables of the `BankAccount` class. Furthermore, protected data can be accessed by all methods of classes in the same package.

Some programmers like the `protected` access feature because it seems to strike a balance between absolute protection (making all instance variables private) and no protection at all (making all instance variables public). However, experience has shown that protected instance variables are subject to the same kinds of problems as public instance variables. The designer of the superclass has no control over the authors of subclasses. Any of the subclass methods can corrupt the superclass data. Furthermore, classes with protected instance variables are hard to modify. Even if the author of the superclass would like to change the data implementation, the protected variables cannot be changed, because someone somewhere out there might have written a subclass whose code depends on them.

In Java, protected instance variables have another drawback—they are accessible not just by subclasses, but also by other classes in the same package (see Special Topic 8.9).

It is best to leave all data private. If you want to grant access to the data to subclass methods only, consider making the *accessor* method protected.

How To 10.1

Developing an Inheritance Hierarchy

When you work with a set of classes, some of which are more general and others more specialized, you want to organize them into an inheritance hierarchy. This enables you to process objects of different classes in a uniform way.

To illustrate the design process, consider an application that presents a quiz and grades the user's responses. A quiz consists of questions, and there are different kinds of questions:

- Fill-in-the-blank
- Choice (single or multiple)
- Numeric (where an approximate answer is ok; e.g., 1.33 when the actual answer is 4/3)
- Free response

Step 1 List the classes that are part of the hierarchy.

From the problem description, we can find these classes:

FillInQuestion (fill in the blank)
ChoiceQuestion (offers answer choices to the user)
MultiChoiceQuestion (offers answer choices to the user; user can pick more than one)
NumericQuestion
FreeResponseQuestion

In addition, we introduce a common superclass Question to model the commonality among these classes.

Step 2 Organize the classes into an inheritance hierarchy.

Draw a UML diagram that shows super- and subclasses. Here is the diagram for our example.

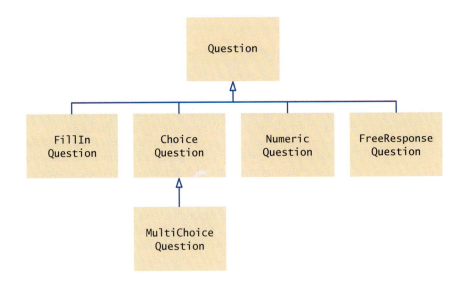

Step 3 Determine the common responsibilities.

In Step 2, you will have identified a class at the root of the hierarchy. That class needs to have sufficient responsibilities to carry out the tasks at hand.

To find out what those tasks are, write pseudocode for processing the objects.

For each question
Display the question to the user.
Get the user response.
Check whether the response is correct.

From the pseudocode, we obtain the following list of common responsibilities that every question must carry out:

Display the question.
Check the response.

Step 4 Decide which methods are overridden in subclasses.

For each subclass and each of the common responsibilities, decide whether the inherited behavior is appropriate or whether it needs to be overridden. Be sure to declare any methods that are inherited or overridden in the root of the hierarchy.

We place the responsibilities common to all questions into the `Question` superclass.

```
public class Question
{
    . . .
    /**
        Displays this question.
    */
    public void display() { . . . }

    /**
        Checks a given response for correctness.
        @param response  the response to check
        @return  true if the response was correct, false otherwise
    */
    public boolean checkAnswer(String response) { . . . }
}
```

The `ChoiceQuestion` class will need to override the `display` method to display all the choices. The `NumericQuestion` class will need to override the `checkAnswer` method, converting the response to a number and checking that it is approximately the same as the expected answer.

From now on, we will only consider the `ChoiceQuestion` in detail. For the other question types, see the programming exercises at the end of this chapter.

Step 5 Define the public interface of each subclass.

Typically, subclasses have responsibilities other than those of the superclass. List those, as well as the methods that need to be overridden. You also need to specify how the objects of the subclasses should be constructed.

With the `ChoiceQuestion`, we need a way of adding choices, like this:

```
ChoiceQuestion question = new ChoiceQuestion(
    "In which country was the inventor of Java born?");
question.addChoice("Australia", false);
question.addChoice("Canada", true);
question.addChoice("Denmark", false);
question.addChoice("United States", false);
```

We then override the `display` method to display those choices in the form

```
1: Australia
2: Canada
3: Denmark
4: United States
```

Here are the methods that we just discovered for the `ChoiceQuestion` class:

```java
public class ChoiceQuestion extends Question
{
   . . .
   /**
      Adds an answer choice to this question.
      @param choice the choice to add
      @param correct true if this is the correct choice, false otherwise
   */
   public void addChoice(String choice, boolean correct)

   public void display() { . . . } // Overrides superclass method
}
```

Step 6 Identify instance variables.

List the instance variables for each class. If you find a instance variable that is common to all classes, be sure to place it in the base of the hierarchy.

All questions have a question text and an answer. We store those values in the `Question` superclass.

```java
public class Question
{
   private String text;
   private String answer;
   . . .
}
```

The `ChoiceQuestion` class needs to store the list of choices.

```java
public class ChoiceQuestion extends Question
{
   private ArrayList<String> choices;
   . . .
}
```

We need to spend some thought on how question objects are constructed. We can supply the question text in the constructor. However, the answer for a choice question is only known when the correct choice is added, so we need a setter method for it:

```java
public class Question
{
   . . .
   /**
      Constructs a question with a given text and an empty answer.
      @param questionText the text of this question
   */
   public Question(String questionText) { . . . }

   /**
      Sets the answer for this question.
      @param correctResponse the answer
   */
   public void setAnswer(String correctResponse) { . . . }
}
```

Step 7 Implement constructors and methods.

The methods of the `Question` class are very straightforward:

```java
public class Question
{
   . . .
```

```java
public Question(String questionText)
{
   text = questionText;
   answer = "";
}

public void setAnswer(String correctResponse)
{
   answer = correctResponse;
}

public boolean checkAnswer(String response)
{
   return response.equals(answer);
}

public void display()
{
   System.out.println(text);
}
}
```

The `ChoiceQuestion` constructor must call the superclass constructor to set the question text:

```java
public ChoiceQuestion(String questionText)
{
   super(questionText);
   choices = new ArrayList<String>();
}
```

The addChoice method sets the answer when the correct choice is added.

```java
public void addChoice(String choice, boolean correct)
{
   choices.add(choice);
   if (correct)
   {
      // Convert choices.size() to string
      String choiceString = "" + choices.size();
      setAnswer(choiceString);
   }
}
```

Finally, the `display` method of the `ChoiceQuestion` class displays the question text, then the choices. Note the call to the superclass method.

```java
public void display()
{
   super.display();
   for (int i = 0; i < choices.size(); i++)
   {
      int choiceNumber = i + 1;
      System.out.println(choiceNumber + ": " + choices.get(i));
   }
}
```

Step 8   Construct objects of different subclasses and process them.

In our sample program, we construct two questions and present them to the user.

```java
public class QuestionDemo
{
   public static void main(String[] args)
   {
```

```
        Question[] quiz = new Question[2];

        quiz[0] = new Question("Who was the inventor of Java?");
        quiz[0].setAnswer("James Gosling");

        ChoiceQuestion question = new ChoiceQuestion(
            "In which country was the inventor of Java born?");
        question.addChoice("Australia", false);
        question.addChoice("Canada", true);
        question.addChoice("Denmark", false);
        question.addChoice("United States", false);
        quiz[1] = question;

        Scanner in = new Scanner(System.in);
        for (Question q : quiz)
        {
            q.display();
            System.out.print("Your answer: ");
            String response = in.nextLine();
            System.out.println(q.checkAnswer(response));
        }
    }
}
```

Program Run

```
Who was the inventor of Java?
Your answer: James Gosling
true
In which country was the inventor of Java born?
1: Australia
2: Canada
3: Denmark
4: United States
Your answer: 4
false
```

The complete program is contained in the ch10/questions directory of your source code.

⊕ **Worked Example 10.1**

Implementing an Employee Hierarchy for Payroll Processing

This Worked Example shows how to implement payroll processing that works for different kinds of employees.

10.7 Object: The Cosmic Superclass

Every class extends the Object class either directly or indirectly.

In Java, every class that is declared without an explicit extends clause automatically extends the class Object. That is, the class Object is the direct or indirect superclass of *every* class in Java (see Figure 7).

⊕ Available online in WileyPLUS and at www.wiley.com/college/horstmann.

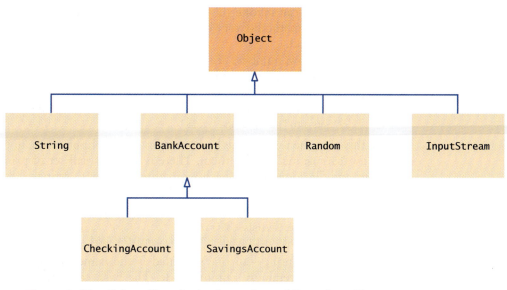

Figure 7 The Object Class Is the Superclass of Every Java Class

Of course, the methods of the Object class are very general. Here are the most useful ones:

Method	Purpose
String toString()	Returns a string representation of the object
boolean equals(Object otherObject)	Tests whether the object equals another object
Object clone()	Makes a full copy of an object

It is a good idea for you to override these methods in your classes.

10.7.1 Overriding the toString Method

In your classes, provide toString methods that describe each object's state.

The toString method returns a string representation for each object. It is useful for debugging. For example,

```
Rectangle box = new Rectangle(5, 10, 20, 30);
String s = box.toString();
   // Sets s to "java.awt.Rectangle[x=5,y=10,width=20,height=30]"
```

In fact, this toString method is called whenever you concatenate a string with an object. Consider the concatenation

```
"box=" + box;
```

On one side of the + concatenation operator is a string, but on the other side is an object reference. The Java compiler automatically invokes the toString method to turn the object into a string. Then both strings are concatenated. In this case, the result is the string

```
"box=java.awt.Rectangle[x=5,y=10,width=20,height=30]"
```

The compiler can invoke the toString method, because it knows that *every* object has a toString method: Every class extends the Object class, and that class provides a toString method.

As you know, numbers are also converted to strings when they are concatenated with other strings. For example,

```
int age = 18;
String s = "Harry's age is " + age;
    // Sets s to "Harry's age is 18"
```

In this case, the toString method is not involved. Numbers are not objects, and there is no toString method for them. There is only a small set of primitive types, however, and the compiler knows how to convert them to strings.

Let's try the toString method for the BankAccount class:

```
BankAccount momsSavings = new BankAccount(5000);
String s = momsSavings.toString();
    // Sets s to something like "BankAccount@d24606bf"
```

That's disappointing—all that's printed is the name of the class, followed by the **hash code**, a seemingly random code. The hash code can be used to tell objects apart—different objects are likely to have different hash codes. (See Chapter 16 for the details.)

We don't care about the hash code. We want to know what is inside the object. But, of course, the toString method of the Object class does not know what is inside the BankAccount class. Therefore, we have to override the method and supply our own version in the BankAccount class. We'll follow the same format that the toString method of the Rectangle class uses: first print the name of the class, and then the values of the instance variables inside brackets.

```
public class BankAccount
{
    . . .
    public String toString()
    {
        return "BankAccount[balance=" + balance + "]";
    }
}
```

This works better:

```
BankAccount momsSavings = new BankAccount(5000);
String s = momsSavings.toString();
    // Sets s to "BankAccount[balance=5000]"
```

10.7.2 Overriding the equals Method

When implementing the equals method, test whether two objects have equal state.

The equals method is called whenever you want to compare whether two objects have the same contents:

```
if (coin1.equals(coin2)) . . .
    // Contents are the same—see Figure 8
```

This is different from the test with the == operator, which tests whether the two references are to the *same object:*

```
if (coin1 == coin2) . . .
    // Objects are the same—see Figure 9
```

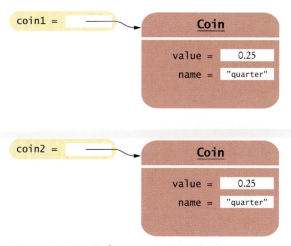

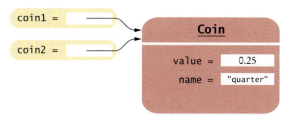

Figure 8   Two References to Equal Objects

Figure 9   Two References to the Same Object

Let us implement the `equals` method for the `Coin` class. You need to override the `equals` method of the `Object` class:

```
public class Coin
{
    . . .
    public boolean equals(Object otherObject)
    {
        . . .
    }
    . . .
}
```

Now you have a slight problem. The `Object` class knows nothing about coins, so it declares the `otherObject` parameter of the `equals` method to have the type `Object`. When overriding the method, you are not allowed to change the parameter type. To overcome this problem, cast the parameter to the class `Coin`:

```
Coin other = (Coin) otherObject;
```

Then you can compare the two coins.

```
public boolean equals(Object otherObject)
{
    Coin other = (Coin) otherObject;
    return name.equals(other.name) && value == other.value;
}
```

Note that you must use `equals` to compare object references, but use `==` to compare numbers.

When you override the `equals` method, you should also override the `hashCode` method so that equal objects have the same hash code—see Chapter 16 for details.

10.7.3 The clone Method

You know that copying an object reference simply gives you two references to the same object:

```
BankAccount account = new BankAccount(1000);
BankAccount account2 = account;
account2.deposit(500);
    // Now both account and account2 refer to a bank account with a balance of 1500
```

> The clone method makes a new object with the same state as an existing object.

What can you do if you actually want to make a copy of an object? That is the purpose of the `clone` method. The `clone` method must return a *new* object that has an identical state to the existing object (see Figure 10).

Implementing the `clone` method is quite a bit more difficult than implementing the `toString` or `equals` methods—see Special Topic 10.6 on page 452 for details.

Let us suppose that someone has implemented the `clone` method for the Bank-Account class. Here is how to call it:

```
BankAccount clonedAccount = (BankAccount) account.clone();
```

The return type of the `clone` method is the class `Object`. When you call the method, you must use a cast to convince the compiler that `account.clone()` really has the same type as `clonedAccount`.

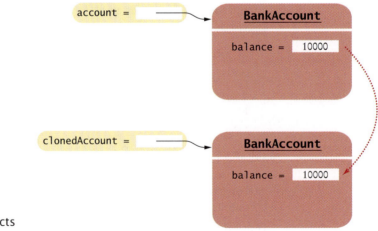

Figure 10
Cloning Objects

SELF CHECK

15. Should the call `x.equals(x)` always return `true`?

16. Can you implement `equals` in terms of `toString`? Should you?

Quality Tip 10.1

Supply toString in All Classes

If you have a class whose toString() method returns a string that describes the object state, then you can simply call System.out.println(x) whenever you need to inspect the current state of an object x. This works because the println method of the PrintStream class invokes x.toString() when it needs to print an object, which is extremely helpful if there is an error in your program and the objects don't behave the way you think they should. You can simply insert a few print statements and peek inside the object state during the program run. Some debuggers can even invoke the toString method on objects that you inspect.

Sure, it is a bit more trouble to write a toString method when you aren't sure your program ever needs one—after all, it might work correctly on the first try. Then again, many programs don't work on the first try. As soon as you find out that yours doesn't, consider adding those toString methods to help you debug the program.

Special Topic 10.4

Inheritance and the toString Method

You just saw how to write a toString method: Form a string consisting of the class name and the names and values of the instance variables. However, if you want your toString method to be usable by subclasses of your class, you need to work a bit harder. Instead of hardcoding the class name, you should call the getClass method to obtain a *class* object, an object of the Class class that describes classes and their properties. Then invoke the getName method to get the name of the class:

```java
public String toString()
{
   return getClass().getName() + "[balance=" + balance + "]";
}
```

Then the toString method prints the correct class name when you apply it to a subclass, say a SavingsAccount.

```java
SavingsAccount momsSavings = . . . ;
System.out.println(momsSavings);
// Prints "SavingsAccount[balance=10000]"
```

Of course, in the subclass, you should override toString and add the values of the subclass instance variables. Note that you must call super.toString to get the superclass instance variables—the subclass can't access them directly.

```java
public class SavingsAccount extends BankAccount
{
   public String toString()
   {
      return super.toString() + "[interestRate=" + interestRate + "]";
   }
}
```

Now a savings account is converted to a string such as SavingsAccount[balance= 10000][interestRate=5]. The brackets show which instance variables belong to the superclass.

Common Error 10.6

Declaring the equals Method with the Wrong Parameter Type

Consider the following, seemingly simpler, version of the equals method for the Coin class:

```java
public boolean equals(Coin other) // Don't do this!
{
   return name.equals(other.name) && value == other.value;
}
```

Here, the parameter of the equals method has the type Coin, not Object.

Unfortunately, this method *does not override* the equals method in the Object class. Instead, the Coin class now has two different equals methods:

```java
boolean equals(Coin other) // Declared in the Coin class
boolean equals(Object otherObject) // Inherited from the Object class
```

This is error-prone because the wrong equals method can be called. For example, consider these variable declarations:

```java
Coin aCoin = new Coin(0.25, "quarter");
Object anObject = new Coin(0.25, "quarter");
```

The call aCoin.equals(anObject) calls the second equals method, which returns false.

The remedy is to ensure that you use the Object type for the explicit parameter of the equals method.

Special Topic 10.5

Inheritance and the equals Method

You just saw how to write an equals method: Cast the otherObject parameter to the type of your class, and then compare the instance variables of the implicit parameter and the other parameter.

But what if someone called coin1.equals(x) where x wasn't a Coin object? Then the bad cast would generate an exception, and the program would die. Therefore, you first want to test whether otherObject really is an instance of the Coin class. The easiest test would be with the instanceof operator. However, that test is not specific enough. It would be possible for otherObject to belong to some subclass of Coin. To rule out that possibility, you should test whether the two objects belong to the *same class*. If not, return false.

```java
if (getClass() != otherObject.getClass()) return false;
```

Moreover, the Java language specification demands that the equals method return false when otherObject is null.

Here is an improved version of the equals method that takes these two points into account:

```java
public boolean equals(Object otherObject)
{
   if (otherObject == null) return false;
   if (getClass() != otherObject.getClass())
      return false;

   Coin other = (Coin) otherObject;
   return name.equals(other.name) && value == other.value;
}
```

When you implement equals in a subclass, you should first call equals in the superclass, like this:

```
public CollectibleCoin extends Coin
{
   private int year;
   . . .
   public boolean equals(Object otherObject)
   {
      if (!super.equals(otherObject)) return false;

      CollectibleCoin other = (CollectibleCoin) otherObject;
      return year == other.year;
   }
}
```

Quality Tip 10.2

Clone Mutable Instance Variables in Accessor Methods

Consider the following class:

```
public class Customer
{
   private String name;
   private BankAccount account;

   public Customer(String aName)
   {
      name = aName;
      account = new BankAccount();
   }

   public String getName()
   {
      return name;
   }

   public BankAccount getAccount()
   {
      return account;
   }
}
```

This class looks very boring and normal, but the getAccount method has a curious property. It *breaks encapsulation*, because anyone can modify the object state without going through the public interface:

```
Customer harry = new Customer("Harry Handsome");
BankAccount account = harry.getAccount();
   // Anyone can withdraw money!
account.withdraw(100000);
```

Maybe that wasn't what the designers of the class had in mind? Maybe they wanted class users only to inspect the account? In such a situation, you should *clone* the object reference:

```
public BankAccount getAccount();
{
```

```
        return (BankAccount) account.clone();
    }
```

Do you also need to clone the getName method? No—that method returns a string, and strings are immutable. It is safe to give out a reference to an immutable object.

Special Topic 10.6

Implementing the clone Method

The Object.clone method is the starting point for the clone methods in your own classes. It creates a new object of the same type as the original object. It also automatically copies the instance variables from the original object to the cloned object. Here is a first attempt to implement the clone method for the BankAccount class:

```java
public class BankAccount
{
    . . .
    public Object clone()
    {
        // Not complete
        Object clonedAccount = super.clone();
        return clonedAccount;
    }
}
```

However, this Object.clone method must be used with care. It only shifts the problem of cloning by one level; it does not completely solve it. Specifically, if an object contains a reference to another object, then the Object.clone method makes a copy of that object reference, not a clone of that object. The figure below shows how the Object.clone method works with a Customer object that has references to a String object and a BankAccount object. As you can see, the Object.clone method copies the references to the cloned Customer object and does not clone the objects to which they refer. Such a copy is called a **shallow copy**.

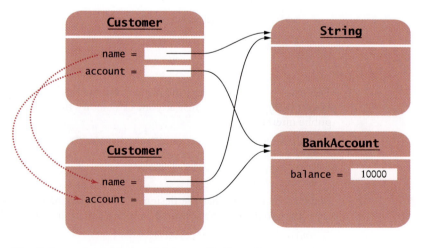

The Object.clone Method Makes a Shallow Copy

There is a reason why the Object.clone method does not systematically clone all sub-objects. In some situations, it is unnecessary. For example, if an object contains a reference to a string, there is no harm in copying the string reference, because Java string objects can never change their contents. The Object.clone method does the right thing if an object contains only numbers, Boolean values, and strings. But it must be used with caution when an object contains references to other objects.

For that reason, there are two safeguards built into the Object.clone method to ensure that it is not used accidentally. First, the method is declared protected (see Special Topic 10.3 on page 439). This prevents you from accidentally calling x.clone() if the class to which x belongs hasn't declared clone to be public.

As a second precaution, Object.clone checks that the object being cloned implements the Cloneable interface. If not, it throws an exception. The Object.clone method looks like this:

```java
public class Object
{
   protected Object clone()
         throws CloneNotSupportedException
   {
      if (this instanceof Cloneable)
      {
         // Copy the instance variables
         . . .
      }
      else
         throw new CloneNotSupportedException();
   }
}
```

Unfortunately, all that safeguarding means that the legitimate callers of Object.clone() pay a price—they must catch that exception (see Chapter 11) *even if their class implements* Cloneable.

```java
public class BankAccount implements Cloneable
{
   . . .
   public Object clone()
   {
      try
      {
         return super.clone();
      }
      catch (CloneNotSupportedException e)
      {
         // Can't happen because we implement Cloneable but we still must catch it.
         return null;
      }
   }
}
```

If an object contains a reference to another mutable object, then you must call clone for that reference. For example, suppose the Customer class has an instance variable of class Bank-Account. You can implement Customer.clone as follows:

```java
public class Customer implements Cloneable
{
   private String name;
   private BankAccount account;
   . . .
   public Object clone()
   {
      try
      {
```

```
            Customer cloned = (Customer) super.clone();
            cloned.account = (BankAccount) account.clone();
            return cloned;
         }
         catch(CloneNotSupportedException e)
         {
            // Can't happen because we implement Cloneable
            return null;
         }
      }
   }
```

Special Topic 10.7

Enumeration Types Revisited

In Special Topic 5.3, we introduced the concept of an enumeration type: a type with a finite number of values. An example is

```
public enum FilingStatus { SINGLE, MARRIED }
```

In Java, enumeration types are classes with special properties. They have a finite number of instances, namely the objects declared inside the braces. For example, there are exactly two objects of the FilingStatus class: FilingStatus.SINGLE and FilingStatus.MARRIED. Since Filing-Status has no public constructor, it is impossible to construct additional objects.

Enumeration classes extend the Enum class, from which they inherit toString and clone methods. The toString method returns a string that equals the object's name. For example, FilingStatus.SINGLE.toString() returns "SINGLE". The clone method returns the given object *without making a copy*. After all, it should not be possible to generate new objects of an enumeration class.

The Enum class inherits the equals method from its superclass, Object. Thus, two enumeration constants are only considered equal when they are identical.

You can add your own methods and constructors to an enumeration class, for example

```
public enum CoinType
{
    private double value;
    PENNY(0.01), NICKEL(0.05), DIME(0.1), QUARTER(0.25);
    CoinType(double aValue) { value = aValue; }
    public double getValue() { return value; }
}
```

This CoinType class has exactly four instances: CoinType.PENNY, CoinType.NICKEL, CoinType.DIME, and CoinType.QUARTER. If you have one of these four CoinType objects, you can apply the getValue method to obtain the coin's value.

Note that there is a major philosophical difference between this CoinType class and the Coin class that we have discussed elsewhere in this chapter. A Coin object represents a particular coin. You can construct as many Coin objects as you like. Different Coin objects can be equal to another. We consider two Coin objects equal when their names and values match. However, CoinType describes a type of coins, not an individual coin. The four CoinType objects are distinct from each other.

Random Fact 10.1

Scripting Languages

Suppose you work for an office where you must help with the bookkeeping. Suppose that every sales person sends in a weekly spreadsheet with sales figures. One of your jobs is to copy and paste the individual figures into a master spreadsheet and then copy and paste the totals into a word processor document that gets e-mailed to several managers. This kind of repetitive work can be intensely boring. Can you automate it?

It would be a real challenge to write a Java program that can help you—you'd have to know how to read a spreadsheet file, how to format a word processor document, and how to send e-mail.

Fortunately, many office software packages include **scripting languages**. These are programming languages that are integrated with the software for the purpose of automating repetitive tasks. The best-known of these scripting languages is Visual Basic Script, which is a part of the Microsoft Office suite. The Macintosh operating system has a language called AppleScript for the same purpose.

In addition, scripting languages are available for many other purposes. JavaScript is used for web pages. (There is no relationship between Java and JavaScript—the name JavaScript was chosen for marketing reasons.) Tcl (short for "tool control language" and pronounced "tickle") is an open source scripting language that has been ported to many platforms and is often used for scripting software test procedures. Shell scripts are used for automating software configuration, backup procedures, and other system administration tasks.

Scripting languages have two features that makes them easier to use than full-fledged programming languages such as Java. First, they are *interpreted*. The interpreter program reads each line of program code and executes it immediately without compiling it first. That makes experimenting much more fun—you get immediate feedback. Also, scripting languages are usually *loosely typed*, meaning you don't have to declare the types of variables. Every variable can hold values of any type. For example, the figure below shows a scripting session with the JavaScript implementation that is included in the Java Development Kit.

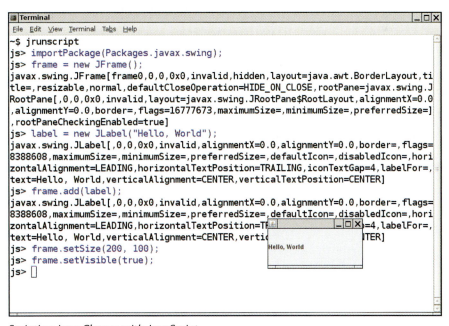

Scripting Java Classes with JavaScript

This version of JavaScript allows you to manipulate Java objects. The script stores frame and label objects in variables that are declared without types. It then calls methods that are executed immediately, without compilation. The frame pops up as soon as the line with the setVisible command is entered. In recent years, authors of computer viruses have discovered how scripting languages simplify their lives. The famous "love bug" is a Visual Basic Script program that is sent as an attachment to an e-mail. The e-mail has an enticing subject line "I love you" and asks the recipient to click on an attachment masquerading as a love letter. In fact, the attachment is a script file that is executed when the user clicks on it. The script creates some damage on the recipient's computer and then, through the power of the scripting language, uses the Outlook e-mail client to mail itself to all addresses found in the address book. Try programming that in Java! By the way, the person suspected of authoring that virus was a student who had submitted a proposal to write a thesis researching how to write such programs. Perhaps not surprisingly, the proposal was rejected by the faculty.

Why do we still need Java if scripting is easy and fun? Scripts often have poor error checking and are difficult to adapt to new circumstances. Scripting languages lack many of the structuring and safety mechanisms (such as classes and type checking by the compiler) that are important for building robust and scalable programs.

10.8 Using Inheritance to Customize Frames

Provide a JFrame subclass for a complex frame.

As you add more user-interface components to a frame, the frame can get quite complex. Your programs will become easier to understand when you use inheritance for complex frames.

To do so, design a subclass of JFrame. Store the components as instance variables. Initialize them in the constructor of your subclass. If the initialization code gets complex, simply add some helper methods.

Here, we carry out this process for the investment viewer program in Chapter 9.

```java
public class InvestmentFrame extends JFrame
{
   private JButton button;
   private JLabel label;
   private JPanel panel;
   private BankAccount account;

   public InvestmentFrame()
   {
      account = new BankAccount(INITIAL_BALANCE);

      // Use instance variables for components
      label = new JLabel("balance: " + account.getBalance());

      // Use helper methods
      createButton();
      createPanel();

      setSize(FRAME_WIDTH, FRAME_HEIGHT);
   }

   private void createButton()
   {
```

```
      button = new JButton("Add Interest");
      ActionListener listener = new AddInterestListener();
      button.addActionListener(listener);
   }

   private void createPanel()
   {
      panel = new JPanel();
      panel.add(button);
      panel.add(label);
      add(panel);
   }
   . . .
}
```

This approach differs from the programs in Chapter 9. In those programs, we simply configured the frame in the main method of a viewer class.

It is a bit more work to provide a separate class for the frame. However, the frame class makes it easier to organize the code that constructs the user-interface elements.

Of course, we still need a class with a main method:

```
public class InvestmentViewer2
{
   public static void main(String[] args)
   {
      JFrame frame = new InvestmentFrame();
      frame.setDefaultCloseOperation(JFrame.EXIT_ON_CLOSE);
      frame.setVisible(true);
   }
}
```

SELF CHECK

17. How many Java source files are required by the investment viewer application when we use inheritance to declare the frame class?

18. Why does the InvestmentFrame constructor call setSize(FRAME_WIDTH, FRAME_HEIGHT), whereas the main method of the investment viewer class in Chapter 9 called frame.setSize(FRAME_WIDTH, FRAME_HEIGHT)?

Special Topic 10.8

Adding the main Method to the Frame Class

Have another look at the InvestmentFrame and InvestmentViewer2 classes. Some programmers prefer to combine these two classes, by adding the main method to the frame class:

```
public class InvestmentFrame extends JFrame
{
   public static void main(String[] args)
   {
      JFrame frame = new InvestmentFrame();
      frame.setDefaultCloseOperation(JFrame.EXIT_ON_CLOSE);
      frame.setVisible(true);
   }

   public InvestmentFrame()
   {
      account = new BankAccount(INITIAL_BALANCE);
```

```
                 // Use instance variables for components
                 label = new JLabel("balance: " + account.getBalance());

                 // Use helper methods
                 createButton();
                 createPanel();

                 setSize(FRAME_WIDTH, FRAME_HEIGHT);
             }
         . . .
     }
```

This is a convenient shortcut that you will find in many programs, but it does muddle the responsibilities between the frame class and the program. Therefore, we do not use this approach in this book.

Summary of Learning Objectives

Explain the notions of inheritance, superclasses, and subclasses.

- Sets of classes can form complex inheritance hierarchies.

Implement subclasses in Java.

- Inheritance is a mechanism for extending existing classes by adding instance variables and methods.
- A subclass inherits the methods of its superclass.
- The instance variables declared in the superclass are present in subclass objects.
- A subclass has no access to private instance variables of its superclass.
- The more general class is called a superclass. The more specialized class that inherits from the superclass is called the subclass.
- Inheriting from a class differs from implementing an interface: The subclass inherits behavior from the superclass.

Describe how a subclass can override methods from its superclass.

- A subclass can inherit a superclass method or override it by providing another implementation.
- Use the super reserved word to call a method of the superclass.

Describe how a subclass can construct its superclass.

- To call the superclass constructor, you use the super reserved word in the first statement of the subclass constructor.

Describe how to convert between class and superclass types.

- Subclass references can be converted to superclass references.
- The instanceof operator tests whether an object belongs to a particular type.

Describe dynamic method lookup and polymorphism.

- When the virtual machine calls an instance method, it locates the method of the implicit parameter's class. This is called dynamic method lookup.
- An abstract method is a method whose implementation is not specified.

- An abstract class is a class that cannot be instantiated.
- Protected features can be accessed by all subclasses and by all classes in the same package.

Provide appropriate overrides of the methods of the Object superclass.
- Every class extends the Object class either directly or indirectly.
- In your classes, provide toString methods that describe each object's state.
- When implementing the equals method, test whether two objects have equal state.
- The clone method makes a new object with the same state as an existing object.

Use inheritance to customize frames.
- Provide a JFrame subclass for a complex frame.

Classes, Objects, and Methods Introduced in this Chapter

```
java.lang.Cloneable                      java.lang.Object
java.lang.CloneNotSupportedException          clone
                                              toString
```

Media Resources

www.wiley.com/
college/
horstmann

- ***Worked Example*** Implementing an Employee Hierarchy for Payroll Processing
- Lab Exercises
- ➕ ***Animation*** Inheritance
- ➕ Practice Quiz
- ➕ Code Completion Exercises

Review Exercises

★ **R10.1** What is the balance of b after the following operations?

```
SavingsAccount b = new SavingsAccount(10);
b.deposit(5000);
b.withdraw(b.getBalance() / 2);
b.addInterest();
```

★ **R10.2** Describe all constructors of the SavingsAccount class. List all methods that are inherited from the BankAccount class. List all methods that are added to the SavingsAccount class.

★★ **R10.3** Can you convert a superclass reference into a subclass reference? A subclass reference into a superclass reference? If so, give examples. If not, explain why not.

★★ **R10.4** Identify the superclass and the subclass in each of the following pairs of classes.

    a. Employee, Manager

    b. Polygon, Triangle

    c. GraduateStudent, Student

    d. Person, Student

    e. Employee, GraduateStudent

    f. BankAccount, CheckingAccount

    g. Vehicle, Car

    h. Vehicle, Minivan

    i. Car, Minivan

    j. Truck, Vehicle

★ **R10.5** Suppose the class Sub extends the class Sandwich. Which of the following assignments are legal?

```
Sandwich x = new Sandwich();
Sub y = new Sub();
```

    a. x = y;

    b. y = x;

    c. y = new Sandwich();

    d. x = new Sub();

★ **R10.6** Draw an inheritance diagram that shows the inheritance relationships between the classes:

- Person
- Employee
- Student
- Instructor
- Classroom
- Object

★★ **R10.7** In an object-oriented traffic simulation system, we have the following classes:

- Vehicle
- Car
- Truck
- Sedan
- Coupe
- PickupTruck
- SportUtilityVehicle
- Minivan
- Bicycle
- Motorcycle

Draw an inheritance diagram that shows the relationships between these classes.

★★ **R10.8** What inheritance relationships would you establish among the following classes?

- Student
- Professor
- TeachingAssistant
- Employee
- Secretary
- DepartmentChair
- Janitor
- SeminarSpeaker
- Person
- Course
- Seminar
- Lecture
- ComputerLab

★★★ **R10.9** Which of these conditions returns true? Check the Java documentation for the inheritance patterns.

> **a.** Rectangle r = new Rectangle(5, 10, 20, 30);
> **b.** if (r instanceof Rectangle) . . .
> **c.** if (r instanceof Point) . . .
> **d.** if (r instanceof Rectangle2D.Double) . . .
> **e.** if (r instanceof RectangularShape) . . .
> **f.** if (r instanceof Object) . . .
> **g.** if (r instanceof Shape) . . .

★★ **R10.10** Explain the two meanings of the super reserved word. Explain the two meanings of the this reserved word. How are they related?

★★★ **R10.11** (Tricky.) Consider the two calls

```java
public class D extends B
{
   public void f()
   {
      this.g(); // 1
   }
   public void g()
   {
      super.g(); // 2
   }
   . . .
}
```

Which of them is an example of polymorphism?

★★★ **R10.12** Consider this program:

```java
public class AccountPrinter
{
   public static void main(String[] args)
   {
      SavingsAccount momsSavings
            = new SavingsAccount(0.5);

      CheckingAccount harrysChecking
            = new CheckingAccount(0);

      . . .
      endOfMonth(momsSavings);
      endOfMonth(harrysChecking);
      printBalance(momsSavings);
      printBalance(harrysChecking);
   }

   public static void endOfMonth(SavingsAccount savings)
   {
      savings.addInterest();
   }

   public static void endOfMonth(CheckingAccount checking)
   {
      checking.deductFees();
   }
```

```
        public static void printBalance(BankAccount account)
        {
            System.out.println("The balance is $"
                + account.getBalance());
        }
    }
```

Do the calls to the endOfMonth methods use dynamic method invocation? Inside the printBalance method, does the call to getBalance use dynamic method invocation?

★ **R10.13** Explain the terms *shallow copy* and *deep copy*.

★ **R10.14** What access attribute should instance variables have? What access attribute should static variables have? How about static final variables?

★ **R10.15** What access attribute should instance methods have? Does the same hold for static methods?

★★ **R10.16** The static variables System.in and System.out are public. Is it possible to overwrite them? If so, how?

★★ **R10.17** Why are public instance variables dangerous? Are public static variables more dangerous than public instance variables?

Programming Exercises

★ **P10.1** Enhance the addInterest method of the SavingsAccount class to compute the interest on the *minimum* balance since the last call to addInterest. *Hint:* You need to modify the withdraw method as well, and you need to add an instance variable to remember the minimum balance.

★★ **P10.2** Add a TimeDepositAccount class to the bank account hierarchy. The time deposit account is just like a savings account, but you promise to leave the money in the account for a particular number of months, and there is a $20 penalty for early withdrawal. Construct the account with the interest rate and the number of months to maturity. In the addInterest method, decrement the count of months. If the count is positive during a withdrawal, charge the withdrawal penalty.

★ **P10.3** Add a class NumericQuestion to the question hierarchy of How To 10.1. If the response and the expected answer differ by no more than 0.01, then accept it as correct.

★★ **P10.4** Add a class FillInQuestion to the question hierarchy of How To 10.1. An object of this class is constructed with a string that contains the answer, surrounded by _ _, for example, "The inventor of Java was _James Gosling_". The question should be displayed as

```
The inventor of Java was _____
```

★ **P10.5** Modify the checkAnswer method of the Question class of How To 10.1 so that it does not take into account different spaces or upper/lowercase characters. For example, the response " JAMES gosling" should match an answer of "James Gosling".

★ **P10.6** Add a class MultiChoiceQuestion to the question hierarchy of How To 10.1 that allows multiple correct choices. The respondent should provide all correct choices, separated by spaces. Provide instructions in the question text.

★ **P10.7** Add a class AnyCorrectChoiceQuestion to the question hierarchy of How To 10.1 that allows multiple correct choices. The respondent should provide any one of the correct choices. The answer string should contain all of the correct choices, separated by spaces.

★ **P10.8** Add a method addText to the Question class of How To 10.1 and provide a different implementation of ChoiceQuestion that calls addText rather than storing an array list of choices.

★★ **P10.9** Provide toString and equals methods for the Question and ChoiceQuestion classes of How To 10.1.

★ **P10.10** Implement a subclass Square that extends the Rectangle class. In the constructor, accept the *x*- and *y*-positions of the *center* and the side length of the square. Call the setLocation and setSize methods of the Rectangle class. Look up these methods in the documentation for the Rectangle class. Also supply a method getArea that computes and returns the area of the square. Write a sample program that asks for the center and side length, then prints out the square (using the toString method that you inherit from Rectangle) and the area of the square.

★ **P10.11** Implement a superclass Person. Make two classes, Student and Instructor, that inherit from Person. A person has a name and a year of birth. A student has a major, and an instructor has a salary. Write the class declarations, the constructors, and the methods toString for all classes. Supply a test program that tests these classes and methods.

If GT ≥ 500,000 gets
by

★★ **P10.12** Make a class Employee with a name and salary. Make a class Manager inherit from Employee. Add an instance variable, named department, of type String. Supply a method toString that prints the manager's name, department, and salary. Make a class Executive inherit from Manager. Supply appropriate toString methods for all classes. Supply a test program that tests these classes and methods.

Key to the
washroom
Boolean

★★★ **P10.13** Reorganize the bank account classes as follows. In the BankAccount class, introduce an abstract method endOfMonth with no implementation. Rename the addInterest and deductFees methods into endOfMonth in the subclasses. Which classes are now abstract and which are concrete? Write a static method void test(BankAccount account) that makes five transactions and then calls endOfMonth. Test it with instances of all concrete account classes.

★★★G **P10.14** Implement an abstract class Vehicle and concrete subclasses Car and Truck. A vehicle has a position on the screen. Write methods draw that draw cars and trucks as follows:

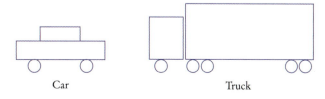

Car   Truck

Then write a method randomVehicle that randomly generates Vehicle references, with an equal probability for constructing cars and trucks, with random positions. Call it 10 times and draw all of them.

★★G P10.15 Write a program that prompts the user for an integer, using a JOptionPane, and then draws as many rectangles at random positions in a component as the user requested. Use inheritance for your frame class.

★★G P10.16 Write a program that asks the user to enter an integer n into a JOptionPane, and then draws an *n*-by-*n* grid. Use inheritance for the frame class.

Programming Projects

Project 10.1 Your task is to program robots with varying behaviors. The robots try to escape a maze, such as the following:

```
*  *******
*       * *
*  ***** *
*  *  *    *
*  *  *** *
*     *     *
***  *  *  *
*         *  *
******* *
```

A robot has a position and a method void move(Maze m) that modifies the position. Provide a common superclass Robot whose move method does nothing. Provide subclasses RandomRobot, RightHandRuleRobot, and MemoryRobot. Each of these robots has a different strategy for escaping. The RandomRobot simply makes random moves. The RightHandRuleRobot moves around the maze so that it's right hand always touches a wall. The MemoryRobot remembers all positions that it has previously occupied and never goes back to a position that it knows to be a dead end.

Project 10.2 Implement the toString, equals, and clone methods for all subclasses of the BankAccount class, as well as the Bank class of Chapter 7. Write unit tests that verify that your methods work correctly. Be sure to test a Bank that holds objects from a mixture of account classes.

Answers to Self-Check Questions

1. To express the common behavior of text fields and text components.
2. Not all bank accounts earn interest.
3. Two instance variables: `balance` and `interestRate`.
4. `deposit`, `withdraw`, `getBalance`, and `addInterest`.
5. `Manager` is the subclass; `Employee` is the superclass.
6. The `SavingsAccount` class inherits the `deposit`, `withdraw`, and `getBalance` methods. The `addInterest` method is new. No methods override superclass methods.
7. It needs to reduce the balance, and it cannot access the `balance` instance variable directly.
8. So that the count can reflect the number of transactions for the following month.
9. It was content to use the superclass constructor without parameters, which sets the balance to zero.
10. No—this is a requirement only for constructors. For example, the `Checking-Account.deposit` method first increments the transaction count, then calls the superclass method.
11. We want to use the method for all kinds of bank accounts. Had we used a parameter of type `SavingsAccount`, we couldn't have called the method with a `CheckingAccount` object.
12. We cannot invoke the `deposit` method on a variable of type `Object`.
13. The object is an instance of `BankAccount` or one of its subclasses.
14. The balance of a is unchanged (you withdraw from and deposit to the same account), and the transaction count is incremented twice.
15. It certainly should—unless, of course, x is `null`.
16. If `toString` returns a string that describes all instance variables, you can simply call `toString` on the implicit and explicit parameters, and compare the results. However, comparing the instance variables is more efficient than converting them into strings.
17. Three: `InvestmentFrameViewer`, `InvestmentFrame`, and `BankAccount`.
18. The `InvestmentFrame` constructor adds the panel to *itself*.

Chapter 11

Input/Output and Exception Handling

CHAPTER GOALS

- To be able to read and write text files
- To learn how to throw and catch exceptions
- To be able to design your own exception classes
- To understand the difference between checked and unchecked exceptions
- To know when and where to catch an exception

This chapter starts with a discussion of file input and output.

Whenever you read or write data, potential errors are to be expected. A file may have been corrupted or deleted, or it may be stored on another computer that was just disconnected from the network. In order to deal with these issues, you need to know about exception handling. This chapter tells you how your programs can report exceptional conditions, and how they can recover when an exceptional condition has occurred.

CHAPTER CONTENTS

11.1 Reading and Writing Text Files

We begin this chapter by discussing the common task of reading and writing files that contain text. Examples are files that are created with a simple text editor, such as Windows Notepad, as well as Java source code and HTML files.

The simplest mechanism for reading text is to use the Scanner class. You already know how to use a Scanner for reading console input. To read input from a disk file, the Scanner class relies on another class, File, which describes disk files and directories. (The File class has many methods that we do not discuss in this book; for example, methods that delete or rename a file.) First construct a File object with the name of the input file, then use the File to construct a Scanner object:

```
File inFile = new File("input.txt");
Scanner in = new Scanner(inFile);
```

> When reading text files, use the Scanner class.

This Scanner object reads text from the file input.txt. You can use the Scanner methods (such as next, nextLine, nextInt, and nextDouble) to read data from the input file.

To write output to a file, you construct a PrintWriter object with the given file name, for example

```
PrintWriter out = new PrintWriter("output.txt");
```

> When writing text files, use the PrintWriter class.

If the output file already exists, it is emptied before the new data are written into it. If the file doesn't exist, an empty file is created. You can also construct a PrintWriter object from a File object. This is useful if you use a file chooser (see Special Topic 11.1).

The PrintWriter class is an enhancement of the PrintStream class that you already know—System.out is a PrintStream object. You can use the familiar print, println, and printf methods with any PrintWriter object:

```
out.print(29.95);
out.println(new Rectangle(5, 10, 15, 25));
out.printf("%10.2f", price);
```

When you are done writing to a file, be sure to *close* the `PrintWriter`:

```
out.close();
```

If your program exits without closing the `PrintWriter`, the disk file may not contain all of the output.

The following program puts these concepts to work. It reads all lines of an input file and sends them to the output file, preceded by *line numbers*. If the input file is

```
Mary had a little lamb
Whose fleece was white as snow.
And everywhere that Mary went,
The lamb was sure to go!
```

then the program produces the output file

```
/* 1 */ Mary had a little lamb
/* 2 */ Whose fleece was white as snow.
/* 3 */ And everywhere that Mary went,
/* 4 */ The lamb was sure to go!
```

The line numbers are enclosed in `/* */` delimiters so that the program can be used for numbering Java source files.

There is one additional issue that we need to tackle. When the input or output file doesn't exist, a `FileNotFoundException` can occur. The compiler insists that we tell it what the program should do when that happens. (In this regard, the `FileNotFoundException` is different from the exceptions that you have already encountered. We will discuss this difference in detail in Section 11.4.) In our sample program, we take the easy way out and acknowledge that the `main` method should simply be terminated if the exception occurs. We label the `main` method like this:

```
public static void main(String[] args) throws FileNotFoundException
```

You will see in the following sections how to deal with exceptions in a more professional way.

ch11/lines/LineNumberer.java

```java
1  import java.io.File;
2  import java.io.FileNotFoundException;
3  import java.io.PrintWriter;
4  import java.util.Scanner;
5
6  /**
7     This program applies line numbers to a file.
8  */
9  public class LineNumberer
10 {
11    public static void main(String[] args) throws FileNotFoundException
12    {
13       // Prompt for the input and output file names
14
15       Scanner console = new Scanner(System.in);
16       System.out.print("Input file: ");
17       String inputFileName = console.next();
18       System.out.print("Output file: ");
19       String outputFileName = console.next();
20
```

```
21      // Construct the Scanner and PrintWriter objects for reading and writing
22
23      File inputFile = new File(inputFileName);
24      Scanner in = new Scanner(inputFile);
25      PrintWriter out = new PrintWriter(outputFileName);
26      int lineNumber = 1;
27
28      // Read the input and write the output
29
30      while (in.hasNextLine())
31      {
32         String line = in.nextLine();
33         out.println("/* " + lineNumber + " */ " + line);
34         lineNumber++;
35      }
36
37      in.close();
38      out.close();
39   }
40 }
```

SELF CHECK

1. What happens when you supply the same name for the input and output files to the LineNumberer program?

2. What happens when you supply the name of a nonexistent input file to the Line-Numberer program?

Common Error 11.1

Backslashes in File Names

When you specify a file name as a string literal, and the name contains backslash characters (as in a Windows file name), you must supply each backslash twice:

```
inFile = new File("c:\\homework\\input.dat");
```

Recall that a single backslash inside quoted strings is an **escape character** that is combined with another character to form a special meaning, such as \n for a newline character. The \\ combination denotes a single backslash.

When a user supplies a file name to a program, however, the user should not type the backslash twice.

Common Error 11.2

Constructing a Scanner with a String

When you construct a PrintWriter with a string, it writes to a file:

```
PrintWriter out = new PrintWriter("output.txt");
```

However, this does *not* work for a Scanner. The statement

```
Scanner in = new Scanner("input.txt"); // ERROR?
```

does *not* open a file. Instead, it simply reads through the string: in.nextLine() returns the string "input.txt". This feature can be useful—see Section 11.2.3 for an example.

You must simply remember to use File objects in the Scanner constructor:

```
Scanner in = new Scanner(new File("input.txt")); // OK
```

Special Topic 11.1

File Dialog Boxes

The JFileChooser dialog box allows users to select a file by navigating through directories.

In a program with a graphical user interface, you will want to use a file dialog box (such as the one shown in the figure below) whenever the users of your program need to pick a file. The JFileChooser class implements a file dialog box for the Swing user interface toolkit.

The JFileChooser class has many options to fine-tune the display of the dialog box, but in its most basic form it is quite simple: Construct a file chooser object; then call the showOpenDialog or showSaveDialog method. Both methods show the same dialog box, but the button for selecting a file is labeled "Open" or "Save", depending on which method you call.

A File object describes a file or directory.

For better placement of the dialog box on the screen, you can specify the user interface component over which to pop up the dialog box. If you don't care where the dialog box pops up, you can simply pass null. The showOpenDialog and showSaveDialog methods return either JFileChooser.APPROVE_OPTION, if the user has chosen a file, or JFileChooser.CANCEL_OPTION, if the user canceled the selection. If a file was chosen, then you call the getSelectedFile method to obtain a File object that describes the file. Here is a complete example:

```
JFileChooser chooser = new JFileChooser();
Scanner in = null;
if (chooser.showOpenDialog(null) == JFileChooser.APPROVE_OPTION)
{
   File selectedFile = chooser.getSelectedFile();
   in = new Scanner(selectedFile);
   . . .
}
```

Open			✕
Look In: ☐ api	▼	⌂ ⌂ ☐	▦ ▤
☐ index-files	☐ allclasses-noframe.html	☐ overview-summa
☐ java	☐ constant-values.html	☐ overview-tree.ht
☐ javax	☐ deprecated-list.html	☐ package-list
☐ org	☐ help-doc.html	☐ serialized-form.h
☐ resources	☐ index.html	☐ stylesheet.css
☐ allclasses-frame.html	☐ overview-frame.html	

File Name:	
Files of Type:	All Files ▼

Open **Cancel**

A JFileChooser Dialog Box

Special Topic 11.2

Reading Web Pages

You can read the contents of a web page with this sequence of commands:

```
String address = "http://java.sun.com/index.html";
URL locator = new URL(address);
Scanner in = new Scanner(locator.openStream());
```

Now simply read the contents of the web page with the Scanner in the usual way. The URL constructor and the openStream method can throw an IOException. You need to tag the main method with throws IOException. (See Section 11.3 for more information on the throws clause.)

Special Topic 11.3

Command Line Arguments

Depending on the operating system and Java development system used, there are different methods of starting a program—for example, by selecting "Run" in the compilation environment, by clicking on an icon, or by typing the name of the program at a prompt in a terminal or shell window. The latter method is called "invoking the program from the command line". When you use this method, you must type the name of the program, but you can also type in additional information that the program can use. These additional strings are called *command line arguments*.

For example, it is convenient to specify the input and output file names for the Line-Numberer program on the command line:

```
java LineNumberer input.txt numbered.txt
```

The strings that are typed after the Java program name are placed into the args parameter of the main method. (Now you finally know the use of the args parameter that you have seen in so many programs!)

For example, with the given program invocation, the args parameter of the LineNumberer.main method has the following contents:

- args[0] is "input.txt"
- args[1] is "numbered.txt"

The main method can then process these parameters, for example:

```
if (args.length >= 1)
    inputFileName = args[0];
```

It is entirely up to the program what to do with the command line argument strings. It is customary to interpret strings starting with a hyphen (-) as program options. For example, we may want to enhance the LineNumberer program so that a -c option places line numbers inside comment delimiters; for example

```
java LineNumberer -c HelloWorld.java HelloWorld.txt
```

If the -c option is missing, the delimiters should not be included. Here is how the main method can analyze the command line arguments:

```
for (String arg : args)
{
    if (arg.startsWith("-")) // It's an option
    {
        if (arg.equals("-c")) useCommentDelimiters = true;
```

> When you launch a program from the command line, you can specify arguments after the program name. The program can access these strings by processing the args parameter of the main method.

```
    }
    else if (inputFileName == null) inputFileName = arg;
    else if (outputFileName == null) outputFileName = arg;
}
```

Should you support command line interfaces for your programs, or should you instead supply a graphical user interface with file chooser dialog boxes? For a casual and infrequent user, the graphical user interface is much better. The user interface guides the user along and makes it possible to navigate the application without much knowledge. But for a frequent user, graphical user interfaces have a major drawback—they are hard to automate. If you need to process hundreds of files every day, you could spend all your time typing file names into file chooser dialog boxes. But it is not difficult to call a program multiple times automatically with different command line arguments. Productivity Hint 7.3 discusses how to use shell scripts (also called batch files) for this purpose.

11.2 Reading Text Input

In the following sections, you will learn how to process complex text input that you often encounter in real life situations.

11.2.1 Reading Words

> The next method reads a word at a time. Call Scanner.useDelimiter to specify a pattern for word boundaries.

In the preceding example program, we read input a line at a time. Sometimes, it is useful to read words rather than lines. For example, consider the loop

```
while (in.hasNext())
{
    String input = in.next();
    System.out.println(input);
}
```

With our sample input, this loop would print a word on every line:

```
Mary
had
a
little
lamb
```

In Java, a *word* is not the same as in English. It is any sequence of characters that is not white space. White space includes spaces, tab characters, and the newline characters that separate lines. For example, the following are considered words:

```
snow.
1729
C++
```

(Note the period after snow—it is considered a part of the word because it is not white space.)

Here is precisely what happens when the next method is executed. Input characters that are *white space* are *consumed*—that is, removed from the input. However, they do not become part of the word. The first character that is not white space becomes the first character of the word. More characters are added until either another white space character occurs, or the end of the input has been reached.

Sometimes, you want to read just the words and discard anything that isn't a letter. You achieve this task by calling the useDelimiter method on your Scanner object as follows:

```
Scanner in = new Scanner(. . .);
in.useDelimiter("[^A-Za-z]+");
```

Here, we set the character pattern that separates words to "any sequence of characters other than letters". (The notation used for describing the character pattern is called a *regular expression*. See Productivity Hint 11.1 on page 477 if you are interested in more details.) With this setting, punctuation and numbers are stripped off from the words returned by the next method.

11.2.2 Processing Lines

> The nextLine method reads a line of input and consumes the newline character at the end of the line.

When each line of a file is a data record, it is often best to read entire lines with the nextLine method:

```
String line = in.nextLine();
```

The nextLine method consumes the next input line (including the newline character) and returns the line without the newline character. You can then take the line apart for further processing.

Here is a typical example of processing lines in a file. A file with population data from the CIA Fact Book site (http://www.cia.gov/library/publications/the-world-factbook/) contains lines such as the following:

```
China   1330044605
India   1147995898
United States 303824646
. . .
```

Because some country names have more than one word, it would be tedious to read this file using the next method. For example, after reading United, how would your program know that it still needs to read another word before reading the population count?

Instead, read each input line into a string. Then use the isDigit and isWhitespace methods to find out where the name ends and the number starts.

Locate the first digit:

```
int i = 0;
while (!Character.isDigit(line.charAt(i))) { i++; }
```

Then extract the country name and population:

```
String countryName = line.substring(0, i);
String population = line.substring(i);
```

However, the country name contains one or more spaces at the end. Use the trim method to remove them:

```
countryName = countryName.trim();
```

The trim method returns the string with all white space at the beginning and end removed.

i starts here   Use trim to remove this space.   i ends here

U	n	i	t	e	d		S	t	a	t	e	s		3	0	3	8	2	4	6	4	6
0	1	2	3	4	5	6	7	8	9	10	11	12	13	14	15	16	17	18	19	20	21	22

`countryName`   `population`

There is another problem. The population is stored in a string, not a number. Use the `Integer.parseInt` method to convert it:

```
int populationValue = Integer.parseInt(population);
```

You need to be careful when calling the `Integer.parseInt` method. Its parameter value must be a string containing the digits of an integer or a `NumberFormatException` occurs. The parameter value may not contain any additional characters. Not even spaces are allowed! In our situation, we happen to know that there won't be any spaces at the beginning of the string, but there might be some at the end. Therefore, we use the `trim` method:

```
int populationValue = Integer.parseInt(population.trim());
```

Here you saw how to break a string into parts by looking at individual characters. Another approach is occasionally easier. Construct a new `Scanner` object to read the characters from a string:

```
Scanner lineScanner = new Scanner(line);
```

Then you can use `lineScanner` like any other `Scanner` object, reading words and numbers:

```
String countryName = lineScanner.next();
while (!lineScanner.hasNextInt())
{
   countryName = countryName + " " + lineScanner.next();
}
int populationValue = lineScanner.nextInt();
```

11.2.3 Reading Numbers

The `nextInt` and `nextDouble` methods consume white space and the next number.

You have used the `nextInt` and `nextDouble` methods of the `Scanner` class many times, but here we will have a look at their behavior in detail. Suppose you call

```
double value = in.nextDouble();
```

The `nextDouble` method recognizes floating-point numbers such as 3.14159, -21, or 1E12 (a billion in scientific notation). However, if there is *no number* in the input, then a `NoSuchElementException` occurs.

Consider an input containing the characters

White space is consumed and the word 21st is read. However, this word is not a properly formatted number. In this situation, an "input mismatch exception" occurs.

To avoid exceptions, use the `hasNextDouble` method to screen the input. For example,

```
if (in.hasNextDouble())
{
    double value = in.nextDouble();
    . . .
}
```

Similarly, you should call the `hasNextInt` method before calling `nextInt`.

Note that the `nextInt` and `nextDouble` methods *do not* consume the white space that follows a number. This can be a problem if you alternate between calling `nextInt`/`nextDouble` and `nextLine`. Suppose a file contains student IDs and names in this format:

```
1729
Harry Morgan
1730
Diana Lin
. . .
```

Now suppose you read the file with these instructions:

```
while (in.hasNextInt())
{
    int studentID = in.nextInt();
    String name = in.nextLine();
    Process the student ID and name
}
```

Initially, the input contains

After the first call to `nextInt`, the input contains

\n	H	a	r	r	y

The call to `nextLine` reads an empty string! The remedy is to add a call to `nextLine` after reading the ID:

```
int studentID = in.nextInt();
in.nextLine(); // Consume the newline
String name = in.nextLine();
```

11.2.4 Reading Characters

To read one character at a time, set the delimiter pattern to the empty string.

Sometimes, you want to read a file one character at a time. You achieve this task by calling the `useDelimiter` method on your `Scanner` object with an empty string:

```
Scanner in = new Scanner(. . .);
in.useDelimiter("");
```

Now each call to `next` returns a string consisting of a single character. Here is how you can process the characters:

```
while (in.hasNext())
{
```

```
        char ch = in.next().charAt(0);
        Process ch
    }
```

3. Suppose the input contains the characters 6,995.0. What is the value of number and input after these statements?

```
int number = in.nextInt();
String input = in.next();
```

4. Suppose the input contains the characters 6,995.00 12. What is the value of price and quantity after these statements?

```
double price = in.nextDouble();
int quantity = in.nextInt();
```

5. Your input file contains a sequence of numbers, but sometimes a value is not available and marked as N/A. How can you read the numbers and skip over the markers?

Productivity Hint 11.1

Regular Expressions

Regular expressions describe character patterns. For example, numbers have a simple form. They contain one or more digits. The regular expression describing numbers is [0-9]+. The set [0-9] denotes any digit between 0 and 9, and the + means "one or more".

The search commands of professional programming editors understand regular expressions. Moreover, several utility programs use regular expressions to locate matching text. A commonly used program that uses regular expressions is *grep* (which stands for "global regular expression print"). You can run grep from a command line or from inside some compilation environments. Grep is part of the UNIX operating system, and versions are available for Windows. It needs a regular expression and one or more files to search. When grep runs, it displays a set of lines that match the regular expression.

Suppose you want to look for all magic numbers (see Quality Tip 4.1) in a file. The command

```
grep [0-9]+ Homework.java
```

lists all lines in the file Homework.java that contain sequences of digits. That isn't terribly useful; lines with variable names x1 will be listed. OK, you want sequences of digits that do *not* immediately follow letters:

```
grep [^A-Za-z][0-9]+ Homework.java
```

The set [^A-Za-z] denotes any characters that are *not* in the ranges A to Z and a to z. This works much better, and it shows only lines that contain actual numbers.

The useDelimiter method of the Scanner class accepts a regular expression to describe delimiters—the blocks of text that separate words. As already mentioned, if you set the delimiter pattern to [^A-Za-z]+, a delimiter is a sequence of one or more characters that are not letters.

For more information on regular expressions, consult one of the many tutorials on the Internet by pointing your search engine to "regular expression tutorial".

How To 11.1

Processing Text Files

Processing text files that contain real data can be surprisingly challenging. This How To gives you step-by-step guidance.

As an example, we will consider this task: Read two country data files, `worldpop.txt` and `worldarea.txt` (supplied with your book code). Both files contain data for the same countries in the same order. Write a file `world_pop_density.txt` that contains country names and population densities (people per square km), with the country names aligned left and the numbers aligned right:

```
Afghanistan                                  50.56
Akrotiri                                    127.64
Albania                                     125.91
Algeria                                      14.18
American Samoa                              288.92
. . .
```

Step 1 Understand the processing task.

As always, you need to have a clear understanding of the task before designing a solution. Can you carry out the task by hand (perhaps with smaller input files)? If not, get more information about the problem.

One important aspect that you need to consider is whether you can process the data as it becomes available, or whether you need to store it first. For example, if you are asked to write out sorted data, you need to first collect all input, perhaps by placing it in an array list. However, it is often possible to process the data "on the go", without storing it.

In our example, we can read each file a line at a time and compute the density for each line because our input files store the population and area data in the same order.

The following pseudocode describes our processing task.

> **While there are more lines to be read**
> **Read a line from each file.**
> **Extract the country name.**
> **population = number following the country name in the line from the first file**
> **area = number following the country name in the line from the second file**
> **If area != 0**
> **density = population / area**
> **Print country name and density.**

Step 2 Determine which files you need to read and write.

This should be clear from the problem. In our example, there are two input files, the population data and the area data, and one output file.

Step 3 Choose a mechanism for obtaining the file names.

There are four options:

- Hard-coding the file names (such as `"worldpop.txt"`)
- Asking the user:
  ```
  Scanner in = new Scanner(System.in);
  System.out.print("Enter filename: ");
  String inFile = in.nextLine();
  ```
- Using command line arguments for the file names (see Special Topic 11.3 on page 472)
- Using a file chooser dialog box (see Special Topic 11.1 on page 471)

In our example, we use hard-coded file names for simplicity.

Step 4 Choose between line, word, and character-based input.

As a rule of thumb, read lines if the input data is grouped by lines. That is the case with tabular data, such as in our example, or when you need to report line numbers.

When gathering data that can be distributed over several lines, then it makes more sense to read words. Keep in mind that you lose all white space when you read words.

Reading characters is mostly useful for tasks that require access to individual characters. Examples include analyzing character frequencies, changing tabs to spaces, or encryption.

Step 5 With line-oriented input, extract the required data.

It is simple to read a line of input with the nextLine method. Then you need to get the data out of that line. You can extract substrings, as described in Section 11.2.2.

Typically, you will use methods such as Character.isWhitespace and Character.isDigit to find the boundaries of substrings.

If you need any of the substrings as numbers, you must convert them, using Integer.parseInt or Double.parseDouble.

Step 6 Use classes and methods to factor out common tasks.

Processing input files usually has repetitive tasks, such as skipping over white space or extracting numbers from strings. It really pays off to isolate these tedious operations from the remainder of the code.

In our example, we have a task that occurs twice: splitting an input line into the country name and the value that follows. We implement a simple CountryValue class for this purpose, using the technique described in Section 11.2.2.

Here is the complete source code.

ch11/population/CountryValue.java

```java
1  /**
2     Describes a value that is associated with a country.
3  */
4  public class CountryValue
5  {
6     private String country;
7     private double value;
8
9     /**
10        Constructs a CountryValue from an input line.
11        @param line a line containing a country name, followed by a value
12     */
13     public CountryValue(String line)
14     {
15        int i = 0; // Locate the start of the first digit
16        while (!Character.isDigit(line.charAt(i))) { i++; }
17        int j = i - 1; // Locate the end of the preceding word
18        while (Character.isWhitespace(line.charAt(j))) { j--; }
19        country = line.substring(0, j + 1); // Extract the country name
20        value = Double.parseDouble(line.substring(i).trim()); // Extract the value
21     }
22
23     /**
24        Gets the country name.
25        @return the country name
26     */
27     public String getCountry() { return country; }
28
```

```
29    /**
30       Gets the associated value.
31       @return the value associated with the country
32    */
33    public double getValue() { return value; }
34 }
```

ch11/population/PopulationDensity.java

```java
1  import java.io.File;
2  import java.io.FileNotFoundException;
3  import java.io.PrintWriter;
4  import java.util.Scanner;
5
6  public class PopulationDensity
7  {
8     public static void main(String[] args) throws FileNotFoundException
9     {
10        // Open input files
11        Scanner in1 = new Scanner(new File("worldpop.txt"));
12        Scanner in2 = new Scanner(new File("worldarea.txt"));
13
14        // Open output file
15        PrintWriter out = new PrintWriter("world_pop_density.txt");
16
17        // Read lines from each file
18        while (in1.hasNextLine() && in2.hasNextLine())
19        {
20           CountryValue population = new CountryValue(in1.nextLine());
21           CountryValue area = new CountryValue(in2.nextLine());
22
23           // Compute and print the population density
24           double density = 0;
25           if (area.getValue() != 0) // Protect against division by zero
26           {
27              density = population.getValue() / area.getValue();
28           }
29           out.printf("%-40s%15.2f\n", population.getCountry(), density);
30        }
31
32        in1.close();
33        in2.close();
34        out.close();
35     }
36 }
```

<table>
<tr><td>⊕ *Worked*
Example 11.1</td><td>

Analyzing Baby Names

In this Worked Example, you will use data from the
Social Security Administration to analyze the most
popular baby names.

</td><td></td></tr>
</table>

⊕ Available online in WileyPLUS and at www.wiley.com/college/horstmann.

11.3 Throwing Exceptions

There are two main aspects to exception handling: *reporting* and *recovery*. A major challenge of error handling is that the point of reporting is usually far apart from the point of recovery. For example, the get method of the ArrayList class may detect that a nonexistent element is being accessed, but it does not have enough information to decide what to do about this failure. Should the user be asked to try a different operation? Should the program be aborted after saving the user's work? These decisions must be made in a different part of the program.

In Java, *exception handling* provides a flexible mechanism for passing control from the point of error reporting to a competent recovery handler. In the remainder of this chapter, we will look into the details of this mechanism.

When you detect an error condition, your job is really easy. You just throw an appropriate exception object, and you are done. For example, suppose someone tries to withdraw too much money from a bank account.

To signal an exceptional condition, use the throw statement to throw an exception object.

```java
public class BankAccount
{
    . . .
    public void withdraw(double amount)
    {
        if (amount > balance)
            // Now what?
        . . .
    }
}
```

First look for an appropriate exception class. The Java library provides many classes to signal all sorts of exceptional conditions. Figure 1 on the next page shows the most useful ones.

Look around for an exception type that might describe your situation. How about the IllegalStateException? Is the bank account in an illegal state for the withdraw operation? Not really—some withdraw operations could succeed. Is the parameter value illegal? Indeed it is. It is just too large. Therefore, let's throw an IllegalArgumentException. (The term **argument** is an alternative term for a parameter value.)

```java
public class BankAccount
{
    public void withdraw(double amount)
    {
        if (amount > balance)
        {
            throw new IllegalArgumentException("Amount exceeds balance");
        }
        balance = balance - amount;
    }
    . . .
}
```

When you throw an exception, the current method terminates immediately.

The statement

```java
throw new IllegalArgumentException("Amount exceeds balance");
```

constructs an object of type IllegalArgumentException and throws that object.

When you throw an exception, execution does not continue with the next statement but with an **exception handler**. For now, we won't worry about the handling of the exception. That is the topic of Section 11.5.

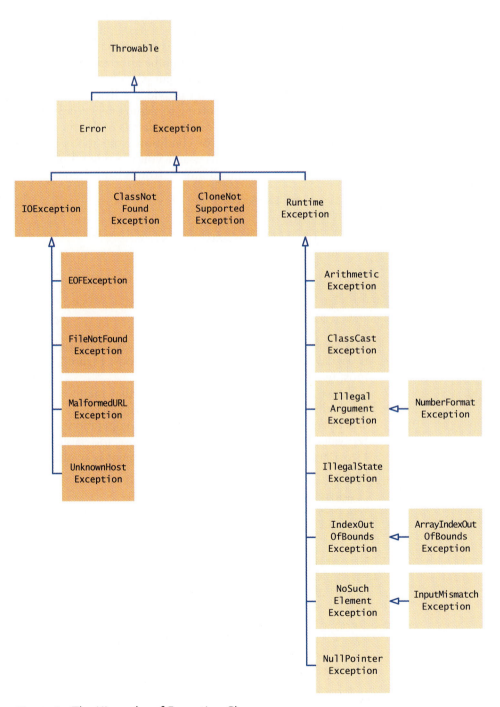

Figure 1 The Hierarchy of Exception Classes

Syntax 11.1   Throwing an Exception

Syntax   throw *exceptionObject*;

Example

Most exception objects can be constructed with an error message.

```
if (amount > balance)
{
    throw new IllegalArgumentException("Amount exceeds balance");
}
balance = balance - amount;
```

A new exception object is constructed, then thrown.

This line is not executed when the exception is thrown.

SELF CHECK

6. How should you modify the deposit method to ensure that the balance is never negative?

7. Suppose you construct a new bank account object with a zero balance and then call withdraw(10). What is the value of balance afterwards?

11.4 Checked and Unchecked Exceptions

There are two kinds of exceptions: *checked* and *unchecked*. Unchecked exceptions extend the class RuntimeException or Error.

Java exceptions fall into two categories, called *checked* and *unchecked* exceptions. When you call a method that throws a **checked exception**, the compiler checks that you don't ignore it. You must tell the compiler what you are going to do about the exception if it is ever thrown. For example, all subclasses of IOException are checked exceptions. On the other hand, the compiler does not require you to keep track of **unchecked exceptions**. Exceptions such as NumberFormatException, IllegalArgument-Exception, and NullPointerException are unchecked exceptions. More generally, all exceptions that belong to subclasses of RuntimeException are unchecked, and all other subclasses of the class Exception are checked. (In Figure 1, the checked exceptions are shaded in a darker color.) There is a second category of internal errors that are reported by throwing objects of type Error. One example is the OutOfMemoryError, which is thrown when all available memory has been used up. These are fatal errors that happen rarely and are beyond your control. They too are unchecked.

Why have two kinds of exceptions? A checked exception describes a problem that is likely to occur at times, no matter how careful you are. The unchecked exceptions, on the other hand, are your fault. For example, an unexpected end of file can be caused by forces beyond your control, such as a disk error or a broken network connection. But you are to blame for a NullPointerException, because your code was wrong when it tried to use a null reference.

Checked exceptions are due to external circumstances that the programmer cannot prevent. The compiler checks that your program handles these exceptions.

The compiler doesn't check whether you handle a NullPointerException, because you should test your references for null before using them rather than install a handler for that exception. The compiler does insist that your program be able to handle error conditions that you cannot prevent.

Actually, those categories aren't perfect. For example, the `Scanner.nextInt` method throws an unchecked `InputMismatchException` if the input does not contain a valid integer. A checked exception would have been more appropriate because the programmer cannot prevent users from entering incorrect input. (The designers of the `Scanner` class made this choice to make it easy to use for beginning programmers.)

As you can see from Figure 1, the majority of checked exceptions occur when you deal with input and output. That is a fertile ground for external failures beyond your control—a file might have been corrupted or removed, a network connection might be overloaded, a server might have crashed, and so on. Therefore, you will need to deal with checked exceptions principally when programming with files and streams.

You have seen how to use the `Scanner` class to read data from a file, by passing a `File` object to the `Scanner` constructor:

```
String filename = . . .;
File inFile = new File(filename);
Scanner in = new Scanner(inFile);
```

However, the `Scanner` constructor can throw a `FileNotFoundException`. The `FileNotFoundException` is a checked exception, so you need to tell the compiler what you are going to do about it. You have two choices. You can handle the exception, using the techniques that you will see in Section 11.5. Or you can simply tell the compiler that you are aware of this exception and that you want your method to be terminated when it occurs. The method that reads input does not usually know what to do about an unexpected error, so that is usually the better option.

To declare that a method should be terminated when a checked exception occurs within it, tag the method with a `throws` clause.

```
public void read(String filename) throws FileNotFoundException
{
    File inFile = new File(filename);
    Scanner in = new Scanner(inFile);
    . . .
}
```

> Add a throws clause to a method that can throw a checked exception.

The `throws` clause in turn signals the caller of your method that it may encounter a `FileNotFoundException`. Then the caller needs to make the same decision—handle the exception, or tell its caller that the exception may be thrown.

If your method can throw exceptions of different types, you separate the exception class names by commas:

```
public void read(String filename)
    throws FileNotFoundException, NoSuchElementException
```

Always keep in mind that exception classes form an inheritance hierarchy. For example, `FileNotFoundException` is a subclass of `IOException`. Thus, if a method can throw both an `IOException` and a `FileNotFoundException`, you only tag it as `throws` `IOException`.

It sounds somehow irresponsible not to handle an exception when you know that it happened. Actually, though, it is usually best not to catch an exception if you don't know how to remedy the situation. After all, what can you do in a low-level read method? Can you tell the user? How? By sending a message to `System.out`? You don't know whether this method is called in a graphical program or an embedded system (such as a vending machine), where the user may never see `System.out`. And even if your users can see your error message, how do you know that they can

Syntax 11.2 The throws Clause

Syntax	*accessSpecifier returnType methodName(parameterType parameterName, . . .)* throws *ExceptionClass, ExceptionClass, . . .*
| *Example* | ```
public void read(String filename)
    throws FileNotFoundException, NoSuchElementException
``` |

You must specify all checked exceptions that this method may throw.

You may also list unchecked exceptions.

understand English? Your class may be used to build an application for users in another country. If you can't tell the user, can you patch up the data and keep going? How? If you set a variable to zero, null, or an empty string, that may just cause the program to break later, with much greater mystery.

Of course, some methods in the program know how to communicate with the user or take other remedial action. By allowing the exception to reach those methods, you make it possible for the exception to be processed by a competent handler.

SELF CHECK

8. Suppose a method calls the Scanner constructor, which can throw a FileNot-FoundException, and the nextInt method of the Scanner class, which can cause a NoSuchElementException or InputMismatchException. Which exceptions should be included in the throws clause?

9. Why is a NullPointerException not a checked exception?

11.5 Catching Exceptions

> In a method that is ready to handle a particular exception type, place the statements that can cause the exception inside a try block, and the handler inside a catch clause.

Every exception should be handled somewhere in your program. If an exception has no handler, an error message is printed, and your program terminates. That may be fine for a student program. But you would not want a professionally written program to die just because some method detected an unexpected error. Therefore, you should install exception handlers for all exceptions that your program might throw.

You install an exception handler with the try/catch statement. Each try block contains one or more statements that may cause an exception. Each catch clause contains the handler for an exception type. Here is an example:

```
try
{
    String filename = . . .;
    File inFile = new File(filename);
    Scanner in = new Scanner(inFile);
    String input = in.next();
    int value = Integer.parseInt(input);
    . . .
```
```

```
    }
    catch (IOException exception)
    {
        exception.printStackTrace();
    }
    catch (NumberFormatException exception)
    {
        System.out.println("Input was not a number");
    }
```

Three exceptions may be thrown in this try block: The Scanner constructor can throw a FileNotFoundException, Scanner.next can throw a NoSuchElementException, and Integer.parseInt can throw a NumberFormatException.

If any of these exceptions is actually thrown, then the rest of the instructions in the try block are skipped. Here is what happens for the various exception types:

- If a FileNotFoundException is thrown, then the catch clause for the IOException is executed. (Recall that FileNotFoundException is a subclass of IOException.)

- If a NumberFormatException occurs, then the second catch clause is executed.

- A NoSuchElementException is *not caught* by any of the catch clauses. The exception remains thrown until it is caught by another try block or the main method terminates.

When the catch (IOException exception) block is executed, then some method in the try block has failed with an IOException. The variable exception contains a reference

Syntax 11.3 Catching Exceptions

Syntax
```
try
{
    statement
    statement
    . . .
}
catch (ExceptionClass exceptionObject)
{
    statement
    statement
    . . .
}
```

This constructor can throw a
FileNotFoundException.

Example
```
try
{
    Scanner in = new Scanner(new File("input.txt"));
    String input = in.next();
    process(input);
}
catch (IOException exception)
{
    System.out.println("Could not open input file");
}
```

This is the exception that was thrown.

When an IOException is thrown, execution resumes here.

Additional catch clauses can appear here.

A FileNotFoundException is a special case of an IOException.

to the exception object that was thrown. The catch clause can analyze that object to find out more details about the failure. For example, you can get a printout of the chain of method calls that lead to the exception, by calling

```
exception.printStackTrace()
```

In these sample catch clauses, we merely inform the user of the source of the problem. A better way of dealing with the exception would be to give the user another chance to provide a correct input—see Section 11.8 for a solution.

It is important to remember that you should place catch clauses only in methods in which you can competently handle the particular exception type.

SELF CHECK

10. Suppose the file with the given file name exists and has no contents. Trace the flow of execution in the try block in this section.

11. Is there a difference between catching checked and unchecked exceptions?

Quality Tip 11.1

Throw Early, Catch Late

When a method detects a problem that it cannot solve, it is better to throw an exception rather than to try to come up with an imperfect fix. For example, suppose a method expects to read a number from a file, and the file doesn't contain a number. Simply using a zero value would be a poor choice because it hides the actual problem and perhaps causes a different problem elsewhere.

Conversely, a method should only catch an exception if it can really remedy the situation. Otherwise, the best remedy is simply to have the exception propagate to its caller, allowing it to be caught by a competent handler.

These principles can be summarized with the slogan "throw early, catch late".

> Throw an exception as soon as a problem is detected. Catch it only when the problem can be handled.

Quality Tip 11.2

Do Not Squelch Exceptions

When you call a method that throws a checked exception and you haven't specified a handler, the compiler complains. In your eagerness to continue your work, it is an understandable impulse to shut the compiler up by squelching the exception:

```
try
{
    File inFile = new File(filename);
    Scanner in = new Scanner(inFile);
    // Compiler complained about FileNotFoundException
    . . .
}
catch (Exception e) {} // So there!
```

The do-nothing exception handler fools the compiler into thinking that the exception has been handled. In the long run, this is clearly a bad idea. Exceptions were designed to transmit problem reports to a competent handler. Installing an incompetent handler simply hides an error condition that could be serious.

11.6 The finally Clause

Occasionally, you need to take some action whether or not an exception is thrown. The `finally` construct is used to handle this situation. Here is a typical situation.

It is important to close a `PrintWriter` to ensure that all output is written to the file. In the following code segment, we open a stream, call one or more methods, and then close the stream:

```
PrintWriter out = new PrintWriter(filename);
writeData(out);
out.close(); // May never get here
```

Now suppose that one of the methods before the last line throws an exception. Then the call to `close` is never executed! Solve this problem by placing the call to `close` inside a `finally` clause:

```
PrintWriter out = new PrintWriter(filename);
try
{
    writeData(out);
}
finally
{
    out.close();
}
```

Syntax 11.4 The finally Clause

Syntax
```
try
{
    statement
    statement
    . . .
}
finally
{
    statement
    statement
    . . .
}
```

Example

This variable must be declared outside the `try` block so that the `finally` clause can access it.

```
PrintWriter out = new PrintWriter(filename);
try
{
    writeData(out);
}
finally
{
    out.close();
}
```

This code may throw exceptions.

This code is always executed, even if an exception occurs.

Once a try block is entered, the statements in a `finally` clause are guaranteed to be executed, whether or not an exception is thrown.

In a normal case, there will be no problem. When the `try` block is completed, the `finally` clause is executed, and the writer is closed. However, if an exception occurs, the `finally` clause is also executed before the exception is passed to its handler.

Use the `finally` clause whenever you need to do some clean up, such as closing a file, to ensure that the clean up happens no matter how the method exits.

It is also possible to have a `finally` clause following one or more `catch` clauses. Then the code in the `finally` clause is executed whenever the try block is exited in any of three ways:

1. After completing the last statement of the try block
2. After completing the last statement of a catch clause, if this try block caught an exception
3. When an exception was thrown in the try block and not caught

However, we recommend that you don't mix `catch` and `finally` clauses in the same try block—see Quality Tip 11.3.

SELF CHECK

12. Why was the out variable declared outside the try block?

13. Suppose the file with the given name does not exist. Trace the flow of execution of the code segment in this section.

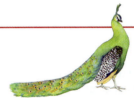

Quality Tip 11.3

Do Not Use catch and finally in the Same try Statement

It is tempting to combine catch and `finally` clauses, but the resulting code can be hard to understand. Instead, you should use a try/`finally` statement to close resources and a separate try/catch statement to handle errors. For example,

```
try
{
    PrintWriter out = new PrintWriter(filename);
    try
    {
        Write output to out
    }
    finally
    {
        out.close();
    }
}
catch (IOException exception)
{
    Handle exception
}
```

Note that the nested statements work correctly if the `PrintWriter` constructor throws an exception—see Exercise R11.18.

Special Topic 11.4

Automatic Resource Management in Java 7

In Java 7, you can use a new form of the try block that automatically closes an object that implements the Closeable interface, such as a PrintWriter or Scanner. Here is the syntax:

```
try (PrintWriter out = new PrintWriter(filename))
{
    Write output to out
}
```

The close method is automatically invoked on the out object when the try block ends, whether or not an exception has occurred. A finally statement is not required.

11.7 Designing Your Own Exception Types

Sometimes none of the standard exception types describe your particular error condition well enough. In that case, you can design your own exception class. Consider a bank account. Let's report an InsufficientFundsException when an attempt is made to withdraw an amount from a bank account that exceeds the current balance.

```
if (amount > balance)
{
    throw new InsufficientFundsException(
        "withdrawal of " + amount + " exceeds balance of " + balance);
}
```

> To describe an error condition, provide a subclass of an existing exception class.

Now you need to provide the InsufficientFundsException class. Should it be a checked or an unchecked exception? Is it the fault of some external event, or is it the fault of the programmer? We take the position that the programmer could have prevented the exceptional condition—after all, it would have been an easy matter to check whether amount <= account.getBalance() before calling the withdraw method. Therefore, the exception should be an unchecked exception and extend the Runtime-Exception class or one of its subclasses.

It is a good idea to extend an appropriate class in the exception hierarchy. For example, we can consider an InsufficientFundsException a special case of an Illegal-ArgumentException. This enables other programmers to catch the exception as an IllegalArgumentException if they are not interested in the exact nature of the problem.

It is customary to provide two constructors for an exception class: a constructor with no parameters and a constructor that accepts a message string describing the reason for the exception. Here is the declaration of the exception class.

```
public class InsufficientFundsException extends IllegalArgumentException
{
    public InsufficientFundsException() {}

    public InsufficientFundsException(String message)
    {
        super(message);
    }
}
```

When the exception is caught, its message string can be retrieved using the get-Message method of the Throwable class.

SELF CHECK

14. What is the purpose of the call super(message) in the second InsufficientFunds-Exception constructor?

15. Suppose you read bank account data from a file. Contrary to your expectation, the next input value is not of type double. You decide to implement a BadData-Exception. Which exception class should you extend?

Quality Tip 11.4

Do Throw Specific Exceptions

When throwing an exception, you should choose an exception class that describes the situation as closely as possible. For example, it would be a bad idea to simply throw a Runtime-Exception object when a bank account has insufficient funds. This would make it far too difficult to catch the exception. After all, if you caught all exceptions of type Runtime-Exception, your catch clause would also be activated by exceptions of the type NullPointer-Exception, ArrayIndexOutOfBoundsException, and so on. You would then need to carefully examine the exception object and attempt to deduce whether the exception was caused by insufficient funds.

If the standard library does not have an exception class that describes your particular error situation, simply provide a new exception class.

11.8 Case Study: A Complete Example

This section walks through a complete example of a program with exception handling. The program asks a user for the name of a file. The file is expected to contain data values. The first line of the file contains the total number of values, and the remaining lines contain the data. A typical input file looks like this:

```
3
1.45
-2.1
0.05
```

What can go wrong? There are two principal risks.

* The file might not exist.
* The file might have data in the wrong format.

Who can detect these faults? The Scanner constructor will throw an exception when the file does not exist. The methods that process the input values need to throw an exception when they find an error in the data format.

What exceptions can be thrown? The Scanner constructor throws a FileNot-FoundException when the file does not exist, which is appropriate in our situation. Finally, when the file data is in the wrong format, we will throw a BadDataException, a custom checked exception class. We use a checked exception because corruption of a data file is beyond the control of the programmer.

Who can remedy the faults that the exceptions report? Only the main method of the DataAnalyzer program interacts with the user. It catches the exceptions, prints appropriate error messages, and gives the user another chance to enter a correct file.

ch11/data/DataAnalyzer.java

```java
1   import java.io.FileNotFoundException;
2   import java.io.IOException;
3   import java.util.Scanner;
4
5   /**
6      This program reads a file containing numbers and analyzes its contents.
7      If the file doesn't exist or contains strings that are not numbers, an
8      error message is displayed.
9   */
10  public class DataAnalyzer
11  {
12     public static void main(String[] args)
13     {
14        Scanner in = new Scanner(System.in);
15        DataSetReader reader = new DataSetReader();
16
17        boolean done = false;
18        while (!done)
19        {
20           try
21           {
22              System.out.println("Please enter the file name: ");
23              String filename = in.next();
24
25              double[] data = reader.readFile(filename);
26              double sum = 0;
27              for (double d : data) sum = sum + d;
28              System.out.println("The sum is " + sum);
29              done = true;
30           }
31           catch (FileNotFoundException exception)
32           {
33              System.out.println("File not found.");
34           }
35           catch (BadDataException exception)
36           {
37              System.out.println("Bad data: " + exception.getMessage());
38           }
39           catch (IOException exception)
40           {
41              exception.printStackTrace();
42           }
43        }
44     }
45  }
```

The catch clauses in the main method give a human-readable error report if the file was not found or bad data was encountered.

The following readFile method of the DataSetReader class constructs the Scanner object and calls the readData method. It is completely unconcerned with any exceptions. If there is a problem with the input file, it simply passes the exception to its caller.

```java
public double[] readFile(String filename) throws IOException
{
   File inFile = new File(filename);
   Scanner in = new Scanner(inFile);
   try
   {
      readData(in);
      return data;
   }
   finally
   {
      in.close();
   }
}
```

The method throws an IOException, the common superclass of FileNotFoundException (thrown by the Scanner constructor) and BadDataException (thrown by the readData method).

Next, here is the readData method of the DataSetReader class. It reads the number of values, constructs an array, and calls readValue for each data value.

```java
private void readData(Scanner in) throws BadDataException
{
   if (!in.hasNextInt())
      throw new BadDataException("Length expected");
   int numberOfValues = in.nextInt();
   data = new double[numberOfValues];

   for (int i = 0; i < numberOfValues; i++)
      readValue(in, i);

   if (in.hasNext())
      throw new BadDataException("End of file expected");
}
```

This method checks for two potential errors. The file might not start with an integer, or it might have additional data after reading all values.

However, this method makes no attempt to catch any exceptions. Plus, if the readValue method throws an exception—which it will if there aren't enough values in the file—the exception is simply passed on to the caller.

Here is the readValue method:

```java
private void readValue(Scanner in, int i) throws BadDataException
{
   if (!in.hasNextDouble())
      throw new BadDataException("Data value expected");
   data[i] = in.nextDouble();
}
```

To see the exception handling at work, look at a specific error scenario.

ANIMATION
Exception Handling

1. DataAnalyzer.main calls DataSetReader.readFile.
2. readFile calls readData.
3. readData calls readValue.
4. readValue doesn't find the expected value and throws a BadDataException.
5. readValue has no handler for the exception and terminates immediately.
6. readData has no handler for the exception and terminates immediately.

7. `readFile` has no handler for the exception and terminates immediately after executing the `finally` clause and closing the `Scanner` object.

8. `DataAnalyzer.main` has a handler for a `BadDataException`. That handler prints a message to the user. Afterwards, the user is given another chance to enter a file name. Note that the statements computing the sum of the values have been skipped.

This example shows the separation between error detection (in the `DataSetReader.readValue` method) and error handling (in the `DataAnalyzer.main` method). In between the two are the `readData` and `readFile` methods, which just pass exceptions along.

ch11/data/DataSetReader.java

```java
 1  import java.io.File;
 2  import java.io.IOException;
 3  import java.util.Scanner;
 4
 5  /**
 6      Reads a data set from a file. The file must have the format
 7      numberOfValues
 8      value1
 9      value2
10      . . .
11  */
12  public class DataSetReader
13  {
14      private double[] data;
15
16      /**
17          Reads a data set.
18          @param filename the name of the file holding the data
19          @return the data in the file
20      */
21      public double[] readFile(String filename) throws IOException
22      {
23          File inFile = new File(filename);
24          Scanner in = new Scanner(inFile);
25
26          try
27          {
28              readData(in);
29              return data;
30          }
31          finally
32          {
33              in.close();
34          }
35      }
36
37      /**
38          Reads all data.
39          @param in the scanner that scans the data
40      */
41      private void readData(Scanner in) throws BadDataException
42      {
43          if (!in.hasNextInt())
44              throw new BadDataException("Length expected");
45          int numberOfValues = in.nextInt();
```

```
46        data = new double[numberOfValues];
47
48        for (int i = 0; i < numberOfValues; i++)
49            readValue(in, i);
50
51        if (in.hasNext())
52            throw new BadDataException("End of file expected");
53    }
54
55    /**
56        Reads one data value.
57        @param in the scanner that scans the data
58        @param i the position of the value to read
59    */
60    private void readValue(Scanner in, int i) throws BadDataException
61    {
62        if (!in.hasNextDouble())
63            throw new BadDataException("Data value expected");
64        data[i] = in.nextDouble();
65    }
66 }
```

ch11/data/BadDataException.java

```
1  import java.io.IOException;
2
3  /**
4      This class reports bad input data.
5  */
6  public class BadDataException extends IOException
7  {
8      public BadDataException() {}
9      public BadDataException(String message)
10     {
11         super(message);
12     }
13 }
```

SELF CHECK

16. Why doesn't the `DataSetReader.readFile` method catch any exceptions?

17. Suppose the user specifies a file that exists and is empty. Trace the flow of execution.

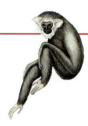

Random Fact 11.1

The Ariane Rocket Incident

The European Space Agency (ESA), Europe's counterpart to NASA, had developed a rocket model called Ariane that it had successfully used several times to launch satellites and scientific experiments into space. However, when a new version, the Ariane 5, was launched on June 4, 1996, from ESA's launch site in Kourou, French Guiana, the rocket veered off course about 40 seconds after liftoff. Flying at an angle of more than 20 degrees, rather than straight up, exerted such an aerodynamic force that the boosters separated, which triggered the automatic self-destruction mechanism. The rocket blew itself up.

The ultimate cause of this accident was an unhandled exception! The rocket contained two identical devices (called inertial reference systems) that processed flight data from

The Explosion of the Ariane Rocket

measuring devices and turned the data into information about the rocket position. The onboard computer used the position information for controlling the boosters. The same inertial reference systems and computer software had worked fine on the Ariane 4.

However, due to design changes to the rocket, one of the sensors measured a larger acceleration force than had been encountered in the Ariane 4. That value, expressed as a floating-point value, was stored in a 16-bit integer (like a short variable in Java). Unlike Java, the Ada language, used for the device software, generates an exception if a floating-point number is too large to be converted to an integer. Unfortunately, the programmers of the device had decided that this situation would never happen and didn't provide an exception handler.

When the overflow did happen, the exception was triggered and, because there was no handler, the device shut itself off. The onboard computer sensed the failure and switched over to the backup device. However, that device had shut itself off for exactly the same reason, something that the designers of the rocket had not expected. They figured that the devices might fail for mechanical reasons, and the chances of two devices having the same mechanical failure was considered remote. At that point, the rocket was without reliable position information and went off course.

Perhaps it would have been better if the software hadn't been so thorough? If it had ignored the overflow, the device wouldn't have been shut off. It would have computed bad data. But then the device would have reported wrong position data, which could have been just as fatal. Instead, a correct implementation should have caught overflow exceptions and come up with some strategy to recompute the flight data. Clearly, giving up was not a reasonable option in this context.

The advantage of the exception-handling mechanism is that it makes these issues explicit to programmers—something to think about when you curse the Java compiler for complaining about uncaught exceptions.

Summary of Learning Objectives

Read and write text that is stored in files.

- When reading text files, use the Scanner class.
- When writing text files, use the PrintWriter class.
- You must close a print stream when you are done writing output.
- The JFileChooser dialog box allows users to select a file by navigating through directories.
- A File object describes a file or directory.
- When you launch a program from the command line, you can specify arguments after the program name. The program can access these strings by processing the args parameter of the main method.

Choose an appropriate mechanism for processing input.

- The `next` method reads a word at a time. Call `Scanner.useDelimiter` to specify a pattern for word boundaries.
- The `nextLine` method reads a line of input and consumes the newline character at the end of the line.
- The `nextInt` and `nextDouble` methods consume white space and the next number.
- To read one character at a time, set the delimiter pattern to the empty string.

Understand when and how to throw an exception.

- To signal an exceptional condition, use the `throw` statement to throw an exception object.
- When you throw an exception, the current method terminates immediately.

Choose between checked and unchecked exceptions.

- There are two kinds of exceptions: *checked* and *unchecked*. Unchecked exceptions extend the class `RuntimeException` or `Error`.
- Checked exceptions are due to external circumstances that the programmer cannot prevent. The compiler checks that your program handles these exceptions.
- Add a `throws` clause to a method that can throw a checked exception.

Use exception handlers to decouple error detection and error reporting.

- In a method that is ready to handle a particular exception type, place the statements that can cause the exception inside a `try` block, and the handler inside a `catch` clause.
- Throw an exception as soon as a problem is detected. Catch it only when the problem can be handled.

Use the `finally` clause to ensure that resources are released when an exception is thrown.

- Once a `try` block is entered, the statements in a `finally` clause are guaranteed to be executed, whether or not an exception is thrown.

Design exception types to describe error conditions.

- To describe an error condition, provide a subclass of an existing exception class.

Classes, Objects, and Methods Introduced in this Chapter

```
java.io.EOFException                  java.lang.RuntimeException
java.io.File                          java.lang.Throwable
java.io.FileNotFoundException            getMessage
java.io.IOException                      printStackTrace
java.io.PrintWriter                   java.util.NoSuchElementException
   close                              java.util.Scanner
java.lang.Error                          close
java.lang.IllegalArgumentException    javax.swing.JFileChooser
java.lang.IllegalStateException          getSelectedFile
java.lang.NullPointerException           showOpenDialog
java.lang.NumberFormatException          showSaveDialog
```

Media Resources

www.wiley.com/
college/
horstmann

- • ***Worked Example*** Analyzing Baby Names
- • Lab Exercises
- ➕ ***Animation*** Exception Handling
- ➕ Practice Quiz
- ➕ Code Completion Exercises

Review Exercises

★★ **R11.1** What happens if you try to open a file for reading that doesn't exist? What happens if you try to open a file for writing that doesn't exist?

★★★ **R11.2** What happens if you try to open a file for writing, but the file or device is write-protected (sometimes called read-only)? Try it out with a short test program.

★ **R11.3** How do you open a file whose name contains a backslash, like `c:\temp\output.dat`?

★★★ **R11.4** What is a command line? How can a program read its command line arguments?

★★ **R11.5** Give two examples of programs on your computer that read arguments from the command line.

★★ **R11.6** If a program Woozle is started with the command

```
java Woozle -Dname=piglet -I\eeyore -v heff.txt a.txt lump.txt
```

what are the values of `args[0]`, `args[1]`, and so on?

★★ **R11.7** What is the difference between throwing an exception and catching an exception?

★★ **R11.8** What is a checked exception? What is an unchecked exception? Is a `NullPointer-Exception` checked or unchecked? Which exceptions do you need to declare with the `throws` reserved word?

★ **R11.9** Why don't you need to declare that your method might throw a `NullPointer-Exception`?

★★ **R11.10** When your program executes a `throw` statement, which statement is executed next?

★ **R11.11** What happens if an exception does not have a matching `catch` clause?

★ **R11.12** What can your program do with the exception object that a `catch` clause receives?

★ **R11.13** Is the type of the exception object always the same as the type declared in the `catch` clause that catches it?

★ **R11.14** What kind of values can you throw? Can you throw a string? An integer?

★★ **R11.15** What is the purpose of the `finally` clause? Give an example of how it can be used.

★★★ **R11.16** What happens when an exception is thrown, the code of a `finally` clause executes, and that code throws an exception of a different kind than the original one? Which one is caught by a surrounding `catch` clause? Write a sample program to try it out.

★★ R11.17 Which exceptions can the next and nextInt methods of the Scanner class throw? Are they checked exceptions or unchecked exceptions?

★★★ R11.18 Suppose the code in Quality Tip 11.3 on page 489 had been condensed to a single try/catch/finally statement:

```
PrintWriter out = new PrintWriter(filename);
try
{
    Write output
}
catch (IOException exception)
{
    Handle exception
}
finally
{
    out.close();
}
```

What is the disadvantage of this version? (*Hint:* What happens when the PrintWriter constructor throws an exception?) Why can't you solve the problem by moving the declaration of the out variable inside the try block?

★★ R11.19 Suppose the program in Section 11.8 reads a file containing the following values:

```
0
1
2
3
```

What is the outcome? How could the program be improved to give a more accurate error report?

★★ R11.20 Can the readFile method in Section 11.8 throw a NullPointerException? If so, how?

Programming Exercises

★★   P11.1 Write a program that asks a user for a file name and prints the number of characters, words, and lines in that file.

★★   P11.2 Write a program that asks the user for a file name and counts the number of characters, words, and lines in that file. Then the program asks for the name of the next file. When the user enters a file that doesn't exist, the program prints the total counts of characters, words, and lines in all processed files and exits.

★★   P11.3 Write a program CopyFile that copies one file to another. The file names are specified on the command line. For example,

```
java CopyFile report.txt report.sav
```

★★   P11.4 Write a program that *concatenates* the contents of several files into one file. For example,

```
java CatFiles chapter1.txt chapter2.txt chapter3.txt book.txt
```

makes a long file, book.txt, that contains the contents of the files chapter1.txt, chapter2.txt, and chapter3.txt. The output file is always the last file specified on the command line.

★★   **P11.5**   Write a program Find that searches all files specified on the command line and prints out all lines containing a reserved word. For example, if you call

```
java Find ring report.txt address.txt Homework.java
```

then the program might print

```
report.txt: has broken up an international ring of DVD bootleggers that
address.txt: Kris Kringle, North Pole
address.txt: Homer Simpson, Springfield
Homework.java: String filename;
```

The reserved word is always the first command line argument.

★★   **P11.6**   Write a program that checks the spelling of all words in a file. It should read each word of a file and check whether it is contained in a word list. A word list is available on most UNIX systems in the file /usr/dict/words. (If you don't have access to a UNIX system, your instructor should be able to get you a copy.) The program should print out all words that it cannot find in the word list.

★★   **P11.7**   Write a program that replaces each line of a file with its reverse. For example, if you run

```
java Reverse HelloPrinter.java
```

then the contents of HelloPrinter.java are changed to

```
retnirPolleH ssalc cilbup
{
)sgra ][gnirtS(niam diov citats cilbup
{
wodniw elosnoc eht ni gniteerg a yalpsiD //

;)"!dlroW ,olleH"(nltnirp.tuo.metsyS
}
}
```

Of course, if you run Reverse twice on the same file, you get back the original file.

★   **P11.8**   Get the data for names in prior decades from the Social Security Administration. Paste the table data in files named babynames80s.txt, etc. Modify the BabyNames.java program so that it prompts the user for a file name. The numbers in the files have comma separators, so modify the program to handle them. Can you spot a trend in the frequencies?

★   **P11.9**   Write a program that reads in babynames.txt and produces two files boynames.txt and girlnames.txt, separating the data for the boys and girls.

★★   **P11.10**   Write a program that reads a file in the same format as babynames.txt and prints all names that are both boy and girl names (such as Alexis or Morgan).

★★★   **P11.11**   Write a program that replaces all tab characters '\t' in a file with the *appropriate* number of spaces. By default, the distance between tab columns should be 3 (the value we use in this book for Java programs) but it can be changed by the user. Expand tabs to the number of spaces necessary to move to the next tab column. That may be *less* than three spaces. For example, consider the line containing "\t|\t||\t|". The first tab is changed to three spaces, the second to two spaces, and the third to one space. Your program should be executed as

```
    java TabExpander filename
```
or
```
    java TabExpander -t tabwidth filename
```

★ **P11.12** Modify the `BankAccount` class to throw an `IllegalArgumentException` when the account is constructed with a negative balance, when a negative amount is deposited, or when an amount that is not between 0 and the current balance is withdrawn. Write a test program that causes all three exceptions to occur and that catches them all.

★★ **P11.13** Repeat Exercise P11.12, but throw exceptions of three exception types that you provide.

★★ **P11.14** Write a program that asks the user to input a set of floating-point values. When the user enters a value that is not a number, give the user a second chance to enter the value. After two chances, quit reading input. Add all correctly specified values and print the sum when the user is done entering data. Use exception handling to detect improper inputs.

★★ **P11.15** Repeat Exercise P11.14, but give the user as many chances as necessary to enter a correct value. Quit the program only when the user enters a blank input.

★ **P11.16** Modify the `DataSetReader` class so that you do not call `hasNextInt` or `hasNextDouble`. Simply have `nextInt` and `nextDouble` throw a `NoSuchElementException` and catch it in the `main` method.

★★ **P11.17** Write a program that reads in a set of coin descriptions from a file. The input file has the format

```
    coinName1 coinValue1
    coinName2 coinValue2
    . . .
```

Add a method

```
    void read(Scanner in) throws FileNotFoundException
```

to the `Coin` class. Throw an exception if the current line is not properly formatted. Then implement a method

```
    static ArrayList<Coin> readFile(String filename)
        throws FileNotFoundException
```

In the `main` method, call `readFile`. If an exception is thrown, give the user a chance to select another file. If you read all coins successfully, print the total value.

★★★ **P11.18** Design a class `Bank` that contains a number of bank accounts. Each account has an account number and a current balance. Add an `accountNumber` field to the `BankAccount` class. Store the bank accounts in an array list. Write a `readFile` method of the `Bank` class for reading a file with the format

```
    accountNumber1  balance1
    accountNumber2  balance2
    . . .
```

Implement `read` methods for the `Bank` and `BankAccount` classes. Write a sample program to read in a file with bank accounts, then print the account with the highest balance. If the file is not properly formatted, give the user a chance to select another file.

Programming Projects

Project 11.1 You can read the contents of a web page with this sequence of commands.

```
String address = "http://java.sun.com/index.html";
URL u = new URL(address);
Scanner in = new Scanner(u.openStream());
. . .
```

Some of these methods may throw exceptions—check out the API documentation. Design a class `LinkFinder` that finds all hyperlinks of the form

```
<a href="link">link text</a>
```

Throw an exception if you find a malformed hyperlink. Extra credit if your program can follow the links that it finds and find links in those web pages as well. (This is the method that search engines such as Google use to find web sites.)

Answers to Self-Check Questions

1. When the `PrintWriter` object is created, the output file is emptied. Sadly, that is the same file as the input file. The input file is now empty and the `while` loop exits immediately.
2. The `Scanner` constructor throws a `FileNotFoundException`, and the program terminates.
3. `number` is 6, `input` is `",995.0"`
4. `price` is set to 6 because the comma is not considered a part of a floating-point number in Java. Then the call to `nextInt` causes an exception, and `quantity` is not set.
5. Read them as strings, and convert those strings to numbers that are not equal to N/A:
```
String input = in.next();
if (!input.equals("N/A"))
{
    double value = Double.parseDouble(input);
    Process value
}
```
6. Throw an exception if the amount being deposited is less than zero.
7. The balance is still zero because the last statement of the `withdraw` method was never executed.
8. You must include the `FileNotFoundException` and you may include the `NoSuchElementException` if you consider it important for documentation purposes. `InputMismatchException` is a subclass of `NoSuchElementException`. It is your choice whether to include it.
9. Because programmers should simply check for `null` pointers instead of trying to handle a `NullPointerException`.
10. The `Scanner` constructor succeeds, and `in` is constructed. Then the call `in.next()` throws a `NoSuchElementException`, and the `try` block is aborted. None of the catch clauses match, so none are executed. If none of the enclosing method calls catch the exception, the program terminates.
11. No—you catch both exception types in the same way, as you can see from the code example on page 485. Recall that `IOException` is a checked exception and `NumberFormatException` is an unchecked exception.

12. If it had been declared inside the try block, its scope would only have extended to the end of the try block, and the finally clause could not have closed it.

13. The PrintWriter constructor throws an exception. The assignment to out and the try block are skipped. The finally clause is not executed. This is the correct behavior because out has not been initialized.

14. To pass the exception message string to the RuntimeException superclass.

15. Because file corruption is beyond the control of the programmer, this should be a checked exception, so it would be wrong to extend RuntimeException or Illegal-ArgumentException. Because the error is related to input, IOException would be a good choice.

16. It would not be able to do much with them. The DataSetReader class is a reusable class that may be used for systems with different languages and different user interfaces. Thus, it cannot engage in a dialog with the program user.

17. DataAnalyzer.main calls DataSetReader.readFile, which calls readData. The call in.hasNextInt() returns false, and readData throws a BadDataException. The read-File method doesn't catch it, so it propagates back to main, where it is caught.

12

Object-Oriented Design

CHAPTER GOALS

- To learn about the software life cycle
- To learn how to discover new classes and methods
- To understand the use of CRC cards for class discovery
- To be able to identify inheritance, aggregation, and dependency relationships between classes
- To master the use of UML class diagrams to describe class relationships
- To learn how to use object-oriented design to build complex programs

To implement a software system successfully, be it as simple as your next homework project or as complex as the next air traffic monitoring system, some amount of planning, design, and testing is required. In fact, for larger projects, the amount of time spent on planning is much higher than the amount of time spent on programming and testing.

If you find that most of your homework time is spent in front of the computer, keying in code and fixing bugs, you are probably spending more time on your homework than you should. You could cut down your total time by spending more on the planning and design phase. This chapter tells you how to approach these tasks in a systematic manner, using the object-oriented design methodology.

CHAPTER CONTENTS

12.1 The Software Life Cycle

The software life cycle encompasses all activities from initial analysis until obsolescence.

In this section we will discuss the **software life cycle**: the activities that take place between the time a software program is first conceived and the time it is finally retired.

A software project usually starts because a customer has a problem and is willing to pay money to have it solved. The Department of Defense, the customer of many programming projects, was an early proponent of a *formal process* for software development. A formal process identifies and describes different phases and gives guidelines for carrying out the phases and when to move from one phase to the next.

A formal process for software development describes phases of the development process and gives guidelines for how to carry out the phases.

Many software engineers break the development process down into the following five phases:

- Analysis
- Design
- Implementation
- Testing
- Deployment

In the *analysis* phase, you decide *what* the project is supposed to accomplish; you do not think about *how* the program will accomplish its tasks. The output of the analysis phase is a *requirements document*, which describes in complete detail what the program will be able to do once it is completed. Part of this requirements document can be a user manual that tells how the user will operate the program to derive the promised benefits. Another part sets performance criteria—how many inputs the program must be able to handle in what time, or what its maximum memory and disk storage requirements are.

In the *design* phase, you develop a plan for how you will implement the system. You discover the structures that underlie the problem to be solved. When you use object-oriented design, you decide what classes you need and what their most important methods are. The output of this phase is a description of the classes and methods, with diagrams that show the relationships among the classes.

In the *implementation* phase, you write and compile program code to implement the classes and methods that were discovered in the design phase. The output of this phase is the completed program.

In the *testing* phase, you run tests to verify that the program works correctly. The output of this phase is a report describing the tests that you carried out and their results.

In the *deployment* phase, the users of the program install it and use it for its intended purpose.

When formal development processes were first established in the early 1970s, software engineers had a very simple visual model of these phases. They postulated that one phase would run to completion, its output would spill over to the next phase, and the next phase would begin. This model is called the **waterfall model** of software development (see Figure 1).

In an ideal world the waterfall model has a lot of appeal: You figure out what to do; then you figure out how to do it; then you do it; then you verify that you did it right; then you hand the product to the customer. When rigidly applied, though, the waterfall model simply did not work. It was very difficult to come up with a perfect requirement specification. It was quite common to discover in the design phase that the requirements were inconsistent or that a small change in the requirements would lead to a system that was both easier to design and more useful for the customer, but the analysis phase was over, so the designers had no choice—they had to take the existing requirements, errors and all. This problem would repeat itself during implementation. The designers may have thought they knew how to solve the problem as efficiently as possible, but when the design was actually implemented, it turned out that the resulting program was not as fast as the designers had thought. The next transition is one with which you are surely familiar. When the program was handed to the quality assurance department for testing, many bugs were found that would best be fixed by reimplementing, or maybe even redesigning, the program, but the waterfall model did not allow for this. Finally, when the customers received the finished product, they were often not at all happy with it. Even though the customers typically were very involved in the analysis phase, often they

> The waterfall model of software development describes a sequential process of analysis, design, implementation, testing, and deployment.

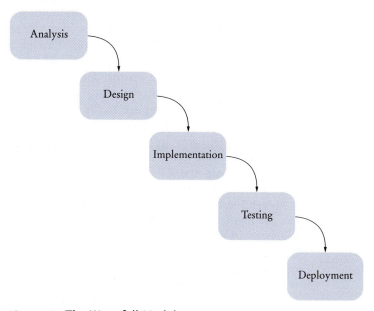

Figure 1 The Waterfall Model

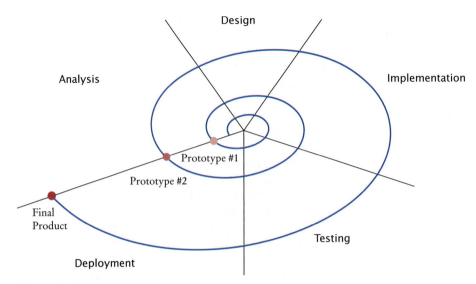

Figure 2 A Spiral Model

themselves were not sure exactly what they needed. After all, it can be very difficult to describe how you want to use a product that you have never seen before. But when the customers started using the program, they began to realize what they would have liked. Of course, then it was too late, and they had to live with what they got.

Having some level of iteration is clearly necessary. There simply must be a mechanism to deal with errors from the preceding phase. A **spiral model**, originally proposed by Barry Boehm in 1988, breaks the development process down into multiple phases (see Figure 2). Early phases focus on the construction of *prototypes*. A prototype is a small system that shows some aspects of the final system. Because prototypes model only a part of a system and do not need to withstand customer abuse, they can be implemented quickly. It is common to build a *user interface prototype* that shows the user interface in action. This gives customers an early chance to become more familiar with the system and to suggest improvements before the analysis is complete. Other prototypes can be built to validate interfaces with external systems, to test performance, and so on. Lessons learned from the development of one prototype can be applied to the next iteration of the spiral.

By building in repeated trials and feedback, a development process that follows the spiral model has a greater chance of delivering a satisfactory system. However, there is also a danger. If engineers believe that they don't have to do a good job because they can always do another iteration, then there will be many iterations, and the process will take a very long time to complete.

Figure 3 shows activity levels in the "Rational Unified Process", a development process methodology by the inventors of UML (see Grady Booch, James Rumbaugh, and Ivar Jacobson, *The Unified Modeling Language User Guide*, Addison-Wesley, 1999). The details are not important, but as you can see, this is a complex process involving multiple iterations.

Even complex development processes with many iterations have not always met with success. In 1999, Kent Beck published an influential book on **Extreme Programming**, a development methodology that strives for simplicity by cutting out

The spiral model of software development describes an iterative process in which design and implementation are repeated.

Extreme Programming is a development methodology that strives for simplicity by removing formal structure and focusing on best practices.

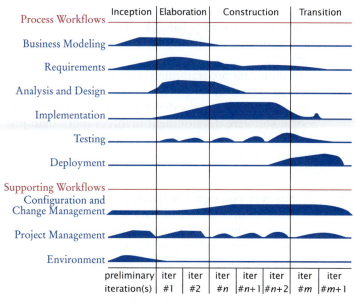

Figure 3   Activity Levels in the Rational Unified Process Methodology

most of the formal trappings of a traditional development methodology and instead focusing on a set of *practices:*

- *Realistic planning:* Customers are to make business decisions, programmers are to make technical decisions. Update the plan when it conflicts with reality.
- *Small releases:* Release a useful system quickly, then release updates on a very short cycle.
- *Metaphor:* All programmers should have a simple shared story that explains the system under development.
- *Simplicity:* Design everything to be as simple as possible instead of preparing for future complexity.
- *Testing:* Both programmers and customers are to write test cases. The system is continuously tested.
- *Refactoring:* Programmers are to restructure the system continuously to improve the code and eliminate duplication.
- *Pair programming:* Put programmers together in pairs, and require each pair to write code on a single computer.
- *Collective ownership:* All programmers have permission to change all code as it becomes necessary.
- *Continuous integration:* Whenever a task is completed, build the entire system and test it.
- *40-hour week:* Don't cover up unrealistic schedules with bursts of heroic effort.
- *On-site customer:* An actual customer of the system is to be accessible to team members at all times.
- *Coding standards:* Programmers are to follow standards that emphasize self-documenting code.

Many of these practices are common sense. Others, such as the pair programming requirement, are surprising. Beck claims that the value of the Extreme Programming approach lies in the synergy of these practices—the sum is bigger than the parts.

In your first programming course, you will not develop systems that are so complex that you need a full-fledged methodology to solve your homework problems. This introduction to the development process should, however, show you that successful software development involves more than just coding. In the remainder of this chapter we will have a closer look at the *design phase* of the software development process.

SELF CHECK

1. Suppose you sign a contract, promising that you will, for an agreed-upon price, design, implement, and test a software package exactly as it has been specified in a requirements document. What is the primary risk you and your customer are facing with this business arrangement?

2. Does Extreme Programming follow a waterfall or a spiral model?

3. What is the purpose of the "on-site customer" in Extreme Programming?

Random Fact 12.1

Programmer Productivity

If you talk to your friends in this programming class, you will find that some of them consistently complete their assignments much more quickly than others. Perhaps they have more experience. However, even when programmers with the same education and experience are compared, wide variations in competence are routinely observed and measured. It is not uncommon to have the best programmer in a team be *five to ten times* as productive as the worst, using any of a number of reasonable measures of productivity.

That is a staggering range of performance among trained professionals. In a marathon race, the best runner will not run five to ten times faster than the slowest one. Software product managers are acutely aware of these disparities. The obvious solution is, of course, to hire only the best programmers, but even in recent periods of economic slowdown the demand for good programmers has greatly outstripped the supply.

Fortunately for all of us, joining the rank of the best is not necessarily a question of raw intellectual power. Good judgment, experience, broad knowledge, attention to detail, and superior planning are at least as important as mental brilliance. These skills can be acquired by individuals who are genuinely interested in improving themselves.

Even the most gifted programmer can deal with only a finite number of details in a given time period. Suppose a programmer can implement and debug one method every two hours, or one hundred methods per month. (This is a generous estimate. Few programmers are this productive.) If a task requires 10,000 methods (which is typical for a medium-sized program), then a single programmer would need 100 months to complete the job. Such a project is sometimes expressed as a "100-man-month" project. But as Fred Brooks explains in his famous book, *The Mythical Man-Month* (Addison-Wesley, 1975), the concept of "man-month" is a myth. One cannot trade months for programmers. One hundred programmers cannot finish the task in one month. In fact, 10 programmers probably couldn't finish it in 10 months. First of all, the 10 programmers need to learn about the project before they can get productive. Whenever there is a problem with a particular method, both the author and its users need to meet and discuss it, taking time away from all of them. A bug in one method may have other programmers twiddling their thumbs until it is fixed.

It is difficult to estimate these inevitable delays. They are one reason why software is often released later than originally promised. What is a manager to do when the delays mount? As Brooks points out, adding more personnel will make a late project even later, because the productive people have to stop working and train the newcomers.

You will experience these problems when you work on your first team project with other students. Be prepared for a major drop in productivity, and be sure to set ample time aside for team communications.

There is, however, no alternative to teamwork. Most important and worthwhile projects transcend the ability of one single individual. Learning to function well in a team is just as important as becoming a competent programmer.

12.2 Discovering Classes

In the design phase of software development, your task is to discover structures that make it possible to implement a set of tasks on a computer. When you use the object-oriented design process, you carry out the following tasks:

In object-oriented design, you discover classes, determine the responsibilities of classes, and describe the relationships between classes.

1. Discover classes.
2. Determine the responsibilities of each class.
3. Describe the relationships between the classes.

A class represents some useful concept. You have seen classes for concrete entities, such as bank accounts, ellipses, and products. Other classes represent abstract concepts, such as streams and windows.

Make a list of candidates for classes, starting with nouns in the task description.

A simple rule for finding classes is to look for *nouns* in the task description. For example, suppose your job is to print an invoice such as the one in Figure 4.

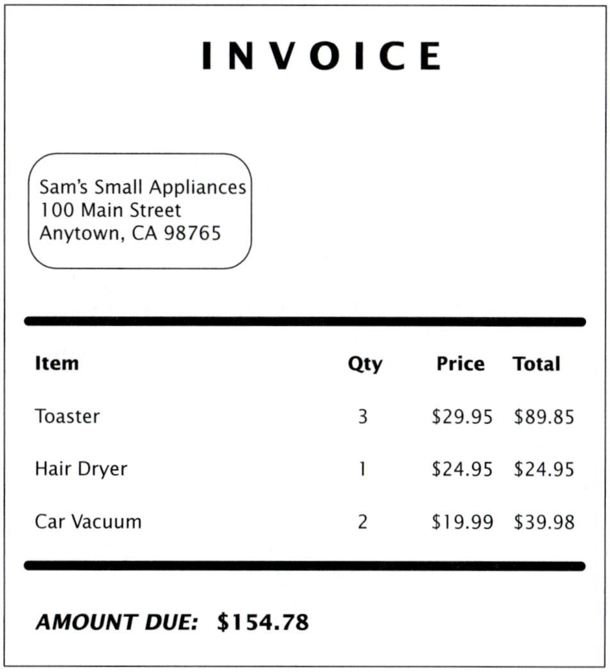

INVOICE

Sam's Small Appliances
100 Main Street
Anytown, CA 98765

Item	Qty	Price	Total
Toaster	3	$29.95	$89.85
Hair Dryer	1	$24.95	$24.95
Car Vacuum	2	$19.99	$39.98

AMOUNT DUE: $154.78

Figure 4
An Invoice

Obvious classes that come to mind are Invoice, LineItem, and Customer. It is a good idea to keep a list of *candidate classes* on a whiteboard or a sheet of paper. As you brainstorm, simply put all ideas for classes onto the list. You can always cross out the ones that weren't useful after all.

When finding classes, keep the following points in mind:

- A class represents a set of objects with the same behavior. Entities with multiple occurrences in your problem description, such as customers or products, are good candidates for objects. Find out what they have in common, and design classes to capture those commonalities.

- Some entities should be represented as objects, others as primitive types. For example, should an address be an object of an Address class, or should it simply be a string? There is no perfect answer—it depends on the task that you want to solve. If your software needs to analyze addresses (for example, to determine shipping costs), then an Address class is an appropriate design. However, if your software will never need such a capability, you should not waste time on an overly complex design. It is your job to find a balanced design; one that is not too limiting or excessively general.

- Not all classes can be discovered in the analysis phase. Most complex programs need classes for tactical purposes, such as file or database access, user interfaces, control mechanisms, and so on.

- Some of the classes that you need may already exist, either in the standard library or in a program that you developed previously. You also may be able to use inheritance to extend existing classes into classes that match your needs.

Once a set of classes has been identified, you need to define the behavior for each class. That is, you need to find out what methods each object needs to do to solve the programming problem. A simple rule for finding these methods is to look for *verbs* in the task description, then match the verbs to the appropriate objects. For example, in the invoice program, a class needs to compute the amount due. Now you need to figure out *which class* is responsible for this method. Do customers compute what they owe? Do invoices total up the amount due? Do the items total themselves up? The best choice is to make "compute amount due" the responsibility of the Invoice class.

An excellent way to carry out this task is the "**CRC card** method." *CRC* stands for "*classes*", "*responsibilities*", "*collaborators*", and in its simplest form, the method works as follows. Use an index card for each *class* (see Figure 5). As you think about verbs in the task description that indicate methods, you pick the card of the class that you think should be responsible, and write that *responsibility* on the card.

> A CRC card describes a class, its responsibilities, and its collaborating classes.

For each responsibility, you record which other classes are needed to fulfill it. Those classes are the **collaborators**.

For example, suppose you decide that an invoice should compute the amount due. Then you write "compute amount due" on the left-hand side of an index card with the title Invoice.

If a class can carry out that responsibility by itself, do nothing further. But if the class needs the help of other classes, write the names of these collaborators on the right-hand side of the card.

To compute the total, the invoice needs to ask each line item about its total price. Therefore, the LineItem class is a collaborator.

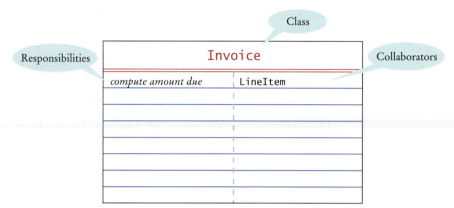

Figure 5 A CRC Card

This is a good time to look up the index card for the LineItem class. Does it have a "get total price" method? If not, add one.

How do you know that you are on the right track? For each responsibility, ask yourself how it can actually be done, using the responsibilities written on the various cards. Many people find it helpful to group the cards on a table so that the collaborators are close to each other, and to simulate tasks by moving a token (such as a coin) from one card to the next to indicate which object is currently active.

Keep in mind that the responsibilities that you list on the CRC card are on a *high level*. Sometimes a single responsibility may need two or more Java methods for carrying it out. Some researchers say that a CRC card should have no more than three distinct responsibilities.

The CRC card method is informal on purpose, so that you can be creative and discover classes and their properties. Once you find that you have settled on a good set of classes, you will want to know how they are related to each other. Can you find classes with common properties, so that some responsibilities can be taken care of by a common superclass? Can you organize classes into clusters that are independent of each other? Finding class relationships and documenting them with diagrams is the topic of the next section.

SELF CHECK

4. Suppose the invoice is to be saved to a file. Name a likely collaborator.

5. Looking at the invoice in Figure 4, what is a likely responsibility of the Customer class?

6. What do you do if a CRC card has ten responsibilities?

12.3 Relationships Between Classes

When designing a program, it is useful to document the relationships between classes. This helps you in a number of ways. For example, if you find classes with common behavior, you can save effort by placing the common behavior into a superclass. If you know that some classes are *not* related to each other, you can assign different programmers to implement each of them, without worrying that one of them has to wait for the other.

You have seen the inheritance relationship between classes many times in this book. Inheritance is a very important relationship, but, as it turns out, it is not the only useful relationship, and it can be overused.

Inheritance is a relationship between a more general class (the superclass) and a more specialized class (the subclass). This relationship is often described as the *is-a* relationship. Every truck is a vehicle. Every savings account is a bank account. Every circle is an ellipse (with equal width and height).

Inheritance is sometimes abused, however. For example, consider a Tire class that describes a car tire. Should the class Tire be a subclass of a class Circle? It sounds convenient. There are quite a few useful methods in the Circle class—for example, the Tire class may inherit methods that compute the radius, perimeter, and center point, which should come in handy when drawing tire shapes. Though it may be convenient for the programmer, this arrangement makes no sense conceptually. It isn't true that every tire is a circle. Tires are car parts, whereas circles are geometric objects. There is a relationship between tires and circles, though. A tire *has a* circle as its boundary. Java lets us model that *has-a* relationship, too. Use an instance variable:

```java
public class Tire
{
    private String rating;
    private Circle boundary;
    . . .
}
```

> Inheritance (the *is-a* relationship) is sometimes inappropriately used when the *has-a* relationship would be more appropriate.

The technical term for this relationship is **aggregation**. Each Tire aggregates a Circle object. In general, a class aggregates another class if its objects have objects of the other class.

Here is another example. Every car *is a* vehicle. Every car *has a* tire (in fact, it has typically four or, if you count the spare, five). Thus, you would use inheritance from Vehicle and use aggregation of Tire objects:

```java
public class Car extends Vehicle
{
    private Tire[] tires;
    . . .
}
```

> Aggregation (the *has-a* relationship) denotes that objects of one class contain references to objects of another class.

In this book, we use the UML notation for class diagrams. You have already seen many examples of the UML notation for inheritance—an arrow with an open triangle pointing to the superclass. In the UML notation, aggregation is denoted by a solid line with a diamond-shaped symbol next to the aggregating class. Figure 6 shows a class diagram with an inheritance and an aggregation relationship.

The aggregation relationship is related to the **dependency** relationship, which you saw in Chapter 8. Recall that a class depends on another if one of its methods *uses* an object of the other class in some way.

> Dependency is another name for the *uses* relationship.

For example, many of our applications depend on the Scanner class, because they use a Scanner object to read input.

Aggregation is a stronger form of dependency. If a class has objects of another class, it certainly uses the other class. However, the converse is not true. For example, a class may use the Scanner class without ever declaring an instance variable of class Scanner. The class may simply construct a local variable of type Scanner, or its methods may receive Scanner objects as parameters. This use is not aggregation

Figure 6
UML Notation for
Inheritance and Aggregation

because the objects of the class don't contain Scanner objects—they just create or receive them for the duration of a single method.

Generally, you need aggregation when an object needs to remember another object *between method calls*.

As you saw in Chapter 8, the UML notation for dependency is a dashed line with an open arrow that points to the dependent class.

The arrows in the UML notation can get confusing. Table 1 shows a summary of the four UML relationship symbols that we use in this book.

You need to be able to distinguish the UML notations for inheritance, interface implementation, aggregation, and dependency.

Table 1   UML Relationship Symbols

Relationship	Symbol	Line Style	Arrow Tip
Inheritance	⟶	Solid	Triangle
Interface Implementation	┈┈▷	Dotted	Triangle
Aggregation	◇───	Solid	Diamond
Dependency	┈┈┈⟩	Dotted	Open

SELF CHECK

7. Consider the Bank and BankAccount classes of Chapter 7. How are they related?

8. Consider the BankAccount and SavingsAccount objects of Chapter 10. How are they related?

9. Consider the BankAccountTester class of Chapter 3. Which classes does it depend on?

How To 12.1   **CRC Cards and UML Diagrams**

Before writing code for a complex problem, you need to design a solution. The methodology introduced in this chapter suggests that you follow a design process that is composed of the following tasks:

- Discover classes.
- Determine the responsibilities of each class.
- Describe the relationships between the classes.

CRC cards and UML diagrams help you discover and record this information.

Step 1   Discover classes.

Highlight the nouns in the problem description. Make a list of the nouns. Cross out those that don't seem to be reasonable candidates for classes.

Step 2   Discover responsibilities.

Make a list of the major tasks that your system needs to fulfill. From those tasks, pick one that is not trivial and that is intuitive to you. Find a class that is responsible for carrying out that task. Make an index card and write the name and the task on it. Now ask yourself how an object of the class can carry out the task. It probably needs help from other objects. Then make CRC cards for the classes to which those objects belong and write the responsibilities on them.

Don't be afraid to cross out, move, split, or merge responsibilities. Rip up cards if they become too messy. This is an informal process.

You are done when you have walked through all major tasks and are satisfied that they can all be solved with the classes and responsibilities that you discovered.

Step 3   Describe relationships.

Make a class diagram that shows the relationships between all the classes that you discovered.

Start with inheritance—the *is-a* relationship between classes. Is any class a specialization of another? If so, draw inheritance arrows. Keep in mind that many designs, especially for simple programs, don't use inheritance extensively.

The "collaborators" column of the CRC cards tell you which classes use others. Draw usage arrows for the collaborators on the CRC cards.

Some dependency relationships give rise to aggregations. For each of the dependency relationships, ask yourself: How does the object locate its collaborator? Does it navigate to it directly because it stores a reference? In that case, draw an aggregation arrow. Or is the collaborator a method parameter or return value? Then simply draw a dependency arrow.

Special Topic 12.1

Attributes and Methods in UML Diagrams

Sometimes it is useful to indicate class *attributes* and *methods* in a class diagram. An **attribute** is an externally observable property that objects of a class have. For example, name and price would be attributes of the Product class. Usually, attributes correspond to instance variables. But they don't have to—a class may have a different way of organizing its data. For example, a GregorianCalendar object from the Java library has attributes day, month, and year, and it would be appropriate to draw a UML diagram that shows these attributes. However, the class doesn't actually have instance variables that store these quantities. Instead, it internally represents all dates by counting the milliseconds from January 1, 1970—an implementation detail that a class user certainly doesn't need to know about.

You can indicate attributes and methods in a class diagram by dividing a class rectangle into three compartments, with the class name in the top, attributes in the middle, and methods in the bottom (see the figure below). You need not list *all* attributes and methods in a particular diagram. Just list the ones that are helpful to understand whatever point you are making with a particular diagram.

Also, don't list as an attribute what you also draw as an aggregation. If you denote by aggregation the fact that a Car has Tire objects, don't add an attribute tires.

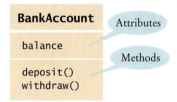

Attributes and Methods in a Class Diagram

Special Topic 12.2

Multiplicities

Some designers like to write *multiplicities* at the end(s) of an aggregation relationship to denote how many objects are aggregated. The notations for the most common multiplicities are:

- any number (zero or more): *
- one or more: 1..*
- zero or one: 0..1
- exactly one: 1

The figure below shows that a customer has one or more bank accounts.

An Aggregation Relationship with Multiplicities

Special Topic 12.3

Aggregation and Association

Some designers find the aggregation or *has-a* terminology unsatisfactory. For example, consider customers of a bank. Does the bank "have" customers? Do the customers "have" bank accounts, or does the bank "have" them? Which of these "has" relationships should be modeled by aggregation? This line of thinking can lead us to premature implementation decisions.

Early in the design phase, it makes sense to use a more general relationship between classes called **association**. A class is associated with another if you can *navigate* from objects of one class to objects of the other class. For example, given a Bank object, you can navigate to Customer objects, perhaps by accessing an instance variable, or by making a database lookup.

The UML notation for an association relationship is a solid line, with optional arrows that show in which directions you can navigate the relationship. You can also add words to the line ends to further explain the nature of the relationship. The figure below shows that you can navigate from Bank objects to Customer objects, but you cannot navigate the other way around. That is, in this particular design, the Customer class has no mechanism to determine in which banks it keeps its money.

Frankly, the differences between aggregation and association are confusing, even to experienced designers. If you find the distinction helpful, by all means use the relationship that you find most appropriate. But don't spend time pondering subtle differences between these concepts. From the practical point of view of a Java programmer, it is useful to know when objects of one class manage objects of another class. The aggregation or *has-a* relationship accurately describes this phenomenon.

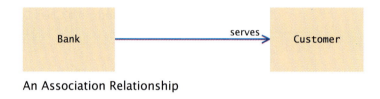

An Association Relationship

12.4 Case Study: Printing an Invoice

In this chapter, we discuss a five-part development process that is particularly well suited for beginning programmers:

1. Gather requirements.
2. Use CRC cards to find classes, responsibilities, and collaborators.
3. Use UML diagrams to record class relationships.
4. Use javadoc to document method behavior.
5. Implement your program.

There isn't a lot of notation to learn. The class diagrams are simple to draw. The deliverables of the design phase are obviously useful for the implementation phase—you simply take the source files and start adding the method code. Of course, as your projects get more complex, you will want to learn more about formal design methods. There are many techniques to describe object scenarios, call sequencing, the large-scale structure of programs, and so on, that are very beneficial even for relatively simple projects. *The Unified Modeling Language User Guide* gives a good overview of these techniques.

In this section, we will walk through the object-oriented design technique with a very simple example. In this case, the methodology may feel overblown, but it is a good introduction to the mechanics of each step. You will then be better prepared for the more complex example that follows.

12.4.1 Requirements

Start the development process by gathering and documenting program requirements.

Before you begin designing a solution, you should gather all requirements for your program in plain English. Write down what your program should do. It is helpful to include typical scenarios in addition to a general description.

The task of our sample program is to print out an invoice. An invoice describes the charges for a set of products in certain quantities. (We omit complexities such as dates, taxes, and invoice and customer numbers.) The program simply prints the billing address, all line items, and the amount due. Each line item contains the description and unit price of a product, the quantity ordered, and the total price.

```
                I N V O I C E

Sam's Small Appliances
100 Main Street
Anytown, CA 98765

Description                  Price  Qty  Total
Toaster                      29.95   3   89.85
Hair dryer                   24.95   1   24.95
Car vacuum                   19.99   2   39.98

AMOUNT DUE: $154.78
```

Also, in the interest of simplicity, we do not provide a user interface. We just supply a test program that adds line items to the invoice and then prints it.

12.4.2 CRC Cards

Use CRC cards to find classes, responsibilities, and collaborators.

When designing an object-oriented program, you need to discover classes. Classes correspond to nouns in the requirements description. In this problem, it is pretty obvious what the nouns are:

```
Invoice          Address
LineItem         Product
Description      Price
Quantity         Total
Amount due
```

(Of course, Toaster doesn't count—it is the description of a LineItem object and therefore a data value, not the name of a class.)

Description and price are attributes of the Product class. What about the quantity? The quantity is not an attribute of a Product. Just as in the printed invoice, let's have a class LineItem that records the product and the quantity (such as "3 toasters").

The total and amount due are computed—not stored anywhere. Thus, they don't lead to classes.

After this process of elimination, we are left with four candidates for classes:

```
Invoice
Address
LineItem
Product
```

Each of them represents a useful concept, so let's make them all into classes.

The purpose of the program is to print an invoice. However, the Invoice class won't necessarily know whether to display the output in System.out, in a text area, or in a file. Therefore, let's relax the task slightly and make the invoice responsible for *formatting* the invoice. The result is a string (containing multiple lines) that can be printed out or displayed. Record that responsibility on a CRC card:

Invoice	
format the invoice	

How does an invoice format itself? It must format the billing address, format all line items, and then add the amount due. How can the invoice format an address? It can't—that really is the responsibility of the Address class. This leads to a second CRC card:

Address	
format the address	

Similarly, formatting of a line item is the responsibility of the LineItem class.

The format method of the Invoice class calls the format methods of the Address and LineItem classes. Whenever a method uses another class, you list that other class as a collaborator. In other words, Address and LineItem are collaborators of Invoice:

Invoice	
format the invoice	Address
	LineItem

When formatting the invoice, the invoice also needs to compute the total amount due. To obtain that amount, it must ask each line item about the total price of the item.

How does a line item obtain that total? It must ask the product for the unit price, and then multiply it by the quantity. That is, the Product class must reveal the unit price, and it is a collaborator of the LineItem class.

Finally, the invoice must be populated with products and quantities, so that it makes sense to format the result. That too is a responsibility of the Invoice class.

We now have a set of CRC cards that completes the CRC card process.

Product	
get description	
get unit price	

LineItem	
format the item	Product
get total price	

Invoice	
format the invoice	Address
add a product and quantity	LineItem
	Product

12.4.3 UML Diagrams

Use UML diagrams to record class relationships.

After you have discovered classes and their relationships with CRC cards, you should record your findings in UML diagrams. The dependency relationships come from the collaboration column on the CRC cards. Each class depends on the classes with which it collaborates. In our example, the Invoice class collaborates with the Address, LineItem, and Product classes. The LineItem class collaborates with the Product class.

Now ask yourself which of these dependencies are actually aggregations. How does an invoice know about the address, line item, and product objects with which it collaborates? An invoice object must hold references to the address and the line items when it formats the invoice. But an invoice object need not hold a reference to a product object when adding a product. The product is turned into a line item, and then it is the item's responsibility to hold a reference to it.

Therefore, the `Invoice` class aggregates the `Address` and `LineItem` classes. The `LineItem` class aggregates the `Product` class. However, there is no *has-a* relationship between an invoice and a product. An invoice doesn't store products directly—they are stored in the `LineItem` objects.

There is no inheritance in this example.

Figure 7 shows the class relationships that we discovered.

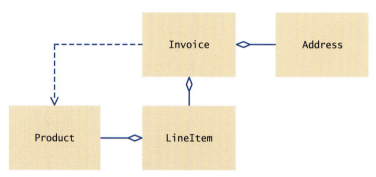

Figure 7 The Relationships Between the Invoice Classes

12.4.4 Method Documentation

The final step of the design phase is to write the documentation of the discovered classes and methods. Simply write a Java source file for each class, write the method comments for those methods that you have discovered, and leave the bodies of the methods blank.

```java
/**
    Describes an invoice for a set of purchased products.
*/
public class Invoice
{
    /**
        Adds a charge for a product to this invoice.
        @param aProduct the product that the customer ordered
        @param quantity the quantity of the product
    */
    public void add(Product aProduct, int quantity)
    {
    }

    /**
        Formats the invoice.
        @return the formatted invoice
    */
    public String format()
    {
```

```
        }
    }

    /**
        Describes a quantity of an article to purchase.
    */
    public class LineItem
    {
        /**
            Computes the total cost of this line item.
            @return the total price
        */
        public double getTotalPrice()
        {
        }

        /**
            Formats this item.
            @return a formatted string of this item
        */
        public String format()
        {
        }
    }

    /**
        Describes a product with a description and a price.
    */
    public class Product
    {
        /**
            Gets the product description.
            @return the description
        */
        public String getDescription()
        {
        }

        /**
            Gets the product price.
            @return the unit price
        */
        public double getPrice()
        {
        }
    }

    /**
        Describes a mailing address.
    */
    public class Address
    {
        /**
            Formats the address.
            @return the address as a string with three lines
        */
        public String format()
        {
        }
    }
```

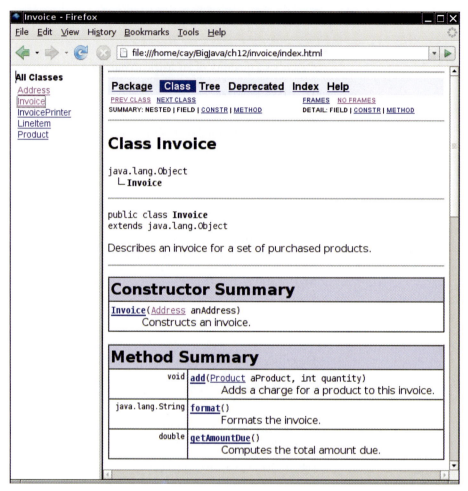

Figure 8 The Class Documentation in HTML Format

Then run the javadoc program to obtain a prettily formatted version of your documentation in HTML format (see Figure 8).

This approach for documenting your classes has a number of advantages. You can share the HTML documentation with others if you work in a team. You use a format that is immediately useful—Java source files that you can carry into the implementation phase. And, most importantly, you supply the comments of the key methods—a task that less prepared programmers leave for later, and then often neglect for lack of time.

12.4.5 Implementation

After completing the design, implement your classes.

After you have completed the object-oriented design, you are ready to implement the classes.

You already have the method parameters and comments from the previous step. Now look at the UML diagram to add instance variables. Aggregated classes yield instance variables. Start with the Invoice class. An invoice aggregates Address and

`LineItem`. Every invoice has one billing address, but it can have many line items. To store multiple `LineItem` objects, you can use an array list. Now you have the instance variables of the `Invoice` class:

```
public class Invoice
{
    private Address billingAddress;
    private ArrayList<LineItem> items;
    . . .
}
```

A line item needs to store a `Product` object and the product quantity. That leads to the following instance variables:

```
public class LineItem
{
    private int quantity;
    private Product theProduct;
    . . .
}
```

The methods themselves are now easy to implement. Here is a typical example. You already know what the `getTotalPrice` method of the `LineItem` class needs to do—get the unit price of the product and multiply it with the quantity.

```
/**
    Computes the total cost of this line item.
    @return the total price
*/
public double getTotalPrice()
{
    return theProduct.getPrice() * quantity;
}
```

We will not discuss the other methods in detail—they are equally straightforward.

Finally, you need to supply constructors, another routine task.

Here is the entire program. It is a good practice to go through it in detail and match up the classes and methods against the CRC cards and UML diagram.

ch12/invoice/InvoicePrinter.java

```
1  /**
2      This program demonstrates the invoice classes by
3      printing a sample invoice.
4  */
5  public class InvoicePrinter
6  {
7      public static void main(String[] args)
8      {
9          Address samsAddress
10             = new Address("Sam's Small Appliances",
11             "100 Main Street", "Anytown", "CA", "98765");
12
13         Invoice samsInvoice = new Invoice(samsAddress);
14         samsInvoice.add(new Product("Toaster", 29.95), 3);
15         samsInvoice.add(new Product("Hair dryer", 24.95), 1);
16         samsInvoice.add(new Product("Car vacuum", 19.99), 2);
17
18         System.out.println(samsInvoice.format());
19     }
20  }
```

ch12/invoice/Invoice.java

```java
1  import java.util.ArrayList;
2
3  /**
4     Describes an invoice for a set of purchased products.
5  */
6  public class Invoice
7  {
8     private Address billingAddress;
9     private ArrayList<LineItem> items;
10
11     /**
12        Constructs an invoice.
13        @param anAddress the billing address
14     */
15     public Invoice(Address anAddress)
16     {
17        items = new ArrayList<LineItem>();
18        billingAddress = anAddress;
19     }
20
21     /**
22        Adds a charge for a product to this invoice.
23        @param aProduct the product that the customer ordered
24        @param quantity the quantity of the product
25     */
26     public void add(Product aProduct, int quantity)
27     {
28        LineItem anItem = new LineItem(aProduct, quantity);
29        items.add(anItem);
30     }
31
32     /**
33        Formats the invoice.
34        @return the formatted invoice
35     */
36     public String format()
37     {
38        String r = "                      I N V O I C E\n\n"
39              + billingAddress.format()
40              + String.format("\n\n%-30s%8s%5s%8s\n",
41              "Description", "Price", "Qty", "Total");
42
43        for (LineItem item : items)
44        {
45           r = r + item.format() + "\n";
46        }
47
48        r = r + String.format("\nAMOUNT DUE: $%8.2f", getAmountDue());
49
50        return r;
51     }
52
```

```
53      /**
54         Computes the total amount due.
55         @return the amount due
56      */
57      public double getAmountDue()
58      {
59         double amountDue = 0;
60         for (LineItem item : items)
61         {
62            amountDue = amountDue + item.getTotalPrice();
63         }
64         return amountDue;
65      }
66   }
```

ch12/invoice/LineItem.java

```
1    /**
2       Describes a quantity of an article to purchase.
3    */
4    public class LineItem
5    {
6       private int quantity;
7       private Product theProduct;
8
9       /**
10         Constructs an item from the product and quantity.
11         @param aProduct the product
12         @param aQuantity the item quantity
13      */
14      public LineItem(Product aProduct, int aQuantity)
15      {
16         theProduct = aProduct;
17         quantity = aQuantity;
18      }
19
20      /**
21         Computes the total cost of this line item.
22         @return the total price
23      */
24      public double getTotalPrice()
25      {
26         return theProduct.getPrice() * quantity;
27      }
28
29      /**
30         Formats this item.
31         @return a formatted string of this line item
32      */
33      public String format()
34      {
35         return String.format("%-30s%8.2f%5d%8.2f",
36            theProduct.getDescription(), theProduct.getPrice(),
37            quantity, getTotalPrice());
38      }
39   }
```

ch12/invoice/Product.java

```java
1   /**
2       Describes a product with a description and a price.
3   */
4   public class Product
5   {
6      private String description;
7      private double price;
8
9      /**
10          Constructs a product from a description and a price.
11          @param aDescription the product description
12          @param aPrice the product price
13      */
14      public Product(String aDescription, double aPrice)
15      {
16         description = aDescription;
17         price = aPrice;
18      }
19
20      /**
21          Gets the product description.
22          @return the description
23      */
24      public String getDescription()
25      {
26         return description;
27      }
28
29      /**
30          Gets the product price.
31          @return the unit price
32      */
33      public double getPrice()
34      {
35         return price;
36      }
37   }
```

ch12/invoice/Address.java

```java
1   /**
2       Describes a mailing address.
3   */
4   public class Address
5   {
6      private String name;
7      private String street;
8      private String city;
9      private String state;
10     private String zip;
11
12     /**
13         Constructs a mailing address.
14         @param aName the recipient name
15         @param aStreet the street
16         @param aCity the city
```

```
17              @param aState  the two-letter state code
18              @param aZip  the ZIP postal code
19           */
20           public Address(String aName, String aStreet,
21                 String aCity, String aState, String aZip)
22           {
23              name = aName;
24              street = aStreet;
25              city = aCity;
26              state = aState;
27              zip = aZip;
28           }
29
30           /**
31              Formats the address.
32              @return  the address as a string with three lines
33           */
34           public String format()
35           {
36              return name + "\n" + street + "\n"
37                    + city + ", " + state + " " + zip;
38           }
39        }
```

S E L F   C H E C K

10. Which class is responsible for computing the amount due? What are its collaborators for this task?

11. Why do the format methods return String objects instead of directly printing to System.out?

12.5 Case Study: An Automatic Teller Machine

12.5.1 Requirements

The purpose of this project is to design a simulation of an automatic teller machine (ATM). The ATM is used by the customers of a bank. Each customer has two accounts: a checking account and a savings account. Each customer also has a customer number and a personal identification number (PIN); both are required to gain access to the accounts. (In a real ATM, the customer number would be recorded on the magnetic strip of the ATM card. In this simulation, the customer will need to type it in.) With the ATM, customers can select an account (checking or savings). The balance of the selected account is displayed. Then the customer can deposit and withdraw money. This process is repeated until the customer chooses to exit.

The details of the user interaction depend on the user interface that we choose for the simulation. We will develop two separate interfaces: a graphical interface that closely mimics an actual ATM (see Figure 9), and a text-based interface that allows you to test the ATM and bank classes without being distracted by GUI programming.

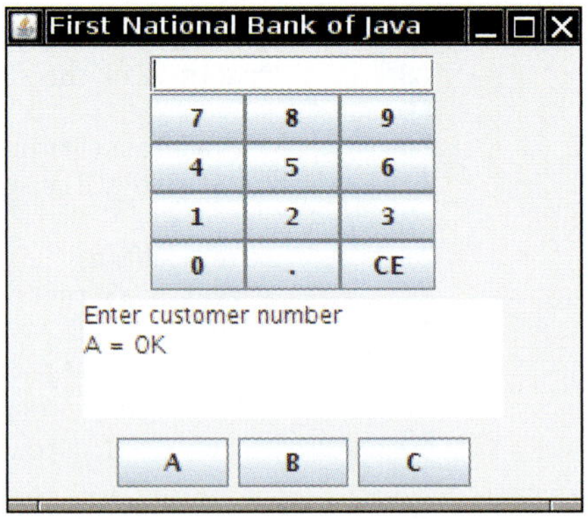

Figure 9
Graphical User Interface
for the Automatic Teller Machine

In the GUI interface, the ATM has a keypad to enter numbers, a display to show messages, and a set of buttons, labeled A, B, and C, whose function depends on the state of the machine.

Specifically, the user interaction is as follows. When the ATM starts up, it expects a user to enter a customer number. The display shows the following message:

```
Enter customer number
A = OK
```

The user enters the customer number on the keypad and presses the A button. The display message changes to

```
Enter PIN
A = OK
```

Next, the user enters the PIN and presses the A button again. If the customer number and ID match those of one of the customers in the bank, then the customer can proceed. If not, the user is again prompted to enter the customer number.

If the customer has been authorized to use the system, then the display message changes to

```
Select Account
A = Checking
B = Savings
C = Exit
```

If the user presses the C button, the ATM reverts to its original state and asks the next user to enter a customer number.

If the user presses the A or B buttons, the ATM remembers the selected account, and the display message changes to

```
Balance = balance of selected account
Enter amount and select transaction
A = Withdraw
B = Deposit
C = Cancel
```

If the user presses the A or B buttons, the value entered in the keypad is withdrawn from or deposited into the selected account. (This is just a simulation, so no money is dispensed and no deposit is accepted.) Afterwards, the ATM reverts to the preceding state, allowing the user to select another account or to exit.

If the user presses the C button, the ATM reverts to the preceding state without executing any transaction.

In the text-based interaction, we read input from `System.in` instead of the buttons. Here is a typical dialog:

```
Enter account number: 1
Enter PIN: 1234
A=Checking, B=Savings, C=Quit: A
Balance=0.0
A=Deposit, B=Withdrawal, C=Cancel: A
Amount: 1000
A=Checking, B=Savings, C=Quit: C
```

In our solution, only the user interface classes are affected by the choice of user interface. The remainder of the classes can be used for both solutions—they are decoupled from the user interface.

Because this is a simulation, the ATM does not actually communicate with a bank. It simply loads a set of customer numbers and PINs from a file. All accounts are initialized with a zero balance.

12.5.2 CRC Cards

We will again follow the recipe of Section 12.2 and show how to discover classes, responsibilities, and relationships and how to obtain a detailed design for the ATM program.

Recall that the first rule for finding classes is "Look for nouns in the problem description". Here is a list of the nouns:

```
ATM
User
Keypad
Display
Display message
Button
State
Bank account
Checking account
Savings account
Customer
Customer number
PIN
Bank
```

Of course, not all of these nouns will become names of classes, and we may yet discover the need for classes that aren't in this list, but it is a good start.

Users and customers represent the same concept in this program. Let's use a class `Customer`. A customer has two bank accounts, and we will require that a `Customer` object should be able to locate these accounts. (Another possible design would make the `Bank` class responsible for locating the accounts of a given customer—see Exercise P12.9.)

A customer also has a customer number and a PIN. We can, of course, require that a customer object give us the customer number and the PIN. But perhaps that isn't so secure. Instead, simply require that a customer object, when given a customer number and a PIN, will tell us whether it matches its own information or not.

Customer
get accounts
match number and PIN

A bank contains a collection of customers. When a user walks up to the ATM and enters a customer number and PIN, it is the job of the bank to find the matching customer. How can the bank do this? It needs to check for each customer whether its customer number and PIN match. Thus, it needs to call the *match number and PIN* method of the Customer class that we just discovered. Because the *find customer* method calls a Customer method, it collaborates with the Customer class. We record that fact in the right-hand column of the CRC card.

When the simulation starts up, the bank must also be able to read account information from a file.

Bank	
find customer	Customer
read customers	

The BankAccount class is our familiar class with methods to get the balance and to deposit and withdraw money.

In this program there is nothing that distinguishes checking accounts from savings accounts. The ATM does not add interest or deduct fees. Therefore, we decide not to implement separate subclasses for checking and savings accounts.

Finally, we are left with the ATM class itself. An important notion of the ATM is the **state**. The current machine state determines the text of the prompts and the function of the buttons. For example, when you first log in, you use the A and B buttons to select an account. Next, you use the same buttons to choose between deposit and withdrawal. The ATM must remember the current state so that it can correctly interpret the buttons.

There are four states:

1. START: Enter customer ID
2. PIN: Enter PIN
3. ACCOUNT: Select account
4. TRANSACT: Select transaction

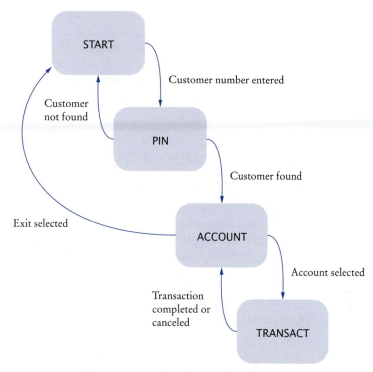

Figure 10 State Diagram for the ATM Class

To understand how to move from one state to the next, it is useful to draw a **state diagram** (Figure 10). The UML notation has standardized shapes for state diagrams. Draw states as rectangles with rounded corners. Draw state changes as arrows, with labels that indicate the reason for the change.

The user must type a valid customer number and PIN. Then the ATM can ask the bank to find the customer. This calls for a *select customer* method. It collaborates with the bank, asking the bank for the customer that matches the customer number and PIN. Next, there must be a *select account* method that asks the current customer for the checking or savings account. Finally, the ATM must carry out the selected transaction on the current account.

ATM	
manage state	Customer
select customer	Bank
select account	BankAccount
execute transaction	

Of course, discovering these classes and methods was not as neat and orderly as it appears from this discussion. When I designed these classes for this book, it took me several trials and many torn cards to come up with a satisfactory design. It is also important to remember that there is seldom one best design.

This design has several advantages. The classes describe clear concepts. The methods are sufficient to implement all necessary tasks. (I mentally walked through every ATM usage scenario to verify that.) There are not too many collaboration dependencies between the classes. Thus, I was satisfied with this design and proceeded to the next step.

12.5.3 UML Diagrams

Figure 11 shows the relationships between these classes, using the graphical user interface. (The console user interface uses a single class `ATMSimulator` instead of the `ATMFrame` and `Keypad` classes.)

To draw the dependencies, use the "collaborator" columns from the CRC cards. Looking at those columns, you find that the dependencies are as follows:

- `ATM` uses `Bank`, `Customer`, and `BankAccount`.
- `Bank` uses `Customer`.
- `Customer` uses `BankAccount`.

It is easy to see some of the aggregation relationships. A bank has customers, and each customer has two bank accounts.

Does the `ATM` class aggregate `Bank`? To answer this question, ask yourself whether an ATM object needs to store a reference to a bank object. Does it need to locate the same bank object across multiple method calls? Indeed it does. Therefore, aggregation is the appropriate relationship.

Does an ATM aggregate customers? Clearly, the ATM is not responsible for storing all of the bank's customers. That's the bank's job. But in our design, the ATM remembers the *current* customer. If a customer has logged in, subsequent commands refer to the same customer. The ATM needs to either store a reference to the customer, or ask the bank to look up the object whenever it needs the current

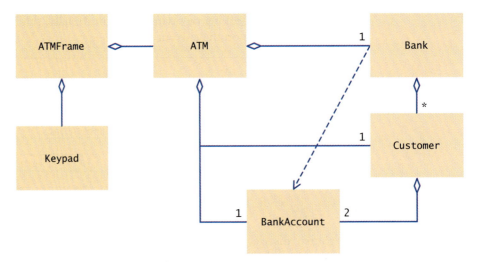

Figure 11 Relationships Between the ATM Classes

customer. It is a design decision: either store the object, or look it up when needed. We will decide to store the current customer object. That is, we will use aggregation. Note that the choice of aggregation is not an automatic consequence of the problem description—it is a design decision.

Similarly, we will decide to store the current bank account (checking or savings) that the user selects. Therefore, we have an aggregation relationship between ATM and BankAccount.

The class diagram is a good tool to visualize dependencies. Look at the GUI classes. They are completely independent from the rest of the ATM system. You can replace the GUI with a console interface, and you can take out the Keypad class and use it in another application. Also, the Bank, BankAccount, and Customer classes, although dependent on each other, don't know anything about the ATM class. That makes sense—you can have banks without ATMs. As you can see, when you analyze relationships, you look for both the absence and presence of relationships.

12.5.4 Method Documentation

Now you are ready for the final step of the design phase: documenting the classes and methods that you discovered. Here is a part of the documentation for the ATM class:

```java
/**
    An ATM that accesses a bank.
*/
public class ATM
{
    . . .
    /**
        Constructs an ATM for a given bank.
        @param aBank  the bank to which this ATM connects
    */
    public ATM(Bank aBank) { }

    /**
        Sets the current customer number
        and sets state to PIN.
        (Precondition: state is START)
        @param number  the customer number
    */
    public void setCustomerNumber(int number) { }

    /**
        Finds customer in bank.
        If found sets state to ACCOUNT, else to START.
        (Precondition: state is PIN)
        @param pin  the PIN of the current customer
    */
    public void selectCustomer(int pin) { }

    /**
        Sets current account to checking or savings. Sets
        state to TRANSACT.
        (Precondition: state is ACCOUNT or TRANSACT)
        @param account  one of CHECKING or SAVINGS
    */
    public void selectAccount(int account) { }
```

```
/**
    Withdraws amount from current account.
    (Precondition: state is TRANSACT)
    @param value the amount to withdraw
*/
    public void withdraw(double value) { }
}
```

Then run the `javadoc` utility to turn this documentation into HTML format.

For conciseness, we omit the documentation of the other classes.

12.5.5 Implementation

Finally, the time has come to implement the ATM simulator. The implementation phase is very straightforward and should take *much less time than the design phase.*

A good strategy for implementing the classes is to go "bottom-up". Start with the classes that don't depend on others, such as `Keypad` and `BankAccount`. Then implement a class such as `Customer` that depends only on the `BankAccount` class. This "bottom-up" approach allows you to test your classes individually. You will find the implementations of these classes at the end of this section.

The most complex class is the `ATM` class. In order to implement the methods, you need to declare the necessary instance variables. From the class diagram, you can tell that the ATM has a bank object. It becomes an instance variable of the class:

```
public class ATM
{
    private Bank theBank;
    . . .
}
```

From the description of the ATM states, it is clear that we require additional instance variables to store the current state, customer, and bank account.

```
public class ATM
{
    private int state;
    private Customer currentCustomer;
    private BankAccount currentAccount;
    . . .
}
```

Most methods are very straightforward to implement. Consider the `selectCustomer` method. From the design documentation, we have the description

```
/**
    Finds customer in bank.
    If found sets state to ACCOUNT, else to START.
    (Precondition: state is PIN)
    @param pin the PIN of the current customer
*/
```

This description can be almost literally translated to Java instructions:

```
public void selectCustomer(int pin)
{
    assert state == PIN;
    currentCustomer = theBank.findCustomer(customerNumber, pin);
```

```
         if (currentCustomer == null)
            state = START;
      else
            state = ACCOUNT;
   }
```

We won't go through a method-by-method description of the ATM program. You should take some time and compare the actual implementation against the CRC cards and the UML diagram.

ch12/atm/ATM.java

```java
 1  /**
 2      An ATM that accesses a bank.
 3  */
 4  public class ATM
 5  {
 6     public static final int CHECKING = 1;
 7     public static final int SAVINGS = 2;
 8
 9     private int state;
10     private int customerNumber;
11     private Customer currentCustomer;
12     private BankAccount currentAccount;
13     private Bank theBank;
14
15     public static final int START = 1;
16     public static final int PIN = 2;
17     public static final int ACCOUNT = 3;
18     public static final int TRANSACT = 4;
19
20     /**
21         Constructs an ATM for a given bank.
22         @param aBank  the bank to which this ATM connects
23     */
24     public ATM(Bank aBank)
25     {
26        theBank = aBank;
27        reset();
28     }
29
30     /**
31         Resets the ATM to the initial state.
32     */
33     public void reset()
34     {
35        customerNumber = -1;
36        currentAccount = null;
37        state = START;
38     }
39
40     /**
41         Sets the current customer number
42         and sets state to PIN.
43         (Precondition: state is START)
44         @param number  the customer number
45     */
46     public void setCustomerNumber(int number)
47     {
```

```
48        assert state == START;
49        customerNumber = number;
50        state = PIN;
51     }
52
53     /**
54        Finds customer in bank.
55        If found, sets state to ACCOUNT, else to START.
56        (Precondition: state is PIN)
57        @param pin the PIN of the current customer
58     */
59     public void selectCustomer(int pin)
60     {
61        assert state == PIN;
62        currentCustomer = theBank.findCustomer(customerNumber, pin);
63        if (currentCustomer == null)
64           state = START;
65        else
66           state = ACCOUNT;
67     }
68
69     /**
70        Sets current account to checking or savings. Sets
71        state to TRANSACT.
72        (Precondition: state is ACCOUNT or TRANSACT)
73        @param account one of CHECKING or SAVINGS
74     */
75     public void selectAccount(int account)
76     {
77        assert state == ACCOUNT || state == TRANSACT;
78        if (account == CHECKING)
79           currentAccount = currentCustomer.getCheckingAccount();
80        else
81           currentAccount = currentCustomer.getSavingsAccount();
82        state = TRANSACT;
83     }
84
85     /**
86        Withdraws amount from current account.
87        (Precondition: state is TRANSACT)
88        @param value the amount to withdraw
89     */
90     public void withdraw(double value)
91     {
92        assert state == TRANSACT;
93        currentAccount.withdraw(value);
94     }
95
96     /**
97        Deposits amount to current account.
98        (Precondition: state is TRANSACT)
99        @param value the amount to deposit
100    */
101    public void deposit(double value)
102    {
103       assert state == TRANSACT;
104       currentAccount.deposit(value);
105    }
106
```

```
107     /**
108         Gets the balance of the current account.
109         (Precondition: state is TRANSACT)
110         @return the balance
111     */
112     public double getBalance()
113     {
114         assert state == TRANSACT;
115         return currentAccount.getBalance();
116     }
117
118     /**
119         Moves back to the previous state.
120     */
121     public void back()
122     {
123         if (state == TRANSACT)
124             state = ACCOUNT;
125         else if (state == ACCOUNT)
126             state = PIN;
127         else if (state == PIN)
128             state = START;
129     }
130
131     /**
132         Gets the current state of this ATM.
133         @return the current state
134     */
135     public int getState()
136     {
137         return state;
138     }
139 }
```

ch12/atm/Bank.java

```
 1   import java.io.File;
 2   import java.io.IOException;
 3   import java.util.ArrayList;
 4   import java.util.Scanner;
 5
 6   /**
 7       A bank contains customers with bank accounts.
 8   */
 9   public class Bank
10   {
11       private ArrayList<Customer> customers;
12
13       /**
14           Constructs a bank with no customers.
15       */
16       public Bank()
17       {
18           customers = new ArrayList<Customer>();
19       }
20
```

```
21    /**
22        Reads the customer numbers and pins
23        and initializes the bank accounts.
24        @param filename the name of the customer file
25    */
26    public void readCustomers(String filename)
27            throws IOException
28    {
29        Scanner in = new Scanner(new File(filename));
30        while (in.hasNext())
31        {
32            int number = in.nextInt();
33            int pin = in.nextInt();
34            Customer c = new Customer(number, pin);
35            addCustomer(c);
36        }
37        in.close();
38    }
39
40    /**
41        Adds a customer to the bank.
42        @param c the customer to add
43    */
44    public void addCustomer(Customer c)
45    {
46        customers.add(c);
47    }
48
49    /**
50        Finds a customer in the bank.
51        @param aNumber a customer number
52        @param aPin a personal identification number
53        @return the matching customer, or null if no customer
54        matches
55    */
56    public Customer findCustomer(int aNumber, int aPin)
57    {
58        for (Customer c : customers)
59        {
60            if (c.match(aNumber, aPin))
61                return c;
62        }
63        return null;
64    }
65 }
```

ch12/atm/Customer.java

```
1   /**
2       A bank customer with a checking and a savings account.
3   */
4   public class Customer
5   {
6       private int customerNumber;
7       private int pin;
8       private BankAccount checkingAccount;
9       private BankAccount savingsAccount;
10
```

```
11      /**
12          Constructs a customer with a given number and PIN.
13          @param aNumber the customer number
14          @param aPin the personal identification number
15      */
16      public Customer(int aNumber, int aPin)
17      {
18          customerNumber = aNumber;
19          pin = aPin;
20          checkingAccount = new BankAccount();
21          savingsAccount = new BankAccount();
22      }
23
24      /**
25          Tests if this customer matches a customer number
26          and PIN.
27          @param aNumber a customer number
28          @param aPin a personal identification number
29          @return true if the customer number and PIN match
30      */
31      public boolean match(int aNumber, int aPin)
32      {
33          return customerNumber == aNumber && pin == aPin;
34      }
35
36      /**
37          Gets the checking account of this customer.
38          @return the checking account
39      */
40      public BankAccount getCheckingAccount()
41      {
42          return checkingAccount;
43      }
44
45      /**
46          Gets the savings account of this customer.
47          @return the checking account
48      */
49      public BankAccount getSavingsAccount()
50      {
51          return savingsAccount;
52      }
53 }
```

The following class implements a console user interface for the ATM.

ch12/atm/ATMSimulator.java

```
1  import java.io.IOException;
2  import java.util.Scanner;
3
4  /**
5      A text-based simulation of an automatic teller machine.
6  */
7  public class ATMSimulator
8  {
9      public static void main(String[] args)
10     {
11         ATM theATM;
```

```
12      try
13      {
14         Bank theBank = new Bank();
15         theBank.readCustomers("customers.txt");
16         theATM = new ATM(theBank);
17      }
18      catch(IOException e)
19      {
20         System.out.println("Error opening accounts file.");
21         return;
22      }
23
24      Scanner in = new Scanner(System.in);
25
26      while (true)
27      {
28         int state = theATM.getState();
29         if (state == ATM.START)
30         {
31            System.out.print("Enter customer number: ");
32            int number = in.nextInt();
33            theATM.setCustomerNumber(number);
34         }
35         else if (state == ATM.PIN)
36         {
37            System.out.print("Enter PIN: ");
38            int pin = in.nextInt();
39            theATM.selectCustomer(pin);
40         }
41         else if (state == ATM.ACCOUNT)
42         {
43            System.out.print("A=Checking, B=Savings, C=Quit: ");
44            String command = in.next();
45            if (command.equalsIgnoreCase("A"))
46               theATM.selectAccount(ATM.CHECKING);
47            else if (command.equalsIgnoreCase("B"))
48               theATM.selectAccount(ATM.SAVINGS);
49            else if (command.equalsIgnoreCase("C"))
50               theATM.reset();
51            else
52                System.out.println("Illegal input!");
53         }
54         else if (state == ATM.TRANSACT)
55         {
56            System.out.println("Balance=" + theATM.getBalance());
57            System.out.print("A=Deposit, B=Withdrawal, C=Cancel: ");
58            String command = in.next();
59            if (command.equalsIgnoreCase("A"))
60            {
61               System.out.print("Amount: ");
62               double amount = in.nextDouble();
63               theATM.deposit(amount);
64               theATM.back();
65            }
66            else if (command.equalsIgnoreCase("B"))
67            {
68               System.out.print("Amount: ");
69               double amount = in.nextDouble();
```

```
70                    theATM.withdraw(amount);
71                    theATM.back();
72                }
73                else if (command.equalsIgnoreCase("C"))
74                    theATM.back();
75                else
76                    System.out.println("Illegal input!");
77            }
78        }
79    }
80 }
```

Program Run

```
Enter account number: 1
Enter PIN: 1234
A=Checking, B=Savings, C=Quit: A
Balance=0.0
A=Deposit, B=Withdrawal, C=Cancel: A
Amount: 1000
A=Checking, B=Savings, C=Quit: C
. . .
```

Here are the user interface classes for the GUI version of the user interface.

ch12/atm/ATMViewer.java

```java
 1  import java.io.IOException;
 2  import javax.swing.JFrame;
 3  import javax.swing.JOptionPane;
 4
 5  /**
 6     A graphical simulation of an automatic teller machine.
 7  */
 8  public class ATM Viewer
 9  {
10     public static void main(String[] args)
11     {
12        ATM theATM;
13
14        try
15        {
16           Bank theBank = new Bank();
17           theBank.readCustomers("customers.txt");
18           theATM = new ATM(theBank);
19        }
20        catch(IOException e)
21        {
22           JOptionPane.showMessageDialog(null, "Error opening accounts file.");
23           return;
24        }
25
26        JFrame frame = new ATMFrame(theATM);
27        frame.setTitle("First National Bank of Java");
28        frame.setDefaultCloseOperation(JFrame.EXIT_ON_CLOSE);
29        frame.setVisible(true);
30     }
31  }
```

ch12/atm/ATMFrame.java

```java
1   import java.awt.FlowLayout;
2   import java.awt.GridLayout;
3   import java.awt.event.ActionEvent;
4   import java.awt.event.ActionListener;
5   import javax.swing.JButton;
6   import javax.swing.JFrame;
7   import javax.swing.JPanel;
8   import javax.swing.JTextArea;
9
10  /**
11     A frame displaying the components of an ATM.
12  */
13  public class ATMFrame extends JFrame
14  {
15     private static final int FRAME_WIDTH = 300;
16     private static final int FRAME_HEIGHT = 300;
17
18     private JButton aButton;
19     private JButton bButton;
20     private JButton cButton;
21
22     private KeyPad pad;
23     private JTextArea display;
24
25     private ATM theATM;
26
27     /**
28        Constructs the user interface of the ATM frame.
29     */
30     public ATMFrame(ATM anATM)
31     {
32        theATM = anATM;
33
34        // Construct components
35        pad = new KeyPad();
36
37        display = new JTextArea(4, 20);
38
39        aButton = new JButton("  A  ");
40        aButton.addActionListener(new AButtonListener());
41
42        bButton = new JButton("  B  ");
43        bButton.addActionListener(new BButtonListener());
44
45        cButton = new JButton("  C  ");
46        cButton.addActionListener(new CButtonListener());
47
48        // Add components
49
50        JPanel buttonPanel = new JPanel();
51        buttonPanel.add(aButton);
52        buttonPanel.add(bButton);
53        buttonPanel.add(cButton);
54
55        setLayout(new FlowLayout());
56        add(pad);
57        add(display);
```

```
58        add(buttonPanel);
59        showState();
60
61        setSize(FRAME_WIDTH, FRAME_HEIGHT);
62     }
63
64     /**
65        Updates display message.
66     */
67     public void showState()
68     {
69        int state = theATM.getState();
70        pad.clear();
71        if (state == ATM.START)
72           display.setText("Enter customer number\nA = OK");
73        else if (state == ATM.PIN)
74           display.setText("Enter PIN\nA = OK");
75        else if (state == ATM.ACCOUNT)
76           display.setText("Select Account\n"
77                 + "A = Checking\nB = Savings\nC = Exit");
78        else if (state == ATM.TRANSACT)
79           display.setText("Balance = "
80                 + theATM.getBalance()
81                 + "\nEnter amount and select transaction\n"
82                 + "A = Withdraw\nB = Deposit\nC = Cancel");
83     }
84
85     class AButtonListener implements ActionListener
86     {
87        public void actionPerformed(ActionEvent event)
88        {
89           int state = theATM.getState();
90           if (state == ATM.START)
91              theATM.setCustomerNumber((int) pad.getValue());
92           else if (state == ATM.PIN)
93              theATM.selectCustomer((int) pad.getValue());
94           else if (state == ATM.ACCOUNT)
95              theATM.selectAccount(ATM.CHECKING);
96           else if (state == ATM.TRANSACT)
97           {
98              theATM.withdraw(pad.getValue());
99              theATM.back();
100          }
101          showState();
102       }
103    }
104
105    class BButtonListener implements ActionListener
106    {
107       public void actionPerformed(ActionEvent event)
108       {
109          int state = theATM.getState();
110          if (state == ATM.ACCOUNT)
111             theATM.selectAccount(ATM.SAVINGS);
112          else if (state == ATM.TRANSACT)
113          {
114             theATM.deposit(pad.getValue());
115             theATM.back();
```

```
116            }
117            showState();
118        }
119    }
120
121    class CButtonListener implements ActionListener
122    {
123        public void actionPerformed(ActionEvent event)
124        {
125            int state = theATM.getState();
126            if (state == ATM.ACCOUNT)
127                theATM.reset();
128            else if (state == ATM.TRANSACT)
129                theATM.back();
130            showState();
131        }
132    }
133 }
```

This class uses layout managers to arrange the text field and the keypad buttons. See Chapter 18 for more information about layout managers.

ch12/atm/KeyPad.java

```
 1  import java.awt.BorderLayout;
 2  import java.awt.GridLayout;
 3  import java.awt.event.ActionEvent;
 4  import java.awt.event.ActionListener;
 5  import javax.swing.JButton;
 6  import javax.swing.JPanel;
 7  import javax.swing.JTextField;
 8
 9  /**
10      A component that lets the user enter a number, using
11      a keypad labeled with digits.
12  */
13  public class KeyPad extends JPanel
14  {
15      private JPanel buttonPanel;
16      private JButton clearButton;
17      private JTextField display;
18
19      /**
20          Constructs the keypad panel.
21      */
22      public KeyPad()
23      {
24          setLayout(new BorderLayout());
25
26          // Add display field
27
28          display = new JTextField();
29          add(display, "North");
30
31          // Make button panel
32
33          buttonPanel = new JPanel();
34          buttonPanel.setLayout(new GridLayout(4, 3));
```

```
35
36        // Add digit buttons
37
38        addButton("7");
39        addButton("8");
40        addButton("9");
41        addButton("4");
42        addButton("5");
43        addButton("6");
44        addButton("1");
45        addButton("2");
46        addButton("3");
47        addButton("0");
48        addButton(".");
49
50        // Add clear entry button
51
52        clearButton = new JButton("CE");
53        buttonPanel.add(clearButton);
54
55        class ClearButtonListener implements ActionListener
56        {
57           public void actionPerformed(ActionEvent event)
58           {
59              display.setText("");
60           }
61        }
62        ActionListener listener = new ClearButtonListener();
63
64        clearButton.addActionListener(new
65              ClearButtonListener());
66
67        add(buttonPanel, "Center");
68     }
69
70     /**
71        Adds a button to the button panel.
72        @param label the button label
73     */
74     private void addButton(final String label)
75     {
76        class DigitButtonListener implements ActionListener
77        {
78           public void actionPerformed(ActionEvent event)
79           {
80
81              // Don't add two decimal points
82              if (label.equals(".")
83                    && display.getText().indexOf(".") != -1)
84                 return;
85
86              // Append label text to button
87              display.setText(display.getText() + label);
88           }
89        }
90
91        JButton button = new JButton(label);
92        buttonPanel.add(button);
```

```
 93          ActionListener listener = new DigitButtonListener();
 94          button.addActionListener(listener);
 95       }
 96
 97       /**
 98          Gets the value that the user entered.
 99          @return the value in the text field of the keypad
100       */
101       public double getValue()
102       {
103          return Double.parseDouble(display.getText());
104       }
105
106       /**
107          Clears the display.
108       */
109       public void clear()
110       {
111          display.setText("");
112       }
113    }
```

In this chapter, you learned a systematic approach for building a relatively complex program. However, object-oriented design is definitely not a spectator sport. To really learn how to design and implement programs, you have to gain experience by repeating this process with your own projects. It is quite possible that you don't immediately home in on a good solution and that you need to go back and reorganize your classes and responsibilities. That is normal and only to be expected. The purpose of the object-oriented design process is to spot these problems in the design phase, when they are still easy to rectify, instead of in the implementation phase, when massive reorganization is more difficult and time consuming.

SELF CHECK

12. Why does the Bank class in this example not store an array list of bank accounts?
13. Suppose the requirements change—you need to save the current account balances to a file after every transaction and reload them when the program starts. What is the impact of this change on the design?

Random Fact 12.2

Software Development—Art or Science?

There has been a long discussion whether the discipline of computing is a science or not. We call the field "computer science", but that doesn't mean much. Calling a discipline a science doesn't automatically make it so. A scientific discipline operates on the *scientific method:* by posing hypotheses and testing them with experiments that are repeatable by other workers in the field. For example, a physicist may have a theory on the makeup of nuclear particles and attempt to confirm or refute that theory by running experiments in a particle collider. If an experiment cannot be confirmed, such as the "cold fusion" research in the early 1990s, then the theory dies a quick death.

Some software developers indeed run experiments. They try out various methods of computing certain results or of configuring computer systems, and measure the differences in performance.

Some computer scientists discover fundamental principles. One class of fundamental results, for instance, states that it is impossible to write certain kinds of computer programs, no matter how powerful the computing equipment is. For example, it is impossible to write a program that takes as its input any two Java program files and as its output prints whether or not these two programs always compute the same results. Such a program would be very handy for grading student homework, but nobody, no matter how clever, will ever be able to write one that works for all input files. However, the majority of computer scientists are not researching the limits of computation.

Some people view software development as an *art* or *craft*. A programmer who writes elegant code that is easy to understand and runs with optimum efficiency can indeed be considered a good craftsman. Calling it an art is perhaps far-fetched, because an art object requires an audience to appreciate it, whereas the program code is generally hidden from the program user.

Others call software development an *engineering discipline*. Just as mechanical engineering is based on the fundamental mathematical principles of statics, computing has certain mathematical foundations. There is more to mechanical engineering than mathematics, such as knowledge of materials and of project planning. The same is true for computing. A *software engineer* needs to know about planning, budgeting, design, test automation, documentation, and source code control, in addition to computer science subjects, such as programming, algorithm design, and database technologies.

In one somewhat worrisome aspect, software development does not have the same standing as other engineering disciplines. There is little agreement as to what constitutes professional conduct in the computer field. Unlike the scientist, whose main responsibility is the search for truth, the software developer must strive to satisfy the conflicting demands of quality, safety, and economy. Engineering disciplines have professional organizations that hold their members to standards of conduct. The computer field is so new that in many cases we simply don't know the correct method for achieving certain tasks. That makes it difficult to set professional standards.

What do you think? Based on your experience, do you consider software development an art, a craft, a science, or an engineering activity?

Summary of Learning Objectives

Describe the software life cycle alternatives for the software development process.

- The software life cycle encompasses all activities from initial analysis until obsolescence.
- A formal process for software development describes phases of the development process and gives guidelines for how to carry out the phases.
- The waterfall model of software development describes a sequential process of analysis, design, implementation, testing, and deployment.
- The spiral model of software development describes an iterative process in which design and implementation are repeated.
- Extreme Programming is a development methodology that strives for simplicity by removing formal structure and focusing on best practices.

Recognize how to discover classes and their responsibilities.

- In object-oriented design, you discover classes, determine the responsibilities of classes, and describe the relationships between classes.
- Make a list of candidates for classes, starting with nouns in the task description.
- A CRC card describes a class, its responsibilities, and its collaborating classes.

Categorize relationships between classes and produce UML diagrams that describe them.

- Inheritance (the *is-a* relationship) is sometimes inappropriately used when the *has-a* relationship would be more appropriate.
- Aggregation (the *has-a* relationship) denotes that objects of one class contain references to objects of another class.
- Dependency is another name for the *uses* relationship.
- You need to be able to distinguish the UML notations for inheritance, interface implementation, aggregation, and dependency.

Apply an object-oriented development process to designing a program.

- Start the development process by gathering and documenting program requirements.
- Use CRC cards to find classes, responsibilities, and collaborators.
- Use UML diagrams to record class relationships.
- Use javadoc comments (with the method bodies left blank) to record the behavior of classes.
- After completing the design, implement your classes.

Media Resources

www.wiley.com/
college/
horstmann

- Lab Exercises
- ➕ Practice Quiz
- ➕ Code Completion Exercises

Review Exercises

★ **R12.1** What is the software life cycle?

★★ **R12.2** List the steps in the process of object-oriented design that this chapter recommends for student use.

★ **R12.3** Give a rule of thumb for how to find classes when designing a program.

★ **R12.4** Give a rule of thumb for how to find methods when designing a program.

★★ **R12.5** After discovering a method, why is it important to identify the object that is *responsible* for carrying out the action?

★ **R12.6** What relationship is appropriate between the following classes: aggregation, inheritance, or neither?

    a. University–Student

    b. Student–TeachingAssistant

    c. Student–Freshman

    d. Student–Professor

    e. Car–Door

    f. Truck–Vehicle

    g. Traffic–TrafficSign

    h. TrafficSign–Color

★★ **R12.7** Every BMW is a vehicle. Should a class BMW inherit from the class Vehicle? BMW is a vehicle manufacturer. Does that mean that the class BMW should inherit from the class VehicleManufacturer?

★★ **R12.8** Some books on object-oriented programming recommend using inheritance so that the class Circle extends the class Point. Then the Circle class inherits the setLocation method from the Point superclass. Explain why the setLocation method need not be overridden in the subclass. Why is it nevertheless not a good idea to have Circle inherit from Point? Conversely, would inheriting Point from Circle fulfill the *is-a* rule? Would it be a good idea?

★ **R12.9** Write CRC cards for the Coin and CashRegister classes described in Section 8.2.

★ **R12.10** Write CRC cards for the Bank and BankAccount classes in Section 7.2.

★★ **R12.11** Draw a UML diagram for the Coin and CashRegister classes described in Section 8.2.

★★★ **R12.12** A file contains a set of records describing countries. Each record consists of the name of the country, its population, and its area. Suppose your task is to write a program that reads in such a file and prints

    • The country with the largest area

    • The country with the largest population

    • The country with the largest population density (people per square kilometer)

Think through the problems that you need to solve. What classes and methods will you need? Produce a set of CRC cards, a UML diagram, and a set of javadoc comments.

★★★ **R12.13** Discover classes and methods for generating a student report card that lists all classes, grades, and the grade point average for a semester. Produce a set of CRC cards, a UML diagram, and a set of javadoc comments.

★★★ **R12.14** Consider a quiz grading system that grades student responses to quizzes. A quiz consists of questions. There are different types of questions, including essay questions and multiple-choice questions. Students turn in submissions for quizzes, and the grading system grades them. Draw a UML diagram for classes Quiz, Question, EssayQuestion, MultipleChoiceQuestion, Student, and Submission.

Programming Exercises

★★ **P12.1** Enhance the invoice-printing program by providing for two kinds of line items: One kind describes products that are purchased in certain numerical quantities (such as "3 toasters"), another describes a fixed charge (such as "shipping: $5.00"). *Hint:* Use inheritance. Produce a UML diagram of your modified implementation.

★★ **P12.2** The invoice-printing program is somewhat unrealistic because the formatting of the LineItem objects won't lead to good visual results when the prices and quantities have varying numbers of digits. Enhance the format method in two ways: Accept an int[] array of column widths as a parameter. Use the NumberFormat class to format the currency values.

★★ **P12.3** The invoice-printing program has an unfortunate flaw—it mixes "application logic", the computation of total charges, and "presentation", the visual appearance of the invoice. To appreciate this flaw, imagine the changes that would be necessary to draw the invoice in HTML for presentation on the Web. Reimplement the program, using a separate InvoiceFormatter class to format the invoice. That is, the Invoice and LineItem methods are no longer responsible for formatting. However, they will acquire other responsibilities, because the InvoiceFormatter class needs to query them for the values that it requires.

★★★ **P12.4** Write a program that teaches arithmetic to a young child. The program tests addition and subtraction. In level 1 it tests only addition of numbers less than 10 whose sum is less than 10. In level 2 it tests addition of arbitrary one-digit numbers. In level 3 it tests subtraction of one-digit numbers with a nonnegative difference. Generate random problems and get the player input. The player gets up to two tries per problem. Advance from one level to the next when the player has achieved a score of five points.

★★★ **P12.5** Design a simple e-mail messaging system. A message has a recipient, a sender, and a message text. A mailbox can store messages. Supply a number of mailboxes for different users and a user interface for users to log in, send messages to other users, read their own messages, and log out. Follow the design process that was described in this chapter.

★★ **P12.6** Write a program that simulates a vending machine. Products can be purchased by inserting coins with a value at least equal to the cost of the product. A user selects a product from a list of available products, adds coins, and either gets the product or gets the coins returned if insufficient money was supplied or if the product is sold out. The machine does not give change if too much money was added. Products can be restocked and money removed by an operator. Follow the design process that was described in this chapter. Your solution should include a class VendingMachine that is not coupled with the Scanner or PrintStream classes.

★★★ **P12.7** Write a program to design an appointment calendar. An appointment includes the date, starting time, ending time, and a description; for example,

```
Dentist 2007/10/1 17:30 18:30
CS1 class 2007/10/2 08:30 10:00
```

Supply a user interface to add appointments, remove canceled appointments, and print out a list of appointments for a particular day. Follow the design process that was described in this chapter. Your solution should include a class Appointment-Calendar that is not coupled with the Scanner or PrintStream classes.

★★★ **P12.8** *Airline seating.* Write a program that assigns seats on an airplane. Assume the airplane has 20 seats in first class (5 rows of 4 seats each, separated by an aisle) and 90 seats in economy class (15 rows of 6 seats each, separated by an aisle). Your program should take three commands: add passengers, show seating, and quit. When passengers are added, ask for the class (first or economy), the number of passengers traveling together (1 or 2 in first class; 1 to 3 in economy), and the seating preference (aisle or window in first class; aisle, center, or window in economy). Then try to find a match and assign the seats. If no match exists, print a message. Your solution should include a class Airplane that is not coupled with the Scanner or PrintStream classes. Follow the design process that was described in this chapter.

★★ **P12.9** Modify the implementations of the classes in the ATM example so that the bank manages a collection of bank accounts and a separate collection of customers. Allow joint accounts in which some accounts can have more than one customer.

★★★ **P12.10** Write a program that administers and grades quizzes. A quiz consists of questions. There are four types of questions: text questions, number questions, choice questions with a single answer, and choice questions with multiple answers. When grading a text question, ignore leading or trailing spaces and letter case. When grading a numeric question, accept a response that is approximately the same as the answer.

A quiz is specified in a text file. Each question starts with a letter indicating the question type (T, N, S, M), followed by a line containing the question text. The next line of a non-choice question contains the answer. Choice questions have a list of choices that is terminated by a blank line. Each choice starts with + (correct) or - (incorrect). Here is a sample file:

```
T
Which Java reserved word is used to declare a subclass?
extends
S
What is the original name of the Java language?
- *7
- C--
+ Oak
- Gosling

M
Which of the following types are supertypes of Rectangle?
- PrintStream
+ Shape
+ RectangularShape
+ Object
- String

N
What is the square root of 2?
1.41421356
```

Your program should read in a quiz file, prompt the user for responses to all questions, and grade the responses. Follow the design process that was described in this chapter.

★★★G **P12.11** Implement a program to teach a young child to read the clock. In the game, present an analog clock, such as the one in Figure 12. Generate random times and display the clock. Accept guesses from the player. Reward the player for correct guesses. After two incorrect guesses, display the correct answer and make a new random time. Implement several levels of play. In level 1, only show full hours. In level 2, show quarter hours. In level 3, show five-minute multiples, and in level 4, show any number of minutes. After a player has achieved five correct guesses at one level, advance to the next level.

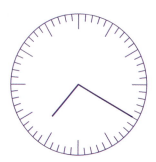

Figure 12   An Analog Clock

★★★G **P12.12** Write a program that can be used to design a suburban scene, with houses, streets, and cars. Users can add houses and cars of various colors to a street. Write more specific requirements that include a detailed description of the user interface. Then, discover classes and methods, provide UML diagrams, and implement your program.

★★★G **P12.13** Write a simple graphics editor that allows users to add a mixture of shapes (ellipses, rectangles, and lines in different colors) to a panel. Supply commands to load and save the picture. Discover classes, supply a UML diagram, and implement your program.

Programming Projects

Project 12.1 Produce a requirements document for a program that allows a company to send out personalized mailings, either by e-mail or through the postal service. Template files contain the message text, together with variable fields (such as Dear [Title] [Last Name] . . .). A database (stored as a text file) contains the field values for each recipient. Use HTML as the output file format. Then design and implement the program.

Project 12.2 Write a tic-tac-toe game that allows a human player to play against the computer. Your program will play many turns against a human opponent, and it will learn. When it is the computer's turn, the computer randomly selects an empty field, except that it won't ever choose a losing combination. For that purpose, your program must keep an array of losing combinations. Whenever the human wins, the immediately preceding combination is stored as losing. For example, suppose that X = computer and 0 = human. Suppose the current combination is

```
 O | X | X
---+---+---
   | O |
---+---+---
   |   |
```

Now it is the human's turn, who will of course choose

```
 O | X | X
---+---+---
   | O |
---+---+---
   |   | O
```

The computer should then remember the preceding combination

```
 O | X | X
---+---+---
   | O |
---+---+---
   |   |
```

as a losing combination. As a result, the computer will never again choose that combination from

```
 O | X |
---+---+---
   | O |
---+---+---
   |   |
```

or

```
 O |   | X
---+---+---
   | O |
---+---+---
   |   |
```

Discover classes and supply a UML diagram before you begin to program.

Answers to Self-Check Questions

1. It is unlikely that the customer did a perfect job with the requirements document. If you don't accommodate changes, your customer may not like the outcome. If you charge for the changes, your customer may not like the cost.

2. An "extreme" spiral model, with lots of iterations.

3. To give frequent feedback as to whether the current iteration of the product fits customer needs.

4. `PrintStream`

5. To produce the shipping address of the customer.

6. Reword the responsibilities so that they are at a higher level, or come up with more classes to handle the responsibilities.

7. Through aggregation. The bank manages bank account objects.

8. Through inheritance.

9. The `BankAccount`, `System`, and `PrintStream` classes.

10. The `Invoice` class is responsible for computing the amount due. It collaborates with the `LineItem` class.

11. This design decision reduces coupling. It enables us to reuse the classes when we want to show the invoice in a dialog box or on a web page.

12. The bank needs to store the list of customers so that customers can log in. We need to locate all bank accounts of a customer, and we chose to simply store them in the customer class. In this program, there is no further need to access bank accounts.

13. The `Bank` class needs to have an additional responsibility: to load and save the accounts. The bank can carry out this responsibility because it has access to the customer objects and, through them, to the bank accounts.

Recursion

CHAPTER GOALS

- To learn about the technique of recursion
- To understand the relationship between recursion and iteration
- To analyze problems that are much easier to solve by recursion than by iteration
- To learn to "think recursively"
- To be able to use recursive helper methods
- To understand when the use of recursion affects the efficiency of an algorithm

Recursion is a powerful technique for reducing complex computational problems to simpler ones. The term "recursion" refers to the fact that the same computation recurs, or occurs repeatedly, as the problem is solved. Recursion is often the most natural way of thinking about a problem, and there are some computations that are very difficult to perform without recursion. This chapter shows you simple and complex examples of recursion and teaches you how to "think recursively".

CHAPTER CONTENTS

13.1 Triangle Numbers

We begin this chapter with a very simple example that demonstrates the power of thinking recursively. In this example, we will look at triangle shapes such as this one:

```
[]
[][]
[][][]
```

We'd like to compute the area of a triangle of width n, assuming that each [] square has area 1. This value is sometimes called the nth *triangle number*. For example, as you can tell from looking at the triangle above, the third triangle number is 6.

You may know that there is a very simple formula to compute these numbers, but you should pretend for now that you don't know about it. The ultimate purpose of this section is not to compute triangle numbers, but to learn about the concept of **recursion** by working through a simple example.

Here is the outline of the class that we will develop:

```java
public class Triangle
{
    private int width;

    public Triangle(int aWidth)
    {
        width = aWidth;
    }

    public int getArea()
    {
        . . .
    }
}
```

If the width of the triangle is 1, then the triangle consists of a single square, and its area is 1. Let's take care of this case first.

```java
public int getArea()
{
    if (width == 1) { return 1; }
    . . .
}
```

To deal with the general case, consider this picture.

```
[]
[][]
[][][]
[][][][]
```

Suppose we knew the area of the smaller, colored triangle. Then we could easily compute the area of the larger triangle as

```
smallerArea + width
```

How can we get the smaller area? Let's make a smaller triangle and ask it!

```
Triangle smallerTriangle = new Triangle(width - 1);
int smallerArea = smallerTriangle.getArea();
```

Now we can complete the getArea method:

```
public int getArea()
{
    if (width == 1) { return 1; }
    Triangle smallerTriangle = new Triangle(width - 1);
    int smallerArea = smallerTriangle.getArea();
    return smallerArea + width;
}
```

Here is an illustration of what happens when we compute the area of a triangle of width 4.

- The getArea method makes a smaller triangle of width 3.
- It calls getArea on that triangle.
    - That method makes a smaller triangle of width 2.
    - It calls getArea on that triangle.
        - That method makes a smaller triangle of width 1.
        - It calls getArea on that triangle.
            - That method returns 1.
        - The method returns smallerArea + width = 1 + 2 = 3.
    - The method returns smallerArea + width = 3 + 3 = 6.
- The method returns smallerArea + width = 6 + 4 = 10.

This solution has one remarkable aspect. To solve the area problem for a triangle of a given width, we use the fact that we can solve the same problem for a lesser width. This is called a *recursive* solution.

The call pattern of a **recursive method** looks complicated, and the key to the successful design of a recursive method is *not to think about it.* Instead, look at the getArea method one more time and notice how utterly reasonable it is. If the width is 1, then, of course, the area is 1. The next part is just as reasonable. Compute the area of the smaller triangle *and don't think about why that works*. Then the area of the larger triangle is clearly the sum of the smaller area and the width.

There are two key requirements to make sure that the recursion is successful:

- Every recursive call must simplify the computation in some way.
- There must be special cases to handle the simplest computations directly.

For a recursion to terminate, there must be special cases for the simplest values.

The getArea method calls itself again with smaller and smaller width values. Eventually the width must reach 1, and there is a special case for computing the area of a triangle with width 1. Thus, the getArea method always succeeds.

Actually, you have to be careful. What happens when you call the area of a triangle with width –1? It computes the area of a triangle with width –2, which computes the area of a triangle with width –3, and so on. To avoid this, the getArea method should return 0 if the width is ≤ 0.

Recursion is not really necessary to compute the triangle numbers. The area of a triangle equals the sum

```
1 + 2 + 3 + . . . + width
```

Of course, we can program a simple loop:

```
double area = 0;
for (int i = 1; i <= width; i++)
{
    area = area + i;
}
```

Many simple recursions can be computed as loops. However, loop equivalents for more complex recursions—such as the one in our next example—can be complex.

Actually, in this case, you don't even need a loop to compute the answer. The sum of the first n integers can be computed as

$$1 + 2 + \cdots + n = n \times (n + 1)/2$$

Thus, the area equals

```
width * (width + 1) / 2
```

Therefore, neither recursion nor a loop is required to solve this problem. The recursive solution is intended as a "warm-up" to introduce you to the concept of recursion.

+ ANIMATION
Tracing a Recursion

ch13/triangle/Triangle.java

```
1  /**
2      A triangular shape composed of stacked unit squares like this:
3      []
4      [][]
5      [][][]
6      . . .
7  */
8  public class Triangle
9  {
10     private int width;
11
12     /**
13         Constructs a triangular shape.
14         @param aWidth the width (and height) of the triangle
15     */
16     public Triangle(int aWidth)
17     {
18         width = aWidth;
19     }
20
```

```
21      /**
22          Computes the area of the triangle.
23          @return the area
24      */
25      public int getArea()
26      {
27          if (width <= 0) { return 0; }
28          if (width == 1) { return 1; }
29          Triangle smallerTriangle = new Triangle(width - 1);
30          int smallerArea = smallerTriangle.getArea();
31          return smallerArea + width;
32      }
33  }
```

ch13/triangle/TriangleTester.java

```
1   public class TriangleTester
2   {
3       public static void main(String[] args)
4       {
5           Triangle t = new Triangle(10);
6           int area = t.getArea();
7           System.out.println("Area: " + area);
8           System.out.println("Expected: 55");
9       }
10  }
```

Program Run

```
Enter width: 10
Area: 55
Expected: 55
```

SELF CHECK

1. Why is the statement if (width == 1) { return 1; } in the getArea method unnecessary?
2. How would you modify the program to recursively compute the area of a square?

Common Error 13.1

Infinite Recursion

A common programming error is an infinite recursion: a method calling itself over and over with no end in sight. The computer needs some amount of memory for bookkeeping for each call. After some number of calls, all memory that is available for this purpose is exhausted. Your program shuts down and reports a "stack overflow".

Infinite recursion happens either because the parameter values don't get simpler or because a special terminating case is missing. For example, suppose the getArea method was allowed to compute the area of a triangle with width 0. If it weren't for the special test, the method would construct triangles with width –1, –2, –3, and so on.

Common Error 13.2

Tracing Through Recursive Methods

Debugging a recursive method can be somewhat challenging. When you set a **breakpoint** in a recursive method, the program stops as soon as that program line is encountered in *any call to the recursive method.* Suppose you want to debug the recursive getArea method of the Triangle class. Debug the TriangleTester program and run until the beginning of the getArea method. Inspect the width instance variable. It is 10.

Remove the breakpoint and now run until the statement return smallerArea + width; (see Figure 1). When you inspect width again, its value is 2! That makes no sense. There was no instruction that changed the value of width. Is that a bug with the debugger?

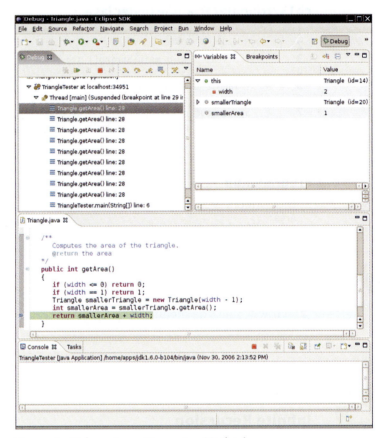

Figure 1 Debugging a Recursive Method

No. The program stopped in the first recursive call to getArea that reached the return statement. If you are confused, look at the **call stack** (top left in the figure). You will see that nine calls to getArea are pending.

You can debug recursive methods with the debugger. You just need to be particularly careful, and watch the call stack to understand which nested call you currently are in.

How To 13.1

Thinking Recursively

To solve a problem recursively requires a different mindset than to solve it by programming a loop. In fact, it helps if you pretend to be a bit lazy, asking others to do most of the work for you. If you need to solve a complex problem, pretend that "someone else" will do most of the heavy lifting and solve the problem for simpler inputs. Then you only need to figure out how you can turn the solutions with simpler inputs into a solution for the whole problem.

To illustrate the technique of recursion, let us consider the following problem. We want to test whether a sentence is a *palindrome*—a string that is equal to itself when you reverse all characters. Typical examples of palindromes are

- A man, a plan, a canal—Panama!

- Go hang a salami, I'm a lasagna hog

and, of course, the oldest palindrome of all:

- Madam, I'm Adam

When testing for a palindrome, we match upper- and lowercase letters, and ignore all spaces and punctuation marks.

We want to implement the isPalindrome method in the following class:

```java
public class Sentence
{
    private String text;

    /**
        Constructs a sentence.
        @param aText a string containing all characters of the sentence
    */
    public Sentence(String aText)
    {
        text = aText;
    }

    /**
        Tests whether this sentence is a palindrome.
        @return true if this sentence is a palindrome, false otherwise
    */
    public boolean isPalindrome()
    {
        . . .
    }
}
```

Step 1   Consider various ways to simplify inputs.

In your mind, fix a particular input or set of inputs for the problem that you want to solve.

Think how you can simplify the inputs in such a way that the same problem can be applied to the simpler input.

When you consider simpler inputs, you may want to remove just a little bit from the original input—maybe remove one or two characters from a string, or remove a small portion of a geometric shape. But sometimes it is more useful to cut the input in half and then see what it means to solve the problem for both halves.

In the palindrome test problem, the input is the string that we need to test. How can you simplify the input? Here are several possibilities:

- Remove the first character.

- Remove the last character.

- Remove both the first and last characters.

- Remove a character from the middle.
- Cut the string into two halves.

These simpler inputs are all potential inputs for the palindrome test.

Step 2 Combine solutions with simpler inputs into a solution of the original problem.

In your mind, consider the solutions of your problem for the simpler inputs that you discovered in Step 1. Don't worry *how* those solutions are obtained. Simply have faith that the solutions are readily available. Just say to yourself: These are simpler inputs, so someone else will solve the problem for me.

Now think how you can turn the solution for the simpler inputs into a solution for the input that you are currently thinking about. Maybe you need to add a small quantity, related to the quantity that you lopped off to arrive at the simpler input. Maybe you cut the original input in half and have solutions for each half. Then you may need to add both solutions to arrive at a solution for the whole.

Consider the methods for simplifying the inputs for the palindrome test. Cutting the string in half doesn't seem a good idea. If you cut

```
"Madam, I'm Adam"
```

in half, you get two strings:

```
"Madam, I"
```
and
```
"'m Adam"
```

Neither of them is a palindrome. Cutting the input in half and testing whether the halves are palindromes seems a dead end.

The most promising simplification is to remove the first *and* last characters. Removing the M at the front and the m at the back yields

```
"adam, I'm Ada"
```

Suppose you can verify that the shorter string is a palindrome. Then *of course* the original string is a palindrome—we put the same letter in the front and the back. That's extremely promising. A word is a palindrome if

- The first and last letters match (ignoring letter case)

and

- The word obtained by removing the first and last letters is a palindrome.

Again, don't worry how the test works for the shorter string. It just works.

There is one other case to consider. What if the first or last letter of the word is not a letter? For example, the string

```
"A man, a plan, a canal, Panama!"
```

ends in a ! character, which does not match the A in the front. But we should ignore nonletters when testing for palindromes. Thus, when the last character is not a letter but the first character is a letter, it doesn't make sense to remove both the first and the last characters. That's not a problem. Remove only the last character. If the shorter string is a palindrome, then it stays a palindrome when you attach a nonletter.

The same argument applies if the first character is not a letter. Now we have a complete set of cases.

- If the first and last characters are both letters, then check whether they match. If so, remove both and test the shorter string.
- Otherwise, if the last character isn't a letter, remove it and test the shorter string.
- Otherwise, the first character isn't a letter. Remove it and test the shorter string.

In all three cases, you can use the solution to the simpler problem to arrive at a solution to your problem.

Step 3   Find solutions to the simplest inputs.

A recursive computation keeps simplifying its inputs. Eventually it arrives at very simple inputs. To make sure that the recursion comes to a stop, you must deal with the simplest inputs separately. Come up with special solutions for them, which is usually very easy.

However, sometimes you get into philosophical questions dealing with *degenerate* inputs: empty strings, shapes with no area, and so on. Then you may want to investigate a slightly larger input that gets reduced to such a trivial input and see what value you should attach to the degenerate inputs so that the simpler value, when used according to the rules you discovered in Step 2, yields the correct answer.

Let's look at the simplest strings for the palindrome test:

- Strings with two characters
- Strings with a single character
- The empty string

We don't have to come up with a special solution for strings with two characters. Step 2 still applies to those strings—either or both of the characters are removed. But we do need to worry about strings of length 0 and 1. In those cases, Step 2 can't apply. There aren't two characters to remove.

The empty string is a palindrome—it's the same string when you read it backwards. If you find that too artificial, consider a string "mm". According to the rule discovered in Step 2, this string is a palindrome if the first and last characters of that string match and the remainder—that is, the empty string—is also a palindrome. Therefore, it makes sense to consider the empty string a palindrome.

A string with a single letter, such as "I", is a palindrome. How about the case in which the character is not a letter, such as "!"? Removing the ! yields the empty string, which is a palindrome. Thus, we conclude that all strings of length 0 or 1 are palindromes.

Step 4   Implement the solution by combining the simple cases and the reduction step.

Now you are ready to implement the solution. Make separate cases for the simple inputs that you considered in Step 3. If the input isn't one of the simplest cases, then implement the logic you discovered in Step 2.

Here is the isPalindrome method.

```java
public boolean isPalindrome()
{
   int length = text.length();

   // Separate case for shortest strings.
   if (length <= 1) { return true; }

   // Get first and last characters, converted to lowercase.
   char first = Character.toLowerCase(text.charAt(0));
   char last = Character.toLowerCase(text.charAt(length - 1));

   if (Character.isLetter(first) && Character.isLetter(last))
   {
      // Both are letters.
      if (first == last)
      {
         // Remove both first and last character.
         Sentence shorter = new Sentence(text.substring(1, length - 1));
         return shorter.isPalindrome();
      }
      else
      {
         return false;
```

```
            }
        }
        else if (!Character.isLetter(last))
        {
            // Remove last character.
            Sentence shorter = new Sentence(text.substring(0, length - 1));
            return shorter.isPalindrome();
        }
        else
        {
            // Remove first character.
            Sentence shorter = new Sentence(text.substring(1));
            return shorter.isPalindrome();
        }
    }
}
```

⊕ **Worked Example 13.1**

Finding Files

In this Worked Example, we find all files with a given extension in a directory tree.

13.2 Recursive Helper Methods

Sometimes it is easier to find a recursive solution if you make a slight change to the original problem.

Sometimes it is easier to find a recursive solution if you change the original problem slightly. Then the original problem can be solved by calling a recursive helper method.

Here is a typical example. Consider the palindrome test of How To 13.1. It is a bit inefficient to construct new Sentence objects in every step. Now consider the following change in the problem. Rather than testing whether the entire sentence is a palindrome, let's check whether a substring is a palindrome:

```
/**
    Tests whether a substring of the sentence is a palindrome.
    @param start the index of the first character of the substring
    @param end the index of the last character of the substring
    @return true if the substring is a palindrome
*/
public boolean isPalindrome(int start, int end)
```

This method turns out to be even easier to implement than the original test. In the recursive calls, simply adjust the start and end parameters to skip over matching letter pairs and characters that are not letters. There is no need to construct new Sentence objects to represent the shorter strings.

```
public boolean isPalindrome(int start, int end)
{
    // Separate case for substrings of length 0 and 1.
    if (start >= end) { return true; }
```

```
      // Get first and last characters, converted to lowercase.
      char first = Character.toLowerCase(text.charAt(start));
      char last = Character.toLowerCase(text.charAt(end));

      if (Character.isLetter(first) && Character.isLetter(last))
      {
         if (first == last)
         {
            // Test substring that doesn't contain the matching letters.
            return isPalindrome(start + 1, end - 1);
         }
         else
         {
            return false;
         }
      }
      else if (!Character.isLetter(last))
      {
         // Test substring that doesn't contain the last character.
         return isPalindrome(start, end - 1);
      }
      else
      {
         // Test substring that doesn't contain the first character.
         return isPalindrome(start + 1, end);
      }
   }
```

You should still supply a method to solve the whole problem—the user of your method shouldn't have to know about the trick with the substring positions. Simply call the helper method with positions that test the entire string:

```
   public boolean isPalindrome()
   {
      return isPalindrome(0, text.length() - 1);
   }
```

Note that this call is *not* a recursive method. The isPalindrome() method calls the helper method isPalindrome(int, int). In this example, we use overloading to declare two methods with the same name. The isPalindrome method without parameters is the method that we expect the public to use. The second method, with two int parameters, is the recursive helper method. If you prefer, you can avoid overloaded methods by choosing a different name for the helper method, such as substringIs-Palindrome.

Use the technique of recursive helper methods whenever it is easier to solve a recursive problem that is equivalent to the original problem—but more amenable to a recursive solution.

S E L F   C H E C K

3. Do we have to give the same name to both isPalindrome methods?

4. When does the recursive isPalindrome method stop calling itself?

13.3 The Efficiency of Recursion

As you have seen in this chapter, recursion can be a powerful tool to implement complex algorithms. On the other hand, recursion can lead to algorithms that perform poorly. In this section, we will analyze the question of when recursion is beneficial and when it is inefficient.

Consider the Fibonacci sequence: a sequence of numbers defined by the equation

$$f_1 = 1$$
$$f_2 = 1$$
$$f_n = f_{n-1} + f_{n-2}$$

That is, each value of the sequence is the sum of the two preceding values. The first ten terms of the sequence are

$$1, 1, 2, 3, 5, 8, 13, 21, 34, 55$$

It is easy to extend this sequence indefinitely. Just keep appending the sum of the last two values of the sequence. For example, the next entry is $34 + 55 = 89$.

We would like to write a function that computes f_n for any value of n. Let us translate the definition directly into a recursive method:

ch13/fib/RecursiveFib.java

```java
1  import java.util.Scanner;
2
3  /**
4     This program computes Fibonacci numbers using a recursive method.
5  */
6  public class RecursiveFib
7  {
8     public static void main(String[] args)
9     {
10        Scanner in = new Scanner(System.in);
11        System.out.print("Enter n: ");
12        int n = in.nextInt();
13
14        for (int i = 1; i <= n; i++)
15        {
16           long f = fib(i);
17           System.out.println("fib(" + i + ") = " + f);
18        }
19     }
20
21     /**
22        Computes a Fibonacci number.
23        @param n an integer
24        @return the nth Fibonacci number
25     */
26     public static long fib(int n)
27     {
28        if (n <= 2) { return 1; }
29        else return fib(n - 1) + fib(n - 2);
30     }
31  }
```

Program Run

```
Enter n: 50
fib(1) = 1
fib(2) = 1
fib(3) = 2
fib(4) = 3
fib(5) = 5
fib(6) = 8
fib(7) = 13
. . .
fib(50) = 12586269025
```

That is certainly simple, and the method will work correctly. But watch the output closely as you run the test program. The first few calls to the fib method are fast. For larger values, though, the program pauses an amazingly long time between outputs.

That makes no sense. Armed with pencil, paper, and a pocket calculator you could calculate these numbers pretty quickly, so it shouldn't take the computer anywhere near that long.

To find out the problem, let us insert **trace messages** into the method:

ch13/fib/RecursiveFibTracer.java

```java
1   import java.util.Scanner;
2
3   /**
4      This program prints trace messages that show how often the
5      recursive method for computing Fibonacci numbers calls itself.
6   */
7   public class RecursiveFibTracer
8   {
9      public static void main(String[] args)
10     {
11        Scanner in = new Scanner(System.in);
12        System.out.print("Enter n: ");
13        int n = in.nextInt();
14
15        long f = fib(n);
16
17        System.out.println("fib(" + n + ") = " + f);
18     }
19
20     /**
21        Computes a Fibonacci number.
22        @param n an integer
23        @return the nth Fibonacci number
24     */
25     public static long fib(int n)
26     {
27        System.out.println("Entering fib: n = " + n);
28        long f;
29        if (n <= 2) { f = 1; }
30        else { f = fib(n - 1) + fib(n - 2); }
31        System.out.println("Exiting fib: n = " + n
32              + " return value = " + f);
33        return f;
34     }
35  }
```

Program Run

```
Enter n: 6
Entering fib: n = 6
Entering fib: n = 5
Entering fib: n = 4
Entering fib: n = 3
Entering fib: n = 2
Exiting fib: n = 2 return value = 1
Entering fib: n = 1
Exiting fib: n = 1 return value = 1
Exiting fib: n = 3 return value = 2
Entering fib: n = 2
Exiting fib: n = 2 return value = 1
Exiting fib: n = 4 return value = 3
Entering fib: n = 3
Entering fib: n = 2
Exiting fib: n = 2 return value = 1
Entering fib: n = 1
Exiting fib: n = 1 return value = 1
Exiting fib: n = 3 return value = 2
Exiting fib: n = 5 return value = 5
Entering fib: n = 4
Entering fib: n = 3
Entering fib: n = 2
Exiting fib: n = 2 return value = 1
Entering fib: n = 1
Exiting fib: n = 1 return value = 1
Exiting fib: n = 3 return value = 2
Entering fib: n = 2
Exiting fib: n = 2 return value = 1
Exiting fib: n = 4 return value = 3
Exiting fib: n = 6 return value = 8
fib(6) = 8
```

Figure 2 shows the call tree for computing fib(6). Now it is becoming apparent why the method takes so long. It is computing the same values over and over. For example, the computation of fib(6) calls fib(4) twice and fib(3) three times. That is very different from the computation we would do with pencil and paper. There we would just write down the values as they were computed and add up the last two to

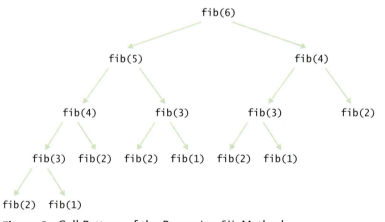

Figure 2 Call Pattern of the Recursive fib Method

get the next one until we reached the desired entry; no sequence value would ever be computed twice.

If we imitate the pencil-and-paper process, then we get the following program.

ch13/fib/LoopFib.java

```
1   import java.util.Scanner;
2
3   /**
4      This program computes Fibonacci numbers using an iterative method.
5   */
6   public class LoopFib
7   {
8      public static void main(String[] args)
9      {
10        Scanner in = new Scanner(System.in);
11        System.out.print("Enter n: ");
12        int n = in.nextInt();
13
14        for (int i = 1; i <= n; i++)
15        {
16           long f = fib(i);
17           System.out.println("fib(" + i + ") = " + f);
18        }
19     }
20
21     /**
22        Computes a Fibonacci number.
23        @param n an integer
24        @return the nth Fibonacci number
25     */
26     public static long fib(int n)
27     {
28        if (n <= 2) { return 1; }
29        long olderValue = 1;
30        long oldValue = 1;
31        long newValue = 1;
32        for (int i = 3; i <= n; i++)
33        {
34           newValue = oldValue + olderValue;
35           olderValue = oldValue;
36           oldValue = newValue;
37        }
38        return newValue;
39     }
40  }
```

Program Run

```
Enter n: 50
fib(1) = 1
fib(2) = 1
fib(3) = 2
fib(4) = 3
fib(5) = 5
fib(6) = 8
fib(7) = 13

. . .

fib(50) = 12586269025
```

This method runs *much* faster than the recursive version.

In this example of the fib method, the recursive solution was easy to program because it exactly followed the mathematical definition, but it ran far more slowly than the iterative solution, because it computed many intermediate results multiple times.

Can you always speed up a recursive solution by changing it into a loop? Frequently, the iterative and recursive solution have essentially the same performance. For example, here is an iterative solution for the palindrome test.

```java
public boolean isPalindrome()
{
    int start = 0;
    int end = text.length() - 1;
    while (start < end)
    {
        char first = Character.toLowerCase(text.charAt(start));
        char last = Character.toLowerCase(text.charAt(end);

        if (Character.isLetter(first) && Character.isLetter(last))
        {
            // Both are letters.
            if (first == last)
            {
                start++;
                end--;
            }
            else
            {
                return false;
            }
        }
        if (!Character.isLetter(last)) { end--; }
        if (!Character.isLetter(first)) { start++; }
    }
    return true;
}
```

This solution keeps two index variables: start and end. The first index starts at the beginning of the string and is advanced whenever a letter has been matched or a nonletter has been ignored. The second index starts at the end of the string and moves toward the beginning. When the two index variables meet, the iteration stops.

Both the iteration and the recursion run at about the same speed. If a palindrome has n characters, the iteration executes the loop between $n/2$ and n times, depending on how many of the characters are letters, since one or both index variables are moved in each step. Similarly, the recursive solution calls itself between $n/2$ and n times, because one or two characters are removed in each step.

In such a situation, the iterative solution tends to be a bit faster, because each recursive method call takes a certain amount of processor time. In principle, it is possible for a smart compiler to avoid recursive method calls if they follow simple patterns, but most compilers don't do that. From that point of view, an iterative solution is preferable.

However, many problems have recursive solutions that are easier to understand and implement correctly than their iterative counterparts. Sometimes there is no obvious iterative solution at all—see the example in the next section. There is a certain elegance and economy of thought to recursive solutions that makes them more appealing. As the computer scientist (and creator of the GhostScript interpreter for the PostScript graphics description language) L. Peter Deutsch put it: "To iterate is human, to recurse divine."

SELF CHECK

5. Is it faster to compute the triangle numbers recursively, as shown in Section 13.1, or is it faster to use a loop that computes `1 + 2 + 3 + . . . + width`?

6. You can compute the factorial function either with a loop, using the definition that $n! = 1 \times 2 \times \ldots \times n$, or recursively, using the definition that $0! = 1$ and $n! = (n - 1)! \times n$. Is the recursive approach inefficient in this case?

13.4 Permutations

> The permutations of a string can be obtained more naturally through recursion than with a loop.

In this section, we will study a more complex example of recursion that would be difficult to program with a simple loop. (As Exercise P13.11 shows, it is possible to avoid the recursion, but the resulting solution is quite complex, and no faster).

We will design a class that lists all permutations of a string. A permutation is simply a rearrangement of the letters in the string. For example, the string "eat" has six permutations (including the original string itself):

```
"eat"
"eta"
"aet"
"ate"
"tea"
"tae"
```

As in the preceding section, we will declare a class that is in charge of computing the answer. In this case, the answer is not a single number but a collection of permuted strings. Here is our generator class:

```
public class PermutationGenerator
{
    public PermutationGenerator(String aWord) { . . . }
    ArrayList<String> getPermutations() { . . . }
}
```

And here is the program that prints out all permutations of the string "eat":

ch13/permute/PermutationGeneratorDemo.java

```
1   import java.util.ArrayList;
2
3   /**
4       This program demonstrates the permutation generator.
5   */
6   public class PermutationGeneratorDemo
7   {
8       public static void main(String[] args)
9       {
10          PermutationGenerator generator = new PermutationGenerator("eat");
11          ArrayList<String> permutations = generator.getPermutations();
12          for (String s : permutations)
13          {
```

```
14              System.out.println(s);
15          }
16      }
17  }
```

Program Run

```
eat
eta
aet
ate
tea
tae
```

Now we need a way to generate the permutations recursively. Consider the string "eat". Let's simplify the problem. First, we'll generate all permutations that start with the letter 'e', then those that start with 'a', and finally those that start with 't'. How do we generate the permutations that start with 'e'? We need to know the permutations of the substring "at". But that's the same problem—to generate all permutations—with a simpler input, namely the shorter string "at". Thus, we can use recursion. Generate the permutations of the substring "at". They are

```
"at"
"ta"
```

For each permutation of that substring, prepend the letter 'e' to get the permutations of "eat" that start with 'e', namely

```
"eat"
"eta"
```

Now let's turn our attention to the permutations of "eat" that start with 'a'. We need to produce the permutations of the remaining letters, "et". They are:

```
"et"
"te"
```

We add the letter 'a' to the front of the strings and obtain

```
"aet"
"ate"
```

We generate the permutations that start with 't' in the same way.

That's the idea. The implementation is fairly straightforward. In the getPermutations method, we loop through all positions in the word to be permuted. For each of them, we compute the shorter word that is obtained by removing the ith letter:

```
String shorterWord = word.substring(0, i) + word.substring(i + 1);
```

We construct a permutation generator to get the permutations of the shorter word, and ask it to give us all permutations of the shorter word.

```
PermutationGenerator shorterPermutationGenerator
      = new PermutationGenerator(shorterWord);
ArrayList<String> shorterWordPermutations
      = shorterPermutationGenerator.getPermutations();
```

Finally, we add the removed letter to the front of all permutations of the shorter word.

```
for (String s : shorterWordPermutations)
{
```

```
        permutations.add(word.charAt(i) + s);
    }
```

As always, we have to provide a special case for the simplest strings. The simplest possible string is the empty string, which has a single permutation—itself.

Here is the complete PermutationGenerator class.

ch13/permute/PermutationGenerator.java

```java
 1  import java.util.ArrayList;
 2
 3  /**
 4     This class generates permutations of a word.
 5  */
 6  public class PermutationGenerator
 7  {
 8     private String word;
 9
10     /**
11        Constructs a permutation generator.
12        @param aWord the word to permute
13     */
14     public PermutationGenerator(String aWord)
15     {
16        word = aWord;
17     }
18
19     /**
20        Gets all permutations of a given word.
21     */
22     public ArrayList<String> getPermutations()
23     {
24        ArrayList<String> permutations = new ArrayList<String>();
25
26        // The empty string has a single permutation: itself
27        if (word.length() == 0)
28        {
29           permutations.add(word);
30           return permutations;
31        }
32
33        // Loop through all character positions
34        for (int i = 0; i < word.length(); i++)
35        {
36           // Form a simpler word by removing the ith character
37           String shorterWord = word.substring(0, i)
38              + word.substring(i + 1);
39
40           // Generate all permutations of the simpler word
41           PermutationGenerator shorterPermutationGenerator
42              = new PermutationGenerator(shorterWord);
43           ArrayList<String> shorterWordPermutations
44              = shorterPermutationGenerator.getPermutations();
45
46           // Add the removed character to the front of
47           // each permutation of the simpler word
48           for (String s : shorterWordPermutations)
49           {
50              permutations.add(word.charAt(i) + s);
```

```
51          }
52      }
53      // Return all permutations
54      return permutations;
55      }
56  }
```

Compare the PermutationGenerator and Triangle classes. Both of them work on the same principle. When they work on a more complex input, they first solve the problem for a simpler input. Then they combine the result for the simpler input with additional work to deliver the results for the more complex input. There really is no particular complexity behind that process as long as you think about the solution on that level only. However, behind the scenes, the simpler input creates even simpler input, which creates yet another simplification, and so on, until one input is so simple that the result can be obtained without further help. It is interesting to think about this process, but it can also be confusing. What's important is that you can focus on the one level that matters—putting a solution together from the slightly simpler problem, ignoring the fact that the simpler problem also uses recursion to get its results.

SELF CHECK

7. What are all permutations of the four-letter word beat?

8. Our recursion for the permutation generator stops at the empty string. What simple modification would make the recursion stop at strings of length 0 or 1?

9. Why isn't it easy to develop an iterative solution for the permutation generator?

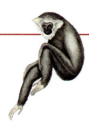

Random Fact 13.1

The Limits of Computation

Have you ever wondered how your instructor or grader makes sure your programming homework is correct? In all likelihood, they look at your solution and perhaps run it with some test inputs. But usually they have a correct solution available. That suggests that there might be an easier way. Perhaps they could feed your program and their correct program into a "program comparator", a computer program that analyzes both programs and determines whether they both compute the same results. Of course, your solution and the program that is known to be correct need not be identical—what matters is that they produce the same output when given the same input.

How could such a program comparator work? Well, the Java compiler knows how to read a program and make sense of the classes, methods, and statements. So it seems plausible that someone could, with some effort, write a program that reads two Java programs, analyzes what they do, and determines whether they solve the same task. Of course, such a program would be very attractive to instructors, because it could automate the grading process. Thus, even though no such program exists today, it might be tempting to try to develop one and sell it to universities around the world.

However, before you start raising venture capital for such an effort, you should know that theoretical computer scientists have proven that it is impossible to develop such a program, *no matter how hard you try.*

There are quite a few of these unsolvable problems. The first one, called the *halting problem,* was discovered by the British researcher Alan Turing in 1936. Because his research occurred before the first actual computer was constructed, Turing had to devise a theoretical device, the *Turing machine,* to explain how computers could work. The Turing machine con-

Alan Turing

sists of a long magnetic tape, a read/write head, and a program that has numbered instructions of the form: "If the current symbol under the head is *x*, then replace it with *y*, move the head one unit left or right, and continue with instruction *n*" (see figure below). Interestingly enough, with only these instructions, you can program just as much as with Java, even though it is incredibly tedious to do so. Theoretical computer scientists like Turing machines because they can be described using nothing more than the laws of mathematics.

Expressed in terms of Java, the halting problem states: "It is impossible to write a program with two inputs, namely the source code of an arbitrary Java program P and a string I, and that decides whether the program *P*, when executed with the input *I*, will halt—that is, the program will not get into an infinite loop with the given input". Of course, for some

Program

Instruction number	If tape symbol is	Replace with	Then move head	Then go to instruction
1	0	2	right	2
1	1	1	left	4
2	0	0	right	2
2	1	1	right	2
2	2	0	left	3
3	0	0	left	3
3	1	1	left	3
3	2	2	right	1
4	1	1	right	5
4	2	0	left	4

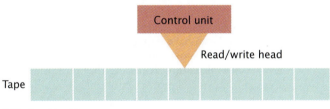

A Turing Machine

kinds of programs and inputs, it is possible to decide whether the program halts with the given input. The halting problem asserts that it is impossible to come up with a single decision-making algorithm that works with all programs and inputs. Note that you can't simply run the program *P* on the input *I* to settle this question. If the program runs for 1,000 days, you don't know that the program is in an infinite loop. Maybe you just have to wait another day for it to stop.

Such a "halt checker", if it could be written, might also be useful for grading homework. An instructor could use it to screen student submissions to see if they get into an infinite loop with a particular input, and then stop checking them. However, as Turing demonstrated, such a program cannot be written. His argument is ingenious and quite simple.

Suppose a "halt checker" program existed. Let's call it *H*. From *H*, we will develop another program, the "killer" program *K*. *K* does the following computation. Its input is a string containing the source code for a program *R*. It then applies the halt checker on the input program *R* and the input string *R*. That is, it checks whether the program *R* halts if its input is its own source code. It sounds bizarre to feed a program to itself, but it isn't impossible. For example, the Java compiler is written in Java, and you can use it to compile itself. Or, as a simpler example, a word counting program can count the words in its own source code.

When *K* gets the answer from *H* that *R* halts when applied to itself, it is programmed to enter an infinite loop. Otherwise *K* exits. In Java, the program might look like this:

```java
public class Killer
{
   public static void main(String[] args)
   {
      String r = read program input;
      HaltChecker checker = new HaltChecker();
      if (checker.check(r, r))
      {
         while (true) { } // Infinite loop
      }
      else
      {
         return;
      }
   }
}
```

Now ask yourself: What does the halt checker answer when asked whether *K* halts when given *K* as the input? Maybe it finds out that *K* gets into an infinite loop with such an input. But wait, that can't be right. That would mean that checker.check(r, r) returns false when r is the program code of *K*. As you can plainly see, in that case, the killer method returns, so K didn't get into an infinite loop. That shows that *K* must halt when analyzing itself, so checker.check(r, r) should return true. But then the killer method doesn't terminate—it goes into an infinite loop. That shows that it is logically impossible to implement a program that can check whether *every* program halts on a particular input.

It is sobering to know that there are *limits* to computing. There are problems that no computer program, no matter how ingenious, can answer.

Theoretical computer scientists are working on other research involving the nature of computation. One important question that remains unsettled to this day deals with problems that in practice are very time-consuming to solve. It may be that these problems are intrinsically hard, in which case it would be pointless to try to look for better algorithms. Such theoretical research can have important practical applications. For example, right now, nobody knows whether the most common encryption schemes used today could be broken by discovering a new algorithm. Knowing that no fast algorithms exist for breaking a particular code could make us feel more comfortable about the security of encryption.

13.5 Mutual Recursions

> In a mutual recursion, a set of cooperating methods calls each other repeatedly.

In the preceding examples, a method called itself to solve a simpler problem. Sometimes, a set of cooperating methods calls each other in a recursive fashion. In this section, we will explore a typical situation of such a mutual recursion. This technique is significantly more advanced than the simple recursion that we discussed in the preceding sections.

We will develop a program that can compute the values of arithmetic expressions such as

```
3+4*5
(3+4)*5
1-(2-(3-(4-5)))
```

Computing such an expression is complicated by the fact that * and / bind more strongly than + and -, and that parentheses can be used to group subexpressions.

Figure 3 shows a set of **syntax diagrams** that describes the syntax of these expressions. To see how the syntax diagrams work, consider the expression 3+4*5. When you enter the *expression* syntax diagram, the arrow points directly to *term*, giving you no alternative but to enter the *term* syntax diagram. The arrow points to *factor*, again giving you no choice. You enter the *factor* diagram, and now you have two choices: to follow the top branch or the bottom branch. Because the first input token is the number 3 and not a (, you must follow the bottom branch. You accept the input token because it matches the *number*. Follow the arrow out of *number* to the end of *factor*. Just like in a method call, you now back up, returning to the end of the *factor* element of the *term* diagram. Now you have another choice—to loop back in the *term* diagram, or to exit. The next input token is a +, and it matches neither the * or the / that would be required to loop back. So you exit, returning to *expression*.

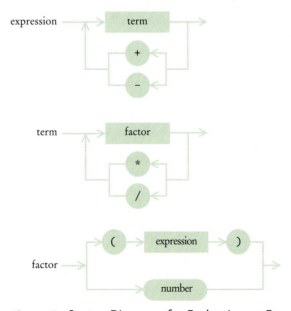

Figure 3 Syntax Diagrams for Evaluating an Expression

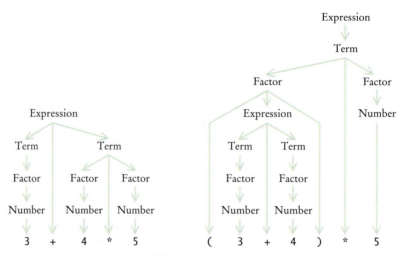

Figure 4 Syntax Trees for Two Expressions

Again, you have a choice, to loop back or to exit. Now the + matches one of the choices in the loop. Accept the + in the input and move back to the *term* element.

In this fashion, an expression is broken down into a sequence of terms, separated by + or -, each term is broken down into a sequence of factors, each separated by * or /, and each factor is either a parenthesized expression or a number. You can draw this breakdown as a tree. Figure 4 shows how the expressions 3+4*5 and (3+4)*5 are derived from the syntax diagram.

Why do the syntax diagrams help us compute the value of the tree? If you look at the syntax trees, you will see that they accurately represent which operations should be carried out first. In the first tree, 4 and 5 should be multiplied, and then the result should be added to 3. In the second tree, 3 and 4 should be added, and the result should be multiplied by 5.

At the end of this section, you will find the implementation of the Evaluator class, which evaluates these expressions. The Evaluator makes use of an Expression-Tokenizer class, which breaks up an input string into tokens—numbers, operators, and parentheses. (For simplicity, we only accept positive integers as numbers, and we don't allow spaces in the input.)

When you call nextToken, the next input token is returned as a string. We also supply another method, peekToken, which allows you to see the next token without consuming it. To see why the peekToken method is necessary, consider the syntax diagram of the factor type. If the next token is a "*" or "/", you want to continue adding and subtracting terms. But if the next token is another character, such as a "+" or "-", you want to stop without actually consuming it, so that the token can be considered later.

To compute the value of an expression, we implement three methods: getExpressionValue, getTermValue, and getFactorValue. The getExpressionValue method first calls getTermValue to get the value of the first term of the expression. Then it checks whether the next input token is one of + or -. If so, it calls getTermValue again and adds or subtracts it.

```java
public int getExpressionValue()
{
```

```
      int value = getTermValue();
      boolean done = false;
      while (!done)
      {
         String next = tokenizer.peekToken();
         if ("+".equals(next) || "-".equals(next))
         {
            tokenizer.nextToken(); // Discard "+" or "-"
            int value2 = getTermValue();
            if ("+".equals(next)) value = value + value2;
            else value = value - value2;
         }
         else
         {
            done = true;
         }
      }
      return value;
   }
```

The getTermValue method calls getFactorValue in the same way, multiplying or dividing the factor values.

Finally, the getFactorValue method checks whether the next input is a number, or whether it begins with a (token. In the first case, the value is simply the value of the number. However, in the second case, the getFactorValue method makes a recursive call to getExpressionValue. Thus, the three methods are mutually recursive.

```
public int getFactorValue()
{
   int value;
   String next = tokenizer.peekToken();
   if ("(".equals(next))
   {
      tokenizer.nextToken(); // Discard "("
      value = getExpressionValue();
      tokenizer.nextToken(); // Discard ")"
   }
   else
   {
      value = Integer.parseInt(tokenizer.nextToken());
   }
   return value;
}
```

To see the mutual recursion clearly, trace through the expression (3+4)*5:

- getExpressionValue calls getTermValue
  - getTermValue calls getFactorValue
    - getFactorValue consumes the (input
    - getFactorValue calls getExpressionValue
      - getExpressionValue returns eventually with the value of 7, having consumed 3 + 4. This is the recursive call.
    - getFactorValue consumes the) input
    - getFactorValue returns 7
  - getTermValue consumes the inputs * and 5 and returns 35
- getExpressionValue returns 35

As always with a recursive solution, you need to ensure that the recursion terminates. In this situation, that is easy to see when you consider the situation in which
`getExpressionValue` calls itself. The second call works on a shorter subexpression than
the original expression. At each recursive call, at least some of the tokens of the
input string are consumed, so eventually the recursion must come to an end.

ch13/expr/Evaluator.java

```java
1   /**
2       A class that can compute the value of an arithmetic expression.
3   */
4   public class Evaluator
5   {
6       private ExpressionTokenizer tokenizer;
7
8       /**
9           Constructs an evaluator.
10          @param anExpression a string containing the expression
11          to be evaluated
12      */
13      public Evaluator(String anExpression)
14      {
15          tokenizer = new ExpressionTokenizer(anExpression);
16      }
17
18      /**
19          Evaluates the expression.
20          @return the value of the expression
21      */
22      public int getExpressionValue()
23      {
24          int value = getTermValue();
25          boolean done = false;
26          while (!done)
27          {
28              String next = tokenizer.peekToken();
29              if ("+".equals(next) || "-".equals(next))
30              {
31                  tokenizer.nextToken(); // Discard "+" or "-"
32                  int value2 = getTermValue();
33                  if ("+".equals(next)) { value = value + value2; }
34                  else { value = value - value2; }
35              }
36              else
37              {
38                  done = true;
39              }
40          }
41          return value;
42      }
43
44      /**
45          Evaluates the next term found in the expression.
46          @return the value of the term
47      */
48      public int getTermValue()
49      {
50          int value = getFactorValue();
51          boolean done = false;
```

```
52          while (!done)
53          {
54             String next = tokenizer.peekToken();
55             if ("*".equals(next) || "/".equals(next))
56             {
57                tokenizer.nextToken();
58                int value2 = getFactorValue();
59                if ("*".equals(next)) { value = value * value2; }
60                else { value = value / value2; }
61             }
62             else
63             {
64                done = true;
65             }
66          }
67          return value;
68       }
69
70       /**
71          Evaluates the next factor found in the expression.
72          @return the value of the factor
73       */
74       public int getFactorValue()
75       {
76          int value;
77          String next = tokenizer.peekToken();
78          if ("(".equals(next))
79          {
80             tokenizer.nextToken(); // Discard "("
81             value = getExpressionValue();
82             tokenizer.nextToken(); // Discard ")"
83          }
84          else
85          {
86             value = Integer.parseInt(tokenizer.nextToken());
87          }
88          return value;
89       }
90    }
```

ch13/expr/ExpressionTokenizer.java

```
1    /**
2       This class breaks up a string describing an expression
3       into tokens: numbers, parentheses, and operators.
4    */
5    public class ExpressionTokenizer
6    {
7       private String input;
8       private int start; // The start of the current token
9       private int end; // The position after the end of the current token
10
11       /**
12          Constructs a tokenizer.
13          @param anInput the string to tokenize
14       */
15       public ExpressionTokenizer(String anInput)
16       {
```

```
17        input = anInput;
18        start = 0;
19        end = 0;
20        nextToken(); //  Find the first token
21     }
22
23     /**
24        Peeks at the next token without consuming it.
25        @return the next token or null if there are no more tokens
26     */
27     public String peekToken()
28     {
29        if (start >= input.length()) { return null; }
30        else { return input.substring(start, end); }
31     }
32
33     /**
34        Gets the next token and moves the tokenizer to the following token.
35        @return the next token or null if there are no more tokens
36     */
37     public String nextToken()
38     {
39        String r = peekToken();
40        start = end;
41        if (start >= input.length()) { return r; }
42        if (Character.isDigit(input.charAt(start)))
43        {
44           end = start + 1;
45           while (end < input.length()
46                 && Character.isDigit(input.charAt(end)))
47           {
48              end++;
49           }
50        }
51        else
52        {
53           end = start + 1;
54        }
55        return r;
56     }
57  }
```

ch13/expr/ExpressionCalculator.java

```
1   import java.util.Scanner;
2
3   /**
4      This program calculates the value of an expression
5      consisting of numbers, arithmetic operators, and parentheses.
6   */
7   public class ExpressionCalculator
8   {
9      public static void main(String[] args)
10     {
11        Scanner in = new Scanner(System.in);
12        System.out.print("Enter an expression: ");
13        String input = in.nextLine();
14        Evaluator e = new Evaluator(input);
15        int value = e.getExpressionValue();
```

```
16          System.out.println(input + "=" + value);
17      }
18  }
```

Program Run

```
Enter an expression: 3+4*5
3+4*5=23
```

SELF CHECK

10. What is the difference between a term and a factor? Why do we need both concepts?

11. Why does the expression parser use mutual recursion?

12. What happens if you try to parse the illegal expression 3+4*)5? Specifically, which method throws an exception?

Summary of Learning Objectives

Understand the control flow in a recursive computation.

- A recursive computation solves a problem by using the solution of the same problem with simpler values.
- For a recursion to terminate, there must be special cases for the simplest values.

Identify recursive helper methods for solving a problem.

- Sometimes it is easier to find a recursive solution if you make a slight change to the original problem.

Contrast the efficiency of recursive and non-recursive algorithms.

- Occasionally, a recursive solution runs much slower than its iterative counterpart. However, in most cases, the recursive solution is only slightly slower.
- In many cases, a recursive solution is easier to understand and implement correctly than an iterative solution.

Review a complex recursion example that cannot be solved with a simple loop.

- The permutations of a string can be obtained more naturally through recursion than with a loop.

Recognize the phenomenon of mutual recursion in a parsing application.

- In a mutual recursion, a set of cooperating methods calls each other repeatedly.

Media Resources

www.wiley.com/
college/
horstmann

- ***Worked Example*** Finding Files
- Lab Exercises
- ⊕ ***Animation*** Tracing a Recursion
- ⊕ Practice Quiz
- ⊕ Code Completion Exercises

Review Exercises

★ **R13.1** Define the terms
   a. Recursion
   b. Iteration
   c. Infinite recursion
   d. Recursive helper method

★★ **R13.2** Outline, but do not implement, a recursive solution for finding the smallest value in an array.

★★ **R13.3** Outline, but do not implement, a recursive solution for sorting an array of numbers. *Hint:* First find the smallest value in the array.

★★ **R13.4** Outline, but do not implement, a recursive solution for generating all subsets of the set $\{1, 2, \ldots, n\}$.

★★★ **R13.5** Exercise P13.12 shows an iterative way of generating all permutations of the sequence $(0, 1, \ldots, n-1)$. Explain why the algorithm produces the correct result.

★ **R13.6** Write a recursive definition of x^n, where $n \geq 0$, similar to the recursive definition of the Fibonacci numbers. *Hint:* How do you compute x^n from x^{n-1}? How does the recursion terminate?

★★ **R13.7** Improve upon Exercise R13.6 by computing x^n as $(x^{n/2})^2$ if n is even. Why is this approach significantly faster? *Hint:* Compute x^{1023} and x^{1024} both ways.

★ **R13.8** Write a recursive definition of $n! = 1 \times 2 \times \ldots \times n$, similar to the recursive definition of the Fibonacci numbers.

★★ **R13.9** Find out how often the recursive version of fib calls itself. Keep a static variable fibCount and increment it once in every call of fib. What is the relationship between fib(n) and fibCount?

★★★ **R13.10** How many moves are required in the "Towers of Hanoi" problem of Exercise P13.13 to move n disks? *Hint:* As explained in the exercise,

$$\text{moves}(1) = 1$$
$$\text{moves}(n) = 2 \cdot \text{moves}(n-1) + 1$$

Programming Exercises

★ **P13.1** Write a recursive method void reverse() that reverses a sentence. For example:

```
Sentence greeting = new Sentence("Hello!");
greeting.reverse();
System.out.println(greeting.getText());
```

prints the string "!olleH". Implement a recursive solution by removing the first character, reversing a sentence consisting of the remaining text, and combining the two.

★★ **P13.2** Redo Exercise P13.1 with a recursive helper method that reverses a substring of the message text.

★   **P13.3** Implement the reverse method of Exercise P13.1 as an iteration.

★★ **P13.4** Use recursion to implement a method boolean find(String t) that tests whether a string is contained in a sentence:

```
Sentence s = new Sentence("Mississippi!");
boolean b = s.find("sip"); // Returns true
```

Hint: If the text starts with the string you want to match, then you are done. If not, consider the sentence that you obtain by removing the first character.

★★ **P13.5** Use recursion to implement a method int indexOf(String t) that returns the starting position of the first substring of the text that matches t. Return –1 if t is not a substring of s. For example,

```
Sentence s = new Sentence("Mississippi!");
int n = s.indexOf("sip"); // Returns 6
```

Hint: This is a bit trickier than the preceding problem, because you must keep track of how far the match is from the beginning of the sentence. Make that value a parameter of a helper method.

★   **P13.6** Using recursion, find the largest element in an array.

```
public class DataSet
{
    public DataSet(int[] values, int first, int last) { . . . }
    public int getMaximum() { . . . }
    . . .
}
```

Hint: Find the largest element in the subset containing all but the last element. Then compare that maximum to the value of the last element.

★   **P13.7** Using recursion, compute the sum of all values in an array.

```
public class DataSet
{
    public DataSet(int[] values, int first, int last) { . . . }
    public int getSum() { . . . }
    . . .
}
```

★★ **P13.8** Using recursion, compute the area of a polygon. Cut off a triangle and use the fact that a triangle with corners (x_1, y_1), (x_2, y_2), (x_3, y_3) has area

$$\frac{\left| x_1 y_2 + x_2 y_3 + x_3 y_1 - y_1 x_2 - y_2 x_3 - y_3 x_1 \right|}{2}$$

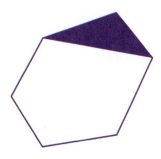

★★★ **P13.9** Implement a SubstringGenerator that generates all substrings of a string. For example, the substrings of the string "rum" are the seven strings

"r", "ru", "rum", "u", "um", "m", ""

Hint: First enumerate all substrings that start with the first character. There are *n* of them if the string has length *n*. Then enumerate the substrings of the string that you obtain by removing the first character.

★★★ **P13.10** Implement a SubsetGenerator that generates all subsets of the characters of a string. For example, the subsets of the characters of the string "rum" are the eight strings

"rum", "ru", "rm", "r", "um", "u", "m", ""

Note that the subsets don't have to be substrings—for example, "rm" isn't a substring of "rum".

★★★ **P13.11** In this exercise, you will change the PermutationGenerator of Section 13.4 (which computed all permutations at once) to a PermutationIterator (which computes them one at a time.)

```
public class PermutationIterator
{
    public PermutationIterator(String s) { . . . }
    public String nextPermutation() { . . . }
    public boolean hasMorePermutations() { . . . }
}
```

Here is how you would print out all permutations of the string "eat":

```
PermutationIterator iter = new PermutationIterator("eat");
while (iter.hasMorePermutations())
{
    System.out.println(iter.nextPermutation());
}
```

Now we need a way to iterate through the permutations recursively. Consider the string "eat". As before, we'll generate all permutations that start with the letter 'e', then those that start with 'a', and finally those that start with 't'. How do we generate the permutations that start with 'e'? Make another PermutationIterator object (called tailIterator) that iterates through the permutations of the substring "at". In the nextPermutation method, simply ask tailIterator what *its* next permutation is, and then add the 'e' at the front. However, there is one special case. When the tail generator runs out of permutations, all permutations that start with the current letter have been enumerated. Then

- Increment the current position.
- Compute the tail string that contains all letters except for the current one.
- Make a new permutation iterator for the tail string.

You are done when the current position has reached the end of the string.

★★★ **P13.12** The following class generates all permutations of the numbers 0, 1, 2, . . ., *n* – 1, without using recursion.

```
public class NumberPermutationIterator
{
    public NumberPermutationIterator(int n)
    {
```

```
            a = new int[n];
            done = false;
            for (int i = 0; i < n; i++) a[i] = i;
        }

        public int[] nextPermutation()
        {
            if (a.length <= 1) { return a; }

            for (int i = a.length - 1; i > 0; i--)
            {
                if (a[i - 1] < a[i])
                {
                    int j = a.length - 1;
                    while (a[i - 1] > a[j]) j--;
                    swap(i - 1, j);
                    reverse(i, a.length - 1);
                    return a;
                }
            }
            return a;
        }

        public boolean hasMorePermutations()
        {
            if (a.length <= 1) { return false; }
            for (int i = a.length - 1; i > 0; i--)
            {
                if (a[i - 1] < a[i]) { return true; }
            }
            return false;
        }

        public void swap(int i, int j)
        {
            int temp = a[i];
            a[i] = a[j];
            a[j] = temp;
        }

        public void reverse(int i, int j)
        {
            while (i < j) { swap(i, j); i++; j--; }
        }
        private int[] a;
    }
```

The algorithm uses the fact that the set to be permuted consists of distinct numbers. Thus, you cannot use the same algorithm to compute the permutations of the characters in a string. You can, however, use this class to get all permutations of the character positions and then compute a string whose ith character is word.charAt(a[i]). Use this approach to reimplement the PermutationIterator of Exercise P13.11 without recursion.

★★ **P13.13** *Towers of Hanoi.* This is a well-known puzzle. A stack of disks of decreasing size is to be transported from the leftmost peg to the rightmost peg. The middle peg can be used as temporary storage (see Figure 5). One disk can be moved at one time, from

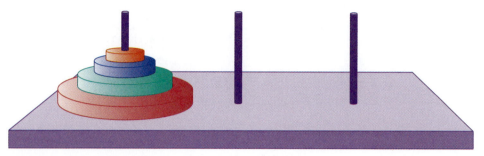

Figure 5 Towers of Hanoi

any peg to any other peg. You can place smaller disks only on top of larger ones, not the other way around.

Write a program that prints the moves necessary to solve the puzzle for *n* disks. (Ask the user for *n* at the beginning of the program.) Print moves in the form

```
Move disk from peg 1 to peg 3
```

Hint: Implement a class `DiskMover`. The constructor takes

- The source peg from which to move the disks (1, 2, or 3)
- The target peg to which to move the disks (1, 2, or 3)
- The number of disks to move

A disk mover that moves a single disk from one peg to another simply has a `nextMove` method that returns a string

```
Move disk from peg source to peg target
```

A disk mover with more than one disk to move must work harder. It needs another `DiskMover` to help it. In the constructor, construct a `DiskMover(source, other, disks - 1)` where `other` is the peg other than `from` and `target`.

The `nextMove` asks that disk mover for its next move until it is done. The effect is to move the first `disks - 1` disks to the other peg. Then the `nextMove` method issues a command to move a disk from the `from` peg to the `to` peg. Finally, it constructs another disk mover `DiskMover(other, target, disks - 1)` that generates the moves that move the disks from the other peg to the target peg.

Hint: It helps to keep track of the state of the disk mover:

- `BEFORE_LARGEST`: The helper mover moves the smaller pile to the other peg.
- `LARGEST`: Move the largest disk from the source to the destination.
- `AFTER_LARGEST`: The helper mover moves the smaller pile from the other peg to the target.
- `DONE`: All moves are done.

Test your program as follows:

```
DiskMover mover = new DiskMover(1, 3, n);
while (mover.hasMoreMoves())
{
    System.out.println(mover.nextMove());
}
```

★★★ **P13.14** *Escaping a Maze.* You are currently located inside a maze. The walls of the maze are indicated by asterisks (*).

```
*  *******
*      *  *
*  *****  *
*  *  *   *
*  *  *** *
*     *   *
*** *  *  *
*      *  *
*******  *
```

Use the following recursive approach to check whether you can escape from the maze: If you are at an exit, return true. Recursively check whether you can escape from one of the empty neighboring locations without visiting the current location. This method merely tests whether there is a path out of the maze. Extra credit if you can print out a path that leads to an exit.

★★★G **P13.15** *The Koch Snowflake.* A snowflake-like shape is recursively defined as follows. Start with an equilateral triangle:

Next, increase the size by a factor of three and replace each straight line with four line segments.

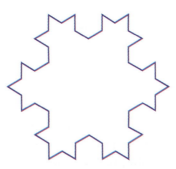

Repeat the process.

Write a program that draws the iterations of this curve. Supply a button that, when clicked, produces the next iteration.

★★ **P13.16** The recursive computation of Fibonacci numbers can be speeded up significantly by keeping track of the values that have already been computed. Provide an implementation of the fib method that uses this strategy. Whenever you return a new value, also store it in an auxiliary array. However, before embarking on a computation, consult the array to find whether the result has already been computed. Compare the running time of your improved implementation with that of the original recursive implementation and the loop implementation.

Programming Projects

Project 13.1 Enhance the expression parser of Section 13.5 to handle more sophisticated expressions, such as exponents, and mathematical functions, such as sqrt or sin.

Project 13.2 Implement a graphical version of the "Towers of Hanoi" program (see Exercise P13.13). Every time the user clicks on a button labeled "Next", draw the next move.

Answers to Self-Check Questions

1. Suppose we omit the statement. When computing the area of a triangle with width 1, we compute the area of the triangle with width 0 as 0, and then add 1, to arrive at the correct area.

2. You would compute the smaller area recursively, then return
   `smallerArea + width + width - 1`.

   [] [] [] []
   [] [] [] []
   [] [] [] []
   [] [] [] []

   Of course, it would be simpler to compute the area simply as width * width. The results are identical because
   $$1 + 0 + 2 + 1 + 3 + 2 + \cdots + n + n - 1 = \frac{n(n+1)}{2} + \frac{(n-1)n}{2} = n^2.$$

3. No—the first one could be given a different name such as substringIsPalindrome.

4. When start >= end, that is, when the investigated string is either empty or has length 1.

5. The loop is slightly faster. Of course, it is even faster to simply compute width * (width + 1) / 2.

6. No, the recursive solution is about as efficient as the iterative approach. Both require $n - 1$ multiplications to compute $n!$.

7. They are b followed by the six permutations of eat, e followed by the six permutations of bat, a followed by the six permutations of bet, and t followed by the six permutations of bea.

8. Simply change if (word.length() == 0) to if (word.length() <= 1), because a word with a single letter is also its sole permutation.

9. An iterative solution would have a loop whose body computes the next permutation from the previous ones. But there is no obvious mechanism for getting the next permutation. For example, if you already found permutations eat, eta, and aet, it is not clear how you use that information to get the next permutation. Actually, there is an ingenious mechanism for doing just that, but it is far from obvious—see Exercise P13.12.

10. Factors are combined by multiplicative operators (* and /), terms are combined by additive operators (+, -). We need both so that multiplication can bind more strongly than addition.

11. To handle parenthesized expressions, such as 2+3*(4+5). The subexpression 4+5 is handled by a recursive call to getExpressionValue.

12. The Integer.parseInt call in getFactorValue throws an exception when it is given the string ")".

Sorting and Searching

CHAPTER GOALS

- To study several sorting and searching algorithms
- To appreciate that algorithms for the same task can differ widely in performance
- To understand the big-Oh notation
- To learn how to estimate and compare the performance of algorithms
- To learn how to measure the running time of a program

Sorting and searching are among the most common tasks in data processing. Of course, the Java library contains methods for carrying out these operations. Nevertheless, studying algorithms for sorting and searching is fruitful because you will learn how to analyze the performance of algorithms and how to choose the best algorithm for a particular task. Sorting and searching are an excellent entry point into the study of algorithm analysis because the tasks themselves are simple to understand. As you will see in this chapter, the most straightforward algorithms do not perform very well, and we can achieve dramatic improvements with more sophisticated algorithms.

CHAPTER CONTENTS

14.1 Selection Sort

In this section, we show you the first of several sorting algorithms. A *sorting algorithm* rearranges the elements of a collection so that they are stored in sorted order. To keep the examples simple, we will discuss how to sort an array of integers before going on to sorting strings or more complex data. Consider the following array a:

[0][1][2][3][4]

11 9 17 5 12

> The selection sort algorithm sorts an array by repeatedly finding the smallest element of the unsorted tail region and moving it to the front.

An obvious first step is to find the smallest element. In this case the smallest element is 5, stored in a[3]. We should move the 5 to the beginning of the array. Of course, there is already an element stored in a[0], namely 11. Therefore we cannot simply move a[3] into a[0] without moving the 11 somewhere else. We don't yet know where the 11 should end up, but we know for certain that it should not be in a[0]. We simply get it out of the way by *swapping* it with a[3].

[0][1][2][3][4]

5 9 17 11 12

Now the first element is in the correct place. In the foregoing figure, the darker color indicates the portion of the array that is already sorted.

Next we take the minimum of the remaining entries a[1] . . . a[4]. That minimum value, 9, is already in the correct place. We don't need to do anything in this case and can simply extend the sorted area by one to the right:

[0][1][2][3][4]

5 9 17 11 12

Repeat the process. The minimum value of the unsorted region is 11, which needs to be swapped with the first value of the unsorted region, 17:

Now the unsorted region is only two elements long, but we keep to the same successful strategy. The minimum value is 12, and we swap it with the first value, 17.

That leaves us with an unprocessed region of length 1, but of course a region of length 1 is always sorted. We are done.

Let's program this algorithm. For this program, as well as the other programs in this chapter, we will use a utility method to generate an array with random entries. We place it into a class ArrayUtil so that we don't have to repeat the code in every example. To show the array, we call the static toString method of the Arrays class in the Java library and print the resulting string.

This algorithm will sort any array of integers. If speed were not an issue, or if there simply were no better sorting method available, we could stop the discussion of sorting right here. As the next section shows, however, this algorithm, while entirely correct, shows disappointing performance when run on a large data set.

Special Topic 14.1 on page 604 discusses insertion sort, another simple sorting algorithm.

ch14/selsort/SelectionSorter.java

```java
1  /**
2      This class sorts an array, using the selection sort
3      algorithm.
4  */
5  public class SelectionSorter
6  {
7      private int[] a;
8
9      /**
10         Constructs a selection sorter.
11         @param anArray the array to sort
12     */
13     public SelectionSorter(int[] anArray)
14     {
15         a = anArray;
16     }
17
18     /**
19         Sorts the array managed by this selection sorter.
20     */
21     public void sort()
22     {
```

```
23        for (int i = 0; i < a.length - 1; i++)
24        {
25            int minPos = minimumPosition(i);
26            swap(minPos, i);
27        }
28    }
29
30    /**
31        Finds the smallest element in a tail range of the array.
32        @param from the first position in a to compare
33        @return the position of the smallest element in the
34        range a[from] . . . a[a.length - 1]
35    */
36    private int minimumPosition(int from)
37    {
38        int minPos = from;
39        for (int i = from + 1; i < a.length; i++)
40            if (a[i] < a[minPos]) minPos = i;
41        return minPos;
42    }
43
44    /**
45        Swaps two entries of the array.
46        @param i the first position to swap
47        @param j the second position to swap
48    */
49    private void swap(int i, int j)
50    {
51        int temp = a[i];
52        a[i] = a[j];
53        a[j] = temp;
54    }
55 }
```

ch14/selsort/SelectionSortDemo.java

```
1  import java.util.Arrays;
2
3  /**
4      This program demonstrates the selection sort algorithm by
5      sorting an array that is filled with random numbers.
6  */
7  public class SelectionSortDemo
8  {
9      public static void main(String[] args)
10     {
11         int[] a = ArrayUtil.randomIntArray(20, 100);
12         System.out.println(Arrays.toString(a));
13
14         SelectionSorter sorter = new SelectionSorter(a);
15         sorter.sort();
16
17         System.out.println(Arrays.toString(a));
18     }
19 }
```

ch14/selsort/ArrayUtil.java

```java
 1  import java.util.Random;
 2
 3  /**
 4     This class contains utility methods for array manipulation.
 5  */
 6  public class ArrayUtil
 7  {
 8     private static Random generator = new Random();
 9
10     /**
11        Creates an array filled with random values.
12        @param length the length of the array
13        @param n the number of possible random values
14        @return an array filled with length numbers between
15        0 and n - 1
16     */
17     public static int[] randomIntArray(int length, int n)
18     {
19        int[] a = new int[length];
20        for (int i = 0; i < a.length; i++)
21           a[i] = generator.nextInt(n);
22
23        return a;
24     }
25  }
```

Typical Output

```
[65, 46, 14, 52, 38, 2, 96, 39, 14, 33, 13, 4, 24, 99, 89, 77, 73, 87, 36, 81]
[2, 4, 13, 14, 14, 24, 33, 36, 38, 39, 46, 52, 65, 73, 77, 81, 87, 89, 96, 99]
```

SELF CHECK

1. Why do we need the temp variable in the swap method? What would happen if you simply assigned a[i] to a[j] and a[j] to a[i]?

2. What steps does the selection sort algorithm go through to sort the sequence 6 5 4 3 2 1?

14.2 Profiling the Selection Sort Algorithm

To measure the performance of a program, you could simply run it and use a stopwatch to measure how long it takes. However, most of our programs run very quickly, and it is not easy to time them accurately in this way. Furthermore, when a program takes a noticeable time to run, a certain amount of that time may simply be used for loading the program from disk into memory and displaying the result (for which we should not penalize it).

In order to measure the running time of an algorithm more accurately, we will create a StopWatch class. This class works like a real stopwatch. You can start it, stop it, and read out the elapsed time. The class uses the System.currentTimeMillis method, which returns the milliseconds that have elapsed since midnight at the start of January 1, 1970. Of course, you don't care about the absolute number of seconds since this historical moment, but the *difference* of two such counts gives us the number of milliseconds of a time interval.

Here is the code for the StopWatch class:

ch14/selsort/StopWatch.java

```java
1   /**
2       A stopwatch accumulates time when it is running. You can
3       repeatedly start and stop the stopwatch. You can use a
4       stopwatch to measure the running time of a program.
5   */
6   public class StopWatch
7   {
8       private long elapsedTime;
9       private long startTime;
10      private boolean isRunning;
11
12      /**
13          Constructs a stopwatch that is in the stopped state
14          and has no time accumulated.
15      */
16      public StopWatch()
17      {
18          reset();
19      }
20
21      /**
22          Starts the stopwatch. Time starts accumulating now.
23      */
24      public void start()
25      {
26          if (isRunning) return;
27          isRunning = true;
28          startTime = System.currentTimeMillis();
29      }
30
31      /**
32          Stops the stopwatch. Time stops accumulating and is
33          is added to the elapsed time.
34      */
35      public void stop()
36      {
37          if (!isRunning) return;
38          isRunning = false;
39          long endTime = System.currentTimeMillis();
40          elapsedTime = elapsedTime + endTime - startTime;
41      }
42
43      /**
44          Returns the total elapsed time.
45          @return the total elapsed time
46      */
47      public long getElapsedTime()
48      {
49          if (isRunning)
50          {
51              long endTime = System.currentTimeMillis();
52              return elapsedTime + endTime - startTime;
53          }
54          else
55              return elapsedTime;
```

```
56        }
57
58        /**
59            Stops the watch and resets the elapsed time to 0.
60        */
61        public void reset()
62        {
63            elapsedTime = 0;
64            isRunning = false;
65        }
66  }
```

Here is how we will use the stopwatch to measure the performance of the sorting algorithm:

ch14/selsort/SelectionSortTimer.java

```java
 1   import java.util.Scanner;
 2
 3   /**
 4       This program measures how long it takes to sort an
 5       array of a user-specified size with the selection
 6       sort algorithm.
 7   */
 8   public class SelectionSortTimer
 9   {
10       public static void main(String[] args)
11       {
12           Scanner in = new Scanner(System.in);
13           System.out.print("Enter array size: ");
14           int n = in.nextInt();
15
16           // Construct random array
17
18           int[] a = ArrayUtil.randomIntArray(n, 100);
19           SelectionSorter sorter = new SelectionSorter(a);
20
21           // Use stopwatch to time selection sort
22
23           StopWatch timer = new StopWatch();
24
25           timer.start();
26           sorter.sort();
27           timer.stop();
28
29           System.out.println("Elapsed time: "
30               + timer.getElapsedTime() + " milliseconds");
31       }
32   }
```

Program Run

```
Enter array size: 100000
Elapsed time: 27880 milliseconds
```

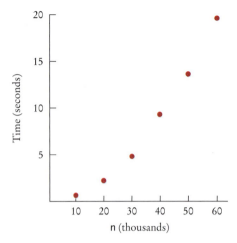

n	Milliseconds
10,000	786
20,000	2,148
30,000	4,796
40,000	9,192
50,000	13,321
60,000	19,299

Figure 1   Time Taken by Selection Sort

By starting to measure the time just before sorting, and stopping the stopwatch just after, you get the time required for the sorting process, without counting the time for input and output.

The table in Figure 1 shows the results of some sample runs. These measurements were obtained with a Intel processor with a clock speed of 2 GHz, running Java 6 on the Linux operating system. On another computer the actual numbers will look different, but the relationship between the numbers will be the same.

The graph in Figure 1 shows a plot of the measurements. As you can see, doubling the size of the data set more than doubles the time needed to sort it.

SELF CHECK

3. Approximately how many seconds would it take to sort a data set of 80,000 values?

4. Look at the graph in Figure 1. What mathematical shape does it resemble?

14.3 Analyzing the Performance of the Selection Sort Algorithm

Let us count the number of operations that the program must carry out to sort an array with the selection sort algorithm. We don't actually know how many machine operations are generated for each Java instruction, or which of those instructions are more time-consuming than others, but we can make a simplification. We will simply count how often an array element is *visited*. Each visit requires about the same amount of work by other operations, such as incrementing subscripts and comparing values.

Let *n* be the size of the array. First, we must find the smallest of *n* numbers. To achieve that, we must visit *n* array elements. Then we swap the elements, which takes two visits. (You may argue that there is a certain probability that we don't need to swap the values. That is true, and one can refine the computation to reflect that observation. As we will soon see, doing so would not affect the overall conclusion.) In the next step, we need to visit only $n - 1$ elements to find the minimum. In the following step, $n - 2$ elements are visited to find the minimum. The last step visits two elements to find the minimum. Each step requires two visits to swap the elements. Therefore, the total number of visits is

$$n + 2 + (n - 1) + 2 + \cdots + 2 + 2 = n + (n - 1) + \cdots + 2 + (n - 1) \cdot 2$$
$$= 2 + \cdots + (n - 1) + n + (n - 1) \cdot 2$$
$$= \frac{n(n + 1)}{2} - 1 + (n - 1) \cdot 2$$

because

$$1 + 2 + \cdots + (n - 1) + n = \frac{n(n + 1)}{2}$$

After multiplying out and collecting terms of n, we find that the number of visits is

$$\tfrac{1}{2}n^2 + \tfrac{5}{2}n - 3$$

We obtain a quadratic equation in n. That explains why the graph of Figure 1 looks approximately like a parabola.

Now simplify the analysis further. When you plug in a large value for n (for example, 1,000 or 2,000), then $\frac{1}{2}n^2$ is 500,000 or 2,000,000. The lower term, $\frac{5}{2}n - 3$, doesn't contribute much at all; it is only 2,497 or 4,997, a drop in the bucket compared to the hundreds of thousands or even millions of comparisons specified by the $\frac{1}{2}n^2$ term. We will just ignore these lower-level terms. Next, we will ignore the constant factor $\frac{1}{2}$. We are not interested in the actual count of visits for a single n. We want to compare the ratios of counts for different values of n. For example, we can say that sorting an array of 2,000 numbers requires four times as many visits as sorting an array of 1,000 numbers:

$$\frac{\left(\frac{1}{2} \cdot 2000^2 \right)}{\left(\frac{1}{2} \cdot 1000^2 \right)} = 4$$

The factor $\frac{1}{2}$ cancels out in comparisons of this kind. We will simply say, "The number of visits is of order n^2". That way, we can easily see that the number of comparisons increases fourfold when the size of the array doubles: $(2n)^2 = 4n^2$.

To indicate that the number of visits is of order n^2, computer scientists often use *big-Oh notation*: The number of visits is $O(n^2)$. This is a convenient shorthand.

In general, the expression $f(n) = O(g(n))$ means that f grows no faster than g, or, more formally, that for all n larger than some threshold, the ratio $f(n)/g(n) \leq C$ for some constant value C. The function g is usually chosen to be very simple, such as n^2 in our example.

To turn an exact expression such as

$$\tfrac{1}{2}n^2 + \tfrac{5}{2}n - 3$$

into big-Oh notation, simply locate the fastest-growing term, n^2, and ignore its constant coefficient, no matter how large or small it may be.

Computer scientists use the big-Oh notation $f(n) = O(g(n))$ to express that the function f grows no faster than the function g.

We observed before that the actual number of machine operations, and the actual amount of time that the computer spends on them, is approximately proportional to the number of element visits. Maybe there are about 10 machine operations (increments, comparisons, memory loads, and stores) for every element visit. The number of machine operations is then approximately $10 \times \frac{1}{2}n^2$. As before, we aren't interested in the coefficient, so we can say that the number of machine operations, and hence the time spent on the sorting, is of the order of n^2 or $O(n^2)$.

The sad fact remains that doubling the size of the array causes a fourfold increase in the time required for sorting it with selection sort. When the size of the array increases by a factor of 100, the sorting time increases by a factor of 10,000. To sort an array of a million entries, (for example, to create a telephone directory) takes 10,000 times as long as sorting 10,000 entries. If 10,000 entries can be sorted in about 1/2 of a second (as in our example), then sorting one million entries requires well over an hour. We will see in the next section how one can dramatically improve the performance of the sorting process by choosing a more sophisticated algorithm.

> Selection sort is an $O(n^2)$ algorithm. Doubling the data set means a fourfold increase in processing time.

SELF CHECK

5. If you increase the size of a data set tenfold, how much longer does it take to sort it with the selection sort algorithm?
6. How large does n need to be so that $\frac{1}{2}n^2$ is bigger than $\frac{5}{2}n - 3$?

Special Topic 14.1

Insertion Sort

Insertion sort is another simple sorting algorithm. In this algorithm, we assume that the initial sequence

    a[0] a[1] . . . a[k]

of an array is already sorted. (When the algorithm starts, we set k to 0.) We enlarge the initial sequence by inserting the next array element, a[k + 1], at the proper location. When we reach the end of the array, the sorting process is complete.

For example, suppose we start with the array

| 11 | 9 | 16 | 5 | 7 |

Of course, the initial sequence of length 1 is already sorted. We now add a[1], which has the value 9. The element needs to be inserted before the element 11. The result is

| 9 | 11 | 16 | 5 | 7 |

Next, we add a[2], which has the value 16. As it happens, the element does not have to be moved.

| 9 | 11 | 16 | 5 | 7 |

We repeat the process, inserting a[3] or 5 at the very beginning of the initial sequence.

| 5 | 9 | 11 | 16 | 7 |

Finally, a[4] or 7 is inserted in its correct position, and the sorting is completed.

The following class implements the insertion sort algorithm:

```java
public class InsertionSorter
{
    private int[] a;

    /**
        Constructs an insertion sorter.
        @param anArray  the array to sort
    */
    public InsertionSorter(int[] anArray)
    {
        a = anArray;
    }

    /**
        Sorts the array managed by this insertion sorter.
    */
    public void sort()
    {
        for (int i = 1; i < a.length; i++)
        {
            int next = a[i];
            // Find the insertion location
            // Move all larger elements up
            int j = i;
            while (j > 0 && a[j - 1] > next)
            {
                a[j] = a[j - 1];
                j--;
            }
            // Insert the element
            a[j] = next;
        }
    }
}
```

How efficient is this algorithm? Let n denote the size of the array. We carry out n − 1 iterations. In the kth iteration, we have a sequence of k elements that is already sorted, and we need to insert a new element into the sequence. For each insertion, we need to visit the elements of the initial sequence until we have found the location in which the new element can be inserted. Then we need to move up the remaining elements of the sequence. Thus, $k + 1$ array elements are visited. Therefore, the total number of visits is

$$2 + 3 + \cdots + n = \frac{n(n + 1)}{2} - 1$$

We conclude that insertion sort is an $O(n^2)$ algorithm, on the same order of efficiency as selection sort.

> Insertion sort is an $O(n^2)$ algorithm.

Insertion sort has a desirable property: Its performance is $O(n)$ if the array is already sorted—see Exercise R14.13. This is a useful property in practical applications, in which data sets are often partially sorted.

Special Topic 14.2

Oh, Omega, and Theta

We have used the big-Oh notation somewhat casually in this chapter, to describe the growth behavior of a function. Strictly speaking, $f(n) = O(g(n))$ means that f grows *no faster* than g.

But it is permissible for f to grow much more slowly. Thus, it is technically correct to state that $f(n) = n^2 + 5n - 3$ is $O(n^3)$ or even $O(n^{10})$.

Computer scientists have invented additional notation to describe the growth behavior of functions more accurately. The expression

$$f(n) = \Omega(g(n))$$

means that f grows at least as fast as g, or, formally, that for all n larger than some threshold, the ratio $f(n)/g(n) \geq C$ for some constant value C. (The Ω symbol is the capital Greek letter omega.) For example, $f(n) = n^2 + 5n - 3$ is $\Omega(n^2)$ or even $\Omega(n)$.

The expression

$$f(n) = \Theta(g(n))$$

means that f and g grow at the same rate—that is, both $f(n) = O(g(n))$ and $f(n) = \Omega(g(n))$ hold. (The Θ symbol is the capital Greek letter theta.)

The Θ notation gives the most precise description of growth behavior. For example, $f(n) = n^2 + 5n - 3$ is $\Theta(n^2)$ but not $\Theta(n)$ or $\Theta(n^3)$.

The Ω and Θ notation is very important for the precise analysis of algorithms. However, in casual conversation it is common to stick with big-Oh, while still giving as good an estimate as one can.

14.4 Merge Sort

In this section, you will learn about the merge sort algorithm, a much more efficient algorithm than selection sort. The basic idea behind merge sort is very simple.

Suppose we have an array of 10 integers. Let us engage in a bit of wishful thinking and hope that the first half of the array is already perfectly sorted, and the second half is too, like this:

| 5 | 9 | 10 | 12 | 17 | 1 | 8 | 11 | 20 | 32 |

Now it is simple to *merge* the two sorted arrays into one sorted array, by taking a new element from either the first or the second subarray, and choosing the smaller of the elements each time:

In fact, you may have performed this merging before if you and a friend had to sort a pile of papers. You and the friend split the pile in half, each of you sorted your half, and then you merged the results together.

That is all well and good, but it doesn't seem to solve the problem for the computer. It still must sort the first and second halves of the array, because it can't very well ask a few buddies to pitch in. As it turns out, though, if the computer keeps dividing the array into smaller and smaller subarrays, sorting each half and merging them back together, it carries out dramatically fewer steps than the selection sort requires.

Let's write a `MergeSorter` class that implements this idea. When the `MergeSorter` sorts an array, it makes two arrays, each half the size of the original, and sorts them recursively. Then it merges the two sorted arrays together:

```java
public void sort()
{
    if (a.length <= 1) return;
    int[] first = new int[a.length / 2];
    int[] second = new int[a.length - first.length];
    // Copy the first half of a into first, the second half into second
    . . .
    MergeSorter firstSorter = new MergeSorter(first);
    MergeSorter secondSorter = new MergeSorter(second);
    firstSorter.sort();
    secondSorter.sort();
    merge(first, second);
}
```

The `merge` method is tedious but quite straightforward. You will find it in the code that follows.

ch14/mergesort/MergeSorter.java

```java
1  /**
2      This class sorts an array, using the merge sort algorithm.
3  */
4  public class MergeSorter
5  {
6      private int[] a;
7
8      /**
9          Constructs a merge sorter.
10         @param anArray the array to sort
11     */
12     public MergeSorter(int[] anArray)
13     {
14         a = anArray;
15     }
16
17     /**
18         Sorts the array managed by this merge sorter.
19     */
20     public void sort()
21     {
22         if (a.length <= 1) return;
23         int[] first = new int[a.length / 2];
24         int[] second = new int[a.length - first.length];
25         // Copy the first half of a into first, the second half into second
26         for (int i = 0; i < first.length; i++) { first[i] = a[i]; }
27         for (int i = 0; i < second.length; i++)
28         {
29             second[i] = a[first.length + i];
30         }
```

```
31        MergeSorter firstSorter = new MergeSorter(first);
32        MergeSorter secondSorter = new MergeSorter(second);
33        firstSorter.sort();
34        secondSorter.sort();
35        merge(first, second);
36     }
37
38     /**
39        Merges two sorted arrays into the array managed by this merge sorter.
40        @param first the first sorted array
41        @param second the second sorted array
42     */
43     private void merge(int[] first, int[] second)
44     {
45        int iFirst = 0;   // Next element to consider in the first array
46        int iSecond = 0;   // Next element to consider in the second array
47        int j = 0;   // Next open position in a
48
49        // As long as neither iFirst nor iSecond past the end, move
50        // the smaller element into a
51        while (iFirst < first.length && iSecond < second.length)
52        {
53           if (first[iFirst] < second[iSecond])
54           {
55              a[j] = first[iFirst];
56              iFirst++;
57           }
58           else
59           {
60              a[j] = second[iSecond];
61              iSecond++;
62           }
63           j++;
64        }
65
66        // Note that only one of the two loops below copies entries
67        // Copy any remaining entries of the first array
68        while (iFirst < first.length)
69        {
70           a[j] = first[iFirst];
71           iFirst++; j++;
72        }
73        // Copy any remaining entries of the second half
74        while (iSecond < second.length)
75        {
76           a[j] = second[iSecond];
77           iSecond++; j++;
78        }
79     }
80  }
```

ch14/mergesort/MergeSortDemo.java

```
1  import java.util.Arrays;
2
3  /**
4     This program demonstrates the merge sort algorithm by
5     sorting an array that is filled with random numbers.
6  */
```

```
 7  public class MergeSortDemo
 8  {
 9     public static void main(String[] args)
10     {
11        int[] a = ArrayUtil.randomIntArray(20, 100);
12        System.out.println(Arrays.toString(a));
13
14        MergeSorter sorter = new MergeSorter(a);
15        sorter.sort();
16        System.out.println(Arrays.toString(a));
17     }
18  }
```

Typical Output

```
[8, 81, 48, 53, 46, 70, 98, 42, 27, 76, 33, 24, 2, 76, 62, 89, 90, 5, 13, 21]
[2, 5, 8, 13, 21, 24, 27, 33, 42, 46, 48, 53, 62, 70, 76, 76, 81, 89, 90, 98]
```

SELF CHECK

7. Why does only one of the two `while` loops at the end of the `merge` method do any work?

8. Manually run the merge sort algorithm on the array 8 7 6 5 4 3 2 1.

14.5 Analyzing the Merge Sort Algorithm

The merge sort algorithm looks a lot more complicated than the selection sort algorithm, and it appears that it may well take much longer to carry out these repeated subdivisions. However, the timing results for merge sort look much better than those for selection sort.

Figure 2 shows a table and a graph comparing both sets of performance data. As you can see, merge sort is a tremendous improvement. To understand why, let us estimate the number of array element visits that are required to sort an array with the merge sort algorithm. First, let us tackle the merge process that happens after the first and second halves have been sorted.

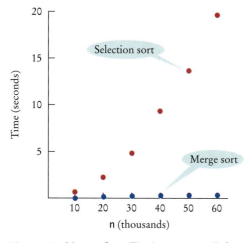

n	Merge Sort (milliseconds)	Selection Sort (milliseconds)
10,000	40	786
20,000	73	2,148
30,000	134	4,796
40,000	170	9,192
50,000	192	13,321
60,000	205	19,299

Figure 2 Merge Sort Timing versus Selection Sort

Each step in the merge process adds one more element to a. That element may come from first or second, and in most cases the elements from the two halves must be compared to see which one to take. We'll count that as 3 visits (one for a and one each for first and second) per element, or $3n$ visits total, where n denotes the length of a. Moreover, at the beginning, we had to copy from a to first and second, yielding another $2n$ visits, for a total of $5n$.

If we let $T(n)$ denote the number of visits required to sort a range of n elements through the merge sort process, then we obtain

$$T(n) = T\left(\frac{n}{2}\right) + T\left(\frac{n}{2}\right) + 5n$$

because sorting each half takes $T(n/2)$ visits. Actually, if n is not even, then we have one subarray of size $(n-1)/2$ and one of size $(n+1)/2$. Although it turns out that this detail does not affect the outcome of the computation, we will nevertheless assume for now that n is a power of 2, say $n = 2^m$. That way, all subarrays can be evenly divided into two parts.

Unfortunately, the formula

$$T(n) = 2T\left(\frac{n}{2}\right) + 5n$$

does not clearly tell us the relationship between n and $T(n)$. To understand the relationship, let us evaluate $T(n/2)$, using the same formula:

$$T\left(\frac{n}{2}\right) = 2T\left(\frac{n}{4}\right) + 5\frac{n}{2}$$

Therefore

$$T(n) = 2 \times 2T\left(\frac{n}{4}\right) + 5n + 5n$$

Let us do that again:

$$T\left(\frac{n}{4}\right) = 2T\left(\frac{n}{8}\right) + 5\frac{n}{4}$$

hence

$$T(n) = 2 \times 2 \times 2T\left(\frac{n}{8}\right) + 5n + 5n + 5n$$

This generalizes from 2, 4, 8, to arbitrary powers of 2:

$$T(n) = 2^k T\left(\frac{n}{2^k}\right) + 5nk$$

Recall that we assume that $n = 2^m$; hence, for $k = m$,

$$T(n) = 2^m T\left(\frac{n}{2^m}\right) + 5nm$$

$$= nT(1) + 5nm$$

$$= n + 5n\log_2(n)$$

Because $n = 2^m$, we have $m = \log_2(n)$.

To establish the growth order, we drop the lower-order term n and are left with $5n \log_2(n)$. We drop the constant factor 5. It is also customary to drop the base of the logarithm, because all logarithms are related by a constant factor. For example,

$$\log_2(x) = \log_{10}(x)/\log_{10}(2) \approx \log_{10}(x) \times 3.32193$$

Hence we say that merge sort is an $O(n \log(n))$ algorithm.

> Merge sort is an $O(n \log(n))$ algorithm. The $n \log(n)$ function grows much more slowly than n^2.

Is the $O(n \log(n))$ merge sort algorithm better than the $O(n^2)$ selection sort algorithm? You bet it is. Recall that it took $100^2 = 10,000$ times as long to sort a million records as it took to sort 10,000 records with the $O(n^2)$ algorithm. With the $O(n \log(n))$ algorithm, the ratio is

$$\frac{1,000,000 \log(1,000,000)}{10,000 \log(10,000)} = 100\left(\frac{6}{4}\right) = 150$$

Suppose for the moment that merge sort takes the same time as selection sort to sort an array of 10,000 integers, that is, 3/4 of a second on the test machine. (Actually, it is much faster than that.) Then it would take about 0.75×150 seconds, or under 2 minutes, to sort a million integers. Contrast that with selection sort, which would take over 2 hours for the same task. As you can see, even if it takes you several hours to learn about a better algorithm, that can be time well spent.

In this chapter we have barely begun to scratch the surface of this interesting topic. There are many sorting algorithms, some with even better performance than merge sort, and the analysis of these algorithms can be quite challenging. These important issues are often revisited in later computer science courses.

SELF CHECK

9. Given the timing data for the merge sort algorithm in the table at the beginning of this section, how long would it take to sort an array of 100,000 values?

10. If you double the size of an array, how much longer will the merge sort algorithm take to sort the new array?

Special Topic 14.3

The Quicksort Algorithm

Quicksort is a commonly used algorithm that has the advantage over merge sort that no temporary arrays are required to sort and merge the partial results.

The quicksort algorithm, like merge sort, is based on the strategy of divide and conquer. To sort a range a[from] . . . a[to] of the array a, first rearrange the elements in the range so that no element in the range a[from] . . . a[p] is larger than any element in the range a[p + 1] . . . a[to]. This step is called *partitioning* the range.

For example, suppose we start with a range

| 5 | 3 | 2 | 6 | 4 | 1 | 3 | 7 |

Here is a partitioning of the range. Note that the partitions aren't yet sorted.

| 3 | 3 | 2 | 1 | 4 | | 6 | 5 | 7 |

You'll see later how to obtain such a partition. In the next step, sort each partition, by recursively applying the same algorithm on the two partitions. That sorts the entire range, because the largest element in the first partition is at most as large as the smallest element in the second partition.

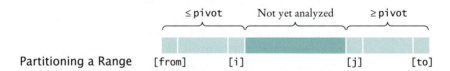

Quicksort is implemented recursively as follows:

```
public void sort(int from, int to)
{
    if (from >= to) return;
    int p = partition(from, to);
    sort(from, p);
    sort(p + 1, to);
}
```

Let us return to the problem of partitioning a range. Pick an element from the range and call it the *pivot*. There are several variations of the quicksort algorithm. In the simplest one, we'll pick the first element of the range, a[from], as the pivot.

Now form two regions a[from] . . . a[i], consisting of values at most as large as the pivot and a[j] . . . a[to], consisting of values at least as large as the pivot. The region a[i + 1] . . . a[j - 1] consists of values that haven't been analyzed yet. (See the figure below.) At the beginning, both the left and right areas are empty; that is, i = from - 1 and j = to + 1.

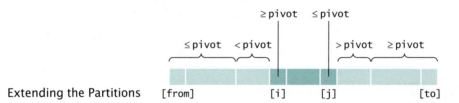

Partitioning a Range

Then keep incrementing i while a[i] < pivot and keep decrementing j while a[j] > pivot. The figure below shows i and j when that process stops.

Extending the Partitions

Now swap the values in positions i and j, increasing both areas once more. Keep going while i < j. Here is the code for the partition method:

```
private int partition(int from, int to)
{
    int pivot = a[from];
    int i = from - 1;
    int j = to + 1;
    while (i < j)
    {
        i++; while (a[i] < pivot) i++;
        j--; while (a[j] > pivot) j--;
        if (i < j) swap(i, j);
    }
    return j;
}
```

On average, the quicksort algorithm is an $O(n \log(n))$ algorithm. Because it is simpler, it runs faster than merge sort in most cases. There is just one unfortunate aspect to the quicksort algorithm. Its *worst-case* run-time behavior is $O(n^2)$. Moreover, if the pivot element is chosen as the first element of the region, that worst-case behavior occurs when the input set is already sorted—a common situation in practice. By selecting the pivot element more cleverly, we can make it extremely unlikely for the worst-case behavior to occur. Such "tuned" quicksort algorithms are commonly used, because their performance is generally excellent. For example, the sort method in the Arrays class uses a quicksort algorithm.

Another improvement that is commonly made in practice is to switch to insertion sort when the array is short, because the total number of operations of insertion sort is lower for short arrays. The Java library makes that switch if the array length is less than 7.

Random Fact 14.1

The First Programmer

Before pocket calculators and personal computers existed, navigators and engineers used mechanical adding machines, slide rules, and tables of logarithms and trigonometric functions to speed up computations. Unfortunately, the tables—for which values had to be computed by hand—were notoriously inaccurate. The mathematician Charles Babbage (1791–1871) had the insight that if a machine could be constructed that produced printed tables automatically, both calculation and typesetting errors could be avoided. Babbage set out to develop a machine for this purpose, which he called a *Difference Engine* because it used successive differences to compute polynomials. For example, consider the function $f(x) = x^3$. Write down the values for $f(1)$, $f(2)$, $f(3)$, and so on. Then take the *differences* between successive values:

```
1
        7
8
        19
27
        37
64
        61
125
        91
216
```

Repeat the process, taking the difference of successive values in the second column, and then repeat once again:

```
1
        7
8           12
        19       6
27          18
        37       6
64          24
        61       6
125         30
        91
216
```

Now the differences are all the same. You can retrieve the function values by a pattern of additions—you need to know the values at the fringe of the pattern and the constant difference. You can try it out yourself: Write the highlighted numbers on a sheet of paper, and fill in the others by adding the numbers that are in the north and northwest positions.

A Replica of Babbage's Difference Engine

This method was very attractive, because mechanical addition machines had been known for some time. They consisted of cog wheels, with ten cogs per wheel, to represent digits, and mechanisms to handle the carry from one digit to the next. Mechanical multiplication machines, on the other hand, were fragile and unreliable. Babbage built a successful prototype of the Difference Engine and, with his own money and government grants, proceeded to build the table-printing machine. However, because of funding problems and the difficulty of building the machine to the required precision, it was never completed.

While working on the Difference Engine, Babbage conceived of a much grander vision that he called the *Analytical Engine*. The Difference Engine was designed to carry out a limited set of computations—it was no smarter than a pocket calculator is today. But Babbage realized that such a machine could be made *programmable* by storing programs as well as data. The internal storage of the Analytical Engine was to consist of 1,000 registers of 50 decimal digits each. Programs and constants were to be stored on punched cards—a technique that was, at that time, commonly used on looms for weaving patterned fabrics.

Ada Augusta, Countess of Lovelace (1815–1852), the only child of Lord Byron, was a friend and sponsor of Charles Babbage. Ada Lovelace was one of the first people to realize the potential of such a machine, not just for computing mathematical tables but for processing data that were not numbers. She is considered by many the world's first programmer. The Ada programming language, a language developed for use in U.S. Department of Defense projects, was named in her honor.

14.6 Searching

Suppose you need to find your friend's telephone number. You look up the friend's name in the telephone book, and naturally you can find it quickly, because the telephone book is sorted alphabetically. Now suppose you have a telephone number and you must know to what party it belongs. You could of course call that number, but suppose nobody picks up on the other end. You could look through the telephone book, a number at a time, until you find the number. That would obviously be a tremendous amount of work, and you would have to be desperate to attempt it.

This thought experiment shows the difference between a search through an unsorted data set and a search through a sorted data set. The following two sections will analyze the difference formally.

If you want to find a number in a sequence of values that occur in arbitrary order, there is nothing you can do to speed up the search. You must simply look through all elements until you have found a match or until you reach the end. This is called a **linear** or **sequential search**.

> A linear search examines all values in an array until it finds a match or reaches the end.

How long does a linear search take? If we assume that the element v is present in the array a, then the average search visits $n/2$ elements, where n is the length of the array. If it is not present, then all n elements must be inspected to verify the absence. Either way, a linear search is an $O(n)$ algorithm.

> A linear search locates a value in an array in $O(n)$ steps.

Here is a class that performs linear searches through an array a of integers. When searching for the value v, the search method returns the first index of the match, or -1 if v does not occur in a.

ch14/linsearch/LinearSearcher.java

```java
1  /**
2      A class for executing linear searches through an array.
3  */
4  public class LinearSearcher
5  {
6     private int[] a;
7
8     /**
9         Constructs the LinearSearcher.
10        @param anArray an array of integers
11    */
12    public LinearSearcher(int[] anArray)
13    {
14       a = anArray;
15    }
16
17    /**
18        Finds a value in an array, using the linear search
19        algorithm.
20        @param v the value to search
21        @return the index at which the value occurs, or -1
22        if it does not occur in the array
23    */
24    public int search(int v)
25    {
26       for (int i = 0; i < a.length; i++)
27       {
28          if (a[i] == v)
29             return i;
30       }
31       return -1;
32    }
33  }
```

ch14/linsearch/LinearSearchDemo.java

```java
 1  import java.util.Arrays;
 2  import java.util.Scanner;
 3
 4  /**
 5      This program demonstrates the linear search algorithm.
 6  */
 7  public class LinearSearchDemo
 8  {
 9     public static void main(String[] args)
10     {
11        int[] a = ArrayUtil.randomIntArray(20, 100);
12        System.out.println(Arrays.toString(a));
13        LinearSearcher searcher = new LinearSearcher(a);
14
15        Scanner in = new Scanner(System.in);
16
17        boolean done = false;
18        while (!done)
19        {
20           System.out.print("Enter number to search for, -1 to quit: ");
21           int n = in.nextInt();
22           if (n == -1)
23              done = true;
24           else
25           {
26              int pos = searcher.search(n);
27              System.out.println("Found in position " + pos);
28           }
29        }
30     }
31  }
```

Typical Output

```
[46, 99, 45, 57, 64, 95, 81, 69, 11, 97, 6, 85, 61, 88, 29, 65, 83, 88, 45, 88]
Enter number to search for, -1 to quit: 11
Found in position 8
```

SELF CHECK

11. Suppose you need to look through 1,000,000 records to find a telephone number. How many records do you expect to search before finding the number?

12. Why can't you use a "for each" loop `for (int element : a)` in the search method?

14.7 Binary Search

Now let us search for an item in a data sequence that has been previously sorted. Of course, we could still do a linear search, but it turns out we can do much better than that.

Consider the following sorted array a. The data set is:

```
[0][1][2][3][4][5][6][7]
 1  5  8  9 12 17 20 32
```

We would like to see whether the value 15 is in the data set. Let's narrow our search by finding whether the value is in the first or second half of the array. The last point in the first half of the data set, a[3], is 9, which is smaller than the value we are looking for. Hence, we should look in the second half of the array for a match, that is, in the sequence:

```
[0][1][2][3][4][5][6][7]
 1  5  8  9 12 17 20 32
```

Now the last value of the first half of this sequence is 17; hence, the value must be located in the sequence:

```
[0][1][2][3][4][5][6][7]
 1  5  8  9 12 17 20 32
```

The last value of the first half of this very short sequence is 12, which is smaller than the value that we are searching, so we must look in the second half:

```
[0][1][2][3][4][5][6][7]
 1  5  8  9 12 17 20 32
```

It is trivial to see that we don't have a match, because 15 ≠ 17. If we wanted to insert 15 into the sequence, we would need to insert it just before a[5].

This search process is called a **binary search**, because we cut the size of the search in half in each step. That cutting in half works only because we know that the sequence of values is sorted.

The following class implements binary searches in a sorted array of integers. The search method returns the position of the match if the search succeeds, or –1 if v is not found in a.

> A binary search locates a value in a sorted array by determining whether the value occurs in the first or second half, then repeating the search in one of the halves.

ch14/binsearch/BinarySearcher.java

```java
 1  /**
 2      A class for executing binary searches through an array.
 3  */
 4  public class BinarySearcher
 5  {
 6      private int[] a;
 7
 8      /**
 9          Constructs a BinarySearcher.
10          @param anArray a sorted array of integers
11      */
12      public BinarySearcher(int[] anArray)
13      {
14          a = anArray;
15      }
16
17      /**
18          Finds a value in a sorted array, using the binary
19          search algorithm.
20          @param v the value to search
21          @return the index at which the value occurs, or -1
22          if it does not occur in the array
23      */
```

```
24    public int search(int v)
25    {
26       int low = 0;
27       int high = a.length - 1;
28       while (low <= high)
29       {
30          int mid = (low + high) / 2;
31          int diff = a[mid] - v;
32
33          if (diff == 0) // a[mid] == v
34             return mid;
35          else if (diff < 0) // a[mid] < v
36             low = mid + 1;
37          else
38             high = mid - 1;
39       }
40       return -1;
41    }
42 }
```

Now let's determine the number of visits to array elements required to carry out a binary search. We can use the same technique as in the analysis of merge sort. Because we look at the middle element, which counts as one visit, and then search either the left or the right subarray, we have

$$T(n) = T\left(\frac{n}{2}\right) + 1$$

Using the same equation,

$$T\left(\frac{n}{2}\right) = T\left(\frac{n}{4}\right) + 1$$

By plugging this result into the original equation, we get

$$T(n) = T\left(\frac{n}{4}\right) + 2$$

That generalizes to

$$T(n) = T\left(\frac{n}{2^k}\right) + k$$

As in the analysis of merge sort, we make the simplifying assumption that n is a power of 2, $n = 2^m$, where $m = \log_2(n)$. Then we obtain

$$T(n) = 1 + \log_2(n)$$

Therefore, binary search is an $O(\log(n))$ algorithm.

> A binary search locates a value in a sorted array in $O(\log(n))$ steps.

That result makes intuitive sense. Suppose that n is 100. Then after each search, the size of the search range is cut in half, to 50, 25, 12, 6, 3, and 1. After seven comparisons we are done. This agrees with our formula, because $\log_2(100) \approx 6.64386$, and indeed the next larger power of 2 is $2^7 = 128$.

Because a binary search is so much faster than a linear search, is it worthwhile to sort an array first and then use a binary search? It depends. If you search the array only once, then it is more efficient to pay for an $O(n)$ linear search than for an $O(n \log(n))$ sort and an $O(\log(n))$ binary search. But if you will be making many searches in the same array, then sorting it is definitely worthwhile.

The Arrays class contains a static binarySearch method that implements the binary search algorithm, but with a useful enhancement. If a value is not found in the array, then the returned value is not –1, but $-k - 1$, where k is the position before which the element should be inserted. For example,

```
int[] a = { 1, 4, 9 };
int v = 7;
int pos = Arrays.binarySearch(a, v);
    // Returns -3; v should be inserted before position 2
```

SELF CHECK

13. Suppose you need to look through a sorted array with 1,000,000 elements to find a value. Using the binary search algorithm, how many records do you expect to search before finding the value?

14. Why is it useful that the Arrays.binarySearch method indicates the position where a missing element should be inserted?

15. Why does Arrays.binarySearch return $-k - 1$ and not $-k$ to indicate that a value is not present and should be inserted before position k?

14.8 Sorting Real Data

> The Arrays class implements a sorting method that you should use for your Java programs.

When you write Java programs, you don't have to implement your own sorting algorithms. The Arrays class contains static sort methods to sort arrays of integers and floating-point numbers. For example, you can sort an array of integers simply as

```
int[] a = . . .;
Arrays.sort(a);
```

That sort method uses the quicksort algorithm—see Special Topic 14.3 on page 611 for more information about that algorithm.

Of course, in application programs, there is rarely a need to search through a collection of integers. However, it is easy to modify these techniques to search through real data.

> The sort method of the Arrays class sorts objects of classes that implement the Comparable interface.

The Arrays class also supplies a static sort method for sorting arrays of objects. However, the Arrays class cannot know how to compare arbitrary objects. Suppose, for example, that you have an array of Coin objects. It is not obvious how the coins should be sorted. You could sort them by their names, or by their values. The Arrays.sort method cannot make that decision for you. Instead, it requires that the objects belong to classes that implement the Comparable interface. That interface has a single method:

```
public interface Comparable
{
    int compareTo(Object otherObject);
}
```

The call

```
a.compareTo(b)
```

must return a negative number if a should come before b, 0 if a and b are the same, and a positive number otherwise.

Several classes in the standard Java library, such as the String and Date classes, implement the Comparable interface.

You can implement the Comparable interface for your own classes as well. For example, to sort a collection of coins, the Coin class would need to implement this interface and declare a compareTo method:

```java
public class Coin implements Comparable
{
    . . .
    public int compareTo(Object otherObject)
    {
        Coin other = (Coin) otherObject;
        if (value < other.value) return -1;
        if (value == other.value) return 0;
        return 1;
    }
    . . .
}
```

When you implement the compareTo method of the Comparable interface, you must make sure that the method defines a **total ordering** relationship, with the following three properties:

- *Antisymmetric:* If a.compareTo(b) $\leq$ 0, then b.compareTo(a) $\geq$ 0
- *Reflexive:* a.compareTo(a) = 0
- *Transitive:* If a.compareTo(b) $\leq$ 0 and b.compareTo(c) $\leq$ 0, then a.compareTo(c) $\leq$ 0

Once your Coin class implements the Comparable interface, you can simply pass an array of coins to the Arrays.sort method:

```java
Coin[] coins = new Coin[n];
// Add coins
. . .
Arrays.sort(coins);
```

The Collections class contains a sort method that can sort array lists.

If the coins are stored in an ArrayList, use the Collections.sort method instead; it uses the merge sort algorithm:

```java
ArrayList<Coin> coins = new ArrayList<Coin>();
// Add coins
. . .
Collections.sort(coins);
```

As a practical matter, you should use the sorting and searching methods in the Arrays and Collections classes and not those that you write yourself. The library algorithms have been fully debugged and optimized. Thus, the primary purpose of this chapter was not to teach you how to implement practical sorting and searching algorithms. Instead, you have learned something more important, namely that different algorithms can vary widely in performance, and that it is worthwhile to learn more about the design and analysis of algorithms.

 **S E L F   C H E C K**

16. Why can't the Arrays.sort method sort an array of Rectangle objects?

17. What steps would you need to take to sort an array of BankAccount objects by increasing balance?

Common Error 14.1

The compareTo Method Can Return Any Integer, Not Just −1, 0, and 1

The call a.compareTo(b) is allowed to return *any* negative integer to denote that a should come before b, not necessarily the value −1. That is, the test

```
if (a.compareTo(b) == -1) // ERROR!
```

is generally wrong. Instead, you should test

```
if (a.compareTo(b) < 0) // OK
```

Why would a compareTo method ever want to return a number other than −1, 0, or 1? Sometimes, it is convenient to just return the difference of two integers. For example, the compareTo method of the String class compares characters in matching positions:

```
char c1 = charAt(i);
char c2 = other.charAt(i);
```

If the characters are different, then the method simply returns their difference:

```
if (c1 != c2) return c1 - c2;
```

This difference is a negative number if c1 is less than c2, but it is not necessarily the number −1.

Special Topic 14.4

The Parameterized Comparable Interface

As of Java version 5, the Comparable interface is a parameterized type, similar to the ArrayList type:

```
public interface Comparable<T>
{
   int compareTo(T other)
}
```

The type parameter specifies the type of the objects that this class is willing to accept for comparison. Usually, this type is the same as the class type itself. For example, the Coin class would implement Comparable<Coin>, like this:

```
public class Coin implements Comparable<Coin>
{
   . . .
   public int compareTo(Coin other)
   {
      if (value < other.value) return -1;
      if (value == other.value) return 0;
      return 1;
   }
   . . .
}
```

The type parameter has a significant advantage: You need not use a cast to convert an Object parameter into the desired type.

Special Topic 14.5

The Comparator Interface

Sometimes, you want so sort an array or array list of objects, but the objects don't belong to a class that implements the Comparable interface. Or, perhaps, you want to sort the array in a different order. For example, you may want to sort coins by name rather than by value.

You wouldn't want to change the implementation of a class just in order to call Arrays.sort. Fortunately, there is an alternative. One version of the Arrays.sort method does not require that the objects belong to classes that implement the Comparable interface. Instead, you can supply arbitrary objects. However, you must also provide a *comparator* object whose job is to compare objects. The comparator object must belong to a class that implements the Comparator interface. That interface has a single method, compare, which compares two objects.

As of Java version 5, the Comparator interface is a parameterized type. The type parameter specifies the type of the compare parameters. For example, Comparator<Coin> looks like this:

```java
public interface Comparator<Coin>
{
    int compare(Coin a, Coin b);
}
```

The call

```java
comp.compare(a, b)
```

must return a negative number if a should come before b, 0 if a and b are the same, and a positive number otherwise. (Here, comp is an object of a class that implements Comparator<Coin>.)

For example, here is a Comparator class for coins:

```java
public class CoinComparator implements Comparator<Coin>
{
    public int compare(Coin a, Coin b)
    {
        if (a.getValue() < b.getValue()) return -1;
        if (a.getValue() == b.getValue()) return 0;
        return 1;
    }
}
```

To sort an array of coins by value, call

```java
Arrays.sort(coins, new CoinComparator());
```

Summary of Learning Objectives

Describe the selection sort algorithm.

- The selection sort algorithm sorts an array by repeatedly finding the smallest element of the unsorted tail region and moving it to the front.

Measure the running time of a method.

- To measure the running time of a method, get the current time immediately before and after the method call.

Use the big-Oh notation to describe the running time of an algorithm.

- Computer scientists use the big-Oh notation $f(n) = O(g(n))$ to express that the function f grows no faster than the function g.
- Selection sort is an $O(n^2)$ algorithm. Doubling the data set means a fourfold increase in processing time.
- Insertion sort is an $O(n^2)$ algorithm.

Describe the merge sort algorithm.

- The merge sort algorithm sorts an array by cutting the array in half, recursively sorting each half, and then merging the sorted halves.

Contrast the running times of the merge sort and selection sort algorithms.

- Merge sort is an $O(n \log(n))$ algorithm. The $n \log(n)$ function grows much more slowly than n^2.

Describe the linear search algorithm and its running time.

- A linear search examines all values in an array until it finds a match or reaches the end.
- A linear search locates a value in an array in $O(n)$ steps.

Describe the binary search algorithm and its running time.

- A binary search locates a value in a sorted array by determining whether the value occurs in the first or second half, then repeating the search in one of the halves.
- A binary search locates a value in a sorted array in $O(\log(n))$ steps.

Use the Java library methods for sorting data.

- The `Arrays` class implements a sorting method that you should use for your Java programs.
- The `sort` method of the `Arrays` class sorts objects of classes that implement the `Comparable` interface.
- The `Collections` class contains a sort method that can sort array lists.

Classes, Objects, and Methods Introduced in This Chapter

```
java.lang.Comparable<T>          java.util.Collections
    compareTo                        binarySearch
java.lang.System                     sort
    currentTimeMillis            java.util.Comparator<T>
java.util.Arrays                     compare
    binarySearch
    sort
    toString
```


Media Resources

*www.wiley.com/
college/
horstmann*

- Lab Exercises
- Practice Quiz
- Code Completion Exercises

Review Exercises

★ **R14.1** What is the difference between searching and sorting?

★★ **R14.2** *Checking against off-by-one errors.* When writing the selection sort algorithm of Section 14.1, a programmer must make the usual choices of < against <=, a.length against a.length - 1, and from against from + 1. This is a fertile ground for off-by-one errors. Conduct code walkthroughs of the algorithm with arrays of length 0, 1, 2, and 3 and check carefully that all index values are correct.

★★ **R14.3** For the following expressions, what is the order of the growth of each?

a. $n^2 + 2n + 1$

b. $n^{10} + 9n^9 + 20n^8 + 145n^7$

c. $(n + 1)^4$

d. $(n^2 + n)^2$

e. $n + 0.001n^3$

f. $n^3 - 1000n^2 + 10^9$

g. $n + \log(n)$

h. $n^2 + n \log(n)$

i. $2^n + n^2$

j. $\dfrac{n^3 + 2n}{n^2 + 0.75}$

★ **R14.4** We determined that the actual number of visits in the selection sort algorithm is

$$T(n) = \tfrac{1}{2}n^2 + \tfrac{5}{2}n - 3$$

We characterized this method as having $O(n^2)$ growth. Compute the actual ratios

$$T(2{,}000)/T(1{,}000)$$
$$T(4{,}000)/T(1{,}000)$$
$$T(10{,}000)/T(1{,}000)$$

and compare them with

$$f(2{,}000)/f(1{,}000)$$
$$f(4{,}000)/f(1{,}000)$$
$$f(10{,}000)/f(1{,}000)$$

where $f(n) = n^2$.

★ **R14.5** Suppose algorithm A takes 5 seconds to handle a data set of 1,000 records. If the algorithm A is an $O(n)$ algorithm, how long will it take to handle a data set of 2,000 records? Of 10,000 records?

★★ **R14.6** Suppose an algorithm takes 5 seconds to handle a data set of 1,000 records. Fill in the following table, which shows the approximate growth of the execution times depending on the complexity of the algorithm.

	$O(n)$	$O(n^2)$	$O(n^3)$	$O(n \log(n))$	$O(2^n)$
1,000	5	5	5	5	5
2,000					
3,000		45			
10,000					

For example, because $3{,}000^2/1{,}000^2 = 9$, the algorithm would take 9 times as long, or 45 seconds, to handle a data set of 3,000 records.

★★ **R14.7** Sort the following growth rates from slowest to fastest growth.

$$O(n) \qquad\qquad O(n \log(n))$$

$$O(n^3) \qquad\qquad O(2^n)$$

$$O(n^n) \qquad\qquad O(\sqrt{n})$$

$$O(\log(n)) \qquad\qquad O(n\sqrt{n})$$

$$O(n^2 \log(n)) \qquad\qquad O(n^{\log(n)})$$

★ **R14.8** What is the growth rate of the standard algorithm to find the minimum value of an array? Of finding both the minimum and the maximum?

★ **R14.9** What is the growth rate of the following method?

```
public static int count(int[] a, int c)
{
   int count = 0;

   for (int i = 0; i < a.length; i++)
   {
      if (a[i] == c) count++;
   }
   return count;
}
```

★★ **R14.10** Your task is to remove all duplicates from an array. For example, if the array has the values

$$4\ 7\ 11\ 4\ 9\ 5\ 11\ 7\ 3\ 5$$

then the array should be changed to

$$4\ 7\ 11\ 9\ 5\ 3$$

Here is a simple algorithm. Look at a[i]. Count how many times it occurs in a. If the count is larger than 1, remove it. What is the growth rate of the time required for this algorithm?

★★ **R14.11** Consider the following algorithm to remove all duplicates from an array. Sort the array. For each element in the array, look at its next neighbor to decide whether it is present more than once. If so, remove it. Is this a faster algorithm than the one in Exercise R14.10?

★★★ **R14.12** Develop an $O(n \log (n))$ algorithm for removing duplicates from an array if the resulting array must have the same ordering as the original array.

★★★ **R14.13** Why does insertion sort perform significantly better than selection sort if an array is already sorted?

★★★ **R14.14** Consider the following speedup of the insertion sort algorithm of Special Topic 14.1 on page 604. For each element, use the enhanced binary search algorithm that yields the insertion position for missing elements. Does this speedup have a significant impact on the efficiency of the algorithm?

Programming Exercises

★ **P14.1** Modify the selection sort algorithm to sort an array of integers in descending order.

★ **P14.2** Modify the selection sort algorithm to sort an array of coins by their value.

★★ **P14.3** Write a program that generates the table of sample runs of the selection sort times automatically. The program should ask for the smallest and largest value of n and the number of measurements and then make all sample runs.

★ **P14.4** Modify the merge sort algorithm to sort an array of strings in lexicographic order.

★★★ **P14.5** Write a telephone lookup program. Read a data set of 1,000 names and telephone numbers from a file that contains the numbers in random order. Handle lookups by name and also reverse lookups by phone number. Use a binary search for both lookups.

★★ **P14.6** Implement a program that measures the performance of the insertion sort algorithm described in Special Topic 14.1 on page 604.

★★★ **P14.7** Write a program that sorts an `ArrayList<Coin>` in decreasing order so that the most valuable coin is at the beginning of the array. Use a `Comparator`.

★★ **P14.8** Consider the binary search algorithm in Section 14.7. If no match is found, the search method returns −1. Modify the method so that if a is not found, the method returns $-k - 1$, where k is the position before which the element should be inserted. (This is the same behavior as `Arrays.binarySearch`.)

★★ **P14.9** Implement the `sort` method of the merge sort algorithm without recursion, where the length of the array is a power of 2. First merge adjacent regions of size 1, then adjacent regions of size 2, then adjacent regions of size 4, and so on.

★★★ **P14.10** Implement the `sort` method of the merge sort algorithm without recursion, where the length of the array is an arbitrary number. Keep merging adjacent regions whose size is a power of 2, and pay special attention to the last area whose size is less.

★★★ **P14.11** Use insertion sort and the binary search from Exercise P14.8 to sort an array as described in Exercise R14.14. Implement this algorithm and measure its performance.

★ **P14.12** Supply a class Person that implements the Comparable interface. Compare persons by their names. Ask the user to input 10 names and generate 10 Person objects. Using the compareTo method, determine the first and last person among them and print them.

★★ **P14.13** Sort an array list of strings by increasing *length*. *Hint:* Supply a Comparator.

★★★ **P14.14** Sort an array list of strings by increasing length, and so that strings of the same length are sorted lexicographically. *Hint:* Supply a Comparator.

Programming Projects

Project 14.1 Write a program that keeps an appointment book. Make a class Appointment that stores a description of the appointment, the appointment day, the starting time, and the ending time. Your program should keep the appointments in a sorted array list. Users can add appointments and print out all appointments for a given day. When a new appointment is added, use binary search to find where it should be inserted in the array list. Do not add it if it conflicts with another appointment.

Project 14.2 Implement a *graphical animation* of sorting and searching algorithms. Fill an array with a set of random numbers between 1 and 100. Draw each array element as a bar, as in Figure 3. Whenever the algorithm changes the array, wait for the user to click the Step button, then call the repaint method. The Run button should run the animation until the animation has finished or the user clicks the Step button again.

Animate selection sort, merge sort, and binary search. In the binary search animation, highlight the currently inspected element and the current values of from and to.

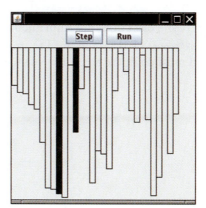

Figure 3
Graphical Animation

Answers to Self-Check Questions

1. Dropping the temp variable would not work. Then a[i] and a[j] would end up being the same value.

2. 1 | 5 4 3 2 6, 1 2 | 4 3 5 6, 1 2 3 4 5 6

3. Four times as long as 40,000 values, or about 50 seconds.

4. A parabola.

5. It takes about 100 times longer.

6. If n is 4, then $\frac{1}{2}n^2$ is 8 and $\frac{5}{2}n - 3$ is 7.

7. When the preceding while loop ends, the loop condition must be false, that is, iFirst >= first.length or iSecond >= second.length (De Morgan's Law).

8. First sort 8 7 6 5. Recursively, first sort 8 7. Recursively, first sort 8. It's sorted. Sort 7. It's sorted. Merge them: 7 8. Do the same with 6 5 to get 5 6. Merge them to 5 6 7 8. Do the same with 4 3 2 1: Sort 4 3 by sorting 4 and 3 and merging them to 3 4. Sort 2 1 by sorting 2 and 1 and merging them to 1 2. Merge 3 4 and 1 2 to 1 2 3 4. Finally, merge 5 6 7 8 and 1 2 3 4 to 1 2 3 4 5 6 7 8.

9. Approximately $100{,}000 \cdot \log(100{,}000) / 50{,}000 \cdot \log(50{,}000) = 2 \cdot 5 / 4.7 = 2.13$ times the time required for 50,000 values. That's $2.13 \cdot 97$ milliseconds or approximately 207 milliseconds.

10. $\dfrac{2n \log(2n)}{n \log(n)} = 2\dfrac{(1 + \log(2))}{\log(n)}$ For $n > 2$, that is a value < 3.

11. On average, you'd make 500,000 comparisons.

12. The search method returns the index at which the match occurs, not the data stored at that location.

13. You would search about 20. (The binary log of 1,024 is 10.)

14. Then you know where to insert it so that the array stays sorted, and you can keep using binary search.

15. Otherwise, you would not know whether a value is present when the method returns 0.

16. The Rectangle class does not implement the Comparable interface.

17. The BankAccount class would need to implement the Comparable interface. Its compareTo method must compare the bank balances.

An Introduction to Data Structures

CHAPTER GOALS

- To learn how to use the linked lists provided in the standard library
- To be able to use iterators to traverse linked lists
- To understand the implementation of linked lists
- To distinguish between abstract and concrete data types
- To know the efficiency of fundamental operations of lists and arrays
- To become familiar with the stack and queue data types

Up to this point, we have used arrays as a one-size-fits-all mechanism for collecting objects. However, computer scientists have developed many different data structures that have varying performance tradeoffs. In this chapter, you will learn about the *linked list*, a data structure that allows you to add and remove elements efficiently, without moving any existing elements. You will also learn about the distinction between concrete and abstract data types. An abstract type spells out the fundamental operations that should be supported efficiently, but it leaves the implementation unspecified. The stack and queue types, introduced at the end of this chapter, are examples of abstract types.

CHAPTER CONTENTS

15.1 Using Linked Lists

A **linked list** is a data structure used for collecting a sequence of objects that allows efficient addition and removal of elements in the middle of the sequence.

To understand the need for such a data structure, imagine a program that maintains a sequence of employee objects, sorted by the last names of the employees. When a new employee is hired, an object needs to be inserted into the sequence. Unless the company happened to hire employees in alphabetical order, the new object probably needs to be inserted somewhere near the middle of the sequence. If we use an array to store the objects, then all objects following the new hire must be moved toward the end.

Conversely, if an employee leaves the company, the object must be removed, and the hole in the sequence needs to be closed up by moving all objects that come after it. Moving a large number of values can involve a substantial amount of processing time. We would like to structure the data in a way that minimizes this cost.

> A linked list consists of a number of nodes, each of which has a reference to the next node.

Rather than storing the values in an array, a linked list uses a sequence of *nodes*. Each node stores a value and a reference to the next node in the sequence (see Figure 1). When you insert a new node into a linked list, only the neighboring node references need to be updated. The same is true when you remove a node. What's the catch? Linked lists allow speedy insertion and removal, but element access can be slow.

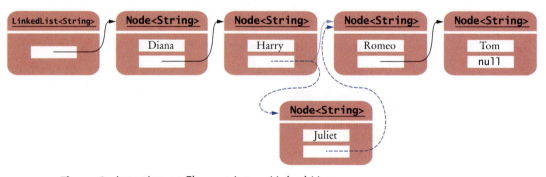

Figure 1 Inserting an Element into a Linked List

630

Adding and removing elements in the middle of a linked list is efficient.

For example, suppose you want to locate the fifth element. You must first traverse the first four. This is a problem if you need to access the elements in arbitrary order. The term "random access" is used in computer science to describe an access pattern in which elements are accessed in arbitrary (not necessarily random) order. In contrast, sequential access visits the elements in sequence. For example, a binary search requires random access, whereas a linear search requires sequential access.

Visiting the elements of a linked list in sequential order is efficient, but random access is not.

Of course, if you mostly visit elements in sequence (for example, to display or print the elements), you don't need to use random access. Use linked lists when you are concerned about the efficiency of inserting or removing elements and you rarely need element access in random order.

The Java library provides a linked list class. In this section you will learn how to use that library class. In the next section you will peek under the hood and see how some of its key methods are implemented.

The `LinkedList` class in the `java.util` package is a **generic class**, just like the `Array-List` class. That is, you specify the type of the list elements in angle brackets, such as `LinkedList<String>` or `LinkedList<Product>`.

The methods shown in Table 1 give you direct access to the first and the last element in the list.

How do you add and remove elements in the middle of the list? The list will not give you references to the nodes. If you had direct access to them and somehow messed them up, you would break the linked list. As you will see in the next section, when you implement some of the linked list operations yourself, keeping all links between nodes intact is not trivial.

You use a list iterator to access elements inside a linked list.

Instead, the Java library supplies a `ListIterator` type. A list **iterator** describes a position anywhere inside the linked list (see Figure 2).

Table 1 LinkedList Methods

`LinkedList<String> lst = new LinkedList<String>();`	An empty list.
`lst.addLast("Harry")`	Adds an element to the end of the list. Same as add.
`lst.addFirst("Sally")`	Adds an element to the beginning of the list. `lst` is now `[Sally, Harry]`.
`lst.getFirst()`	Gets the element stored at the beginning of the list; here `"Sally"`.
`lst.getLast()`	Gets the element stored at the end of the list; here `"Harry"`.
`String removed = lst.removeFirst();`	Removes the first element of the list and returns it. `removed` is `"Sally"` and `lst` is `[Harry]`. Use `removeLast` to remove the last element.
`ListIterator<String> iter = lst.listIterator()`	Provides an iterator for visiting all list elements (see Table 2 on page 634).

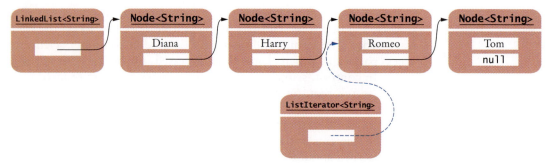

Figure 2 A List Iterator

Conceptually, you should think of the iterator as pointing between two elements, just as the cursor in a word processor points between two characters (see Figure 3). In the conceptual view, think of each element as being like a letter in a word processor, and think of the iterator as being like the blinking cursor between letters.

You obtain a list iterator with the `listIterator` method of the `LinkedList` class:

```
LinkedList<String> employeeNames = . . .;
ListIterator<String> iterator = employeeNames.listIterator();
```

Note that the iterator class is also a generic type. A `ListIterator<String>` iterates through a list of strings; a `ListIterator<Product>` visits the elements in a `LinkedList<Product>`.

Initially, the iterator points before the first element. You can move the iterator position with the `next` method:

```
iterator.next();
```

The `next` method throws a `NoSuchElementException` if you are already past the end of the list. You should always call the method `hasNext` before calling `next`—it returns `true` if there is a next element.

```
if (iterator.hasNext())
    iterator.next();
```

The `next` method returns the element that the iterator is passing. When you use a `ListIterator<String>`, the return type of the `next` method is `String`. In general, the return type of the `next` method matches the type parameter of the list.

You traverse all elements in a linked list of strings with the following loop:

```
while (iterator.hasNext())
{
    String name = iterator.next();
    Do something with name
}
```

As a shorthand, if your loop simply visits all elements of the linked list, you can use the "for each" loop:

```
for (String name : employeeNames)
{
    Do something with name
}
```

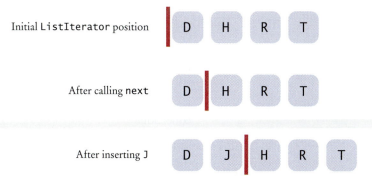

Figure 3 A Conceptual View of the List Iterator

Then you don't have to worry about iterators at all. Behind the scenes, the for loop uses an iterator to visit all list elements (see Special Topic 15.1 on page 635).

The nodes of the LinkedList class store two links: one to the next element and one to the previous one. Such a list is called a **doubly linked list**. You can use the previous and hasPrevious methods of the ListIterator interface to move the iterator position backwards.

The add method adds an object after the iterator, then moves the iterator position past the new element.

```
iterator.add("Juliet");
```

You can visualize insertion to be like typing text in a word processor. Each character is inserted after the cursor, and then the cursor moves past the inserted character (see Figure 3). Most people never pay much attention to this—you may want to try it out and watch carefully how your word processor inserts characters.

The remove method removes the object that was returned by the last call to next or previous. For example, the following loop removes all names that fulfill a certain condition:

```
while (iterator.hasNext())
{
   String name = iterator.next();
   if (name fulfills condition)
      iterator.remove();
}
```

ANIMATION
List Iterators

You have to be careful when using the remove method. It can be called only once after calling next or previous. The following is an error:

```
iterator.next();
iterator.next();
iterator.remove();
iterator.remove(); // Error: You cannot call remove twice.
```

You cannot call remove immediately after a call to add:

```
iter.add("Fred");
iter.remove(); // Error: Can only call remove after calling next or previous
```

If you call the remove method improperly, it throws an IllegalStateException.

Table 2 summarizes the methods of the ListIterator interface.

Table 2 Methods of the `ListIterator` Interface

`String s = iter.next();`	Assume that `iter` points to the beginning of the list `[Sally]` before calling next. After the call, s is `"Sally"` and the iterator points to the end.
`iter.hasNext()`	Returns `false` because the iterator is at the end of the collection.

`if (iter.hasPrevious())`
`{`
   `s = iter.previous();`
`}`
	hasPrevious returns true because the iterator is not at the beginning of the list.

`iter.add("Diana");`	Adds an element before the iterator position. The list is now `[Diana, Sally]`.
`iter.next();` `iter.remove();`	remove removes the last element returned by next or previous. The list is again `[Diana]`.

Here is a sample program that inserts strings into a list and then iterates through the list, adding and removing elements. Finally, the entire list is printed. The comments indicate the iterator position.

ch15/uselist/ListTester.java

```java
1   import java.util.LinkedList;
2   import java.util.ListIterator;
3
4   /**
5      A program that tests the LinkedList class.
6   */
7   public class ListTester
8   {
9      public static void main(String[] args)
10     {
11        LinkedList<String> staff = new LinkedList<String>();
12        staff.addLast("Diana");
13        staff.addLast("Harry");
14        staff.addLast("Romeo");
15        staff.addLast("Tom");
16
17        // | in the comments indicates the iterator position
18
19        ListIterator<String> iterator = staff.listIterator(); // |DHRT
20        iterator.next(); // D|HRT
21        iterator.next(); // DH|RT
22
23        // Add more elements after second element
24
25        iterator.add("Juliet"); // DHJ|RT
26        iterator.add("Nina"); // DHJN|RT
27
28        iterator.next(); // DHJNR|T
29
```

```
30      // Remove last traversed element
31
32      iterator.remove(); // DHJN|T
33
34      // Print all elements
35
36      for (String name : staff)
37         System.out.print(name + " ");
38      System.out.println();
39      System.out.println("Expected: Diana Harry Juliet Nina Tom");
40   }
41 }
```

Program Run

```
Diana Harry Juliet Nina Tom
Expected: Diana Harry Juliet Nina Tom
```

SELF CHECK

1. Do linked lists take more storage space than arrays of the same size?
2. Why don't we need iterators with arrays?

Special Topic 15.1

The `Iterable` Interface and the "For Each" Loop

You can use the "for each" loop

```
for (Type variable : collection)
```

with any of the collection classes in the standard Java library. This includes the `ArrayList` and `LinkedList` classes as well as the library classes which will be discussed in Chapter 16. In fact, the "for each" loop can be used with any class that implements the `Iterable` interface:

```
public interface Iterable<E>
{
    Iterator<E> iterator();
}
```

The interface has a type parameter E, denoting the element type of the collection. The single method, iterator, yields an object that implements the `Iterator<E>` interface. That interface has methods

```
boolean hasNext();
E next();
```

The `ListIterator` interface that you saw in the preceding section is a subinterface of `Iterator` with additional methods (such as `add` and `previous`).

The compiler translates a "for each" loop into an equivalent loop that uses an iterator. The loop

```
for (Type variable : collection)
    body
```

is equivalent to

```
Iterator<Type> iter = collection.iterator();
while (iter.hasNext())
{
```

```
    Type variable = iter.next();
    body
}
```

The `ArrayList` and `LinkedList` classes implement the `Iterable` interface. If your own classes implement the `Iterable` interface, you can use them with the "for each" loop as well—see Exercise P15.19.

15.2 Implementing Linked Lists

In the last section you saw how to use the linked list class supplied by the Java library. In this section, we will look at the implementation of a simplified version of this class. This shows you how the list operations manipulate the links as the list is modified.

To keep this sample code simple, we will not implement all methods of the linked list class. We will implement only a singly linked list, and the list class will supply direct access only to the first list element, not the last one. Our list will not use a type parameter. We will simply store raw `Object` values and insert casts when retrieving them. The result will be a fully functional list class that shows how the links are updated in the `add` and `remove` operations and how the iterator traverses the list.

A `Node` object stores an object and a reference to the next node. Because the methods of both the linked list class and the iterator class have frequent access to the `Node` instance variables, we do not make the instance variables of the `Node` class private. Instead, we make `Node` a private inner class of the `LinkedList` class. Because none of the `LinkedList` methods returns a `Node` object, it is safe to leave the instance variables public.

```java
public class LinkedList
{
    . . .
    class Node
    {
        public Object data;
        public Node next;
    }
}
```

Our `LinkedList` class holds a reference `first` to the first node (or `null`, if the list is completely empty).

A linked list object holds a reference to the first node, and each node holds a reference to the next node.

```java
public class LinkedList
{
    private Node first;
    . . .
    public LinkedList()
    {
        first = null;
    }

    public Object getFirst()
    {
        if (first == null)
            throw new NoSuchElementException();
```

```
        return first.data;
    }
}
```

Now let us turn to the `addFirst` method (see Figure 4). When a new node is added to the list, it becomes the head of the list, and the node that was the old list head becomes its next node:

```java
public class LinkedList
{
    . . .
    public void addFirst(Object element)
    {
        Node newNode = new Node();     1
        newNode.data = element;
        newNode.next = first;          2
        first = newNode;               3
    }
    . . .
}
```

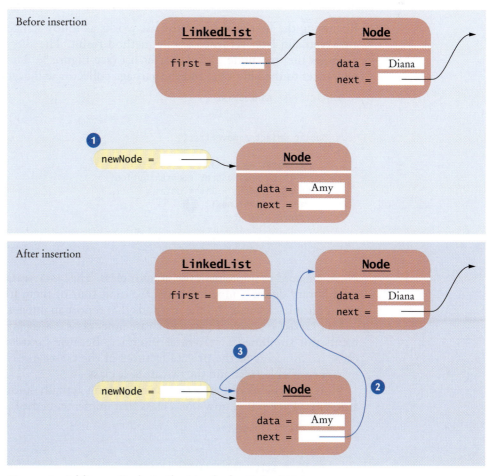

Figure 4 Adding a Node to the Head of a Linked List

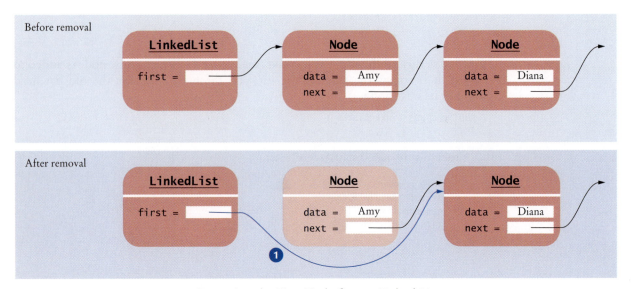

Figure 5 Removing the First Node from a Linked List

Removing the first element of the list works as follows. The data of the first node are saved and later returned as the method result. The successor of the first node becomes the first node of the shorter list (see Figure 5). Then there are no further references to the old node, and the garbage collector will eventually recycle it.

```java
public class LinkedList
{
   . . .
   public Object removeFirst()
   {
      if (first == null)
         throw new NoSuchElementException();
      Object element = first.data;
      first = first.next; ❶
      return element;
   }
   . . .
}
```

Next, we need to implement the iterator class. The ListIterator interface in the standard library declares nine methods. We omit four of them (the methods that move the iterator backwards and the methods that report an integer index of the iterator).

Our LinkedList class declares a private inner class LinkedListIterator, which implements our simplified ListIterator interface. Because LinkedListIterator is an inner class, it has access to the private features of the LinkedList class—in particular, the instance variable first and the private Node class.

Note that clients of the LinkedList class don't actually know the name of the iterator class. They only know it is a class that implements the ListIterator interface.

```java
public class LinkedList
{
   . . .
   public ListIterator listIterator()
   {
      return new LinkedListIterator();
```

```
      }

      class LinkedListIterator implements ListIterator
      {
         private Node position;
         private Node previous;
         . . .
         public LinkedListIterator()
         {
            position = null;
            previous = null;
         }
      }
      . . .
   }
```

A list iterator object has a reference to the last visited node.

Each iterator object has a reference, position, to the last visited node. We also store a reference to the last node before that, previous. We will need that reference to adjust the links properly in the remove method.

The next method is simple. The position reference is advanced to position.next, and the old position is remembered in previous. There is a special case, however—if the iterator points before the first element of the list, then the old position is null, and position must be set to first.

```
   class LinkedListIterator implements ListIterator
   {
      . . .
      public Object next()
      {
         if (!hasNext())
            throw new NoSuchElementException();
         previous = position; // Remember for remove

         if (position == null)
            position = first;
         else
            position = position.next;

         return position.data;
      }
      . . .
   }
```

The next method is supposed to be called only when the iterator is not yet at the end of the list, so we declare the hasNext method accordingly. The iterator is at the end if the list is empty (that is, first == null) or if there is no element after the current position (position.next == null).

```
   class LinkedListIterator implements ListIterator
   {
      . . .
      public boolean hasNext()
      {
         if (position == null)
            return first != null;
         else
            return position.next != null;
      }
      . . .
   }
```

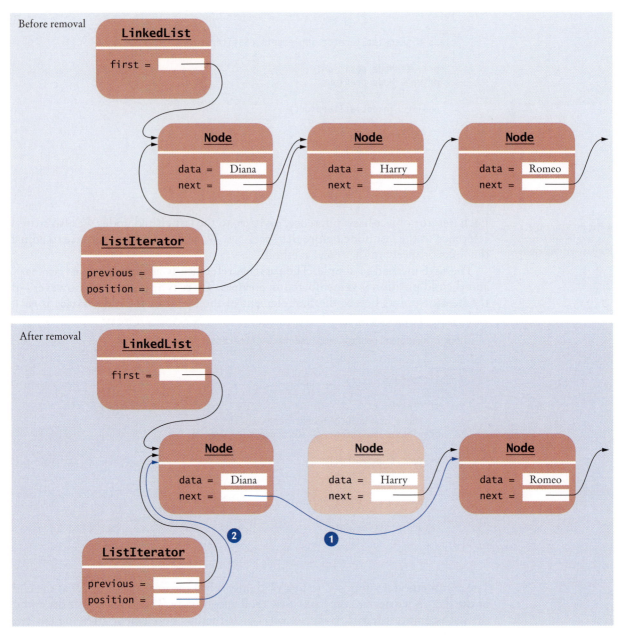

Figure 6 Removing a Node from the Middle of a Linked List

Implementing operations that modify a linked list is challenging— you need to make sure that you update all node references correctly.

Removing the last visited node is more involved. If the element to be removed is the first element, we just call removeFirst. Otherwise, an element in the middle of the list must be removed, and the node preceding it needs to have its next reference updated to skip the removed element (see Figure 6). If the previous reference equals position, then this call to remove does not immediately follow a call to next, and we throw an IllegalStateException.

According to the declaration of the remove method, it is illegal to call remove twice in a row. Therefore, the remove method sets the position reference to previous.

```
class LinkedListIterator implements ListIterator
{
   . . .
   public void remove()
   {
      if (previous == position)
         throw new IllegalStateException();
      if (position == first)
      {
         removeFirst();
      }
      else
      {
         previous.next = position.next;        1
      }
      position = previous;        2
   }
   . . .
}
```

The set method changes the data stored in the previously visited element. Its implementation is straightforward because our linked lists can be traversed in only one direction. The linked list implementation of the standard library must keep track of whether the last iterator movement was forward or backward. For that reason, the standard library forbids a call to the set method following an add or remove method. That restriction is unnecessary in our implementation, and we do not enforce it.

```
public void set(Object element)
{
   if (position == null)
      throw new NoSuchElementException();
   position.data = element;
}
```

Finally, the most complex operation is the addition of a node. You insert the new node after the node last visited by the iterator (see Figure 7).

```
class LinkedListIterator implements ListIterator
{
   . . .
   public void add(Object element)
   {
      if (position == null)
      {
         addFirst(element);
         position = first;
      }
      else
      {
         Node newNode = new Node();
         newNode.data = element;
         newNode.next = position.next;        1
         position.next = newNode;        2
         position = newNode;        3
      }
      previous = position;        4
   }
   . . .
}
```

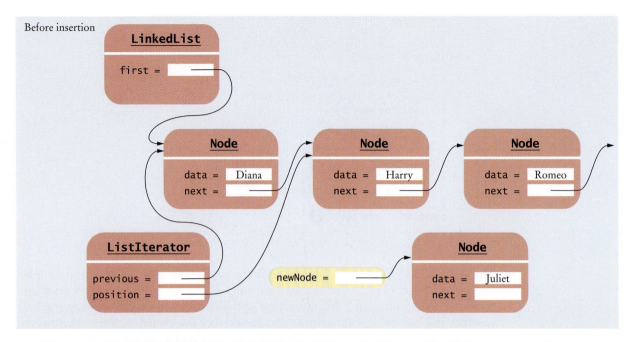

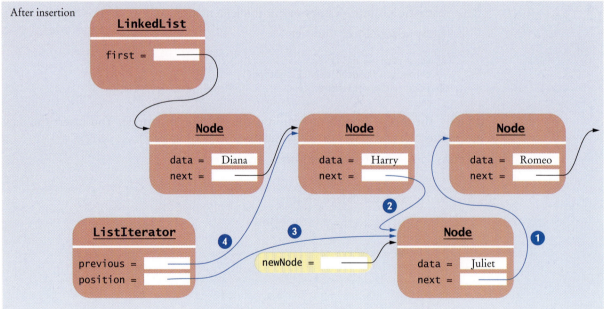

Figure 7 Adding a Node to the Middle of a Linked List

At the end of this section is the complete implementation of our LinkedList class.

You now know how to use the LinkedList class in the Java library, and you have had a peek "under the hood" to see how linked lists are implemented.

ch15/impllist/LinkedList.java

```java
1   import java.util.NoSuchElementException;
2
3   /**
4      A linked list is a sequence of nodes with efficient
5      element insertion and removal. This class
6      contains a subset of the methods of the standard
7      java.util.LinkedList class.
8   */
9   public class LinkedList
10  {
11     private Node first;
12
13     /**
14        Constructs an empty linked list.
15     */
16     public LinkedList()
17     {
18        first = null;
19     }
20
21     /**
22        Returns the first element in the linked list.
23        @return the first element in the linked list
24     */
25     public Object getFirst()
26     {
27        if (first == null)
28           throw new NoSuchElementException();
29        return first.data;
30     }
31
32     /**
33        Removes the first element in the linked list.
34        @return the removed element
35     */
36     public Object removeFirst()
37     {
38        if (first == null)
39           throw new NoSuchElementException();
40        Object element = first.data;
41        first = first.next;
42        return element;
43     }
44
45     /**
46        Adds an element to the front of the linked list.
47        @param element the element to add
48     */
49     public void addFirst(Object element)
50     {
51        Node newNode = new Node();
52        newNode.data = element;
53        newNode.next = first;
54        first = newNode;
55     }
56
```

```java
 57    /**
 58       Returns an iterator for iterating through this list.
 59       @return an iterator for iterating through this list
 60    */
 61    public ListIterator listIterator()
 62    {
 63       return new LinkedListIterator();
 64    }
 65
 66    class Node
 67    {
 68       public Object data;
 69       public Node next;
 70    }
 71
 72    class LinkedListIterator implements ListIterator
 73    {
 74       private Node position;
 75       private Node previous;
 76
 77       /**
 78          Constructs an iterator that points to the front
 79          of the linked list.
 80       */
 81       public LinkedListIterator()
 82       {
 83          position = null;
 84          previous = null;
 85       }
 86
 87       /**
 88          Moves the iterator past the next element.
 89          @return the traversed element
 90       */
 91       public Object next()
 92       {
 93          if (!hasNext())
 94             throw new NoSuchElementException();
 95          previous = position; // Remember for remove
 96
 97          if (position == null)
 98             position = first;
 99          else
100             position = position.next;
101
102          return position.data;
103       }
104
105       /**
106          Tests if there is an element after the iterator position.
107          @return true if there is an element after the iterator position
108       */
109       public boolean hasNext()
110       {
111          if (position == null)
112             return first != null;
113          else
114             return position.next != null;
115       }
```

```
116
117        /**
118            Adds an element before the iterator position
119            and moves the iterator past the inserted element.
120            @param element  the element to add
121        */
122        public void add(Object element)
123        {
124            if (position == null)
125            {
126                addFirst(element);
127                position = first;
128            }
129            else
130            {
131                Node newNode = new Node();
132                newNode.data = element;
133                newNode.next = position.next;
134                position.next = newNode;
135                position = newNode;
136            }
137            previous = position;
138        }
139
140        /**
141            Removes the last traversed element. This method may
142            only be called after a call to the next() method.
143        */
144        public void remove()
145        {
146            if (previous == position)
147                throw new IllegalStateException();
148
149            if (position == first)
150            {
151                removeFirst();
152            }
153            else
154            {
155                previous.next = position.next;
156            }
157            position = previous;
158        }
159
160        /**
161            Sets the last traversed element to a different value.
162            @param element  the element to set
163        */
164        public void set(Object element)
165        {
166            if (position == null)
167                throw new NoSuchElementException();
168            position.data = element;
169        }
170    }
171 }
```

ch15/impllist/ListIterator.java

```java
1   /**
2      A list iterator allows access to a position in a linked list.
3      This interface contains a subset of the methods of the
4      standard java.util.ListIterator interface. The methods for
5      backward traversal are not included.
6   */
7   public interface ListIterator
8   {
9      /**
10        Moves the iterator past the next element.
11        @return the traversed element
12     */
13     Object next();
14
15     /**
16        Tests if there is an element after the iterator position.
17        @return true if there is an element after the iterator position
18     */
19     boolean hasNext();
20
21     /**
22        Adds an element before the iterator position
23        and moves the iterator past the inserted element.
24        @param element the element to add
25     */
26     void add(Object element);
27
28     /**
29        Removes the last traversed element. This method may
30        only be called after a call to the next() method.
31     */
32     void remove();
33
34     /**
35        Sets the last traversed element to a different value.
36        @param element the element to set
37     */
38     void set(Object element);
39   }
```

SELF CHECK

3. Trace through the addFirst method when adding an element to an empty list.

4. Conceptually, an iterator points between elements (see Figure 3). Does the position reference point to the element to the left or to the element to the right?

5. Why does the add method have two separate cases?

Special Topic 15.2

Static Inner Classes

You first saw the use of inner classes for event handlers. Inner classes are useful in that context, because their methods have the privilege of accessing private data members of outer-class objects. The same is true for the LinkedListIterator inner class in the sample code for this section. The iterator needs to access the first instance variable of its linked list.

However, the Node inner class has no need to access the outer class. In fact, it has no methods. Thus, there is no need to store a reference to the outer list class with each Node object. To suppress the outer-class reference, you can declare the inner class as static:

```
public class LinkedList
{
    . . .
    private static class Node
    {
        . . .
    }
}
```

The purpose of the reserved word static in this context is to indicate that the inner-class objects do not depend on the outer-class objects that generate them. In particular, the methods of a static inner class cannot access the outer-class instance variables. Declaring the inner class static is efficient, because its objects do not store an outer-class reference.

However, the LinkedListIterator class cannot be a static inner class. It frequently references the first element of the enclosing LinkedList.

15.3 Abstract Data Types

An abstract data type defines the fundamental operations on the data but does not specify an implementation.

There are two ways of looking at a linked list. One way is to think of the concrete implementation of such a list as a sequence of node objects with links between them (see Figure 8).

On the other hand, you can think of the *abstract* concept that underlies the linked list. In the abstract, a linked list is an ordered sequence of data items that can be traversed with an iterator (see Figure 9).

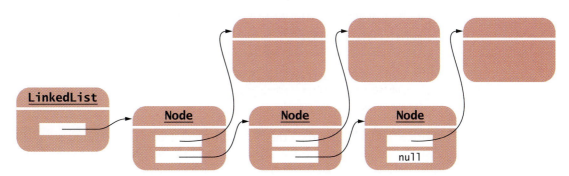

Figure 8   A Concrete View of a Linked List

Figure 9   An Abstract View of a List

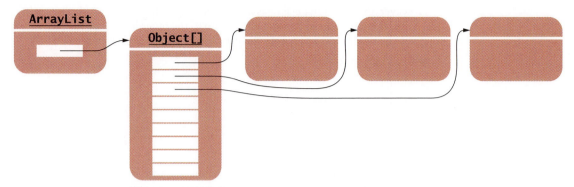

Figure 10 A Concrete View of an Array List

Figure 11 An Abstract View of an Array

Similarly, there are two ways of looking at an array list. Of course, an array list has a concrete implementation: a partially filled array of object references (see Figure 10). But you don't usually think about the concrete implementation when using an array list. You take the abstract point of view. An array list is an ordered sequence of data items, each of which can be accessed by an integer index (see Figure 11).

The concrete implementations of a linked list and an array list are quite different. The abstractions, on the other hand, seem to be similar at first glance. To see the difference, consider the public interfaces stripped down to their minimal essentials.

An array list allows *random access* to all elements. You specify an integer index, and you can get or set the corresponding element.

```
public class ArrayList
{
   . . .
   public Object get(int index) { . . . }
   public void set(int index, Object element) { . . . }
   . . .
}
```

With a linked list, on the other hand, element access is a bit more complex. A linked list allows *sequential access*. You need to ask the linked list for an iterator. Using that iterator, you can easily traverse the list elements one at a time. But if you want to go to a particular element, say the 100th one, you first have to skip all elements before it.

```
public class LinkedList
{
   . . .
   public ListIterator listIterator() { . . . }
   . . .
}
```

```
public interface ListIterator
{
    Object next();
    boolean hasNext();
    void add(Object element);
    void remove();
    void set(Object element);
    . . .
}
```

Here we show only the *fundamental* operations on array lists and linked lists. Other operations can be composed from these fundamental operations. For example, you can add or remove an element in an array list by moving all elements beyond the insertion or removal index, calling get and set multiple times.

Of course, the ArrayList class has methods to add and remove elements in the middle, even if they are slow. Conversely, the LinkedList class has get and set methods that let you access any element in the linked list, albeit very inefficiently, by performing repeated sequential accesses.

In fact, the term ArrayList signifies that its implementors wanted to combine the interfaces of an array and a list. Somewhat confusingly, both the ArrayList and the LinkedList class implement an interface called List that declares operations both for random access and for sequential access.

That terminology is not in common use outside the Java library. Instead, let us adopt a more traditional terminology. We will call the abstract types *array* and *list*. The Java library provides concrete implementations ArrayList and LinkedList for these abstract types. Other concrete implementations are possible in other libraries. In fact, Java arrays are another implementation of the abstract array type.

To understand an abstract data type completely, you need to know not just its fundamental operations but also their relative efficiency.

In an abstract list, an element can be added or removed in constant time (assuming that the iterator is already in the right position). A fixed number of node references need to be modified to add or remove a node, regardless of the size of the list. Using the big-Oh notation, an operation that requires a bounded amount of time, regardless of the total number of elements in the structure, is denoted as $O(1)$. Random access in an abstract array also takes $O(1)$ time.

Adding or removing an arbitrary element in an abstract array of size n takes $O(n)$ time, because on average $n/2$ elements need to be moved. Random access in an abstract list takes $O(n)$ time because on average $n/2$ elements need to be skipped.

Table 3 shows this information for abstract arrays and lists.

An abstract list is an ordered sequence of items that can be traversed sequentially and that allows for $O(1)$ insertion and removal of elements at any position.

An abstract array is an ordered sequence of items with $O(1)$ random access via an integer index.

Table 3 Efficiency of Operations for the Abstract Array and List Types

Operation	Abstract Array	Abstract List
Random access	$O(1)$	$O(n)$
Linear traversal step	$O(1)$	$O(1)$
Add/remove an element	$O(n)$	$O(1)$

Why consider abstract types at all? If you implement a particular algorithm, you can tell what operations you need to carry out on the data structures that your algorithm manipulates. You can then determine the abstract type that supports those operations efficiently, without being distracted by implementation details.

For example, suppose you have a sorted collection of items and you want to locate items using the binary search algorithm (see Section 14.7). That algorithm makes a random access to the middle of the collection, followed by other random accesses. Thus, fast random access is essential for the algorithm to work correctly. Once you know that an abstract array supports fast random access and an abstract list does not, you then look for concrete implementations of the abstract array type. You won't be fooled into using a LinkedList, even though the LinkedList class actually provides get and set methods.

In the next section, you will see additional examples of abstract data types.

SELF CHECK

6. What is the advantage of viewing a type abstractly?

7. How would you sketch an abstract view of a doubly linked list? A concrete view?

8. How much slower is the binary search algorithm for an abstract list compared to the linear search algorithm?

Random Fact 15.1

Standardization

You encounter the benefits of standardization every day. When you buy a light bulb, you can be assured that it fits the socket without having to measure the socket at home and the light bulb in the store. In fact, you may have experienced how painful the lack of standards can be if you have ever purchased a flashlight with nonstandard bulbs. Replacement bulbs for such a flashlight can be difficult and expensive to obtain.

Programmers have a similar desire for standardization. Consider the important goal of platform independence for Java programs. After you compile a Java program into class files, you can execute the class files on any computer that has a Java virtual machine. For this to work, the behavior of the virtual machine has to be strictly defined. If virtual machines don't all behave exactly the same way, then the slogan of "write once, run anywhere" turns into "write once, debug everywhere". In order for multiple implementors to create compatible virtual machines, the virtual machine needed to be *standardized*. That is, someone needed to create a definition of the virtual machine and its expected behavior.

Who creates standards? Some of the most successful standards have been created by volunteer groups such as the Internet Engineering Task Force (IETF) and the World Wide Web Consortium (W3C). You can find the Requests for Comment (RFC) that standardize many of the Internet protocols at the IETF site, http://www.ietf.org/rfc.html. For example, RFC 822 standardizes the format of e-mail, and RFC 2616 defines the Hypertext Transmission Protocol (HTTP) that is used to serve web pages to browsers. The W3C standardizes the Hypertext Markup Language (HTML), the format for web pages—see http://www.w3c.org. These standards have been instrumental in the creation of the World Wide Web as an open platform that is not controlled by any one company.

Many programming languages, such as C++ and Scheme, have been standardized by independent standards organizations, such as the American National Standards Institute (ANSI) and the International Organization for Standardization—called ISO for short (not an acronym; see http://www.iso.ch/iso/en/aboutiso/introduction/whatisISO.html). ANSI and ISO are associations of industry professionals who develop standards for everything from car tires and credit card shapes to programming languages.

When a company invents a new technology, it has an interest in its invention becoming a standard, so that other vendors produce tools that work with the invention and thus increase its likelihood of success. On the other hand, by handing over the invention to a standards committee, the company may lose control over the standard. For that reason, the Java standard is developed by the "Java Community Process", an industry consortium controlled by Sun Microsystems, the inventor of Java.

Of course, many important pieces of technology aren't standardized at all. Consider the Windows operating system. Although Windows is often called a de-facto standard, it really is no standard at all. Nobody has ever attempted to define formally what the Windows operating system should do. The behavior changes at the whim of its vendor. That suits Microsoft just fine, because it makes it impossible for a third party to create its own version of Windows.

As a computer professional, there will be many times in your career when you need to make a decision whether to support a particular standard. Consider a simple example. In this chapter, we use the LinkedList class from the standard Java library. However, many computer scientists dislike this class because the interface muddies the distinction between abstract lists and arrays, and the iterators are clumsy to use. Should you use the LinkedList class in your own code, or should you implement a better list? If you do the former, you have to deal with a design that is less than optimal. If you do the latter, other programmers may have a harder time understanding your code because they aren't familiar with your list class.

15.4 Stacks and Queues

In this section we will consider two common abstract data types that allow insertion and removal of items at the ends only, not in the middle. A **stack** lets you insert and remove elements at only one end, traditionally called the *top* of the stack. To visualize a stack, think of a stack of books (see Figure 12).

> A stack is a collection of items with "last in, first out" retrieval.

New items can be added to the top of the stack. Items are removed at the top of the stack as well. Therefore, they are removed in the order that is opposite from the order in which they have been added, called *last in, first out* or *LIFO* order. For example, if you add items A, B, and C and then remove them, you obtain C, B, and A. Traditionally, the addition and removal operations are called push and pop.

> A queue is a collection of items with "first in, first out" retrieval.

A **queue** is similar to a stack, except that you add items to one end of the queue (the *tail*) and remove them from the other end of the queue (the *head*). To visualize

Figure 12
A Stack of Books

Figure 13   A Queue

a queue, simply think of people lining up (see Figure 13). People join the tail of the queue and wait until they have reached the head of the queue. Queues store items in a *first in, first out* or *FIFO* fashion. Items are removed in the same order in which they have been added.

There are many uses of queues and stacks in computer science. The Java graphical user interface system keeps an event queue of all events, such as mouse and keyboard events. The events are inserted into the queue whenever the operating system notifies the application of the event. Events are removed and passed to event listeners in the order in which they were inserted. Another example is a print queue. A printer may be accessed by several applications, perhaps running on different computers. If each of the applications tried to access the printer at the same time, the printout would be garbled. Instead, each application places all bytes that need to be sent to the printer into a file and inserts that file into the print queue. When the printer is done printing one file, it retrieves the next one from the queue. Therefore, print jobs are printed using the "first in, first out" rule, which is a fair arrangement for users of the shared printer.

Stacks are used when a "last in, first out" rule is required. For example, consider an algorithm that attempts to find a path through a maze. When the algorithm encounters an intersection, it pushes the location on the stack, and then it explores the first branch. If that branch is a dead end, it returns to the location at the top of the stack and explores the next untried branch. If all branches are dead ends, it pops the location off the stack, revealing a previously encountered intersection. Another important example is the **run-time stack** that a processor or virtual machine keeps to organize the variables of nested methods. Whenever a new method is called, its parameters and local variables are pushed onto a stack. When the method exits, they are popped off again. This stack makes recursive method calls possible.

There is a Stack class in the Java library that implements the abstract stack type and the push and pop operations.

Table 4 Working with Queues and Stacks	
`Queue<Integer> q = new LinkedList<Integer>();`	The `LinkedList` class implements the `Queue` interface.
`q.add(1); q.add(2); q.add(3);`	Adds to the tail of the queue; q is now `[1, 2, 3]`.
`int head = q.remove();`	Removes the head of the queue; head is set to 1 and q is `[2, 3]`.
`head = q.peek();`	Gets the head of the queue without removing it; head is set to 2.
`Stack<Integer> s = new Stack<Integer>();`	Constructs an empty stack.
`s.push(1); s.push(2); s.push(3);`	Adds to the top of the stack; s is now `[1, 2, 3]`.
`int top = s.pop();`	Removes the top of the stack; top is set to 3 and s is now `[1, 2]`.
`head = s.peek();`	Gets the top of the stack without removing it; head is set to 2.

The `Queue` interface in the standard Java library has methods `add` to add an element to the tail of the queue, `remove` to remove the head of the queue, and `peek` to get the head element of the queue without removing it.

The standard library provides a number of queue classes for programs in which multiple activities, called threads, run in parallel. These queues are useful for sharing work between threads. We do not discuss those classes in this book. The `LinkedList` class also implements the `Queue` interface, and you can use it when a queue is required:

```
Queue<String> q = new LinkedList<String>();
```

Table 4 shows how to use the stack and queue methods in Java.

The `Stack` class in the Java library uses an array list to implement a stack. Exercise P15.15 shows how to use a linked list instead.

You would definitely not want to use an array list to implement a queue. Removing the first element of an array list is inefficient—all other elements must be moved toward the beginning. A queue can be efficiently implemented as a linked list. Moreover, Exercise P15.16 shows you how to implement a queue efficiently as a "circular" array, in which all elements stay at the position at which they were inserted, but the index values that denote the head and tail of the queue change when elements are added and removed.

In this chapter, you have seen the two most fundamental abstract data types, arrays and lists, and their concrete implementations. You also learned about the stack and queue types. In the next chapter, you will see additional data types that require more sophisticated implementation techniques.

SELF CHECK

9. Draw a sketch of the abstract queue type, similar to Figures 9 and 11.

10. Why wouldn't you want to use a stack to manage print jobs?

⊕ Worked   **A Reverse Polish Notation Calculator**
Example 15.1

Worked Example 15.1 shows how to use a stack for implementing a "Reverse Polish Notation" calculator.

Random Fact 15.2

Reverse Polish Notation

In the 1920s, the Polish mathematician Jan Łukasiewicz realized that it is possible to dispense with parentheses in arithmetic expressions, provided that you write the operators *before* their arguments, for example, + 3 4 instead of 3 + 4. Thirty years later, Australian computer scientist Charles Hamblin noted that an even better scheme would be to have the operators *follow* the operands. This was termed **reverse Polish notation** or RPN.

Reverse Polish notation might look strange to you, but that is just an accident of history. Had earlier mathematicians realized its advantages, today's schoolchildren might be using it and not worry about precedence rules and parentheses.

Standard Notation	Reverse Polish Notation
3 + 4	3 4 +
3 + 4 × 5	3 4 5 × +
3 × (4 + 5)	3 4 5 + ×
(3 + 4) × (5 + 6)	3 4 + 5 6 + ×
3 + 4 + 5	3 4 + 5 +

In 1972, Hewlett-Packard introduced the HP 35 calculator that used reverse Polish notation. The calculator had no keys labeled with parentheses or an equals symbol. There is just a key labeled ENTER to push a number onto a stack. For that reason, Hewlett-Packard's marketing department used to refer to their product as "the calculators that have no equal".

Figure 14
The Calculator with No Equal

⊕ Available online in WileyPLUS and at www.wiley.com/college/horstmann.

Over time, calculator vendors have adapted to the standard algebraic notation rather than forcing its users to learn a new notation. However, those users who have made the effort to learn reverse Polish notation tend to be fanatic proponents, and to this day, some Hewlett-Packard calculator models still support it.

Summary of Learning Objectives

Describe the linked list data structure and the use of list iterators.

- A linked list consists of a number of nodes, each of which has a reference to the next node.
- Adding and removing elements in the middle of a linked list is efficient.
- Visiting the elements of a linked list in sequential order is efficient, but random access is not.
- You use a list iterator to access elements inside a linked list.

Explain how linked lists are implemented.

- A linked list object holds a reference to the first node, and each node holds a reference to the next node.
- A list iterator object has a reference to the last visited node.
- Implementing operations that modify a linked list is challenging— you need to make sure that you update all node references correctly.

Describe the notion of abstract data types and the behavior of the abstract list and array types.

- An abstract data type defines the fundamental operations on the data but does not specify an implementation.
- An abstract list is an ordered sequence of items that can be traversed sequentially and that allows for $O(1)$ insertion and removal of elements at any position.
- An abstract array is an ordered sequence of items with $O(1)$ random access via an integer index.
- A stack is a collection of items with "last in, first out" retrieval.
- A queue is a collection of items with "first in, first out" retrieval.

Classes, Objects, and Methods Introduced in this Chapter

java.util.Collection<E>	*java.util.LinkedList<E>*	*java.util.ListIterator<E>*
add	addFirst	add
contains	addLast	hasPrevious
iterator	getFirst	previous
remove	getLast	set
size	removeFirst	
java.util.Iterator<E>	removeLast	
hasNext	*java.util.List<E>*	
next	listIterator	
remove		

Media Resources

www.wiley.com/
college/
horstmann

- • **_Worked Example_** A Reverse Polish Notation Calculator
- • Lab Exercises
- ✚ **_Animation_** List Iterators
- ✚ Practice Quiz
- ✚ Code Completion Exercises

Review Exercises

★ **R15.1** Explain what the following code prints. Draw pictures of the linked list after each step. Just draw the forward links, as in Figure 1.

```
LinkedList<String> staff = new LinkedList<String>();
staff.addFirst("Harry");
staff.addFirst("Diana");
staff.addFirst("Tom");
System.out.println(staff.removeFirst());
System.out.println(staff.removeFirst());
System.out.println(staff.removeFirst());
```

★ **R15.2** Explain what the following code prints. Draw pictures of the linked list after each step. Just draw the forward links, as in Figure 1.

```
LinkedList<String> staff = new LinkedList<String>();
staff.addFirst("Harry");
staff.addFirst("Diana");
staff.addFirst("Tom");
System.out.println(staff.removeLast());
System.out.println(staff.removeFirst());
System.out.println(staff.removeLast());
```

★ **R15.3** Explain what the following code prints. Draw pictures of the linked list after each step. Just draw the forward links, as in Figure 1.

```
LinkedList<String> staff = new LinkedList<String>();
staff.addFirst("Harry");
staff.addLast("Diana");
staff.addFirst("Tom");
System.out.println(staff.removeLast());
System.out.println(staff.removeFirst());
System.out.println(staff.removeLast());
```

★ **R15.4** Explain what the following code prints. Draw pictures of the linked list and the iterator position after each step.

```
LinkedList<String> staff = new LinkedList<String>();
ListIterator<String> iterator = staff.listIterator();
iterator.add("Tom");
iterator.add("Diana");
iterator.add("Harry");
iterator = staff.listIterator();
if (iterator.next().equals("Tom"))
    iterator.remove();
while (iterator.hasNext())
    System.out.println(iterator.next());
```

★ **R15.5** Explain what the following code prints. Draw pictures of the linked list and the iterator position after each step.

```
LinkedList<String> staff = new LinkedList<String>();
ListIterator<String> iterator = staff.listIterator();
iterator.add("Tom");
iterator.add("Diana");
iterator.add("Harry");
iterator = staff.listIterator();
iterator.next();
iterator.next();
iterator.add("Romeo");
iterator.next();
iterator.add("Juliet");
iterator = staff.listIterator();
iterator.next();
iterator.remove();
while (iterator.hasNext())
    System.out.println(iterator.next());
```

★★ **R15.6** The linked list class in the Java library supports operations addLast and removeLast. To carry out these operations efficiently, the LinkedList class has an added reference last to the last node in the linked list. Draw a "before/after" diagram of the changes of the links in a linked list under the addLast and removeLast methods.

★★ **R15.7** The linked list class in the Java library supports bidirectional iterators. To go backward efficiently, each Node has an added reference, previous, to the predecessor node in the linked list. Draw a "before/after" diagram of the changes of the links in a linked list under the addFirst and removeFirst methods that shows how the previous links need to be updated.

★★ **R15.8** What advantages do lists have over arrays? What disadvantages do they have?

★★ **R15.9** Suppose you needed to organize a collection of telephone numbers for a company division. There are currently about 6,000 employees, and you know that the phone switch can handle at most 10,000 phone numbers. You expect several hundred lookups against the collection every day. Would you use an array or a list to store the information?

★★ **R15.10** Suppose you needed to keep a collection of appointments. Would you use a list or an array of Appointment objects?

★ **R15.11** Suppose you write a program that models a card deck. Cards are taken from the top of the deck and given out to players. As cards are returned to the deck, they are placed on the bottom of the deck. Would you store the cards in a stack or a queue?

★ **R15.12** Suppose the strings "A" . . . "Z" are pushed onto a stack. Then they are popped off the stack and pushed onto a second stack. Finally, they are all popped off the second stack and printed. In which order are the strings printed?

★ **R15.13** Consider the following algorithm for traversing a maze such as the one shown below.

Make the cell at the entrance the current cell. Take the following actions, then repeat:

• If the current cell is adjacent to the exit, stop.
• Mark the current cell as visited.

- Add all unvisited neighbors to the north, east, south, and west to a queue.
- Remove the next element from the queue and make it the current cell.

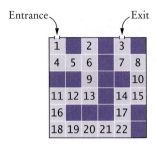

In which order will the cells of the sample maze be visited?

★ **R15.14** Repeat Exercise R15.13, using a stack instead of a queue.

Programming Exercises

★★ **P15.1** Using only the public interface of the linked list class, write a method

```
public static void downsize(LinkedList<String> staff)
```

that removes every other employee from a linked list.

★★ **P15.2** Using only the public interface of the linked list class, write a method

```
public static void reverse(LinkedList<String> staff)
```

that reverses the entries in a linked list.

★★★ **P15.3** Add a method reverse to our implementation of the LinkedList class that reverses the links in a list. Implement this method by directly rerouting the links, not by using an iterator.

★ **P15.4** Add a method size to our implementation of the LinkedList class that computes the number of elements in the list, by following links and counting the elements until the end of the list is reached.

★ **P15.5** Add an instance variable currentSize to our implementation of the LinkedList class. Modify the add and remove methods of both the linked list and the list iterator to update the currentSize variable so that it always contains the correct size. Change the size method of the preceding exercise so that it simply returns the value of this instance variable.

★★ **P15.6** The linked list class of the standard library has an add method that allows efficient insertion at the end of the list. Implement this method for the LinkedList class in Section 15.2. Add an instance variable to the linked list class that points to the last node in the list. Make sure the other mutator methods update that variable.

★★★ **P15.7** Repeat Exercise P15.6, but use a different implementation strategy. Remove the reference to the first node in the LinkedList class, and make the next reference of the last node point to the first node, so that all nodes form a cycle. Such an implementation is called a *circular linked list*.

★★★ **P15.8** Reimplement the LinkedList class of Section 15.2 so that the Node and LinkedList-Iterator classes are not inner classes.

★★★ **P15.9** Add an instance variable previous to the Node class in Section 15.2, and supply previous and hasPrevious methods in the iterator.

★★ **P15.10** The LISP language, created in 1960, implements linked lists in a very elegant way. You will explore a Java analog in this set of exercises. The key observation is that the *tail* of an abstract list—that is, the list with its head node removed—is also a list. The tail of that list is again a list, and so on, until you reach the empty list. Here is a Java interface for such as list:

```
public interface LispList
{
   boolean isEmpty();
   Object head();
   LispList tail();
   . . .
}
```

There are two kinds of lists, empty lists and nonempty lists:

```
public class EmptyList extends LispList { ... }
public class NonEmptyList extends LispList { ... }
```

These classes are quite trivial. The EmptyList class has no instance variables. Its head and tail methods simply throw an UnsupportedOperationException, and its isEmpty method returns true. The NonEmptyList class has instance variables for the head and tail.

Here is one way of making a lisp list with three elements:

```
LispList list = new NonEmptyList("A", new NonEmptyList("B",
   new NonEmptyList("C", new EmptyList())));
```

This is a bit tedious, and it is a good idea to supply a convenience method cons that calls the constructor, as well as a static variable NIL that is an instance of an empty list. Then our list construction becomes

```
LispList list = NIL.cons("C").cons("B").cons("A");
```

Note that you need to build up the list starting from the (empty) tail.

To see the elegance of this approach, consider the implementation of a toString method that produces a string containing all list elements. The method must be implemented by both subclasses:

```
public class EmptyList
{
   ...
   public String toString() { return ""; }
}

public class NonEmptyList
{
   ...
   public String toString() { return head() + " " + tail().toString(); }
}
```

Note that no if statement is required. A list is either empty or nonempty, and the correct toString method is invoked due to polymorphism.

In this exercise, complete the LispList interface and the EmptyList and NonEmptyList classes. Write a test program that constructs a list and prints it.

★ **P15.11** Add a method `length` to the `LispList` interface of Exercise P15.10 that returns the length of the list. Implement the method in the `EmptyList` and `NonEmptyList` classes.

★★ **P15.12** Add a method

```
LispList merge(LispList other)
```

to the `LispList` interface of Exercise P15.10 that returns the length of the list. Implement the method in the `EmptyList` and `NonEmptyList` classes. When merging two lists, alternate between the elements, then add the remainder of the longer list. For example, merging the lists with elements 1 2 3 4 and 5 6 yields 1 5 2 6 3 4.

★ **P15.13** Add a method

```
boolean contains(Object obj)
```

to the `LispList` interface of Exercise P15.10 that returns true if the list contains an element that equals `obj`.

★★★ **P15.14** The standard Java library implements a `Stack` class, but in this exercise you are asked to provide your own implementation. Do not implement type parameters. Use an `Object[]` array to hold the stack elements. When the array fills up, allocate an array of twice the size and copy the values to the larger array.

★ **P15.15** Implement a `Stack` class by using a linked list to store the elements. Do not implement type parameters.

★★ **P15.16** Implement a queue as a *circular array* as follows: Use two index variables `head` and `tail` that contain the index of the next element to be removed and the next element to be added. After an element is removed or added, the index is incremented (see Figure 15 on page 661).

After a while, the `tail` element will reach the top of the array. Then it "wraps around" and starts again at 0—see Figure 16 on page 661. For that reason, the array is called "circular".

```java
public class CircularArrayQueue
{
    private int head;
    private int tail;
    private int theSize;
    private Object[] elements;

    public CircularArrayQueue(int capacity) { . . . }
    public void add(Object x) { . . . }
    public Object remove() { . . . }
    public int size() { . . . }
}
```

This implementation supplies a *bounded* queue—it can eventually fill up. See the next exercise on how to remove that limitation.

★★★ **P15.17** The queue in Exercise P15.16 can fill up if more elements are added than the array can hold. Improve the implementation as follows. When the array fills up, allocate a larger array, copy the values to the larger array, and assign it to the `elements` instance variable. *Hint:* You can't just copy the elements into the same position of the new array. Move the head element to position 0 instead.

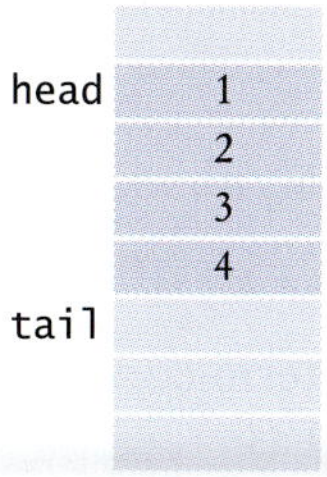

Figure 15
Adding and Removing
Queue Elements

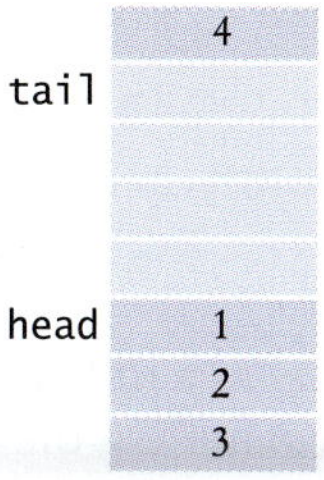

Figure 16
A Queue That Wraps Around
the End of the Array

★★ **P15.18** Modify the insertion sort algorithm of Special Topic 14.1 to sort a linked list.

★★ **P15.19** Modify the Invoice class of Chapter 12 so that it implements the Iterable<LineItem>
interface. Then demonstrate how an Invoice object can be used in a "for each" loop.

★ **P15.20** In a paint program, a "flood fill" fills all empty pixels of a drawing with a given
color, stopping when it reaches occupied pixels. In this exercise, you will implement
a simple variation of this algorithm, flood-filling a 10 × 10 array of integers that are
initially 0. Prompt for the starting row and column. Push the (row, column) pair on
a stack. (You will need to provide a simple Pair class.)

Then repeat the following operations until the stack is empty.

- Pop off the (row, column) pair from the top of the stack.
- If it has not yet been filled, fill it now. (Fill in numbers 1, 2, 3, and so on, to
  show the order in which the square is filled.)
- Push the coordinates of any unfilled neighbors in the north, east, south, or
  west direction on the stack.

When you are done, print the entire array.

★ **P15.21** Repeat Exercise P15.20, but use a queue instead.

★★ **P15.22** Use a stack to enumerate all permutations of a string. Suppose you want to find all
permutations of the string meat. Push the string +meat on the stack. Now repeat the
following operations until the stack is empty.

- Pop off the top of the stack.
- If that string ends in a + (such as tame+), remove the + and print the string
- Otherwise, remove each letter in turn from the right of the +, insert it just
  before the +, and push the resulting string on the stack. For example, after
  popping e+mta, you push em+ta, et+ma, and ea+mt.

★★ **P15.23** Repeat Exercise P15.22, but use a queue instead.

★★G **P15.24** Write a program to display a linked list graphically. Draw each element of the list as
a box, and indicate the links with line segments. Draw an iterator as in Figure 3.
Supply buttons to move the iterator and to add and remove elements.

Programming Projects

Project 15.1 Implement a class Polynomial that describes a polynomial such as

$$p(x) = 5x^{10} + 9x^7 - x - 10$$

Store a polynomial as a linked list of terms. A term contains the coefficient and the power of x. For example, you would store $p(x)$ as

$$(5, 10), (9, 7), (-1, 1), (-10, 0)$$

Supply methods to add, multiply, and print polynomials, and to compute the derivative of a polynomial.

Project 15.2 Make the list implementation of this chapter as powerful as the implementation of the Java library. (Do not implement type parameters, though.)

- Provide bidirectional iteration.
- Make Node a static inner class.
- Implement the standard List and ListIterator interfaces and provide the missing methods. (*Tip:* You may find it easier to extend AbstractList instead of implementing all List methods from scratch.)

Project 15.3 Implement the following algorithm for the evaluation of arithmetic expressions.

Each operator has a *precedence*. The + and - operators have the lowest precedence, * and / have a higher (and equal) precedence, and ∧ (which denotes "raising to a power" in this exercise) has the highest. For example,

    3 * 4 ∧ 2 + 5

should mean the same as

    (3 * (4 ∧ 2)) + 5

with a value of 53.

In your algorithm, use two stacks. One stack holds numbers, the other holds operators. When you encounter a number, push it on the number stack. When you encounter an operator, push it on the operator stack if it has higher precedence than the operator on the top of the stack. Otherwise, pop an operator off the operator stack, pop two numbers off the number stack, and push the result of the computation on the number stack. Repeat until the top of the operator stack has lower precedence. At the end of the expression, clear the stack in the same way. For example, here is how the expression 3 * 4 ∧ 2 + 5 is evaluated:

	Expression: 3 * 4 ∧ 2 + 5			
1	Remaining expression:	* 4 ∧ 2 + 5	Number stack	Operator stack
			3	
2	Remaining expression:	4 ∧ 2 + 5	Number stack	Operator stack
			3	*
3	Remaining expression:	∧ 2 + 5	Number stack	Operator stack
			4	
			3	*

4	Remaining expression:	2 + 5	Number stack	Operator stack
			4	∧
			3	*

5	Remaining expression:	+ 5	Number stack	Operator stack
			2	
			4	∧
			3	*

6	Remaining expression:	+ 5	Number stack	Operator stack
			16	
			3	*

7	Remaining expression:	5	Number stack	Operator stack
			48	+

8	Remaining expression:		Number stack	Operator stack
			5	
			48	+

9	Remaining expression:		Number stack	Operator stack
			53	

You should enhance this algorithm to deal with parentheses. Also, make sure that subtractions and divisions are carried out in the correct order. For example, 12 - 5 - 3 should yield 4.

Answers to Self-Check Questions

1. Yes, for two reasons. You need to store the node references, and each node is a separate object. (There is a fixed overhead to store each object in the virtual machine.)

2. An integer index can be used to access any array location.

3. When the list is empty, first is null. A new Node is allocated. Its data instance variable is set to the newly inserted object. It's next instance variable is set to null because first is null. The first instance variable is set to the new node. The result is a linked list of length 1.

4. It points to the element to the left. You can see that by tracing out the first call to next. It leaves position to point to the first node.

5. If position is null, we must be at the head of the list, and inserting an element requires updating the first reference. If we are in the middle of the list, the first reference should not be changed.

6. You can focus on the essential characteristics of the data type without being distracted by implementation details.

7. The abstract view would be like Figure 9, but with arrows in both directions. The concrete view would be like Figure 8, but with references to the previous node added to each node.

8. To locate the middle element takes $n / 2$ steps. To locate the middle of the subinterval to the left or right takes another $n / 4$ steps. The next lookup takes $n / 8$ steps. Thus, we expect almost n steps to locate an element. At this point, you are better off just making a linear search that, on average, takes $n / 2$ steps.

9.

10. Stacks use a "last in, first out" discipline. If you are the first one to submit a print job and lots of people add print jobs before the printer has a chance to deal with your job, they get their printouts first, and you have to wait until all other jobs are completed.

Advanced Data Structures

CHAPTER GOALS

- To learn about the set and map data types
- To understand the implementation of hash tables
- To be able to program hash functions
- To learn about binary trees
- To become familiar with the heap data structure
- To learn how to implement the priority queue data type
- To understand how to use heaps for sorting

In this chapter we study data structures that are more complex than arrays or lists. These data structures take control of organizing their elements, rather than keeping them in a fixed position. In return, they can offer better performance for adding, removing, and finding elements.

You will learn about the abstract set and map data types and the implementations that the standard library offers for these abstract types. You will see how two completely different implementations—hash tables and trees—can be used to implement these abstract types efficiently.

CHAPTER CONTENTS

16.1 Sets

In the preceding chapter you encountered two important data structures: arrays and lists. Both have one characteristic in common: These data structures keep the elements in the same order in which you inserted them. However, in many applications, you don't really care about the order of the elements in a collection. For example, a server may keep a collection of objects representing available printers (see Figure 1). The order of the objects doesn't really matter.

In mathematics, such an unordered collection is called a **set**. You have probably learned some set theory in a course in mathematics, and you may know that sets are a fundamental mathematical notion.

> A set is an unordered collection of distinct elements. Elements can be added, located, and removed.

But what does that mean for data structures? If the data structure is no longer responsible for remembering the order of element insertion, can it give us better performance for some of its operations? It turns out that it can indeed, as you will see later in this chapter.

Let's list the fundamental operations on a set:

- Adding an element
- Removing an element
- Locating an element (Does the set contain a given object?)
- Listing all elements (not necessarily in the order in which they were added)

> Sets don't have duplicates. Adding a duplicate of an element that is already present is silently ignored.

In mathematics, a set rejects duplicates. If an object is already in the set, an attempt to add it again is ignored. That's useful in many programming situations as well. For example, if we keep a set of available printers, each printer should occur at most once in the set. Thus, we will interpret the add and remove operations of sets just as we do in mathematics: Adding an element has no effect if the element is already in the set, and attempting to remove an element that isn't in the set is silently ignored.

Of course, we could use a linked list or array list to implement a set. But adding, removing, and containment testing would be $O(n)$ operations, because they all have to do a linear search through the list. (Adding requires a search through the list to make sure that we don't add a duplicate.) As you will see later in this chapter, there are data structures that can handle these operations much more quickly.

Figure 1
A Set of Printers

The HashSet and TreeSet classes both implement the Set interface.

In fact, there are two different data structures for this purpose, called *hash tables* and *trees*. The standard Java library provides set implementations based on both data structures, called HashSet and TreeSet. Both of these data structures implement the Set interface (see Figure 2).

When you want to use a set in your program, you must choose between these implementations. In order to use a HashSet, the elements must provide a hashCode method. We discuss this method in Sections 16.3 and 16.4. Many classes in the standard library implement these methods, for example String, Integer, Point, Rectangle, Color, and all the collection classes. Therefore, you can form a HashSet<String>, HashSet<Rectangle>, or even a HashSet<HashSet<Integer>>.

The TreeSet class uses a different strategy for arranging its elements. Elements are kept in sorted order. In order to use a TreeSet, the element type should implement the Comparable interface (see Section 15.8). The String and Integer classes fulfill this requirement, but many other classes do not. You can also construct a TreeSet with a Comparator (see Special Topic 15.5).

As a rule of thumb, use a hash set unless you want to visit the set elements in sorted order.

Now let's look at using a set of strings. First, construct the set, either as

```
Set<String> names = new HashSet<String>();
```
or
```
Set<String> names = new TreeSet<String>();
```

Note that we store the reference to the HashSet<String> or TreeSet<String> object in a Set<String> variable. After you construct the collection object, the implementation no longer matters; only the interface is important.

Adding and removing set elements is straightforward:

```
names.add("Romeo");
names.remove("Juliet");
```

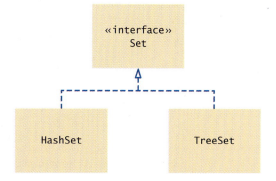

Figure 2
Set Classes and Interfaces in
the Standard Library

The `contains` method tests whether an element is contained in the set:

```
if (names.contains("Juliet")) . . .
```

Finally, to list all elements in the set, get an iterator. As with list iterators, you use the `next` and `hasNext` methods to step through the set.

```
Iterator<String> iter = names.iterator();
while (iter.hasNext())
{
    String name = iter.next();
    Do something with name
}
```

Or, as with arrays and lists, you can use the "for each" loop instead of explicitly using an iterator:

```
for (String name : names)
{
    Do something with name
}
```

> **To visit all elements in a set, use an iterator.**

> **A set iterator visits elements in seemingly random order (HashSet) or sorted order (TreeSet).**

> **You cannot add an element to a set at an iterator position.**

Note that the elements are *not* visited in the order in which you inserted them. When you use a hash set, the elements are visited in a seemingly random order—see Section 16.5 for the reason. With a tree set, elements are visited in sorted order.

There is an important difference between the `Iterator` that you obtain from a set and the `ListIterator` that a list yields. The `ListIterator` has an `add` method to add an element at the list iterator position. The `Iterator` interface has no such method. It makes no sense to add an element at a particular position in a set, because the set can order the elements any way it likes. Thus, you always add elements directly to a set, never to an iterator of the set.

However, you can remove a set element at an iterator position, just as you do with list iterators.

Also, the `Iterator` interface has no `previous` method to go backwards through the elements. Because the elements are not ordered, it is not meaningful to distinguish between "going forward" and "going backward". The following test program shows a practical application of sets. We read in all words from a dictionary file that contains correctly spelled words and place them into a set. We then read all words from a document into a second set—here, the book "Alice in Wonderland". Finally, we print all words from that set that are not in the dictionary set. These are the potential misspellings. (As you can see from the output, we used an American dictionary, and words with British spelling, such as *clamour*, are flagged as potential errors.)

ch16/spellcheck/SpellCheck.java

```java
1   import java.util.HashSet;
2   import java.util.Scanner;
3   import java.util.Set;
4   import java.io.File;
5   import java.io.FileNotFoundException;
6
7   /**
8       This program checks which words in a file are not present in a dictionary.
9   */
10  public class SpellCheck
11  {
12      public static void main(String[] args)
13          throws FileNotFoundException
```

```
14    {
15        // Read the dictionary and the document
16
17        Set<String> dictionaryWords = readWords("words");
18        Set<String> documentWords = readWords("alice30.txt");
19
20        // Print all words that are in the document but not the dictionary
21
22        for (String word : documentWords)
23        {
24            if (!dictionaryWords.contains(word))
25            {
26                System.out.println(word);
27            }
28        }
29    }
30
31    /**
32        Reads all words from a file.
33        @param filename the name of the file
34        @return a set with all lowercased words in the file. Here, a
35        word is a sequence of upper- and lowercase letters.
36    */
37    public static Set<String> readWords(String filename)
38        throws FileNotFoundException
39    {
40        Set<String> words = new HashSet<String>();
41        Scanner in = new Scanner(new File(filename));
42        // Use any characters other than a-z or A-Z as delimiters
43        in.useDelimiter("[^a-zA-Z]+");
44        while (in.hasNext())
45        {
46            words.add(in.next().toLowerCase());
47        }
48        return words;
49    }
50 }
```

Program Run

```
neighbouring
croqueted
pennyworth
dutchess
comfits
xii
dinn
clamour
. . .
```

SELF CHECK

1. Arrays and lists remember the order in which you added elements; sets do not. Why would you want to use a set instead of an array or list?

2. Why are set iterators different from list iterators?

3. Suppose you changed line 18 of the SpellCheck program to use a TreeSet instead of a HashSet. How would the output change?

4. When would you choose a tree set over a hash set?

Quality Tip 16.1

Use Interface References to Manipulate Data Structures

It is considered good style to store a reference to a HashSet or TreeSet in a variable of type Set.

```
Set<String> names = new HashSet<String>();
```

This way, you have to change only one line if you decide to use a TreeSet instead.

Also, methods that operate on sets should specify parameters of type Set:

```
public static void print(Set<String> s)
```

Then the method can be used for all set implementations.

In theory, we should make the same recommendation for linked lists, namely to save LinkedList references in variables of type List. However, in the Java library, the List interface is common to both the ArrayList and the LinkedList class. In particular, it has get and set methods for random access, even though these methods are very inefficient for linked lists. You can't write efficient code if you don't know whether random access is efficient or not. This is plainly a serious design error in the standard library, and I cannot recommend using the List interface for that reason. (To see just how embarrassing that error is, have a look at the source code for the binarySearch method of the Collections class. That method takes a List parameter, but binary search makes no sense for a linked list. The code then clumsily tries to discover whether the list is a linked list, and then switches to a linear search!)

The Set interface and the Map interface, which you will see in the next section, are well-designed, and you should use them.

16.2 Maps

A map is a data type that keeps associations between *keys* and *values*. Figure 3 gives a typical example: a map that associates names with colors. This map might describe the favorite colors of various people.

> A map keeps associations between key and value objects.

Mathematically speaking, a map is a function from one set, the *key set*, to another set, the *value set*. Every key in the map has a unique value, but a value may be associated with several keys.

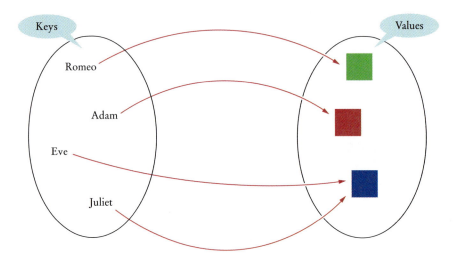

Figure 3 A Map

The HashMap and TreeMap classes both implement the Map interface.

Just as there are two kinds of set implementations, the Java library has two implementations for maps: HashMap and TreeMap. Both of them implement the Map interface (see Figure 4). As with sets, you need to decide which of the two to use. As a rule of thumb, use a hash map unless you want to visit the keys in sorted order.

After constructing a HashMap or TreeMap, you should store the reference to the map object in a Map reference:

```
Map<String, Color> favoriteColors = new HashMap<String, Color>();
```

or

```
Map<String, Color> favoriteColors = new TreeMap<String, Color>();
```

Use the put method to add an association:

```
favoriteColors.put("Juliet", Color.RED);
```

You can change the value of an existing association, simply by calling put again:

```
favoriteColors.put("Juliet", Color.BLUE);
```

The get method returns the value associated with a key.

```
Color julietsFavoriteColor = favoriteColors.get("Juliet");
```

If you ask for a key that isn't associated with any values, then the get method returns null.

To remove a key and its associated value, use the remove method:

```
favoriteColors.remove("Juliet");
```

To find all keys and values in a map, iterate through the key set and find the values that correspond to the keys.

Sometimes you want to enumerate all keys in a map. The keySet method yields the set of keys. You can then ask the key set for an iterator and get all keys. From each key, you can find the associated value with the get method. Thus, the following instructions print all key/value pairs in a map m:

```
Set<String> keySet = m.keySet();
for (String key : keySet)
{
    Color value = m.get(key);
    System.out.println(key + " : " + value);
}
```

When you use a hash map, the keys are visited in a seemingly random order. With a tree map, keys are visited in sorted order. The following sample program shows a map in action.

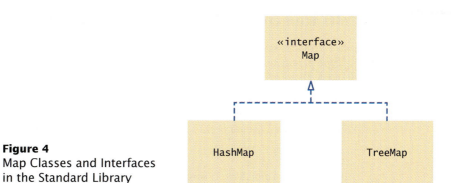

Figure 4
Map Classes and Interfaces
in the Standard Library

ch16/map/MapDemo.java

```java
1   import java.awt.Color;
2   import java.util.HashMap;
3   import java.util.Map;
4   import java.util.Set;
5
6   /**
7      This program demonstrates a map that maps names to colors.
8   */
9   public class MapDemo
10  {
11     public static void main(String[] args)
12     {
13        Map<String, Color> favoriteColors = new HashMap<String, Color>();
14        favoriteColors.put("Juliet", Color.BLUE);
15        favoriteColors.put("Romeo", Color.GREEN);
16        favoriteColors.put("Adam", Color.RED);
17        favoriteColors.put("Eve", Color.BLUE);
18
19        // Print all keys and values in the map
20
21        Set<String> keySet = favoriteColors.keySet();
22        for (String key : keySet)
23        {
24           Color value = favoriteColors.get(key);
25           System.out.println(key + " : " + value);
26        }
27     }
28  }
```

Program Run

```
Romeo : java.awt.Color[r=0,g=255,b=0]
Eve : java.awt.Color[r=0,g=0,b=255]
Adam : java.awt.Color[r=255,g=0,b=0]
Juliet : java.awt.Color[r=0,g=0,b=255]
```

SELF CHECK

5. What is the difference between a set and a map?

6. Why is the collection of the keys of a map a set?

Special Topic 16.1

Enhancements to Collection Classes in Java 7

Java 7 provides several syntactical conveniences for working with collection classes.

Type parameters in constructors can be inferred from variable types. You no longer have to repeat them in the variable declaration and the constructor. For example,

```java
Set<String> names = new HashSet<>(); // Constructs a HashSet<String>
Map<String, Integer> scores = new TreeMap<>(); // Constructs a TreeMap<String, Integer>
```

You can obtain *collection literals* of type List, Set, and Map, with the following syntax:

```java
["Tom", "Diana", "Harry"];
{ 2, 3, 5, 7, 11 };
{ "Juliet" : Color.BLUE, "Romeo" : Color.GREEN, "Eve" : Color.BLUE };
```

These objects are immutable: you cannot change the contents of the list, set, or map literal. The objects are instances of classes that implements the List, Set, and Map interfaces, but you don't know what those classes are.

You can pass collection or map literals to methods, for example

```
names.addAll(["Tom", "Diana", "Harry"]);
```

If you want to store a literal in a variable, you must use the interface type for the variable declaration:

```
List<String> friends = ["Tom", "Diana", "Harry"];
```

Alternatively, you can initialize a collection with a literal:

```
ArrayList<String> friends = new ArrayList<>(["Tom", "Diana", "Harry"]);
```

This works because all Java collection and map classes have constructors that copy entries from another collection or map.

Finally, you can use the [] operator instead of the get, set, or put methods. For example,

```
String name = names[0];
names[0] = "Fred";
scores["Fred"] = 13;
int score = scores["Fred"];
```

How To 16.1

Choosing a Container

Suppose you need to store objects in a container. You have now seen a number of different data structures. This How To reviews how to pick an appropriate container for your application.

Step 1 Determine how you access the values.

You store values in a container so that you can later retrieve them. How do you want to access individual values? You have several choices.

- Values are accessed by an integer position. Use an ArrayList. Go to Step 2, then stop.
- Values are accessed by a key that is not a part of the object. Use a map.
- It doesn't matter. Values are always accessed "in bulk", by traversing the collection and doing something with each value.

Step 2 Determine the element types of key/value types.

For a list or set, determine the type of the elements that you want to store. For example, if you collect a set of books, then the element type is Book.

Similarly, for a map, determine the types of the keys and the associated values. If you want to look up books by ID, you can use a Map<Integer, Book> or Map<String, Book>, depending on your ID type.

Step 3 Determine whether element or key order matters.

When you visit elements from a container or keys from a map, do you care about the order in which they are visited? You have several choices.

- Elements or keys must be sorted. Use a TreeSet or TreeMap. Go to Step 6.
- Elements must be in the same order in which they were inserted. Your choice is now narrowed down to a LinkedList or ArrayList.
- It doesn't matter. As long as you get to visit all elements, you don't care in which order. If you chose a map in Step 1, use a HashMap and go to Step 5.

Step 4 For a collection, determine which operations must be fast.

You have several choices.
- Finding elements must be fast. Use a HashSet and go to Step 5.
- Adding and removing elements at the beginning or middle must be fast. Use a LinkedList.
- It doesn't matter. You only insert at the end, or collect so few elements that you aren't concerned about speed. Then use an ArrayList.

Step 5 For hash sets and maps, decide whether you need to implement the equals and hashCode methods.

If your elements or keys belong to a class that someone else provided, check whether the class implements hashCode and equals methods. If so, you are all set. This is the case for most classes in the standard Java library, such as String, Integer, Rectangle, and so on.

If not, decide whether you can compare the elements by identity. Are all elements distinct in your program? That is, can it never happen that you have two different elements with the same instance variables? In that case, you need not do anything—the hashCode and equals methods of the Object class are appropriate.

If you need to implement your own equals and hashCode methods, turn to Section 16.4.

Step 6 If you use a tree, decide whether to supply a comparator.

Look at the class of the set elements or map keys. Does that class implement the Comparable interface? If so, is the sort order given by the compareTo method the one you want? If yes, then you don't need to do anything further. This is the case for many classes in the standard library, in particular for String and Integer.

If no, then your element class must implement the Comparable interface, or you must provide a class that implements the Comparator interface. See Section 14.8 for the details.

⊕ **Worked Example 16.1**

Word Frequency

In this Worked Example, we read a text file and print a list of all words in the file in alphabetical order, together with a count that indicates how often each word occurred in the file

---

16.3 Hash Tables

In this section, you will see how the technique of **hashing** can be used to find elements in a data structure quickly, without making a linear search through all elements. Hashing gives rise to the **hash table**, which can be used to implement sets and maps.

A **hash function** is a function that computes an integer value, the **hash code**, from an object, in such a way that different objects are likely to yield different hash codes. The Object class has a hashCode method that other classes need to override. The call

A hash function computes an integer value from an object.

```
int h = x.hashCode();
```

computes the hash code of the object x.

⊕ Available online in WileyPLUS and at www.wiley.com/college/horstmann.

Table 1	Sample Strings and Their Hash Codes		
String	Hash Code	String	Hash Code
"Adam"	2035631	"Joe"	74656
"Eve"	70068	"Juliet"	−2065036585
"Harry"	69496448	"Katherine"	2079199209
"Jim"	74478	"Sue"	83491

Table 1 shows some examples of strings and their hash codes. You will see in Section 16.4 how these values are obtained.

> A good hash function minimizes *collisions*—identical hash codes for different objects.

It is possible for two or more distinct objects to have the same hash code; this is called a *collision*. For example, the strings "VII" and "Ugh" happen to have the same hash code. These collisions are very rare for strings (see Exercise P16.6).

Section 16.5 explains how you should override the hashCode method for other classes.

A hash code is used as an array index into a hash table. In the simplest implementation of a hash table, you could make an array and insert each object at the location of its hash code (see Figure 5).

If there are no collisions, it is a very simple matter to find out whether an object is already present in the set or not. Compute its hash code and check whether the array position with that hash code is already occupied. This doesn't require a search through the entire array!

Of course, it is not feasible to allocate an array that is large enough to hold all possible integer index positions. Therefore, we must pick an array of some reasonable size and then reduce the hash code to fall inside the array:

```java
int h = x.hashCode();
if (h < 0) h = -h;
position = h % buckets.length;
```

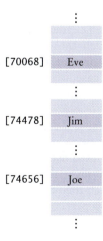

Figure 5
A Simplistic Implementation
of a Hash Table

Figure 6

A Hash Table with Buckets to Store Elements with the Same Hash Code

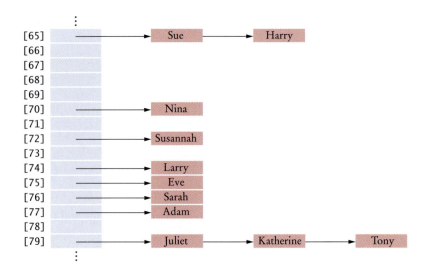

After reducing the hash code modulo a smaller array size, it becomes even more likely that several objects will collide. In order to handle collisions, we will store all colliding elements in a "bucket", a linked list of elements with the same position value (see Figure 6).

Here is the algorithm for finding an object x in a hash table.

> A hash table can be implemented as an array of *buckets*—sequences of nodes that hold elements with the same hash code.

1. Compute the hash code and reduce it modulo the table size. This gives an index h into the hash table.

2. Iterate through the elements of the bucket at position h. For each element of the bucket, check whether it is equal to x.

3. If a match is found among the elements of that bucket, then x is in the set. Otherwise, it is not.

Adding an element is a straightforward extension of the algorithm for finding an object. First compute the hash code to locate the bucket in which the element should be inserted. Try finding the object in that bucket. If it is already present, do nothing. Otherwise, insert it.

Removing an element is equally simple. First compute the hash code to locate the bucket in which the element should be inserted. Try finding the object in that bucket. If it is present, remove it. Otherwise, do nothing.

> If there are no or only a few collisions, then adding, locating, and removing hash table elements takes constant or $O(1)$ time.

In the best case, in which there are no collisions, all buckets either are empty or have a single element. Then adding, finding, and removing elements takes constant or $O(1)$ time.

More generally, for this algorithm to be effective, the bucket sizes must be small. (In the worst case, where all elements end up in the same bucket, a hash table degenerates into a linked list!)

In order to reduce the chances for collisions, you should make a hash table somewhat larger than the number of elements that you expect to insert. An excess capacity of about 30 percent is typically recommended. According to some researchers, the hash table size should be chosen to be a prime number to minimize the number of collisions.

At the end of this section you will find the code for a simple implementation of a hash set. That implementation takes advantage of the AbstractSet class, which already implements most of the methods of the Set interface.

In this implementation you must specify the size of the hash table. In the standard library, you don't need to supply a table size. If the hash table gets too full, a new table of twice the size is created, and all elements are inserted into the new table.

ch16/hashtable/HashSet.java

```java
import java.util.AbstractSet;
import java.util.Iterator;
import java.util.NoSuchElementException;

/**
    A hash set stores an unordered collection of objects, using
    a hash table.
*/
public class HashSet extends AbstractSet
{
    private Node[] buckets;
    private int size;

    /**
        Constructs a hash table.
        @param bucketsLength the length of the buckets array
    */
    public HashSet(int bucketsLength)
    {
        buckets = new Node[bucketsLength];
        size = 0;
    }

    /**
        Tests for set membership.
        @param x an object
        @return true if x is an element of this set
    */
    public boolean contains(Object x)
    {
        int h = x.hashCode();
        if (h < 0) h = -h;
        h = h % buckets.length;

        Node current = buckets[h];
        while (current != null)
        {
            if (current.data.equals(x)) return true;
            current = current.next;
        }
        return false;
    }
```

```
44      /**
45         Adds an element to this set.
46         @param x an object
47         @return true if x is a new object, false if x was
48         already in the set
49      */
50      public boolean add(Object x)
51      {
52         int h = x.hashCode();
53         if (h < 0) h = -h;
54         h = h % buckets.length;
55
56         Node current = buckets[h];
57         while (current != null)
58         {
59            if (current.data.equals(x))
60               return false; // Already in the set
61            current = current.next;
62         }
63         Node newNode = new Node();
64         newNode.data = x;
65         newNode.next = buckets[h];
66         buckets[h] = newNode;
67         size++;
68         return true;
69      }
70
71      /**
72         Removes an object from this set.
73         @param x an object
74         @return true if x was removed from this set, false
75         if x was not an element of this set
76      */
77      public boolean remove(Object x)
78      {
79         int h = x.hashCode();
80         if (h < 0) h = -h;
81         h = h % buckets.length;
82
83         Node current = buckets[h];
84         Node previous = null;
85         while (current != null)
86         {
87            if (current.data.equals(x))
88            {
89               if (previous == null) buckets[h] = current.next;
90               else previous.next = current.next;
91               size--;
92               return true;
93            }
94            previous = current;
95            current = current.next;
96         }
97         return false;
98      }
99
```

```
100   /**
101      Returns an iterator that traverses the elements of this set.
102      @return a hash set iterator
103   */
104   public Iterator iterator()
105   {
106      return new HashSetIterator();
107   }
108
109   /**
110      Gets the number of elements in this set.
111      @return the number of elements
112   */
113   public int size()
114   {
115      return size;
116   }
117
118   class Node
119   {
120      public Object data;
121      public Node next;
122   }
123
124   class HashSetIterator implements Iterator
125   {
126      private int bucket;
127      private Node current;
128      private int previousBucket;
129      private Node previous;
130
131      /**
132         Constructs a hash set iterator that points to the
133         first element of the hash set.
134      */
135      public HashSetIterator()
136      {
137         current = null;
138         bucket = -1;
139         previous = null;
140         previousBucket = -1;
141      }
142
143      public boolean hasNext()
144      {
145         if (current != null && current.next != null)
146            return true;
147         for (int b = bucket + 1; b < buckets.length; b++)
148            if (buckets[b] != null) return true;
149         return false;
150      }
151
152      public Object next()
153      {
154         previous = current;
155         previousBucket = bucket;
156
```

```
157          if (current == null || current.next == null)
158          {
159             // Move to next bucket
160             bucket++;
161
162             while (bucket < buckets.length
163                   && buckets[bucket] == null)
164                bucket++;
165             if (bucket < buckets.length)
166                current = buckets[bucket];
167             else
168                throw new NoSuchElementException();
169          }
170          else // Move to next element in bucket
171             current = current.next;
172          return current.data;
173       }
174
175       public void remove()
176       {
177          if (previous != null && previous.next == current)
178             previous.next = current.next;
179          else if (previousBucket < bucket)
180             buckets[bucket] = current.next;
181          else
182             throw new IllegalStateException();
183          current = previous;
184          bucket = previousBucket;
185       }
186    }
187 }
```

ch16/hashtable/HashSetDemo.java

```
1  import java.util.Iterator;
2  import java.util.Set;
3
4  /**
5     This program demonstrates the hash set class.
6  */
7  public class HashSetDemo
8  {
9     public static void main(String[] args)
10    {
11       Set names = new HashSet(101); // 101 is a prime
12
13       names.add("Harry");
14       names.add("Sue");
15       names.add("Nina");
16       names.add("Susannah");
17       names.add("Larry");
18       names.add("Eve");
19       names.add("Sarah");
20       names.add("Adam");
21       names.add("Tony");
22       names.add("Katherine");
23       names.add("Juliet");
```

```
24        names.add("Romeo");
25        names.remove("Romeo");
26        names.remove("George");
27
28        Iterator iter = names.iterator();
29        while (iter.hasNext())
30            System.out.println(iter.next());
31    }
32 }
```

Program Run

```
Harry
Sue
Nina
Susannah
Larry
Eve
Sarah
Adam
Juliet
Katherine
Tony
```

S E L F   C H E C K

7. If a hash function returns 0 for all values, will the HashSet work correctly?

8. What does the hasNext method of the HashSetIterator do when it has reached the end of a bucket?

16.4 Computing Hash Codes

A hash function computes an integer hash code from an object, so that different objects are likely to have different hash codes. Let us first look at how you can compute a hash code from a string. Clearly, you need to combine the character values of the string to yield some integer. You could, for example, add up the character values:

```
int h = 0;
for (int i = 0; i < s.length(); i++)
   h = h + s.charAt(i);
```

However, that would not be a good idea. It doesn't scramble the character values enough. Strings that are permutations of another (such as "eat" and "tea") all have the same hash code.

Here is the method the standard library uses to compute the hash code for a string.

```
final int HASH_MULTIPLIER = 31;
int h = 0;
for (int i = 0; i < s.length(); i++)
   h = HASH_MULTIPLIER * h + s.charAt(i);
```

For example, the hash code of "eat" is

```
31 * (31 * 'e' + 'a') + 't' = 100184
```

The hash code of "tea" is quite different, namely

```
31 * (31 * 't' + 'e') + 'a' = 114704
```

(Use the Unicode table from Appendix A to look up the character values: 'a' is 97, 'e' is 101, and 't' is 116.)

For your own classes, you should make up a hash code that combines the hash codes of the instance variables in a similar way. For example, let us implement a hashCode method for the Coin class. There are two instance variables: the coin name and the coin value. First, compute their hash code. You know how to compute the hash code of a string. To compute the hash code of a floating-point number, first wrap the floating-point number into a Double object, and then compute its hash code.

> When implementing the hashCode method, combine the hash codes for the instance variables.

```
class Coin
{
   public int hashCode()
   {
      int h1 = name.hashCode();
      int h2 = new Double(value).hashCode();
      . . .
   }
}
```

Then combine the two hash codes.

```
final int HASH_MULTIPLIER = 29;
int h = HASH_MULTIPLIER * h1 + h2;
return h;
```

Use a prime number as the hash multiplier—it scrambles the values better.

If you have more than two instance variables, then combine their hash codes as follows:

```
int h = HASH_MULTIPLIER * h1 + h2;
h = HASH_MULTIPLIER * h + h3;
h = HASH_MULTIPLIER * h + h4;
. . .
return h;
```

If one of the instance variables is an integer, just use the integer value as its hash code.

When you add objects of your class into a hash table, you need to double-check that the hashCode method is *compatible* with the equals method of your class. Two objects that are equal must yield the same hash code:

> Your hashCode method must be compatible with the equals method.

- If x.equals(y), then x.hashCode() == y.hashCode()

After all, if x and y are equal to each other, then you don't want to insert both of them into a set—sets don't store duplicates. But if their hash codes are different, x and y may end up in different buckets, and the add method would never notice that they are actually duplicates.

Of course, the converse of the compatibility condition is generally not true. It is possible for two objects to have the same hash code without being equal.

For the Coin class, the compatibility condition holds. We define two coins to be equal to each other if their names and values are equal. In that case, their hash codes will also be equal, because the hash code is computed from the hash codes of the name and value instance variables.

You get into trouble if your class provides an equals method but not a hashCode method. Suppose we forget to provide a hashCode method for the Coin class. Then it inherits the hash code method from the Object superclass. That method computes a hash code from the *memory location* of the object. The effect is that any two objects are very likely to have a different hash code.

```
Coin coin1 = new Coin(0.25, "quarter");
Coin coin2 = new Coin(0.25, "quarter");
```

Now coin1.hashCode() is derived from the memory location of coin1, and coin2.hashCode() is derived from the memory location of coin2. Even though coin1.equals(coin2) is true, their hash codes differ.

If a class provides neither equals nor hashCode, then objects are compared by identity.

However, if you provide *neither* equals *nor* hashCode, then there is no problem. The equals method of the Object class considers two objects equal only if their memory location is the same. That is, the Object class has compatible equals and hashCode methods. Of course, then the notion of equality is very restricted: Only identical objects are considered equal. That is not necessarily a bad notion of equality: If you want to collect a set of coins in a purse, you may not want to lump coins of equal value together.

Whenever you use a hash set, you need to make sure that an appropriate hash function exists for the type of the objects that you add to the set. Check the equals method of your class. It tells you when two objects are considered equal. There are two possibilities. Either equals has been provided or it has not been provided. If equals has not been provided, only identical objects are considered equal. In that case, don't provide hashCode either. However, if the equals method has been provided, look at its implementation. Typically, two objects are considered equal if some or all of the instance variables are equal. Sometimes, not all instance variables are used in the comparison. Two Student objects may be considered equal if their studentID variables are equal. Implement the hashCode method to combine the hash codes of the instance variables that are compared in the equals method.

In a hash map, only the keys are hashed.

When you use a HashMap, only the keys are hashed. They need compatible hashCode and equals methods. The values are never hashed or compared. The reason is simple—the map only needs to find, add, and remove keys quickly.

ch16/hashcode/Coin.java

```java
1  /**
2     A coin with a monetary value.
3  */
4  public class Coin
5  {
6     private double value;
7     private String name;
8
9     /**
10       Constructs a coin.
11       @param aValue the monetary value of the coin
12       @param aName the name of the coin
13    */
14    public Coin(double aValue, String aName)
15    {
```

```java
16          value = aValue;
17          name = aName;
18       }
19
20       /**
21          Gets the coin value.
22          @return the value
23       */
24       public double getValue()
25       {
26          return value;
27       }
28
29       /**
30          Gets the coin name.
31          @return the name
32       */
33       public String getName()
34       {
35          return name;
36       }
37
38       public boolean equals(Object otherObject)
39       {
40          if (otherObject == null) return false;
41          if (getClass() != otherObject.getClass()) return false;
42          Coin other = (Coin) otherObject;
43          return value == other.value && name.equals(other.name);
44       }
45
46       public int hashCode()
47       {
48          int h1 = name.hashCode();
49          int h2 = new Double(value).hashCode();
50          final int HASH_MULTIPLIER = 29;
51          int h = HASH_MULTIPLIER * h1 + h2;
52          return h;
53       }
54
55       public String toString()
56       {
57          return "Coin[value=" + value + ",name=" + name + "]";
58       }
59    }
```

ch16/hashcode/CoinHashCodePrinter.java

```java
1    import java.util.HashSet;
2    import java.util.Set;
3
4    /**
5       A program that prints hash codes of coins.
6    */
7    public class CoinHashCodePrinter
8    {
9       public static void main(String[] args)
10      {
```

```
11          Coin coin1 = new Coin(0.25, "quarter");
12          Coin coin2 = new Coin(0.25, "quarter");
13          Coin coin3 = new Coin(0.05, "nickel");
14
15          System.out.println("hash code of coin1=" + coin1.hashCode());
16          System.out.println("hash code of coin2=" + coin2.hashCode());
17          System.out.println("hash code of coin3=" + coin3.hashCode());
18
19          Set<Coin> coins = new HashSet<Coin>();
20          coins.add(coin1);
21          coins.add(coin2);
22          coins.add(coin3);
23
24          for (Coin c : coins)
25             System.out.println(c);
26       }
27    }
```

Program Run

```
hash code of coin1=-1513525892
hash code of coin2=-1513525892
hash code of coin3=-1768365211
Coin[value=0.25,name=quarter]
Coin[value=0.05,name=nickel]
```

SELF CHECK

9. What is the hash code of the string "to"?
10. What is the hash code of new Integer(13)?

Common Error 16.1

Forgetting to Provide hashCode

When putting elements into a hash table, make sure that the hashCode method is provided. (The only exception is that you don't need to provide hashCode if equals isn't provided either. In that case, distinct objects of your class are considered different, even if they have matching contents.)

If you forget to implement the hashCode method, then you inherit the hashCode method of the Object class. That method computes a hash code of the memory location of the object. For example, suppose that you do *not* provide the hashCode method of the Coin class. Then the following code is likely to fail:

```
Set<Coin> coins = new HashSet<Coin>();
coins.add(new Coin(0.25, "quarter"));
// The following comparison will probably fail if hashCode not provided
if (coins.contains(new Coin(0.25, "quarter"))
   System.out.println("The set contains a quarter.");
```

The two Coin objects are constructed at different memory locations, so the hashCode method of the Object class will probably compute different hash codes for them. (As always with hash codes, there is a small chance that the hash codes happen to collide.) Then the contains method will inspect the wrong bucket and never find the matching coin.

The remedy is to provide a hashCode method in the Coin class.

16.5 Binary Search Trees

A set implementation is allowed to rearrange its elements in any way it chooses so that it can find elements quickly. Suppose a set implementation *sorts* its entries. Then it can use **binary search** to locate elements quickly. Binary search takes $O(\log(n))$ steps, where n is the size of the set. For example, binary search in an array of 1,000 elements is able to locate an element in at most 10 steps by cutting the size of the search interval in half in each step.

If we use an array to store the elements of a set, inserting or removing an element is an $O(n)$ operation. In this section, you will see how tree-shaped data structures can keep elements in sorted order with more efficient insertion and removal.

A linked list is a one-dimensional data structure. In a linked list, a node has only one successor. You can imagine that all nodes are arranged in line. In contrast, a **tree** is made of nodes that have references to multiple nodes, called the child nodes. Because the child nodes can also have children, the data structure has a tree-like appearance. It is traditional to draw the tree upside down, like a family tree or hierarchy chart (see Figure 7). In keeping with the tree image, the node at the top is called the *root node*, and the nodes without children are called *leaf nodes*. In a **binary tree**, every node has at most two children (called the *left* and *right children*); hence the name *binary*.

> A binary tree consists of nodes, each of which has at most two child nodes.

Finally, a **binary search tree** is constructed to have this important property:

- The data values of *all* descendants to the left of *any* node are less than the data value stored in that node, and *all* descendants to the right have greater data values.

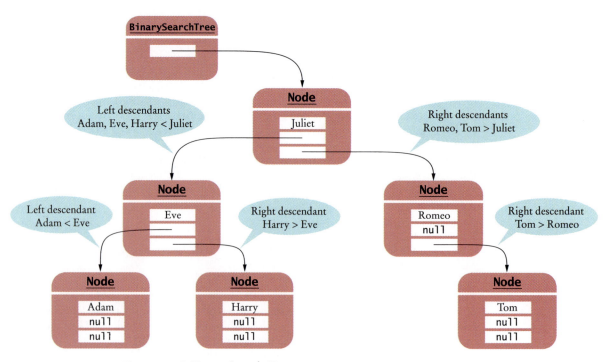

Figure 7 A Binary Search Tree

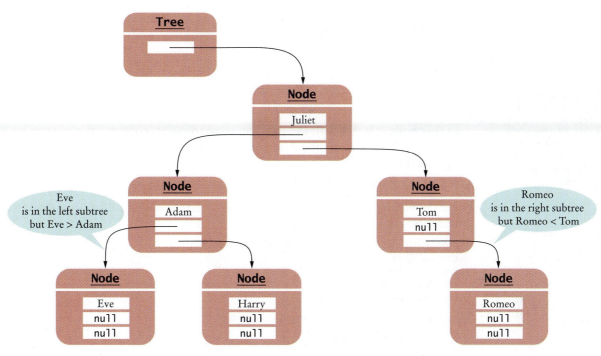

Figure 8 A Binary Tree That Is Not a Binary Search Tree

All nodes in a binary search tree fulfill the property that the descendants to the left have smaller data values than the node data value, and the descendants to the right have larger data values.

The tree in Figure 7 has this property. To verify the binary search property, you must check each node. Consider the node "Juliet". All descendants to the left have data before "Juliet". All descendants on the right have data after "Juliet". Move on to "Eve". There is a single descendant to the left, with data "Adam" before "Eve", and a single descendant to the right, with data "Harry" after "Eve". Check the remaining nodes in the same way.

Figure 8 shows a binary tree that is not a binary search tree. Look carefully—the root node passes the test, but its two children do not.

Let us implement these tree classes. Just as you needed classes for lists and their nodes, you need one class for the tree, containing a reference to the *root node,* and a separate class for the nodes. Each node contains two references (to the left and right child nodes) and an instance variable data. At the fringes of the tree, one or two of the child references can be null. The data variable has type Comparable, not Object, because you must be able to compare the values in a binary search tree in order to place them into the correct position.

```java
public class BinarySearchTree
{
   private Node root;

   public BinarySearchTree() { . . . }
   public void add(Comparable obj) { . . . }
   . . .
   class Node
   {
      public Comparable data;
      public Node left;
      public Node right;
```

```
            public void addNode(Node newNode) { . . . }
        . . .
    }
}
```

To insert data into the tree, use the following algorithm:

> To insert a value into a binary search tree, keep comparing the value with the node data and follow the nodes to the left or right, until reaching a null node.

- If you encounter a non-null node reference, look at its data value. If the data value of that node is larger than the one you want to insert, continue the process with the left child. If the existing data value is smaller, continue the process with the right child.
- If you encounter a null node reference, replace it with the new node.

For example, consider the tree in Figure 9. It is the result of the following statements:

```
BinarySearchTree tree = new BinarySearchTree();
tree.add("Juliet"); ❶
tree.add("Tom"); ❷
tree.add("Diana"); ❸
tree.add("Harry"); ❹
```

We want to insert a new element Romeo into it.

```
tree.add("Romeo"); ❺
```

Start with the root node, Juliet. Romeo comes after Juliet, so you move to the right subtree. You encounter the node Tom. Romeo comes before Tom, so you move to the left subtree. But there is no left subtree. Hence, you insert a new Romeo node as the left child of Tom (see Figure 10).

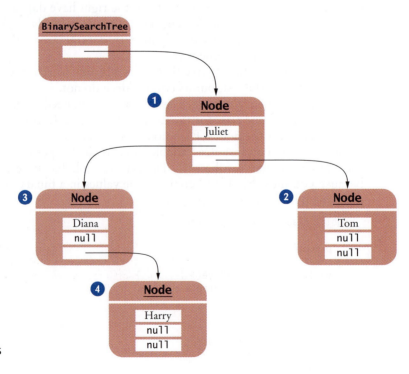

Figure 9
Binary Search Tree
After Four Insertions

Figure 10
Binary Search Tree
After Five Insertions

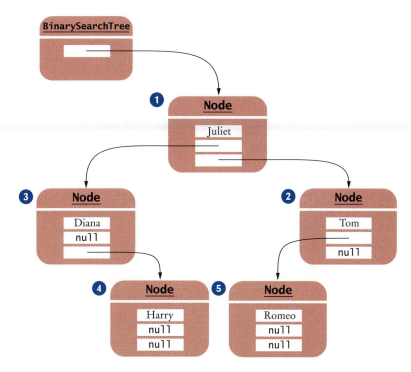

You should convince yourself that the resulting tree is still a binary search tree. When Romeo is inserted, it must end up as a right descendant of Juliet—that is what the binary search tree condition means for the root node Juliet. The root node doesn't care where in the right subtree the new node ends up. Moving along to Tom, the right child of Juliet, all it cares about is that the new node Romeo ends up somewhere on its left. There is nothing to its left, so Romeo becomes the new left child, and the resulting tree is again a binary search tree.

Here is the code for the add method of the BinarySearchTree class:

```
public void add(Comparable obj)
{
   Node newNode = new Node();
   newNode.data = obj;
   newNode.left = null;
   newNode.right = null;
   if (root == null) root = newNode;
   else root.addNode(newNode);
}
```

If the tree is empty, simply set its root to the new node. Otherwise, you know that the new node must be inserted somewhere within the nodes, and you can ask the root node to perform the insertion. That node object calls the addNode method of the Node class, which checks whether the new object is less than the object stored in the node. If so, the element is inserted in the left subtree; if not, it is inserted in the right subtree:

```
class Node
{
   . . .
   public void addNode(Node newNode)
   {
```

```
            int comp = newNode.data.compareTo(data);
            if (comp < 0)
            {
               if (left == null) left = newNode;
               else left.addNode(newNode);
            }
            else if (comp > 0)
            {
               if (right == null) right = newNode;
               else right.addNode(newNode);
            }
         }
         . . .
      }
```

Let's trace the calls to addNode when inserting Romeo into the tree in Figure 9. The first call to addNode is

```
root.addNode(newNode)
```

Because root points to Juliet, you compare Juliet with Romeo and find that you must call

```
root.right.addNode(newNode)
```

The node root.right is Tom. Compare the data values again (Tom vs. Romeo) and find that you must now move to the left. Since root.right.left is null, set root.right.left to newNode, and the insertion is complete (see Figure 10).

Unlike a linked list or an array, and like a hash table, a binary tree has no *insert positions.* You cannot select the position where you would like to insert an element into a binary search tree. The data structure is *self-organizing;* that is, each element finds its own place.

We will now discuss the removal algorithm. Our task is to remove a node from the tree. Of course, we must first *find* the node to be removed. That is a simple matter, due to the characteristic property of a binary search tree. Compare the data value to be removed with the data value that is stored in the root node. If it is smaller, keep looking in the left subtree. Otherwise, keep looking in the right subtree.

Let us now assume that we have located the node that needs to be removed. First, let us consider an easy case, when that node has only one child (see Figure 11).

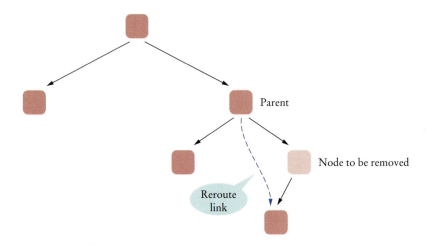

Figure 11
Removing a Node
with One Child

When removing a node with only one child from a binary search tree, the child replaces the node to be removed.

When removing a node with two children from a binary search tree, replace it with the smallest node of the right subtree.

In a balanced tree, all paths from the root to the leaves have about the same length.

To remove the node, simply modify the parent link that points to the node so that it points to the child instead.

If the node to be removed has no children at all, then the parent link is simply set to null.

The case in which the node to be removed has two children is more challenging. Rather than removing the node, it is easier to replace its data value with the next larger value in the tree. That replacement preserves the binary search tree property. (Alternatively, you could use the largest element of the left subtree—see Exercise P16.21).

To locate the next larger value, go to the right subtree and find its smallest data value. Keep following the left child links. Once you reach a node that has no left child, you have found the node containing the smallest data value of the subtree. Now remove that node—it is easily removed because it has at most one child to the right. Then store its data value in the original node that was slated for removal. Figure 12 shows the details. You will find the complete code at the end of this section.

At the end of this section, you will find the source code for the BinarySearchTree class. It contains the add and remove methods that we just described, as well as a find method that tests whether a value is present in a binary search tree, and a print method that we will analyze in the following section.

Now that you have seen the implementation of this data structure, you may well wonder whether it is any good. Like nodes in a list, nodes are allocated one at a time. No existing elements need to be moved when a new element is inserted or removed; that is an advantage. How fast insertion and removal are, however, depends on the shape of the tree. These operations are fast if the tree is *balanced* (see Figure 13).

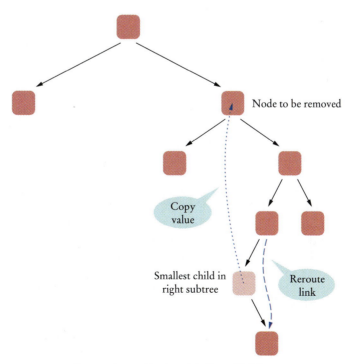

Figure 12 Removing a Node with Two Children

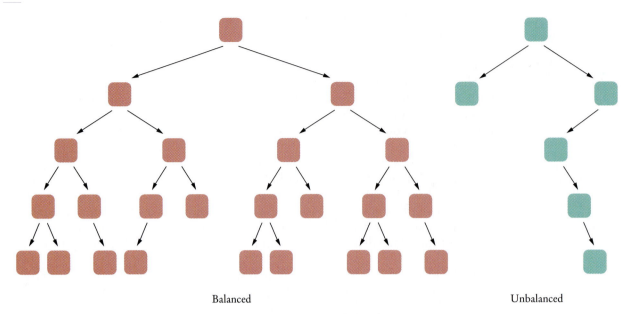

Balanced   Unbalanced

Figure 13 Balanced and Unbalanced Trees

Adding, finding, and removing an element in a tree set is proportional to the height of the tree.

In a balanced tree, all paths from the root to one of the leaf nodes (that is, nodes without children) have approximately the same length. The number of nodes in the longest of these paths is called the *height* of the tree. The trees in Figure 13 have height 5.

Because the operations of finding, adding, and removing an element process the nodes along a path from the root to a leaf, their execution time is proportional to the height of the tree, and not to the total number of nodes in the tree.

A tree of height h can have up to $n = 2^h - 1$ nodes. For example, a completely filled tree of height 4 has $1 + 2 + 4 + 8 = 15 = 2^4 - 1$ nodes. In other words, $h = \log_2 (n + 1)$ for a completely filled tree. For a balanced tree, we still have $h \approx \log_2 n$. For example, the height of a tree with 1,000 nodes is approximately 10 (because 1024 = 2^{10}). A tree with 1,000,000 nodes has height approximately 20. In such a tree, you can find any element in about 20 steps. That is a lot faster than traversing the 1,000,000 elements of a list.

If a binary search tree is balanced, then adding, locating, or removing an element takes $O(\log(n))$ time.

On the other hand, if the tree happens to be *unbalanced*, then binary tree operations can be slow—in the worst case, as slow as insertion into a linked list.

If new elements are fairly random, the resulting tree is likely to be well balanced. However, if the incoming elements happen to be in sorted order already, then the resulting tree is completely unbalanced. Each new element is inserted at the end, and the entire tree must be traversed every time to find that end!

Binary search trees work well for random data, but if you suspect that the data in your application might be sorted or have long runs of sorted data, you should not use a binary search tree. There are more sophisticated tree structures whose methods keep trees balanced at all times. In these tree structures, one can guarantee that finding, adding, and removing elements takes $O(\log(n))$ time. The standard Java library uses *red-black trees*, a special form of balanced binary trees, to implement sets and maps.

ch16/tree/BinarySearchTree.java

```java
1   /**
2       This class implements a binary search tree whose
3       nodes hold objects that implement the Comparable
4       interface.
5   */
6   public class BinarySearchTree
7   {
8       private Node root;
9
10      /**
11          Constructs an empty tree.
12      */
13      public BinarySearchTree()
14      {
15          root = null;
16      }
17
18      /**
19          Inserts a new node into the tree.
20          @param obj the object to insert
21      */
22      public void add(Comparable obj)
23      {
24          Node newNode = new Node();
25          newNode.data = obj;
26          newNode.left = null;
27          newNode.right = null;
28          if (root == null) root = newNode;
29          else root.addNode(newNode);
30      }
31
32      /**
33          Tries to find an object in the tree.
34          @param obj the object to find
35          @return true if the object is contained in the tree
36      */
37      public boolean find(Comparable obj)
38      {
39          Node current = root;
40          while (current != null)
41          {
42              int d = current.data.compareTo(obj);
43              if (d == 0) return true;
44              else if (d > 0) current = current.left;
45              else current = current.right;
46          }
47          return false;
48      }
49
50      /**
51          Tries to remove an object from the tree. Does nothing
52          if the object is not contained in the tree.
53          @param obj the object to remove
54      */
55      public void remove(Comparable obj)
56      {
57          // Find node to be removed
58
```

```
59      Node toBeRemoved = root;
60      Node parent = null;
61      boolean found = false;
62      while (!found && toBeRemoved != null)
63      {
64         int d = toBeRemoved.data.compareTo(obj);
65         if (d == 0) found = true;
66         else
67         {
68            parent = toBeRemoved;
69            if (d > 0) toBeRemoved = toBeRemoved.left;
70            else toBeRemoved = toBeRemoved.right;
71         }
72      }
73
74      if (!found) return;
75
76      // toBeRemoved contains obj
77
78      // If one of the children is empty, use the other
79
80      if (toBeRemoved.left == null || toBeRemoved.right == null)
81      {
82         Node newChild;
83         if (toBeRemoved.left == null)
84            newChild = toBeRemoved.right;
85         else
86            newChild = toBeRemoved.left;
87
88         if (parent == null) // Found in root
89            root = newChild;
90         else if (parent.left == toBeRemoved)
91            parent.left = newChild;
92         else
93            parent.right = newChild;
94         return;
95      }
96
97      // Neither subtree is empty
98
99      // Find smallest element of the right subtree
100
101     Node smallestParent = toBeRemoved;
102     Node smallest = toBeRemoved.right;
103     while (smallest.left != null)
104     {
105        smallestParent = smallest;
106        smallest = smallest.left;
107     }
108
109     // smallest contains smallest child in right subtree
110
111     // Move contents, unlink child
112
113     toBeRemoved.data = smallest.data;
114     if (smallestParent == toBeRemoved)
115        smallestParent.right = smallest.right;
116     else
117        smallestParent.left = smallest.right;
```

```
118    }
119
120    /**
121        Prints the contents of the tree in sorted order.
122    */
123    public void print()
124    {
125        if (root != null)
126            root.printNodes();
127        System.out.println();
128    }
129
130    /**
131        A node of a tree stores a data item and references
132        to the child nodes to the left and to the right.
133    */
134    class Node
135    {
136        public Comparable data;
137        public Node left;
138        public Node right;
139
140        /**
141            Inserts a new node as a descendant of this node.
142            @param newNode  the node to insert
143        */
144        public void addNode(Node newNode)
145        {
146            int comp = newNode.data.compareTo(data);
147            if (comp < 0)
148            {
149                if (left == null) left = newNode;
150                else left.addNode(newNode);
151            }
152            if (comp > 0)
153            {
154                if (right == null) right = newNode;
155                else right.addNode(newNode);
156            }
157        }
158
159        /**
160            Prints this node and all of its descendants
161            in sorted order.
162        */
163        public void printNodes()
164        {
165            if (left != null)
166                left.printNodes();
167            System.out.print(data + " ");
168            if (right != null)
169                right.printNodes();
170        }
171    }
172 }
```

11. What is the difference between a tree, a binary tree, and a balanced binary tree?

12. Give an example of a string that, when inserted into the tree of Figure 10, becomes a right child of Romeo.

16.6 Binary Tree Traversal

Now that the data are inserted in the tree, what can you do with them? It turns out to be surprisingly simple to print all elements in sorted order. You *know* that all data in the left subtree of any node must come before the node and before all data in the right subtree. That is, the following algorithm will print the elements in sorted order:

1. Print the left subtree.
2. Print the data.
3. Print the right subtree.

Let's try this out with the tree in Figure 10 on page 689. The algorithm tells us to

1. Print the left subtree of Juliet; that is, Diana and descendants.
2. Print Juliet.
3. Print the right subtree of Juliet; that is, Tom and descendants.

How do you print the subtree starting at Diana?

1. Print the left subtree of Diana. There is nothing to print.
2. Print Diana.
3. Print the right subtree of Diana, that is, Harry.

That is, the left subtree of Juliet is printed as

    Diana Harry

The right subtree of Juliet is the subtree starting at Tom. How is it printed? Again, using the same algorithm:

1. Print the left subtree of Tom, that is, Romeo.
2. Print Tom.
3. Print the right subtree of Tom. There is nothing to print.

Thus, the right subtree of Juliet is printed as

    Romeo Tom

Now put it all together: the left subtree, Juliet, and the right subtree:

    Diana Harry Juliet Romeo Tom

The tree is printed in sorted order.

Now we can implement the print method. You need a worker method printNodes of the Node class:

```
class Node
{
    . . .
    public void printNodes()
    {
        if (left != null)
            left.printNodes();
        System.out.print(data + " ");

        if (right != null)
            right.printNodes();
    }
    . . .
}
```

To print the entire tree, start this recursive printing process at the root, with the following method of the `BinarySearchTree` class.

```
public class BinarySearchTree
{
    . . .
    public void print()
    {
        if (root != null)
            root.printNodes();
        System.out.println();
    }
    . . .
}
```

To visit all elements in a tree, visit the root and recursively visit the subtrees. We distinguish between preorder, inorder, and postorder traversal.

This visitation scheme is called *inorder traversal* (visit the left subtree, the root, the right subtree). There are two other common traversal schemes, called *preorder traversal* and *postorder traversal*.

In preorder traversal,

- Visit the root,
- Visit the left subtree,
- Visit the right subtree.

In postorder traversal,

- Visit the left subtree,
- Visit the right subtree,
- Visit the root.

These two visitation schemes will not print the tree in sorted order. However, they are important in other applications of binary trees. Here is an example.

In Chapter 13, we presented an algorithm for parsing arithmetic expressions such as

```
(3 + 4) * 5
3 + 4 * 5
```

It is customary to draw these expressions in tree form—see Figure 14. If all operators have two arguments, then the resulting tree is a binary tree. Its leaves store numbers, and its interior nodes store operators.

Note that the expression trees describe the order in which the operators are applied.

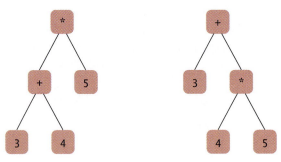

Figure 14 Expression Trees

This order becomes visible when applying the postorder traversal of the expression tree. The first tree yields

3 4 + 5 *

whereas the second tree yields

3 4 5 * +

You can interpret these sequences as expressions in "reverse Polish notation" (see Special Topic 15.1), or equivalently, instructions for a stack-based calculator (see Worked Example 15.1).

> Postorder traversal of an expression tree yields the instructions for evaluating the expression on a stack-based calculator.

SELF CHECK

13. What are the inorder traversals of the two trees in Figure 14?
14. Are the trees in Figure 14 binary search trees?

16.7 Priority Queues

In Section 15.4, you encountered two common abstract data types: stacks and queues. Another important abstract data type, the **priority queue**, collects elements, each of which has a *priority*. A typical example of a priority queue is a collection of work requests, some of which may be more urgent than others. Unlike a regular queue, the priority queue does not maintain a first-in, first-out discipline. Instead, elements are retrieved according to their priority. In other words, new items can be inserted in any order. But whenever an item is removed, that item has highest priority.

> When removing an element from a priority queue, the element with the highest priority is retrieved.

It is customary to give low values to high priorities, with priority 1 denoting the highest priority. The priority queue extracts the *minimum* element from the queue.

For example, consider this sample code:

```
PriorityQueue<WorkOrder> q = new PriorityQueue<WorkOrder>();
q.add(new WorkOrder(3, "Shampoo carpets"));
q.add(new WorkOrder(1, "Fix overflowing sink"));
q.add(new WorkOrder(2, "Order cleaning supplies"));
```

When calling q.remove() for the first time, the work order with priority 1 is removed. The next call to q.remove() removes the work order whose priority is highest among those remaining in the queue—in our example, the work order with priority 2.

The standard Java library supplies a `PriorityQueue` class that is ready for you to use. Later in this chapter, you will learn how to supply your own implementation.

Keep in mind that the priority queue is an *abstract* data type. You do not know how a priority queue organizes its elements. There are several concrete data structures that can be used to implement priority queues.

Of course, one implementation comes to mind immediately. Just store the elements in a linked list, adding new elements to the head of the list. The `remove` method then traverses the linked list and removes the element with the highest priority. In this implementation, adding elements is quick, but removing them is slow.

Another implementation strategy is to keep the elements in sorted order, for example in a binary search tree. Then it is an easy matter to locate and remove the largest element. However, another data structure, called a heap, is even more suitable for implementing priority queues.

16.8 Heaps

A heap is an almost completely filled tree in which the values of all nodes are at most as large as those of their descendants.

A **heap** (or, for greater clarity, *min-heap*) is a binary tree with two special properties.

1. A heap is *almost completely filled:* all nodes are filled in, except the last level may have some nodes missing toward the right (see Figure 15).
2. The tree fulfills the *heap property:* all nodes store values that are at most as large as the values stored in their descendants (see Figure 16).

It is easy to see that the heap property ensures that the smallest element is stored in the root.

A heap is superficially similar to a binary search tree, but there are two important differences.

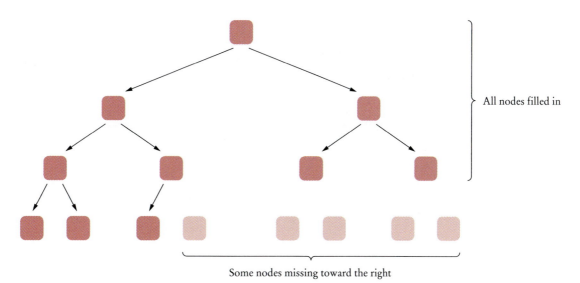

All nodes filled in

Some nodes missing toward the right

Figure 15 An Almost Completely Filled Tree

Figure 16
A Heap

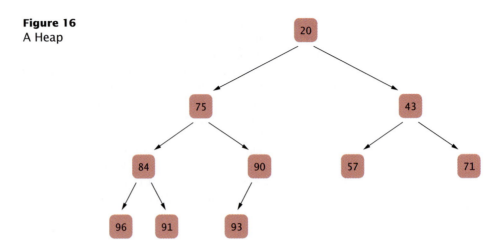

1. The shape of a heap is very regular. Binary search trees can have arbitrary shapes.
2. In a heap, the left and right subtrees both store elements that are larger than the root element. In contrast, in a binary search tree, smaller elements are stored in the left subtree and larger elements are stored in the right subtree.

Suppose you have a heap and want to insert a new element. Afterwards, the heap property should again be fulfilled. The following algorithm carries out the insertion (see Figure 17).

1. First, add a vacant slot to the end of the tree.
2. Next, demote the parent of the empty slot if it is larger than the element to be inserted. That is, move the parent value into the vacant slot, and move the vacant slot up. Repeat this demotion as long as the parent of the vacant slot is larger than the element to be inserted. (See Figure 17 continued.)

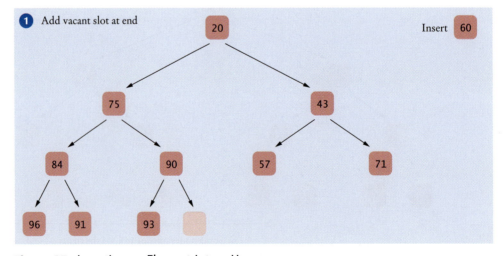

Figure 17 Inserting an Element into a Heap

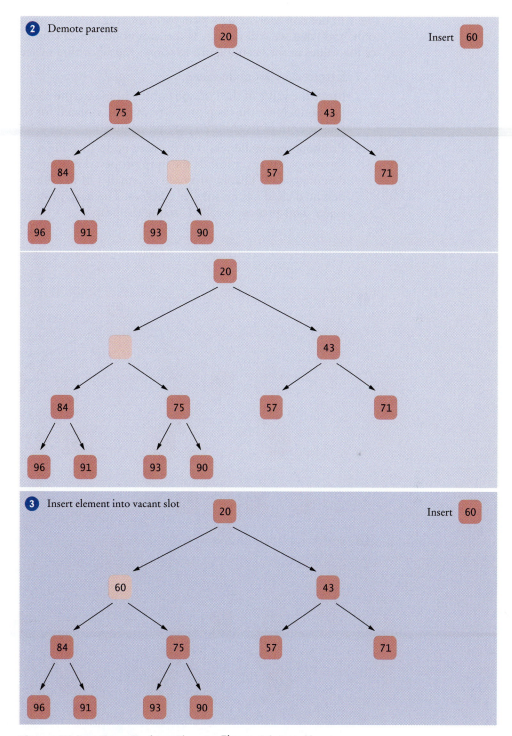

Figure 17 (continued) Inserting an Element into a Heap

3. At this point, either the vacant slot is at the root, or the parent of the vacant slot is smaller than the element to be inserted. Insert the element into the vacant slot.

We will not consider an algorithm for removing an arbitrary node from a heap. The only node that we will remove is the root node, which contains the minimum of all of the values in the heap. Figure 18 shows the algorithm in action.

1. Extract the root node value.

2. Move the value of the last node of the heap into the root node, and remove the last node. Now the heap property may be violated for the root node, because one or both of its children may be smaller.

3. Promote the smaller child of the root node. (See Figure 18 continued.) Now the root node again fulfills the heap property. Repeat this process with the demoted child. That is, promote the smaller of its children. Continue until the demoted child has no smaller children. The heap property is now fulfilled again. This process is called "fixing the heap".

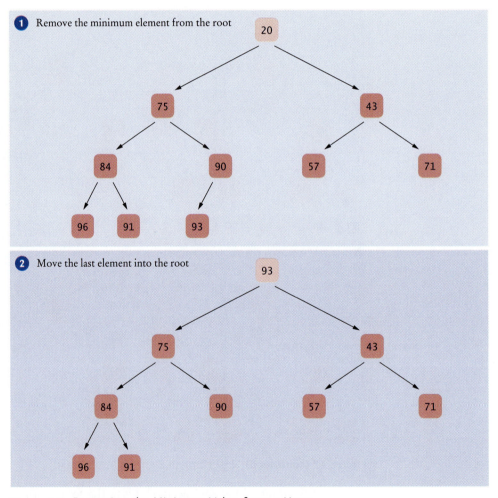

Figure 18 Removing the Minimum Value from a Heap

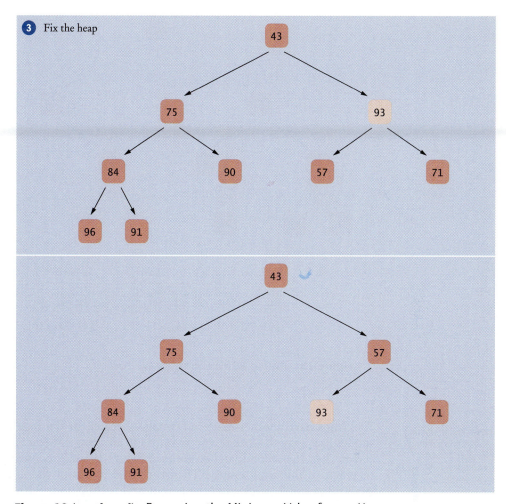

3 Fix the heap

Figure 18 (continued) Removing the Minimum Value from a Heap

Inserting and removing heap elements is very efficient. The reason lies in the balanced shape of a heap. The insertion and removal operations visit at most h nodes, where h is the height of the tree. A heap of height h contains at least 2^{h-1} elements, but less than 2^h elements. In other words, if n is the number of elements, then

$$2^{h-1} \leq n < 2^h$$

or

$$h - 1 \leq \log_2(n) < h$$

Inserting or removing a heap element is an $O(\log(n))$ operation.

This argument shows that the insertion and removal operations in a heap with n elements take $O(\log(n))$ steps.

Contrast this finding with the situation of binary search trees. When a binary search tree is unbalanced, it can degenerate into a linked list, so that in the worst case insertion and removal are $O(n)$ operations.

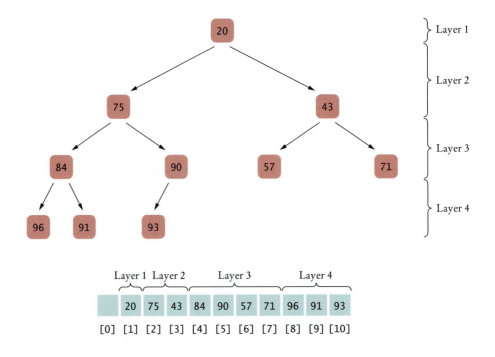

Figure 19 Storing a Heap in an Array

The regular layout of a heap makes it possible to store heap nodes efficiently in an array.

Heaps have another major advantage. Because of the regular layout of the heap nodes, it is easy to store the node values in an array or array list. First store the first layer, then the second, and so on (see Figure 19). For convenience, we leave the 0 element of the array empty. Then the child nodes of the node with index i have index $2 \cdot i$ and $2 \cdot i + 1$, and the parent node of the node with index i has index $i/2$. For example, as you can see in Figure 19, the children of node 4 are nodes 8 and 9, and the parent is node 2.

Storing the heap values in an array may not be intuitive, but it is very efficient. There is no need to allocate individual nodes or to store the links to the child nodes. Instead, child and parent positions can be determined by very simple computations.

The program at the end of this section contains an implementation of a heap. For greater clarity, the computation of the parent and child index positions is carried out in methods getParentIndex, getLeftChildIndex, and getRightChildIndex. For greater efficiency, the method calls could be avoided by using expressions index / 2, 2 * index, and 2 * index + 1 directly.

In this section, we have organized our heaps such that the smallest element is stored in the root. It is also possible to store the largest element in the root, simply by reversing all comparisons in the heap-building algorithm. If there is a possibility of misunderstanding, it is best to refer to the data structures as min-heap or max-heap.

The test program demonstrates how to use a min-heap as a priority queue.

ch16/pqueue/MinHeap.java

```java
import java.util.*;

/**
   This class implements a heap.
*/
public class MinHeap
{
   private ArrayList<Comparable> elements;

   /**
      Constructs an empty heap.
   */
   public MinHeap()
   {
      elements = new ArrayList<Comparable>();
      elements.add(null);
   }

   /**
      Adds a new element to this heap.
      @param newElement the element to add
   */
   public void add(Comparable newElement)
   {
      // Add a new leaf
      elements.add(null);
      int index = elements.size() - 1;

      // Demote parents that are larger than the new element
      while (index > 1
            && getParent(index).compareTo(newElement) > 0)
      {
         elements.set(index, getParent(index));
         index = getParentIndex(index);
      }

      // Store the new element in the vacant slot
      elements.set(index, newElement);
   }

   /**
      Gets the minimum element stored in this heap.
      @return the minimum element
   */
   public Comparable peek()
   {
      return elements.get(1);
   }

   /**
      Removes the minimum element from this heap.
      @return the minimum element
   */
   public Comparable remove()
   {
      Comparable minimum = elements.get(1);
```

```
58        // Remove last element
59        int lastIndex = elements.size() - 1;
60        Comparable last = elements.remove(lastIndex);
61
62        if (lastIndex > 1)
63        {
64           elements.set(1, last);
65           fixHeap();
66        }
67
68        return minimum;
69     }
70
71     /**
72        Turns the tree back into a heap, provided only the root
73        node violates the heap condition.
74     */
75     private void fixHeap()
76     {
77        Comparable root = elements.get(1);
78
79        int lastIndex = elements.size() - 1;
80        // Promote children of removed root while they are smaller than last
81
82        int index = 1;
83        boolean more = true;
84        while (more)
85        {
86           int childIndex = getLeftChildIndex(index);
87           if (childIndex <= lastIndex)
88           {
89              // Get smaller child
90
91              // Get left child first
92              Comparable child = getLeftChild(index);
93
94              // Use right child instead if it is smaller
95              if (getRightChildIndex(index) <= lastIndex
96                    && getRightChild(index).compareTo(child) < 0)
97              {
98                 childIndex = getRightChildIndex(index);
99                 child = getRightChild(index);
100             }
101
102             // Check if larger child is smaller than root
103             if (child.compareTo(root) < 0)
104             {
105                // Promote child
106                elements.set(index, child);
107                index = childIndex;
108             }
109             else
110             {
111                // Root is smaller than both children
112                more = false;
113             }
114          }
115          else
116          {
```

```
117                    // No children
118                 more = false;
119              }
120          }
121
122          // Store root element in vacant slot
123          elements.set(index, root);
124       }
125
126       /**
127          Returns the number of elements in this heap.
128       */
129       public int size()
130       {
131          return elements.size() - 1;
132       }
133
134       /**
135          Returns the index of the left child.
136          @param index the index of a node in this heap
137          @return the index of the left child of the given node
138       */
139       private static int getLeftChildIndex(int index)
140       {
141          return 2 * index;
142       }
143
144       /**
145          Returns the index of the right child.
146          @param index the index of a node in this heap
147          @return the index of the right child of the given node
148       */
149       private static int getRightChildIndex(int index)
150       {
151          return 2 * index + 1;
152       }
153
154       /**
155          Returns the index of the parent.
156          @param index the index of a node in this heap
157          @return the index of the parent of the given node
158       */
159       private static int getParentIndex(int index)
160       {
161          return index / 2;
162       }
163
164       /**
165          Returns the value of the left child.
166          @param index the index of a node in this heap
167          @return the value of the left child of the given node
168       */
169       private Comparable getLeftChild(int index)
170       {
171          return elements.get(2 * index);
172       }
173
```

```
174    /**
175        Returns the value of the right child.
176        @param index  the index of a node in this heap
177        @return the value of the right child of the given node
178    */
179    private Comparable getRightChild(int index)
180    {
181        return elements.get(2 * index + 1);
182    }
183
184    /**
185        Returns the value of the parent.
186        @param index  the index of a node in this heap
187        @return the value of the parent of the given node
188    */
189    private Comparable getParent(int index)
190    {
191        return elements.get(index / 2);
192    }
193  }
```

ch16/pqueue/WorkOrder.java

```
1    /**
2        This class encapsulates a work order with a priority.
3    */
4    public class WorkOrder implements Comparable
5    {
6        private int priority;
7        private String description;
8
9        /**
10            Constructs a work order with a given priority and description.
11            @param aPriority  the priority of this work order
12            @param aDescription  the description of this work order
13        */
14        public WorkOrder(int aPriority, String aDescription)
15        {
16            priority = aPriority;
17            description = aDescription;
18        }
19
20        public String toString()
21        {
22            return "priority=" + priority + ", description=" + description;
23        }
24
25        public int compareTo(Object otherObject)
26        {
27            WorkOrder other = (WorkOrder) otherObject;
28            if (priority < other.priority) return -1;
29            if (priority > other.priority) return 1;
30            return 0;
31        }
32  }
```

ch16/pqueue/HeapDemo.java

```java
1  /**
2      This program demonstrates the use of a heap as a priority queue.
3  */
4  public class HeapDemo
5  {
6      public static void main(String[] args)
7      {
8          MinHeap q = new MinHeap();
9          q.add(new WorkOrder(3, "Shampoo carpets"));
10         q.add(new WorkOrder(7, "Empty trash"));
11         q.add(new WorkOrder(8, "Water plants"));
12         q.add(new WorkOrder(10, "Remove pencil sharpener shavings"));
13         q.add(new WorkOrder(6, "Replace light bulb"));
14         q.add(new WorkOrder(1, "Fix broken sink"));
15         q.add(new WorkOrder(9, "Clean coffee maker"));
16         q.add(new WorkOrder(2, "Order cleaning supplies"));
17
18         while (q.size() > 0)
19             System.out.println(q.remove());
20     }
21 }
```

Program Run

```
priority=1, description=Fix broken sink
priority=2, description=Order cleaning supplies
priority=3, description=Shampoo carpets
priority=6, description=Replace light bulb
priority=7, description=Empty trash
priority=8, description=Water plants
priority=9, description=Clean coffee maker
priority=10, description=Remove pencil sharpener shavings
```

SELF CHECK

15. The software that controls the events in a user interface keeps the events in a data structure. Whenever an event such as a mouse move or repaint request occurs, the event is added. Events are retrieved according to their importance. What abstract data type is appropriate for this application?

16. Could we store a binary search tree in an array so that we can quickly locate the children by looking at array locations 2 * index and 2 * index + 1?

16.9 The Heapsort Algorithm

> The heapsort algorithm is based on inserting elements into a heap and removing them in sorted order.

Heaps are not only useful for implementing priority queues, they also give rise to an efficient sorting algorithm, heapsort. In its simplest form, the algorithm works as follows. First insert all elements to be sorted into the heap, then keep extracting the minimum.

This algorithm is an $O(n \log(n))$ algorithm: each insertion and removal is $O(\log(n))$, and these steps are repeated n times, once for each element in the sequence that is to be sorted.

> Heapsort is an $O(n \log(n))$ algorithm.

The algorithm can be made a bit more efficient. Rather than inserting the elements one at a time, we will start with a sequence of values in an array. Of course, that array does not represent a heap. We will use the procedure of "fixing the heap" that you encountered in the preceding section as part of the element removal algorithm. "Fixing the heap" operates on a binary tree whose child trees are heaps but whose root value may not be smaller than the descendants. The procedure turns the tree into a heap, by repeatedly promoting the smallest child value, moving the root value to its proper location.

Of course, we cannot simply apply this procedure to the initial sequence of unsorted values—the child trees of the root are not likely to be heaps. But we can first fix small subtrees into heaps, then fix larger trees. Because trees of size 1 are automatically heaps, we can begin the fixing procedure with the subtrees whose roots are located in the next-to-last level of the tree.

The sorting algorithm uses a generalized `fixHeap` method that fixes a subtree:

```
void fixHeap(int rootIndex, int lastIndex)
```

The subtree is specified by the index of its root and of its last node.

The `fixHeap` method needs to be invoked on all subtrees whose roots are in the next-to-last level. Then the subtrees whose roots are in the next level above are fixed, and so on. Finally, the fixup is applied to the root node, and the tree is turned into a heap (see Figure 20).

That repetition can be programmed easily. Start with the *last* node on the next-to-lowest level and work toward the left. Then go to the next higher level. The node index values then simply run backwards from the index of the last node to the index of the root.

```
int n = a.length - 1;
for (int i = (n - 1) / 2; i >= 0; i--)
   fixHeap(i, n);
```

It can be shown that this procedure turns an arbitrary array into a heap in $O(n)$ steps.

Note that the loop ends with index 0. When working with a given array, we don't have the luxury of skipping the 0 entry. We consider the 0 entry the root and adjust the formulas for computing the child and parent index values.

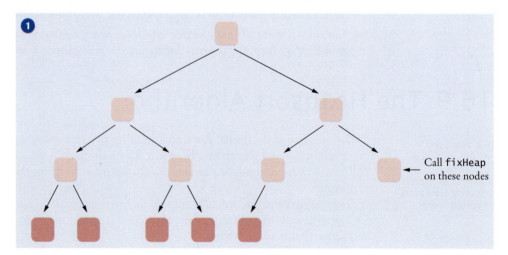

Figure 20 Turning a Tree into a Heap

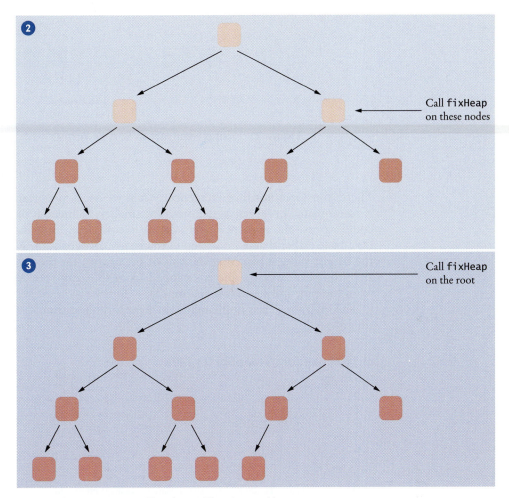

Figure 20 (continued) Turning a Tree into a Heap

After the array has been turned into a heap, we repeatedly remove the root element. Recall from the preceding section that removing the root element is achieved by placing the last element of the tree in the root and calling the fixHeap method. Because we call the $O(\log(n))$ fixHeap method n times, this process requires $O(n \log(n))$ steps.

Rather than moving the root element into a separate array, we can *swap* the root element with the last element of the tree and then reduce the tree length. Thus, the removed root ends up in the last position of the array, which is no longer needed by the heap. In this way, we can use the same array both to hold the heap (which gets shorter with each step) and the sorted sequence (which gets longer with each step).

```
while (n > 0)
{
   swap(0, n);
   n--;
   fixHeap(0, n);
}
```

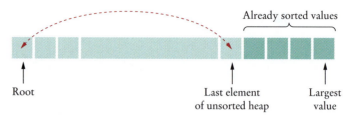

Figure 21 Using Heapsort to Sort an Array

There is just a minor inconvenience. When we use a min-heap, the sorted sequence is accumulated in reverse order, with the smallest element at the end of the array. We could reverse the sequence after sorting is complete. However, it is easier to use a max-heap rather than a min-heap in the heapsort algorithm. With this modification, the largest value is placed at the end of the array after the first step. After the next step, the next-largest value is swapped from the heap root to the second position from the end, and so on (see Figure 21).

The following class implements the heapsort algorithm.

ch16/heapsort/HeapSorter.java

```java
1  /**
2      This class applies the heapsort algorithm to sort an array.
3  */
4  public class HeapSorter
5  {
6     private int[] a;
7
8     /**
9         Constructs a heap sorter that sorts a given array.
10         @param anArray an array of integers
11     */
12     public HeapSorter(int[] anArray)
13     {
14        a = anArray;
15     }
16
17     /**
18         Sorts the array managed by this heap sorter.
19     */
20     public void sort()
21     {
22        int n = a.length - 1;
23        for (int i = (n - 1) / 2; i >= 0; i--)
24           fixHeap(i, n);
25        while (n > 0)
26        {
27           swap(0, n);
28           n--;
29           fixHeap(0, n);
30        }
31     }
32
```

```java
 33   /**
 34      Ensures the heap property for a subtree, provided its
 35      children already fulfill the heap property.
 36      @param rootIndex the index of the subtree to be fixed
 37      @param lastIndex the last valid index of the tree that
 38      contains the subtree to be fixed
 39   */
 40   private void fixHeap(int rootIndex, int lastIndex)
 41   {
 42      // Remove root
 43      int rootValue = a[rootIndex];
 44
 45      // Promote children while they are larger than the root
 46
 47      int index = rootIndex;
 48      boolean more = true;
 49      while (more)
 50      {
 51         int childIndex = getLeftChildIndex(index);
 52         if (childIndex <= lastIndex)
 53         {
 54            // Use right child instead if it is larger
 55            int rightChildIndex = getRightChildIndex(index);
 56            if (rightChildIndex <= lastIndex
 57                  && a[rightChildIndex] > a[childIndex])
 58            {
 59               childIndex = rightChildIndex;
 60            }
 61
 62            if (a[childIndex] > rootValue)
 63            {
 64               // Promote child
 65               a[index] = a[childIndex];
 66               index = childIndex;
 67            }
 68            else
 69            {
 70               // Root value is larger than both children
 71               more = false;
 72            }
 73         }
 74         else
 75         {
 76            // No children
 77            more = false;
 78         }
 79      }
 80
 81      // Store root value in vacant slot
 82      a[index] = rootValue;
 83   }
 84
 85   /**
 86      Swaps two entries of the array.
 87      @param i the first position to swap
 88      @param j the second position to swap
 89   */
 90   private void swap(int i, int j)
 91   {
```

```
92       int temp = a[i];
93       a[i] = a[j];
94       a[j] = temp;
95    }
96
97    /**
98       Returns the index of the left child.
99       @param index the index of a node in this heap
100      @return the index of the left child of the given node
101   */
102   private static int getLeftChildIndex(int index)
103   {
104      return 2 * index + 1;
105   }
106
107   /**
108      Returns the index of the right child.
109      @param index the index of a node in this heap
110      @return the index of the right child of the given node
111   */
112   private static int getRightChildIndex(int index)
113   {
114      return 2 * index + 2;
115   }
116 }
```

SELF CHECK

17. Which algorithm requires less storage, heapsort or merge sort?
18. Why are the computations of the left child index and the right child index in the HeapSorter different than in MinHeap?

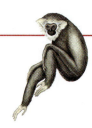

Random Fact 16.1

Software Piracy

As you read this, you have written a few computer programs, and you have experienced firsthand how much effort it takes to write even the humblest of programs. Writing a real software product, such as a financial application or a computer game, takes a lot of time and money. Few people, and fewer companies, are going to spend that kind of time and money if they don't have a reasonable chance to make more money from their effort. (Actually, some companies give away their software in the hope that users will upgrade to more elaborate paid versions. Other companies give away the software that enables users to read and use files but sell the software needed to create those files. Finally, there are individuals who donate their time, out of enthusiasm, and produce programs that you can copy freely.)

When selling software, a company must rely on the honesty of its customers. It is an easy matter for an unscrupulous person to make copies of computer programs without paying for them. In most countries that is illegal. Most governments provide legal protection, such as copyright laws and patents, to encourage the development of new products. Countries that tolerate widespread piracy have found that they have an ample cheap supply of foreign software, but no local manufacturers willing to design good software for their own citizens, such as word processors in the local script or financial programs adapted to the local tax laws.

When a mass market for software first appeared, vendors were enraged by the money they lost through piracy. They tried to fight back by various schemes to ensure that only the legitimate owner could use the software. Some manufacturers used *key disks:* disks with special patterns of holes burned in by a laser, which couldn't be copied. Others used *dongles:* devices that are attached to a printer port. Legitimate users hated these measures. They paid for the software, but they had to suffer through the inconvenience of inserting a key disk every time they started the software or having multiple dongles stick out from their computer. In the United States, market pressures forced most vendors to give up on these copy protection schemes, but they are still commonplace in other parts of the world.

Because it is so easy and inexpensive to pirate software, and the chance of being found out is minimal, you have to make a moral choice for yourself. If a package that you would really like to have is too expensive for your budget, do you steal it, or do you stay honest and get by with a more affordable product?

Of course, piracy is not limited to software. The same issues arise for other digital products as well. You may have had the opportunity to obtain copies of songs or movies without payment. Or you may have been frustrated by a copy protection device on your music player that made it difficult for you to listen to songs that you paid for. Admittedly, it can be difficult to have a lot of sympathy for a musical ensemble whose publisher charges a lot of money for what seems to have been very little effort on their part, at least when compared to the effort that goes into designing and implementing a software package. Nevertheless, it seems only fair that artists and authors receive some compensation for their efforts. How to pay artists, authors, and programmers fairly, without burdening honest customers, is an unsolved problem at the time of this writing, and many computer scientists are engaged in research in this area.

Summary of Learning Objectives

Describe the abstract set type and its implementations in the Java library.

- A set is an unordered collection of distinct elements. Elements can be added, located, and removed.
- Sets don't have duplicates. Adding a duplicate of an element that is already present is silently ignored.
- The HashSet and TreeSet classes both implement the Set interface.
- To visit all elements in a set, use an iterator.
- A set iterator visits elements in seemingly random order (HashSet) or sorted order (TreeSet).
- You cannot add an element to a set at an iterator position.

Describe the abstract map type and its implementations in the Java library.

- A map keeps associations between key and value objects.
- The HashMap and TreeMap classes both implement the Map interface.
- To find all keys and values in a map, iterate through the key set and find the values that correspond to the keys.

Explain the implementation of a hash table and its performance characteristics.

- A hash function computes an integer value from an object.
- A good hash function minimizes *collisions*—identical hash codes for different objects.

- A hash table can be implemented as an array of *buckets*—sequences of nodes that hold elements with the same hash code.
- If there are no or only a few collisions, then adding, locating, and removing hash table elements takes constant or $O(1)$ time.

Develop a `hashCode` method that is appropriate for a given class.

- When implementing the `hashCode` method, combine the hash codes for the instance variables.
- Your `hashCode` method must be compatible with the `equals` method.
- If a class provides neither `equals` nor `hashCode`, then objects are compared by identity.
- In a hash map, only the keys are hashed.

Explain the implementation of a binary search tree and its performance characteristics.

- A binary tree consists of nodes, each of which has at most two child nodes.
- All nodes in a binary search tree fulfill the property that the descendants to the left have smaller data values than the node data value, and the descendants to the right have larger data values.
- To insert a value into a binary search tree, keep comparing the value with the node data and follow the nodes to the left or right, until reaching a `null` node.
- When removing a node with only one child from a binary search tree, the child replaces the node to be removed.
- When removing a node with two children from a binary search tree, replace it with the smallest node of the right subtree.
- In a balanced tree, all paths from the root to the leaves have about the same length.
- Adding, finding, and removing an element in a tree set is proportional to the height of the tree.
- If a binary search tree is balanced, then adding, locating, or removing an element takes $O(\log(n))$ time.

Describe preorder, inorder, and postorder tree traversal.

- To visit all elements in a tree, visit the root and recursively visit the subtrees. We distinguish between preorder, inorder, and postorder traversal.
- Postorder traversal of an expression tree yields the instructions for evaluating the expression on a stack-based calculator.

Describe the behavior of the priority queue data type.

- When removing an element from a priority queue, the element with the highest priority is retrieved.

Describe the heap data structure and the efficiency of its operations.

- A heap is an almost completely filled tree in which the values of all nodes are at most as large as those of their descendants.
- Inserting or removing a heap element is an $O(\log(n))$ operation.
- The regular layout of a heap makes it possible to store heap nodes efficiently in an array.

Describe the heapsort algorithm and its run-time performance.

- The heapsort algorithm is based on inserting elements into a heap and removing them in sorted order.
- Heapsort is an $O(n \log(n))$ algorithm.

Classes, Objects, and Methods Introduced in this Chapter

```
java.util.Collection<E>          java.util.Map<K, V>        java.util.PriorityQueue<E>
   contains                         get                         remove
   remove                           keySet                   java.util.Set<E>
   size                             put                      java.util.TreeMap<K, V>
java.util.HashMap<K, V>             remove                   java.util.TreeSet<K, V>
java.util.HashSet<K, V>
```

Media Resources

www.wiley.com/
college/
horstmann

- ***Worked Example*** Word Frequency
- Lab Exercises
- ⊕ Practice Quiz
- ⊕ Code Completion Exercises

Review Exercises

★ **R16.1** What is the difference between a set and a map?

★ **R16.2** What implementations does the Java library provide for the abstract set type?

★★ **R16.3** What are the fundamental operations on the abstract set type? What additional methods does the Set interface provide? (Look up the interface in the API documentation.)

★★ **R16.4** The union of two sets *A* and *B* is the set of all elements that are contained in *A*, *B*, or both. The intersection is the set of all elements that are contained in *A* and *B*. How can you compute the union and intersection of two sets, using the four fundamental set operations described on page 666?

★★ **R16.5** How can you compute the union and intersection of two sets, using some of the methods that the java.util.Set interface provides? (Look up the interface in the API documentation.)

★ **R16.6** Can a map have two keys with the same value? Two values with the same key?

★ **R16.7** A map can be implemented as a set of (*key*, *value*) pairs. Explain.

★★ **R16.8** When implementing a map as a hash set of (*key*, *value*) pairs, how is the hash code of a pair computed?

★ **R16.9** Verify the hash codes of the strings "Jim" and "Joe" in Table 1.

★ **R16.10** From the hash codes in Table 1, show that Figure 6 accurately shows the locations of the strings if the hash table size is 101.

★ **R16.11** What is the difference between a binary tree and a binary search tree? Give examples of each.

★ **R16.12** What is the difference between a balanced tree and an unbalanced tree? Give examples of each.

★ **R16.13** The following elements are inserted into a binary search tree. Make a drawing that shows the resulting tree after each insertion.

```
Adam
Eve
Romeo
Juliet
Tom
Diana
Harry
```

★★ **R16.14** Insert the elements of Exercise R16.13 in opposite order. Then determine how the BinarySearchTree.print method prints out both the tree from Exercise R16.13 and this tree. Explain how the printouts are related.

★★ **R16.15** Consider the following tree. In which order are the nodes printed by the Binary-SearchTree.print method? The numbers identify the nodes. The data stored in the nodes is not shown.

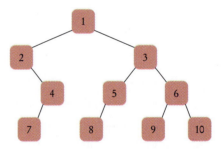

★★ **R16.16** Could a priority queue be implemented efficiently as a binary search tree? Give a detailed argument for your answer.

★★★ **R16.17** Will preorder, inorder, or postorder traversal print a heap in sorted order? Why or why not?

★★★ **R16.18** Prove that a heap of height h contains at least 2^{h-1} elements but less than 2^h elements.

★★★ **R16.19** Suppose the heap nodes are stored in an array, starting with index 1. Prove that the child nodes of the heap node with index i have index $2 \cdot i$ and $2 \cdot i + 1$, and the parent heap node of the node with index i has index $i/2$.

★★ **R16.20** Simulate the heapsort algorithm manually to sort the array

```
11 27 8 14 45 6 24 81 29 33
```

Show all steps.

Programming Exercises

★ **P16.1** Write a program that reads text from System.in and breaks it up into individual words. Insert the words into a tree set. At the end of the input file, print all words, followed by the size of the resulting set. This program determines how many unique words a text file has.

★ **P16.2** Insert the 13 standard colors that the Color class declares (that is, Color.PINK, Color.GREEN, and so on) into a set. Prompt the user to enter a color by specifying red, green, and blue integer values between 0 and 255. Then tell the user whether the resulting color is in the set.

★★ **P16.3** Implement the *sieve of Eratosthenes:* a method for computing prime numbers, known to the ancient Greeks. Choose an *n*. This method will compute all prime numbers up to *n*. First insert all numbers from 2 to *n* into a set. Then erase all multiples of 2 (except 2); that is, 4, 6, 8, 10, 12, ... Erase all multiples of 3; that is, 6, 9, 12, 15, ... Go up to $\sqrt{n}$. Then print the set.

★ **P16.4** Insert all words from a large file (such as the novel "War and Peace", which is available on the Internet) into a hash set and a tree set. Time the results. Which data structure is faster?

★★★ **P16.5** Write a program that reads a Java source file and produces an index of all identifiers in the file. For each identifier, print all lines in which it occurs.
Hint: Call in.useDelimiter("[^A-Za-z0-9_]+"). Then each call to next returns a string consisting only of letters, numbers, and underscores.

★★ **P16.6** Try to find two words with the same hash code in a large file, such as the /usr/share/dict/words file on a Linux system. Keep a Map<Integer, HashSet<String>>. When you read in a word, compute its hash code *h* and put the word in the set whose key is *h*. Then iterate through all keys and print the sets whose size is > 1.

★★ **P16.7** Write a program that keeps a map in which both keys and values are strings—the names of students and their course grades. Prompt the user of the program to add or remove students, to modify grades, or to print all grades. The printout should be sorted by name and formatted like this:

```
Carl: B+
Joe: C
Sarah: A
```

★★★ **P16.8** Reimplement Exercise P16.7 so that the keys of the map are objects of class Student. A student should have a first name, a last name, and a unique integer ID. For grade changes and removals, lookup should be by ID. The printout should be sorted by last name. If two students have the same last name, then use the first name as tie breaker. If the first names are also identical, then use the integer ID. *Hint:* Use two maps.

★★★ **P16.9** Add a debug method to the HashSet implementation in Section 16.4 that prints the nonempty buckets of the hash table. Run the test program at the end of Section 16.4. Call the debug method after all additions and removals and verify that Figure 6 accurately represents the state of the hash table.

★★ **P16.10** Supply compatible hashCode and equals methods to the Student class described in Exercise P16.8. Test the hash code by adding Student objects to a hash set.

★ **P16.11** Supply compatible hashCode and equals methods to the BankAccount class of Chapter 7. Test the hashCode method by printing out hash codes and by adding BankAccount objects to a hash set.

★ **P16.12** A labeled point has *x*- and *y*-coordinates and a string label. Provide a class Labeled-Point with a constructor LabeledPoint(int x, int y, String label) and hashCode and equals methods. Two labeled points are considered the same when they have the same location and label.

★ **P16.13** Reimplement the LabeledPoint class of Exercise P16.12 by storing the location in a java.awt.Point object. Your hashCode and equals methods should call the hashCode and equals methods of the Point class.

★ **P16.14** Modify the LabeledPoint class of Exercise P16.13 so that it implements the Comparable interface. Sort points first by their *x*-coordinates. If two points have the same *x*-coordinate, sort them by their *y*-coordinates. If two points have the same *x*- and *y*-coordinates, sort them by their label. Write a tester program that checks all cases.

★★ **P16.15** Design a data structure IntSet that can hold a set of integers. Hide the private implementation: a binary search tree of Integer objects. Provide the following methods:

- A constructor to make an empty set
- void add(int x) to add x if it is not present
- void remove(int x) to remove x if it is present
- void print() to print all elements currently in the set
- boolean contains(int x) to test whether x is present

★★ **P16.16** Reimplement the set class from Exercise P16.15 by using a TreeSet<Integer>. In addition to the methods specified in Exercise P16.15, supply an iterator method yielding an object that supports *only* the hasNext/next methods.

The next method should return an int, not an object. For that reason, you cannot simply return the iterator of the tree set.

★ **P16.17** Reimplement the set class from Exercise P16.15 by using a TreeSet<Integer>. In addition to the methods specified in Exercise P16.15, supply methods

```
IntSet union(IntSet other)
IntSet intersection(IntSet other)
```

that compute the union and intersection of two sets.

★ **P16.18** Write a method of the BinarySearchTree class

```
Comparable smallest()
```

that returns the smallest element of a tree. You will also need to add a method to the Node class.

★★★ **P16.19** Change the BinarySearchTree.print method to print the tree as a tree shape. You can print the tree sideways. Extra credit if you instead display the tree with the root node centered on the top.

★ **P16.20** Implement methods that use preorder and postorder traversal to print the elements in a binary search tree.

★★★ **P16.21** In the BinarySearchTree class, modify the remove method so that a node with two children is replaced by the largest child of the left subtree.

★★ **P16.22** Suppose an interface `Visitor` has a single method

```
void visit(Object obj)
```

Supply methods

```
void inOrder(Visitor v)
void preOrder(Visitor v)
void postOrder(Visitor v)
```

to the `BinarySearchTree` class. These methods should visit the tree nodes in the specified traversal order and apply the `visit` method to the data of the visited node.

★★ **P16.23** Apply Exercise P16.22 to compute the average value of the elements in a binary search tree filled with `Integer` objects. That is, supply an object of an appropriate class that implements the `Visitor` interface.

★★ **P16.24** Modify the implementation of the `MinHeap` class so that the parent and child index positions and elements are computed directly, without calling helper methods.

★★★ **P16.25** Modify the implementation of the `MinHeap` class so that the 0 element of the array is not wasted.

★ **P16.26** Time the results of heapsort and merge sort. Which algorithm behaves better in practice?

Programming Projects

Project 16.1 Implement a `BinaryTreeSet` class that uses a `TreeSet` to store its elements. You will need to implement an iterator that iterates through the nodes in sorted order. This iterator is somewhat complex, because sometimes you need to backtrack. You can either add a reference to the parent node in each `Node` object, or have your iterator object store a stack of the visited nodes.

Project 16.2 Implement an expression evaluator that uses a parser to build an expression tree, such as in Section 16.7. (Note that the resulting tree is a binary tree but not a binary search tree.) Then use postorder traversal to evaluate the expression, using a stack for the intermediate results.

Project 16.3 Program an animation of the heapsort algorithm, displaying the tree graphically and stopping after each call to `fixHeap`.

Answers to Self-Check Questions

1. Efficient set implementations can quickly test whether a given element is a member of the set.
2. Sets do not have an ordering, so it doesn't make sense to add an element at a particular iterator position, or to traverse a set backwards.
3. The words would be listed in sorted order.
4. When it is desirable to visit the set elements in sorted order.
5. A set stores elements. A map stores associations between keys and values.

6. The ordering does not matter, and you cannot have duplicates.

7. Yes, the hash set will work correctly. All elements will be inserted into a single bucket.

8. It locates the next bucket in the bucket array and points to its first element.

9. $31 \times 116 + 111 = 3707$.

10. 13.

11. In a tree, each node can have any number of children. In a binary tree, a node has at most two children. In a balanced binary tree, all nodes have approximately as many descendants to the left as to the right.

12. For example, Sarah. Any string between Romeo and Tom will do.

13. For both trees, the inorder traversal is 3 + 4 * 5.

14. No—for example, consider the children of +. Even without looking up the Unicode codes for 3, 4, and +, it is obvious that + isn't between 3 and 4.

15. A priority queue is appropriate because we want to get the important events first, even if they have been inserted later.

16. Yes, but a binary search tree isn't almost filled, so there may be holes in the array. We could indicate the missing nodes with null elements.

17. Heapsort requires less storage because it doesn't need an auxiliary array.

18. The MinHeap wastes the 0 entry to make the formulas more intuitive. When sorting an array, we don't want to waste the 0 entry, so we adjust the formulas instead.

Generic Programming

CHAPTER GOALS

- To understand the objective of generic programming
- To be able to implement generic classes and methods
- To understand the execution of generic methods in the virtual machine
- To know the limitations of generic programming in Java

Generic programming involves the design and implementation of data structures and algorithms that work for multiple types. You are already familiar with the generic ArrayList class that can be used to collect elements of arbitrary types. In this chapter, you will learn how to implement your own generic classes.

CHAPTER CONTENTS

17.1 Generic Classes and Type Parameters

Generic programming is the creation of programming constructs that can be used with many different types. For example, the Java library programmers who implemented the ArrayList class used the technique of generic programming. As a result, you can form array lists that collect elements of different types, such as Array-List<String>, ArrayList<BankAccount>, and so on.

The LinkedList class that we implemented in Section 15.2 is also an example of generic programming—you can store objects of any class inside a LinkedList. That LinkedList class achieves genericity by using *inheritance.* It uses references of type Object and is therefore capable of storing objects of any class. In contrast, the Array-List class is a *generic class:* a class with a **type parameter** that is used to specify the type of the objects that you want to store. (Note that only our LinkedList implementation of Chapter 15 uses inheritance. The standard Java library has a generic LinkedList class that uses type parameters.)

> In Java, generic programming can be achieved with inheritance or with type parameters.

When declaring a generic class, you specify a type variable for each type parameter. Here is how the standard Java library declares the ArrayList class, using the type variable E for the element type:

> A generic class has one or more type parameters.

```java
public class ArrayList<E>
{
    public ArrayList() { . . . }
    public void add(E element) { . . . }
    . . .
}
```

Here, E is a type variable, not a Java reserved word. You could use another name, such as ElementType, instead of E. However, it is customary to use short, uppercase names for type parameters.

> Type parameters can be instantiated with class or interface types.

In order to use a generic class, you need to *instantiate* the type parameter, that is, supply an actual type. You can supply any class or interface type, for example

```java
ArrayList<BankAccount>
ArrayList<Measurable>
```

However, you cannot substitute any of the eight primitive types for a type parameter. It would be an error to declare an ArrayList<double>. Use the corresponding wrapper class instead, such as ArrayList<Double>.

When you instantiate a generic class, the type that you supply replaces all occurrences of the type variable in the declaration of the class. For example, the add method for ArrayList<BankAccount> has the type variable E replaced with the type BankAccount:

```
public void add(BankAccount element)
```

Contrast that with the add method of the LinkedList class in Chapter 15:

```
public void add(Object element)
```

The add method of the generic ArrayList class is safer. It is impossible to add a String object into an ArrayList<BankAccount>, but you can accidentally add a String into a LinkedList that is intended to hold bank accounts.

```
ArrayList<BankAccount> accounts1 = new ArrayList<BankAccount>();
LinkedList accounts2 = new LinkedList(); // Should hold BankAccount objects
accounts1.add("my savings"); // Compile-time error
accounts2.add("my savings"); // Not detected at compile time
```

The latter will result in a class cast exception when some other part of the code retrieves the string, believing it to be a bank account:

```
BankAccount account = (BankAccount) accounts2.getFirst(); // Run-time error
```

Type parameters make generic code safer and easier to read.

Code that uses the generic ArrayList class is also easier to read. When you spot an ArrayList<BankAccount>, you know right away that it must contain bank accounts. When you see a LinkedList, you have to study the code to find out what it contains.

In Chapters 15 and 16, we used inheritance to implement generic linked lists, hash tables, and binary trees, because you were already familiar with the concept of inheritance. Using type parameters requires new syntax and additional techniques—those are the topic of this chapter.

SELF CHECK

1. The standard library provides a class HashMap<K, V> with key type K and value type V. Declare a hash map that maps strings to integers.
2. The binary search tree class in Chapter 16 is an example of generic programming because you can use it with any classes that implement the Comparable interface. Does it achieve genericity through inheritance or type parameters?

17.2 Implementing Generic Types

In this section, you will learn how to implement your own generic classes. We will write a very simple generic class that stores *pairs* of objects, each of which can have an arbitrary type. For example,

```
Pair<String, Integer> result = new Pair<String, Integer>("Harry Morgan", 1729);
```

The getFirst and getSecond methods retrieve the first and second values of the pair.

```
String name = result.getFirst();
Integer number = result.getSecond();
```

This class can be useful when you implement a method that computes two values at the same time. A method cannot simultaneously return a String and an Integer, but it can return a single object of type Pair<String, Integer>.

The generic Pair class requires two type parameters, one for the type of the first element and one for the type of the second element.

We need to choose variables for the type parameters. It is considered good form to use short uppercase names for type variables, such as those in the following table:

Type Variable	Meaning
E	Element type in a collection
K	Key type in a map
V	Value type in a map
T	General type
S, U	Additional general types

Type variables of a generic class follow the class name and are enclosed in angle brackets.

You place the type variables for a generic class after the class name, enclosed in angle brackets (< and >):

```
public class Pair<T, S>
```

When you declare the instance variables and methods of the Pair class, use the variable T for the first element type and S for the second element type:

```
public class Pair<T, S>
{
    private T first;
    private S second;

    public Pair(T firstElement, S secondElement)
    {
        first = firstElement;
        second = secondElement;
    }
    public T getFirst() { return first; }
    public S getSecond() { return second; }
}
```

Use type parameters for the types of generic instance variables, method parameters, and return values.

Some people find it simpler to start out with a regular class, choosing some actual types instead of the type parameters. For example,

```
public class Pair // Here we start out with a pair of String and Integer values
{
    private String first;
    private Integer second;

    public Pair(String firstElement, Integer secondElement)
    {
        first = firstElement;
        second = secondElement;
    }
    public String getFirst() { return first; }
    public Integer getSecond() { return second; }
}
```

Now it is an easy matter to replace all String types with the type variable S and all Integer types with the type variable T.

This completes the declaration of the generic Pair class. It is ready to use whenever you need to form a pair of two objects of arbitrary types. The following sample program shows how to make use of a Pair for returning two values from a method.

Syntax 17.1   Declaring a Generic Class

Syntax	*accessSpecifier* class *GenericClassName*<*TypeVariable₁*, *TypeVariable₂*, . . .>

$$\text{accessSpecifier } \texttt{class } \textit{GenericClassName}<\textit{TypeVariable}_1, \textit{TypeVariable}_2, . . .>$$

```
{
    instance variables
    constructors
    methods
}
```

Example

Supply a variable for each type parameter.

```
public class Pair<T, S>
{
    private T first;          Instance variables with a variable data type
    private S second;
    . . .
    public T getFirst() { return first; }
    . . .
}
```

A method with a variable return type

ch17/pair/Pair.java

```java
 1  /**
 2      This class collects a pair of elements of different types.
 3  */
 4  public class Pair<T, S>
 5  {
 6      private T first;
 7      private S second;
 8
 9      /**
10          Constructs a pair containing two given elements.
11          @param firstElement the first element
12          @param secondElement the second element
13      */
14      public Pair(T firstElement, S secondElement)
15      {
16          first = firstElement;
17          second = secondElement;
18      }
19
20      /**
21          Gets the first element of this pair.
22          @return the first element
23      */
24      public T getFirst() { return first; }
25
26      /**
27          Gets the second element of this pair.
28          @return the second element
29      */
30      public S getSecond() { return second; }
31
32      public String toString() { return "(" + first + ", " + second + ")"; }
33  }
```

ch17/pair/PairDemo.java

```java
1  public class PairDemo
2  {
3     public static void main(String[] args)
4     {
5        String[] names = { "Tom", "Diana", "Harry" };
6        Pair<String, Integer> result = firstContaining(names, "a");
7        System.out.println(result.getFirst());
8        System.out.println("Expected: Diana");
9        System.out.println(result.getSecond());
10       System.out.println("Expected: 1");
11    }
12
13    /**
14       Gets the first String containing a given string, together
15       with its index.
16       @param strings an array of strings
17       @param sub a string
18       @return a pair (strings[i], i) where strings[i] is the first
19       strings[i] containing str, or a pair (null, -1) if there is no
20       match.
21    */
22    public static Pair<String, Integer> firstContaining(
23       String[] strings, String sub)
24    {
25       for (int i = 0; i < strings.length; i++)
26       {
27          if (strings[i].contains(sub))
28          {
29             return new Pair<String, Integer>(strings[i], i);
30          }
31       }
32       return new Pair<String, Integer>(null, -1);
33    }
34 }
```

Program Run

```
Diana
Expected: Diana
1
Expected: 1
```

SELF CHECK

3. How would you use the generic Pair class to construct a pair of strings "Hello" and "World"?

4. What is the difference between an ArrayList<Pair<String, Integer>> and a Pair<ArrayList<String>, Integer>?

17.3 Generic Methods

> A generic method is a method with a type parameter.

A generic method is a method with a type parameter. Such a method can occur in a class that in itself is not generic. You can think of it as a template for a set of methods that differ only by one or more types. For example, we may want to declare a method that can print an array of any type:

```java
public class ArrayUtil
{
   /**
      Prints all elements in an array.
      @param a the array to print
   */
   public <T> static void print(T[] a)
   {
      . . .
   }
   . . .
}
```

As described in the previous section, it is often easier to see how to implement a generic method by starting with a concrete example. This method prints the elements in an array of *strings*.

```java
public class ArrayUtil
{
   public static void print(String[] a)
   {
      for (String e : a)
         System.out.print(e + " ");
      System.out.println();
   }
   . . .
}
```

Supply the type parameters of a generic method between the modifiers and the method return type.

In order to make the method into a generic method, replace String with a type parameter, say E, to denote the element type of the array. Add a type parameter list, enclosed in angle brackets, between the modifiers (public static) and the return type (void):

```java
public static <E> void print(E[] a)
{
   for (E e : a)
      System.out.print(e + " ");
   System.out.println();
}
```

Syntax 17.2   Declaring a Generic Method

Syntax   modifiers <TypeVariable₁, TypeVariable₂, . . .> returnType methodName(parameters)
              {
                 body
              }

Example

Supply the type variable before the return type.

```java
public static <E> void print(E[] a)
{
   for (E e : a)
      System.out.print(e + " ");
   System.out.println();
}
```

Local variable with a variable data type

When you call the generic method, you need not specify which type to use for the type parameter. (In this regard, generic methods differ from generic classes.) Simply call the method with appropriate parameters, and the compiler will match up the type parameters with the parameter types. For example, consider this method call:

```
Rectangle[] rectangles = . . .;
ArrayUtil.print(rectangles);
```

> When calling a generic method, you need not instantiate the type parameters.

The type of the `rectangles` parameter is `Rectangle[]`, and the type of the parameter variable is `E[]`. The compiler deduces that `E` is `Rectangle`.

This particular generic method is a static method in an ordinary class. You can also declare generic methods that are not static. You can even have generic methods in generic classes.

As with generic classes, you cannot replace type parameters with primitive types. The generic `print` method can print arrays of any type *except* the eight primitive types. For example, you cannot use the generic `print` method to print an array of type `int[]`. That is not a major problem. Simply implement a `print(int[] a)` method in addition to the generic `print` method.

SELF CHECK

5. Exactly what does the generic `print` method print when you pass an array of `BankAccount` objects containing two bank accounts with zero balances?

6. Is the `getFirst` method of the `Pair` class a generic method?

17.4 Constraining Type Parameters

> Type parameters can be constrained with bounds.

It is often necessary to specify what types can be used in a generic class or method. Consider a generic `min` method that finds the smallest element in an array list of objects. How can you find the smallest element when you know nothing about the element type? You need to have a mechanism for comparing array elements. One solution is to require that the elements belong to a type that implements the `Comparable` interface. In this situation, we need to *constrain* the type parameter.

```
public static <E extends Comparable> E min(E[] a)
{
   E smallest = a[0];
   for (int i = 1; i < a.length; i++)
      if (a[i].compareTo(smallest) < 0) smallest = a[i];
   return smallest;
}
```

You can call `min` with a `String[]` array but not with a `Rectangle[]` array—the `String` class implements `Comparable`, but `Rectangle` does not.

The `Comparable` bound is necessary for calling the `compareTo` method. Had it been omitted, then the `min` method would not have compiled. It would have been illegal to call `compareTo` on `a[i]` if nothing is known about its type. (Actually, the `Comparable` interface is itself a generic type, but for simplicity we do not supply a type parameter. See Special Topic 17.1 on page 731 for more information.)

Very occasionally, you need to supply two or more type bounds. Then you separate them with the & character, for example

```
<E extends Comparable & Cloneable>
```

The extends reserved word, when applied to type parameters, actually means "extends or implements". The bounds can be either classes or interfaces, and the type parameter can be replaced with a class or interface type.

S E L F   C H E C K

7. How would you constrain the type parameter for a generic BinarySearchTree class?

8. Modify the min method to compute the minimum of an array of elements that implements the Measurable interface of Chapter 9.

Common Error 17.1

Genericity and Inheritance

If SavingsAccount is a subclass of BankAccount, is ArrayList<SavingsAccount> a subclass of Array-List<BankAccount>? Perhaps surprisingly, it is not. Inheritance of type parameters does not lead to inheritance of generic classes. There is no relationship between ArrayList<Savings-Account> and ArrayList<BankAccount>.

This restriction is necessary for type checking. Without the restriction, it would be possible to add objects of unrelated types to a collection. Suppose it was possible to assign an ArrayList<SavingsAccount> object to a variable of type ArrayList<BankAccount>:

```
ArrayList<SavingsAccount> savingsAccounts = new ArrayList<SavingsAccount>();
ArrayList<BankAccount> bankAccounts = savingsAccounts;
    // Not legal, but suppose it was
BankAccount harrysChecking = new CheckingAccount();
    // CheckingAccount is another subclass of BankAccount
bankAccounts.add(harrysChecking); // OK—can add BankAccount object
```

But bankAccounts and savingsAccounts refer to the same array list! If the assignment was legal, we would be able to add a CheckingAccount into an ArrayList<SavingsAccount>.

In many situations, this limitation can be overcome by using wildcards—see Special Topic 17.1.

Special Topic 17.1

Wildcard Types

It is often necessary to formulate subtle constraints of type parameters. Wildcard types were invented for this purpose. There are three kinds of wildcard types:

Name	Syntax	Meaning
Wildcard with lower bound	? extends B	Any subtype of B
Wildcard with upper bound	? super B	Any supertype of B
Unbounded wildcard	?	Any type

A wildcard type is a type that can remain unknown. For example, we can declare the following method in the `LinkedList<E>` class:

```java
public void addAll(LinkedList<? extends E> other)
{
   ListIterator<E> iter = other.listIterator();
   while (iter.hasNext()) add(iter.next());
}
```

The method adds all elements of other to the end of the linked list.

The `addAll` method doesn't require a specific type for the element type of other. Instead, it allows you to use any type that is a subtype of E. For example, you can use `addAll` to add a `LinkedList<SavingsAccount>` to a `LinkedList<BankAccount>`.

To see a wildcard with a super bound, have another look at the `min` method of the preceding section. Recall that `Comparable` is a generic interface; the type parameter of the `Comparable` interface specifies the parameter type of the `compareTo` method.

```java
public interface Comparable<T>
{
   int compareTo(T other)
}
```

Therefore, we might want to specify a type bound:

```java
public static <E extends Comparable<E>> E min(E[] a)
```

However, this bound is too restrictive. Suppose the `BankAccount` class implements `Comparable<BankAccount>`. Then the subclass `SavingsAccount` also implements `Comparable<BankAccount>` and *not* `Comparable<SavingsAccount>`. If you want to use the `min` method with a `SavingsAccount` array, then the type parameter of the `Comparable` interface should be *any supertype* of the array element type:

```java
public static <E extends Comparable<? super E>> E min(E[] a)
```

Here is an example of an unbounded wildcard. The `Collections` class declares a method

```java
public static void reverse(List<?> list)
```

You can think of that declaration as a shorthand for

```java
public static <T> void reverse(List<T> list)
```

17.5 Type Erasure

The virtual machine erases type parameters, replacing them with their bounds or `Objects`.

Because generic types are a fairly recent addition to the Java language, the virtual machine that executes Java programs does not work with generic classes or methods. Instead, type parameters are "erased", that is, they are replaced with ordinary Java types. Each type parameter is replaced with its bound, or with `Object` if it is not bounded.

For example, the generic class `Pair<T, S>` turns into the following raw class:

```java
public class Pair
{
   private Object first;
   private Object second;

   public Pair(Object firstElement, Object secondElement)
   {
      first = firstElement;
      second = secondElement;
```

```
    }
    public Object getFirst() { return first; }
    public Object getSecond() { return second; }
}
```

As you can see, the type parameters T and S have been replaced by Object. The result is an ordinary class.

The same process is applied to generic methods. After erasing the type parameter, the min method of the preceding section turns into an ordinary method. Note that in this example, the type parameter is replaced with its bound, the Comparable interface:

```
public static Comparable min(Comparable[] a)
{
    Comparable smallest = a[0];
    for (int i = 1; i < a.length; i++)
        if (a[i].compareTo(smallest) < 0) smallest = a[i];
    return smallest;
}
```

You cannot construct objects or arrays of a generic type.

Knowing about type erasure helps you understand limitations of Java generics. For example, you cannot construct new objects of a generic type. The following method, which tries to fill an array with copies of default objects, would be wrong:

```
public static <E> void fillWithDefaults(E[] a)
{
    for (int i = 0; i < a.length; i++)
        a[i] = new E(); // ERROR
}
```

To see why this is a problem, carry out the type erasure process, as if you were the compiler:

```
public static void fillWithDefaults(Object[] a)
{
    for (int i = 0; i < a.length; i++)
        a[i] = new Object(); // Not useful
}
```

Of course, if you start out with a Rectangle[] array, you don't want it to be filled with Object instances. But that's what the code would do after erasing types.

In situations such as this one, the compiler will report an error. You then need to come up with another mechanism for solving your problem. In this particular example, you can supply a default object:

```
public static <E> void fillWithDefaults(E[] a, E defaultValue)
{
    for (int i = 0; i < a.length; i++)
        a[i] = defaultValue;
}
```

Similarly, you cannot construct an array of a generic type.

```
public class Stack<E>
{
    private E[] elements;
    . . .
    public Stack()
    {
        elements = new E[MAX_SIZE]; // Error
    }
}
```

Because the array construction expression `new E[]` would be erased to `new Object[]`, the compiler disallows it. A remedy is to use an array list instead:

```
public class Stack<E>
{
   private ArrayList<E> elements;
   . . .
   public Stack()
   {
      elements = new ArrayList<E>(); // Ok
   }
   . . .
}
```

Another solution is to use an array of objects and provide a cast when reading elements from the array:

```
public class Stack<E>
{
   private Object[] elements;
   private int size;
   . . .
   public Stack()
   {
      elements = new Object[MAX_SIZE]; // Ok
   }
   . . .
   public E pop()
   {
      size--;
      return (E) elements[size];
   }
}
```

The cast `(E)` generates a warning because it cannot be checked at run time.

These limitations are frankly awkward. It is hoped that a future version of Java will no longer erase types so that the current restrictions that are the consequence of erasure can be lifted.

SELF CHECK

9. What is the erasure of the `print` method in Section 17.3?

10. Could the `Stack` example be implemented as follows?

```
public class Stack<E>
{
   private E[] elements;
   . . .
   public Stack()
   {
      elements = (E[]) new Object[MAX_SIZE];
   }
   . . .
}
```

Common Error 17.2

Using Generic Types in a Static Context

You cannot use type parameters to declare static variables, static methods, or static inner classes. For example, the following would be illegal:

```java
public class LinkedList<E>
{
    private static E defaultValue; // ERROR
    . . .
    public static List<E> replicate(E value, int n) { . . . } // ERROR
    private static class Node { public E data; public Node next; } // ERROR
}
```

In the case of static variables, this restriction is very sensible. After the generic types are erased, there is only a single variable LinkedList.defaultValue, whereas the static variable declaration gives the false impression that there is a separate variable for each LinkedList<E>.

For static methods and inner classes, there is an easy workaround; simply add a type parameter:

```java
public class LinkedList<E>
{
    . . .
    public static <T> List<T> replicate(T value, int n) { . . . } // OK
    private static class Node<T> { public T data; public Node<T> next; } // OK
}
```

Summary of Learning Objectives

Describe generic classes and type parameters.

- In Java, generic programming can be achieved with inheritance or with type parameters.
- A generic class has one or more type parameters.
- Type parameters can be instantiated with class or interface types.
- Type parameters make generic code safer and easier to read.

Implement generic classes and interfaces.

- Type variables of a generic class follow the class name and are enclosed in angle brackets.
- Use type parameters for the types of generic instance variables, method parameters, and return values.

Implement generic methods.

- A generic method is a method with a type parameter.
- Supply the type parameters of a generic method between the modifiers and the method return type.
- When calling a generic method, you need not instantiate the type parameters.

Specify constraints on type parameters.

- Type parameters can be constrained with bounds.

Recognize how erasure of type parameters places limitations on generic programming in Java.

- The virtual machine erases type parameters, replacing them with their bounds or Objects.
- You cannot construct objects or arrays of a generic type.

Media Resources

www.wiley.com/
college/
horstmann

- Lab Exercises
- ⊕ Practice Quiz
- ⊕ Code Completion Exercises

Review Exercises

★ **R17.1** What is a type parameter?

★ **R17.2** What is the difference between a generic class and an ordinary class?

★ **R17.3** What is the difference between a generic class and a generic method?

★ **R17.4** Find an example of a non-static generic method in the standard Java library.

★★ **R17.5** Find four examples of a generic class with two type parameters in the standard Java library.

★★ **R17.6** Find an example of a generic class in the standard library that is not a collection class.

★ **R17.7** Why is a bound required for the type parameter T in the following method?

```
<T extends Comparable> int binarySearch(T[] a, T key)
```

★★ **R17.8** Why is a bound not required for the type parameter E in the HashSet<E> class?

★ **R17.9** What is an ArrayList<Pair<T, T>>?

★★ **R17.10** Explain the type bounds of the following method of the Collections class:

```
public static <T extends Comparable<? super T>> void sort(List<T> a)
```

Why doesn't T extends Comparable or T extends Comparable<T> suffice?

★ **R17.11** What happens when you pass an ArrayList<String> to a method with parameter ArrayList? Try it out and explain.

★★★ **R17.12** What happens when you pass an ArrayList<String> to a method with parameter ArrayList, and the method stores an object of type BankAccount into the array list? Try it out and explain.

★★ R17.13 What is the result of the following test?

```
ArrayList<BankAccount> accounts = new ArrayList<BankAccount>();
if (accounts instanceof ArrayList<String>) . . .
```

Try it out and explain.

★★ R17.14 The `ArrayList<E>` class in the standard Java library must manage an array of objects of type `E`, yet it is not legal to construct a generic array of type `E[]` in Java. Locate the implementation of the `ArrayList` class in the library source code that is a part of the JDK. Explain how this problem is overcome.

Programming Exercises

★ P17.1 Modify the generic `Pair` class so that both values have the same type.

★ P17.2 Add a method `swap` to the `Pair` class of Exercise P17.1 that swaps the first and second elements of the pair.

★★ P17.3 Implement a static generic method `PairUtil.swap` whose parameter is a `Pair` object, using the generic class declared in Section 17.2. The method should return a new pair, with the first and second element swapped.

★★ P17.4 Write a static generic method `PairUtil.minmax` that computes the minimum and maximum elements of an array of type `T` and returns a pair containing the minimum and maximum value. Require that the array elements implement the `Measurable` interface of Chapter 9.

★★ P17.5 Repeat the problem of Exercise P17.4, but require that the array elements implement the `Comparable` interface.

★★★ P17.6 Repeat the problem of Exercise P17.5, but refine the bound of the type parameter to extend the generic `Comparable` type.

★★ P17.7 Implement a generic version of the binary search algorithm.

★★★ P17.8 Implement a generic version of the merge sort algorithm. Your program should compile without warnings.

P17.9 Implement a generic version of the `LinkedList` class of Chapter 15.

★★ P17.10 Implement a generic version of the `BinarySearchTree` class of Chapter 16.

★★ P17.11 Turn the `HashSet` implementation of Chapter 16 into a generic class. Use an array list instead of an array to store the buckets.

★★ P17.12 Provide suitable `hashCode` and `equals` methods for the `Pair` class of Section 17.2 and implement a `HashMap` class, using a `HashSet<Pair<K, V>>`.

★★★ P17.13 Implement a generic version of the permutation generator in Section 13.2. Generate all permutations of a `List<E>`.

★★ P17.14 Write a generic static method `print` that prints the elements of any object that implements the `Iterable<E>` interface. The elements should be separated by commas. Place your method into an appropriate utility class.

Programming Projects

Project 17.1 Design and implement a generic version of the DataSet class of Chapter 9 that can be used to analyze data of any class that implements the Measurable interface. Make the Measurable interface generic as well. Supply an addAll method that lets you add all values from another data set with a compatible type. Supply a generic Measurer<T> interface to allow the analysis of data whose classes don't implement the Measurable type.

Project 17.2 Turn the MinHeap class of Chapter 16 into a generic class. As with the TreeSet class of the standard library, allow a Comparator to compare queue elements. If no comparator is supplied, assume that the element type implements the Comparable interface.

Answers to Self-Check Questions

1. HashMap<String, Integer>
2. It uses inheritance.
3. new Pair<String, String>("Hello", "World")
4. An ArrayList<Pair<String, Integer>> contains multiple pairs, for example [(Tom, 1), (Harry, 3)]. A Pair<ArrayList<String>, Integer> contains a list of strings and a single integer, such as ([Tom, Harry], 1).
5. The output depends on the implementation of the toString method in the BankAccount class.
6. No—the method has no type parameters. It is an ordinary method in a generic class.
7. public class BinarySearchTree<E extends Comparable>
8.
```
public static <E extends Measurable> E min(E[] a)
{
    E smallest = a[0];
    for (int i = 1; i < a.length; i++)
        if (a[i].getMeasure() < smallest.getMeasure())
            smallest = a[i];
    return smallest;
}
```
9.
```
public static void print(Object[] a)
{
    for (Object e : a)
        System.out.print(e + " ");
    System.out.println();
}
```
10. This code compiles (with a warning), but it is a poor technique. In the future, if type erasure no longer happens, the code will be *wrong*. The cast from Object[] to String[] will cause a class cast exception.

Graphical User Interfaces

CHAPTER GOALS

G To become familiar with common user-interface components, such as text components, radio buttons, check boxes, and menus

G To understand the use of layout managers to arrange user-interface components in a container

G To build programs that handle events from user-interface components

• To learn how to browse the Java documentation

In this chapter, we will delve more deeply into graphical user interface programming. The graphical applications with which you are familiar have many visual gadgets for information entry: text components, buttons, scroll bars, menus, and so on. In this chapter, you will learn how to use the most common user-interface components in the Java Swing user-interface toolkit. Swing has many more components than can be mastered in a first course, and even the basic components have advanced options that can't be covered here. In fact, few programmers try to learn everything about a particular user-interface component. It is more important to understand the concepts and to search the Java documentation for the details. This chapter walks you through one example to show you how the Java documentation is organized and how you can rely on it for your programming.

18.1 Processing Text Input

We start our discussion of graphical user interfaces with text input. Of course, a graphical application can receive text input by calling the showInputDialog method of the JOptionPane class, but popping up a separate dialog box for each input is not a natural user interface. Most graphical programs collect text input through **text fields** (see Figure 1). In this section, you will learn how to add text fields to a graphical application, and how to read what the user types into them.

The JTextField class provides a text field. When you construct a text field, you need to supply the width—the approximate number of characters that you expect the user to type.

> Use JTextField components to provide space for user input. Place a JLabel next to each text field.

```
final int FIELD_WIDTH = 10;
final JTextField rateField = new JTextField(FIELD_WIDTH);
```

Users can type additional characters, but then a part of the contents of the field becomes invisible.

You will want to label each text field so that the user knows what to type into it. Construct a JLabel object for each label:

```
JLabel rateLabel = new JLabel("Interest Rate: ");
```

You want to give the user an opportunity to enter all information into the text fields before processing it. Therefore, you should supply a button that the user can press to indicate that the input is ready for processing.

When that button is clicked, its actionPerformed method reads the user input from the text field, using the getText method of the JTextField class. The getText method returns a String object. In our sample program, we turn the string into a number, using the Double.parseDouble method. After updating the account, we show the balance in another label.

```
class AddInterestListener implements ActionListener
{
    public void actionPerformed(ActionEvent event)
    {
        double rate = Double.parseDouble(rateField.getText());
        double interest = account.getBalance() * rate / 100;
        account.deposit(interest);
        resultLabel.setText("balance: " + account.getBalance());
    }
}
```

The following application is a useful prototype for a graphical user-interface front end for arbitrary calculations. You can easily modify it for your own needs. Place

740

Figure 1   An Application with a Text Field

other input components into the frame. Change the contents of the `actionPerformed` method to carry out other calculations. Display the result in a label.

ch18/textfield/InvestmentViewer3.java

```java
1  import javax.swing.JFrame;
2
3  /**
4     This program displays the growth of an investment.
5  */
6  public class InvestmentViewer3
7  {
8     public static void main(String[] args)
9     {
10        JFrame frame = new InvestmentFrame();
11        frame.setDefaultCloseOperation(JFrame.EXIT_ON_CLOSE);
12        frame.setVisible(true);
13     }
14  }
```

ch18/textfield/InvestmentFrame.java

```java
1  import java.awt.event.ActionEvent;
2  import java.awt.event.ActionListener;
3  import javax.swing.JButton;
4  import javax.swing.JFrame;
5  import javax.swing.JLabel;
6  import javax.swing.JPanel;
7  import javax.swing.JTextField;
8
9  /**
10    A frame that shows the growth of an investment with variable interest.
11 */
12 public class InvestmentFrame extends JFrame
13 {
14    private static final int FRAME_WIDTH = 450;
15    private static final int FRAME_HEIGHT = 100;
16
17    private static final double DEFAULT_RATE = 5;
18    private static final double INITIAL_BALANCE = 1000;
19
20    private JLabel rateLabel;
21    private JTextField rateField;
22    private JButton button;
23    private JLabel resultLabel;
24    private JPanel panel;
25    private BankAccount account;
26
```

```
27    public InvestmentFrame()
28    {
29       account = new BankAccount(INITIAL_BALANCE);
30
31       // Use instance variables for components
32       resultLabel = new JLabel("balance: " + account.getBalance());
33
34       // Use helper methods
35       createTextField();
36       createButton();
37       createPanel();
38
39       setSize(FRAME_WIDTH, FRAME_HEIGHT);
40    }
41
42    private void createTextField()
43    {
44       rateLabel = new JLabel("Interest Rate: ");
45
46       final int FIELD_WIDTH = 10;
47       rateField = new JTextField(FIELD_WIDTH);
48       rateField.setText("" + DEFAULT_RATE);
49    }
50
51    private void createButton()
52    {
53       button = new JButton("Add Interest");
54
55       class AddInterestListener implements ActionListener
56       {
57          public void actionPerformed(ActionEvent event)
58          {
59             double rate = Double.parseDouble(rateField.getText());
60             double interest = account.getBalance() * rate / 100;
61             account.deposit(interest);
62             resultLabel.setText("balance: " + account.getBalance());
63          }
64       }
65
66       ActionListener listener = new AddInterestListener();
67       button.addActionListener(listener);
68    }
69
70    private void createPanel()
71    {
72       panel = new JPanel();
73       panel.add(rateLabel);
74       panel.add(rateField);
75       panel.add(button);
76       panel.add(resultLabel);
77       add(panel);
78    }
79 }
```

SELF CHECK

1. What happens if you omit the first JLabel object?
2. If a text field holds an integer, what expression do you use to read its contents?

18.2 Text Areas

Use a JTextArea to show multiple lines of text.

In the preceding section, you saw how to construct text fields. A text field holds a single line of text. To display multiple lines of text, use the JTextArea class.

When constructing a text area, you can specify the number of rows and columns:

```
final int ROWS = 10;
final int COLUMNS = 30;
JTextArea textArea = new JTextArea(ROWS, COLUMNS);
```

Use the setText method to set the text of a text field or text area. The append method adds text to the end of a text area. Use newline characters to separate lines, like this:

```
textArea.append(account.getBalance() + "\n");
```

If you want to use a text field or text area for display purposes only, call the set-Editable method like this

```
textArea.setEditable(false);
```

Now the user can no longer edit the contents of the field, but your program can still call setText and append to change it.

As shown in Figure 2, the JTextField and JTextArea classes are subclasses of the class JTextComponent. The methods setText and setEditable are declared in the JText-Component class and inherited by JTextField and JTextArea. However, the append method is declared in the JTextArea class.

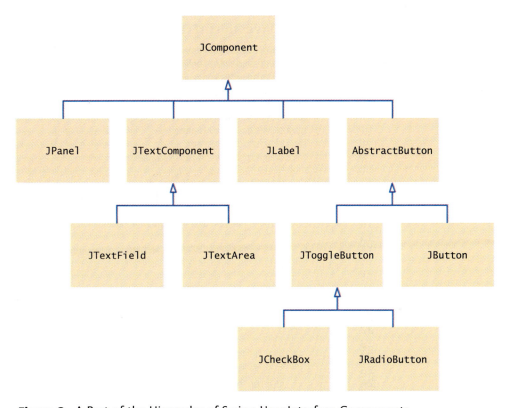

Figure 2 A Part of the Hierarchy of Swing User-Interface Components

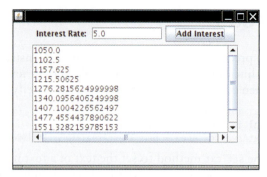

Figure 3 The Investment Application with a Text Area

You can add scroll bars to any component with a JScrollPane.

To add scroll bars to a text area, use a JScrollPane, like this:

```
JTextArea textArea = new JTextArea(ROWS, COLUMNS);
JScrollPane scrollPane = new JScrollPane(textArea);
```

Then add the scroll pane to the panel. Figure 3 shows the result.

The following sample program puts these concepts together. A user can enter numbers into the interest rate text field and then click on the "Add Interest" button). The interest rate is applied, and the updated balance is appended to the text area. The text area has scroll bars and is not editable.

This program is similar to the previous investment viewer program, but it keeps track of all the bank balances, not just the last one.

ch18/textarea/InvestmentFrame.java

```java
1   import java.awt.event.ActionEvent;
2   import java.awt.event.ActionListener;
3   import javax.swing.JButton;
4   import javax.swing.JFrame;
5   import javax.swing.JLabel;
6   import javax.swing.JPanel;
7   import javax.swing.JScrollPane;
8   import javax.swing.JTextArea;
9   import javax.swing.JTextField;
10
11  /**
12     A frame that shows the growth of an investment with variable interest.
13  */
14  public class InvestmentFrame extends JFrame
15  {
16     private static final int FRAME_WIDTH = 400;
17     private static final int FRAME_HEIGHT = 250;
18
19     private static final int AREA_ROWS = 10;
20     private static final int AREA_COLUMNS = 30;
21     private static final double DEFAULT_RATE = 5;
22     private static final double INITIAL_BALANCE = 1000;
23
24     private JLabel rateLabel;
25     private JTextField rateField;
26     private JButton button;
```

```
27      private JTextArea resultArea;
28      private JPanel panel;
29      private BankAccount account;
30
31   public InvestmentFrame()
32   {
33      account = new BankAccount(INITIAL_BALANCE);
34      resultArea = new JTextArea(AREA_ROWS, AREA_COLUMNS);
35      resultArea.setEditable(false);
36
37      // Use helper methods
38      createTextField();
39      createButton();
40      createPanel();
41
42      setSize(FRAME_WIDTH, FRAME_HEIGHT);
43   }
44
45   private void createTextField()
46   {
47      rateLabel = new JLabel("Interest Rate: ");
48
49      final int FIELD_WIDTH = 10;
50      rateField = new JTextField(FIELD_WIDTH);
51      rateField.setText("" + DEFAULT_RATE);
52   }
53
54   private void createButton()
55   {
56      button = new JButton("Add Interest");
57
58      class AddInterestListener implements ActionListener
59         {
60            public void actionPerformed(ActionEvent event)
61            {
62               double rate = Double.parseDouble(rateField.getText());
63               double interest = account.getBalance() * rate / 100;
64               account.deposit(interest);
65               resultArea.append(account.getBalance() + "\n");
66            }
67         }
68
69      ActionListener listener = new AddInterestListener();
70      button.addActionListener(listener);
71   }
72
73   private void createPanel()
74   {
75      panel = new JPanel();
76      panel.add(rateLabel);
77      panel.add(rateField);
78      panel.add(button);
79      JScrollPane scrollPane = new JScrollPane(resultArea);
80      panel.add(scrollPane);
81      add(panel);
82   }
83 }
```

3. What is the difference between a text field and a text area?

4. Why did the InvestmentFrame program call resultArea.setEditable(false)?

5. How would you modify the InvestmentFrame program if you didn't want to use scroll bars?

18.3 Layout Management

> User-interface components are arranged by placing them inside containers.

Up to now, you have had limited control over the layout of user-interface components. You learned how to add components to a panel. The panel arranged the components from the left to the right. However, in many applications, you need more sophisticated arrangements.

> Each container has a layout manager that directs the arrangement of its components.

In Java, you build up user interfaces by adding components into containers such as panels. Each container has its own **layout manager**, which determines how the components are laid out.

By default, a JPanel uses a **flow layout**. A flow layout simply arranges its components from left to right and starts a new row when there is no more room in the current row.

> Three useful layout managers are the border layout, flow layout, and grid layout.

Another commonly used layout manager is the **border layout**. The border layout groups components into five areas: center, north, west, south, and east (see Figure 4). Not all of the areas need to be occupied.

The border layout is the default layout manager for a frame (or, more technically, the frame's content pane). But you can also use the border layout in a panel:

```
panel.setLayout(new BorderLayout());
```

Now the panel is controlled by a border layout, not the flow layout. When adding a component, you specify the position, like this:

> When adding a component to a container with the border layout, specify the NORTH, EAST, SOUTH, WEST, or CENTER position.

```
panel.add(component, BorderLayout.NORTH);
```

The **grid layout** is a third layout that is sometimes useful. The grid layout arranges components in a grid with a fixed number of rows and columns, resizing each of the components so that they all have the same size. Like the border layout, it also expands each component to fill the entire allotted area. (If that is not desirable, you need to place each component inside a panel.) Figure 5 shows a number pad panel that uses a grid layout. To create a grid layout, you supply the number of rows and columns in the constructor, then add the components, row by row, left to right:

> The content pane of a frame has a border layout by default. A panel has a flow layout by default.

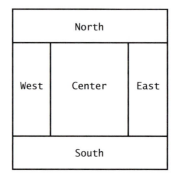

Figure 4
Components Expand to Fill Space in the Border Layout

Figure 5
The Grid Layout

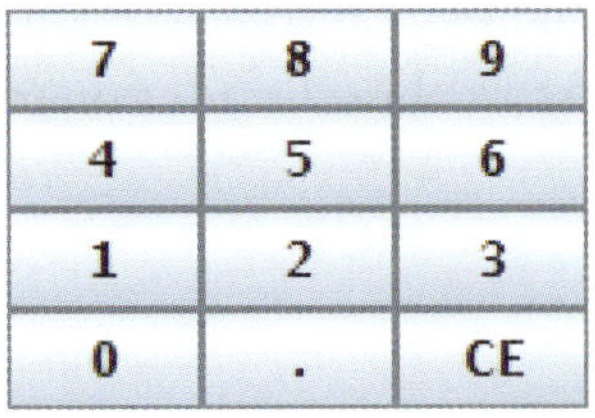

```
JPanel buttonPanel = new JPanel();
buttonPanel.setLayout(new GridLayout(4, 3));
buttonPanel.add(button7);
buttonPanel.add(button8);
buttonPanel.add(button9);
buttonPanel.add(button4);
. . .
```

Sometimes you want to have a tabular arrangement of the components where columns have different sizes or one component spans multiple columns. A more complex layout manager called the *grid bag layout* can handle these situations. The grid bag layout is quite complex to use, however, and we do not cover it in this book; see, for example, Cay S. Horstmann and Gary Cornell, *Core Java 2 Volume 1: Fundamentals,* 8th edition (Prentice Hall, 2008), for more information. Java 6 introduces a group layout that is designed for use by interactive tools—see Productivity Hint 18.1 on page 757.

Fortunately, you can create acceptable-looking layouts in nearly all situations by nesting panels. You give each panel an appropriate layout manager. Panels don't have visible borders, so you can use as many panels as you need to organize your components. Figure 6 shows an example. The keypad buttons are contained in a panel with grid layout. That panel is itself contained in a larger panel with border layout. The text field is in the northern position of the larger panel. The following code produces this arrangement:

```
JPanel keypadPanel = new JPanel();
keypadPanel.setLayout(new BorderLayout());
buttonPanel = new JPanel();
buttonPanel.setLayout(new GridLayout(4, 3));
buttonPanel.add(button7);
buttonPanel.add(button8);
// . . .
keypadPanel.add(buttonPanel, BorderLayout.CENTER);
JTextField display = new JTextField();
keypadPanel.add(display, BorderLayout.NORTH);
```

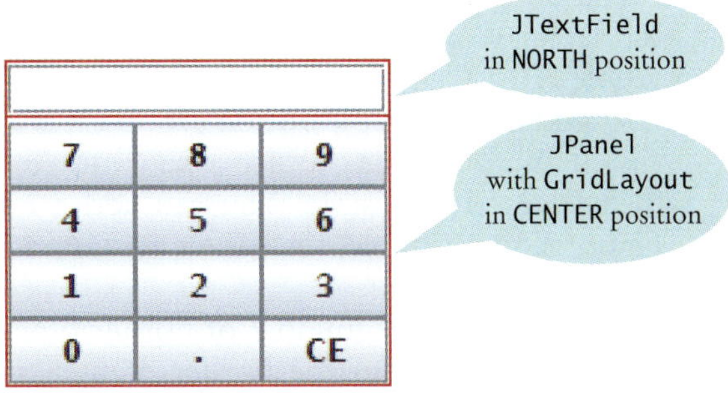

JTextField
in NORTH position

JPanel
with GridLayout
in CENTER position

Figure 6
Nesting Panels

6. How do you add two buttons to the north area of a frame?

7. How can you stack three buttons on top of each other?

18.4 Choices

In the following sections, you will see how to present a finite set of choices to the user. Which Swing component you use depends on whether the choices are mutually exclusive or not, and on the amount of space you have for displaying the choices.

18.4.1 Radio Buttons

For a small set of mutually exclusive choices, use a group of radio buttons or a combo box.

If the choices are mutually exclusive, use a set of **radio buttons**. In a radio button set, only one button can be selected at a time. When the user selects another button in the same set, the previously selected button is automatically turned off. (These buttons are called radio buttons because they work like the station selector buttons on a car radio: If you select a new station, the old station is automatically deselected.) For example, in Figure 7, the font sizes are mutually exclusive. You can select small, medium, or large, but not a combination of them.

Add radio buttons into a ButtonGroup so that only one button in the group is on at any time.

To create a set of radio buttons, first create each button individually, and then add all buttons of the set to a ButtonGroup object:

```
JRadioButton smallButton = new JRadioButton("Small");
JRadioButton mediumButton = new JRadioButton("Medium");
JRadioButton largeButton = new JRadioButton("Large");

ButtonGroup group = new ButtonGroup();
group.add(smallButton);
group.add(mediumButton);
group.add(largeButton);
```

Note that the button group does *not* place the buttons close to each other on the container. The purpose of the button group is simply to find out which buttons to turn off when one of them is turned on. It is still your job to arrange the buttons on the screen.

The isSelected method is called to find out whether a button is currently selected or not. For example,

```
if (largeButton.isSelected()) { size = LARGE_SIZE; }
```

Because users will expect one radio button in a radio button group to be selected, call setSelected(true) on the default radio button before making the enclosing frame visible.

You can place a border around a panel to group its contents visually.

If you have multiple button groups, it is a good idea to group them together visually. It is a good idea to use a panel for each set of radio buttons, but the panels themselves are invisible. You can add a *border* to a panel to make it visible. In Figure 7, for example, the panels containing the Size radio buttons and Style check boxes have borders.

There are a large number of border types. We will show only a couple of variations and leave it to the border enthusiasts to look up the others in the Swing

Figure 7
A Combo Box,
Check Boxes, and
Radio Buttons

documentation. The `EtchedBorder` class yields a border with a three-dimensional, etched effect. You can add a border to any component, but most commonly you apply it to a panel:

```
JPanel panel = new JPanel();
panel.setBorder(new EtchedBorder());
```

If you want to add a title to the border (as in Figure 7), you need to construct a `TitledBorder`. You make a titled border by supplying a basic border and then the title you want. Here is a typical example:

```
panel.setBorder(new TitledBorder(new EtchedBorder(), "Size"));
```

18.4.2 Check Boxes

For a binary choice, use a check box.

A check box is a user-interface component with two states: checked and unchecked. You use a group of check boxes when one selection does not exclude another. For example, the choices for "Bold" and "Italic" in Figure 7 are not exclusive. You can choose either, both, or neither. Therefore, they are implemented as a set of separate check boxes. Radio buttons and check boxes have different visual appearances. Radio buttons are round and have a black dot when selected. Check boxes are square and have a check mark when selected.

You construct a check box by giving the name in the constructor:

```
JCheckBox italicCheckBox = new JCheckBox("Italic");
```

Because check box settings do not exclude each other, you do not place a set of check boxes inside a button group.

As with radio buttons, you use the `isSelected` method to find out whether a check box is currently checked or not.

18.4.3 Combo Boxes

For a large set of choices, use a combo box.

If you have a large number of choices, you don't want to make a set of radio buttons, because that would take up a lot of space. Instead, you can use a **combo box**. This component is called a combo box because it is a combination of a list and a text field. The text field displays the name of the current selection. When you click on the arrow to the right of the text field of a combo box, a list of selections drops down, and you can choose one of the items in the list (see Figure 8).

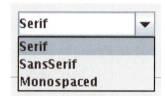

Figure 8
An Open Combo Box

If the combo box is *editable*, you can also type in your own selection. To make a combo box editable, call the setEditable method.

You add strings to a combo box with the addItem method.

```
JComboBox facenameCombo = new JComboBox();
facenameCombo.addItem("Serif");
facenameCombo.addItem("SansSerif");
. . .
```

You get the item that the user has selected by calling the getSelectedItem method. However, because combo boxes can store other objects in addition to strings, the getSelectedItem method has return type Object. Hence you must cast the returned value back to String.

```
String selectedString = (String) facenameCombo.getSelectedItem();
```

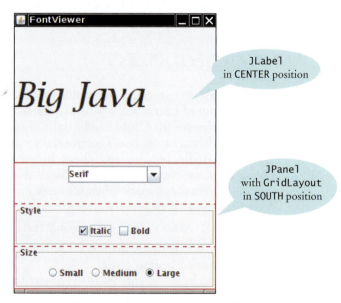

Figure 9 The Components of the FontViewerFrame

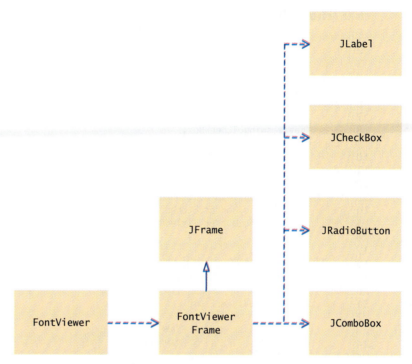

Figure 10 Classes of the Font Viewer Program

You can select an item for the user with the setSelectedItem method.

Radio buttons, check boxes, and combo boxes generate an ActionEvent whenever the user selects an item. In the following program, we don't care which component was clicked—all components notify the same listener object. Whenever the user clicks on any one of them, we simply ask each component for its current content, using the isSelected and getSelectedItem methods. We then redraw the text sample with the new font.

Figure 9 shows how the components are arranged in the frame. Figure 10 shows the relationships between the classes used in the font viewer program.

ch18/choice/FontViewer.java

```java
1   import javax.swing.JFrame;
2
3   /**
4       This program allows the user to view font effects.
5   */
6   public class FontViewer
7   {
8       public static void main(String[] args)
9       {
10          JFrame frame = new FontViewerFrame();
11          frame.setDefaultCloseOperation(JFrame.EXIT_ON_CLOSE);
12          frame.setTitle("FontViewer");
13          frame.setVisible(true);
14      }
15  }
```

ch18/choice/FontViewerFrame.java

```java
1   import java.awt.BorderLayout;
2   import java.awt.Font;
3   import java.awt.GridLayout;
4   import java.awt.event.ActionEvent;
5   import java.awt.event.ActionListener;
6   import javax.swing.ButtonGroup;
7   import javax.swing.JButton;
8   import javax.swing.JCheckBox;
9   import javax.swing.JComboBox;
10  import javax.swing.JFrame;
11  import javax.swing.JLabel;
12  import javax.swing.JPanel;
13  import javax.swing.JRadioButton;
14  import javax.swing.border.EtchedBorder;
15  import javax.swing.border.TitledBorder;
16
17  /**
18     This frame contains a text field and a control panel
19     to change the font of the text.
20  */
21  public class FontViewerFrame extends JFrame
22  {
23     private static final int FRAME_WIDTH = 300;
24     private static final int FRAME_HEIGHT = 400;
25
26     private JLabel sampleField;
27     private JCheckBox italicCheckBox;
28     private JCheckBox boldCheckBox;
29     private JRadioButton smallButton;
30     private JRadioButton mediumButton;
31     private JRadioButton largeButton;
32     private JComboBox facenameCombo;
33     private ActionListener listener;
34
35     /**
36        Constructs the frame.
37     */
38     public FontViewerFrame()
39     {
40        // Construct text sample
41        sampleField = new JLabel("Big Java");
42        add(sampleField, BorderLayout.CENTER);
43
44        // This listener is shared among all components
45        class ChoiceListener implements ActionListener
46        {
47           public void actionPerformed(ActionEvent event)
48           {
49              setSampleFont();
50           }
51        }
52
53        listener = new ChoiceListener();
54
55        createControlPanel();
56        setSampleFont();
57        setSize(FRAME_WIDTH, FRAME_HEIGHT);
58     }
```

```
59
60    /**
61        Creates the control panel to change the font.
62    */
63    public void createControlPanel()
64    {
65        JPanel facenamePanel = createComboBox();
66        JPanel sizeGroupPanel = createCheckBoxes();
67        JPanel styleGroupPanel = createRadioButtons();
68
69        // Line up component panels
70
71        JPanel controlPanel = new JPanel();
72        controlPanel.setLayout(new GridLayout(3, 1));
73        controlPanel.add(facenamePanel);
74        controlPanel.add(sizeGroupPanel);
75        controlPanel.add(styleGroupPanel);
76
77        // Add panels to content pane
78
79        add(controlPanel, BorderLayout.SOUTH);
80    }
81
82    /**
83        Creates the combo box with the font style choices.
84        @return the panel containing the combo box
85    */
86    public JPanel createComboBox()
87    {
88        facenameCombo = new JComboBox();
89        facenameCombo.addItem("Serif");
90        facenameCombo.addItem("SansSerif");
91        facenameCombo.addItem("Monospaced");
92        facenameCombo.setEditable(true);
93        facenameCombo.addActionListener(listener);
94
95        JPanel panel = new JPanel();
96        panel.add(facenameCombo);
97        return panel;
98    }
99
100   /**
101       Creates the check boxes for selecting bold and italic styles.
102       @return the panel containing the check boxes
103   */
104   public JPanel createCheckBoxes()
105   {
106       italicCheckBox = new JCheckBox("Italic");
107       italicCheckBox.addActionListener(listener);
108
109       boldCheckBox = new JCheckBox("Bold");
110       boldCheckBox.addActionListener(listener);
111
112       JPanel panel = new JPanel();
113       panel.add(italicCheckBox);
114       panel.add(boldCheckBox);
115       panel.setBorder(new TitledBorder(new EtchedBorder(), "Style"));
116
117       return panel;
```

```
118     }
119
120     /**
121         Creates the radio buttons to select the font size.
122         @return the panel containing the radio buttons
123     */
124     public JPanel createRadioButtons()
125     {
126         smallButton = new JRadioButton("Small");
127         smallButton.addActionListener(listener);
128
129         mediumButton = new JRadioButton("Medium");
130         mediumButton.addActionListener(listener);
131
132         largeButton = new JRadioButton("Large");
133         largeButton.addActionListener(listener);
134         largeButton.setSelected(true);
135
136         // Add radio buttons to button group
137
138         ButtonGroup group = new ButtonGroup();
139         group.add(smallButton);
140         group.add(mediumButton);
141         group.add(largeButton);
142
143         JPanel panel = new JPanel();
144         panel.add(smallButton);
145         panel.add(mediumButton);
146         panel.add(largeButton);
147         panel.setBorder(new TitledBorder(new EtchedBorder(), "Size"));
148
149         return panel;
150     }
151
152     /**
153         Gets user choice for font name, style, and size
154         and sets the font of the text sample.
155     */
156     public void setSampleFont()
157     {
158         // Get font name
159         String facename
160             = (String) facenameCombo.getSelectedItem();
161
162         // Get font style
163
164         int style = 0;
165         if (italicCheckBox.isSelected())
166         {
167             style = style + Font.ITALIC;
168         }
169         if (boldCheckBox.isSelected())
170         {
171             style = style + Font.BOLD;
172         }
173
174         // Get font size
175
176         int size = 0;
```

```
177
178        final int SMALL_SIZE = 24;
179        final int MEDIUM_SIZE = 36;
180        final int LARGE_SIZE = 48;
181
182        if (smallButton.isSelected()) { size = SMALL_SIZE; }
183        else if (mediumButton.isSelected()) { size = MEDIUM_SIZE; }
184        else if (largeButton.isSelected()) { size = LARGE_SIZE; }
185
186        // Set font of text field
187
188        sampleField.setFont(new Font(facename, style, size));
189        sampleField.repaint();
190     }
191  }
```

SELF CHECK

8. What is the advantage of a `JComboBox` over a set of radio buttons? What is the disadvantage?

9. Why do all user-interface components in the `FontViewerFrame` class share the same listener?

10. Why was the combo box placed inside a panel? What would have happened if it had been added directly to the control panel?

How To 18.1

Laying Out a User Interface

A graphical user interface is made up of components such as buttons and text fields. The Swing library uses containers and layout managers to arrange these components. This How To explains how to group components into containers and how to pick the right layout managers.

Step 1   Make a sketch of your desired component layout.

Draw all the buttons, labels, text fields, and borders on a sheet of paper. Graph paper works best.

Here is an example—a user interface for ordering pizza. The user interface contains

- Three radio buttons
- Two check boxes
- A label: "Your Price:"
- A text field
- A border

```
┌─ Size ──────────┐
│  ● Small          │      ☑ Pepperoni
│  ○ Medium         │
│  ○ Large          │      ☑ Anchovies
└───────────────────┘

        Your Price:  ┌──────────────┐
                     └──────────────┘
```

Step 2   Find groupings of adjacent components with the same layout.

Usually, the component arrangement is complex enough that you need to use several panels, each with its own layout manager. Start by looking at adjacent components that are arranged top to bottom or left to right. If several components are surrounded by a border, they should be grouped together.

Here are the groupings from the pizza user interface:

Size
- Small
- Medium
- Large

✓ Pepperoni

✓ Anchovies

Your Price:

Step 3 Identify layouts for each group.

When components are arranged horizontally, choose a flow layout. When components are arranged vertically, use a grid layout with one column.

In the pizza user interface example, you would choose

- A (3, 1) grid layout for the radio buttons
- A (2, 1) grid layout for the check boxes
- A flow layout for the label and text field

Step 4 Group the groups together.

Look at each group as one blob, and group the blobs together into larger groups, just as you grouped the components in the preceding step. If you note one large blob surrounded by smaller blobs, you can group them together in a border layout.

You may have to repeat the grouping again if you have a very complex user interface. You are done if you have arranged all groups in a single container.

For example, the three component groups of the pizza user interface can be arranged as:

- A group containing the first two component groups, placed in the center of a container with a border layout.

- The third component group, in the southern area of that container.

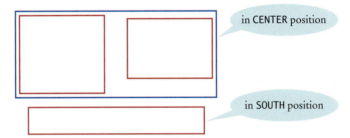

in CENTER position

in SOUTH position

In this step, you may run into a couple of complications. The group "blobs" tend to vary in size more than the individual components. If you place them inside a grid layout, the grid layout forces them all to be the same size. Also, you occasionally would like a component from one group to line up with a component from another group, but there is no way for you to communicate that intent to the layout managers.

These problems can be overcome by using more sophisticated layout managers or implementing a custom layout manager. However, those techniques are beyond the scope of this book. Sometimes, you may want to start over with Step 1, using a component layout that is easier to manage. Or you can decide to live with minor imperfections of the layout. Don't worry about achieving the perfect layout—after all, you are learning programming, not user-interface design.

Step 5 Write the code to generate the layout.

This step is straightforward but potentially tedious, especially if you have a large number of components.

Start by constructing the components. Then construct a panel for each component group and set its layout manager if it is not a flow layout (the default for panels). Add a border to the panel if required. Finally, add the components to their panels. Continue in this fashion until you reach the outermost containers, which you add to the frame.

Here is an outline of the code required for the pizza user interface.

```
JPanel radioButtonPanel = new JPanel();
radioButtonPanel.setLayout(new GridLayout(3, 1));
radioButton.setBorder(new TitledBorder(new EtchedBorder(), "Size"));
radioButtonPanel.add(smallButton);
radioButtonPanel.add(mediumButton);
radioButtonPanel.add(largeButton);

JPanel checkBoxPanel = new JPanel();
checkBoxPanel.setLayout(new GridLayout(2, 1));
checkBoxPanel.add(pepperoniButton());
checkBoxPanel.add(anchoviesButton());

JPanel pricePanel = new JPanel(); // Uses FlowLayout by default
pricePanel.add(new JLabel("Your Price:"));
pricePanel.add(priceTextField);

JPanel centerPanel = new JPanel(); // Uses FlowLayout
centerPanel.add(radioButtonPanel);
centerPanel.add(checkBoxPanel);

// Frame uses BorderLayout by default
add(centerPanel, BorderLayout.CENTER);
add(pricePanel, BorderLayout.SOUTH);
```

Of course, you also need to add event handlers to the components. See How To 10.1.

Productivity Hint 18.1

Use a GUI Builder

As you have seen, implementing even a simple graphical user interface in Java is quite tedious. You have to write a lot of code for constructing components, using layout managers, and providing event handlers. Most of the code is boring and repetitive.

A GUI builder takes away much of the tedium. Most GUI builders help you in three ways:

- You drag and drop components onto a panel. The GUI builder writes the layout management code for you.

- You customize components with a dialog box, setting properties such as fonts, colors, text, and so on. The GUI builder writes the customization code for you.

- You provide event handlers by picking the event to process and providing just the code snippet for the listener method. The GUI builder writes the boilerplate code for attaching a listener object.

Java 6 introduced `GroupLayout`, a powerful layout manager that was specifically designed to be used by GUI builders. The free NetBeans development environment, available from `http://netbeans.org`, makes use of this layout manager—see Figure 11.

If you need to build a complex user interface, you will find that learning to use a GUI builder is a very worthwhile investment. You will spend less time writing boring code, and you will have more fun designing your user interface and focusing on the functionality of your program.

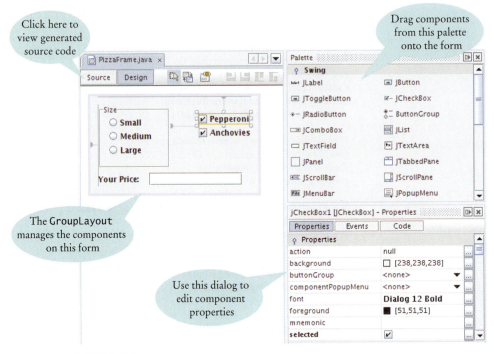

Figure 11 A GUI Builder

18.5 Menus

A frame contains a menu bar. The menu bar contains menus. A menu contains submenus and menu items.

Anyone who has ever used a graphical user interface is familiar with pull-down menus (see Figure 12). In Java it is easy to create these menus.

The container for the top-level menu items is called a *menu bar*. A *menu* is a collection of *menu items* and more menus (submenus). You add menu items and submenus with the add method:

```
JMenuItem fileExitItem = new JMenuItem("Exit");
fileMenu.add(fileExitItem);
```

Menu items generate action events.

A menu item has no further submenus. When the user selects a menu item, the menu item sends an action event. Therefore, you want to add a listener to each menu item:

```
fileExitItem.addActionListener(listener);
```

You add action listeners only to menu items, not to menus or the menu bar. When the user clicks on a menu name and a submenu opens, no action event is sent.

Figure 12
Pull-Down Menus

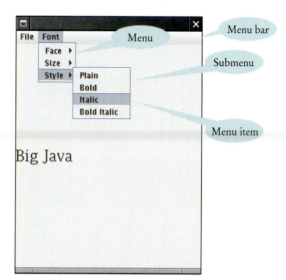

The following program builds up a small but typical menu and traps the action events from the menu items. To keep the program readable, it is a good idea to use a separate method for each menu or set of related menus. Have a look at the create-FaceItem method, which creates a menu item to change the font face. The same listener class takes care of three cases, with the name parameters varying for each menu item. The same strategy is used for the createSizeItem and createStyleItem methods.

ch18/menu/FontViewer2.java

```java
1  import javax.swing.JFrame;
2
3  /**
4     This program uses a menu to display font effects.
5  */
6  public class FontViewer2
7  {
8     public static void main(String[] args)
9     {
10        JFrame frame = new FontViewer2Frame();
11        frame.setDefaultCloseOperation(JFrame.EXIT_ON_CLOSE);
12        frame.setVisible(true);
13     }
14  }
```

ch18/menu/FontViewer2Frame.java

```java
1   import java.awt.BorderLayout;
2   import java.awt.Font;
3   import java.awt.GridLayout;
4   import java.awt.event.ActionEvent;
5   import java.awt.event.ActionListener;
6   import javax.swing.ButtonGroup;
7   import javax.swing.JButton;
8   import javax.swing.JCheckBox;
9   import javax.swing.JComboBox;
10  import javax.swing.JFrame;
```

```
11  import javax.swing.JLabel;
12  import javax.swing.JMenu;
13  import javax.swing.JMenuBar;
14  import javax.swing.JMenuItem;
15  import javax.swing.JPanel;
16  import javax.swing.JRadioButton;
17  import javax.swing.border.EtchedBorder;
18  import javax.swing.border.TitledBorder;
19
20  /**
21     This frame has a menu with commands to change the font
22     of a text sample.
23  */
24  public class FontViewer2Frame extends JFrame
25  {
26     private static final int FRAME_WIDTH = 300;
27     private static final int FRAME_HEIGHT = 400;
28
29     private JLabel sampleField;
30     private String facename;
31     private int fontstyle;
32     private int fontsize;
33
34     /**
35        Constructs the frame.
36     */
37     public FontViewer2Frame()
38     {
39        // Construct text sample
40        sampleField = new JLabel("Big Java");
41        add(sampleField, BorderLayout.CENTER);
42
43        // Construct menu
44        JMenuBar menuBar = new JMenuBar();
45        setJMenuBar(menuBar);
46        menuBar.add(createFileMenu());
47        menuBar.add(createFontMenu());
48
49        facename = "Serif";
50        fontsize = 24;
51        fontstyle = Font.PLAIN;
52
53        setSampleFont();
54        setSize(FRAME_WIDTH, FRAME_HEIGHT);
55     }
56
57     /**
58        Creates the File menu.
59        @return the menu
60     */
61     public JMenu createFileMenu()
62
63     {
64        JMenu menu = new JMenu("File");
65        menu.add(createFileExitItem());
66        return menu;
67     }
68
```

```
69       /**
70          Creates the File->Exit menu item and sets its action listener.
71          @return the menu item
72       */
73       public JMenuItem createFileExitItem()
74       {
75          JMenuItem item = new JMenuItem("Exit");
76          class MenuItemListener implements ActionListener
77          {
78             public void actionPerformed(ActionEvent event)
79             {
80                System.exit(0);
81             }
82          }
83          ActionListener listener = new MenuItemListener();
84          item.addActionListener(listener);
85          return item;
86       }
87
88       /**
89          Creates the Font submenu.
90          @return the menu
91       */
92       public JMenu createFontMenu()
93       {
94          JMenu menu = new JMenu("Font");
95          menu.add(createFaceMenu());
96          menu.add(createSizeMenu());
97          menu.add(createStyleMenu());
98          return menu;
99       }
100
101      /**
102         Creates the Face submenu.
103         @return the menu
104      */
105      public JMenu createFaceMenu()
106      {
107         JMenu menu = new JMenu("Face");
108         menu.add(createFaceItem("Serif"));
109         menu.add(createFaceItem("SansSerif"));
110         menu.add(createFaceItem("Monospaced"));
111         return menu;
112      }
113
114      /**
115         Creates the Size submenu.
116         @return the menu
117      */
118      public JMenu createSizeMenu()
119      {
120         JMenu menu = new JMenu("Size");
121         menu.add(createSizeItem("Smaller", -1));
122         menu.add(createSizeItem("Larger", 1));
123         return menu;
124      }
125
```

```java
126    /**
127       Creates the Style submenu.
128       @return the menu
129    */
130    public JMenu createStyleMenu()
131    {
132       JMenu menu = new JMenu("Style");
133       menu.add(createStyleItem("Plain", Font.PLAIN));
134       menu.add(createStyleItem("Bold", Font.BOLD));
135       menu.add(createStyleItem("Italic", Font.ITALIC));
136       menu.add(createStyleItem("Bold Italic", Font.BOLD
137             + Font.ITALIC));
138       return menu;
139    }
140
141    /**
142       Creates a menu item to change the font face and set its action listener.
143       @param name the name of the font face
144       @return the menu item
145    */
146    public JMenuItem createFaceItem(final String name)
147    {
148       JMenuItem item = new JMenuItem(name);
149       class MenuItemListener implements ActionListener
150       {
151          public void actionPerformed(ActionEvent event)
152          {
153             facename = name;
154             setSampleFont();
155          }
156       }
157       ActionListener listener = new MenuItemListener();
158       item.addActionListener(listener);
159       return item;
160    }
161
162    /**
163       Creates a menu item to change the font size
164       and set its action listener.
165       @param name the name of the menu item
166       @param ds the amount by which to change the size
167       @return the menu item
168    */
169    public JMenuItem createSizeItem(String name, final int ds)
170    {
171       JMenuItem item = new JMenuItem(name);
172       class MenuItemListener implements ActionListener
173       {
174          public void actionPerformed(ActionEvent event)
175          {
176             fontsize = fontsize + ds;
177             setSampleFont();
178          }
179       }
180       ActionListener listener = new MenuItemListener();
181       item.addActionListener(listener);
182       return item;
183    }
184
```

```
185    /**
186        Creates a menu item to change the font style
187        and set its action listener.
188        @param name the name of the menu item
189        @param style the new font style
190        @return the menu item
191    */
192    public JMenuItem createStyleItem(String name, final int style)
193    {
194        JMenuItem item = new JMenuItem(name);
195        class MenuItemListener implements ActionListener
196        {
197            public void actionPerformed(ActionEvent event)
198            {
199                fontstyle = style;
200                setSampleFont();
201            }
202        }
203        ActionListener listener = new MenuItemListener();
204        item.addActionListener(listener);
205        return item;
206    }
207
208    /**
209        Sets the font of the text sample.
210    */
211    public void setSampleFont()
212    {
213        Font f = new Font(facename, fontstyle, fontsize);
214        sampleField.setFont(f);
215        sampleField.repaint();
216    }
217 }
```

SELF CHECK

11. Why do JMenu objects not generate action events?

12. Why is the name parameter in the createFaceItem method declared as final?

How To 18.2

Implementing a Graphical User Interface (GUI)

A GUI program allows users to supply inputs and specify actions. The textfield/Investment-Viewer3 program has only one input and one action. More sophisticated programs have more interesting user interactions, but the basic principles are the same.

Step 1 Enumerate the actions that your program needs to carry out.

For example, the investment viewer has a single action, to add interest. Other programs may have different actions, perhaps for making deposits, inserting coins, and so on.

Step 2 For each action, enumerate the inputs that you need.

For example, the investment viewer has a single input: the interest rate. Other programs may have different inputs, such as amounts of money, product quantities, and so on.

Step 3 For each action, enumerate the outputs that you need to show.

The investment viewer has a single output: the current balance. Other programs may show different quantities, messages, and so on.

Step 4   Supply the user-interface components.

Use buttons or menus for actions, text components for inputs, choice components to present finite sets of choices, and labels for outputs. Implement your own components to produce graphical output, such as charts or drawings.

Step 5   Use layout managers for layout.

Add the required components to a frame, using the techniques of How To 18.1.

Step 6   Supply event handler classes.

For each button, choice component, or menu item, you need to add an object of a listener class. The listener classes must implement the `ActionListener` interface. Supply a class for each action (or group of related actions), and put the instructions for the action in the `actionPerformed` method.

```
class Button1Listener implements ActionListener
{
   public void actionPerformed(ActionEvent event)
   {
      // button1 action goes here
      . . .
   }
}
```

Remember to declare any local variables accessed by the listener methods as `final`.

Step 7   Make listener objects and attach them to the event sources.

For action events, the event source is a button or other user-interface component, or a timer. You need to add a listener object to each event source, like this:

```
ActionListener listener1 = new Button1Listener();
button1.addActionListener(listener1);
```

18.6 Exploring the Swing Documentation

You should learn to navigate the API documentation to find out more about user-interface components.

In the preceding sections, you saw the basic properties of the most common user-interface components. We purposefully omitted many options and variations to simplify the discussion. You can go a long way by using only the simplest properties of these components. If you want to implement a more sophisticated effect, you can look inside the Swing documentation. You will probably find the documentation quite intimidating at first glance, though. The purpose of this section is to show you how you can use the documentation to your advantage without becoming overwhelmed.

As an example, consider a program for mixing colors by specifying the red, green, and blue values. How can you specify the colors? Of course, you could supply three text fields, but sliders would be more convenient for users of your program (see Figure 13).

The Swing user-interface toolkit has a large set of user-interface components. How do you know if there is a slider? You can buy a book that illustrates all Swing components. Or you can run the sample application included in the Java Development Kit that shows off all Swing components (see Figure 14). Or you can look at the names of all of the classes that start with J and decide that `JSlider` may be a good candidate.

Figure 13
A Color Viewer

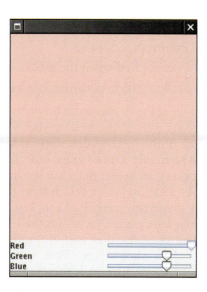

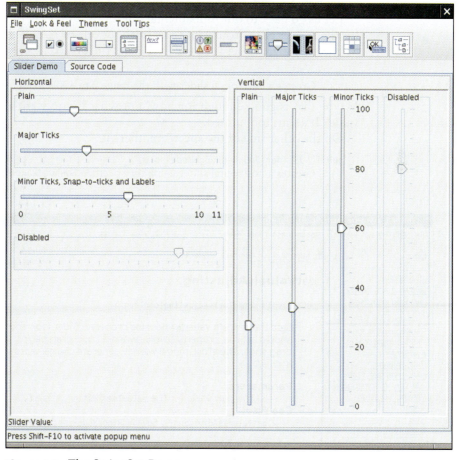

Figure 14 The SwingSet Demo

Next, you need to ask yourself a few questions:

- How do I construct a JSlider?
- How can I get notified when the user has moved it?
- How can I tell to which value the user has set it?

When you look at the documentation of the JSlider class, you will probably not be happy. There are over 50 methods in the JSlider class and over 250 inherited methods, and some of the method descriptions look downright scary, such as the one in Figure 15. Apparently some folks out there are concerned about the valueIsAdjusting property, whatever that may be, and the designers of this class felt it necessary to supply a method to tweak that property. Until you too feel that need, your best bet is to ignore this method. As the author of an introductory book, it pains me to tell you to ignore certain facts. But the truth of the matter is that the Java library is so large and complex that nobody understands it in its entirety, not even the designers of Java themselves. You need to develop the ability to separate fundamental concepts from ephemeral minutiae. For example, it is important that you understand the concept of event handling. Once you understand the concept, you can ask the question, "What event does the slider send when the user moves it?" But it is not important that you memorize how to set tick marks or that you know how to implement a slider with a custom look and feel.

Let us go back to our fundamental questions. In Java 6, there are six constructors for the JSlider class. You want to learn about one or two of them. You must strike a balance somewhere between the trivial and the bizarre. Consider

```
public JSlider()
```
        Creates a horizontal slider with the range 0 to 100 and an initial value of 50.

Maybe that is good enough for now, but what if you want another range or initial value? It seems too limited.

On the other side of the spectrum, there is

```
public JSlider(BoundedRangeModel brm)
```
        Creates a horizontal slider using the specified BoundedRangeModel.

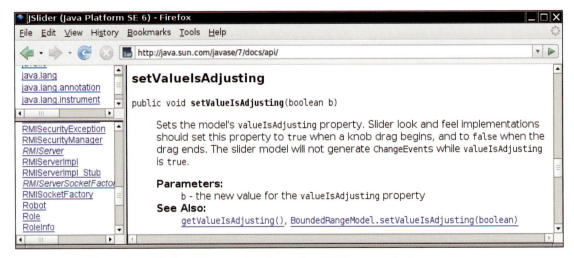

Figure 15 A Mysterious Method Description from the API Documentation

Whoa! What is that? You can click on the BoundedRangeModel link to get a long explanation of this class. This appears to be some internal mechanism for the Swing implementors. Let's try to avoid this constructor if we can. Looking further, we find

```
public JSlider(int min, int max, int value)
     Creates a horizontal slider using the specified min, max, and value.
```

This sounds general enough to be useful and simple enough to be usable. You might want to stash away the fact that you can have vertical sliders as well.

Next, you want to know what events a slider generates. There is no addActionListener method. That makes sense. Adjusting a slider seems different from clicking a button, and Swing uses a different event type for these events. There is a method

```
public void addChangeListener(ChangeListener l)
```

Click on the ChangeListener link to find out more about this interface. It has a single method

```
void stateChanged(ChangeEvent e)
```

Apparently, that method is called whenever the user moves the slider. What is a ChangeEvent? Once again, click on the link, to find out that this event class has *no* methods of its own, but it inherits the getSource method from its superclass EventObject. The getSource method tells us which component generated this event, but we don't need that information—we know that the event came from the slider.

Now let's make a plan: Add a change event listener to each slider. When the slider is changed, the stateChanged method is called. Find out the new value of the slider. Recompute the color value and repaint the color panel. That way, the color panel is continually repainted as the user moves one of the sliders.

To compute the color value, you will still need to get the current value of the slider. Look at all the methods that start with get. Sure enough, you find

```
public int getValue()
     Returns the slider's value.
```

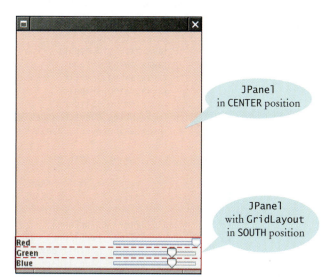

Figure 16
The Components of
the ColorViewerFrame

Figure 17
Classes of the Color
Viewer Program

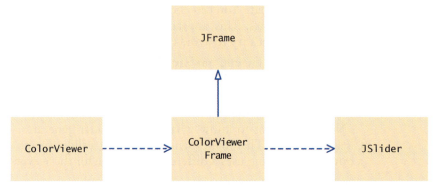

Now you know everything you need to write the program. The program uses one new Swing component and one event listener of a new type. After having mastered the basics, you may want to explore the capabilities of the component further, for example by adding tick marks—see Exercise P18.17.

Figure 16 shows how the components are arranged in the frame. Figure 17 shows the UML diagram.

ch18/slider/ColorViewer.java

```java
1   import javax.swing.JFrame;
2
3   public class ColorViewer
4   {
5      public static void main(String[] args)
6      {
7         ColorViewerFrame frame = new ColorViewerFrame();
8         frame.setDefaultCloseOperation(JFrame.EXIT_ON_CLOSE);
9         frame.setVisible(true);
10     }
11  }
```

ch18/slider/ColorViewerFrame.java

```java
1   import java.awt.BorderLayout;
2   import java.awt.Color;
3   import java.awt.GridLayout;
4   import javax.swing.JFrame;
5   import javax.swing.JLabel;
6   import javax.swing.JPanel;
7   import javax.swing.JSlider;
8   import javax.swing.event.ChangeListener;
9   import javax.swing.event.ChangeEvent;
10
11  public class ColorViewerFrame extends JFrame
12  {
13     private static final int FRAME_WIDTH = 300;
14     private static final int FRAME_HEIGHT = 400;
15
16     private JPanel colorPanel;
17     private JSlider redSlider;
18     private JSlider greenSlider;
19     private JSlider blueSlider;
```

```
20
21      public ColorViewerFrame()
22      {
23         colorPanel = new JPanel();
24
25         add(colorPanel, BorderLayout.CENTER);
26         createControlPanel();
27         setSampleColor();
28         setSize(FRAME_WIDTH, FRAME_HEIGHT);
29      }
30
31      public void createControlPanel()
32      {
33         class ColorListener implements ChangeListener
34         {
35            public void stateChanged(ChangeEvent event)
36            {
37               setSampleColor();
38            }
39         }
40
41         ChangeListener listener = new ColorListener();
42
43         redSlider = new JSlider(0, 255, 255);
44         redSlider.addChangeListener(listener);
45
46         greenSlider = new JSlider(0, 255, 175);
47         greenSlider.addChangeListener(listener);
48
49         blueSlider = new JSlider(0, 255, 175);
50         blueSlider.addChangeListener(listener);
51
52         JPanel controlPanel = new JPanel();
53         controlPanel.setLayout(new GridLayout(3, 2));
54
55         controlPanel.add(new JLabel("Red"));
56         controlPanel.add(redSlider);
57
58         controlPanel.add(new JLabel("Green"));
59         controlPanel.add(greenSlider);
60
61         controlPanel.add(new JLabel("Blue"));
62         controlPanel.add(blueSlider);
63
64         add(controlPanel, BorderLayout.SOUTH);
65      }
66
67      /**
68         Reads the slider values and sets the panel to
69         the selected color.
70      */
71      public void setSampleColor()
72      {
73         // Read slider values
74
75         int red = redSlider.getValue();
76         int green = greenSlider.getValue();
77         int blue = blueSlider.getValue();
78
```

```
79          // Set panel background to selected color
80
81          colorPanel.setBackground(new Color(red, green, blue));
82          colorPanel.repaint();
83      }
84  }
```

SELF CHECK

13. Suppose you want to allow users to pick a color from a color dialog box. Which class would you use? Look in the API documentation.

14. Why does a slider emit change events and not action events?

Summary of Learning Objectives

Use text fields for reading text input.

- Use JTextField components to provide space for user input. Place a JLabel next to each text field.

Use text areas for reading and displaying multi-line text.

- Use a JTextArea to show multiple lines of text.
- You can add scroll bars to any component with a JScrollPane.

Learn how to arrange multiple components in a container.

- User-interface components are arranged by placing them inside containers. Containers can be placed inside larger containers.
- Each container has a layout manager that directs the arrangement of its components.
- When adding a component to a container with the border layout, specify the NORTH, EAST, SOUTH, WEST, or CENTER position.
- The content pane of a frame has a border layout by default. A panel has a flow layout by default.

Select among the Swing components for presenting choices to the user.

- For a small set of mutually exclusive choices, use a group of radio buttons or a combo box.
- Add radio buttons into a ButtonGroup so that only one button in the group is on at any time.
- You can place a border around a panel to group its contents visually.
- For a binary choice, use a check box.
- For a large set of choices, use a combo box.
- Radio buttons, check boxes, and combo boxes generate action events, just as buttons do.

Implement menus in a Swing program.

- A frame contains a menu bar. The menu bar contains menus. A menu contains submenus and menu items.
- Menu items generate action events.
- You should learn to navigate the API documentation to find out more about user-interface components.

Classes, Objects, and Methods Introduced in this Chapter

```
java.awt.BorderLayout              javax.swing.JMenuBar
    CENTER                             add
    EAST                           javax.swing.JMenuItem
    NORTH                          javax.swing.JRadioButton
    SOUTH                          javax.swing.JScrollPane
    WEST                           javax.swing.JSlider
java.awt.Container                     addChangeListener
    setLayout                          getValue
java.awt.FlowLayout                javax.swing.JTextArea
java.awt.Font                          append
java.awt.GridLayout                javax.swing.JTextField
javax.swing.AbstractButton         javax.swing.border.EtchedBorder
    isSelected                     javax.swing.border.TitledBorder
    setSelected                    javax.swing.event.ChangeEvent
javax.swing.ButtonGroup            javax.swing.event.ChangeListener
    add                                stateChanged
javax.swing.ImageIcon              javax.swing.text.JTextComponent
javax.swing.JCheckBox                  getText
javax.swing.JComboBox                  isEditable
    addItem                            setEditable
    getSelectedItem                    setText
    isEditable
    setEditable
javax.swing.JComponent
    setBorder
    setFont
javax.swing.JFrame
    setJMenuBar
javax.swing.JMenu
    add
```

Media Resources

www.wiley.com/ college/ horstmann

- Lab Exercises
- ⊕ Practice Quiz
- ⊕ Code Completion Exercises

Review Exercises

★G R18.1 What is the difference between a label, a text field, and a text area?

★★G R18.2 Name a method that is declared in JTextArea, a method that JTextArea inherits from JTextComponent, and a method that JTextArea inherits from JComponent.

★G R18.3 Can you use a flow layout for the components in a frame? If yes, how?

★G R18.4 What is the advantage of a layout manager over telling the container "place this component at position (x, y)"?

★★G R18.5 What happens when you place a single button into the CENTER area of a container that uses a border layout? Try it out, by writing a small sample program, if you aren't sure of the answer.

★★G R18.6 What happens if you place multiple buttons directly into the SOUTH area, without using a panel? Try it out, by writing a small sample program, if you aren't sure of the answer.

★★G R18.7 What happens when you add a button to a container that uses a border layout and omit the position? Try it out and explain.

★★G R18.8 What happens when you try to add a button to another button? Try it out and explain.

★★G R18.9 The ColorViewerFrame uses a grid layout manager. Explain a drawback of the grid that is apparent from Figure 16 on page 767. What could you do to overcome this drawback?

★★★G R18.10 What is the difference between the grid layout and the grid bag layout?

★★★G R18.11 Can you add icons to check boxes, radio buttons, and combo boxes? Browse the Java documentation to find out. Then write a small test program to verify your findings.

★G R18.12 What is the difference between radio buttons and check boxes?

★G R18.13 Why do you need a button group for radio buttons but not for check boxes?

★G R18.14 What is the difference between a menu bar, a menu, and a menu item?

★G R18.15 When browsing through the Java documentation for more information about sliders, we ignored the JSlider constructor with no parameters. Why? Would it have worked in our sample program?

★G R18.16 How do you construct a vertical slider? Consult the Swing documentation for an answer.

★★G R18.17 Why doesn't a JComboBox send out change events?

★★★G R18.18 What component would you use to show a set of choices, just as in a combo box, but so that several items are visible at the same time? Run the Swing demo application or look at a book with Swing example programs to find the answer.

★★G R18.19 How many Swing user-interface components are there? Look at the Java documentation to get an approximate answer.

★★G R18.20 How many methods does the `JProgressBar` component have? Be sure to count inherited methods. Look at the Java documentation.

Programming Exercises

★G P18.1 Write a graphical application front end for a bank account class. Supply text fields and buttons for depositing and withdrawing money, and for displaying the current balance in a label.

★G P18.2 Write a graphical application front end for an `Earthquake` class. Supply a text field and button for entering the strength of the earthquake. Display the earthquake description in a label.

★G P18.3 Write a graphical application front end for a `DataSet` class. Supply text fields and buttons for adding floating-point values, and display the current minimum, maximum, and average in a label.

★G P18.4 Write an application with three labeled text fields, one each for the initial amount of a savings account, the annual interest rate, and the number of years. Add a button "Calculate" and a read-only text area to display the result, namely, the balance of the savings account after the end of each year.

★★G P18.5 In the application from Exercise P18.4, replace the text area with a bar chart that shows the balance after the end of each year.

★★★G P18.6 Write a program that contains a text field, a button "Add Value", and a component that draws a bar chart of the numbers that a user typed into the text field.

★★★G P18.7 Write a program that draws a clock face with a time that the user enters in two text fields (one for the hours, one for the minutes).

Hint: You need to determine the angles of the hour hand and the minute hand. The angle of the minute hand is easy: The minute hand travels 360 degrees in 60 minutes. The angle of the hour hand is harder; it travels 360 degrees in 12×60 *minutes*.

★G P18.8 Write an application with three buttons labeled "Red", "Green", and "Blue" that changes the background color of a panel in the center of the frame to red, green, or blue.

★★G P18.9 Add icons to the buttons of Exercise P18.8.

★★G P18.10 Write a calculator application. Use a grid layout to arrange buttons for the digits and for the $+ - \times \div$ operations. Add a text field to display the result.

★G P18.11 Write an application with three radio buttons labeled "Red", "Green", and "Blue" that changes the background color of a panel in the center of the frame to red, green, or blue.

★G **P18.12** Write an application with three check boxes labeled "Red", "Green", and "Blue" that adds a red, green, or blue component to the background color of a panel in the center of the frame. This application can display a total of eight color combinations.

★G **P18.13** Write an application with a combo box containing three items labeled "Red", "Green", and "Blue" that changes the background color of a panel in the center of the frame to red, green, or blue.

★G **P18.14** Write an application with a Color menu and menu items labeled "Red", "Green", and "Blue" that changes the background color of a panel in the center of the frame to red, green, or blue.

★G **P18.15** Write a program that displays a number of rectangles at random positions. Supply buttons "Fewer" and "More" that generate fewer or more random rectangles. Each time the user clicks on "Fewer", the count should be halved. Each time the user clicks on "More", the count should be doubled.

★★G **P18.16** Modify the program of Exercise P18.15 to replace the buttons with a slider to generate fewer or more random rectangles.

★★G **P18.17** In the slider test program, add a set of tick marks to each slider that show the exact slider position.

★★★G **P18.18** Enhance the font viewer program to allow the user to select different fonts. Research the API documentation to find out how to find the available fonts on the user's system.

Programming Projects

Project 18.1 Write a program that lets users design charts such as the following:

```
┌─────────────────────────────────────────┐
│ Golden Gate                             │
└─────────────────────────────────────────┘
┌──────────────────────┐
│ Brooklyn            │
└──────────────────────┘
┌─────────────────────────────┐
│ Delaware Memorial         │
└─────────────────────────────┘
┌──────────────────────────────────┐
│ Mackinac                       │
└──────────────────────────────────┘
```

Use appropriate components to ask for the length, label, and color, then apply them when the user clicks an "Add Item" button. Allow the user to switch between bar charts and pie charts.

Project 18.2 Write a program that displays a scrolling message in a panel. Use a timer for the scrolling effect. In the timer's action listener, move the starting position of the message and repaint. When the message has left the window, reset the starting position to the other corner. Provide a user interface to customize the message text, font, foreground and background colors, and the scrolling speed and direction.

Answers to Self-Check Questions

1. Then the text field is not labeled, and the user will not know its purpose.

2. `Integer.parseInt(textField.getText())`

3. A text field holds a single line of text; a text area holds multiple lines.

4. The text area is intended to display the program output. It does not collect user input.

5. Don't construct a `JScrollPane` but add the `resultArea` object directly to the frame.

6. First add them to a panel, then add the panel to the north end of a frame.

7. Place them inside a panel with a `GridLayout` that has three rows and one column.

8. If you have many options, a set of radio buttons takes up a large area. A combo box can show many options without using up much space. But the user cannot see the options as easily.

9. When any of the component settings is changed, the program simply queries all of them and updates the label.

10. To keep it from growing too large. It would have grown to the same width and height as the two panels below it.

11. When you open a menu, you have not yet made a selection. Only `JMenuItem` objects correspond to selections.

12. The parameter variable is accessed in a method of an inner class.

13. `JColorChooser`.

14. Action events describe one-time changes, such as button clicks. Change events describe continuous changes.

Streams and Binary Input/Output

CHAPTER GOALS

- To become familiar with the concepts of text and binary formats
- To learn about encryption
- To understand when to use sequential and random file access
- To be able to read and write objects using serialization

In this chapter you will learn more about how to write Java programs that interact with disk files and other sources of bytes and characters. You will learn about text and binary formats, and about sequential and random access to the data in a file. We will discuss how you can use object serialization to save and load complex objects with very little effort. As an application of file processing, you will study a program for encrypting and decrypting sensitive data.

19.1 Readers, Writers, and Streams

There are two fundamentally different ways to store data: in *text* format or *binary* format. In text format, data items are represented in human-readable form, as a sequence of *characters*. For example, in text form, the integer 12,345 is stored as the sequence of five characters:

    '1' '2' '3' '4' '5'

In binary form, data items are represented in **bytes**. A byte is composed of 8 **bits** and can denote one of 256 values. For example, in binary format, the integer 12,345 is stored as a sequence of four bytes:

    0 0 48 57

(because $12,345 = 48 \cdot 256 + 57$).

The Java library provides two sets of classes for handling input and output. *Streams* handle binary data. *Readers* and *writers* handle data in text form. Figure 1 shows a part of the hierarchy of the Java classes for input and output.

Text input and output are more convenient for humans, because it is easier to produce input (just use a text editor) and it is easier to check that output is correct (just look at the output file in an editor). However, binary storage is more compact and more efficient.

If you store information in text form, as a sequence of characters, you should use the Reader and Writer classes and their subclasses to process input and output. If you store information in binary form, as a sequence of bytes, you use the InputStream and OutputStream classes and their subclasses.

To read text data from a disk file, you create a FileReader object:

    FileReader reader = new FileReader("input.txt");

> Streams access sequences of bytes. Readers and writers access sequences of characters.

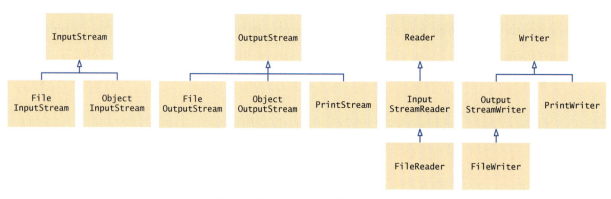

Figure 1 Java Classes for Input and Output

To read binary data from a disk file, you create a `FileInputStream` object instead:

```
FileInputStream inputStream = new FileInputStream("input.bin");
```

Similarly, you use `FileWriter` and `FileOutputStream` objects to write data to a disk file in text or binary form respectively:

```
FileWriter writer = new FileWriter("output.txt");
FileOutputStream outputStream = new FileOutputStream("output.bin");
```

Why use two sets of classes? Characters are made up of bytes, but there is some variation *how* each character is represented. For example, the character 'e' may be a single byte 69 or a two-byte sequence 0 69, depending on whether you use the UTF-8 or UTF-16 encoding. (These are two different methods of representing Unicode characters as bytes.) The character 'é' is encoded as 195 169 or 0 223 under those encodings. There is also a plethora of encoding schemes used in countries around the world. The `Reader` and `Writer` classes have the responsibility of converting between bytes and characters. By default, these classes use the default character encoding of the computer executing the program. It is also possible to specify particular encodings, but we will not use that feature in this chapter.

In Chapter 11, you learned how to work with text files. In that chapter, you used the `Scanner` class. When constructing a `Scanner` from a `File` object, the `Scanner` automatically constructs a `FileReader`. You also know how to write text output to `System.out` or another `PrintStream`. It is a bit inconsistent that you don't need a `PrintWriter` for writing text. This is a historical accident—`System.out` and the `PrintStream` class were a feature of Java 1.0, and the reader/writer classes were only added in Java 1.1.

> Use `FileReader`, `FileWriter`, `FileInputStream`, and `FileOutputStream` classes to read and write disk files.

SELF CHECK

1. Suppose you need to read an image file that contains color values for each pixel in the image. Will you use a `Reader` or an `InputStream`?

2. Special Topic 11.2 introduced the `openStream` method of the `URL` class, which returns an `InputStream`:

```
URL locator = new URL("http://bigjava.com/index.html");
InputStream in = locator.openStream();
```

Why doesn't the `URL` class provide a `Reader` instead?

19.2 Binary Input and Output

In this section, you will learn how to process binary data. The `InputStream` class has a method, `read`, to read a single byte at a time. (The `FileInputStream` class overrides this method to obtain the characters from a disk file.) However, the `read` method actually returns an `int` so that it can signal either that a byte has been read or that the end of input has been reached. At the end of input, `read` returns -1. Otherwise it returns the byte (as an integer between 0 and 255).

You should test the return value and, if it is not -1, cast it to a byte:

```
InputStream in = . . .;
int next = in.read();
byte b;
if (next != -1)
   b = (byte) next;
```

> The `InputStream.read` method returns an integer, either –1 to indicate end of input, or a byte between 0 and 255.

The
OutputStream.write
method writes a
single byte.

Similarly, the OutputStream class has a write method to write a single byte.

```
OutputStream out = . . .;
byte b = . . .;
out.write(b);
```

When you are done writing to the file, you should close it:

```
out.close();
```

These basic methods are the only input and output methods that the input and output stream classes provide. The Java stream package is built on the principle that each class should have a very focused responsibility. The job of an input stream is to get bytes, not to analyze them. If you want to read numbers, strings, or other objects, you have to combine the class with other classes whose responsibility is to group individual bytes or characters together into numbers, strings, and objects. You will see an example of those classes in Section 19.4.

As an application of a task that involves reading and writing individual bytes, we will implement an *encryption* program. The program scrambles the bytes in a file so that the file is unreadable except to those who know the decryption method and the secret keyword. Ignoring over 2000 years of progress in the field of encryption, we will use a method familiar to Julius Caesar. The person performing any encryption chooses an *encryption key*; here the key is a number between 1 and 255 that indicates the shift to be used in encrypting each byte. (Julius Caesar used a key of 3, replacing A with D, B with E, and so on—see Figure 2).

To decrypt, simply use the negative of the encryption key. For example, to decrypt a message encoded with a key of 3, use a key of –3.

In this program we read each byte separately, encrypt it, and write the encrypted byte.

```
int next = in.read();
if (next == -1)
    done = true;
else
{
    byte b = (byte) next;
    byte c = encrypt(b);
    out.write(c);
}
```

In a more complex encryption program, you would read a block of bytes, encrypt the block, and write it out.

Try out the program on a file of your choice. You will find that the encrypted file is unreadable. In fact, because the newline characters are transformed, you may not be able to read the encrypted file in a text editor. To decrypt, simply run the program again and supply the negative of the encryption key.

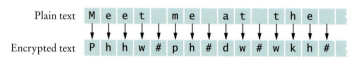

Figure 2 The Caesar Cipher

ch19/caesar/CaesarCipher.java

```java
1   import java.io.InputStream;
2   import java.io.OutputStream;
3   import java.io.IOException;
4
5   /**
6      This class encrypts files using the Caesar cipher.
7      For decryption, use an encryptor whose key is the
8      negative of the encryption key.
9   */
10  public class CaesarCipher
11  {
12     private int key;
13
14     /**
15        Constructs an cipher object with a given key.
16        @param aKey the encryption key
17     */
18     public CaesarCipher(int aKey)
19     {
20        key = aKey;
21     }
22
23     /**
24        Encrypts the contents of a stream.
25        @param in the input stream
26        @param out the output stream
27     */
28     public void encryptStream(InputStream in, OutputStream out)
29           throws IOException
30     {
31        boolean done = false;
32        while (!done)
33        {
34           int next = in.read();
35           if (next == -1) done = true;
36           else
37           {
38              byte b = (byte) next;
39              byte c = encrypt(b);
40              out.write(c);
41           }
42        }
43     }
44
45     /**
46        Encrypts a byte.
47        @param b the byte to encrypt
48        @return the encrypted byte
49     */
50     public byte encrypt(byte b)
51     {
52        return (byte) (b + key);
53     }
54  }
```

ch19/caesar/CaesarEncryptor.java

```java
 1  import java.io.File;
 2  import java.io.FileInputStream;
 3  import java.io.FileOutputStream;
 4  import java.io.InputStream;
 5  import java.io.IOException;
 6  import java.io.OutputStream;
 7  import java.util.Scanner;
 8
 9  /**
10     This program encrypts a file, using the Caesar cipher.
11  */
12  public class CaesarEncryptor
13  {
14     public static void main(String[] args)
15     {
16        Scanner in = new Scanner(System.in);
17        try
18        {
19           System.out.print("Input file: ");
20           String inFile = in.next();
21           System.out.print("Output file: ");
22           String outFile = in.next();
23           System.out.print("Encryption key: ");
24           int key = in.nextInt();
25
26           InputStream inStream = new FileInputStream(inFile);
27           OutputStream outStream = new FileOutputStream(outFile);
28
29           CaesarCipher cipher = new CaesarCipher(key);
30           cipher.encryptStream(inStream, outStream);
31
32           inStream.close();
33           outStream.close();
34        }
35        catch (IOException exception)
36        {
37           System.out.println("Error processing file: " + exception);
38        }
39     }
40  }
```

S E L F   C H E C K

3. Why does the read method of the InputStream class return an int and not a byte?

4. Decrypt the following message: Khoor/#Zruog$.

5. Can you use the sample program from this section to encrypt a binary file, for example, an image file?

Common Error 19.1

Negative byte Values

In Java, the byte type is a *signed* type. There are 256 values of the byte type, from –128 to 127. The starting bit of the byte is the **sign bit**. If it is on, the number is negative. In converting an integer into a byte, only the least significant byte of the integer is taken, and the remaining bytes are ignored. The result can be negative even if the integer is positive.

For example,

```
int n = 233; // Binary 00000000 00000000 00000000 11101001
byte b = (byte) n; // Binary 11101001, sign bit is on
if (b == n) . . . // Not true! b is negative, n is positive
```

When the byte is converted back to an integer, then the result is still negative. In particular, it is different from the original.

Here is an even trickier case. Consider this test:

```
int next = in.read();
byte b = (byte) next;
if (b == 'é') . . .
```

This test is *never* true, even if next was equal to the Unicode value for the 'é' character. That Unicode value happens to be 233, but a single byte is always a value between −128 and 127. American readers won't be too concerned, because all characters and symbols used in American English have Unicode values in the "safe" range between 1 and 127, but international programmers who use characters with Unicode values between 128 and 255 find this a source of frustration.

Random Fact 19.1

Encryption Algorithms

The exercises at the end of this chapter give a few algorithms to encrypt text. Don't actually use any of those methods to send secret messages to your lover. Any skilled cryptographer can break those schemes in a very short time—that is, reconstruct the original text without knowing the secret keyword.

In 1978 Ron Rivest, Adi Shamir, and Leonard Adleman introduced an encryption method that is much more powerful. The method is called RSA encryption, after the last names of its inventors. The exact scheme is too complicated to present here, but it is not difficult to follow. You can find the details in Bruce Schneier's *Applied Cryptography* (John Wiley & Sons, 1994).

RSA is a remarkable encryption method. There are two keys: a public key and a private key. (See the figure below.) You can print the public key on your business card (or in your e-mail signature block) and give it to anyone. Then anyone can send you messages that only you can decrypt. Even though everyone else knows the public key, and even if they intercept all the messages coming to you, they cannot break the scheme and actually read the messages. In 1994, hundreds of researchers, collaborating over the Internet, cracked an RSA message encrypted with a 129-digit key. Messages encrypted with a key of 230 digits or more are expected to be secure.

The inventors of the algorithm obtained a patent for it. That means that for a period of 20 years, anyone using it had to seek a license from the inventors. They have given permission for most noncommercial usage, but companies that implemented RSA in a product that they sold had to get the patent holder's permission and pay substantial royalties. The RSA patent expired on September 20, 2000, so you are now free to use the algorithm without restriction.

A patent is a deal that society makes with an inventor. For a period of 20 years after the filing date, the inventor has an exclusive right to its commercialization, may collect royalties from others wishing to manufacture the invention, and may even stop competitors from marketing it altogether. In return, the inventor must publish the invention, so that others may learn from it, and must relinquish all claims to it after the protection period ends. The presumption is that, in the absence of patent law, inventors would be reluctant to go through the trouble of inventing, or they would try to cloak their techniques to prevent others from copying their devices.

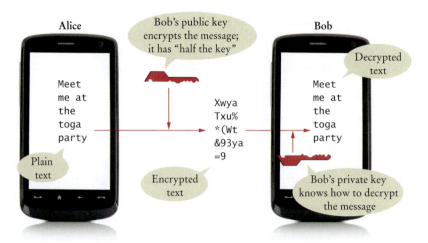

Public Key Encryption

What do you think? Are patents a fair deal? Unquestionably, some companies have chosen not to implement RSA, and instead chose a less capable method, because they could not or would not pay the royalties. Thus, it seems that the patent may have hindered, rather than advanced, commerce. Had there not been patent protection, would the inventors have published the method anyway, thereby giving the benefit for society without the cost of the 20-year monopoly? In this case, the answer is probably yes; the inventors were academic researchers, who live on salaries rather than sales receipts and are usually rewarded for their discoveries by a boost in their reputation and careers. Would their followers have been as active in discovering (and patenting) improvements? There is no way of knowing.

Further, is an algorithm even patentable in the first place? Or is it a mathematical fact that belongs to nobody? The patent office did take the latter attitude for a long time. The RSA inventors and many others described their inventions in terms of imaginary electronic devices, rather than algorithms, to circumvent that restriction. Nowadays, the patent office will award software patents.

There is another fascinating aspect to the RSA story. A programmer named Phil Zimmermann developed a program called PGP (for *Pretty Good Privacy*). PGP implements RSA. That is, you can have it generate a pair of public and private keys, publish the public key, receive encrypted messages from others who use their copy of PGP and your public key, and decrypt them with your private key. Even though the encryption can be performed on any personal computer, decryption is not feasible even with the most powerful computers. You can get a copy of a free PGP implementation from the GNU project at http://www.gnupg.org.

The existence of PGP bothers the government to no end. They worry that criminals use the package to correspond by e-mail and that the police cannot tap those "conversations". Foreign governments can send communications that the National Security Agency (the premier electronic spy organization of the United States) cannot decipher. In the 1990s, the U.S. government unsuccessfully attempted to standardize on a different encryption scheme, called Skipjack, to which government organizations hold a decryption key that—of course—they promise not to use without a court order. There have been serious proposals to make it illegal to use any other encryption method in the United States. At one time, the government considered charging Zimmermann with breaching another law that forbids the unauthorized export of munitions as a crime and defines cryptographic technology as "munitions". They made the argument that, even though Zimmermann never exported the program, he should have known that it would immediately spread through the Internet when he released it in the United States.

What do you think? Will criminals and terrorists be harder to detect and convict once encryption of e-mail and phone conversations is widely available? Should the government therefore have a backdoor key to any legal encryption method? Or is this a gross violation of our civil liberties? Is it even possible to put the genie back into the bottle at this time?

19.3 Random Access

Reading a file sequentially from beginning to end can be inefficient. In this section, you will learn how to directly access arbitrary locations in a file. Consider a file that contains a set of bank accounts. We want to change the balances of some of the accounts. Of course, we can read all account data into an array list, update the information that has changed, and save the data out again. If the data set in the file is very large, we may end up doing a lot of reading and writing just to update a handful of records. It would be better if we could locate the changed information in the file and just replace it.

This is quite different from the file access you programmed in Chapter 11, where you read from a file, starting at the beginning and reading the entire contents until you reached the end. That access pattern is called **sequential access**. Now we would like to access specific locations in a file and change only those locations. This access pattern is called **random access** (see Figure 3). There is nothing "random" about random access—the term simply means that you can read and modify any byte stored at any location in the file.

Only disk files support random access; the System.in and System.out streams, which are attached to the keyboard and the terminal window, do not. Each disk file has a special **file pointer** position. Normally, the file pointer is at the end of the file, and any output is appended to the end. However, if you move the file pointer to the middle of the file and write to the file, the output overwrites what is already there. The next read command starts reading input at the file pointer location. You can move the file pointer just beyond the last byte currently in the file but no further.

In Java, you use a RandomAccessFile object to access a file and move a file pointer. To open a random access file, you supply a file name and a string to specify the *open mode*. You can open a file either for reading only ("r") or for reading and writing ("rw"). For example, the following command opens the file bank.dat for both reading and writing:

```
RandomAccessFile f = new RandomAccessFile("bank.dat", "rw");
```

> In sequential file access, a file is processed one byte at a time. Random access allows access at arbitrary locations in the file, without first reading the bytes preceding the access location.

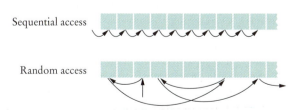

Figure 3 Sequential and Random Access

The method call

```
f.seek(n);
```

moves the file pointer to byte n counted from the beginning of the file. To find out the current position of the file pointer (counted from the beginning of the file), use

```
n = f.getFilePointer();
```

Because files can be very large, the file pointer values are long integers. To determine the number of bytes in a file, use the length method:

```
long fileLength = f.length();
```

In the example program at the end of this section, we use a random access file to store a set of bank accounts, each of which has an account number and a current balance. The test program lets you pick an account and deposit money into it.

If you want to manipulate a data set in a file, you have to pay special attention to the formatting of the data. Suppose you just store the data as text. Say account 1001 has a balance of $900, and account 1015 has a balance of 0.

We want to deposit $100 into account 1001. Suppose we place the file pointer to the first character of the old value.

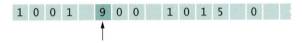

If we now simply write out the new value, the result is

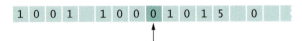

That is not working too well. The update is overwriting the space that separates the values.

In order to be able to update values in a file, you must give each value a *fixed* size that is sufficiently large. As a result, every record in the file has the same size. This has another advantage: It is then easy to skip quickly to, say, the 50th record, without having to read the first 49 records in. Just set the file pointer to 49 × the record size.

When storing numbers in a file with fixed record sizes, it is easier to access them in binary form, rather than text form. For that reason, the RandomAccessFile class stores binary data. The readInt and writeInt methods read and write integers as four-byte quantities. The readDouble and writeDouble methods process double-precision floating-point numbers as eight-byte quantities.

```
double x = f.readDouble();
f.writeDouble(x);
```

If we save the account number as an integer and the balance as a double value, then each bank account record consists of 12 bytes: 4 bytes for the integer and 8 bytes for the double-precision floating-point value.

Now that we have determined the file layout, we can implement our random access file methods. In the program at the end of this section, we use a BankData class to translate between the random access file format and bank account objects. The size method determines the total number of accounts by dividing the file length by the size of a record.

```java
public int size() throws IOException
{
    return (int) (file.length() / RECORD_SIZE);
}
```

To read the nth account in the file, the read method positions the file pointer to the offset n * RECORD_SIZE, then reads the data, and constructs a bank account object:

```java
public BankAccount read(int n) throws IOException
{
    file.seek(n * RECORD_SIZE);
    int accountNumber = file.readInt();
    double balance = file.readDouble();
    return new BankAccount(accountNumber, balance);
}
```

Writing an account works the same way:

```java
public void write(int n, BankAccount account) throws IOException
{
    file.seek(n * RECORD_SIZE);
    file.writeInt(account.getAccountNumber());
    file.writeDouble(account.getBalance());
}
```

The test program asks the user to enter an account number and an amount to deposit. If the account does not currently exist, it is created. The money is deposited, and then the user can choose to continue or quit. The bank data are saved and reloaded when the program is run again.

ch19/random/BankSimulator.java

```java
1   import java.io.IOException;
2   import java.util.Scanner;
3
4   /**
5       This program demonstrates random access. You can access
6       existing accounts and deposit money, or create new accounts.
7       The accounts are saved in a random access file.
8   */
9   public class BankSimulator
10  {
11      public static void main(String[] args) throws IOException
12      {
13          Scanner in = new Scanner(System.in);
14          BankData data = new BankData();
15          try
16          {
17              data.open("bank.dat");
18
19              boolean done = false;
20              while (!done)
21              {
22                  System.out.print("Account number: ");
23                  int accountNumber = in.nextInt();
24                  System.out.print("Amount to deposit: ");
25                  double amount = in.nextDouble();
26
```

```
27              int position = data.find(accountNumber);
28              BankAccount account;
29              if (position >= 0)
30              {
31                 account = data.read(position);
32                 account.deposit(amount);
33                 System.out.println("New balance: " + account.getBalance());
34              }
35              else // Add account
36              {
37                 account = new BankAccount(accountNumber, amount);
38                 position = data.size();
39                 System.out.println("Adding new account.");
40              }
41              data.write(position, account);
42
43              System.out.print("Done? (Y/N) ");
44              String input = in.next();
45              if (input.equalsIgnoreCase("Y")) done = true;
46           }
47        }
48        finally
49        {
50           data.close();
51        }
52     }
53 }
```

ch19/random/BankData.java

```
1  import java.io.IOException;
2  import java.io.RandomAccessFile;
3
4  /**
5     This class is a conduit to a random access file
6     containing savings account data.
7  */
8  public class BankData
9  {
10    private RandomAccessFile file;
11
12    public static final int INT_SIZE = 4;
13    public static final int DOUBLE_SIZE = 8;
14    public static final int RECORD_SIZE = INT_SIZE + DOUBLE_SIZE;
15
16    /**
17       Constructs a BankData object that is not associated with a file.
18    */
19    public BankData()
20    {
21       file = null;
22    }
23
24    /**
25       Opens the data file.
26       @param filename the name of the file containing savings
27       account information
28    */
```

```java
29  public void open(String filename)
30          throws IOException
31  {
32      if (file != null) file.close();
33      file = new RandomAccessFile(filename, "rw");
34  }
35
36  /**
37      Gets the number of accounts in the file.
38      @return the number of accounts
39  */
40  public int size()
41          throws IOException
42  {
43      return (int) (file.length() / RECORD_SIZE);
44  }
45
46  /**
47      Closes the data file.
48  */
49  public void close()
50          throws IOException
51  {
52      if (file != null) file.close();
53      file = null;
54  }
55
56  /**
57      Reads a savings account record.
58      @param n the index of the account in the data file
59      @return a savings account object initialized with the file data
60  */
61  public BankAccount read(int n)
62          throws IOException
63  {
64      file.seek(n * RECORD_SIZE);
65      int accountNumber = file.readInt();
66      double balance = file.readDouble();
67      return new BankAccount(accountNumber, balance);
68  }
69
70  /**
71      Finds the position of a bank account with a given number.
72      @param accountNumber the number to find
73      @return the position of the account with the given number,
74      or –1 if there is no such account
75  */
76  public int find(int accountNumber)
77          throws IOException
78  {
79      for (int i = 0; i < size(); i++)
80      {
81          file.seek(i * RECORD_SIZE);
82          int a = file.readInt();
83          if (a == accountNumber) // Found a match
84              return i;
85      }
86      return -1; // No match in the entire file
87  }
```

```
88
89      /**
90          Writes a savings account record to the data file.
91          @param n the index of the account in the data file
92          @param account the account to write
93      */
94      public void write(int n, BankAccount account)
95              throws IOException
96      {
97          file.seek(n * RECORD_SIZE);
98          file.writeInt(account.getAccountNumber());
99          file.writeDouble(account.getBalance());
100     }
101 }
```

Program Run

```
Account number: 1001
Amount to deposit: 100
Adding new account.
Done? (Y/N) N
Account number: 1018
Amount to deposit: 200
Adding new account.
Done? (Y/N) N
Account number: 1001
Amount to deposit: 1000
New balance: 1100.0
Done? (Y/N) Y
```

SELF CHECK

6. Why doesn't System.out support random access?

7. What is the advantage of the binary format for storing numbers? What is the disadvantage?

19.4 Object Streams

In the program of Section 19.3, you read BankAccount objects by reading each input value separately. Actually, there is an easier way. The ObjectOutputStream class can save entire objects out to disk, and the ObjectInputStream class can read them back in. Objects are saved in binary format; hence, you use streams and not writers.

For example, you can write a BankAccount object to a file as follows:

```
BankAccount b = . . .;
ObjectOutputStream out = new ObjectOutputStream(
    new FileOutputStream("bank.dat"));
out.writeObject(b);
```

> Use object streams to save and restore all instance variables of an object automatically.

The object output stream automatically saves all instance variables of the object to the stream. When reading the object back in, you use the readObject method of the ObjectInputStream class. That method returns an Object reference, so you need to remember the types of the objects that you saved and use a cast:

```
ObjectInputStream in = new ObjectInputStream(
    new FileInputStream("bank.dat"));
BankAccount b = (BankAccount) in.readObject();
```

The `readObject` method can throw a `ClassNotFoundException`—it is a checked exception, so you need to catch or declare it.

You can do even better than that, though. You can store a whole bunch of objects in an array list or array, or inside another object, and then save that object:

```
ArrayList<BankAccount> a = new ArrayList<BankAccount>();
// Now add many BankAccount objects into a
out.writeObject(a);
```

With one instruction, you can save the array list and *all the objects that it references*. You can read all of them back with one instruction:

```
ArrayList<BankAccount> a = (ArrayList<BankAccount>) in.readObject();
```

Of course, if the Bank class contains an `ArrayList` of bank accounts, then you can simply save and restore a `Bank` object. Then its array list, and all the `BankAccount` objects that it contains, are automatically saved and restored as well. The sample program at the end of this section uses this approach.

This is a truly amazing capability that is highly recommended.

To place objects of a particular class into an object stream, the class must implement the `Serializable` interface. That interface has no methods, so there is no effort involved in implementing it:

```
class BankAccount implements Serializable
{
    . . .
}
```

Objects saved to an object stream must belong to classes that implement the Serializable interface.

The process of saving objects to a stream is called **serialization** because each object is assigned a serial number on the stream. If the same object is saved twice, only the serial number is written out the second time. When the objects are read back in, duplicate serial numbers are restored as references to the same object.

Here is a sample program that puts serialization to work. The `BankAccount` and `Bank` classes are identical to those of Chapter 7, except that they both implement the `Serializable` interface. Run the program several times. Whenever the program exits, it saves the `Bank` object (and all bank account objects that the bank contains) into a file `bank.dat`. When the program starts again, the file is loaded, and the changes from the preceding program run are automatically reflected. However, if the file is missing (either because the program is running for the first time, or because the file was erased), then the program starts with a new bank.

ch19/serial/SerialDemo.java

```java
1  import java.io.File;
2  import java.io.IOException;
3  import java.io.FileInputStream;
4  import java.io.FileOutputStream;
5  import java.io.ObjectInputStream;
6  import java.io.ObjectOutputStream;
7
```

```
8  /**
9      This program demonstrates serialization of a Bank object.
10     If a file with serialized data exists, then it is loaded.
11     Otherwise the program starts with a new bank.
12     Bank accounts are added to the bank. Then the bank
13     object is saved.
14  */
15  public class SerialDemo
16  {
17     public static void main(String[] args)
18           throws IOException, ClassNotFoundException
19     {
20        Bank firstBankOfJava;
21
22        File f = new File("bank.dat");
23        if (f.exists())
24        {
25           ObjectInputStream in = new ObjectInputStream(
26                 new FileInputStream(f));
27           firstBankOfJava = (Bank) in.readObject();
28           in.close();
29        }
30        else
31        {
32           firstBankOfJava = new Bank();
33           firstBankOfJava.addAccount(new BankAccount(1001, 20000));
34           firstBankOfJava.addAccount(new BankAccount(1015, 10000));
35        }
36
37        // Deposit some money
38        BankAccount a = firstBankOfJava.find(1001);
39        a.deposit(100);
40        System.out.println(a.getAccountNumber() + ":" + a.getBalance());
41        a = firstBankOfJava.find(1015);
42        System.out.println(a.getAccountNumber() + ":" + a.getBalance());
43
44        ObjectOutputStream out = new ObjectOutputStream(
45              new FileOutputStream(f));
46        out.writeObject(firstBankOfJava);
47        out.close();
48     }
49  }
```

Program Run

```
1001:20100.0
1015:10000.0
```

Second Program Run

```
1001:20200.0
1015:10000.0
```

SELF CHECK

8. Why is it easier to save an object with an `ObjectOutputStream` than a `RandomAccessFile`?

9. What do you have to do to the `Coin` class so that its objects can be saved in an `ObjectOutputStream`?

How To 19.1   **Using Files and Streams**

Suppose your program needs to process data in files. This How To walks you through the steps that are involved.

Step 1   Select a data format.

The most important question you need to ask yourself concerns the format to use for saving your data.

- Does your program manipulate text, such as a plain text files? Then use readers and writers.
- Does your program update portions of a file? Then use random access.
- Does your program read or write individual bytes of binary data, such as image files or encrypted data? Then use streams.
- Does your program save and restore objects? Then use object streams.

Step 2   Use scanners and writers if you are processing text.

Use a scanner to read the input.

```
Scanner in = new Scanner(new File("input.txt"));
```

Then use the familiar methods next, nextInt, and so on. See Chapter 11 for details.
To write output, turn the file output stream into a PrintWriter:

```
PrintWriter out = new PrintWriter("output.txt");
```

Then use the familiar print and println methods:

```
out.println(text);
```

Step 3   Use the RandomAccessFile class if you need random access.

The RandomAccessFile class has methods for moving a file pointer to an arbitrary position:

```
file.seek(position);
```

You can then read or write individual bytes, characters, binary integers, and binary floating-point numbers.

Step 4   Use streams if you are processing bytes.

Use this loop to process input one byte at a time:

```
InputStream in = new FileInputStream("input.bin");
boolean done = false;
while (!done)
{
   int next = in.read();
   if (next = -1)
      done = true;
   else
   {
      byte b = (byte) next;
      Process input
   }
}
```

Similarly, write the output one byte at a time:

```
OutputStream out = new FileOutputStream("output.bin");
. . .
while (. . .)
{
```

```
          byte b = . . .;
          out.write(b);
      }
      out.close();
```

Use binary streams only if you are ready to process the input one byte at a time. This makes sense for encryption/decryption or processing the pixels in an image. In other situations, binary streams are not appropriate.

Step 5 Use object streams if you are processing objects.

First go through your classes and tag them with implements Serializable. You don't need to add any additional methods.

Also go to the online API documentation to check that the library classes that you are using implement the Serializable interface. Fortunately, many of them do. In particular, String and ArrayList are serializable.

Next, put all the objects you want to save into a class (or an array or array list—but why not make another class containing that?).

Saving all program data is a trivial operation:

```
ProgramData data = . . .;
ObjectOutputStream out = new ObjectOutputStream(new FileOutputStream("program.dat"));
out.writeObject(data);
out.close();
```

Similarly, to restore the program data, you use an ObjectInputStream and call

```
ProgramData data = (ProgramData) in.readObject();
```

The readObject method can throw a ClassNotFoundException. You must catch or declare that exception.

Summary of Learning Objectives

Describe the Java class hierarchy for handling input and output.

- Streams access sequences of bytes. Readers and writers access sequences of characters.
- Use FileReader, FileWriter, FileInputStream, and FileOutputStream classes to read and write disk files.

Write programs that carry out input and output of binary data.

- The InputStream.read method returns an integer, either -1 to indicate end of input, or a byte between 0 and 255.
- The OutputStream.write method writes a single byte.

Describe random access and use the RandomAccessFile class.

- In sequential file access, a file is processed one byte at a time. Random access allows access at arbitrary locations in the file, without first reading the bytes preceding the access location.
- A file pointer is a position in a random access file. Because files can be very large, the file pointer is of type long.
- The RandomAccessFile class reads and writes numbers in binary form.

Use object streams to automatically read and write entire objects.

- Use object streams to save and restore all instance variables of an object automatically.
- Objects saved to an object stream must belong to classes that implement the `Serializable` interface.

Classes, Objects, and Methods Introduced in this Chapter

```
java.io.FileInputStream          java.io.RandomAccessFile
java.io.FileOutputStream            getFilePointer
java.io.FileReader                  length
java.io.FileWriter                  readChar
java.io.InputStream                 readDouble
   close                            readInt
   read                             seek
java.io.ObjectInputStream           writeChar
   readObject                       writeChars
java.io.ObjectOutputStream          writeDouble
   writeObject                      writeInt
java.io.OutputStream             java.io.Serializable
   close
   write
```

Media Resources

www.wiley.com/ college/ horstmann

- Lab Exercises
- Practice Quiz
- Code Completion Exercises

Review Exercises

★   **R19.1** What is the difference between a stream and a reader?

★   **R19.2** How can you open a file for both reading and writing in Java?

★★   **R19.3** What happens if you try to write to a file reader? What happens if you try to write to a random access file that you opened only for reading? Try it out if you don't know.

★   **R19.4** How can you break the Caesar cipher? That is, how can you read a document that was encrypted with the Caesar cipher, even though you don't know the key?

★★   **R19.5** What happens if you try to save an object that is not serializable in an object stream? Try it out and report your results.

★★   **R19.6** Of the classes in the `java.lang` and `java.io` packages that you have encountered in this book, which implement the `Serializable` interface?

★★ **R19.7** Why is it better to save an entire `ArrayList` to an object stream instead of programming a loop that writes each element?

★ **R19.8** What is the difference between sequential access and random access?

★ **R19.9** What is the file pointer in a file? How do you move it? How do you tell the current position? Why is it a long integer?

★ **R19.10** How do you move the file pointer to the first byte of a file? To the last byte? To the exact middle of the file?

★★ **R19.11** What happens if you try to move the file pointer past the end of a file? Can you move the file pointer of `System.in`? Try it out and report your results.

Programming Exercises

★★ **P19.1** *Random monoalphabet cipher.* The Caesar cipher, which shifts all letters by a fixed amount, is far too easy to crack. Here is a better idea. For the key, don't use numbers but words. Suppose the key word is FEATHER. Then first remove duplicate letters, yielding FEATHR, and append the other letters of the alphabet in reverse order. Now encrypt the letters as follows:

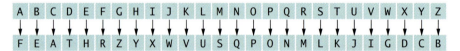

Write a program that encrypts or decrypts a file using this cipher. The key word is specified with the -k command line option. The -d command line option specifies decryption. For example,

```
java Encryptor -d -k FEATHER encrypt.txt output.txt
```

decrypts a file using the keyword FEATHER. It is an error not to supply a keyword.

★ **P19.2** *Letter frequencies.* If you encrypt a file using the cipher of Exercise P19.1, it will have all of its letters jumbled up, and will look as if there is no hope of decrypting it without knowing the keyword. Guessing the keyword seems hopeless, too. There are just too many possible keywords. However, someone who is trained in decryption will be able to break this cipher in no time at all. The average letter frequencies of English letters are well known. The most common letter is E, which occurs about 13% of the time. Here are the average frequencies of the letters.

A	8%	H	4%	O	7%	V	1%
B	<1%	I	7%	P	3%	W	2%
C	3%	J	<1%	Q	<1%	X	<1%
D	4%	K	<1%	R	8%	Y	2%
E	13%	L	4%	S	6%	Z	<1%
F	3%	M	3%	T	9%		
G	2%	N	8%	U	3%		

Write a program that reads an input file and prints the letter frequencies in that file. Such a tool will help a code breaker. If the most frequent letters in an encrypted file are H and K, then there is an excellent chance that they are the encryptions of E and T.

★★   **P19.3**   *Vigenère cipher.* The trouble with a monoalphabetic cipher is that it can be easily broken by frequency analysis. The so-called Vigenère cipher overcomes this problem by encoding a letter into one of several cipher letters, depending on its position in the input document. Choose a keyword, for example TIGER. Then encode the first letter of the input text like this:

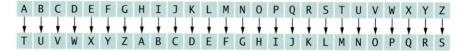

That is, the encoded alphabet is just the regular alphabet shifted to start at T, the first letter of the keyword TIGER. The second letter is encrypted according to the map

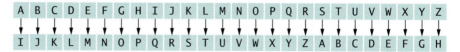

The third, fourth, and fifth letters in the input text are encrypted using the alphabet sequences beginning with characters G, E, and R. Because the key is only five letters long, the sixth letter of the input text is encrypted in the same way as the first.

Write a program that encrypts or decrypts an input text according to this cipher. Use command line arguments as in Exercise P19.1.

★★   **P19.4**   *Playfair cipher.* Another way of thwarting a simple letter frequency analysis of an encrypted text is to encrypt pairs of letters together. A simple scheme to do this is the Playfair cipher. You pick a keyword and remove duplicate letters from it. Then you fill the keyword, and the remaining letters of the alphabet, into a 5 × 5 square. (Because there are only 25 squares, I and J are considered the same letter.) Here is such an arrangement with the keyword PLAYFAIR:

```
P L A Y F
I R B C D
E G H K M
N O Q S T
U V W X Z
```

To encrypt a letter pair, say AT, look at the rectangle with corners A and T:

```
P L A Y F
I R B C D
E G H K M
N O Q S T
U V W X Z
```

The encoding of this pair is formed by looking at the other two corners of the rectangle—in this case, FQ. If both letters happen to be in the same row or column, such as GO, simply swap the two letters. Decryption is done in the same way.

Write a program that encrypts or decrypts an input text according to this cipher. Use command line arguments as in Exercise P19.1.

★   **P19.5**   Write a program that opens a binary file and prints all ASCII characters from that file, that is, all bytes with values between 32 and 126. Print a new line after every 64 characters. What happens when you use your program with word processor documents? With Java class files?

★★ **P19.6** Modify the `BankSimulator` program so that it is possible to delete an account. To delete a record from the data file, fill the record with zeroes.

★★ **P19.7** The data file in Exercise P19.6 may end up with many deleted records that take up space. Write a program that compacts such a file, moving all active records to the beginning and shortening the file length. *Hint:* Use the `setLength` method of the `RandomAccessFile` class to truncate the file length. Look up the method's behavior in the API documentation.

★★★ **P19.8** Write a program that manipulates a database of product records. Records are stored in a binary file. Each record consists of these items:
- Product name: 30 characters at two bytes each = 60 bytes
- Price: one `double` = 8 bytes
- Quantity: one `int` = 8 bytes

The program should allow the user to add a record, find a record that matches a product name, and change the price and quantity of a product by a given amount.

★★ **P19.9** Enhance the `SerialDemo` program to demonstrate that it can save and restore a bank that contains a mixture of savings and checking accounts.

★★G **P19.10** Implement a graphical user interface for the `BankSimulator` program in Section 19.3.

★★G **P19.11** This exercise is a continuation of Exercise P10.14. When the program starts, it should look to see whether a file is present that contains a serialized array of vehicles. If so, it redisplays them. Otherwise, it generates random vehicles, writes them to a file, and displays them.

Programming Projects

Project 19.1 Write a graphical application in which the user clicks on a panel to add shapes (rectangles, ellipses, cars, etc.) at the mouse click location. The shapes are stored in an array list. When the user selects File->Save from the menu, save the selection of shapes in a file. When the user selects File->Open, load in a file. Use serialization.

Project 19.2 Write a toolkit that helps a cryptographer decrypt a file that was encrypted using a monoalphabet cipher. A monoalphabet cipher encrypts each character separately. Examples are the Caesar cipher and the cipher in Exercise P19.1. Analyze the letter frequencies as in Exercise P19.2. Use brute force to try all Caesar cipher keys, and check the output against a dictionary file. Allow the cryptographer to enter some substitutions and show the resulting text, with the unknown characters represented as ?. Try out your toolkit by decrypting files that you get from your classmates.

Answers to Self-Check Questions

1. Image data is stored in a binary format—try loading an image file into a text editor, and you won't see much text. Therefore, you should use an `InputStream`.

2. For HTML files, a reader would be useful. But URLs can also point to binary files, such as `http://bigjava.com/cover.jpg`.

3. It returns a special value of `-1` to indicate that no more input is available. If the return type had been `byte`, no special value would have been available that is distinguished from a legal data value.

4. It is `"Hello, World!"`, encrypted with a key of 3.

5. Yes—the program uses streams and encrypts each byte.

6. Suppose you print something, and then you call `seek(0)`, and print again to the same location. It would be difficult to reflect that behavior in the console window.

7. Advantage: The numbers use a fixed amount of storage space, making it possible to change their values without affecting surrounding data. Disadvantage: You cannot read a binary file with a text editor.

8. You can save the entire object with a single `writeObject` call. With a `RandomAccessFile`, you have to save each instance variable separately.

9. Add `implements Serializable` to the class definition.

Multithreading

CHAPTER GOALS

- To understand how multiple threads can execute in parallel
- To learn how to implement threads
- To understand race conditions and deadlocks
- To avoid corruption of shared objects by using locks and conditions
- To be able to use threads for programming animations

It is often useful for a program to carry out two or more tasks at the same time. For example, a web browser can load multiple images on a web page at the same time. Or an animation program can show moving figures, with separate tasks computing the positions of each separate figure.

In this chapter, you will see how you can implement this behavior by running tasks in multiple threads, and how you can ensure that the tasks access shared data in a controlled fashion.

CHAPTER CONTENTS

20.1 Running Threads

A thread is a
program unit that
is executed
concurrently with
other parts of
the program.

A **thread** is a program unit that is executed independently of other parts of the program. The Java virtual machine executes each thread for a short amount of time and then switches to another thread. This gives the illusion of executing the threads in parallel to each other. Actually, if a computer has multiple central processing units (CPUs), then some of the threads *can* run in parallel, one on each processor.

Running a thread is simple in Java—follow these steps:

1. Implement a class that implements the Runnable interface. That interface has a single method called run:

   ```
   public interface Runnable
   {
      void run();
   }
   ```

2. Place the code for your task into the run method of your class.

   ```
   public class MyRunnable implements Runnable
   {
      public void run()
      {
         Task statements
         . . .
      }
   }
   ```

3. Create an object of your subclass.

   ```
   Runnable r = new MyRunnable();
   ```

4. Construct a Thread object from the runnable object.

   ```
   Thread t = new Thread(r);
   ```

5. Call the start method to start the thread.

   ```
   t.start();
   ```

Let us look at a concrete example. We want to print ten greetings of "Hello, World!", one greeting every second. We will add a time stamp to each greeting to see when it is printed.

```
Mon Dec 28 23:12:03 PST 2009 Hello, World!
Mon Dec 28 23:12:04 PST 2009 Hello, World!
Mon Dec 28 23:12:05 PST 2009 Hello, World!
Mon Dec 28 23:12:06 PST 2009 Hello, World!
Mon Dec 28 23:12:07 PST 2009 Hello, World!
Mon Dec 28 23:12:08 PST 2009 Hello, World!
Mon Dec 28 23:12:09 PST 2009 Hello, World!
Mon Dec 28 23:12:10 PST 2009 Hello, World!
Mon Dec 28 23:12:11 PST 2009 Hello, World!
Mon Dec 28 23:12:12 PST 2009 Hello, World!
```

> The start method of the Thread class starts a new thread that executes the run method of the associated Runnable object.

Using the instructions for creating a thread, define a class that implements the Runnable interface:

```java
public class GreetingRunnable implements Runnable
{
   private String greeting;

   public GreetingRunnable(String aGreeting)
   {
      greeting = aGreeting;
   }

   public void run()
   {
      Task statements
      . . .
   }
}
```

The run method should loop ten times through the following task actions:

- Print a time stamp.
- Print the greeting.
- Wait a second.

Get the time stamp by constructing an object of the java.util.Date class. Its default constructor produces a date that is set to the current date and time.

```java
Date now = new Date();
System.out.println(now + " " + greeting);
```

To wait a second, we use the static sleep method of the Thread class. The call

```java
Thread.sleep(milliseconds)
```

> The sleep method puts the current thread to sleep for a given number of milliseconds.

puts the current thread to sleep for a given number of milliseconds. In our case, it should sleep for 1,000 milliseconds, or one second.

There is, however, one technical problem. Putting a thread to sleep is potentially risky—a thread might sleep for so long that it is no longer useful and should be terminated. As you will see in Section 20.2, to terminate a thread, you interrupt it. When a sleeping thread is interrupted, an InterruptedException is generated. You need to catch that exception in your run method and terminate the thread.

> When a thread is interrupted, the most common response is to terminate the run method.

The simplest way to handle thread interruptions is to give your run method the following form:

```java
public void run()
{
   try
   {
      Task statements
```

```
        }
        catch (InterruptedException exception)
        {
        }
        Clean up, if necessary
    }
```

We follow that structure in our example. Here is the complete code for our runnable class:

ch20/greeting/GreetingRunnable.java

```
 1   import java.util.Date;
 2
 3   /**
 4      A runnable that repeatedly prints a greeting.
 5   */
 6   public class GreetingRunnable implements Runnable
 7   {
 8      private static final int REPETITIONS = 10;
 9      private static final int DELAY = 1000;
10
11      private String greeting;
12
13      /**
14         Constructs the runnable object.
15         @param aGreeting the greeting to display
16      */
17      public GreetingRunnable(String aGreeting)
18      {
19         greeting = aGreeting;
20      }
21
22      public void run()
23      {
24         try
25         {
26            for (int i = 1; i <= REPETITIONS; i++)
27            {
28               Date now = new Date();
29               System.out.println(now + " " + greeting);
30               Thread.sleep(DELAY);
31            }
32         }
33         catch (InterruptedException exception)
34         {
35         }
36      }
37   }
```

To start a thread, first construct an object of the runnable class.

```
    Runnable r = new GreetingRunnable("Hello, World!");
```

Then construct a thread and call the start method.

```
    Thread t = new Thread(r);
    t.start();
```

Now a new thread is started, executing the code in the run method of your runnable class in parallel with any other threads in your program.

In the GreetingThreadRunner program, we start two threads: one that prints "Hello, World!" and one that prints "Goodbye, World!"

ch20/greeting/GreetingThreadRunner.java

```java
 1  /**
 2      This program runs two greeting threads in parallel.
 3  */
 4  public class GreetingThreadRunner
 5  {
 6     public static void main(String[] args)
 7     {
 8        GreetingRunnable r1 = new GreetingRunnable("Hello, World!");
 9        GreetingRunnable r2 = new GreetingRunnable("Goodbye, World!");
10        Thread t1 = new Thread(r1);
11        Thread t2 = new Thread(r2);
12        t1.start();
13        t2.start();
14     }
15  }
```

Program Run

```
Mon Dec 28 12:04:46 PST 2009 Hello, World!
Mon Dec 28 12:04:46 PST 2009 Goodbye, World!
Mon Dec 28 12:04:47 PST 2009 Hello, World!
Mon Dec 28 12:04:47 PST 2009 Goodbye, World!
Mon Dec 28 12:04:48 PST 2009 Hello, World!
Mon Dec 28 12:04:48 PST 2009 Goodbye, World!
Mon Dec 28 12:04:49 PST 2009 Hello, World!
Mon Dec 28 12:04:49 PST 2009 Goodbye, World!
Mon Dec 28 12:04:50 PST 2009 Hello, World!
Mon Dec 28 12:04:50 PST 2009 Goodbye, World!
Mon Dec 28 12:04:51 PST 2009 Hello, World!
Mon Dec 28 12:04:51 PST 2009 Goodbye, World!
Mon Dec 28 12:04:52 PST 2009 Goodbye, World!
Mon Dec 28 12:04:52 PST 2009 Hello, World!
Mon Dec 28 12:04:53 PST 2009 Hello, World!
Mon Dec 28 12:04:53 PST 2009 Goodbye, World!
Mon Dec 28 12:04:54 PST 2009 Hello, World!
Mon Dec 28 12:04:54 PST 2009 Goodbye, World!
Mon Dec 28 12:04:55 PST 2009 Hello, World!
Mon Dec 28 12:04:55 PST 2009 Goodbye, World!
```

The thread scheduler runs each thread for a short amount of time, called a time slice.

Because both threads are running in parallel, the two message sets are interleaved. However, if you look closely, you will find that the two threads aren't *exactly* interleaved. Sometimes, the second thread seems to jump ahead of the first thread. This shows an important characteristic of threads. The thread scheduler gives no guarantee about the order in which threads are executed. Each thread runs for a short amount of time, called a **time slice**. Then the scheduler activates another thread. However, there will always be slight variations in running times, especially when calling operating system services (such as input and output). Thus, you should expect that the order in which each thread gains control is somewhat random.

SELF CHECK

1. What happens if you change the call to the `sleep` method in the `run` method to `Thread.sleep(1)`?

2. What would be the result of the program if the `main` method called

   ```
   r1.run();
   r2.run();
   ```

   instead of starting threads?

Quality Tip 20.1

Use the `Runnable` Interface

In Java, you can define the task statements of a thread in two ways. As you have seen already, you can place the statements into the `run` method of a class that implements the `Runnable` interface. Then you use an object of that class to construct a `Thread` object. You can also form a subclass of the `Thread` class, and place the task statements into the `run` method of your subclass:

```java
public class MyThread extends Thread
{
   public void run()
   {
      Task statements
      . . .
   }
}
```

Then you construct an object of the subclass and call the `start` method:

```java
Thread t = new MyThread();
t.start();
```

This approach is marginally easier than using a `Runnable`, and it also seems quite intuitive. However, if a program needs a large number of threads, or if a program executes in a resource-constrained device, such as a cell phone, it can be quite expensive to construct a separate thread for each task. Special Topic 20.1 on page 806 shows how to use a *thread pool* to overcome this problem. A thread pool uses a small number of threads to execute a larger number of runnables.

The `Runnable` interface is designed to encapsulate the concept of a sequence of statements that can run in parallel with other tasks, without equating it with the concept of a thread, a potentially expensive resource that is managed by the operating system.

Special Topic 20.1

Thread Pools

A program that creates a huge number of short-lived threads can be inefficient. Threads are managed by the operating system, and there is a space and run-time cost for each thread that is created. This cost can be reduced by using a *thread pool*. A thread pool creates a number of threads and keeps them alive. When you add a `Runnable` object to the thread pool, the next idle thread executes its run method.

For example, the following statements submit two runnables to a thread pool:

```java
Runnable r1 = new GreetingRunnable("Hello, World!");
Runnable r2 = new GreetingRunnable("Goodbye, World!");
ExecutorService pool = Executors.newFixedThreadPool(MAX_THREADS);
```

```
pool.execute(r1);
pool.execute(r2);
```

If many runnables are submitted for execution, then the pool may not have enough threads available. In that case, some runnables are placed in a queue until a thread is idle. As a result, the cost of creating threads is minimized. However, the runnables that are run by a particular thread are executed sequentially, not in parallel.

Thread pools are particularly important for server programs, such as database and web servers, that repeatedly execute requests from multiple clients. Rather than spawning a new thread for each request, the requests are implemented as runnable objects and submitted to a thread pool.

20.2 Terminating Threads

A thread terminates when its run method terminates.

A thread terminates when the run method of the associated runnable object returns. This is the normal way of terminating a thread—implement the run method so that it returns when it determines that no more work needs to be done.

However, sometimes you need to terminate a running thread. For example, you may have several threads trying to find a solution to a problem. As soon as the first one has succeeded, you may want to terminate the other ones. In the initial release of the Java library, the Thread class had a stop method to terminate a thread. However, that method is now *deprecated*—computer scientists have found that stopping a thread can lead to dangerous situations when multiple threads share objects. (We will discuss access to shared objects in Section 20.3.) Instead of simply stopping a thread, you should notify the thread that it should be terminated. The thread needs to cooperate, by releasing any resources that it is currently using and doing any other required cleanup. In other words, a thread should be in charge of terminating itself.

To notify a thread that it should clean up and terminate, you use the interrupt method.

```
t.interrupt();
```

The run method can check whether its thread has been interrupted by calling the interrupted method.

This method does not actually cause the thread to terminate—it merely sets a boolean variable in the thread data structure.

The run method can check whether that flag has been set, by calling the static interrupted method. In that case, it should do any necessary cleanup and exit. For example, the run method of the GreetingRunnable could check for interruptions at the beginning of each loop iteration:

```
public void run()
{
    for (int i = 1;
            i <= REPETITIONS && !Thread.interrupted();
            i++)
    {
        Do work
    }
    Clean up
}
```

However, if a thread is sleeping, it can't execute code that checks for interruptions. Therefore, the sleep method is terminated with an InterruptedException whenever a sleeping thread is interrupted. The `sleep` method also throws an `InterruptedException` when it is called in a thread that is already interrupted. If your `run` method calls `sleep` in each loop iteration, simply use the `InterruptedException` to find out whether the thread is terminated. The easiest way to do that is to surround the entire work portion of the `run` method with a try block, like this:

```java
public void run()
{
   try
   {
      for (int i = 1; i <= REPETITIONS; i++)
      {
         Do work
         Sleep
      }
   }
   catch (InterruptedException exception)
   {
   }
   Clean up
}
```

Strictly speaking, there is nothing in the Java language specification that says that a thread must terminate when it is interrupted. It is entirely up to the thread what it does when it is interrupted. Interrupting is a general mechanism for getting the thread's attention, even when it is sleeping. However, in this chapter, we will always terminate a thread that is being interrupted.

SELF CHECK

3. Suppose a web browser uses multiple threads to load the images on a web page. Why should these threads be terminated when the user hits the "Back" button?

4. Consider the following runnable.

```java
public class MyRunnable implements Runnable
{
   public void run()
   {
      try
      {
         System.out.println(1);
         Thread.sleep(1000);
         System.out.println(2);
      }
      catch (InterruptedException exception)
      {
         System.out.println(3);
      }
      System.out.println(4);
   }
}
```

Suppose a thread with this runnable is started and immediately interrupted.

```java
Thread t = new Thread(new MyRunnable());
t.start();
t.interrupt();
```

What output is produced?

Quality Tip 20.2

Check for Thread Interruptions in the run Method of a Thread

By convention, a thread should terminate itself (or at least act in some other well-defined way) when it is interrupted. You should implement your threads to follow this convention.

Simply put the thread action inside a try block that catches the InterruptedException. That exception occurs when your thread is interrupted while it is not running, for example inside a call to sleep. When you catch the exception, do any required cleanup and exit the run method.

Some programmers don't understand the purpose of the InterruptedException and, out of ignorance and desperation, muzzle it by surrounding only the call to sleep inside a try block.

```java
public void run()
{
   while (. . .)
   {
      . . .
      try
      {
         Thread.sleep(delay);
      }
      catch (InterruptedException exception) {} // DON'T
      . . .
   }
}
```

Don't do that. If you do, users of your thread class can't get your thread's attention by interrupting it. It is just as easy to place the entire thread action inside a single try block. Then interrupting the thread terminates the thread action.

```java
public void run()
{
   try
   {
      while (. . .)
      {
         . . .
         Thread.sleep(delay);
         . . .
      }
   }
   catch (InterruptedException exception) {} // OK
}
```

20.3 Race Conditions

When threads share access to a common object, they can conflict with each other. To demonstrate the problems that can arise, we will investigate a sample program in which multiple threads manipulate a bank account.

We construct a bank account that starts out with a zero balance. We create two sets of threads:

- Each thread in the first set repeatedly deposits $100.
- Each thread in the second set repeatedly withdraws $100.

Here is the run method of the DepositRunnable class:

```java
public void run()
{
   try
   {
      for (int i = 1; i <= count; i++)
      {
         account.deposit(amount);
         Thread.sleep(DELAY);
      }
   }
   catch (InterruptedException exception)
   {
   }
}
```

The WithdrawRunnable class is similar—it withdraws money instead.

The deposit and withdraw methods of the BankAccount class have been modified to print messages that show what is happening. For example, here is the code for the deposit method:

```java
public void deposit(double amount)
{
   System.out.print("Depositing " + amount);
   double newBalance = balance + amount;
   System.out.println(", new balance is " + newBalance);
   balance = newBalance;
}
```

You can find the complete source code at the end of this section.

Normally, the program output looks somewhat like this:

```
Depositing 100.0, new balance is 100.0
Withdrawing 100.0, new balance is 0.0
Depositing 100.0, new balance is 100.0
Depositing 100.0, new balance is 200.0
Withdrawing 100.0, new balance is 100.0
. . .
Withdrawing 100.0, new balance is 0.0
```

In the end, the balance should be zero. However, when you run this program repeatedly, you may sometimes notice messed-up output, like this:

```
Depositing 100.0Withdrawing 100.0, new balance is 100.0
, new balance is -100.0
```

And if you look at the last line of the output, you will notice that the final balance is not always zero. Clearly, something problematic is happening.

You may have to try the program several times to see this effect.

Here is a scenario that explains how a problem can occur.

1. A deposit thread executes the lines

```java
System.out.print("Depositing " + amount);
double newBalance = balance + amount;
```

   in the deposit method of the BankAccount class. The value of the balance variable is still 0, and the value of the newBalance local variable is 100.

2. Immediately afterward, the deposit thread reaches the end of its time slice, and the second thread gains control.

3. A withdraw thread calls the withdraw method, which prints a message and withdraws $100 from the balance variable. It is now −100.

4. The withdraw thread goes to sleep.

5. The deposit thread regains control and picks up where it was interrupted. It now executes the lines

```
System.out.println(", new balance is " + newBalance);
balance = newBalance;
```

The value of balance is now 100 (see Figure 1).

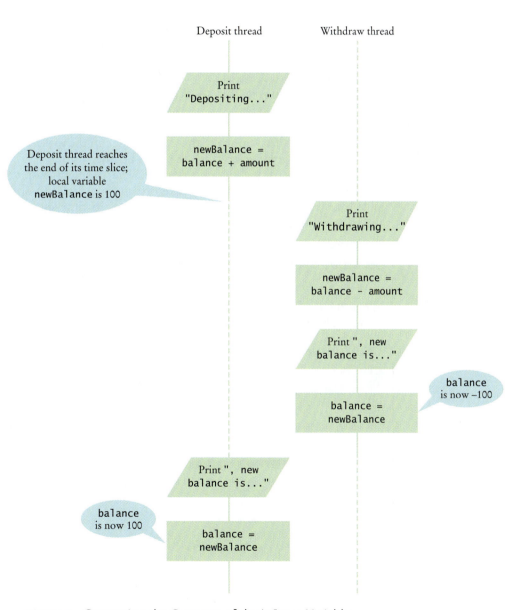

Figure 1 Corrupting the Contents of the balance Variable

Thus, not only are the messages interleaved, but the balance is wrong. The balance after a withdrawal and deposit should again be 0, not 100. Because the deposit method was interrupted, it used the *old* balance (before the withdrawal) to compute the value of its local newBalance variable. Later, when it was activated again, it used that newBalance value to overwrite the changed balance variable.

As you can see, each thread has its own local variables, but all threads share access to the balance instance variable. That shared access creates a problem. This problem is often called a **race condition**. All threads, in their race to complete their respective tasks, manipulate a shared variable, and the end result depends on which of them happens to win the race.

> A race condition occurs if the effect of multiple threads on shared data depends on the order in which the threads are scheduled.

You might argue that the reason for this problem is that we made it too easy to interrupt the balance computation. Suppose the code for the deposit method is reorganized like this:

```java
public void deposit(double amount)
{
    balance = balance + amount;
    System.out.print("Depositing " + amount
            + ", new balance is " + balance);
}
```

Suppose further that you make the same change in the withdraw method. If you run the resulting program, everything seems to be fine.

However, that is a *dangerous illusion*. The problem hasn't gone away; it has become much less frequent, and, therefore, more difficult to observe. It is still possible for the deposit method to reach the end of its time slice after it has computed the right-hand-side value

```java
balance + amount
```

but before it performs the assignment

```java
balance = the right-hand-side value
```

When the method regains control, it finally carries out the assignment, putting the wrong value into the balance variable.

ch20/unsynch/BankAccountThreadRunner.java

```java
1  /**
2     This program runs threads that deposit and withdraw
3     money from the same bank account.
4  */
5  public class BankAccountThreadRunner
6  {
7     public static void main(String[] args)
8     {
9        BankAccount account = new BankAccount();
10       final double AMOUNT = 100;
11       final int REPETITIONS = 100;
12       final int THREADS = 100;
13
14       for (int i = 1; i <= THREADS; i++)
15       {
16          DepositRunnable d = new DepositRunnable(
17                account, AMOUNT, REPETITIONS);
18          WithdrawRunnable w = new WithdrawRunnable(
19                account, AMOUNT, REPETITIONS);
20
```

```
21              Thread dt = new Thread(d);
22              Thread wt = new Thread(w);
23
24              dt.start();
25              wt.start();
26          }
27      }
28  }
```

ch20/unsynch/DepositRunnable.java

```java
1   /**
2       A deposit runnable makes periodic deposits to a bank account.
3   */
4   public class DepositRunnable implements Runnable
5   {
6      private static final int DELAY = 1;
7      private BankAccount account;
8      private double amount;
9      private int count;
10
11     /**
12         Constructs a deposit runnable.
13         @param anAccount the account into which to deposit money
14         @param anAmount the amount to deposit in each repetition
15         @param aCount the number of repetitions
16     */
17     public DepositRunnable(BankAccount anAccount, double anAmount,
18             int aCount)
19     {
20        account = anAccount;
21        amount = anAmount;
22        count = aCount;
23     }
24
25     public void run()
26     {
27        try
28        {
29           for (int i = 1; i <= count; i++)
30           {
31              account.deposit(amount);
32              Thread.sleep(DELAY);
33           }
34        }
35        catch (InterruptedException exception) {}
36     }
37  }
```

ch20/unsynch/WithdrawRunnable.java

```java
1   /**
2       A withdraw runnable makes periodic withdrawals from a bank account.
3   */
4   public class WithdrawRunnable implements Runnable
5   {
6      private static final int DELAY = 1;
7      private BankAccount account;
```

```java
 8     private double amount;
 9     private int count;
10
11     /**
12         Constructs a withdraw runnable.
13         @param anAccount the account from which to withdraw money
14         @param anAmount the amount to withdraw in each repetition
15         @param aCount the number of repetitions
16     */
17     public WithdrawRunnable(BankAccount anAccount, double anAmount,
18           int aCount)
19     {
20         account = anAccount;
21         amount = anAmount;
22         count = aCount;
23     }
24
25     public void run()
26     {
27         try
28         {
29            for (int i = 1; i <= count; i++)
30            {
31                account.withdraw(amount);
32                Thread.sleep(DELAY);
33            }
34         }
35         catch (InterruptedException exception) {}
36     }
37 }
```

ch20/unsynch/BankAccount.java

```java
 1 /**
 2     A bank account has a balance that can be changed by
 3     deposits and withdrawals.
 4 */
 5 public class BankAccount
 6 {
 7     private double balance;
 8
 9     /**
10         Constructs a bank account with a zero balance.
11     */
12     public BankAccount()
13     {
14         balance = 0;
15     }
16
17     /**
18         Deposits money into the bank account.
19         @param amount the amount to deposit
20     */
21     public void deposit(double amount)
22     {
23         System.out.print("Depositing " + amount);
24         double newBalance = balance + amount;
25         System.out.println(", new balance is " + newBalance);
26         balance = newBalance;
```

```
27        }
28
29        /**
30            Withdraws money from the bank account.
31            @param amount  the amount to withdraw
32        */
33        public void withdraw(double amount)
34        {
35            System.out.print("Withdrawing " + amount);
36            double newBalance = balance - amount;
37            System.out.println(", new balance is " + newBalance);
38            balance = newBalance;
39        }
40
41        /**
42            Gets the current balance of the bank account.
43            @return  the current balance
44        */
45        public double getBalance()
46        {
47            return balance;
48        }
49    }
```

Program Run

```
Depositing 100.0, new balance is 100.0
Withdrawing 100.0, new balance is 0.0
Depositing 100.0, new balance is 100.0
Withdrawing 100.0, new balance is 0.0
. . .
Withdrawing 100.0, new balance is 400.0
Depositing 100.0, new balance is 500.0
Withdrawing 100.0, new balance is 400.0
Withdrawing 100.0, new balance is 300.0
```

SELF CHECK

5. Give a scenario in which a race condition causes the bank balance to be −100 after one iteration of a deposit thread and a withdraw thread.

6. Suppose two threads simultaneously insert objects into a linked list. Using the implementation in Chapter 15, explain how the list can be damaged in the process.

20.4 Synchronizing Object Access

To solve problems such as the one that you observed in the preceding section, use a **lock object**. The lock object is used to control the threads that want to manipulate a shared resource.

The Java library defines a Lock interface and several classes that implement this interface. The ReentrantLock class is the most commonly used lock class, and the only one that we cover in this book. (**Locks** are a feature added in Java version 5.0. Earlier versions of Java have a lower-level facility for thread synchronization—see Special Topic 20.2 on page 823).

Typically, a lock object is added to a class whose methods access shared resources, like this:

```
public class BankAccount
{
    private Lock balanceChangeLock;
    . . .
    public BankAccount()
    {
        balanceChangeLock = new ReentrantLock();
        . . .
    }
}
```

All code that manipulates the shared resource is surrounded by calls to lock and unlock the lock object:

```
balanceChangeLock.lock();
Manipulate the shared resource
balanceChangeLock.unlock();
```

However, this sequence of statements has a potential flaw. If the code between the calls to lock and unlock throws an exception, the call to unlock never happens. This is a serious problem. After an exception, the current thread continues to hold the lock, and no other thread can acquire it. To overcome this problem, place the call to unlock into a finally clause:

```
balanceChangeLock.lock();
try
{
    Manipulate the shared resource
}
finally
{
    balanceChangeLock.unlock();
}
```

For example, here is the code for the deposit method:

```
public void deposit(double amount)
{
    balanceChangeLock.lock();
    try
    {
        System.out.print("Depositing " + amount);
        double newBalance = balance + amount;
        System.out.println(", new balance is " + newBalance);
        balance = newBalance;
    }
    finally
    {
        balanceChangeLock.unlock();
    }
}
```

By calling the lock method, a thread acquires a Lock object. Then no other thread can acquire the lock until the first thread releases the lock.

When a thread calls the lock method, it *owns the lock* until it calls the unlock method. If a thread calls lock while another thread owns the lock, it is temporarily deactivated. The thread scheduler periodically reactivates such a thread so that it can again try to acquire the lock. If the lock is still unavailable, the thread is again deactivated. Eventually, when the lock is available because the original thread unlocked it, the waiting thread can acquire the lock.

Figure 2
Visualizing Object Locks

One way to visualize this behavior is to imagine that the lock object is the lock of an old-fashioned telephone booth and the threads are people wanting to make telephone calls (see Figure 2). The telephone booth can accommodate only one person at one time. If the booth is empty, then the first person wanting to make a call goes inside and closes the door. If another person wants to make a call and finds the booth occupied, then the second person needs to wait until the first person leaves the booth. If multiple people want to gain access to the telephone booth, they all wait outside. They don't necessarily form an orderly queue; a randomly chosen person may gain access when the telephone booth becomes available again.

With the ReentrantLock class, a thread can call the lock method on a lock object that it already owns. This can happen if one method calls another, and both start by locking the same object. The thread gives up ownership if the unlock method has been called as often as the lock method.

By surrounding the code in both the deposit and withdraw methods with lock and unlock calls, we ensure that our program will always run correctly. Only one thread at a time can execute either method on a given object. Whenever a thread acquires the lock, it is guaranteed to execute the method to completion before the other thread gets a chance to modify the balance of the same bank account object.

SELF CHECK

7. If you construct two BankAccount objects, how many lock objects are created?

8. What happens if we omit the call unlock at the end of the deposit method?

20.5 Avoiding Deadlocks

A deadlock occurs if no thread can proceed because each thread is waiting for another to do some work first.

You can use lock objects to ensure that shared data are in a consistent state when several threads access them. However, locks can lead to another problem. It can happen that one thread acquires a lock and then waits for another thread to do some essential work. If that other thread is currently waiting to acquire the same lock, then neither of the two threads can proceed. Such a situation is called a **deadlock** or **deadly embrace**. Let's look at an example.

Suppose we want to disallow negative bank balances in our program. Here's a naive way of doing that. In the run method of the WithdrawRunnable class, we can check the balance before withdrawing money:

```
if (account.getBalance() >= amount)
    account.withdraw(amount);
```

This works if there is only a single thread running that withdraws money. But suppose we have multiple threads that withdraw money. Then the time slice of the current thread may expire after the check account.getBalance() >= amount passes, but before the withdraw method is called. If, in the interim, another thread withdraws more money, then the test was useless, and we still have a negative balance.

Clearly, the test should be moved inside the withdraw method. That ensures that the test for sufficient funds and the actual withdrawal cannot be separated. Thus, the withdraw method could look like this:

```
public void withdraw(double amount)
{
    balanceChangeLock.lock();
    try
    {
        while (balance < amount)
            Wait for the balance to grow
            . . .
    }
    finally
    {
        balanceChangeLock.unlock();
    }
}
```

But how can we wait for the balance to grow? We can't simply call sleep inside the withdraw method. If a thread sleeps after acquiring a lock, it blocks all other threads that want to use the same lock. In particular, no other thread can successfully execute the deposit method. Other threads will call deposit, but they will simply be blocked until the withdraw method exits. But the withdraw method doesn't exit until it has funds available. This is the deadlock situation that we mentioned earlier.

To overcome this problem, we use a **condition object**. Condition objects allow a thread to temporarily release a lock, so that another thread can proceed, and to regain the lock at a later time.

In the telephone booth analogy, suppose that the coin reservoir of the telephone is completely filled, so that no further calls can be made until a service technician removes the coins. You don't want the person in the booth to go to sleep with the door closed. Instead, think of the person leaving the booth temporarily. That gives another person (hopefully a service technician) a chance to enter the booth.

Each condition object belongs to a specific lock object. You obtain a condition object with the newCondition method of the Lock interface. For example,

```java
public class BankAccount
{
    private Lock balanceChangeLock;
    private Condition sufficientFundsCondition;
    . . .
    public BankAccount()
    {
        balanceChangeLock = new ReentrantLock();
        sufficientFundsCondition = balanceChangeLock.newCondition();
        . . .
    }
}
```

It is customary to give the condition object a name that describes the condition that you want to test (such as "sufficient funds"). You need to implement an appropriate test. For as long as the test is not fulfilled, call the await method on the condition object:

```java
public void withdraw(double amount)
{
    balanceChangeLock.lock();
    try
    {
        while (balance < amount)
            sufficientFundsCondition.await();
        . . .
    }
    finally
    {
        balanceChangeLock.unlock();
    }
}
```

Calling await on a condition object makes the current thread wait and allows another thread to acquire the lock object.

When a thread calls await, it is not simply deactivated in the same way as a thread that reaches the end of its time slice. Instead, it is in a blocked state, and it will not be activated by the thread scheduler until it is unblocked. To unblock, another thread must execute the signalAll method *on the same condition object*. The signalAll method unblocks all threads waiting on the condition. They can then compete with all other threads that are waiting for the lock object. Eventually, one of them will gain access to the lock, and it will exit from the await method.

In our situation, the deposit method calls signalAll:

```java
public void deposit(double amount)
{
    balanceChangeLock.lock();
    try
    {
        . . .
        sufficientFundsCondition.signalAll();
    }
    finally
    {
        balanceChangeLock.unlock();
    }
}
```

A waiting thread is blocked until another thread calls signalAll or signal on the condition object for which the thread is waiting.

The call to signalAll notifies the waiting threads that sufficient funds *may be* available, and that it is worth testing the loop condition again.

In the telephone booth analogy, the thread calling await corresponds to the person who enters the booth and finds that the phone doesn't work. That person then leaves the booth and waits outside, depressed, doing absolutely nothing, even as other people enter and leave the booth. The person knows it is pointless to try again. At some point, a service technician enters the booth, empties the coin reservoir, and shouts a signal. Now all the waiting people stop being depressed and again compete for the telephone booth.

There is also a signal method, which randomly picks just one thread that is waiting on the object and unblocks it. The signal method can be more efficient, but it is useful only if you know that *every* waiting thread can actually proceed. In general, you don't know that, and signal can lead to deadlocks. For that reason, we recommend that you always call signalAll.

The await method can throw an InterruptedException. The withdraw method propagates that exception, because it has no way of knowing what the thread that calls the withdraw method wants to do if it is interrupted.

With the calls to await and signalAll in the withdraw and deposit methods, we can launch any number of withdrawal and deposit threads without a deadlock. If you run the sample program, you will note that all transactions are carried out without ever reaching a negative balance.

ch20/synch/BankAccountThreadRunner.java

```java
1  /**
2      This program runs threads that deposit and withdraw
3      money from the same bank account.
4  */
5  public class BankAccountThreadRunner
6  {
7      public static void main(String[] args)
8      {
9          BankAccount account = new BankAccount();
10         final double AMOUNT = 100;
11         final int REPETITIONS = 100;
12         final int THREADS = 100;
13
14         for (int i = 1; i <= THREADS; i++)
15         {
16             DepositRunnable d = new DepositRunnable(
17                 account, AMOUNT, REPETITIONS);
18             WithdrawRunnable w = new WithdrawRunnable(
19                 account, AMOUNT, REPETITIONS);
20
21             Thread dt = new Thread(d);
22             Thread wt = new Thread(w);
23
24             dt.start();
25             wt.start();
26         }
27     }
28 }
```

ch20/synch/BankAccount.java

```java
1   import java.util.concurrent.locks.Condition;
2   import java.util.concurrent.locks.Lock;
3   import java.util.concurrent.locks.ReentrantLock;
4
5   /**
6      A bank account has a balance that can be changed by
7      deposits and withdrawals.
8   */
9   public class BankAccount
10  {
11     private double balance;
12     private Lock balanceChangeLock;
13     private Condition sufficientFundsCondition;
14
15     /**
16        Constructs a bank account with a zero balance.
17     */
18     public BankAccount()
19     {
20        balance = 0;
21        balanceChangeLock = new ReentrantLock();
22        sufficientFundsCondition = balanceChangeLock.newCondition();
23     }
24
25     /**
26        Deposits money into the bank account.
27        @param amount the amount to deposit
28     */
29     public void deposit(double amount)
30     {
31        balanceChangeLock.lock();
32        try
33        {
34           System.out.print("Depositing " + amount);
35           double newBalance = balance + amount;
36           System.out.println(", new balance is " + newBalance);
37           balance = newBalance;
38           sufficientFundsCondition.signalAll();
39        }
40        finally
41        {
42           balanceChangeLock.unlock();
43        }
44     }
45
46     /**
47        Withdraws money from the bank account.
48        @param amount the amount to withdraw
49     */
50     public void withdraw(double amount)
51           throws InterruptedException
52     {
53        balanceChangeLock.lock();
54        try
55        {
56           while (balance < amount)
57              sufficientFundsCondition.await();
58           System.out.print("Withdrawing " + amount);
```

```
59              double newBalance = balance - amount;
60              System.out.println(", new balance is " + newBalance);
61              balance = newBalance;
62          }
63          finally
64          {
65              balanceChangeLock.unlock();
66          }
67      }
68
69      /**
70          Gets the current balance of the bank account.
71          @return the current balance
72      */
73      public double getBalance()
74      {
75          return balance;
76      }
77  }
```

Program Run

```
Depositing 100.0, new balance is 100.0
Withdrawing 100.0, new balance is 0.0
Depositing 100.0, new balance is 100.0
Depositing 100.0, new balance is 200.0
. . .
Withdrawing 100.0, new balance is 100.0
Depositing 100.0, new balance is 200.0
Withdrawing 100.0, new balance is 100.0
Withdrawing 100.0, new balance is 0.0
```

SELF CHECK

9. What is the essential difference between calling `sleep` and `await`?

10. Why is the `sufficientFundsCondition` object an instance variable of the `BankAccount` class and not a local variable of the `withdraw` and `deposit` methods?

Common Error 20.1

Calling `await` Without Calling `signalAll`

It is intuitively clear when to call `await`. If a thread finds out that it can't do its job, it has to wait. But once a thread has called `await`, it temporarily gives up all hope and doesn't try again until some other thread calls `signalAll` on the condition object for which the thread is waiting. In the telephone booth analogy, if the service technician who empties the coin reservoir doesn't notify the waiting people, they'll wait forever.

A common error is to have threads call `await` without matching calls to `signalAll` by other threads. Whenever you call `await`, ask yourself which call to `signalAll` will signal your waiting thread.

Common Error 20.2

Calling `signalAll` Without Locking the Object

The thread that calls `signalAll` must own the lock that belongs to the condition object on which `signalAll` is called. Otherwise, an `IllegalMonitorStateException` is thrown.

In the telephone booth analogy, the service technician must shout the signal while *inside* the telephone booth after emptying the coin reservoir.

In practice, this should not be a problem. Remember that `signalAll` is called by a thread that has just changed the state of some shared data in a way that may benefit waiting threads. That change should be protected by a lock in any case. As long as you use a lock to protect all access to shared data, and you are in the habit of calling `signalAll` after every beneficial change, you won't run into problems. But if you use `signalAll` in a haphazard way, you may encounter the `IllegalMonitorStateException`.

Special Topic 20.2

Object Locks and Synchronized Methods

The `Lock` and `Condition` classes were added in Java version 5.0. They overcome limitations of the thread synchronization mechanism in earlier Java versions. In this note, we discuss that classic mechanism.

Every Java object has one built-in lock and one built-in condition variable. The lock works in the same way as a `ReentrantLock` object. However, to acquire the lock, you call a **synchronized method**.

You simply tag all methods that contain thread-sensitive code (such as the `deposit` and `withdraw` methods of the `BankAccount` class) with the `synchronized` reserved word.

```java
public class BankAccount
{
    public synchronized void deposit(double amount)
    {
        System.out.print("Depositing " + amount);
        double newBalance = balance + amount;
        System.out.println(", new balance is " + newBalance);
        balance = newBalance;
    }

    public synchronized void withdraw(double amount)
    {
        . . .
    }
    . . .
}
```

When a thread calls a synchronized method on a `BankAccount` object, it owns that object's lock until it returns from the method and thereby unlocks the object. When an object is locked by one thread, no other thread can enter a synchronized method for that object. When another thread makes a call to a synchronized method for that object, the other thread is automatically deactivated, and it needs to wait until the first thread has unlocked the object again.

In other words, the `synchronized` reserved word automatically implements the lock/try/finally/unlock idiom for the built-in lock.

The object lock has a single condition variable that you manipulate with the `wait`, `notifyAll`, and `notify` methods of the `Object` class. If you call `x.wait()`, the current thread is added to the set of threads that is waiting for the condition of the object x. Most commonly, you will call wait(), which makes the current thread wait on this. For example,

```
public synchronized void withdraw(double amount)
      throws InterruptedException
{
   while (balance < amount)
      wait();
   . . .
}
```

The call notifyAll() unblocks all threads that are waiting for this:

```
public synchronized void deposit(double amount)
{
   . . .
   notifyAll();
}
```

This classic mechanism is undeniably simpler than using explicit locks and condition variables. However, there are limitations. Each object lock has one condition variable, and you can't test whether another thread holds the lock. If these limitations are not a problem, by all means, go ahead and use the synchronized reserved word. If you need more control over threads, the Lock and Condition interfaces give you additional flexibility.

Special Topic 20.3

The Java Memory Model

In a computer with multiple CPUs, you have to be particularly careful when multiple threads access shared data. Because modern processors are quite a bit faster than RAM memory, each CPU has its own *memory cache* that stores copies of frequently used memory locations. If a thread changes shared data, another thread may not see the change until both processor caches are synchronized. The same effect can happen even on a computer with a single CPU—occasionally, memory values are cached in CPU registers.

The Java language specification contains a set of rules, called the *memory model*, that describes under which circumstances the virtual machine must ensure that changes to shared data are visible in other threads. One of the rules states the following:

- If a thread changes shared data and then releases a lock, and another thread acquires the same lock and reads the same data, then it is guaranteed to see the changed data.

However, if the first thread does not release a lock, then the virtual machine is not required to write cached data back to memory. Similarly, if the second thread does not acquire the lock, the virtual machine is not required to refresh its cache from memory.

Thus, you should always use locks or synchronized methods when you access data that is shared among multiple threads, even if you are not concerned about race conditions.

20.6 Case Study: Algorithm Animation

One popular use for thread programming is animation. A program that displays an animation shows different objects moving or changing in some way as time progresses. This is often achieved by launching one or more threads that compute how parts of the animation change.

You can use the Swing Timer class for simple animations without having to do any thread programming—see Exercise P20.12 for an example. However, more advanced animations are best implemented with threads.

In this section, you will see a particular kind of animation, namely the visualization of the steps of an algorithm. Algorithm animation is an excellent technique for gaining a better understanding of how an algorithm works. Many algorithms can be animated—type "Java algorithm animation" into your favorite web search engine, and you'll find lots of links to web pages with animations of various algorithms.

> Use a separate thread for running the algorithm that is being animated.

All algorithm animations have a similar structure. The algorithm runs in a separate thread that periodically updates an image of the current state of the algorithm and then pauses so that the user can view the image. After a short amount of time, the algorithm thread wakes up again and runs to the next point of interest in the algorithm. It then updates the image and pauses again. This sequence is repeated until the algorithm has finished.

Let's take the selection sort algorithm of Chapter 14 as an example. That algorithm sorts an array of values. It first finds the smallest element, by inspecting all elements in the array, and bringing the smallest element to the leftmost position. It then finds the smallest element among the remaining elements and brings it into the second position. It keeps going in that way. As the algorithm progresses, the sorted part of the array grows.

How can you visualize this algorithm? It is useful to show the part of the array that is already sorted in a different color. Also, we want to show how each step of the algorithm inspects another element in the unsorted part. That demonstrates why the selection sort algorithm is so slow—it first inspects all elements of the array, then all but one, and so on. If the array has n elements, the algorithm inspects

$$n + (n-1) + (n-2) + \cdots = n(n-1)/2 = O(n^2)$$

elements. To demonstrate that, we mark the currently visited element in red.

Thus, the algorithm state is described by three items:

- The array of values
- The size of the already sorted area
- The currently marked element

> The algorithm state needs to be safely accessed by the algorithm and painting threads.

This state is accessed by two threads: the thread that sorts the array and the thread that paints the frame. We use a lock to synchronize access to the shared state.

Finally, we add a component instance variable to the algorithm class and augment the constructor to set it. That instance variable is needed for repainting the component and finding out the dimensions of the component when drawing the algorithm state.

```java
public class SelectionSorter
{
    private JComponent component;
    . . .
    public SelectionSorter(int[] anArray, JComponent aComponent)
    {
        a = anArray;
        sortStateLock = new ReentrantLock();
        component = aComponent;
    }
}
```

Figure 3
A Step in the Animation of
the Selection Sort Algorithm

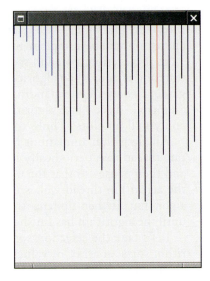

At each point of interest, the algorithm needs to pause so that the user can admire
the graphical output. We supply the pause method shown below, and call it at various
places in the algorithm. The pause method repaints the component and sleeps
for a small delay that is proportional to the number of steps involved.

```
public void pause(int steps) throws InterruptedException
{
   component.repaint();
   Thread.sleep(steps * DELAY);
}
```

We add a draw method to the algorithm class that can draw the current state of the
data structure, with the items of special interest highlighted. The draw method is specific
to the particular algorithm. This draw method draws the array elements as a
sequence of sticks in different colors. The already sorted portion is blue, the marked
position is red, and the remainder is black (see Figure 3).

```
public void draw(Graphics2D g2)
{
   sortStateLock.lock();
   try
   {
      int deltaX = component.getWidth() / a.length;
      for (int i = 0; i < a.length; i++)
      {
         if (i == markedPosition)
            g2.setColor(Color.RED);
         else if (i <= alreadySorted)
            g2.setColor(Color.BLUE);
         else
            g2.setColor(Color.BLACK);
         g2.draw(new Line2D.Double(i * deltaX, 0,
               i * deltaX, a[i]));
      }
   }
   finally
   {
```

```
                    sortStateLock.unlock();
            }
        }
```

You need to update the special positions as the algorithm progresses and pause the animation whenever something interesting happens. The pause should be proportional to the number of steps that are being executed. For a sorting algorithm, pause one unit for each visited array element.

Here is the minimumPosition method from Chapter 14, before the animation code is inserted.

```
public int minimumPosition(int from)
{
    int minPos = from;
    for (int i = from + 1; i < a.length; i++)
        if (a[i] < a[minPos]) minPos = i;
    return minPos;
}
```

After each iteration of the for loop, update the marked position of the algorithm state; then pause the program. To measure the cost of each step fairly, pause for two units of time, because two array elements were inspected.

```
public int minimumPosition(int from)
        throws InterruptedException
{
    int minPos = from;
    for (int i = from + 1; i < a.length; i++)
    {
        sortStateLock.lock();
        try
        {
            if (a[i] < a[minPos]) minPos = i;
            markedPosition = i;
        }
        finally
        {
            sortStateLock.unlock();
        }
        pause(2);
    }
    return minPos;
}
```

The sort method is augmented in the same way. You will find the code at the end of this section. This concludes the modification of the algorithm class. Let us now turn to the component class.

The component's paintComponent method calls the draw method of the algorithm object.

```
public class SelectionSortComponent extends JComponent
{
    private SelectionSorter sorter;
    . . .
    public void paintComponent(Graphics g)
    {
        if (sorter == null) return;
        Graphics2D g2 = (Graphics2D) g;
```

```
        sorter.draw(g2);
     }
   }
```

The `startAnimation` method constructs a `SelectionSorter` object, which supplies a new array and the `this` reference to the component that displays the sorted values. Then the method constructs a thread that calls the sorter's sort method.

```
public void startAnimation()
{
   int[] values = ArrayUtil.randomIntArray(30, 300);
   sorter = new SelectionSorter(values, this);

   class AnimationRunnable implements Runnable
   {
      public void run()
      {
         try
         {
            sorter.sort();
         }
         catch (InterruptedException exception)
         {
         }
      }
   }

   Runnable r = new AnimationRunnable();
   Thread t = new Thread(r);
   t.start();
}
```

The class for the program that displays the animation is at the end of this section. Run the program and the animation starts.

Exercise P20.7 asks you to animate the merge sort algorithm of Chapter 14. If you do that exercise, then start both programs and run them in parallel to see which algorithm is faster. Actually, you may find the result surprising. If you build fair delays into the merge sort animation to account for the copying from and to the temporary array, you will find that it doesn't perform all that well for small arrays. But if you increase the array size, then the advantage of the merge sort algorithm becomes clear.

ch20/animation/SelectionSortViewer.java

```
 1  import java.awt.BorderLayout;
 2  import javax.swing.JButton;
 3  import javax.swing.JFrame;
 4
 5  public class SelectionSortViewer
 6  {
 7     public static void main(String[] args)
 8     {
 9        JFrame frame = new JFrame();
10
11        final int FRAME_WIDTH = 300;
12        final int FRAME_HEIGHT = 400;
13
```

```
14         frame.setSize(FRAME_WIDTH, FRAME_HEIGHT);
15         frame.setDefaultCloseOperation(JFrame.EXIT_ON_CLOSE);
16
17         final SelectionSortComponent component
18             = new SelectionSortComponent();
19         frame.add(component, BorderLayout.CENTER);
20
21         frame.setVisible(true);
22         component.startAnimation();
23      }
24   }
```

ch20/animation/SelectionSortComponent.java

```
 1   import java.awt.Graphics;
 2   import java.awt.Graphics2D;
 3   import javax.swing.JComponent;
 4
 5   /**
 6      A component that displays the current state of the selection sort algorithm.
 7   */
 8   public class SelectionSortComponent extends JComponent
 9   {
10      private SelectionSorter sorter;
11
12      /**
13         Constructs the component.
14      */
15      public SelectionSortComponent()
16      {
17         int[] values = ArrayUtil.randomIntArray(30, 300);
18         sorter = new SelectionSorter(values, this);
19      }
20
21      public void paintComponent(Graphics g)
22      {
23         Graphics2D g2 = (Graphics2D)g;
24         sorter.draw(g2);
25      }
26
27      /**
28         Starts a new animation thread.
29      */
30      public void startAnimation()
31      {
32         class AnimationRunnable implements Runnable
33         {
34            public void run()
35            {
36               try
37               {
38                  sorter.sort();
39               }
40               catch (InterruptedException exception)
41               {
42               }
43            }
44         }
```

```
45
46        Runnable r = new AnimationRunnable();
47        Thread t = new Thread(r);
48        t.start();
49     }
50  }
```

ch20/animation/SelectionSorter.java

```
 1   import java.awt.Color;
 2   import java.awt.Graphics2D;
 3   import java.awt.geom.Line2D;
 4   import java.util.concurrent.locks.Lock;
 5   import java.util.concurrent.locks.ReentrantLock;
 6   import javax.swing.JComponent;
 7
 8   /**
 9       This class sorts an array, using the selection sort algorithm.
10   */
11   public class SelectionSorter
12   {
13      private static final int DELAY = 100;
14
15      private int[] a;
16      private Lock sortStateLock;
17
18      // The component is repainted when the animation is paused
19      private JComponent component;
20
21      // These instance variables are needed for drawing
22      private int markedPosition = -1;
23      private int alreadySorted = -1;
24
25      /**
26          Constructs a selection sorter.
27          @param anArray the array to sort
28          @param aComponent the component to be repainted when the animation
29          pauses
30      */
31      public SelectionSorter(int[] anArray, JComponent aComponent)
32      {
33         a = anArray;
34         sortStateLock = new ReentrantLock();
35         component = aComponent;
36      }
37
38      /**
39          Sorts the array managed by this selection sorter.
40      */
41      public void sort()
42            throws InterruptedException
43      {
44         for (int i = 0; i < a.length - 1; i++)
45         {
46            int minPos = minimumPosition(i);
47            sortStateLock.lock();
48            try
49            {
```

```
50              swap(minPos, i);
51              // For animation
52              alreadySorted = i;
53           }
54           finally
55           {
56              sortStateLock.unlock();
57           }
58           pause(2);
59        }
60     }
61
62     /**
63        Finds the smallest element in a tail range of the array.
64        @param from  the first position in a to compare
65        @return  the position of the smallest element in the
66        range a[from] . . . a[a.length - 1]
67     */
68     private int minimumPosition(int from)
69           throws InterruptedException
70     {
71        int minPos = from;
72        for (int i = from + 1; i < a.length; i++)
73        {
74           sortStateLock.lock();
75           try
76           {
77              if (a[i] < a[minPos]) minPos = i;
78              // For animation
79              markedPosition = i;
80           }
81           finally
82           {
83              sortStateLock.unlock();
84           }
85           pause(2);
86        }
87        return minPos;
88     }
89
90     /**
91        Swaps two entries of the array.
92        @param i  the first position to swap
93        @param j  the second position to swap
94     */
95     private void swap(int i, int j)
96     {
97        int temp = a[i];
98        a[i] = a[j];
99        a[j] = temp;
100    }
101
102    /**
103       Draws the current state of the sorting algorithm.
104       @param g2  the graphics context
105    */
106    public void draw(Graphics2D g2)
107    {
```

```
108        sortStateLock.lock();
109        try
110        {
111           int deltaX = component.getWidth() / a.length;
112           for (int i = 0; i < a.length; i++)
113           {
114              if (i == markedPosition)
115                 g2.setColor(Color.RED);
116              else if (i <= alreadySorted)
117                 g2.setColor(Color.BLUE);
118              else
119                 g2.setColor(Color.BLACK);
120              g2.draw(new Line2D.Double(i * deltaX, 0,
121                    i * deltaX, a[i]));
122           }
123        }
124        finally
125        {
126           sortStateLock.unlock();
127        }
128     }
129
130     /**
131        Pauses the animation.
132        @param steps  the number of steps to pause
133     */
134     public void pause(int steps)
135           throws InterruptedException
136     {
137        component.repaint();
138        Thread.sleep(steps * DELAY);
139     }
140  }
```

SELF CHECK

11. Why is the draw method added to the SelectionSorter class and not the SelectionSortComponent class?

12. Would the animation still work if the startAnimation method simply called sorter.sort() instead of spawning a thread that calls that method?

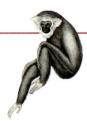

Random Fact 20.1

Embedded Systems

An **embedded system** is a computer system that controls a device. The device contains a processor and other hardware and is controlled by a computer program. Unlike a personal computer, which has been designed to be flexible and run many different computer programs, the hardware and software of an embedded system are tailored to a specific device. Computer-controlled devices are becoming increasingly common, ranging from washing machines to medical equipment, automobile engines, and spacecraft.

Several challenges are specific to programming embedded systems. Most importantly, a much higher standard of quality control applies. Vendors are often unconcerned about bugs in personal computer software, because they can always make you install a patch or upgrade to the next version. But in an embedded system, that is not an option. Few consumers would

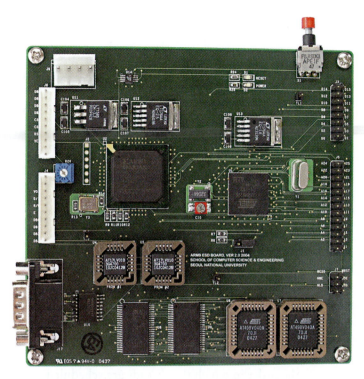

Figure 4 The Controller of an Embedded System

feel comfortable upgrading the software in their washing machines or automobile engines. If you ever handed in a programming assignment that you believed to be correct, only to have the instructor or grader find bugs in it, then you know how hard it is to write software that can reliably do its task for many years without a chance of changing it.

Quality standards are especially important in devices whose failure would destroy property or human life—see Random Facts 7.2 and 11.1.

Many personal computer purchasers buy computers that are fast and have a lot of storage, because the investment is paid back over time when many programs are run on the same equipment. But the hardware for an embedded device is not shared—it is dedicated to one device. A separate processor, memory, and so on, are built for every copy of the device (see Figure 4). If it is possible to shave a few pennies off the manufacturing cost of every unit, the savings can add up quickly for devices that are produced in large volumes. Thus, the embedded-system programmer has a much larger economic incentive to conserve resources than the programmer of desktop software. Unfortunately, trying to conserve resources usually makes it harder to write programs that work correctly.

Generally, embedded systems are written in lower-level programming languages to avoid the overhead of a complex run-time system. The Java run-time system, with its safety mechanisms, garbage collector, support for multithreading, and so on, would be too costly to add to every washing machine. However, some devices are now being built with a scaled-down version of Java: the Java 2 Micro Edition. Examples are smart cell phones and onboard computers for automobiles. The Java 2 Micro Edition is a good candidate for devices that are connected to a network and that need to be able to run new applications safely. For example, you can download a program into a Java-enabled cell phone and be assured that it cannot corrupt other parts of the cell phone software.

Summary of Learning Objectives

Describe how multiple threads execute concurrently.

- A thread is a program unit that is executed concurrently with other parts of the program.
- The start method of the Thread class starts a new thread that executes the run method of the associated Runnable object.
- The sleep method puts the current thread to sleep for a given number of milliseconds.
- When a thread is interrupted, the most common response is to terminate the run method.
- The thread scheduler runs each thread for a short amount of time, called a time slice.

Choose appropriate mechanisms for terminating threads.

- A thread terminates when its run method terminates.
- The run method can check whether its thread has been interrupted by calling the interrupted method.

Recognize the causes and effects of race conditions.

- A race condition occurs if the effect of multiple threads on shared data depends on the order in which the threads are scheduled.

Use locks to control access to resources that are shared by multiple threads.

- By calling the lock method, a thread acquires a Lock object. Then no other thread can acquire the lock until the first thread releases the lock.

Explain how deadlocks occur and how they can be avoided with condition objects.

- A deadlock occurs if no thread can proceed because each thread is waiting for another to do some work first.
- Calling await on a condition object makes the current thread wait and allows another thread to acquire the lock object.
- A waiting thread is blocked until another thread calls signalAll or signal on the condition object for which the thread is waiting.

Use multiple threads to display an animation of an algorithm.

- Use a separate thread for running the algorithm that is being animated.
- The algorithm state needs to be safely accessed by the algorithm and painting threads.

Media Resources

wwwwiley.com/ college/ horstmann

- Lab Exercises
- ⊕ Practice Quiz
- ⊕ Code Completion Exercises

Classes, Objects, and Methods Introduced in this Chapter

```
java.lang.InterruptedException          java.util.Date
java.lang.Object                        java.util.concurrent.locks.Condition
   notify                                  await
   notifyAll                               signal
   wait                                    signalAll
java.lang.Runnable                      java.util.concurrent.locks.Lock
   run                                      lock
java.lang.Thread                           newCondition
   interrupted                              unlock
   sleep                                 java.util.concurrent.locks.ReentrantLock
   start
```

Review Exercises

★ **R20.1** Run a program with the following instructions:

```
GreetingRunnable r1 = new GreetingRunnable("Hello, World!");
GreetingRunnable r2 = new GreetingRunnable("Goodbye, World!");
r1.run();
r2.run();
```

Note that the threads don't run in parallel. Explain.

★★★ **R20.2** In the program of Section 20.1, is it possible that both threads are sleeping at the same time? Is it possible that neither of the two threads is sleeping at a particular time? Explain.

★★★ **R20.3** In Java, a graphical user interface program has more than one thread. Explain how you can prove that.

★★★ **R20.4** Why is the stop method for stopping a thread deprecated? How do you terminate a thread?

★ **R20.5** Give an example of why you would want to terminate a thread.

★★ **R20.6** Suppose you surround each call to the sleep method with a try/catch block to catch an InterruptedException and ignore it. What problem do you create?

★★ **R20.7** What is a race condition? How can you avoid it?

★★ **R20.8** What is a deadlock? How can you avoid it?

★ **R20.9** What is the difference between a thread that sleeps by calling sleep and a thread that waits by calling await?

★ **R20.10** What happens when a thread calls await and no other thread calls signalAll or signal?

★★ **R20.11** In the algorithm animation program of Section 20.6, we do not use any conditions. Why not?

Programming Exercises

★★★ **P20.1** Implement a Queue class whose add and remove methods are synchronized. Supply one thread, called the producer, which keeps inserting strings into the queue as long as there are fewer than 10 elements in it. When the queue gets too full, the thread waits. As sample strings, simply use time stamps new Date().toString(). Supply a second thread, called the consumer, that keeps removing and printing strings from the queue as long as the queue is not empty. When the queue is empty, the thread waits. Both the consumer and producer threads should run for 100 iterations.

★ **P20.2** Enhance Exercise P20.1 by supplying a variable number of producer and consumer threads. Prompt the program user for the numbers.

★ **P20.3** Reimplement Exercise P20.2 by using the ArrayBlockingQueue class from the standard library.

★★ **P20.4** Write a program WordCount that counts the words in one or more files. Start a new thread for each file. For example, if you call

```
java WordCount report.txt address.txt Homework.java
```

then the program might print

```
address.txt: 1052
Homework.java: 445
report.txt: 2099
```

★★ **P20.5** Write a program Find that searches all files specified on the command line and prints out all lines containing a reserved word. Start a new thread for each file. For example, if you call

```
java Find Buff report.txt address.txt Homework.java
```

then the program might print

```
report.txt: Buffet style lunch will be available at the
address.txt: Buffet, Warren|11801 Trenton Court|Dallas|TX
Homework.java: BufferedReader in;
address.txt: Walters, Winnie|59 Timothy Circle|Buffalo|MI
```

★★ **P20.6** Add a condition to the deposit method of the BankAccount class, restricting deposits to $100,000 (the insurance limit of the U.S. government). The method should block until sufficient money has been withdrawn by another thread. Test your program with a large number of deposit threads.

★★★ **P20.7** Implement the merge sort algorithm of Chapter 14 by spawning a new thread for each smaller MergeSorter. *Hint:* Use the join method of the Thread class to wait for the spawned threads to finish. Look up the method's behavior in the API documentation.

★★G **P20.8** Modify the car viewer of Chapter 3 so that the cars are moving. Use a separate thread for each car.

★★★G **P20.9** Modify Exercise P20.8 so that the cars change direction when they hit an edge of the window.

★G **P20.10** Enhance the SelectionSorter of Section 20.6 so that the current minimum is painted in yellow.

★★G **P20.11** Enhance the SelectionSortViewer of Section 20.6 so that the sorting only starts when the user clicks a "Start" button.

★★G **P20.12** Instead of using a thread and a pause method, use the Timer class of Chapter 9 to animate an algorithm. Whenever the timer sends out an action event, run the algorithm to the next step and display the state. That requires a more extensive recoding of the algorithm. You need to implement a runToNextStep method that is capable of running the algorithm one step at a time. Add sufficient instance variables to the algorithm to remember where the last step left off. For example, in the case of the selection sort algorithm, if you know the values of alreadySorted and markedPosition, you can determine the next step.

★★★G **P20.13** Implement an animation of the merge sort algorithm of Chapter 14. Reimplement the algorithm so that the recursive calls sort the elements inside a subrange of the the original array, rather than in their own arrays:

```
public void mergeSort(int from, int to)
{
   if (from == to) return;
   int mid = (from + to) / 2;
   mergeSort(from, mid);
   mergeSort(mid + 1, to);
   merge(from, mid, to);
}
```

The merge method merges the sorted ranges a[from] . . . a[mid] and a[mid + 1] . . . a[to]. Merge the ranges into a temporary array, then copy back the temporary array into the combined range.

Pause in the merge method whenever you inspect an array element. Color the range a[from] . . . a[to] in blue and the currently inspected element in red.

★★★G **P20.14** Enhance Exercise P20.13 so that it shows two frames, one for a merge sorter and one for a selection sorter. They should both sort arrays with the same values.

Programming Projects

Project 20.1 Implement a program that animates multiple sorting algorithms running in parallel. For each algorithm, provide buttons to pause and resume the animation, and to execute a single step. Provide sliders to control the animation speed.

Project 20.2 Implement a program that animates multiple robots moving through a maze. Each robot should be animated by its own thread, moving to an adjacent unoccupied maze position and then sleeping. Use locking to ensure that no two robots occupy the same cell of the maze.

Answers to Self-Check Questions

1. The messages are printed about one millisecond apart.
2. The first call to run would print ten "Hello" messages, and then the second call to run would print ten "Goodbye" messages.
3. If the user hits the "Back" button, the current web page is no longer displayed, and it makes no sense to expend network resources to fetch additional image data.
4. The run method prints the values 1, 3, and 4. The call to interrupt merely sets the interruption flag, but the sleep method immediately throws an InterruptedException.
5. There are many possible scenarios. Here is one:
   a. The first thread loses control after the first print statement.
   b. The second thread loses control just before the assignment balance = newBalance.
   c. The first thread completes the deposit method.
   d. The second thread completes the withdraw method.
6. One thread calls addFirst and is preempted just before executing the assignment first = newLink. Then the next thread calls addFirst, using the old value of first. Then the first thread completes the process, setting first to its new link. As a result, the links are not in sequence.
7. Two, one for each bank account object. Each lock protects a separate balance variable.
8. When a thread calls deposit, it continues to own the lock, and any other thread trying to deposit or withdraw money in the same bank account is blocked forever.
9. A sleeping thread is reactivated when the sleep delay has passed. A waiting thread is only reactivated if another thread has called signalAll or signal.
10. The calls to await and signal/signalAll must be made *to the same object*.
11. The draw method uses the array values and the values that keep track of the algorithm's progress. These values are available only in the SelectionSorter class.
12. Yes, provided you only show a single frame. If you modify the SelectionSortViewer program to show two frames, you want the sorters to run in parallel.

Internet Networking

CHAPTER GOALS

- To understand the concept of sockets
- To learn how to send and receive data through sockets
- To implement network clients and servers
- To communicate with web servers and server-side applications through the Hypertext Transfer Protocol (HTTP)

You probably have quite a bit of experience with the **Internet**: the global network that links together millions of computers. In particular, you use the Internet whenever you browse the World Wide Web. Note that the Internet is not the same as the "Web". The World Wide Web is only one of many services offered over the Internet. E-mail, another popular service, also uses the Internet, but its implementation differs from that of the Web. In this chapter, you will see what goes on "under the hood" when you send an e-mail message or when you retrieve a web page from a remote server. You will also learn how to write your own programs that fetch data from sites across the Internet and how to write server programs that can serve information to other programs.

CHAPTER CONTENTS

21.1 The Internet Protocol

The *Internet* is a worldwide collection of networks, routing equipment, and computers using a common set of protocols to define how each party will interact with each other.

Computers can be connected with each other through a variety of physical media. In a computer lab, for example, computers are connected by network cabling. Electrical impulses representing information flow across the cables. If you use a DSL modem to connect your computer to the Internet, the signals travel across a regular telephone wire, encoded as tones. On a wireless network, signals are sent by transmitting a modulated radio frequency. The physical characteristics of these transmissions differ widely, but they ultimately consist of sending and receiving streams of zeroes and ones along the network connection.

These zeroes and ones represent two kinds of information: *application data,* the data that one computer actually wants to send to another, and *network protocol data,* the data that describe how to reach the intended recipient and how to check for errors and data loss in the transmission. The protocol data follow certain rules set forth by a particular **network protocol**. Various protocols have been developed for local area networks, such as Microsoft Networking, Novell NetWare, or Apple-Talk. The *Internet Protocol (IP),* on the other hand, was developed to enable different local area networks to communicate with each other and has become the basis for connecting computers around the world over the Internet. We will discuss IP in this chapter.

Suppose that a computer A wants to send data to a computer B, both on the Internet. The computers aren't connected directly with a cable, as they could be if both were on the same local area network. Instead, A may be someone's home computer and connected to an *Internet service provider (ISP),* which is in turn connected to an *Internet access point;* B might be a computer on a local area network belonging to a large firm that has an Internet access point of its own, which may be half a world away from A. The Internet itself, finally, is a complex collection of pathways on which a message can travel from one Internet access point to, eventually, any other Internet access point (see Figure 1). Those connections carry millions of messages, not just the data that A is sending to B.

For the data to arrive at its destination, it must be marked with a *destination address.* In IP, addresses are denoted by sequences of four numbers, each one byte (that is, between 0 and 255); for example, 130.65.86.66. (Because there aren't enough four-byte addresses for all devices that would like to connect to the Internet, these addresses will be extended to sixteen bytes in the near future.) In order to send data, A needs to know the Internet address of B and include it in the protocol portion when sending the data across the Internet. The routing software that is distributed across the Internet can then deliver the data to B.

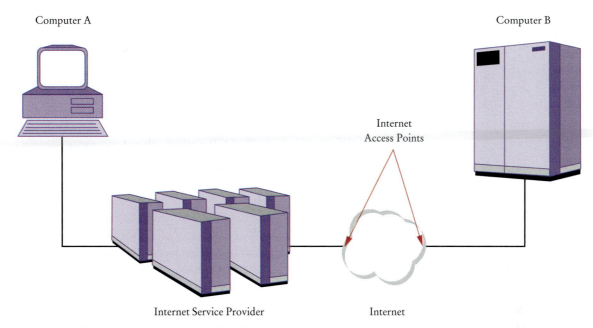

Figure 1   Two Computers Communicating Across the Internet

Of course, addresses such as 130.65.86.66 are not easy to remember. You would not be happy if you had to use number sequences every time you sent e-mail or requested information from a web server. On the Internet, computers can have so-called *domain names* that are easier to remember, such as cs.sjsu.edu or horstmann.com. A special service called the *Domain Naming Service (DNS)* translates between domain names and Internet addresses. Thus, if computer A wants to have information from horstmann.com, it first asks the DNS to translate this domain name into a numeric Internet address; then it includes the numeric address with the request.

One interesting aspect of IP is that it breaks large chunks of data up into more manageable *packets*. Each packet is delivered separately, and different packets that are part of the same transmission can take different routes through the Internet. Packets are numbered, and the recipient reassembles them in the correct order.

The Internet Protocol has just one function—to attempt to deliver data from one computer to another across the Internet. If some data get lost or garbled in the process, IP has safeguards built in to make sure that the recipient is aware of that unfortunate fact and doesn't rely on incomplete data. However, IP has no provision for retrying an incomplete transmission. That is the job of a higher-level protocol, the *Transmission Control Protocol (TCP)*. This protocol attempts reliable delivery of data, with retries if there are failures, and it notifies the sender whether or not the attempt succeeded. Most, but not all, Internet programs use TCP for reliable delivery. (Exceptions are "streaming media" services, which bypass the slower TCP for the highest possible throughput and tolerate occasional information loss. However, the most popular Internet services—the World Wide Web and e-mail—use TCP.) TCP is independent of the Internet Protocol; it could in principle be used with another lower-level network protocol. However, in practice, TCP over IP (often called TCP/IP) is the most commonly used combination. We will focus on TCP/IP networking in this chapter.

TCP/IP is the abbreviation for *Transmission Control Protocol over Internet Protocol*, the pair of communication protocols used to establish reliable transmission of data between two computers on the Internet.

A computer that is connected to the Internet may have programs for many different purposes. For example, a computer may run both a web server program and a mail server program. When data are sent to that computer, they need to be marked so that they can be forwarded to the appropriate program. TCP uses *port numbers* for this purpose. A port number is an integer between 0 and 65,535. The sending computer must know the port number of the receiving program and include it with the transmitted data. Some applications use "well-known" port numbers. For example, by convention, web servers use port 80, whereas mail servers running the Post Office Protocol (POP) use port 110. TCP packets, therefore, must contain

> A TCP connection requires the Internet addresses and port numbers of both end points.

- The Internet address of the recipient.
- The port number of the recipient.
- The Internet address of the sender.
- The port number of the sender.

You can think of a TCP connection as a "pipe" between two computers that links the two ports together. Data flow in either direction through the pipe. In practical programming situations, you simply establish a connection and send data across it without worrying about the details of the TCP/IP mechanism. You will see how to establish such a connection in Section 21.3.

SELF CHECK

1. What is the difference between an IP address and a domain name?
2. Why do some streaming media services not use TCP?

21.2 Application Level Protocols

> HTTP, or *Hypertext Transfer Protocol*, is the protocol that defines communication between web browsers and web servers.

In the preceding section you saw how the TCP/IP mechanism can establish an Internet connection between two ports on two computers so that the two computers can exchange data. Each Internet application has a different *application protocol*, which describes how the data for that particular application are transmitted.

Consider, for example, HTTP: the **Hypertext Transfer Protocol**, which is used for the World Wide Web. Suppose you type a web address, called a **Uniform Resource Locator** (URL, often pronounced like "Earl"), such as `http://horstmann.com/index.html`, into the address window of your browser and ask the browser to load the page.

> An URL, or *Uniform Resource Locator*, is a pointer to an information resource (such as a web page or an image) on the World Wide Web.

The browser now takes the following steps:

1. It examines the part of the URL between the double slash and the first single slash ("`horstmann.com`"), which identifies the computer to which you want to connect. Because this part of the URL contains letters, it must be a domain name rather than an Internet address, so the browser sends a request to a DNS server to obtain the Internet address of the computer with domain name `horstmann.com`.

2. From the `http:` prefix of the URL, the browser deduces that the protocol you want to use is HTTP, which by default uses port 80.

3. It establishes a TCP/IP connection to port 80 at the Internet address it obtained in Step 1.

4. It deduces from the `/index.html` suffix that you want to see the file `/index.html`, so it sends a request, formatted as an HTTP command, through the connection that was established in Step 3. The request looks like this:

```
GET /index.html HTTP/1.1
Host: horstmann.com
blank line
```

(The host is needed because a web server can host multiple domains with the same Internet address.)

5. The web server running on the computer whose Internet address is the one the browser obtained in Step 1 receives the request and decodes it. It then fetches the file `/index.html` and sends it back to the browser on your computer.

6. The browser displays the contents of the file. Because it happens to be an HTML file, the browser translates the HTML tags into fonts, bullets, separator lines, and so on. If the HTML file contains images, then the browser makes more `GET` requests, one for each image, through the same connection, to fetch the image data. (Appendix F contains a summary of the most frequently used HTML tags.)

You can try the following experiment to see this process in action. The "Telnet" program enables a user to type characters for sending to a remote computer and view characters that the remote computer sends back. On Windows, you need to enable the Telnet program in the control panel. UNIX, Linux, and Mac OS X systems normally have Telnet preinstalled.

For this experiment, you want to start Telnet with a host of `horstmann.com` and port 80. To start the program from the command line, simply type

```
telnet horstmann.com 80
```

Table 1 HTTP Commands	
Command	Meaning
GET	Return the requested item
HEAD	Request only the header information of an item
OPTIONS	Request communications options of an item
POST	Supply input to a server-side command and return the result
PUT	Store an item on the server
DELETE	Delete an item on the server
TRACE	Trace server communication

Once the program starts, type very carefully, without making any typing errors and without hitting the backspace key,

```
GET / HTTP/1.1
Host: horstmann.com
```

Then hit the Enter key twice.

The first / denotes the root page of the web server. Note that there are spaces before and after the first /, but there are no spaces in HTTP/1.1.

On Windows, you will not see what you type, so you should be extra careful when typing in the commands.

The server now sends a response to the request—see Figure 2. The response, of course, consists of the root web page that you requested. The Telnet program is not a browser and does not understand HTML tags, so it simply displays the HTML file—text, tags, and all.

> The Telnet program is a useful tool for establishing test connections with servers.

The GET command is one of the commands of HTTP. Table 1 shows the other commands of the protocol. As you can see, the protocol is pretty simple.

> The HTTP GET command requests information from a web server. The web server returns the requested item, which may be a web page, an image, or other data.

By the way, be sure not to confuse HTML with HTTP. **HTML** is a *document format* (with commands such as <h1> or <ul>) that describes the structure of a document, including headings, bulleted lists, images, hyperlinks, and so on. **HTTP** is a *protocol* (with commands such as GET and POST) that describes the command set for web server requests. Web *browsers* know how to display HTML documents and how to issue HTTP commands. Web *servers* know nothing about HTML. They merely understand HTTP and know how to fetch the requested items. Those items may be HTML documents, GIF or JPEG images, or any other data that a web browser can display.

```
~$ telnet horstmann.com 80
Trying 67.210.118.65...
Connected to horstmann.com.
Escape character is '^]'.
GET / HTTP/1.1
Host: horstmann.com

HTTP/1.1 200 OK
Date: Thu, 17 Sep 2009 14:33:55 GMT
Server: Apache/1.3.41 (Unix) Sun-ONE-ASP/4.0.2 mod_fastcgi/2.4.6 mod_log_byte
.2 mod_bwlimited/1.4 mod_auth_passthrough/1.8 FrontPage/5.0.2.2635 mod_ssl/2.
1 OpenSSL/0.9.7a
Last-Modified: Tue, 25 Aug 2009 00:05:05 GMT
ETag: "305e572-19fe-4a932ab1"
Accept-Ranges: bytes
Content-Length: 6654
Content-Type: text/html

<?xml version="1.0" encoding="us-ascii"?>
<!DOCTYPE html PUBLIC "-//W3C//DTD XHTML 1.0 Strict//EN"
        "http://www.w3.org/TR/xhtml1/DTD/xhtml1-strict.dtd">
<html xmlns="http://www.w3.org/1999/xhtml">
<head>
  <meta http-equiv="content-type" content="text/html; charset=us-ascii" />
  <title>Cay Horstmann's Home Page</title>
```

Figure 2 Using Telnet to Connect to a Web Server

Figure 3
A Sample POP Session

```
+OK San Quentin State POP server
USER harryh
+OK Password required for harryh
PASS secret
+OK harryh has 2 messages (320 octets)
STAT
+OK 2 320
RETR 1
+OK 120 octets
the message is included here
DELE 1
+OK message 1 deleted
QUIT
+OK POP server signing off
```

Black = mail client requests
Color = mail server responses

HTTP is just one of many application protocols in use on the Internet. Another commonly used protocol is the Post Office Protocol (POP), which is used to download received messages from e-mail servers. To *send* messages, you use yet another protocol called the Simple Mail Transfer Protocol (SMTP). We don't want to go into the details of these protocols, but Figure 3 gives you a flavor of the commands used by the Post Office Protocol.

Both HTTP and POP use plain text, which makes it particularly easy to test and debug client and server programs (see How To 21.1 on page 855).

SELF CHECK

3. Why don't you need to know about HTTP when you use a web browser?
4. Why is it important that you don't make typing errors when you type HTTP commands in Telnet?

21.3 A Client Program

In this section you will see how to write a Java program that establishes a TCP connection to a server, sends a request to the server, and prints the response.

In the terminology of TCP/IP, there is a **socket** on each side of the connection (see Figure 4). In Java, a client establishes a socket with a call

> A socket is an object that encapsulates a TCP connection. To communicate with the other end point of the connection, use the input and output streams attached to the socket.

```
Socket s = new Socket(hostname, portnumber);
```

For example, to connect to the HTTP port of the server horstmann.com, you use

```
final int HTTP_PORT = 80;
Socket s = new Socket("horstmann.com", HTTP_PORT);
```

The socket constructor throws an UnknownHostException if it can't find the host.

Once you have a socket, you obtain its input and output streams:

```
InputStream instream = s.getInputStream();
OutputStream outstream = s.getOutputStream();
```

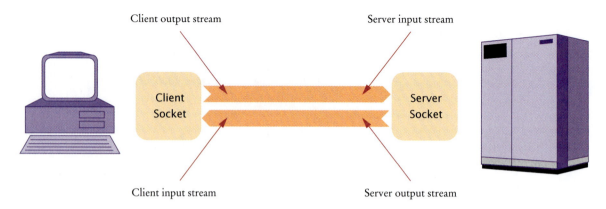

Figure 4 Client and Server Sockets

When you send data to outstream, the socket automatically forwards it to the server. The socket catches the server's response, and you can read the response through instream (see Figure 4).

When you are done communicating with the server, you should close the socket:

When transmission over a socket is complete, remember to close the socket.

```
s.close();
```

In Chapter 19, you saw that the InputStream and OutputStream classes are used for reading and writing bytes. If you want to communicate with the server by sending and receiving text, you should turn the streams into scanners and writers, as follows:

For text protocols, turn the socket streams into scanners and writers.

```
Scanner in = new Scanner(instream);
PrintWriter out = new PrintWriter(outstream);
```

A print writer **buffers** the characters that you send to it. That is, characters are not immediately sent to their destination. Instead, they are placed into an array. When the array is full, then the print writer sends all characters in the array to its destination. The advantage of buffering is increased performance—it takes some amount of time to contact the destination and send it data, and it is expensive to pay for that contact time for every character. However, when communicating with a server that responds to requests, you want to make sure that the server gets a complete request at a time. Therefore, you need to *flush* the buffer manually whenever you send a command:

```
out.print(command);
out.flush();
```

Flush the writer attached to a socket at the end of every command. Then the command is sent to the server, even if the writer's buffer is not completely filled.

The flush method empties the buffer and forwards all waiting characters to the destination.

The WebGet program at the end of this section lets you retrieve any item from a web server. You need to specify the host and the item from the command line. For example,

```
java WebGet horstmann.com /
```

The / item denotes the root page of the web server that listens to port 80 of the host horstmann.com. Note that there is a space before the /.

The program simply establishes a connection to the host, sends a GET command to the host, and then receives input from the server until the server closes its connection.

ch21/webget/WebGet.java

```java
import java.io.InputStream;
import java.io.IOException;
import java.io.OutputStream;
import java.io.PrintWriter;
import java.net.Socket;
import java.util.Scanner;

/**
    This program demonstrates how to use a socket to communicate
    with a web server. Supply the name of the host and the
    resource on the command-line, for example,
    java WebGet horstmann.com index.html.
*/
public class WebGet
{
    public static void main(String[] args) throws IOException
    {
        // Get command-line arguments

        String host;
        String resource;

        if (args.length == 2)
        {
            host = args[0];
            resource = args[1];
        }
        else
        {
            System.out.println("Getting / from horstmann.com");
            host = "horstmann.com";
            resource = "/";
        }

        // Open socket

        final int HTTP_PORT = 80;
        Socket s = new Socket(host, HTTP_PORT);

        // Get streams

        InputStream instream = s.getInputStream();
        OutputStream outstream = s.getOutputStream();

        // Turn streams into scanners and writers

        Scanner in = new Scanner(instream);
        PrintWriter out = new PrintWriter(outstream);

        // Send command

        String command = "GET " + resource + " HTTP/1.1\n"
            + "Host: " + host + "\n\n";
        out.print(command);
```

```
55      out.flush();
56
57      // Read server response
58
59      while (in.hasNextLine())
60      {
61          String input = in.nextLine();
62          System.out.println(input);
63      }
64
65      // Always close the socket at the end
66
67      s.close();
68      }
69 }
```

Program Run

```
Getting / from horstmann.com
HTTP/1.1 200 OK
Date: Thu, 17 Sep 2009 14:15:04 GMT
Server: Apache/1.3.41 (Unix) Sun-ONE-ASP/4.0.2
. . .
Content-Length: 6654
Content-Type: text/html

<html>
<head><title>Cay Horstmann's Home Page</title></head>
<body>
<h1>Welcome to Cay Horstmann's Home Page</h1>
. . .
</body>
</html>
```

SELF CHECK

5. What happens if you call WebGet with a nonexistent resource, such as wombat.html at horstmann.com?

6. How do you open a socket to read e-mail from the POP server at e-mail.sjsu.edu?

21.4 A Server Program

Now that you have seen how to write a network client, we will turn to the server side. In this section we will develop a server program that enables clients to manage a set of bank accounts in a bank.

Whenever you develop a server application, you need to specify some application-level protocol that clients can use to interact with the server. For the purpose of this example, we will create a "Simple Bank Access Protocol". Table 2 shows the protocol format. Of course, this is just a toy protocol to show you how to implement a server.

The server program waits for clients to connect to a particular port. We choose port 8888 for this service. This number has not been preassigned to another service,

Table 2 A Simple Bank Access Protocol

Client Request	Server Response	Description
BALANCE n	n and the balance	Get the balance of account n
DEPOSIT n a	n and the new balance	Deposit amount a into account n
WITHDRAW n a	n and the new balance	Withdraw amount a from account n
QUIT	None	Quit the connection

so it is unlikely to be used by another server program. To listen to incoming connections, you use a *server socket*. To construct a server socket, you need to supply the port number.

```
ServerSocket server = new ServerSocket(8888);
```

The accept method of the ServerSocket class waits for a client connection. When a client connects, then the server program obtains a socket through which it communicates with the client.

```
Socket s = server.accept();
BankService service = new BankService(s, bank);
```

The BankService class carries out the service. This class implements the Runnable interface, and its run method will be executed in each thread that serves a client connection. The run method gets a scanner and writer from the socket in the same way as we discussed in the preceding section. Then it executes the following method:

```
public void doService() throws IOException
{
   while (true)
   {
      if (!in.hasNext()) return;
      String command = in.next();
      if (command.equals("QUIT")) return;
      executeCommand(command);
   }
}
```

The executeCommand method processes a single command. If the command is DEPOSIT, then it carries out the deposit.

```
int account = in.nextInt();
double amount = in.nextDouble();
bank.deposit(account, amount);
```

The WITHDRAW command is handled in the same way. After each command, the account number and new balance are sent to the client:

```
out.println(account + " " + bank.getBalance(account));
```

The doService method returns to the run method if the client closed the connection or the command equals "QUIT". Then the run method closes the socket and exits.

Let us go back to the point where the server socket accepts a connection and constructs the BankService object. At this point, we could simply call the run method.

But then our server program would have a serious limitation: only one client could connect to it at any point in time. To overcome that limitation, server programs spawn a new thread whenever a client connects. Each thread is responsible for serving one client.

Our `BankService` class implements the `Runnable` interface. Therefore, the server program simply starts a thread with the following instructions:

```
Thread t = new Thread(service);
t.start();
```

The thread dies when the client quits or disconnects and the `run` method exits. In the meantime, the `BankServer` loops back to accept the next connection.

```
while (true)
{
    Socket s = server.accept();
    BankService service = new BankService(s, bank);
    Thread t = new Thread(service);
    t.start();
}
```

The server program never stops. When you are done running the server, you need to kill it. For example, if you started the server in a shell window, hit Ctrl+C.

To try out the program, run the server. Then use Telnet to connect to `localhost`, port number 8888. Start typing commands. Here is a typical dialog (see Figure 5):

```
DEPOSIT 3 1000
3 1000.0
WITHDRAW 3 500
3 500.0
QUIT
```

Alternatively, you can use a client program that connects to the server. You will find a sample client program at the end of this section.

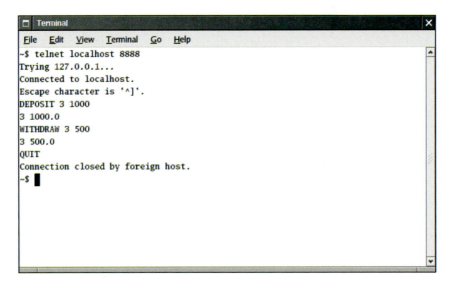

Figure 5 Using the Telnet Program to Connect to the Bank Server

ch21/bank/BankServer.java

```java
1   import java.io.IOException;
2   import java.net.ServerSocket;
3   import java.net.Socket;
4
5   /**
6       A server that executes the Simple Bank Access Protocol.
7   */
8   public class BankServer
9   {
10      public static void main(String[] args) throws IOException
11      {
12         final int ACCOUNTS_LENGTH = 10;
13         Bank bank = new Bank(ACCOUNTS_LENGTH);
14         final int SBAP_PORT = 8888;
15         ServerSocket server = new ServerSocket(SBAP_PORT);
16         System.out.println("Waiting for clients to connect . . . ");
17
18         while (true)
19         {
20            Socket s = server.accept();
21            System.out.println("Client connected.");
22            BankService service = new BankService(s, bank);
23            Thread t = new Thread(service);
24            t.start();
25         }
26      }
27   }
```

ch21/bank/BankService.java

```java
1   import java.io.InputStream;
2   import java.io.IOException;
3   import java.io.OutputStream;
4   import java.io.PrintWriter;
5   import java.net.Socket;
6   import java.util.Scanner;
7
8   /**
9       Executes Simple Bank Access Protocol commands
10      from a socket.
11  */
12  public class BankService implements Runnable
13  {
14      private Socket s;
15      private Scanner in;
16      private PrintWriter out;
17      private Bank bank;
18
19      /**
20          Constructs a service object that processes commands
21          from a socket for a bank.
22          @param aSocket the socket
23          @param aBank the bank
24      */
25      public BankService(Socket aSocket, Bank aBank)
26      {
```

```
27          s = aSocket;
28          bank = aBank;
29       }
30
31       public void run()
32       {
33          try
34          {
35             try
36             {
37                in = new Scanner(s.getInputStream());
38                out = new PrintWriter(s.getOutputStream());
39                doService();
40             }
41             finally
42             {
43                s.close();
44             }
45          }
46          catch (IOException exception)
47          {
48             exception.printStackTrace();
49          }
50       }
51
52       /**
53          Executes all commands until the QUIT command or the
54          end of input.
55       */
56       public void doService() throws IOException
57       {
58          while (true)
59          {
60             if (!in.hasNext()) return;
61             String command = in.next();
62             if (command.equals("QUIT")) return;
63             else executeCommand(command);
64          }
65       }
66
67       /**
68          Executes a single command.
69          @param command the command to execute
70       */
71       public void executeCommand(String command)
72       {
73          int account = in.nextInt();
74          if (command.equals("DEPOSIT"))
75          {
76             double amount = in.nextDouble();
77             bank.deposit(account, amount);
78          }
79          else if (command.equals("WITHDRAW"))
80          {
81             double amount = in.nextDouble();
82             bank.withdraw(account, amount);
```

```
83          }
84          else if (!command.equals("BALANCE"))
85          {
86             out.println("Invalid command");
87             out.flush();
88             return;
89          }
90          out.println(account + " " + bank.getBalance(account));
91          out.flush();
92       }
93    }
```

ch21/bank/Bank.java

```
1    /**
2        A bank consisting of multiple bank accounts.
3    */
4    public class Bank
5    {
6       private BankAccount[] accounts;
7
8       /**
9           Constructs a bank account with a given number of accounts.
10          @param size the number of accounts
11      */
12      public Bank(int size)
13      {
14         accounts = new BankAccount[size];
15         for (int i = 0; i < accounts.length; i++)
16            accounts[i] = new BankAccount();
17      }
18
19      /**
20          Deposits money into a bank account.
21          @param accountNumber the account number
22          @param amount the amount to deposit
23      */
24      public void deposit(int accountNumber, double amount)
25      {
26         BankAccount account = accounts[accountNumber];
27         account.deposit(amount);
28      }
29
30      /**
31          Withdraws money from a bank account.
32          @param accountNumber the account number
33          @param amount the amount to withdraw
34      */
35      public void withdraw(int accountNumber, double amount)
36      {
37         BankAccount account = accounts[accountNumber];
38         account.withdraw(amount);
39      }
40
```

```
41      /**
42          Gets the balance of a bank account.
43          @param accountNumber the account number
44          @return the account balance
45      */
46      public double getBalance(int accountNumber)
47      {
48          BankAccount account = accounts[accountNumber];
49          return account.getBalance();
50      }
51  }
```

ch21/bank/BankClient.java

```
1   import java.io.InputStream;
2   import java.io.IOException;
3   import java.io.OutputStream;
4   import java.io.PrintWriter;
5   import java.net.Socket;
6   import java.util.Scanner;
7
8   /**
9       This program tests the bank server.
10  */
11  public class BankClient
12  {
13      public static void main(String[] args) throws IOException
14      {
15          final int SBAP_PORT = 8888;
16          Socket s = new Socket("localhost", SBAP_PORT);
17          InputStream instream = s.getInputStream();
18          OutputStream outstream = s.getOutputStream();
19          Scanner in = new Scanner(instream);
20          PrintWriter out = new PrintWriter(outstream);
21
22          String command = "DEPOSIT 3 1000\n";
23          System.out.print("Sending: " + command);
24          out.print(command);
25          out.flush();
26          String response = in.nextLine();
27          System.out.println("Receiving: " + response);
28
29          command = "WITHDRAW 3 500\n";
30          System.out.print("Sending: " + command);
31          out.print(command);
32          out.flush();
33          response = in.nextLine();
34          System.out.println("Receiving: " + response);
35
36          command = "QUIT\n";
37          System.out.print("Sending: " + command);
38          out.print(command);
39          out.flush();
40
41          s.close();
42      }
43  }
```

Program Run

```
Sending: DEPOSIT 3 1000
Receiving: 3 1000.0
Sending: WITHDRAW 3 500
Receiving: 3 500.0
Sending: QUIT
```

SELF CHECK

7. Why didn't we choose port 80 for the bank server?
8. Can you read data from a server socket?

How To 21.1

Designing Client/Server Programs

The bank server of this section is a typical example of a client/server program. A web browser/web server is another example. Follow these steps when designing a client/server application.

Step 1 Determine whether it really makes sense to implement a stand-alone server and a matching client.

Many times it makes more sense to build a web application instead. Chapter 24 discusses the construction of web applications in detail. For example, the bank application of this section could easily be turned into a web application, using an HTML form with Withdraw and Deposit buttons. However, programs for chat or peer-to-peer file sharing cannot easily be implemented as web applications.

Step 2 Design a communication protocol.

Figure out exactly what messages the client and server send to each other and what the success and error responses are.

With each request and response, ask yourself how the *end of data* is indicated.

- Do the data fit on a single line? Then the end of the line serves as the data terminator.
- Can the data be terminated by a special line (such as a blank line after the HTTP header or a line containing a period in SMTP)?
- Does the sender of the data close the socket? That's what a web server does at the end of a GET request.
- Can the sender indicate how many bytes are contained in the request? Web browsers do that in POST requests.

Use text, not binary data, for the communication between client and server. A text-based protocol is easier to debug.

Step 3 Implement the server program.

The server listens for socket connections and accepts them. It starts a new thread for each connection. Supply a class that implements the Runnable interface. The run method receives commands, interprets them, and sends responses back to the client.

Step 4 Test the server with the Telnet program.

Try out all commands in the communication protocol.

Step 5 Once the server works, write a client program.

The client program interacts with the program user, turns user requests into protocol commands, sends the commands to the server, receives the response, and displays the response for the program user.

21.5 URL Connections

The URLConnection class makes it easy to communicate with a web server without having to issue HTTP commands.

In Section 21.3, you saw how to use sockets to connect to a web server and how to retrieve information from the server by sending HTTP commands. However, because HTTP is such an important protocol, the Java library contains an URLConnection class, which provides convenient support for the HTTP. The URLConnection class takes care of the socket connection, so you don't have to fuss with sockets when you want to retrieve from a web server. As an additional benefit, the URLConnection class can also handle FTP, the *file transfer protocol*.

The URLConnection class makes it very easy to fetch a file from a web server given the file's URL as a string. First, you construct an URL object from the URL in the familiar format, starting with the http or ftp prefix. Then you use the URL object's openConnection() method to get the URLConnection object itself.

```
URL u = new URL("http://horstmann.com/index.html");
URLConnection connection = u.openConnection();
```

Then you call the getInputStream method to obtain an input stream:

```
InputStream instream = connection.getInputStream();
```

You can turn the stream into a scanner in the usual way, and read input from the scanner.

The URLConnection and HttpURLConnection classes can give you additional information about HTTP requests and responses.

The URLConnection class can give you additional useful information. To understand those capabilities, we need to have a closer look at HTTP requests and responses. You saw in Section 21.2 that the command for getting an item from the server is

```
GET item HTTP/1.1
Host: hostname
blank line
```

You may have wondered why you need to provide a blank line. This blank line is a part of the general request format. The first line of the request is a command, such as GET or POST. The command is followed by *request properties* (such as Host:). Some commands—in particular, the POST command—send input data to the server. The reason for the blank line is to denote the boundary between the request property section and the input data section.

A typical request property is If-Modified-Since. If you request an item with

```
GET item HTTP/1.1
Host: hostname
If-Modified-Since: date
blank line
```

the server sends the item only if it is newer than the date. Browsers use this feature to speed up redisplay of previously loaded web pages. When a web page is loaded, the browser stores it in a *cache* directory. When the user wants to see the same web page again, the browser asks the server to get a new page only if it has been modified since the date of the cached copy. If it hasn't been, the browser simply redisplays the cached copy and doesn't spend time downloading another identical copy.

The URLConnection class has methods to set request properties. For example, you can set the If-Modified-Since property with the setIfModifiedSince method:

```
connection.setIfModifiedSince(date);
```

You need to set request properties before calling the getInputStream method. The URLConnection class then sends to the web server all the request properties that you set.

Similarly, the response from the server starts with a status line followed by a set of response parameters. The response parameters are terminated by a blank line and followed by the requested data (for example, an HTML page). Here is a typical response:

```
HTTP/1.1 200 OK
Date: Tue, 24 Aug 2010 00:15:48 GMT
Server: Apache/1.3.3 (Unix)
Last-Modified: Sat, 26 Jun 2010 20:53:38 GMT
Content-Length: 4813
Content-Type: text/html
blank line
requested data
```

Normally, you don't see the response code. However, you may have run across bad links and seen a page that contained a response code 404 Not Found. (A successful response has status 200 OK.)

To retrieve the response code, you need to cast the URLConnection object to the HttpURLConnection subclass. You can retrieve the response code (such as the number 200 in this example, or the code 404 if a page was not found) and response message with the getResponseCode and getResponseMessage methods:

```
HttpURLConnection httpConnection = (HttpURLConnection) connection;
int code = httpConnection.getResponseCode(); // e.g., 404
String message = httpConnection.getResponseMessage(); // e.g., "Not found"
```

As you can see from the response example, the server sends some information about the requested data, such as the content length and the content type. You can request this information with methods from the URLConnection class:

```
int length = connection.getContentLength();
String type = connection.getContentType();
```

You need to call these methods after calling the getInputStream method.

To summarize: You don't need to use sockets to communicate with a web server, and you need not master the details of the HTTP protocol. Simply use the URLConnection and HttpURLConnection classes to obtain data from a web server, to set request parameters, or to obtain response information.

The program at the end of this section puts the URLConnection class to work. The program fulfills the same purpose as that of Section 21.3 — to retrieve a web page from a server — but it works at a higher level of abstraction. There is no longer a need to issue an explicit GET command. The URLConnection class takes care of that. Similarly, the parsing of the HTTP request and response headers is handled transparently to the programmer. Our sample program takes advantage of that fact. It checks whether the server response code is 200. If not, it exits. You can try that out by testing the program with a bad URL, like http://horstmann.com/wombat.html. Then the program prints a server response, such as 404 Not Found.

This program completes our introduction into Internet programming with Java. You have seen how to use sockets to connect client and server programs. You also saw how to use the higher-level `URLConnection` class to obtain information from web servers.

ch21/urlget/URLGet.java

```java
 1  import java.io.InputStream;
 2  import java.io.IOException;
 3  import java.io.OutputStream;
 4  import java.io.PrintWriter;
 5  import java.net.HttpURLConnection;
 6  import java.net.URL;
 7  import java.net.URLConnection;
 8  import java.util.Scanner;
 9
10  /**
11      This program demonstrates how to use an URL connection
12      to communicate with a web server. Supply the URL on
13      the command-line, for example
14      java URLGet http://horstmann.com/index.html.
15  */
16  public class URLGet
17  {
18     public static void main(String[] args) throws IOException
19     {
20        // Get command-line arguments
21
22        String urlString;
23        if (args.length == 1)
24           urlString = args[0];
25        else
26        {
27           urlString = "http://horstmann.com/";
28           System.out.println("Using " + urlString);
29        }
30
31        // Open connection
32
33        URL u = new URL(urlString);
34        URLConnection connection = u.openConnection();
35
36        // Check if response code is HTTP_OK (200)
37
38        HttpURLConnection httpConnection
39              = (HttpURLConnection) connection;
40        int code = httpConnection.getResponseCode();
41        String message = httpConnection.getResponseMessage();
42        System.out.println(code + " " + message);
43        if (code != HttpURLConnection.HTTP_OK)
44           return;
45
46        // Read server response
47
48        InputStream instream = connection.getInputStream();
49        Scanner in = new Scanner(instream);
50
```

```
51        while (in.hasNextLine())
52        {
53            String input = in.nextLine();
54            System.out.println(input);
55        }
56    }
57 }
```

Program Run

```
Using http://horstmann.com/
200 OK
<html>
<head><title>Cay Horstmann's Home Page</title></head>
<body>
<h1>Welcome to Cay Horstmann's Home Page</h1>
. . .
</body>
</html>
```

S E L F   C H E C K

9. Why is it better to use an `URLConnection` instead of a socket when reading data from a web server?

10. What happens if you use the `URLGet` program to request an image (such as `http://horstmann.com/cay-tiny.gif`)?

Productivity Hint 21.1

Use High-Level Libraries

When you communicate with a web server to obtain data, you have two choices. You can make a socket connection and send `GET` and `POST` commands to the server over the socket. Or you can use the `URLConnection` class and have it issue the commands on your behalf.

Similarly, to communicate with a mail server, you can write programs that send SMTP and POP commands, or you can learn how to use the Java mail extensions. (See `http://java.sun.com/products/javamail/index.html` for more information on the Java Mail API.)

In such a situation, you may be tempted to use the low-level approach and send commands over a socket connection. It seems simpler than learning a complex set of classes. However, that simplicity is often deceptive. Once you go beyond the simplest cases, the low-level approach usually requires hard work. For example, to send binary mail attachments, you may need to master complex data encodings. The high-level libraries have all that knowledge built in, so you don't have to reinvent the wheel.

For that reason, you should not actually use sockets to connect to web servers. Always use the `URLConnection` class instead. Why did this book teach you about sockets if you aren't expected to use them? There are two reasons. Some client programs don't communicate with web or mail servers, and you may need to use sockets when a high-level library is not available. And, just as importantly, knowing what the high-level library does under the hood helps you understand it better. For the same reason, you saw in Chapter 15 how to implement linked lists, even though you probably will never program your own lists and will just use the `LinkedList` class.

Summary of Learning Objectives

Describe the IP and TCP protocols.

- The Internet is a worldwide collection of networks, routing equipment, and computers using a common set of protocols to define how each party will interact with each other.
- TCP/IP is the abbreviation for Transmission Control Protocol over Internet Protocol, the pair of communication protocols used to establish reliable transmission of data between two computers on the Internet.
- A TCP connection requires the Internet addresses and port numbers of both end points.

Describe the HTTP protocol.

- HTTP, or Hypertext Transfer Protocol, is the protocol that defines communication between web browsers and web servers.
- An URL, or Uniform Resource Locator, is a pointer to an information resource (such as a web page or an image) on the World Wide Web.
- The Telnet program is a useful tool for establishing test connections with servers.
- The HTTP GET command requests information from a web server. The web server returns the requested item, which may be a web page, an image, or other data.

Implement programs that use network sockets for reading data.

- A socket is an object that encapsulates a TCP connection. To communicate with the other end point of the connection, use the input and output streams attached to the socket.
- When transmission over a socket is complete, remember to close the socket.
- For text protocols, turn the socket streams into scanners and writers.
- Flush the writer attached to a socket at the end of every command. Then the command is sent to the server, even if the writer's buffer is not completely filled.

Implement programs that serve data over a network.

- The ServerSocket class is used by server applications to listen for client connections.

Use the URLConnection class to read data from a web server.

- The URLConnection class makes it easy to communicate with a web server without having to issue HTTP commands.
- The URLConnection and HttpURLConnection classes can give you additional information about HTTP requests and responses.

Classes, Objects, and Methods Introduced in this Chapter

```
java.net.HttpURLConnection          java.net.Socket                java.net.URLConnection
    getResponseCode                     close                          getContentLength
    getResponseMessage                  getInputStream                 getContentType
java.net.ServerSocket                   getOutputStream                getInputsetIfModifiedSince
    accept                          java.net.URL
    close                               openConnection
```

Media Resources

www.wiley.com/
college/
horstmann

- ● Lab Exercises
- ➕ Practice Quiz
- ➕ Code Completion Exercises

Review Exercises

★   **R21.1**   What is a server? What is a client? How many clients can connect to a server at one time?

★   **R21.2**   What is a socket? What is the difference between a Socket object and a ServerSocket object?

★   **R21.3**   Under what circumstances would an UnknownHostException be thrown?

★★ **R21.4**   What happens if the Socket constructor's second parameter is not the same as the port number at which the server waits for connections?

★   **R21.5**   When a socket is created, which Internet address is used?
- **a.** The address of the computer to which you want to connect
- **b.** The address of your computer
- **c.** The address of your ISP

★   **R21.6**   What is the purpose of the accept method of the ServerSocket class?

★   **R21.7**   After a socket establishes a connection, what mechanism will your client program use to read data from the server computer?
- **a.** The Socket will fill a buffer with bytes.
- **b.** You will use a Reader obtained from the Socket.
- **c.** You will use an InputStream obtained from the Socket.

★   **R21.8**   Why is it not common to work directly with the InputStream and OutputStream objects obtained from a Socket object?

★   **R21.9**   When a client program communicates with a server, it sometimes needs to flush the output stream. Explain why.

★   **R21.10** What is the difference between HTTP and HTML?

★   **R21.11** How can you communicate with a web server without using sockets?

★   **R21.12** What is the difference between an URL instance and an URLConnection instance?

★   **R21.13** What is an URL? How do you create an object of class URL? How do you connect to an URL?

Programming Exercises

★   **P21.1** Modify the WebGet program to print only the HTTP header of the returned HTML page. The HTTP header is the beginning of the response data. It consists of several lines, such as

```
HTTP/1.1 200 OK
Date: Tue, 15 Jun 2010 16:10:34 GMT
Server: Apache/1.3.19 (Unix)
Cache-Control: max-age=86400
Expires: Wed, 16 Jun 2010 16:10:34 GMT
Connection: close
Content-Type: text/html
```

followed by a blank line.

★   **P21.2** Modify the WebGet program to print only the *title* of the returned HTML page. An HTML page has the structure

```
<html><head><title> . . . </title></head><body> . . . </body></html>
```

For example, if you run the program by typing at the command line java WebGet horstmann.com /, the output should be the title of the root web page at horstmann.com, such as Cay Horstmann's Home Page.

★★ **P21.3** Modify the BankServer program so that it can be terminated more elegantly. Provide another socket on port 8889 through which an administrator can log in. Support the commands LOGIN *password*, STATUS, PASSWORD *newPassword*, LOGOUT, and SHUTDOWN. The STATUS command should display the total number of clients that have logged in since the server started.

★★ **P21.4** Modify the BankServer program to provide complete error checking. For example, checking to make sure that there is enough money in the account when withdrawing. Send appropriate error reports back to the client. Enhance the protocol to be similar to HTTP, in which each server response starts with a number indicating the success or failure condition, followed by a string with response data or an error description.

★★ **P21.5** Write a client application that executes an infinite loop that does the following: (*a*) prompts the user for a number, (*b*) sends that value to the server, (*c*) receives the number, and (*d*) displays the new number. Also write a server that executes an infinite loop whose body accepts a client connection, reads a number from the client, computes its square root, and writes the result to the client.

★★ **P21.6** Implement a client-server program in which the client will print the date and time given by the server. Two classes should be implemented: DateClient and DateServer. The DateServer simply prints new Date().toString() whenever it accepts a connection and then closes the socket.

★★ **P21.7** Write a program to display the protocol, host, port, and file components of an URL. *Hint:* Look at the API documentation of the URL class.

★★★ **P21.8** Write a simple web server that recognizes only the GET request (without the Host: request parameter and blank line). When a client connects to your server and sends a command, such as GET *filename* HTTP/1.1, then return a header

```
HTTP/1.1 200 OK
```

followed by a blank line and all lines in the file. If the file doesn't exist, return 404 Not Found instead.

Your server should listen to port 8080. Test your web server by starting up your web browser and loading a page, such as localhost:8080/c:\cs1\myfile.html.

★★★   **P21.9**   Write a chat server and client program. The chat server accepts connections from clients. Whenever one of the clients sends a chat message, it is displayed for all other clients to see. Use a protocol with three commands: LOGIN *name*, CHAT *message*, and LOGOUT.

★★   **P21.10**   A query such as

        http://aa.usno.navy.mil/cgi-bin/aa_moonphases.pl?year=2011

returns a page containing the moon phases in a given year. Write a program that asks the user for a year, month, and day and then prints the phase of the moon on that day.

Programming Projects

Project 21.1   Write a program that allows several people to play a networked game. Each player connects to a game server. Each player's move is transmitted to the game server. The game server checks that the move is valid and informs all client programs of the updated game status.

You can either implement your favorite multiplayer game, or simply use Poker (see http://www.rgpfaq.com/basic-rules.html for the rules). Extra credit if your code is structured to separate the generic mechanism that is required for all games and the specific rules of a particular game.

Project 21.2   Write a program that allows a user to query the *CIA World Fact Book* (http://www.cia.gov/cia/publications/factbook) for facts about a country, such as the size, average income, capital city, and so on. To get the answers for user queries, connect to the web site, retrieve the web page, and extract the requested information. You will find that task simpler if you access the text version of the fact book.

Answers to Self-Check Questions

1. An IP address is a numerical address, consisting of four or sixteen bytes. A domain name is an alphanumeric string that is associated with an IP address.
2. TCP is reliable but somewhat slow. When sending sounds or images in real time, it is acceptable if a small amount of the data is lost. But there is no point in transmitting data that is late.
3. The browser software translates your requests (typed URLs and mouse clicks on links) into HTTP commands that it sends to the appropriate web servers.
4. Some Telnet implementations send all keystrokes that you type to the server, including the backspace key. The server does not recognize a character sequence such as G W Backspace E T as a valid command.

5. The program makes a connection to the server, sends the GET request, and prints the error message that the server returns.

6. `Socket s = new Socket("e-mail.sjsu.edu", 110);`

7. Port 80 is the standard port for HTTP. If a web server is running on the same computer, then one can't open a server socket on an open port.

8. No, a server socket just waits for a connection and yields a regular `Socket` object when a client has connected. You use that socket object to read the data that the client sends.

9. The `URLConnection` class understands the HTTP protocol, freeing you from assembling requests and analyzing response headers.

10. The bytes that encode the images are displayed on the console, but they will appear to be random gibberish.

Relational Databases

CHAPTER GOALS

- To understand how relational databases store information
- To learn how to query a database with the Structured Query Language (SQL)
- To connect to a database with Java Database Connectivity (JDBC)
- To write database programs that insert, update, and query data in a relational database

In Chapter 19 you saw how to store data in a file. When you store data, you will want to be able to add more data items, remove data, change data items, and find items that match certain criteria. However, if you have a lot of data, it can be difficult to carry out these operations quickly and efficiently. Because data storage is such a common task, special *database management systems (DBMS)* have been invented that let the programmer think in terms of the data rather than file storage. In this chapter you will learn how to use SQL, the Structured Query Language, to query and update information in a relational database, and how to access database information from Java programs.

CHAPTER CONTENTS

22.1 Organizing Database Information

22.1.1 Database Tables

A relational database stores information in tables. Each table column has a name and a data type.

A relational database stores information in *tables*. Figure 1 shows a typical table. As you can see, each *row* in this table corresponds to a product. The *column headers* correspond to attributes of the product: the product code, description, and unit price. Note that all items in a particular column have the same type: product codes and descriptions are strings, unit prices are floating-point numbers. The allowable column types differ somewhat from one database to another. Table 1 shows types that are commonly available in relational databases that follow the SQL (for Structured Query Language; often pronounced "sequel") standard.

SQL (Structured Query Language) is a command language for interacting with a database.

Most relational databases follow the SQL standard. There is no relationship between SQL and Java—they are different languages. However, as you will see later in this chapter, you can use Java to send SQL commands to a database. You will see in the next section how to use SQL commands to carry out queries, but there are other SQL commands.

For example, here is the SQL command to create a product table:

```
CREATE TABLE Product
(
    Product_Code CHAR(7),
    Description VARCHAR(40),
    Price DECIMAL(10, 2)
)
```

Product

Product_Code	Description	Price
116-064	Toaster	24.95
257-535	Hair dryer	29.95
643-119	Car vacuum	19.99

Figure 1 A Product Table in a Relational Database

Table 1	Some Standard SQL Types and Their Corresponding Java Types
SQL Data Type	Java Data Type
INTEGER or INT	int
REAL	float
DOUBLE	double
DECIMAL(*m*, *n*)	Fixed-point decimal numbers with *m* total digits and *n* digits after the decimal point; similar to BigDecimal.
BOOLEAN	boolean
VARCHAR(*n*)	Variable-length String of length up to *n*
CHARACTER(*n*) or CHAR(*n*)	Fixed-length String of length *n*

Use the SQL commands CREATE TABLE and INSERT INTO to add data to a database.

Unlike Java, SQL is not case sensitive. For example, you could spell the command create table instead of CREATE TABLE. However, as a matter of convention, we will use uppercase letters for SQL keywords and mixed case for table and column names.

To insert rows into the table, use the INSERT INTO command. Issue one command for each row, such as

```
INSERT INTO Product
   VALUES ('257-535', 'Hair dryer', 29.95)
```

SQL uses single quotes ('), not double quotes, to delimit strings. What if you have a string that contains a single quote? Rather than using an escape sequence (such as \') as in Java, you just write the single quote twice, such as

```
'Sam''s Small Appliances'
```

If you create a table and subsequently want to remove it, use the DROP TABLE command. For example,

```
DROP TABLE Test
```

22.1.2 Linking Tables

If you have objects whose instance variables are strings, numbers, dates, or other types that are permissible as table column types, then you can easily store them as rows in a database table. For example, consider a Java class Customer:

```java
public class Customer
{
   private String name;
   private String address;
   private String city;
   private String state;
   private String zip;
   . . .
}
```

Customer

Name	Address	City	State	Zip
VARCHAR(40)	VARCHAR(40)	VARCHAR(30)	CHAR(2)	CHAR(5)
Sam's Small Appliances	100 Main Street	Anytown	CA	98765

Figure 2   A Customer Table

It is simple to come up with a database table structure that allows you to store customers—see Figure 2.

For other objects, it is not so easy. Consider an invoice. Each invoice object contains a reference to a customer object.

```
public class Invoice
{
    private int invoiceNumber;
    private Customer theCustomer;
    . . .
}
```

Because Customer isn't a standard SQL type, you might consider simply entering all the customer data into the invoice table—see Figure 3. However, this is not a good idea. If you look at the sample data in Figure 3, you will notice that Sam's Small Appliances had two invoices, number 11731 and 11733. Yet all information for the customer was *replicated* in two rows.

This replication has two problems. First, it is wasteful to store the same information multiple times. If the same customer places many orders, then the replicated information can take up a lot of space. More importantly, the replication is *dangerous*. Suppose the customer moves to a new address. Then it would be an easy mistake to update the customer information in some of the invoice records and leave the old address in place in others.

In a Java program, neither of these problems occurs. Multiple Invoice objects can contain references to a single shared Customer object.

Invoice

Invoice_ Number	Customer_ Name	Customer_ Address	Customer_ City	Customer_ State	Customer_ Zip	...
INTEGER	VARCHAR(40)	VARCHAR(40)	VARCHAR(30)	CHAR(2)	CHAR(5)	...
11731	Sam's Small Appliances	100 Main Street	Anytown	CA	98765	...
11732	Electronics Unlimited	1175 Liberty Ave	Pleasantville	MI	45066	...
11733	Sam's Small Appliances	100 Main Street	Anytown	CA	98765	...

Figure 3   A Poor Design for an Invoice Table with Replicated Customer Data

Invoice

Invoice_ Number	Customer_ Number	Payment
INTEGER	INTEGER	DECIMAL(10, 2)
11731	3175	0
11732	3176	249.95
11733	3175	0

Customer

Customer_ Number	Name	Address	City	State	Zip
INTEGER	VARCHAR(40)	VARCHAR(40)	VARCHAR(30)	CHAR(2)	CHAR(5)
3175	Sam's Small Appliances	100 Main Street	Anytown	CA	98765
3176	Electronics Unlimited	1175 Liberty Ave	Pleasantville	MI	45066

Figure 4   Two Tables for Invoice and Customer Data

> You should avoid rows with replicated data. Instead, distribute the data over multiple tables.

The first step in achieving the same effect in a database is to organize your data into multiple tables as in Figure 4. Dividing the columns into two tables solves the replication problem. The customer data are no longer replicated—the Invoice table contains no customer information, and the Customer table contains a single record for each customer. But how can we refer to the customer to which an invoice is issued? Notice in Figure 4 that there is now a Customer_Number column in *both* the Customer table and the Invoice table. Now all invoices for Sam's Small Appliances share only the customer number. The two tables are *linked* by the Customer_Number field. To find out more details about this customer, you need to use the customer number to look up the customer in the Customer table.

Note that the customer number is a *unique identifier*. We introduced the customer number because the customer name by itself may not be unique. For example, there may well be multiple Electronics Unlimited stores in various locations. Thus, the customer name alone does not uniquely identify a record (a row of data), so we cannot use the name as a link between the two tables.

> A primary key is a column (or set of columns) whose value uniquely specifies a table record.

In database terminology, a column (or combination of columns) that uniquely identifies a row in a table is called a **primary key**. In our Customer table, the Customer_Number column is a primary key. Not all database tables need a primary key. You need a primary key if you want to establish a link from another table. For example, the Customer table needs a primary key so that you can link customers to invoices.

> A foreign key is a reference to a primary key in a linked table.

When a primary key is linked to another table, the matching column (or combination of columns) in that table is called a **foreign key**. For example, the Customer_Number in the Invoice table is a foreign key, linked to the primary key in the Customer table. Unlike primary keys, foreign keys need not be unique. For example, in our Invoice table we have several records that have the same value for the Customer_Number foreign key.

22.1.3 Implementing Multi-Valued Relationships

Each invoice is linked to exactly one customer. That is called a *single-valued* relationship. On the other hand, each invoice has many line items. (As in Chapter 12, a *line item* identifies the product, quantity, and unit price.) Thus, there is a *multi-valued* relationship between invoices and line items. In the Java class, the LineItem objects are stored in an array list:

```
public class Invoice
{
    private int invoiceNumber;
    private Customer theCustomer;
    private ArrayList<LineItem> items;
    private double payment;
    . . .
}
```

However, in a relational database, you need to store the information in tables. Surprisingly many programmers, when faced with this situation, commit a major faux pas and replicate columns, one for each line item, as in the Figure 5 below.

Clearly, this design is not satisfactory. What should we do if there are more than three line items on an invoice? Perhaps we should have 10 line items instead? But that is wasteful if the majority of invoices have only a couple of line items, and it still does not solve our problem for the occasional invoice with lots of line items.

Instead, distribute the information into two tables: one for invoices and another for line items. Link each line item back to its invoice with an Invoice_Number foreign key in the LineItem table—see Figure 6.

Invoice

Invoice_ Number	Customer_ Number	Product_ Code1	Quantity1	Product_ Code2	Quantity2	Product_ Code3	Quantity3	Payment
INTEGER	INTEGER	CHAR(7)	INTEGER	CHAR(7)	INTEGER	CHAR(7)	INTEGER	DECIMAL(10, 2)
11731	3175	116-064	3	257-535	1	643-119	2	0

Figure 5 A Poor Design for an Invoice Table with Replicated Columns

LineItem

Invoice_Number	Product_Code	Quantity
INTEGER	CHAR(7)	INTEGER
11731	116-064	3
11731	257-535	1
11731	643-119	2
11732	116-064	10
11733	116-064	2
11733	643-119	1

Invoice

Invoice_Number	Customer_Number	Payment
INTEGER	INTEGER	DECIMAL(10, 2)
11731	3175	0
11732	3176	249.50
11733	3175	0

Figure 6 Linked Invoice and LineItem Tables Implement a Multi-Valued Relationship

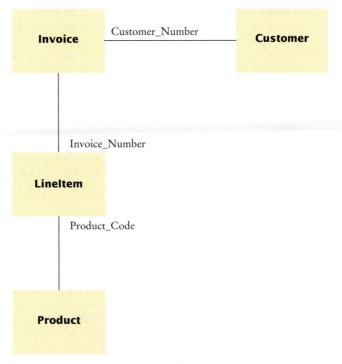

Figure 7 The Links Between the Tables in the Sample Database

> Implement one-to-many relationships with linked tables, not replicated columns.

Our database now consists of four tables:

- Invoice
- Customer
- LineItem
- Product

Figure 7 shows the links between these tables. In the next section you will see how to query this database for information about invoices, customers, and products. The queries will take advantage of the links between the tables.

SELF CHECK

1. Would a telephone number be a good primary key for a customer table?
2. In the database of Section 22.1.3, what are all the products that customer 3176 ordered?

Productivity Hint 22.1

Stick with the Standard

The Java language is highly standardized. You will rarely find compilers that allow you to specify Java code that differs from the standard, and if they do, it is always a compiler bug. However, SQL implementations are often much more forgiving. For example, many SQL vendors allow you to use a Java-style escape sequence such as

```
'Sam\'s Small Appliances'
```

in a SQL string. The vendor probably thought that this would be "helpful" to programmers who are familiar with Java or C. (The C language uses the same escape mechanism for denoting special characters.)

However, this is an illusion. Deviating from the standard limits portability. Suppose you later want to move your database code to another vendor, perhaps to improve performance or to lower the cost of the database software. If the other vendor hasn't implemented a particular deviation, then your code will no longer work and you need to spend time fixing it.

To avoid these problems, you should stick with the standard. With SQL, you cannot rely on your database to flag all errors—some of them may be considered "helpful" extensions. That means that you need to *know* the standard and have the discipline to follow it. (See *A Guide to the SQL Standard: A User's Guide to the Standard Database Language*, by Chris J. Date and Hugh Darwen (Addison-Wesley, 1996), for more information.)

Productivity Hint 22.2

Avoid Unnecessary Data Replication

It is very common for beginning database designers to replicate data. When replicating data in a table, ask yourself if you can move the replicated data into a separate table and use a key, such as a code or ID number, to link the tables.

Consider this example in an Invoice table:

Invoice

...	Product_Code	Description	Price	...
...	CHAR(7)	VARCHAR(40)	DECIMAL(10, 2)	...
...	116-064	Toaster	24.95	...
...	116-064	Toaster	24.95	...
...	...	...	...	...

As you can see, some product information is replicated. Is this replication an error? It depends. The product description for the product with code 116-064 is always going to be "Toaster". Therefore, that correspondence should be stored in an external Product table.

The product price, however, can change over time. When it does, the old invoices don't automatically use the new price. Thus, it makes sense to store the price that the customer was actually charged in an Invoice table. The current list price, however, is best stored in an external Product table.

Special Topic 22.1

Primary Keys and Indexes

Recall that a **primary key** is a column (or combination of columns) that uniquely identifies a row in a table. When a table has a primary key, then the database can build an *index file:* a file that stores information on how to access a row quickly when the primary key is known. Indexing can greatly increase the speed of database queries.

If the primary key is contained in a single column, then you can tag the column with the PRIMARY KEY attribute, like this:

```
CREATE TABLE Product
(
    Product_Code CHAR(7) PRIMARY KEY,
    Description VARCHAR(40),
    Price DECIMAL(10, 2)
)
```

If the primary key is contained in multiple columns, then add a PRIMARY KEY clause to the end of the CREATE TABLE command, like this:

```
CREATE TABLE LineItem
(
    Invoice_Number INTEGER,
    Product_Code CHAR(7),
    Quantity INTEGER,
    PRIMARY KEY (Invoice_Number, Product_Code)
)
```

Occasionally, one can speed queries up by building *secondary indexes:* index files that index other column sets, which are not necessarily unique. That is an advanced technique that we will not discuss here.

Productivity Hint 22.3

Don't Replicate Columns in a Table

If you find yourself numbering columns in a table with suffixes 1, 2, and so forth (such as Quantity1, Quantity2, Quantity3), then you are probably on the wrong track. How do you know there are exactly three quantities? In that case, it's time for another table.

Add a table to hold the information for which you replicated the columns. In that table, add a column that links back to a key in the first table, such as the invoice number in our example. By using an additional table, you can implement a multi-valued relationship.

22.2 Queries

Let's assume that the tables in our database have been created and that records have been inserted. Once a database is filled with data, you will want to *query* the database for information, such as

- What are the names and addresses of all customers?
- What are the names and addresses of all customers in California?
- What are the names and addresses of all customers who buy toasters?
- What are the names and addresses of all customers with unpaid invoices?

In this section you will learn how to formulate simple and complex queries in SQL. We will use the data shown in Figure 8 for our examples.

Invoice

Invoice_ Number	Customer_ Number	Payment
INTEGER	INTEGER	DECIMAL(10, 2)
11731	3175	0
11732	3176	249.50
11733	3175	0

LineItem

Invoice_ Number	Product_ Code	Quantity
INTEGER	CHAR(7)	INTEGER
11731	116-064	3
11731	257-535	1
11731	643-119	2
11732	116-064	10
11733	116-064	2
11733	643-119	1

Product

Product_Code	Description	Price
CHAR(7)	VARCHAR(40)	DECIMAL(10, 2)
116-064	Toaster	24.95
257-535	Hair dryer	29.95
643-119	Car vacuum	19.99

Customer

Customer_ Number	Name	Address	City	State	Zip
INTEGER	VARCHAR(40)	VARCHAR(40)	VARCHAR(30)	CHAR(2)	CHAR(5)
3175	Sam's Small Appliances	100 Main Street	Anytown	CA	98765
3176	Electronics Unlimited	1175 Liberty Ave	Pleasantville	MI	45066

Figure 8 A Sample Database

22.2.1 Simple Queries

Use the SQL SELECT command to query a database.

In SQL, you use the SELECT command to issue queries. For example, the command to select all data from the Customer table is

```
SELECT * FROM Customer
```

The result is

Customer_ Number	Name	Address	City	State	Zip
3175	Sam's Small Appliances	100 Main Street	Anytown	CA	98765
3176	Electronics Unlimited	1175 Liberty Ave	Pleasantville	MI	45066

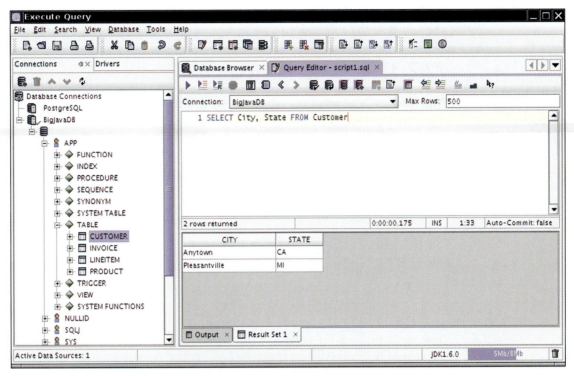

Figure 9 An Interactive SQL Tool

The outcome of the query is a *view*—a set of rows and columns that provides a "window" through which you can see some of the database data. If you select all rows and columns from a single table, of course you get a view into just that table.

Many database systems have tools that let you issue interactive SQL commands—Figure 9 shows a typical example. When you issue a SELECT command, the tool displays the resulting view. You may want to skip ahead to Section 22.3 and install a database. Or perhaps your computer lab has a database installed already. Then you can run the interactive SQL tool of your database and try out some queries.

22.2.2 Selecting Columns

Often, you don't care about all columns in a table. Suppose your traveling salesperson is planning a trip to all customers. To plan the route, the salesperson wants to know the cities and states of all customers. Here is the query:

```
SELECT City, State FROM Customer
```

The result is

City	State
Anytown	CA
Pleasantville	MI

As you can see, the syntax for selecting columns is straightforward. Simply specify the names of the columns you want, separated by commas.

22.2.3 Selecting Subsets

You just saw how you can restrict a view to show selected columns. Sometimes you want to select certain rows that fit a particular criterion. For example, you may want to find all customers in California. Whenever you want to select a subset, you use the WHERE clause, followed by the condition that describes the subset. Here is an example.

```
SELECT * FROM Customer WHERE State = 'CA'
```

The result is

Customer_Number	Name	Address	City	State	Zip
3175	Sam's Small Appliances	100 Main Street	Anytown	CA	98765

You have to be a bit careful with expressing the condition in the WHERE clause, because SQL syntax differs from the Java syntax. As you already know, in SQL you use single quotes to delimit strings, such as 'CA'. You also use a single =, not a double ==, to test for equality. To test for inequality, you use the <> operator. For example

```
SELECT * FROM Customer WHERE State <> 'CA'
```

selects all customers that are *not* in California.

You can match patterns with the LIKE operator. The right-hand side must be a string that can contain the special symbols _ (match exactly one character) and % (match any character sequence). For example, the expression

```
Name LIKE '_o%'
```

matches all strings whose second character is an "o". Thus, "Toaster" is a match but "Crowbar" is not.

You can combine expressions with the logical connectives AND, OR, and NOT. (Do not use the Java &&, ||, and ! operators.) For example,

```
SELECT *
   FROM Product
   WHERE Price < 100
      AND Description <> 'Toaster'
```

selects all products with a price less than 100 that are not toasters.

Of course, you can select both row and column subsets, such as

```
SELECT Name, City FROM Customer WHERE State = 'CA'
```

22.2.4 Calculations

Suppose you want to find out *how many* customers there are in California. Use the COUNT function:

```
SELECT COUNT(*) FROM Customer WHERE State = 'CA'
```

In addition to the COUNT function, there are four other functions: SUM, AVG (average), MAX, and MIN.

The * means that you want to calculate entire records. That is appropriate only for the COUNT function. For other functions, you have to access a specific column. Put the column name inside the parentheses:

```
SELECT AVG(Price) FROM Product
```

22.2.5 Joins

The queries that you have seen so far all involve a single table. However, usually, the information that you want is distributed over multiple tables. For example, suppose you are asked to find all invoices that include a line item for a car vacuum. From the Product table, you can issue a query to find the product code:

```
SELECT Product_Code
    FROM Product
    WHERE Description = 'Car vacuum'
```

You will find out that the car vacuum has product code 643-119. Then you can issue a second query

```
SELECT Invoice_Number
    FROM LineItem
    WHERE Product_Code = '643-119'
```

But it makes sense to combine these two queries so that you don't have to keep track of the intermediate result. When combining queries, note that the two tables are linked by the Product_Code field. We want to look at matching rows in both tables. In other words, we want to restrict the search to rows where

```
Product.Product_Code = LineItem.Product_Code
```

Here, the syntax

TableName.ColumnName

denotes the column in a particular table. Whenever a query involves multiple tables, you should specify both the table name and the column name. Thus, the combined query is

```
SELECT LineItem.Invoice_Number
    FROM Product, LineItem
    WHERE Product.Description = 'Car vacuum'
        AND Product.Product_Code = LineItem.Product_Code
```

The result is

Invoice_Number
11731
11733

A join is a query that involves multiple tables.

In this query, the FROM clause contains the names of multiple tables, separated by commas. (It doesn't matter in which order you list the tables.) Such a query is often called a **join** because it involves joining multiple tables.

You may want to know in what cities hair dryers are popular. Now you need to add the Customer table to the query—it contains the customer addresses. The customers are referenced by invoices, so you need that table as well. Here is the complete query:

```
SELECT Customer.City, Customer.State, Customer.Zip
   FROM Product, LineItem, Invoice, Customer
   WHERE Product.Description = 'Hair dryer'
      AND Product.Product_Code = LineItem.Product_Code
      AND LineItem.Invoice_Number = Invoice.Invoice_Number
      AND Invoice.Customer_Number = Customer.Customer_Number
```

The result is

City	State	Zip
Anytown	CA	98765

Whenever you formulate a query that involves multiple tables, remember to:

- List all tables that are involved in the query in the FROM clause.
- Use the *TableName.ColumnName* syntax to refer to column names.
- List all join conditions (*TableName1.ColumnName1 = TableName2.ColumnName2*) in the WHERE clause.

As you can see, these queries can get a bit complex. However, databases are very good at answering these queries (see Productivity Hint 22.4 on page 892). One remarkable aspect of SQL is that you tell the database *what* you want, not *how* it should find the answer. It is entirely up to the database to come up with a plan for how to find the answer to your query in the shortest number of steps. Commercial database manufacturers take great pride in coming up with clever ways to speed up queries: query optimization strategies, caching of prior results, and so on. In this regard, SQL is a very different language from Java. SQL statements are descriptive and leave it to the database to determine how to execute them. Java statements are prescriptive—you spell out exactly the steps you want your program to carry out.

22.2.6 Updating and Deleting Data

The UPDATE and DELETE SQL commands modify the data in a database.

Up to now, you have been shown how to formulate increasingly complex SELECT queries. The outcome of a SELECT query is a *result set* that you can view and analyze. Two related statement types, UPDATE and DELETE, don't produce a result set. Instead, they modify the database. The DELETE statement is the easier of the two. It simply deletes the rows that you specify. For example, to delete all customers in California, you issue the statement

```
DELETE FROM Customer WHERE State = 'CA'
```

The UPDATE query allows you to update columns of all records that fulfill a certain condition. For example, here is how you can add another unit to the quantity of every line item in invoice number 11731.

```
UPDATE LineItem
   SET Quantity = Quantity + 1
   WHERE Invoice_Number = '11731'
```

You can update multiple column values by specifying multiple update expressions in the SET clause, separated by commas.

Both the DELETE and the UPDATE statements return a value, namely the number of rows that are deleted or updated.

SELF CHECK

3. How do you query the names of all customers that are not from Alaska or Hawaii?

4. How do you query all invoice numbers of all customers in Hawaii?

Common Error 22.1

Joining Tables Without Specifying a Link Condition

If you select data from multiple tables without a restriction, the result is somewhat surprising—you get a result set containing *all combinations* of the values, whether or not one of the combinations exists with actual data. For example, the query

```
SELECT Invoice.Invoice_Number, Customer.Name
    FROM Invoice, Customer
```

returns the result set

Invoice.Invoice_Number	Customer.Name
11731	Sam's Small Appliances
11732	Sam's Small Appliances
11733	Sam's Small Appliances
11731	Electronics Unlimited
11732	Electronics Unlimited
11733	Electronics Unlimited

As you can see, the result set contains all six combinations of invoice numbers (11731, 11732, 11733) and customer names (Sam's Small Appliances and Electronics Unlimited), even though three of those combinations don't occur with real invoices. You need to supply a WHERE clause to restrict the set of combinations. For example,

```
SELECT Invoice.Invoice_Number, Customer.Name
    FROM Invoice, Customer
    WHERE Invoice.Customer_Number = Customer.Customer_Number
```

yields

Invoice.Invoice_Number	Customer.Name
11731	Sam's Small Appliances
11732	Electronics Unlimited
11733	Sam's Small Appliances

Random Fact 22.1

Databases and Privacy

Most companies use computers to keep huge databases of customer records and other business information. Databases not only lower the cost of doing business, they improve the quality of service that companies can offer. Nowadays it is almost unimaginable how time-consuming it used to be to withdraw money from a bank branch or to make travel reservations.

As these databases became ubiquitous, they started creating problems for citizens. Consider the "no fly list" maintained by the U.S. government, which lists names used by suspected terrorists. On March 1, 2007, Professor Walter Murphy, a constitutional scholar of Princeton University and a decorated former Marine, was denied a boarding pass. The airline employee asked him, "Have you been in any peace marches? We ban a lot of people from flying because of that." As Murphy tells it, "I explained that I had not so marched but had, in September 2006, given a lecture at Princeton, televised and put on the Web, highly critical of George Bush for his many violations of the constitution. 'That'll do it,' the man said."

We do not actually know if Professor Murphy's name was on the list because he was critical of the Bush administration or because some other potentially dangerous person had traveled under the same name. Travelers with similar misfortunes had serious difficulties trying to get themselves off the list.

Problems such as these have become commonplace. Companies and the government routinely merge multiple databases, derive information about us that may be quite inaccurate, and then use that information to make decisions. An insurance company may deny coverage, or charge a higher premium, if it finds that you have too many relatives with a certain disease. You may be denied a job because of a credit or medical report. You do not usually know what information about yourself is stored or how it is used. In cases where the information can be checked—such as credit reports—it is often difficult to correct errors.

Another issue of concern is privacy. Most people do something, at one time or another in their lives, that they do not want everyone to know about. As judge Louis Brandeis wrote in 1928, "Privacy is the right to be alone—the most comprehensive of rights, and the right most valued by civilized man." When employers can see your old Facebook posts, divorce lawyers have access to tollroad records, and Google mines your e-mails and searches to present you "targeted" advertising, you have little privacy left.

The 1948 "universal declaration of human rights" by the United Nations states, "No one shall be subjected to arbitrary interference with his privacy, family, home or correspondence,

If you pay road or bridge tolls with an electronic pass, your records may not be private.

nor to attacks upon his honour and reputation. Everyone has the right to the protection of the law against such interference or attacks." The United States has surprisingly few legal protections against privacy invasion, apart from federal laws protecting student records and video rentals (the latter was passed after a Supreme Court nominee's video rental records were published). Other industrialized countries have gone much further and recognize every citizen's right to control what information about themselves should be communicated to others and under what circumstances.

22.3 Installing a Database

A wide variety of database systems are available. Among them are

- Production-quality databases, such as Oracle, IBM DB2, Microsoft SQL Server, PostgreSQL, or MySQL.
- Lightweight Java databases, such as Apache Derby.
- Desktop databases, such as Microsoft Access.

Which one should you choose for learning database programming? That depends greatly on your available budget, computing resources, and experience with installing complex software. In a laboratory environment with a trained administrator, it makes a lot of sense to install a production-quality database. Lightweight Java databases are much easier to install and work on a variety of platforms. This makes them a good choice for the beginner. Desktop databases have limited SQL support and can be difficult to configure for Java programming.

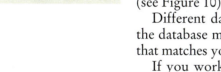

You need a JDBC (Java Database Connectivity) driver to access a database from a Java program.

In addition to a database, you need a *JDBC driver*. The acronym JDBC stands for Java Database Connectivity, the name of the technology that enables Java programs to interact with databases. When your Java program issues SQL commands, the driver forwards them to the database and lets your program analyze the results (see Figure 10).

Different databases require different drivers, which may be supplied by either the database manufacturer or a third party. You need to locate and install the driver that matches your database.

If you work in a computing laboratory, someone will have installed a database for you, and you should ask your lab for instructions on how to use it. If you install your own database, we recommend that you start out with the lightweight Apache Derby database. Java 6 includes Apache Derby, branded as "JavaDB". If you use an earlier version of Java, you can download Apache Derby from http://db.apache.org/derby/.

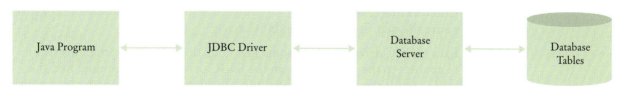

Figure 10 JDBC Architecture

You should run a test program to check that your database is working correctly. You will find the code for the test program at the end of this section. The following section describes the implementation of the test program in detail.

If you use Apache Derby, then follow these simple instructions.

1. Locate the JDBC driver file `derby.jar` and copy it into the `ch22/test` directory of the companion code for this book.

2. Open a shell window, change to the `ch22/test` directory, and run

   ```
   javac TestDB.java
   java -classpath derby.jar;. TestDB database.properties
   ```

   If you run Linux, UNIX, or Mac OS X, change the semicolon to a colon:

   ```
   java -classpath derby.jar:. TestDB database.properties
   ```

3. If you followed the test instructions precisely, you should see one line of output with the name "Romeo". You may then skip the remainder of this section.

If you install a database other than the one included with Java, you will need to set aside some time to carry out the installation process. Detailed instructions for installing a database vary widely. Here we give you a general sequence of steps on how to install a database and test your installation.

1. Install the database program.

2. Start the database. With most database systems (but not some of the light-weight Java database systems), you need to start the database server before you can carry out any database operations. Read the installation instructions for details.

3. Set up user accounts. This typically involves running an administration program, logging in as administrator with a default administration account, and adding user names and passwords. If you are the only user of the database, you may simply be able to use a default account. Again, details vary greatly among databases, and you should consult the documentation.

4. Run a test. Locate the program that allows you to execute interactive SQL instructions. Run the program and issue the following SQL instructions:

   ```
   CREATE TABLE Test (Name VARCHAR(20))
   INSERT INTO Test VALUES ('Romeo')
   SELECT * FROM Test
   DROP TABLE Test
   ```

   At this point, you should get a display that shows a single row and column of the Test database, containing the string "Romeo". If not, carefully read the documentation of your SQL tool to see how you need to enter SQL statements. For example, with some SQL tools, you need a special terminator for each SQL statement.

Next, locate the JDBC driver and run a sample Java program to verify that the installation was successful.

Here are the steps for testing the JDBC driver.

1. Every JDBC driver contains some Java code that your Java programs require to connect to the database. From the JDBC driver documentation, find the *class path* for the driver. Here is a typical example—the class path component

Make sure the JDBC driver is on the class path when you launch the Java program.

for the Apache Derby JDBC driver that is included in the Java Development kit.

```
c:\jdk1.6.0\db\lib\derby.jar
```

One version of the Oracle database uses a class path

```
/usr/local/oracle/jdbc/classes111b.zip
```

You will find this information in the documentation of your database system.

2. If your JDBC driver is not fully compliant with the JDBC4 standard, you need to know the name of the driver class. For example, the Oracle database uses a driver

```
oracle.jdbc.driver.OracleDriver
```

Your database documentation will have this information.

3. Find the name of the *database URL* that your driver expects. All database URLs have the format

   jdbc:*subprotocol*:*driver-specific data*

   The subprotocol is a code that identifies the driver manufacturer, such as mckoi or oracle. The driver-specific data encode the database name and the location of the database. Here are typical examples:

```
jdbc:derby:InvoiceDB;create=true
jdbc:oracle:thin:@larry.mathcs.sjsu.edu:1521:InvoiceDB
```

   Again, consult your JDBC driver information for details on the format of the database URL and how to specify the database that you use.

To connect to the database, you need to specify a database URL, user name, and password.

4. In order to run the TestDB.java program at the end of this section, edit the file database.properties and supply

   • The driver class name (if required).
   • The database URL.
   • Your database user name.
   • Your database password.

   With lightweight Java databases such as Apache Derby, you usually specify a blank user name and password.

5. Compile the program as

```
javac TestDB.java
```

6. Run the program as

   java -classpath *driver_class_path*;. TestDB database.properties

   In UNIX/Linux/Mac OS X, use a : separator in the class path:

   java -classpath *driver_class_path*:. TestDB database.properties

   If everything works correctly, you will get an output that lists all data in the Test table. If you followed the test instructions precisely, you will see one line of output with the name "Romeo".

Here is the test program. We will explain the Java instructions of this program in the following section.

ch22/test/TestDB.java

```java
1   import java.io.File
2   import java.sql.Connection;
3   import java.sql.ResultSet;
4   import java.sql.Statement;
5
6   /**
7      Tests a database installation by creating and querying
8      a sample table. Call this program as
9      java -classpath driver_class_path;. TestDB database.properties
10  */
11  public class TestDB
12  {
13     public static void main(String[] args) throws Exception
14     {
15        if (args.length == 0)
16        {
17           System.out.println(
18                 "Usage: java -classpath driver_class_path"
19                 + File.pathSeparator
20                 + ". TestDB database.properties");
21           return;
22        }
23        else
24           SimpleDataSource.init(args[0]);
25
26        Connection conn = SimpleDataSource.getConnection();
27        try
28        {
29           Statement stat = conn.createStatement();
30
31           stat.execute("CREATE TABLE Test (Name VARCHAR(20))");
32           stat.execute("INSERT INTO Test VALUES ('Romeo')");
33
34           ResultSet result = stat.executeQuery("SELECT * FROM Test");
35           result.next();
36           System.out.println(result.getString("Name"));
37
38           stat.execute("DROP TABLE Test");
39        }
40        finally
41        {
42           conn.close();
43        }
44     }
45  }
```

ch22/test/SimpleDataSource.java

```java
1   import java.sql.Connection;
2   import java.sql.DriverManager;
3   import java.sql.SQLException;
4   import java.io.FileInputStream;
5   import java.io.IOException;
6   import java.util.Properties;
7
8   /**
9      A simple data source for getting database connections.
10  */
```

```
11  public class SimpleDataSource
12  {
13     private static String url;
14     private static String username;
15     private static String password;
16
17     /**
18         Initializes the data source.
19         @param fileName the name of the property file that
20         contains the database driver, URL, username, and password
21     */
22     public static void init(String fileName)
23           throws IOException, ClassNotFoundException
24     {
25        Properties props = new Properties();
26        FileInputStream in = new FileInputStream(fileName);
27        props.load(in);
28
29        String driver = props.getProperty("jdbc.driver");
30        url = props.getProperty("jdbc.url");
31        username = props.getProperty("jdbc.username");
32        if (username == null) username = "";
33        password = props.getProperty("jdbc.password");
34        if (password == null) password = "";
35        if (driver != null)
36           Class.forName(driver);
37     }
38
39     /**
40         Gets a connection to the database.
41         @return the database connection
42     */
43     public static Connection getConnection() throws SQLException
44     {
45        return DriverManager.getConnection(url, username, password);
46     }
47  }
```

ch22/test/database.properties (for Apache Derby)

```
1  jdbc.url=jdbc:derby:BigJavaDB;create=true
2  # With other databases, you may need to add entries such as these
3  # jdbc.username=admin
4  # jdbc.password=secret
5  # jdbc.driver=org.apache.derby.jdbc.EmbeddedDriver
```

S E L F   C H E C K

5. After installing a database system, how can you test that it is properly installed?

6. You are starting a Java database program to use the Apache Derby database and get the following error message:

   ```
   Exception in thread "main" java.sql.SQLException: No suitable driver found for
   jdbc:derby:BigJavaDB;create=true
   ```

   What is the most likely cause of this error?

22.4 Database Programming in Java

22.4.1 Connecting to the Database

Use a Connection object to access a database from a Java program.

To connect to a database, you need an object of the Connection class. The following shows you how to obtain such a connection. With older versions of the JDBC standard, you first need to manually load the database driver class. Starting with JDBC4 (which is a part of Java 6), the driver is loaded automatically. If you use Java 6 or later and a fully JDBC4 compatible driver, you can skip the loading step. Otherwise, use the following code:

```
String driver = . . .;
Class.forName(driver); // Load driver
```

Next, you ask the DriverManager for a connection. You need to initialize the url, username, and password strings with the values that apply to your database.

```
String url = . . .;
String username = . . .;
String password = . . .;
Connection conn = DriverManager.getConnection(url, username, password);
```

When you are done issuing your database commands, close the database connection by calling the close method:

```
conn.close();
```

This is actually a somewhat simplistic view of connection management. Two problems occur in practice. Larger programs (such as the bank example in Section 22.5) need to connect to the database from many classes. You don't want to propagate the database login information to a large number of classes. Also, it is usually not feasible to use a single connection for all database requests. In particular, as you will see in Chapter 24, a container for Java server pages can run many simultaneous web page requests from different browsers. Each page request needs its own database connection. But because opening a database connection is quite slow and page requests come so frequently, database connections need to be pooled rather than closed and reopened. The details can be complex, and there is currently no standard implementation available.

It is always a good idea to decouple connection management from the other database code. We supply a SimpleDataSource class for this purpose. You can find the implementation at the end of the preceding section. This class is a very simple tool for connection management. At the beginning of your program, call the static init method with the name of the database configuration file, for example

```
SimpleDataSource.init("database.properties");
```

The configuration file is a text file that may contain the following lines:

```
jdbc.driver= . . .
jdbc.url= . . .
jdbc.username= . . .
jdbc.password= . . .
```

The init method uses the Properties class, which is designed to make it easy to read such a file.

The Properties class has a load method to read a file of key/value pairs from a stream:

```
Properties props = new Properties();
FileInputStream in = new FileInputStream(fileName);
props.load(in);
```

The getProperty method returns the value of a given key:

```
String driver = props.getProperty("jdbc.driver");
```

You don't actually have to think about this—the init method takes care of the details. Whenever you need a connection, call

```
Connection conn = SimpleDataSource.getConnection();
```

You need to close the connection by calling

```
conn.close();
```

when you are done using it.

Real-world connection managers have slightly different methods, but the basic principle is the same.

22.4.2 Executing SQL Statements

A Connection object can create Statement objects that are used to execute SQL commands.

Once you have a connection, you can use it to create Statement objects. You need Statement objects to execute SQL statements.

```
Statement stat = conn.createStatement();
```

The execute method of the Statement class executes a SQL statement. For example,

```
stat.execute("CREATE TABLE Test (Name VARCHAR(20))");
stat.execute("INSERT INTO Test VALUES ('Romeo')");
```

The result of a SQL query is returned in a ResultSet object.

To issue a query, use the executeQuery method of the Statement class. The query result is returned as a ResultSet object. For example,

```
String query = "SELECT * FROM Test";
ResultSet result = stat.executeQuery(query);
```

You will see in the next section how to use the ResultSet object to analyze the result of the query.

For UPDATE statements, you can use the executeUpdate method. It returns the number of rows affected by the statement:

```
String command = "UPDATE LineItem"
    + " SET Quantity = Quantity + 1"
    + " WHERE Invoice_Number = '11731'";
int count = stat.executeUpdate(command);
```

If your statement has variable parts, then you should use a PreparedStatement instead.

```
String query = "SELECT * WHERE Account_Number = ?";
PreparedStatement stat = conn.prepareStatement(query);
```

The ? symbols in the query string denote variables that you fill in when you make an actual query. You call a set method for that purpose, for example

```
stat.setString(1, accountNumber);
```

The first parameter of the set methods denotes the variable position: 1 is the first ?, 2 the second, and so on. There are also methods setInt and setDouble for setting numerical variables. After you set all variables, you call executeQuery or executeUpdate.

Finally, you can use the generic execute method to execute arbitrary SQL statements. It returns a boolean value to indicate whether the SQL command yields a result set. If so, you can obtain it with the getResultSet method. Otherwise, you can get the update count with the getUpdateCount method.

```
String command = . . .;
boolean hasResultSet = stat.execute(command);
if (hasResultSet)
{
    ResultSet result = stat.getResultSet();
    . . .
}
else
{
    int count = stat.getUpdateCount();
    . . .
}
```

You can reuse a Statement or PreparedStatement object to execute as many SQL commands as you like. However, for each statement, you should only have one active ResultSet. If your program needs to look at several result sets at the same time, then you need to create multiple Statement objects.

When you are done using a ResultSet, you should close it before issuing a new query on the same statement.

```
result.close();
```

When you are done with a Statement object, you should close it. That automatically closes the associated result set.

```
stat.close();
```

When you close a connection, it automatically closes all statements and result sets.

22.4.3 Analyzing Query Results

A ResultSet lets you fetch the query result, one row at a time. You iterate through the rows, and for each row, you can inspect the column values. Like the collection iterators that you saw in Chapter 15, the ResultSet class has a next method to visit the next row. However, the behavior of the next method is somewhat different. The next method does not return any data but a boolean value that indicates whether more data are available. Moreover, when you first get a result set from the executeQuery method, no row data are available. You need to call next to move to the first row. This appears curious, but it makes the iteration loop simple:

```
while (result.next())
{
    Inspect column data from the current row
}
```

If the result set is completely empty, then the first call to result.next() returns false, and the loop is never entered. Otherwise, the first call to result.next() fetches the data for the first row from the database. As you can see, the loop ends when the next method returns false, which indicates that all rows have been fetched.

Once the result set object has fetched a particular row, you can inspect its columns. Various get methods return the column value formatted as a number, string, date, and so on. In fact, for each data type, there are two get methods. One of them has an integer parameter that indicates the column position. The other has a string parameter for the column name. For example, you can fetch the product code as

```
String productCode = result.getString(1);
```

or

```
String productCode = result.getString("Product_Code");
```

Note that the integer index starts at one, not at zero; that is, getString(1) inspects the first column. Database column indexes are different from array subscripts.

Accessing a column by an integer index is marginally faster and perfectly acceptable if you explicitly named the desired columns in the SELECT statement, such as

```
SELECT Invoice_Number FROM Invoice WHERE Payment = 0
```

However, if you make a SELECT * query, it is a good idea to use a column name instead of a column index. It makes your code easier to read, and you don't have to update the code when the column layout changes.

In the preceding example, you saw the getString method in action. To fetch a number, use the getInt and getDouble methods instead, for example

```
int quantity = result.getInt("Quantity");
double unitPrice = result.getDouble("Price");
```

22.4.4 Result Set Meta Data

Meta data are data about an object. Result set meta data describe the properties of a result set.

When you have a result set from an unknown table, you may want to know the names of the columns. You can use the ResultSetMetaData class to find out about properties of a result set. Start by requesting the meta data object from the result set:

```
ResultSetMetaData metaData = result.getMetaData();
```

Then you can get the number of columns with the getColumnCount method. The getColumnLabel method gives you the column name for each column. Finally, the getColumnDisplaySize method returns the column width, which is useful if you want to print table rows and have the columns line up. Note that the indexes for these methods start with 1. For example,

```
for (int i = 1; i <= metaData.getColumnCount(); i++)
{
   String columnName = metaData.getColumnLabel(i);
   int columnSize = metaData.getColumnDisplaySize(i);
   . . .
}
```

ExecSQL.java is a useful program that puts these concepts to work. The program reads a file containing SQL statements and executes them all. When a statement has a result set, the result set is printed, using the result set meta data to determine the column count and column labels.

For example, suppose you have the following file:

ch22/exec/Product.sql

```
1   CREATE TABLE Product
2       (Product_Code CHAR(7), Description VARCHAR(40), Price DECIMAL(10, 2))
3   INSERT INTO Product VALUES ('116-064', 'Toaster', 24.95)
4   INSERT INTO Product VALUES ('257-535', 'Hair dryer', 29.95)
5   INSERT INTO Product VALUES ('643-119', 'Car vacuum', 19.95)
6   SELECT * FROM Product
```

Run the Exec.SQL program as

```
java -classpath derby.sql;. ExecSQL database.properties Product.sql
```

The program executes the statements in the Product.sql file and prints out the result of the SELECT query.

You can also use the Exec.SQL program as an interactive testing tool. Run

```
java -classpath derby.sql;. ExecSQL database.properties
```

Then type in SQL commands at the command line. Every time you hit the Enter key, the command is executed.

ch22/exec/ExecSQL.java

```java
 1  import java.sql.Connection;
 2  import java.sql.ResultSet;
 3  import java.sql.ResultSetMetaData;
 4  import java.sql.Statement;
 5  import java.sql.SQLException;
 6  import java.io.File;
 7  import java.io.IOException;
 8  import java.util.Scanner;
 9
10  /**
11     Executes all SQL statements in a file or the console.
12  */
13  public class ExecSQL
14  {
15     public static void main (String[] args)
16           throws SQLException, IOException, ClassNotFoundException
17     {
18        if (args.length == 0)
19        {
20           System.out.println(
21                 "Usage: java -classpath driver_class_path"
22                 + File.pathSeparator
23                 + ". ExecSQL propertiesFile [SQLcommandFile]");
24           return;
25        }
26
27        SimpleDataSource.init(args[0]);
28
29        Scanner in;
30        if (args.length > 1)
31           in = new Scanner(new File(args[1]));
32        else
33           in = new Scanner(System.in);
34
35        Connection conn = SimpleDataSource.getConnection();
36        try
37        {
38           Statement stat = conn.createStatement();
39           while (in.hasNextLine())
40           {
41              String line = in.nextLine();
42              try
43              {
44                 boolean hasResultSet = stat.execute(line);
```

```
45              if (hasResultSet)
46              {
47                  ResultSet result = stat.getResultSet();
48                  showResultSet(result);
49                  result.close();
50              }
51          }
52          catch (SQLException ex)
53          {
54              System.out.println(ex);
55          }
56      }
57      }
58      finally
59      {
60          conn.close();
61      }
62   }
63
64   /**
65      Prints a result set.
66      @param result the result set
67   */
68   public static void showResultSet(ResultSet result)
69          throws SQLException
70   {
71      ResultSetMetaData metaData = result.getMetaData();
72      int columnCount = metaData.getColumnCount();
73
74      for (int i = 1; i <= columnCount; i++)
75      {
76        if (i > 1) System.out.print(", ");
77        System.out.print(metaData.getColumnLabel(i));
78      }
79      System.out.println();
80
81      while (result.next())
82      {
83        for (int i = 1; i <= columnCount; i++)
84        {
85            if (i > 1) System.out.print(", ");
86            System.out.print(result.getString(i));
87        }
88        System.out.println();
89      }
90   }
91 }
```

S E L F   C H E C K

7. Suppose you want to test whether there are any customers in Hawaii. Issue the statement

   ```
   ResultSet result = stat.executeQuery("SELECT * FROM Customer WHERE State = 'HI'");
   ```

   Which Boolean expression answers your question?

8. Suppose you want to know how many customers are in Hawaii. What is an efficient way to get this answer?

Quality Tip 22.1

Don't Hardwire Database Connection Parameters into Your Program

It is considered inelegant to hardwire the database parameters into a program.

```java
public class MyProg
{
    public static void main(String[] args)
    {
        // Don't do this:
        String driver = "oracle.jdbc.driver.OracleDriver";
        String url = "jdbc:oracle:thin:@larry.mathcs.sjsu.edu:1521:InvoiceDB";
        String username = "admin";
        String password = "secret";
        . . .
    }
}
```

If you want to change to a different database, you must locate these strings, update them, and recompile.

Instead, place the strings into a separate configuration file. The `SimpleDataSource.java` file reads in a configuration file with the database connection parameters. To connect to a different database, you simply supply a different configuration file name on the command line.

Common Error 22.2

Delimiters in Manually Constructed Queries

Suppose you need to issue the following query with different names.

```sql
SELECT * FROM Customer WHERE Name = customerName
```

Many students try to construct a `SELECT` statement manually, like this:

```java
String customerName = . . . ;
String query = "SELECT * FROM Customer WHERE Name = '" + customerName + "'";
ResultSet result = stat.executeQuery(query);
```

However, this code will fail if the name contains single quotes, such as `"Sam's Small Appliances"`. The query string has a syntax error: a mismatched quote.

The remedy is to use a `PreparedStatement` instead:

```java
String query = "SELECT * FROM Customer WHERE Name = ?";
PreparedStatement stat = conn.prepareStatement(query);
stat.setString(1, aName);
ResultSet result = stat.executeQuery(query);
```

Productivity Hint 22.4

Let the Database Do the Work

You now know how to issue a SQL query from a Java program and iterate through the result set. A common error that students make is to iterate through one table at a time to find a result. For example, suppose you want to find all invoices that contain car vacuums. You could use the following plan:

1. Issue the query SELECT * FROM Product and iterate through the result set to find the product code for a car vacuum.
2. Issue the query SELECT * FROM LineItem and iterate through the result set to find the line items with that product code.

However, that plan is *extremely inefficient*. Such a program does in very slow motion what a database has been designed to do quickly.

Instead, you should let the database do all the work. Give the complete query to the database:

```
SELECT LineItem.Invoice_Number
    FROM Product, LineItem
    WHERE Product.Description = 'Car vacuum'
        AND Product.Product_Code = LineItem.Product_Code
```

Then iterate through the result set to read off all invoice numbers.

Beginners are often afraid of issuing complex SQL queries. However, you are throwing away a major benefit of a relational database if you don't take advantage of SQL.

22.5 Case Study: A Bank Database

In this section, we will develop a complete database program. We will reimplement the ATM simulation of Chapter 12, storing the customer and account data in a database. Recall that in the simulation, every customer has a customer number, a PIN, and two bank accounts: a checking account and a savings account. We'll store the information in two tables:

BankCustomer

Customer_Number	PIN	Checking_Account_Number	Savings_Account_Number
INTEGER	INTEGER	INTEGER	INTEGER

Account

Account_Number	Balance
INTEGER	DECIMAL(10, 2)

The Bank class now needs to connect to the database whenever it is asked to find a customer. Here is the implementation of the method that finds a customer. The method makes a query

```
SELECT * FROM BankCustomer WHERE Customer_Number = . . .
```

It then checks that the PIN matches, and it constructs a Customer object. This method turns the row-and-column information of the database into object-oriented data.

```
public Customer findCustomer(int customerNumber, int pin)
    throws SQLException
{
```

```
        Connection conn = SimpleDataSource.getConnection();
        try
        {
            Customer c = null;
            PreparedStatement stat = conn.prepareStatement(
                    "SELECT * FROM BankCustomer WHERE Customer_Number = ?");
            stat.setInt(1, customerNumber);

            ResultSet result = stat.executeQuery();
            if (result.next() && pin == result.getInt("PIN"))
                c = new Customer(customerNumber,
                        result.getInt("Checking_Account_Number"),
                        result.getInt("Savings_Account_Number"));
            return c;
        }
        finally
        {
            conn.close();
        }
    }
```

Note that the method throws a SQLException. Why don't we catch that exception and return null if an exception occurs? There are many potential reasons for a SQL exception, and the Bank class doesn't want to hide the exception details. But the Bank class also doesn't know anything about the user interface of the application, so it can't display information about the exception to the user. By throwing the exception to the caller, the information can reach the part of the program that interacts with the user.

The BankAccount class in this program is quite different from the implementation you have seen throughout the book. Now we do not store the balance of the bank account in the object; instead, we look it up from the database:

```
public double getBalance() throws SQLException
{
    Connection conn = SimpleDataSource.getConnection();
    try
    {
        double balance = 0;
        PreparedStatement stat = conn.prepareStatement(
                "SELECT Balance FROM Account WHERE Account_Number = ?");
        stat.setInt(1, accountNumber);
        ResultSet result = stat.executeQuery();
        if (result.next())
            balance = result.getDouble(1);
        return balance;
    }
    finally
    {
        conn.close();
    }
}
```

The deposit and withdraw operations immediately update the database as well:

```
public void deposit(double amount)
        throws SQLException
{
    Connection conn = SimpleDataSource.getConnection();
    try
    {
```

```
        PreparedStatement stat = conn.prepareStatement(
            "UPDATE Account"
            + " SET Balance = Balance + ?"
            + " WHERE Account_Number = ?");
        stat.setDouble(1, amount);
        stat.setInt(2, accountNumber);
        stat.executeUpdate();
    }
    finally
    {
        conn.close();
    }
}
```

It seems somewhat inefficient to connect to the database whenever the bank balance is accessed, but it is much safer than storing it in an object. Suppose you have two instances of the ATM program running at the same time. Then it is possible that both programs modify the same bank account. If each of them copied the bank balances from the database into objects, then the modifications made by one user would not be seen by the other.

You can try out this simultaneous access yourself, simply by running two instances of the ATM simulation. Alternatively, you can modify the main method of the ATMViewer class to pop up two ATM frames.

The source code for the modified ATM application follows. The source code for the ATM and ATMSimulator/ATMViewer classes is only changed minimally, by adding code to deal with the SQLException. The Customer class is unchanged. We do not list those classes, but you will find them in the atm folder of your book code.

This example completes our chapter on Java database programming. You have seen how you can use SQL to query and update data in a database and how the JDBC library makes it easy for you to issue SQL commands in a Java program.

ch22/atm/Bank.java

```
 1  import java.sql.Connection;
 2  import java.sql.ResultSet;
 3  import java.sql.PreparedStatement;
 4  import java.sql.SQLException;
 5
 6  /**
 7      A bank consisting of multiple bank accounts.
 8  */
 9  public class Bank
10  {
11      /**
12          Finds a customer with a given number and PIN.
13          @param customerNumber the customer number
14          @param pin the personal identification number
15          @return the matching customer, or null if none found
16      */
17      public Customer findCustomer(int customerNumber, int pin)
18          throws SQLException
19      {
20          Connection conn = SimpleDataSource.getConnection();
21          try
22          {
```

```
23        Customer c = null;
24        PreparedStatement stat = conn.prepareStatement(
25            "SELECT * FROM BankCustomer WHERE Customer_Number = ?");
26        stat.setInt(1, customerNumber);
27
28        ResultSet result = stat.executeQuery();
29        if (result.next() && pin == result.getInt("PIN"))
30          c = new Customer(customerNumber,
31              result.getInt("Checking_Account_Number"),
32              result.getInt("Savings_Account_Number"));
33        return c;
34     }
35     finally
36     {
37        conn.close();
38     }
39   }
40 }
```

ch22/atm/BankAccount.java

```
1  import java.sql.Connection;
2  import java.sql.ResultSet;
3  import java.sql.PreparedStatement;
4  import java.sql.SQLException;
5
6  /**
7     A bank account has a balance that can be changed by
8     deposits and withdrawals.
9  */
10 public class BankAccount
11 {
12    private int accountNumber;
13
14    /**
15       Constructs a bank account with a given balance.
16       @param anAccountNumber  the account number
17    */
18    public BankAccount(int anAccountNumber)
19    {
20       accountNumber = anAccountNumber;
21    }
22
23    /**
24       Deposits money into a bank account.
25       @param amount  the amount to deposit
26    */
27    public void deposit(double amount)
28          throws SQLException
29    {
30       Connection conn = SimpleDataSource.getConnection();
31       try
32       {
33          PreparedStatement stat = conn.prepareStatement(
34              "UPDATE Account"
35              + " SET Balance = Balance + ?"
36              + " WHERE Account_Number = ?");
37          stat.setDouble(1, amount);
```

```java
38              stat.setInt(2, accountNumber);
39              stat.executeUpdate();
40          }
41          finally
42          {
43              conn.close();
44          }
45      }
46
47      /**
48          Withdraws money from a bank account.
49          @param amount the amount to withdraw
50      */
51      public void withdraw(double amount)
52              throws SQLException
53      {
54          Connection conn = SimpleDataSource.getConnection();
55          try
56          {
57              PreparedStatement stat = conn.prepareStatement(
58                  "UPDATE Account"
59                  + " SET Balance = Balance - ?"
60                  + " WHERE Account_Number = ?");
61              stat.setDouble(1, amount);
62              stat.setInt(2, accountNumber);
63              stat.executeUpdate();
64          }
65          finally
66          {
67              conn.close();
68          }
69      }
70
71      /**
72          Gets the balance of a bank account.
73          @return the account balance
74      */
75      public double getBalance()
76              throws SQLException
77      {
78          Connection conn = SimpleDataSource.getConnection();
79          try
80          {
81              double balance = 0
82              PreparedStatement stat = conn.prepareStatement(
83                  "SELECT Balance FROM Account WHERE Account_Number = ?");
84              stat.setInt(1, accountNumber);
85              ResultSet result = stat.executeQuery();
86              if (result.next())
87                  balance = result.getDouble(1);
88              return balance;
89          }
90          finally
91          {
92              conn.close();
93          }
94      }
95  }
```

9. Why doesn't the Bank class store an array of Customer objects?

10. Why do the BankAccount methods throw an SQLException instead of catching it?

Special Topic 22.2

Transactions

An important part of database processing is *transaction handling.* A **transaction** is a set of database updates that should either succeed in its entirety or not happen at all. For example, consider a banking application that transfers money from one account to another. This operation involves two steps: reducing the balance of one account and increasing the balance of another account. No software system is perfect, and there is always the possibility of an error. The banking application, the database program, or the network connection between them could exhibit an error right after the first part—then the money would be withdrawn from the first account but never deposited to the second account. Clearly, this would be very bad. There are many other similar situations. For example, if you change an airline reservation, you don't want to give up your old seat until the new one is confirmed.

What all these situations have in common is that there is a set of database operations that are grouped together to carry out the transaction. All operations in the group must be carried out together—a partial completion cannot be tolerated. In SQL, you use the COMMIT and ROLLBACK commands to manage transactions. For example, to transfer money from one account to another, you issue the commands

```
UPDATE Account SET Balance = Balance - 1000
   WHERE Account_Number = '95667-2574'
UPDATE Account SET Balance = Balance + 1000
   WHERE Account_Number = '82041-1196'
COMMIT
```

The COMMIT command makes the updates permanent. Conversely, the ROLLBACK command undoes all changes up to the last COMMIT.

When you program with JDBC, by default the JDBC library automatically commits all database updates. That is convenient for simple programs, but it is not what you want for transaction processing. Thus, you should first turn the autocommit mode off:

```
Connection conn = . . .;
conn.setAutoCommit(false);
Statement stat = conn.createStatement();
```

Then issue the updates that form the transaction and call the commit method of the Statement class.

```
stat.executeUpdate(
     "UPDATE Account SET Balance = Balance - "
     + amount + " WHERE Account_Number = " + fromAccount);
stat.executeUpdate(
     "UPDATE Account SET Balance = Balance + "
     + amount + " WHERE Account_Number = " + toAccount);
conn.commit();
```

Conversely, if you encounter an error, then call the rollback method. This typically happens in an exception handler:

```
try
{
   . . .
}
catch (Exception ex)
{
```

```
        conn.rollback();
    }
```

You may wonder how a database can undo updates when a transaction is rolled back. The database actually stores your changes in a set of temporary tables. If you make queries within a transaction, the information in the temporary tables is merged with the permanent data for the purpose of computing the query result, giving you the illusion that the updates have already taken place. When you commit the transaction, the temporary data are made permanent. When you execute a rollback, the temporary tables are simply discarded.

Special Topic 22.3

Object-Relational Mapping

Database tables store rows that contain strings, numbers, and other fundamental data types, but not arbitrary objects. In Sections 22.1.2 and 22.1.3, you learned how to translate object references into database relationships. An object-relational mapper automates this process. The Java Enterprise Edition contains such a mapper. You add annotations to the Java classes that describe the relationships. The rules are simple:

- Add @Entity to every class that should be stored in the database.
- Each entity class needs an ID that is annotated with @Id.
- Relationships between classes are expressed with @OneToOne, @OneToMany, @ManyToOne, and @ManyToMany.

Here are the annotations for the invoice classes. A customer can have many invoices, but each invoice has exactly one customer. This is expressed by the @ManyToOne annotation. Conversely, each line item is contained in exactly one invoice, but each invoice can have many line items. This is expressed by the @OneToMany relationship.

```
@Entity public class Invoice
{
    @Id private int id;
    @ManyToOne private Customer theCustomer;
    @OneToMany private List<LineItem> items;
    private double payment;
    . . .
}

@Entity public class LineItem
{
    @Id private int id;
    @ManyToOne private Product theProduct;
    private int quantity
    . . .
}

@Entity public class Product
{
    @Id private int id;
    private String description;
    private double price;
    . . .
}

@Entity public class Customer
{
```

```
        @Id private int id;
        private String name;
        private String address;
        private String city;
        private String state;
        private String zip;
        . . .
    }
```

The object-relational mapper processes the annotations and produces a database table layout. You don't have to worry exactly how the data are stored in the database. For example, to store a new invoice, simply build up the Java object and call

```
    entityManager.persist(invoice);
```

As a result of this call, the data for the invoice and line items are automatically stored in the various database tables.

To read data from the database, you do not use SQL—after all, you do not know the exact table layout. Instead, you formulate a query in an object-oriented query language. A typical query looks like this:

```
    SELECT x FROM Invoice x WHERE x.id = 11731
```

The result is a Java object of type Invoice. The references to the customer and line item objects have been automatically populated with the proper data from various tables.

Object-relational mapping technology is powerful and convenient. However, you still need to understand the underlying principles of relational databases in order to specify efficient mappings and queries.

Summary of Learning Objectives

Develop strategies for storing data in a database.

- A relational database stores information in tables. Each table column has a name and a data type.
- SQL (Structured Query Language) is a command language for interacting with a database.
- Use the SQL commands CREATE TABLE and INSERT INTO to add data to a database.
- You should avoid rows with replicated data. Instead, distribute the data over multiple tables.
- A primary key is a column (or set of columns) whose value uniquely specifies a table record.
- A foreign key is a reference to a primary key in a linked table.
- Implement one-to-many relationships with linked tables, not replicated columns.

Use SQL to query and update a database.

- Use the SQL SELECT command to query a database.
- The WHERE clause selects data that fulfill a condition.
- A join is a query that involves multiple tables.
- The UPDATE and DELETE SQL commands modify the data in a database.

Install a database system and test that you can connect to it from a Java program.
- You need a JDBC (Java Database Connectivity) driver to access a database from a Java program.
- Make sure the JDBC driver is on the class path when you launch the Java program.
- To connect to the database, you need to specify a database URL, user name, and password.

Write Java programs that access and update database records.
- Use a `Connection` object to access a database from a Java program.
- A `Connection` object can create `Statement` objects that are used to execute SQL commands.
- The result of a SQL query is returned in a `ResultSet` object.
- Meta data are data about an object. Result set meta data describe the properties of a result set.

Classes, Objects, and Methods Introduced in this Chapter

```
java.io.File
    pathSeparator
java.lang.Class
    forName
java.sql.Connection
    close
    commit
    createStatement
    prepareStatement
    rollback
    setAutoCommit
java.sql.DriverManager
    getConnection
```

```
java.sql.PreparedStatement
    execute
    executeQuery
    executeUpdate
    setDouble
    setInt
    setString
java.sql.ResultSet
    close
    getDouble
    getInt
    getMetaData
    getString
    next
```

```
java.sql.ResultSetMetaData
    getColumnCount
    getColumnDisplaySize
    getColumnLabel
java.sql.SQLException
java.sql.Statement
    close
    execute
    executeQuery
    executeUpdate
    getResultSet
    getUpdateCount
java.util.Properties
    getProperty
    load
```

Media Resources

*www.wiley.com/
college/
horstmann*

- Lab Exercises
- ⊕ Practice Quiz
- ⊕ Code Completion Exercises

Review Exercises

★ **R22.1** Design a set of database tables to store people and cars. A person has a name, a unique driver license number, and an address. Every car has a unique vehicle identification number, manufacturer, type, and year. Every car has one owner, but one person can own multiple cars.

★ **R22.2** Design a set of database tables to store library books and patrons. A book has an ISBN (International Standard Book Number), an author, and a title. The library may have multiple copies of each book, each with a different book ID. A patron has a name, a unique ID, and an address. A book may be checked out by at most one patron, but one patron can check out multiple books.

★ **R22.3** Design a set of database tables to store sets of coins in purses. Each purse has an owner name and a unique ID. Each coin type has a unique name and a value. Each purse contains some quantity of coins of a given type.

★ **R22.4** Design a set of database tables to store students, classes, professors, and classrooms. Each student takes zero or more classes. Each class has one professor, but a professor can teach multiple classes. Each class has one classroom.

★ **R22.5** Give SQL commands to create a Book table, with columns for the ISBN, author, and title, and to insert all textbooks that you are using this semester.

★ **R22.6** Give SQL commands to create a Car table, with columns for the vehicle identification number, manufacturer, model, and year of each car, and to insert all cars that your family members own.

★ **R22.7** Give a SQL query that lists all products in the invoice database of Section 22.2.

★ **R22.8** Give a SQL query that lists all customers in California.

★ **R22.9** Give a SQL query that lists all customers in California or Nevada.

★ **R22.10** Give a SQL query that lists all customers not in Hawaii.

★★ **R22.11** Give a SQL query that lists all customers who have an unpaid invoice.

★★ **R22.12** Give a SQL query that lists all products that have been purchased by a customer in California.

★★ **R22.13** Give a SQL query that lists all line items that are part of invoice number 11731.

★★ **R22.14** Give a SQL query that computes the sum of all quantities that are part of invoice number 11731.

★★★ **R22.15** Give a SQL query that computes the total cost of all line items in invoice number 11731.

★★ **R22.16** Give a SQL update statement that raises all prices by 10 percent.

★★ **R22.17** Give a SQL statement that deletes all customers in California.

★★ **R22.18** Pick a database system (such as DB2, Oracle, Postgres, or SQL Server) and determine from the web documentation:
- What JDBC driver do you need? Is it automatically discovered?
- What is the database URL?

★ **R22.19** What is the difference between a Connection and a Statement?

★ **R22.20** Of the SQL commands introduced in this chapter, which yield result sets, which yield an update count, and which yield neither?

★ **R22.21** How is a ResultSet different from an Iterator?

Programming Exercises

★ **P22.1** Write a Java program that creates a Coin table with coin names and values; inserts coin types penny, nickel, dime, quarter, half dollar, and dollar; and prints out the sum of the coin values. Use CREATE TABLE, INSERT, and SELECT SUM SQL commands.

★ **P22.2** Write a Java program that creates a Car table with car manufacturers, models, model years, and fuel efficiency ratings. Insert several cars. Print out the average fuel efficiency. Use CREATE TABLE, INSERT, and SELECT AVG SQL commands.

★★ **P22.3** Reimplement the bank data program from Section 19.3 using a database table for the bank accounts.

★★ **P22.4** Improve the ExecSQL program and make the columns of the output line up. *Hint:* Use the getColumnDisplaySize method of the ResultSetMetaData class.

★★ **P22.5** Write a Java program that uses the database tables from the invoice database in Section 22.2. Prompt the user for an invoice number and print out the invoice, formatted as in Chapter 12.

★★ **P22.6** Write a Java program that uses the database tables from the invoice database in Section 22.2. Produce a report that lists all customers, their invoices, the amounts paid, and the unpaid balances.

★★ **P22.7** Write a Java program that uses a library database of books and patron data, as described in Exercise R22.2. Patrons should be able to check out and return books. Supply commands to print the books that a patron has checked out and to find who has checked out a particular book. Create and populate Patron and Book tables before running the program.

★★ **P22.8** Write a Java program that creates a grade book for a class. Create and populate Student and Grade tables before running the program. The program should be able to display all grades for a given student. It should allow the instructor to add a new grade (such as "Homework 4: 100") or modify an existing grade.

★★★ **P22.9** Write a program that assigns seats on an airplane as described in Exercise P12.8. Keep the seating information in a database.

★★★ **P22.10** Write a program that keeps an appointment calendar in a database. An appointment includes a description, a date, the starting time, and the ending time; for example,

```
Dentist 2007/10/1 17:30 18:30
CS1 class 2007/10/2 08:30 10:00
```

Supply a user interface to add appointments, remove canceled appointments, and print out a list of appointments for a particular day.

★ **P22.11** Modify the ATM simulation program of Section 22.5 so that the program pops up two ATM frames. Verify that the database can be accessed simultaneously by two users.

Programming Projects

Project 22.1 Implement a message board application that stores users and messages in a database. Users can post messages, reply to messages, and view posted messages. Provide views that list the messages by topic, by user, and by posting date. Allow the user to view all replies to a given message.

Project 22.2 Implement a group calendar application that stores users, groups, and event dates in a database. Users can join groups. Meetings and other events can be scheduled, and individuals and groups can be added as participants. Users can accept or reject invitations to events. Provide views that show all events of a user in a given time interval, and all users for an event, showing whether they have accepted or rejected the invitation.

Answers to Self-Check Questions

1. The telephone number for each customer may not be unique—the same number might be shared by roommates. Even if the number were unique, however, it can change when a customer moves. In that situation, both the primary and all foreign keys would need to be updated. Therefore, a customer ID is a better choice.

2. Customer 3176 ordered ten toasters.

3. `SELECT Name FROM Customer WHERE State <> 'AK' AND State <> 'HI'`

4. `SELECT Invoice.Invoice_Number FROM Invoice, Customer`
   `    WHERE Invoice.Customer_Number = Customer.Customer_Number`
   `    AND Customer.State = 'HI'`

5. Connect to the database with a program that lets you execute SQL instructions. Try creating a small database table, adding a record, and selecting all records. Then drop the table again.

6. You didn't set the class path correctly. The JAR file containing the JDBC driver must be on the class path.

7. `result.next()`. If there is at least one result, then `next` returns `true`.

8. `ResultSet result = stat.executeQuery(`
   `        "SELECT COUNT(*) FROM Customer WHERE State = 'HI'");`
   `result.next();`
   `int count = result.getInt(1);`

   Note that the following alternative is significantly slower if there are many such customers.

   `ResultSet result = stat.executeQuery(`
   `        "SELECT * FROM Customer WHERE State = 'HI'");`
   `while (result.next()) count++; // Inefficient`

9. The customer data are stored in the database. The `Bank` class is now merely a conduit to the data.

10. The methods are not equipped to handle the exception. What could they do? Print an error report? To the console or a GUI window? In which language?

Chapter **23**

XML

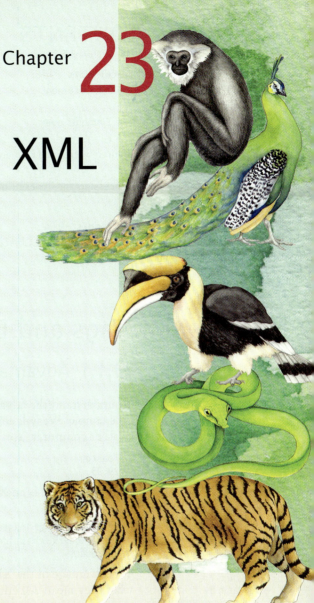

CHAPTER GOALS

- Understanding XML elements and attributes
- Understanding the concept of an XML parser
- Being able to read and write XML documents
- Being able to design Document Type Definitions for XML documents

In this chapter, you will learn about the **Extensible Markup Language (XML)**, a mechanism for encoding data that is independent of any programming language. XML allows you to encode complex data in a form that the recipient can easily parse. XML is very popular for data exchange. It is simple enough that a wide variety of programs can easily generate XML data. XML data has a nested structure, so you can use it to describe hierarchical data sets—for example, an invoice that contains many items, each of which consists of a product and a quantity. Because the XML format is standardized, libraries for parsing the data are widely available and—as you will see in this chapter—easy to use for a programmer.

It is particularly easy to read and write XML documents in Java. In fact, it is generally easier to use XML than it is to use an "ad hoc" file format. Thus, using XML makes your programs easier to write and more professional.

CHAPTER CONTENTS

23.1 XML Tags and Documents

23.1.1 Advantages of XML

> XML allows you to encode complex data, independent from any programming language, in a form that the recipient can easily parse.

To understand the advantages of using XML for encoding data, let's look at a typical example. We will encode product descriptions, so that they can be transferred to another computer. Your first attempt might be a naïve encoding like this:

```
Toaster
29.95
```

In contrast, here is an XML encoding of the same data:

```
<product>
    <description>Toaster</description>
    <price>29.95</price>
</product>
```

> XML files are readable by computer programs and by humans.

The advantage of the XML version is clear: You can look at the data and understand what they mean. Of course, this is a benefit for the programmer, not for a computer program. A computer program has no understanding of what a "price" is. As a programmer, you still need to write code to extract the price as the content of the price element. Nevertheless, the fact that an XML document is comprehensible by humans is a huge advantage for program development.

> XML-formatted data files are resilient to change.

A second advantage of the XML version is that it is *resilient to change*. Suppose the product data change, and an additional data item is introduced, to denote the manufacturer. In the naïve format, the manufacturer might be added after the price, like this:

```
Toaster
29.95
General Appliances
```

A program that can process the old format might get confused when reading a sequence of products in the new format. The program would think that the price is followed by the name of the next product. Thus, the program needs to be updated to work with both the old and new data formats. As data get more complex, programming for multiple versions of a data format can be difficult and time-consuming.

When using XML, on the other hand, it is easy to add new elements:

```
<product>
    <description>Toaster</description>
    <price>29.95</price>
    <manufacturer>General Appliances</manufacturer>
</product>
```

Now a program that processes the new data can still extract the old information in the same way—as the contents of the description and price elements. The program need not be updated, and it can tolerate different versions of the data format.

23.1.2 Differences Between XML and HTML

If you know HTML, you may have noticed that the XML format of the product data looked somewhat like HTML code. However, there are some differences that we will discuss in this section.

Let's start with the similarities. The XML tag pairs, such as <price> and </price> look just like HTML tag pairs, for example <li> and </li>. Both in XML and in HTML, tags are enclosed in angle brackets < >, and a start-tag is paired with an end-tag that starts with a slash / character.

However, web browsers are quite permissive about HTML. For example, you can omit an end-tag </li> and the browser will try to figure out what you mean. In XML, this is not permissible. When writing XML, pay attention to the following rules:

- In XML, you *must* pay attention to the letter case of the tags; for example, <li> and <LI> are different tags that bear no relation to each other.

- Every start-tag *must* have a matching end-tag. You cannot omit tags, such as </li>. However, if a tag has no end-tag, it must end in />, for example

    ```
    <img src="hamster.jpeg"/>
    ```

    When the parser sees the />, it knows not to look for a matching end-tag.

- Finally, attribute values must be enclosed in quotes. For example,

    ```
    <img src="hamster.jpeg" width=400 height=300/>
    ```

    is not acceptable. You must use

    ```
    <img src="hamster.jpeg" width="400" height="300"/>
    ```

Moreover, there is an important conceptual difference between HTML and XML. HTML has one specific purpose: to describe web documents. In contrast, XML is an *extensible* syntax that can be used to specify many different kinds of data. For example, the VRML language uses the XML syntax to describe virtual reality scenes. The MathML language uses the XML syntax to describe mathematical formulas. You can use the XML syntax to describe your own data, such as product records or invoices.

Most people who first see XML wonder how an XML document looks inside a browser. However, that is *not* generally a useful question to ask. Most data that are encoded in XML have nothing to do with browsers. For example, it would probably not be exciting to display an XML document with nothing but product records (such as the ones in the previous section) in a browser. Instead, you will learn in this chapter how to write programs that analyze XML data. XML does not tell you how to display data; it is merely a convenient format for representing data.

XML describes the meaning of data, not how to display them.

23.1.3 The Structure of an XML Document

In this section, you will see the rules for properly formatted XML. In XML, text and tags are combined into a *document*. The XML standard recommends that every XML document start with a declaration

```
<?xml version="1.0"?>
```

Next, the XML document contains the actual data. The data are contained in a root element. For example,

```
<?xml version="1.0"?>
<invoice>
    more data
</invoice>
```

The root element is an example of an XML element. An element has one of two forms:

<elementName> content </elementName>

or

<elementName/>

In the first case, the element has content—elements, text, or a mixture of both. A good example is a paragraph in an HTML document:

```
<p>Use XML for <strong>robust</strong> data formats.</p>
```

The p element contains

1. The text: "Use XML for "
2. A strong child element
3. More text: " data formats."

For XML files that contain documents in the traditional sense of the term, the mixture of text and elements is useful. The XML specification calls this type of content *mixed content*. But for files that describe data sets—such as our product data—it is better to stick with elements that contain *either* other elements or text. Content that consists only of elements is called *element content*.

An element can have *attributes*. For example, the a element of HTML has an href attribute that specifies the URL of a hyperlink:

```
<a href="http://java.sun.com"> . . . </a>
```

An attribute has a name (such as href) and a value. In XML, the value must be enclosed in single or double quotes.

An element can have multiple attributes, for example

```
<img src="hamster.jpeg" width="400" height="300"/>
```

And, as you have already seen, an element can have both attributes and content.

```
<a href="http://java.sun.com">Sun's Java web site</a>
```

Programmers often wonder whether it is better to use attributes or child elements. For example, should a product be described as

```
<product description="Toaster" price="29.95"/>
```

or

```
<product>
```

```
        <description>Toaster</description>
        <price>29.95</price>
    </product>
```

The former is shorter. However, it violates the spirit of attributes. Attributes are intended to provide information *about* the element content. For example, the price element might have an attribute currency that helps interpret the element content. The content 29.95 has a different interpretation in the element

```
    <price currency="USD">29.95</price>
```

than it does in the element

```
    <price currency="EUR">29.95</price>
```

You have now seen the components of an XML document that are needed to use XML for encoding data. There are other XML constructs for more specialized situations—see `http://www.xml.com/axml/axml.html` for more information. In the next section, you will see how to use Java to parse XML documents.

SELF CHECK

1. Write XML code with a student element and child elements name and id that describe you.
2. What does your browser do when you load an XML file, such as the items.xml file that is contained in the companion code for this book?
3. Why does HTML use the src attribute to specify the source of an image instead of `<img>hamster.jpeg</img>`?

How To 23.1

Designing an XML Document Format

This How To walks you through the process of designing an XML document format. You will see in Section 23.4 how to formally describe the format with a document type definition. Right now, we focus on an informal definition of the document content. The "output" of this activity is a sample document.

Step 1   Gather the data that you must include in the XML document.

Write them on a sheet of paper. If at all possible, work from some real-life examples. For example, suppose you need to design an XML document for an invoice. A typical invoice has

- An invoice number
- A shipping address
- A billing address
- A list of items ordered

If possible, gather some actual invoices. Decide which features of the actual invoices you need to include in your XML document.

Step 2   Analyze which data elements need to be refined.

Continue refinement until you reach data values that can be described by single strings or numbers. Make a note of all data items that you discovered during the refinement process. When done, you should have a list of data elements, some of which can be broken down further and some of which are simple enough to be described by a single string or number.

For example, the "shipping address" actually contains the customer name, street, city, state, and ZIP code.

The "list of items ordered" contains items. Each item contains a product and the quantity ordered. Each product contains the product name and price.

Thus, our list now contains

- Address
- Name
- Street
- City
- State
- ZIP code
- List of items ordered
- Item
- Product
- Description
- Price
- Quantity

Keep breaking the data items down until each of them can be described by a single *string* or *number*. For example, an address cannot be described by a single string, but a city can be described by a single string.

Step 3   Come up with a suitable element name that describes the entire XML document.

This element becomes the root element. For example, the invoice data would be contained in an element named `invoice`.

Step 4   Come up with suitable element names for the top-level decomposition that you found in Step 1.

These become the children of the root element. For example, the `invoice` element has children

- `address`
- `items`

Step 5   Repeat this process to give names to the other elements that you discovered in Step 2.

As you do this, make a comprehensive example that shows all elements at work. For the invoice problem, here is an example.

```
<invoice>
  <address>
     <name>ACME Computer Supplies Inc.</name>
     <street>1195 W. Fairfield Rd.</street>
     <city>Sunnyvale</city>
     <state>CA</state>
     <zip>94085</zip>
  </address>
  <items>
     <item>
        <product>
           <description>Ink Jet Refill Kit</description>
           <price>29.95</price>
        </product>
        <quantity>8</quantity>
     </item>
     <item>
        <product>
```

```
                    <description>4-port Mini Hub</description>
                    <price>19.95</price>
                </product>
                <quantity>4</quantity>
            </item>
        </items>
    </invoice>
```

Step 6   Check that the document doesn't have mixed content.

That is, make sure each element has as its children either additional elements or text, but not both. If necessary, add more child elements to wrap any text.

For example, suppose the product element looked like this:

```
<product>
    <description>Ink Jet Refill Kit</description>
    29.95
</product>
```

Perhaps someone thought it was "obvious" that the last entry was the price. However, following Quality Tip 23.2 on page 912, it is best to wrap the price inside a price element, like this:

```
<product>
    <description>Ink Jet Refill Kit</description>
    <price>29.95</price>
</product>
```

Quality Tip 23.1

Prefer XML Elements over Attributes

Attributes are shorter than elements. For example,

```
<product description="Toaster" price="29.95"/>
```

seems simpler than

```
<product>
    <description>Toaster</description>
    <price>29.95</price>
</product>
```

There is the temptation to use attributes because they are "easier to type". But of course, you don't type XML documents, except for testing purposes. In real-world situations, XML documents are generated by programs.

Attributes are less flexible than elements. Suppose we want to add a currency indication to the value. With elements, that's easy to do:

```
<price currency="USD">29.95</price>
```

or even

```
<price>
    <currency>USD</currency>
    <amount>29.95</amount>
</price>
```

With attributes, you are stuck—you can't refine the structure. Of course, you could use

```
<product description="Toaster" price="USD 29.95"/>
```

But then your program has to parse the string USD 29.95 and manually take it apart. That's just the kind of tedious and error-prone coding that XML is designed to avoid.

In HTML, there is a simple rule when using attributes. All strings that are not part of the displayed text are attributes. For example, consider a link.

```
<a href="http://java.sun.com">The Java web page</a>
```

The text inside the a element, The Java web page, is part of what the user sees on the web page, but the href attribute value http://java.sun.com is not displayed on the page.

Of course, HTML is a little different from the XML documents that you construct to describe data, such as product lists, but the same basic rule applies. Anything that's a part of your data should not be an attribute. An attribute is appropriate only if it tells something *about* the data but isn't a part of the data itself. If you find yourself engaged in metaphysical discussions to determine whether an item is part of the data or tells something about the data, make the item an element, not an attribute.

Quality Tip 23.2

Avoid Children with Mixed Elements and Text

The children of an element can be

1. Elements
2. Text
3. A mixture of both

In HTML, it is common to mix elements and text, for example

```
<p>Use XML for <strong>robust</strong> data formats.</p>
```

But when describing data sets, you should not mix elements and text. For example, you should not do the following:

```
<price>
   <currency>USD</currency>
   29.95
</price>
```

Instead, the children of an element should be either text

```
<price>29.95</price>
```

or elements

```
<price>
   <currency>USD</currency>
   <amount>29.95</amount>
</price>
```

There is an important reason for this design rule. As you will see later in this chapter, you can specify much stricter rules for elements that have only child elements than for elements whose children can contain text.

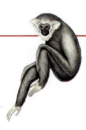

Random Fact 23.1

Word Processing and Typesetting Systems

You have almost certainly used a *word processor* for writing letters or reports. A word processor is a program to write and edit documents made up of text and images. The text can contain characters in various fonts. It can be arranged in paragraphs, tables, and footnotes.

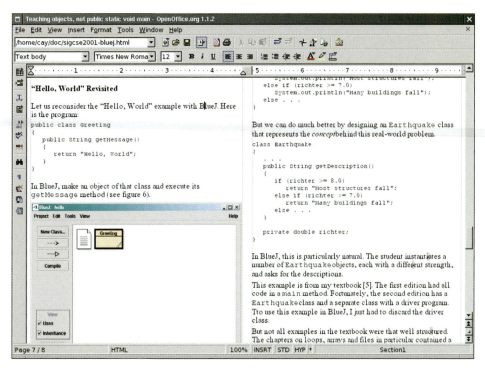

Figure 1 A "What You See Is What You Get" Word Processor

Paragraphs can be formatted in various ways, such as ragged right (that is, the left ends of the lines of text are aligned under each other, but the right ends aren't), centered, and fully justified (that is, both the left and right ends of the lines are aligned). What is characteristic of modern word processors is their "what you see is what you get" operation. You enter text and commands, using the keyboard and the mouse. The computer screen instantly shows what the printed document will look like (see Figure 1).

However, there are disadvantages to the "what you see is what you get" (WYSIWYG, pronounced *wis-ee-wig*) nature of a word processor. You may labor to arrange various related images and tables on the same page. Later, you find that you need to add a couple of paragraphs on the preceding page. Now half of the material moves to the next page, and you have do the arranging all over again. It would have been more useful if you could have told the word processor your intention, namely: "Always keep these images and tables together on the same page". In general, "what you see is what you get" programs are very good in letting you arrange material, but they don't know *why* you arranged the material in a certain way. Thus, they can't keep the arrangement when your document changes. Some people call these programs "what you see is all you've got".

More fundamentally, "what you see is what you get" programs break down when you need to publish the same material in multiple ways. You may want to format product information as a product parts list and an advertising brochure. Or you may want to publish the information in printed form, on the Web, and in spoken form for telephone retrieval. Now you no longer want to "get" a single result, so it isn't as helpful to see what you get. Instead, it becomes much more important to visualize the *structure* of the information.

A program for editing structured text needs to capture three pieces of information:

- The text itself
- The structural element (paragraph, bulleted list, heading, and so on) to which each part of the text belongs
- The rules for formatting the structural elements

To make it easy to interchange structured documents between computer systems, the structural information is often encoded in *markup tags*. For example, XML and HTML use tags that are enclosed in angle brackets, such as the familiar <p>, <ul>, and <h1> tags.

In the 1970s, when publishers began to move away from traditional manual typesetting to computer-based typesetting, the result at first was inferior quality, particularly for mathematical formulas. Arranging the symbols in complex formulas in a way that makes mathematical sense is an art that requires practice and good judgment, and the first typesetting programs were definitely not up to the job. Frustrated by this situation, the famous computer scientist Donald Knuth of Stanford University decided to do something about it and invented a typesetting program that he called T$_E$X (pronounced "tek" because the "X" is a capital Greek chi). Input to that program consists of text with markup tags that start with a backslash; curly braces {} for grouping; and other special markup symbols, such as _ and ∧ to indicate subscript and superscript. For example, to specify a summation, you type

```
\sum_{i=1}^n i^2
```

The T$_E$X program typesets the summation as shown in Figure 2. Note that the expression is formatted one way when it occurs inside text and another way when it appears as part of a displayed formula.

A markup tag such as <h1> in HTML or \sum in T$_E$X is mainly beneficial for exchanging documents among different computer systems. Only the most hardened HTML or T$_E$X authors produce the markup by hand. For HTML in particular, many programs are available that display the structure of an HTML document and allow authors to edit both text and structure in a convenient way that combines the benefits of visual feedback and structure editing.

A sum inside text: $\sum_{i=1}^{n} i^2$

The same sum as a displayed formula:

$$\sum_{i=1}^{n} i^2$$

Figure 2 A Formula Typeset in the T$_E$X Typesetting System

23.2 Parsing XML Documents

A parser is a program that reads a document, checks whether it is syntactically correct, and takes some action as it processes the document.

A streaming parser reports the building blocks of an XML document. A tree-based parser builds a document tree.

To read and analyze the contents of an XML document, you need an XML **parser**. A parser is a program that reads a document, checks whether it is syntactically correct, and takes some action as it processes the document.

Two kinds of XML parsers are in common use. *Streaming parsers* read the XML input one token at a time and report what they encounter: a start tag, text, an end tag, and so on. In contrast, a *tree-based parser* builds a tree that represents the parsed document. Once the parser is done, you can analyze the tree.

Streaming parsers are more efficient for handling large XML documents whose tree structure would require large amounts of memory. Tree-based parsers, however, are easier to use for most applications—the parse tree gives you a complete overview of the data, whereas a streaming parser gives you the information in bits and pieces.

In this section, you will learn how to use a tree-based parser that produces a tree structure according to the DOM (Document Object Model) standard. The DOM standard defines interfaces and methods to analyze and modify the tree structure that represents an XML document.

In order to parse an XML document into a DOM tree, you need a Document-Builder. To get a DocumentBuilder object, first call the static newInstance method of the DocumentBuilderFactory class, then call the newDocumentBuilder method on the factory object.

> A DocumentBuilder can read an XML document from a file, URL, or input stream. The result is a Document object, which contains a tree.

```
DocumentBuilderFactory factory = DocumentBuilderFactory.newInstance();
DocumentBuilder builder = factory.newDocumentBuilder();
```

Once you have a DocumentBuilder, you can read a document. To read a document from a file, first construct a File object from the file name, then call the parse method of the DocumentBuilder class.

```
String fileName = . . .;
File f = new File(fileName);
Document doc = builder.parse(f);
```

If the document is located on the Internet, use an URL:

```
String urlName = . . .;
URL u = new URL(urlName);
Document doc = builder.parse(u);
```

You can also read a document from an arbitrary input stream:

```
InputStream in = . . .;
Document doc = builder.parse(in);
```

Once you have created a new document or read a document from a file, you can inspect and modify it.

> An XPath describes a node or node set, using a notation similar to that for directory paths.

The easiest method for inspecting a document is the *XPath* syntax. An XPath describes a node or set of nodes, using a syntax that is similar to directory paths. For example, consider the following XPath, applied to the document in Figure 3 and Figure 4:

```
/items/item[1]/quantity
```

```xml
<?xml version="1.0"?>
<items>
   <item>
      <product>
         <description>Ink Jet Refill Kit</description>
         <price>29.95</price>
      </product>
      <quantity>8</quantity>
   </item>
   <item>
      <product>
         <description>4-port Mini Hub</description>
         <price>19.95</price>
      </product>
      <quantity>4</quantity>
   </item>
</items>
```

Figure 3 An XML Document

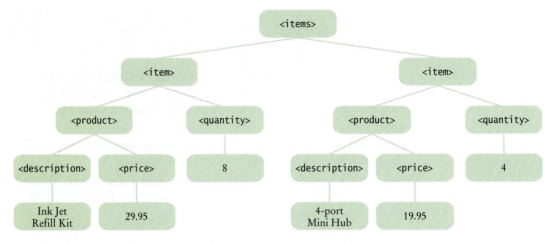

Figure 4 The Tree View of the Document

This XPath selects the quantity of the first item, that is, the value 8. (In XPath, array positions start with 1. Accessing `/items/item[0]` would be an error.)

Similarly, you can get the price of the second product as

```
/items/item[2]/product/price
```

To get the number of items, use the XPath expression

```
count(/items/item)
```

In our example, the result is 2.

The total number of children can be obtained as

```
count(/items/*)
```

In our example, the result is again 2 because the items element has exactly two children.

To select attributes, use an @ followed by the name of the attribute. For example,

```
/items/item[2]/product/price/@currency
```

would select the currency price attribute if it had one.

Finally, if you have a document with variable or unknown structure, you can find out the name of a child with an expression such as the following:

```
name(/items/item[1]/*[1])
```

The result is the name of the first child of the first item, or product.

That is all you need to know about the XPath syntax to analyze simple documents. (See Table 1 for a summary.) There are many more options in the XPath syntax that we do not cover here. If you are interested, look up the specification (http:/ /www.w3.org/TR/xpath) or work through the online tutorial (http://www.zvon.org/xxl/ XPathTutorial/General/examples.html).

To evaluate an XPath expression in Java, first create an XPath object:

```
XPathFactory xpfactory = XPathFactory.newInstance();
XPath path = xpfactory.newXPath();
```

Then call the evaluate method, like this:

```
String result = path.evaluate(expression, doc)
```

Table 1 XPath Syntax Summary		
Syntax Element	Purpose	Example
name	Matches an element	`item`
/	Separates elements	`/items/item`
[*n*]	Selects a value from a set	`/items/item[1]`
@*name*	Matches an attribute	`price/@currency`
*	Matches anything	`/items/*[1]`
count	Counts matches	`count(/items/item)`
name	The name of a match	`name(/items/*[1])`

Here, *expression* is an XPath expression and `doc` is the `Document` object that represents the XML document. For example, the statement

```
String result = path.evaluate("/items/item[2]/product/price", doc)
```

sets `result` to the string `"19.95"`.

Now you have all the tools that you need to read and analyze an XML document. The example program at the end of this section puts these techniques to work. (The program uses the `LineItem` and `Product` classes from Chapter 12.) The class `ItemListParser` can parse an XML document that contains a list of product descriptions. Its `parse` method takes the file name and returns an array list of `LineItem` objects:

```
ItemListParser parser = new ItemListParser();
ArrayList<LineItem> items = parser.parse("items.xml");
```

The `ItemListParser` class translates each XML element into an object of the corresponding Java class. We first get the number of items:

```
int itemCount = Integer.parseInt(path.evaluate("count(/items/item)", doc));
```

For each item element, we gather the product data and construct a `Product` object:

```
String description = path.evaluate(
      "/items/item[" + i + "]/product/description", doc);
double price = Double.parseDouble(path.evaluate(
      "/items/item[" + i + "]/product/price", doc));
Product pr = new Product(description, price);
```

Then we construct a `LineItem` object in the same way, and add it to the `items` array list. Here is the complete source code.

ch23/parser/ItemListParser.java

```
1  import java.io.File;
2  import java.io.IOException;
3  import java.util.ArrayList;
4  import javax.xml.parsers.DocumentBuilder;
```

```
 5  import javax.xml.parsers.DocumentBuilderFactory;
 6  import javax.xml.parsers.ParserConfigurationException;
 7  import javax.xml.xpath.XPath;
 8  import javax.xml.xpath.XPathExpressionException;
 9  import javax.xml.xpath.XPathFactory;
10  import org.w3c.dom.Document;
11  import org.xml.sax.SAXException;
12
13  /**
14     An XML parser for item lists.
15  */
16  public class ItemListParser
17  {
18     private DocumentBuilder builder;
19     private XPath path;
20
21     /**
22        Constructs a parser that can parse item lists.
23     */
24     public ItemListParser()
25           throws ParserConfigurationException
26     {
27        DocumentBuilderFactory dbfactory
28              = DocumentBuilderFactory.newInstance();
29        builder = dbfactory.newDocumentBuilder();
30        XPathFactory xpfactory = XPathFactory.newInstance();
31        path = xpfactory.newXPath();
32     }
33
34     /**
35        Parses an XML file containing an item list.
36        @param fileName the name of the file
37        @return an array list containing all items in the XML file
38     */
39     public ArrayList<LineItem> parse(String fileName)
40           throws SAXException, IOException, XPathExpressionException
41     {
42        File f = new File(fileName);
43        Document doc = builder.parse(f);
44
45        ArrayList<LineItem> items = new ArrayList<LineItem>();
46        int itemCount = Integer.parseInt(path.evaluate(
47              "count(/items/item)", doc));
48        for (int i = 1; i <= itemCount; i++)
49        {
50           String description = path.evaluate(
51                 "/items/item[" + i + "]/product/description", doc);
52           double price = Double.parseDouble(path.evaluate(
53                 "/items/item[" + i + "]/product/price", doc));
54           Product pr = new Product(description, price);
55           int quantity = Integer.parseInt(path.evaluate(
56                 "/items/item[" + i + "]/quantity", doc));
57           LineItem it = new LineItem(pr, quantity);
58           items.add(it);
59        }
60        return items;
61     }
62  }
```

ch23/parser/ItemListParserDemo.java

```
 1  import java.util.ArrayList;
 2
 3  /**
 4     This program parses an XML file containing an item list.
 5     It prints out the items that are described in the XML file.
 6  */
 7  public class ItemListParserDemo
 8  {
 9     public static void main(String[] args) throws Exception
10     {
11        ItemListParser parser = new ItemListParser();
12        ArrayList<LineItem> items = parser.parse("items.xml");
13        for (LineItem anItem : items)
14           System.out.println(anItem.format());
15     }
16  }
```

Program Run

```
Ink Jet Refill Kit        29.95   8   239.6
4-port Mini Hub           19.95   4   79.8
```

SELF CHECK

4. What is the result of evaluating the XPath statement /items/item[1]/product/ price in the XML document of Figure 4?

5. Which XPath statement yields the name of the root element of any XML document?

Common Error 23.1

XML Elements Describe Objects, Not Classes

When you convert XML documents to Java classes, you need to determine a class for each element type. A common mistake is to make a separate class for each XML element. For example, consider a slightly different invoice description, with separate shipping and billing addresses:

```
<invoice>
   <shipto>
      <name>ACME Computer Supplies Inc.</name>
      <street>1195 W. Fairfield Rd.</street>
      <city>Sunnyvale</city>
      <state>CA</state>
      <zip>94085</state>
   </shipto>
   <billto>
      <name>ACME Computer Supplies Inc.</name>
      <street>P.O. Box 11098</street>
      <city>Sunnyvale</city>
      <state>CA</state>
      <zip>94080-1098</zip>
   </billto>
   <items>
   . . .
   </items>
</invoice>
```

Should you have a class Shipto to match the shipto element and another class Billto to match the billto element? That makes no sense, because both of them have the same contents: elements that describe an address.

Instead, you should think of the XML element as the value of an instance variable and then determine an appropriate class. For example, an invoice object has instance variables

- billto, of type Address
- shipto, also of type Address

Note that you don't see the classes in the XML document. There is no notion of a class Address in the XML document describing an invoice. To make element classes explicit, you use an XML schema—see Special Topic 23.1 on page 938 for more information.

Random Fact 23.2

Grammars, Parsers, and Compilers

Grammars are very important in many areas of computer science to describe the structure of computer programs or data formats. To introduce the concept of a grammar, consider this set of rules for a set of simple English language sentences:

1. A sentence has a noun phrase followed by a verb and another noun phrase.
2. A noun phrase consists of an article followed by an adjective list followed by a noun.
3. An adjective list consists of an adjective or an adjective followed by an adjective list.
4. Articles are "a" and "the".
5. Adjectives are "quick", "brown", "lazy", and "hungry".
6. Nouns are "fox", "dog", and "hamster".
7. Verbs are "jumps over" and "eats".

Here are two sentences that follow these rules:

- The quick brown fox jumps over the lazy dog.
- The hungry hamster eats a quick brown fox.

Symbolically, these rules can be expressed by a formal grammar:

```
<sentence> ::= <noun-phrase> <verb> <noun-phrase>
<noun-phrase> ::= <article> <adjective-list> <noun>
<adjective-list> ::= <adjective> | <adjective> <adjective-list>
<article> ::= a | the
<adjective> ::= quick | brown | lazy | hungry
<noun> ::= fox | dog | hamster
<verb> ::= jumps over | eats
```

Here the symbol ::= means "can be replaced with" and | separates alternate choices. For example, <article> can be replaced with "a" or "the".

The grammar symbols, such as <noun>, happen to be enclosed in angle brackets just like XML tags, but they are different from tags. One purpose of a grammar is to produce strings that are valid according to the grammar, by starting with the start symbol (<sentence> in this example) and applying replacement rules until the resulting string is free from symbols. See the table on the facing page for an example of the replacement process.

If you have a grammar and a string, such as "the hungry hamster eats a quick brown fox" or "a brown jumps over hamster quick lazy", you can parse the sentence: that is, check whether the sentence is described by the grammar rules and, if it is, show how it can be derived from the start symbol. One way to show the derivation is to construct a **parse tree** (see Figure 5).

String	Rule
<sentence>	Start
<noun-phrase> <verb> <noun-phrase>	1
<noun-phrase> eats <noun-phrase>	7
<article> <adjective-list> <noun> eats <noun-phrase>	2
the <adjective-list> <noun> eats <noun-phrase>	4
the <adjective> <noun> eats <noun-phrase>	3
the hungry <noun> eats <noun-phrase>	5
the hungry hamster eats <noun-phrase>	6
the hungry hamster eats <article> <adjective-list> <noun>	2
the hungry hamster eats a <adjective-list> <noun>	4
the hungry hamster eats a <adjective> <adjective-list> <noun>	3
the hungry hamster eats a quick <adjective-list> <noun>	5
the hungry hamster eats a quick <adjective> <noun>	3
the hungry hamster eats a quick brown <noun>	5
the hungry hamster eats a quick brown fox	6

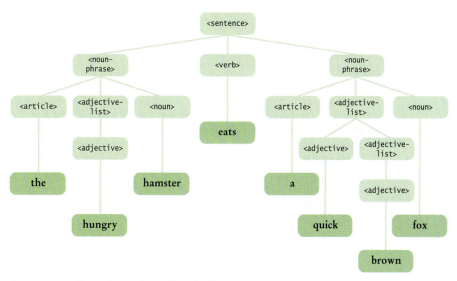

Figure 5 A Parse Tree for a Simple Sentence

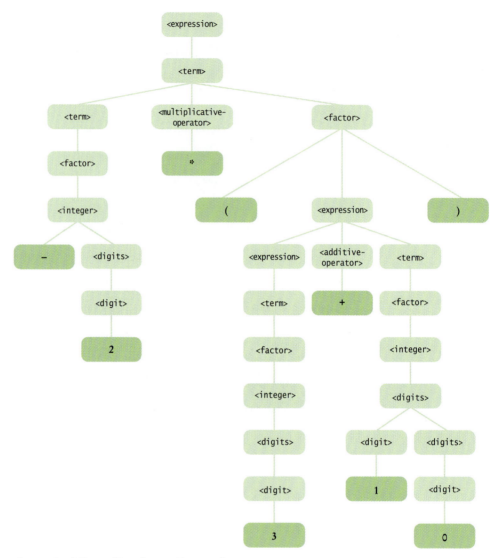

Figure 6 A Parse Tree for an Expression

A **parser** is a program that reads strings and decides whether the input conforms to the rules of a certain grammar. Some parsers—such as the DOM XML parser—build a parse tree in the process or report an error message when a parse tree cannot be constructed. Other parsers—such as the SAX XML parser—call user-specified methods whenever a part of the input was successfully parsed.

The most important use for parsers is inside compilers for programming languages. Just as our grammar can describe (some) simple English language sentences, the valid "sentences" in a programming language can be described by a grammar. The actual grammar for the Java programming language occupies about 15 pages in *The Java Language Specification* (http://java.sun.com/docs/book/jls). To give a flavor of a small subset of such a grammar, here is a grammar that describes arithmetic expressions.

```
<expression> ::= <term> | <expression> <additive-operator> <term>
<additive-operator> ::= + | -
<term> ::= <factor> | <term> <multiplicative-operator> <factor>
```

```
<multiplicative-operator> ::= * | /
<factor> ::= <integer> | ( <expression> )
<integer> ::= <digits> | - <digits>
<digits> ::= <digit> | <digit> <digits>
<digit> ::= 0 | 1 | 2 | 3 | 4 | 5 | 6 | 7 | 8 | 9
```

An example of a valid expression in this grammar is

```
-2 * (3 + 10)
```

Figure 6 shows the parse tree for this expression.

In a compiler, parsing the program source is the first step toward generating code that the target processor (the Java virtual machine in the case of Java) can execute. Writing a parser is a challenging and interesting task. You may at one point in your studies take a course in compiler construction, in which you learn how to write a parser and how to generate code from the parsed input. Fortunately, to use XML you don't have to know how the parser does its job. You simply ask the XML parser to read the XML input and then process the resulting Document tree.

23.3 Creating XML Documents

In the preceding section, you saw how to read an XML file into a Document object and how to analyze the contents of that object. In this section, you will see how to do the opposite—build up a Document object and then save it as an XML file. Of course, you can also generate an XML file simply as a sequence of print statements. However, that is not a good idea—it is easy to build an illegal XML document in this way, as when data contain special characters such as < or &.

Recall that you needed a DocumentBuilder object to read in an XML document. You also need such an object to create a new, empty document. Thus, to create a new document, first make a document builder factory, then a document builder, and finally the empty document:

```
DocumentBuilderFactory factory = DocumentBuilderFactory.newInstance();
DocumentBuilder builder = factory.newDocumentBuilder();
Document doc = builder.newDocument();
// An empty document
```

> The Document interface has methods to create elements and text nodes.

Now you are ready to insert nodes into the document. You use the createElement method of the Document interface to create the elements that you need.

```
Element priceElement = doc.createElement("price");
```

You set element attributes with the setAttribute method. For example,

```
priceElement.setAttribute("currency", "USD");
```

You have to work a bit harder for inserting text. First create a text node:

```
Text textNode = doc.createTextNode("29.95");
```

Then add the text node to the element:

```
priceElement.appendChild(textNode);
```

Figure 7 shows the DOM interfaces for XML document nodes. To construct the tree structure of a document, it is a good idea to use a set of helper methods.

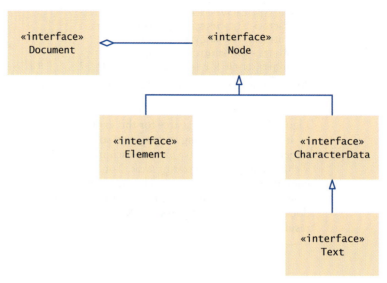

Figure 7 UML Diagram of DOM Interfaces Used in This Chapter

We start out with a helper method that creates an element with text:

```
private Element createTextElement(String name, String text)
{
    Text t = doc.createTextNode(text);
    Element e = doc.createElement(name);
    e.appendChild(t);
    return e;
}
```

Using this helper method, we can construct a price element like this:

```
Element priceElement = createTextElement("price", "29.95");
```

Next, we write a helper method to create a product element from a Product object:

```
private Element createProduct(Product p)
{
    Element e = doc.createElement("product");
    e.appendChild(createTextElement("description", p.getDescription()));
    e.appendChild(createTextElement("price", "" + p.getPrice()));
    return e;
}
```

This helper method is called from the createItem helper method:

```
private Element createItem(LineItem anItem)
{
    Element e = doc.createElement("item");
    e.appendChild(createProduct(anItem.getProduct()));
    e.appendChild(createTextElement("quantity", "" + anItem.getQuantity()));
    return e;
}
```

A helper method

```
private Element createItems(ArrayList<LineItem> items)
```

for the items element is implemented in the same way—see the program listing at the end of this section.

Now you build the document as follows:

```
ArrayList<LineItem> items = . . .;
doc = builder.newDocument();
Element root = createItems(items);
doc.appendChild(root);
```

Once you have built the document, you will want to write it to a file. The DOM standard provides the `LSSerializer` interface for this purpose. Unfortunately, the DOM standard uses very generic methods, which makes the code that is required to obtain a serializer object look like a "magic incantation":

```
DOMImplementation impl = doc.getImplementation();
DOMImplementationLS implLS
      = (DOMImplementationLS) impl.getFeature("LS", "3.0");
LSSerializer ser = implLS.createLSSerializer();
```

Once you have the serializer object, you simply use the `writeToString` method:

```
String str = ser.writeToString(doc);
```

By default, the `LSSerializer` produces an XML document without spaces or line breaks. As a result, the output looks less pretty, but it is actually more suitable for parsing by another program because it is free from unnecessary white space.

If you want white space, you use yet another magic incantation after creating the serializer:

```
ser.getDomConfig().setParameter("format-pretty-print", true);
```

Here is an example program that shows how to build and print an XML document.

ch23/builder/ItemListBuilder.java

```
 1  import java.util.ArrayList;
 2  import javax.xml.parsers.DocumentBuilder;
 3  import javax.xml.parsers.DocumentBuilderFactory;
 4  import javax.xml.parsers.ParserConfigurationException;
 5  import org.w3c.dom.Document;
 6  import org.w3c.dom.Element;
 7  import org.w3c.dom.Text;
 8
 9  /**
10     Builds a DOM document for an array list of items.
11  */
12  public class ItemListBuilder
13  {
14     private DocumentBuilder builder;
15     private Document doc;
16
17     /**
18        Constructs an item list builder.
19     */
20     public ItemListBuilder()
21           throws ParserConfigurationException
22     {
23        DocumentBuilderFactory factory
24              = DocumentBuilderFactory.newInstance();
25        builder = factory.newDocumentBuilder();
26     }
27
```

```java
28    /**
29       Builds a DOM document for an array list of items.
30       @param items the items
31       @return a DOM document describing the items
32    */
33    public Document build(ArrayList<LineItem> items)
34    {
35       doc = builder.newDocument();
36       doc.appendChild(createItems(items));
37       return doc;
38    }
39
40    /**
41       Builds a DOM element for an array list of items.
42       @param items the items
43       @return a DOM element describing the items
44    */
45    private Element createItems(ArrayList<LineItem> items)
46    {
47       Element e = doc.createElement("items");
48
49       for (LineItem anItem : items)
50          e.appendChild(createItem(anItem));
51
52       return e;
53    }
54
55    /**
56       Builds a DOM element for an item.
57       @param anItem the item
58       @return a DOM element describing the item
59    */
60    private Element createItem(LineItem anItem)
61    {
62       Element e = doc.createElement("item");
63
64       e.appendChild(createProduct(anItem.getProduct()));
65       e.appendChild(createTextElement(
66          "quantity", "" + anItem.getQuantity()));
67
68       return e;
69    }
70
71    /**
72       Builds a DOM element for a product.
73       @param p the product
74       @return a DOM element describing the product
75    */
76    private Element createProduct(Product p)
77    {
78       Element e = doc.createElement("product");
79
80       e.appendChild(createTextElement(
81          "description", p.getDescription()));
82       e.appendChild(createTextElement(
83          "price", "" + p.getPrice()));
84
85       return e;
86    }
```

```
87
88      private Element createTextElement(String name, String text)
89      {
90         Text t = doc.createTextNode(text);
91         Element e = doc.createElement(name);
92         e.appendChild(t);
93         return e;
94      }
95   }
```

ch23/builder/ItemListBuilderDemo.java

```java
1    import java.util.ArrayList;
2    import org.w3c.dom.DOMImplementation;
3    import org.w3c.dom.Document;
4    import org.w3c.dom.ls.DOMImplementationLS;
5    import org.w3c.dom.ls.LSSerializer;
6
7    /**
8       This program demonstrates the item list builder. It prints the XML
9       file corresponding to a DOM document containing a list of items.
10   */
11   public class ItemListBuilderDemo
12   {
13      public static void main(String[] args) throws Exception
14      {
15         ArrayList<LineItem> items = new ArrayList<LineItem>();
16         items.add(new LineItem(new Product("Toaster", 29.95), 3));
17         items.add(new LineItem(new Product("Hair dryer", 24.95), 1));
18
19         ItemListBuilder builder = new ItemListBuilder();
20         Document doc = builder.build(items);
21         DOMImplementation impl = doc.getImplementation();
22         DOMImplementationLS implLS
23            = (DOMImplementationLS) impl.getFeature("LS", "3.0");
24         LSSerializer ser = implLS.createLSSerializer();
25         String out = ser.writeToString(doc);
26
27         System.out.println(out);
28      }
29   }
```

This program uses the Product and LineItem classes from Chapter 12. The LineItem class has been modified by adding getProduct and getQuantity methods.

Program Run

```
<?xml version="1.0" encoding="UTF-8"?><items><item><product>
<description>Toaster</description><price>29.95</price></product>
<quantity>3</quantity></item><item><product><description>Hair dryer
</description><price>24.95</price></product><quantity>1</quantity>
</item></items>
```

SELF CHECK

6. Suppose you need to construct a Document object that represents an XML document other than an item list. Which methods from the ItemListBuilder class can you reuse?

7. How would you write a document to the file output.xml?

How To 23.2 Writing an XML Document

What is the best way to write an XML document? This How To shows you how to produce a Document object and generate an XML document from it.

Step 1 Provide the outline of a document builder class.

To construct the Document object from an object of some class, you should implement a class such as this one:

```java
public class MyBuilder
{
    private DocumentBuilder builder;
    private Document doc;

    public Document build(SomeClass x) { . . . }
    . . .
    private Element createTextElement(String name, String text)
    {
        Text t = doc.createTextNode(text);
        Element e = doc.createElement(name);
        e.appendChild(t);
        return e;
    }
}
```

Step 2 Look at the format of the XML document that you want to create.

Consider all elements, except for those that only have text content. Find the matching Java classes. In the ItemListBuilder example, we ignore quantity, description, and price because they have text content. The remaining elements and their Java classes are

- product – Product
- item – LineItem
- items – ArrayList<LineItem>

Step 3 For each element in Step 2, add a helper method to your builder class.

Each helper method has the form

```java
private Element createElementName(ClassForElement x)
```

For example,

```java
public class MyBuilder
{
    . . .
    public Document build(ArrayList<LineItem> x) { . . . }
    private Element createProduct(Product x)  { . . . }
    private Element createItem(LineItem x)  { . . . }
    private Element createItems(ArrayList<LineItem> x)  { . . . }
}
```

Step 4 Implement the helper methods.

For each element, call the helper methods of its children. However, if a child has text content, call createTextElement instead.

For example, the item element has two children: product and quantity. The former has a helper method, and the latter has text content. Therefore, the createItem method calls create-Product and createTextElement:

```java
private Element createItem(LineItem anItem)
{
```

```
        Element e = doc.createElement("item");
        e.appendChild(createProduct(anItem.getProduct()));
        e.appendChild(createTextElement("quantity", "" + anItem.getQuantity()));
        return e;
    }
```

You may find it helpful to implement the helper methods "bottom up", starting with the simplest method (such as createProduct) and finishing with the method for the root element (createItems).

Step 5   Finish off your builder by writing a constructor and the build method.

```
public class MyBuilder
{
    public MyBuilder() throws ParserConfigurationException
    {
        DocumentBuilderFactory factory = DocumentBuilderFactory.newInstance();
        builder = factory.newDocumentBuilder();
    }
    public Document build(ClassForRootElement x)
    {
        doc = builder.newDocument();
        doc.appendChild(createRootElementName(x));
        return doc;
    }
    . . .
}
```

Step 6   Use a class, such as the LSSerializer, to convert the Document to a string.

For example,

```
Invoice x = . . .;
InvoiceBuilder builder = new InvoiceBuilder();
Document doc = builder.build(x);
LSSerializer ser = . . .;
String str = ser.writeToString(doc);
```

23.4 Validating XML Documents

In this section you will learn how to specify rules for XML documents of a particular type. There are several mechanisms for this purpose. The oldest and simplest mechanism is a Document Type Definition (DTD), the topic of this section. We discuss other mechanisms in Special Topic 23.1 on page 938.

23.4.1 Document Type Definitions

Consider a document of type items. Intuitively, items denotes a sequence of item elements. Each item element contains a product and a quantity. A product contains a description and a price. Each of these elements contains text describing the product's description, price, and quantity. The purpose of a DTD is to formalize this description.

Table 2	Replacements for Special Characters	
Character	Encoding	Name
<	&lt;	Less than (left angle bracket)
>	&gt;	Greater than (right angle bracket)
&	&amp;	Ampersand
'	&apos;	Apostrophe
"	&quot;	Quotation mark

A DTD is a sequence of rules that describes the valid child elements and attributes for each element type.

A DTD is a sequence of rules that describes

- The valid attributes for each element type
- The valid child elements for each element type

Let us first turn to child elements. The valid child elements of an element are described by an ELEMENT rule:

```
<!ELEMENT items (item*)>
```

This means that an item list must contain a sequence of 0 or more item elements.

As you can see, the rule is delimited by <! . . .>, and it contains the name of the element whose children are to be constrained (items), followed by a description of what children are allowed.

Next, let us turn to the definition of an item node:

```
<!ELEMENT item (product, quantity)>
```

This means that the children of an item node must be a product node, followed by a quantity node.

The definition for a product is similar:

```
<!ELEMENT product (description, price)>
```

Finally, here are the definitions of the three remaining node types:

```
<!ELEMENT quantity (#PCDATA)>
<!ELEMENT description (#PCDATA)>
<!ELEMENT price (#PCDATA)>
```

The symbol #PCDATA refers to text, called "parsed character data" in XML terminology. The character data can contain any characters. However, certain characters, such as < and &, have special meaning in XML and need to be replaced if they occur in character data. Table 2 shows the replacements for special characters.

The complete DTD for an item list has six rules, one for each element type:

```
<!ELEMENT items (item*)>
<!ELEMENT item (product, quantity)>
<!ELEMENT product (description, price)>
<!ELEMENT quantity (#PCDATA)>
<!ELEMENT description (#PCDATA)>
<!ELEMENT price (#PCDATA)>
```

Let us have a closer look at the descriptions of the allowed children. Table 3 shows the expressions used to describe the children of an element. The EMPTY reserved word

Table 3 Regular Expressions for Element Content

Rule Description	Element Content
EMPTY	No children allowed
$(E*)$	Any sequence of 0 or more elements E
$(E+)$	Any sequence of 1 or more elements E
$(E?)$	Optional element E (0 or 1 occurrences allowed)
$(E_1, E_2, \ldots)$	Element E_1, followed by $E_2, \ldots$
$(E_1 \mid E_2 \mid \ldots)$	Element E_1 or E_2 or $\ldots$
(#PCDATA)	Text only
(#PCDATA $\mid E_1 \mid E_2 \ldots$)*	Any sequence of text and elements $E_1, E_2, \ldots$, in any order
ANY	Any children allowed

is self-explanatory: an element that is declared as EMPTY may not have any children. For example, the HTML DTD defines the img element to be EMPTY—an image has only attributes, specifying the image source, size, and placement, and no children.

More interesting child rules can be formed with the **regular expression** operations (* + ? , |). (See Table 3 and Figure 8. Also see Productivity Hint 11.1 for more information on regular expressions.) You have already seen the * ("0 or more") and , (sequence) operations. The children of an items element are 0 or more item elements, and the children of an item are a sequence of product and description elements.

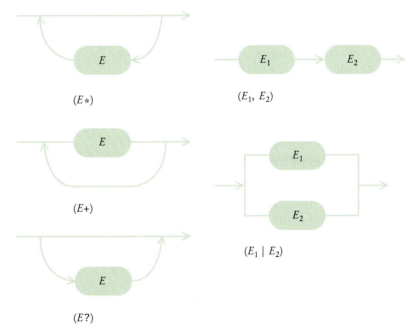

Figure 8
DTD Regular
Expression Operations

You can also combine these operations to form more complex expressions. For example,

```
<!ELEMENT section (title, (paragraph | (image, title?))+)
```

defines an element section whose children are:

1. A title element
2. A sequence of one or more of the following:
   - paragraph elements
   - image elements followed by optional title elements

Thus,

```
<section>
    <title/>
    <paragraph/>
    <image/>
    <title/>
    <paragraph/>
</section>
```

is valid, but

```
<section>
    <paragraph/>
    <paragraph/>
    <title/>
</section>
```

is not—there is no starting title, and the title at the end doesn't follow an image.

You already saw the (#PCDATA) rule. It means that the children can consist of any character data. For example, in our product list DTD, the description element can have any character data inside.

You can also allow *mixed content*—any sequence of character data and specified elements. However, in mixed content, you have no control over the order in which the elements appear. As explained in Quality Tip 23.2 on page 912, you should avoid mixed content for DTDs that describe data sets. This feature is intended for documents that contain both text and markup instructions, such as HTML pages.

Finally, you can allow a node to have children of any type—you should avoid that for DTDs that describe data sets.

You now know how to specify what children a node may have. A DTD also gives you control over the allowed attributes of an element. An attribute description looks like this:

```
<!ATTLIST Element Attribute Type Default>
```

The most useful attribute type descriptions are listed in Table 4. The CDATA type describes any sequence of character data. As with #PCDATA, certain characters, such as

Table 4 Common Attribute Types

Type Description	Attribute Type
CDATA	Any character data
$(V_1 \mid V_2 \mid \ . \ . \ . \ )$	One of $V_1, V_2, \ldots$

< and &, need to be encoded (as <, & and so on). There is no practical difference between the CDATA and #PCDATA types. Simply use CDATA in attribute declarations and #PCDATA in element declarations.

Rather than allowing arbitrary attribute values, you can specify a finite number of choices. For example, you may want to restrict a currency attribute to U.S. dollar, euro, and Japanese yen. Then use the following declaration:

```
<!ATTLIST price currency (USD | EUR | JPY) #REQUIRED>
```

You can use letters, numbers, and the hyphen (-) and underscore (_) characters for the attribute values.

There are other type descriptions that are less common in practice. You can find them in the XML reference (http://www.xml.com/axml/axml.html).

The attribute type description is followed by a "default" declaration. The reserved words that can appear in a "default" declaration are listed in Table 5.

For example, this attribute declaration describes that each price element must have a currency attribute whose value is any character data:

```
<!ATTLIST price currency CDATA #REQUIRED>
```

To fulfill this declaration, each price element must have a currency attribute, such as <price currency="USD">. A price without a currency would not be valid.

For an optional attribute, you use the #IMPLIED reserved word instead.

```
<!ATTLIST price currency CDATA #IMPLIED>
```

That means that you can supply a currency attribute in a price element, or you can omit it. If you omit it, then the application that processes the XML data implicitly assumes some default currency.

A better choice would be to supply the default value explicitly:

```
<!ATTLIST price currency CDATA "USD">
```

That means that the currency attribute is understood to mean USD if the attribute is not specified. An XML parser will then report the value of currency as USD if the attribute was not specified.

Finally, you can state that an attribute can only be identical to a particular value. For example, the rule

```
<!ATTLIST price currency CDATA #FIXED "USD">
```

means that a price element must either not have a currency attribute at all (in which case the XML parser will report its value as USD), or specify the currency attribute as USD. Naturally, this kind of rule is not very common.

Table 5 Attribute Defaults

Default Declaration	Explanation
#REQUIRED	Attribute is required
#IMPLIED	Attribute is optional
V	Default attribute, to be used if attribute is not specified
#FIXED V	Attribute must either be unspecified or contain this value

You have now seen the most common constructs for DTDs. Using these constructs, you can define your own DTDs for XML documents that describe data sets. In the next section, you will see how to specify which DTD an XML document should use, and how to have the XML parser check that a document conforms to its DTD.

23.4.2 Specifying a DTD in an XML Document

When you reference a DTD with an XML document, you can instruct the parser to check that the document follows the rules of the DTD. That way, the parser can check errors in the document.

In the preceding section you saw how to develop a DTD for a class of XML documents. The DTD specifies the permitted elements and attributes in the document. An XML document has two ways of referencing a DTD:

> An XML document can contain its DTD or refer to a DTD that is stored elsewhere.

1. The document may contain the DTD.

2. The document may refer to a DTD that is stored elsewhere.

A DTD is introduced with the DOCTYPE declaration. If the document contains its DTD, then the declaration looks like this:

```
<!DOCTYPE rootElement [ rules ]>
```

For example, an item list can include its DTD like this:

```
<?xml version="1.0"?>
<!DOCTYPE items [

<!ELEMENT items (item*)>
<!ELEMENT item (product, quantity)>
<!ELEMENT product (description, price)>
<!ELEMENT quantity (#PCDATA)>
<!ELEMENT description (#PCDATA)>
<!ELEMENT price (#PCDATA)>

]>
<items>
   <item>
      <product>
         <description>Ink Jet Refill Kit</description>
         <price>29.95</price>
      </product>
      <quantity>8</quantity>
   </item>
   <item>
      <product>
         <description>4-port Mini Hub</description>
         <price>19.95</price>
      </product>
      <quantity>4</quantity>
   </item>
</items>
```

However, if the DTD is more complex, then it is better to store it outside the XML document. In that case, you use the SYSTEM reserved word inside the DOCTYPE declaration to indicate that the system that hosts the XML processor must locate the DTD.

The SYSTEM reserved word is followed by the location of the DTD. For example, a DOCTYPE declaration might point to a local file

When referencing an external DTD, you must supply an URL for locating the DTD.

```
<!DOCTYPE items SYSTEM "items.dtd">
```

Alternatively, the resource might be an URL anywhere on the Web:

```
<!DOCTYPE items SYSTEM "http://www.mycompany.com/dtds/items.dtd">
```

For commonly used DTDs, the DOCTYPE declaration can contain a PUBLIC reserved word. For example,

```
<!DOCTYPE faces-config PUBLIC
    "-//Sun Microsystems, Inc.//DTD JavaServer Faces Config 1.0//EN"
    "http://java.sun.com/dtd/web-facesconfig_1_0.dtd">
```

A program parsing the DTD can look at the public identifier. If it is a familiar identifier, then it need not spend time retrieving the DTD from the URL.

23.4.3 Parsing and Validation

When you include a DTD with an XML document, then you can tell the parser to *validate* the document. That means that the parser will check that all child elements and attributes of an element conform to the ELEMENT and ATTLIST rules in the DTD. If a document is invalid, then the parser reports an error. To turn on validation, you use the setValidating method of the DocumentBuilderFactory class before calling the newDocumentBuilder method:

When your XML document has a DTD, you can request validation when parsing.

```
DocumentBuilderFactory factory = DocumentBuilderFactory.newInstance();
factory.setValidating(true);
DocumentBuilder builder = factory.newDocumentBuilder();
Document doc = builder.parse(. . .);
```

Validation can simplify your code for processing XML documents. For example, if the DTD specifies that the child elements of each item element are product and quantity elements in that order, then you can rely on that fact and don't need to put tedious checks in your code.

When you parse an XML file with a DTD, tell the parser to ignore white space.

If the parser has access to the DTD, it can make another useful improvement. By default, the parser converts all spaces in the input document to text, even if the spaces are only used to logically line up elements. As a result, the document contains text nodes that are wasteful and can be confusing when you analyze the document tree.

To make the parser ignore white space, call the setIgnoringElementContentWhitespace method of the DocumentBuilderFactory class.

```
factory.setValidating(true);
factory.setIgnoringElementContentWhitespace(true);
```

Finally, if the parser has access to the DTD, it can fill in default values for attributes. For example, suppose a DTD defines a currency attribute for a price element:

```
<!ATTLIST price currency CDATA "USD">
```

If a document contains a price element without a currency attribute, then the parser can supply the default:

```
String attributeValue = priceElement.getAttribute("currency");
    // Gets "USD" if no currency specified
```

This concludes our discussion of XML. You now know enough XML to put it to work for describing data formats. Whenever you are tempted to use a "quick and dirty" file format, you should consider using XML instead. By using XML for data interchange, your programs become more professional, robust, and flexible. This chapter covers the most important aspects of XML for everyday programming. For more advanced features that can be useful in specialized situations, please see http://www.xml.com/axml/axml.html. Furthermore, XML technology is still undergoing rapid change at the time of this writing. Therefore, it is a good idea to check out the latest developments. Good web sites are http://www.w3c.org/xml, the W3C XML web site, and http://java.sun.com/xml, the Sun Microsystems XML web site.

SELF CHECK

8. How can a DTD specify that the `quantity` element in an `item` is optional?

9. How can a DTD specify that a `product` element can contain a `description` and a `price` element, in any order?

10. How can a DTD specify that the `description` element has an optional attribute `language`?

How To 23.3

Writing a DTD

You write a DTD to describe a set of XML documents of the same type. The DTD specifies which elements contain child elements (and the order in which they may appear) and which elements contain text. It also specifies which elements may have attributes, which attributes are required, and which defaults are used for missing attributes.

These rules are for DTDs that describe program data. DTDs that describe narrative text generally have a much more complex structure.

Step 1 Get or write a couple of sample XML documents.

For example, if you wanted to make a DTD for XML documents that describe an invoice, you could study samples such as the one in How To 23.1 on page 909.

Step 2 Make a list of all elements that can occur in the XML document.

In the invoice example, they are
- `invoice`
- `address`
- `name`
- `street`
- `city`
- `state`
- `zip`
- `items`
- `item`
- `product`
- `description`
- `quantity`

Step 3 For each of the elements, decide whether its children are elements or text.

Following Quality Tip 23.2 on page 912, it is best to avoid elements whose children are a mixture of both. In the invoice example, the following elements have element content:

- invoice
- address
- items
- item
- product

The remainder contain text.

Step 4 For elements that contain text, the DTD rule is

```
<!ELEMENT elementName (#PCDATA)>
```

Thus, we have the following simple rules for the invoice elements that contain text:

```
<!ELEMENT name (#PCDATA)>
<!ELEMENT street (#PCDATA)>
<!ELEMENT city (#PCDATA)>
<!ELEMENT state (#PCDATA)>
<!ELEMENT zip (#PCDATA)>
<!ELEMENT quantity (#PCDATA)>
<!ELEMENT description (#PCDATA)>
```

Step 5 For each element that contains other elements, make a list of the possible child elements.

Here are the lists in the invoice example:

invoice
- address
- items

address
- name
- street
- city
- state
- zip

items
- item

item
- product
- quantity

product
- description
- price

Step 6 For each of those elements, decide in which order the child elements should occur and how often they should occur.

Then form the rule

```
<!ELEMENT elementName child1 count1, child2 count2, . . .>
```

where each *count* is one of the following:

Quantity	Count
0 or 1	?
1	omit
0 or more	*
1 or more	+

In the invoice example, the `items` element can contain any number of items, so the rule is

```
<!ELEMENT items (item*)>
```

In the remaining cases, each child element occurs exactly once. That leads to the rules

```
<!ELEMENT invoice (address, items)>
<!ELEMENT address (name, street, city, state, zip)>
<!ELEMENT item (product, quantity)>
<!ELEMENT product (descripton, price)>
```

Step 7   Decide whether any elements should have attributes.

Following Quality Tip 23.1 on page 911, it is best to avoid attributes altogether or to minimize the use of attributes. Because we have no good reason to add attributes in the invoice example, our invoice is complete without attributes.

Special Topic 23.1

Schema Languages

Several mechanisms have been developed to deal with the limitations of DTDs. DTDs cannot express certain details about the structure of an XML document. For example, you can't force an element to contain just a number or a date—any text string is allowed for a (#PCDATA) element.

The XML Schema specification is one mechanism for overcoming these limitations. An XML schema is like a DTD in that it is a set of rules that documents of a particular type need to follow, but a schema can contain far more precise rule descriptions.

Here is just a hint of how an XML schema is specified. For each element, you specify the element name and the type. For example, this definition restricts the contents of `quantity` to an integer.

```
<xsd:element name="quantity" type="xsd:integer"/>
```

Note that an XML schema is itself written in XML—unlike a DTD, which uses a completely different syntax. (The `xsd:` prefix is a *name space* prefix to denote that `xsd:element` and `xsd:integer` are part of the XML Schema Definition name space. See Special Topic 23.2 on page 939 for more information about name spaces.)

In XML Schema, you can define complex types, much as you define classes in Java. Here is the definition of an `Address` type:

```
<xsd:complexType name="Address">
   <xsd:sequence>
      <xsd:element name="name" type="xsd:string"/>
      <xsd:element name="street" type="xsd:string"/>
      <xsd:element name="city" type="xsd:string"/>
      <xsd:element name="state" type="xsd:string"/>
      <xsd:element name="zip" type="xsd:string"/>
   </xsd:sequence>
</xsd:complexType>
```

Then you can specify that an invoice should have `shipto` and `billto` instance variables that are both of type `Address`:

```
<xsd:element name="shipto" type="Address"/>
<xsd:element name="billto" type="Address"/>
```

These examples show that an XML schema can be more precise than a DTD.

The XML Schema specification has many advanced features—see the W3C web site, www.w3c.org/xml, for details. However, some programmers find that specification overly complex and instead use a competing standard called Relax NG—see www.relaxng.org. Relax NG is simpler than XML Schema, and it shares a feature with DTDs: a compact notation that is not XML. For example, in Relax NG, you simply write

```
element quantity { xsd:integer }
```

to denote that quantity is an element containing an integer. The designers of Relax NG realized that XML, despite its many advantages, is not always the best notation for humans.

Special Topic 23.2

Other XML Technologies

This chapter covers the subset of the XML 1.0 specification that is most useful for common programming situations. Since version 1.0 of the XML specification was released, there has been a huge amount of interest in advanced XML technologies. A number of useful technologies have recently been standardized. Among them are:

- Schema Definitions
- Name Spaces
- XHTML
- XSL and Transformations

Special Topic 23.1 contains more information about schema definitions.

Name spaces were invented to ensure that many different people and organizations can develop XML documents without running into conflicts with element names. For example, if you look inside Special Topic 23.1, you will see that XML Schema definitions have element names that are prefixed with a tag xsd:, such as

```
<xsd:element name="city" type="xsd:string"/>
```

That way, the tag and attribute names, such as element and string, don't conflict with other names. In that regard, name spaces are similar to Java packages. However, a name space prefix such as xsd: is just a shortcut for the actual name space identifier, which is a much longer, unique string. For example, the full name space for XML Schema definitions is http://www.w3.org/2000/08/XMLSchema. Each schema definition starts out with the statement

```
<xsd:schema xmlns:xsd="http://www.w3.org/2000/08/XMLSchema">
```

which binds the xsd prefix to the full name space.

XHTML is the most recent recommendation of the W3C for formatting web pages. Unlike HTML, XHTML is fully XML-compliant. Once web-editing tools switch to XHTML, it will become much easier to write programs that parse web pages. The XHTML standard has been carefully designed to be backwards compatible with existing browsers.

While XHTML documents are intended to be viewed by browsers, general XML documents are not designed to be viewed at all. Nevertheless, it is often desirable to *transform* an XML document into a viewable form. XSL (Extensible Stylesheet Language) was created for this purpose. A style sheet indicates how to change an XML document into an HTML document, or even a completely different format, such as PDF.

For more information on these and other emerging technologies, see the W3C web site, http://www.w3.org/xml.

Summary of Learning Objectives

Describe the purpose of XML and the structure of an XML document.

- XML allows you to encode complex data, independent from any programming language, in a form that the recipient can easily parse.
- XML files are readable by computer programs and by humans.
- XML-formatted data files are resilient to change.
- XML describes the meaning of data, not how to display them.
- An XML document starts out with an XML declaration and contains elements and text.
- An element can contain text, child elements, or both (mixed content). For data descriptions, avoid mixed content.
- Elements can have attributes. Use attributes to describe how to interpret the element content.

Use a parser and the XPath language to process an XML document.

- A parser is a program that reads a document, checks whether it is syntactically correct, and takes some action as it processes the document.
- A streaming parser reports the building blocks of an XML document. A tree-based parser builds a document tree.
- A DocumentBuilder can read an XML document from a file, URL, or input stream. The result is a Document object, which contains a tree.
- An XPath describes a node or node set, using a notation similar to that for directory paths.

Write Java programs that create XML documents.

- The Document interface has methods to create elements and text nodes.
- Use an LSSerializer to write a DOM document.

Explain the use of DTDs for validating XML documents.

- A DTD is a sequence of rules that describes the valid child elements and attributes for each element type.
- An XML document can contain its DTD or refer to a DTD that is stored elsewhere.
- When referencing an external DTD, you must supply an URL for locating the DTD.
- When your XML document has a DTD, you can request validation when parsing.
- When you parse an XML file with a DTD, tell the parser to ignore white space.

Media Resources

www.wiley.com/
college/
horstmann

- Lab Exercises
- ⊕ Practice Quiz
- ⊕ Code Completion Exercises

Classes, Objects, and Methods Introduced in this Chapter

```
javax.xml.parsers.DocumentBuilder          org.w3c.dom.DOMConfiguration
   newDocument                                setParameter
   parse                                    org.w3c.dom.DOMImplementation
javax.xml.parsers.DocumentBuilderFactory     getFeature
   newDocumentBuilder                       org.w3c.dom.Element
   newInstance                                getAttribute
   setIgnoringElementContentWhitespace        setAttribute
   setValidating                            org.w3c.dom.ls.DOMImplementationLS
javax.xml.xpath.XPath                          createLSSerializer
   evaluate                                 org.w3c.dom.ls.LSSerializer
javax.xml.xpath.XPathExpressionException       getDomConfig
javax.xml.xpath.XPathFactory                   writeToString
   newInstance
   newXPath
org.w3c.dom.Document
   createElement
   createTextNode
   getImplementation
```

Review Exercises

★ **R23.1** Give some examples to show the differences between XML and HTML.

★ **R23.2** Design an XML document that describes a bank account.

★ **R23.3** Draw a tree view for the XML document you created in Exercise R23.2.

★ **R23.4** Write the XML document that corresponds to the parse tree in Figure 5.

★ **R23.5** Write the XML document that corresponds to the parse tree in Figure 6.

★ **R23.6** Make an XML document describing a book, with child elements for the author name, the title, and the publication year.

★ **R23.7** Add a description of the book's language to the document of the preceding exercise. Should you use an element or an attribute?

★★ **R23.8** What is mixed content? What problems does it cause?

★ **R23.9** Design an XML document that describes a purse containing three quarters, a dime, and two nickels.

★★ **R23.10** Explain why a paint program, such as Microsoft Paint, is a WYSIWYG program that is also "what you see is all you've got".

★★ **R23.11** Consider the XML file

```
<purse>
  <coin>
    <value>0.5</value>
    <name lang="en">half dollar</name>
  </coin>
  <coin>
```

```
            <value>0.25</value>
            <name lang="en">quarter</name>
        </coin>
    </purse>
```

What are the values of the following XPath expressions?

a. `/purse/coin[1]/value`

b. `/purse/coin[2]/name`

c. `/purse/coin[2]/name/@lang`

d. `name(/purse/coin[2]/*[1])`

e. `count(/purse/coin)`

f. `count(/purse/coin[2]/name)`

★★ **R23.12** With the XML file of Exercise R23.11, give XPath expressions that yield:

    a. the value of the first coin.

    b. the number of coins.

    c. the name of the first child element of the first coin element.

    d. the name of the first attribute of the first coin's name element. (The expression @* selects the attributes of an element.)

    e. the value of the lang attribute of the second coin's name element.

★★ **R23.13** Design a DTD that describes a bank with bank accounts.

★★ **R23.14** Design a DTD that describes a library patron who has checked out a set of books. Each book has an ID number, an author, and a title. The patron has a name and telephone number.

★★ **R23.15** Write the DTD file for the following XML document

```
<?xml version="1.0"?>
<productlist>
    <product>
        <name>Comtrade Tornado</name>
        <price currency="USD">2495</price>
        <score>60</score>
    </product>
    <product>
        <name>AMAX Powerstation 75</name>
        <price>2999</price>
        <score>62</score>
    </product>
</productlist>
```

★★ **R23.16** Design a DTD for invoices, as described in How To 23.3 on page 936.

★★★ **R23.17** Design a DTD for simple English sentences, as described in Random Fact 23.2 on page 920.

★★★ **R23.18** Design a DTD for arithmetic expressions, as described in Random Fact 23.2 on page 920.

Programming Exercises

★★ **P23.1** Write a program that can read XML files, such as

```
<purse>
  <coin>
    <value>0.5</value>
    <name>half dollar</name>
  </coin>
  . . .
</purse>
```

Your program should construct a Purse object and print the total value of the coins in the purse.

★★★ **P23.2** Building on Exercise P23.1, make the program read an XML file as described in that exercise. Then print an XML file of the form

```
<purse>
  <coins>
    <coin>
      <value>0.5</value>
      <name>half dollar</name>
    </coin>
    <quantity>3</quantity>
  </coins>
  <coins>
    <coin>
      <value>0.25</value>
      <name>quarter</name>
    </coin>
    <quantity>2</quantity>
  </coins>
</purse>
```

★★ **P23.3** Repeat Exercise P23.1, using a DTD for validation.

★★ **P23.4** Write a program that can read XML files, such as

```
<bank>
  <account>
    <number>3</number>
    <balance>1295.32</balance>
  </account>
  . . .
</bank>
```

Your program should construct a Bank object and print the total value of the balances in the accounts.

★★ **P23.5** Repeat Exercise P23.4, using a DTD for validation.

★★ **P23.6** Enhance Exercise P23.4 as follows: First read the XML file in, then add 10 percent interest to all accounts, and write an XML file that contains the increased account balances.

★★★ **P23.7** Write a DTD file that describes documents that contain information about countries: name of the country, its population, and its area. Create an XML file that has five different countries. The DTD and XML should be in different files. Write a program that uses the XML file you wrote and prints:

- The country with the largest area.
- The country with the largest population.
- The country with the largest population density (people per square kilometer).

★★ **P23.8** Write a parser to parse invoices using the invoice structure described in How To 23.1 on page 909. The parser should parse the XML file into an `Invoice` object and print out the invoice in the format used in Chapter 12.

★★ **P23.9** Modify Exercise P23.8 to support separate shipping and billing addresses. Supply a modified DTD with your solution.

★★ **P23.10** Write a document builder that turns an invoice object, as defined in Chapter 12, into an XML file of the format described in How To 23.1 on page 909.

★★★ **P23.11** Modify Exercise P23.10 to support separate shipping and billing addresses.

★G **P23.12** Write a program that can read an XML document of the form

```
<rectangle>
    <x>5</x>
    <y>10</y>
    <width>20</width>
    <height>30</height>
</rectangle>
```

and draw the shape in a window.

★G **P23.13** Write a program that can read an XML document of the form

```
<ellipse>
    <x>5</x>
    <y>10</y>
    <width>20</width>
    <height>30</height>
</ellipse>
```

and draw the shape in a window.

★★G **P23.14** Write a program that can read an XML document of the form

```
<rectangularshape shape="ellipse">
    <x>5</x>
    <y>10</y>
    <width>20</width>
    <height>30</height>
</rectangularshape>
```

Support shape attributes `"rectangle"`, `"roundrectangle"`, and `"ellipse"`.

Draw the shape in a window.

★★G **P23.15** Write a program that can read an XML document of the form

```
<polygon>
    <point>
        <x>5</x>
        <y>10</y>
    </point>
    . . .
```

```
</polygon>
```

and draw the shape in a window.

★★★G **P23.16** Write a program that can read an XML document of the form

```
<drawing>
   <rectangle>
      <x>5</x>
      <y>10</y>
      <width>20</width>
      <height>30</height>
   </rectangle>
   <line>
      <x1>5</x1>
      <y1>10</y1>
      <x2>25</x2>
      <y2>40</y2>
   </line>
   <message>
      <text>Hello, World!</text>
      <x>20</x>
      <y>30</y>
   </message>
</drawing>
```

and show the drawing in a window.

★★★G **P23.17** Repeat Exercise P23.16, using a DTD for validation.

Programming Projects

Project 23.1 Following Exercise P12.7, design an XML format for the appointments in an appointment calendar. Write a program that first reads in a file with appointments, then another file of the format

```
<commands>
   <add>
      <appointment>
         . . .
      </appointment>
   </add>
   . . .
   <remove>
      <appointment>
         . . .
      </appointment>
   </remove>
</commands>
```

Your program should process the commands and then produce an XML file that consists of the updated appointments.

Project 23.2 Write a program to simulate an airline seat reservation system, using XML documents. Reference Exercise P12.8 for the airplane seat information. The program reads a seating chart, in an XML format of your choice, and a command file, in an XML format of your choice, similar to the command file of the preceding exercise. Then the program processes the commands and produces an updated seating chart.

Answers to Self-Check Questions

1. Your answer should look similar to this:

```
<student>
    <name>James Bond</name>
    <id>007</id>
</student>
```

2. Most browsers display a tree structure that indicates the nesting of the tags. Some browsers display nothing at all because they can't find any HTML tags.

3. The text `hamster.jpg` is never displayed, so it should not be a part of the document. Instead, the `src` attribute tells the browser where to find the image that should be displayed.

4. 29.95.

5. `name(/*[1])`.

6. The `createTextElement` method is useful for creating other documents.

7. First construct a string, as described, and then use a `PrintWriter` to save the string to a file.

8. `<!ELEMENT item (product, quantity?)>`

9. `<!ELEMENT product ((description, price) | (price, description))>`

10. `<!ATTLIST description language CDATA #IMPLIED>`

Web Applications

CHAPTER GOALS

- To understand the web application concept
- To learn the syntactical elements of the JavaServer Faces web application framework
- To learn about navigation in web applications
- To build three-tier web applications

Web applications are a new type of software that has become very important in recent years. Applications for a wide variety of purposes, such as e-mail, banking, shopping, and playing games, run on servers and interact with users through a web browser. Developing web-based user interfaces is more complex and challenging than writing graphical user interfaces. Until recently, only primitive technologies (such as Java servlets) were available for this purpose. Fortunately, more capable frameworks for web programming have emerged that are roughly analogous to the Swing framework for client-side user interface programming. In this chapter, you will learn how to write web applications using the **JavaServer Faces (JSF)** framework.

CHAPTER CONTENTS

24.1 The Architecture of a Web Application

A **web application** is an application whose user interface is displayed in a web browser. The application program resides on the web server. The user fills out form elements and clicks on buttons and links. The user inputs are transmitted over the Internet to the server, and the server program updates the web page that the user sees (see Figure 1).

> The user interface of a web application is displayed in a web browser.

The browser sends information to the server using the HTTP protocol that was described in Sections 21.2 and 21.5. The server responds by sending a new web page in HTML format.

The web pages that are used in a web application contain forms: groups of elements to collect user input, such as text fields and buttons. For example, here is the HTML code for a simple form that prompts for a user name and password.

```html
<html>
   <head>
      <title>A Simple Form</title>
   </head>
   <body>
      <form action="login.xhtml" method="POST">
         <p>
            User name:
            <input type="text" name="username" />
            Password:
            <input type="password" name="passwd" />
            <input type="submit" name="login" value="Log in"/>
         </p>
      </form>
   </body>
</html>
```

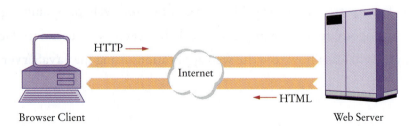

Figure 1 The Architecture of a Web Application

948

Figure 2 A Simple Form

Figure 2 shows the form. Note that there are three input elements: a text field, a password field, and a submit button. (The HTML tags are summarized in Appendix F.)

When a form is submitted, the names and values of the form elements are sent to the web server.

When a submit button is pressed, the form data is submitted to the server. The data is formatted according to the rules of the HTTP protocol, using the POST request type. The form data consists of the names and values of the form elements, formatted in a special way, called "URL encoding". In our example form, the returned data has the following form:

```
POST /login.xhtml HTTP/1.1
Content-Type: application/x-www-form-urlencoded
Content-Length: 46
blank line
username=jqpublic&passwd=secret&login=Log%20in
```

The web server analyzes the request and sends a new HTML page to the browser. The new page might tell the user that the login was successful and ask the user to specify another action. Alternatively, the new page might tell the user that the login failed.

This simple example illustrates why it is difficult to implement a web application. Imagine what the server program has to do. At any time, it might receive a request with form data. At that point, the server program has to remember which form it has last sent to the client. It then needs to analyze the submitted data, decide what form to show next, and produce the HTML tags for that form.

Upon receiving the form data, the web server sends a new web page to the browser.

There are multiple challenges. As described in Special Topic 24.1 on page 955, the HTTP protocol is stateless—there is no memory of which form was last sent when a new request is received. Generating the HTML tags for a form is tedious. Perhaps most importantly, an application that consists of response strategies for a large number of request types is very hard to comprehend without additional structure.

In order to overcome these challenges, various web application frameworks have been developed. A web application framework hides the low-level details of analyzing HTTP and generating HTML from the application programmer. In this chapter, you will learn about the **JavaServer Faces** (JSF) framework, the web framework that is a part of the Java Enterprise Edition. You can think of JSF as "Swing for the Web". Both Swing and JSF handle the tedious details of capturing user input and painting text fields and buttons. Swing captures mouse and keyboard events and paints pixels in a frame. JSF handles form-posting events and paints by emitting HTML code. This chapter describes JSF 2.0, an improvement to the original JSF framework, that became available in 2009.

1. Why are two different protocols (HTML and HTTP) required by a web application?

2. How can a web application know which user is trying to log in when the information of the sample login screen is submitted?

24.2 The Architecture of a JSF Application

In the following sections, we give an overview of the architecture of a JSF application and show a very simple sample application.

24.2.1 JSF Pages

The user interface of a JSF application is described by a set of *JSF pages.* Each JSF page has the following structure:

```
<?xml version="1.0" encoding="UTF-8"?>
<html xmlns="http://www.w3.org/1999/xhtml"
    xmlns:h="http://java.sun.com/jsf/html">
    <h:head>
        <title>Page title</title>
    </h:head>
    <h:body>
        <h:form>
            Page contents
        </h:form>
    </h:body>
</html>
```

A JavaServer Faces (JSF) page contains HTML and JSF tags.

You can think of this as the required "plumbing", similar to the `public static void main` incantation that is required for every Java program. If you compare this page with the HTML page from the preceding section, you will notice that the main elements are very similar to a regular HTML page, but several elements (`head`, `body`, and `form`) are JSF tags with an `h:` prefix. Following is a complete example of a JSF page. Figure 3 shows the result of executing the program.

Figure 3 Executing the `time` Web Application

ch24/time/index.xhtml

```
1   <?xml version="1.0" encoding="UTF-8"?>
2   <html xmlns="http://www.w3.org/1999/xhtml"
3       xmlns:h="http://java.sun.com/jsf/html">
4       <h:head>
5           <title>The time application</title>
6       </h:head>
7       <h:body>
8           <h:form>
9               <p>
10                  The current time is #{timeBean.time}
11              </p>
12          </h:form>
13      </h:body>
14  </html>
```

> The JSF container converts a JSF page to an HTML page, replacing all JSF tags with text and HTML tags.

The purpose of a JSF page is to *generate* an HTML page. The basic process is as follows:

* The HTML tags that are present in the JSF page (such as title and p) are retained. These are the *static* part of the page: the formatting instructions that do not change.

* The JSF tags are translated into HTML. This translation is *dynamic:* it depends on the state of Java objects that are associated with the tags. In our example, the expression #{timeBean.time} has been replaced by dynamically generated text, namely the current time.

Figure 4 shows the basic process. The browser requests a JSF page. The page is processed by the **JSF container,** the server-side software that implements the JSF framework. The JSF container translates all JSF tags into text and HTML tags, yielding a pure HTML page. That page is transmitted to the client browser. The browser displays the page.

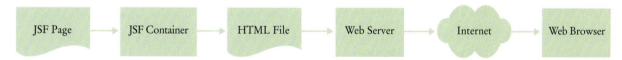

Figure 4 The JSF Container Rewrites the Requested Page

24.2.2 Managed Beans

The expression #{timeBean.time} is called a **value expression.** Value expressions invoke method calls on Java objects, which are called *managed beans.*

> A managed bean is an object that is controlled by the JSF container.

These objects are called "managed" because they are controlled by the JSF container. The container creates a managed bean when it is first used in a value expression. The *scope* of the managed bean determines which clients can access the object and how long the object stays alive.

In this chapter, we only consider managed beans with *session scope*. A session-scoped object can be accessed by all requests from the same browser. If multiple users are simultaneously accessing a JSF application, each of them is given a separate object. This is a good default for simple web applications.

Here is the code for the TimeBean class. Note the following:

- You declare a session-scoped managed bean with the annotations @ManagedBean and @SessionScoped.

- The name of the bean in a value expression is the class name with the first letter changed to lowercase, e.g., timeBean.

- The value expression timeBean.time calls the getTime method. You will see the reason in the next section.

- The getTime method uses the DateFormat class to format the current time, producing a string such as 9:00:00 AM.

- When deploying the application, all class files must be placed inside the WEB-INF/ classes directory. Because many application servers also require that classes be contained in a package, we place our classes inside the bigjava package. For that reason, the class is contained in the WEB-INF/classes/bigjava directory.

ch24/time/WEB-INF/classes/bigjava/TimeBean.java

```java
1   package bigjava;
2
3   import java.text.DateFormat;
4   import java.util.Date;
5   import java.util.TimeZone;
6   import javax.faces.bean.ManagedBean;
7   import javax.faces.bean.SessionScoped;
8
9   @ManagedBean
10  @SessionScoped
11  public class TimeBean
12  {
13      private DateFormat timeFormatter;
14
15      /**
16          Initializes the formatter.
17      */
18      public TimeBean()
19      {
20          timeFormatter = DateFormat.getTimeInstance();
21      }
22
23      /**
24          Read-only time property.
25          @return the formatted time
26      */
27      public String getTime()
28      {
29          Date time = new Date();
30          String timeString = timeFormatter.format(time);
31          return timeString;
32      }
33  }
```

24.2.3 Separation of Presentation and Business Logic

The JSF technology enables the separation of presentation and business logic.

We will look at value expressions and managed beans in more detail in the next section. The key observation is that every JSF application has two parts: *presentation* and *business logic*.

The term "presentation" refers to the user interface of the web application: the arrangement of the text, images, buttons, and so on. The *business logic* is the part of the application that is independent of the visual presentation. In commercial applications, it contains the rules that are used for business decisions: what products to offer, how much to charge, to whom to extend credit, and so on. In our example, we simulated the business logic with a TimeBean object.

JSF pages define the presentation logic. Managed beans define the business logic. Value expressions tie the two together.

The separation of presentation logic and business logic is very important when designing web applications. Some web technologies place the code for the business logic right into the web page. However, this quickly turns into a serious problem. Programmers are rarely skilled in web design (as you can see from the boring web pages in this chapter). Graphic designers don't usually know much about programming and find it very challenging to improve web pages that contain a lot of code. JSF solves this problem. In JSF, the graphic designer only sees the elements that make up the presentation logic. It is easy to take a boring JSF page and make it pretty by adding banners, icons, and so on.

24.2.5 Deploying a JSF Application

To run a JSF application, you need a server with a **JSF container**. We suggest that you use the GlassFish application server, http://glassfish.dev.java.net, which has, together with many other features that you can ignore, a JSF container and a convenient administration interface.

To deploy a JSF application, follow these steps:

1. Make a separate directory tree for each web application.
2. Place JSF pages (such as index.xhtml) into the root directory of the application's directory tree.
3. Create a WEB-INF subdirectory in your application directory.
4. Place all Java classes inside a classes subdirectory of the WEB-INF directory. Note that you should place your classes into a package.
5. Place the file web.xml (which is shown below) inside the WEB-INF subdirectory. Some servers need the web.xml file to configure the JSF container. We also turn on development mode, which gives better error messages.
6. Zip up all application files into a file with extension .war (Web Archive). This is easily achieved by running the jar command from the command line, after changing to the application directory. For example,

```
cd time
jar cvf time.war .
```

The period (.) denotes the current directory. The jar command creates an archive time.war consisting of all files in all subdirectories of the current directory.

7. Make sure the application server is started. The application server listens to web requests, typically on port 8080.

8. Deploy the application to the application server. With GlassFish, this can be achieved either through the administrative interface or simply by copying the WAR file into a special deployment directory. By default, this is the subdirectory `domains/domain1/autodeploy` inside the GlassFish installation directory.

9. Point your browser to an URL such as `http://localhost:8080/time/faces/index.xhtml`. Note the `faces` part in the URL. If you forget this part, the file will not be processed by the JSF container.

Figure 5 shows the directory structure for the application.

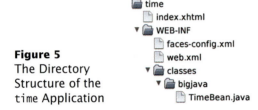

Figure 5
The Directory
Structure of the
`time` Application

ch24/time/WEB-INF/web.xml

```xml
1  <?xml version="1.0" encoding="UTF-8"?>
2  <web-app xmlns:xsi="http://www.w3.org/2001/XMLSchema-instance"
3      xmlns="http://java.sun.com/xml/ns/javaee"
4      xmlns:web="http://java.sun.com/xml/ns/javaee/web-app_2_5.xsd"
5      xsi:schemaLocation="http://java.sun.com/xml/ns/javaee
6          http://java.sun.com/xml/ns/javaee/web-app_2_5.xsd"
7      version="2.5">
8      <servlet>
9          <servlet-name>Faces Servlet</servlet-name>
10         <servlet-class>javax.faces.webapp.FacesServlet</servlet-class>
11     </servlet>
12     <servlet-mapping>
13         <servlet-name>Faces Servlet</servlet-name>
14         <url-pattern>/faces/*</url-pattern>
15     </servlet-mapping>
16     <welcome-file-list>
17         <welcome-file>faces/index.xhtml</welcome-file>
18     </welcome-file-list>
19     <context-param>
20         <param-name>javax.faces.PROJECT_STAGE</param-name>
21         <param-value>Development</param-value>
22     </context-param>
23  </web-app>
```

SELF CHECK

3. What steps are required to add the image of a clock to the `time` application? (The clock doesn't have to show the correct time.)

4. Does a Swing program automatically separate presentation and business logic?

5. Why does the WAR file need to be deployed to the application server?

Special Topic 24.1

Session State and Cookies

You may recall from Chapter 21 that HTTP is a *stateless* protocol. A browser sends a request to a web server. The web server sends the reply and then disconnects. This is different from other protocols, such as POP, where the mail client logs into the mail server and stays connected until it has retrieved all e-mail messages. In contrast, a browser makes a new connection to the web server for each web page, and the web server has no way of knowing that those connections originate from the same browser. This makes it difficult to implement web applications. For example, in a shopping application, it is essential to track which requests came from a particular shopper.

Cookies were invented to overcome this restriction. A cookie consists of a small string that the web server sends to a browser, and that the browser sends back to the same server with all further requests. That way, the server can tie the stream of requests together. The JSF container matches up the cookies with the beans that have session scope. When a browser request contains a cookie, the value expressions in the JSF page refer to the matching beans.

You may have heard some privacy advocates complaining about cookies. Cookies are not inherently evil. When used to establish a session or to remember login information, they can make web applications more user-friendly. But when cookies are used to track your identity while you surf the Web, there can be privacy concerns. For example, Figure 6 shows some of the cookies that my browser held on a particular day. I have no recollection of visiting the advertising sites, so it is a bit disconcerting to see that my browser communicated with them.

Some people turn off cookies, and then web applications need to use another scheme to establish a session, typically by embedding a session identifier in the request URL or a hidden field of a form. The JSF session mechanism automatically switches to URLs with session identifiers if the client browser doesn't support cookies.

Figure 6
Viewing the Cookies
in a Browser

24.3 JavaBeans Components

Properties of a software component can be accessed without having to write Java code.

A JavaBean is a class that exposes properties through its get and set methods.

A *software component* is an entity that encapsulates functionality and can be plugged into a software system without programming. A managed bean is an example of a software component. When we added the timeBean object to the web application, we did not write Java code to construct the object or to call its methods.

Some programming languages have explicit support for components, but Java does not. Instead, in Java, you use a programming convention to implement components. A **JavaBean** is a Java class that follows this convention. A JavaBean exposes **properties**—values of the component that can be accessed without programming.

Just about any Java class can be a JavaBean—there are only two requirements.

- A JavaBean must have a constructor with no parameters.
- A JavaBean must have methods for accessing the component properties that follow the get/set naming convention. For example, to get or set a property named city, the methods must be called getCity and setCity.

In general, if the name of the property is *propertyName*, and its type is *Type*, then the associated methods must be of the form

```
public Type getPropertyName()
public void setPropertyName(Type newValue)
```

Note that the name of a property starts with a lowercase letter (such as city), but the corresponding methods have an uppercase letter (getCity). The only exception is that property names can be all capitals, such as ID or URL, with corresponding methods getID or setURL.

If a property has only a get method, then it is a *read-only* property. If it has only a set method, then it is a *write-only* property.

A JavaBean can have additional methods, but they are not connected with properties.

Here is a simple example of a bean class that formats the time for a given city, which we will further develop in the next section.

```
public class TimeZoneBean
{
   // Instance variables
   . . .
   // Required constructor with no parameters
   public TimeZoneBean() { . . . }

   // city property
   public String getCity() { . . . }
   public void setCity(String newValue) { . . . }

   // read-only time property
   public String getTime() { . . . }

   // Other methods
   . . .
}
```

This bean has two properties: city and time.

You should *not* make any assumptions about the internal representation of properties in the bean class. The getter and setter methods may simply read or write an instance variable. But they may also do other work. An example is the getTime method from the TimeBean in the preceding section; it formats the current time.

When a property name is used in a value expression that is included in the JSF page, then the get method is involved. For example, when the string

```
The current time is #{timeBean.time}
```

is rendered, the JSF container calls the getTime method of the session's TimeBean instance.

When a property name is used in an h:inputText tag (that, is the equivalent of an HTML input field or a JTextField), the situation is more complex. Consider this example:

```
<h:inputText value="#{timeZoneBean.city}"/>
```

When the JSF page is first displayed, the getCity method is called, and the current value of the city property is displayed. But after the user submits the page, the setCity method is called. It sets the city property to the value that the user typed into the input field.

> In the value expression of an output tag, only the property getter is called.

> In the value expression of an input tag, the property setter is called when the page is submitted.

SELF CHECK

6. Is the Random class a JavaBean?

7. What work does the setCity method of the TimeZoneBean do?

24.4 Navigation Between Pages

In most web applications, users will want to move between different pages. For example, a shopping application might have a login page, a page to show products for sale, and a checkout page that shows the shopping cart. In this section, you will learn how to enable users to navigate from one page to another.

Consider our sample timezone program. If the time computation uses the time zone *at the server location*, it will not be very useful when the user is in another time zone. Therefore, we will prompt for the city in which the user is located. When the user clicks the submit button, we move to the page next.xhtml and display the time in the user's time zone (see Figure 7). However, if no time zone is available for the city, we display the page error.xhtml.

> The outcome string of an action determines the next page that the JSF container sends to the browser.

A button yields an *outcome*, a string that determines the next page. Unless specified otherwise, the next page is the outcome string with the .xhtml extension added. For example, if the outcome string is error, the next page is error.xhtml. (It is possible to specify a different mapping from outcomes to pages, but there is no need to do so for a simple application.)

In many situations, the next page depends on the result of some computation. In our example, we need different outcomes depending on the city that the user entered. To achieve this flexibility, you specify a **method expression** as the action attribute:

```
<h:commandButton value="Submit" action="#{timeZoneBean.checkCity}"/>
```

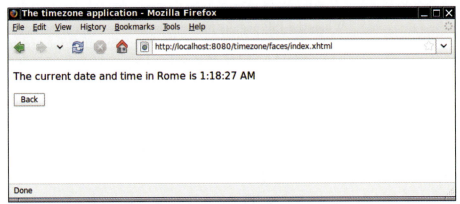

Figure 7 The `timezone` Application

A method expression specifies a bean and a method that should be invoked on the bean.

A method expression consists of the name of a bean and the name of a method. When the form is submitted, the JSF container calls `timeZoneBean.checkCity()`. The `checkCity` method returns the outcome string:

```
public class TimeZoneBean
{
    . . .
    public String checkCity()
    {
        zone = getTimeZone(city);
        if (zone == null) return "error";
        return "next";
    }
}
```

If the next page does not depend on a computation, then you set the `action` attribute of the button to a fixed outcome string, like this:

```
<h:commandButton value="Back" action="index"/>
```

If a button has no `action` attribute, or if the action outcome is `null`, then the current page is redisplayed.

We can now complete our time zone application. The Java library contains a convenient `TimeZone` class that knows about time zones across the world. A time zone is identified by a string such as "America/Los_Angeles" or "Asia/Tokyo". The static method getAvailableIDs returns a string array containing all IDs:

```
String[] ids = TimeZone.getAvailableIDs();
```

There are several hundred time zone IDs. (We are using time zones in this example because the TimeZone class gives us an interesting data source with lots of data. Later in this chapter, you will see how to access data from a database, but of course that's more complex.)

The static getTimeZone method returns a TimeZone object for a given ID string:

```
String id = "America/Los_Angeles";
TimeZone zone = TimeZone.getTimeZone(id);
```

Once you have a TimeZone object, you can use it in conjunction with a DateFormat object to get a time string in that time zone.

```
DateFormat timeFormatter = DateFormat.getTimeInstance();
timeFormatter.setTimeZone(zone);
Date now = new Date();
// Suppose the server is in New York, and it's noon there
System.out.println(timeFormatter.format(now));
// Prints 9:00:00 AM
```

Of course, we don't expect the user to know about time zone ID strings, such as "America/Los_Angeles". Instead, we assume that the user will simply enter the city name. The time zone bean will check whether that string, with spaces replaced by underscores, appears at the end of one of the valid time zone IDs.

Here is the code for the bean class.

ch24/timezone/WEB-INF/classes/bigjava/TimeZoneBean.java

```java
1   package bigjava;
2
3   import java.text.DateFormat;
4   import java.util.Date;
5   import java.util.TimeZone;
6   import javax.faces.bean.ManagedBean;
7   import javax.faces.bean.SessionScoped;
8
9   /**
10     This bean formats the local time of day for a given date
11     and city.
12   */
13   @ManagedBean
14   @SessionScoped
15   public class TimeZoneBean
16   {
17      private DateFormat timeFormatter;
18      private String city;
19      private TimeZone zone;
20
21      /**
22        Initializes the formatter.
23      */
24      public TimeZoneBean()
25      {
26         timeFormatter = DateFormat.getTimeInstance();
27      }
```

```
28
29      /**
30          Setter for city property.
31          @param aCity the city for which to report the local time
32      */
33      public void setCity(String aCity)
34      {
35          city = aCity;
36      }
37
38      /**
39          Getter for city property.
40          @return the city for which to report the local time
41      */
42      public String getCity()
43      {
44          return city;
45      }
46
47      /**
48          Read-only time property.
49          @return the formatted time
50      */
51      public String getTime()
52      {
53          if (zone == null) return "not available";
54          timeFormatter.setTimeZone(zone);
55          Date time = new Date();
56          String timeString = timeFormatter.format(time);
57          return timeString;
58      }
59
60      /**
61          Action for checking a city.
62          @return "next" if time zone information is available for the city,
63          "error" otherwise
64      */
65      public String checkCity()
66      {
67          zone = getTimeZone(city);
68          if (zone == null) return "error";
69          return "next";
70      }
71
72      /**
73          Looks up the time zone for a city.
74          @param aCity the city for which to find the time zone
75          @return the time zone or null if no match is found
76      */
77      private static TimeZone getTimeZone(String aCity)
78      {
79          String[] ids = TimeZone.getAvailableIDs();
80          for (int i = 0; i < ids.length; i++)
81              if (timeZoneIDmatch(ids[i], aCity))
82                  return TimeZone.getTimeZone(ids[i]);
83          return null;
84      }
85
```

```
86   /**
87       Checks whether a time zone ID matches a city.
88       @param id  the time zone ID (e.g., "America/Los_Angeles")
89       @param aCity  the city to match (e.g., "Los Angeles")
90       @return  true if the ID and city match
91   */
92   private static boolean timeZoneIDmatch(String id, String aCity)
93   {
94       String idCity = id.substring(id.indexOf('/') + 1);
95       return idCity.replace('_', ' ').equals(aCity);
96   }
97 }
```

Here is the JSF page for setting the city. The h:inputText tag produces an input field and the h:commandButton tag produces a button. (We discuss its action attribute in the next section.) When the user clicks the button, the browser sends the form values (that is, the contents of the input field) back to the web application. The web application calls the setCity method on the bean because the input field has a #{timeZone-Bean.city} value expression.

ch24/timezone/index.xhtml

```
1   <?xml version="1.0" encoding="UTF-8"?>
2   <html xmlns="http://www.w3.org/1999/xhtml"
3       xmlns:h="http://java.sun.com/jsf/html">
4       <h:head>
5           <title>The timezone application</title>
6       </h:head>
7       <h:body>
8           <h:form>
9               <p>
10                  Set time zone:
11                  <h:inputText value="#{timeZoneBean.city}"/>
12              </p>
13              <p>
14                  <h:commandButton value="Submit"
15                      action="#{timeZoneBean.checkCity}"/>
16              </p>
17          </h:form>
18      </h:body>
19  </html>
```

The next JSF page shows the result, using two value expressions that display the city and time properties. These expressions invoke the getCity and getTime methods of the bean class.

ch24/timezone/next.xhtml

```
1   <?xml version="1.0" encoding="UTF-8"?>
2   <html xmlns="http://www.w3.org/1999/xhtml"
3       xmlns:h="http://java.sun.com/jsf/html">
4       <h:head>
5           <title>The timezone application</title>
6       </h:head>
```

```
 7    <h:body>
 8      <h:form>
 9        <p>
10          The current time in #{timeZoneBean.city} is #{timeZoneBean.time}
11        </p>
12        <p>
13          <h:commandButton value="Back" action="index"/>
14        </p>
15      </h:form>
16    </h:body>
17  </html>
```

Figure 8 shows the directory structure of the timezone application.

Figure 8 The Directory Structure of the timezone Application

SELF CHECK

8. What tag would you need to add to error.xhtml so that the user can click on a button labeled "Help" and see help.xhtml?

9. Which page would be displayed if the checkCity method returned null?

How To 24.1

Designing a Managed Bean

A managed bean is just a regular Java class, with three special characteristics.

• The bean must have a constructor with no parameters

• Methods of the form

  Type get*PropertyName*()
  void set*PropertyName*(*Type* x)

  define properties that can be accessed from JSF pages.

• Methods of the form

  String *methodName*()

  can be used to specify command actions.

Here are step-by-step instructions for designing a managed bean class.

Step 1   Decide on the responsibility of the bean.

When designing a JSF application, it is tempting to stuff all code into a single bean class. Some development environments even encourage this approach. However, from a software engineering perspective, it is best to come up with different beans for different responsibilities. For example, a shopping application might have a UserBean to describe the current user, a SiteBean to describe how the user visits the shopping site, and a ShoppingCart-Bean that holds the items that the user is purchasing.

Step 2   Discover the properties that the bean should expose.

A property is an entity that you want to access or modify from your JSF pages. For example, a UserBean might have properties firstName, lastName, and password.

Sometimes, you have to resort to a bit of trickery. For example, consider adding an item to the shopping cart. You could use a property items, but it would be cumbersome to access all items in a JSF page and then set items to a new collection that contains one additional element. Instead, you can design a property addedItem. When that property is set, the setAddedItem method of your bean adds its value to the collection of items.

Step 3   Settle on the type and access permissions for each property.

Properties that are only used to generate output can be read-only. Properties that are used in h:inputText and other input tags must have read-write access.

Step 4   Define action methods for navigation.

Your action methods can carry out arbitrary tasks in order to react to the user inputs. The only limitation is that they don't have access to the form data. Everything that the user entered on the form must have already been set as a bean property.

The return value is the name of the next page to be displayed, or null if you want to redisplay the current page.

Step 5   Implement the constructor with no parameters.

It initializes any instance variables that are reused whenever the bean's computation is executed. Examples are formatters, random number generators, and so on.

Step 6   Implement the get and set methods for all properties.

Most get and set methods simply get or set an instance variable. However, you can carry out arbitrary computations in these methods if it is convenient. For example, a get method may retrieve information from a database instead of an instance variable.

Step 7   Supply any needed helper methods.

Your bean can have methods that are not property getters and setters. For example, the Time-ZoneBean has helper methods to look up the time zone for a city.

24.5 JSF Components

There are JSF components for text input, choices, buttons, and images.

In this section, you will see the most useful user interface components that you can place on a JSF form. Table 1 shows a summary. For a comprehensive discussion of all JSF components, see *Core JavaServer Faces*, 3rd ed., by David Geary and Cay Horstmann (Sun Microsystems Press/Prentice Hall, 2010).

The value attribute of an input component denotes the value that the user supplies.

Each component has a value attribute that allows you to connect the component value with a bean property, for example

```
<h:inputSecret value="#{user.password}"/>
```

The h:inputTextArea component has attributes to specify the rows and columns, such as

```
<h:inputTextArea value="#{user.comment}" rows="10" cols="40"/>
```

			Table 1 Common JSF Components		

Component	JSF Tag	Common Attributes	Example
Text Field	`h:inputText`	value	12345678901234567890
Password Field	`h:inputSecret`	value	**********
Text Area	`h:inputTextArea`	value rows cols	line one line two line three
Radio Button Group	`h:selectOneRadio`	value layout	○ Cheese ⦿ Pickle ○ Mustard ○ Lettuce ○ Onions
Checkbox	`h:selectOneCheckbox`	value	Receive email: ☑
Checkbox Group	`h:selectManyCheckbox`	value layout	☑ Cheese ☐ Pickle ☑ Mustard ☐ Lettuce ☐ Onions
Menu	`h:selectOneMenu` `h:selectManyMenu`	value	Cheese Pickle Mustard Lettuce
Image	`h:graphicImage`	value	
Submit Button	`h:commandButton`	value action	press me

The radio button and checkbox groups allow you to specify horizontal or vertical layout:

```
<h:selectOneRadio value="#{burger.topping}" layout="lineDirection">
```

In European languages, `lineDirection` means horizontal and `pageDirection` means vertical. However, in some languages, lines are written top-to-bottom, and the meanings are reversed.

Button groups and menus are more complex than the other user interface components. They require you to specify two properties:

- the collection of possible choices
- the actual choice

The `value` attribute of the component specifies the actual choice to be displayed. The collection of possible choices is defined by a nested `f:selectItems` tag, like this:

```
<h:selectOneRadio value="#{creditCardBean.expirationMonth}"
    layout="pageDirection">
  <f:selectItems value="#{creditCardBean.monthChoices}"/>
</h:selectOneRadio>
```

Use an `f:selectItems` tag to specify all choices for a component that allows selection from a list of choices.

When you use the f:selectItems tag, you need to add the namespace declaration

```
xmlns:f="http://java.sun.com/jsf/core"
```

to the html tag at the top of your JSF page.

The value of the f:selectItems tag must have a type that can describe a list of choices. There are several types that you can use, but the easiest—and the only one that we will discuss—is a Map. The keys of the map are the *labels*—the strings that are displayed next to each choice. The corresponding map values are the *label values*—the values that correspond to the selection. For example, a choice map for months would map January to 1, February to 2, and so on:

```java
public class CreditCardBean
{
    . . .
    public Map<String, Integer> getMonthChoices()
    {
        Map<String, Integer> choices = new LinkedHashMap<String, Integer>();
        choices.put("January", 1);
        choices.put("February", 2);
        . . .
        return choices;
    }
}
```

Here, we use a LinkedHashMap because we want to visit entries in the order in which they are inserted. This is more useful than a HashMap, which would visit the labels in random order or a TreeMap, which would visit them in alphabetical order (starting with April!).

The type of the value property of the component enclosing the f:selectItems tag must match the type of the map value. For example, creditCardBean.expirationMonth must be an integer, not a string. If multiple selections are allowed, the type of the value property must be a list or array of matching types. For example, if one could choose multiple months, a selectManyRadio component would have a value property with a type such as int[] or ArrayList<Integer>.

SELF CHECK

10. Which JSF components can be used to give a user a choice between "AM/PM" and "military" time?

11. How would you supply a set of choices for a credit card expiration year to a h:selectOneMenu component?

24.6 A Three-Tier Application

A three-tier application has separate tiers for presentation, business logic, and data storage.

In the final JSF example, you will see a web application with a very common structure. In this example, we will use a database for information storage. We will enhance the time zone example by storing additional cities that are not known to the TimeZone class in a database. Such an application is called a **three-tier application** because it consists of three separate layers or tiers (see Figure 9):

- The presentation tier: the web browser
- The "business logic" tier: the JSF container, the JSF pages, and the JavaBeans
- The storage tier: the database

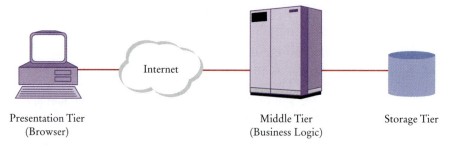

Figure 9 Three-Tier Architecture

Contrast the three-tier architecture with the more traditional *client-server* or *two-tier architecture* that you saw in the database programs of Chapter 22. In that architecture, one of the tiers is the database server, which is accessed by multiple client programs on desktops. Each client program has a presentation layer—usually with a specially programmed graphical user interface—and business logic code. (See Figure 10.) When the business logic changes, a new client program must be distributed over all desktops. In contrast, in a three-tier application, the business logic resides on a server. When the logic changes, the server code is updated, while the presentation tier—the browser—remains unchanged. That is much simpler to manage than updating multiple desktops.

In our example, we will have a single database table, CityZone, with city and time zone names (see Figure 11).

ch24/multizone/sql/CityZone.sql

```
1  CREATE TABLE CityZone (City VARCHAR(40), Zone VARCHAR(40))
2  INSERT INTO CityZone VALUES ('San Francisco', 'America/Los_Angeles')
3  INSERT INTO CityZone VALUES ('Hamburg', 'Europe/Rome')
4  SELECT * FROM CityZone
```

If the TimeZoneBean can't find the city among the standard time zone IDs, it makes a database query:

```
SELECT Zone FROM CityZone WHERE City = the requested city
```

If there is a matching entry in the database, that time zone is returned.

To query the database, the bean needs a Connection object. In Chapter 22, we used the static getConnection method of the DriverManager class to obtain a database connection. However, JSF containers have a better mechanism for configuring a database in one central location so that multiple web applications can access it.

Figure 10 Two-Tier Client-Server Architecture

Figure 11
The CityZone Table

CityZone

City	Zone
San Francisco	America/Los_Angeles
Hamburg	Europe/Rome
. . .	. . .

The GlassFish application server includes the Derby database. It has a predefined data source with the resource name jdbc/__default. In your bean code, you declare an instance variable of type DataSource and tag it with a @Resource annotation, like this:

```
@Resource(name="jdbc/__default")
private DataSource source;
```

You can use the administrative interface of GlassFish to define other data sources.

When the application server loads the web application, it automatically initializes this instance variable. Whenever you need a database connection, call

```
Connection conn = source.getConnection();
try
{
    Use the connection
}
finally
{
    conn.close();
}
```

You define data sources in the JSF container and use resource annotations to initialize them.

The application server provides an additional service: it *pools* database connections. When a pooled connection is closed, it is not physically terminated but instead returned to a queue and given out again to another caller of the getConnection method. Pooling avoids the overhead of creating new database connections. In a web application, it would be particularly inefficient to connect to the database with every web request. Connection pooling is completely automatic.

In order to make the application more interesting, we enhanced the TimeZoneBean so that it manages a list of cities. You can add cities to the list and remove a selected city (see Figure 12).

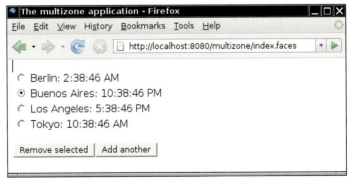

Figure 12 The multizone Application Shows a List of Cities

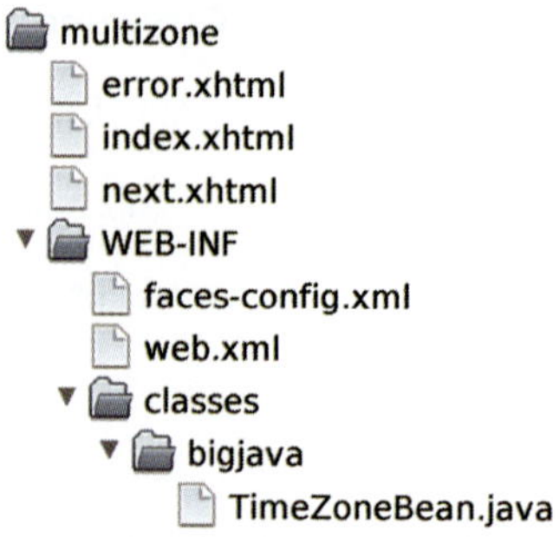

Figure 13
The Directory Structure of the `multizone` Application

```
multizone
    error.xhtml
    index.xhtml
    next.xhtml
    WEB-INF
        faces-config.xml
        web.xml
        classes
            bigjava
                TimeZoneBean.java
```

You will find the code for this web application at the end of this section. Figure 13 shows the directory structure of the application.

You have now seen how to use the JavaServer Faces technology to build web applications. JSF takes care of low-level details so that you don't have to think about HTML forms and the HTTP protocol. Instead, you can focus on the presentation and business logic of your application.

ch24/multizone/index.xhtml

```
1   <?xml version="1.0" encoding="UTF-8"?>
2   <html xmlns="http://www.w3.org/1999/xhtml"
3      xmlns:h="http://java.sun.com/jsf/html">
4      <h:head>
5         <title>The multizone application</title>
6      </h:head>
7      <h:body>
8         <h:form>
9            <p>
10              Enter city:
11              <h:inputText value="#{timeZoneBean.cityToAdd}"/>
12           </p>
13           <p>
14              <h:commandButton value="Submit"
15                    action="#{timeZoneBean.addCity}"/>
16           </p>
17        </h:form>
18     </h:body>
19  </html>
```

ch24/multizone/next.xhtml

```
1   <?xml version="1.0" encoding="UTF-8"?>
2   <html xmlns="http://www.w3.org/1999/xhtml"
3      xmlns:f="http://java.sun.com/jsf/core"
4      xmlns:h="http://java.sun.com/jsf/html">
5      <h:head>
6         <title>The multizone application</title>
7      </h:head>
8      <h:body>
9         <h:form>
10           <p>
11              <h:selectOneRadio value="#{timeZoneBean.cityToRemove}"
12                 layout="pageDirection">
13                 <f:selectItems value="#{timeZoneBean.citiesAndTimes}"/>
14              </h:selectOneRadio>
15           </p>
```

```
16          <p>
17              <h:commandButton value="Remove selected"
18                  action="#{timeZoneBean.removeCity}"/>
19              <h:commandButton value="Add another" action="index"/>
20          </p>
21      </h:form>
22    </h:body>
23  </html>
```

ch24/multizone/error.xhtml

```
1   <?xml version="1.0" encoding="UTF-8"?>
2   <html xmlns="http://www.w3.org/1999/xhtml"
3       xmlns:h="http://java.sun.com/jsf/html">
4       <h:head>
5           <title>The multizone application</title>
6       </h:head>
7       <h:body>
8           <h:form>
9               <p>
10                  Sorry, no information is available for #{timeZoneBean.cityToAdd}.
11              </p>
12              <p>
13                  <h:commandButton value="Back" action="index"/>
14              </p>
15          </h:form>
16      </h:body>
17  </html>
```

ch24/multizone/WEB-INF/classes/bigjava/TimeZoneBean.java

```
1   package bigjava;
2
3   import java.sql.Connection;
4   import java.sql.PreparedStatement;
5   import java.sql.ResultSet;
6   import java.sql.SQLException;
7   import java.text.DateFormat;
8   import java.util.ArrayList;
9   import java.util.Date;
10  import java.util.Map;
11  import java.util.TimeZone;
12  import java.util.TreeMap;
13  import java.util.logging.Logger;
14  import javax.annotation.Resource;
15  import javax.faces.bean.ManagedBean;
16  import javax.faces.bean.SessionScoped;
17  import javax.sql.DataSource;
18
19  /**
20      This bean formats the local time of day for a given date
21      and city.
22  */
23  @ManagedBean
24  @SessionScoped
25  public class TimeZoneBean
26  {
27      @Resource(name="jdbc/__default")
28      private DataSource source;
```

```
29
30      private DateFormat timeFormatter;
31      private ArrayList<String> cities;
32      private String cityToAdd;
33      private String cityToRemove;
34
35      /**
36          Initializes the formatter.
37      */
38      public TimeZoneBean()
39      {
40          timeFormatter = DateFormat.getTimeInstance();
41          cities = new ArrayList<String>();
42      }
43
44      /**
45          Setter for cityToAdd property.
46          @param city the city to add to the list of cities
47      */
48      public void setCityToAdd(String city)
49      {
50          cityToAdd = city;
51      }
52
53      /**
54          Getter for cityToAdd property.
55          @return the city to add to the list of cities
56      */
57      public String getCityToAdd()
58      {
59          return cityToAdd;
60      }
61
62      /**
63          Setter for the cityToRemove property.
64          @param city the city to remove from the list of cities
65      */
66      public void setCityToRemove(String city)
67      {
68          cityToRemove = city;
69      }
70
71      /**
72          Getter for the cityToRemove property.
73          @return the city to remove from the list of cities
74      */
75      public String getCityToRemove()
76      {
77          return cityToRemove;
78      }
79
80      /**
81          Read-only citiesAndTimes property.
82          @return a map containing the cities and formatted times
83      */
84      public Map<String, String> getCitiesAndTimes()
85      {
86          Date time = new Date();
87          Map<String, String> result = new TreeMap<String, String>();
```

```
88          for (int i = 0; i < cities.size(); i++)
89          {
90             String city = cities.get(i);
91             String label = city + ": ";
92             TimeZone zone = getTimeZone(city);
93             if (zone != null)
94             {
95                timeFormatter.setTimeZone(zone);
96                String timeString = timeFormatter.format(time);
97                label = label + timeString;
98             }
99             else
100               label = label + "unavailable";
101            result.put(label, city);
102         }
103
104         return result;
105      }
106
107      /**
108         Action for adding a city.
109         @return "next" if time zone information is available for the city,
110         "error" otherwise
111      */
112      public String addCity()
113      {
114         TimeZone zone = getTimeZone(cityToAdd);
115         if (zone == null) return "error";
116         cities.add(cityToAdd);
117         cityToRemove = cityToAdd;
118         cityToAdd = "";
119         return "next";
120      }
121
122      /**
123         Action for removing a city.
124         @return null if there are more cities to remove, "index" otherwise
125      */
126      public String removeCity()
127      {
128         cities.remove(cityToRemove);
129         if (cities.size() > 0) return null;
130         else return "index";
131      }
132
133      /**
134         Looks up the time zone for a city.
135         @param city the city for which to find the time zone
136         @return the time zone or null if no match is found
137      */
138      private TimeZone getTimeZone(String city)
139      {
140         String[] ids = TimeZone.getAvailableIDs();
141         for (int i = 0; i < ids.length; i++)
142            if (timeZoneIDmatch(ids[i], city))
143               return TimeZone.getTimeZone(ids[i]);
144         try
145         {
146            String id = getZoneNameFromDB(city);
```

```
147            if (id != null)
148                return TimeZone.getTimeZone(id);
149        }
150        catch (Exception ex)
151        {
152            Logger.global.info("Caught in TimeZone.getTimeZone: "
153                    + ex);
154        }
155        return null;
156    }
157
158    private String getZoneNameFromDB(String city)
159            throws SQLException
160    {
161        if (source == null)
162        {
163            Logger.global.info("No database connection");
164            return null;
165        }
166        Connection conn = source.getConnection();
167        try
168        {
169            PreparedStatement stat = conn.prepareStatement(
170                    "SELECT Zone FROM CityZone WHERE City=?");
171            stat.setString(1, city);
172            ResultSet result = stat.executeQuery();
173            if (result.next())
174                return result.getString(1);
175            else
176                return null;
177        }
178        finally
179        {
180            conn.close();
181        }
182    }
183
184    /**
185        Checks whether a time zone ID matches a city.
186        @param id the time zone ID (e.g., "America/Los_Angeles")
187        @param city the city to match (e.g., "Los Angeles")
188        @return true if the ID and city match
189    */
190    private static boolean timeZoneIDmatch(String id, String city)
191    {
192        String idCity = id.substring(id.indexOf('/') + 1);
193        return idCity.replace('_', ' ').equals(city);
194    }
195 }
```

SELF CHECK

12. Why don't we just keep a database connection as an instance variable in the TimeZoneBean?

13. Why does the removeCity method of the TimeZoneBean return null or "index", depending on the size of the cities instance variable?

Special Topic 24.2

AJAX

In Section 24.1, you learned that a web application receives an HTTP request from the browser and then sends back an HTML form. The cycle repeats when the user submits the next form data. Web application designers and users dislike the "page flip"—the visual discontinuity between pages that is often accompanied by a significant delay, as the browser waits for the new form tags.

The AJAX (Asynchronous JavaScript and XML) technology, invented in 2005, aims to solve this problem. In an AJAX application, the browser does not merely display an HTML page, but it also executes code written in the JavaScript language. The JavaScript code continuously communicates with the server program and updates parts of the HTML page.

One example of an AJAX application is the Google Maps™ mapping service—see Figure 14. In a traditional map application, the user might click on a "move North" button and then wait until the browser receives the new map image and displays it in a new page. The Google Maps application uses AJAX to fetch only the needed tiles, and it fluidly rearranges the tiles in the current page, without the dreaded page flip.

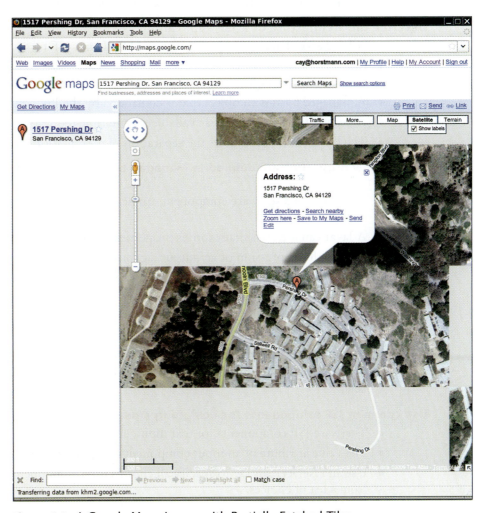

Figure 14 A Google Maps Image with Partially-Fetched Tiles

AJAX applications are much more difficult to program than regular web applications. Frameworks are being proposed to handle these additional challenges. JSF 2 supports AJAX, giving the web application programmer the benefit of producing a pleasant user experience without having to worry about the intricate details of the JavaScript communication channel. The book's companion code contains a modification of the multizone application that uses AJAX. When you click one of the buttons, the page is updated without a page flip.

Summary of Learning Objectives

Describe the architecture of a web application.

- The user interface of a web application is displayed in a web browser.
- When a form is submitted, the names and values of the form elements are sent to the web server.
- Upon receiving the form data, the web server sends a new web page to the browser.

Describe the architecture of a JSF application.

- A JavaServer Faces (JSF) page contains HTML and JSF tags.
- The JSF container converts a JSF page to an HTML page, replacing all JSF tags with text and HTML tags.
- A managed bean is an object that is controlled by the JSF container.
- A bean with session scope is available for multiple requests by the same browser.
- The JSF technology enables the separation of presentation and business logic.

Explain how properties are defined in managed beans and accessed in value expressions.

- Properties of a software component can be accessed without having to write Java code.
- A JavaBean is a class that exposes properties through its get and set methods.
- In the value expression of an output tag, only the property getter is called.
- In the value expression of an input tag, the property setter is called when the page is submitted.

Implement navigation between pages.

- The outcome string of an action determines the next page that the JSF container sends to the browser.
- A method expression specifies a bean and a method that should be invoked on the bean.

Use common JSF components for designing a user interface.

- There are JSF components for text input, choices, buttons, and images.
- The value attribute of an input component denotes the value that the user supplies.
- Use an f:selectItems tag to specify all choices for a component that allows selection from a list of choices.

Develop applications that use JSF and a database.

- A three-tier application has separate tiers for presentation, business logic, and data storage.
- You define data sources in the JSF container and use resource annotations to initialize them.

Classes, Objects, and Methods Introduced in this Chapter

```
java.text.DateFormat                java.util.TimeZone
   format                              getAvailableIDs
   getTimeInstance                     getTimeZone
   setTimeZone                      javax.sql.DataSource
java.util.LinkedHashMap                 getConnection
```

Media Resources

*www.wiley.com/
college/
horstmann*

- Lab Exercises
- ➕ Practice Quiz

Review Exercises

★ **R24.1** What is the difference between a JSF page and a JSF container?

★ **R24.2** What is a bean?

★ **R24.3** What is a bean property?

★ **R24.4** Is a JButton a bean? Why or why not?

★ **R24.5** What is the software engineering purpose of using beans in conjunction with JSF pages?

★★ **R24.6** How are variables in the JSF expression language different from variables in Java programs?

★★ **R24.7** What are the choices for the scope of a bean? What is the default? When should you choose which scope?

★★ **R24.8** How can you implement error checking in a JSF application? Explain, using a login page as an example.

★★ **R24.9** What input elements can you place on a JSF form? What are their Swing equivalents?

★ **R24.10** What is the difference between a client-server application and a three-tier application?

Programming Exercises

★ **P24.1** Write a JSF application that reports the values of the following system properties of the web server:
  - The Java version (java.version)
  - The operating system name (os.name)
  - The operating system version (os.version)

  Supply a bean that uses the getProperties method of the System class.

★ **P24.2** Write a JSF application that simulates two rolls of a die, producing an output such as "Rolled a 4 and a 6". When the user reloads the page, a new pair of values should be displayed. Supply a bean that encapsulates a Random object.

★★ **P24.3** Enhance Exercise P24.2 by producing a web page that shows images of the rolled dice. Find GIF images of dice with numbers 1 through 6 on the front, and generate an HTML page that references the appropriate images. *Hint:* Use the tag <h:graphic-Image value=*imageURL*/> and take advantage of the fact that you can embed a value expression into regular text, such as "/image#{*expression*}.gif".

★ **P24.4** Write a web application that allows a user to specify six lottery numbers. Generate your own combination on the server, and then print out both combinations together with a count of matches.

★★ **P24.5** Add error checking to Exercise P24.4. If the lottery numbers are not within the correct range, or if there are duplicates, show an appropriate message and allow the user to fix the error.

★★★ **P24.6** Personalize the time zone application of Section 24.3. Prompt the user to log in and specify a city to be stored in a profile. The next time the user logs in, the time of their favorite city is displayed automatically. Store users, passwords, and favorite cities in a database. You need a logout button to switch users.

★★★ **P24.7** Extend Exercise P24.6 so that a user can choose multiple cities and all cities chosen by the user are remembered on the next login.

★★★ **P24.8** Write a web version of the ExecSQL utility of Chapter 22. Allow users to type arbitrary SQL queries into a text area. Then submit the query to the database and display the result.

★★★ **P24.9** Produce a web front end for the ATM program in Chapter 12.

★★★ **P24.10** Produce a web front end for the appointment calendar application of Exercise P12.7.

★★★ **P24.11** Produce a web front end for the airline reservation program of Exercise P12.8.

Programming Projects

Project 24.1 Write a shopping cart application. A database contains items that can be purchased and their prices, descriptions, and available quantities. If the user wants to check out, ask for the user account. If the user does not yet have an account, create one. The user name and address should be stored with the account in the database.

Display an invoice as the last process in the checkout step. When the user has confirmed the purchase, update the quantities in the warehouse.

Project 24.2 Write a web-based grade book application that your instructor might use to manage student grades in this course. Your application should have one account for the instructor, and one account for each student. Instructors can enter and view grades for all students. Students can only see their own grades and their ranking within the course. Implement the features that your instructor uses for determining the course grade (such as dropping the lowest quiz score, counting homework as 30% of the total grade, and so on.) All information should be stored in a database.

Answers to Self-Check Questions

1. Each protocol has a specific purpose. HTML describes the appearance of a page; it would be useless for sending requests from a browser to a server. HTTP describes a request; it cannot describe the appearance of a page.

2. The data of the POST request contain a portion username=*the name supplied by the user*&password=*the password supplied by the user.*

3. Place an image file, say clock.gif, into the time directory, and add a tag `<img src="clock.gif"/>` to the index.xhtml file.

4. No—it is possible (and sadly common) for programmers to place the business logic into the frame and component classes of the user interface.

5. The application server knows nothing about the files on your computer. You need to hand it the WAR file with all the application's pages, code, and configuration files so that it can execute the application when it receives a web request.

6. Technically, yes. It has a constructor with no parameters. However, it has no methods with names that start with get or set, so it exposes no properties.

7. There is no way of knowing without looking at the source code. Perhaps it simply executes a statement city = newValue, setting an instance variable of the bean class. But the method may also do other work, for example checking whether the city name is valid or storing the name in a database.

8. Add the tag `<h:commandButton value="Help" action="help"/>` to error.xhtml.

9. The current page would be redisplayed.

10. h:selectOneRadio, h:selectOneMenu, or h:selectOneCheckbox

11. You would need a bean with a property such as the following:
```
public Map<String, Integer> getYearChoices()
{
    Map<String, Integer> choices = new TreeMap<String, Integer>();
    choices.put("2003", 2003);
    choices.put("2004", 2004);
    . . .
    return choices;
}
```
Then supply a tag `<f:selectItems value="#{creditCard.yearChoices}"/>`.

12. Then the database connection would be kept open for the entire session.

13. As long as there are cities, the next.xhtml page is redisplayed. If all cities are removed, it is pointless to display the next.xhtml page, so the application navigates to the index.xhtml page.

The Basic Latin and Latin-1 Subsets of Unicode

This appendix lists the Unicode characters that are most commonly used for processing Western European languages. A complete listing of Unicode characters can be found at http://unicode.org.

Table 1 Selected Control Characters			
Character	Code	Decimal	Escape Sequence
Tab	'\u0009'	9	'\t'
Newline	'\u000A'	10	'\n'
Return	'\u000D'	13	'\r'
Space	'\u0020'	32	

Table 2 The Basic Latin (ASCII) Subset of Unicode

Char.	Code	Dec.	Char.	Code	Dec.	Char.	Code	Dec.
			@	'\u0040'	64	`	'\u0060'	96
!	'\u0021'	33	A	'\u0041'	65	a	'\u0061'	97
"	'\u0022'	34	B	'\u0042'	66	b	'\u0062'	98
#	'\u0023'	35	C	'\u0043'	67	c	'\u0063'	99
$	'\u0024'	36	D	'\u0044'	68	d	'\u0064'	100
%	'\u0025'	37	E	'\u0045'	69	e	'\u0065'	101
&	'\u0026'	38	F	'\u0046'	70	f	'\u0066'	102
'	'\u0027'	39	G	'\u0047'	71	g	'\u0067'	103
(	'\u0028'	40	H	'\u0048'	72	h	'\u0068'	104
)	'\u0029'	41	I	'\u0049'	73	i	'\u0069'	105
*	'\u002A'	42	J	'\u004A'	74	j	'\u006A'	106
+	'\u002B'	43	K	'\u004B'	75	k	'\u006B'	107
,	'\u002C'	44	L	'\u004C'	76	l	'\u006C'	108
-	'\u002D'	45	M	'\u004D'	77	m	'\u006D'	109
.	'\u002E'	46	N	'\u004E'	78	n	'\u006E'	110
/	'\u002F'	47	O	'\u004F'	79	o	'\u006F'	111
0	'\u0030'	48	P	'\u0050'	80	p	'\u0070'	112
1	'\u0031'	49	Q	'\u0051'	81	q	'\u0071'	113
2	'\u0032'	50	R	'\u0052'	82	r	'\u0072'	114
3	'\u0033'	51	S	'\u0053'	83	s	'\u0073'	115
4	'\u0034'	52	T	'\u0054'	84	t	'\u0074'	116
5	'\u0035'	53	U	'\u0055'	85	u	'\u0075'	117
6	'\u0036'	54	V	'\u0056'	86	v	'\u0076'	118
7	'\u0037'	55	W	'\u0057'	87	w	'\u0077'	119
8	'\u0038'	56	X	'\u0058'	88	x	'\u0078'	120
9	'\u0039'	57	Y	'\u0059'	89	y	'\u0079'	121
:	'\u003A'	58	Z	'\u005A'	90	z	'\u007A'	122
;	'\u003B'	59	[	'\u005B'	91	{	'\u007B'	123
<	'\u003C'	60	\	'\u005C'	92	|	'\u007C'	124
=	'\u003D'	61	]	'\u005D'	93	}	'\u007D'	125
>	'\u003E'	62	^	'\u005E'	94	~	'\u007E'	126
?	'\u003F'	63	_	'\u005F'	95			

Table 3   The Latin-1 Subset of Unicode

Char.	Code	Dec.	Char.	Code	Dec.	Char.	Code	Dec.
			À	'\u00C0'	192	à	'\u00E0'	224
¡	'\u00A1'	161	Á	'\u00C1'	193	á	'\u00E1'	225
¢	'\u00A2'	162	Â	'\u00C2'	194	â	'\u00E2'	226
£	'\u00A3'	163	Ã	'\u00C3'	195	ã	'\u00E3'	227
¤	'\u00A4'	164	Ä	'\u00C4'	196	ä	'\u00E4'	228
¥	'\u00A5'	165	Å	'\u00C5'	197	å	'\u00E5'	229
¦	'\u00A6'	166	Æ	'\u00C6'	198	æ	'\u00E6'	230
§	'\u00A7'	167	Ç	'\u00C7'	199	ç	'\u00E7'	231
¨	'\u00A8'	168	È	'\u00C8'	200	è	'\u00E8'	232
©	'\u00A9'	169	É	'\u00C9'	201	é	'\u00E9'	233
ª	'\u00AA'	170	Ê	'\u00CA'	202	ê	'\u00EA'	234
«	'\u00AB'	171	Ë	'\u00CB'	203	ë	'\u00EB'	235
¬	'\u00AC'	172	Ì	'\u00CC'	204	ì	'\u00EC'	236
-	'\u00AD'	173	Í	'\u00CD'	205	í	'\u00ED'	237
®	'\u00AE'	174	Î	'\u00CE'	206	î	'\u00EE'	238
¯	'\u00AF'	175	Ï	'\u00CF'	207	ï	'\u00EF'	239
°	'\u00B0'	176	Ð	'\u00D0'	208	ð	'\u00F0'	240
±	'\u00B1'	177	Ñ	'\u00D1'	209	ñ	'\u00F1'	241
²	'\u00B2'	178	Ò	'\u00D2'	210	ò	'\u00F2'	242
³	'\u00B3'	179	Ó	'\u00D3'	211	ó	'\u00F3'	243
´	'\u00B4'	180	Ô	'\u00D4'	212	ô	'\u00F4'	244
µ	'\u00B5'	181	Õ	'\u00D5'	213	õ	'\u00F5'	245
¶	'\u00B6'	182	Ö	'\u00D6'	214	ö	'\u00F6'	246
·	'\u00B7'	183	×	'\u00D7'	215	÷	'\u00F7'	247
¸	'\u00B8'	184	Ø	'\u00D8'	216	ø	'\u00F8'	248
¹	'\u00B9'	185	Ù	'\u00D9'	217	ù	'\u00F9'	249
º	'\u00BA'	186	Ú	'\u00DA'	218	ú	'\u00FA'	250
»	'\u00BB'	187	Û	'\u00DB'	219	û	'\u00FB'	251
¼	'\u00BC'	188	Ü	'\u00DC'	220	ü	'\u00FC'	252
½	'\u00BD'	189	Ý	'\u00DD'	221	ý	'\u00FD'	253
¾	'\u00BE'	190	Þ	'\u00DE'	222	þ	'\u00FE'	254
¿	'\u00BF'	191	ß	'\u00DF'	223	ÿ	'\u00FF'	255

Java Operator Summary

The Java operators are listed in groups of decreasing precedence in the table below. The horizontal lines in the table indicate a change in operator precedence. For example, z = x - y; means z = (x - y); because = has lower precedence than -.

The prefix unary operators, conditional operator, and the assignment operators associate right-to-left. All other operators associate left-to-right.

Operator	Description	Associativity
.	Access class feature	
[]	Array subscript	Left to right
()	Function call	
++	Increment	
--	Decrement	
!	Boolean *not*	
~	Bitwise *not*	
+ *(unary)*	(Has no effect)	Right to left
- *(unary)*	Negative	
(*TypeName*)	Cast	
new	Object allocation	
*	Multiplication	
/	Division or integer division	Left to right
%	Integer remainder	
+	Addition, string concatenation	Left to right
-	Subtraction	

Operator	Description	Associativity
<<	Shift left	
>>	Right shift with sign extension	Left to right
>>>	Right shift with zero extension	
<	Less than	
<=	Less than or equal	
>	Greater than	Left to right
>=	Greater than or equal	
instanceof	Tests whether an object's type is a given type or a subtype thereof	
==	Equal	Left to right
!=	Not equal	
&	Bitwise *and*	Left to right
^	Bitwise exclusive *or*	Left to right
|	Bitwise *or*	Left to right
&&	Boolean "short circuit" *and*	Left to right
||	Boolean "short circuit" *or*	Left to right
? :	Conditional	Right to left
=	Assignment	Right to left
op=	Assignment with binary operator (*op* is one of +, -, *, /, &, |, ^, <<, >>, >>>)	

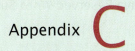

Appendix C

Java Reserved Word Summary

Reserved Word	Description
abstract	An abstract class or method
assert	An assertion that a condition is fulfilled
boolean	The Boolean type
break	Breaks out of the current loop or labeled statement
byte	The 8-bit signed integer type
case	A label in a switch statement
catch	The handler for an exception in a try block
char	The 16-bit Unicode character type
class	Defines a class
const	Not used
continue	Skip the remainder of a loop body
default	The default label in a switch statement
do	A loop whose body is executed at least once
double	The 64-bit double-precision floating-point type
else	The alternative clause in an if statement
enum	An enumeration type
extends	Indicates that a class is a subclass of another class
final	A value that cannot be changed after it has been initialized, a method that cannot be overridden, or a class that cannot be extended
finally	A clause of a try block that is always executed
float	The 32-bit single-precision floating-point type
for	A loop with initialization, condition, and update expressions
goto	Not used

Reserved Word	Description
if	A conditional branch statement
implements	Indicates that a class realizes an interface
import	Allows the use of class names without the package name
instanceof	Tests whether an object's type is a given type or a subtype thereof
int	The 32-bit integer type
interface	An abstract type with only abstract methods and constants
long	The 64-bit integer type
native	A method implemented in non-Java code
new	Allocates an object
package	A collection of related classes
private	A feature that is accessible only by methods of the same class
protected	A feature that is accessible only by methods of the same class, a subclass, or another class in the same package
public	A feature that is accessible by all methods
return	Returns from a method
short	The 16-bit integer type
static	A feature that is defined for a class, not for individual instances
strictfp	Use strict rules for floating-point computations
super	Invoke the superclass constructor or a superclass method
switch	A selection statement
synchronized	A block of code that is accessible to only one thread at a time
this	The implicit parameter of a method; or invocation of another constructor of the same class
throw	Throws an exception
throws	The exceptions that a method may throw
transient	Instance variables that should not be serialized
try	A block of code with exception handlers or a finally handler
void	Tags a method that doesn't return a value
volatile	A variable that may be accessed by multiple threads without synchronization
while	A loop statement

The Java Library

This appendix lists all classes and methods from the standard Java library that are used in this book.

In the following inheritance hierarchy, superclasses that are not used in this book are shown in gray type. Some classes implement interfaces not covered in this book; they are omitted. Classes are sorted first by package, then alphabetically within a package.

```
java.awt.Shape
java.io.Serializable
java.lang.Cloneable
java.lang.Object
    java.awt.BorderLayout implements Serializable
    java.awt.Color implements Serializable
    java.awt.Component implements Serializable
        java.awt.Container
            javax.swing.JComponent
                javax.swing.AbstractButton
                    javax.swing.JButton
                    javax.swing.JMenuItem
                        javax.swing.JMenu
                    javax.swing.JToggleButton
                        javax.swing.JCheckBox
                        javax.swing.JRadioButton
                javax.swing.JComboBox
                javax.swing.JFileChooser
                javax.swing.JLabel
                javax.swing.JMenuBar
                javax.swing.JPanel
                javax.swing.JOptionPane
                javax.swing.JScrollPane
                javax.swing.JSlider
                javax.swing.text.JTextComponent
                    javax.swing.JTextArea
                    javax.swing.JTextField
            java.awt.Panel
                java.applet.Applet
                    javax.swing.JApplet
        java.awt.Window
            java.awt.Frame
                javax.swing.JFrame
    java.awt.Dimension2D
        java.awt.Dimension implements Cloneable, Serializable
    java.awt.FlowLayout implements Serializable
    java.awt.Font implements Serializable
```

```
java.awt.Graphics
   java.awt.Graphics2D;
java.awt.GridLayout implements Serializable
java.awt.event.MouseAdapter implements MouseListener
java.awt.geom.Line2D implements Cloneable, Shape
   java.awt.geom.Line2D.Double implements Serializable
java.awt.geom.Point2D implements Cloneable
   java.awt.geom.Point2D.Double implements Serializable
java.awt.geom.RectangularShape implements Cloneable, Shape
   java.awt.geom.Rectangle2D
      java.awt.Rectangle implements Serializable
   java.awt.geom.Ellipse2D
      java.awt.geom.Ellipse2D.Double implements Serializable
java.io.File implements Comparable<File>, Serializable
java.io.InputStream
   java.io.FileInputStream
   java.io.ObjectInputStream
java.io.OutputStream
   java.io.FileOutputStream
   java.io.FilterOutputStream
      java.io.PrintStream
   java.io.ObjectOutputStream
java.io.RandomAccessFile
java.io.Serializable
java.io.Writer
   java.io.PrintWriter
java.lang.Boolean implements Comparable<Boolean>, Serializable
java.lang.Character implements Comparable<Character>, Serializable
java.lang.Class implements Serializable
java.lang.Math
java.lang.Number implements Serializable
   java.math.BigDecimal implements Comparable<BigDecimal>
   java.math.BigInteger implements Comparable<BigInteger>
   java.lang.Double implements Comparable<Double>
   java.lang.Integer implements Comparable<Integer>
java.lang.String implements Comparable<String>, Serializable
java.lang.System
java.lang.Thread implements Runnable
java.lang.Throwable
  java.lang.Error
  java.lang.Exception
     java.lang.CloneNotSupportedException
     java.lang.InterruptedException
     java.io.IOException
        java.io.EOFException
        java.io.FileNotFoundException
     java.lang.RuntimeException
        java.lang.IllegalArgumentException
           java.lang.NumberFormatException
        java.lang.IllegalStateException
        java.util.NoSuchElementException
           java.util.InputMismatchException
        java.lang.NullPointerException
     java.sql.SQLException
     javax.xml.xpath.XPathException
        javax.xml.xpath.XPathExpressionException
java.net.ServerSocket
java.net.Socket
java.net.URL implements Serializable
```

```
java.net.URLConnection
   java.net.HttpURLConnection
java.sql.DriverManager
java.text.Format implements Cloneable, Serializable
   java.text.DateFormat
java.util.AbstractCollection<E>
   java.util.AbstractList<E>
      java.util.AbstractSequentialList<E>
         java.util.LinkedList<E> implements Cloneable, List<E>, Serializable
         java.util.ArrayList<E> implements Cloneable, List<E>, Serializable
      java.util.AbstractQueue<E>
         java.util.PriorityQueue<E> implements Serializable
      java.util.AbstractSet<E>
         java.util.HashSet<E> implements Cloneable, Serializable, Set<E>
         java.util.TreeSet<E> implements Cloneable, Serializable, SortedSet<E>
java.util.AbstractMap<K, V>
   java.util.HashMap<K, V> implements Cloneable, Map<K, V>, Serializable
      java.util.LinkedHashMap<K, V>
   java.util.TreeMap<K, V> implements Cloneable, Serializable, Map<K, V>
java.util.Arrays
java.util.Collections
java.util.Calendar
   java.util.GregorianCalendar
java.util.Date implements Serializable
java.util.Dictionary<K, V>
   java.util.Hashtable<K, V>
      java.util.Properties implements Serializable
java.util.EventObject implements Serializable
   java.awt.AWTEvent
      java.awt.event.ActionEvent
      java.awt.event.ComponentEvent
         java.awt.event.InputEvent
            java.awt.event.MouseEvent
   javax.swing.event.ChangeEvent
java.util.Random implements Serializable
java.util.Scanner
java.util.TimeZone implements Cloneable, Serializable
java.util.concurrent.locks.ReentrantLock implements Lock, Serializable
java.util.logging.Level implements Serializable
java.util.logging.Logger
javax.swing.ButtonGroup implements Serializable
javax.swing.ImageIcon implements Serializable
javax.swing.Timer implements Serializable
javax.swing.border.AbstractBorder implements Serializable
   javax.swing.border.EtchedBorder
   javax.swing.border.TitledBorder
javax.xml.parsers.DocumentBuilder
javax.xml.parsers.DocumentBuilderFactory
javax.xml.xpath.XPathFactory
java.lang.Comparable<T>
java.lang.Runnable
java.sql.Connection
java.sql.ResultSet
java.sql.ResultSetMetaData
java.sql.Statement
   java.sql.PreparedStatement
java.util.Collection<E>
   java.util.List<E>
   java.util.Set<E>
      java.util.SortedSet<E>
```

```
java.util.Comparator<T>
java.util.EventListener
    java.awt.event.ActionListener
    java.awt.event.MouseListener
    javax.swing.event.ChangeListener
java.util.Iterator<E>
    java.util.ListIterator<E>
java.util.Map<K, V>
java.util.concurrent.locks.Condition
java.util.concurrent.locks.Lock
javax.xml.xpath.XPath
org.w3c.dom.DOMConfiguration
org.w3c.dom.DOMImplementaton
org.w3c.dom.Node
    org.w3c.dom.CharacterData
        org.w3c.dom.Text
    org.w3c.dom.Document
    org.w3c.dom.Element
org.w3c.dom.ls.DOMImplementationLS
org.w3c.dom.ls.LSSerializer
```

In the following descriptions, the phrase "this object" ("this component", "this container", and so forth) means the object (component, container, and so forth) on which the method is invoked (the implicit parameter, this).

Package java.applet

Class java.applet.Applet

- void **destroy**()
  This method is called when the applet is about to be terminated, after the last call to stop.
- void **init**()
  This method is called when the applet has been loaded, before the first call to start. Applets override this method to carry out applet-specific initialization and to read applet parameters.
- void **start**()
  This method is called after the init method and each time the applet is revisited.
- void **stop**()
  This method is called whenever the user has stopped watching this applet.

Package java.awt

Class java.awt.BorderLayout

- **BorderLayout**()
  This constructs a border layout. A border layout has five regions for adding components, called "North", "East", "South", "West", and "Center".
- static final int CENTER
  This value identifies the center position of a border layout.
- static final int EAST
  This value identifies the east position of a border layout.
- static final int NORTH
  This value identifies the north position of a border layout.
- static final int SOUTH
  This value identifies the south position of a border layout.
- static final int WEST
  This value identifies the west position of a border layout.

Class java.awt.Color

- **Color**(int red, int green, int blue)
  This creates a color with the specified red, green, and blue values between 0 and 255.
  Parameters: red   The red component
  green   The green component
  blue   The blue component

Class java.awt.Component

- void **addMouseListener**(MouseListener listener)
  This method adds a mouse listener to the component.
  Parameters: listener The mouse listener to be added

- int **getHeight**()
  This method gets the height of this component.
  Returns: The height in pixels.

- int **getWidth**()
  This method gets the width of this component.
  Returns: The width in pixels.

- void **repaint**()
  This method repaints this component by scheduling a call to the paint method.

- void **setPreferredSize**(Dimension preferredSize)
  This method sets the preferred size of this component.

- void **setSize**(int width, int height)
  This method sets the size of this component.
  Parameters: width the component width
  height   the component height

- void **setVisible**(boolean visible)
  This method shows or hides the component.
  Parameters: visible true to show the component, or false to hide it

Class java.awt.Container

- void **add**(Component c)
- void **add**(Component c, Object position)
  These methods add a component to the end of this container. If a position is given, the layout manager is called to position the component.
  Parameters: c The component to be added
  position An object expressing position information for the layout manager

- void **setLayout**(LayoutManager manager)
  This method sets the layout manager for this container.
  Parameters: manager A layout manager

Class java.awt.Dimension

- **Dimension**(int width, int height)
  This constructs a Dimension object with the given width and height.
  Parameters: width The width
  height The height

Class java.awt.FlowLayout

- **FlowLayout**()
  This constructs a new flow layout. A flow layout places as many components as possible in a row, without changing their size, and starts new rows when necessary.

Class java.awt.Font

- **Font**(String name, int style, int size)

  This constructs a font object from the specified name, style, and point size.

  Parameters: name   The font name, either a font face name or a logical font name, which must be one of "Dialog", "DialogInput", "Monospaced", "Serif", or "SansSerif"

  style   One of Font.PLAIN, Font.ITALIC, Font.BOLD, or Font.ITALIC+Font.BOLD

  size   The point size of the font

Class java.awt.Frame

- void **setTitle**(String title)

  This method sets the frame title.

  Parameters: title   The title to be displayed in the border of the frame

Class java.awt.Graphics

- void **setColor**(Color c)

  This method sets the current color. From now on, all graphics operations use this color.

  Parameters: c   The new drawing color

Class java.awt.Graphics2D

- void **draw**(Shape s)

  This method draws the outline of the given shape. Many classes—among them Rectangle and Line2D.Double—implement the Shape interface.

  Parameters: s   The shape to be drawn

- void **drawString**(String s, int x, int y)
- void **drawString**(String s, float x, float y)

  These methods draw a string in the current font.

  Parameters: s   The string to draw

  x,y   The basepoint of the first character in the string

- void **fill**(Shape s)

  This method draws the given shape and fills it with the current color.

  Parameters: s   The shape to be filled

Class java.awt.GridLayout

- **GridLayout**(int rows, int cols)

  This constructor creates a grid layout with the specified number of rows and columns. The components in a grid layout are arranged in a grid with equal widths and heights. One, but not both, of rows and cols can be zero, in which case any number of objects can be placed in a row or in a column, respectively.

  Parameters: rows   The number of rows in the grid

  cols   The number of columns in the grid

Class java.awt.Rectangle

- **Rectangle**()

  This constructs a rectangle with a top-left corner at (0, 0) and width and height set to 0.

- **Rectangle**(`int x, int y, int width, int height`)
  This constructs a rectangle with given top-left corner and size.
  Parameters: `x,y` The top-left corner
  `width` The width
  `height` The height

- `double` **getHeight**()
- `double` **getWidth**()
  These methods get the height and width of the rectangle.

- `double` **getX**()
- `double` **getY**()
  These methods get the x- and y-coordinates of the top-left corner of the rectangle.

- `void` **grow**(`int dw, int dh`)
  This method adjusts the width and height of this rectangle.
  Parameters: `dw` The amount to add to the width (can be negative)
  `dh` The amount to add to the height (can be negative)

- `Rectangle` **intersection**(`Rectangle other`)
  This method computes the intersection of this rectangle with the specified rectangle.
  Parameters: `other` A rectangle
  Returns: The largest rectangle contained in both `this` and `other`

- `void` **setLocation**(`int x, int y`)
  This method moves this rectangle to a new location.
  Parameters: `x,y` The new top-left corner

- `void` **setSize**(`int width, int height`)
  This method sets the width and height of this rectangle to new values.
  Parameters: `width` The new width
  `height` The new height

- `void` **translate**(`int dx, int dy`)
  This method moves this rectangle.
  Parameters: `dx` The distance to move along the x-axis
  `dy` The distance to move along the y-axis

- `Rectangle` **union**(`Rectangle other`)
  This method computes the union of this rectangle with the specified rectangle. This is not the set-theoretic union but the smallest rectangle that contains both `this` and `other`.
  Parameters: `other` A rectangle
  Returns: The smallest rectangle containing both `this` and `other`

Interface java.awt.Shape

The `Shape` interface describes shapes that can be drawn and filled by a `Graphics2D` object.

Package java.awt.event

Interface java.awt.event.ActionListener

- `void` **actionPerformed**(`ActionEvent e`)
  The event source calls this method when an action occurs.

Class java.awt.event.MouseEvent

- `int` **getX**()
  This method returns the horizontal position of the mouse as of the time the event occurred.
  Returns: The x-position of the mouse
- `int` **getY**()
  This method returns the vertical position of the mouse as of the time the event occurred.
  Returns: The y-position of the mouse

Interface java.awt.event.MouseListener

- `void` **mouseClicked**(MouseEvent e)
  This method is called when the mouse has been clicked (that is, pressed and released in quick succession).
- `void` **mouseEntered**(MouseEvent e)
  This method is called when the mouse has entered the component to which this listener was added.
- `void` **mouseExited**(MouseEvent e)
  This method is called when the mouse has exited the component to which this listener was added.
- `void` **mousePressed**(MouseEvent e)
  This method is called when a mouse button has been pressed.
- `void` **mouseReleased**(MouseEvent e)
  This method is called when a mouse button has been released.

Package java.awt.geom

Class java.awt.geom.Ellipse2D.Double

- `Ellipse2D.Double`(double x, double y, double w, double h)
  This constructs an ellipse from the specified coordinates.
  Parameters: x, y   The top-left corner of the bounding rectangle
  w   The width of the bounding rectangle
  h   The height of the bounding rectangle

Class java.awt.geom.Line2D

- `double` **getX1**()
- `double` **getX2**()
- `double` **getY1**()
- `double` **getY2**()
  These methods get the requested coordinate of an endpoint of this line.
  Returns: The x- or y-coordinate of the first or second endpoint
- `void` **setLine**(double x1, double y1, double x2, double y2)
  This methods sets the endpoints of this line.
  Parameters: x1, y1   A new endpoint of this line
  x2, y2   The other new endpoint

Class `java.awt.geom.Line2D.Double`

- **Line2D.Double**(double x1, double y1, double x2, double y2)
  This constructs a line from the specified coordinates.
  Parameters: x1, y1 One endpoint of the line
  x2, y2 The other endpoint
- **Line2D.Double**(Point2D p1, Point2D p2)
  This constructs a line from the two endpoints.
  Parameters: p1, p2 The endpoints of the line

Class `java.awt.geom.Point2D`

- double **getX**()
- double **getY**()
  These methods get the requested coordinates of this point.
  Returns: The x- or y-coordinate of this point
- void **setLocation**(double x, double y)
  This method sets the x- and y-coordinates of this point.
  Parameters: x, y The new location of this point

Class `java.awt.geom.Point2D.Double`

- **Point2D.Double**(double x, double y)
  This constructs a point with the specified coordinates.
  Parameters: x, y The coordinates of the point

Class `java.awt.geom.RectangularShape`

- int **getHeight**()
- int **getWidth**()
  These methods get the height or width of the bounding rectangle of this rectangular shape.
  Returns: The height or width, respectively
- double **getCenterX**()
- double **getCenterY**()
- double **getMaxX**()
- double **getMaxY**()
- double **getMinX**()
- double **getMinY**()
  These methods get the requested coordinate value of the corners or center of the bounding rectangle of this shape.
  Returns: The center, maximum, or minimum x- and y-coordinates

Package java.io

Class java.io.EOFException

- **EOFException**(String message)

  This constructs an "end of file" exception object.

  Parameters: message   The detail message

Class java.io.File

- **File**(String name)

  This constructs a File object that describes a file (which may or may not exist) with the given name.

  Parameters: name   The name of the file

- static final String pathSeparator

  The sytem-dependent separator between path names. A colon (:) in Linux or Mac OS X; a semicolon (;) in Windows.

Class java.io.FileInputStream

- **FileInputStream**(File f)

  This constructs a file input stream and opens the chosen file. If the file cannot be opened for reading, a FileNotFoundException is thrown.

  Parameters: f   The file to be opened for reading

- **FileInputStream**(String name)

  This constructs a file input stream and opens the named file. If the file cannot be opened for reading, a FileNotFoundException is thrown.

  Parameters: name   The name of the file to be opened for reading

Class java.io.FileNotFoundException

This exception is thrown when a file could not be opened.

Class java.io.FileOutputStream

- **FileOutputStream**(File f)

  This constructs a file output stream and opens the chosen file. If the file cannot be opened for writing, a FileNotFoundException is thrown.

  Parameters: f   The file to be opened for writing

- **FileOutputStream**(String name)

  This constructs a file output stream and opens the named file. If the file cannot be opened for writing, a FileNotFoundException is thrown.

  Parameters: name   The name of the file to be opened for writing

Class java.io.InputStream

- void **close**()

  This method closes this input stream (such as a FileInputStream) and releases any system resources associated with the stream.

- int **read**()
  This method reads the next byte of data from this input stream.
  Returns: The next byte of data, or -1 if the end of the stream is reached.

Class java.io.InputStreamReader

- **InputStreamReader**(InputStream in)
  This constructs a reader from a specified input stream.
  Parameters: in The stream to read from

Class java.io.IOException

This type of exception is thrown when an input/output error is encountered.

Class java.io.ObjectInputStream

- **ObjectInputStream**(InputStream in)
  This constructs an object input stream.
  Parameters: in The stream to read from
- Object **readObject**()
  This method reads the next object from this object input stream.
  Returns: The next object

Class java.io.ObjectOutputStream

- **ObjectOutputStream**(OutputStream out)
  This constructs an object output stream.
  Parameters: out The stream to write to
- Object **writeObject**(Object obj)
  This method writes the next object to this object output stream.
  Parameters: obj The object to write

Class java.io.OutputStream

- void **close**()
  This method closes this output stream (such as a FileOutputStream) and releases any system resources associated with this stream. A closed stream cannot perform output operations and cannot be reopened.
- void **write**(int b)
  This method writes the lowest byte of b to this output stream.
  Parameters: b The integer whose lowest byte is written

Class java.io.PrintStream/Class java.io.PrintWriter

- **PrintStream**(String name)
- **PrintWriter**(String name)
  This constructs a PrintStream or PrintWriter and opens the named file. If the file cannot be opened for writing, a FileNotFoundException is thrown.
  Parameters: name The name of the file to be opened for writing
- void **close**()
  This method closes this stream or writer and releases any associated system resources.

- void **print**(int x)
- void **print**(double x)
- void **print**(Object x)
- void **print**(String x)
- void **println**()
- void **println**(int x)
- void **println**(double x)
- void **println**(Object x)
- void **println**(String x)

These methods print a value to this PrintStream or PrintWriter. The println methods print a newline after the value. Objects are printed by converting them to strings with their toString methods.

Parameters: x   The value to be printed

- PrintStream **printf**(Sting format, Object... values)
- Printwriter **printf**(Sting format, Object... values)

This method prints the format string to this PrintStream or PrintWriter, substituting the given values for placeholders that start with %.

Parameters: format   The format string

values   The values to be printed. You can supply any number of values

Returns: The implicit parameter

Class java.io.RandomAccessFile

- **RandomAccessFile**(String name, String mode)

This method opens a named random access file for reading or read/write access.

Parameters: name   The file name

mode   "r" for reading or "rw" for read/write access

- long **getFilePointer**()

This method gets the current position in this file.

Returns: The current position for reading and writing

- long **length**()

This method gets the length of this file.

Returns: The file length

- char **readChar**()
- double **readDouble**()
- int **readInt**()

These methods read a value from the current position in this file.

Returns: The value that was read from the file

- void **seek**(long position)

This method sets the position for reading and writing in this file.

Parameters: position   The new position

- void **writeChar**(int x)
- void **writeChars**(String x)
- void **writeDouble**(double x)
- void **writeInt**(int x)

These methods write a value to the current position in this file.

Parameters: x   The value to be written

Interface java.io.Serializable

A class should implement this interface in order to enable serialization of objects.

Package `java.lang`

Class `java.lang.Boolean`

- **Boolean**`(boolean value)`
  This constructs a wrapper object for a `boolean` value.
  Parameters: `value` The value to store in this object
- `boolean` **booleanValue**`()`
  This method returns the `boolean` value stored in this `Boolean` object.
  Returns: The Boolean value of this object

Class `java.lang.Character`

- `static boolean` **isDigit**`(ch)`
  This method tests whether a given character is a Unicode digit.
  Parameters: `ch` The character to test
  Returns: `true` if the character is a digit
- `static boolean` **isLetter**`(ch)`
  This method tests whether a given character is a Unicode letter.
  Parameters: `ch` The character to test
  Returns: `true` if the character is a letter
- `static boolean` **isLowerCase**`(ch)`
  This method tests whether a given character is a lowercase Unicode letter.
  Parameters: `ch` The character to test
  Returns: `true` if the character is a lowercase letter
- `static boolean` **isUpperCase**`(ch)`
  This method tests whether a given character is an uppercase Unicode letter.
  Parameters: `ch` The character to test
  Returns: `true` if the character is an uppercase letter

Class `java.lang.Class`

- `static Class` **forName**`(String className)`
  This method loads a class with a given name. Loading a class initializes its static fields.
  Parameters: `className` The name of the class to load
  Returns: The type descriptor of the class

Interface `java.lang.Cloneable`

A class implements this interface to indicate that the `Object.clone` method is allowed to make a shallow copy of its instance variables.

Class `java.lang.CloneNotSupportedException`

This exception is thrown when a program tries to use `Object.clone` to make a shallow copy of an object of a class that does not implement the `Cloneable` interface.

Interface java.lang.Comparable<T>

- int **compareTo**(T other)

  This method compares this object with the other object.

  Parameters: other   The object to be compared

  Returns: A negative integer if this object is less than the other, zero if they are equal, or a positive integer otherwise

Class java.lang.Double

- **Double**(double value)

  This constructs a wrapper object for a double-precision floating-point number.

  Parameters: value   The value to store in this object

- double **doubleValue**()

  This method returns the floating-point value stored in this Double wrapper object.

  Returns: The value stored in the object

- static double **parseDouble**(String s)

  This method returns the floating-point number that the string represents. If the string cannot be interpreted as a number, a NumberFormatException is thrown.

  Parameters: s   The string to be parsed

  Returns: The value represented by the string parameter

Class java.lang.Error

This is the superclass for all unchecked system errors.

Class java.lang.IllegalArgumentException

- **IllegalArgumentException**()

  This constructs an IllegalArgumentException with no detail message.

Class java.lang.IllegalStateException

This exception is thrown if the state of an object indicates that a method cannot currently be applied.

Class java.lang.Integer

- **Integer**(int value)

  This constructs a wrapper object for an integer.

  Parameters: value   The value to store in this object

- int **intValue**()

  This method returns the integer value stored in this wrapper object.

  Returns: The value stored in the object

- static int **parseInt**(String s)

  This method returns the integer that the string represents. If the string cannot be interpreted as an integer, a NumberFormatException is thrown.

  Parameters: s   The string to be parsed

  Returns: The value represented by the string parameter

- `static Integer` **`parseInt`**`(String s, int base)`
  This method returns the integer value that the string represents in a given number system. If the string cannot be interpreted as an integer, a `NumberFormatException` is thrown.
  Parameters: s The string to be parsed
  base The base of the number system (such as 2 or 16)
  Returns: The value represented by the string parameter
- `static String` **`toString`**`(int i)`
- `static String` **`toString`**`(int i, int base)`
  This method creates a string representation of an integer in a given number system. If no base is given, a decimal representation is created.
  Parameters: i An integer number
  base The base of the number system (such as 2 or 16)
  Returns: A string representation of the number parameter in the specified number system
- `static final int MAX_VALUE`
  This constant is the largest value of type `int`.
- `static final int MIN_VALUE`
  This constant is the smallest (negative) value of type `int`.

Class `java.lang.InterruptedException`

This exception is thrown to interrupt a thread, usually with the intent of terminating it.

Class `java.lang.Math`

- `static double` **`abs`**`(double x)`
  This method returns the absolute value $|x|$.
  Parameters: x A floating-point value
  Returns: The absolute value of the parameter
- `static double` **`acos`**`(double x)`
  This method returns the angle with the given cosine, $\cos^{-1} x \in [0, \pi]$.
  Parameters: x A floating-point value between −1 and 1
  Returns: The arc cosine of the parameter, in radians
- `static double` **`asin`**`(double x)`
  This method returns the angle with the given sine, $\sin^{-1} x \in [-\pi/2, \pi/2]$.
  Parameters: x A floating-point value between −1 and 1
  Returns: The arc sine of the parameter, in radians
- `static double` **`atan`**`(double x)`
  This method returns the angle with the given tangent, $\tan^{-1} x\ (-\pi/2, \pi/2)$.
  Parameters: x A floating-point value
  Returns: The arc tangent of the parameter, in radians
- `static double` **`atan2`**`(double y, double x)`
  This method returns the arc tangent, $\tan^{-1} (y/x) \in (-\pi, \pi)$. If x can equal zero, or if it is necessary to distinguish "northwest" from "southeast" and "northeast" from "southwest", use this method instead of atan(y/x).
  Parameters: y,x Two floating-point values
  Returns: The angle, in radians, between the points (0,0) and (x,y)

- `static double` **`ceil`**`(double x)`

  This method returns the smallest integer $\geq x$ (as a `double`).

  Parameters: x   A floating-point value

  Returns: The "ceiling integer" of the parameter

- `static double` **`cos`**`(double radians)`

  This method returns the cosine of an angle given in radians.

  Parameters: radians   An angle, in radians

  Returns: The cosine of the parameter

- `static double` **`exp`**`(double x)`

  This method returns the value e^x, where e is the base of the natural logarithms.

  Parameters: x   A floating-point value

  Returns: e^x

- `static double` **`floor`**`(double x)`

  This method returns the largest integer $\leq x$ (as a `double`).

  Parameters: x   A floating-point value

  Returns: The "floor integer" of the parameter

- `static double` **`log`**`(double x)`
- `static double` **`log10`**`(double x)`

  This method returns the natural (base e) or decimal (base 10) logarithm of x, $\ln x$.

  Parameters: x   A number greater than 0.0

  Returns: The natural logarithm of the parameter

- `static int` **`max`**`(int x, int y)`
- `static double` **`max`**`(double x, double y)`

  These methods return the larger of the given parameter values.

  Parameters: x, y   Two integers or floating-point values

  Returns: The maximum of the parameter values

- `static int` **`min`**`(int x, int y)`
- `static double` **`min`**`(double x, double y)`

  These methods return the smaller of the given parameter values.

  Parameters: x, y   Two integers or floating-point values

  Returns: The minimum of the parameter values

- `static double` **`pow`**`(double x, double y)`

  This method returns the value x^y ($x > 0$, or $x = 0$ and $y > 0$, or $x < 0$ and y is an integer).

  Parameters: x, y   Two floating-point values

  Returns: The value of the first parameter raised to the power of the second parameter

- `static long` **`round`**`(double x)`

  This method returns the closest `long` integer to the parameter.

  Parameters: x   A floating-point value

  Returns: The value of the parameter rounded to the nearest `long` value

- `static double` **`sin`**`(double radians)`

  This method returns the sine of an angle given in radians.

  Parameters: radians   An angle, in radians

  Returns: The sine of the parameter

- `static double` **`sqrt`**`(double x)`

  This method returns the square root of x, $\sqrt{x}$.

  Parameters: x   A nonnegative floating-point value

  Returns: The square root of the parameter

- static double **tan**(double radians)
  This method returns the tangent of an angle given in radians.
  Parameters: radians   An angle, in radians
  Returns: The tangent of the parameter
- static double **toDegrees**(double radian)
  This method converts radians to degrees.
  Parameters: radians   An angle, in radians
  Returns: The angle in degrees
- static double **toRadians**(double degrees)
  This methods converts degrees to radians.
  Parameters: degrees   An angle, in degrees
  Returns: The angle in radians
- static final double E
  This constant is the value of e, the base of the natural logarithms.
- static final double PI
  This constant is the value of π.

Class java.lang.NullPointerException

This exception is thrown when a program tries to use an object through a null reference.

Class java.lang.NumberFormatException

This exception is thrown when a program tries to parse the numerical value of a string that is not a number.

Class java.lang.Object

- protected Object **clone**()
  This constructs and returns a shallow copy of this object whose instance variables are copies of the instance variables of this object. If an instance variable of the object is an object reference itself, only the reference is copied, not the object itself. However, if the class does not implement the Cloneable interface, a CloneNotSupportedException is thrown. Subclasses should redefine this method to make a deep copy.
  Returns: A copy of this object
- boolean **equals**(Object other)
  This method tests whether this and the other object are equal. This method tests only whether the object references are to the same object. Subclasses should redefine this method to compare the instance variables.
  Parameters: other   The object with which to compare
  Returns: true if the objects are equal, false otherwise
- void **notify**()
  This method notifies one of the threads that is currently on the wait list for the lock of this object.
- void **notifyAll**()
  This method notifies all of the threads that are currently on the wait list for the lock of this object.

- String **toString**()

  This method returns a string representation of this object. This method produces only the class name and locations of the objects. Subclasses should redefine this method to print the instance variables.

  Returns: A string describing this object

- void **wait**()

  This method blocks the currently executing thread and puts it on the wait list for the lock of this object.

Interface `java.lang.Runnable`

- void **run**()

  This method should be overridden to define the tasks to be carried out when this runnable is executed.

Class `java.lang.RuntimeException`

This is the superclass for all unchecked exceptions.

Class `java.lang.String`

- int **compareTo**(String other)

  This method compares this string and the other string lexicographically.

  Parameters: other The other string to be compared

  Returns: A value less than 0 if this string is lexicographically less than the other, 0 if the strings are equal, and a value greater than 0 otherwise.

- boolean **equals**(String other)
- boolean **equalsIgnoreCase**(String other)

  These methods test whether two strings are equal, or whether they are equal when letter case is ignored.

  Parameters: other The other string to be compared

  Returns: true if the strings are equal

- static String **format**(String format, Object... values)

  This method formats the given string by substituting placeholders that start with % with the given values.

  Parameters: format The string with the placeholders

  values The values to be substituted for the placeholders

  Returns: The formatted string, with the placeholders replaced by the given values

- int **length**()

  This method returns the length of this string.

  Returns: The count of characters in this string

- String **replace**(String match, String replacement)

  This method replaces matching substrings with a given replacement.

  Parameters: match The string whose matches are to be replaced

  replacement The string with which matching substrings are replaced

  Returns: A string that is identical to this string, with all matching substrings replaced by the given replacement

- String **substring**(int begin)
- String **substring**(int begin, int pastEnd)

  These methods return a new string that is a substring of this string, made up of all characters starting at position begin and up to either position pastEnd - 1, if it is given, or the end of the string.

  Parameters: begin The beginning index, inclusive

  pastEnd The ending index, exclusive

  Returns: The specified substring

- String **toLowerCase**()

  This method returns a new string that consists of all characters in this string converted to lowercase.

  Returns: A string with all characters in this string converted to lowercase

- String **toUpperCase**()

  This method returns a new string that consists of all characters in this string converted to uppercase.

  Returns: A string with all characters in this string converted to uppercase

Class java.lang.System

- static void **arraycopy**(Object from, int fromStart, Object to, int toStart, int count)

  This method copies values from one array to the other. (The array parameters are of type Object because you can convert an array of numbers to an Object but not to an Object[].)

  Parameters: from The source array

  fromStart Start position in the source array

  to The destination array

  toStart Start position in the destination data

  count The number of array elements to be copied

- static long **currentTimeMillis**()

  This method returns the difference, measured in milliseconds, between the current time and midnight, Universal Time, January 1, 1970.

  Returns: The current time in milliseconds

- static void **exit**(int status)

  This method terminates the program.

  Parameters: status Exit status. A nonzero status code indicates abnormal termination

- static final InputStream in

  This object is the "standard input" stream. Reading from this stream typically reads keyboard input.

- static final PrintStream out

  This object is the "standard output" stream. Printing to this stream typically sends output to the console window.

Class java.lang.Thread

- boolean **interrupted**()

  This method tests whether another thread has called the interrupt method on the current thread.

  Returns: true if the thread has been interrupted

- static void **sleep**(int millis)
  This method puts the calling thread to sleep.
  Parameters: millis   the number of millseconds to sleep
- void **start**()
  This method starts the thread and executes its run method.

Class java.lang.Throwable

This is the superclass of exceptions and errors.

- **Throwable**()
  This constructs a Throwable with no detail message.
- String **getMessage**()
  This method gets the message that describes the exception or error.
  Returns: The message
- void **printStackTrace**()
  This method prints a stack trace to the "standard error" stream. The stack trace contains a printout of this object and of all calls that were pending at the time it was created.

Package java.math

Class java.math.BigDecimal

- **BigDecimal**(String value)
  This constructs an arbitrary-precision floating-point number from the digits in the given string.
  Parameters: value   A string representing the floating-point number
- BigDecimal **add**(BigDecimal other)
- BigDecimal **multiply**(BigDecimal other)
- BigDecimal **subtract**(BigDecimal other)
  These methods return a BigDecimal whose value is the sum, difference, product, or quotient of this number and the other.
  Parameters: other   The other number
  Returns: The result of the arithmetic operation

Class java.math.BigInteger

- **BigInteger**(String value)
  This constructs an arbitrary-precision integer from the digits in the given string.
  Parameters: value   A string representing an arbitrary-precision integer
- BigInteger **add**(BigInteger other)
- BigInteger **divide**(BigInteger other)
- BigInteger **mod**(BigInteger other)
- BigInteger **multiply**(BigInteger other)
- BigInteger **subtract**(BigInteger other)
  These methods return a BigInteger whose value is the sum, difference, product, quotient, or remainder of this number and the other.
  Parameters: other   The other number
  Returns: The result of the arithmetic operation

Package `java.net`

Class `java.net.HttpURLConnection`

- int **getResponseCode**()
  This method gets the response status code from this connection. A value of HTTP_OK indicates success.
  Returns: The HTTP response code

- String **getResponseMessage**()
  This method gets the response message of this connection's HTTP request.
  Returns: The message, such as "OK" or "File not found"

- static int HTTP_OK
  This response code indicates a successful fulfillment of the request.

Class `java.net.ServerSocket`

- **ServerSocket**(int port)
  This constructs a server socket that listens to the given port.
  Parameters: port The port number to listen to

- Socket **accept**()
  This method waits for a client to connect to the port to which this server socket listens. When a connection occurs, the method returns a socket through which the server can communicate with the client.
  Returns: The socket through which the server can communicate with the client

- void **close**()
  This method closes the server socket. Clients can no longer connect.

Class `java.net.Socket`

- **Socket**(String host, int port)
  This constructs a socket that connects to a server.
  Parameters: host The host name
  port The port number to connect to

- void **close**()
  This method closes the connection with the server.

- InputStream **getInputStream**()
  This method gets the input stream through which the client can read the information that the server sends.
  Returns: The input stream associated with this socket

- OutputStream **getOutputStream**()
  This method gets the output stream through which the client can send information to the server.
  Returns: The output stream associated with this socket

Class `java.net.URL`

- `URL(String s)`
  This constructs an URL object from a string containing the URL.
  Parameters: s   The URL string, such as `"http://java.sun.com/index.html"`

- `InputStream openStream()`
  This method gets the input stream through which the client can read the information that the server sends.
  Returns: The input stream associated with this URL

Class `java.net.URLConnection`

- `URLConnection(URL u)`
  This constructs an URLConnection object from an URL object.
  Parameters: u   The resource to which you intend to connect

- `int getContentLength()`
  This method gets the value of the `content-length` header of this URL connection.
  Returns: The number of bytes in the content that the server is sending

- `String getContentType()`
  This method gets the value of the `content-type` header of this URL connection.
  Returns: The MIME type of the content that the server is sending, such as `"text/plain"` or `"image/gif"`

- `InputStream getInputStream()`
  This method gets the input stream through which the client can read the information that the server sends.
  Returns: The input stream associated with this URL

- `void setIfModifiedSince(Date d)`
  This method instructs the connection to request that the server send data only if the content has been modified since a given date.
  Parameters: d   The modification date

Package `java.sql`

Interface `java.sql.Connection`

- `void close()`
  This method closes the connection with the database.

- `void commit()`
  This method commits all database changes since the last call to `commit` or `rollback`.

- `Statement createStatement()`
  This method creates a statement object, which can be used to issue database commands.
  Returns: A statement object

- `PreparedStatement prepareStatement(String command)`
  This method creates a prepared statement for a SQL command that is issued repeatedly.
  Parameters: command   The SQL command
  Returns: The statement object for setting parameters and executing the call

- `void rollback()`
  This method abandons all database changes since the last call to `commit` or `rollback`.

- void **setAutoCommit**(boolean b)

  This method sets the auto commit mode. By default, it is true. If it is set to false, then transactions are indicated with calls to commit or rollback. Creates a prepared statement for a SQL command that is issued repeatedly.

  Parameters: command The SQL command
                       b The desired auto commit mode

Class java.sql.DriverManager

- static Connection **getConnection**(String url, String username, String password)

  This method obtains a connection to the database specified in the database URL.

  Parameters: url The database URL
                     username The database user name
                     password The password for the database user

  Returns: A connection to the database

Interface java.sql.PreparedStatement

- boolean **execute**()

  This method executes this prepared statement.

  Returns: true if the execution yielded a result set

- ResultSet **executeQuery**()

  This method executes this prepared query.

  Returns: The query result

- int **executeUpdate**()

  This method executes this prepared update command.

  Returns: The number of records affected by the update

- void **setDouble**(int index, double value)

  This method sets a floating-point parameter for a call of this prepared statement.

  Parameters: index The parameter index (starting with 1)
                   value The parameter value

- void **setInt**(int index, int value)

  This method sets an integer parameter for a call of this prepared statement.

  Parameters: index The parameter index (starting with 1)
                   value The parameter value

- void **setString**(int index, String value)

  This method sets a string parameter for a call of this prepared statement.

  Parameters: index The parameter index (starting with 1)
                   value The parameter value

Interface java.sql.ResultSet

- void **close**()

  This method closes the result set.

- double **getDouble**(int column)

  This method returns the floating-point value at the cursor row and the given column.

  Parameters: column The column index (starting with 1)

  Returns: The data value

- `double` **getDouble**`(String columnName)`
  This method returns the floating-point value at the cursor row and the given column.
  Parameters: columnName   The column name
  Returns: The data value
- `int` **getInt**`(int column)`
  This method returns the integer value at the cursor row and the given column.
  Parameters: column   The column index (starting with 1)
  Returns: The data value
- `int` **getInt**`(String columnName)`
  This method returns the integer value at the cursor row and the given column.
  Parameters: columnName   The column name
  Returns: The data value
- `ResultSetMetaData` **getMetaData**`()`
  This method returns the meta data associated with this result set.
  Returns: The meta data
- `String` **getString**`(int column)`
  This method returns the value at the cursor row and the given column.
  Parameters: column   The column index (starting with 1)
  Returns: The data value, as a string
- `String` **getString**`(String columnName)`
  This method returns the value at the cursor row and the given column.
  Parameters: columnName   The column name
  Returns: The data value, as a string
- `boolean` **next**`()`
  This method positions the cursor to the next row. You must call next once before calling any of the get methods to move the cursor to the first row.
  Returns: true if the cursor has been positioned on a row, false at the end of the result set

Interface java.sql.ResultSetMetaData

- `int` **getColumnCount**`()`
  This method returns the number of columns of this result set.
  Returns: The number of columns
- `int` **getColumnDisplaySize**`(int column)`
  This method returns the number of characters that should be used to display the specified column in this result set.
  Parameters: column   The column index (starting with 1)
  Returns: The number of characters that should be used to display this column
- `String` **getColumnLabel**`(int column)`
  This method returns the label for a column in this result set.
  Parameters: column   The column index (starting with 1)
  Returns: The column label

Class java.sql.SQLException

This exception is thrown when a database error occurs.

Interface `java.sql.Statement`

- `void close()`
  This method closes this statement.
- `boolean execute(String command)`
  This method executes a SQL command.
  Parameters: command The command to execute
  Returns: true if the execution yielded a result set
- `ResultSet executeQuery(String command)`
  This method executes a SQL query.
  Parameters: command The query command to execute
  Returns: The query result
- `int executeUpdate(String command)`
  This method executes a SQL update command.
  Parameters: command The update command to execute
  Returns: The number of records affected by the update
- `ResultSet getResultSet()`
  This method gets the result of the last command.
  Returns: The query result from the last command
- `int getUpdateCount()`
  This method gets the update count of the last command.
  Returns: The number of records affected by the last command

Package `java.text`

Class `java.text.DateFormat`

- `String format(Date aDate)`
  This method formats a date.
  Parameters: aDate The date to format
  Returns: A string containing the formatted date
- `static DateFormat getTimeInstance()`
  This method returns a formatter that formats only the time portion of a date.
  Returns: The formatter object
- `void setTimeZone(TimeZone zone)`
  This method sets the time zone to be used when formatting dates.
  Parameters: zone The time zone to use

Package `java.util`

Class `java.util.ArrayList<E>`

- `ArrayList()`
  This constructs an empty array list.

- boolean **add**(E element)

  This method appends an element to the end of this array list.

  Parameters: element   The element to add

  Returns: true (This method returns a value because it overrides a method in the List interface.)

- void **add**(int index, E element)

  This method inserts an element into this array list.

  Parameters: index   Insert position

  element   The element to insert

- E **get**(int index)

  This method gets the element at the specified position in this array list.

  Parameters: index   Position of the element to return

  Returns: The requested element

- E **remove**(int index)

  This method removes the element at the specified position in this array list and returns it.

  Parameters: index   Position of the element to remove

  Returns: The removed element

- E **set**(int index, E element)

  This method replaces the element at a specified position in this array list.

  Parameters: index   Position of element to replace

  element   Element to be stored at the specified position

  Returns: The element previously at the specified position

- int **size**()

  This method returns the number of elements in this array list.

  Returns: The number of elements in this array list

Class java.util.Arrays

- static int **binarySearch**(Object[] a, Object key)

  This method searches the specified array for the specified object using the binary search algorithm. The array elements must implement the Comparable interface. The array must be sorted in ascending order.

  Parameters: a   The array to be searched

  key   The value to be searched for

  Returns: The position of the search key, if it is contained in the array; otherwise, −*index* − 1, where *index* is the position where the element may be inserted

- static T[] **copyOf**(T[] a, int newLength)

  This method copies the elements of the array a, or the first newLength elements if a.length < newLength, into an array of length newLength and returns that array. T can be a primitive type, class, or interface type.

  Parameters: a   The array to be copied

  key   The value to be searched for

  Returns: The position of the search key, if it is contained in the array; otherwise, −*index* − 1, where *index* is the position where the element may be inserted

- `static void` **`sort`**`(Object[] a)`
  This method sorts the specified array of objects into ascending order. Its elements must implement the `Comparable` interface.
  Parameters: a The array to be sorted

- `static String` **`toString`**`(T[] a)`
  This method creates and returns a string containing the array elements. *T* can be a primitive type, class, or interface type.
  Parameters: a An array
  Returns: A string containing a comma-separated list of string representations of the array elements, surrounded by brackets.

Class java.util.Calendar

- `int` **`get`**`(int field)`
  This method returns the value of the given field.
  Parameters: One of `Calendar.YEAR`, `Calendar.MONTH`, `Calendar.DAY_OF_MONTH`, `Calendar.HOUR`, `Calendar.MINUTE`, `Calendar.SECOND`, or `Calendar.MILLISECOND`

Interface java.util.Collection<E>

- `boolean` **`add`**`(E element)`
  This method adds an element to this collection.
  Parameters: element The element to add
  Returns: true if adding the element changes the collection

- `boolean` **`contains`**`(E element)`
  This method tests whether an element is present in this collection.
  Parameters: element The element to find
  Returns: true if the element is contained in the collection

- `Iterator` **`iterator`**`()`
  This method returns an iterator that can be used to traverse the elements of this collection.
  Returns: An object of a class implementing the `Iterator` interface

- `boolean` **`remove`**`(E element)`
  This method removes an element from this collection.
  Parameters: element The element to remove
  Returns: true if removing the element changes the collection

- `int` **`size`**`()`
  This method returns the number of elements in this collection.
  Returns: The number of elements in this collection

Class java.util.Collections

- `static <T> int` **`binarySearch`**`(List<T> a, T key)`
  This method searches the specified list for the specified object using the binary search algorithm. The list elements must implement the `Comparable` interface. The list must be sorted in ascending order.
  Parameters: a The list to be searched
  key The value to be searched for
  Returns: The position of the search key, if it is contained in the list; otherwise, −*index* − 1, where *index* is the position where the element may be inserted

- static <T> void **sort**(T[] a)
  This method sorts the specified list of objects into ascending order. Its elements must implement the Comparable interface.
  Parameters: a   The list to be sorted

Interface java.util.Comparator<T>

- int **compare**(T first, T second)
  This method compares the given objects.
  Parameters: first, second   The objects to be compared
  Returns: A negative integer if the first object is less than the second, zero if they are equal, or a positive integer otherwise

Class java.util.Date

- **Date**()
  This constructs an object that represents the current date and time.

Class java.util.EventObject

- Object **getSource**()
  This method returns a reference to the object on which this event initially occurred.
  Returns: The source of this event

Class java.util.GregorianCalendar

- **GregorianCalendar**()
  This constructs a calendar object that represents the current date and time.

- **GregorianCalendar**(int year, int month, int day)
  This constructs a calendar object that represents the start of the given date.
  Parameters: year, month, day   The given date

Class java.util.HashMap<K, V>

- **HashMap**<K, V>()
  This constructs an empty hash map.

Class java.util.HashSet<E>

- **HashSet**<E>()
  This constructs an empty hash set.

Class java.util.InputMismatchException

This exception is thrown if the next available input item does not match the type of the requested item.

Interface java.util.Iterator<E>

- boolean **hasNext**()
  This method checks whether the iterator is past the end of the list.
  Returns: true if the iterator is not yet past the end of the list

- E **next**()
  This method moves the iterator over the next element in the linked list. This method throws an exception if the iterator is past the end of the list.
  Returns: The object that was just skipped over

- void **remove**()
  This method removes the element that was returned by the last call to next or previous. This method throws an exception if there was an add or remove operation after the last call to next or previous.

Class java.util.LinkedHashMap<K, V>

- **LinkedHashMap**<K, V>()
  This constructs an empty linked hash map. The iterator of a linked hash map visits the entries in the order in which they were added to the map.

Class java.util.LinkedList<E>

- void **addFirst**(E element)
- void **addLast**(E element)
  These methods add an element before the first or after the last element in this list.
  Parameters: element   The element to be added

- E **getFirst**()
- E **getLast**()
  These methods return a reference to the specified element from this list.
  Returns: The first or last element

- E **removeFirst**()
- E **removeLast**()
  These methods remove the specified element from this list.
  Returns: A reference to the removed element

Interface java.util.List<E>

- ListIterator<E> **listIterator**()
  This method gets an iterator to visit the elements in this list.
  Returns: An iterator that points before the first element in this list

Interface java.util.ListIterator<E>

Objects implementing this interface are created by the listIterator methods of list classes.

- void **add**(E element)
  This method adds an element after the iterator position and moves the iterator after the new element.
  Parameters: element   The element to be added

- boolean **hasPrevious**()
  This method checks whether the iterator is before the first element of the list.
  Returns: true if the iterator is not before the first element of the list

- E **previous**()
  This method moves the iterator over the previous element in the linked list. This method throws an exception if the iterator is before the first element of the list.
  Returns: The object that was just skipped over

- void **set**(E element)
  This method replaces the element that was returned by the last call to next or previous. This method throws an exception if there was an add or remove operation after the last call to next or previous.
  Parameters: element   The element that replaces the old list element

Interface java.util.Map<K, V>

- V **get**(K key)
  Gets the value associated with a key in this map.
  Parameters: key   The key for which to find the associated value
  Returns: The value associated with the key, or null if the key is not present in the table

- Set<K> **keySet**()
  This method returns all keys in the table of this map.
  Returns: A set of all keys in the table of this map

- V **put**(K key, V value)
  This method associates a value with a key in this map.
  Parameters: key   The lookup key
              value   The value to associate with the key
  Returns: The value previously associated with the key, or null if the key was not present in the table

- V **remove**(K key)
  This method removes a key and its associated value from this map.
  Parameters: key   The lookup key
  Returns: The value previously associated with the key, or null if the key was not present in the table

Class java.util.NoSuchElementException

This exception is thrown if an attempt is made to retrieve a value that does not exist.

Class java.util.PriorityQueue<E>

- **PriorityQueue**<E>()
  This constructs an empty priority queue. The element type E must implement the Comparable interface.

- E **remove**()
  This method removes the smallest element in the priority queue.
  Returns: The removed value

Class java.util.Properties

- String **getProperty**(String key)
  This method gets the value associated with a key in this properties map.
  Parameters: key   The key for which to find the associated value
  Returns: The value, or null if the key is not present in the table

- void **load**(InputStream in)
  This method loads a set of key/value pairs into this properties map from a stream.
  Parameters: in   The stream from which to read the key/value pairs (it must be a sequence of lines of the form key=value)

Class java.util.Random

- **Random**()
  This constructs a new random number generator.

- double **nextDouble**()
  This method returns the next pseudorandom, uniformly distributed floating-point number between 0.0 (inclusive) and 1.0 (exclusive) from this random number generator's sequence.
  Returns: The next pseudorandom floating-point number

- int **nextInt**(int n)
  This method returns the next pseudorandom, uniformly distributed integer between 0 (inclusive) and the specified value (exclusive) drawn from this random number generator's sequence.
  Parameters: n Number of values to draw from
  Returns: The next pseudorandom integer

Class java.util.Scanner

- **Scanner**(File in)
- **Scanner**(InputStream in)
- **Scanner**(Reader in)
  These construct a scanner that reads from the given file, input stream, or reader.
  Parameters: in The file, input stream, or reader from which to read

- void **close**()
  This method closes this scanner and releases any associated system resources.

- boolean **hasNext**()
- boolean **hasNextDouble**()
- boolean **hasNextInt**()
- boolean **hasNextLine**()
  These methods test whether it is possible to read any non-empty string, a floating-point value, an integer, or a line, as the next item.
  Returns: true if it is possible to read an item of the requested type, false otherwise (either because the end of the file has been reached, or because a number type was tested and the next item is not a number)

- String **next**()
- double **nextDouble**()
- int **nextInt**()
- String **nextLine**()
  These methods read the next whitespace-delimited string, floating-point value, integer, or line.
  Returns: The value that was read

- Scanner **useDelimiter**(String pattern)
  Sets the pattern for the delimiters between input tokens.
  Parameters: pattern A regular expression for the delimiter pattern
  Returns: This scanner

Interface java.util.Set<E>

This interface describes a collection that contains no duplicate elements.

Class `java.util.TimeZone`

- `static String[]` **`getAvailableIDs`**`()`
  This method gets the supported time zone IDs.
  Returns: An array of ID strings
- `static TimeZone` **`getTimeZone`**`(String id)`
  This method gets the time zone for a time zone ID.
  Parameters: id   The time zone ID, such as `"America/Los_Angeles"`
  Returns: The time zone object associated with the ID, or `null` if the ID is not supported

Class `java.util.TreeMap<K, V>`

- **`TreeMap`**`<K, V>()`
  This constructs an empty tree map. The iterator of a `TreeMap` visits the entries in sorted order.

Class `java.util.TreeSet<E>`

- **`TreeSet`**`<E>()`
  This constructs an empty tree set.

Package `java.util.concurrent.locks`

Interface `java.util.concurrent.locks.Condition`

- `void` **`await`**`()`
  This method blocks the current thread until it is signalled or interrupted.
- `void` **`signal`**`()`
  This method unblocks one thread that is waiting on this condition.
- `void` **`signalAll`**`()`
  This method unblocks all threads that are waiting on this condition.

Interface `java.util.concurrent.locks.Lock`

- `void` **`lock`**`()`
  This method causes the current thread to acquire this lock. The thread blocks if the lock is not available.
- `Condition` **`newCondition`**`()`
  This method creates a new condition object for this lock.
  Returns: The condition object
- `void` **`unlock`**`()`
  This method causes the current thread to relinquish this lock.

Class `java.util.concurrent.locks.ReentrantLock`

- **`ReentrantLock`**`()`
  This constructs a new reentrant lock.

Package `java.util.logging`

Class `java.util.logging.Level`

- `static final int ALL`
  This value indicates logging of all messages.
- `static final int INFO`
  This value indicates informational logging.
- `static final int NONE`
  This value indicates logging of no messages.

Class `java.util.logging.Logger`

- `static Logger getGlobal()`
  This method gets the global logger. For Java 5 and 6, use `getLogger("global")` instead.
  Returns: The global logger that, by default, displays messages with level *INFO* or a higher severity on the console.
- `void info(String message)`
  This method logs an informational message.
  Parameters: `message` The message to log
- `void setLevel(Level aLevel)`
  This method sets the logging level. Logging messages with a lesser severity than the current level are ignored.
  Parameters: `aLevel` The minimum level for logging messages

Package `javax.swing`

Class `javax.swing.AbstractButton`

- `void addActionListener(ActionListener listener)`
  This method adds an action listener to the button.
  Parameters: `listener` The action listener to be added
- `boolean isSelected()`
  This method returns the selection state of the button.
  Returns: `true` if the button is selected
- `void setSelected(boolean state)`
  This method sets the selection state of the button. This method updates the button but does not trigger an action event.
  Parameters: `state` `true` to select, `false` to deselect

Class `javax.swing.ButtonGroup`

- `void add(AbstractButton button)`
  This method adds the button to the group.
  Parameters: `button` The button to add

Class javax.swing.ImageIcon

- **ImageIcon**(String filename)
  This constructs an image icon from the specified graphics file.
  Parameters: filename   A string specifying a file name

Class javax.swing.JButton

- **JButton**(String label)
  This constructs a button with the given label.
  Parameters: label   The button label

Class javax.swing.JCheckBox

- **JCheckBox**(String text)
  This constructs a check box, having the given text, initially deselected. (Use the setSelected() method to make the box selected; see the javax.swing.AbstractButton class.)
  Parameters: text   The text displayed next to the check box

Class javax.swing.JComboBox

- **JComboBox**()
  This constructs a combo box with no items.
- void **addItem**(Object item)
  This method adds an item to the item list of this combo box.
  Parameters: item   The item to add
- Object **getSelectedItem**()
  This method gets the currently selected item of this combo box.
  Returns: The currently selected item
- boolean **isEditable**()
  This method checks whether the combo box is editable. An editable combo box allows the user to type into the text field of the combo box.
  Returns: true if the combo box is editable
- void **setEditable**(boolean state)
  This method is used to make the combo box editable or not.
  Parameters: state   true to make editable, false to disable editing

Class javax.swing.JComponent

- protected void **paintComponent**(Graphics g)
  Override this method to paint the surface of a component. Your method needs to call super.paintComponent(g).
  Parameters: g   The graphics context used for drawing
- void **setBorder**(Border b)
  This method sets the border of this component.
  Parameters: b   The border to surround this component
- void **setFont**(Font f)
  Sets the font used for the text in this component.
  Parameters: f   A font

Class javax.swing.JFileChooser

- **JFileChooser**()
  This constructs a file chooser.

- File **getSelectedFile**()
  This method gets the selected file from this file chooser.
  Returns: The selected file

- int **showOpenDialog**(Component parent)
  This method displays an "Open File" file chooser dialog box.
  Parameters: parent The parent component or null
  Returns: The return state of this file chooser after it has been closed by the user: either APPROVE_OPTION or CANCEL_OPTION. If APPROVE_OPTION is returned, call getSelectedFile() on this file chooser to get the file

- int **showSaveDialog**(Component parent)
  This method displays a "Save File" file chooser dialog box.
  Parameters: parent The parent component or null
  Returns: The return state of the file chooser after it has been closed by the user: either APPROVE_OPTION or CANCEL_OPTION

Class javax.swing.JFrame

- void **setDefaultCloseOperation**(int operation)
  This method sets the default action for closing the frame.
  Parameters: operation The desired close operation. Choose among
  DO_NOTHING_ON_CLOSE, HIDE_ON_CLOSE (the default), DISPOSE_ON_CLOSE, or
  EXIT_ON_CLOSE

- void **setJMenuBar**(JMenuBar mb)
  This method sets the menu bar for this frame.
  Parameters: mb The menu bar. If mb is null, then the current menu bar is removed

- static final int EXIT_ON_CLOSE
  This value indicates that when the user closes this frame, the application is to exit.

Class javax.swing.JLabel

- **JLabel**(String text)
- **JLabel**(String text, int alignment)
  These containers create a JLabel instance with the specified text and horizontal alignment.
  Parameters: text The label text to be displayed by the label
  alignment One of SwingConstants.LEFT, SwingConstants.CENTER, or
  SwingConstants.RIGHT

Class javax.swing.JMenu

- **JMenu**()
  This constructs a menu with no items.

- JMenuItem **add**(JMenuItem menuItem)
  This method appends a menu item to the end of this menu.
  Parameters: menuItem The menu item to be added
  Returns: The menu item that was added

Class javax.swing.JMenuBar

- **JMenuBar**()
  This constructs a menu bar with no menus.
- JMenu **add**(JMenu menu)
  This method appends a menu to the end of this menu bar.
  Parameters: menu   The menu to be added
  Returns: The menu that was added

Class javax.swing.JMenuItem

- **JMenuItem**(String text)
  This constructs a menu item.
  Parameters: text   The text to appear in the menu item

Class javax.swing.JOptionPane

- static String **showInputDialog**(Object prompt)
  This method brings up a modal input dialog box, which displays a prompt and waits for the user to enter an input in a text field, preventing the user from doing anything else in this program.
  Parameters: prompt   The prompt to display
  Returns: The string that the user typed
- static void **showMessageDialog**(Component parent, Object message)
  This method brings up a confirmation dialog box that displays a message and waits for the user to confirm it.
  Parameters: parent   The parent component or null
  message   The message to display

Class javax.swing.JPanel

This class is a component without decorations. It can be used as an invisible container for other components.

Class javax.swing.JRadioButton

- **JRadioButton**(String text)
  This constructs a radio button having the given text that is initially deselected. (Use the setSelected() method to select it; see the javax.swing.AbstractButton class.)
  Parameters: text   The string displayed next to the radio button

Class javax.swing.JScrollPane

- **JScrollPane**(Component c)
  This constructs a scroll pane around the given component.
  Parameters: c   The component that is decorated with scroll bars

Class javax.swing.JSlider

- **JSlider**(int min, int max, int value)
  This constructor creates a horizontal slider using the specified minimum, maximum, and value.
  Parameters: min The smallest possible slider value
  max The largest possible slider value
  value The initial value of the slider

- void **addChangeListener**(ChangeListener listener)
  This method adds a change listener to the slider.
  Parameters: listener The change listener to add

- int **getValue**()
  This method returns the slider's value.
  Returns: The current value of the slider

Class javax.swing.JTextArea

- **JTextArea**()
  This constructs an empty text area.

- **JTextArea**(int rows, int columns)
  This constructs an empty text area with the specified number of rows and columns.
  Parameters: rows The number of rows
  columns The number of columns

- void **append**(String text)
  This method appends text to this text area.
  Parameters: text The text to append

Class javax.swing.JTextField

- **JTextField**()
  This constructs an empty text field.

- **JTextField**(int columns)
  This constructs an empty text field with the specified number of columns.
  Parameters: columns The number of columns

Class javax.swing.Timer

- **Timer**(int millis, ActionListener listener)
  This constructs a timer that notifies an action listener whenever a time interval has elapsed.
  Parameters: millis The number of milliseconds between timer notifications
  listener The object to be notified when the time interval has elapsed

- void **start**()
  This method starts the timer. Once the timer has started, it begins notifiying its listener.

- void **stop**()
  This method stops the timer. Once the timer has stopped, it no longer notifies its listener.

Package javax.swing.border

Class javax.swing.border.EtchedBorder

- `EtchedBorder()`
  This constructor creates a lowered etched border.

Class javax.swing.border.TitledBorder

- `TitledBorder(Border b, String title)`
  This constructor creates a titled border that adds a title to a given border.
  Parameters: b   The border to which the title is added
  title   The title the border should display

Package javax.swing.event

Class javax.swing.event.ChangeEvent

Components such as sliders emit change events when they are manipulated by the user.

Interface javax.swing.event.ChangeListener

- `void stateChanged(ChangeEvent e)`
  This event is called when the event source has changed its state.
  Parameters: e   A change event

Package javax.swing.text

Class javax.swing.text.JTextComponent

- `String getText()`
  This method returns the text contained in this text component.
  Returns: The text
- `boolean isEditable()`
  This method checks whether this text component is editable.
  Returns: true if the component is editable
- `void setEditable(boolean state)`
  This method is used to make this text component editable or not.
  Parameters: state   true to make editable, false to disable editing
- `void setText(String text)`
  This method sets the text of this text component to the specified text. If the text is empty, the old text is deleted.
  Parameters: text   The new text to be set

Package `javax.xml.parsers`

Class `javax.xml.parsers.DocumentBuilder`

- Document **newDocument**()
  This constructs a new document object.
  Returns: An empty document

- Document **parse**(File in)
  This method parses an XML document in a file.
  Parameters: in The file containing the document
  Returns: The parsed document

- Document **parse**(InputStream in)
  This method parses an XML document in a stream.
  Parameters: in The stream containing the document
  Returns: The parsed document

Class `javax.xml.parsers.DocumentBuilderFactory`

- DocumentBuilder **newDocumentBuilder**()
  This method creates a new document builder object.
  Returns: The document builder

- static DocumentBuilderFactory **newInstance**()
  This method creates a new document builder factory object.
  Returns: The document builder factory object

- void **setIgnoringElementContentWhitespace**(boolean b)
  This method sets the parsing mode for ignoring white space in element content for all document builders that are generated from this factory.
  Parameters: b true if white space should be ignored

- void **setValidating**(boolean b)
  This method sets the validation mode for all document builders that are generated from this factory.
  Parameters: b true if documents should be validated during parsing

Package `javax.xml.xpath`

Interface `javax.xml.xpath.XPath`

- String **evaluate**(String path, Object context)
  This method evaluates the given path expression in the given context.
  Parameters: path An XPath expression
  context The starting context for the evaluation, such as a document, node, or node list
  Returns: The result of the evaluation

Class `javax.xml.xpath.XPathExpressionException`

This exception is thrown when an XPath expression cannot be evaluated.

Class `javax.xml.xpath.XPathFactory`

- `static XPathFactory` **`newInstance`**`()`
  This method returns a factory instance that can be used to construct XPath objects.
  Returns: An XPathFactory instance
- `XPath` **`newXPath`**`()`
  This method returns an XPath object that can be used to evaluate XPath expressions.
  Returns: An XPath object

Package `org.w3c.dom`

Interface `org.w3c.dom.Document`

- `Element` **`createElement`**`(String tagName)`
  This method creates a new document element with a given tag.
  Parameters: `tagName`   The name of the XML tag
  Returns: The created element
- `Text` **`createTextNode`**`(String text)`
  This method creates a text node with the given text.
  Parameters: `text`   The text for the text node
  Returns: The created text node
- `DOMImplementation` **`getImplementation`**`()`
  This method returns the `DOMImplementation` object associated with this document.

Interface `org.w3c.dom.DOMConfiguration`

- `void` **`setParameter`**`(String name, Object value)`
  This method sets the value of a configuration parameter.
  Parameters: `name`   The name of the parameter to set
               `value`   The new value or `null` to unset the parameter

Interface `org.w3c.dom.DOMImplementation`

- `Object` **`getFeature`**`(String feature, String version)`
  This method gets an object that implements a specialized API (such as loading and saving of DOM trees).
  Parameters: `feature`   The feature version (such as "LS")
               `version`   The version number (such as "3.0")
  Returns: The feature object

Interface `org.w3c.dom.Element`

- `String` **`getAttribute`**`(String attributeName)`
  This method returns the value of a given attribute.
  Parameters: `attributeName`   The name of the XML attribute
  Returns: The attribute value, or the empty string "" if that attribute does not exist for this element

- void **setAttribute**(String name, String value)
  This method sets the value of a given attribute.
  Parameters: name   The name of the XML attribute
                    value   The desired value of the XML attribute

Interface org.w3c.dom.Text

This interface describes a node that contains the textual content of an XML element.

Package org.w3c.dom.ls

Interface org.w3c.dom.ls.DOMImplementationLS

- LSSerializer **createLSSerializer**()
  This method creates a serializer object that can be used to convert a DOM tree to a string or stream.
  Returns: The serializer object

Interface org.w3c.dom.ls.LSSerializer

- DOMConfiguration **getDomConfig**()
  This method gets the configuration object that allows customization of the serializer behavior.
- String **writeToString**(Node root)
  This method converts the DOM tree starting at the given node to a string.
  Parameters: node   The root node of the tree
  Returns: The string representation of the tree

Java Syntax Summary

In this syntax summary, we use a monospaced font for actual Java reserved words and tokens such as `while`. An italic font denotes language constructs such as *condition* or *variable*. Items enclosed in brackets [ ] are optional. Items separated by vertical bars | are alternatives. Do not include the brackets or vertical bars in your code!

The summary reflects the parts of the Java language that were covered in this book. For a full overview of the Java syntax, see `http://java.sun.com/docs/books/jls/`.

As always, please be careful to distinguish an ellipsis . . . from the ... token. The latter appears twice in this appendix in the "variable parameters" discussion in the "Methods" section.

Types

A type is a primitive type or a reference type. The primitive types are

- The numeric types `int`, `long`, `short`, `char`, `byte`, `float`, `double`
- The `boolean` type

The reference types are

- Classes such as `String` or `Employee`
- Enumeration types such as `enum Sex { FEMALE, MALE }`
- Interfaces such as `Comparable`
- Array types such as `Employee[]` or `int[][]`

Variables

Local variable declarations have the form

    [final] *Type* *variableName* [= *initializer*];

Examples:

```
int n;
double x = 0;
String harry = "Harry Handsome";
Rectangle box = new Rectangle(5, 10, 20, 30);
int[] a = { 1, 4, 9, 16, 25 };
```

The variable name consists only of letters, numbers, and underscores. It must begin with a letter or underscore. Names are case-sensitive: totalscore, TOTALSCORE, and totalScore are three different variables.

The scope of a local variable extends from the point of its definition to the end of the enclosing block.

A variable that is declared as final can have its value set only once.

Instance variables will be discussed under "Classes".

Expressions

An *expression* is a variable, a method call, or a combination of subexpressions joined by operators. Examples are:

```
x
Math.sin(x)
x + Math.sin(x)
x * (1 + Math.sin(x))
x++
x == y
x == y && (z > 0 || w > 0)
p.x
e.getSalary()
v[i]
```

Operators can be *unary*, *binary*, or *ternary*. A unary operator acts on a single expression, such as x++. A binary operator combines two expressions, such as x + y. A ternary operator combines three expressions. Java has one ternary operator, ? : (see Special Topic 5.1).

Unary operators can be *prefix* or *postfix*. A prefix operator is written before the expression on which it operates, as in -x. A postfix operator is written after the expression on which it operates, such as x++.

Operators are ranked by *precedence* levels. Operators with a higher precedence bind more strongly than operators with a lower precedence. For example, * has a higher precedence than +, so x + y * z is the same as x + (y * z), even though the + comes first.

Most operators are *left-associative*. That is, operators of the same precedence are evaluated from the left to right. For example, x - y + z is interpreted as (x - y) + z, not x - (y + z). The exceptions are the unary prefix operators and the assignment operator which are right-associative. For example, z = y = Math.sin(x) means the same as z = (y = Math.sin(x)).

Appendix B has a list of all Java operators.

Classes

The syntax for a *class* is

```
[public] [abstract|final] class ClassName
      [extends SuperClassName]
      [implements InterfaceName₁, InterfaceName₂, . . .]
   {
```

> *feature₁*
> *feature₂*
>   . . .
> }

Each *feature* is either a declaration of the form

> *modifiers constructor|method|instance variable|class*

or an initialization block

> [static] { *body* }

See the section "Constructors" for more information about initialization blocks.

Potential *modifiers* include public, private, protected, static, and final.

An *instance variable* declaration has the form

> *Type variableName* [= *initializer*];

A *constructor* has the form

> *ClassName*(*parameter₁*, *parameter₂*, . . .)
>   [throws *ExceptionType₁*, *ExceptionType₂*, . . .]
> {
>   *body*
> }

A *method* has the form

> *Type methodName*(*parameter₁*, *parameter₂*, . . .)
>   [throws *ExceptionType₁*, *ExceptionType₂*, . . .]
> {
>   *body*
> }

An *abstract method* has the form

> abstract *Type methodName*(*parameter₁*, *parameter₂*, . . .);

Here is an example:

```java
public class Point
{
    private double x;
    private double y;

    public Point()
    {
        x = 0; y = 0;
    }

    public Point(double xx, double yy)
    {
        x = xx; y = yy;
    }

    public double getX()
    {
        return x;
    }

    public double getY()
    {
        return y;
    }
}
```

A class can have both instance variables and static variables. Each object of the class has a separate copy of the instance variables. There is only a one per-class copy of the static variables.

A class that is declared as abstract cannot be instantiated. That is, you cannot construct objects of that class.

A class that is declared as final cannot be extended.

Interfaces

The syntax for an interface is

```
[public] interface InterfaceName
        [extends InterfaceName₁, InterfaceName₂, . . .]
{
    feature₁
    feature₂
    . . .
}
```

Each feature has the form

modifiers method|instance variable

Potential modifiers are public, static, final. However, modifiers are never necessary because methods are automatically public and instance variables are automatically public static final.

An instance variable declaration has the form

Type variableName = initializer;

A method declaration has the form

Type methodName(parameter₁, parameter₂, . . .);

Here is an example:

```
public interface Measurable
{
    int CM_PER_INCH = 2.54;

    int getMeasure();
}
```

Enumeration Types

The syntax for an enumeration type is

```
[public] enum EnumerationTypeName
{
    constant₁, constant₂, . . .;
    feature₁
    feature₂
    . . .
}
```

Each constant is a constant name, followed by optional construction parameters.

constantName[(parameter₁, parameter₂, . . .)]

The semicolon after the constants is only required if the enumeration declares additional features. An enumeration can have the same features as a class. Each feature has the form

modifiers method|*instance variable*

Potential modifiers are `public`, `static`, `final`.

Here are two examples:

```
public enum Suit { HEARTS, DIAMONDS, SPADES, CLUBS };
public enum Card
{
   TWO(2), THREE(3), FOUR(4), FIVE(5), SIX(6),
        SEVEN(7), EIGHT(8), NINE(9), TEN(10),
        JACK(10), QUEEN(10), KING(10), ACE(11);
   private int value;

   public void Card(int aValue) { value = aValue; }
   public int getValue() { return value; }
}
```

Methods

A method definition has the form

modifiers Type methodName(parameter$_1$, parameter$_2$, . . ., parameter$_n$)
   [throws *ExceptionType$_1$, ExceptionType$_2$, . . .*]
{
   body
}

The return type *Type* is any Java type, or the special type `void` to indicate that the method returns no value.

Each *parameter* has the form

[`final`] *Type parameterName*

A method has *variable parameters* if the last parameter has the special form

Type... *parameterName*

Such a method can be called with a sequence of values of the given type of any length. The parameter variable with the given name is an array of the given type that holds the parameter values. For example, the method

```
public static double sum(double... values)
{
   double s = 0;
   for (double v : values) s = s + v;
   return s;
}
```

can be called as

```
double result = sum(1, -2.5, 3.14);
```

In Java, all parameters are passed by *value*. Each parameter is a local variable whose scope extends to the end of the method body. It is initialized with a copy of the value supplied in the call. That value may be a primitive type or a reference type. If it is a reference type, invoking a mutator on the reference will modify the object whose reference has been passed to the method.

Changing the value of the parameter variable has no effect outside the method. Tagging the parameter as `final` disallows such a change altogether. This is commonly done to allow access of the parameter from an inner class declared in the method.

Java distinguishes between *instance* methods and *static* methods. Instance methods have a special parameter, the *implicit* parameter, supplied in the method call with the syntax

implicitParameterValue.methodName(parameterValue$_1$, parameterValue$_2$, . . .)

Example:

```
harry.setSalary(30000)
```

The type of the implicit parameter must be the same as the type of the class containing the method definition. A static method does not have an implicit parameter.

In the method body, the `this` variable is initialized with a copy of the implicit parameter value. Using an instance variable name without qualification means to access the instance variable of the implicit parameter. For example,

```
public void setSalary(double s)
{
   salary = s; // i.e., this.salary = s
}
```

By default, Java uses *dynamic method lookup*. The virtual machine determines the class to which the implicit parameter object belongs and invokes the method declared in that class. However, if a method is invoked on the special variable `super`, then the method declared in the superclass is invoked on `this`. For example,

```
public class MyPanel extends JPanel
{
   . . .
   public void paintComponent(Graphics g)
   {
      super.paintComponent(g);
      // Calls JPanel.paintComponent
      . . .
   }
   . . .
}
```

The `return` statement causes a method to exit immediately. If the method type is not `void`, you must return a value. The syntax is

```
return [value];
```

For example,

```
public double getSalary()
{
   return salary;
}
```

A method can call itself. Such a method is called *recursive:*

```
public static int factorial(int n)
{
```

```
      if (n <= 1) return 1;
         return n * factorial(n - 1);
   }
```

Constructors

A constructor definition has the form

modifiers *ClassName*(*parameter₁*, *parameter₂*, . . .)
    [throws *ExceptionType₁*, *ExceptionType₂*, . . .]
{
   body
}

You invoke a constructor to allocate and construct a new object with a `new` expression

new *ClassName*(*parameterValue₁*, *parameterValue₂*, . . .)

A constructor can call the body of another constructor of the same class with the syntax

this(*parameterValue₁*, *parameterValue₂*, . . .)

For example,

```
public Employee()
{
   this("", 0);
}
```

It can call a constructor of its superclass with the syntax

super(*parameterValue₁*, *parameterValue₂*, . . .)

The call to `this` or `super` must be the first statement in the constructor.
    Arrays are constructed with the syntax

new *ArrayType* [= { *initializer₁*, *initializer₂*, . . . }]

For example,

```
new int[] = { 1, 4, 9, 16, 25 }
```

When an object is constructed, the following actions take place:

- All instance variables are initialized with 0, `false`, or `null`.

- The initializers and initialization blocks are executed in the order in which they are declared.

- The body of the constructor is invoked.

When a class is loaded, the following actions take place:

- All static variables are initialized with 0, `false`, or `null`.

- The initializers of static variables and static initialization blocks are executed in the order in which they are declared.

Statements

A *statement* is one of the following:

- An expression followed by a semicolon
- A branch or loop statement
- A `return` statement
- A `throw` statement
- A block, that is, a group of variable declarations and statements enclosed in braces {. . .}
- A `try` block

Java has two branch statements (`if` and `switch`), three loop statements (`while`, `for`, and `do`), and two mechanisms for nonlinear control flow (`break` and `continue`).

The `if` statement has the form

```
if (condition) statement₁ [else statement₂]
```

If the *condition* is true, then the first *statement* is executed. Otherwise, the second *statement* is executed.

The `switch` statement has the form

```
switch (expression)
{
    group₁:
    group₂:
    . . .
      [default:
       statement₁
       statement₂
       . . .]
}
```

Where each *group* has the form

```
case constant₁
case constant₂
. . .
    statement₁
    statement₂
    . . .
```

The *expression* must be an integer or an enumeration type. Depending on its value, control is transferred to the first statement following the matching `case` label, or to the first statement following the `default` label if none of the `case` labels match. Execution continues with the next statement until a `break` or `return` statement is encountered, an exception is thrown, or the end of the `switch` is reached. Execution skips over any case labels.

The `while` loop has the form

```
while (condition) statement
```

The *statement* is executed while the *condition* is true.

The `for` loop has the form

```
for (initExpression|variableDeclaration;
        condition;
        updateExpression₁, updateExpression₂, . . .)
    statement
```

The initialization expression or the variable declaration are executed once. While the *condition* remains true, the loop *statement* and the *updateExpressions* are executed. Examples:

```
for (i = 0; i < 10; i++)
    sum = sum + i;
for (int i = 0, j = 9; i < 10; i++, j--)
    a[j] = b[i];
```

The enhanced `for` loop or "for each" loop has the form

```
for (Type variable : array|iterableObject)
    statement
```

When this loop traverses an array, it is equivalent to

```
for (int i = 0; i < array.length; i++)
{
    Type variable = array[i];
    statement
}
```

Otherwise, the *iterableObject* must belong to a class that implements the `Iterable` interface. Then the loop is equivalent to

```
Iterator i = iterableObject.iterator();
while (i.hasNext())
{
    Type variable = i.next();
    statement
}
```

The `do` loop has the form

```
do statement while (condition);
```

The *statement* is repeatedly executed until the *condition* is no longer true. In contrast to a `while` loop, the statement of a `do` loop is executed at least once.

The `break` statement exits the innermost enclosing `while`, `do`, `for`, or `switch` statement (not counting `if` or block statements).

Any statement (including `if` and block statements) can be tagged with a label:

```
label: statement
```

The labeled `break` statement

```
break label;
```

exits the labeled statement.

The `continue` statement skips past the end of the *statement* part of a `while`, `do`, or `for` loop. In the case of the `while` or `do` loop, the loop *condition* is executed next. In the case of the `for` loop, the *updateExpressions* are executed next.

The labeled `continue` statement

```
continue label;
```

skips past the end of the *statement* part of a `while`, `do`, or `for` loop with the matching label.

Exceptions

The `throw` statement

> throw *expression*;

abruptly terminates the current method and resumes control inside the innermost matching `catch` clause of a surrounding `try` block. The *expression* must evaluate to a reference to an object of a subclass of `Throwable`.

The try statement has the form

```
try tryBlock
[catch (ExceptionType₁ exceptionVariable₁) catchBlock₁
catch (ExceptionType₂ exceptionVariable₂) catchBlock₂
. . .]
[finally finallyBlock]
```

- The try statement must have at least one `catch` or `finally` clause.
- All blocks are block statements in the usual sense, that is, { . . . }-delimited statement sequences.

The statements in the *tryBlock* are executed. If one of them throws an exception object whose type is a subtype of one of the types in the `catch` clauses, then its *catchBlock* is executed. As soon as the catch block is entered, that exception is handled.

If the *tryBlock* exits for any reason at all (because all of its statements executed completely; because one of its statements was a `break`, `continue`, or `return` statement; or because an exception was thrown), then the *finallyBlock* is executed.

If the *finallyBlock* was entered because an exception was thrown and it itself throws another exception, then that exception masks the prior exception.

Packages

A class can be placed in a package by putting the package declaration

> package *packageName*;

as the first non-`import` declaration of the source file.

A package name has the form

> *identifier₁.identifier₂*. . . .

For example,

```
java.util
com.horstmann.bigjava
```

A fully qualified name of a class is

> *packageName.ClassName*

Classes can always be referenced by their fully qualified class names. However, this can be inconvenient. For that reason, you can reference imported classes by just their *ClassName*. All classes in the package `java.lang` and in the package of the current source file are always imported. To import additional classes, use an `import` directive

> import *packageName.ClassName*;

or

```
import packageName.*;
```

The second version imports all classes in the package.

Generic Types and Methods

A generic type is declared with one or more *type parameters*, placed after the type name:

modifiers class|interface *TypeName*<*typeParameter₁*, *typeParameter₂*, . . .>

Similarly, a generic method is declared with one or more type parameters, placed *before* the method's return type:

modifiers <*typeParameter₁*, *typeParameter₂*, . . .> *returnType methodName*

Each type parameter has the form

typeParameterName [extends *bound₁* & *bound₂* & . . .]

For example,

```
public class BinarySearchTree<T extends Comparable>
public interface Comparator<T>
public <T extends Comparable & Cloneable> T cloneMin(T[] values)
```

Type parameters can be used in the definition of the generic type or method as if they were regular types. They can be replaced with any types that match the bounds. For example, the BinarySearchTree<String> type substitutes the String type for the type parameter T.

Type parameters can also be replaced with *wildcard types*. A wildcard type has the form

? [super|extends *Type*]

It denotes a specific type that is unknown at the time that is declared. For example, Comparable<? super Rectangle> is a type Comparable<S> for a specific type S, which can be Rectangle or a supertype such as RectangularShape or Shape.

Comments

There are three kinds of comments:

```
/* comment */
// one-line-comment
/** documentationComment */
```

The one-line comment extends to the end of the line. The other comments can span multiple lines and extend to the */ delimiter.

Documentation comments are further explained in Appendix H.

HTML
Summary

A Brief Introduction to HTML

A web page is written in a language called HTML (Hypertext Markup Language). Like Java code, HTML code is made up of text that follows certain strict rules. When a browser reads a web page, the browser *interprets* the code and *renders* the page, displaying characters, fonts, paragraphs, tables, and images.

HTML files are made up of text and *tags* that tell the browser how to render the text. Nowadays, there are dozens of HTML tags—see Table 1 for a summary of the most important tags. Fortunately, you need only a few to get started. Most HTML tags come in pairs consisting of an opening tag and a closing tag, and each pair applies to the text between the two tags. Here is a typical example of a tag pair:

```
Java is an <i>object-oriented</i> programming language.
```

The tag pair `<i>  </i>` directs the browser to display the text inside the tags in *italics*:

Java is an *object-oriented* programming language.

The closing tag is just like the opening tag, but it is prefixed by a slash (/). For example, bold-faced text is delimited by `<b>  </b>`, and a paragraph is delimited by the tag pair `<p>  </p>`.

```
<p><b>Java</b> is an <i>object-oriented</i> programming language.</p>
```

The result is the paragraph

Java is an *object-oriented* programming language.

Another common construct is a bulleted list. For example:

Java is

- object-oriented
- safe
- platform-independent

Here is the HTML code to display it:

```
<p>Java is</p>
<ul><li>object-oriented</li>
<li>safe</li>
<li>platform-independent</li></ul>
```

Each item in the list is delimited by `<li>  </li>` (for "list item"), and the whole list is surrounded by `<ul>  </ul>` (for "unnumbered list").

Table 1   Selected HTML Tags

Tag	Meaning	Children	Commonly Used Attributes
html	HTML document	head, body	
head	Head of an HTML document	title	
title	Title of an HTML document		
body	Body of an HTML document		
h1 . . . h6	Heading level 1 . . . 6		
p	Paragraph		
ul	Unnumbered list	li	
ol	Ordered list	li	
dl	Definition list	dt, dd	
li	List item		
dt	Term to be defined		
dd	Definition data		
table	Table	tr	
tr	Table row	th, td	
th	Table header cell		
td	Table cell data		
a	Anchor		href, name
img	Image		src, width, height
applet	Applet		code, width, height
pre	Preformatted text		
hr	Horizontal rule		
br	Line break		
i or em	Italic		
b or strong	Bold		
tt or code	Typewriter or code font		
s or strike	Strike through		
u	Underline		
super	Superscript		

Tang 1	Selected HTML Tags, continued		

Tag	Meaning	Children	Commonly Used Attributes
sub	Subscript		
form	Form		action, method
input	Input field		type, name, value, size, checked
select	Combo box style selector	option	name
option	Option for selection		
textarea	Multiline text area		name, rows, cols

As in Java code, you can freely use white space (spaces and line breaks) in HTML code to make it easier to read. For example, you can lay out the code for a list as follows:

```
<p>Java is</p>
<ul>
<li>object-oriented</li>
<li>safe</li>
<li>platform-independent</li>
</ul>
```

The browser ignores the white space.

If you omit a tag (such as a </li>), most browsers will try to guess the missing tags—sometimes with differing results. It is always best to include all tags.

You can include images in your web pages with the img tag. In its simplest form, an image tag has the form

```
<img src="hamster.jpeg"/>
```

This code tells the browser to load and display the image that is stored in the file hamster.jpeg. This is a slightly different type of tag. Rather than text inside a tag pair <img> </img>, the img tag uses an attribute to specify a file name. Attributes have names and values. For example, the src attribute has the value "hamster.jpeg". Table 2 contains commonly used attributes.

It is considered polite to use several additional attributes with the img tag, namely the *image size* and an *alternate description*:

```
<img src="hamster.jpeg" width="640" height="480"
alt="A photo of Harry, the Horrible Hamster"/>
```

These additional attributes help the browser lay out the page and display a temporary description while gathering the data for the image (or if the browser cannot display images, such as a voice browser for blind users). Users with slow network connections really appreciate this extra effort.

Because there is no closing </img> tag, we put a slash / before the closing >. This is not a requirement of HTML, but it is a requirement of the emerging XHTML standard, the XML-based successor to HTML. See www.w3c.org/TR/xhtml1 for more information on XHTML.

	Table 2 Selected HTML Attributes	
Attribute	Description	Commonly Contained in Element
name	Name of form element or anchor	input, select, textarea, a
href	Hyperlink reference	a
src	Source (as of an image)	img
code	Applet code	applet
width, height	Width, height of image or applet	img, applet
rows, cols	Rows, columns of text area	textarea
type	Type of input field, such as text, password, checkbox, radio, submit, hidden	input
value	Value of input field, or label of submit button	input
size	Size of text field	input
checked	Check radio button or checkbox	input
action	URL of form action	form
method	GET or POST	form

The most important tag in web pages is the `<a> </a>` tag pair, which makes the enclosed text into a *link* to another file. The links between web pages are what makes the Web into, well, a web. The browser displays a link in a special way (for example, underlined text in blue color). Here is the code for a typical link:

```
<a href="http://java.sun.com">Java</a> is an object-oriented
programming language.
```

When the viewer of the web page clicks on the word <u>Java</u>, the browser loads the web page located at `java.sun.com`. (The value of the `href` attribute is a *Universal Resource Locator* (URL), which tells the browser where to go. The prefix `http:`, for *Hypertext Transfer Protocol*, tells the browser to fetch the file as a web page. Other protocols allow different actions, such as `ftp:` to download a file, `mailto:` to send e-mail to a user, and `file:` to view a local HTML file.)

Finally, the `applet` tag includes an applet in a web page. To display an applet, you need first to write and compile a Java file to generate the applet code—see Special Topic 2.2. Then you tell the browser how to find the code for the applet and how much screen space to reserve for the applet. Here is an example:

```
<applet code="HamsterApplet.class" width="400" height="300">An
animation of Harry, the Horrible Hamster</applet>
```

The text between the `<applet>` and `</applet>` tags is only displayed in lieu of the actual applet by browsers that can't run Java applets.

Table 3	Selected HTML Entities	
Entity	Description	Appearance
&lt;	Less than	<
&gt;	Greater than	>
&amp;	Ampersand	&
&quot;	Quotation mark	"
	Nonbreaking space	
&copy;	Copyright symbol	©

You have noticed that tags are enclosed in angle brackets (less-than and greater-than signs). What if you want to show an angle bracket on a web page? HTML provides the notations < and > to produce the < and > symbols, respectively. Other codes of this kind produce symbols such as accented letters. The & (ampersand) symbol introduces these codes; to get that symbol itself, use &. See Table 3 for a summary.

You may already have created web pages with a web editor that works like a word processor, giving you a WYSIWYG (what you see is what you get) view of your web page. But the tags are still there, and you can see them when you load the HTML file into a text editor. If you are comfortable using a WYSIWYG web editor, and if your editor can insert applet tags, you don't need to memorize HTML tags at all. But many programmers and professional web designers prefer to work directly with the tags at least some of the time, because it gives them more control over their pages.

Tool Summary

In this summary, we use a monospaced font for actual commands such as javac. An italic font denotes descriptions of tool command components such as *options*. Items enclosed in brackets [...] are optional. Items separated by vertical bars | are alternatives. Do not include the brackets or vertical bars when typing the commands.

The Java Compiler

javac [*options*] *sourceFile*$_1$|@*fileList*$_1$ *sourceFile*$_2$|@*fileList*$_2$ . . .

A file list is a text file that contains one file name per line. For example,

File Greeting.list

```
1  Greeting.java
2  GreetingTest.java
```

Then you can compile all files with the command

javac @Greeting.list

The Java compiler options are summarized in Table 1.

Table 1 Common Compiler Options	
Option	**Description**
-classpath *locations* or -cp *locations*	The compiler is to look for classes on this path, overriding the CLASSPATH environment variable. If neither is specified, the current directory is used. Each *location* is a directory, JAR file, or ZIP file. Locations are separated by a platform-dependent separator (: on Unix, ; on Windows).
-sourcepath *locations*	The compiler is to look for source files on this path. If not specified, source files are searched in the class path.
-d *directory*	The compiler places files into the specified directory.
-g	Generate debugging information.
-verbose	Include information about all classes that are being compiled (useful for troubleshooting).
-deprecation	Give detailed information about the usage of deprecated messages.
-Xlint:*errorType*	Carry out additional error checking. If you get warnings about unchecked conversions, compile with the -Xlint:unchecked option.

The Java Virtual Machine Launcher

The following command loads the given class and starts its `main` method, passing it an array containing the provided command line arguments.

java [*options*] *ClassName* [*argument₁ argument₂* . . .]

The following command loads the main class of the given JAR file and starts its `main` method, passing it an array containing the provided command line arguments.

java [*options*] -jar *jarFileName* [*argument₁ argument₂* . . .]

The Java virtual machine options are summarized in Table 2.

Table 2	Common Virtual Machine Launcher Options
Option	**Description**
-classpath *locations* or -cp *locations*	Look for classes on this path, overriding the CLASSPATH environment variable. If neither is specified, the current directory is used. Each *location* is a directory, JAR file, or ZIP file. Locations are separated by a platform-dependent separator (: on Unix, ; on Windows).
-verbose	Trace class loading
-D*property=value*	Set a system property that you can retrieve with the System.getProperties method.

The Applet Viewer

appletviewer *url₁ url₂* . . .

The *urls* are searched for applets, and each applet is displayed in a separate window. An applet should be specified as an HTML tag of the form

```
<applet
   code=appletClassFile
   width=pixels
   height=pixels
   [codebase=relativeURL]>
   <param name=parameterName₁ value=parameterValue₁>
   <param name=parameterName₂ value=parameterValue₂>
   . . .
</applet>
```

The codebase parameter is an URL that is relative to the URL of the HTML file containing the applet or object tag.

The JAR Tool

To combine one or more files into a JAR (Java Archive) file, use the command

    jar cvf *jarFile* *file₁* *file₂* . . .

The resulting JAR file can be included in a class path.

To build a program that can be launched with java -jar, you must create a *manifest file*, such as

File myprog.mf

```
1   Main-Class: com/horstmann/MyProg
```

The manifest must specify the path name of the class file that launches the application, but with the .class extension removed. Then build the JAR file as

    jar cvfm *jarFile* *manifestFile* *file₁* *file₂* . . .

You can also use JAR as a replacement for a ZIP utility, simply to compress and bundle a set of files for any purpose. Then you may want to suppress the generation of the JAR manifest, with the command

    jar cvfM *jarFile* *file₁* *file₂* . . .

To extract the contents of a JAR file into the current directory, use

    jar xvf *jarFile*

To see the files contained in a JAR file without extracting the files, use

    jar tvf *jarFile*

javadoc Summary

Setting Documentation Comments in Source

A documentation comment is delimited by /** and */. You can comment

- Classes
- Methods
- Instance variables

Each comment is placed *immediately above* the feature it documents.

Each /** . . . */ documentation comment contains introductory text followed by tagged documentation. A tag starts with an @ character, such as @author or @param. Tags are summarized in Table 1. The *first sentence* of the introductory text should be a summary statement. The javadoc utility automatically generates summary pages that extract these sentences.

Table 1 Common javadoc Tags

Tag	Description
@param *parameter explanation*	A parameter of a method. Use a separate tag for each parameter.
@return *explanation*	The return value of a method.
@throws *exceptionType explanation*	An exception that a method may throw. Use a separate tag for each exception.
@deprecated	A feature that remains for compatibility but that should not be used for new code.
@see *packageName.ClassName* @see *packageName.ClassName* *#methodName(Type$_1$, Type$_2$, . . .)* @see *packageName.ClassName#variableName*	A reference to a related documentation entry.
@author	The author of a class or interface. Use a separate tag for each author.
@version	The version of a class or interface.

You can use HTML tags such as em for emphasis, code for a monospaced font, img for images, ul for bulleted lists, and so on.

Here is a typical example. The summary sentence (in color) will be included with the method summary.

```
/**
    Withdraws money from the bank account. Increments the
    transaction count.
    @param amount  the amount to withdraw
    @return  the balance after the withdrawal
    @throws IllegalArgumentException  if the balance is not sufficient
*/
public double withdraw(double amount)
{
    if (balance - amount < minimumBalance)
        throw new IllegalArgumentException();
    balance = balance - amount;
    transactions++;
    return balance;
}
```

Generating Documentation from Commented Source

To extract the comments, run the javadoc program:

javadoc [*options*] *sourceFile*$_1$| *packageName*$_1$| @*fileList*$_1$
    sourceFile$_2$| *packageName*$_2$| @*fileList*$_2$ . . .

See the documentation of the javac command in Appendix F for an explanation of file lists. Commonly used options are summarized in Table 2.

To document all files in the current directory, use (all on one line)

javadoc -link http://java.sun.com/javase/7/docs/api
    -d docdir *.java

Table 2 Common javadoc Command Line Options	
Option	**Description**
-link *URL*	Link to another set of Javadoc files. You should include a link to the standard library documentation, either locally or at http://java.sun.com/javase/7/docs/api .
-d *directory*	Store the output in *directory*. This is a useful option, because it keeps your current directory from being cluttered up with javadoc files.
-classpath *locations*	Look for classes on the specified paths, overriding the CLASSPATH environment variable. If neither is specified, the current directory is used. Each *location* is a directory, JAR file, or ZIP file. Locations are separated by a platform-dependent separator (: Unix, ; Windows).
-sourcepath *locations*	Look for source files on the specified paths. If not specified, source files are searched in the class path.
-author, -version	Include author, version information in the documentation. This information is omitted by default.

Number Systems

Binary Numbers

Decimal notation represents numbers as powers of 10, for example

$$1729_{\text{decimal}} = 1 \times 10^3 + 7 \times 10^2 + 2 \times 10^1 + 9 \times 10^0$$

There is no particular reason for the choice of 10, except that several historical number systems were derived from people's counting with their fingers. Other number systems, using a base of 12, 20, or 60, have been used by various cultures throughout human history. However, computers use a number system with base 2 because it is far easier to build electronic components that work with two values, which can be represented by a current being either off or on, than it would be to represent 10 different values of electrical signals. A number written in base 2 is also called a *binary* number.

For example,

$$1101_{\text{binary}} = 1 \times 2^3 + 1 \times 2^2 + 0 \times 2^1 + 1 \times 2^0 = 8 + 4 + 1 = 13$$

For digits after the "decimal" point, use negative powers of 2.

$$1.101_{\text{binary}} = 1 \times 2^0 + 1 \times 2^{-1} + 0 \times 2^{-2} + 1 \times 2^{-3}$$
$$= 1 + \frac{1}{2} + \frac{1}{8}$$
$$= 1 + 0.5 + 0.125 = 1.625$$

In general, to convert a binary number into its decimal equivalent, simply evaluate the powers of 2 corresponding to digits with value 1, and add them up. Table 1 shows the first powers of 2.

To convert a decimal integer into its binary equivalent, keep dividing the integer by 2, keeping track of the remainders. Stop when the number is 0. Then write the remainders as a binary number, starting with the *last* one.

For example,

$$100 \div 2 = 50 \text{ remainder } 0$$
$$50 \div 2 = 25 \text{ remainder } 0$$
$$25 \div 2 = 12 \text{ remainder } 1$$
$$12 \div 2 = 6 \text{ remainder } 0$$
$$6 \div 2 = 3 \text{ remainder } 0$$
$$3 \div 2 = 1 \text{ remainder } 1$$
$$1 \div 2 = 0 \text{ remainder } 1$$

Table 1 Powers of Two	
Power	**Decimal Value**
2^0	1
2^1	2
2^2	4
2^3	8
2^4	16
2^5	32
2^6	64
2^7	128
2^8	256
2^9	512
2^{10}	1,024
2^{11}	2,048
2^{12}	4,096
2^{13}	8,192
2^{14}	16,384
2^{15}	32,768
2^{16}	65,536

Therefore, $100_{\text{decimal}} = 1100100_{\text{binary}}$.

Conversely, to convert a fractional number less than 1 to its binary format, keep multiplying by 2. If the result is greater than 1, subtract 1. Stop when the number is 0. Then use the digits before the decimal points as the binary digits of the fractional part, starting with the *first* one. For example,

$$0.35 \cdot 2 = 0.7$$
$$0.7 \cdot 2 = 1.4$$
$$0.4 \cdot 2 = 0.8$$
$$0.8 \cdot 2 = 1.6$$
$$0.6 \cdot 2 = 1.2$$
$$0.2 \cdot 2 = 0.4$$

Here the pattern repeats. That is, the binary representation of 0.35 is 0.01 0110 0110 0110 . . .

To convert any floating-point number into binary, convert the whole part and the fractional part separately.

Two's Complement Integers

To represent negative integers, there are two common representations, called "signed magnitude" and "two's complement". Signed magnitude notation is simple: use the leftmost bit for the sign (0 = positive, 1 = negative). For example, when using 8-bit numbers,

$$-13 = 10001101_{\text{signed magnitude}}$$

However, building circuitry for adding numbers gets a bit more complicated when one has to take a sign bit into account. The two's complement representation solves this problem.

To form the two's complement of a number,

- Flip all bits.
- Then add 1.

For example, to compute −13 as an 8-bit value, first flip all bits of 00001101 to get 11110010. Then add 1:

$$-13 = 11110011_{\text{two's complement}}$$

Now no special circuitry is required for adding two numbers. Simply follow the normal rule for addition, with a carry to the next position if the sum of the digits and the prior carry is 2 or 3. For example,

```
       1 1111 111
+13      0000 1101
-13      1111 0011
       ─────────────
       1 0000 0000
```

But only the last 8 bits count, so +13 and −13 add up to 0, as they should.

In particular, −1 has two's complement representation 1111 . . . 1111, with all bits set.

The leftmost bit of a two's complement number is 0 if the number is positive or zero, 1 if it is negative.

Two's complement notation with a given number of bits can represent one more negative number than positive numbers. For example, the 8-bit two's complement numbers range from −128 to +127.

This phenomenon is an occasional cause for a programming error. For example, consider the following code:

```
byte b = . . . .;
if (b < 0) b = (byte) -b;
```

This code does not guarantee that b is nonnegative afterwards. If b happens to be −128, then computing its negative again yields −128. (Try it out—take 10000000, flip all bits, and add 1.)

IEEE Floating-Point Numbers

The Institute for Electrical and Electronics Engineering (IEEE) defines standards for floating-point representations in the IEEE-754 standard. Figure 1 shows how single-precision (float) and double-precision (double) values are decomposed into

- A sign bit
- An exponent
- A mantissa

Floating-point numbers use scientific notation, in which a number is represented as

$$b_0.b_1b_2b_3\ldots \times 2^e$$

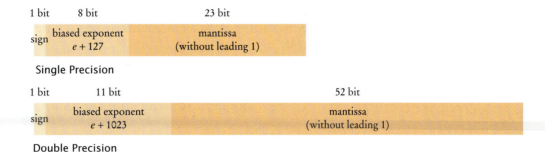

Single Precision

Double Precision

Figure 1   IEEE Floating-Point Representation

In this representation, e is the exponent, and the digits $b_0.b_1b_2b_3\ldots$ form the mantissa. The *normalized* representation is the one where $b_0 \neq 0$. For example,

$$100_{\text{decimal}} = 1100100_{\text{binary}} = 1.100100_{\text{binary}} \times 2^6$$

Because in the binary number system the first bit of a normalized representation must be 1, it is not actually stored in the mantissa. Therefore, you always need to add it on to represent the actual value. For example, the mantissa 1.100100 is stored as 100100.

The exponent part of the IEEE representation uses neither signed magnitude nor two's complement representation. Instead, a bias is added to the actual exponent. The bias is 127 for single-precision numbers, 1023 for double-precision numbers. For example, the exponent $e = 6$ would be stored as 133 in a single-precision number.

Thus,

$$100_{\text{decimal}} = \boxed{0\ 10000101\ 10010000000000000000000}\ {}_{\text{single-precision IEEE}}$$

In addition, there are several special values. Among them are:

- *Zero:* biased exponent = 0, mantissa = 0.
- *Infinity:* biased exponent = 11...1, mantissa = ±0.
- *NaN* (not a number): biased exponent = 11...1, mantissa ≠ ±0.

Hexadecimal Numbers

Because binary numbers can be hard to read for humans, programmers often use the hexadecimal number system, with base 16. The digits are denoted as 0, 1, ..., 9, A, B, C, D, E, F (see Table 2).

Four binary digits correspond to one hexadecimal digit. That makes it easy to convert between binary and hexadecimal values. For example,

$$11\,|\,1011\,|\,0001_{\text{binary}} = 3B1_{\text{hexadecimal}}$$

In Java, hexadecimal numbers are used for Unicode character values, such as \u03B1 (the Greek lowercase letter alpha). Hexadecimal integers are denoted with a 0x prefix, such as 0x3B1.

Table 2	Hexadecimal Digits	
Hexadecimal	**Decimal**	**Binary**
0	0	0000
1	1	0001
2	2	0010
3	3	0011
4	4	0100
5	5	0101
6	6	0110
7	7	0111
8	8	1000
9	9	1001
A	10	1010
B	11	1011
C	12	1100
D	13	1101
E	14	1110
F	15	1111

Bit and Shift Operations

There are four bit operations in Java: the unary negation (~) and the binary and (&), or (|), and exclusive or (^), often called xor.

Tables 1 and 2 show the truth tables for the bit operations in Java. When a bit operation is applied to integer values, the operation is carried out on corresponding bits.

Table 1	The Unary Negation Operation
a	~a
0	1
1	0

Table 2	The Binary And, Or, and Xor Operations			
a	b	a & b	a | b	a ^ b
0	0	0	0	0
0	1	0	1	1
1	0	0	1	1
1	1	1	1	0

For example, suppose we want to compute 46 & 13. First convert both values to binary. $46_{decimal} = 101110_{binary}$ (actually 00000000000000000000000000101110 as a 32-bit integer), and $13_{decimal} = 1101_{binary}$. Now combine corresponding bits:

```
    0.....0101110
&   0.....0001101
    ─────────────
    0.....0001100
```

The answer is $1100_{binary} = 12_{decimal}$.

You sometimes see the | operator being used to combine two bit patterns. For example, Font.BOLD is the value 1, Font.ITALIC is 2. The binary or combination Font.BOLD | Font.ITALIC has both the bold and the italic bit set:

$$
\begin{array}{r}
0.\,.\,.\,.\,.\,0000001 \\
| \quad 0.\,.\,.\,.\,.\,0000010 \\
\hline
0.\,.\,.\,.\,.\,0000011
\end{array}
$$

Don't confuse the & and | bit operators with the && and || operators. The latter work only on boolean values, not on bits of numbers.

Besides the operations that work on individual bits, there are three *shift* operations that take the bit pattern of a number and shift it to the left or right by a given number of positions. There are three shift operations: shift left (<<), right shift with sign extension (>>), and right shift with zero extension (>>>).

The left shift moves all bits to the left, filling in zeroes in the least significant bits. Shifting to the left by n bits yields the same result as multiplication by 2^n. The right shift with sign extension moves all bits to the right, propagating the sign bit. Therefore, the result is the same as integer division by 2^n, both for positive and negative values. Finally, the right shift with zero extension moves all bits to the right, filling in zeroes in the most significant bits. (See Figure 1.)

Note that the right-hand-side value of the shift operators is reduced modulo 32 (for int values) or 64 (for long values) to determine the actual number of bits to shift.

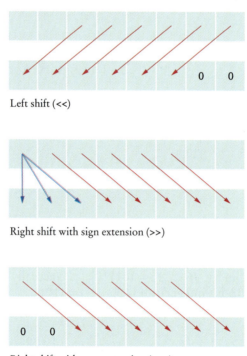

Left shift (<<)

Right shift with sign extension (>>)

Right shift with zero extension (>>>)

Figure 1   The Shift Operations

For example, `1 << 35` is the same as `1 << 3`. Actually shifting 1 by 35 bits to the left would make no sense—the result would be 0.

The expression

```
1 << n
```

yields a bit pattern in which the nth bit is set (where the 0 bit is the least significant bit).

To set the nth bit of a number, carry out the operation

```
x = x | 1 << n
```

To check whether the nth bit is set, execute the test

```
if ((x & 1 << n) != 0) . . .
```

Note that the parentheses around the & are required—the & operator has a lower precedence than the relational operators.

UML
Summary

In this book, we use a very restricted subset of the UML notation. This appendix lists the components of the subset.

For a complete discussion of the UML notation, see *The Unified Modeling Language User Guide,* Grady Booch, James Rumbaugh, and Ivar Jacobson (Addison-Wesley, 2005, 1999).

CRC Cards

CRC cards are used to describe in an informal fashion the responsibilities and collaborators for a class. Figure 1 shows a typical CRC card.

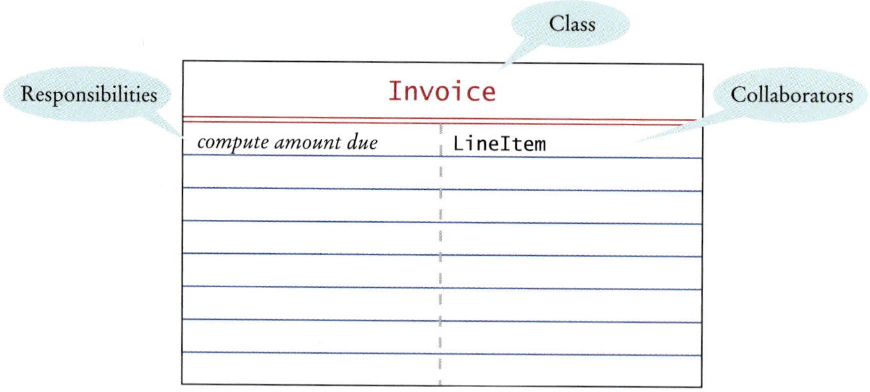

Figure 1   Typical CRC Card

UML Diagrams

Figure 2 shows the UML notation for classes and interfaces. You can optionally supply attributes and methods in a class diagram, as in Figure 3.

Figure 2
UML Symbols for Classes and Interfaces

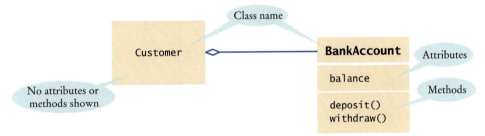

Figure 3   Attributes and Methods in a Class Diagram

Figure 4   An Aggregation Relationship with Multiplicities

Table 1 shows the arrows used to indicate relationships between classes. Multiplicity can be indicated in a diagram, as in Figure 4.

Table 1 UML Relationship Symbols			
Relationship	Symbol	Line Style	Arrow Tip
Inheritance	——————▷	Solid	Triangle
Interface Implementation	- - - - - - -▷	Dotted	Triangle
Aggregation	◇———————	Solid	Diamond
Dependency	- - - - - - ->	Dotted	Open

Dependencies between objects are described by a dependency diagram. Figure 5 is a typical example.

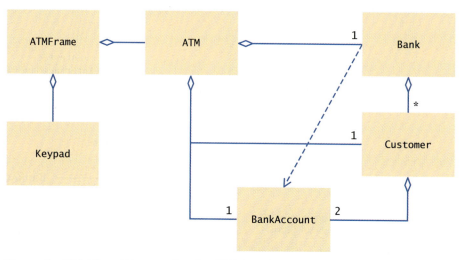

Figure 5 UML Class Diagram for the ATM Simulation

State diagrams are used when an object goes through a discrete set of states that affects its behavior (see Figure 6).

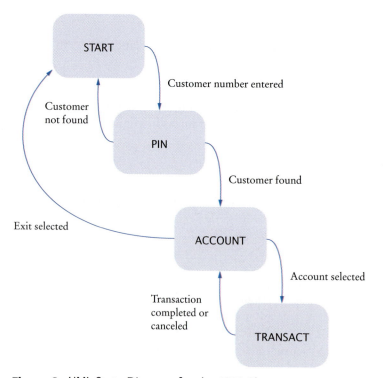

Figure 6 UML State Diagram for the ATM Class

Java Language Coding Guidelines

Introduction

This coding style guide is a simplified version of one that has been used with good success both in industrial practice and for college courses.

A style guide is a set of mandatory requirements for layout and formatting. Uniform style makes it easier for you to read code from your instructor and classmates. You will really appreciate that if you do a team project. It is also easier for your instructor and your grader to grasp the essence of your programs quickly.

A style guide makes you a more productive programmer because it *reduces gratuitous choice*. If you don't have to make choices about trivial matters, you can spend your energy on the solution of real problems.

In these guidelines, several constructs are plainly outlawed. That doesn't mean that programmers using them are evil or incompetent. It does mean that the constructs are not essential and can be expressed just as well or even better with other language constructs.

If you already have programming experience, in Java or another language, you may be initially uncomfortable at giving up some fond habits. However, it is a sign of professionalism to set aside personal preferences in minor matters and to compromise for the benefit of your group.

These guidelines are necessarily somewhat dull. They also mention features that you may not yet have seen in class. Here are the most important highlights:

- Tabs are set every three spaces.
- Variable and method names are lowercase, with occasional upperCase characters in the middle.
- Class names start with an Uppercase letter.
- Constant names are UPPERCASE, with an occasional UNDER_SCORE.
- There are spaces after keywords and surrounding binary operators.
- Braces must line up horizontally or vertically.
- No magic numbers may be used.
- Every method, except for main and overridden methods, must have a comment.
- At most 30 lines of code may be used per method.
- No continue or break is allowed.
- All non-final variables must be private.

Note to the instructor: Of course, many programmers and organizations have strong feelings about coding style. If this style guide is incompatible with your own preferences or with local custom, please feel free to modify it. For that purpose, this coding style guide is available in electronic form at www.wiley.com/college/horstmann and in the WileyPLUS course for this book.

Source Files

Each Java program is a collection of one or more source files. The executable program is obtained by compiling these files. Organize the material in each file as follows:

- `package` statement, if appropriate
- `import` statements
- A comment explaining the purpose of this file
- A `public` class
- Other classes, if appropriate

The comment explaining the purpose of this file should be in the format recognized by the `javadoc` utility. Start with a `/**`, and use the `@author` and `@version` tags:

```
/**
    COPYRIGHT (C) 2010 Harry Morgan. All Rights Reserved.
    Classes to manipulate widgets.
    Solves CS101 homework assignment #3
    @author  Harry Morgan
    @version 1.01 2010-02-15
*/
```

Classes

Each class should be preceded by a class comment explaining the purpose of the class.

First list all public features, then all private features.

Within the public and private sections, use the following order:

1. Instance variables
2. Static variables
3. Constructors
4. Instance methods
5. Static methods
6. Inner classes

Leave a blank line after every method.

All non-`final` variables must be private. (However, instance variables of a private inner class may be public.) Methods and final variables can be either public or private, as appropriate.

All features must be tagged `public` or `private`. Do not use the default visibility (that is, package visibility) or the `protected` attribute.

Avoid static variables (except `final` ones) whenever possible. In the rare instance that you need static variables, you are permitted one static variable per class.

Methods

Every method (except for `main`) starts with a comment in `javadoc` format.

```
/**
   Convert calendar date into Julian day.
   Note: This algorithm is from Press et al., Numerical Recipes
   in C, 2nd ed., Cambridge University Press, 1992.
   @param day  day of the date to be converted
   @param month  month of the date to be converted
   @param year  year of the date to be converted
   @return  the Julian day number that begins at noon of the
   given calendar date.
*/
public static int getJulianDayNumber(int day, int month, int year)
{
   . . .
}
```

Parameter names must be explicit, especially if they are integers or Boolean:

```
public Employee remove(int d, double s)
   // Huh?
public Employee remove(int department, double severancePay)
   // OK
```

Methods must have at most 30 lines of code. The method signature, comments, blank lines, and lines containing only braces are not included in this count. This rule forces you to break up complex computations into separate methods.

Variables and Constants

Do not define all variables at the beginning of a block:

```
{
   double xold; // Don't
   double xnew;
   boolean done;
   . . .
}
```

Define each variable just before it is used for the first time:

```
{
   . . .
   double xold = Integer.parseInt(input);
   boolean done = false;
   while (!done)
   {
      double xnew = (xold + a / xold) / 2;
      . . .
   }
   . . .
}
```

Do not define two variables on the same line:

```java
int dimes = 0, nickels = 0; // Don't
```

Instead, use two separate definitions:

```java
int dimes = 0; // OK
int nickels = 0;
```

In Java, constants must be defined with the keyword `final`. If the constant is used by multiple methods, declare it as `static final`. It is a good idea to define static final variables as `private` if no other class has an interest in them.

Do not use *magic numbers!* A magic number is a numeric constant embedded in code, without a constant definition. Any number except −1, 0, 1, and 2 is considered magic:

```java
if (p.getX() < 300) // Don't
```

Use `final` variables instead:

```java
final double WINDOW_WIDTH = 300;
. . .
if (p.getX() < WINDOW_WIDTH) // OK
```

Even the most reasonable cosmic constant is going to change one day. You think there are 365 days per year? Your customers on Mars are going to be pretty unhappy about your silly prejudice. Make a constant

```java
public static final int DAYS_PER_YEAR = 365;
```

so that you can easily produce a Martian version without trying to find all the 365s, 364s, 366s, 367s, and so on, in your code.

When declaring array variables, group the `[]` with the type, not the variable.

```java
int[] values; // OK
int values[]; // Ugh—this is an ugly holdover from C
```

When using collections, use type parameters and not "raw" types.

```java
ArrayList<String> names = new ArrayList<String>(); // OK
ArrayList names = new ArrayList(); // Not OK
```

Control Flow

The `if` Statement

Avoid the "if . . . if . . . else" trap. The code

```java
if ( . . . )
   if ( . . . ) . . .;
else . . .;
```

will not do what the indentation level suggests, and it can take hours to find such a bug. Always use an extra pair of { . . . } when dealing with "if . . . if . . . else":

```java
if ( . . . )
{
   if ( . . . ) . . .;
} // { . . . } are necessary
else . . .;
```

```
if ( . . . )
{
   if ( . . . ) . . .;
   else . . .;
} // { . . . } not necessary, but they keep you out of trouble
```

The for Statement

Use `for` loops only when a variable runs from somewhere to somewhere with some constant increment/decrement:

```
for (int i = 0; i < a.length; i++)
   System.out.println(a[i]);
```

Or, even better, use the "for each" loop:

```
for (int e : a)
   System.out.println(e);
```

Do not use the `for` loop for weird constructs such as

```
for (a = a / 2; count < ITERATIONS; System.out.println(xnew))
   // Don't
```

Make such a loop into a `while` loop. That way, the sequence of instructions is much clearer.

```
a = a / 2;
while (count < ITERATIONS) // OK
{
   . . .
   System.out.println(xnew);
}
```

Nonlinear Control Flow

Avoid the `switch` statement, because it is easy to fall through accidentally to an unwanted case. Use `if/else` instead.

Avoid the `break` or `continue` statements. Use another `boolean` variable to control the execution flow.

Exceptions

Do not tag a method with an overly general exception specification:

```
Widget readWidget(Reader in) throws Exception // Bad
```

Instead, specifically declare any checked exceptions that your method may throw:

```
Widget readWidget(Reader in)
      throws IOException, MalformedWidgetException // Good
```

Do not "squelch" exceptions:

```
try
{
   double price = in.readDouble();
}
catch (Exception e)
{ } // Bad
```

Beginners often make this mistake "to keep the compiler happy". If the current method is not appropriate for handling the exception, simply use a `throws` specification and let one of its callers handle it.

Lexical Issues

Naming Conventions

The following rules specify when to use upper- and lowercase letters in identifier names.

- All variable and method names are in lowercase (maybe with an occasional upperCase in the middle); for example, `firstPlayer`.
- All constants are in uppercase (maybe with an occasional UNDER_SCORE); for example, `CLOCK_RADIUS`.
- All class and interface names start with uppercase and are followed by lowercase letters (maybe with an occasional UpperCase letter); for example, `BankTeller`.
- Generic type variables are in uppercase, usually a single letter.

Names must be reasonably long and descriptive. Use `firstPlayer` instead of `fp`. No drppng f vwls. Local variables that are fairly routine can be short (`ch`, `i`) as long as they are really just boring holders for an input character, a loop counter, and so on. Also, do not use `ctr`, `c`, `cntr`, `cnt`, `c2` for variables in your method. Surely these variables all have specific purposes and can be named to remind the reader of them (for example, `current`, `next`, `previous`, `result`, . . .). However, it is customary to use single-letter names, such as `T` or `E` for generic types.

Indentation and White Space

Use tab stops every three columns. That means you will need to change the tab stop setting in your editor!

Use blank lines freely to separate parts of a method that are logically distinct.

Use a blank space around every binary operator:

```
x1 = (-b - Math.sqrt(b * b - 4 * a * c)) / (2 * a);
// Good

x1=(-b-Math.sqrt(b*b-4*a*c))/(2*a);
// Bad
```

Leave a blank space after (and not before) each comma or semicolon. Do not leave a space before or after a parenthesis or bracket in an expression. Leave spaces around the (. . .) part of an `if`, `while`, `for`, or `catch` statement.

```
if (x == 0) y = 0;

f(a, b[i]);
```

Every line must fit in 80 columns. If you must break a statement, add an indentation level for the continuation:

```
a[n] = ..............................................
          + .................;
```

Start the indented line with an operator (if possible).

If the condition in an `if` or `while` statement must be broken, be sure to brace the body in, even if it consists of only one statement:

```
if ( ......................................................
      && .................
      || .......... )
{
    . . .
}
```

If it weren't for the braces, it would be hard to separate the continuation of the condition visually from the statement to be executed.

Braces

Opening and closing braces must line up, either horizontally or vertically:

```
while (i < n) { System.out.println(a[i]); i++; }

while (i < n)
{
    System.out.println(a[i]);
    i++;
}
```

Some programmers don't line up vertical braces but place the { behind the keyword:

```
while (i < n) { // DON'T
    System.out.println(a[i]);
    i++;
}
```

Doing so makes it hard to check that the braces match.

Unstable Layout

Some programmers take great pride in lining up certain columns in their code:

```
firstRecord = other.firstRecord;
lastRecord  = other.lastRecord;
cutoff      = other.cutoff;
```

This is undeniably neat, but the layout is not stable under change. A new variable name that is longer than the preallotted number of columns requires that you move all entries around:

```
firstRecord = other.firstRecord;
lastRecord  = other.lastRecord;
cutoff      = other.cutoff;
marginalFudgeFactor = other.marginalFudgeFactor;
```

This is just the kind of trap that makes you decide to use a short variable name like `mff` instead. Use a simple layout that is easy to maintain as your programs change.

Abstract array   An ordered sequence of items that can be efficiently accessed at random through an integer index.

Abstract class   A class that cannot be instantiated.

Abstract list   An ordered sequence of items that can be traversed sequentially and that allows for efficient insertion and removal of elements at any position.

Abstract method   A method with a name, parameter types, and return type but without an implementation.

Abstraction   The process of finding the essential feature set for a building block of a program such as a class.

Access specifier   A reserved word that indicates the accessibility of a feature, such as private or public.

Accessor method   A method that accesses an object but does not change it.

Actual parameter   The expression supplied for a formal parameter of a method by the caller.

ADT (Abstract Data Type)   A specification of the fundamental operations that characterize a data type, without supplying an implementation.

Aggregation   The *has-a* relationship between classes.

Algorithm   An unambiguous, executable, and terminating specification of a way to solve a problem.

Anonymous class   A class that does not have a name.

Anonymous object   An object that is not stored in a named variable.

API (Application Programming Interface)   A code library for building programs.

API Documentation   Information about each class in the Java library.

Applet   A graphical Java program that executes inside a web browser or applet viewer.

Argument   An actual parameter in a method call, or one of the values combined by an operator.

Array   A collection of values of the same type stored in contiguous memory locations, each of which can be accessed by an integer index.

Array list   A Java class that implements a dynamically-growable array of objects.

Assertion   A claim that a certain condition holds in a particular program location.

Assignment   Placing a new value into a variable.

Association   A relationship between classes in which one can navigate from objects of one class to objects of the other class, usually by following object references.

Asymmetric bounds   Bounds that include the starting index but not the ending index.

Attribute   A named property that an object is responsible for maintaining.

Auto-boxing   Automatically converting a primitive type value into a wrapper type object.

Balanced tree   A tree in which each subtree has the property that the number of descendants to the left is approximately the same as the number of descendants to the right.

Big-Oh notation   The notation $g(n) = O(f(n))$, which denotes that the function g grows at a rate that is bounded by the growth rate of the function f with respect to n. For example, $10n^2 + 100n - 1000 = O(n^2)$.

Binary file   A file in which values are stored in their binary representation and cannot be read as text.

Binary operator   An operator that takes two arguments, for example + in $x + y$.

Binary search   A fast algorithm for finding a value in a sorted array. It narrows the search down to half of the array in every step.

Binary search tree   A binary tree in which *each* subtree has the property that all left descendants are smaller than the value stored in the root, and all right descendants are larger.

Binary tree   A tree in which each node has at most two child nodes.

Bit   Binary digit; the smallest unit of information, having two possible values: 0 and 1. A data element consisting of n bits has 2^n possible values.

Black-box testing   Testing a method without knowing its implementation.

Block   A group of statements bracketed by {}.

Blocked thread   A thread that cannot proceed because it is waiting for some external event.

Boolean operator   See **Logical operator**

Boolean type   A type with two possible values: true and false.

Border layout   A layout management scheme in which components are placed into the center or one of the four borders of their container.

Boundary test case   A test case involving values that are at the outer boundary of the set of legal values. For example, if a function is expected to work for all nonnegative integers, then 0 is a boundary test case.

Bounds error   Trying to access an array element that is outside the legal range.

Breakpoint   A point in a program, specified in a debugger, at which the debugger stops executing the program and lets the user inspect the program state.

break statement   A statement that terminates a loop or switch statement.

Bucket   In a hash table, a set of values with the same hash code.

Buffer   A temporary storage location for holding values that have been produced (for example, characters typed by the user) and are waiting to be consumed (for example, read a line at a time).

Buffered input   Input that is gathered in batches, for example, a line at a time.

Bug   A programming error.

Byte   A number made up of eight bits. Essentially all currently manufactured computers use a byte as the smallest unit of storage in memory.

Bytecode   Instructions for the Java virtual machine.

Callback   A mechanism for specifying a block of code so it can be executed at a later time.

Call by reference   A method call mechanism in which the method receives the memory location of a variable supplied as an actual parameter. Call by reference enables a method to change the contents of the original variable so that the change remains in effect after the method returns.

Call by value A method call mechanism in which the method receives a copy of the contents of a variable supplied as an actual parameter. Java uses only call by value. If a parameter variable's type is a class, its value is an object reference, so the method can alter that object but cannot make the parameter variable refer to a different object.

Call stack The ordered set of all methods that currently have been called but not yet terminated, starting with the current method and ending with main.

Case sensitive Distinguishing upper- and lowercase characters.

Cast Explicitly converting a value from one type to a different type. For example, the cast from a floating-point number x to an integer is expressed in Java by the cast notation (int) x.

catch clause A part of a try block that is executed when a matching exception is thrown by any statement in the try block.

Central processing unit (CPU) The part of a computer that executes the machine instructions.

Character A single letter, digit, or symbol.

Check box A user-interface component that can be used for a binary selection.

Checked exception An exception that the compiler checks. All checked exceptions must be declared or caught.

Class A programmer-defined data type.

Class method See **Static method**

Class path The set of directories and archives that the virtual machine searches for class files.

Client A computer program or system that issues requests to a server and processes the server responses.

Cloning Making a copy of an object so the copy's state can be modified independently of the original object.

Code coverage A measure of the amount of source code that has been executed during testing.

Cohesion A class is cohesive if its features support a single abstraction.

Collaborator A class on which another class depends.

Combo box A user-interface component that combines a text field with a drop-down list of selections.

Command line The line the user types to start a program in DOS or UNIX or a command window in Windows. It consists of the program name followed by any necessary arguments.

Comment An explanation to help the human reader understand a section of a program; ignored by the compiler.

Compiler A program that translates code in a high-level language (such as Java) to machine instructions (such as bytecode for the Java virtual machine).

Compile-time error An error that is detected when a program is compiled.

Component See **User-interface component**

Compound statement A statement such as if or while that is made up of several parts such as a condition and a body.

Concatenation   Placing one string after another to form a new string.

Concrete class   A class that can be instantiated.

Condition object   An object that manages threads that currently cannot proceed.

Console program   A Java program that does not have a graphical window. A console program reads input from the keyboard and writes output to the terminal screen.

Constant   A value that cannot be changed by a program. In Java, constants are defined with the reserved word final.

Construction   Setting a newly allocated object to an initial state.

Constructor   A method that initializes a newly instantiated object.

Container   A user-interface component that can hold other components and present them together to the user. Also, a data structure, such as a list, that can hold a collection of objects and present them individually to a program.

Content pane   The part of a Swing frame that holds the user-interface components of the frame.

Coupling   The degree to which classes are related to each other by dependency.

CRC card   An index card representing a class that lists its responsibilities and collaborating classes.

De Morgan's Law   A law about logical operations that describes how to negate expressions formed with *and* and *or* operations.

Deadlock   A state in which no thread can proceed because each thread is waiting for another to do some work first.

Deadly embrace   A set of blocked threads, each of which could only be unblocked by the action of other threads in the set.

Debugger   A program that lets a user run another program one or a few steps at a time, stop execution, and inspect the variables in order to analyze it for bugs.

Default constructor   A constructor that is invoked with no parameters.

Dependency   The *uses* relationship between classes, in which one class needs services provided by another class.

Dictionary ordering   See **Lexicographic ordering**

Directory   A structure on a disk that can hold files or other directories; also called a folder.

Documentation comment   A comment in a source file that can be automatically extracted into the program documentation by a program such as javadoc.

Dot notation   The notation *object.method(parameters)* or *object.variable* used to invoke a method or access a variable.

Doubly linked list   A linked list in which each link has a reference to both its predecessor and successor links.

DTD (Document Type Definition)   A sequence of rules that describes the legal child elements and attributes for each element type in an SGML or XML document.

Dynamic method lookup   Selecting a method to be invoked at run time. In Java, dynamic method lookup considers the class of the implicit parameter object to select the appropriate method.

Editor   A program for writing and modifying text files.

Embedded system The processor, software, and supporting circuitry that is included in a device other than a computer.

Encapsulation The hiding of implementation details.

End of file The condition that is true when all characters of a file have been read. Note that there is no special "end of file character". When composing a file on the keyboard, you may need to type a special character to tell the operating system to end the file, but that character is not part of the file.

Enumeration type A type with a finite number of values, each of which has its own symbolic name.

Escape character A character in text that is not taken literally but has a special meaning when combined with the character or characters that follow it. The \ character is an escape character in Java strings.

Event See **User-interface event**

Event class A class that contains information about an event, such as its source.

Event adapter A class that implements an event listener interface by defining all methods to do nothing.

Event handler A method that is executed when an event occurs.

Event listener An object that is notified by an event source when an event occurs.

Event source An object that can notify other classes of events.

Exception A class that signals a condition that prevents the program from continuing normally. When such a condition occurs, an object of the exception class is thrown.

Exception handler A sequence of statements that is given control when an exception of a particular type has been thrown and caught.

Explicit parameter A parameter of a method other than the object on which the method is invoked.

Expression A syntactical construct that is made up of constants, variables, method calls, and operators combining them.

Extension The last part of a file name, which specifies the file type. For example, the extension .java denotes a Java file.

Extreme Programming A development methodology that strives for simplicity, by removing formal structure and focusing on best practices.

Fibonacci numbers The sequence of numbers 1, 1, 2, 3, 5, 8, 13, . . ., in which every term is the sum of its two predecessors.

File A sequence of bytes that is stored on disk.

File pointer The position within a random-access file of the next byte to be read or written. It can be moved so as to access any byte in the file.

finally clause A part of a try block that is executed no matter how the try block is exited.

Flag See **Boolean type**

Floating-point number A number that can have a fractional part.

Flow layout A layout management scheme in which components are laid out left to right.

Flushing a stream Sending all characters that are still held in a buffer to its destination.

Folder See **Directory**

Font A set of character shapes in a particular style and size.

Foreign key A reference to a primary key in a linked table.

Formal parameter A variable in a method definition; it is initialized with an actual parameter value when the method is called.

Frame A window with a border and a title bar.

Garbage collection Automatic reclamation of memory occupied by objects that are no longer referenced.

Generic class A class with one or more type parameters.

Generic method A method with one or more type parameters.

Generic programming Providing program components that can be reused in a wide variety of situations.

goto statement A statement that transfers control to some other statement, which is tagged with a label. Java does not have a goto statement.

Grammar A set of rules that specifies which sequences of tokens are legal for a particular document set.

Graphics context A class through which a programmer can cause shapes to appear on a window or off-screen bitmap.

grep The "global regular expression print" search program, useful for finding all strings matching a pattern in a set of files.

Grid layout A layout management scheme in which components are placed into a two-dimensional grid.

GUI (Graphical User Interface) A user interface in which the user supplies inputs through graphical components such as buttons, menus, and text fields.

Hash code A value that is computed by a hash function.

Hash collision Two different objects for which a hash function computes identical values.

Hash function A function that computes an integer value from an object in such a way that different objects are likely to yield different values.

Hash table A data structure in which elements are mapped to array positions according to their hash function values.

Hashing Applying a hash function to a set of objects.

Heap A balanced binary tree that is used for implementing sorting algorithms and priority queues.

Heapsort algorithm A sorting algorithm that inserts the values to be sorted into a heap.

HTML (Hypertext Markup Language) The language in which web pages are described.

HTTP (Hypertext Transfer Protocol) The protocol that defines communication between web browsers and web servers.

IDE (Integrated Development Environment) A programming environment that includes an editor, compiler, and debugger.

Immutable class A class without a mutator method.

Implementing an interface Implementing a class that defines all methods specified in the interface.

Implicit parameter   The object on which a method is invoked. For example, in the call x.f(y), the object x is the implicit parameter of the method f.

Importing a class or package   Indicating the intention of referring to a class, or all classes in a package, by the simple name rather than the qualified name.

Inheritance   The *is-a* relationship between a more general superclass and a more specialized subclass.

Initialization   Setting a variable to a well-defined value when it is created.

Inner class   A class that is defined inside another class.

Instance method   A method with an implicit parameter; that is, a method that is invoked on an instance of a class.

Instance of a class   An object whose type is that class.

Instance variable   A variable defined in a class for which every object of the class has its own value.

Instantiation of a class   Construction of an object of that class.

Integer   A number that cannot have a fractional part.

Integer division   Taking the quotient of two integers and discarding the remainder. In Java the / symbol denotes integer division if both arguments are integers. For example, 11/4 is 2, not 2.75.

Interface   A type with no instance variables, only abstract methods and constants.

Internet   A worldwide collection of networks, routing equipment, and computers using a common set of protocols that define how participants interact with each other.

Interpreter   A program that reads a set of codes and carries out the commands specified by them.

Iterator   An object that can inspect all elements in a container such as a linked list.

JavaBean   A class with a default constructor that exposes properties through its get and set methods.

javadoc   The documentation generator in the Java SDK. It extracts documentation comments from Java source files and produces a set of linked HTML files.

JavaServer Faces (JSF)   A framework for developing web applications that aids in the separation of user interface and program logic.

JDBC (Java Database Connectivity)   The technology that enables a Java program to interact with relational databases.

JDK   The Java software development kit that contains the Java compiler and related development tools.

Join   A database query that involves multiple tables.

JSF container   A program that executes JSF applications.

JVM   The Java Virtual Machine.

Layout manager   A class that arranges user-interface components inside a container.

Lazy evaluation   Deferring the computation of a value until it is needed, thereby avoiding the computation if the value is never needed.

Legacy code   Software that has existed for a long time and that continues to operate.

Lexicographic ordering   Ordering strings in the same order as in a dictionary, by skipping all matching characters and comparing the first non matching characters of both strings. For example, "orbit" comes before "orchid" in lexicographic ordering. Note that in Java, unlike a dictionary, the ordering is case-sensitive: Z comes before a.

Library   A set of precompiled classes that can be included in programs.

Linear search   Searching a container (such as an array or list) for an object by inspecting each element in turn.

Linked list   A data structure that can hold an arbitrary number of objects, each of which is stored in a link object, which contains a pointer to the next link.

Local variable   A variable whose scope is a block.

Lock   A data structure to regulate the scheduling of multiple threads. Once a thread has acquired a lock, other threads that also wish to acquire it must wait until the first thread relinquishes it.

Lock object   An object that allows a single thread to execute a section of a program.

Logging   Sending messages that trace the progress of a program to a file or window.

Logical operator   An operator that can be applied to Boolean values. Java has three logical operators: &&, ||, and !.

Logic error   An error in a syntactically correct program that causes it to act differently from its specification. (A form of run-time error.)

Loop   A sequence of instructions that is executed repeatedly.

Loop and a half   A loop whose termination decision is neither at the beginning nor at the end.

Loop invariant   A statement about the program state that is preserved when the statements in the loop are executed once.

Machine code   Instructions that can be executed directly by the CPU.

Magic number   A number that appears in a program without explanation.

`main` **method**   The method that is first called when a Java application executes.

Managed bean   A JavaBean that is managed by a JSF container.

Map   A data structure that keeps associations between key and value objects.

Markup   Information about data that is added as humanly readable instructions. An example is the tagging of HTML documents with elements such as <h1> or <b>.

Memory location   A value that specifies the location of data in computer memory.

Merge sort   A sorting algorithm that first sorts two halves of a data structure and then merges the sorted subarrays together.

Meta data   Data that describe properties of a data set.

Method   A sequence of statements that has a name, may have formal parameters, and may return a value. A method can be invoked any number of times, with different values for its parameters.

Method expression   In JSF, an expression describing a bean and a method that is to be applied to the bean at a later time.

Method signature   The name of a method and the types of its parameters.

Mixed content   In XML, a markup element that contains both text and other elements.

Mock object   An object that is used during program testing, replacing another object and providing similar behavior. Usually, the mock object is simpler to implement or provides better support for testing.

Mutator method   A method that changes the state of an object.

Mutual recursion   Cooperating methods that call each other.

Name clash   Accidentally using the same name to denote two program features in a way that cannot be resolved by the compiler.

Navigation rule   In JSF, a rule that describes when to move from one web page to another.

Negative test case   A test case that is expected to fail. For example, when testing a root-finding program, an attempt to compute the square root of −1 is a negative test case.

Nested block   A block that is contained inside another block.

Nested loop   A loop that is contained in another loop.

Network protocol   A set of rules that must be followed by programs that communicate over a network.

new operator   An operator that allocates new objects.

Newline   The '\n' character, which indicates the end of a line.

Null reference   A reference that does not refer to any object.

Number literal   A constant value in a program this is explicitly written as a number, such as −2 or 6.02214115E23.

Object   A value of a class type.

Object-oriented design   Designing a program by discovering objects, their properties, and their relationships.

Object reference   A value that denotes the location of an object in memory. In Java, a variable whose type is a class contains a reference to an object of that class.

Off-by-one error   A common programming error in which a value is one larger or smaller than it should be.

Opening a file   Preparing a file for reading or writing.

Operating system   The software that launches application programs and provides services (such as a file system) for those programs.

Operator   A symbol denoting a mathematical or logical operation, such as + or &&.

Operator associativity   The rule that governs in which order operators of the same precedence are executed. For example, in Java the - operator is left-associative because a - b - c is interpreted as (a - b) - c, and = is right-associative because a = b = c is interpreted as a = (b = c).

Operator precedence   The rule that governs which operator is evaluated first. For example, in Java the && operator has a higher precedence than the || operator. Hence a || b && c is interpreted as a || (b && c). (See Appendix B.)

Oracle   A program that predicts how another program should behave.

Overloading   Giving more than one meaning to a method name.

Overriding   Redefining a method in a subclass.

Package   A collection of related classes. The import statement is used to access one or more classes in a package.

Package access Accessibility by methods of classes in the same package.

Panel A user-interface component with no visual appearance. It can be used to group other components.

Parallel arrays Arrays of the same length, in which corresponding elements are logically related.

Parameter An item of information that is specified to a method when the method is called. For example, in the call `System.out.println("Hello, World!")`, the parameters are the implicit parameter `System.out` and the explicit parameter `"Hello, World!"`.

Parameter passing Specifying expressions to be actual parameter values for a method when it is called.

Parameter variable A variable of a method that is initialized with a parameter value when the method is called.

Parse tree A tree structure that shows how a string conforms to rules of a grammar.

Parser A program that reads a document, checks whether it is syntactically correct, and takes some action as it processes the document.

Partially filled array An array that is not filled to capacity, together with a companion variable that indicates the number of elements actually stored.

Permutation A rearrangement of a set of values.

Polymorphism Selecting a method among several methods that have the same name on the basis of the actual types of the implicit parameters.

Positive test case A test case that a method is expected to handle correctly.

Postcondition A condition that is true after a method has been called.

Postfix operator A unary operator that is written after its argument.

Precondition A condition that must be true when a method is called if the method is to work correctly.

Predicate method A method that returns a Boolean value.

Prefix operator A unary operator that is written before its argument.

Prepared statement A SQL statement with a precomputed query strategy.

Primary key A column (or combination of columns) whose value uniquely specifies a table record.

Primitive type In Java, a number type or `boolean`.

Priority queue An abstract data type that enables efficient insertion of elements and efficient removal of the smallest element.

Private feature A feature that is accessible only by methods of the same class or an inner class.

Project A collection of source files and their dependencies.

Prompt A string that tells the user to provide input.

Property A named value that is managed by a component.

Protected feature A feature that is accessible by a class, its inner classes, its subclasses, and the other classes in the same package.

Pseudocode A high-level description of the actions of a program or algorithm, using a mixture of English and informal programming language syntax.

Pseudorandom number A number that appears to be random but is generated by a mathematical formula.

Public feature A feature that is accessible by all classes.

Public interface The features (methods, variables, and nested types) of a class that are accessible to all clients.

Qualified name A name that is made unambiguous because it starts with the package name.

Queue A collection of items with "first in, first out" retrieval.

Quicksort A generally fast sorting algorithm that picks an element, called the pivot, partitions the sequence into the elements smaller than the pivot and those larger than the pivot, and then recursively sorts the subsequences.

Race condition A condition in which the effect of multiple threads on shared data depends on the order in which the threads are scheduled.

Radio button A user-interface component that can be used for selecting one of several options.

RAM (random-access memory) Electronic circuits in a computer that can store code and data of running programs.

Random access The ability to access any value directly without having to read the values preceding it.

Reader In the Java input/output library, a class from which to read characters.

Recursion A method for computing a result by decomposing the inputs into simpler values and applying the same method to them.

Recursive method A method that can call itself with simpler values. It must handle the simplest values without calling itself.

Redirection Linking the input or output of a program to a file instead of the keyboard or display.

Reference See **Object reference**

Regression testing Keeping old test cases and testing every revision of a program against them.

Regular expression A string that defines a set of matching strings according to their content. Each part of a regular expression can be a specific required character; one of a set of permitted characters such as [abc], which can be a range such as [a-z]; any character not in a set of forbidden characters, such as [^0-9]; a repetition of one or more matches, such as [0-9]+, or zero or more, such as [ACGT]; one of a set of alternatives, such as and|et|und; or various other possibilities. For example, "[A-Za-z][0-9]+" matches "Cloud9" or "007" but not "Jack".

Relational database A data repository that stores information in tables and retrieves data as the result of queries that are formulated in terms of table relationships.

Relational operator An operator that compares two values, yielding a Boolean result.

Reserved word A word that has a special meaning in a programming language and therefore cannot be used as a name by the programmer.

Return value The value returned by a method through a return statement.

Reverse Polish notation   A style of writing expressions in which the operators are written following the operands, such as 2 3 4   + for 2 + 3   4.

Roundoff error   An error introduced by the fact that the computer can store only a finite number of digits of a floating-point number.

Runnable thread   A thread that can proceed provided it is given a time slice to do work.

Run-time error   An error in a syntactically correct program that causes it to act differently from its specification.

Run-time stack   The data structure that stores the local variables of all called methods as a program runs.

Scope   The part of a program in which a variable is defined.

Scripting language   A programming language that favors rapid development over execution speed and code maintainability.

Selection sort   A sorting algorithm in which the smallest element is repeatedly found and removed until no elements remain.

Sentinel   A value in input that is not to be used as an actual input value but to signal the end of input.

Sequential access   Accessing values one after another without skipping over any of them.

Sequential search   See **Linear search**

Serialization   The process of saving an object, and all the objects that it references, to a stream.

Server   A computer program or system that receives requests from a client, obtains or computes the requested information, and sends it to the client.

Session   A sequence of page requests from the same browser to the same web server.

Set   An unordered collection that allows efficient addition, location, and removal of elements.

Shadowing   Hiding a variable by defining another one with the same name.

Shallow copy   Copying only the reference to an object.

Shell script   A file that contains commands for running programs and manipulating files. Typing the name of the shell script file on the command line causes those commands to be executed.

Shell window   A window for interacting with an operating system through textual commands.

Short circuit evaluation   Evaluating only a part of an expression if the remainder cannot change the result.

Side effect   An effect of a method other than returning a value.

Sign bit   The bit of a binary number that indicates whether the number is positive or negative.

Signature   See **Method signature**

Simple statement   A statement consisting of a single expression.

Single-stepping   Executing a program in the debugger one statement at a time.

Socket   An object that encapsulates a TCP/IP connection. To communicate with the other endpoint of the connection, you use the input and output streams attached to the socket.

Software life cycle All activities related to the creation and maintenance of the software from initial analysis until obsolescence.

Source code Instructions in a programming language that need to be translated before execution on a computer.

Source file A file containing instructions in a programming language such as Java.

Spiral model An iterative process model of software development in which design and implementation are repeated.

SQL (Structured Query Language) A command language for interacting with a database.

Stack A data structure with "last in, first out" retrieval. Elements can be added and removed only at one position, called the top of the stack.

Stack trace A printout of the call stack, listing all currently pending method calls.

State The current value of an object, which is determined by the cumulative action of all methods that were invoked on it.

State diagram A diagram that depicts state transitions and their causes.

Statement A syntactical unit in a program. In Java a statement is either a simple statement, a compound statement, or a block.

Static method A method with no implicit parameter.

Static variable A variable defined in a class that has only one value for the whole class, which can be accessed and changed by any method of that class.

Stored procedures A database procedure that is executed in the database kernel.

Stream An abstraction for a sequence of bytes from which data can be read or to which data can be written.

String A sequence of characters.

Stub A method with no or minimal functionality.

Subclass A class that inherits variables and methods from a superclass but adds instance variables, adds methods, or redefines methods.

Superclass A general class from which a more specialized class (a subclass) inherits.

Swing A Java toolkit for implementing graphical user interfaces.

Symmetric bounds Bounds that include the starting index and the ending index.

Synchronized block A block of code that is controlled by a lock. To start execution, a thread must acquire the lock. Upon completion, it relinquishes the lock.

Synchronized method A method that is controlled by a lock. In order to execute the method, the calling thread must acquire the lock.

Syntax Rules that define how to form instructions in a particular programming language.

Syntax diagram A graphical representation of grammar rules.

Syntax error An instruction that does not follow the programming language rules and is rejected by the compiler. (A form of compile-time error.)

Tab character The '\t' character, which advances the next character on the line to the next one of a set of fixed positions known as tab stops.

TCP/IP (Transmission Control Protocol/Internet Protocol)   The pair of communication protocols that is used to establish reliable transmission of data between two computers on the Internet.

Ternary operator   An operator with three arguments. Java has one ternary operator, a ? b : c.

Test coverage   The instructions of a program that are executed in a set of test cases.

Test harness   A program that calls a function that needs to be tested, supplying parameters and analyzing the function's return value.

Test suite   A set of test cases for a program.

Text field   A user-interface component that allows a user to provide text input.

Text file   A file in which values are stored in their text representation.

Thread   A program unit that is executed independently of other parts of the program.

Three-tier application   An application that is composed of separate tiers for presentation logic, business logic, and data storage.

Throwing an exception   Indicating an abnormal condition by terminating the normal control flow of a program and transferring control to a matching catch clause.

throws specifier   Indicates the types of the checked exceptions that a method may throw.

Time slicing   Scheduling threads by giving each thread a small amount of time in which to do its work, then giving control to another thread.

Token   A sequence of consecutive characters from an input source that belongs together for the purpose of analyzing the input. For example, a token can be a sequence of characters other than white space.

Total ordering   An ordering relationship in which all elements can be compared to each other.

Trace message   A message that is printed during a program run for debugging purposes.

Transaction   A set of database operations that should either succeed in their entirety, or not happen at all.

Tree   A data structure consisting of nodes, each of which has a list of child nodes, and one of which is distinguished as the root node.

try block   A block of statements that contains exception processing clauses. A try block contains at least one catch or finally clause.

Turing machine   A very simple model of computation that is used in theoretical computer science to explore computability of problems.

Two-dimensional array   A tabular arrangement of elements in which an element is specified by a row and a column index.

Type   A named set of values and the operations that can be carried out with them.

Type parameter   A parameter in a generic class or method that can be replaced with an actual type.

Type variable   A variable in the declaration of a generic type that can be instantiated with a type.

Unary operator   An operator with one argument.

Unchecked exception   An exception that the compiler doesn't check.

Unicode   A standard code that assigns code values consisting of two bytes to characters used in scripts around the world. Java stores all characters as their Unicode values.

Unified Modeling Language (UML)   A notation for specifying, visualizing, constructing, and documenting the artifacts of software systems.

Uninitialized variable   A variable that has not been set to a particular value. In Java, using an uninitialized local variable is a syntax error.

Unit test   A test of a method by itself, isolated from the remainder of the program.

URL (uniform resource locator)   A pointer to an information resource (such as a web page or an image) on the World Wide Web.

User-interface component   A building block for a graphical user interface, such as a button or a text field. User-interface components are used to present information to the user and allow the user to enter information to the program.

User-interface event   A notification to a program that a user action such as a key press, mouse move, or menu selection has occurred.

Value expression   In JSF, an expression describing a bean and a property that is to be accessed at a later time.

Variable   A symbol in a program that identifies a storage location that can hold different values.

Virtual machine   A program that simulates a CPU that can be implemented efficiently on a variety of actual machines. A given program in Java bytecode can be executed by any Java virtual machine, regardless of which CPU is used to run the virtual machine itself.

Visual programming   Programming by arranging graphical elements on a form, setting program behavior by selecting properties for these elements, and writing only a small amount of "glue" code linking them.

void   A reserved word indicating no type or an unknown type.

Watch window   A window in a debugger that shows the current values of selected variables.

Waterfall model   A sequential process model of software development, consisting of analysis, design, implementation, testing, and deployment.

Web application   An application that executes on a web server and whose user interface is displayed in a web browser.

White-box testing   Testing methods by taking their implementations into account, in contrast to black-box testing; for example, by selecting boundary test cases and ensuring that all branches of the code are covered by some test case.

White space   Any sequence of only space, tab, and newline characters.

Wrapper class   A class that contains a primitive type value, such as Integer.

Writer   In the Java input/output library, a class to which characters are to be sent.

XML (Extensible Markup Language)   A simple format for structured data in which the structure is indicated by markup instructions.

INDEX

Page references followed by *t* indicate material in tables. Java library classes are indexed under java, as for example "java.util.Scanner class."

ILLUSTRATION CREDITS

Chapter 12 Page 509: Booch/Jacobson/Rumbaugh, *The Unified Modeling Language Reference Manual*, pg. 41, © 1999 by Addison Wesley Longman, Inc. Reproduced by permission of Pearson Education, Inc.

Chapter 13 Page 577: Science Photo Library/Photo Researchers, Inc.

Chapter 14 Page 614: Topham/The Image Works.

Chapter 15 Page 652: Photodisc/Punchstock.
Page 654: Courtesy Nigel Tout.

Chapter 19 Page 784: Anna Khomulo/iStockphoto.

Chapter 20 Page 817: Creatas/Punchstock.
Page 833: Courtesy of Professor Naehyuck Chang, Computer Systems Lab, Department of Computer Engineering, Seoul National University.

Chapter 22 Page 880: Greg Nicholas/iStockphoto.

Chapter 24 Page 973: Google Earth™ mapping service screenshot © Google, Inc., reprinted with permission.

Animation Icon james steidl/iStockphoto.